THE PILLAR NEW TESTAMENT COMMENTARY

General Editor

D. A. CARSON

The Gospel according to
LUKE

James R. Edwards

WILLIAM B. EERDMANS PUBLISHING COMPANY

GRAND RAPIDS, MICHIGAN / CAMBRIDGE, U.K.

APOLLOS
NOTTINGHAM, ENGLAND

Published 2015 in the United States of America by

Wm. B. Eerdmans Publishing Co.

2140 Oak Industrial Drive N.E., Grand Rapids, Michigan 49505 /

P.O. Box 163, Cambridge CB3 9PU U.K.

www.eerdmans.com

and in the United Kingdom by

APOLLOS

Norton Street, Nottingham,

England NG7 3HR

Printed in the United States of America

26 25 24 23   7 6 5 4 3

Library of Congress Cataloging-in-Publication Data

Edwards, James R.

The gospel according to Luke / James R. Edwards.

pages   cm. — (The Pillar New Testament commentary)

ISBN 978-0-8028-3735-6 (cloth: alk. paper)

1. Bible. Luke — Commentaries.   I. Title.

BS2595.53.E39   2015

226.4´07 — dc23

2014043605

British Library Cataloguing in Publication Data

A catalogue record for this book is available from the British Library.

ISBN 978-1-78359-268-5

To my family

Contents

INDEXES

Editor's Preface

Commentaries have specific aims, and this series is no exception. Designed for serious pastors and teachers of the Bible, the Pillar commentaries seek above all to make clear the text of Scripture as we have it. The scholars writing these volumes interact with the most important informed contemporary debate, but avoid getting mired in undue technical detail. Their ideal is a blend of rigorous exegesis and exposition, with an eye alert both to biblical theology and to the contemporary relevance of the Bible, without confusing the commentary and the sermon.

The rationale for this approach is that the vision of "objective scholarship" (a vain chimera) may actually be profane. God stands over against us; we do not stand in judgment of him. When God speaks to us through his Word, those who profess to know him must respond in an appropriate way, and that is certainly different from a stance in which the scholar projects an image of autonomous distance. Yet this is no surreptitious appeal for uncontrolled subjectivity. The writers of this series aim for an even-handed openness to the text that is the best kind of "objectivity" of all.

If the text is God's Word, it is appropriate that we respond with reverence, a certain fear, a holy joy, a questing obedience. These values should be reflected in the way Christians write. With these values in place, the Pillar commentaries will be warmly welcomed not only by pastors, teachers, and students, but by general readers as well.

*   *   *

The challenges associated with writing a good commentary on one of the canonical Gospels are well known. I briefly articulated a handful of them in the Preface to James Edwards's excellent commentary on Mark (also in the Pillar series). By adding this commentary on Luke, Dr. Edwards has successfully navigated two further challenges: first, he has ensured that Luke speaks in his own voice, and not merely as a slightly-longer-Mark; and second, he has not forgotten that Luke's Gospel is the first volume of a two-volume work, such that one must be aware of Luke's companion volume, the Acts of the Apostles, lurking just around the corner. Above all, this commentary carefully explores Luke's witness to Jesus, never losing sight of the fact that whatever we may reasonably infer about Luke himself, or his readers, Luke's first aim is to talk about Jesus. Again and again Dr. Edwards displays a sure-footed exegesis that helps readers grapple with the text of Scripture, simultaneously engendering deepening knowledge and grateful reverence.

D. A. CARSON

Author's Preface

It is my hope that this commentary will be for church, academy, and personal reading a window of understanding and insight into the Third Gospel. The following practical information will assist readers in a profitable use of the work as a whole. I have followed *The SBL Handbook of Style* in matters relating to bibliographic formatting and abbreviations of source works, both ancient and modern.[1] Readers will find a complete list of all abbreviations used in the commentary, beginning on p. xii. A list of Frequently Cited Works beginning on p. xxiv provides full bibliographies of works referenced occasionally or regularly in footnotes. When a Frequently Cited Work is referenced, I include the author's last name, a key word from the title in *italic* print, and page number(s). When a source is cited that is not in the Frequently Cited Works, I include full bibliographical reference. Dates in the Christian era are normally given by year alone (without A.D. or C.E.), but dates prior to the Christian era are signified by B.C. Scripture references of only chapter and verse (or verse[s] alone) without identifying book refer to Luke; all other Scripture references (including those to Acts) are identified by book, chapter, and verse. In accordance with the editorial policy of the Pillar series, all Scripture citations in the commentary, unless otherwise noted, follow the New International Version (NIV) of the Bible. All English translations of foreign language sources, ancient or modern, are my own, unless otherwise noted. For computer-assisted research I have relied on BibleWorks 7. The commentary on Luke 1–21 was prepared on the basis of the Greek text of Nestle-Aland[27], and chaps. 22–24 on Nestle-Aland[28], which became available to me in 2013.

Literature on the NT, as in virtually all fields, has become voluminous, but unlike most other fields, literature on the NT has twenty centuries of momentum behind it. A Gospel commentator stands at the intersection of many

---

1. *The SBL Handbook of Style: For Ancient Near Eastern, Biblical, and Early Christian Studies* (ed. P. Alexander, J. Kutsko, J. Ernest, S. Decker-Lucke, and D. Petersen; Peabody: Hendrickson Publishers, 1999).

exciting fields of knowledge, including archaeology, ancient languages, epigraphy, ancient manuscripts, ancient history and social customs, alertness to the theological intention of an author, and the way the church has understood that theological intention over the ages. The scope of the task is both stimulating and humbling. Regarding the last-mentioned field above, the page constraints of the commentary have dictated that the various ways the text of Luke has been received in the past two millennia, commonly called "reception history," be treated cursorily. Readers interested in this aspect of Lukan research will find François Bovon's three-volume commentary in the Hermeneia Series comprehensive and illuminating.

I am grateful to God for energy and inspiration to write this commentary, and to the assistance of many friends and colleagues in the process of its writing. I wish first of all to thank Don Carson, general editor of the Pillar series, who arranged through somewhat unusual circumstances for me to return to the series and contribute, in addition to the commentary on the Second Gospel, now the commentary on the Third. The superb editorial eye and hand of Craig Noll at Eerdmans have improved the manuscript at countless points. Financial resources available to the Bruner-Welch Chair of Theology, which I occupy, enabled me to hire four competent and industrious Whitworth University students as research assistants. My gratitude and indebtedness to Amy Erickson, Travis Niles, Rachel Toone, and Joshua Mikelson are enduring. My colleagues in the Theology Department, particularly Jerry Sittser, Adam Neder, and Jonathan Moo, have been helpful, encouraging, and forbearing conversation partners in the writing of this commentary. The interest and insights of students in my course on the Gospel of Luke at Whitworth University and of members of the adult Bible class at Whitworth Community Presbyterian Church, where I taught on Luke for several years, have informed and enriched this commentary in delightful and substantive ways.

I dedicate this book to my family, whose prayers, support, understanding, and encouragement have meant more than they can know: to my daughter, Corrie, and her husband, Shane, and their sons Anders, Mathias, and Soren; to my son, Mark, and his wife, Janine, and their daughter, Adeline, and son, Elias; and to my sister Diana and her family. Above all, I dedicate this book to my wife, Janie, whose abiding dedication throughout the writing of the commentary has been a gift of grace.

JAMES R. EDWARDS

Abbreviations

1 Apol.	Justin Martyr, *First Apology*
1 Chr	1 Chronicles
1 Clem.	*1 Clement,* Apostolic Fathers
1 Cor	1 Corinthians
1 En.	*1 Enoch (Ethiopic Apocalypse),* OT Pseudepigrapha
1 Esd	1 Esdras, OT Apocrypha
1 Kgs	1 Kings
1 Macc	1 Maccabees, OT Apocrypha
1 Pet	1 Peter
1Q28b	*Rule of Benedictions,* DSS
1QapGen	*Genesis Apocryphon,* DSS
1QH	*Hodayot,* DSS
1QM	*War Scroll,* DSS
1QpHab	*Pesher on Habakkuk,* DSS
1QS	*Rule of the Congregation, Manual of Discipline,* DSS
1QSa	Appendix A *(Rule of the Congregation)* to 1QS, DSS
1 Sam	1 Samuel
1 Thess	1 Thessalonians
1 Tim	1 Timothy
2 Apoc. Jas.	*2 Apocalypse of James,* Nag Hammadi Codices
2 Bar.	*2 Baruch (Syriac Apocalypse),* OT Pseudepigrapha
2 Chr	2 Chronicles
2 Clem.	*2 Clement,* Apostolic Fathers
2 Cor	2 Corinthians
2 En.	*2 Enoch (Slavonic Apocalypse),* OT Pseudepigrapha
2 Esd	2 Esdras, OT Apocrypha
2 Kgs	2 Kings
2 Macc	2 Maccabees, OT Apocrypha
2 Pet	2 Peter
2 Sam	2 Samuel
2 Thess	2 Thessalonians
2 Tim	2 Timothy

3 Bar	*3 Baruch (Greek Apocalypse)*, OT Pseudepigrapha
3 En.	*3 Enoch (Hebrew Apocalypse)*, OT Pseudepigrapha
3 Macc	3 Maccabees, OT Apocrypha
4 Ezra	*4 Ezra*, OT Pseudepigrapha
4 Macc	4 Maccabees, OT Apocrypha
4Q175 (4QFlor)	*Messianic Anthology*, DSS
4Q246	*An Aramaic Apocalypse*, DSS
4Q394-98 (4QMMT)	*Halakhic Letter*, DSS
4QT Levi (4Q540-41)	*Testament of Levi*, DSS
4QT Naph (4Q215)	*Testament of Naphtali*, DSS
11Q13	*Melchizedek*, DSS
11Q19 (11QT)	*Temple Scroll*, DSS
AB	Anchor Bible
ABD	*Anchor Bible Dictionary.* Edited by D. Freedman. 6 vols. Doubleday, 1992.
ACCS	Ancient Christian Commentary on Scripture NT 3, *Luke*, by A. Just, InterVarsity Press, 2003
Acts Pet.	*Acts of Peter*, NT Apocrypha and Pseudepigrapha
Acts Pil.	*Acts of Pilate*, NT Apocrypha and Pseudepigrapha
Acts Thom.	*Acts of Thomas*, NT Apocrypha and Pseudepigrapha
Aen.	Virgil, *The Aeneid*
Ag. Ap.	Josephus, *Against Apion*
Anab.	Arrian, *Anabasis*
AnBib	Analecta biblica
Ann.	Tacitus, *Annals*
Ant.	Josephus, *Antiquities of the Jews*
ANTC	Abingdon New Testament Commentary
Anti.-Marc. Prolog.	*Anti-Marcionite Prologue*
Ap.	Plato, *Apology*
APAW	Abhandlungen der königlichen preussischen Akademie der Wissenschaft
Ap. Jas.	*Apocryphon of James*, Nag Hammadi Codices
Apoc. Ab.	*Apocalypse of Abraham*, OT Pseudepigrapha
Apoc. Dan.	*Apocalypse of Daniel*, OT Pseudepigrapha
Apoc. Pet.	*Apocalypse of Peter*, NT Apocrypha and Pseudepigrapha
Apoc. Zeph.	*Apocalypse of Zephaniah*, OT Pseudepigrapha
Apol.	Plato, *Apology of Socrates*
Apos. Con.	*Apostolic Constitutions*, NT Apocrypha and Pseudepigrapha
Ar.	Aramaic
Ascen. Isa.	*Ascension of Isaiah*, OT Pseudepigrapha
As. Mos.	*Assumption of Moses*, OT Pseudepigrapha
ASNU	Acta seminarii neotestamentica upsaliensis
ATANT	Abhandlungen zur Theologie des Alten und Neuen Testaments
Aug.	Suetonius, "Deified Augustus," *Lives of the Caesars*

BA	*Biblical Archaeologist*
BAR	*Biblical Archaeological Review*
Bar	Baruch, OT Apocrypha
Barn.	*Epistle of Barnabas,* Apostolic Fathers
BBB	Bonner biblische Beiträge
b. Ber.	*Berakot,* Babylonian Talmud
b. B. Qam.	*Baba Qamma,* Babylonian Talmud
BBR	*Bulletin for Biblical Research*
B.C.	Before Christ
BDAG	F. W. Danker, W. Bauer, W. F. Arndt, and F. W. Gingrich. *Greek-English Lexicon of the New Testament and Other Early Christian Literature.* 3rd ed. Chicago, 2000.
BDF	F. Blass, A. Debrunner, and R. Funk. *A Greek Grammar of the New Testament and Other Early Christian Literature.* Chicago, 1967.
BECNT	Baker Exegetical Commentary on the New Testament
Ben.	Benediction
BETL	Bibliotheca ephemeridum theologicarum lovaniensium
b. Ḥag.	*Ḥagigah,* Babylonian Talmud
BHT	Beiträge zur historischen Theologie
Bib	*Biblica*
Bib. hist.	Diodorus Siculus, *Bibliotheca historica*
BibKir	*Bibel und Kirche*
BiTS	Biblical Tools and Studies
BJS	Brown Judaic Studies
b. Meg.	*Megillah,* Babylonian Talmud
b. Ned.	*Nedarim,* Babylonian Talmud
b. Nid.	*Niddah,* Babylonian Talmud
BNTC	Black's New Testament Commentary
b. Pesaḥ.	*Pesaḥim,* Babylonian Talmud
b. Qidd.	*Qiddušin,* Babylonian Talmud
BRev	*Bible Review*
b. Šabb.	*Šabbat,* Babylonian Talmud
b. Sanh.	*Sanhedrin,* Babylonian Talmud
b. Soṭah	*Soṭah,* Babylonian Talmud
b. Suk.	*Sukkah,* Babylonian Talmud
b. Taʿan.	*Taʿanit,* Babylonian Talmud
BTZ	*Berliner Theologische Zeitschrift*
b. Yoma	*Yoma,* Babylonian Talmud
Byz	Byzantine Greek textual tradition
c.	century
ca.	*circa,* about
Caes.	Plutarch, "Caesar," *Lives of the Noble Greeks and Romans*
Cant	Song of Solomon
CBQ	*Catholic Biblical Quarterly*

CBQMS	Catholic Biblical Quarterly Monograph Series
CD	*Damascus Document,* DSS
Cels.	Origen, *Against Celsus*
cf.	compare
CGTC	Cambridge Greek Testament Commentary
chap(s).	chapter(s)
Cher.	Philo, "On the Cherubim"
ChrCent.	*Christian Century*
Chron.	Eusebius, *Chronicle*
Civ.	Augustine, *City of God*
cm	centimeter(s)
Col	Colossians
Comm. Acts	Ephrem the Syrian, *Commentary on Acts*
Comm. Ezech.	Jerome, *Commentary on Ezekiel*
Comm. Isa.	Jerome, *Commentary on Isaiah*
Comm. Jo.	Origen, *Commentary on John*
Comm. Luc.	Cyril of Alexandria, *Commentary on Luke*
Comm. Matt.	Origen or Jerome, *Commentary on Matthew*
Comm. Mich.	Jerome, *Commentary on Micah*
Comm. Rom.	Origen, *Commentary on Romans*
Comm. Tat. Diates.	Ephrem the Syrian, *Commentary on Tatian's Diatessaron*
Conf.	Augustine, *The Confessions*
Contempl.	Philo, *On the Contemplative Life*
d.	died
Dan	Daniel
Decl.	Quintilian, *Declamationes*
Demon.	Isocrates, *To Demonicus*
Deut	Deuteronomy
Dial.	Justin Martyr, *Dialogue with Trypho*
Diatr.	Epictetus, *Dissertations*
Did.	*Didache,* Apostolic Fathers
Diogn.	*Epistle of Diognetus,* Apostolic Fathers
DSS	Dead Sea Scrolls
Eccl	Ecclesiastes
ed.	edited (by), editor, edition
EDNT	*Exegetical Dictionary of the New Testament.* Edited by H. Balz and G. Schneider. 3 vols. Eerdmans, 1990
EECh	*Encyclopedia of the Early Church.* Edited by A. di Berardino. Translated by A. Walford. 2 vols. Cambridge, 1992.
e.g.	*exempli gratia,* for example
Eg. Pap.	*Egerton Papyrus*
EKKNT	Evangelisch-katholischer Kommentar zum Neuen Testament
Embassy	Philo, *On the Embassy to Gaius*
Ench.	*Enchiridion*

EncJud.	*Encyclopaedia Judaica.* Keter Publishing, 1971
Eng.	English
Ep.	Seneca, *Epistles*
Ep. Ap.	*Epistula Apostolorum,* NT Apocrypha and Pseudepigrapha
Eph	Ephesians
Eph.	Ignatius, *Letter to the Ephesians,* Apostolic Fathers
Epict. Diss.	Arrian, *Discourses of Epictetus*
Epist.	Jerome, *Letters*
Ep. Pet. Phil.	*Epistle of Peter to Philip,* Nag Hammadi Codices
Ep. Tra.	Pliny the Younger, *Epistle to Trajan*
esp.	especially
Esth	Esther
ETL	*Ephemerides theologicae Lovanienses*
EvT	*Evangelische Theologie*
Exod	Exodus
Exod. Rab.	*Exodus Rabbah*
Exp. Luc.	Ambrose, *Exposition on the Gospel according to Luke*
ExpTim	*Expository Times*
Ezek	Ezekiel
FC	Fathers of the Church
Flor.	Apuleius, *Florida*
Frag.	Fragment
FRLANT	Forschungen zur Religion und Literatur des Alten und Neuen Testaments
Fr. Luc.	Origen, *Fragments of Luke*
𝕲	Septuagint, Greek translation of Hebrew OT
Gal	Galatians
Gaud.	Augustine, *Against Gaudentius the Donatist Bishop*
Gen	Genesis
Gen. Rab.	*Genesis Rabbah*
Geogr.	Strabo, *Geography*
Gk.	Greek
Gk. Apoc. Ezra	*Greek Apocalypse of Ezra,* OT Pseudepigrapha
GNT	Grundrisse zum Neuen Testament
Gos. Eb.	*Gospel of the Ebionites,* NT Apocrypha and Pseudepigrapha
Gos. Heb.	*Gospel of the Hebrews,* NT Apocrypha and Pseudepigrapha
Gos. Mani	*Gospel of Mani*
Gos. Mary	*Gospel of Mary,* NT Apocrypha and Pseudepigrapha
Gos. Naz.	*Gospel of the Nazarenes,* NT Apocrypha and Pseudepigrapha
Gos. Pet.	*Gospel of Peter,* NT Apocrypha and Pseudepigrapha
Gos. Phil.	*Gospel of Philip,* Nag Hammadi Codices
Gos. Thom.	*Gospel of Thomas,* Nag Hammadi Codices
ha	hectare(s)
Hab	Habakkuk

Haer.	Irenaeus, *Against Heresies*
Hag	Haggai
HALOT	L. Koehler, W. Baumgartner, and J. J. Stamm. *The Hebrew and Aramaic Lexicon of the Old Testament.* Translated by M. E. J. Richardson. Brill, 1995.
HCNT	*A Hellenistic Commentary to the New Testament.* Edited by M. Boring, K. Berger, and C. Colpe. Abingdon, 1995
Heb	Hebrews
Heb.	Hebrew
Herm. Man.	*Shepherd of Hermas, Mandate,* Apostolic Fathers
Herm. Sim.	*Shepherd of Hermas, Similitude,* Apostolic Fathers
Herm. Vis.	*Shepherd of Hermas, Visions,* Apostolic Fathers
Hist.	Herodotus or Tacitus, *Histories*
Hist. an.	Aristotle, *History of Animals*
Hist. eccl.	Eusebius or Sozomen, *Church History*
Hist. pass. Dom.	*History of the Lord's Passion.* Anonymous, fourteenth c.
Hist. Pelop. War	Thucydides, *History of the Peloponnesian War*
HNT	Handbuch zum Neuen Testament
Hom.	Homily/homilies
Hom. Jer.	Origen, *Homilies on Jeremiah*
Hom. Luc.	Origen, *Homilies on Luke*
Hos	Hosea
HTKNT	Herders theologischer Kommentar zum Neuen Testament
HTR	*Harvard Theological Review*
HTS	Harvard Theological Studies
HvTSt	*Hervormde teologiese studies*
ibid.	*ibidem,* in the same place
ICC	International Critical Commentary
IDB	*The Interpreter's Dictionary of the Bible.* Edited by G. Buttrick. 4 vols. plus suppl. Abingdon Press, 1962
Idol.	Tertullian, *Idolatry*
IEJ	*Israel Exploration Journal*
incl.	including
Inf. Gos. Thom.	*Infancy Gospel of Thomas,* NT Apocrypha and Pseudepigrapha
Int	*Interpretation*
Isa	Isaiah
IVP	InterVarsity Press
JAMA	*Journal of the American Medical Association*
Jas	James
JBL	*Journal of Biblical Literature*
JBR	*Journal of Bible and Religion*
JBTh	*Jahrbuch für Biblische Theologie*
Jdt	Judith, OT Apocrypha
Jer	Jeremiah

JerusalemPersp	*Jerusalem Perspective*
JETS	*Journal of the Evangelical Theological Society*
JJS	*Journal of Jewish Studies*
Jos. Asen.	*Joseph and Asenath,* OT Pseudepigrapha
Josh	Joshua
JSNT	*Journal for the Study of the New Testament*
JSNTSup	*Journal for the Study of the New Testament,* Supplement Series
JSP	*Journal for the Study of the Pseudepigrapha*
JTS	*Journal of Theological Studies*
Jub.	*Jubilees*
Judg	Judges
Jul.	Suetonius, "Deified Julius," *Lives of the Caesars*
J.W.	Josephus, *The Jewish War*
KEK	Kritisch-exegetischer Kommentar über das Neue Testament (Meyer-Kommentar)
kg	kilogram(s)
KJV	King James Version of the Bible
km	kilometer(s)
Lam	Lamentations
Lat.	Latin
LCL	Loeb Classical Library
LEC	Library of Early Christianity
Let. Aris.	*Letter of Aristeas,* OT Pseudepigrapha
Lev	Leviticus
Life	Josephus, *Life*
lit.	literally
LNTS	Library of New Testament Studies
LSJ	H. Liddell, R. Scott, J. Jones, and R. McKenzie. *A Greek-English Lexicon.* Oxford, 1968
LXX	Septuagint, Greek translation of Hebrew OT
m	meter(s)
m. 'Abot	*'Abot,* Mishnah
Magn.	Ignatius, *Letter to the Magnesians,* Apostolic Fathers.
Mal	Malachi
Marc.	Tertullian or Epiphanius, *Against Marcion*
Mart. Isa.	*Martyrdom of Isaiah,* OT Pseudepigrapha
Mart. Pol.	*Martyrdom of Polycarp,* Apostolic Fathers
Matt	Gospel of Matthew
m. B. Bat.	*Baba Batra,* Mishnah
m. Bek.	*Bekorot,* Mishnah
m. Ber.	*Berakot,* Mishnah
m. B. Qam.	*Baba Qamma,* Mishnah
Med.	Marcus Aurelius, *Meditations*
Mek. Exod.	*Mekilta on Exodus*

Mem.	Xenophon, *Memorabilia*
Mem. Apost.	*Memoria of Apostles,* NT Apocrypha and Pseudepigrapha
m. Giṭ.	*Giṭṭin,* Mishnah
m. Ḥag.	*Ḥagigah,* Mishnah
Mic	Micah
Midr. Esth.	*Midrash on Esther*
m. Kel.	*Kelim,* Mishnah
m. Ker.	*Keritot,* Mishnah
m. Ketub.	*Ketubbot,* Mishnah
m. Kil.	*Kil'ayim,* Mishnah
m. Menaḥ.	*Menaḥot,* Mishnah
m. Mid.	*Middot,* Mishnah
m. Miqw.	*Miqwa'ot,* Mishnah
m. Naz.	*Nazir,* Mishnah
m. Ned.	*Nedarim,* Mishnah
m. Neg.	*Nega'im,* Mishnah
m. Nid.	*Niddah,* Mishnah
m. 'Ohal.	*'Ohalot,* Mishnah
Mor.	Plutarch, *Moralia*
Mos.	Philo, *On the Life of Moses*
m. Pe'ah	*Pe'ah,* Mishnah
m. Pesaḥ.	*Pesaḥim,* Mishnah
m. Qidd.	*Qiddušin,* Mishnah
m. Roš Haš.	*Roš Haššanah,* Mishnah
m. Šabb.	*Šabbat,* Mishnah
m. Sanh.	*Sanhedrin,* Mishnah
m. Šebu.	*Šebu'ot,* Mishnah
m. Šeqal.	*Šeqalim,* Mishnah
m. Soṭah	*Soṭah,* Mishnah
m. Sukkah	*Sukkah,* Mishnah
MT	Masoretic Text
m. Ta'an.	*Ta'anit,* Mishnah
m. Tamid	*Tamid,* Mishnah
m. Ṭehar.	*Ṭeharot,* Mishnah
Mur. Can.	*Muratorian Canon*
m. Yad.	*Yadayim,* Mishnah
m. Yoma	*Yoma,* Mishnah
m. Zabim	*Zabim,* Mishnah
m. Zebaḥ.	*Zebaḥim,* Mishnah
n.	note/footnote
NAB	New American Bible
Nah	Nahum
Nat.	Pliny the Elder, *Natural History*
NCB	New Century Bible
n.d.	no date

NEB	New English Bible
Neh	Nehemiah
NIBC	New International Biblical Commentary
NICNT	New International Commentary on the New Testament
NIGTC	New International Greek Testament Commentary
NIV	New International Version of the Bible
NovT	*Novum Testamentum*
NovTSup	Supplements to *Novum Testamentum*
nr.	number
NRSV	New Revised Standard Version of the Bible
n.s.	new series
NT	New Testament
NTApoc.	*New Testament Apocrypha.* Edited by W. Schneemelcher. Translated by R. Mcl. Wilson. 2 vols. Rev. ed. James Clarke & Co.; Westminster/John Knox Press, 1991
NTD	Das Neue Testament Deutsch
NTS	*New Testament Studies*
NTTS	New Testament Tools and Studies
Num	Numbers
Obad	Obadiah
Od.	Homer, *Odyssey*
ODCC	*The Oxford Dictionary of the Christian Church*
Odes Sol.	*Odes of Solomon,* OT Pseudepigrapha
Or.	Origen, *On Prayer*
OT	Old Testament
OTP	*Old Testament Pseudepigrapha.* Edited by J. Charlesworth. 2 vols. Doubleday, 1985
p(p).	page(s)
Paed.	Clement of Alexandria, *Christ the Educator*
Pan.	Epiphanius, *Panarion*
par.	parallel(s)
Pelag.	Jerome, *Against the Pelagians, Three Dialogues*
PG	Patrologia graeca. Edited by J.-P. Migne. 162 vols. 1857-86
PGL	*Patristic Greek Lexicon.* Edited by G. W. H. Lampe. 1968.
Phd.	Plato, *Phaedo*
Phil	Philippians
Phil.	Polycarp, *To the Philippians,* Apostolic Fathers
Phld.	Ignatius, *To the Philadelphians,* Apostolic Fathers
Phlm	Philemon
PilNTC	Pillar New Testament Commentary
PNTC	Penguin New Testament Commentary
Pol.	Ignatius, *Letter to Polycarp,* Apostolic Fathers
P.Oxy.	Oxyrhynchus Papyrus
Pr Azar	Prayer of Azariah, OT Apocrypha
Princ.	Origen, *First Principles*

Pr Man	Prayer of Manasseh, OT Apocrypha
Prot. Jas.	*Protoevangelium of James,* NT Apocrypha and Pseudepigrapha
Protr.	Clement of Alexandria, *Exhortation to the Greeks*
Prov	Proverbs
Ps(s)	Psalm(s)
Ps.-Clem.	*Pseudo-Clementines,* NT Apocrypha and Pseudepigrapha
Pss. Sol.	*Psalms of Solomon,* OT Pseudepigrapha
QE 1	Philo, *Questions and Answers on Exodus 1*
Quis div.	Clement of Alexandria, *Salvation of the Rich Man*
R.	Rabbi
Rab. Exod.	*Rabbah on Exodus*
Rab. Lev.	*Rabbah on Leviticus*
Rab. Perd.	Cicero, *In Defense of Rabinius*
RB	*Revue Biblique*
Refut. Om. Haer.	Hippolytus, *Refutation of All Heresies*
Regn. Tyr.	Dio Chrysostom, *Kingship and Tyranny*
Rep.	Plato, *The Republic*
Rev	Revelation
rev.	revised
RevQ	*Revue de Qumran*
RIDA	*Revue internationale des droits de l'antiquité*
Rom	Romans
Rom.	Ignatius, *Letter to the Romans,* Apostolic Fathers
RSV	Revised Standard Version of the Bible
SBT	Studies in Biblical Theology
SciEsp	*Science et Esprit*
SHBC	Smyth and Helwys Biblical Commentary
Sib. Or.	*Sibylline Oracles*
Sipre Deut.	*Sifre on Deuteronomy*
Sir	Ecclesiasticus, or Wisdom of Jesus Ben-Sira, OT Apocrypha
SJLA	Studies in Judaism in Late Antiquity
SJT	*Scottish Journal of Theology*
Smyrn.	Ignatius, *Letter to the Smyrneans,* Apostolic Fathers
SNT(SU)	Studien zum Neuen Testament (und seiner Umwelt)
SNTSMS	Society for New Testament Studies Monograph Series
SP	Sacra Pagina
Spec.	Philo, *Special Laws*
SQE	*Synopsis Quattuor Evangeliorum.* Edited by K. Aland. 5th ed. Württemburgische Bibelanstalt, 1968.
Str-B	*Kommentar zum Neuen Testament aus dem Talmud und Midrasch.* Edited by H. Strack and P. Billerbeck. 6 vols. Beck Verlag, 1926
Strom.	Clement of Alexandria, *Miscellanies*
StudNeot	Studia Neotestamentica

Sull.	Plutarch, *Life of Sulla*
Sus	Susannah, OT Apocrypha
Sym.	Symmachus
Symp.	Plato or Xenophon, *Symposium*
T. Ab.	*Testament of Abraham,* OT Pseudepigrapha
T. Adam	*Testament of Adam,* OT Pseudepigrapha
TAVO	*Tübinger Atlas des Vorderen Orients* (Wiesbaden)
T. Benj.	*Testament of Benjamin,* OT Pseudepigrapha
t. B. Qam	*Baba Qamma,* Babylonian Talmud
TCGNT	B. Metzger. *A Textual Commentary on the Greek New Testament.* 2nd ed. United Bible Societies, 1994
T. Dan	*Testament of Dan,* OT Pseudepigrapha
TDNT	*Theological Dictionary of the New Testament.* Edited by G. Kittel and G. Friedrich. Translated by G. Bromiley. 9 vols. Eerdmans, 1964.
TDOT	*Theological Dictionary of the Old Testament.* Edited by G. Botterweck and H. Ringgren. 15 vols. Eerdmans, 1974-
Testim. Truth	*Testimony of Truth,* Nag Hammadi Codices
Tg. Isa.	*Targum of Isaiah*
Tg. Jon.	*Targum Jonathan*
Tg. Yer. 1	*Targum Yerusalmi 1*
θ	Theodotion version of the Septuagint
Theoph.	Eusebius, *Divine Manifestation*
THKNT	Theologische Handkommentar zum Neuen Testament
Thom. Cont.	*Book of Thomas the Contender,* Nag Hammadi Codices
Tib.	Suetonius, "Tiberius," *Lives of the Caesars*
T. Iss.	*Testament of Issachar,* OT Pseudepigrapha
T. Job	*Testament of Job,* OT Pseudepigrapha
T. Jud.	*Testament of Judah,* OT Pseudepigrapha
t. Kil.	*Kil'ayim,* Tosefta
T. Levi	*Testament of Levi,* OT Pseudepigrapha
TLG	Thesaurus Linguae Graecae
T. Mos.	*Testament of Moses,* OT Pseudepigrapha
T. Naph.	*Testament of Naphtali,* OT Pseudepigrapha
Tob	Tobit
Trad. Ap.	Hippolytus, *The Apostolic Tradition*
Trall.	Ignatius, *Letter to the Trallians,* Apostolic Fathers
trans.	translated (by), translator, translation
Treat. Res.	*Treatise on the Resurrection,* Nag Hammadi Codices
Treat. Seth	*Second Treatise of the Great Seth,* Nag Hammadi Codices
Tri. Trac.	*Tripartite Tractate,* Nag Hammadi Codices
TS	*Theological Studies*
T. Sim.	*Testament of Simeon,* OT Pseudepigrapha
T. Sol.	*Testament of Solomon,* OT Pseudepigrapha
t. Soṭah	*Soṭah,* Tosefta

TU	Texte und Untersuchungen
TWNT	*Theologisches Wörterbuch zum Neuen Testament.* Edited by
	G. Kittel and G. Friedrich. 9 vols. Stuttgart, 1932-79
TynBul	*Tyndale Bulletin*
TZ	*Theologische Zeitschrift*
T. Zeb.	*Testament of Zebulun,* OT Pseudepigrapha
UBS	United Bible Society
v(v).	verse(s)
Verr.	Cicero, *In Verrem*
Vir. ill.	Jerome, *The Lives of Illustrious Men*
Virt.	Philo, *On Virtue*
Vita	Josephus, *Life*
Vita Apol.	Philostratus, *Life of Apollonius*
Vita Pyth.	Iamblicus, *Life of Pythagoras*
vol(s).	volume(s)
WBC	Word Biblical Commentary
Wis	Wisdom of Solomon, OT Apocrypha
WordWorld	*Word and World*
WUNT	Wissenschaftliche Untersuchungen zum Neuen Testament
y. Ber.	*Berakot,* Jerusalem Talmud
y. Šebu.	*Šebuʿot,* Jerusalem Talmud
Zech	Zechariah
ZECS	Zondervan Exegetical Commentary Series
ZEE	*Zeitschrift für evangelische Ethik*
Zeph	Zephaniah
ZNW	*Zeitschrift für die neutestamentliche Wissenschaft*
ZTK	*Zeitschrift für Theologie und Kirche*

Frequently Cited Works

Bailey, Kenneth E. *Jesus through Middle Eastern Eyes: Cultural Studies in the Gospels.* Downers Grove: IVP Academic, 2008.

Barth, Karl. *Church Dogmatics.* Edited by G. Bromiley and T. Torrance. 13 vols. Edinburgh: T&T Clark, 1956-75.

Bengel, John Albert. *Gnomon of the New Testament.* Translated by Andrew Fausset. Edinburgh: T&T Clark, 1873.

Bock, Darrell L. *Luke 1:1–9:50.* BECNT. Grand Rapids: Baker Academic, 1994.

———. *Luke 9:51–24:53.* BECNT. Grand Rapids: Baker Academic, 1996.

Bovon, François. *Das Evangelium nach Lukas 1,1–9,50.* EKKNT 3/1. Zürich: Benziger/Neukirchener Verlag, 1989.

———. *Das Evangelium nach Lukas 9,51–14,35.* 2nd ed. EKKNT 3/2. Zürich: Neukirchener/Patmos Verlag, 2008.

———. *Das Evangelium nach Lukas 15,1–19,27.* EKKNT 3/3. Zürich: Neukirchener/Patmos Verlag, 2001.

———. *Das Evangelium nach Lukas 19,28–24:53.* EKKNT 3/4. Zürich: Neukirchener/Patmos Verlag, 2009.

———. *Luke 1: A Commentary on the Gospel of Luke 1:1–9:50.* Translated by Christine M. Thomas. Minneapolis: Fortress Press, 2002.

———. *Luke the Theologian. Fifty-Five Years of Research (1950-2005).* 2nd ed. Waco: Baylor University Press, 2006.

Brown, Raymond E. *The Birth of the Messiah: A Commentary on the Infancy Narratives in Matthew and Luke.* New York: Image, Doubleday, 1977.

———. *The Death of the Messiah: From Gethsemane to the Grave.* 2 vols. New York: Doubleday, 1994.

Cadbury, Henry J. *The Making of Luke-Acts.* Peabody: Hendrickson Publishers, 1999.

Caird, G. B. *Saint Luke.* PNTC. Middlesex: Penguin Books, 1963.

Dalman, Gustaf. *Sacred Sites and Ways: Studies in the Topography of the Gospels.* Translated by P. Levertoff. London: SCPC, 1935.

Deissmann, Adolf. *Light from the Ancient East.* Translated by L. Strachan. London: Hodder & Stoughton, 1927.

Denaux, Adelbert, Rita Corstjens, and Hellen Mardaga. *The Vocabulary of Luke: An Alphabetical Presentation and a Survey of Characteristic and Noteworthy Words and Word Groups in Luke's Gospel.* BiTS 10. Leuven: Peeters, 2009.

Edwards, James R. *The Gospel according to Mark*. PilNTC. Grand Rapids: Eerdmans, 2002.

———. *The Hebrew Gospel and the Development of the Synoptic Tradition*. Grand Rapids: Eerdmans, 2009.

Ellis, E. Earle. *The Gospel of Luke*. NCB. Greenwood: Attic Press, 1977.

Evans, Craig A. *Ancient Texts for New Testament Studies: A Guide to the Background Literature*. Peabody: Hendrickson Publishers, 2005.

———. *Luke*. NIBC. Peabody: Hendrickson Publishers, 1990.

Fitzmyer, Joseph A., S.J. *The Gospel according to Luke (I–IX)*. AB 28. Garden City: Doubleday, 1981.

———. *The Gospel according to Luke (X–XXIV)*. AB 28A. Garden City: Doubleday, 1985.

Freeman-Grenville, G. S. P., R. Chapman, and J. Taylor. *The Onomasticon by Eusebius of Caesarea*. Jerusalem: Carta, 2003.

García Martínez, Florentino, and Eibert J. C. Tigchelaar. *The Dead Sea Scrolls: Study Edition*. Leiden: Brill, 1997/98.

Garland, David E. *Zondervan Exegetical Commentary on the New Testament: Luke*. ZECS. Grand Rapids: Zondervan, 2011.

Geldenhuys, Norval. *Commentary on the Gospel of Luke*. NICNT. Grand Rapids: Eerdmans, 1993.

Green, Joel B. *The Gospel of Luke*. NICNT. Grand Rapids: Eerdmans, 1997.

Grundmann, Walter. *Das Evangelium nach Lukas*. THKNT 3. Berlin: Evangelische Verlagsanstalt, 1974.

Harnack, Adolf von. *Luke the Physician*. London: Williams & Norgate, 1908.

Hengel, Martin. *The Four Gospels and the One Gospel of Jesus Christ*. Translated by J. Bowden. Harrisburg: Trinity Press International, 2000.

Isaak, John Paul. "Luke." In *Africa Bible Commentary*. Nairobi: WordAlive Publishers, 2006.

Jeremias, Joachim. *Jerusalem in the Time of Jesus*. Translated by F. H. and C. H. Cave. Philadelphia: Fortress Press, 1989.

———. *Die Sprache des Lukasevangeliums*. KEK. Göttingen: Vandenhoeck & Ruprecht, 1980.

Johnson, Luke Timothy. *The Gospel of Luke*. SP 3. Collegeville: Liturgical Press, 1991.

Just, Arthur A., Jr. *Luke*. ACCS 3. Downers Grove: InterVarsity Press, 2003.

Kealy, Sean P. *The Interpretation of the Gospel of Luke*. Vol. 1: *From Apostolic Times through the Nineteenth Century*. SBEC 63. Lewiston: Edwin Mellen Press, 2005.

Keck, Leander E., and J. Louis Martyn, eds. *Studies in Luke-Acts*. Nashville: Abingdon Press, 1966.

Klein, Hans. *Das Lukasevangelium*. KEK I/3. Göttingen: Vandenhoeck & Ruprecht, 2006.

Klostermann, Erich. *Das Lukasevangelium*. 3rd ed. HNT 5. Tübingen: Mohr Siebeck, 1975.

Lagrange, M.-J. *Évangile selon Saint Luc*. 2nd ed. Paris: J. Gabalda, 1921.

Lampe, G. W. H. *A Patristic Greek Lexicon*. Oxford: Clarendon Press, 1961.

Leaney, A. R. C. *The Gospel according to St Luke*. 2nd ed. BNTC. London: Adam & Charles Black, 1976.

Lohmeyer, Ernst. *Das Evangelium des Markus*. Göttingen: Vandenhoeck & Ruprecht, 1953.

Marshall, I. Howard. *The Gospel of Luke: A Commentary on the Greek Text*. NIGTC. Grand Rapids: Eerdmans, 1978.

Metzger, Bruce M. *A Textual Commentary on the Greek New Testament.* 2nd ed. Stuttgart: Deutsche Bibelgesellschaft, 1994.

Moessner, David P. *Lord of the Banquet: The Literary and Theological Significance of the Lukan Travel Narrative.* Harrisburg: Trinity Press International, 1989.

Murphy-O'Connor, Jerome. *The Holy Land: An Archaeological Guide from Earliest Times to 1700.* 4th ed. Oxford: Oxford University Press, 1998.

Neyrey, Jerome H., ed. *The Social World of Luke-Acts: Models for Interpretation.* Peabody: Hendrickson Publishers, 1991.

Nolland, John. *Luke 1:1–9:20.* WBC 35A. Dallas: Word Books, 1993.

———. *Luke 9:21–18:34.* WBC 35B. Dallas: Word Books, 1993.

———. *Luke 18:35–24:53.* WBC 35C. Dallas: Word Books, 1993.

Origen. *Homilies on Luke.* Translated by Joseph T. Lienhard, S.J. FC 94. Washington, D.C.: Catholic University of America Press, 1996.

Orton, David E., ed. *The Composition of Luke's Gospel: Selected Studies from Novum Testamentum.* Leiden: Brill, 1999.

Pixner, Bargil, O.S.B. *Mit Jesus in Jerusalem. Seine ersten und letzten Tage in Judäa.* Rosh Pina: Corazin Publishing, 1996.

———. *With Jesus through Galilee according to the Fifth Gospel.* Translated by C. Botha and D. Foster. Rosh Pina: Corazin Publishing, 1992.

Plummer, Alfred. *A Critical and Exegetical Commentary on the Gospel according to S. Luke.* 5th ed. ICC. Edinburgh: T&T Clark, 1900.

Rengstorf, Karl Heinrich. *Das Evangelium nach Lukas.* NTD 3. Göttingen: Vandenhoeck & Ruprecht, 1937.

Rowe, C. Kavin. *Early Narrative Christology: The Lord in the Gospel of Luke.* Grand Rapids: Baker Academic, 2009.

Schlatter, Adolf. *Das Evangelium des Lukas. Aus seinen Quellen erklärt.* Stuttgart: Calwer Verlag, 1960.

———. *Die Evangelien nach Markus und Lukas.* Erläuterung zum Neuen Testament 2. Stuttgart: Calwer Verlag, 1961.

Schürer, Emil. *The History of the Jewish People in the Age of Jesus Christ.* Edited by G. Vermes, F. Millar, M. Black, and P. Vermes. 4 vols. Edinburgh: T&T Clark, 1993.

Schürmann, Heinz. *Das Lukasevangelium 1,1–9,50.* HTKNT 3. Freiburg: Herder, 1969.

Schweizer, Eduard. *Das Evangelium nach Lukas.* NTD 3. Göttingen: Vandenhoeck & Ruprecht, 1982.

Smyth, H. W. *Greek Grammar.* Rev. G. Messing. Cambridge: Harvard University Press, 1984.

Synopsis Quattuor Evangeliorum. Edited by K. Aland. 5th ed. Stuttgart: Württembergische Bibelanstalt, 1968.

Talbert, Charles. *Reading Luke: A Literary and Theological Commentary on the Third Gospel.* New York: Crossroad, 1982.

Tannehill, Robert C. *Luke.* ANTC. Nashville: Abingdon Press, 1996.

———. *The Narrative Unity of Luke-Acts: A Literary Interpretation.* Vol. 1: *The Gospel according to Luke.* Philadelphia: Fortress Press, 1986.

Vinson, Richard B. *Luke.* SHBC. Macon: Smyth & Helwys, 2008.

Wolter, Michael. *Das Lukasevangelium.* HNT 5. Tübingen: Mohr Siebeck, 2008.

Zahn, Theodor. *Das Evangelium des Lukas.* 4th ed. Leipzig: Deichert Verlag, 1930.

Introduction

The Gospel of Luke begins with a personal testimony of its author, and I should like to claim the same precedent at the outset of this commentary. It is my understanding that Luke understands Jesus of Nazareth to be the incarnation of the eternal God within human history, who was sent "in the fullness of time" in fulfillment of God's promises to Israel, and that his death as the righteous Servant of God effects the salvation of both Jews and Gentiles, to which the church — which Luke treats in his sequel in Acts — bears saving witness. I have sought to write an understandable and, when possible, insightful exposition of this wonderful evangelical narrative by following a narrow ridge between exegesis and interpretation. With regard to the former, I attempt to give adequate attention to data that make the text as intelligible as possible, and with regard to the latter, to consider the data in terms of their potential meaning for faith and discipleship. The Gospel is determined by both historical and theological purposes, and its proper understanding and interpretation require attention to both purposes. Through these, God's inspiring breath and providential hand were and are manifested to accomplish their divine purpose in Jesus, the Messiah and Son of God. May those who read Luke's story of Jesus concur with the two disciples at Emmaus, "Did not our hearts burn within us as Jesus talked with us on the way and opened to us the Scriptures?" (Luke 24:32).

Important thematic issues related to the Third Gospel, which otherwise might appear in the Introduction, are discussed in **excursuses** at relevant points in the commentary. These include discussions of Luke's infancy narratives (1:5) and the relation of the infancy narratives to the body of the Third Gospel (2:46-52), Pharisees (5:17), Son of Man (5:26), Luke's use of Elijah-Elisha typology in his presentation of Jesus' Galilean ministry (7:15-17), Christ/Messiah (9:18-21), the mission of Jesus as the way of salvation (9:51), Jerusalem in the Third Gospel (13:34-35), Luke's use of pairs, and especially male-female pairs, in the Gospel (14:1), Son of God (22:66-71), Herod Antipas and Pontius Pilate (23:1), and Luke's depiction of the universal scope of the gospel (24:44-49). Many

1

additional historical, exegetical, and geographic subthemes are identified in **bold** print and discussed more briefly at relevant points in the commentary.

The Introduction proper will address textual, linguistic, and historical issues that I consider important for understanding the Third Gospel. These include the testimony to the Gospel of Luke in early Christianity, questions related to Lukan authorship, date and place of composition, Luke's use of sources, the narrative structure of the Gospel, and an epilogue on Marcion.

1. TESTIMONY OF EARLY CHRISTIANITY
TO THE GOSPEL OF LUKE

The earliest certain references to the Third Gospel occur in the first half of the second century. Seven quotations in *2 Clem.* are close enough in wording to assume their derivation from Luke. *2 Clem.* is usually assigned a date of post-120, thus indicating that Luke was known and quoted by the first half of the second century.[1] At roughly the same time, Marcion (d. ca. 160) was excommunicated from the church in Rome for producing a violently altered version of the Third Gospel (see **9. Epilogue on Marcion**, pp. 19-22). Marcion's choice of Luke from among the other three Gospels presupposes a fourfold Gospel tradition established well before his time, and certainly in Rome, where he taught. In the wake of Marcion's mutilation of Luke — and often in reaction to it — a chorus of voices in the latter half of the second century either mention the Third Gospel or quote from it, including Irenaeus (ca. 130-200; *Haer.* 3.1; 3.14), Justin Martyr (ca. 100-165; *1 Apol.* 34; *Dial.* 78, 88, 100, 103, 105, 106), Tatian (d. ca. 160; Diatessaron), Clement of Alexandria (ca. 150-215; *Strom.* 1.1), Tertullian (ca. 160-225; throughout *Marc.*), and the *Mur. Can.* (ca. 170-80). Second-century antagonists of Christianity, including Celsus (Origen, *Cels.* 2.32) and the gnostics Basilides and Valentinus (Clement of Alexandria, *Strom.* 4.9), were also acquainted with the Third Gospel.

From Irenaeus onward the four symbolical creatures of Rev 4:6-7 and Ezek 1:4-21 surrounding the throne of God in heaven — the lion, ox, man, and eagle — were interpreted with reference to the Gospels. Whether the Seer of

---

1. *2 Clem.* 2:4 → Luke 5:32; *2 Clem.* 3:2 → Luke 12:8; *2 Clem.* 4:2 → Luke 6:46; *2 Clem.* 6:1 → Luke 16:13; *2 Clem.* 6:2 → Luke 9:25; *2 Clem.* 9:11 → Luke 8:21; *2 Clem.* 13:4 → Luke 6:27, 28, 32. See W. Pratscher, *The Apostolic Fathers: An Introduction* (Waco: Baylor University Press, 2010), 76. Bock, *Luke 1:1–9:50,* 5, sees allusions to Luke in *1 Clem.* 13:2 and 48:4 (46:8 could be added). If Bock is correct, these would be references to the Third Gospel in the late first century (*1 Clem.* was written ca. 95). I am not persuaded, however, that the verbal similarity in these three allusions in *1 Clem.* is close enough to the corresponding passages in Luke to argue for their reliance on Luke. The degree of verbal similarity could also derive from similar oral tradition.

the Revelation intended the four creatures to signify the Gospels cannot be proven, but the four creatures reappear in Rev 5:6-8 with reference to the Lamb holding a book, which corresponds coincidentally if not intentionally with the function of the Gospels. Three of the creatures are variously ascribed to Matt, Mark, and John, but throughout church history the ox (or calf) is consistently ascribed to the Third Gospel. According to Irenaeus, the ox, like the fatted calf sacrificed at the return of the Prodigal Son, signified "the sacrificial and sacerdotal order" of the Son of God (*Haer.* 3.11.8).

Another reference of Irenaeus is among the earliest and most important to the Gospel of Luke:

> Matthew also issued a written Gospel among the Hebrews in their own dialect, while Peter and Paul were preaching in Rome, and laying the foundations of the Church. After their departure, Mark, the disciple and interpreter of Peter, also handed down to us in writing what had been preached by Peter. Luke also, the companion of Paul, recorded in a book the gospel preached by him. Afterwards, John, the disciple of the Lord, who also had leaned on his breast, himself published a Gospel during his residence at Ephesus in Asia (*Haer.* 3.1.1).

Irenaeus is not announcing a new conclusion about the Gospels, but appealing to a tradition established much earlier, perhaps even in the late first century. In response to the novelty — and heresy — of Marcion's expurgated text of Luke, Irenaeus resorts to a precedent from antiquity, namely, the fourfold Gospel tradition, which for him and all authoritative proponents of the orthodox tradition was an established and unalterable article of Christian faith. Also important in Irenaeus's report is the order of the Gospels, which corresponds to the chronological order of their composition: Hebrew Matthew written first (the name "Matthew" may have been later transferred to the First Gospel), followed by Mark, Luke, and John. This order is retained by Origen in the third century, by Eusebius and Athanasius in the fourth, and by nearly all later church fathers, as well as by the great uncial manuscripts of the fourth and fifth centuries, including Codex Vaticanus (B), Sinaiticus (א), Alexandrinus (A), and Ephraemi (C). A revised "Western order" (Matt, John, Luke, Mark) arises in the third century but does not prevail over the tradition identified with Irenaeus, which determined the sequence of the Gospels in subsequent Christian history.[2] In both orders Luke remains, literally, the "Third Gospel," composed after and indebted to its two predecessors, the Hebrew Gospel of Matthew and Mark.[3]

---

2. On the testimony of Irenaeus and the "Western order," see Hengel, *The Four Gospels,* 38-47.

3. Only in Codex Claromontanus (D 06) and the so-called Cheltenham-Canon (both from the 4th c.) does Luke appear fourth in the Gospel sequence.

Luke is the third Gospel in other respects as well. It is the third most frequently quoted Gospel in the early church — quoted less frequently than Matt and John, but more frequently than Mark. It is the third most frequently expounded commentary among the Fathers, expounded less frequently than Matt and John, but more frequently than Mark. Origen (185-254), Ambrose (339-97), and Cyril of Jerusalem (375-444) all left Greek commentaries on the Third Gospel, and a fourth in Latin from late antiquity stems from the Venerable Bede (673-735). The Greek text of Luke is also the third best attested in the NT, better than Mark, but not as well attested as Matt and John.[4] With respect to textual attestation, the oldest extant manuscript witness to Luke, $\mathfrak{p}^4$ (ca. 200), preserves excerpts of Luke 1–6; and $\mathfrak{p}^{75}$ (also ca. 200) contains substantial portions of the entire Gospel, as does $\mathfrak{p}^{45}$ (slightly later in the third c.). The earliest complete copies of Luke appear in the great uncial parchments of the fourth and fifth centuries: Codex Sinaiticus (ℵ), Alexandrinus (A), Vaticanus (B [but with significant lacunae]), and Ephraemi (C).

2. TITLE OF THE GOSPEL

It was customary in Jewish synagogue services to preface sacred readings by their titles or names of authors as verification of their authenticity and authority. An anonymous sacred text, according to Martin Hengel, was something of a contradiction in terms, for an unprovenanced text that lacked a name guaranteeing its authority was an uninspired text.[5] The name of the author of the Third Gospel is not given in the Gospel itself, nor can it be derived by implication from the Gospel (something true of all four Gospels). We have no evidence, however, that the Third Gospel circulated anonymously (something also true of all four Gospels). Its earliest title appears at the end of papyrus $\mathfrak{p}^{75}$ — *Euangelion kata Loukan,* "Gospel according to Luke." This same title identifies the Gospel in nearly all uncial manuscripts either at the beginning (D K L W Γ Δ Θ Ξ Ψ) or end (ℵ A) of the Gospel. Codex Vaticanus (B), in contrast, entitles the Gospel simply *kata Loukan* at the end of the text, and both Vaticanus and Sinaiticus include the same abbreviated title at the head of each codex page.[6] The important point in these titles is that all contain the name "Luke," and as far as we know, the Third Gospel never circulated

---

4. See Kealy, *Interpretation of the Gospel of Luke,* 28.

5. Hengel, *The Four Gospels,* 37.

6. The Third Gospel is entitled "The Holy Gospel according to Luke" in two minuscule manuscripts (seventh and thirteenth c.) and "The Beginning of the Gospel according to Luke" in a twelfth-c. minuscule.

under any name other than "Luke."[7] This is more significant than it might appear, for, unlike the First and Fourth Gospels, which circulated under the names of apostles, the Second and Third Gospels circulated under the names of nonapostles. It is unlikely that the early church would have assigned authorship of a Gospel to a nonapostle — i.e., to an "uncredentialed" author — unless he was known to be its author.[8]

3. AUTHORSHIP

3.1. Lukan Authorship

Greek *Loukas* is a shortened form of both Greek *Loukios* and Latin *Lucanus*.[9] The identity of the bearer of this name must be gleaned from three NT references and a half-dozen patristic references.[10] The NT references occur in lists of acquaintances at the conclusion of Pauline letters. In Col 4:14 Luke is called "beloved physician," in Phlm 24 Paul names Luke in a list of "fellow workers," and in 2 Tim 4:10-11 Paul writes that "only Luke is with me." All three references place Luke in Paul's company when he is in prison. With minor exceptions, this meager information is repeated among patristic writers in the first four Christian centuries. On two points the witness to Luke from NT and patristic sources is unanimous. First, none of the sources claims that Luke was an apostle or knew Jesus "in the flesh." The testimony to Luke in all sources assumes, and in some instances explicitly states (*Mur. Can.;* Tertullian, *Marc.* 4.2.2), that Luke's Gospel was indebted to the testimony of others rather than to personal experience of its author.

The second and most constitutive patristic datum is that Luke was a follower and long-time traveling companion of Paul (*Mur. Can.;* Tertullian, *Marc.* 4.2.2; Eusebius, *Hist. eccl.* 3.4.6; Jerome, *Vir. ill.* 7.1), who was praised by Paul (Origen, *Comm. Matt.* [Eusebius, *Hist. eccl.* 6.25.6]) but also inferior to

7. On the titles of the Gospels and the theory of anonymous circulation, see Hengel, *The Four Gospels*, 48-56.

8. See F. F. Bruce, *The Acts of the Apostles: The Greek Text, with Introduction and Commentary* (Grand Rapids: Eerdmans, 1951; repr., 1984), 4.

9. See Deissmann, *Light from the Ancient East*, 435; Lagrange, *Luc*, 1; Fitzmyer, *Luke (I–IX)*, 42.

10. Col 4:14; 2 Tim 4:11; Phlm 24; *Mur. Can.* (ca. 170-80); Irenaeus (130-200; *Haer.* 3.1.14); Tertullian (160-225; *Marc.* 4.2.2); *Anti-Marc. Prolog.* (early 3rd c.); Origen (185-254; *Comm. Matt.* [cited in Eusebius, *Hist. eccl.* 6.25.6); Eusebius (ca. 260-340; *Hist. eccl.* 3.4.6-7); Jerome (345-419; *Vir. ill.* 7). For original Greek and Latin texts of the patristic sources, see *SQE* 532-48.

him (Tertullian, *Marc.* 4.2.2). Irenaeus describes the bond between Luke and Paul as "inseparable." Theodor Zahn was surely correct in concluding that Marcion would never have adopted Luke as his preferred Gospel had not its author been acknowledged as the protégé of Paul.[11] Irenaeus is also the first to contend that the "we"-passages in Acts (16:10-17; 20:5-15; 21:1-18; 27:1–28:16) document Luke's attendance in the Pauline mission (*Haer.* 3.14.1).[12] Following this lead, Eusebius and Jerome report that Luke wrote the Gospel on the basis of what he had heard, but Acts on the basis of what he had seen. So indebted was Luke to Paul for the content of the Gospel, declare Eusebius and Jerome, that Pauline references to "my gospel" (Rom 2:16; 16:25; 2 Tim 2:8) should be understood as references to the Gospel of Luke rather than to Paul's proclamation (Eusebius, *Hist. eccl.* 3.4.7; Jerome, *Vir. ill.* 7.4). This final claim appears fanciful, for Paul seldom references the historical Jesus in his epistles. Indeed, he is indifferent to such (2 Cor 5:16), for the gospel was revealed to him by the exalted Jesus (Gal 1:12).

Modern scholars sometimes challenge Luke's association with Paul on the grounds that characteristic features of Pauline theology, especially regarding natural theology, the law, Christology, and eschatology, are either muted or absent from the profile of Paul in Acts. Others have responded to this challenge more completely than I can afford to here.[13] I would suggest only that the differences between the Paul of Acts and the Paul of the epistles, although not essential, may in fact argue in favor of Luke's association with Paul.[14] Moderns know Paul primarily from his epistles, and hence as a theologian, whereas Luke knew a Paul who is no longer accessible to moderns — Paul the pastor and charismatic founder of Christian communities on the mission field.[15] This latter perspective prevails in Acts, doubtless due to Luke's experience of Paul on the mission field.

Further information about Luke, though not unanimous, emerges from

---

11. Zahn, *Lukas*, 2.

12. In the *Purgatorio* (canto 29, lines 133-41), Dante places Luke and Paul as climactic counterparts in the Heavenly Pageant. Following the church triumphant, the Griffon (symbol of Christ as both divine and human), the three theological virtues and four cardinal virtues, and the seven elders (symbols of the remaining books of the NT), "come two, side by side / different in dress, but both / by the same massive bearing dignified. / One showed he was a follower of the art / of great Hippocrates, whom Nature made / to heal the creatures dearest to her heart. / The other, his counterpart, carried a blade / so sharp and bright that at the sight of it, / even across the stream, I was afraid" (John Ciardi trans.).

13. See, e.g., Ellis, *Luke,* 44-51; Fitzmyer, *Luke (I–IX),* 47-51.

14. Ellis, *Luke,* 50, makes the important observation that one who knew Paul, as did Luke, would be more likely to offer an independent testimony to the apostle than would a postapostolic admirer.

15. An insight suggested by M. Hengel, *Between Paul and Jesus* (Philadelphia: Fortress Press, 1983), 110.

patristic witnesses. It is widely agreed that Luke consulted with "other apostles" in addition to Paul in the writing of his Gospel, as he testifies in his prologue (1:2; Irenaeus [*Haer.* 3.14.1], *Anti-Marc. Prolog.,* Eusebius [*Hist. eccl.* 3.4.6], Jerome [*Vir. ill.* 7.5], perhaps Tertullian [*Marc.* 4.2.2]). It is also assumed and often acknowledged that the Book of Acts is Luke's sequel to the Gospel (Irenaeus [*Haer.* 3.14.1], *Anti-Marc. Prolog.,* Eusebius [*Hist. eccl.* 2.22.1; 3.4.6], Jerome [*Vir. ill.* 7.2]). Several Fathers agree that Luke was a physician, as Col. 4:14 attests (*Mur. Can., Anti-Marc. Prolog.,* Eusebius [*Hist. eccl.* 3.4.6], and Jerome [*Vir. ill.* 7.1]). Finally, *Anti-Marc. Prolog.,* Eusebius (*Hist. eccl.* 3.4.6), and Jerome (*Vir. ill.* 7.1) identify Luke as a native of Antioch. This final point is the first datum presented so far that is not supplied in the NT references or reasonably deducible from the "we"-passages in Acts.[16]

3.2. Comparison of External Testimony of the Early Church to Internal Evidence in Luke-Acts

The foregoing details generally correlate positively with the Third Gospel. The Lukan prologue declares what is echoed throughout the patristic testimony, that Luke was not an apostle nor personally present during the ministry of Jesus, but dependent for his information in the Gospel on others who were "eye-witnesses and servants of the word" (1:2). Luke's association with Paul can be similarly corroborated. By Pauline testimony, Luke is thrice identified in his entourage (Col 4:14; Phlm 24; 2 Tim 4:11), and the "we"-passages in Acts are still best explained as personal testimony of Luke, perhaps even from his travel diary.[17] We will see numerous points in the commentary where the vocabulary, themes, and theological emphases of the Third Gospel exhibit notable and sometimes unmistakable correspondences with Pauline literature. Luke-Acts thus offers significant internal evidence in support of the early Christian consensus of Luke's association with Paul.

That the Book of Acts is a sequel to the Third Gospel remains a virtually assured result of Christian scholarship, ancient and modern. Both volumes are addressed to "Theophilus" (1:3; Acts 1:1), Acts references the Third Gospel as its prequel (Acts 1:1), the vocabulary of Luke-Acts can be ascribed to the

---

16. Codex Bezae (D) introduces a "we"-passage (italicized) at Acts 11:28, "In these days prophets came down from Jerusalem to Antioch. *And there was much rejoicing. When we gathered together,* one of the prophets named Agabus said. . . ." If "we"-passages refer to Luke, this passage associates him with Antioch. If Eusebius and Jerome derived the association of Luke with Antioch from a version of Acts represented by Codex Bezae, this detail would also derive from the NT.

17. For a critical discussion and defense of the "we"-passages as a reference to Luke, see Tannehill, *Luke,* 21-24.

same author with a high degree of statistical probability, and the thematic and organizational development of both documents exhibit numerous parallels that argue in favor of a single author. That Luke was a physician may also be reasonably assumed. This particular datum derives from Col 4:14 and is reaffirmed in *Mur. Can.,* Jerome, and Eusebius. More than a century ago Harnack asserted that whole narratives in the Third Gospel are determined by medical themes, and that many stories and much vocabulary of the Third Evangelist are colored by medical and technical terminology.[18] This overstates the case considerably.[19] Nevertheless, challenges to Luke's medical profession are invariably directed to overstatements or degree of certainty rather than to the datum itself.[20] That Luke was a doctor cannot be proven, nor would his being so materially affect our understanding of the Gospel. Nevertheless, details in the descriptions of illnesses and healings in the Third Gospel, and the unsentimental sensitivity with which Jesus attends the sick, are what we would expect from a medical professional.

3.3. Luke: Jew or Gentile?

It is commonly assumed that Luke is the only Gentile author in the NT.[21] Fewer biblical data have been more widely assumed on the basis of less evidence than this particular datum. Occasional patristic sources report that Luke wrote for Gentile converts (*Anti-Marc. Prolog.,* Origen [*Comm. Matt.,* cited in Eusebius, *Hist. eccl.* 6.25.6]), but only Jerome (*Vir. ill.* 7.1) implies that Luke was a Gentile. He does so by identifying Luke as the unnamed brother of Titus in 2 Cor 8:18, the latter of whom was a Gentile (Gal 2:3). This would obviously make Luke a Gentile and settle the matter. Paul does not identify Luke as the brother of Titus in 2 Cor 8:18, however, and Jerome offers no evidence for his assertion of such. This seems to relegate this particular testimony to the category of conjecture. The otherwise wholesale silence in the patristic tradition on Luke's ethnicity could be taken as an argument in favor of Luke's Jewishness, for if he were Jewish, as were all other NT authors, it would be unremarkable and thus go unmentioned. It would be difficult to imagine the Fathers leaving

18. Harnack, *Luke the Physician,* esp. 175-98.

19. E.g., "Very nearly all of the alterations and additions which the third evangelist has made in the Markan text are most simply and surely explained from the professional interest of a physician" (*Luke the Physician,* 187).

20. So H. Cadbury, *The Style of Literary Method of Luke* (HTS 6; Cambridge: Harvard University Press, 1920).

21. Note W. Kümmel's wholesale assertion, "Upon the basis of the Gospel of Luke, only one thing can be said with certainty about its author — he was a Gentile Christian" (*Introduction to the New Testament*[14] [Nashville: Abingdon Press, 1966], 104-5).

unmentioned his Gentile ethnicity, however, which would distinguish him from all other NT authors.

The sole NT datum on which the assumption of Luke's Gentile ethnicity rests is an inference in Col. In Col 4:10-11 the author lists Aristarchus; Mark, the cousin of Barnabas; Jesus, called Justus, as "being of the circumcision [group]," i.e., Jews. Immediately following in vv. 12-13 Epaphras is introduced as "one of you, the servant of Christ," commending him for his dedicated and sacrificial service on behalf of the Colossians. "One of you" ostensibly means "one of you *Gentiles*," thus differentiating Epaphras from the three Jews mentioned in vv. 10-11. In v. 14 the greetings conclude with reference to "Luke, the beloved physician, and Demas." The argument that Luke was a Gentile is made on the basis of association with Epaphras: since Epaphras is identified as Gentile (v. 12), the names that follow (Luke and Demas) are also reckoned Gentile. This may be a justifiable inference, but it is not a necessary inference, for unlike the foregoing names (Aristarchus, Mark, Jesus [Justus], and Epaphras), the ethnicity of Luke and Demas is not specified. Moreover, in Phlm 23-24 Paul again mentions Epaphras, Mark, Aristarchus, Demas, and Luke as either fellow prisoners or fellow workers, but with no reference to their ethnicities. In 2 Tim 4:10-11 Paul again mentions Demas, Luke, and Mark, along with three other names, again without reference to ethnicities. The indifference to ethnicity in these last two passages raises questions about its exactness in the first passage. The case is further complicated by mention of *Loukios* (NIV, "Lucius") in Acts 13:1 and Rom 16:21. *Loukas,* it will be recalled, is a shortened form of *Loukios.* If *Loukios* refers to the same *Loukas* in Col 4:14, 2 Tim 4:11, and Phlm 24, then the case for Luke's Gentile ethnicity is scuttled, for in Rom 16:21 *Loukios* is identified as a "fellow Jew." Origen (*Comm. Rom.* 10:39) and Ephrem the Syrian (*Comm. Acts* 12:25–13:3) accepted the *Loukios* of Rom 16:21 as the same *Loukas* who traveled with Paul and authored the Third Gospel. *Loukios* and *Loukas* may not be the same person, of course. It might be asked why Paul would refer to the same person by two different names. This is a fair question, but it does not settle the question, for in multilingual first-century Palestinian culture, it was not uncommon to refer to the same person by different names (e.g., Peter/Cephas in Gal 2:7, 9).

The inference of Col 4:10-14 that Luke was a Gentile is thus far from secure. It is further complicated by the testimony of Epiphanius (*Pan.* 51.11.6), who identified Luke as one of the seventy(-two) Jews sent out by Jesus in Luke 10. The historical value of this witness may be debatable, but the fact remains that three Fathers (Origen, Ephrem, and Epiphanius) specify Luke's Jewishness, and only Jerome suggests his Gentile ethnicity. Moreover, and more important from my perspective, is the fact that the most constitutive element of the Third Gospel is its portrayal of Jesus as the fulfillment of God's sovereign mission to Israel. In contrast to the popular conception of Luke as the Gentile/

Greek Gospel, the primary purpose of the Third Gospel is to present Jesus as Messiah, and thus Israel's long-awaited savior, into whom Gentiles are also engrafted. The Third Gospel is characterized, moreover, by pronounced and repeated reliance on Hebraisms in its construction (see **7. Luke's Sources**). Hengel observes that no ancient non-Jewish author reports on Judaism, Jewish worship in synagogue and temple, and Jewish practices and parties with greater knowledge, accuracy, and positiveness than does Luke.[22] To be sure, this does not necessitate Luke being a Jew. (Hengel himself regards Luke a Gentile.) A Gentile outsider might penetrate to the essence of Israel in a way that a Jewish insider might miss because of its familiarity. Especially if Luke was tutored by Paul, he would share Paul's conviction of Jesus' fulfillment of the divine plan in the fullness of time (Gal 4:4). The above evidence and arguments are thus not conclusive against Luke being a Gentile, but they seem to argue more decidedly for his being a Jew. At the very least, the Gentile birth certificate that has so freely been issued to Luke in popular tradition should be reconsidered in light of the above.[23]

3.4. The Tradition of Luke as Artist

In the Middle Ages, Luke emerged as patron saint of artists and painters. The association of an apostle with the enterprise of art may have influenced the development of Christian art in the West much more than is recognized. The tradition antedates the Middle Ages, however. A fourteenth-century writer, Nicephoros Kallistos, attributed to a sixth-century Byzantine, Theodoros Anagnostes (Lector), the memory that "an image of the Mother of God [was] painted by the apostle Luke."[24] An ancient picture of the Virgin that has been in the Church of Santa Maria Maggiore in Rome since 1204, when it was brought there following the sack of Constantinople in the Fourth Crusade, has some claim to being the image attested by Theodoros. All known portraits attributed to Luke portray him painting the Virgin Mary. The many Byzantine images of

---

22. M. Hengel, "Zur urchristlichen Geschichtsschreibung," in *Studien zum Urchristentum (Kleine Schriften VI)* (WUNT 234; Tübingen: Mohr Siebeck, 2008), 51.

23. For arguments in favor of Luke's Gentile ethnicity, see Plummer, *Luke*, xvii-xx; J. B. Lightfoot, *Saint Paul's Epistles to the Colossians and to Philemon* (Grand Rapids: Zondervan, n.d.), 241; Fitzmyer, *Luke (I–IX),* 41-47. For arguments in favor of Luke's Jewishness, see Deissmann, *Light from the Ancient East*, 435-38; Ellis, *Luke*, 51-53; R. Martin, *Colossians* (Grand Rapids: Zondervan, 1972), 146; J. Jervell, *Die Apostelgeschichte* (KEK 3; Göttingen: Vandenhoeck & Ruprecht, 1998), 50ff.; M. Parsons, "Who Wrote the Gospel of Luke?" *BRev* 17/2 (2001): 12-20; Wolter, *Lukasevangelium*, 9-10. Older scholars who favored Luke's Jewishness are A. Schlatter, B. Reicke, W. F. Albright, E. C. Selwyn, B. S. Easton, A. H. McNeile, and C. F. Burney.

24. PG 86:165.

the Madonna and Child attributed to him indicate that the tradition of Luke as artist was established by late antiquity. Precisely why Luke is remembered as patron of artists is unknown. The suggestion that the association derives from his literary artistry, and especially his use of verbal imagery in parables and illustrations, is worthy of consideration.[25]

4. DATE OF COMPOSITION

The date of composition is neither given nor suggested in the Third Gospel. Information regarding dating must be tentatively inferred from Luke-Acts. The Lukan prologue mentions the existence of many accounts prior to the Gospel (1:1), and it can be taken for near-certain that the Gospel of Mark, which can be dated to approximately 65 (plus or minus five years), was one of these accounts. The Third Gospel must have been written later than that date, but how much later cannot be said with any degree of certainty.

A case for an early date shortly after Mark is made on the basis (1) that the two passages in Luke that mention the fall of Jerusalem (19:43-44; 21:20-24) do not reflect the actual conditions of the Jewish War in 66-70; (2) that the use of the present tense in Acts 6:13-14 indicates the temple was still standing when Stephen was stoned; and (3) that Acts concludes while Paul is still alive. These data are cited in favor of a pre-70 date of composition of both Luke and Acts.[26] These arguments, neither separately nor combined, seem persuasive. The references to the fall of Jerusalem in Luke 19 and 21 seem to many, myself included, to betray particulars of the Jewish War of 66-70. The present tense in Acts 6:13-14 quite plausibly refers to the time reference of Stephen's martyrdom rather than to Luke's authorship. With reference to the dating of Luke, it is difficult to know how much weight should be ascribed to the fact that Acts concludes with Paul alive in Rome, for the primary purpose of Acts was to chart the extension of the gospel to Rome rather than write a biography of Paul.

A case for a date of Luke-Acts between 70 and 80 is made on other grounds. The producing of "many accounts" of Jesus' life (1:1) would seem to presuppose a lapse of several decades. Paul, who writes in the 50s, makes no allusion to any Gospel known to us, thus giving the impression of writing before the composition of the Gospels. The reference to John before James in

25. On Luke as artist, see Plummer, *Luke*, xxi-xxii; M. Parsons, "Who Wrote the Gospel of Luke?" *BRev* 17/2 (2001): 12-20; Kealy, *Interpretation of the Gospel of Luke*, 18-19.

26. This case has been made recently by A. Mittelstaedt, *Lukas als Historiker: Zur Datierung des lukanischen Doppelwerkes* (Tübingen: Francke, 2005), who argues for a date of composition of Luke ca. 59, and Acts ca. 62.

8:51 and 9:28, which is contrary to their birth order and customary mention in apostolic lists, and the further mention of John without James in 22:8, may suggest that Luke wrote after the death of James in 62, when John's reputation was second only to that of Peter. Above all, references to the impending destruction of Jerusalem in 19:43-44, and especially 21:20-24, with the description of a Roman defense perimeter *(circumvallatio),* the encirclement of Jerusalem by Roman armies, and the subjugation and "trampling by Gentiles" (21-24), seem to presuppose the sacking of Jerusalem by the Roman Tenth Legion (Fretensis) in 70. These observations, and particularly the last, argue — if not conclusively, at least plausibly — for a post-70 date of Luke-Acts. I would provisionally place their composition a decade or slightly more after Mark, perhaps in the late seventies.[27]

5. PLACE OF COMPOSITION

The place of origin of the Third Gospel may have ceased to be known to the ancient church at a relatively early date. That Luke was a native of Antioch is attested by the *Anti-Marc. Prolog.,* Eusebius, and Jerome,[28] the latter two of whom also attest that he wrote Acts from Rome (Eusebius, *Chron.;* Jerome, *Vir. ill.* 7.2). This latter suggestion is not surprising, for Acts ends with Paul (and ostensibly Luke) in Rome. Both the *Anti-Marc. Prolog.* and Jerome *(Comm. Matt.)* report that the Third Gospel was produced in Achaia (and Boeotia, according to Jerome).[29] Jerome's omission of this particular datum in his authoritative discussion of Luke in *Vir. ill.* 7 raises questions about its certainty in his thinking.[30] No further mention of place of origin is given by Jerome or any other patristic writer. Modern scholars have suggested Antioch, Caesarea Maritima, Ephesus, Philippi, Corinth, and Rome as places of origin of the Third Gospel, but without consensus. For two reasons I regard Antioch as the strongest of these suggestions. First, the well-attested patristic tradition associating Luke with Antioch might account for the mention of (Syrian) Antioch in Acts more than a dozen times. Second, and more important in my judgment, the frequency of Semitisms in the Third Gospel, as I shall argue in section 7,

27. Ellis, *Luke,* 55-60, offers a balanced presentation of evidence related to dating.

28. The reading of Codex Bezae at Acts 11:28 sets this first "we"-passage in Antioch as well.

29. Jerome omits this datum in *Vir. ill.* 7. Bovon, *Lukas 1,1–9,50,* 23, argues that Luke's precise knowledge of Philippi and its Roman institutions recommends Macedonia, directly north of Achaia, as the place of origin of Luke-Acts.

30. The *Anti-Marc. Prolog.* also attests that Luke died in Boeotia at age seventy (or eighty)-four.

suggests a Hebrew source of the Third Gospel. The discovery of unusually high numbers of Semitic inscriptions in Syria[31] offers additional evidence in favor of a composition of the Third Gospel (and perhaps the Hebrew Gospel itself) in Syria. Evidence connecting Luke with Antioch, though admittedly limited, is thus early, varied, and not unreasonable.

6. REFLECTIONS ON THE TESTIMONY TO THE THIRD GOSPEL IN EARLY CHRISTIANITY

Luke-Acts is the largest literary corpus in the NT, constituting nearly one-third of its total volume. The second largest NT corpus, the Pauline epistles, is still 15 percent shorter than Luke-Acts. Readers may find it puzzling that so little is known about such a major NT author, and disappointing that the discussion of authorship, date, and place of origin does not appreciably advance their understanding of the Third Gospel. A comment of C. S. Lewis, that "things need to be treated at length not in so far as they are great but in so far as they are complicated," is appropriate in this regard.[32] Things are complicated regarding the Third Gospel because the questions we ask are not satisfied by the paucity of material available to answer them. The material is particularly scarce regarding personal details about the author of the Luke-Acts. The interests of the early church were for the most part directed elsewhere than to personal details about authors. Jerome's *Lives of Illustrious Men,* for example, a comprehensive survey of 135 early Christian leaders, is in general more complete with regard to bibliographies than biographies. To the extent that the early church indulged in the quest for private lives, it did so with apostolic "pillars" (Gal 2:9) like Peter, James, John, and Paul. With regard to a secondary figure like Luke, the chief concern was to legitimate his Gospel by the authority of the apostle Paul, as the Gospel of Mark was legitimated by the authority of the apostle Peter. Like unsigned masterpieces, the Second and Third Gospels are identified and to some extent legitimated by their relation to greater apostolic authorities rather than by personal details of their authors and circumstances of their composition.

Let us turn, then, from the person of Luke to the purpose and achievement of his Gospel. The Gospel of Luke is the only first-century Christian document in which its author explicitly declares its purpose, that readers would "know the certainty of the things they have been taught" (1:4). Its purpose,

---

31. Deissmann, *Light from the Ancient East,* 11.

32. C. S. Lewis, *English Literature in the Sixteenth Century, Excluding Drama* (Oxford: Clarendon Press, 1954), Preface.

broadly speaking, is apologetic — to set forth a convincing narrative of the truth of the Christian gospel. Luke is the first Evangelist to present the gospel of Jesus Christ as a two-part story of salvation, beginning with the story of Jesus as the fulfillment of the OT messianic expectation,[33] and concluding with the expansion of the gospel into the Gentile world of the Roman Empire. In the Gospel, Luke defends Christ and the apostles (= church) against Jewish polemic as the legitimate heir of the promises to Israel; in Acts, Luke seeks to allay Roman fears that "the Way" is politically subversive by demonstrating that proclamation of the gospel and the resultant formation of Christian communities do not constitute a spiritual or moral reaction against culture but rather constitute a positive and indeed redemptive force within culture, both Jewish and Roman.

7. LUKE'S SOURCES

The subject of the sources of the Gospels has been rigorously investigated and debated by scholars in the past two centuries. A complete resolution of the question has not been achieved and, given the limited evidence at our disposal, may not be achievable, although some particulars have commanded wider support than others. Two particulars that have commanded widest support, with which I agree, are that Mark is the earliest of the Gospels, and that Mark is a chief source of both Matt and Luke. The quest for sources is closely related to a study of style and vocabulary, and in this regard the Third Gospel offers the most advantageous conditions of any of the four Gospels, for Luke can be compared not only to Mark (as can Matt), but also to the Book of Acts, which offers a long and more independent Lukan sequel. To be sure, Acts also relies on prior sources and is not "purely" Lukan, but its literary character is more uniform and less encumbered than is the Third Gospel's, thus providing a fairly reliable template of Lukan style.[34] Acts thus aids in identifying Lukan vocabulary and style in the Third Gospel and differentiating it from Mark. In addition, the prologue of the Third Gospel refers to "many accounts" on which the author relied for his narrative. When stylistic changes occur in portions of Luke that are not reliant on Mark, and that differ appreciably from the diction

---

33. I do not follow Ellis, *Luke,* 16-18, who portrays the relationship between Christianity and Judaism in terms of a hostile dichotomy. Based on the presentation of Jesus in the Third Gospel from start (1:32; 2:29-32) to finish (24:44-47) as the Messiah foretold by the prophets, on Luke's more sympathetic portrayal of Pharisaism, and on his apparent reliance on a Hebrew source for much of the Gospel, I understand the Third Gospel to offer a more positive portrayal of Christianity as the fulfillment of Israel.

34. Jeremias, *Sprache des Lukasevangeliums,* 6.

characteristic of Acts, it becomes possible to hypothesize that Luke is being influenced by one of these unnamed sources. In a separate volume on this subject I have examined the stylistic variations of the Third Gospel, especially in its non-Markan portions.[35] On the basis of this analysis I believe it possible to identify a second major source of the Third Gospel in addition to Mark and, with somewhat less certainty, a third and minor source as well. The following discussion will briefly summarize the conclusions of this prior research, in hopes that readers who desire fuller evidence will consult *The Hebrew Gospel and the Development of the Synoptic Tradition*.

The second major source that Luke utilizes in addition to Mark appears to be a Hebrew source, which I shall reference frequently in the commentary. This source is evidenced by a disproportionately high occurrence of Semitisms in the roughly one-half of the Third Gospel (ca. 550 vv.) not shared in common with Matt and/or Mark. A Semitism is a Greek word, phrase, or expression that can best — and sometimes only — be explained as the result of a prior Semitic (Hebrew or Aramaic) exemplar. This unique Lukan material, commonly referred to as Special Luke, exhibits a fourfold increase in Semitisms in comparison with portions of Luke shared in common with Matt and/or Mark. Such Semitisms include words, grammatical forms, phrases, and idioms (such as "divine passives") that ostensibly derive from a Hebrew original. The Semitisms in Special Luke are prolific and undisguised and have been recognized by nearly all major linguistic analyses of the Third Gospel, although they are customarily explained as "Septuagintisms," i.e., Lukan imitations of the language and style of the LXX. Semitisms in the Third Gospel cannot be properly explained as Septuagintisms, however, for some of them do not occur in the LXX, and others that may occur in the LXX occur too infrequently to constitute an imitable pattern. Nor do Hebraisms appear to be Aramaisms, as is often supposed, or to derive from an Aramaic spoken *Vorlage*. They appear, rather, to derive from a genuine Hebrew-language source, perhaps with some Mishnaic influence. Lukan Semitisms are thus most plausibly explained by reliance on a gospel composed in Hebrew.

The unusually high concentration of Semitisms in Special Luke is attended by a second and corroborating line of evidence from the patristic era. Two dozen Fathers and early Christian sources in the first nine centuries of the Christian era refer to the existence of a Hebrew Gospel, known variously as "The Gospel that is written in Hebrew," the Gospel used by "the Ebionites," or "The Gospel of the Nazarenes." Of the various sources that mention the Hebrew Gospel, ten preserve *quotations* from it. Some, such as Ignatius of Antioch or Sedulius Scottus, preserve single quotations; others like Origen or Epiphanius preserve several; and Jerome preserves twenty-two quotations. All

35. Edwards, *Hebrew Gospel*.

told, some seventy-five references to or quotations of the Hebrew Gospel — a fairly sizable corpus of material — are preserved from the patristic era. When the quotations are compared with the Synoptic Gospels, they exhibit a clearer and stronger correspondence with Special Luke than with portions of Luke shared by Matt and/or Mark, or with material unique to Matt and Mark. The comparative data from the patristic era suggest that Hebraic portions of the Third Gospel are indebted to the same source that is quoted and identified by the Fathers, the Hebrew Gospel.

The Lukan prologue constitutes a third corroborating line of evidence related to Semitic influence in Special Luke. In the prologue, Luke identifies the authors of the various accounts on which he relies as "eyewitnesses and servants of the word" (1:2). That description can only mean disciples within Jesus' apostolic circle. According to a dozen Fathers, the Hebrew Gospel was composed by such an eyewitness, the apostle Matthew.[36] Thus the mention or quotation of the Hebrew Gospel by two dozen early Christian sources, the high percentage of patristic quotations of the Hebrew Gospel that correspond to Special Luke, and the testimony of a dozen early Christian sources to the authorship of the Hebrew source by the apostle Matthew combine in support of the thesis that Luke's Semitisms derive from his use of an original Hebrew Gospel.

The Hebrew Gospel was known and cited extensively in the early centuries of Christianity, and it circulated widely throughout the Roman Empire. NT canonical discussions show no evidence that the Hebrew Gospel was considered canonical, nor does any Father argue for its canonicity. Nevertheless, the Hebrew Gospel was assigned by Eusebius, as it was earlier by Origen, to a category of six or eight "disputed" books, thus indicating its generally high repute.[37] Moreover, the Hebrew Gospel is cited by the Fathers more frequently and positively alongside canonical texts than is any noncanonical document. The foregoing intersecting lines of evidence form the basis for my conclusion, which is represented in the exposition of this commentary, that Luke relied on a Hebrew source for the composition of his Gospel in addition to the Gospel of Mark, and that this Hebrew text is the chief source for the majority of material in the Gospel that is not dependent on Mark.

It is likely that Luke utilized a third source in the composition of his Gospel, although this source (or combination of sources) cannot be identified with the same probability and specificity that Mark and the Hebrew Gospel

---

36. Canonical Greek Matt is largely free from Hebraisms and should not be confused with the Hebrew Gospel, which many Fathers attribute to the apostle Matthew. Since the Hebrew Gospel and canonical Matthew were both addressed to Jewish audiences, it may be that the author of the former was later connected to canonical Greek Matt.

37. *Hist. eccl.* 3.25.5.

can be. Approximately 175 verses in Luke do not appear to derive either from
the Hebrew Gospel or from Mark. These verses, which for the most part are
also present in one form or another in Matt, could be accounted for in various
ways, none of which is conclusive. I refer to these verses simply as the Double
Tradition.

The Double Tradition constitutes the core of what is traditionally called
"Q," the hypothetical source of Jesus' sayings that is accepted in varying degrees by many NT scholars. I refer to this material as the Double Tradition
rather than "Q," because the "Q"-hypothesis is defined by two assumptions
that I find untenable. First, some of the 175 verses are narrative rather than
sayings (e.g., 4:1-13; 7:6-10), and at least one of them extends into the Passion
Narrative (22:62). This suggests that the Double Tradition was a more or less
complete Gospel, including sayings, narrative, and passion, unlike the "Q"-
hypothesis, which posits an early source of Jesus' sayings without historical
narrative and without a passion account. Second, and more important, I find
no evidence in early Christianity of the existence of a specialized source of
Jesus' sayings that corresponds to the assumptions of the "Q" hypothesis. *Gos.
Thom.* is, to be sure, a collection of Jesus' sayings, but it was not accepted by
any branch of apostolic Christianity that we know of.[38] *Did.* is also a collection of sayings, but its sayings are attributed to the apostles rather than to
Jesus, and they are a compilation not of a special sayings source but of the
Gospels, Epistles (both Pauline and General), and OT. The formation of the
gospel tradition constitutes an important subtheme of patristic literature. The
absence of any reference in that literature to a compilation of Jesus' sayings
in early Christianity makes it highly unlikely that such a compilation existed.
Given the high esteem, even reverence, in which the words of Jesus were held
from apostolic times onward, it is virtually impossible to imagine that, had an
anthology of his sayings existed, it would not be mentioned by any ancient
Christian source.[39]

The Double Tradition appears to be the skeletal remnants of one of the
several "accounts" that Luke credits to his predecessors (1:1). The roughly 175
verses that Luke and Matt share in common may come from one of these
sources (or from a combination of them). The Double Tradition exhibits minor differences from characteristic Lukan style, although it is generally absent Hebraisms and thus unrelated to the Hebrew Gospel. Whether Luke and

---

38. Eusebius, *Hist. eccl.* 3.25.6, writes: "As for the writings put forward by heretics under
the name of the apostles, containing gospels such as those of Peter and Thomas and Matthias,
and some others besides, or Acts such as those of Andrew and John and the other apostles,
none of these has any who belonged to the succession of the orthodox who ever thought it
right to refer to in his writings."

39. For further challenges to the "Q" hypothesis, see Ellis, *Luke,* 21-24.

Matt received the Double Tradition from an independent source, or whether, which I think more likely, Matt received it from Luke, cannot be said with any certainty.

8. NARRATIVE STRUCTURE

The prologue (1:1-4) is a metanarrative of the Gospel, instructing readers in Luke's use of prior sources in the composition of the Gospel, the character of the Gospel, and his intention as author to assure readers of the reliability of his testimony.

A transition to the infancy narratives of John and Jesus is marked by a distinct change in style in 1:5. In the infancy narrative, Luke 1:5–2:52 alternates between John and Jesus in narrating their annunciations, births, circumcisions, and coming of age. Similarly, both Mary and Zechariah dedicate hymns, the Magnificat, 1:46-55, and Benedictus, 1:67-79, respectively, to their offspring foretold by Gabriel. An episode of Jesus' visit to the temple in Jerusalem as a twelve-year-old — the only story of his youth in the canonical Gospels — is appended to the infancy narrative (2:41-52).

The body of the Gospel commences at 3:1 after an interval of some thirty years, at which point the Lukan narrative begins to correspond with the Gospel of Mark. The commencement of the ministries of John and Jesus is again introduced in alternating fashion, beginning with John's call, ministry in the wilderness, and arrest (3:1-20), followed by Jesus' baptism, genealogy, and temptation in the wilderness (3:21–4:13). Henceforth, Luke focuses exclusively on the ministry of Jesus, which in the Third Gospel is roughly divided into three parts — the Galilean ministry (4:14–9:50), the mission of Jesus and the way of salvation (9:51–18:34), and the passion in Jerusalem (18:35–24:53). The Galilean ministry begins with Jesus' programmatic sermon in Nazareth (4:14-30) and extends to 9:50. Capernaum becomes the home base of Jesus' itinerant ministry of healing and teaching, which transpires primarily in the northwest quadrant of the Sea of Galilee. Jesus calls twelve apostles into a special relation with himself (6:12-16), but he is followed by others as well, including women (8:1-3), who attend him and are tutored by him. He attracts extraordinary crowds in Galilee (6:17), but also opposition, particularly from Pharisees and scribes. The Twelve become the increasing focus of Jesus' Galilean ministry, as evidenced by their first mission (9:1-6) and the challenge for them to understand the necessity of suffering in the fulfillment of his messianic role (9:22), which he refers to as his exodus (9:31).

The second phase of Jesus' ministry occupies the central section of Luke, extending from Jesus setting his face to go to Jerusalem in 9:51 until the fourth passion prediction in 18:31-34. This central section consists almost entirely of teachings and parables of Jesus, with virtually no narrative context, geographic references, or place-names. Jesus' teaching and parables continue to focus on discipleship, not only on the Twelve as in the Galilean ministry, but on all disciples in relation to mission, conflicts, dangers, and the kingdom of God. The instruction of the central section prepares for, and must be understood in the context of, the repeated refrain of the necessity of Jesus going to Jerusalem (9:31, 51, 53; 13:22, 33; 17:11; 18:31). Its overall theme is the mission of Jesus as the way of salvation. Jesus' "way" will become the earliest description of the Christian movement in the Acts sequel (9:2; 13:10; 16:17; 18:25-26; 19:9, 23; 22:4; 24:14, 22).

The third and final section of the Gospel narrates Jesus' passion and resurrection, including his arrival in Jerusalem, teaching in the temple, arrest, trials, crucifixion, burial, and resurrection (18:35–24:53). In contrast to the mission and way of Jesus in the central section, the Passion Narrative, like the Galilean ministry in 4:14–9:50, resumes place-names, specific movements, and identifying data. Jesus is no longer an itinerant preacher but a resident teacher in the temple of Jerusalem. There he not only proclaims the word of God but is increasingly opposed by the temple authorities, the chief priests and scribes. The concrete events of the passion — the prayer on the Mount of Olives; the arrest; trials by the Sanhedrin, Antipas, and Pilate; and crucifixion and death — are presented by Luke as the fulfillment of Jesus' "exodus," announced earlier on the Mount of Transfiguration (9:31). This *exodos* is the necessary consequence of the *hodos,* the "way" of Jesus to Jerusalem as Messiah and Righteous Sufferer (23:47).

The Gospel concludes with four passion interpretations (24:7, 26, 44, 46) in which the resurrected Jesus confesses himself to be "the fulfillment of all that was written in the law of Moses and the prophets and Psalms" (24:44), as foretold by the angel Gabriel at his annunciation (1:31-35). Luke concludes the Gospel with the ascension of Jesus, the same event with which he commences his sequel of the early church in the Book of Acts.

9. EPILOGUE ON MARCION

The first interpreter of Luke known to us is Marcion, who altered the text of the Third Gospel violently in support of his heterodox theological views.[40] A native of Pontus and wealthy shipowner, Marcion became a benefactor and bishop in

---

40. For helpful overviews of Marcion, see A. von Harnack, *Die Entstehung der christlichen Theologie und des kirchlichen Dogmas* (Gotha: Klotz Verlag, 1927), 63-64; G. Krüger, "Mar-

the church in Rome, from which he was excommunicated in 144 for espous-
ing a radical separation of law and grace. The most extreme example of that
distinction was his teaching that the creator God was an inferior and wrathful
demiurge in contrast to the good God and Father of Jesus. Marcion was a disciple of Cerdo, a Syrian gnostic teacher, and Marcion's Docetism, in particular,
corresponds with that of his gnostic tutor. In other respects, however, particularly in his lack of interest in metaphysical questions and religious cosmology,
Marcion espoused a tradition independent of Gnosticism. Unlike most of his
contemporaries, Marcion refused to interpret the OT allegorically. Without the
aid of allegory to alleviate offensive elements of retributive justice, wars, dietary
regulations, and low morality in parts of the OT, Marcion concluded that the
God of the OT and the morality of Judaism were offensive and irreconcilable
with the character of the God of the NT and the morality of Jesus of Nazareth.

Marcion believed that Paul alone had received the true gospel (Gal 1:12),
and that Paul, in contrast to Peter, James, and John, was the only true apostle,
to which the Third Gospel bore witness. Marcion thus ascribed the Third Gospel to Pauline tradition, referring to it generically as "the gospel," i.e., the only
true Gospel, in contrast to Matt, Mark, and John. Marcion did not accept Paul
or Luke unaltered, however. His "mutilations," to quote Irenaeus (*Haer.* 3.11.7;
3.12.12), consisted of various deletions, *but no additions,*[41] thus "purging the
Gospel of Luke of all Jewish leaven"[42] by rejecting the entire OT and all the NT
with the exception of the epistles of Paul. Virtually all orthodox Fathers of the
second and subsequent centuries vigorously denounced Marcion (d. c. 160)
as an archheretic.[43]

The following chart identifies the main sections or verses of Luke omitted by Marcion. Although Marcion's biblical hermeneutic cannot be reduced
to a single or simple formula, two primary criteria appear to be responsible for
the majority of his excisions of Luke. Those in *italic* font indicate material or
sayings that reflect positively on the OT and Jews. By far the most important
excision is Luke 1:1–4:28, which, with the exception of 3:1, is wholly expurgated
from Marcion's version of Luke. The omission of Luke's critical introductory

---

cion, Marcionites," *New Schaff-Herzog Religious Encyclopedia,* 7:172-74; B. Aland, "Marcion-
Marcionites-Marcionism," *EECh* 2:523-24; J. Clabeaux, "Marcion," *ABD* 4:514-16.

41. For a defense of the view that Marcion altered Luke (and not the reverse), see
T. Zahn, *Geschichte des neutestamentlichen Kanons* (Erlangen: Verlag Deichert, 1888), 1:681,
713; A. von Harnack, *Marcion: Das Evangelium vom Fremden Gott* (2nd ed.; TU 45; Darmstadt:
Wissenschaftliche Buchgesellschaft, 1996), 240; D. Roth, "Marcion's Gospel and Luke: The
History of Research in Current Debate," *JBL* 127/3 (2008): 513-27.

42. M. Hengel, *The Four Gospels,* 32.

43. A. von Harnack, *Geschichte der altchristlichen Literatur bis Eusebius* (2nd ed.;
Leipzig: Hinrichs Verlag, 1958), 1:191-97, offers a survey of the more than two dozen patristic
antagonists of Marcion.

chapters severed all links with the OT in accounting for the origin of Jesus and the Christian gospel.[44] Marcion's "gospel" begins with Jesus descending directly from an unknown God to Capernaum, free from ancestry and intercourse tainted by Judaism. Anti-Jewish excisions continued after 4:28, as the italicized material indicates, though in less radical and more selective fashion. A second and lesser category of excised material is signified in **bold** font, indicating material omitted because it reflected negatively on Jesus and the disciples. Excisions in regular font indicate a smaller third category for which neither of the above reasons, nor any other, is apparent.

Chapter	Verses omitted	Content omitted
1	*1-80*	*Predications of births of John and Jesus*
2	*1-52*	*Birth of Jesus*
3	*1b-38*	*John's preaching; Jesus' baptism and genealogy*
4	*1-27*[45]	*Jesus' temptation, Nazareth sermon*
5	*39*	*Old wine being better*
6	19b	Jesus has power to heal all
	23a	Rejoice in that day and be glad
7	29-35	Difference between Jesus and John the Baptizer
8	**19**	**Mother and brothers of Jesus approach him in crowd**
	40-42a; 49-56	*Healing of Jairus's daughter*
9	26b	Jesus comes in the glory of the Father and angels
	27	**Some standing here will not taste death until the kingdom arrives**
	31	*Jesus' "exodus" in Jerusalem*
10	*12-15*	*Better for Sodom, Tyre, Sidon than for unreceptive cities*
11	*29-32*	*Jonah and Queen of Sheba as examples for disciples*
	42	*Pharisees who tithe*
	49-51	*Blood of prophets, including blood of Abel*
12	6-7	Sayings about sparrows and hairs of one's head
	24	God's care for ravens that neither sow nor reap
	27-28	*Lilies of the field that are adorned like Solomon*
13	*1-9*	*Victims of Pilate and Tower of Siloam; parable of fig tree*
	29-35	*Pharisees warn Jesus to flee from Herod Antipas*

44. Irenaeus, *Haer.* 1.27.2, writes that Marcion "mutilates the Gospel which is according to Luke, removing all that is written respecting the generation of the Lord, and setting aside a great deal of the teaching of the Lord, in which the Lord is recorded as most clearly confessing that the maker of this universe is his Father."

45. Except v. 16 (partially) and v. 23a.

14		nothing omitted
15	*11-32*	*Parable of Prodigal Son*
16		nothing omitted
17	**7-10**	**Even servants who do their master's will are still unworthy**
18	31-33	Final passion prediction of Jesus' suffering in Jerusalem
19	*9*	*Salvation comes to Zacchaeus, a "son of Abraham"*
	27	**Slaying of enemies of nobleman**
	29-46	*Jesus' triumphal entry and remorse over Jerusalem*
20	*9-18*	*Parable of Vineyard and chosen cornerstone*
	37-38	*Resurrection attested by Moses, Abraham, Isaac, and Jacob*
21	18	No hair of your head will perish
	21-24	*Let Judeans flee destruction befalling Jerusalem*
22	**3**	**Satan enters Judas Iscariot, one of the Twelve**
	14	Apostles recline with Jesus at Last Supper
	16-18	**Jesus will not eat and drink until arrival of the kingdom of God**
	35-38	**Jesus instructs disciples to sell garments and buy swords**
	49-51	**Cutting off ear of high priest's servant at Jesus' arrest**
	70	**Jesus equivocates before high priest that he is God's Son**
23	*34*	*Jesus prays for forgiveness of those who crucify him*
	43	**Jesus says to penitent thief, "Today, you will be in paradise"**
24		nothing omitted[46]

---

46. The above excisions, assembled in Zahn, *Neutestamentlichen Kanons*, 1:704, are documented in anti-Marcionite writers of the second and third centuries. Zahn entertains the possibility that Marcion's version may have been further abridged.

CHAPTER ONE

Heavenly Announcements of John and Jesus

Luke 1:1-80

THE PROLOGUE (1:1-4)

Luke prefaces his Gospel with a formal introduction composed in the best Greek in the NT, which differs perceptibly from the language and style of the remainder of his Gospel.[1] Luke's introductory dedication bears similarities to introductions of other academic Hellenistic works, especially in history and science,[2] but he is the only Evangelist in the NT who offers such for his Gospel. The prologue of the Third Gospel is the most important testimony in the first century to the prehistory of the Gospels,[3] and it offers unique insight into Luke's craft as author and Evangelist. Unlike the other Evangelists, Luke begins not with the gospel but with a description of the hermeneutical task before him. His gospel is rooted in eyewitness testimony and prior written sources, and he identifies the recipient of the work by name, "the most excellent Theophilus" (v. 3). Every meaningful proclamation of the gospel requires an interpreter, and Luke stands as a hermeneutical bridge between his sources and his audience.

1 "Many have undertaken to draw up an account of the things that have been fulfilled among us." Luke's Gospel is not a pioneer or novel effort, but dependent on "many" who have gone before him. Like all mediators of

---

1. Of the forty-three words in the prologue, a dozen are typical of introductions of Hellenistic works (Grundmann, *Lukas*, 43).

2. For discussions and examples of Hellenistic introductions, see Klostermann, *Lukasevangelium,* 1-2; Marshall, *Luke,* 39; Klein, *Lukasevangelium,* 76-78; and esp. L. Alexander, "Luke's Preface in the Context of Greek Preface-Writing," in Orton, *Composition of Luke's Gospel,* 90-116. A close analogy to Luke's prologue (and probably indebted to it) is the second-c. *Diogn.* 1, which, like 1:1-4, declares the intention to instruct the recipient in the essentials of the Christian faith and addresses him with the title "Most Excellent" *(kratiste).*

3. B. Gerhardsson, "The Gospel Tradition," in *The Interrelations of the Gospels: A Symposium Led by M.-E. Boismard, W. R. Farmer, F. Neirynck, Jerusalem 1984* (ed. D. Dungan; BETL 95; Leuven: University Press, 1990), 534-37.

the gospel in the postapostolic era, Luke is dependent on authoritative tradition for his narrative. Luke does not identify the "many" before him, but as noted in the Introduction, and as we shall see repeatedly in the commentary, two of Luke's sources were doubtless the Gospel of Mark and the Hebrew Gospel. Several early church fathers interpreted v. 1 as a disparagement of the prior traditions, a point of view occasionally followed by modern commentators. The prologue does not suggest that the previous narratives were defective, however. They too were indebted to "eyewitnesses and servants of the word" (v. 2), and they may possibly have been Luke's inspiration. The Greek for "draw up an account" (v. 1) means to organize a complete and orderly record, to make a coherent narrative. The aorist middle of the Greek infinitive *anataxasthai* may intensify the sense, implying the personal investment and assiduousness of the "many" who contributed to the conversion of oral testimony into written tradition.[4] The Greek noun *diēgēsis*, "account," occurs only here in the NT. The singular is important: Luke does not say there were "many accounts," but *one* gospel narrative, of which there are various versions. The noun and its verbal form *diēgeisthai*, also a distinctive Lukan word (8:39; 9:10; Acts 8:33; 9:27; 12:17; only three times elsewhere in the NT), mean "to recount a narrative."[5] *Diēgēsis* is a "historical-literary term which appears both in Jewish-Hellenistic literature and among Greek authors,"[6] thus a *written* narrative. The various versions of the account known to Luke and Theophilus were thus written.

The subject of the account is "the things that have been fulfilled among us." Luke's Gospel is not a testimony of his ideas, or even of his faith. It narrates *events that have been brought to completion among us,* i.e., the concrete and saving acts of God that have been fulfilled in Jesus Christ. The gospel is not a noble moral proclamation, nor can it be reduced to a set of abstract teachings and truths. It is not something that Luke or any witness can take credit for. The passive voice of the Greek verb translated "the things that have been fulfilled"

---

4. G. Delling, *anatassō, TWNT* 8:32-33.

5. A variant form of the verb occurs in Acts 15:3, also meaning to set forth a narrative of events. G. E. Lessing, "New Hypothesis on the Evangelists as Merely Human Historians," in *Philosophical and Theological Writings* (trans. and ed. H. Nisbet; Cambridge Texts in the History of Philosophy; Cambridge: University Press, 2005), §§45-47, suggests the first two verses of the prologue preserve the name of the Hebrew Gospel: "A Narrative of the Things That Have Been Fulfilled among Us, as Handed Down to Us by Those Who from the Beginning Were Eyewitnesses and Ministers of the Word." The "many" who transmitted the witness in the Hebrew Gospel were the Twelve, and vv. 3-4 announce Luke's particular agency. Lessing concludes: "This much is certain: Luke himself had before him the Hebrew document, the Gospel of the Nazarenes, and he transferred if not all, at least most of it, into his gospel, only in a somewhat different order and in somewhat better language" (§48).

6. Hengel, *The Four Gospels,* 100, 415; G. Delling, *anatassō, TWNT* 8:32-33.

means a history of what *God has done,* to which the proper human responses are belief and proclamation. Since Luke admits he was not an "eyewitness and servant of the word" (v. 2), the references to "us" in vv. 1, 2 probably mean "the things that have been fulfilled among us *Christians*."[7]

2 The narratives prior to Luke were written from a closer perspective than his, for "they were handed down to us by those who from the first were eyewitnesses and servants of the word." The Greek word behind "handed down" *(paradidonai)* is the standard term for authoritative oral tradition in early Christianity.[8] "Eyewitnesses" must signify the twelve apostles, although perhaps not exclusively.[9] V. 2 thus alludes to "Scripture and tradition" — eyewitness testimony and authentic tradition stemming from it, the two primary sources of authority recognized in all three major branches of Christianity.[10] The eyewitnesses on whom Luke relies recount events "from the first." A similar phrase appears in Acts 1:22 with reference to the necessary credentials of an apostle, which "began with John's baptism to the time when Jesus was taken up from us." "From the first" carries a similar sense here, signifying participation of eyewitnesses in Jesus' complete earthly ministry.[11] If eyewitness testimony includes the Gospel of Mark, then it must refer to the authority of the apostle Peter, to whom the Second Evangelist, who was not an apostle, was indebted for his Gospel. Eyewitness testimony would also include the Hebrew Gospel, which throughout the early church was attributed to the testimony of the apostle Matthew. "Eyewitnesses and servants of the word" should be understood as a single concept and company of followers. Eyewitness of the Christ-event alone would not qualify one for this particular company, for Antipas, Pilate, members of the Sanhedrin, and countless individuals saw Jesus of Nazareth but did not respond in faith and become "servants of the word." The eyewitnesses here referred to are endowed with foundational importance for the Christian faith, for they not only saw the word, which here must refer

---

7. So Lagrange, *Luc,* 4.

8. "This personal link of the Jesus tradition with particular tradents, or more precisely their memory and missionary preaching, on which more or less emphasis is put, is historically undeniable" (M. Hengel, *The Four Gospels,* 143).

9. The inescapable sense of 1:2, in the words of R. Bauckham, *Jesus and the Eyewitnesses: The Gospels as Eyewitness Testimony* (Grand Rapids: Eerdmans, 2006), 119, is "a claim that the eyewitnesses had been present throughout the events from the appropriate commencement of the author's history onward."

10. Perhaps for this reason Athanasius explicitly imitates Luke 1:1-4 in the prologue to his famous Thirty-Ninth Festal Letter (367), in which for the first time in Christian history he identifies all twenty-seven books of the NT (and only them) as authoritative and canonical. For the text of the Festal Letter, see Kealy, *Interpretation of the Gospel of Luke,* 72.

11. In his celebrated testimony to Jesus, Josephus, *Ant.* 18.64, appeals to a similar tradition deriving from Jesus, namely, when he was condemned to be crucified "those who in the first place had come to love [Jesus] did not give up their affection for him."

to both the "word and deed" of Jesus (so 24:19; also John 15:27; Acts 1:21-22), but embraced its claim by becoming "servants of the word." In Acts 6:4 Luke likewise describes the ministry of the Twelve "in service of the word." The word of the gospel does not belong to believers, but rather believers belong to the gospel and serve it (Rom 6:17). A witness does not seek mastery over the word but submits in service to the word.

3-4 Luke is neither the origin nor the authority of the material present in his Gospel, but rather a significant link in the hermeneutical chain. In Acts 1:1 he refers to the Third Gospel as a work that he *made*. The middle Greek form *epoiēsamēn* implies Luke's solemn responsibility for the final product presented to Theophilus. For the first time in v. 3 Luke addresses his own role in his Gospel, literally in Greek *edoxe kamoi*, "It seemed good also to me" (NIV "With this in mind"). This seems a very modest way to speak of what we regard as divine inspiration. "It seemed good also to me" may strike us as tentative or equivocal. *Edoxe* was widespread in official Hellenistic Greek inscriptions (e.g., "it pleased [*edoxe*] the council and citizenry . . .") as an attestation of the authority of the body politic. Luke's use of this term is thus not tentative, but the authoritative foundation of five pillars of assurance.[12] First, the material in the Third Gospel bears the imprimatur of Luke's personal "investigation." The Greek verb *parakolouthein* means "to follow someone," especially an authority figure. Luke has not waited for a bolt of inspiration but has carefully followed the course of events by personal investment and investigation. Second, Luke has investigated "everything," i.e., all available evidence relevant to the history. Third, he has done so "from the beginning." The events upon which his testimony rests occupied a significant time span, which Luke has followed from the outset. Fourth, Luke claims for his Gospel the important criterion of *akribōs*, "carefully," or perhaps better, "accurately," a term that includes the ideas of completeness and exactness. Finally, Luke claims to present the whole as "an orderly account."[13] Exactly how literally this phrase should be taken is debatable.[14] It seems significant that Luke chooses a term *(kathexēs)* that signifies a proper narrative *sequence and order,* a term Luke uses similarly in Acts 11:4. Luke claims for his work what Papias claimed of the Gospel of Mark, that its primary contribution was with reference to "arrangement" of material (Gk. *syntassein*).[15] In terms of modern source analysis, Luke's claim would include his integration of Markan material and the Hebrew Gospel. According

---

12. Luke uses the same term to similar effect in Acts 15:22, 25, 28, (34).

13. On *kathexēs,* "orderly," see Tannehill, *Narrative Unity of Luke-Acts,* 9-12.

14. See J. V. Bartlet, "The Sources of St. Luke's Gospel," in *Studies in the Synoptic Problem* (ed. W. Sanday; Oxford: Clarendon, 1911), 354; Marshall, *Luke,* 43; Klostermann, *Lukasevangelium,* 3.

15. Eusebius, *Hist. eccl.* 3.39.15.

to Luke's testimony, his primary contribution to the apostolic tradition consists in matters of sequence and order more than in content and substance. The Third Gospel is not a mere concatenation of disparate information, but a presentation of the life of Jesus in such a way that readers can know the *meaning* of Jesus.

The foregoing is necessary for Theophilus, the recipient of the gospel, to "know the certainty of the things you have been taught" (v. 4). Authority in Christian faith is not based in the piety or the subjective state of the believer, but in the authenticity of a historical record that can be tested by objective canons of truth. Luke does not base the credibility of his Gospel in religious inspiration, but in the presentation of a history that can withstand historical scrutiny.[16] Thus, Luke assures Theophilus of the veracity of the "many" prior accounts, which were the source of his initial knowledge of the gospel.

The identity of Theophilus is no longer known to us. The name itself, which means "lover of God" in Greek, was often taken by the Fathers as a metaphor of the reader. "If you love God, it was written to you," said Ambrose.[17] The intentionality with which Luke sets forth his apologia in vv. 1-3 seems rather superfluous if he is writing only for metaphoric readers, however. It does not appear to have been a custom in antiquity to dedicate books to imaginary persons.[18] Theophilus is probably a historic person, although the name could be a pseudonym to protect the recipient from detection or persecution.[19] "Most excellent" (Gk. *kratiste*) implies a man of status and honor, and probably of wealth. It was customary in the ancient world to dedicate works to patrons, whose role would include paying for publication and dissemination of the work. The honorary title could indicate that Theophilus was a Roman official (e.g., Acts 23:26; 24:3; 26:25), but this is less certain than often assumed. The title was not unique to political office but was used of any person of rank and status. Nor was "Theophilus" exclusively a Gentile name; Caiaphas's successor once removed who ruled the Sanhedrin as high priest in the latter 30s bore the very name.[20] Whether Theophilus

---

16. Several Latin copyists, dissatisfied that Luke makes no reference to divine inspiration, added *et spiritui sancto* in v. 3, ". . . it seemed good also to me *and to the Holy Spirit*. . . ." This addition comes from Acts 15:28, however (see B. Metzger, *TCGNT*, 108).

17. *Exp. Luc.* 1.12 (cited from A. Just, *Luke*, 4).

18. L. Alexander, *The Preface to Luke's Gospel: Literary Convention and Social Context in Luke 1.1-4 and Acts 1.1* (SNTSMS 78; Cambridge: University Press, 1993), 188.

19. M. Hengel, *The Four Gospels*, 40, suggests "Perhaps 'Theophilus,' the 'friend of God,' was a prominent Roman whose real name had to be kept secret. That would explain why Luke ends his second book with the arrival of Paul in Rome. From now on the recipient knows the story himself."

20. Theophilus (Heb. *Yedidiah*) was appointed high priest by Vitellius, Roman governor of Syria from 37 to 41, after which he was removed by King Agrippa (*Ant.* 19.297).

was a convert or simply an informed observer in not clear from vv. 3-4. In the NT, the Greek word for "taught," *katēchein,* can mean to inform (Acts 21:21) or to instruct in the content of the faith (Gal 6:6). In church tradition *catechetics* is instruction of believers in the substance and meaning of the faith, but this meaning is premature for Luke's day. Since Luke bases his prologue on historical inquiry and evidence rather than on faith, it seems possible to take Theophilus as a seeker, an individual who is open but not necessarily committed to the gospel.[21]

Luke's elegant prologue is dedicated to historical investigation that can be corroborated by human testimony apart from appeals to divine inspiration, Christian terminology, or religious claims. In the sequel to his Gospel, Luke speaks of the resurrected Jesus presenting himself to the disciples in "many convincing proofs" (*pollois tekmēriois,* Acts 1:3).[22] Without using the same word in the prologue, Luke imputes equal veracity to the eyewitness sources of his Gospel. The essential underpinning of Christian mission and proclamation is not a myth, philosophy, or religious or moral system, but *human witness* to the saving significance of Jesus Christ (24:48; Acts 1–8). Loveday Alexander argues that Luke has consciously rooted his prologue in the language of academic discourse typical of scientific treatises.[23] In the prologue, Luke testifies

---

Theophilus's brother Jonathan, both appointed and deposed by Vitellius, had preceded him as high priest from 36 to 37 (*Ant.* 18.123). Josephus reports that Agrippa proposed to restore Jonathan to the priesthood but that Jonathan refused, volunteering in his place Mattathias, son of Theophilus, who served as high priest until war broke out against Rome in 66 (*Ant.* 19.313-16). Jonathan testified against Cumanus, Roman governor of Judea from 48 to 52, for his slaughter of Samaritan Jews (*J.W.* 2.240) and was later sent to appear before Caesar in Rome (*J.W.* 2.243). Jonathan became the first Jewish authority to be murdered by the Sicarii (*J.W.* 2.256). His death at the hands of the Sicarii was instigated by Felix, Roman governor of Judea from 52 to 60 C.E., because of his "incessant rebukes" of Roman authority, according to Josephus (*Ant.* 20.162-65). For a summary of Jonathan's rule, see E. Schürer, *Jewish People in the Age of Jesus Christ,* 1:459. The above intrigues are reviewed only to suggest that the high priest Theophilus, who fits the time frame of Luke's writing, is not an impossible candidate as recipient of the Third Gospel. The Hebrew Gospel, on which Luke depended, would bear a special testimony to a person such as Theophilus. A high priest who had been removed from office by King Agrippa, who was brother of a high priest (Jonathan) deposed by Rome and later killed by Jewish insurrectionists, and who was father of a high priest (Mattathias) who suffered the ravages of the Jewish War may have had more reason to be open to the alternative Christian gospel than the average Jewish leader.

21. See Schlatter, *Lukas,* 16; and H. Beyer, *katēcheō, TWNT* 3:638-40.

22. Gk. *tekmērion,* which occurs similarly in *Ant.* 5.39 and 17.128, means the ability to supply demonstrable proof.

23. "It is in fact possible to go through Luke's preface word by word and find parallels in the scientific tradition for virtually every feature" (L. Alexander, "Luke's Preface in the Context of Greek Preface-Writing," in Orton, *Composition of Luke's Gospel,* 102).

that his role as an Evangelist is to bear responsible testimony to what God has done in human history in the life of Jesus of Nazareth.[24]

EXCURSUS: LUKE'S INFANCY NARRATIVES (1–2)

The prologue announces that Luke "carefully investigated everything from the beginning" (1:3). In correspondence with his claim, Luke charts the most far-reaching example of family planning in human history, stretching from Adam to Jesus (3:23-38). The specifics of the divine plan culminate with the infancy narratives of John and Jesus, and with them the introduction of the age of salvation. Luke was breaking new ground in this regard, for although infancy narratives existed of some of Israel's past heroes — Enoch (*1 En.* 106), Moses (Exod 2:1-10; *Ant.* 2.215), Samuel (1 Sam 1–3), Samson (Judg 13; *Ant.* 2.276-85) — of no canonical OT prophet was an infancy narrative preserved.[25] The only other canonical Gospel to provide a lineage and birth narrative of Jesus is Matt, but unlike Matt's narrative, which is told from Joseph's perspective, Luke's is told from Mary's, and Luke's is a fuller birth narrative of both John and Jesus, composing 10 percent of the length of the Gospel. Luke 1–2 is set forth with literary artistry, in terms of both language and composition. If Mary is one of the eyewitness sources mentioned in 1:2, her testimony has been so absorbed as to be indistinguishable from Luke's hand. Luke narrates births of Jesus and John in parallel succession, and nowhere more so than in their respective annunciations (John, 1:5-25; Jesus, 1:26-38). Both are announced by the angel Gabriel; both births are miraculous; both sets of parents receive the angelic proclamation in the face of besetting human circumstances and are bewildered by it; the names and divine destinies of both sons are announced; both sets of parents query how such things can happen; both are assured of the divine determination of the events; both are given signs; and both play no active role in the fulfillment of the annunciations except to trust and retire to their respective habitations. The two annunciations occur in isolation from each other, but they intersect with Mary's visit to Elizabeth when both acknowledge in their own bodies (1:44!) the same agency of the Holy Spirit of God within them. The respective announcements may be diagrammed thus:

---

24. On Luke 1:1-4, see Cadbury, *Making of Luke-Acts,* 194-204; and esp. M. Hengel, "Der Lukasprolog und seine Augenzeugen: Die Apostel, Petrus, und die Frauen," in *Memory in the Bible and Antiquity: The Fifth Durham-Tübingen Research Symposium (Durham, September 2004)* (ed. S. Barton, L. Stuckenbruck, and B. Wold; WUNT 212; Tübingen: Mohr Siebeck, 2007), 195-242.

25. See Grundmann, *Lukas,* 46; Schweizer, *Lukas,* 11. In Jer 1, Jeremiah was called as a youth, although no details of his youth are preserved.

Birth of John foretold   Birth of Jesus foretold
to Zechariah and Elizabeth   to Mary and Joseph
(1:5-25)   (1:26-38)

Rejoicing of Mary and Elizabeth together
(1:39-56)[26]

The second major division of Luke's infancy narrative, also set in parallel succession, comprises the birth and infancy narratives of John and Jesus and may be thus diagrammed:

Birth, circumcision,   Birth, circumcision,
naming of John   naming of Jesus
(1:57-66)   (2:1-21)

Greeting of John   Greeting of Jesus
by inspired Zechariah   by inspired Simeon and Anna
(1:67-80)   (2:22-40)

Boy Jesus in the temple
(2:41-52)[27]

Further details are shared in common in the birth stories: the result of both births is great joy; both births evoke remarkable responses from third parties; both are also the subjects of beatitudes; and both grow in the strength and purpose of God. The balance in the annunciation narrative is not maintained in the birth and childhood stories, however. Once John's circumcision and naming are given, the narrative spotlight falls fully on Jesus, including the contrast between his humble birth and Caesar's megalomania, the attendance of a company of shepherds and a canticle of angels, miraculous prophecies in the temple, and his own announcement in the temple twelve years later that he must be about his Father's business. The parallelism in the infancy narrative is thus asymmetric. The asymmetry is not a mistake on Luke's part, nor intended to avert a possible

---

26. Wolter, *Lukasevangelium,* 71, sees the following chiasmus in Luke 1:
    A[1] Annunciation of birth of John to Zechariah (1:8-23)
      B[1] Annunciation of birth of Jesus to Mary (1:26-38)
        AB John and Elizabeth respond to the visit of Mary (1:40-45)
      B[2] Mary responds with a hymn of praise (1:46-55)
    A[2] Zechariah responds with a hymn of praise (1:67-79).
    27. This schema (with the exception of the boy Jesus in the temple) follows that of M. Dibelius, "Jungfrausohn und Krippenkind: Untersuchungen zur Geburtsgeschichte Jesu im Lukas-Evangelium," in *Botschaft und Geschichte: Gesammelte Aufsätze von Martin Dibelius* (Tübingen: Mohr, 1953), 1:1-78.

rivalry between John and Jesus, but necessitated by theological realities. John is the "preparer" (1:17), the forerunner of the Son of God and Savior; his side of the equation cannot claim equal or even similar weight to that of Jesus. "[Jesus] must become greater, [John] must become less" (John 3:30).[28]

The effect of the infancy narratives is to demonstrate that the births of John and Jesus flow out of Israel's saving history, and that the birth of Jesus marks the fulfillment of it. Luke's literary style is saturated with Semitisms, and the infancy narratives reverberate with OT echoes.[29] A child is born to an old couple, as was the case with Abraham and Sarah (1:7 and Gen 18:11). The barrenness of Elizabeth repeats the barrenness of Sarah (1:36 and Gen 11:30; 16:1), Rebecca (Gen 25:21), Rachel (Gen 29:31; 30:1), the wife of Manoah (Judg 13:2), and Hannah (1 Sam 1:2). Elizabeth responds to her unexpected pregnancy as does Rachel to the birth of Joseph (1:25 and Gen 30:23). Angels announce the births of John and Jesus as they did OT portents (1:8-20, 26-38; 2:8-14 and Gen 18:1-15; Dan 9:21). Mary's Magnificat echoes Hannah's song (1:46-55 and 1 Sam 2:1-10).[30] Luke's infancy narrative throbs with the literary and theological pulse of OT expectation. The OT, however, leaves the story of Israel unfinished, pending a resolution of its outstanding problems and paradoxes. Gabriel's annunciations in Luke 1–2 revive suspended and failed expectations, gathering great joy and hope as they announce the culmination of God's saving intervention not simply in Israel, but in all human history through the medium of Israel's historic fulfillment. The allusions of the infancy narrative do not simply repeat former stories and outcomes, however, as do the decrees of Mount Olympus, for example, which Homer transposes onto the fall of Troy. They herald new possibilities. The infancy narrative awakens readers not to the inevitable, but to expectation and hope. The allusions are beacons of light guiding the feet of those living in darkness and in the shadow of death (1:79) as they proceed into the precarious territory of God's radical intervention into the Roman world in the birth of a savior, who is Christ the Lord (2:11).

THE BIRTH OF JOHN (1:5-25)

5-7 "In the time of Herod king of Judea . . ." (v. 5). With these exact words, according to Epiphanius (ca. 315-403), the Hebrew Gospel began what may

28. For further elaboration of the infancy narratives, see A. Plummer, *Luke*, 6-7; E. Klostermann, *Lukasevangelium*, 3; J. Fitzmyer, *Luke (I–IX)*, 313-21; F. Bovon, *Gospel of Luke 1:1–9:50*, 29.
29. On Semitisms in Luke, see Edwards, *Hebrew Gospel*, 292-332.
30. Wolter, *Lukasevangelium*, 70.

have been the first written Gospel of Jesus Christ.[31] Evidence of Luke's reliance on this primitive document ebbs and flows throughout the Third Gospel, but nowhere is its contribution more evident than in the first two chapters, which are studded with Hebraisms.[32] **Herod**, an Idumaean by birth but a Jew by religion, ruled Palestine from 34 to 4 B.C. Romans did not normally allow puppet rulers to bear the title "king," but they recognized Herod's abilities and made an exception in his case.[33] Endowed with strength, stamina, and shrewdness, with a gift for taking strategic risks and landing on his feet, a passionate builder, artistically sensitive and sensuous, but barbarically cruel to his enemies, real or imagined, Herod managed to prosper in an era of political intrigue and dangerous liaisons by political sagacity and a veneer of cultural grandeur.[34] The *ruins* of Herod's buildings are still today more impressive than anything, ancient or modern, that visitors to Israel are likely to see. Nevertheless, despite his influence on the history, politics, and architecture of the first century, Herod lacked greatness of character and spirit and as a consequence did not change history. Herod sought in vain to immortalize himself and his reign, but at his death in 4 B.C. an angel announces the dawn of a new kingdom that will have no end (1:33).[35]

Luke begins his Gospel in the temple in Jerusalem that Herod began building in 20 B.C., but that would not be completed until A.D. 66. The temple in Jerusalem plays a singularly important role of commencing (v. 5) and concluding (24:49) the Third Gospel. The temple commemorated the presence of God more definitively than any other place in Israel or Judaism, and here

31. Epiphanius, *Pan.* 30.13.6; 30.14.3. On the testimony of Epiphanius to the Hebrew Gospel, see Edwards, *Hebrew Gospel,* 65-76.

32. Grundmann, *Lukas,* 23, writes, "The transition from the prologue (1:1-4) to the infancy narrative in v. 5 makes immediately apparent that Luke preserves in large measure the narrative style of his predecessors and allows their Semitic rudiments unmistakably to shine through."

33. "[Mark Antony] gave the throne to Herod, and Augustus, after his victory [over Antony at Actium] increased his power" (Tacitus, *Hist.* 5.9.3).

34. On Herod, see Josephus, *Ant.* 14.158–17.199; E. Schürer, *History of the Jewish People,* 1:287-329. For a modern scholarly treatment of this fascinating and appalling historical figure, see P. Richardson, *Herod: King of the Jews and Friend of the Romans* (Columbia: University of South Carolina Press, 1996).

35. The role of Herod the Great is accented differently in the infancy narratives of Matt and Luke. Matt casts Jesus' infancy in terms of the fulfillment of the OT, particularly its messianic prophecies. The second chapter of Matt is dominated by the figure of Herod (mentioned 9x), perhaps because Matt sees several messianic prophecies fulfilled in relation to Herod in 2:6, 15, 18. Luke is also interested in casting Jesus' infancy in light of the fulfillment of the OT, but more in terms of the fulfillment of salvation history rather than of messianic prophecy. Luke assigns Herod a negligible role in salvation history and correspondingly mentions him but once (1:5) in the infancy narrative.

Luke commences the story of the fulfillment of salvation history through the crucified and risen Messiah.[36] A priest named Zechariah (Heb. "remembered by God"), who belonged to the division of Abijah, "was chosen by lot, according to the custom of the priesthood, to go to the temple of the Lord and burn incense" (v. 9). The **Israelite priesthood** was divided into twenty-four classes or divisions, each of which needed to be available for the major festivals of Passover, Pentecost (Feast of Weeks), Day of Atonement, and Feast of Booths, and thereafter for service in the temple for one week, twice annually. The order of service of the various divisions was prescribed in 1 Chr 24:7-18 (further, 1 Esd 1:2, 15; Josephus, *Ant.* 7.366). According to *Let. Aris.* (92-95), priestly duties included officiating at worship, burning incense, celebrating liturgy, accepting sacrifices and offerings, hearing confessions, and above all butchery of animals for sacrifice. Each of the divisions was named after a family from which it had descended (Ezra 10:16-22; Neh 12:1-21), and each was presided over by a "head" or "officer." Some divisions were more prestigious than others; Abijah was a lesser division that served in the eighth week of each semester. The divisions represented a remarkable feat of organization and orchestration. Tractate *Ta'anit* in the Jerusalem Talmud numbers 1,000 priests per division, 24,000 total. Whether actual numbers were that high is unknown, but priestly divisions required large numbers of able-bodied men to offer the various sacrifices, which during Passover, for example, required the slaughter of no fewer than 100,000 lambs in the temple within a period of a few hours.[37]

Zechariah's wife "was also a descendent of Aaron" (v. 5) and, like Aaron's wife, was named Elizabeth (the Hellenized form of Heb. Elisheba; Exod 6:23). The ancestry of the prospective wife of a priest was carefully researched in order to verify that the woman was, ideally, the daughter of a priest or Levite, or at the least of undisputed Israelite background.[38] Luke begins his Gospel in the temple of Jerusalem with two protagonists from the priestly caste. The Third Gospel contains more references to the temple than do the other three. In commencing and concluding the Third Gospel in the temple, Luke signals to his audience, including Gentile readers, that the good news proclaimed to the nations has its source in Israel, and that the church, which comprises both Jews and Gentiles, is not a separate will and work of God but a divine germination that springs from the seed of Israel.

V. 5 establishes the impeccable credentials of Zechariah and Elizabeth.

---

36. M. Hengel, *Between Jesus and Paul* (trans. J. Bowden; Philadelphia: Fortress Press, 1983), 101.

37. On the priestly divisions and their services, see Str-B 2:55-70; E. Schürer, *History of the Jewish People*, 2:7-56; E. P. Sanders, *The Historical Figure of Jesus* (London: Penguin Press, 1993), 41-43. The work of slaughtering, skinning, and processing animal sacrifices occasionally overwhelmed the priests (2 Chr 29:34).

38. Str-B 2:68-71.

Vv. 6-7, however, relate two things about them that allow us as readers to identify with them. Zechariah and Elizabeth are more than title bearers and functional figures; they are persons of moral integrity. "Both were upright in the sight of God, observing all the Lord's commandments and regulations." This language identifies them with another ancestry, not of the Aaronic priesthood, but of the great protagonists of Israel's faith: of Noah, who was righteous before God (Gen 7:1), and of Abraham, who obeyed God's voice and kept all his commandments (Gen 26:5). Jesus declared that love of God and neighbor fulfills the law and prophets (10:25-27; Mark 12:28-31), and Zechariah and Elizabeth fulfill that ideal. In calling them blameless (v. 6), Luke does not imply that Zechariah and Elizabeth have no need of the righteousness of Christ (e.g., Phil 3:7-11), but rather, as Paul confesses of himself in Phil 3:4-6, that they had fulfilled the summary commands of Torah (Num 36:13; Deut 4:40; Josh 22:5) and prophets (Ezek 36:27).[39]

Because of advanced age and Elizabeth's barrenness, the couple is childless (v. 7). The exemplary piety and integrity of the couple, in other words, have gone unrewarded. This second datum strikes a tender nerve in readers, moving them from moral respect to unanticipated empathy with this otherwise remote couple. Zechariah and Elizabeth replay the anxious story of Abraham and Sarah, who were also old (Gen 18:11) and childless (Gen 11:30). The severe fate of Abraham and Sarah is now shared by a similar though more righteous couple. In the third century, both Origen and Rabbi Levi noted that, whenever Scripture pronounces a woman barren, God later gave her the holy son for whom she longed.[40] The predicament of Zechariah and Elizabeth now becomes an existential challenge not only to the aged couple, but also to the faith and hope of Luke's readers.

8-12   As Zechariah officiated, "he was chosen by lot, according to the custom of the priesthood, to go into the temple of the Lord and burn incense" (v. 9). The altar of incense was approximately twenty inches (0.5 m) square and forty inches (1.0 m) high, covered with gold, and placed in the Court of Israel, also known as the Holy Place, directly before the curtain separating the Holy of Holies from the Holy Place (Heb 9:2-7). The only furnishings in the Holy Place were the altar of incense, the golden lampstand, and the table of showbread (Exod 40:22-28), "three most wonderful works of art, universally renowned," according to Josephus (*J.W.* 5.216). Twice daily, morning and afternoon, priests burned incense (consisting of gum, resin, onycha, galbanum,

---

39. The reminder of Str-B 1:814 is relevant in this regard: "That a person possessed the ability without exception to fulfill God's commandments was so firmly rooted in rabbinic teaching, that in all seriousness the rabbis spoke of people who had kept the entire Torah from A to Z."

40. So Sarah, Rebecca, Rachel, and Hannah: Str-B 1:71; A. Just, *Luke,* 7.

frankincense, and salt, according to Exod 30:34-38) on the altar of incense as a perpetual offering to the Lord (Exod 30:1-10). Only priests who had not previously done so were eligible for the inexpressible honor of officiating at the altar of incense. Bearing a lidded ladle with approximately a gallon of incense (3.6 liters), the priest, accompanied by a second priest bearing coals in a similar ladle, entered the Court of Israel, offered the incense, prostrated himself, and retired. Following the sacrifice, priests pronounced the Aaronic blessing (Num 6:24-26) on the steps of the sanctuary. The recitation of the blessing was the only time that a priest was permitted to vocalize the divine name YHWH instead of substituting Adonai.[41] Zechariah's service took place while "all the assembled worshipers were praying outside" (v. 10), during which, according to Jewish tradition, they chanted, "God of mercy, come into your holy sanctuary and receive with pleasure the offering of your people."[42] Luke's frequent references to "all the people"[43] are a hallmark of his narrative, signifying the universal significance of the gospel. Whether Zechariah's officiating was at the morning or at the afternoon sacrifice is not indicated, nor does the crowd of worshipers, which may have been equally great at either sacrifice, argue for one over the other.[44]

As Zechariah performs his sacrifice, "an angel of the Lord appeared to him, standing at the right side of the altar of incense" (v. 11). A holy heavenly creature appears to a holy priest who is standing in a holy place and performing a holy sacrifice. Holiness might appear as a prerequisite for an encounter with the ineffable, perhaps even suggesting that the angelic vision is Zechariah's reward. Despite his cultic proprieties, Zechariah lacks the most important quality of a disciple — belief (v. 20). The angel (Gk. *angelos*, "heavenly messenger") is standing not to Zechariah's right, but to the right of the altar of incense. The altar symbolizes God's presence, and the right side is the all-important station of authority and exaltation. The position of the messenger, like the position of Jesus standing at the right hand of God Almighty (Acts 7:55-56), invests the message with divine legitimacy (Ps 110:1; Rev 5:7). The angel does not immediately identify himself. Only after the prophetic annunciation of vv. 13-17, and after due account of Zechariah's fears and inadequacies, does Gabriel, whose name means "God's Mighty One," reveal his identity (v. 19). The word of God, not the credentials of its messenger, is its own source of authority.

The Greek word *ōphthē* (v. 11; NIV "appeared") is a technical term in the

---

41. The incense sacrifice is thoroughly prescribed in Exod 30 and *m. Tamid.* Further, see Josephus, *Ant.* 3.147; Str-B 1:71-77; E. Schürer, *History of the Jewish People,* 2:302-6.

42. Str-B 2:79.

43. 1:10; 2:1, 10, 31; 3:3, 21; 4:25, 37; 6:17, 19, 26; 7:17, 29; 8:47; 9:13; 12:30; 13:17; 18:43; 20:45; 21:38; 24:19, 47. On this preferred Lukan expression, see Jeremias, *Sprache des Lukasevangeliums,* 30-31.

44. Str-B 2:75-77, assumes the morning sacrifice.

Greek Bible for divine and angelic appearances (Gen 12:7; 17:1; 26:24; Mark 9:4).[45] The angelic appearance is strongly reminiscent of similar appearances to Gideon (Judg 6:12) and Daniel (Dan. 9:21, to whom Gabriel appeared at the time of evening sacrifice). The first thing mentioned after the appearance of the angel is Zechariah's seizure by fear. The first Greek word used to describe Zechariah's reaction, *tarassein* (NIV "startled"), means to throw into turmoil and confusion; the second, *phobos* (NIV gripped with "fear"), a stronger term, means fright and terror. Throughout Scripture, angelic appearances reduce humans, like Zechariah, to *status horribilis et terribilis* (e.g., Judg 13:6). Zechariah's piety and righteousness are no shield from the terror of standing in the presence of a divine messenger; indeed, they may heighten it, for genuine piety and righteousness are always mindful of sinfulness and unworthiness before God.

13-20   Gabriel responds to Zechariah's fear with divine assurance, "Do not fear, Zechariah, your prayer has been heard" (v. 13).[46] The childlessness of Zechariah and Elizabeth is not unknown to God, nor have their prayers with respect to it been unheard or forgotten by God (18:1). The promise that Elizabeth will bear a son and call him John (v. 13) repeats verbatim (except for name changes) the divine promise to Sarah in Gen 17:19. The birth of Isaac fulfilled the long-awaited promise of God to form a new people in the call of Abraham (Gen 12:1-3). The promise of a son to Zechariah in the same formula presages a new eschatological people of the Son of God who will receive the throne of his father David (v. 32). The child will be named "John," which in Hebrew (Jochanan) means "God is gracious." The name signifies that the childlessness and insufficiency of the aged couple have been relieved not by their piety or merit, but by divine grace. V. 14 could be translated either, "There will be joy and delight to you" (NRSV), or "He will be a joy and delight to you" (NIV). The latter reading is preferable because (1) the preceding (v. 13) and following (v. 15) verses both refer to John; and (2) vv. 14, 15 both begin with Greek *estai* (future, third-person singular), which in v. 15 refers to John. Hence, v. 14 probably refers to John. The child will bring joy to his parents and to "many." Whether "many" should be understood as a Semitic reference to "all" (so Isa 52:14-15; 53:11-12; Rom 5:12-21; Heb 12:15),[47] or in a more restricted sense, is not clear. The angelic prophecy clearly imputes vicarious agency to John, however, for through him the lives of many will be

---

45. M. Wolter, *Lukasevangelium,* 77.

46. In his interpretation of the Third Gospel, Theophylact of Euboea (ca. 1050–ca. 1125) observes that the prayer of Zechariah at the altar of incense would not have been for a son but rather for the sins of the people. On account of his prayer on behalf of others, however, God answered the deeper prayer of his own heart for a son. See Kealy, *Interpretation of the Gospel of Luke,* 159.

47. See J. Jeremias, *polloi, TWNT* 6:540-42.

affected. Prophecies of God's imminent action often arouse the dread of judgment and punishment. Gabriel's prophecy, however, results in *agalliasis* — joy, gladness, exaltation (v. 14). In the LXX, the Greek word *agalliasis* translates several different Hebrew words in the MT, all of which signify either joy in God or in God's eschatological fulfillment. In the NT this rather infrequent term likewise carries a sense of joy in God, especially in God's consummate saving act in Jesus Christ.[48] The first angelic prophecy in Luke is thus, literally, the gospel — "good news."

The remainder of Gabriel's prophecy in vv. 15-17 amplifies v. 14 by giving reasons for the elation attending John's birth. Like Jesus (v. 32), John will be "great"; but also like Jesus, his greatness will be "in the sight of the Lord" (v. 15) rather than greatness according to a human scale of measurement. The reference to his avoidance of wine and alcohol (v. 15) is a quotation from Num 6:3, where abstinence from alcohol is a condition for fulfillment of a Nazirite vow. It is unlikely that v. 15 implies that John will be a Nazirite, however, for John is not said to fulfill three Nazirite distinctives: not cutting his hair, undergoing a prescribed thirty-day initiation vow, avoiding contact with the dead.[49] John's abstinence from "wine and fermented drink" (v. 15) is better understood in light of the priestly regulations required in Lev 10:9, which, like the similar prohibition of the boy Samuel (1 Sam 1:11), signified personal commitment "to make ready a people for the Lord" (v. 17). Ascetic qualities will not be John's only, or chief, credentials, however. His abstention from alcohol may indicate his acknowledgment of being "filled with the Holy Spirit," which does not depend on his choice or virtue, but on God's prevenient election in the womb of his mother (v. 15). Others also had been set apart from their mothers' wombs by God's Spirit — Samson (Judg 13), the Servant of the Lord (Isa 49:1), Jeremiah (Jer 1:5), Paul (Gal 1:15) — but whereas they were intermediary links in God's plan, John is the final link preparing the way for one whose "kingdom will never end" (v. 33). Form critics frequently drove a wedge between John and Jesus, portraying John as the last prophet of the old era rather than a herald of the new.[50] In the gospel tradition, however, the advent of Jesus is linked inseparably with John. Even the Fourth Gospel, which introduces the incarnation in relation to the preexistent, eternal Word, commences Jesus' earthly ministry in relation to John (John 1). The annunciation of Gabriel, likewise, identifies John as "the

48. R. Bultmann, *agalliaomai, agalliasis,* *TWNT* 1:18-20; A. Weiser, *agalliaō, agalliasis,* *EDNT* 1:7-8.

49. On Nazirites, see Num 6; Judg 13, 16; *m. Naz.;* J. C. Rylaarsdam, "Nazirite," *IDB* 3:526-27. Moreover, the mother of Samson was forbidden alcoholic drink (Judg 13:14), although Samson himself, the foremost Nazirite, was not.

50. E.g., H. Conzelmann, *The Theology of Saint Luke* (trans. G. Buswell; London: SPCK, 1960), 22-23.

one who will go before the Lord in the spirit and power of Elijah" (v. 17) and introduce the joyful evangelical era (v. 14). John's peerless role is enabled and orchestrated by the Holy Spirit, who is mentioned a dozen times in Luke (compared to 5x in Matt, and 4x each in Mark and John). More than any other, the Third Evangelist identifies the Spirit as the executive director of the saving work of God in the Incarnation.

The Holy Spirit will call and animate John "in the spirit and power of Elijah" (v. 17; see Mal 3:1) for the purpose of completing the work of Elijah (Mal 4:6; Sir 48:10) — "to return the people of Israel to the Lord their God" (v. 16), "the hearts of the fathers to their children," "the disobedient to the wisdom of the righteous," "to make ready a people prepared for the Lord" (v. 17). The work ascribed to John will exceed that of a religious and moral reformer. The latter may change behaviors, but John's mission will be animated by "spirit and power" (v. 17) and result in *conversion*. Where divisions reach their deepest and most destructive levels, John's mission will turn the hearts of parents to children, reconcile families, and transform strong-willed rebellion to righteousness. John's mission will not stop with individual change but will effect the formation of a new society, turning Israel back to God. The mantle of the great prophet who prepares Israel to meet its God has fallen to John. Elijah is often assumed to have been the forerunner of the Messiah. In pre-Christian Jewish texts preserved in the OT and intertestamental literature, however, Elijah is actually portrayed as the forerunner of *God*.[51] In prophesying that "[John] will go before him" (v. 17; NIV "before the Lord"), Gabriel indicates that John will not simply herald the Messiah, but God himself, who will appear in Jesus.[52]

Gabriel's prophecy in vv. 13-17 again recalls Abraham and Sarah. To Zechariah and Elizabeth, as to aged Abraham and Sarah, a divine promise comes that a yet-unborn son will begin a new world order. No wonder Zechariah remonstrates. Abraham remonstrated his childlessness to God in practically the same words (Gen 15:8). Zechariah and Elizabeth are too old for children, and his wife is barren. The good news announced by Gabriel seems impossible of fulfillment, unbelievable. Zechariah's protest, "How can I be sure of this?" (v. 18), seems to presuppose a *sign* of confirmation. The angel does not offer a sign, but rather his name as a verification of his message, "I am Gabriel." Gabriel's self-disclosure, prefaced by an emphatic "I am" (Gk. *ego eimi*), is a pledge to Zechariah in this fragile moment. Angels are infrequent in canonical Jewish literature, but Gabriel, along with Michael and Raphael, always belongs to a select group of heavenly messengers who attend God's

---

51. M. Öhler, "The Expectation of Elijah and the Presence of the Kingdom of God," *JBL* 118 (1999): 641-76.

52. So too Grundmann, *Lukas*, 51; Wolter, *Lukasevangelium*, 81.

throne and are intimately knowledgeable of his will (Isa 63:9; Ezek 6:1; *Jub.* 1:27; 1Q28b 4:25; *1 En.* 20; Rev 8:2). Zechariah's remonstration that he and his wife are old betrays an element of doubt, however. Gabriel therefore reinforces his authority by announcing that he belongs to God's inner circle, and that he was sent by God with the announcement of good news. The passive voice of the verb "was sent" (v. 19) is important: Gabriel is not self-appointed but stands before Zechariah at the command and commission of God Almighty. Luke does not use the noun for "good news" *(to euangelion)* in his Gospel (and only twice in Acts). He prefers the verbal form in v. 19 and in its other ten occurrences in the Third Gospel (and fifteen occurrences in Acts). The verbal form connotes vitality and transformative energy, the *enactment* of "good news," with the corresponding description of the early Christian movement as "the way" in Acts.[53]

Gabriel's final word is not related to the prophecy about John but is directed to Zechariah's request for a sign (vv. 18-20). In the NT the request for a sign is frequently regarded as a lack of faith (11:16; Mark 8:11-13; Acts 13:11; 1 Cor 1:22). A sign capable of removing all doubt may remove faith itself. In the OT signs often appear in more neutral or even positive lights. Others before Zechariah, and not unlike him, had asked God for signs, but without being punished (Abraham, Gen 15:2; Moses, Exod 4:1; Gideon, Judg 6:36-40; Samuel, 1 Sam 10:2; Hezekiah, 2 Kgs 20:8). God even insisted that a timorous Israelite king request a sign (Isa 7:11). Zechariah's request in v. 18 is similar to Mary's in v. 34 and in itself does not appear objectionable. Gabriel's spiritual discernment, however, understands it as an expression of disbelief (v. 20), and as a consequence Zechariah is rendered mute until the birth of the child. Gabriel's sentence results in an impairment that disqualifies Zechariah from further priestly duty.[54] Disbelief is not the result of Zechariah's feelings, doubts, temperament, or circumstances, but of personal choice. The divine word is given as an invitation to choose faith, and the choice of faith awakens further faith. Not unlike Jacob (Gen 32:22-32), Zechariah reminds us that one does not contend with God and leave unchanged. The purpose of Gabriel's judgment is not to annul the choice of Zechariah, nor does it result in his fall from grace or halt the fulfillment of God's promise. It is a remedial work of the Spirit — a severe mercy — that will enable faith. The "spiritual experience" of believers is not the determining factor in the life of

---

53. Acts 9:2; 13:10; 16:17; 18:25, 26; 19:9, 23; 22:4; 24:14, 22.

54. On physical defects that disqualified priests, see Lev 21:16-23, esp. v. 21: "No descendant of Aaron the priest who has any defect is to come near to present the offerings made to the Lord by fire." On deaf-*mute* per se, see *m. Bek.* 7:6. J. A. Bengel, *Gnomon*, 2:15, interprets the disqualification from the priesthood allegorically: "This constitutes the prelude of the termination of the ceremonial law, now that Christ is coming."

discipleship, but rather the concrete promises of God, "which will come true at their appointed time" (v. 20).

21-25   Zechariah was not alone at the altar of incense. Other priests officiated in the Court of Israel with him, but Luke focuses on Zechariah alone. As the crowd awaits his exit and pronouncement of the benediction (Num 6:24-26; Sir 50:19-21), suspense grows, even a sense of danger (Dan 10:7). After all, no one can look on the face of God and live (Exod 33:20), and the incense altar is near the Holy of Holies, where God is numinously present. If a messenger of God smites a mortal with fear (v. 12), how much more so the unmediated presence of God? When Zechariah emerged "he could not speak [the benediction] to them" (v. 22). The worshipers are aware that in fulfilling his priestly duties Zechariah has seen a supernatural vision, for that is the meaning of the Greek *optasia* (v. 22). Luke accentuates his muteness with alliteration: *dianeuein . . . diamenein* (v. 22; NIV "he kept making signs to them, but he remained unable to speak"). Zechariah's term of service expired on the Sabbath, but his muteness would effectively terminate his temple duties in any case. At the end of the week, Zechariah and Elizabeth returned home. Outside Jerusalem itself, the main residence of priests and Levites in Jesus' day was Jericho, where half of each priestly division resided while the other half served in Jerusalem.[55] Jericho cannot have been the home of Zechariah, however, for Jericho lay in the Jordan valley, and Zechariah and Elizabeth lived in an unspecified Judean hill town (1:39). There, after becoming pregnant, Elizabeth "hid herself for five months" (v. 24, lit. in Greek). No known Palestinian custom calls for such seclusion. In Greek, v. 25 begins with a limited explanation, "*For thus* the Lord has done to me in these days in which he has looked down to remove my disgrace among people" (my translation). In Elizabeth's day childlessness, which was often attributed to a woman's fault, was regarded a social humiliation, if not an adverse judgment of God. Elizabeth, however, is aware that God has shown grace to *her,* and not simply to her husband or for his sake. Her circumstance repeats that of Rachel at the birth of Joseph, and with Rachel she confesses, "God has taken away my disgrace" (Gen 30:23). She hides herself for five months until her pregnancy is obvious and her disgrace removed. "[God] hears the prayer of an individual and, through him — because he is a priest — the prayer of a nation. He takes away the disgrace of an individual and, through her, the disgrace of Israel."[56] Something is at hand "in these days" (v. 25) that has not happened before: a people is being prepared for the Lord (v. 17). Something "unknown to historical knowledge" is about to be proclaimed: a universal way of salvation.[57]

55. Str-B 2:66.
56. F. Bovon, *Luke 1:1–9:50,* 41.
57. Augustine, *Civ.* 10.32.

THE BIRTH OF JESUS (1:26-38)

Luke sets the annunciation of Jesus' birth in close parallelism with the annunciation of John's birth. Both annunciations contain five elements common with most angelic birth announcements in the OT:

1. Entrance of heavenly messenger (1:11//1:28)
2. Perplexity of recipient (1:12//1:29)
3. Deliverance of heavenly message (1:13-17//1:30-33)
4. Objection of recipient (1:18//1:34)
5. Reassurance and sign (1:19//1:35-37).[58]

The two annunciations are narrated independently of one another, yet both are governed by the one divine purpose of inaugurating God's eschatological kingdom. The two annunciations are thus narrative elements of a single story, which Luke signifies by their sequential placement and parallel details. The overarching metanarrative does not absorb and dissolve the particulars of the two annunciations, however, but accentuates the unique elements of each in the purpose of God.

The history of religions school, which so influenced nineteenth- and twentieth-century biblical interpretation, often compared and even attributed Mary's conception to the many stories of gods consorting with earthly woman in the myths, sagas, and stories of the ancient Near East. A judicious comparison of the virginal conception of Jesus with the various stories of gods consorting with earthly women reveals significant differences. The amorous exploits of Zeus and other Olympian gods all involve acts of sexual intercourse (which the annunciation of Mary does not), whereas female virginity plays no role in classical mythology (as it does in the annunciation of Mary). Stories of celestial amours with earthly women were much less common in Judaism, but they were not unknown, as is evidenced by a rabbinic legend of an angel who impersonated an impotent rabbi in order to impregnate his pious wife.[59] Another category of conceptions involves preternatural circumstances surrounding births of mythic heroes of the past or founders of religious cults, including births of religious figures such as Osiris,[60] legendary figures of the mythic past such as Romulus and Numa Pompilius,[61] or historic heroes such as Alexander[62] and Caesar Augustus.[63] The mothers of Alexander and Augustus

58. See Fitzmyer, *Luke (I–IX)*, 335; Brown, *Birth*, 292-98.
59. Str-B 2:98-99.
60. Plutarch, *Mor.*
61. Both of which are discussed in Plutarch, *Lives of the Noble Grecians and Romans.*
62. Plutarch, *Lives of the Noble Grecians and Romans.*
63. Suetonius, *Aug.* 94.

were both reported to have been mythically impregnated by serpents.[64] The purpose of such birth wonders is directed less to the actual births, which are often shrouded in obscurity, than to account for the extraordinary achievements of their respective heroes in later life. Another class of conceptions, reflected in Philo, for example, focuses on "the seed of generation" involved in human conceptions as the agency of divine mystery.[65] The focus here is on the divine mystery of all human generation rather than on the uniqueness of a particular birth, as is the case with the annunciations of John and Jesus. A final category of miraculous conceptions in *Prot. Jas.*[66] and *Sib. Or.,*[67] for instance, demonstrates unmistakable parallels to the annunciation of Mary. The similarities in these two accounts, the first deriving from the second century and the relevant sections in the *Sib. Or.* later than that, are due to reliance on Luke. To sum up, the annunciation of Mary bears a thematic similarity to the genre of wondrous conceptions in pagan antiquity, but its character and detail are not close enough to any such accounts to posit a derivation from them. C. S. Lewis's understanding of the incarnation as the "true myth" that sums up and transcends earlier mythological intimations offers an intriguing insight for contemplating the thematic similarities between Mary's conception and wondrous births of antiquity.[68]

The Jewish thought-world clearly provided concepts and vocabulary that influenced 1:26-38. Salient elements of Isa 9:6-7 are evident in Gabriel's prophecy, including the birth of a son, his greatness, messianic rule "on the throne of David," and eternal governance as Mighty God in peace and justice. The

---

64. Of Alexander's conception, Dryden wrote:

> A dragon's fiery form belied the god;
> Sublime on radiant spires he rode
> When he to fair Olympia prest,
> And while he sought her snowy breast,
> Then round her slender waist he curl'd,
> And stamp'd an image of himself, a sovereign of the world.
>
> John Dryden, "Alexander's Feast, or the Power of Music"

65. Philo, *Cher.* 43-47.

66. W. Schneemelcher, *NTApoc.* 1:421-39.

67. *Sib. Or.* have a long and complex textual history, evolving from pre- to post-Christian times. The paragraph on the incarnation in 8.456-80 is post-Christian and reflects Luke 1–2, John 1:14, and Matt 2. See J. Charlesworth, *OTP* 1.327-472; and John J. Collins, "Sibylline Oracles," *ABD* 6:2-6.

68. C. S. Lewis, "Myth Became Fact," in *God in the Dock: Essays on Theology and Ethics* (ed. W. Hooper; Grand Rapids: Eerdmans, 1972), 63-67. "We must not be ashamed of the mythical radiance resting on our theology. We must not be nervous about 'parallels' and 'Pagan Christs': they *ought* to be there — it would be a stumbling block if they weren't. We must not, in false spirituality, withhold our imaginative welcome. If God chooses to be mythopoeic . . . shall we refuse to be *mythopathic?*" (p. 67).

same expectation of a heavenly kingdom ruled by a "Son of the Most High" is present in the Dead Sea Scrolls. The following three phrases from 4Q246 are particularly reminiscent of 1:32-33: "[He] will be great," "he will be called Son of God and Son of the Most High," and "his kingdom will be an everlasting kingdom." Like Gabriel's annunciation, this Qumran text heralds a coming Son of God who will rule God's kingdom in truth and justice. Although 4Q246 is earlier than Luke, it is not likely that it has influenced Luke directly. Rather, the Qumran text provides an(other) instance of the influence of Isa 9 on the various traditions and branches of Judaism. Indeed, the influence of Isa 9 is greater on 4Q246 than on 1:30-35.[69] The influence of Isa 9 may have overflowed the banks of Judaism and reached the Roman world as well. Virgil's *Fourth Eclogue,* written perhaps a century before the Third Gospel, predicts the birth of a boy who will introduce a golden age in the Roman world and "reign over a world in peace" and justice. Sections of *Sib. Or.* (e.g., 3.367-80), which date from the second-century B.C., resemble Isa 9 fairly closely. *Sib. Or.* was popular in Rome in Virgil's day and could have inspired both the hopes and the language of the *Fourth Eclogue* and *Aen.* 6.792-94, in both of which Virgil foretells a Son of God who will establish a glorious age. Patristic and medieval theologians commonly regarded the *Fourth Eclogue* as an example of divine prophecy in the pagan world. If Virgil was influenced by Isa 9 via *Sib. Or.,* as he may have been, then there is more than a grain of truth in the suspicions of older theologians.[70]

26-27 The temporal reference in v. 26 refers to "the sixth month" of Elizabeth's pregnancy and connects the annunciations of John and Jesus. The reappearance of Gabriel, again "sent from God" (see v. 19), further connects the annunciations. The passive voice indicates that Gabriel is not on an elective mission, but obeying God's commission. Calling, mission, and obedience characterize both celestial and earthly service of the divine. The fact that **Nazareth** must be identified as "a town in Galilee" indicates its obscurity (see, e.g., John 1:46). Nazareth is not mentioned in the OT, Josephus, rabbinic literature, Mishnah, or Talmud. Nazareth is mentioned in the NT a dozen times, but it does not appear in a writer outside the NT until Julius Africanus, who writes two centuries after Jesus' birth. No church was built in Nazareth until the era of Constantine (325). Archaeological excavations have uncovered a series of grottoes under the Churches of the Annunciation and St. Joseph that date to the time of Jesus. The evidence indicates a hamlet of earthen dwellings without independent political importance cut into sixty acres (25 ha) of rocky hillside,

---

69. On 4Q246, see García Martínez and Tigchelaar, *Dead Sea Scrolls,* 1:493-94; and John J. Collins, "A Pre-Christian 'Son of God' among the Dead Sea Scrolls," *BRev* 9/3 (1993): 34-38.

70. For a discussion of the *Fourth Eclogue,* see R. Brown, *Birth,* 564-70.

with a total population of perhaps five hundred people, at the most. Nazareth appears to have been a vibrant village, producing wheat, wine, oil, fruit, honey, and millet. Nor was it entirely isolated, for three and a half miles (6 km) south lay the showcase city of Sepphoris, where major traffic routes converged, affording Nazareth a window of access and influence to the Hellenistic world.[71]

In introducing Mary, Luke twice refers to her as a "virgin" (v. 27). Despite the similarities of the annunciations of Zechariah and Mary to OT precedents, this is a new feature, for neither Sarah, Hagar, Rachel, nor the wife of Manoah was a virgin. The Greek word for "virgin," *parthenos*, means a young woman of marriageable age (Matt 25:1, 7, 11), with the accent on virginity (e.g., 1 Cor. 7, where it refers to the virgin state of unmarried men and women). *Parthenos* usually translates Heb. *bethulah*, which in its fifty occurrences in the OT consistently means a woman who has not experienced sexual intercourse.[72] "Pledged to be married" (again in 2:5) means that Mary had exchanged marital consent with Joseph, but had not been taken to his house. Isolated church fathers understood "descendent of David" to refer to Mary rather than Joseph, but this is unlikely. "Descendent of David" (Gk. lit. "house of David") immediately follows the reference to Joseph and ostensibly modifies it, as it does again in 2:4 and Matt 1:20. The natural sense of the phrase is that Mary was engaged to be married "to a man named Joseph, of the house of David." Although Mary is the protagonist in this story, Luke mentions Joseph's name first, perhaps to accentuate the Davidic ancestry of Jesus through Joseph (so too 3:23).

28-33 It was normally taboo for a man to greet an unknown woman in Judaism.[73] To approach and greet an engaged woman might even be understood to challenge the fiancé's authority. Gabriel's mission of informing an unmarried and ineligible young woman in an insignificant village that she will bear a child is fraught with social obstacles. How ironic, therefore, the address of Gabriel: "Greetings, you who are highly favored! The Lord is with you" (v. 28).[74] What in Mary's circumstances is favorable? Origen marveled at Gabriel's address, finding nothing like it in all Scripture.[75] Aquinas marveled that the

---

71. On Nazareth, see Dalman, *Sacred Sites and Ways,* 57-78; J. Strange, "Nazareth," *ABD* 4:1050-51; J. Murphy-O'Connor, *The Holy Land,* 374-77.

72. See BDAG, 777; J. A. Fitzmyer, "Parthenos," *EDNT* 3:39-40. In Isa 7:14 the Hebrew behind *parthenos* (LXX) is *almah,* which occurs nine times in the OT, usually as "virgin," but occasionally as "young woman" without reference to sexual experience (Prov. 30:19). Given the importance of female virginity prior to marriage in the OT, however, it seems probable that *almah* also widely connoted virginity.

73. Str-B 2:99.

74. A number of manuscripts add "Blessed are you among women" to Gabriel's greeting, but this addition, which is not as well attested as the shorter reading, was probably inserted by later copyists from 1:42 (see Metzger, *TCGNT,* 108).

75. *Hom. Luc.* 6.7.

angelic blessing is the first instance in Scripture of an angel showing reverence to a human being.[76] The word for "greetings" (Gk. *chaire*) is the customary Greek greeting, but the word for "highly favored" *(kecharitōmenē)* occurs only here and in Eph 1:6. This second word is derived from the Greek word for "grace" and is more important, for in the NT grace is reserved solely for divine acts. *Kecharitōmenē* (perfect passive participle) carries the sense, "you who have been favored with grace," with the accent on anticipatory or prevenient grace. Mary is not earning God's favor, but like Gideon (Judg 6:12), in this unusual address and unusual visitation, she is receiving God's predetermined blessing. The assurance that "the Lord is with you," which also can be found in Judg 6:12 and Ruth 2:4, is almost certainly a declaration rather than the expression of a wish (i.e., "May the Lord be with you").[77] It assures Mary of a factual condition: God is with her. It does not direct her attention to a *what* (a set of outcomes), but to a *whom* — to the personal agency of *the Lord who is with you,* recalling perhaps God's revelation to Moses in Exod 3 as the God who hears and sees and knows, the "with-you-God" who breaks into the human arena. Like Moses, Mary is the recipient of God's unexpected, undeserved, and overwhelming grace. Bengel captured the surprise of the annunciation in saying that Mary is "not the mother of grace, but the daughter of grace."[78]

Like Zechariah (1:12) and virtually all recipients of angelic visitations in Scripture, Mary is "greatly troubled" (v. 29). The Greek word describing her fear *(diatarassein),* occurring only here in the NT, is stronger than the word describing the fear *(tarassein)* that both Zechariah (1:12) and Herod the Great (Matt 2:3) experienced. Ironically, Mary, the quintessential model of faith, is more greatly perplexed by the presence of God than are persons of lesser faith, or of no faith. Some ancient manuscripts (A, C, Θ) attribute her fear to what she *saw.* This is probably a later attempt to explain her fear, as is her vain search for the source of the voice in *Prot. Jas.* 11.1. The Western text (D) adds that Mary "wondered *in herself* what kind of greeting this might be" (v. 29). The reflexive "in herself" could be original, for this is a frequent expression in Luke that appears to have originated from his Hebrew source.[79] Luke explicitly states that Mary's perplexity is due to Gabriel's *words* (v. 29). The unexpectedness of God choosing one so unlikely and unimportant is confounding and perplexing. It is not something Mary finds assuring. Only in wrestling with the word may Mary become "a servant of the word" (1:2).

76. Thomas, *On the Hail Mary (On the Angelic Salutation):* "It was written in praise of Abraham that he received angels hospitably and that he showed them reverence. But it was never heard that an angel showed reverence to a man until he saluted the blessed virgin, saying reverently, 'Hail'" (cited in Kealy, *Interpretation of the Gospel of Luke,* 228).

77. See Brown, *Birth,* 288.

78. Bengel, *Gnomon,* 2:216.

79. Edwards, *Hebrew Gospel,* 139.

Gabriel addresses Mary directly and personally: "Do not be afraid, Mary, you have found favor with God" (v. 30). Gabriel charged Zechariah likewise not to be afraid (1:13), and in the Midrash on Gen 18:11 the angel Michael charged the same of Sarah.[80] Gabriel's word does not seek to calm Mary's emotions, but to assure her of the work to which God calls her. The Greek word behind "favor" is *charis,* "grace." The assurance that Mary has "found favor with God" repeats the essence of v. 28, that Mary, for reasons she cannot fathom, stands in God's grace (see Gen 6:8; Exod 33:16; Prov 12:2).

Gabriel's commission of Mary in v. 31 is virtually identical to his commission of Zechariah in 1:13, but it is intensified in two ways — first by addressing Mary directly and personally in second person, "you," and second, by instructing that Mary rather than Joseph will name the child. The almighty male has been bypassed in both the procreative process and in the naming of the son. The closest OT parallel to Gabriel's commission of Mary is not the charge of Manoah and his wife (Judg 13:3), not even the famous wording of Isa 7:14, but the angelic annunciation to Hagar: "You are now with child and you will bear a son and you will call his name Ishmael, because the Lord has heard you in your humiliation" (Gen 16:11). In the Magnificat, Mary will confess that God looked on her humiliation (1:48), as he had on Hagar's. Luke cast Zechariah and Elizabeth according to the patri- and matriarchal models of Abraham and Sarah, but he casts Mary in the plight of Hagar. Even in their prayers for progeny, Zechariah and Elizabeth, like Abraham and Sarah, have a wealth of personal and material resources to rely on. Not so Mary. Like Hagar, she is more alone and vulnerable, with fewer resources in which to trust except for the promise of Gabriel itself. The foreseeable outcome of a pregnancy in her state will be expulsion from Joseph's house, as Hagar was expelled from Abraham's. Mary herself will need to live by the name of her son Jesus, which means "[God] will save."

V. 31 does not explicitly declare a virginal conception. Not surprisingly, some scholars interpret v. 31 to imply a normal or even illegitimate pregnancy. One scholar argues that Mary's reference to "humiliation" in the Magnificat (1:48) is an outcry of injustice that recalls the rape and seduction of a betrothed virgin in Deut 22:23-27.[81] This cannot represent Luke's intention. A virginal conception, though not clearly stated, is clearly implied. Mary is called a virgin twice in v. 27, and in v. 34 she questions how she can become pregnant apart from sexual intercourse. Luke's later allusion to Jesus as the "supposed" son of

---

80. Str-B 2:99.
81. J. Schaberg, *The Illegitimacy of Jesus: A Feminist Theological Interpretation of the Infancy Narratives* (San Francisco: Harper & Row, 1987). For a critique of Schaberg's thesis, see D. Landry, "Narrative Logic in the Annunciation to Mary (Luke 1:26-38)," *JBL* 114/1 (1995): 65-79.

Joseph (3:23) implies a nonnatural conception. Elizabeth's pregnancy is due to divine intervention (1:13), and Mary's can scarcely be considered less so. Above all, Mary's response in v. 38 is not an outcry of injustice but a believing and humble submission to Gabriel's pronouncement. Nothing in the account supports a theory of divine sexual violation. To be sure, there is no mention of Mary's perpetual virginity in the annunciation, but the annunciation unmistakably informs her that as a virgin she will conceive a child, and that her conception is the result of the gracious, joyful, and saving intervention of God.[82]

Vv. 32-33 record five declarations of Gabriel, all joined by the Greek copulative *kai* ("and"), that will characterize the saving intervention of God in Jesus.[83] First, Jesus will be "great." John's greatness was in the sight of God (1:15), but Jesus' greatness is unqualified and absolute. Especially in the LXX, greatness without a qualifier is an attribute of God alone (Pss 48:2; 86:10; 135:5; 145:3). Gabriel attributes this quality to Jesus.[84] Second, Jesus "will be called the Son of the Most High." "Most High" is an early appellation of Melchizedek for God, Heb. *El Elyon* (Gen 14:18; Heb 7:1). In the OT and later Judaism, *El Elyon* and "Most High" (Gk. *hypsistos*) became an exclusive name for the one true God, emphasizing his majesty and supremacy over all.[85] This divine epithet is also ascribed to Jesus. Third, "the Lord God will give him the throne of his father David." The "Son of the Most High" is not an episodic work of God, but the revelation of the one who will fulfill the messianic ideal of David set forth in Isa 9:6, and especially in 2 Sam 7. Indeed, the four attributes of Nathan's dynastic oracle in 2 Sam 7 are here applied to Jesus: great name (2 Sam 7:9//v. 32), messianic throne (2 Sam 7:13//v. 32), divine sonship (2 Sam 7:14//v. 32), eternal kingdom (2 Sam 7:16//v. 33).[86] Fourth, the Son's reign will last forever. Eternal rule over Zion, which Mic 4:7 ascribes to God, is ascribed to Mary's son in the annunciation. In contrast to King Herod's futile attempts to establish a dynasty in perpetuity, the Messiah-Son "will reign over the house of Jacob (= Israel) forever." Finally, the reign of the Messiah-Son will found a kingdom that will never end. Eternality is an attribute of God, and in the OT only God's kingdom is eternal (Isa 9:7; Dan 7:14; Ps 145:13; Heb 7:24; etc.). All five divine declarations of Gabriel, four of which alone characterize God, are applied expressly to Jesus. The two great redemptive offices in Israel, the

---

82. For a thorough examination and defense of the virginal conception, see Brown, *Birth*, 298-309, 534-43.

83. So Wolter, *Lukasevangelium*, 89.

84. Fitzmyer, *Luke (I–IX)*, 325.

85. In the NT "Most High" is used by Gentiles (Mark 5:7; Luke 8:28; Acts 16:17), angels (Luke 1:32, 35, 76; 2:14), Jesus (6:35), and Jews (Matt 21:9 par.; Acts 7:48) to accentuate the uniqueness of God. Further, see G. Bertram, *hypsistos, TWNT* 8:617.

86. Fitzmyer, *Luke (I–IX)*, 338.

Messiah and Son of God, will in Mary's womb converge in the incarnation of Jesus, who will finally and fully complete the redemption of Israel.

34-35   Gabriel's glad tidings in vv. 30-33 do not relieve Mary's perplexity, however. They heighten it. Like all mortals, Mary's understanding is determined by *human* reality and possibility. She knows that children cannot be conceived apart from sexual intercourse, and that in Israel they ought not be conceived outside marriage. As an unmarried woman who has not had sexual intercourse, Mary takes exception to Gabriel's announcement, "How will this be, since I am a virgin?" (v. 34). The original Greek literally reads, "since I am not knowing a man [husband]." The word for "know" (Gk. *ginōskein*) is the normal Hebrew circumlocution implying sexual intercourse (Gen 19:8; Num 31:17; Judg 11:39). Mary's response is nearly identical to Zechariah's in v. 18, but whereas Zechariah's implied disbelief, Mary's does not. She understands the annunciation to mean that she will conceive a child as an unmarried woman who is not involved in a sexual relation. Her response contains a hint of what Kierkegaard wrestles with in the sacrifice of Isaac (Gen 22): God seems to command or promise something that violates his own rules.[87] *Prot. Jas.* 13.1–16.2, a later romance based on Luke 1–2, underscores this same dilemma by having Joseph and Mary undergo the test of adultery by drinking (and surviving) the bitter potion of Num 5:11-31.

Gabriel addresses Mary directly in her quandary: "The Holy Spirit will come upon you, and the power of the Most High will overshadow you. So the holy one to be born will be called the Son of God" (v. 35). Gabriel's message contains three substantives — Holy Spirit, power of the Most High, and Son of God — but "power of the Most High" should probably be understood in apposition to Holy Spirit and thus synonymous with it. The combination of spirit and power is typical and important in Luke, and they are often used interchangeably (1:17; 4:14; Acts 1:8; 6:5, 8; 10:38).[88] V. 35 thus addresses the Holy Spirit and Jesus as the Son of God. Jesus Christ is the Son of God because of a union of the Holy Spirit, the power of the Most High, in the person of Mary. The NIV translation, "So the holy one to be born will be called the Son of God," is grammatically possible, but more preferable is, "So the one to be born will be holy, called the Son of God" (see similar construction in 2:23). The holiness of the child is the result of his generation by the Holy Spirit. Gabriel's pronouncement does not address the preexistence of the Son before the incarnation, but the wording that Jesus will be *called* Son of God, not that he will *become* such, can be taken to support preexistence.

Critically important in understanding the glorious eschatological pro-

---

87. S. Kierkegaard, *Fear and Trembling* (trans. W. Lowrie; Princeton: Princeton University Press, 1974). Kierkegaard discusses this issue under the rubric of "the teleological suspension of the ethical" (Problem I, pp. 64-71).

88. Brown, *Birth*, 290.

nouncement of v. 35 is the word "overshadow" (Gk. *episkiazein*), which recalls the divine cloud that overshadowed the tabernacle in Exod 40:35 (LXX). When all work on the tabernacle had been completed (Exod 40:33), God overshadowed *(episkiazein)* it and infused it with his presence and glory. In the tabernacle, God chose to materialize and localize himself within a particular time and space. Luke uses this otherwise inconsequential word, which occurs in only three other places in the OT, to describe the divine overshadowing of Mary (v. 35). The divine cloud that established his presence in a place now does so in a *person*. The divine overshadowing of the earthly tabernacle was a *foreshadowing* of the living tabernacle, the incarnation. John's inimitable declaration that "the Word became flesh and dwelt among us" (John 1:14) repeats this motif, for the Greek word behind "dwelt," *skēnoun* — "to pitch a tent" — recalls the tabernacle. *Episkiazein* reappears at the transfiguration (9:34-36) when the divine cloud overshadows *them* — Jesus and Peter, James, and John — signifying divine empowerment of the apostles for mission, an event recalled in 2 Pet 1:16-18. The divine cloud that guided the Israelites in the wilderness and infused the tabernacle at Sinai completes the drama of salvation by infusing Mary's womb with Jesus, the Son of God, and through Jesus, the apostolic community of faith.[89]

36-38   The effect of vv. 36-38 is to inform Mary that her miraculous conception, and the mighty prophecies associated with it, are not isolated, but part of the divine purpose extending as far back as Abraham and Sarah. Gabriel's concluding word first connects the annunciation of Mary with the annunciation of Elizabeth, who is called *syngenis* in Greek, a "relative" (NIV). *Syngenis* is often interpreted as a familial relation (e.g., "sister" or "cousin"), but that is overly specific. It more appropriately signifies a "kinswoman" in the same tribe or clan.[90] The description of Elizabeth's conception is narrated in terms reminiscent of God's earlier miraculous work in Sarah (Gen 18:14). Sarah's archetypical example is further recalled in v. 37, where the vanquishing of Elizabeth's barrenness is described in the same expression as the vanquishing of Sarah's barrenness: "For nothing is impossible with God" (Gen 18:14).

---

89. The discussion of the Divine Shadow in Brown, *Birth*, 327-28 underestimates this creative motif, and also the significant use of *episkiazein* with reference to it. Irenaeus, *Haer.* 3.11.3, captures the uniqueness of the incarnation by contrasting it to all forms of Greek and Gnostic religion: "According to the opinion of none of the heretics [Valentinus, Basilides, Marcion, etc.] was the Word of God made flesh. For if any one carefully examines the systems of them all, he will find that the Word of God is brought in by all of them not as having become incarnate [Lat. *sine carne*] and impassible, as is also the Christ from above. Others consider him to have been manifested as a transfigured man; but they maintain him to have been neither born nor to have become incarnate, while others hold that he did not assume a human form at all, but that, as a dove, he did descend upon that Jesus who was born from Mary."

90. So BDAG, 950 and the long note in Lagrange, *Luc*, 37.

"I am the Lord's servant," Mary answered. "May it be to me as you have said" (v. 38). "Servant" is too discreet for Greek *doulē,* which denotes "female slave." When Mary responds to Gabriel, "Let it be to me as you have said," she surrenders herself absolutely to God's will. In the ancient world, slavery (for which *doulos/ē* was the generic word) signified total belonging and submission. "Slave" accurately represents Mary's will, for despite her perplexity, she chooses to comply with grace. Let God's will be done! Her response is perhaps the best definition of faith in the Bible — the desire for God's word to become reality in our lives. The infancy narratives, as we have seen, are securely stitched with cross references and allusions to Israel's story, especially as embodied by Abraham and Sarah. There is no cross reference to the OT in v. 38, however. No one in Israel ever responded to God as does Mary. Mary demands no outside proofs or signs that the impossible shall be made possible. She receives God's word in abandonment and trust. The troubling word of v. 29 has become the sustaining word, the sole sufficiency of her life. For the first time in the divine-human encounter, God has found a worthy partner. "There never was a time when Israel encountered its God as Mary encountered Jesus, when it was willing to trust Him and therefore to dedicate itself wholeheartedly and unreservedly to Him."[91] Years later, in deep distress on the Mount of Olives, Jesus will pray in words closely reminiscent of Mary's, "Not my will, but yours be done" (22:42).

The annunciation of Mary signifies a new creation for Luke, and it is narrated accordingly. John's annunciation is set in close parallelism to the birth of Isaac, but the birth of the Messiah is likened to the creation of Adam. The annunciation presents Jesus as the second Adam, for Luke will trace Jesus' lineage as Son of God back to Adam the "son of God" (3:38). In the early church Mary was acknowledged as a second Eve, whose willing obedience as "the servant of the Lord" (v. 38) reverses Eve's disobedience.[92] The overshadowing Spirit of God, who created the world from chaos and who later localized God's presence in the tabernacle, overshadows Mary to bring forth the new Adam in God's image, who is "holy, called Son of God" (1:35). The church fathers, especially, recognized that, in incarnating his Son not in the priestly womb of Elizabeth but in the common human womb of Mary, God was "refashioning again the whole human race" and providing its savior.[93]

The annunciation narratives of John and Jesus complement each other,

91. K. Barth, *Church Dogmatics,* 2/2:464.

92. So Irenaeus, *Haer.* 5.19.1, "If [Eve] disobeyed God, yet Mary was persuaded to be obedient to God, in order that the Virgin Mary might become the advocate (Lat. *advocata*) of the virgin Eve. And thus, as the human race fell into bondage to death by means of a virgin, so it is rescued by a virgin; virginal disobedience having been balanced in the opposite scale by virginal obedience."

93. From the *Exaposteilarion of the Annunciation,* in A. Just, *Luke,* 16.

but they also exhibit powerful countercurrents beneath their surface complementarities. Zechariah and Elizabeth have proper credentials; Mary has none. The first annunciation is set in the Jerusalem temple, the center of Jewish religion, culture, and economics; the second in rustic Nazareth. Zechariah enjoys the status of a priest; Mary is unmarried, and to be unmarried or widowed in Israel was to know bitterness (Ruth 1:20). The old couple is well connected and financially secure; Mary is neither. Zechariah and Elizabeth are likened to noble Abraham and Sarah; Mary to outcast and vulnerable Hagar. The countercurrents of irony continue in the respective responses of Zechariah and Mary to the divine word. Zechariah responds on the basis of human possibilities: he and Elizabeth are too old for children, and he doubts the heavenly promise. Mary responds on the basis of divine possibilities: she hears the heavenly promise and asks, How can it be? The mystery of divine grace is at work *in spite of* and *because of* these complexities and contrarieties, and through them it ushers in the dawn of salvation.

PRAISE FROM THE DEPTHS OF BEING (1:39-56)

Vv. 39-56 describe Mary's visit to Elizabeth during their respective pregnancies, followed by Mary's hymn of praise to God, called the Magnificat. The visitation and Magnificat resound with praise and elation: greeting (*aspazesthai/ aspasmos*, vv. 40, 41, 44), glorification (*megalynein*, v. 46), rejoicing (*agalliasis/ agallian*, vv. 44, 47), blessing (*eulogein*, vv. 42 [2x]; *makaria/makarizein*, vv. 45, 48), mercy (*eleos*, vv. 50, 54), and uplifting (*hypsoun*, v. 52). The Greek word for "rejoicing" (*agallian/agalliasis*) is known only in biblical and early church Greek. The joy experienced by Mary and Elizabeth is exhibited by John's leaping with joy (*skirtan*, vv. 41, 44) in utero at Mary's greeting. The visitation is an embryo of the church, for the Gospel and Acts repeatedly emphasize that God's saving plan brings disparate and divided peoples together in fellowship, joy, and mission. Until now Luke has developed the annunciation of John (1:5-25) and of Jesus (1:26-38) in two separate lines of revelation. In the meeting of Mary and Elizabeth the two separate lines converge, revealing the two annunciations to be the complementary work of the foreordaining God. The ancients, and Hebrews in particular, located the soul not high in the head, or even in the heart, but in the deep center of the body. Mary and Elizabeth experience saving knowledge in the depths of their soul — Elizabeth in her exuberant womb, and Mary in her soul. What they experience further informs readers of the divine purpose at work in John and Jesus.

39-45 "At that time" Mary arose and visited Elizabeth at her home in the hill country of Judea. The time reference — literally in Greek, "in those days" — is a Hebraic expression used only by Luke in the NT. It signifies an indeterminate time.[94] The two Greek words for "arose" (*anistasthai;* NIV "got ready") and "went" (*poreuesthai;* NIV "hurried") are particularly Lukan, the latter occurring eighty-eight times in Luke-Acts, often indicating going according to a plan of salvation.[95] We do not know Mary's age. Schweizer suggests she was espoused at the onset of puberty, between twelve and fourteen years of age,[96] but whether girls were normally espoused so young is uncertain. Mary journeys to "the hill country of Judea" to visit Elizabeth. Priests normally lived in Jerusalem or in surrounding towns in order to be near the temple, where, in addition to the major religious festivals, they served twice annually for one week at a time. Zechariah's town is left anarthrous ("*a* town"), unnamed and unknown to us (also 1:65).[97] Jerusalem and its environs lay more than sixty rocky-and-hilly miles (95 km) south of Nazareth, where Mary received the annunciation, thus requiring a two- or three-day journey to reach Elizabeth. Mary's haste in visiting Elizabeth appears to be the result of her "obedience to the plan revealed to her by the angel."[98] Mary apparently journeyed alone, for Joseph is unmentioned in either the visitation or the Magnificat, and she returned alone to *her* house (so the Gk. v. 56), implying that she was still unmarried at the time. Luke does not inform us when Mary and Joseph married, although their marriage is assumed when they journey to Bethlehem for Jesus' birth (2:4-5). The sequence of names in vv. 39-40 parallels that of 1:26-27, and in both cases the critical person (Elizabeth and Mary, respectively) is mentioned last.

At the greeting of Mary, "the baby leaped in [Elizabeth's] womb, and Elizabeth was filled with the Holy Spirit" (v. 41). The kicking infant and filling with Holy Spirit signify divine causation. The Greek word for "leaped," *skirtan,* occurring in the NT only in 1:41, 44, and 6:23, connotes the skipping and frisking of sheep and young animals (*Herm. Sim.* 6.2.3),[99] thus "leaped for joy" in v. 44 (likewise 6:23; Wis 19:9). The infant in Elizabeth's womb kicks when hearing Mary's greeting; the announcement of the birth of the Messiah thus causes John delight even in utero, and his reflex announces the eschatological joy coming into the world in Jesus.[100] The kick of the infant may further recall Gen 25:22, where the "jostling" and "struggling" (Heb. *ratsats*) of Jacob

---

94. Gk. *en tais hēmerais tautais* translates Heb. *bayyamim ha'eleh* (e.g., Zech 8:9, 15). The phrase occurs in the NT only in 1:39; 6:12; 24:18 and Acts 1:15.

95. Bovon, *Luke 1:1–9:50,* 58.

96. So Schweizer, *Lukas,* 34.

97. The legend that Ain Karim was the birthplace of John, popular among the Crusaders, is no earlier than the sixth c., and thus late. See Plummer, *Luke,* 28; Lagrange, *Luc,* 41.

98. Brown, *Birth,* 331.

99. G. Fitzer, *skirtaō,* TDNT 7:401-2.

100. Wolter, *Lukasevangelium,* 97.

and Esau in Rebecca's womb is translated in the LXX by *skirtan*. If Rebecca's conception and pregnancy inform 1:41, 44, as they have earlier portions of the chapter, then Luke may employ this word to alert readers that, like Jacob, the ministry of John will bring contention to Israel (3:7-17).

At the greeting of Mary, Elizabeth is also filled with the Holy Spirit (v. 41). John is filled with the Holy Spirit from his conception (1:15), Elizabeth at the moment she hears the joyful news of Mary (1:41), and Zechariah at the Benedictus (1:67). That God would endow an infant in utero and an elderly mother-to-be with the Holy Spirit before a priest illustrates Mary's testimony in the Magnificat that the humble and needy are favored over the powerful and privileged (1:52-53). The three family members are filled by the Holy Spirit not for their own benefit but to empower them for witness. Elizabeth's message is one of veneration of Mary. The Greek of v. 42, "she cried aloud in a great cry" — a redundancy of unrestrained joy — is a remarkable transformation from her earlier disgrace and concealment (v. 24). The benediction, "Blessed are you among women, and blessed is the child you will bear!" (v. 42), does not confer a blessing but acknowledges an existing state of blessedness (so too vv. 45, 48).[101] The first half of the blessing is similar to blessings pronounced on other women in Israel (11:27; Deut 28:4; Judg 5:24). It does not declare Mary the most blessed of all women, nor does it praise Mary for any particular virtue. The second half of the blessing on "the fruit of your womb," literally in Greek, is the more important, for this Hebraic formulation recognizes that the child in Mary's womb is the work of God's saving grace.

Vv. 43-45 generally repeat the foregoing conversation. Indeed, if they were placed before v. 42 the conversation would proceed more logically. Three things are apparent in these verses. First, from v. 43 onward, the visitation and Magnificat focus no longer on Elizabeth but exclusively on Mary and Jesus. Second, Elizabeth's reference to Mary as "the mother of my Lord" (v. 43) is significant because the "Lord" (Gk. *kyrios*), which in the LXX is the default rendering of YHWH, clearly refers to Jesus. What is conceived in Mary's womb can be described only in the language proper to Israel's unique and incomparable God.[102] Finally, the word for "blessed" (v. 45; Gk. *makaria*), the same word used in the Beatitudes (Matt 5:3-11), was originally a sociological term meaning a member of the upper class. To be blessed by God is to be a member of his upper caste. The blessing of Mary in v. 45 as "she who has believed what

---

101. See the discussion in Brown, *Birth*, 333.

102. Rowe, *Early Narrative Christology*, 48-49, writes: "In the birth-infancy narrative of Luke, Jesus' life cannot be thought of apart from the Power of the Most High, because it is the Holy Spirit . . . who begins the new baby's life as [the Lord]. God's life is now bound up with Jesus' life to such a great extent and with such intensity that they share the name/title *kyrios*."

the Lord has said" must be understood against the background of Zechariah's disbelief of what the Lord said in 1:20. When a divinely ordained entity — whether priest, temple, church, or denomination — fails to trust God, God's work does not fail. God raises up a surrogate from the least imaginable quarter to believe and receive his word. Mary is thus the epitome of true faith, for she trusts in that which does not yet exist on the basis of God's promise.

46-56   The **Magnificat** is Mary's hymn of praise in response to God's gracious election of her to be the mother of the Messiah. It receives its name from the opening line of the hymn in the Latin Vulgate, *Magnificat anima mea Dominum*, "My soul magnifies the Lord" (v. 46). Hymns of praise are embedded in the literature of ancient Israel: in the Psalms, OT narrative literature (e.g., 1 Sam 2:1-10; 1 Chr 16:8-36), the Hodayot of the Dead Sea Scrolls, the *Psalms of Solomon* of the Pseudepigrapha, and the NT (e.g., Luke 1:68-79; Rev 18:21–19:3). The Magnificat belongs to the genre of a thanksgiving of an individual in need. The thanksgiving, which addresses God in third person, praises God for gracious deliverance. In the Magnificat God is the subject of every verb except in vv. 47 and 48b. Almost all lines in the Magnificat have parallels in earlier Israelite hymns, but the Magnificat is not modeled on a single earlier hymn, not even Hannah's hymn of praise in 1 Samuel 2:1-10 or *Pss. Sol.*, its closest parallels.[103] The language of the Magnificat, like the language of the Psalms in general, can be understood with reference to Mary, but the figures of speech speak to and for anyone who has experienced God's extraordinary deliverance.[104] Like so much material in the infancy narratives, Luke may have received the Magnificat from the Hebrew Gospel. Modern scholarship is overwhelmingly pessimistic that the Magnificat derives from Mary's hand.[105] The general nature of the Magnificat certainly allows for the possibility that it originated in an unknown source. The dogmatism with which modern scholarship denies Marian authorship is curious, however. Anyone familiar with twentieth-century literature of oppression — Holocaust literature, antislave and civil rights literature in America, or literature of apartheid from South Africa, for example — will not find it terribly difficult to imagine that a marginalized young peasant woman steeped in the psalms of Israel could have composed what we know as the Magnificat.

---

103. For parallels with canonical OT literature, see Brown, *Birth*, 358-60; for parallels with *Pss. Sol.*, see Bovon, *Lukas 1,1–9,50*, 82-83. Nolland, *Luke 1:1–9:20*, 74, speaks of the "fresh coinage" of OT language, allusions, and motifs that "evokes more generally the whole thought world of OT faith." R. Simons, "The Magnificat: Cento, Psalm or Imitatio?" *TynBul* 60/1 (2009): 25-46, argues that the Magnificat is a Quintilian-like *imitation* of the style, but not the exact content, of OT hymns.

104. On the structure of the Magnificat, see Brown, *Birth*, 355-57; Plummer, *Luke*, 30-31.

105. E.g., Brown, *Birth*, 340: "Virtually no serious scholar would argue today that the Magnificat was composed by Mary." On the contrary, R. Simons, "The Magnificat," 43, posits that "the Magnificat is something that Mary could plausibly have spoken."

Although v. 46 attributes the Magnificat to Mary, three Latin manuscripts from the fourth to eighth centuries, and one manuscript each from
Irenaeus and Origen, attribute it to Elizabeth.[106] In itself, this is not impressive
textual evidence. A century ago, however, a number of scholars favored the
name of Elizabeth in v. 46 on the basis of *lectio difficilior,* i.e., they could not
explain why a scribe would have altered the name from Mary to Elizabeth
unless Elizabeth, the more difficult name, were original. For the most part,
the language and figures of speech cannot resolve the question, for they are
general enough to speak of either Mary or Elizabeth. Nevertheless, phrases
like "the humiliation of his servant woman" and "all generations will call me
blessed," (v. 48), coupled with the sustained emphasis on God's solidarity with
and aid of the needy, seem to fit rural Mary better than aristocratic Elizabeth.
Elizabeth's name may have been substituted for Mary's since she is the speaker
and last person named in vv. 39-45. These reasons, combined with the otherwise overwhelming textual attestation to Mary, argue for Mary as the hymnist.

"Soul" and "spirit" in vv. 46-47 do not refer to different aspects of human
personality, but to the same deep center of human existence with two different
words, as was common in Hebrew poetry. Only twice in Luke does the word
"savior" appear: in v. 47 with reference to God, and in 2:11 with reference to
Jesus. Luke is fully prepared to transfer without alteration divine attributes and
nomenclature to Jesus. The Greek word behind "humble state" in v. 48 *(tapeinō-
sis)* in both the LXX and NT often connotes social and economic deprivation.[107]
"Servant" (v. 48) is again (see at 1:38) too respectable; the Greek *doulē,* "female
slave," is more derogatory, connoting total submission and belonging. The word
for "blessed" (v. 48; *makarizein*) is the same word used in the Beatitudes of
Matt 5:3-11. "The Mighty One" in v. 49 derives from the Greek *dynatos,* which
in the LXX often denotes a king as a rescuing hero (Ps 120:4; Zeph 3:17). A
similar metaphor occurs in "mighty deeds performed with his arm" in v. 51.
The "arm" of God, a Semitism, is used throughout the exodus narratives to
refer to God's redemption of captive Israel from Egypt. No human attitude
falls more severely under God's judgment than haughtiness and "pride" (v. 51),
which causes humanity to forget God (Deut 8:14). Pride competes with God,
refusing to acknowledge his sovereignty.[108] The powerful and wealthy are inclined to pride; hence, God tears down "rulers from their thrones" (v. 52) and
sends "the rich away empty" (v. 53). God's remembrance and aid of "his servant
Israel" (v. 54) recalls the Servant Songs of Isa 40–55, where Israel is frequently
called God's servant (Heb. *ebed,* Gk. *pais*). Because the Servant of Yahweh for-

---

106. For a complete review of the textual tradition, see Lagrange, *Luc,* 44-45; Brown,
Birth, 334-36; Metzger, *TCGNT,* 109.

107. W. Grundmann, *tapeinos, TWNT* 8:1-27.

108. Str-B 2:101-6.

sakes presumption, power, and prestige, casting his fate irrevocably on God, God rescues and vindicates him, making him "a light for the Gentiles [who] will bring my salvation to the ends of the earth" (Isa 49:6). This covenant promise and age-old hope of Israel comes to fruition in Mary, who fulfills the promise "to Abraham and his descendents" (v. 55). Luke concludes the hymn with the historical note that "Mary stayed with Elizabeth for about three months" — i.e., until John was born (see v. 26) — "and then returned home" (v. 56).

The essence of the Magnificat does not consist in its particular language or figures of speech, but in its revolutionary blueprint of divine favor. It is a hymn not of the proud, but of the powerless; not of just deserts, but of unexpected grace; not of a world fully controlled and determined by human powers, but overturned by divine comedy. God is the subject of nearly every verb, and the verbs are all transitive: they do not declare who God is, but what God *does* as the powerful deliverer of the needy and oppressed. God does not turn away from want and oppression, but toward both in compassion and rescuing intervention. In most religions a meeting with God requires the low to ascend high, sinners to become saints. The Magnificat reverses all protocol and expectations: God who is high becomes low. He sees human need and initiates a revolution that reorders reality: the transcendent God intercedes on behalf of a lowly young woman and calls her blessed; the Almighty gives mercy to those who fear him and scatters the strong, proud, and rich, while filling the hungry and needy with all good things. The reversal of expectations announced in the Magnificat will reappear throughout Luke-Acts.[109] Feminist and liberation theologies tend to read the Magnificat largely in economic, political, and social terms, whereas traditional theology often spiritualizes it. The language and imagery of the Magnificat come from Israel's religious, social, political, and ethnic life and thus include both the physical and the spiritual. Perhaps most significant of all, the Almighty restructures cosmic reality through the unmighty. The God of the Magnificat advocates the small, insignificant, and needy. God's salvific intrusion in the incarnation does not erase, but includes the lowly state of Mary and "the fruit of her womb."[110]

THE BIRTH OF JOHN AND THE SONG OF ZECHARIAH (1:57-80)

With this section Luke begins the second major division of the infancy narrative by placing the birth, circumcision, and naming of John (1:57-66) and

---

109. See R. Simons, "The Magnificat," 41-42.
110. On this final point, see Schweizer, *Lukas,* 24.

Jesus (2:1-21) in parallel succession. Both sets of stories are also followed by canticles — the Benedictus (1:67-79) in the case of John, and the Nunc Dimittis (2:28-32) in the case of Jesus. The parallelism in the birth stories is less exact than in the preceding annunciations, however, particularly in the Benedictus, which is longer and more exalted than the corresponding Nunc Dimittis. The Benedictus clearly celebrates and completes more than the birth of John. Its length, sublimity, and placement distinguish it as the consummation of Luke's long introductory chapter. In the annunciations of John and Jesus, and in the birth of John, God is to be blessed and praised, for "he has come to his people and redeemed them" (1:68).

Elizabeth's Baby (1:57-66)

57-58   "When it was time for Elizabeth to have her baby, she gave birth to a son" (v. 57). This verse resumes the narrative of Elizabeth that was suspended at v. 25. Stylistically, Luke's Greek is Hebraic. Thematically, Luke again places Elizabeth in correspondence with Rebecca: in v. 41 John in utero was likened to Jacob and Esau in Rebecca's womb (Gen 25:22); in v. 57 John's birth is described in terms reminiscent of the births of Jacob and Esau (Gen 25:24). The literal wording of v. 57 is "the time was fulfilled." To readers familiar with biblical language this phrase suggests the great overture of the incarnation as described in the birth of Jesus in 2:6, and by Paul in Gal 4:6.

The surprising news of John's birth breaks forth among relatives and friends of Zechariah and Elizabeth, and the region is swept up in their joy. The joy of the community is a fulfillment of Gabriel's promise to Zechariah, that "many will rejoice because of his birth" (1:14). The description of vv. 57-58 may foreshadow the Christian community (see also at v. 38), for the fulfillment of God's promises is a source of joy to others no less than to the specific recipient(s) of the promise.

59-66   Ironically, the community poses a threat to the promise in which it rejoices and requires of Elizabeth and Zechariah a first obedience of faith. It was not normal in Judaism to name a son after his father. If a boy bore a family name, it was more likely to be the name of his grandfather. Why the community assumes the child should bear the name of his father is not apparent, although Lagrange's suggestion that the age and infirmity of Zechariah make him the child's virtual grandfather is worthy of consideration.[111] V. 59 implies that the naming of John coincides with his circumcision on the eighth day, although the imperfect tense of Greek *kalein* (v. 59, "they were calling him") suggests that "Zechariah" was applied to the child before the circum-

---

111. Lagrange, *Saint Luc*, 55.

cision. Normally in Israel the name of a child was given at birth (Gen 21:1-3; 25:24-26). The delay in naming John until his circumcision — and likewise in naming Jesus (2:21) — was unusual in Judaism at this time. The Talmud is familiar with this custom in the third and subsequent centuries, but v. 59 and 2:21 are the earliest examples in Judaism of naming a boy at his circumcision.[112]

Circumcision is the sign and condition par excellence of the covenant of God with Abraham (Gen 17:9-14). So important was circumcision that it was one of the few observances permitted on a Sabbath. Circumcision was prescribed for the eighth day (Gen 17:12; Lev 12:3; *m. Šabb.* 19:5), which was still observed if it fell on Sabbath. Circumcision could be performed by a layman, even a woman (Exod 4:25; 1 Macc 1:60; 2 Macc 6:10; *Ant.* 12.256), although it was customarily performed by a priest trained in the operation.[113] The OT does not explicitly state why circumcision became the sign and condition of the covenant, although it probably signified a rejection of paganism. Sacred and cult prostitution (of both sexes) were commonly practiced in the ancient Near East as a means of venerating the divine. Surgically reconfiguring the penis through circumcision was a visible and tangible "sign of the covenant in your flesh" (Gen 17:13). It signified that human sexuality in Israel, contrary to its ubiquitous practice in pagan cultures, was not the means of accessing divine powers and properties. Rather, like all human capacities and abilities, sexuality also belonged to the one saving covenant of the God of Israel, the sign of which was circumcision.

At John's circumcision the community expects him to be named Zechariah, but his mother protests, "No! He is to be called John" (v. 60). We need not infer that Elizabeth, like Zechariah, knows the child's name by divine revelation. Even in his muteness Zechariah surely communicated the name and its importance to his wife. The name of John, a shortened form of the Hebrew "Jochanan," means "God's gracious gift," but the expectation of the community pressures the aged couple to forsake the name — and perhaps the gift. Elizabeth and Zechariah must affirm the divine will announced by Gabriel against the expectations of their community. Luke alerts readers that faith is expressed in allegiance to God's will, even when that will contrasts with the pressures of family, relatives, and friends (14:26!).

The community turns to Zechariah to resolve the conflict, "making signs . . . to find out what he would like to name the child" (v. 62). Luke implies that Zechariah is deaf as well as mute. Bengel suggests that the crowd motioned rather than spoke, out of deference to Zechariah's inability to speak.[114]

---

112. Str-B 2:107.

113. Str-B 4/1:23-40 provides a full discussion of the rite of circumcision in Israel.

114. Bengel, *Gnomon*, 2:23, "To one dumb it is more convenient that he should see persons making signs, than that he should hear them speaking, inasmuch as he is not able to reply to them by word of mouth."

Curiously, the exact wording of 1:22 is that Zechariah's vision in the temple affected his *hearing* as well as his speech.[115] Zechariah signals for a "writing tablet" (v. 63) — probably a boxwood tablet covered with wax — on which he etches with a pointed instrument, "His name is John."[116] Bengel notes that in this, the first instance of writing in the NT, the subject is grace.[117] Zechariah's wording is instructive: he does not say his name *shall be* John, but *is* John — already determined and announced by divine decree (1:13). Discipleship in this instance requires that Zechariah *declare,* not decide! The community was "**astonished**" (v. 63). The Greek word *thaumazein,* "to be amazed or astonished," is a preferred term in Luke, usually describing the reaction of crowds rather than of disciples or opponents of Jesus. Luke uses the term thirteen times as a positive reference to Jesus, especially to his miracles or teachings or to something done by Jesus, including astonishment at the empty tomb (24:12). Amazement is not faith, however. Its four occurrences in Mark 5:20; 6:6; 15:5, 44, for instance, signify bewilderment that does not lead to faith. In Rev 13:3; 17:6, 7, 8 four more occurrences describe fascination with the satanic beast. Likewise in Luke, *thaumazein* is a sense of awe that may grow into faith if it leads to knowing and following Jesus.[118]

When Zechariah verifies the name, his mouth is "immediately" opened. In regaining his speech, Zechariah experiences the miraculous reversal of his punishment in v. 20. NIV supplies a clarifying addition in v. 64, "his tongue *was loosed,*" but the Greek of the verse can be adequately translated as written, "Immediately, his mouth and tongue were opened, and he began to speak, praising God."[119] The one who disbelieved (1:20) now believes, and his first response is to praise God. "Praising" (v. 64) is in the imperfect tense in Greek, implying *continued* praising — as Luke will illustrate in the Benedictus.[120]

115. A literal rendering of the Greek of 1:22 reads: "When [Zechariah] came out [of the temple] he was unable to speak to them, and they knew that he had seen a vision in the temple; and he was nodding to them and was remaining deaf [*kōphos*]." The reading of the NIV, ". . . he remained unable to *speak*" is an interpretation rather than an exact translation. Plummer, *Luke,* 37, makes the interesting suggestion that if "made signs" (v. 62) and "asked" (v. 63) were transposed, the problem would be resolved. Did Luke (or an early scribe) accidently switch the two verbs?

116. So Ezek 37:16, 20; *4 Ezra* 14:24. Str-B 2:108-10 notes that the written expression of a mute person held legal status in Judaism.

117. For "John" means "God's gracious gift"; Bengel, *Gnomon,* 2:24.

118. See G. Bertram, *thaumazō, TWNT* 3:27-42; F. Annen, *thaumazō, EDNT* 2:134-35.

119. The reading of the Western text (D) of v. 64, "And immediately his tongue was loosed and all marveled; and his mouth was opened," may have been influenced by Mark 7:35. My translation is based on the practice of a compound subject of similar kind taking a singular verb in Koine Greek.

120. The Greek word used for "praise" in v. 64, *eulogein,* is the verbal form of the first word of the Benedictus, *eulogētos* (v. 68).

News of the birth and naming of John spread "throughout the hill country of Judea" (v. 65), implying a larger area than the similar designation in 1:39. Like Zechariah (1:12) and Mary (1:30) earlier, everyone is filled with "awe" (Gk. *phobos*). This word regularly describes the fear and reverence that befall humans in the immanence of the spiritual world. Ancient Jews experienced the divine nearness not unlike moderns experience a high-voltage transformer — as something awesome and startling. The NIV rendering of v. 65, "people were talking about these things," is less adequate than "all these things were being spoken of throughout the hill country of Judea." The passive voice properly stresses the magnitude of the *event* rather than the people who reported it. All who heard of it "set these things in their heart" (lit., v. 66). The expression is a Hebraism, meaning that the events reached — and were registered — in the core of their being.

The miracle of John's birth does not bring closure for the community but arouses a question, the answer to which alone can move the hearts and minds of the people from astonishment to faith. "What then is this child going to be?" (v. 66). The first clue to the answer is that the "hand of the Lord" was with John.[121] "Hand of the Lord" is a metaphor for God's activity in creation and redemption occurring more than 200 times in the OT; its single most frequent use refers to deliverance of Israel from Egypt (e.g., Exod 14:31).[122] "Hand of God" does not occur in the NT independently of its OT connotations. It is not used by Luke with reference to Jesus, for example, where it would appear appropriate (e.g., 4:32; 5:17; 6:19). But in Acts 11:21 Luke repeats the phrase "the hand of God being with [him/them]" in virtually the same Greek phrase. In both instances it signifies the commencement of God's epic work: in John as the introducer of the Messiah in 1:66, and in the commencement of the Gentile mission in Acts 11:21. In v. 66 "hand of God" signifies that John's birth is in continuity and character with the manifestation of God's redemptive activity in the history of Israel. The metaphor assures readers of God's presence with John. It does not assure the fulfillment of human hopes and expectations, however, for it can denote divine judgment and punishment (Acts 13:11), and it will not spare John from imprisonment and death (3:20; 9:9). "Hand of God" does not tell us what will happen, but it does make clear *who* directs the drama, which Zechariah heralds in the Benedictus.

---

121. Several Western manuscripts (D, some Italian and Syriac witnesses) omit *ēn* in the final Greek clause of v. 66, thus making the clause part of the question, i.e., "What then is this child going to be, for the hand of the Lord (is) with him?" These manuscripts mistakenly imagine the final clause to be part of the previous question, whereas it is an observation made by Luke (elsewhere 2:50; 3:15; 7:39; 16:14; 20:20; 23:12). See Metzger, *TCGNT,* 109-10.

122. On "hand of God," see esp. E. Lohse, *cheir, TWNT* 9:416-17, 420.

Benedictus (1:67-80)

Although Zechariah is the first recipient of an angelic annunciation (1:11), he is, following John (1:15) and Elizabeth (1:41), the last to be filled with the Holy Spirit (v. 67), which issues forth in the Benedictus and consummates the birth announcements of chap. 1.[123] The Benedictus is similar to the Magnificat (1:46-55), although the Magnificat is modeled on the Psalms, whereas the Benedictus is modeled on the prophets and rightly called a prophecy (v. 67).[124] Taking its name from the Latin translation of the first word in Greek, *eulogētos* (= "blessed"; Lat. *benedictus*), the Benedictus is Zechariah's hymn to "the hand of the Lord" (v. 66) after the recovery of his speech (v. 64). The first part of the Benedictus, set in past tense and third person, declares God's faithfulness to the covenant with Abraham (vv. 68-75);[125] the second, set in future tense and second person, foretells the redemption promised to Israel that is signified in the birth of John (vv. 76-79). The occasion of the Benedictus is an eight-day-old infant, whose appearance Zechariah celebrates in the *past* tense. So certain are God's presence and activity that both can be referred to as already at hand and accomplished (i.e., "he has . . . redeemed his people and raised up a horn of salvation for us" (vv. 68-69). God's saving activity is not an abstraction or limited to momentous

123. Irenaeus, *Haer.* 3.10.2, captures the inspiration of the Benedictus with particular theological insight: "Zechariah, when he had recovered from the state of dumbness which he suffered on account of unbelief, was filled with a new spirit and blessed God in a new manner. For all things had entered upon a new phase, the Word arranging after a new manner the advent in the flesh, that he might win back to God that human nature which had departed from God; and therefore people were taught to worship not a new God, but the one God after a new fashion."

124. For OT parallels to the elements and phrases of the Benedictus, see Plummer, *Luke*, 38-39; Klostermann, *Lukasevangelium*, 25; Brown, *Birth*, 386-89.

125. Schweizer, *Lukas*, 27 sees the covenant with Abraham as the crux of a seven-part chiasmus in the Benedictus:

    A^1 visited (68b)
        B^1 people (68b)
            C^1 salvation (69)
                D^1 prophets (70)
                    E^1 enemies (71)
                        F^1 hand (71)
                            G^1 our fathers (72)
                            G^2 our father (73)
                      F^2 hand (74)
                    E^2 enemies (74)
                D^2 prophet (76)
            C^2 salvation (77a)
        B^2 people (77a)
    A^2 visited (78b).

events but is focused in a person, indeed a child, who will become a "prophet of the Most High" (v. 76) to prepare the way for the "Son of the Most High" (v. 32).

67-75   God is worthy of being blessed because he has repeatedly revealed himself as Israel's redeemer. The word "visited" (v. 68; Gk. *episkeptesthai;* NIV "had come") is a load-bearing OT term (Heb. *paqad*) that appears in the NT predominantly in Luke-Acts. God is regularly the subject of the term, which conveys his oversight (Ruth 1:6; Isa 23:17; Ps 80:14) or punishment (Ps 89:33[32]; Sir 2:14) of Israel. God's supreme visitation in the OT was the saving deliverance of the exodus (Gen 50:24-25; Exod 3:16). Israel's experience of the divine was thus not a mere "God consciousness" but a concrete historical revelation of God in space and time.[126] God visits his people to redeem them (v. 68), and he redeems them so they may serve him (v. 74). "Horn" (v. 69) is a Hebrew metaphor for power and might (Deut 33:17; Ps 75:10); "horn of salvation" thus connotes the power of salvation (2 Sam 22:3; Ps 18:3[2]). In the OT, God is nowhere spoken of as "raising up" a horn of salvation, but the "horn of salvation" in v. 69 has been personally "raised up" by God from the "house of his servant David." This metaphor is thus not a reference to salvation in general but to its specific fulfillment of the long-awaited hope of Israel's Messiah. Salvation is not, as Marcion imagined, an arbitrary occurrence, like a powerful but random lightning bolt. Rather, salvation stands in continuity with God's historic work in Israel, as revealed in the establishment of the Davidic monarchy (v. 69), the holy prophets through whom God spoke (v. 70), and the holy covenant sworn to Abraham (vv. 72-73). "Covenant" appears in Luke only with reference to Abraham (1:72; 22:20; Acts 3:25; 7:8), again signifying the continuity of old and new covenants, and the fulfillment of the former by the latter.[127] In Gen 22:16 God swore an oath to Abraham because "you have not withheld your son, your only son" (similarly, Lev 23:24; Ps 105:8-9). God will now fulfill that oath by not withholding his Son, his only Son. The two effects of the salvation proclaimed by Zechariah will be deliverance "from our enemies and from the hand of all who hate us" (vv. 71, 74) and mercy (v. 72; Gk. *eleos;* Heb. *hesed*) — God's covenant faithfulness and loving-kindness. Both effects will enable God's covenant people "to serve him without fear in holiness and righteousness all our days" (vv. 74-75). The rabbinic tradition recognized that God could be served in either fear or love, but service in love was superior to service in fear.[128] The word for "serve" (v. 74; Gk. *latreuein*)

---

126. Tannehill, *Narrative Unity of Luke-Acts,* 87: "In 1:68, 78 God's visitation is associated with the redemption, salvation, and dawning from on high which fulfill the messianic hope and the promise to Abraham."

127. Bovon, *Luke 1:1–9:50,* 74: "The Lord remains faithful; he will not forget. His covenant is holy because it is *his* covenant."

128. Str-B 2:112.

connotes priestly service in worship (Exod 3:12), fulfilling the ancient ideal that Israel would be "a kingdom of priests" (Exod 19:6). "The priesthood of all believers" is thus intimated in the Benedictus. True service of God in vv. 74-75 includes both a pure heart ("holiness"), and the outward practice of virtue ("righteousness").[129] Summarizing the train of thought in vv. 68-75, God will make good the promise sworn to Abraham and ratified through the holy prophets by raising up the horn of salvation in the house of David through his servant Jesus, who will rescue his people from enemies and equip them for service in holiness and righteousness.

76-79   In v. 76 the panorama of salvation history comes to concrete focus in a "Thou." Some Jewish traditions (e.g., Judges, *Pss. Sol., War Scroll* at Qumran), not unlike humanity as a whole perhaps, longed for a Maccabean "thou," a warrior-deliverer who would defeat, avenge, and vindicate. The Benedictus does not celebrate weapons and war. It celebrates a child (vv. 59, 66, 76, 80), addressed intimately — "you, my child." This child will be the true eschatological harbinger, a "prophet of the Most High" who will prepare the way of the Lord (v. 76). Who the "Lord" refers to is not entirely clear.[130] V. 76b reflects Isa 40:3 and Mal 3:1, both of which refer to God, but the coming God is now announced as the "Son of the Most High" (1:32), the "horn of salvation for us in the house of his servant David" (v. 69). Mark 1:2-3 applies these very references from Isa and Mal to Jesus. A significant battery of clues thus prejudices readers to take "Lord" as a reference to Jesus. The ambiguity of "Lord" may be as important as it is undeniable, for this title, which in the OT is used jealously and exclusively of YHWH, is now daringly employed in a way appropriate to Jesus! John is not referred to as a "baptizer" in the Benedictus. His primary function is, as Eastern Orthodoxy emphasizes, *prodromos,* the Forerunner who "will give his people the knowledge of salvation through the forgiveness of their sins" (v. 77). The forgiveness of sins comes not through John, but through the salvation that he makes known. The interplay of Forerunner and Fulfiller, "prophet of Most High" and "Son of Most High," again signifies that the incarnation of Jesus Christ is not a random and unprecedented innovation of God, but the *fulfillment* of a purposeful chain of saving events in Israel in which John is the penultimate link.

The salvation proclaimed by John in v. 78 issues from the depths of God, *splanchna eleous* in Greek, literally, "the bowels of God's unfailing mercy" (NIV "tender mercy of our God").[131] God's salvation will appear in a visitation of

---

129. Lagrange, *Luc,* 60-61.

130. Commentators are divided whether "Lord" refers to God (Lagrange, *Luc,* 61; Brown, *Birth,* 380) or Jesus (Grundmann, *Lukas,* 73; Fitzmyer, *Luke [I–IX],* 385-86).

131. Note Bovon's insight in *Luke 1:1–9:50,* 76: "Seldom has the compassion of God been declared in so personal and experiential a manner as the source and motive of salvation history."

"the rising sun" (v. 78). "Visitation" repeats the same verb with which the Benedictus began in v. 68, though here it is future rather than past tense.[132] The image of the "rising one" or "dawning one" (v. 78; NIV "rising sun"; lit. "a rising [or dawning] from on high") repeats an OT metaphor for the coming of the Messiah (Jer 23:5; Zech 3:8; 6:12; *T. Levi* 4:4).[133] The phraseology of 78b implies an individual, thus "the Dawning One from on high will visit us," recalling the messianic prophecy of Num 24:17, "A star will arise from Jacob."[134] V. 79 likewise recalls the messianic imagery of Isa 9:2 (also Isa 42:6-7; Ps 106:10), where Messiah will "shine on those living in darkness and in the shadow of death" to bring "the way of peace" (v. 79).[135] Whereas Isaiah lamented that "the way of peace they do not know, and there is no justice in their paths" (59:8), the Dawning One will "guide our feet into the way of peace" (v. 79).

80   The report that he "grew and became strong in spirit" concludes the birth of John. By the early third century, statements such as this could be cited in favor of monasticism. Origen, for example, took v. 80 to imply that John became a monk, "an athlete of God."[136] "Spirit" should probably be understood to refer to "character" rather than "Holy Spirit," in conformity with Luke's similar stereotype in 2:40, 52. John will dwell "in the wilderness" until his appearance to baptize in preparation for Jesus' public ministry in 3:2. Especially in the immediate aftermath of the discovery of the Dead Sea Scrolls, scholars often suggested that "wilderness" implied a sojourn of John with the Qumran Covenanters.[137] This is unlikely. John's father was a temple priest (against whom the Covenanters polemicized); his dress was that of a prophet (not of an Essene); his baptismal ablution was administered but once (not daily as at Qumran); he called all to repentance (not simply the desert elect); and he did not require the same (degree of) legal observance as did the Covenanters.[138] "Wilderness" refers to remote and uninhabited regions away from powers of influence, long familiar to Israel's prophets and holy men.

---

132. The aorist *epeskepsato,* although well attested in v. 78, is probably due to scribal intention to assimilate the verb to the tense of the same verb in v. 68. Since all finite verbs in 76-78 are future, and since *episkepsetai* (fut.) is also well attested in the manuscript tradition, the "visitation" in v. 78 should probably be understood to refer to the coming "rising sun," which is a messianic metaphor. See Metzger, *TCGNT,* 110; Wolter, *Lukasevangelium,* 116; contra Brown, *Birth,* 373.

133. Str-B 2:113.

134. The messianic imagery of Num 24:17 is already apparent in *T. Levi* 4:4. Further, Klostermann, *Lukasevangelium,* 28; Bovon, *Luke 1:1–9:50,* 76.

135. For a full discussion of the messianic metaphor of v. 78, see Wolter, *Lukasevangelium,* 116-17.

136. Origen, *Hom. Luc.* 11.3.

137. E.g., Caird, *Luke,* 59; Grundmann, *Lukas,* 74; still today Fitzmyer, *Luke (I–IX),* 388-89.

138. See Schweizer, *Lukas,* 29.

The Greek phrase *en tais erēmois* is significant, occurring only four times in all Scripture (1:80; 5:16, Sir 9:7; Ezek 13:4).[139] In 5:16 it refers to Jesus' refuge in the wilderness for prayer and communion with God at the outset of his ministry (similarly, Mark 1:45). In the wilderness, too, John prepares the way for Jesus' ministry. John remains "in the wilderness" until his "public installation" (*anadeixis;* NIV "appeared publicly"). This Greek technical term signifies public recognition of a duly-appointed official.[140] Such prestige is associated with important places (cities and temples) and important functions (those of magistrates and officials). God's commissioning and installation, ironically, fall not upon a man of prominence in a center of power, but upon a child who grows up in the wilderness.

---

139. The more usual *en tē erēmō* occurs hundreds of times in the Greek Bible.
140. H. Schlier, *anadeixis, TWNT* 2:31.

CHAPTER TWO

Birth and Boyhood of Jesus

Luke 2:1-52

THE BIRTH OF JESUS (2:1-20)

The births of John and Jesus, as foretold by the angel Gabriel in chap. 1, are fulfilled in 1:57-66 and 2:1-20, respectively. Luke's distinctive style, which retains its Hebraic influence, is continued in chap. 2,[1] but in chap. 2 the narrative focuses exclusively on Jesus. Mary is the only character from chap. 1 to reappear in chap. 2,[2] but with new characteristics and emphases. The theologically rich annunciation of 1:26-38 is not further developed in chap. 2; indeed, the miraculous conception by the Holy Spirit and virgin birth are left unmentioned. The significance of Jesus is now defined in terms of soteriology (2:11) rather than divine sonship and Davidic kinship (1:31-35).[3] I do not regard these differences as evidence of a new source but rather of a new context. The new context is set by Caesar Augustus's imperial plan to number and tax the Roman world. Within this plan the story of Mary and Joseph appears as a subsidiary tableau. The census of Augustus and the birth of Jesus are narrated with decorum appropriate to solemn events. The disarming intrusion of God into the world in the birth of Jesus stands in sharp contrast to the imperial ambitions of Caesar Augustus. God does not break into the world in a world leader, Führer, or cosmic hero — all of which Caesar Augustus epitomized. God penetrates the defensive armor of the world by sending his Son as a child, not to the well-connected and established, but to shepherds who live on the precarious margins of society. Beginning with *Prot. Jas.* (17–18) and continuing

---

1. In addition to the distinctive and numerous Hebraisms in Luke 1–2, no fewer than forty-six of the sixty-two favorite words of Luke also appear in the first two chapters, as well as Lukan stylistic elements, such as his use of conjunctions, articular infinitives, prepositions, and the article. For Hebraisms, see Edwards, *Hebrew Gospel*, 294-99; for stylistic elements, see P. Minear, "Luke's Use of the Birth Stories," in Keck and Martyn, eds., *Studies in Luke-Acts*, 114.

2. The angel that announces Jesus' birth in 2:9 is presumed to be Gabriel, but he is not named.

3. On the new accents in Luke 2, see Brown, *Birth*, 408-14; Bovon, *Lukas 1,1–9,50*, 115.

with predictable regularity in modern Christmas pageants, the birth of Jesus is often sentimentalized — winter cold, a poor and pregnant couple turned away from an inn, adoring ox and ass presiding over the manger. These romantic embellishments are absent from Luke's sober narrative, which reflects the *Realpolitik* of imperial Rome and Caesar's regulations requiring a pregnant woman to make an arduous journey in order to be enrolled and taxed in the town of her husband's birth.

1-3 The beginning of chap. 2 ("It happened in those days a decree went out from Caesar Augustus," v. 1) parallels the beginning of chap. 1 ("It happened in the days of Herod, King of Judea," 1:5). Both statements are strongly Hebraic and may derive from an original Hebrew source. The story of Jesus, like that of Israel as a whole, does not begin, "Once upon a time," but "In those days." The biblical story is not a myth, but a record of divine activity in historical time. "In those days" is a Hebraism utilized by Luke for an indeterminate passage of time (also 4:2; Acts 2:18; 7:41; 9:37), here designating the approximate time of Jesus' birth. The word for "decree" (Gk. *dogma*) means an official public ordinance, whether of the Roman Empire (v. 1; Acts 17:7), the church (Acts 16:4; *Did.* 11:3), or Mosaic law (Eph 2:15; Col 2:14). "Decree" is made the subject of v. 1, thus attributing the hardship laid on the shoulders of Joseph and Mary to an official dogma rather than directly to Caesar Augustus. Oppression from *systems* is not a modern invention. The Greek word for "census," *apographesthai,* means "to enroll or register," here specifically for a census. The form of the Greek word allows a translation that is either passive ("for the whole world to be enrolled") or middle ("for the whole world to present itself for enrollment"). The middle makes the registration more humiliating and onerous, whereas the passive emphasizes the aspect of subjugation. Jews were exempt from serving in the Roman army; hence, the census was introduced for the purposes of taxation, not of military conscription. The census, as specified in v. 1, was not local but universal, extending throughout *orbis terrarum,* the entire Roman Empire.

The sovereign who decreed the census was **Caesar Augustus**.[4] Augustus was born in 63 B.C., the son of Julius Caesar's nephew, and named Octavian. Octavian joined Mark Antony after the assassination of Julius Caesar in 44 B.C. to punish and defeat Brutus and Cassius at Philippi in 42. Octavian became the sole ruler of the Roman Empire after defeating Antony and Cleopatra at Actium in 31. He was granted the title "Augustus" ("majestic," "holy") by the Roman Senate in 27, after which he reigned with unrivaled supremacy until his death in A.D. 14. Luke is the only NT author to refer to a Roman emperor by name, here by the honorific title "Augustus" (Latin, for Gk. *se-*

---

4. See Suetonius, *Aug.,* 1.150-309. The information in the following paragraph is summarized from Suetonius and augmented by notes 5-6.

bastos, "reverenced").[5] Augustus built the Roman Forum, founded libraries, sponsored lavish spectacles for the populace, and boasted that he had found Rome "built in brick but left it in marble."[6] Augustus was the first emperor to encourage a cult to deify his name and reign. According to legend, Augustus, like Alexander the Great, had been miraculously conceived by a serpent. An inscription discovered at Priene and dated to 9 B.C. hails Augustus as a god whose "birthday signaled the beginning of good news [Gk. *euangelion*] for the world."[7] Another inscription from Halicarnassus, now preserved in the British Museum, celebrates his reign thus:

> [Augustus] is the father of his divine homeland Rome, inherited from his father Zeus, and a savior of the common folk. His foresight not only fulfilled the entreaties of all people, but surpassed them, making peace for land and sea, while cities bloom with order, harmony, and good seasons; the productivity of all things is good and at its prime, there are fond hopes for the future and good will during the present which fills all men, so that they ought to bear pleasing sacrifices and hymns.[8]

These inscriptions identify Augustus as God, Son of God, and savior, and they associate him with peace, hope, and good news. Significantly, these titles and terms are applied to Jesus in the angelic announcement to the shepherds in vv. 10-11, declaring Jesus to be the divine alternative to the imperial ideology and cult (see further discussion at 2:11).[9]

Luke mentions Augustus with reference to "the first census that took place while Quirinius was governor of Syria" (v. 2). The **census** provides the narrative means to move Joseph and Mary from their home in Nazareth to Bethlehem, where Jesus was born. Mention of the word "census" should alert readers to danger, for in the OT only God legitimately counts his people.[10]

---

5. Luke identifies three emperors by name: Augustus (2:1), Tiberius (3:1), and Claudius (Acts 11:28; 18:2).

6. Suetonius, "Deified Augustus," 28.3. For a full picture of Augustus, see the *Res Gestae* (reproduced in C. K. Barrett, *The New Testament Background: Selected Documents* [New York: Harper Torchbooks, 1961], 1-5), a personal chronicle of Augustus's achievements and importance written at age seventy-six, a year before his death.

7. Deissmann, *Light from the Ancient East,* 366-67. The Priene inscription, discovered by German archaeologists in the late nineteenth c., is now in Berlin.

8. Cited from H. Kleinknecht, *Pantheion: Religiöse Texte des Griechentums* (Tübingen: Mohr Siebeck, 1959), 40.

9. K. Yamazaki-Ransom, *The Roman Empire in Luke's Narrative* (LNTS 404; New York: T&T Clark, 2010), 83; similarly C. Kavin Rowe, *World Upside Down: Reading Acts in the Graeco-Roman Age* (Oxford: University Press, 2009).

10. In Num 1 and 26 God legitimately institutes censuses of the people, but in 2 Sam 24 and 1 Chr 21 David and Satan, respectively, institute censuses — with disastrous consequences.

"The first census" is somewhat ambiguous. It could mean (1) the first general imperial census, (2) the first imperial census in Syria and Judea, or (3) the first census imposed by Quirinius. We know of neither empire-wide censuses nor of further censuses taken by Quirinius. This makes option 2 preferable, suggesting this was the first census instituted by Augustus, which was organized by Quirinius specifically for Judea.[11] According to Luke, (1) the census was decreed by Caesar Augustus (v. 1); (2) Herod the Great was still alive (1:5); (3) the census encompassed the entire Roman Empire (v. 1); (4) it was superintended by Quirinius, governor of Syria (v. 2); and (5) it required Joseph (and Mary?) to travel from Nazareth to Bethlehem, the city of his (and her?) birth, to be registered (v. 3). Since Herod the Great died in 4 B.C. and Luke implies that Jesus was born prior to Herod's death, this would also place the census of 2:1-2 prior to 4 B.C. This combined information cannot easily be reconciled with that of the Jewish historian Josephus, a contemporary of Luke and our main source of information about the census.[12] According to Josephus, (1) Quirinius was made governor of Syria by Augustus in A.D. 6 (*Ant.* 18.2; confirmed by Tacitus, *Ann.* 30.30; Suetonius, *Tib.* 49);[13] (2) Quirinius was sent to Syria to liquidate the estate of Archaelaus (who was deposed in A.D. 6) and to impose a census in order to annex Judea under Coponius as prefect (*Ant.* 17.355; 18.1-2; *J.W.* 2.117); and (3) Judas the Galilean and Saddok, a Pharisee, formed a freedom-fighting movement (later identified with the Zealots) in opposition to the Roman census and annexation (*Ant.* 18.4-10; 20.102). Josephus and Luke thus agree on a census that was administered by Quirinius, but they disagree on its date, extent, and requirement to register in one's city of birth.

Can this conundrum be resolved? Most of the related historical data can be accounted for, but the date of the census remains unresolved. Enrollment in one's place of birth was not stipulated in Roman law, but it is imaginable that Herod may have added such a stipulation in deference to Jewish custom.[14]

---

11. Schürer, *History of the Jewish People,* 1:406-7.

12. Literature on the census is immense. For bibliographies and discussions, see L. Feldman, *Josephus: Jewish Antiquities* (LCL; Cambridge: Harvard University Press, 1969), 9.556-57; Schürer, *History of the Jewish People,* 1:399-437; Leaney, *Luke,* 44-48; Marshall, *Luke,* 99-102; Nolland, *Luke 1:1–9:20,* 99-102; Brown, *Birth,* 547-56; Klein, *Lukasevangelium,* 131-33.

13. On Quirinius, see D. S. Potter, "Quirinius," *ABD* 5:588-89. It is not known how long Quirinius ruled as governor of Syria after his appointment in A.D. 6, but he was back in Rome in 12.

14. So too Plummer, *Luke,* 51, and subsequent scholars. A decree of C. Vibius Maximus, dated to 104, required absentees to return to their home towns for a census in Egypt. Some scholars imagine a similar requirement for the census in Judea (e.g., Marshall, *Luke,* 101). The Egyptian census is of dubious relevance, however, since (1) it occurred a century after the census of Quirinius, and (2) there is no evidence of its custom being practiced in Palestine. An alternative suggestion is that Mary and Joseph returned to Bethlehem because, as descendents of David, they owned land there. This suggestion, which derives from Eusebius, *Hist. eccl.* 3.20,

Regarding extent of the census, there is no evidence of an empire-wide census at any time in Roman history.[15] Regional censuses were enforced at various times and places in the history of the empire, such as the one at the annexation of Judea under Quirinius. How literally Luke intended "entire Roman world" we cannot say, but he uses "whole inhabited world" (Acts 11:28; NIV "entire Roman world") to refer to a widespread (although not universal) famine, and he may possibly use "entire Roman world" similarly for an "event that covered much of the Roman Empire."[16] This leaves the date of the census as the major problem. Lagrange attempts to resolve the issue by translating *prōtē* (v. 2) as "before" rather than "first," i.e., "This census took place *before* the one that took place under Quirinius governor of Syria."[17] This suggestion attempts to defend the historicity of the account, but it is grammatically offensive. The near-universal denotation of *prōtē* (and clearly its connotation in v. 2) is "first in sequence" rather than "before" (which would require *proteros*).[18] Others have argued that Quirinius served twice as governor of Syria, once during Herod's lifetime and once in A.D. 6, and that v. 2 refers to the first term of service.[19] Roman records indicate that Sentius Saturninus served as governor of Syria from 9 to 6 B.C., Quinctilius Verus from 6 to 4 B.C., unknown governor(s) from 3 B.C. to A.D. 6, and P. Sulpicius Quirinius afterward.[20] The career history

---

is wistfully speculative. Eusebius mentions certain unnamed members of the family of Judas (brother of Jesus? Mark 6:3) owning "property," but he makes no mention of Mary or Joseph, or that the property was in Bethlehem.

15. "No regular census was taken in Republican times of the nations subject to Rome" (Schürer, *History of the Jewish People,* 1:401). The dual purposes of a census (taxation and military conscription) had lost their significance in the Roman Republic, according to Schürer, since Italy and the colonies no longer paid direct taxes, nor were they liable to universal conscription.

16. So Bock, *Luke 1:1–9:50,* 202.

17. Lagrange, *Luc,* 67-68. "Ce recensement fut antérieur à celui qui eut lieu Quirinius étant gouverneur de Syrie."

18. Nearly three columns of lexical evidence in BDAG, 892-94 give no instances of *prōtē* meaning "before." Schürer, *History of the Jewish People,* 1:416, "Josephus knows nothing of a Roman census in Palestine during the reign of Herod; he refers to the census of A.D. 6/7 as something new and unprecedented."

19. F. F. Bruce, *The Acts of the Apostles: The Greek Text, with Notes and Commentary* (Grand Rapids: Eerdmans, 1984), 148, cites evidence in favor of this option. Schürer, *History of the Jewish People,* 1:420-27, discusses the issue at length and finds an earlier governorship of Quirinius implausible. He concludes that "there is no alternative but to recognize that the evangelist based his statement on uncertain information." It is sometimes further argued that Quirinius is the officer mentioned in an inscription from Tibur, which alludes to the career of a senator in the reign of Augustus. The inscription does not name the senator, however, and preserves only parts of his career. A relationship between the officer in the Tibur inscription and an earlier governorship of Quirinius is highly speculative. See D. Potter, "Quirinius," *ABD* 5:588.

20. Tertullian (*Marc.* 4.19), writing ca. 200, discreetly corrected Luke 2:2 by attributing the census to Saturninus.

of Quirinius is well documented and does not include an earlier governorship of Syria during the unspecified governorship(s) of 3 B.C. to A.D. 6.

The conundrum is made more curious by the fact that a reference to "the census" in Acts essentially agrees with Josephus. Recording a speech of Gamaliel I, Luke writes that "Judas the Galilean appeared in the days of the census and led a band of people in revolt" (Acts 5:37). Judas the Galilean, as Josephus informs us (*Ant.* 18.4-10), founded a militant protest movement in reaction to the census in A.D. 6 under Quirinius. Luke does not mention Quirinius in Acts 5:37, but his reference to *the* census would appear to recall the census of 2:2 associated with Quirinius. Why Luke twice refers to the same event, the latter in essential correspondence with external historical records and the former at variance from them, remains a mystery. Given available evidence related to the matter, it appears that the reference to Quirinius in Luke 2:2 is a conflation of the census of Quirinius with the death of Herod the Great. The two events were easy to conflate, for the death of Herod and the census of Quirinius were both epic events, and both incited massive protests that were violently suppressed by the Roman army.[21] A full resolution of the historical problems related to the dating of the census of Quirinius seems impossible on the basis of current historical knowledge.[22]

4-7 Bethlehem lies some seventy miles (110 km) due south of Nazareth, the home of Joseph and Mary (2:39). Luke properly speaks of going *up* from Nazareth (1,600 feet [500 m] above sea level) to Bethlehem (2,300 feet [700 m] above sea level). "City of David" normally refers to Jerusalem (see further at 2:11), but here it is used with unusual specificity to refer to the place of David's birth (John 7:42; 1 Sam 16:4; 20:6; Mic 5:1-2), thus anchoring Joseph "to the house and line of David" (v. 4), i.e., the ancestry of David. The description of Mary, "who was pledged to be married to [Joseph] and was expecting a child" (v. 5), is slightly redundant (see 1:27). Some scholars suggest that her reintroduction here is evidence of a different source.[23] This suggestion seems overly pedantic. The first reference occurred almost sixty verses earlier, and its repetition is here advisable from a narrative standpoint. The reference also advances the plot in subtle step-repetition: in 1:27 Mary is a virgin engaged to Joseph, and in 2:5 she is still engaged, but now pregnant. Luke repeats Mary's

---

21. R. Syme, "The Titulus Tiburtinus," in *Vestigia: Akten des VI Internationalen Kongresses für griechische und lateinische Epigraphik, 1972* (Beiträge zur Alten Geschichte 17; Munich: Beck'sche Verlag, 1972), 600; Leaney, *Luke*, 47; Brown, *Birth*, 555.

22. Bock, *Luke 1:1–9:50*, 903-9, surveys historical evidence related to the census at length and urges against "premature" judgment of the matter.

23. In addition to Mary's reintroduction, Bovon, *Lukas 1,1–9,50*, 115, also notes that she understands the birth by the shepherd's announcement (2:19-20) rather than by the previous annunciation of 1:26-38. Brown, *Birth*, 396-97, likewise suspects another source for Luke 2 than for Luke 1.

unchanged marital status in order to highlight the fulfillment of the divine promise (1:31) in her pregnancy (2:5).[24] The journey from Nazareth to Bethlehem leaves Mary and Joseph — an unmarried and pregnant couple traveling together in a Jewish milieu — in a shocking social liaison.[25] Some ancient manuscripts attempted to alleviate the scandal by altering Mary's status to "Joseph's wife," or alternatively, "betrothed to him as a wife." The NIV translation is surely correct, however, for it is unlikely that a later scribe would expose the Holy Family to the social impropriety of vv. 4-5 unless it corresponded with Luke's original wording. Why Mary is traveling with Joseph in such a socially and physically precarious situation has been much discussed. Was she, too, of Davidic ancestry and thus required to appear in Bethlehem? Did she own property in Bethlehem and likewise need to appear in person? Neither suggestion seems probable. Joseph alone is identified as a descendent of David (v. 4), and the property hypothesis is based on a fictional reading of Eusebius.[26] Luke reports only that Mary attended Joseph "because she was pregnant" (v. 5).[27] This seems reasonable enough; Mary needs the protection of Joseph during her pregnancy and delivery, even if it entails the ordeal of obligatory travel.

Jesus is popularly imagined to have been born the first night Joseph and Mary arrived in Bethlehem. This understanding first arises in the romantic *Prot. Jas.* 17–18, in which Mary gives birth in a cave on the way to Bethlehem. Luke, however, implies that Joseph and Mary had been in Bethlehem for a length of time, and "while they were there, the time came for the baby to be born" (v. 6). The birth of Jesus is more than a reproductive event; it is the *fulfillment* of a divine promise (1:31), described in the same terminology as the births of John in 1:57 and of Esau and Jacob in Gen 25:24. The wrapping of a newborn in cloths is an ancient Jewish custom (Ezek 16:4) that continues even today in villages in Syria and Palestine. A "manger" is a feed trough for stable animals — cattle, sheep, goats. "Because there was no room for him in the inn" (KJV) is indelibly etched in Christian vernacular, but it is misleading. The Greek word *katalyma* does not refer to an "inn" or "hotel" (in the Parable of the Good Samarian, 10:34, the Greek word *pandocheian* means "inn" or "hotel"). Archaeology, even more than lexicography,[28] has helped define

24. Similarly, Wolter, *Lukasevangelium,* 124-25.

25. Bovon, *Lukas 1,1–9,50,* 120.

26. Eusebius, *Hist. eccl.* 3:20, records that grandsons of Judas (presumably Jesus' brother [Mark 6:3]) were interrogated before the emperor Domitian (81-96) about "how much property they had." Eusebius does not locate the property in Bethlehem, however, or attribute it to Mary.

27. Plummer, *Luke,* 53, "*ousē* introduces, not a mere fact, but the reason for what has just been stated; he took her with him, '*because* she was with child.'"

28. In the LXX, *katalyma* translates five different Hebrew words in the MT (*HALOT* 1:588). It is a general term for "lodging" of various sorts, frequently connoting a shelter, such as a caravanserai, where travelers unloaded burdens.

katalyma properly as a "guest room" (so NIV). The footprint of a typical first-century Palestine dwelling was a rectangle divided into three spaces: a large central room with a stable for animals on one end and a guest room *(katalyma)* on the other. All three rooms normally had separate entrances. The *katalyma* was an attached guest room separated from the central room by a solid wall.[29] The stable was separated from the central room by a half-wall, thus allowing the family to feed animals without going outdoors. When Joseph and Mary arrived in Bethlehem, the guest rooms in homes were already occupied, and hence the newborn Jesus was swaddled and placed in a manger. The manger was within sight, sound, and reach of the central room. Kenneth Bailey is correct in saying that, despite improvised arrangements, Middle Eastern hospitality, then as now, would have ensured that Mary, Joseph, and Jesus were properly cared for.[30]

Most early church fathers believed in Mary's perpetual virginity. Consequently, they did not understand "firstborn son" (v. 7; *prōtotokos*) to refer to Jesus as the first of later siblings, but, as the incarnate and resurrected Jesus, to the firstborn of redeemed humanity (e.g., John 1:12).[31] From a lexical perspective, however, the primary referent of *prōtotokos* is to birth order.[32] Had Luke intended to imply either Mary's perpetual virginity or that Jesus was her only son, he could have used *monogenēs,* "only (begotten) son." Early Christian tradition freely ascribed further children to Joseph and Mary (Mark 6:3). Indeed, Luke's use of "firstborn" seems to indicate that in his day there was no dogma that Jesus was an only child.[33] The use of *prōtotokos* may not be limited to birth order, however. It may be reminiscent of Exodus 4:22, where God declares, "Israel is my firstborn son." If so, Jesus is the fulfillment of the OT ideal:

---

29. A self-contained guest room provided separate lodgings for family and guests, protecting them from suspicions of promiscuity. Thus *m. Ketub.* 1:5, "If in Judea a man ate in the house of his father-in-law and had not witnesses he may not lodge a virginity suit against [his wife-to-be], since he has (already) remained alone with her."

30. On *katalyma,* see Plummer, *Luke,* 54; J. Martin, *Exploring Bible Times* (Amarillo: Bible World Seminars, 1993), 5-8; Bailey, *Jesus through Middle Eastern Eyes,* 25-36; and esp. Brown, *Birth,* 100-101. In contrast to the above view, J. Jeremias, *poimēn, TWNT* 6:490, argues on the basis of archaeological excavations under the Church of the Nativity in Bethlehem and the testimony of several church fathers that Jesus was born in a cave owned by the shepherds themselves. Jeremias's theory is not as far removed from the "guest room" theory as might be imagined, since many Palestinian homes were dug into hillsides and were thus partial cave dwellings. In a freestanding domicile, however, the description of *katalyma* in the above commentary is the proper understanding of "guest room."

31. See A. Just, *Luke,* 38.

32. BDAG, 894; LSJ, 1545.

33. Plummer, *Luke,* 53; Brown, *Birth,* 398. Bovon, *Lukas 1,1–9,50,* 121, however, understands *prōtotokos* with reference to divine sonship: "In any case, Luke sets Jesus in a preeminent relation to God, not in relationship to later siblings."

he is the true Son of God, through whom Israel will reappropriate its original divine sonship. It may also identify Jesus over against Caesar Augustus, who as *divus Augustus* promoted himself as a son of God.

8-14 The infancy narrative reaches a second christological highpoint, in addition to the Annunciation (1:26-38), in the angelic announcement to the shepherds in vv. 8-14, each verse of which (with the exception of v. 12) was utilized as text in Handel's *Messiah*. The announcement begins with the introduction of **shepherds**, who represented one of the meaner demographic elements in Palestinian society. Luke mentions two characteristics of shepherds: living outside in open country (the literal meaning of *agraulountes*) and taking turns in night watches. Nomadic shepherds who were separated from human communities and culture for long periods of time were inevitably subjected to suspicion and scorn. Popular lore accused them of failing to observe the difference between "mine" and "thine." Because they could prey on lonely travelers, they were often suspected of practicing "the craft of robbers" (*m. Qidd.* 4:14). Their prolonged absences — and ill-repute — disqualified them from being legal witnesses. A third-century rabbi, commenting on Ps 23, said, "There is no more despised occupation in the world than that of shepherds."[34] Along with gamblers and tax collectors, herdsmen were regularly listed among despised trades by Mishnah and Talmud.[35] In contrast to this negative assessment, the NT holds shepherds in generally high esteem. Indeed, the shepherd becomes a symbol of God himself in Luke 15:4-6 (as earlier in Ezek 34:11-16). The radical re-presentation of shepherds in the NT may, as Jeremias suggests, be due to the life of Jesus himself, the Good Shepherd, who knows the sheep by name (John 10:3) and lays down his life for the flock (John 10:11-13).[36]

"In the same countryside" (v. 8; NIV "field nearby") suggests a location of the shepherds near Bethlehem. According to the Mishnah, livestock within a certain circumference of Jerusalem were reserved for sacrifice in the Jerusalem temple.[37] Bethlehem lay within that circumference, and the shepherds may have tended flocks appointed for that purpose. In general, shepherds spent warmer, drier months (March-November) further afield, and colder, wetter months (November-March) nearer towns and cities. Proximity to Bethlehem could speak for a winter birth of Jesus; a census, however, would more likely be scheduled for July-August, when harvests were complete. The

---

34. Str-B 2:113-14.

35. E.g., *m. Qidd.* 4:14; *b. Sanh.* 25b. On shepherds in first-c. Palestine, see Str-B 1:113-14; Jeremias, *Jerusalem in the Time of Jesus*, 303-6; Brown, *Birth*, 420-24.

36. J. Jeremias, *poimēn*, *TWNT* 6:489.

37. *m. Šeqal.* 7:4. The outer limit of the area is designated as Migdal Eder (Gen 35:21). Although not certainly identified, the name means "Tower of the Flock," which in Mic 4:8 appears in the vicinity of Mount Zion.

dearth of information on the date of Jesus' birth may indicate that NT writers themselves did not know when he was born.

The appearance of the angel to the shepherds exemplifies the proclamation of "good news to the poor" (Isa 61:1). Luke will quote the same verse twice again (4:18; 7:22) as a defining characteristic of Jesus' ministry. According to Mic 5:1-4, a "ruler over Israel" will arise in Bethlehem and "shepherd his flock in the strength of the Lord." The shepherds are ordained to be the first to hear of the savior's birth and recognize the Good Shepherd in Bethlehem. The Greek word for "appeared" (v. 9; *epestē*) is commonly used of heavenly appearances and visions in classical Greek.[38] The "angel of the Lord" is not identified in v. 9, but the same expression is used of Gabriel in 1:11, and presumably indicates Gabriel here. With the angel of the Lord appears "the glory of the Lord" (v. 9). The Hebrew word for "glory," *kabod,* means "weight," that which is heavy and substantial, whereas the Greek word for "glory," *doxa,* is nonmaterial, meaning "splendor" or "brightness." Despite the different connotations of *kabod* and *doxa,* both are associated with radiant light.[39] Luke describes the flash of light at Paul's conversion (Acts 26:13) with the same word for the radiance of the Lord here. The antiphony between light and darkness may reflect Isa 9:2, for Luke artfully contrasts human darkness in v. 8 and divine light in v. 9. He further contrasts "great fear" at the appearance of the angel in v. 9 (also 1:13) with "great joy" in v. 10. "Joy," a major motif in the Third Gospel, is not an emotion caused by auspicious circumstances but by the presence and work of God — in salvation (1:14; 2:10; 15:7, 10), spiritual works (10:17), and the resurrection of Jesus (24:41, 52). An angelic appearance that simply impressed the shepherds with brilliance would have left them in fear. The purpose of the angelic appearance is not to stun or dazzle, but "to bring you good news" (v. 10). The use of "good news" (Gk. *euangelizesthai*) subtly counteracts Caesar's self-promotion by use of the same word (see the discussion of vv. 1-3 above). The proclamation of joy is not a general announcement of euphoria, but good news specifically and personally "to *you*" — the shepherds — and for "all the people" (on "all people," see note at 1:10).

The angelic proclamation reaches a climax, "Today in the city of David a Savior has been born to you; he is the Messiah, the Lord" (v. 11). It is natural to take "City of David" with reference to Bethlehem, since David was a native of Bethlehem (1 Sam 17:12-15) and Mary and Joseph are in Bethlehem for Jesus' birth (v. 4). "City of David" almost certainly refers to Jerusalem, however, and associates Jesus' birth with it. The epithet occurs forty-five times in the OT, always with reference to "Zion," i.e., to Jerusalem as either the cultic heart of Israel (ark and temple) or as the seat of royal power of the kings of Judah. In

---

38. Plummer, *Luke,* 55.

39. 9:31-32; Exod 16:10; 24:16; 40:34-35; Ezek 1:28; 3:12, 23; 2 Cor 3:18.

the NT "City of David" occurs only in 2:4, 11. The former reference specifically refers to Bethlehem, but v. 11 is better taken with reference to Jerusalem, thus associating the birth of Jesus with the two most tangible expressions of God's presence in Israel — the *place* of God's presence in the temple, and the *line* of God's presence through the kings. The former theme will reappear in 23:45, when the temple curtain is rent asunder at Jesus' death on the cross. With regard to the royal dynasty of Judah, beginning with David (1 Kgs 2:10), "city of David" occurs twenty-eight times in the OT with reference to Jerusalem as the final resting place of the kings of Judah.[40] As a burial epithet "city of David" connects Jesus directly with the royal and filial theology of the monarchy (2 Sam 7:12-14; Ps 2:7); the burial place of Israel's monarchs is now declared the birthplace of Israel's Messiah.

The angelic proclamation is emphatically existential ("today") and personal ("for you," v. 11). "Today" belongs to the lexicon of Luke's load-bearing theological vocabulary. Its occurrence here announces Jesus' advent; in 4:21 it is the first word of Jesus' inaugural sermon in Nazareth; at 23:43 it is the final promise of Jesus from the cross, "Today you will be with me in paradise." The angel identifies the newborn Jesus as Messiah, Lord, and Savior. The first two titles appear in tandem, "Messiah-Lord" in Greek, a construction found nowhere else in the NT. "Messiah" (Gk. *Christos,* "Christ") means God's anointed Davidic-king. "Lord" (Gk. *kyrios*) is the standard LXX translation of the Hebrew Tetragrammaton, YHWH. One would expect the construction to read "Messiah *of* the Lord," as is prevalent throughout the LXX.[41] Significantly, in this first occurrence of "Messiah" in Luke, it appears with "Lord." The apposition of "Messiah-Lord" is similar to the apposition of "Christ-King" in 23:2;[42] both convey that Jesus is not simply the Messiah *of* the Lord, but the Messiah who *is* the Lord.[43] The attribution to the newborn Jesus of a title reserved exclusively for God in the OT corroborates the high Christology of the annunciation, where Jesus is called Son of God (1:35). Although "Savior" is less exalted than either "Son of God" or "Lord," it is more remarkable in this context. It would have been sufficient for Luke to say, "The Messiah, the Lord, was born today in the city of David." The identification of the Messiah-Lord as "savior" counteracts the claims and cult of Caesar Augustus in v. 1, who repeatedly promoted himself as "savior of the common

40. The remaining two references to "city of David" refer to the placement of the ark of the covenant in the temple of Jerusalem (1 Chr 15:1; 2 Chr 8:11). All thirty references to the epithet in the OT refer to Jerusalem, and none to Bethlehem.

41. A few manuscripts change the reading to "Messiah of the Lord," but the chief textual witnesses favor "Messiah-Lord"; see Metzger, *TCGNT,* 110.

42. Gk. *christon basilea.*

43. Ps 110:1 also uses "Lord" in two senses and may have influenced Luke's usage of the term here. On "Christ-Lord," see Rowe, *Early Narrative Christology,* 49-55.

folk" and "savior of the world."[44] In an official litany of accomplishments known as *Res Gestae*, Caesar Augustus postured as a "savior" who inaugurated a new and propitious age of peace,[45] order, and prosperity, fulfilling the longings of humanity.[46] The NT, and particularly the Gospels, are sparing in attributing *sōtēr*, "savior," to Jesus, perhaps to avoid its rampant association with the emperor cult.[47] We noted in the discussion of the Halicarnassus and Priene inscriptions (see discussion at v. 1) that the titles ascribed to Caesar Augustus — Son of God, savior, bringer of peace, hope, and good news — are all attributed by Luke to the newborn Jesus, as a divine alternative to the Roman imperial political-theology. The attribution of *sōtēr* to Jesus in v. 11 is a direct challenge to that political-theology. Contrary to imperial propaganda, the true Son of God and Savior of the world — and thus the ultimate good news for the world — are not contained in a decree of Caesar but in the divine proclamation from heaven. The Savior is not mighty Augustus in Rome, but an infant lying in a feed trough in the city of David.[48]

The angelic promise does not remain an abstraction but is instantiated in a sign, "a baby wrapped in cloths and lying in a manger" (v. 12). Luke's combination of word and sign in the infancy narratives, a combination repeated with greater precision in the revelation of the resurrected Jesus through Scripture and breaking of bread in 24:25-32, anticipates the categories of "word and sacrament" in later theology. Divine word in human flesh clearly presupposes incarnation. In contrast to the Fourth Gospel, Luke and the Synoptics are skeptical about the value of signs for faith. The only sign promised by Jesus in the Third Gospel is the dubious sign of Jonah in 11:29-30. The sign announced

---

44. In a comment of relevance for v. 11, Suetonius, *Aug.* 53, says that Augustus "always shrank from the title of Lord." Augustus favored the term "savior," however, which may account for Luke's inclusion of it in v. 11.

45. According to Venerable Bede, God sent Jesus Christ into the world during the Pax Romana because he is the Pax Mundi; see Just, *Luke*, 37. Also Brown, *Birth*, 414-15.

46. E. Lohmeyer, *Christuskult und Kaiserkult* (Tübingen: Mohr Siebeck, 1919), 17-20. For a fuller discussion of the emperor cult, see J. Edwards, *Is Jesus the Only Savior?* (Grand Rapids: Eerdmans, 2005), 123-32.

47. "Savior" does not occur in Matthew or Mark, only twice in Luke (1:47; 2:11), and once in John (4:42). It is largely avoided by Paul as well (only Eph 5:23; Phil 3:20). Its most frequent occurrences are found in the Pastorals (10x) and 2 Pet (5x).

48. Bovon, *Lukas 1,1–9,50*, 116-18 (so too Brown, *Birth*, 424), suggests that the Caesar-Christ contrast is "Luke's gentle counterpropaganda that Jesus, not Augustus, was the Savior." The infancy narrative may be more than "gentle counterpropaganda." Both Caesar and Christ are called "savior" (2:11); Caesar delivers a "decree," the angels a "proclamation" (2:13); Caesar enrolls "the entire Roman world," Christ "all the people" (2:10); both Caesar and Christ deliver "good news" (2:10); both deliver "peace" (2:14); both are called "firstborn" (2:7); the father of Caesar is Zeus, the Father of Jesus is the "Highest God" (1:32); Caesar promises fond hopes for the future, Jesus a kingdom without end (1:33).

by the angel is itself dubious: a newborn is commonplace, and a newborn in a manger is primitive, if not brutish.[49] Apart from the angelic announcement, this sign could easily be overlooked or mistaken for something other than it is. Without the divine word, who would imagine that in this humble person and place, *Immanuel,* "God is with us"?[50]

The angelic herald is like an announcer standing on stage before a curtain. The curtain rises, and "suddenly a great company of the heavenly host appeared with the angel" (v. 13). "Suddenly" (Gk. *exaiphnēs*) indicates that what follows is not humanly induced but divinely given. The Greek word for "company," *stratia,* denoted a military unit, an army. This army is huge (Gk. *plēthos;* NIV "great"), regimented, and marshaled for the praise and purposes of God. The Greek word for "praise," *ainein,* occurs only eight times in the NT, six of them in Luke-Acts. *Ainein* augments Luke's central theme of *joy,* reminding believers that the eschatological community of God, both the church triumphant and the church militant, is by nature doxological, ultimately determined by its celebration of God. Bengel notes the paradox of an army deployed for peace rather than war.[51]

> The heavenly army chants:
> "Glory to God in the highest heaven,
>   And on earth peace among those of good will."

The angelic song does not proclaim a mystical union of heaven and earth. Rather, it celebrates two sovereign works of God: one in heaven, and one on earth. Rather than being mystically amalgamated, God's activity is praised in both: glory in heaven, and peace on earth; glory to God, and peace to humanity.[52] A minority of Greek manuscripts, and older English translations, rendered the final phrase as "good will among men," i.e., the peace of God rests on people of good will. This translation, although deeply engrained in public memory, is probably incorrect. Textual support is decidedly superior for the NIV translation ("peace to those on whom his favor rests").

---

49. Jerome, who was not adverse to scatological imagery, captures the irony of the manger scene: "He found no room in the Holy of Holies that shone with gold, precious stones, pure silk and silver. He is not born in the midst of gold and riches, but in the midst of dung, in a stable where our sins were filthier than the dung. He is born on a dunghill in order to lift up those who come from it: 'From the dunghill he lifts up the poor' (Ps 113:7)" (Just, *Luke,* 39).

50. Further on word and sign, Bovon, *Lukas 1,1–9,50,* 126-27.

51. Bengel, *Gnomon,* 2:30.

52. "In the highest heaven" is sometimes mistaken to mean "in the highest degree." This is not the sense of *hypsistos,* a frequent and important word in Luke (1:32, 35, 76; 2:14; 6:35; 8:28; 19:38), which refers specifically to God and God's place in the universe. See the discussion at 1:32 and, further, G. Bertram, *hypsistos, TWNT* 8:617-19; Brown, *Birth,* 403-5.

Moreover, the translation adopted by NIV is the more difficult reading (and hence to be preferred). Finally, the word for "favor" (Gk. *eudokia, eudokein*) means *God's* saving pleasure rather than humanity's good will whenever used in Luke (2:14; 3:22; 10:21; 12:32). The meaning is "not that divine peace can be bestowed only where human good will is already present, but that at the birth of the Saviour God's peace rests on those whom he has chosen in accord with his good pleasure."[53]

15-20 Various church fathers interpreted the visit of the shepherds to Bethlehem as a metaphor of bishops tending the church, thus "shepherds of the church," similar to Ezek 34.[54] Luke does not intend the shepherds allegorically, however, but in all their rustic reality. The construction of v. 15 in Greek places "angels" at the end of the first clause and "shepherds" at the beginning of the second. The syntax of angels-shepherds thus repeats the contrast between heaven and earth (v. 14), a contrast that in the incarnation is resolved and united in Jesus, the Son of God in human flesh. The use of the Greek imperfect tense, "the shepherds *were* saying among themselves," in an otherwise aorist narrative emphasizes repeated discourse, i.e., they could not stop talking about it. The word for "thing" (v. 15; Gk. *to rhēma*) is a Hebraism, a translation of Hebrew *dabar,* which means both "word" and "thing." The shepherds are thus impelled to visit the child because of the spectacle of the heavenly army in vv. 13-14 and because of what "the Lord made known to us." This last phrase indicates that the shepherds take the angel's report as the word of the Lord himself. The narrative is thus driven by the divine announcement of Jesus' birth rather than simply by the visit of the shepherds.

The "thing" the shepherds seek and find is "Mary and Joseph, and the baby, who was lying in the manger" (v. 16). It is unusual for Mary to be mentioned before her husband Joseph. This suggests that Mary's preeminence as mother of the Messiah was already acknowledged when Luke wrote (so too Matt 2:11). Luke-Acts is attentive to the nature of communities, and particularly the joy they experience in the proclamation and mission of the gospel. The birth of Jesus creates such a community in his own family, and he is first encountered by a community of shepherd outsiders. Ironically, the shepherds, who were disqualified from serving as witnesses in legal cases in Judaism, are qualified to be the first witnesses of the gospel, not because of any innate abilities (see their *demerits* at v. 8), but because of "the word that had been told them" (v. 17). It is not witnesses who invoke the word, but the *Word* that calls, creates, and empowers witnesses. The shepherds are also, although in a different way from Luke and his predecessors, "servants of the word" (1:2), indebted to make known "this child" (v. 17).

---

53. Metzger, *TCGNT,* 111; further, see Bovon, *Lukas 1,1–9,50,* 128-29; Brown, *Birth,* 403-5.
54. See Just, *Luke,* 40-42.

The testimony of the shepherds results in three responses: the amazement of hearers (v. 18), the pondering of Mary (v. 19), and praise of the community (v. 20). Amazement (see discussion of term at 1:63) is normally in
Luke, as here, a group response. Amazement is not evoked by a spectacle, but
by a report directed specifically "to them," the hearers (v. 18). Amazement
is not itself faith, but hearing a testimony of God's word directed to oneself
can be a first step in faith. Mary, by contrast, is not amazed but "ponders" in
her heart (v. 19; NIV "treasured"). In 1:66 the crowd ponders in its heart the
meaning of John's birth, but only Mary ponders Jesus' birth. The word for
"ponder," *syntērein,* means to "preserve," "treasure," "protect and defend." The
same word is used in the LXX of Jacob's puzzling over the meaning of Joseph's
dreams (Gen 37:11). This word is in the imperfect tense, connoting something
ongoing; thus, "to ruminate," even "to wrestle with." In addition to pondering,
Mary "interpreted" events in her heart. Greek *symballein* means to scrutinize
difficult events, often with divine aid, for right understanding.[55] Mary is the
only adult mentioned in Luke 1–2 who later appears in the Gospel. Already
in the report of the shepherds, she becomes a model of faith for Luke; like the
good seed in the parable of the Sower (8:15), Mary "hears the word, holds it
fast, and preserves a good crop."[56] Finally, the shepherds return to their tasks,
"glorifying and praising God for all they had heard and seen" (v. 20). Hearing
precedes seeing as an avenue of faith. Their joy is not innate within themselves, but *gaudium extra eos* — the result of what "they had been told." The
description of the visit of the shepherds to the Holy Family already contains
Lukan clues regarding the nature of the community formed by the gospel. The
gospel does not result, as does Caesar's ambition to enroll "the entire Roman
world" (v. 1) and promote his pretense of deity, in despotism, subjection, or
blind obedience. The new community of the manger results in the coming
together of disparate groups who hear and speak, marvel and ponder, glorify
and praise, and return to useful work in the world.[57]

SIMEON AND ANNA RECEIVE JESUS
IN THE TEMPLE (2:21-40)

The circumcision, naming, and presentation of Jesus in the temple in 2:21-40
are the counterpart to the circumcision and naming of John in 1:57-80. In
both accounts, hymns are dedicated to the infants: the longer Benedictus by

---

55. Brown, *Birth,* 406-7.
56. Brown, *Birth,* 428-30.
57. See Bovon, *Lukas 1,1–9,50,* 131-32.

Zechariah in 1:68-79 and a shorter Nunc Dimittus by Simeon in 2:29-32. The significance of 2:21-40 exceeds its correspondence with 1:57-80, however. Luke insightfully frames the reception of Jesus in the temple by the repetition of Greek *prosdechesthai,* a word that combines the ideas of "receiving, welcoming" and "waiting in expectation." Simeon is introduced as a righteous man "*waiting* for the consolation of Israel" (2:25). Anna is likewise described as a devout prophetess who spoke about Jesus "to all who were *awaiting* the redemption of Jerusalem" (2:38). Half of all occurrences of *prosdechesthai* in the NT occur in Luke-Acts, testifying to the steadfast faith of common people in the fulfillment of the messianic hope.[58] The recognition and reception of Jesus occurs, appropriately, in the temple in Jerusalem, where Israel's most sacred beliefs and hopes were enshrined. The people involved, however, are not obviously appropriate. No high priest or member of the Sanhedrin, nor any other temple official, whether priest or Levite, receives Jesus. Rather, Jesus is received by two otherwise unknown persons who never again appear in Scripture, who, although they occupy no temple office, embody the sincere faith of the temple. The long-awaited but unfulfilled messianic hope led some in Judaism to compromise with Roman Realpolitik, others to militant opposition of the same, others to utopian dreams, and still others to flight, separation, seclusion, and resignation. Simeon and Anna follow a less celebrated but more difficult course: they *wait in faith* (Isa 7:9), trusting in the God of the promise — and in his timing. They exemplify the poor who hunger for the kingdom of God, and who may be despised for doing so (6:20-22). Their steadfast courage to await God's promise rather than take refuge in spiritual counterfeits results in their seeing in the baby Jesus the dawn of God's salvation (2:30).[59] Simeon and Anna epitomize Jewish piety in Israel's most holy place. That they recognize and proclaim Jesus not only as Israel's Messiah, but also as a light to Gentiles, indicates that the Gentile mission is not an addendum to salvation history but constituent of it.

21-24   Like John, Jesus is circumcised and named on the eighth day after his birth (on naming and circumcision, see at 1:59). The delay in naming a boy until his circumcision was unusual in Judaism at this time; indeed, 1:59 and 2:21 are two of the earliest examples in Judaism of naming a boy at his circumcision. The circumcision and naming of Jesus do not play the prominent role they do for John (1:57-66), but they are nevertheless a "fulfillment" (v. 21; Gk. *pimplanai;* NIV "when it was time"). *Eplēsthēsan* occurs twenty-two times in Luke-Acts (only three times elsewhere in the NT), signifying the development of events in accordance with God's plan. Jesus' submission

---

58. See 2:25, 38; 12:36; 15:2; 23:51; Acts 23:21; 24:15.

59. On awaiting the messianic hope and living in quiet expectation, see Schweizer, *Lukas,* 40, and Wolter, *Lukasevangelium,* 134.

to circumcision signifies his full identification with humanity ("in the likeness of sinful humanity," Rom 8:3), indeed, his full identification with *Jewish* humanity ("made like Abraham's descendents in every way," Heb 2:17). Paul captures both aspects of Jesus' identification in Gal 4:4 — "born of a woman, born under the law." "Jesus" is a Greek name related to the Hebrew word *yasha,* meaning "help," "deliverance," or "salvation." Matt 1:21 identifies the name expressly with salvation, whereas in 1:31-33 Luke identifies the name with divine sonship and Davidic kingship.[60] The declaration of Jesus' name to Mary *before* she conceived (1:31 and 2:21) is similar to Gen 1, where the word of God is the creative precondition of material reality.

"The purification rites required by the Law of Moses" (v. 22) mark another stage of "fulfillment" (again *pimplanai*). According to Torah, the mother of a male infant was unclean for seven days postpartum, and she was required to remain at home and avoid contact with holy foods, persons, or places for an additional thirty-three days. The period of uncleanness thus totaled forty days. If the child was a girl, the period of uncleanness was twice as long.[61] Scholars sometimes judge Luke's description of the purification and presentation of Jesus in the temple as confused or contrary to Mosaic law. Already in the OT, however, the custom of offering all firstborn males to the Lord (Exod 13:2, 12, 15) was transferred specifically to the Levites (Num 8:15-19). Luke's description of Jesus' purification and presentation may be the result of the evolution in legal protocol related to purification of birth mothers and offerings for the firstborn. Vv. 22-24 generally reflect the protocol of Lev 12, where a birth mother's purification is followed by an offering in the temple. Luke departs from Lev 12 in two respects, both of which can be explained by his interest in highlighting Jesus rather than Mary. The first is the reference to "their purification" (v. 22; NIV "the purification"). Torah required only the purification of the mother, but Exod 34:19-20 requires also the redemption of the firstborn, which Luke appears to include in the purification of Mary, thus *their* purification.[62] The second departure concerns the offering of "a pair of doves or two young pigeons" (v. 24). This offering, which was prescribed for Israelites of humble means and thus identifies Mary and Joseph with the lower economic classes in Palestine, was prescribed for the purification of a birth mother (Lev 5:11; 12:8). Luke ascribes this offering to the presentation of Jesus in the temple (v. 22) in a manner reminiscent of the presentation of Samuel at the sanctuary in Shiloh (1 Sam 1:22-24). The two exceptions to the protocol

---

60. For the etymology of the name, see Fitzmyer, *Luke (I–IX),* 347, and *HALOT* 1:448-49.

61. Exod 13:2, 12, 15; Lev 12:2-5; Num 8:15-17; Str-B 2:119-20.

62. Lagrange, *Luc,* 82, captures Luke's sense: "To summarize, the thought of Luke is clear. He is occupied throughout with Jesus, the center of the entire scene, who is necessarily to be included with Mary in the plural pronoun." Similarly, Vinson, *Luke,* 66-67.

set forth in Lev 12 thus accentuate the presentation, even *manifestation*, of Jesus in the temple.[63]

25-35 Luke's emphasis on the reception of Jesus in the temple exceeds the foregoing account of the purification rites of mother and child. Simeon and Anna are introduced as otherwise unknown individuals, although Anna's credentials and piety in vv. 36-37 exceed those of Simeon, who is simply called "righteous and devout" (v. 25). Typical of the Third Gospel, the Greek word for "Jerusalem" follows the Hebraic rather than the Hellenistic spelling, thus implying a Hebraic source of the name.[64] The receptions of Simeon and Anna are told sequentially, but their combined witness is necessary to complete Luke's narrative effect. Simeon and Anna represent male and female awaiting redemption in Christ,[65] both espouse the same messianic hope (vv. 25, 38), and their joint witness is necessary to establish valid testimony in accordance with Torah (Deut 19:15). In some respects, Simeon and Anna understand and receive the good news of the advent of Jesus more laudably than does Mary.[66]

Simeon (or Simon) was a common name in Israel, deriving from the second of Jacob's twelve sons (Gen 29:33), who became the eponymous ancestor of the tribe of Simeon. *Prot. Jas.* introduces Simeon as a priest, and *Acts Pil.* as a great teacher, but these are later apocryphal accounts of doubtful historical value.[67] It has also been proposed that the Simeon of v. 25 was the son of Hillel and father of Gamaliel, and was also president of the Sanhedrin in A.D. 13, but this too is conjectural.[68] Were Simeon a character of note, we might expect Luke to give his credentials, as he does of Anna in vv. 36-37. Luke does not cite Simeon's credentials, but rather his character and the Spirit's guidance of him. Luke mentions three times the presentation of Jesus in the temple according

---

63. Fitzmyer, *Luke (I–IX)*, 420-21, offers a plausible and helpful interpretation of vv. 22-24 as a "manifestation of Jesus."

64. Of the thirty-one references to "Jerusalem" in Luke, twenty-seven follow the Hebraic *Ierousalēm*, and only four (2:22; 13:22; 19:28; 23:7) the Hellenistic *Hierosolyma*. Neither Mark nor John uses the Hebraic spelling of Jerusalem, and Matt uses it only once (20:17, when following Luke's usage of the same in 13:22). For a full discussion of the spelling in both Luke and Acts, see Edwards, *Hebrew Gospel*, 136-38.

65. This was already recognized in the early church; so Venerable Bede (Just, *Luke*, 48). On Luke's penchant for pairs, and esp. male-female pairs, see excursus at 14:1.

66. Luke portrays Mary as "greatly troubled" (1:29) at the annunciation, "mulling over" (Gk. *symballein;* TNIV "pondered") the report of the shepherds (2:19), and (along with Joseph) failing to "understand what [Jesus] was saying to them" (2:50). On the joint witness of Simeon and Anna, see B. Witherington III, "Mary, Simeon, or Anna: Who First Recognized Jesus as Messiah?" *BRev* 21/5 (2005): 12-14, 51.

67. *Prot. Jas.* 24.4; *Acts Pil.* 16.2 (in 17.1 it is reported that Jesus raised Simeon's two sons from the dead).

68. A. Cutler, "Does Simeon of Luke 2 Refer to Simeon the Son of Hillel?" *JBR* 34 (1966): 29-35. Contra the thesis, see Brown, *Birth*, 437-38; Fitzmyer, *Luke (I–IX)*, 426.

to the law of Moses (vv. 22-24), and also mentions three times that Simeon is led by the Holy Spirit to see and confess the Christ child (vv. 25-27). It is important to remember that, in Judaism, prophecy was attributed to the influence of the Holy Spirit.[69] The references to Torah and Holy Spirit thus invoke the witness of law and prophets to the infant Jesus.[70] Simeon is indeed "righteous and devout" (v. 25), but the influence of the Spirit rather than his moral piety prompts him to recognize and confess Jesus in the temple.[71] Simeon is the sixth person in the infancy narratives to be indwelt by the Holy Spirit (John, 1:15; Mary, 1:35; Jesus, 1:35; Elizabeth, 1:41; Zechariah, 1:67). The outpouring of the Holy Spirit on the chief characters in Luke 1–2 stands in marked contrast to the sparing references to the Spirit in the OT and signifies that the birth of Jesus is the divine fulfillment of the messianic hope (Isa 61:1).[72] Luke summarizes Simeon's life as an embodiment of the faithful expectation of "the consolation of Israel" (v. 25; so too Isa 40:1; 52:9; 66:12-13). Contrary to Israel's traditional expectation, Simeon does not hope simply for the comfort and vindication of Jerusalem. He awaits God's Messiah. For Simeon, "faith in Christ is the legitimate answer to the legitimate Jewish expectation."[73]

Divine superintendence of Simeon is repeated in vv. 26-27. The Greek *chrēmatizein* (v. 26; NIV "revealed") means to impart a divine message;[74] thus, the revelation to Simeon is no less God's word than was the angelic annunciation to the shepherds (v. 13). The revelation that Simeon "would not die before he had seen the Lord's Messiah" (v. 26) recalls similar wording in the Book of Tobit.[75] For

---

69. Str-B 2:126-38.

70. So Brown, *Birth*, 452.

71. Unlike Judith, who received God's favor because of her piety (*eusebēs*, Jdt 8:31), Simeon, who is also pious and devout, is superintended by God's Holy Spirit.

72. On the role of the (Holy) Spirit in the OT and rabbinic Judaism, see Str-B 2:126-38. Of particular interest in v. 25 is the word "devout" (Gk. *eulabēs*). This word occurs only in Luke-Acts (2:25; Acts 2:5; 8:2; 22:12), and belongs to Luke's unique vocabulary. Nevertheless, Codex Sinaiticus and five minuscule manuscripts read *eusebēs* ("pious") instead of *eulabēs*. Although manuscript evidence clearly favors the latter, a fourth-c. inscription (thus roughly the same date as Sinaiticus) recently discovered in the Kidron Valley in Jerusalem paraphrases Luke 2:25 thus: "The tomb of Simeon who was(?) . . . an old man most righteous and pious [*eusebēs*], who awaited the consolation of the people." The site of the inscription, Absalom's Pillar, was from a very early time associated in Christian tradition with the burials of Simeon, Zechariah, and James the brother of Jesus. Six words in the inscription (incl. *eusebēs*) agree with the Sinaiticus version of Luke 2:25, suggesting that *eusebēs* has a stronger claim to originality than is often supposed. On the inscription, see D. C. Parker, *An Introduction to the New Testament Manuscripts and Their Texts* (Cambridge: University Press, 2008), 128-29. On the find site, see E. Puech, "Le Tombeau de Siméon et Zacharie dans la vallée de Josaphat," *RB* 111 (2004): 563-77.

73. Bovon, *Lukas 1,1–9,50*, 141. Similarly, Green, *Luke*, 146.

74. BDAG, 1089; B. Reicke, *"chrēmatizō," TWNT* 9:469-71.

75. When Anna sees the return of her son Tobias, she falls upon his neck and exclaims,

the third time, Luke notes the influence of the Holy Spirit on Simeon: "moved by the Spirit, [Simeon] went into the temple courts" (v. 27). This is not a reference to a state of ecstasy (so Rev 1:10), but to the influence of *the* Spirit referred to in the previous two verses. The innermost temple court in which Simeon could meet with Mary and the child would be the Court of Women. That Luke refers to "the parents" of Jesus rather than simply to Mary is certainly no argument against the virgin birth. How else should Luke refer to Joseph who, though not the biological father of Jesus, faithfully fulfilled the duties of husband to Mary and father to Jesus? In the presence of Jesus, Simeon's first response of faith is not to speak but to touch: "Simeon took him in his arms and praised God" (v. 28). The Greek word for "take" is not the expected *lambanein* but a less frequent form of the word for awaiting the messianic hope above, thus achieving a play on words: in receiving *(dechesthai)* Jesus into his arms, Simeon is in fact receiving *(prosdechesthai)* the consolation of Israel (v. 25). Simeon's reception of Jesus symbolizes the ideal hope that Israel will receive and embrace Jesus as Messiah. Simeon is a "true Israelite" (John 1:47) and thus a prototype of all Israel who finds salvation in the Redeemer from Zion (Rom 11:26).

The exclamation of Simeon when he receives Jesus into his arms constitutes Luke's final infancy hymn. Shorter than the Magnificat (1:46-55) and Benedictus (1:68-79), and more personal than the Gloria in Excelsis (2:14), the Nunc Dimittis (2:29-32) is a doxology of confidence in God.[76] The Nunc Dimittis has been a standard element in evening prayer liturgies from the fourth century onward.[77] The doxology echoes the trust, hope, and universalism of the Servant of the Lord passages of Isa (esp. 40:5; 42:6; 46:13; 49:6; and 52:9-10).[78] The force of the first word in Greek, *nyn* ("now"), repeats the idea of "today" in 2:11, signaling that a new stage has been completed in the divine plan. The Nunc Dimittis is an "I-Thou" doxology between Simeon, a trusting servant, and God, a benevolent Master. Simeon employs the vocabulary of slave manumission ("release," "slave," and "master," v. 29) to depict his impending death as a willing resignation to the sovereign will of God.[79] Simeon is

---

"Now that I have seen you, my child, I am ready to die." Thereafter, Anna's husband, Tobit, sings a veritable Nunc Dimittis to Tobias (Tob 11:9-15).

76. The name derives from the Latin, "Nunc dimittis servum tuum Domine" ("Lord, now dismiss your servant").

77. *Apos. Con.* 7.48, an ancient collection of ecclesiastical law of Syrian origin, dated to the second half of the fourth c., preserves the earliest evidence of the Nunc Dimittis in evening prayer liturgies. See K. L. Schmidt, "Apostolic Constitution and Canons," *The New Schaff-Herzog Encyclopedia of Religious Knowledge*, 1:245-46.

78. Brown, *Birth*, 456-60, and Green, *Luke*, 147, provide helpful discussions of the linguistic and thematic relationships of the Nunc Dimittis with Second Isaiah.

79. The Greek word for "release/dismiss," *apolyein*, is also used of death in LXX Gen 15:2; Num 20:29; Tob 3:6; 2 Macc 7:9.

ready to die because his "eyes have seen [God's] salvation" (v. 30). God cannot be seen by human eyes, but God's concrete activity in the world of time and space can be. The word Luke uses for "salvation" is not *sōtēria,* but a variant, *sōtērion,* meaning "pertaining to salvation." In seeing the Christ child, Simeon sees everything that God ordains pertaining to salvation. *Sōtērion,* which occurs frequently in the LXX but only four times in the NT, plays a special role in Luke-Acts: it depicts the first human response to Jesus from the mouth of Simeon (2:30) and the final testimony to Jesus from Paul (Acts 28:28), both of which are delivered to Jewish audiences.

Because the good news is not "done in a corner" (Acts 26:26), Christian proclamation is not a private affair, but rather public proclamation for all people, "prepared in the sight of all nations" (v. 31). "Nations" carries national and political connotations, but the original Greek reads "all the people," a favorite expression of Luke (see at 1:10) denoting absolute universality. V. 32 defines "all the people" as "Gentiles" and "Israel." It was rare in any genre of ancient literature to see Gentiles and Jews placed in positive apposition to one another, and rarer still to see Gentiles mentioned *before* Israel.[80] Coming from a righteous Jew, standing in the holy temple, and quoting from the prophet Isaiah, Simeon's declaration is invested with the imprimatur of divine authority. In declaring God's messianic salvation as light to the *Gentiles* (Isa 42:6; 49:6), Simeon recovers a long-neglected but seminal truth of Judaism, namely, that Israel was not the terminus of God's revelation, but the conduit of God's revelation to all humanity.[81] A "light for revelation to the Gentiles" does not mean that God has rejected Israel; Israel is and ever remains God's people (Rom 11:29). But Jesus the Messiah reveals the heart of God and the essence of Israel's Scriptures and prophecy (24:26-27, 44-46). The reception of Jesus as Messiah enlightens Simeon to declare that "the glory of your people Israel" (v. 32) must now and ever more include Gentiles.

"The child's father and mother marveled at what was said about him" (v. 33). Luke's wording identifies Mary and Joseph by their relationship to Jesus, not his to them. It is Jesus who determines the family. Several manuscripts replace "the child's father" with "Joseph," but this is a later change, doubtless motivated by the desire to safeguard the doctrine of the virgin birth.[82] The parents of Jesus are less knowledgeable about Jesus than are the shepherds (2:17-19),

80. Bovon, *Lukas 1,1–9,50,* 145, translates v. 32 as "a light for the revelation of Gentiles [not *to* Gentiles], and for the glory of your people Israel." He defends this translation because (1) it agrees with Isa 42:6 and 49:6, (2) the genitive following "revealed" indicates the content of the revelation, not its recipient, and (3) the Greek text makes Gentiles and Israel linguistically parallel.

81. Str-B 2:139 notes that "the Biblical texts in Isa 42:6 and 49:6 that support this truth are almost never mentioned in rabbinic literature."

82. Metzger, *TCGNT,* 111-12; Brown, *Birth,* 440.

Simeon (vv. 29-35), and Anna (v. 38). Like other people, Jesus' parents must also come to know him through his life and teaching. Contrary to protocol, Simeon does not bless the child, perhaps because he knows that Jesus is the Son of the Most High (1:32). Instead, he blesses Mary — but with a severe mercy. "This child is destined to cause the falling and rising of many in Israel, and to be a sign that will be spoken against" (v. 34).[83] Bengel rightly recognizes that signs are ordinarily given to resolve contradictions, but "*this* sign shall be an object of contradiction."[84] Simeon's prophecy repeats the theme of Isaiah's prophecy to King Ahaz in Isa 8:14-15. The Greek *keitai* (v. 34; NIV "destined") in Simeon's prophecy is critical: Jesus will not happen to be an occasion of division, he is "appointed" for that purpose (so too Rom 9:33; 1 Pet 2:6-8). The prophetic word causes offense and division, and the Word become flesh no less so (12:51-53!). The gospel provokes a *krisis,* "crisis" (John 3:19). The Son of God, like the cloud of divine presence in Exod 14:20, brings darkness to one side and light to another (similarly, 2 Cor 2:15-16; 4:3-4). The Greek word for "spoken against," *antilegein,* occurs eleven times in the NT, seven of which occur in Luke with reference to *Jewish* resistance.[85] This word, like so many others in the infancy narrative (see n. 140 below), provides thematic bookends for Luke-Acts: in Jerusalem, Simeon witnesses that Jesus will cause offense in Israel (2:34); in Rome, Jews will be offended by the proclamation of the gospel by Paul (Acts 28:22). Thus, the witness is delivered from "Jerusalem . . . to the ends of the earth" (Acts 1:8). Jesus will not provoke a general, impersonal crisis, but he will divide his chosen followers (6:16) and pierce the heart of his mother (v. 35). The Greek word for "sword," *romphaia,* designates a broad double-edged sword.[86] Ephrem the Syrian interpreted the sword allegorically of Mary removing the sword that guarded paradise after the fall (Gen 3:24).[87] Ambrose and many Western Fathers likewise interpreted the sword in accordance with its use in Isaiah's Servant of the Lord passages, as the sharp and incisive word of God.[88] These allegorical interpretations blunt the force of v. 35. The Greek syntax of v. 35 shifts Mary emphatically to the front of the sentence, meaning "*Your* very soul will be pierced by a sword." Luke intends the sword, similar to the prophetic word of Ezek 5:1-2; 6:8-9; 12:14-16; 14:17, to signify the test that will befall the world in the life of Jesus, a test that will pierce the soul of his own mother (John 19:25) and will climax in the cross

83. The Greek text of v. 34 is closer to the Hebrew than LXX wording of Isa 8:15, suggesting Lukan reliance on a Hebraic exemplar.

84. Bengel, *Gnomon,* 2:35.

85. Origen, *Hom. Luc.* 17.4-5, saw in 2:34 an explanation for the opposition of Marcionites, Ebionites, heretics, and other detractors of the gospel.

86. In contrast to the common smaller, single-edged *machaira,* BDAG, 907; Vinson, *Luke,* 71-72.

87. See Just, *Luke,* 51.

88. Thus Isa 49:2, "The [Lord] made my mouth like a sharpened sword."

of Calvary.[89] The use of *dialogismoi* (v. 35; NIV "thoughts") further supports this interpretation. All thirteen occurrences of this word in the NT refer to thoughts that resist or oppose the divine will. The appearance of the incarnate Son of God is like a catalyst in a chemical solution; it brings to light such thoughts, even provokes them, throwing faith and disbelief into stark relief.

36-40   The prophecy of Simeon is followed by that of Anna, thus establishing the reception of Jesus by a requisite second witness in Judaism (Deut 19:15). In placing Anna and Simeon together, Luke anticipates the outpouring of God's Spirit at Pentecost "on your sons and daughters, who will prophesy" (Acts 2:17).[90] Anna is not a female clone of Simeon, but a unique witness. The sight of the Messiah makes Simeon long for death, but it seems to vivify Anna.[91] Simeon is introduced by character virtues ("righteous and devout," v. 25), but Anna is identified by offices, relations, and commitments.[92] As prophetess, Anna occupies a position in the NT hierarchy of offices second only to that of apostle (1 Cor 12:29; Eph 2:20; 4:11). Miriam (Exod 15:20), Deborah (Judg 4:14), Huldah (2 Kgs 22:14//2 Chr 34:22), and Isaiah's wife (Isa 8:3) are named prophetesses in the OT,[93] but Anna is one of only two named prophetesses in the NT (the other, Jezebel, Rev 2:20). Female prophets in the NT exceed this latter number, however, for unnamed women prophesy in Acts 2:17; 21:9 and 1 Cor 11:5. Anna is identified as the daughter of Phanuel and of the tribe of Asher, both of which may hold significance for Luke's readers. Equally possible, Phanuel and the tribe of Asher may derive from the source of the infancy narrative, perhaps from the Hebrew Gospel. As one of the ten "lost tribes," Asher might also represent the lost (albeit within Israel) whom Jesus came to restore. Anna does not simply visit the temple, as does Simeon, but "she never left the temple but worshiped night and day, fasting and praying." (v. 37). Fasting is a form of "religious protest, an assertion that all is not well,"[94] and thus a religious observance in character with awaiting the redemption of Jerusalem. The description of Anna's temple residency leads one scholar to query whether she belonged to an order of widows who performed special functions in the temple.[95]

89. For further discussions of this position, see esp. Brown, *Birth,* 462-64; Klostermann, *Lukasevangelium,* 44; and Bovon, *Lukas 1,1–9,50,* 147-48.

90. So Brown, *Birth,* 466.

91. So Plummer, *Luke,* 71.

92. Bovon, *Lukas 1,1–9,50,* 148-49, sees two different cultural norms represented in the respective introductions of Simeon and Anna. Simeon is identified by internal characteristics (who he is), whereas Anna's identity is linked to externals — family, tribe, age, and habits.

93. Rabbinic tradition added the names of Sarah, Hannah, Abigail, and Esther to the list of OT prophetesses (Str-B 2:140).

94. So Green, *Luke,* 151.

95. B. Witherington III, "Mary, Simeon, or Anna: Who First Recognized Jesus as Messiah?" *BRev* 21/5 (2005): 14.

Anna's precise age is ambiguous, because the Greek wording of "eighty-four years" (vv. 36-37) could be taken either as the length of her widowhood (so NIV) or her total age. If the former is correct, then Anna is over a hundred years old. Vv. 36-37 echo the description of Judith's age (who lived to 105, Jdt 8:6; 16:22-23), and Luke may intend a similar age for Anna. Whatever her exact age, she belongs to a company of witnesses in the infancy narratives, all of whom (with the exception of Mary and the shepherds) are old. In the ancient world, old age was revered and honorable (e.g., Gen 47:7-10). This was also true of the audience to which Luke wrote. To say a witness was old implied a witness that was *credible*. Anna's response to the Christ child, like Simeon's, is an I-Thou response. God answered Anna's prayer in old age, and in response she makes a public expression of gratitude.[96] In Greek, "gave thanks" and "spoke" (v. 38) are both in the imperfect tense, meaning that Anna *continued* giving thanks and testimony after the event.[97]

Vv. 39-40 effectually conclude the infancy narratives. Luke specifies that Mary and Joseph fulfilled all righteousness related to the birth of Jesus, thus validating Jesus' messianic status. The reference to fulfilling "the law of the Lord" (v. 39) rather than the law of Moses may emphasize that, rather than fulfilling mere legal requirements, the events related to the births of John and Jesus fulfilled true righteousness.[98] The emphases on temple and Torah fulfillment throughout Luke 1–2, along with the concomitant activity of the Holy Spirit, betray no conflict between law and gospel. Temple and Torah provide the necessary witness and categories by which to receive and understand the incarnation, and the incarnation reveals the true and proper intent of the OT witness and categories.

From Bethlehem, Jesus' family returns to Nazareth (see at 1:26), where he was raised. V. 40 summarizes twelve years of Jesus' life. Luke refers to the growth and maturity of Jesus in v. 40 in virtually the same words that he used to describe the growth and maturity of John in 1:80, thus implying a normal childhood of Jesus. Several apocryphal gospels attribute miraculous powers to a precocious and peevish preadolescent Jesus,[99] but apart from the isolated

96. The Greek word for "gave thanks" (*anthomologeisthai,* v. 38), occurring only here in the Greek Bible, means to thank publicly.

97. On "looking forward to the redemption of Jerusalem," see introduction to this section. Good manuscript evidence exists for "Jerusalem" without a preposition (either "in" or "of"; see Metzger, *TCGNT,* 112). This unusual Greek construction may be a Hebraism.

98. As examples of true righteousness in Luke 1–2, Green, *Luke,* 144, gives the following: exemplary piety, presence and inspiration of the Holy Spirit, hope for deliverance, joy, exultation, praise, peace, Savior and salvation, advance preparation, universalism, dawning, light, sifting of Israel, and social transposition. Similarly, see Bovon, *Lukas 1,1–9,50,* 150-51.

99. Esp. *Prot. Jas.* and *Inf. Gos. Thom.* See O. Cullmann, "Infancy Gospels," *NTApoc.* 1:414-69.

story of the twelve-year-old Jesus in the temple (2:41-52), neither Luke nor any other Evangelist or reputable early Christian source reports on the early years of Jesus. The omission in Matt, Mark, Luke (with the exception of 2:41-52), and John of Jesus' childhood and adolescence — a time span that typically plays a formative role in biographies — is a clue to the nature of the "gospel" genre. Gospels are not comprehensive biographies in the modern sense, but selective accounts of Jesus' life and teaching between the baptism and resurrection that claim — and proclaim — *saving* significance.

A BOY IN HIS FATHER'S HOUSE (2:41-52)

Throughout the infancy narratives, Luke presents the annunciations, births, circumcisions, namings, and growth of John and Jesus in complementary cycles. The story of young Jesus in the temple, the only story of his youth among the four canonical Gospels, has no counterpart in the complementary cycles, however. Beginning in mid-second century, various **apocryphal Gospels** attempted to fill in the "lost years" of Jesus' youth.[100] Many of these accounts are extant only in fragmentary form, although *Prot. Jas.* and *Inf. Gos. Thom.*, two of the most popular and widely circulated, survive complete. The Jesus of the apocryphal gospels is by and large a miracle- and magic-working Jesus, and the combination of these exceptional powers with the impulses and temperament of a preadolescent result in both comedy and calamity.[101] The apocryphal Jesus often stands in unsavory contrast to the Jesus of the canonical Gospels, but the unsavory characteristics themselves often testify to theological interests of their creators. The attribution of divine powers to young Jesus, for example, defended him in popular Christian imagination against Arianism (that Jesus is less than God) and adoptionism (that Jesus did not become Son of God until his baptism or resurrection). Apocryphal gospels achieved widespread

---

100. For a complete collection of apocryphal infancy stories of Jesus and discussions of their provenance, see B. Ehrman and Z. Pleše, *The Apocryphal Gospels: Texts and Translations* (Oxford: University Press, 2011), 3-193. For *Inf. Gos. Thom.*, see P. Mirecki, "The Infancy Gospel of Thomas," *ABD* 6:540-44.

101. In *Inf. Gos. Thom.* (not to be confused with the Coptic *Gos. Thom.*), the twelve-year-old Jesus cleans a pool and brings twelve clay pigeons to life, strikes dead the son of a scribe, strikes dead a young boy who accidently bumps into him, strikes his accusers blind, confuses his grammar teacher with mystical teachings, laughs as a heavenly redeemer then heals those whom he earlier blinded, raises a playmate to life who perished in a fall, heals the foot of a boy injured with an ax, and stretches a piece of wood that Joseph cut too short. In other stories, Jesus saves a dyer from financial ruin by retrieving cloths from a cauldron, each dyed to customer satisfaction, and changes rude children into goats (but restoring them when they repent).

popularity and influence in late antiquity and the Middle Ages.[102] *Inf. Gos. Thom.*, for example, is extant in no fewer than thirteen languages.

In contrast to the preoccupation with the marvelous and miraculous in apocryphal narratives, 2:41-52 is narrated with restraint, historical verisimilitude, psychological subtlety, and theological introspection. Where Luke derived the story of Jesus in the temple we cannot say for sure, but it does not derive from the battery of apocryphal infancy narratives, all of which date from a century later (at the earliest). It is an anomaly among the canonical Gospels, which many scholars attribute to an "independent tradition" incorporated by Luke after the completion of the body of the gospel.[103] I am rather certain this is not the case. The reference of Jesus to "my Father's house" (2:49) complements the theme of divine sonship elsewhere in the Third Gospel (see excursus on Son of God at 22:66-71), and Hebraisms exist in high numbers in 2:41-52.[104] There is no linguistic or theological reason to attribute 2:41-52 to a source other than that of the infancy narrative as a whole, which likely derives, at least in part, from the Hebrew Gospel. Luke has of course employed the story in accord with his evangelical purposes. Jesus appears only at the conclusion of the narrative both as the object of Mary's mild rebuke and, in his response, as her mentor. It is not necessary to assume that Luke portrays the preteen Jesus as an omniscient Son of God. Luke's two signature clues of divine guidance — references to prayer and/or the Holy Spirit — are both absent from the pericope. Throughout the narrative (vv. 40, 49, 52), Jesus is presented as a boy of unusual wisdom and nearness to God, whose spiritual endowments and understanding are similar to those of Simeon (v. 25) and Anna (vv. 36-37). He displays remarkable understanding of Torah, but his spiritual understanding exceeds both Torah and temple. In response to Mary's reprimand for causing anguish to "your father" (v. 48), Jesus testifies to a prior and higher obedience to "my Father" (v. 49).[105] His filial relation to God as Father is the alpha and omega of the gospel, both his first (2:49) and last word (24:49) in the Third Gospel.

41-45 "Every year Jesus' parents went to Jerusalem for the Festival of

---

102. A series of fourteenth-c. mosaics in the Chora Church in Istanbul, for example, detail the life of the Virgin Mary as presented in *Prot. Jas.*

103. E.g., R. Bultmann, *The History of the Synoptic Tradition* (trans. J. Marsh; New York: Harper & Row, 1972), 300-301; B. van Iersel, "The Finding of Jesus in the Temple: Some Observations on the Original Form of Luke ii 41-51a," in Orton, *Composition of Luke's Gospel*, 1-13; Brown, *Birth*, 472-95, and "Infancy Narratives in the NT Gospels," *ABD* 3:410-15.

104. Fitzmyer, *Luke (I–IX)*, 435, is incorrect in asserting that Semitisms decrease in 2:41-52. There are no fewer than ten Hebraisms in the pericope; see Edwards, *Hebrew Gospel*, 294-99.

105. For further reflections on the relationship between Torah obedience and Jesus' filial consciousness, see Bovon, *Lukas 1,1–9,50*, 162.

Passover" (v. 41). Jesus' family continues to exhibit the same Torah obedience exhibited by Zechariah, Simeon, and Anna. The family's annual Passover pilgrimage to Jerusalem functions as a veiled anticipation of the fulfillment of Jesus' messianic destiny, for "went" *(poreuesthai)* is often used with reference to Jesus' divinely ordained journey to Jerusalem in the Third Gospel (e.g., 9:51). Some Greek textual witnesses in v. 41 (see vv. 33, 43) attempted to safeguard the doctrine of the virgin birth by replacing "Jesus' parents" with "Joseph and Mary."[106] Jewish males were obligated by Torah to appear in Jerusalem for the three major Jewish festivals: Passover, Pentecost (Feast of Weeks), and Tabernacles (Exod 23:17; 34:23; Deut 16:16). Women and children were not required to attend, but as this story indicates, many customarily did (also 1 Sam 1–2). In theory, the city of Jerusalem belonged not only to the tribe of Judah but equally to all twelve tribes of Israel. As a consequence, homeowners were obliged to accommodate festival pilgrims without cost.[107] One can imagine that this theological ideal was not always observed. Luke does not explicitly say this was Jesus' first pilgrimage to Jerusalem, but it may have been. It would have been dangerous for Jesus to travel to Jerusalem earlier when Archelaus was tetrarch of Judea (Matt 2:22), and Jesus was at least ten years old when Archelaus was removed from office in A.D. 6.[108]

Introducing a twelve-year-old boy to the Passover in Jerusalem (v. 42) was associated with the obligation of a father to teach his son Torah.[109] The rabbinic tradition was generally agreed that a son should begin learning Torah no later than puberty, that is, about age twelve.[110] The Passover celebration required a full week of observance in Jerusalem. V. 43 reads literally, "when [Jesus' family] had completed the days [of Passover]," again indicating the family's Torah faithfulness in observing the whole festival. The reference to "the *boy* Jesus" staying behind in Jerusalem reflects awareness of his growth: in v. 16 Jesus is mentioned as a "baby" *(brephos),* in v. 40 as a "child" *(paidion),* in v. 43 as a "boy" *(pais),* and in v. 52 as "Jesus."[111]

---

106. Metzger, *TCGNT,* 112.

107. Str-B 2:144.

108. See Bengel, *Gnomon,* 2:37. Herod died in 4 B.C. If Jesus was born in 6 B.C. (see Matt 2:16), he would have been twelve years old when Archelaus was deposed.

109. Of the six references to "Jerusalem" in the infancy narrative, this is the only Hellenistic spelling of the word, suggesting, perhaps, that it was a later addition to the text. On the Hebraic versus Hellenistic spelling of "Jerusalem" in Luke, see n. 64.

110. Str-B 2:144-47. Thus Josephus (*Ant.* 5.348) says that Samuel became a prophet at age twelve, although his age is not mentioned in Scripture. *M. Nid.* 6:11-12 declared an Israelite a full man, and thus a *bar mitzvah* ("son of the commandment"), when two pubic hairs appeared. Later Judaism declared that a young Jew attained legal majority on his thirteenth birthday (Schürer, *History of the Jewish People,* 2:421).

111. Noted by Plummer, *Luke,* 78.

In the flurry of Passover activities, "Jesus *stayed behind* in Jerusalem" (v. 43). Of this his parents are unaware. "Thinking he was in their company, they traveled on for a day" (v. 44). The Greek word for "thinking," *nomizein,* occurs in Luke only here and in 3:23, both times meaning "supposing something mistakenly." How easy for moral people, religiously observant people, even his own family, to suppose Jesus is with them. This story is a reminder that moral and religious rectitude do not equate to fellowship with Jesus. Mary and Joseph have observed all the law requires, but they have left Jesus behind. At the end of the first day's journey, roughly twenty to twenty-five miles (30-40 km) from Jerusalem,[112] Mary and Joseph "looked everywhere" (v. 45; Gk. *anazētein*) in the caravan but did not find Jesus. Modern readers who think in terms of nuclear families may think Mary and Joseph negligent in leaving Jerusalem without knowing where Jesus was. The travel caravan itself functioned as a quasi-family (the Greek word for "company," *synodia,* sometimes means "family"). Moreover, women and children may have traveled separately, meeting the men only at the evening caravanserai. It was easy for Mary and Joseph to assume that Jesus was with the other parent, or with other members of the company.[113] That Jesus' separation was his choice rather than his parents' oversight is confirmed by Mary's reprimand, "Why have you treated us like this?" (v. 48).

46-52 Vv. 43-45 make readers more informed than Mary and Joseph, who do not know that Jesus remained in Jerusalem.[114] The search for Jesus probably does not require an additional three days, for a search of the temple, and even Jerusalem, would not require so much time. "After three days" (v. 46) is more likely inclusive, i.e., a day for the outbound trip, a day to return, and finding Jesus on the third day in the temple.[115] Through the examples of Zechariah, Simeon, and Anna, Luke has shown that God reveals the new covenant in the heart of the old. It is thus not surprising that Mary and Joseph discover Jesus in the temple. Their doing so is a reminder to Luke's Gentile readers that salvation comes to them not from outside Israel or as an addendum to Israel, but from the Messiah of Israel. The word for "**temple**," *hieron,* refers to the entire temple complex rather than the sanctuary proper, which is signified by Greek *naos.* Herod's temple was Israel's third temple (following the temples of Solomon and Zerubbabel), begun in 20 B.C., but still under construction in Jesus' day. It comprised four divisions — Court of Gentiles, Court of Women,

112. Str-B 2:149.

113. See Str-B 2:149; Plummer, *Luke,* 75. Epictetus, *Diatr.* 4.1.91, writes of a group of travelers waiting until a sufficient company gathered in order to proceed through an area endangered by robbers.

114. Wolter, *Lukasevangelium,* 148.

115. Ambrose saw the three days during which Jesus was lost as an allegory of the three days in the tomb (Just, *Luke,* 54).

Court of Israel, and Holy of Holies — all of which were contained on the Temple Mount, an open-air quadrangle of thirty-five acres (14 ha) measuring roughly 500 by 325 yards (450 × 300 m). The chief purpose of the temple was the sacrifice of animals for the Israelite cult, but it also functioned as a bank, depository for legal documents, market where animals were purchased and money exchanged, meeting place of the Sanhedrin, and other functions related to Jewish religious and social life.[116] The temple complex consisted of many buildings (21:5; Mark 13:1), including a synagogue; we can picture Jesus in the latter conversing with the teachers as described in v. 46.[117] It was normal for a Jewish rabbi to teach several student apprentices "who sat at the teacher's feet" (Acts 22:3). The scene is reversed in v. 46, where a twelve-year-old Jesus is found sitting "in the midst of the teachers." No ordinary student, his mastery of Torah makes him a full conversation partner with temple teachers.[118] In *Inf. Gos. Thom.* 19.2, Jesus does not converse with the elders and teachers but "silences" them (see 20:26), thus suggesting that he terminates and supplants Israel. In Luke's narrative, Jesus does not supplant Israel but instructs it in the proper understanding of Torah and temple. Those who heard Jesus' "understanding and answers" were "amazed" (v. 47). His "wisdom" (v. 40) and "understanding" (v. 47) recall the "spirit of wisdom and understanding" that will rest upon the Messiah (Isa 11:2).[119] The Greek word for "amazed," *existanai,* a favorite Lukan word, describes the wonder that befalls people through miraculous works of God or proclamation of the gospel. Luke describes the response to Paul's first sermon after his conversion (Acts 9:21) in the exact words of v. 47, "Everyone who heard him was amazed."[120]

Jesus' parents are not "amazed" *(existanai)* but "astonished" (v. 48; Gk. *ekplēssein*), which in this context connotes marvel and exasperation. In the male-dominated temple one would expect Joseph rather than Mary to address Jesus. Perhaps Mary's spiritual bond with Jesus (1:30-35) compels her to speak.

---

116. Knowledge of Herod's temple depends on three ancient sources: Josephus (*Ant.* 15.391-425), Mishnah *(m. Mid.),* and the *Temple Scroll* (11QT) in the DSS. For modern reconstructions and discussions of Herod's temple, see J. Patrich, "Reconstructing the Magnificent Temple Herod Built," *BRev* 4/5 (October 1988): 16-29; K. Ritmeyer and L. Ritmeyer, "Reconstructing Herod's Temple Mount in Jerusalem," *BAR* 15/6 (November-December 1989): 23-42; and E. Meyers and M. Chancey, *Alexander to Constantine: Archaeology of the Land of the Bible* (New Haven: Yale University Press, 2012), 53-61.

117. *M. Yoma* 7:1 speaks of the high priest reading from a Torah scroll in the *synagogue* on the Temple Mount; further, see Str-B 2:150.

118. *M. 'Abot* 6:6 lists forty-eight ways in which learning of Torah exceeds either the priesthood or kingship, one of which is "asking and giving answers," as does Jesus in v. 46.

119. So Tannehill, *Luke,* 76.

120. Lagrange, *Luc,* 47, describes *existanai,* "amazed," as the natural human response to a supernatural occurrence.

She addresses him not as *pais* (v. 43, "boy, young man"), but with a more juvenile and subservient term, *teknon* (v. 48; "child," NIV "Son"). "Why have you treated us like this? Your father and I have been anxiously searching for you" (v. 48). Ironically, Jesus is less familiar found than he was lost. Mary expects Jesus to be and remain the son she and Joseph have known in the past. Her reproach expresses less concern for Jesus than for what he has done to *them*.[121] The Greek word for "anxiously searching," *odynan*, means "to cause pain, torment, anguish." Mary's distress is a first fulfillment of Simeon's prophecy that a "sword will pierce her soul" (v. 35).[122]

The "dramatic nucleus" of the narrative is v. 49,[123] exposing the faulty assumptions and even misunderstandings of the parents, as well as Jesus' true relationship to God. "Why were you searching for me? Did you not know I had to be in my Father's house?" Jesus is not surprised that his parents came back for him; he is surprised that they did not know where to find him.[124] Two points in his response deserve consideration, the first of which is the meaning of "house." The NIV rendering, "my Father's house," is an interpretation rather than translation of an unusual and ambiguous Greek expression. It is certainly not improper, as many commentators note, to understand the expression as a reference to the temple.[125] If Jesus had meant (only) "house," however, there was a clearer way to say it (so 16:27).[126] The expression *en tois tou patros mou*, which occurs only here in the Bible, literally means "about the things [e.g., business, affairs] of my Father." This suggests a more comprehensive understanding of God. Although it includes a reference to God's abode, it also incorporates the *mission* of the God whom Jesus knows as "my Father."[127]

The second and more essential point in Jesus' reply is the reference to "my Father." Similar to the situation with Zechariah and Elizabeth in 1:59-63, Jesus "must" (v. 49; Gk. *dei*) align himself with God's purpose over against claims of his family. Luke illustrates this in a masterful contrast between "your

---

121. So Wolter, *Lukasevangelium*, 149.

122. Plummer, *Luke*, 77.

123. Green, *Luke*, 156.

124. Plummer, *Luke*, 77. Similarly, Bengel, *Gnomon*, 2:38-39, "[Jesus] did not blame them, because they lost Him; but because they thought it necessary to seek for Him; and He intimates both that He was not lost, and that He could [not] have been found anywhere else but in the temple."

125. Irenaeus, *Haer.* 5.36.2, uses the same phrase to refer to house. In support of the meaning "house," Wolter, *Lukasevangelium*, 149-50, notes insightfully that "Father's house" fits with searching for Jesus, but "Father's business" does not.

126. The inclusiveness of the Greek is preserved in Delitzsch's Hebrew NT, *ehyeh baasher leabi*, "I will be about that of my Father."

127. For a full discussion of the various translational options, see Fitzmyer, *Luke (I–IX)*, 443-44.

father" (both here and in 3:23), and "my Father."[128] Mary reprimands Jesus for causing anguish to his father Joseph (v. 48). To this Jesus responds that he must be in the house of his Father God (v. 49). Judaism believed Messiah would know God directly and innately without the revelation of Torah or prophecy.[129] In identifying God as his Father, and in addressing God intimately and exclusively as "*my* Father," Jesus fulfills the messianic ideal.[130] Luke earlier referred to Mary as "the mother of the Lord" (1:43). Even this sublime distinction, and Mary's maternal ties, must yield to Jesus' heavenly Father.[131] The first (2:49) and last (24:49) words of Jesus in the Gospel of Luke refer to God as his Father. Jesus' intimate and filial relation to God as Father is the center and sum of his life and ministry.[132]

The story of Jesus in the temple bears subtle witness to his two natures, the divine and human. The all-too-human separation of a child from his parents in a crowd, and the equally human panic of the parents, attests to the humanity of the characters. Nevertheless, this very human boy is at home in the temple and natively identifies with the work of God, whom he calls "my Father." Two fathers are mentioned in the account, one human, one divine, and Jesus is the son of both. His parents "did not understand what he was saying to them" (v. 50), nor do we. Faith and understanding are not guaranteed by the privilege of proximity to Torah, angels, God, or even Jesus. Zechariah was visited by Gabriel, yet he disbelieved (1:20); Mary (and Joseph) received more revelation than he, yet they do not understand. The story of Jesus is the story of the inscrutable and unfathomable ways of God. This story is not understood in a flash of insight. Time, struggle, even suffering are required of the parents of Jesus, as of all people, if they are to know and follow Jesus. "Not understanding" forms another inclusio of Luke-Acts: it characterizes Mary and Joseph in the temple, the disciples on the way to Jerusalem (18:34), the disciples at the end of the gospel (24:45), and the final response of Jewish leaders in Acts (28:26). Lack of understanding is not a final verdict, nor does it alone jeopardize salvation. Jesus himself does not understand the ways of the Father (22:42) — and according to the other Gospels, he experiences the abandonment of God (Mark 15:34; Matt 27:46). Unlike Gnosticism, which bases salvation on knowledge, Christian faith is based on trust in a final *Nev-*

---

128. B. van Iersel, "The Finding of Jesus in the Temple: Some Observations on the Original Form of Luke ii 41-51a," in Orton, *Composition of Luke's Gospel*, 13.

129. Str-B 2:152.

130. Church fathers often saw in Jesus' response a declaration of co-eternality with God (see Just, *Luke*, 55). The category and nomenclature of co-eternality, however, derive from later Christological debates of the third and fourth centuries.

131. So Fitzmyer, *Luke (I–IX)*, 438.

132. Bovon, *Lukas 1,1–9,50*, 155. For Jesus' references to God as Father in Luke, see 2:49; 10:21-22; 11:2; 22:29, 42; 23:34, 46; 24:49.

ertheless — that salvation depends not on human wisdom and understanding, but on God's inscrutable grace.

The journey from Jerusalem (elevation ca. 2,600 feet [800 m]) to Nazareth (ca. 1,300 feet [400 m]) would have taken three to four days and is properly described as "down" (v. 51). The "two-natures theme" continues to the end of the story, for this boy, with his filial consciousness of God, returns to village life and submission to his parents. A mundane ending is a proper ending if Jesus, the Son of God, is truly human. Jesus, who is truly good and godly, spends his youth in a town where popular opinion thought nothing good could be found (John 1:46).[133] The Greek word for his response to his parents, *hypotassein,* is the strongest term in the NT for submission, meaning "to subject" or "to subordinate." Its Greek construction (finite verb plus participle) connotes habitual obedience throughout his youth. V. 51 is the last reference to Joseph in Luke, suggesting perhaps that Joseph died before Jesus' public ministry began. The sole reference to Mary's activity during Jesus' youth is that she "kept" (Gk. *diatērein*) "all these things in her heart" (v. 51). The Greek word recalls Jacob's remembrance of the stories of his son Joseph (Gen 37:11) and is perhaps a reminder that, when the ways of God are perplexing, Mary can *keep* the gospel even when she cannot understand it. Like Samuel (1 Sam 2:26) and John (1:80), Jesus "grew up, increased in wisdom, and in favor with God and people" (v. 52). The final perspective in the infancy narratives belongs to God. In addition to "angels, shepherds, Simeon, Anna, and many others . . . , Luke adds God's own point of view concerning Jesus. He enjoys divine favor."[134] The summary description of Jesus' youth parallels that of John (1:80), but with one exception. We are not told that John enjoyed favor with people (because of his austerity?). Jesus does. The final word of the infancy narratives thus testifies to the purpose of the incarnation: to bring salvation to *people.*

EXCURSUS: THE RELATION OF THE INFANCY NARRATIVE
TO THE BODY OF THE THIRD GOSPEL

NT scholars have devoted considerable attention to the relation of the infancy narrative to the body of the Third Gospel. This interest has been generated, above all, by the influence of twentieth-century form criticism, which endeavored to identify and isolate the earliest discernible units of tradition, usually oral but sometimes written, from which the Gospels were composed. Luke's infancy narrative has become the subject of standing debate in this regard, not

133. An insight derived from Bengel, *Gnomon,* 2:39-40.
134. Green, *Luke,* 158.

simply because Matthew and Luke are the only Gospels (canonical as well as gnostic and apocryphal) prefaced with infancy narratives, but because Luke's infancy narrative is such a substantial part of the Third Gospel, representing more than 10 percent of its length. Two factors, above all, have fueled the debate. First, several data appear to cast doubt on the literary integrity of the infancy narrative in relation to the remainder of the Gospel. Second, these and other data have influenced much twentieth-century German scholarship, and Hans Conzelmann, in particular, an important modern German interpreter of Luke, to discount or deny an organic relationship between the infancy narrative and the body of the Gospel. I wish to focus particularly on the first point, which lies at the root of the skepticism of much German and subsequent English-speaking scholarship regarding the unity of the Third Gospel.

Raymond Brown summarizes the relevant evidence against the original unity of the Third Gospel in the following points: (1) The solemn beginning at 3:1-2 looks like the original beginning of Luke; (2) Mark and John also begin their Gospels with the baptism; (3) Acts 1:22 presents the baptism as the beginning of the gospel; (4) the genealogy in Luke 3 suggests no original infancy narrative; (5) the infancy narrative has not influenced the Gospel in a major way; (6) if the infancy narrative were lost, we would not suspect its existence; (7) there is no precedent in classical historians for supplying infancy narratives to well-known figures.[135]

Five of these objections can be quickly and reasonably dismissed, in my judgment. Regarding #2, the precedents of Mark and John are of dubious relevance, since Luke freely departs from Mark's Gospel nearly half the time, and he almost never follows John's Gospel. Regarding #3, Acts 1:22 identifies the time span between Jesus' baptism and ascension as the critical criterion for the selection of an *apostle,* but as the Gospel of Matthew indicates, which includes an infancy narrative, and as the Gospel of John further indicates, which commences before time itself, the baptism of Jesus was not a determining criterion for a *gospel.* Regarding #4, to judge Luke in error for not following Matthew in placing the genealogy in the infancy narrative is irrelevant. Like all Evangelists, Luke arranges material according to his own purposes, which in its present location (3:21–4:13) creates a powerful threefold witness to Jesus' divine sonship. Regarding #6, the argument that something would not be missed if it were absent presupposes its own conclusion. Regarding #7, the lack of infancy stories in classical biographies is relatively unimportant, since Luke is writing a gospel, not a classical biography; and in the one instance that he follows classical biographical protocol (1:1-4), he amends it for his own purposes.

This leaves #1 and #5. With regard to the latter, to assert that Luke's

---

135. Brown, *Birth,* 239-43. Further on the possibility of the infancy narrative as a later appendix to the Third Gospel, see Fitzmyer, *Luke (I–IX),* 311.

infancy narrative has no affect on the body of the gospel is significantly mistaken. Structurally, Luke transitions to the body of the Gospel in the same "leapfrog" style he utilized in the infancy narrative: thus, the youth of John in 1:80 skips over 2:1-52 and resumes in 3:1-20; the youth of Jesus in 2:40-52 skips over 3:1-20 and resumes in 3:21-22.[136] Likewise, in 3:2 John is not referred as "the Baptist" (so Matt 3:1//Mark 1:4), but uniquely as "the son of Zechariah," in agreement with 1:13, 62, 67. Verbally, the infancy narrative and body of the Gospel are strongly knit together. Paul Minear provides a list of fifty-five "words or phrases which appear both in the birth narratives and in the rest of Luke-Acts, and which are found more often in these two books than in the rest of the New Testament."[137] Henry Cadbury cites six phrases in Luke 1–2 that reappear either verbatim or nearly verbatim in the remainder of Luke-Acts.[138] Most important, Joachim Jeremias devotes one-third of his meticulous examination of the vocabulary of Luke to the vocabulary of chaps. 1–2 and the influence of that vocabulary on the remainder of the Gospel.[139]

In addition to these structural and verbal bonds, the infancy narrative and body of the Third Gospel are spanned by strategic thematic and theological bridges. In the commentary on Luke 1–2 we noted Luke's proclivity to bracket key theological words/ideas in the infancy narrative with the same at the end of the Gospel or the end of Acts. These inclusios are numerous and striking.[140] The Third Evangelist is widely considered a respectable historian but sometimes judged a less respectable theologian, especially in comparison to Paul or John.[141] Luke's prescient inclusios challenge such dismissals of his theological substance by revealing a global theological architecture between

---

136. Noted by Schweizer, *Lukas*, 44.

137. "Luke's Use of the Birth Stories," in Keck and Martyn, eds., *Studies in Luke-Acts,* 113. Similarly, Plummer, *Luke*, lxx, shows that vocabulary from two random passages (1:52-56; 2:41-47) occurs frequently elsewhere in Luke-Acts, but nowhere else in the NT.

138. "Four Features of Lucan Style," in Keck and Martyn, eds., *Studies in Luke-Acts,* 96.

139. *Sprache des Lukasevangeliums*, 15-102.

140. "Temple" (Gk. *naos*, 1:9, 21, 22; 23:45), "trouble" (*tarassein,* 1:12; 24:38), "go before" (*proerchesthai,* 1:17; 22:47), "doubt" (*dialogiz-,* 1:29; 24:38), "remember" (*mimnēskesthai,* 1:54; 24:8), "redemption" (*lytrō-,* 1:68; 2:38; 21:28; 24:21), "visitation" (*episkep-,* 1:68, 78; 7:16; 19:44), "remission of sins" (*aphesis hamartiōn,* 1:77; 3:3; 4:18; 24:47), "overshadow" (*episkiazein;* 1:35; 9:34), "Messiah–Son of God" (1:32, 35; 22:67, 70), "Messiah-Lord" (2:11; Acts 2:36), "glorifying God" (*doxazein ton theon,* 2:20; 23:47), awaiting and expectation (*prosdechesthai;* 2:25, 38; Acts 24:15), "salvation" (*sōtērion;* 2:30; Acts 28:28), "oppose" (*antilegein;* 2:34; Acts 28:22), "an angel appeared to him" (1:11; 22:43), Jesus and the Father (2:49; 24:49), "not understanding" (*synienai;* 2:50; 18:34; 24:45; Acts 28:26), "glory to God and peace on earth/in heaven" (2:14; 19:38), a snare and cause of stumbling (2:34; 20:18), and Jesus as descendent and fulfiller of Davidic lineage (1:27, 32, 69; 2:4, 11; 20:41-44).

141. This judgment is sometimes heard from Protestant German scholars, for whom Lutheran theological canons set a standard of theological reputability.

the infancy narrative and the Third Gospel, and also between the infancy narrative and the Book of Acts.[142]

In light of this architectural framework we may consider the final objection (#1), that 3:1-2 appears to be the original beginning of the Third Gospel. It is clear that 3:1-2 marks a major transition, but why must it commence an *UrLukas?* The Gospel of Mark begins with the baptism of Jesus by John, and Luke follows Mark consciously in 3:1–9:50. But Luke also follows other sources (1:1-4), the most important of which, in my judgment, was the Hebrew Gospel. The prevalence of Hebraisms provides special evidence for the influence of the Hebrew Gospel in chaps. 1–2, 9:51–19:27, and 24.[143] The case for the unity of the Third Gospel is much more substantive than the case against it.

––––––––––––––––

142. Brown, *Birth,* 243-44, concedes that no essential theological differences exist between the infancy narrative and the body of the Third Gospel.

143. See Edwards, *Hebrew Gospel,* chap. 4 and Appendix II.

CHAPTER THREE

The Forerunner and the Son of God
Inaugurate the Kingdom of God

Luke 3:1–4:13

THE WORD OF GOD IN WORLD HISTORY (3:1-20)

The public ministry of the Messiah begins with the two protagonists of the infancy narrative, John (3:1-20) and Jesus (3:21–4:13), again in tandem. Like Matthew, Mark, and John, and like the earliest formulation of the gospel in the kerygma (Acts 1:22; 10:37), Luke anchors the commencement of Jesus' ministry with the figure of John. The description of John in 3:1-20 is an introductory tableau on the larger stage of the Jesus-story. Luke's introduction of John is the longest of the Gospels, and more than twice the length of Josephus's account of John (*Ant.* 18.116-19). It is also absent several referents common to John in the other Gospels. John is not called "the Baptist" (so Matt 3:1; Mark 1:4; John 1:28; 3:23); there is no mention of Elijah in reference to John, or of his primitive dress and diet (so Matt 3:4; Mark 1:6; John 1:21); and although Luke notes John's arrest, there is no account of his martyrdom (Matt 14:3-12; Mark 6:17-29; also Justin Martyr, *Dial.* 49.4-5). Luke has pruned the figure of John to his primary fruit-bearing stock as the forerunner of the Messiah (1:17, 76; Acts 13:24).

In the prologue (1:1-4), Luke testifies to having utilized eyewitness sources in the composition of his Gospel. Here, in 3:1-20, we have likely a tapestry of all Luke's known or putative sources. Vv. 3-6 and 16b-20 appear indebted to Mark 1:2-8; the warnings of 7-9 also appear in Matt 3:7-10 and thus derive from the Double Tradition (i.e., the roughly 175 vv. that appear in Matt and Luke, but not Mark); and vv. 10-16a, which are unique to Luke and contain two Hebraisms, may derive from the Hebrew Gospel. The official introduction in vv. 1-2 may be Luke's addition, although it is important to recall that the Hebrew Gospel also named Herod and Caiaphas in the introduction of John.[1] From these various sources Luke has carefully woven a unified story-line. The

---

1. According to Epiphanius, *Pan.* 30.14.3, the Hebrew Gospel began: "It came to pass in the days of Herod king of Judaea, when Caiaphas was chief priest, a certain man named John came baptizing a baptism of repentance in the Jordan River."

sweeping list of names and titles in vv. 1-2 suddenly focuses on the Spartan figure of John, son of Zechariah, to whom "the word of God came." The word of God forms the backbone of Luke's ensuing picture of John in 3:1-20. John's ministry of baptism (v. 3) and the proclamation that accompanies it (vv. 7-9) embody the prophetic word of Isa 40 (vv. 4-6). Three unlikely groups of hearers in vv. 10-14 respond to John's prophetic call for repentance, each asking, "What shall we do?" Repentance is not an end in itself, but rather a prelude to receiving the More Powerful One (vv. 15-17). After centuries of God's word being received only indirectly, Israel hears God's word directly and compellingly in John's mission and preaching.[2] It is not a word John receives from Torah, rabbinic tradition, or even prophecy. Rather, "the word of God came to John." God's word to John is penultimate rather than final, however, for John is the divinely ordained forerunner who introduces the More Powerful One to come (v. 16; 1:17).

1-2 The historical formality with which Luke introduces the public ministry of Jesus has no equal in any other Gospel, canonical or apocryphal. Matt 3:1, Mark 1:4, and John 1:19-23 begin with incidental references to John's baptism in the wilderness as a prelude to the appearance of Jesus. Anyone unacquainted with the beginnings of the Christian movement will not learn from these accounts who John was, when he appeared, where Judea is, or what baptism is about. Matt, Mark, and John, in other words, presuppose pertinent information on the part of the readers and are written to audiences already familiar with John. Luke, by contrast, dates the appearance of John precisely, and locates his preaching with reference to a Roman emperor, one governor and three tetrarchs of Palestine, and two high priests in Jerusalem. Matt, Mark, and John introduce Jesus in the context of provincial Jewish messianic expectations; Luke introduces the gospel in the context of world history.[3] Origen rightly recognized that the names of Roman and Jewish leaders in 3:1-2 signified the universality of the gospel.[4] Luke takes the world and its history seri-

---

2. On the cessation of the spirit of prophecy at the death of the great writing prophets, see n. 56.

3. The closest historical parallel to 3:1-2 is found in Thucydides, *Hist. Pelop. War* 2.2.1, "In the fifteenth year [of the armistice concluded after the conquest of Euboea], in the forty-eighth year of the priestess-ship of Chrysis at Argos, in the ephorate of Aenesias at Sparta, in the last month but two of the archonship of Pythodorus at Athens, and six months after the battle of Potidaea, just at the beginning of spring, a Theban force came . . ." (trans. R. Crawley). For less elaborate historical introductions, see Jer 1:1-3; Josephus, *Ant.* 18.106.

4. *Hom. Luc.* 21.1-2. Marcion cited 3:1 to argue that the Christ who revealed salvation to the nations in the days of Tiberius was sent by the superior God, whereas the Messiah expected by Jews to restore Israel was a fiction of the inferior and malevolent creator-god, the Demiurge (Tertullian, *Marc.* 4.6). Marcion's Christ, ordained only to save Gentiles, represents the flip side of Zionism's Messiah, ordained only to save Israel. 3:1-2 correctly sails between these two

ously: if God enters human history authentically in Jesus of Nazareth, then his word must be made known to historical persons through historical processes. The process begins with "the word of God that came to John son of Zechariah in the wilderness" (v. 2).

Tiberius Caesar succeeded Caesar Augustus (27 B.C.–A.D. 14) and reigned as Roman Emperor from 14 to 37. Tiberius's reign was blighted by suspicions and paranoia of Roman military and political leaders, and by intolerance of foreign cults, including Jews, whom he expelled from Rome in 19. Tiberius's personal adviser, Sejanus, a Roman of nonsenatorial rank, deepened resentment against the emperor by staging show-trials against his suspected rivals. Not surprisingly, the death of Tiberius brought rejoicing to Rome and the empire.[5] The "fifteenth year of the reign of Tiberius" (3:1) would date John's appearance to 28, if the date is reckoned from the death of Augustus (d. 19 Aug. 14).[6] Tiberius was made coregent with Augustus in the last two years of the latter's reign. If the date is reckoned from the coregency, John's appearance would be as early as 26, although this date is less likely.[7] If Jesus was born shortly before Herod's death in 4 B.C., then he would have been "about thirty years old" (3:23) when John began preaching in 26-28.

In addition to Tiberius Caesar, Luke mentions a Roman governor and three tetrarchs. Pontius Pilate (see further at 23:1) was "governor," or prefect, of Judea from 26 to 36.[8] Following the death of Herod the Great in 4 B.C., Rome,

---

magnetic poles, which throughout its history have erroneously pulled the Christian church to one extreme or the other. Jesus, the messianic Son of God (1:32-33), is the one revelation and redeemer of both Jews and Gentiles.

5. Josephus, *Ant.* 18.225-27: "[Tiberius] had inflicted fearful wrongs in greater numbers on the Roman nobles than any other one man, for he was always quick to anger and relentless in action, even if his grounds for conceiving hatred of a man made no sense. It was his bent to turn savage in every case that he decided; and he inflicted the death penalty even for the slightest offences. And so, though the report that [the Romans] had of his death gave them pleasure, they were prevented from enjoying it as much as they would have liked by fear of the dire consequences that they foresaw if hope played them false" (trans. L. Feldman, *Josephus,* LCL 9:139). For a succinct and informative review of Tiberius's reign, see S. Carroll, "Tiberius," *ABD* 6:549-50.

6. Any part of a year was usually counted as a full year; hence, twenty-eight rather than twenty-nine.

7. Plummer argues for twenty-eight because (1) Tiberius was associated with Augustus only in his last two years, but not co-emperor (Suetonius, *Tib.,* 21); (2) when Augustus died, Tiberius was not regarded by himself or by others as emperor (Tacitus, *Ann.* 1.5-7); and (3) "No instance is known of reckoning the reign of Tiberius from his association with Augustus" (*Luke,* 82).

8. Various titles were used of Roman governors. Josephus, writing in Greek, uses *hēgemōn* ("ruler"), *epitropos* ("guardian/governor"), and *eparchos* ("prefect"). The NT uses only the first term of Pilate, and Philo the second. Tacitus, writing in Latin, uses *procurator.* A

finding no successor among Herod's sons capable of sole rule, subdivided Palestine into three "tetrarchies," assigning one each to his sons, Archelaus, Herod Antipas, and Philip.[9] "Herod tetrarch of Galilee" plays a significant role in the Third Gospel.[10] Also known as Herod Antipas to differentiate him from his father, Antipas ruled over Galilee and Perea from his father's death in 4 B.C. until A.D. 39. Antipas, under whom John was beheaded (9:9), was the son of Malthace, probably the fourth of Herod the Great's ten wives. Philip, the half-brother of Antipas, received the regions of Iturea and Traconitis (and Batanea and Paneas, according to Josephus, *Ant.* 17.189), to the northeast of the Sea of Galilee. The reference to "Abilene" is not entirely certain, but it was presumably the region of "Abila" northwest of Mount Hermon, which Josephus ascribes to Lysanias.[11]

In addition to Roman rulers, Luke includes the names of Annas and Caiaphas as high priest. Annas was so influential that the first-century Jewish high-priesthood could without exaggeration be called the high-priesthood of Annas. Annas (also spelled "Ananus") was himself high priest from 6 to 15; his son Eleazar succeeded him as high priest in 16-17; his son-in-law Caiaphas (John 18:13) from 18 to 36 (before whom Jesus appeared, 22:54); a second son Jonathan in 36-37; a third son Theophilus following 37 (see chap. 1, n. 20); a fourth son Matthias sometime between 41 and 44; and a fifth son Ananus in 62, shortly before the outbreak of the Jewish War.[12] The reference to Annas as "high priest" in the singular (NIV "high priesthood") both here and in Acts 4:6 — when he is mentioned in lists of more than one high priest and at a time when he himself no longer personally occupied the office — testifies to his dynastic influence over the office in the first century. High priests, all of whom in the NT belonged to the sect of the Sadducees (see at 20:27), presided over the Sanhedrin. When the title occurs in the plural, as it often does in the Gospels, it refers to predecessors and family members who were associated with the office of high priest.

During this pantheon of offices and rulers, "the word of God came to John son of Zechariah in the wilderness" (v. 2). Luke's wording closely imitates Jer 1:1-3, implying that John too is a prophet. The "word of God" is John's driv-

---

Latin inscription discovered in Caesarea Maritima in 1961 refers to Pilate specifically as *praefectus,* "prefect." This seems to be the proper title of pre-Claudian governors. See D. Schwartz, "Pontius Pilate," *ABD* 5:397.

9. "Tetrarchy" (lit. "ruler of a fourth part") derives from Philip of Macedon's division of Thessaly into four districts, called tetrarchies. Archelaus was banished in 6, after which his district was incorporated into Judea, which was ruled by a Roman prefect.

10. See excursus on Herod Antipas at 23:1.

11. *Ant.* 19.275; *J.W.* 2.215. Further, see Schürer, *History of the Jewish People,* 1:568-69; S. Carroll, "Lysanias," *ABD* 4:425.

12. Josephus, *Ant.* 20.198.

ing and defining force. Greek *rhēma,* "word," may connote a less full revelation than *logos,* which normally characterizes the word of God taught and lived in Jesus. The proclamation of Jeremiah was addressed to Israelite kings, but the word of God proclaimed by John reflects a universal understanding of God's relation to the world. Mystery religions, which dotted the shoreline of the eastern Mediterranean, freely surrendered the geopolitical world mentioned in 3:1-2 to hostile cosmic powers and retreated instead into a world of magic, mysterious rites, and the individual psyche in hopes of release and redemption in another world.[13] Rather than surrendering the state to hostile cosmic powers, Roman religion tended to deify the state — at least the *Roman* state. Rome's various gods and goddesses were less the objects of worship than the servants, protectors, and guarantors of *res populi Romani.* Especially in the emperor cult, which was coming into full bloom shortly after Luke wrote, the fusion of state and cult was so complete that the emperor (esp. during the reigns of Domitian, Nerva, Trajan, and Hadrian from 81 to 138) was both the object of worship and the chief priest responsible for worship, the *pontifex maximus.*[14] In Greek religion, the gods and goddesses perpetuated the schemes and intrigues of the Olympian heights in earthly "spheres of influence," often with irrevocable and fatal finality. Of the many and varied ancient religions, Judaism alone acknowledged the authentic reality of the heavenly and earthly worlds, and the necessity of morality and redemption in the latter. Judaism was thus closer than were other religions to the theological conception of 3:1-2, but Judaism's attitude toward the secular world was ambiguous, exhibiting both antipathy and accommodation to the Roman Empire.

The vision of 3:1-2 surpasses each of the above religious perspectives. Unlike mystery religions, the world and its social institutions are not abandoned in favor of the deification of the individual psyche. Unlike Roman religion, the reality of the sovereign God is not collapsed into the state. Unlike Greek religion, the world is not to be trifled with by gods and goddesses who, apart from their eternality, are no better (and often worse) than humans. Unlike more militant forms of Judaism, the Roman world must not inevitably be destroyed for the will of God to triumph. With the possible exception of Isa 40–55 and the prophet Jonah, there was little if any precedent in the ancient

13. See E. Schweizer, "Das hellenistische Weltbild als Produkt der Weltangst," in *Neo-testamentica* (Zürich: Zwingli Verlag, 1963), 15-27; J. Edwards, *Is Jesus the Only Savior?* (Grand Rapids: Eerdmans, 2005), 132-39.

14. E. Lohmeyer, *Christuskult und Kaiserkult* (Tübingen: Mohr Siebeck, 1919), 17-18, writes: "The Caesar-cult encompassed the totality of the Roman Empire. Since the empire was seen as the image of the cosmos or world-order, it was therefore believed to be universal and eternal. As the ruler of the world, Caesar was at the same time lord of the world. This universal state-religion was grounded in the one central thought that the emperor was in some way the incarnation of deity, and that he was the visible, earthly manifestation of the revealed God."

world for Luke's understanding of the word of God bearing witness in and to the world through a prophet like John.

3:1-2 thus does not simply date the appearance of John, although it does so with a precision that finds no equal in the NT. If dating were the point, the reference to the fifteenth year of Tiberius's reign would suffice.[15] Rather, the historical solemnity of 3:1-2 signifies that the gospel makes a genuine appearance in the world as a promise of salvation. The gospel does not only break forth during the reigns of the named rulers, it must also be proclaimed *to* them (1 Tim 3:16). A personal judgment about Jesus and the gospel will be required of nearly all the officials mentioned in 3:1-2. John will appear before Herod Antipas, as will Jesus, who also will appear before Caiaphas, Annas, and Pilate. In Acts, Paul will appear before far-flung rulers and officials, including Caesar in Rome (Acts 25:12; Phil 4:22). Paul will testify to one such ruler that divine revelation "was not done in a corner" (Acts 26:26). In John's appearance at the Jordan and Jesus' ministry in Galilee and Jerusalem, the word of God enters the *public* domain; hence the witness to God's word is *public* witness, "to the ends of the earth" (Acts 1:8), to proclaim the name of Christ "to the Gentiles and their kings and to the people of Israel" (Acts 9:15).[16]

3-6 The word of God appears among the powerful and prestigious, but not to them. With acid irony, Luke reports that "the word of God came to John son of Zechariah in the wilderness" (v. 2). The names before John are accompanied by titles and offices: emperor, prefect, tetrarch, high priest. John has no title or office. The names before John are associated with places of importance: Rome, Sepphoris, Jerusalem. John lives in a place with no name, "in the wilderness." People must leave their comforts and securities and *go out* to the wilderness. In Israel's history the wilderness represents a place of testing, repentance, and grace. God brought deliverance to fledgling Israel in the wilderness of Sinai following the exodus (Exod 15–20), and thereafter the wilderness, both literally (Elijah, 1 Kgs 17:2-3) and figuratively (Jer 2:2-3; Hos 2:14-23) became a place of prophetic hope.[17] The reference to John preaching in "all the country around the Jordan" (v. 3) is particularly revealing. This

---

15. Ignatius, *Magn.* 11, finds Pilate's less-specific tenure sufficient to date the Christ-event: ". . . be convinced of the birth and passion and resurrection which took place at the time of the procuratorship of Pontius Pilate."

16. It is important to remember that when Luke was writing, Christianity was "a negligible speck within the vastness of the Roman political order" (L. T. Johnson, *Among the Gentiles: Greco-Roman Religion and Christianity* [New Haven: Yale University Press, 2009], 140). Luke's setting of the Christian gospel in the context of world history thus foresees a reality that would become apparent to the Roman political order only some three centuries later with the Christianization of the Roman Empire under Constantine.

17. On the wilderness motif in Scripture, see U. Mauser, *Christ in the Wilderness* (SBT; London: SCM Press, 1963), 46-52.

Greek phrase repeats verbatim the description of the territory chosen by Lot in Gen 13:10; 19:25. Within this territory lay Sodom and Gomorrah, places synonymous with detestable practices and destruction.[18] The gospel is thus not directed primarily to or reserved exclusively for the Gentile and Jewish potentates of vv. 1-2. Its primary destination, rather, is the once-forsaken region of Sodom, to which John is first directed. The mission of Jesus "to seek and save the lost" (19:10) is already anticipated in the ministry of John.

As a symbol of moral and spiritual regeneration John calls people to **baptism**. "Baptism," from Greek *baptein,* means "to dip fully, to plunge or immerse." Rites of sacred baths and ritual washings are known throughout the ancient Near East. In pre-Christian Judaism, repentance was a necessary prerequisite of the *eschaton,* when God would cleanse his people by a holy spirit (*Jub.* 1:22-25). Although *mikva'ot* (ritual washings before worship) were constitutive elements of Judaism (see *m. Miqw.*), and although there is some evidence for proselyte baptism in Judaism, the chief example of ritual washings in Judaism derived from Qumran, where daily lustrations symbolized the eschatological cleansing of God. "[God] will sprinkle over him the spirit of truth like lustral water (in order to cleanse him) from all the abhorrences of deceit and from the defilement of the unclean spirit" (1QS 4:21-22).[19] Whether, and to what extent, John's baptism reflects these various water-rite precursors is much debated. In several important respects his baptism differs from our understanding of proselyte baptism and Qumran washings. The latter were self-washings, whereas John's baptism was administered to the penitent by John. John and the word of God he proclaims are integral for effectual baptism.[20] Proselyte baptism and Qumran washings were rites of initiation into faith communities, whereas John's baptism signified moral and spiritual renewal. Some scholars suppose that John had either been associated with or influenced by the Essenes.[21] There is no evidence in the NT that John was associated with Qumran, and the NT descriptions of John's baptism, although not exact, generally locate it north of Qumran, along the Jordan River near Galilee.[22] John's baptism more likely recalls and revives God's foundational

18. For references to the "reversed" world of Sodom in the OT, the apocryphal and pseudepigraphical literature, Josephus, Philo, Qumran, and Talmud, see M. J. Mulder, "Sodom and Gomorrah," *ABD* 6:99-103.

19. A. Oepke, *baptō, TDNT* 1:528-29.

20. See Vinson, *Luke,* 89-90.

21. On the possible influence of Qumran on John, see O. Betz, "Was John the Baptist an Essene?" *BRev* 6/6 (1990): 18-25. Betz believes that John was raised at Qumran and strongly influenced by it, but that he later left the sect to preach to a wider community of Jews. John's association with Qumran remains conjectural, however, and the differences between John and the Essenes are more numerous and striking than their similarities.

22. The precise location of John's baptism is uncertain. Mark 1:5 and Matt 3:6 locate

covenant with Israel at Sinai, in which the entire people were summoned to be "a kingdom of priests and a holy nation" (Exod 19:6; also 1 Pet 2:9). Israelites signified acceptance of their covenant relationship with God by washing their clothes and purifying themselves before entering into the covenant at Sinai (Exod 19:10). John's baptism corresponds favorably with the essential elements of preparation for the Day of the Lord in the original Sinai covenant, although it appears more inclusive than the Sinai covenant, and certainly more inclusive than Qumran lustrations, for John baptized not just the religious elite but all Jews who came to him.

Unlike the rites of the mystery religions, John's rite of repentance is, as the Greek *kēryssein* indicates, "*publicly* proclaimed." *Kēryssein*, connoting "official announcement," becomes the major term to describe the gospel proclamation of the early church. It declares the powerful, prophetic, and authoritative inbreaking of divine redemption in Jesus Christ. The redemptive work of God is not something different from the proclamation, but radically present *in* it.[23] John's proclamation is thus about God's action and an appropriate human reaction in repentance and reformation.[24] John's proclamation incorporated "Old Testament prophecy itself, which knows that there is no grace without judgment, no salvation without repentance, and no forgiveness without a claim on the human will."[25]

"**Repentance**" (Gk. *metanoia*) is a compound word meaning "to change one's mind" or "to alter one's understanding." It combines both rational decision and willful act as opposed to emotive feeling alone. This basic sense is sharpened by the concept of repentance and conversion in the OT, particularly in the prophets.[26] The Benedictus defined the mission of John as

---

John's baptism at the Jordan River, without further specificity. Luke 3:3 reports that John "went into all the country around the Jordan," implying that he baptized at more than one place on the river and perhaps on the tributaries flowing into it. B. Pixner suggests that John baptized at various places associated with Elijah (*With Jesus through Galilee*, 19-20). The Fourth Gospel locates John baptizing at "Aenon near Salim, because there was plenty of water" (John 3:23). Both Aenon and Salim lie immediately to the west of the Jordan, some twenty-five miles south of the Sea of Galilee. This locates John's baptism in the Decapolis, close to Galilee. For a thorough discussion of the question, see R. Riesner, "Bethany beyond the Jordan (John 1:28): Topography, Theology, and History in the Fourth Gospel," *TynBul* 38 (1987): 29-63.

23. See G. Friedrich, *kērysso̅*, *TWNT* 3:701-3.

24. See E. Lohmeyer, *Das Evangelium des Markus*, 13-15; and J. Marcus, *The Way of the Lord* (Edinburgh: T&T Clark, 1992), 18-31, who argue that in the NT the object of the verb *kēryssein*, "proclaim," is an action of God.

25. Schweizer, *Lukas*, 47.

26. *Metanoia* and *metanoein* occur infrequently in the LXX, normally as translations of Heb. *naham*, "to regret" or "to be remorseful." The conditions of John's preaching of repentance, particularly as preserved in 3:7-9 and Matt 3:7-10, reveal a pattern more reminiscent of Heb. *shub*, "to turn," which occurs in the MT more than a thousand times.

"bringing knowledge of salvation through the forgiveness of sins" (1:77). In the only reference to John's baptism in Josephus, the centrality of repentance is underscored. "[John] exhorted the Jews to lead righteous lives, to practice justice towards their fellows and piety towards God, and so doing to join in baptism."[27] According to Luke, John's proclamation of repentance entails turning away from sin (including bearing of moral "fruits," vv. 7-14) and turning to the promise of the More Powerful One to come (vv. 15-17). The messianic expectation makes John's call to repentance especially urgent, for repentance is the essential prerequisite for preparing people to receive the redemptive work of God in the More Powerful One (v. 16).[28] John's baptism of repentance not only prepared for the Messiah, it lived on in the apostolic church (24:47; Acts 13:24).[29]

Luke interprets John's baptism by quoting more fully from Isa than do either Matt 3:3 or Mark 1:2-3. The quotation is prefaced by "as it is written" (v. 4), an authoritative formula for both Gentile and Jewish readers. The formula frequently carries legal force in Hellenistic introductions to laws or declarations, and in the OT it imputes the authority of God, Torah, king, or prophet to an appended saying.[30] The quotation in vv. 4-6 closely follows Isa 40:3-5 (LXX). "A voice of one calling in the wilderness" in the opening line provides an appropriate description of John's ministry (v. 2).[31] Two departures from the Isa text are notable. First, the LXX reads "make straight paths for our God" (Isa 40:3), whereas Luke reads "make straight paths for *him* (3:4), referring to Jesus.[32] Already in Luke's day, terminology and categories that had historically been attributed only to God were attributed to Jesus. A high Christology (if not its precise formulation) is already present in first-century Christianity. Second, Luke ends the quotation by omitting "the glory of the Lord will be seen" (Isa 40:5 LXX), perhaps because Jesus has not yet appeared. Luke concludes with "And all people shall see God's salvation" (v. 6; Isa 40:5 LXX). The word for "salvation," *sōtērion,* the same word used in Simeon's prophecy (2:30) and Acts 28:28, is an inclusio of Luke's two-volume work. "All people" is literally "all

---

27. *Ant.* 18.116-18. John's ministry of baptism was known as far as Ephesus (Acts 19:3).

28. H. Merklein, *metanoia, EDNT* 2:415-19; J. Behm, *metanoeō, TDNT* 4:1000-1001.

29. Geldenhuys, *Luke,* 141-42, notes that "preaching of repentance must always be an inherent element in the Gospel-preaching of the church. . . . Without [it] . . . the message of the church would degenerate into sentiment."

30. G. Schrenk, *graphō, TDNT* 1:747-49.

31. "In the wilderness" in the MT modifies "way" rather than "voice": "A voice of one calling: 'In the wilderness prepare the way for the Lord.'" *Barn.* 9:3 follows the LXX rather than the MT.

32. Rowe, *Early Narrative Christology,* 70-77, takes the Isa quotation, and esp. the reference to "him" (3:4), to refer to the eschatological coming of God that is identified with the coming of Jesus.

flesh" in Greek, which in the NT usually refers to sinful humanity (Rom 3:20), and in the OT sometimes to animals as well (Gen 6:19).[33] John's proclamation is addressed not only to religious and moral humanity — to humanity in its ideal state — but to *all flesh*. Sinful humanity, even nonhuman flesh (1 Cor 15:39), will see God's salvation.

7-9   Following the Isa quotation, John's proclamation in vv. 7-9 closely parallels Matt 3:7-10. Matt's version addresses John's sermon to "Pharisees and Sadducees," but Luke addresses it broadly "to the crowds." The tone and content of vv. 7-9 are forceful and uncompromising, with no close parallel in the OT and early Jewish literature. The tectonic metaphor of filling valleys and moving mountains signifies the radical and fundamental act of repentance, which alters the landscape of personal and social life. Indicting people as a "brood of vipers" (v. 7) and warning them that "the wood is about to be cast into the fire" (v. 9) may not strike modern readers as "good news" (so v. 18). Peasants and tax collectors acknowledge its rightness (7:29), however, even if religious elites do not (7:30). In harmony with a chorus of OT psalmists and prophets, and with Jesus, Paul, and the NT church, John warns of the "coming wrath" of God (v. 7).[34] God's wrath does not compromise or contradict his goodness and holiness. His wrath promotes his steadfast goodness, for truth is by nature intolerant of error, as love is of indifference and hate, and goodness is of evil. In the NT God's wrath is not final and irrevocable, but a penultimate warning of the consequences of rejecting the divine will. The object of the warning is not to destroy but to effect repentance and renewal.[35] Hence, the ax lies at the root of the trees (v. 9), but it has not (yet) felled them.[36] The proper response to God's impending wrath is "to make fruits worthy of repentance" (v. 8). The plural "fruits" (in contrast to the singular in Matt 3:8) suggests attention to particular acts rather than focus on general character improvement. The command to "do/make fruits worthy of repentance" (v. 8) is instructive. In nature, fruit is borne, not made. The metaphor of fruit suggests that repentance is not a purely human endeavor, but cooperation with divine activity. Similar to Paul's later warning in Rom 2:25-29, John warns against pretensions

---

33. Plummer, *Luke,* 87-88.

34. The article on God's wrath in G. Stählin, *orgē, TWNT* 5:382-448, is a veritable monograph on the subject.

35. The second-c. *Herm. Sim.* 4.4, however, employs the same imagery of the final judgment: "But the heathen and sinners — the withered trees which you saw — will be found to be such, dried and fruitless in that world, and they shall be burnt up like wood and shall be made manifest, because their conduct was wicked in their lives. For the sinners shall be burnt, because they sinned and did not repent, and the heathen shall be burnt, because they did not know their Creator."

36. In a parable on this theme (13:6-9), Jesus teaches that the object of God's wrath is grace, not destruction.

and presumptions of righteousness — of having "Abraham as our father" — rather than demonstrating true moral righteousness.[37] Recalling the imagery of Isa 51:1-2, John makes a trenchant wordplay on the Hebrew (not Aramaic) words for "stones" and "sons": "I tell you, out of these stones [*abanim*] God can raise up sons [*banim*] for Abraham" (v. 8). Abraham is mentioned fifteen times in the Third Gospel, playing an especially important role as the father of the family of salvation. Especially included in Abraham's family are hurting people and outcasts: a woman afflicted for eighteen years is called a "daughter of Abraham" (13:16); Lazarus sits in the lap of father Abraham (16:24); and Zacchaeus, a tax collector, is called a "son of Abraham" (19:9).

10-14 Vv. 10-14 derive from Luke's special material. The placement of this material immediately following John's preaching may signify that proclamation of the word of God should engage hearers in concrete action. John's preaching is direct and uncompromising, but it does not damn hearers. Rather, it provokes the question, "What should we do?" (vv. 10, 12, 14), from three different constituencies: crowds, tax collectors, and soldiers. The question is phrased in the imperfect tense (*epērōtōn*, vv. 10, 14), indicating it was the typical response to John's preaching — and by correlation the objective of all Christian preaching.[38] All three groups were ethnically Jewish, but they were disparaged as functional outsiders by respectable Jews.[39] The crowds are the first and most generic constituency (v. 10), the *am ha'arets,* "people of the land," whose ethnicity was often suspect or disdained (Ezra 9:1-2; Neh 10:30-31), particularly by Pharisees (John 7:49). John commands them to share life's two basic necessities — clothing and food — with those in need (12:23; Gen 28:20; Deut 10:18). The word for "shirt," *chitōn,* refers to a long undergarment with sleeves worn directly over the skin, over which a heavier outer garment, the *himation,* was worn. Plummer believes the *chitōn* was the easier of the two to surrender, for one could still wear the outer garment.[40] But in calling for the *chitōn,* John calls hearers to sacrifice their innermost garment.

John orders **tax collectors** not to "collect more than they were required to" (v. 13). This requirement was easier to do in most walks of life than in the Roman tax system. Land and poll taxes were collected directly by the Romans, but taxes on transported goods were contracted out to local collectors. Most of the local collaborators were ethnic but not observant Jews, since Torah-conscious Jews could not be expected to transact business with Gentiles.[41]

---

37. Josephus, *Ant.* 18.117, also recognized that John's baptism was not a means of gaining pardon but of signifying moral righteousness.

38. The same question appears throughout Luke-Acts (3:10, 12, 14; 10:25; 18:18; Acts 2:37; 16:30; 22:10).

39. *HCNT,* 194.

40. Plummer, *Luke,* 90-91.

41. Josephus, *J.W.* 2.285-88, records a story in which the Jews of Caesarea called on a

Tax collectors made bids in advance to collect taxes in a given area, and their profit came from what they could extort from their constituents, a portion of which stayed in their own pockets.[42] The Mishnah describes tax collectors making daily rounds, "exacting payment of men with or without their consent" (*m. 'Abot* 3:17). The Roman tax system depended on graft and greed, and it attracted individuals who were not adverse to such means.[43] An honest tax collector was, in principle, a starving tax collector.

Tax collectors were despised and hated. Mishnah and Talmud preserve scathing judgments of them from later periods, lumping them together with thieves and murderers. A Jew who collected taxes was a cause of disgrace to his family, expelled from the synagogue, and disqualified as a judge or witness in court (*b. Sanh.* 25b). The touch of a tax collector rendered a house unclean (*m. Ṭehar.* 7:6; *m. Ḥag.* 3:6). Jews were forbidden from receiving money, including alms, from tax collectors, since tax revenues were deemed robbery. Jewish contempt of tax collectors is epitomized in the ruling that Jews could lie to tax collectors with impunity (*m. Ned.* 3:4) — a ruling with which the houses of Hillel and Shammai, who normally stood poles apart, both agreed. Tax collectors were tangible reminders of the Roman domination, detested alike for its injustice and Gentile uncleanness. Not a few Jewish extremists, including one of Jesus' disciples (6:15), considered submission to the Roman tax system an act of treason (20:20-26).

Roman legions were not stationed in Palestine in the first century, and Palestinian Jews were exempt from serving in the Roman army. The "soldiers" in v. 14 therefore may have been enlisted Jews in the service of Herod Antipas rather than Roman soldiers.[44] This may be the reason why "soldiers" (v. 14) is a Greek participle *(strateuomenoi),* meaning "those in service," rather than the noun *stratiōtai,* which connoted "(Roman) soldiers." The order not to extort money by force or threat of violence (v. 14; *diaseiein*) and not to intimidate or exert pressure on people for personal gain (v. 14; *sykophantein*) was a big expectation of soldiers. Soldiers bore arms, and they were under military rather than civilian authorities. Both realities enabled and even encouraged aggres-

---

tax collector named John to intercede for them with Florus, prefect of Judea from 64 to 66. John's wealth was such that he produced a bribe for Florus amounting to some eight talents of silver (over $40,000).

42. Note Philo's description of a tax collector ca. 40, only a decade after Jesus' death. "Capito is the tax collector for Judea, and he holds the population in contempt. When he came there he was a poor man, but he has amassed much wealth in various forms by defrauding and embezzling the people" (*Embassy,* 199).

43. On the Roman tax system in Palestine, see E. Schürer, *History of the Jewish People,* 1:372-76.

44. Josephus, *Ant.* 14.204. Josephus, *Ant.* 18.113, 119, mentions Antipas's army, presumably of Jewish soldiers. On the soldiers' identity, see Fitzmyer, *Luke (I–IX),* 470.

siveness with civilians and in seeking pay raises. One can fairly ask how tax collectors and soldiers could comply with John's commands. John does not ground his commands in Torah or rabbinic tradition. Unlike Judaism before and the early church after, he does not require tax collectors and soldiers to desist or be rejected.[45] He does not require them to leave occupations and workplaces where there are moral compromises, to practice pacifism, or to retreat into religious insularity. John grounds his commands in self-evident moral standards. His instructions assume that, even in difficult and compromising circumstances, there are ways to behave decently and morally. He does not expect the crowds, tax collectors, and soldiers to change social structures, but, like yeast and leaven, to humanize them by just and honorable behavior. John's counsel anticipates Jesus' quintessential moral maxim, "Do to others as you would have them do to you" (6:31).

15-17   The description of the anticipation produced by John's preaching is similar in wording to the anticipation when Zechariah was delayed in the temple (1:21). The effect of John's preaching on his hearers, like the effect of Gabriel's announcement to Mary (1:29), is described in Greek *dialogizesthai* (v. 15), "to consider or ponder thoughtfully." That people imagined John to be the Messiah indicates that his baptism and preaching aroused hearers to more than moral reform. "John answered them all" (v. 16), i.e., he publicly refuted messianic expectations, declaring that his water baptism would be superseded by a greater baptism from "one more powerful," whose sandals John is unworthy to untie. A sandal lace was an insignificant article of clothing; and "untying sandal thongs" may have been an Israelite saying related to menial work (Gen 14:23). Unfastening shoes and sandals, at any rate, like the washing of feet, was the work of slaves, indeed of *non-Hebrew* slaves.[46] This figure of speech impressed itself in the memory of the early church as a testimony of John's humility and subordination vis-à-vis Jesus (Acts 13:25).

John's allusion to the More Powerful One rather than Messiah, as the crowds expected, is revealing. The More Powerful One does not bear a particularly close resemblance to Messiah. John's requirement to make fruits of repentance (v. 8) and his description of righteous judgment (v. 17) do correspond with Jewish messianic expectations. The image of the "winnowing fork" in the hand of Messiah, separating wheat from chaff, one for the barn and the other for the fire, is a particularly graphic image of eternal judgment. But many predictable messianic expectations are absent from John's proclamation.[47]

---

45. In the Jewish tradition, a list of forbidden occupations is provided in *m. Qidd.* 4.14; in the early church, in Hippolytus, *Trad. Ap.* 16.

46. Str-B 1:121; 2.557.

47. Typical components of Jewish messianic expectations that are absent in John's preaching include (1) the return of Elijah at the end of days to establish purity in doctrine and

John also includes elements that are not common messianic expectations, in particular his declaration that the Coming One will baptize in the Holy Spirit and fire (v. 16). In messianic discussions, Jews typically differentiated between "this present age" and "the [messianic] age to come." John makes no reference to a messianic "age." He focuses rather on a *person* — the More Powerful One to come. This nonspecific designation seems to forestall popular messianic expectations and open the door to a different and fuller understanding of the Coming One, which Luke will develop in Son of God categories rather than messianic categories in 3:21–4:13.

The reference to baptism with "the Holy Spirit and fire" (v. 16) causes modern readers, like John's hearers, to reflect and ponder. The Holy Spirit is obviously a divine figure; hence, baptism of the More Powerful One will not be a symbolic baptism of cleansing with water, but immersion into the power and person of God. "Fire" is less obvious. Some consider it a reference to the tongues of fire at Pentecost, when the Holy Spirit anointed believers with new languages.[48] If this is its meaning, however, we might expect "fire" to appear in Acts 1:5 (and 11:16) in the immediate prelude to Pentecost. Fire is often a symbol of divine judgments (as in the following v. 17). Origen understood "fire" as a second baptism, a "fiery bath" through which believers must pass before entering eternal life.[49] A second baptism is not taught in Scripture, however. "Holy Spirit and fire" seem to refer to a dual character of baptism as both a purification and a refinement, perhaps recalling again the "falling and rising" motif in 2:34 (similarly Isa 4:4-5; 32:15; 44:3; Ezek 36:25-26; Mal 3:2-3).[50]

18-20   John exhorted people in "many other words" (v. 18). The Greek reads, "John exhorted the people in many and various *things*," indicating that, in his portrayal of John, as in the composition of his Gospel (1:1), Luke drew upon a larger pool of sources (see John 20:30; 21:25). In making the word of God (v. 2) the organizing principle for John's message and ministry, Luke makes John the forerunner of the Word of God himself. Luke's preferred description of the gospel is the verb *euangelizesthai*, "to proclaim good news" (24x in Luke-Acts). In striking contrast, Mark never uses the verb form of

---

teaching in Israel; (2) elaborate signs before the Messiah's return; (3) revelation of the Messiah on the pinnacle of the temple, whence he would declare salvation; (4) protracted war with and final military defeat of the kings of the nations, esp. the sacrilegious Roman Empire; (5) future rule of the world by Israel; (6) final and full possession of the land of Israel; (7) rule of Messiah as king of peace in Jerusalem; (8) rich blessing of Israel; and (9) the flourishing of life, both human and animal, in the land. See Str-B 4/2:799-1015.

48. So Bovon, *Lukas 1,1–9,50*, 177.

49. *Hom. Luc.* 24.2; 26.1-3.

50. So Fitzmyer, *Luke (I–IX)*, 473-75. See also Marshall, *Luke*, 146-48; Bock, *Luke 1:1–9:50*, 321-24; and Schweizer, *Lukas*, 49, who writes: "Where the Spirit makes a person capable of receiving God's judgment, there judgment is turned into blessing."

"gospel," and Matt only once (11:5). Luke, in contrast, avoids the noun form of "gospel" (*euangelion;* only twice, Acts 15:7; 20:24). The verbal rather than nominal form defines the gospel in terms of divine activity. One may be surprised to hear John's stern proclamation called good news. It is good not because it is "nice" (a word that never occurs in Scripture!), but because it is *true.*

In vv. 18-19 Luke summarizes John's preaching in three verbs: he *exhorts* all, he *proclaims good news* to the penitent, and he *reproves* (NIV "rebukes") the impenitent.[51] The Greek form of the word "reproved," *elenchomenos,* occurs only twice again in the Greek Bible (Prov. 3:11; Heb 12:5), both with reference to *divine* reproof. Already in v. 19 the name of a ruler mentioned in 3:1-2 reappears. Herod the tetrarch is convicted by John's preaching "because of his marriage to Herodias . . . and all the other evil things he had done" (on Herod Antipas, see excursus at 23:1). Like his father, Herod the Great, Herod Antipas was shrewd and pitiless, as attested in Jesus' reference to him as "that fox" (13:32). Also like his father, he was a lover of luxury and magnificent architecture, as seen even today in the ruins of Tiberias and Sepphoris, his two showcase cities in Galilee. Antipas was also chaotic in marital relations — although in this respect less chaotic than his father. He persuaded Herodias, wife of his half-brother Herod Philip (not the tetrarch Philip of 3:1), son of Herod the Great's third wife Mariamne II, to divorce her husband and marry him. According to both the NT and Josephus, the evil genius of Herodias surpassed that of Antipas in the plot she hatched to execute John.[52] On top of these evils, Antipas "added this to them all: he locked John up in prison" (v. 20). John's ministry and proclamation have already elicited a judgment from one of "the kings of the nations," as Jesus predicts in 22:25. In reporting John's imprisonment before Jesus' baptism, Luke obviously disrupts strict narrative chronology. He apparently does so in anticipation of John's martyrdom in 9:7-9 and, more important, to grant Jesus unrivaled attention in the baptism.

THE MANIFESTATION OF THE SON OF GOD (3:21–4:13)

In the Third Gospel, the baptism, genealogy, and testing of Jesus in the wilderness are unified by the common theme of the Son of God. In the baptism, Jesus is addressed by God as "my Son, whom I love" (3:22); the genealogy reveals that, although Jesus is presumed to be the son of Joseph (3:23), his true ancestry must be traced through "Adam, the son of God" (3:38); and in the wilderness temptation by the devil the divine sonship of Jesus (4:3, 9) is

---

51. Plummer, *Luke,* 96.
52. Mark 6:14-29; Josephus, *Ant.* 18.136.

put to the test. The concentration of Son of God terminology in these three pericopes is significant because the title appears only sparingly in Luke.[53] Four of its nine occurrences are clustered in 3:21–4:13. The baptism, genealogy, and temptation unite to clarify and confirm the annunciation promises to Mary in 1:26-38. John was announced as the divinely appointed "prophet of the Most High" (1:76) who would go before "him" (1:17) or the "Lord" (1:76). John's task as forerunner is clear, but *whom* he precedes is less clear, for "him" and "Lord" can refer equally to Jesus and God. In the annunciation Jesus is identified as the eternal messianic ruler over the house of David, conceived by and filled with the Holy Spirit, who is "the Son of the Most High," "the Son of God" (1:31-35). These prophecies are fulfilled in Jesus' investiture as the Son of God in the baptism, they are confirmed in the divine credentials of his genealogy, and they are tested and proved in his wilderness temptations. In the angelic prophecies, divine sonship is held in indivisible unity with the Spirit of God, and in 3:21–4:13 Jesus is declared the Son of God (3:22, 38; 4:3, 9) who is anointed, indwelt, guided, and empowered by the Spirit of God (3:16, 22; 4:1 [2x], 14).

21-22   John's role as forerunner of Jesus is developed in more detail in the Third Gospel than in any other Gospel. The superstructure of the Gospel of Luke rests upon the alternating annunciations of John and Jesus in the first two chapters. Ironically, however, Luke never records a meeting of John and Jesus. They met at Jesus' baptism, of course, but Luke does not record their meeting or mention John's name in the baptism. The only recorded conversation between Jesus and John in the Third Gospel transpires through the mediation of John's disciples when he was in prison (7:18-23). In 3:20 John is effectively removed from the plot by Luke, and unlike the other Gospels (Matt 3:13; Mark 1:9; John 1:29), there is no overlap in their ministries at the baptism. For Luke, John is less important as a *baptizer* (title occurs only at 7:20, 33) than as the *preparer* of the way of Jesus (1:17; 3:16; 7:19-20, 27).

Three events transpire at the baptism of Jesus that in Jewish tradition signified the inauguration of God's eschatological kingdom: heaven was opened, the Holy Spirit descended on Jesus, and a voice from heaven spoke to Jesus. The prophet Isaiah (64:1) was the first to speak of the rending of the heaven and return of God in the messianic age. Subsequent Jewish tradition elaborated Isaiah's imagery. The *T. Levi*, composed perhaps in 250 B.C., anticipates the baptismal scene by mentioning all three eschatological signs:

> The heavens will be opened,
> and from the temple of glory sanctification will come upon him,
> with a fatherly voice, as from Abraham to Isaac.
> And the glory of the Most High shall burst forth upon him.

---

53. Only nine times: 1:35; 3:22, 38; 4:3, 9, 41; 8:28; 9:35; 22:70.

And the spirit of understanding and sanctification
Shall rest upon him [in the water].
For he shall give the majesty of the Lord to those who are his sons in
   truth forever.[54]

A similar passage from *T. Jud.* speaks of the messianic king as the Star of Jacob, upon whom "the heavens will be opened . . . to pour out the spirit as a blessing of the Holy Father."[55] Second Temple Judaism commonly believed that, with the cessation of the great OT prophets, the Holy Spirit had ceased speaking directly to God's people.[56] The absence of the Spirit quenched prophecy, and God was believed to speak to the faithful only in a distant echo, a *bat-qol* (Heb. "daughter of a voice"). The opening of heaven at the baptism inaugurates the long-awaited return of God's Spirit, not in a prophet but in God's very Son.

The second sign attending the baptism is the descent of the Holy Spirit. Likening the Spirit of God to a dove is unusual in Judaism, but not wholly unknown.[57] In Philo the dove symbolizes the wisdom and word of God; in the targum to Gen 1:2 the Spirit brooding over the water is seen as a dove (*b. Ḥag.* 15a); and in *Odes Sol.* 24:1 a dove flutters over the head of Messiah (this last passage likely reveals Christian influence). Luke's depiction of the Spirit descending in "bodily form like a dove" (3:22) is more specific than Matt 3:16 and Mark 1:10. The Greek word *eidos,* "form," unlike the more common words *morphē* or *schēma,* stresses visibility. Luke's simile suggests that the Spirit's descent on Jesus *looked* like the descent of a dove. Such concrete imagery underscores the objectivity of the event. The descent of the Spirit on Jesus is not depicted as a metaphor of enlightenment or a mystical experience, but as an empirical reality.[58]

---

54. *T. Levi* 18:6-8; Charlesworth, *OTP* 1:795.

55. *T. Jud.* 24:1-3; Charlesworth, *OTP* 1:801.

56. Ps 74:9; *T. Benj.* 9:2; *2 Bar.* 85:3; 1 Macc 4:46; 9:27; 14:41; Josephus, *Ag. Ap.* 1.41. See J. Jeremias, *New Testament Theology* (trans. J. Bowden; New York: Scribners, 1971), 80-81. See Str-B 1:125-34; 2.128-34, for further evidence that, at the death of the last prophets, Haggai, Zechariah, and Malachi, the Spirit of prophecy disappeared from Israel and communicated henceforth only occasionally through an inferior *bat-qol*. Qumran was an exception to this belief, however. For a counterview that the rabbis did not deny the presence of the Holy Spirit in Second Temple Judaism but that they were indifferent to it, partly owing to their desire to defend their authority from the challenge of nascent Christianity, see F. Greenspahn, "Why Prophecy Ceased," *JBL* 108 (1989): 17-35.

57. Str-B 1:124-25.

58. Note R. Bultmann's judgment: "There is not so much as a word about the inner experience of Jesus. . . . Matthew and Luke are quite right to take Mark's story as the description of an objective happening" (*The History of the Synoptic Tradition* [trans. J. Marsh; rev. ed.; New York: Harper & Row, 1963], 247-48). Further on the objectivity of Luke's account, see Lagrange, *Luc,* 115; Wolter, *Lukasevangelium,* 170; and esp. Rengstorf, *Lukas,* 47-48.

The final eschatological sign is the declaration from heaven, "You are my Son, whom I love; with you I am well pleased." Only here and in the transfiguration (excepting John 12:28) do we see direct divine discourse with Jesus in the Gospels, in each instance of which God addresses Jesus as "my Son." A wealth of OT imagery lies behind the divine declaration. A clear antecedent is Isa 49:3, where the servant of the Lord is declared, "You are my servant, Israel, in whom I will display my splendor." The syntactic parallelism between this declaration and the voice at the baptism is immediately apparent. Like Isaiah's Servant, the ministry of Jesus will be fraught with opposition and seeming defeat, but his vicarious service will also be "a light for the Gentiles that my salvation may reach to the ends of the earth" (Isa 49:6; see Luke 2:32; Acts 1:8; 13:47).[59]

The voice from heaven identifies Jesus as God's Son, thus also echoing the enthronement of the Israelite king in Ps 2:7. The filial intimacy and obedience that were imperfectly foreshadowed by the king are perfectly fulfilled in Jesus. Jesus is also the perfect fulfillment of the original concept of sonship that was linked to Israel's call in Exod 4:22-23. This text is particularly relevant to Luke's baptismal narrative, which portrays Jesus as *primus inter pares,* "with all the people" (3:21). Yet another antecedent to the divine voice is the concept of the *beloved* Son. Abraham's deep love for Isaac, even in God's command to sacrifice Isaac on Mount Moriah, is a clear prototype of the heavenly declaration to Jesus (Gen 22:2, 12, 16). The divine proclamation expresses the steadfast love of the Father for the Son, as well as their essential unity. Other NT writers (Heb 11:17-19; Rom 4:24-25; 8:32) and early Fathers (*Barn.* 7:3 onward) also saw in the sacrifice of Isaac the prefiguration of the sacrifice of Jesus.

The three eschatological signs — opening of heaven, descent of Spirit, and divine voice — signify a divine event. Another divine event, the vision to Cornelius in Acts 10, will be narrated by Luke similarly and in virtually the same terminology.[60] Luke's baptismal narrative consists of a single Greek sentence beginning with a finite verb, *egeneto* ("it happened"), followed by six verbs in either participial or infinitival moods describing *what* happened. The three eschatological signs are included in the scene, of course, but they are more muted than in Matt 3:13-17 and Mark 1:9-11. Luke's first unique emphasis in the baptism occurs with mention that "all the people" (*hapanta ton laon,* emphatic in Greek) were being baptized. "The people," who earlier inquired of John whether he was Messiah (vv. 15-16), are now present in even greater

---

59. On the possible influence of Isa 49 on the baptismal narrative and ministry of Jesus, see J. Edwards, "The Servant of the Lord and the Gospel of Mark," in *Biblical Interpretation in Early Christian Gospels,* vol. 1: *The Gospel of Mark* (ed. T. Hatina; LNTS 304; London: T&T Clark, 2006), 49-63.

60. Common to the baptism (3:21-22) and the vision of Cornelius (Acts 10:11-13) are (1) the *opening of heaven,* (2) a *descent* from heaven, and (3) a *voice that came* from heaven. The Greek words for the foregoing italicized English words are identical in both accounts.

numbers — "all the people" — with Jesus at his baptism (v. 21).[61] For Luke, the corporate nature of baptism supersedes Jesus' baptism, which is mentioned rather incidentally.[62] Luke embeds Jesus' baptism within the larger phenomenon of the baptism of the crowds, thereby shifting the baptism from a solo event of Jesus to a communal event of God's people. Luke's second emphasis is the mention of Jesus' prayer, which occurs neither in Matt nor in Mark. Throughout Luke-Acts, key developments in salvation history are set in the context of prayer.[63] After the baptism, *while* Jesus prays, the Father anoints Jesus with the Holy Spirit and declares him the Beloved Son. The Spirit of God enables Jesus to embrace his identity as the Son of God and to assume his vocation as the Servant of God.[64]

Some readers infer that Jesus was adopted as Son of God at the baptism, i.e., elevated from human to divine status. The presence of an alternative reading in the divine declaration in 3:22, "You are my Beloved Son, *today I have begotten you,*" may seem to support this inference.[65] Several reasons argue strongly against an adoptionist understanding of the baptism, however. The textual evidence favoring the received reading, "You are my Beloved Son, in whom I am well pleased" is vastly superior to the alternate longer reading, with "today I have begotten you."[66] More important, Luke would scarcely compromise or contradict the preexistence of Jesus' divine sonship announced by Ga-

---

61. So F. Hahn, *Christologische Hoheitstitel: Ihre Geschichte im frühen Christentum* (4th ed.; FRLANT 83; Göttingen: Vandenhoeck & Ruprecht, 1974), 318-19; A. George, "Jésus Fils de Dieu dans L'Évangile selon Saint Luc," *RB* 72/2 (1965): 187.

62. Plummer, *Luke*, 98, among many others, notes, "It is remarkable that this, which seems to us to be the main fact, should be expressed thus incidentally by a participle."

63. Divine revelations typically follow prayer in Luke-Acts, including Zechariah (1:9-11), Anna (2:37-38), Cornelius (Acts 10:2-6), Peter (10;9-16), Paul (9:11-12; 22:17-21), and the prophets and teachers of the church in Antioch (13:2). In Jesus' ministry, prayer precedes the bestowal of the Holy Spirit and declaration of divine Sonship at the baptism (3:21-22), the choice of the Twelve (6:12), the confession of Peter (9:18), the transfiguration (9:28-29), the temptation in Gethsemane (22:41), and the crucifixion (23:46). See Klein, *Lukasevangelium,* 410; Tannehill, *Narrative Unity of Luke-Acts,* 56-57.

64. See Green, *Luke,* 184.

65. Codex Bezae (D, 5th cent.) is the chief textual witness for the alternate reading. B. Ehrman, *Misquoting Jesus: The Story behind Who Changed the Bible and Why* (New York: Oxford University Press, 2005), 175, argues that "today I have begotten you" was the original reading of Luke, later omitted by orthodox scribes in order to avert the theological heresy of adoptionism. Ehrman's argument is based in his own assumption rather than in historical evidence. "Today I have begotten you," although widely disseminated in the first three centuries, is absent from the most numerous and important manuscripts and is properly regarded by the majority of scholars as a later accommodation to Ps 2:7. See Lagrange, *Luc,* 115-16; Metzger, *TCGNT,* 112-13.

66. See Lagrange, *Luc,* 115-16; Metzger, *TCGNT,* 112-13; Klein, *Lukasevangelium,* 171.

briel (1:31-35) with an insinuation of adoptionism at the baptism.[67] "You are my Beloved Son" implies a permanent status, not an apotheosis. Third, even when accepting the variant, which it often did, the early church did not interpret the baptismal account as adoptionist.[68] Finally, an adoptionist understanding of 3:22 stands at variance from the plenary NT witness to the preexistence of Jesus.[69] Rengstorf aptly concludes, "The voice of God does not establish Jesus' divine sonship; it presupposes it."[70]

If Jesus was the incarnate Son of God and sinless (Heb 4:15), why did he submit to "a baptism of repentance for the forgiveness of sins" (3:3)? This question exercised the church from its earliest days.[71] Matt 3:14-15 registers a protest from John against baptizing the morally righteous Jesus. Two quotations from the Hebrew Gospel record similar objections to the baptism of Jesus.[72] The emphasis on the baptism of the crowds, rather than on Jesus alone, mitigates this particular problem in Luke. The baptism of Jesus with "all the people" emphasizes his identification with sinners, indeed his vicarious baptism on behalf of them. In the dispute between Moses and Pharaoh in Egypt, Moses refers to Israel as "God's firstborn son" (Exod 4:22-23). Early in Israel's history, "Son of God" is thus defined in corporate rather than individual terms, a description of Israel rather than a single Israelite — although it will take Jesus, the True Israelite, to restore the ideal of Israel. Israel failed to fulfill the ideal, but the ideal was not forsaken by God. In the baptism, Jesus — the true Son and thus Israel reduced to one — stands in the water with sinners as himself the "firstborn Son" to redeem and restore the original ideal of divine sonship (Rom 8:29). As the Beloved Son in whom God is pleased and on whom God's

---

67. See, e.g., J. Bieneck, *Sohn Gottes als Christusbezeichnung der Synoptiker* (ATANT; Zürich: Zwingli Verlag, 1951), 59-60; G. Ladd, *A Theology of the New Testament* (Grand Rapids: Eerdmans, 1974), 164.

68. See J. G. Machen, *The Virgin Birth of Christ* (New York: Harper & Brothers, 1930), 51-55; B. M. F. van Iersel, *"Der Sohn" in den synoptischen Jesusworten: Christusbezeichnung der Gemeinde oder Selbstbezeichnung Jesu?* (NovTSup 3; Leiden: Brill, 1964), 88-89; and esp. L. Legrand, "L'arrière-plan néotestamentaire de Lc 1,35," *RB* 70/2 (1963): 167, who accepts the D-reading but rejects an adoptionist interpretation.

69. E.g., John 1:1; 17:5; Phil 2:6-11; Col 1:15-20; Heb 13:8; Rev 1:8.

70. K. H. Rengstorf, *Das Evangelium nach Lukas* (NTD; Göttingen: Vandenhoeck & Ruprecht, 1965), 27: "Die Gottesstimme setzt nicht erst Jesu Sohnschaft, sondern setzt sie voraus."

71. Plummer, *Luke,* 100-101, discusses four options: (1) Jesus wished to honor John, (2) he desired for John to declare his messiahship, (3) he accepted baptism as a transition from private life to public ministry, (4) he saw baptism as a consecration of himself for ministry. Plummer favors #4.

72. An Epiphanius quotation from *Pan.* 30.13.8 agrees with Matt 3:14-15, whereas Jerome preserves a quotation from the Hebrew Gospel in *Pelag.* 3.2 with an objection of Jesus, "What sin have I committed that I should go and be baptized by [John]?"

Holy Spirit rests (1:35; 3:22), Jesus is both the model of Israel's sonship and the means of its fulfillment. In Jesus, the Son of God endowed with the Spirit of God, "all people will see God's salvation" (3:6).

23-38   Luke's genealogy includes many features that are unique to genealogies in both Jewish and Christian literature. No other gospel — canonical, apocryphal, or gnostic — includes a genealogy of Jesus between the baptism and temptation, as does the Third Gospel. Similarly, it is unusual to find a genealogy within a narrative rather than before it. Exod 6:14-27 is an exception, but as a rule Jewish genealogies appear at the introduction rather than in the body of a narrative. The sequence of Luke's genealogy is also unusual. Major genealogies in Scripture, including Matt 1:1-17, list names from past to present,[73] whereas Luke's genealogy is ordered from present to past. Jewish genealogies occasionally follow Luke's order, although those that do are never as long and comprehensive as Luke's.[74] In contrast to Matt, Luke's genealogy mentions no women, there are no explicative words in addition to names, and Luke traces the genealogy back to Adam, in fact, to God, whereas Matthew begins with Abraham. Most unusual, all known genealogies trace back to a human figure, but Luke's alone traces back to God.[75]

Luke's exceptions to the well-established protocol of genealogies reinforce the dual foci of the baptism: Jesus, the Son of God, stands in solidarity with humanity. Jesus' baptism with "all the people" (3:21) connects him spatially with humanity; the seventy-seven human names in the genealogy connect him temporally with humanity. Salvation history flows inevitably and consummately to Jesus. By inserting the genealogy between baptism and temptation, Luke accentuates Jesus' divine sonship. By placing Jesus in a human lineage that begins with "son of God," Luke signals his dual identity, human yet divine, both son of man and Son of God.

The genealogy commences with a salient Hebraism, *kai autos ēn Iēsous archomenos,* "now Jesus himself was beginning" (v. 23).[76] In contrast to the incidental mention of Jesus' baptism in 3:21, his person is introduced prominently here. The NIV rendering "he began his ministry" (v. 23) is somewhat free and misleading. The original Greek lacks "his ministry," and "begin" is not

---

73. E.g., Gen 5:1-32; 11:10-26; Ruth 4:18-22; above all, the frequent genealogies in 1–2 Chr list names past to present.

74. Wolter, *Lukasevangelium*, 174. See, e.g., Ezra 7:1-5; Jdt 8:1; Josephus, *Ant.* 1.79.

75. M. Johnson, *The Purpose of the Biblical Genealogies, with Special Reference to the Setting of the Genealogies of Jesus* (SNTSMS 8; Cambridge: University Press, 1969), 237, "There is no known parallel in the OT or in Rabbinic texts for a genealogy to begin with or culminate with the naming of God." On Luke's genealogy in general, see Brown, *Birth*, 84-94; Fitzmyer, *Luke (I–IX),* 491-504.

76. On the *kai autos* construction, see Edwards, *Hebrew Gospel,* 134; Jeremias, *Sprache des Lukasevangeliums,* 37-38.

a simple past, but an emphatic periphrastic participial construction directing attention exclusively to Jesus. Jesus himself, and not simply his ministry, is the beginning of all that God ordains to do in the world. At the beginning of all things stands the Word, according to John 1:1; at the beginning of the consummation of salvation history stands Jesus, according to Luke. The reference to Jesus' age, "about thirty years old," may recall the age at which Jewish males could commence temple service (Num 4:3), or more specifically, the ages of Joseph (Gen 41:46) and David (2 Sam 5:4) when they commenced to rule.[77]

Jesus is "supposedly" (NIV "so it was thought") the son of Joseph, but his genuine pedigree derives from Adam, the "son of God" (v. 38). The word for "suppose," *nomizein,* is a favorite Lukan word, occurring nine times in Luke-Acts, in all but one instance of supposing wrongly.[78] This reinforces and furthers the point made in 2:48-49: Jesus is adequately understood not as Joseph's son but only as God's Son. In Greek, *nomizein* occurs precisely where "son of" should occur, inviting readers to find Jesus' true and ultimate Father in "the son of God" (v. 38).[79]

---

77. Jesus being thirty years of age is also preserved in the Hebrew Gospel (Epiphanius, *Pan.* 30.13.2-3), Irenaeus (*Haer.* 2.22.4), and Clement of Alexandria (*Strom.* 1.21). Origen, *Hom. Luc.* 28.5, sees Jesus' age as a typological fulfillment of Joseph's beginning to rule Egypt at age thirty. "During the time of plenty, Joseph gathered in the wheat, so that during the time of famine he would have some to distribute. I think that Joseph's age of thirty came before as a type of the Savior's thirty years. This second Joseph did not gather in the kind of wheat that the first Joseph did in Egypt. He, Jesus, gathers in true and heavenly wheat." In the second c. Valentinus attempted to incorporate Jesus into his greater gnostic system by arguing that the thirty years of Jesus' life correlated with the thirty aeons of ultimate reality (Irenaeus, *Haer.* 1.1.3).

78. 2:44; 3:23; Acts 7:25; 8:20; 14:19; 16:13, 27; 17:29; 21:29. Acts 16:13 is the only positive use of *nomizein.*

79. By the second c. the NT testimony that Joseph was not Jesus' true father led to scurrilous rumors of Jesus' paternity. Celsus, a pagan detractor of Christianity, defamed Jesus as a bastard who was fathered not by Joseph but by a Roman soldier named Panthera (or Pandera or Pantira) who seduced Mary (Origen, *Cels.* 1.32, 69). Celsus probably heard this rumor from Jewish polemicists, who promoted it as an explanation of the Christian doctrine of the virgin birth (see G. Dalman, *Jesus Christ in the Talmud, Mishnah, Zohar, and the Liturgy of the Synagogue* [trans. A. W. Streane; Cambridge: Deighton, Bell, 1893], 7-8, 19-25). In the Middle Ages, the *Toledot Jesu* expanded this fabrication into a long and lurid scene of the seduction of Mary by Joseph Pandera (see G. Schlichting, *Ein jüdisches Leben Jesu* [WUNT 24; Tübingen: Mohr Siebeck, 1982], 53-67). During the 1930s and 1940s several prominent German theologians joined the pro-Nazi Institute for Research into and Elimination of Jewish Influence in German Church Life to revive the Pandera story as a way of arguing that Jesus was an Aryan rather than a Jew (see R. Ericksen, *Theologians under Hitler: Gerhard Kittel, Paul Althaus, and Emanuel Hirsch* [New Haven: Yale University Press, 1985], 164-65; most recently, *Gratwanderungen — das "Entjudungsinstitut" in Eisenach: Eine Dokumentation zur Ausstellung des Martin-Luther-Gymnasiums Eisenach* [ed. B. Reichert; Eisenach: Wartburg Verlag, 2013]). The fiction lives on today (though without reference to the Nazi institute!) in J. Tabor, *The Jesus*

The genealogy contains actually seventy-eight names, including God. The names from Abraham to Adam (vv. 34-38) repeat the genealogies of Gen 5:1-32 and 11:10-26, in reverse order. The names from David to Abraham (vv. 31-34) parallel closely the same names in Matt 1:2-6, again in reverse order. The list of names from Joseph to David (vv. 23-31) is unique, however, for only two names (Zerubbabel, Shealtiel) in the Greek text of Nestle-Aland[28] match the corresponding names in Matt 1:6-16. Moreover, between Joseph and David, Matt lists twenty-four generations, whereas Luke lists forty.

The differences in Matt's and Luke's genealogies from David to Jesus perplexed the church from its earliest days. The most radical attempt to harmonize the two accounts is Codex Bezae's (5th c.) wholesale deletion of Luke's forty names and substitution in reverse order of Matt's twenty-four names. Others, such as Julius Africanus (d. ca. 250), followed by Eusebius (d. ca. 340), posit a "complicated but accurate" hypothesis that the different names derive from the practice of second marriages or Levirate marriage (whereby a man raises up children by the wife of a deceased brother).[80] This solution fails to explain why such practices did not affect the generations from Adam to David, but altered them unrecognizably from David to Joseph. The most frequent explanation of the early church was that Luke preserved Mary's genealogy from David to Joseph, whereas Matt preserved Joseph's. This is a possible explanation, but there is no extant genealogy of Mary with which to verify it. Lagrange asks fairly, "Is it proper to sacrifice the principles of normative interpretation to achieve a forced harmonization?"[81] These explanations, some plausible and others contrived, indicate that the discrepancies between the two genealogies are not easily resolved. If there were a satisfying resolution, we should expect the painstaking genealogists of the early church to have discovered it.[82]

Without presuming to resolve all discrepancies between Matt's and Luke's genealogies, I would propose the following hypothesis with reference to the most difficult of the problems, namely, Luke's omission of the name of every Davidic ruler between Jesus and David (except Zerubbabel and Shealtiel). Even Solomon is omitted. Similarly, in the sweep of salvation history in Paul's speech in Pisidian Antioch (Acts 13:16-37), Luke makes a millennial

---

Dynasty: The Hidden History of Jesus, His Royal Family, and the Birth of Christianity (New York: Simon & Schuster, 2006), 63-81.

80. Eusebius, *Hist. eccl.* 1.7. Following Africanus, Eusebius explains the different fathers of Joseph (in Matt, Jacob; in Luke, Eli) thus, "Eli and Jacob were step-brothers with the same mother. When Eli died without children, Jacob raised up seed for him, begetting Joseph as his own natural son but the legal son of Eli. Thus Joseph was the son of both" (1.7.16).

81. For a discussion and critique of this popular theory, see Lagrange, *Luc*, 118-20.

82. See the helpful discussion of Marshall, *Luke*, 157-59, who concludes, "The problem caused by the existence of two genealogies is insoluble with the evidence presently at our disposal."

leap from David (again omitting Solomon) to Jesus. In both Paul's speech and Luke's genealogy, Jesus is placed in direct relationship to David, without intervening — and unfaithful — Davidic rulers. The effect of both of these genealogical revisions is to distinguish Jesus as the only and true heir of "the throne of David his father" (1:32), who "will reign over the house of Jacob forever" (1:32).[83]

Luke ends his genealogy not simply with the first man, but with God, the "terminus beyond which there is none."[84] Luke's genealogy starts and finishes with two beginnings: Jesus as the beginning (v. 23) and God as the beginning (v. 38). The Messiah sent by God is thus not like Melchizedek, who appears mysteriously without father or mother (Gen 14:18-20; Heb 7:3), or like the savior posited by Marcion, without any human credentials by which he may be known. Jesus, rather, is a son of Adam, indeed the "last Adam" (Rom 5:14; 1 Cor 15:22, 45-49), truly human with a truly human ancestry. In tracing Jesus' ancestry through Adam to God, Luke implies that "Son of God" applies to Jesus as it did to Adam before the fall, at which point he lost the ability to pass on the honor of divine sonship to his descendents.[85] In placing the genealogy between the baptism and the temptation, Luke fully intends readers to recognize Jesus as the Son of God through Adam. But the divine sonship is transmitted through a long list of names. All human history, in fact, intervenes between Jesus' sonship (v. 23) and God's fatherhood (v. 38). In the genealogy Jesus is "the Son [who is] the firstborn among many brothers and sisters" (Rom 8:29), who stands in solidarity with humanity — sinful humanity — which he came to redeem.[86]

4:1-13   Jesus' encounter with the devil in the wilderness is a narrative without parallel in the OT, intertestamental literature, Dead Sea Scrolls, or rabbinic literature. All three Synoptic gospels position the temptation to signify a confirmation of Jesus' baptismal vocation and a prelude to his public ministry. All three Synoptics also presuppose a parallel between the testing of Jesus and the testing of Israel in the wilderness. Both tests occur in the wilderness, both

---

83. I am indebted to Wolter, *Lukasevangelium*, 175-76, for this essential hypothesis.

84. Bengel, *Gnomon*, 2:48.

85. Irenaeus, *Haer.* 3.22.3-4, cites Luke's genealogy as evidence of the doctrines of both recapitulation and regeneration. Luke's genealogy, notes Irenaeus, "connects the end with the beginning, implying that it is he who has summed up in himself all nations dispersed from Adam downwards, and all languages and generations of people, together with Adam himself. . . . Therefore Luke, commencing the genealogy with the Lord, carried it back to Adam, indicating that it was the Lord who regenerated them into the Gospel of Life, and not they him."

86. Thus Caird, *Luke*, 77-78: "By calling Adam son of God [Luke] makes a link between the baptism and God's purpose in creation. Man was designed for that close filial relationship to God which was exemplified in Jesus, and which Jesus was to share with those who became his disciples."

are about obedience, and both share the elements of hunger, bread, the number "forty," and water (Red Sea/Israelites; Jordan River/Jesus) in common.[87] Nor is the devil the protagonist of the story; indeed, the devil's name is omitted in vv. 5 and 9, where we should expect it. The temptation narrative, rather, resumes the two foci of the baptism: the direction of the Holy Spirit, and Jesus' identity as Son of God. The Spirit is twice mentioned in the first verse as the one who fills Jesus and leads him to be tested by the devil. The Greek word *peirasmos,* which can be translated either "tempt" (Jas 1:13) or "test" (Rev 2:2), is doubly appropriate in 4:1-13, for in one and the same event the devil *tempts* Jesus to defect from his divine commission, and the Holy Spirit *proves* Jesus and prepares him for it (e.g., 1 Cor 11:19).[88] Jesus is tested not because he lacks God's presence or vocation, but precisely because he possesses both through the fullness of the Holy Spirit (v. 1).[89] The Son of God is not exempt from temptation; indeed, because he does not succumb, he faces *greater* temptation than any mortal. The Spirit orchestrates the wilderness test to determine whether Jesus, the Son, will use his divine nature and power to further his own interests, or whether he will dedicate them to "the things of his Father" (2:49). The test of Jesus as the Son of God is thus a test of whether he will be the Servant of God. Lohmeyer captures this truth insightfully: "The devil addressed Jesus as the Son of God, but Jesus answered with the duties of a common man. This is the meaning of his sonship, not to stand above human beings, but to live among them; not, as God, to be different, but as a man like them to carry out his commission as the Son of God."[90]

The narrative of Jesus' testing appears in 4:1-13 and Matt 4:1-11, both of approximately the same length and in approximately the same wording. The abbreviated temptation narrative in Mark 1:12-13 cannot be the source of the same narrative in Matt and Luke, and the paucity of Hebraisms does not recommend the Hebrew Gospel as its source. The narrative appears to derive from the Double Tradition. The major difference between Luke and Matt is the order of the three temptations, which in Matt's more familiar sequence is (1) bread, (2) temple, (3) kingdoms. The inversion of the last two in Luke's narrative appears to disrupt Matt's superior sequence, where each temptation increases in importance. Luke's bread-kingdoms-temple sequence reflects his

---

87. J. Dupont, *Les tentations de Jésus au désert* (StudNeot 4; Paris: Brouwer, 1968), 20-30.

88. Plummer, *Luke,* 107. Likewise, Str-B 1:135, "In the rabbinic perspective, the purpose of trials [*Versuchungen*] is the authentication of that which is tested and the glorification of God's righteousness."

89. Schweizer, *Lukas,* 54, writes, "According to Scripture, it is precisely those who are called by God who are assailed, pulled back and forth between their God, whom they cannot deny, and the world, in which they suffer."

90. E. Lohmeyer, *Das Evangelium nach Matthäus* (KEK; Göttingen: Vandenhoeck & Ruprecht, 1956), 57.

unique theological emphasis, however. By beginning with bread and ending with the temple, "Son of God" appears in the first and last temptations in Luke (Matt's sequence omits "Son of God" in the final temptation). Perhaps more important, concluding the temptation in the temple of Jerusalem conforms with the narrative teleology of the Third Gospel, which flows irrevocably and climactically to its consummation in the temple of Jerusalem. In the central section of the Gospel, Jesus eight times declares the necessity of his going to Jerusalem (9:31, 51, 53; 13:22, 33; 17:11; 18:31; 19:28). This emphasis far exceeds that of any other Gospel. The temptation of Jesus as "Son of God" to jump from the temple prepares for a fourth and perhaps greatest test, no longer in the wilderness but in Jerusalem itself, where Jesus, the "Messiah of God," is tempted to forsake his salvific mission by coming down from the cross and saving himself (23:35).[91]

The Holy Spirit plays a more prominent role in Luke's temptation narrative than in the temptation narratives of Matt or Mark.[92] As Jesus returned from the Jordan "full of the Holy Spirit," he "was being led by the Spirit in the wilderness" to be tested (v. 1). "Was being led," imperfect passive tense in Greek, emphasizes the Spirit's purposeful intervention. "*In* the wilderness" (not "into the wilderness," Matt 4:1; Mark 1:12) recalls the nearly forty references in the Pentateuch to the temptation of the Israelites "in the wilderness." The traditional site of the temptation is the precipitous badlands to the south and east of Jerusalem, but the Greek word *erēmos* can refer to the country-side of Galilee as well (4:42). Without further identification, the site of the temptation is indeterminate. The severity of the temptation is signified by the number "forty," which in Scripture often connotes suffering.[93] The temptation begins only *after* forty days of fasting. "When the days had been completed" (v. 2) signals the transition from fasting to temptation. The Greek word for "completed," *syntelein,* meaning "to finish, accomplish, bring to completion," occurs in Luke only in the temptation narrative (4:2, 13). Temptation is normally viewed as a sign of God's absence, or an aberration of his will. Luke uses this word, however, as it is used in Gen 2:2 (LXX) of the purposive completion of creation, to consummate the commissioning of Jesus as the Son of God and the perfecting of his mission.[94]

---

91. A point well made by Tannehill, *Narrative Unity of Luke-Acts,* 59-60.

92. Jeremias, *Sprache des Lukasevangeliums,* 114-15.

93. Moses (Deut 9:9) and Elijah (1 Kgs 19:8) fasted for forty days; the flood lasted forty days and nights (Gen 7:4, 12); the Israelites wandered in the wilderness for forty years (Num 14:33; 32:13); Ezekiel must bear the iniquity of Judah for forty days (Ezek 4:6); and offenders received forty lashings as a maximum (Deut 25:1-3). See Plummer, *Luke,* 108-9.

94. Bengel, *Gnomon,* 2:50, sees the test of Jesus as a vicarious model for believers: "There is no temptation against which believers cannot both derive arms of defence, and learn the way to contend, from the temptation of our Lord."

In the temptation narrative, Luke refers to the devil as *diabolos* rather than Satan. In its verb form, *diaballein* means "to inform on" or "accuse," and in its four uses in the LXX (Dan 3:8; 6:25[24]; 2 Macc 3:11; 4 Macc 4:1) "to accuse *falsely*." *Diabolos* — the devil — is thus "the misrepresenter, the slanderer." In Judaism the devil was traditionally associated with three functions: to lead people astray, accuse them wrongly before God, and cause death as the punishment for sin.[95] In the temptation narrative, only the first of these functions is apparent. Otherwise, the devil appears to befriend Jesus, even advocate his cause. The devil of the temptation does not fulfill the diabolical stereotype of hideousness, terrible evil, and destructive cruelty. The devil does not make the earth ugly or bad, but more agreeable. The enticements are deceptive, however, for by nature the devil is and can only be the adversary of God.

The first temptation addresses Jesus at his point of obvious need — his hunger. "If you are the Son of God, tell this stone to become bread" (v. 3). In Greek, "Son of God" is anarthrous, and thus sometimes taken to imply that Jesus was *a* son of God rather than *the* Son of God in an ontological sense. This conclusion is unsustainable on grammatical grounds, for in Koine Greek a definite predicate nominative omits the article when it precedes the verb, as it does in vv. 3, 9.[96] The Son of God tempted in the wilderness is the same Son of God baptized at the Jordan. Geldenhuys suggests that "if" intends to cast doubt in Jesus' mind whether he is God's Son,[97] but that seems unlikely in light of the baptism. Following his momentous experience at the Jordan, Jesus can be in no doubt that he is God's Son. The devil thus affirms Jesus' divine sonship, but tempts him to deploy it for purposes other than God's will. The three temptations do not entice Jesus to do things we normally associate with sin; indeed, the first and second — to provide bread and to promote the Son of God to earthly rule — seem especially reasonable. Origen understood the reasonableness of the temptation: "Since he had taken on flesh, the Lord was tempted first with every temptation that men were to be tempted with."[98] The

---

95. Str-B 1:139. See O. Böcher, *diabolos, EDNT* 1:297-98.

96. E. C. Colwell, "A Definite Rule for the Use of the Article in the Greek New Testament," *JBL* 52 (1933): 12-21; R. Bratcher, "A Note on *Huios Theou* in Mark 15:39," *ExpTim* 80 (1968): 27-28. The attempt of E. S. Johnson Jr, "Is Mark 15:39 the Key to Mark's Christology?" *JSNT* 31 (1987): 4-7, to refute Colwell's rule is unsuccessful, for although there are some exceptions, as there are to any grammatical rule, a high percentage of cases supports Colwell's rule — and *all* uses of Son of God in the Gospels support it. When *huios* ("son") or *huios theou* ("Son of God") precedes the verb in the Gospels, it is always anarthrous (Matt 4:3; 8:29; 14:33; 27:40, 43; 27:54; Mark 5:7; 15:39; Luke 1:35; 4:3, 9; 8:28); and when the substantive follows the verb, it takes the definite article (Matt 3:17; 11:27; 16:16; 17:5; 21:37; 26:63; Luke 3:22; 4:41; 9:35; 10:22; 20:13; 22:70).

97. Geldenhuys, *Luke,* 159.

98. Origen, *Hom. Luc.* 29.3. Origen continues, "If the Son of God is God made man for

restraint and focus of Jesus in response to the temptation is instructive. He does not exert his superior power or expose the devil's deception. He invokes the Word of God, thus obliging the devil to face his ultimate adversary. "It is written, 'People do not live on bread alone.'" "It is written" is a technical expression implying the full authority of God.[99] The quotation agrees verbatim with Deut 8:3, in which Moses reminded the Israelites in the wilderness that they should trust God's word rather than the manna he gave them.[100] The Word of God is to Jesus what bread is to a human being (see John 4:34).

The second temptation is a spectacular contrast to the mundane offer of bread. Jesus is promised absolute earthly power if he will worship the devil (vv. 5-7). The omission of the setting on "a very high mountain" (see Matt 4:8),[101] and especially the reference to "in an instant" (Gk. lit. "in a moment of time"), implies something visionary or imaginary. It is thus more spiritual than the physical version of the temptation in Matt 4:8-9.[102] The devil shows Jesus "all the kingdoms of the inhabited earth" *(oikoumenē),* much like God displayed the Promised Land to Moses from Mount Nebo (Deut 34:1-4). Luke enhances the grandeur of the temptation by noting "all the authority and splendor" of the kingdoms (v. 6). The temptation begins and ends with emphatic promises: "To you I will give it. . . . It will all be yours" (vv. 6-7). The devil makes five references to himself, and three to Jesus, but none to God. In resisting this temptation, Jesus rejects the traditional Jewish concept of a messianic earthly ruler.[103] Significantly, *oikoumenē* ("inhabited world") in v. 5 recalls the same word used to describe the rule of Caesar Augustus (2:1). According to the second temptation, Caesar's claim — or any claim — to absolute political authority looks like a

---

you, and is tempted, then you, who are man by nature, should not complain if perhaps you are tempted" (29.6).

99. On this expression, see at 2:23.

100. Several important manuscripts, including A, D, Θ, Ψ, append the remaining words of Deut 8:3 to the quotation, "but on every word that comes from the mouth of God." The addition is probably an assimilation to Matt 4:4. See Metzger, *TCGNT,* 113.

101. The addition of this phrase in A, Θ, Ψ, D, W, and ℵ[1] is probably also an assimilation to Matt 4:8. Five patristic references in the Hebrew Gospel to the seizure of Jesus by the maternal Holy Spirit and his being taken to a high mountain are often considered relevant to the second temptation (third in Matthew); see Origen, *Comm. Jo.* 2.12.87; *Hom. Jer.* 15.4; Jerome, *Comm. Mich.* 7:7; *Comm. Isa.* 40:9-11; *Comm. Ezech.* 16:13. Several of the texts identify Mount Tabor as the site of the temptation. See the discussion of this site at 9:28-36. Also Edwards, *Hebrew Gospel,* 56-59.

102. *2 Bar.* 76:3 contains a similar vision: "Therefore, go up to the top of this mountain, and all countries of this earth will pass before you, as well as the likeness of the inhabited world, and the top of the mountains, and the depths of the valleys, and the depths of the seas, and the number of rivers, so that you may see that which you leave and whither you go."

103. Geldenhuys, *Luke,* 162.

diabolical claim.[104] The devil claims this authority has been given to him by God (v. 6) and thus presumes to commandeer God's authority to decide and divide. In one sense this is true, for the devil exercises real power in this world (e.g., John 14:30). But ultimately it is not true, for the devil's power is not equal to God's, but entirely subordinate to it. The devil possesses power only as long as the sovereignty of God allows.[105] The devil promises "a religious experience" to those who worship him (v. 7). The devil parades as "an angel of light" (2 Cor 11:14), and hence satanic influence extends beyond the mundane world to the spiritual world as well. Worship per se is thus not necessarily a Christian activity. The one proper worship response is to "worship the Lord your God and serve him only" (v. 8). This is a quotation from Deut 6:13 (also 10:20), but Luke and Matt 4:10 both alter it, first by substituting "worship" *(proskynein)* for "fear" *(phobeisthai),* doubtless because of the specific temptation to worship a false god rather than the one true God. Second, "only" is inserted into the quotation, most likely as a result of Jesus' uncompromising emphasis on worship of God alone (e.g., Exod 20:3).[106]

Luke's third and final temptation concludes in Jerusalem, which exerts a strong gravitational pull throughout the Third Gospel.[107] Matt 4:5 places this temptation second, identifying the site simply as "the holy city," but for Luke the temptation in the temple forms the climax of the temptation narrative. The word for "temple," *hieron,* denotes the entire temple complex rather than the central sanctuary *(naos).* Concrete imagery replaces the conceptual imagery of the second temptation. Jesus is placed on the *pterygion* of the temple, a Greek word that literally means "wing"; the *pterygion* of the temple is thus its highest and most exposed point, its "pinnacle" or "edge." From "the wing

---

104. See Green, *Luke,* 194.

105. See Kazuhiko Yamazaki-Ransom, *The Roman Empire in Luke's Narrative* (LNTS 404; New York: T&T Clark, 2010), 95-97.

106. Bengel, *Gnomon,* 2:50, notes the subtlety in the devil's promise: "This assertion [vv. 6-7] is not altogether false. Satan had great power before his fall: and the portion of power which he retains since his fall, he turns to evil account. The Tempter confesses that he is not the founder or creator of these kingdoms. Therefore he did not demand the highest degree of adoration or worship; and yet Jesus shows that even an inferior degree of worship cannot be given to any creature, much less to Satan."

107. See the excursus "The Mission of Jesus as the Way of Salvation" at 9:51. The spelling of "Jerusalem," *Ierousalēm,* corresponds to the Hebraic spelling of the city, as is usual in Luke. Matt. 4:5 reads "holy city" rather than "Jerusalem," but Codex 566 contains the following scholion at Matt 4:5: "The Jewish [Gospel] does not read 'into the holy city,' but 'in Jerusalem.'" The "Jewish [Gospel]" was identified by Constantin Tischendorf, *Notitia editionis codicis bibliorum sinaitici* (Leipzig: F. A. Brockhaus, 1860), 58, as "no other source than the gospel of the Hebrews . . . that celebrated writing." This is one of several examples of a later editor (or editors) correcting canonical Greek Matthew with readings from the Hebrew Gospel, which Luke ostensibly preserves.

of the temple" James the Just was thrown to his death in A.D. 62, according to Hegesippus.[108] The precise extremity of the temple is not identifiable, but the definite article suggests an obvious point. The most obvious point from which to throw a person to his death would be the southeast corner of the temple, which plunges 150 feet (45 m) to the Kidron Valley.[109] Jesus is commanded, "If you are the Son of God, throw yourself down from here" (v. 9). Jesus is again addressed as "the Son of God," with the assurance from Ps 91:11-12 that God's angels will protect him from injury. The devil, like heretics, said Origen, is quick to quote Scripture. "Whenever you hear quotations from the Scriptures, be careful of trusting the speaker immediately. Consider the person: what sort of a life he leads, what sort of opinions he holds, what sort of intention he has. Otherwise, he might pretend that he is holy and not be holy."[110] The final temptation is a plea for Jesus to promote his divine sonship by means of a spectacle or sensation. For the third and final time, Jesus counters the devil with the authority of Scripture, "Do not put the Lord your God to the test" (Deut 6:16). Jesus appeals to God as *kyrios,* "Lord." The devil may quote Scripture, but Jesus is *bound* to Scripture because it is the expressed will of the sovereign Lord.[111]

The temptation concludes in v. 13, the Greek of which emphasizes the comprehensive nature of the ordeal to which Jesus has been subjected, "When the devil finished *every* temptation" (in contrast to NIV "When the devil had finished all this tempting"). Especially in the Jewish world the number three signified completeness, totality, finality, and that significance is intended in the threefold temptation narrative.[112] In the three temptations, says Bengel, the devil "expended all his weapons of offence."[113] The temptations to provide for bodily necessities, assume cosmocratic authority, and prove oneself through spectacular signs are in one degree or another common to all human temptations. The first Adam succumbed to temptation, but the Second Adam, who was tested far more exhaustively and severely, emerged victorious.[114] Having done so, Jesus embarks on his public ministry "in the power of the Spirit"

---

108. Eusebius, *Hist. eccl.* 2.23.11.

109. For a full note on the term, see Wolter, *Lukasevangelium,* 183. Josephus, *Ant.* 15.412, describes the height as "dizzying."

110. Origen, *Hom. Luc.* 31.3.

111. So J. Bieneck, *Sohn Gottes als Christusbezeichnung der Synoptiker* (Zürich: Zwingli Verlag, 1951), 64.

112. G. Delling, *treis, TWNT* 8:221.

113. Bengel, *Gnomon,* 2:50.

114. So Geldenhuys, *Luke,* 158, "Although [Jesus] had found Himself in the most un-favourable circumstances when the devil launched his most ruthless attacks against Him, He was nevertheless victorious. What a contrast this forms with Adam, who fell although he was living at that time under the most favourable circumstances."

(v. 14). The devil has not yet been vanquished, however. A temporal, though not final, victory has been achieved, for a final temptation awaits him in the passion in Jerusalem (22:53; 23:35-37).[115]

The temptation narrative, as noted earlier, has no parallel in Jewish tradition. Jewish tradition, of course, knew of satanic temptation, but not of the temptation of Messiah.[116] The fact that no known prototype of the temptation of Jesus exists makes it unlikely that the temptation narrative was a later Christian invention.[117] The quotations from Deut 6 and 8 provide readers with a hermeneutical key to understand Jesus' temptation in light of Israel's temptation, but they do not supply a genre for the temptation narrative as a whole. Jesus himself is the only plausible source of the narrative. Many modern readers, including modern Christians, find talk of the devil intellectually embarrassing. As a consequence, the temptation is commonly interpreted metaphorically. Ancient Jews, however, believed in an evil force, both superhuman and personal, that contended with and distorted God's created ideal. They believed this power to be real, although not ultimate. We know that Jesus shared this belief, and we cannot doubt that Luke shared it. The temptation narrative is not presented as a dream, vision, myth, or parable, but as a historical occurrence in which an intentional and deadly earnest personification of evil attempts, using both natural and supernatural means, to mislead the incarnate Son of God from his salvific mission in the world.[118]

115. H. Conzelmann, *Die Mitte der Zeit* (6th ed.; BHT 17; Tübingen: Mohr Siebeck, 1977), 22, understood this phrase to signify a "Satan-free epoch" in which Jesus could carry out his ministry. This does not seem to represent Luke's intent. Throughout his ministry, Jesus encounters individuals (8:2; 13:16; Acts 10:38; 26:18) who are oppressed by Satan. The incarnation succeeds in this world not because Satan is absent but because Jesus is "the stronger one" who vanquishes the enemy (3:16; 11:21-22).

116. R. Bultmann, *The History of the Synoptic Tradition* (trans. J. Marsh; New York: Harper & Row, 1972), 256-57.

117. Bultmann, *The History of the Synoptic Tradition*, 254-55, postulates that the temptation was fashioned from rabbinic disputations, although he cannot say what is asserted and defended in the disputation!

118. Lagrange, *Luc*, 134.

CHAPTER FOUR

Beginnings of the Galilean Ministry

Luke 4:14–5:11

JESUS DELIVERS THE KEYNOTE ADDRESS
OF HIS MINISTRY (4:14-30)

The most frequent way in which divine revelation is expressed in Scripture is not in visions or wondrous works but in prophetic proclamation of the word of God. Luke begins the public ministry of Jesus with such a procla-mation, which, like its OT counterparts, is equally revelatory. The Synoptic Gospels often refer to Jesus as a teacher, and they frequently preserve ex-amples of his teachings, sayings, and parables. 4:16-30 is the only summary report of a sermon of Jesus in the Gospels, however. The sermon occurs in a typical worship service; indeed, 4:16-30 is the earliest known account of a Jewish synagogue service.[1] The sermon contains two elements character-istic of the angelic pronouncements in the infancy narrative: the citation of an OT promise, and an identification of its fulfillment. In commencing Jesus' public ministry in a synagogue, Luke reinforces the leitmotif of the Gospel, that the history of salvation is to be found in the history of Israel. "Israel" is not coterminous with "Jews," however. It includes them, of course, for the history began in the call to Abraham and was carried forth in his Jewish descendents. It was not limited to them, however, but was destined through them to include "all peoples on earth" (Gen 12:1-3). The history of salvation in Israel thus commences with the saving line of Jews and ends with its extension to all nations, Gentiles. Both Jews and Gentiles are thus divinely ordained constituents of "Israel." This point is made gravely clear in Jesus' citation of two models of faith in the OT, the widow of Zarephath and Naaman the Syrian, both of whom were Gentiles. By identifying Gentiles as models of faith in a sermon to Jews, Jesus made the revolutionary point that salvation is not limited for Jews, but also includes Gentiles. The sermon in Nazareth effectively anchors the Gentile mission, not in the later conversion

---

1. Marshall, *Luke,* 181.

of Cornelius (Acts 10), as often supposed, but in the initial proclamation of the gospel by Jesus himself.[2] The inaugural sermon in Nazareth sets forth major theological and missional themes contained in Luke-Acts, and the rejection of Jesus at Nazareth over "the Gentile question" in the Gospel sets the stage for Paul's rejection on the same grounds in Acts.

14-15   Jesus returns from the temptation in the wilderness not as a limping survivor, but "in the power of the Spirit" (v. 14), as the righteous one vindicated by God (2 Pet 2:9). Fidelity to the divine will does not leave one depleted and exhausted, but spiritually empowered.[3] In the infancy narrative the Holy Spirit was active *through* Zechariah (1:67), John (1:15), Elizabeth (1:41), Mary (1:35), and Simeon (2:25) so that the Spirit might be active *in* Jesus the Son of God in his conception (1:35), baptism (3:22), temptation (4:1), and public ministry (4:18). First-century Jews believed that the Holy Spirit ceased speaking directly to God's people at the end of the prophetic era in Israel (see at 3:22). In Jesus the power and righteousness of the Spirit are again active in the world to consummate the divine will. John left human society and went out into the wilderness (3:3-7); the Spirit returns Jesus from the wilderness to human society, to "Galilee . . . and through the whole countryside" (v. 14). The Greek word for "countryside," *perichōros,* repeats the same word of 3:3, which in Gen 13:10 (LXX) describes the land of Sodom that was chosen by Lot. This territory, which had become a byword of depravity and divine wrath, is the starting point of Jesus' redemptive ministry. His ministry consisted of itinerant "teaching in their synagogues." The reference to "*their* synagogues" (v. 15) occurs only this once in Luke, but its repeated use in Mark (1:23, 39) and especially Matt (4:23; 9:35; 10:17; 12:9; 13:54: 23:34) suggests a certain distance between Jesus and the synagogue.[4]

The Greek imperfect tense *edidasken* ("he was teaching") connotes the central role that **teaching** played in Jesus' ministry. Moderns are often more impressed by acts of compassion or ministries of "presence" than they are by teaching and preaching. In Luke's theology of the word, teaching and proclamation are the essential forms of divine revelation. A good deed, even miracle, can be misunderstood; and even if properly understood may not evoke a commitment. Teaching involves a word. A word is capable of greater precision and penetration than any other symbol of reality. God created all things by

---

2. J. Siker, " 'First to the Gentiles': A Literary Analysis of Luke 4:16-30," *JBL* 111/1 (1992): 73-90.

3. Origen, *Hom. Luc.* 32.1, comments on Jesus' empowerment by the Spirit thus: "When [Jesus] fought and overcame the three temptations . . . then see what is written of the Spirit, emphatically and carefully. The passage says, 'Jesus returned in the power of the Spirit.' 'Power' has been added, because he had trodden down the dragon and conquered the tempter in hand-to-hand combat."

4. Jeremias, *Sprache des Lukasevangeliums,* 119.

the word, brought Israel into existence and sustained it through the prophetic word, and through Jesus, who both *is* the Word of God and *declares* the word of God, God offers salvation to all. Through the word of Jesus, God speaks; and through Jesus as both the speech and act of God, hearers *communicate* — literally, they are built up and fortified — with God.[5]

16-24   3:1–9:50 consists primarily of Markan material that Luke has taken over and both augmented and expanded by material from the Hebrew Gospel and the Double Tradition. Included in Luke's reliance on Mark is his general adherence to Mark's sequence of events. Both Mark and Matt set Jesus' visit to Nazareth near the midpoint of his career, but Luke, in his most striking departure from Mark's narrative sequence, places the sermon in Nazareth at the outset of Jesus' ministry. The many Hebraisms in 4:16-30 attest to the Lukan expansion of Mark 6:1-6 with material from the Hebrew Gospel.[6] Luke has not disguised his transposition of the Nazareth narrative, for the first mention of Capernaum, in 4:23, assumes a prior ministry of Jesus there. The bold repositioning of Jesus' sermon in Nazareth, and its dramatic expansion in comparison with its parallels in Mark 6:1-6 and Matt 13:54-58, distinguishes it as the programmatic cornerstone of Jesus' ministry. The literary artistry of the sermon is as evident as is its placement. Luke narrates the sermon in a series of parallel phrases that climax in the central declaration, "The Spirit of the Lord is on me."

> A   into the synagogue (v. 16)
>   B   he stood up to read (v. 16)
>   C   the scroll was handed to him (v. 17)
>   D   [he unrolled] the scroll (v. 17)
>   E   "The Spirit of the Lord is upon me" (v. 18).
>   D[1] he rolled up the scroll (v. 20)
>   C[1] he gave [the scroll] back (v. 20)
>   B[1] he sat down (v. 20)
> A[1] in the synagogue (v. 20).[7]

Unlike modern crescendos that climax in the last expression, the "chiastic" structure places the key idea or term in the middle, to which foregoing statements proceed and from which subsequent ones recede.

The Greek *ēn tethrammenos* (v. 16; NIV "brought up") confirms what readers of the infancy narrative already know, that Jesus was "born and

---

5. On the word of God in Luke, see Bovon, *Lukas 1,1–9,50*, 230-31.

6. See Edwards, *Hebrew Gospel*, 300-301.

7. On the chiastic structure, see J. Siker, "'First to the Gentiles': A Literary Analysis of Luke 4:16-30," *JBL* 111/1 (1992): 76-79.

raised" in Nazareth (1:26; 2:4, 39, 51; Acts 7:21; 22:3).[8] Jesus was not returning to Nazareth as a visitor, but as a native son who knew Nazareth better than it knew him. The **synagogue** was the religious, social, and educational nucleus of a Jewish community. Unlike the temple in Jerusalem, where animals were sacrificed on the altar by priests, Jewish synagogues, according to rabbinic nomenclature, were "assembly halls" or auditoriums, which functioned primarily as worship centers where Torah was read and expounded, and secondarily as community centers, guesthouses, and perhaps schools for children. There was but one temple in Jerusalem, whereas synagogues, the Greek derivation of which simply means "gathering places," could be found throughout the Mediterranean world wherever ten or more Jewish males, thirteen years of age or older, were present. Synagogues abounded in first-century Galilee and have been excavated in Nazareth, Capernaum, Bethsaida, Chorazin, Gennesaret, Magdala, and Gamla.[9] The official in charge of a synagogue was the "ruler of the synagogue," a position that included the responsibilities of librarian, worship committee, custodian, and perhaps schoolteacher. The ruler of the synagogue did not preach or expound Torah, however, which meant that Sabbath teaching and exposition fell to the laity, and on this occasion to Jesus.

A typical Jewish synagogue was outfitted with benches around its perimeter where women were separated from men, and where the latter were seated according to rank and importance. Candlesticks, musical instruments (esp. horns and trumpets), and floor coverings were standard decor in synagogues. A Torah cupboard and a podium, both elevated on a dais, commanded the focal point near the front and center of the synagogue. During worship, a Torah scroll was first produced from the Torah chest, followed by a scroll from the prophets, both of which were read aloud from the adjacent podium (Acts 13:15). Scripture was read from a standing position, but the expository sermon that followed was delivered from a seated position. A minister (Heb. *hasan hakeneset*; Gk. *hypēretēs*) who retrieved scrolls from the Torah cupboard and returned them to it presided over the service. Scripture readings were not the prerogative of particular individuals or officers, but could be assigned to any member of the congregation, including minors.[10] The narrative in v. 17

---

8. On Nazareth, see at 1:26. Wolter, *Lukasevangelium,* 190, describes *ēn tethrammenos* as "a technical biographical expression that includes the span of life from nursing infant to adulthood."

9. The vast majority of Judean Jews resettled in the north after the two Jewish Revolts of 66-70 and 132-35, increasing both the number and significance of Galilean synagogues.

10. On synagogues and their services, see S. Cohen, *From the Maccabees to the Mishnah* (LEC; Philadelphia: Westminster Press, 1987), 111-15; G. Moore, *Judaism in the First Centuries of the Christian Era* (New York: Schocken, 1971), 1:29-36, 281-307; Str-B 4/1:115-88; Schürer, *History of the Jewish People,* 2:423-54; Klein, *Lukasevangelium,* 187-88; E. Meyers and M. Chancey,

commences between the reading of Torah and prophets, and preserves key liturgical elements — standing to read, unrolling the scroll,[11] services of the minister, and seated proclamation — in their proper order. Jesus' keynote address, in other words, is not delivered in an elite Qumran worship service or experimental service of the heterodox Samaritan Jews, but in a mainline Jewish synagogue.

There is no evidence that Jewish lectionary readings were prescribed as early as the first century. V. 17 therefore probably implies that Jesus personally chose the reading from Isa 61:1-2. Commentators often point to the importance of Isa 61 at Qumran, claiming it was applied to the Teacher of Righteousness (1QH 18:14) or cited with reference to the year of jubilee (11QMelch = 11Q13). Both Qumran texts make only faint and passing references to Isa 61, however, as does rabbinic literature as a whole.[12] Isa 61, along with the Servant of the Lord texts (Isa 42:1-4; 49:1-6; 52:13–53:12), are widely read by Christians as self-evident messianic texts, but they were not considered so in Judaism. In Judaism then, as now, the exposition of these texts was infrequent and unremarkable.[13] In reading from Isa 61, Jesus selected a text about an enigmatic Servant uniquely possessed by God's Spirit that carried no particular messianic associations in the ears of his hearers.[14] He immediately applied this text to himself in a one-line sermon, "Today this scripture is fulfilled in your hearing." The first word of Jesus' public ministry is not his own word, but a prophetic word from Scripture proclaiming Israel's Spirit-filled Redeemer. The reference to "scripture" (Gk. *graphē*) appears in Luke only here and in the vocabulary of Jesus as resurrected Lord. In both instances Jesus declares himself the *fulfillment* of Scripture, and in the resurrection discourse its authoritative *interpreter* (24:27), who opens the eyes of the disciples to understand its fulfillment in him (24:32, 44-45).

Alexander to Constantine: Archaeology of the Land of the Bible (New Haven: Yale University Press, 2012), 203-38.

11. Several weighty manuscripts (A, B, L, W, Ξ) read "opened" *(anoixas)* rather than "unrolled" *(anaptyxas)* in v. 17, but the former is probably an explanatory substitution of a later era when the codex had replaced the scroll in liturgical worship. See Metzger, *TCGNT,* 114.

12. On its paucity in rabbinic literature, see Str-B 2:156. Isa 61:1-2 is expressly attributed to Jesus, the Servant of the Lord, in *Barn.* 15.9, however.

13. The lack of evidence of an ancient Jewish messianic understanding of the Servant of the Lord passages is discussed in Schürer, *History of the Jewish People,* 2:547-49. The exposition of these same texts remains unremarkable in contemporary Judaism. A. Heschel's otherwise important study of prophecy does not mention Isa. 61:1-2 in his chap. "Second Isaiah" (*The Prophets* [New York: Harper Torchbooks, 1969], 1:145-58); and to the figure of the Suffering Servant, Heschel devotes three brief and nondescript paragraphs.

14. C. Westermann, *Isaiah 40–66: A Commentary* (trans. D. Stalker; Philadelphia: Westminster Press, 1969), 367, writes of Isa 61, "To the best of our knowledge, this was the last occasion in the history of Israel on which a prophet expressed his certainty of having been sent by God with a message to his nation with such freedom and conviction."

Luke has made repeated references in the infancy, baptismal, and temptation narratives to the Spirit's preparation for Jesus as Messiah and Son of God. At the outset of his ministry Jesus acknowledges and appropriates God's endowment of himself: "The Spirit of the Lord is on me." The text of Isa 61:1-2 quoted in vv. 18-19 closely follows the LXX, although "binding up the brokenhearted" has been omitted, and a line from Isa 58:6, "to set the oppressed free," has been added. These changes probably derive from the hand of Luke.[15] The Isaiah quotation defines the one on whom the Spirit rests by two main verbs: "anointed" and "sent." The anointing and sending of the Spirit-filled Servant is further elaborated in a series of infinitives: "to bring good news to the poor," "to proclaim remission to captives," "to send the wounded away in freedom," and "to proclaim the year of the Lord's favor." A text from Qumran ascribes a similar list of ministries — "freeing prisoners, giving sight to the blind, straightening out the twisted" — not to Messiah or the Servant of the Lord, but to the "Lord God" (4Q521). Jesus, in other words, applies a text to himself that the Qumran Covenanters applied only to God. The effect of the eight-line quotation is to assert that the Servant, with whom Jesus self-identifies, has been anointed by the Spirit and sent to proclaim the evangelical, forgiving, and liberating *word* of God.[16] The first word of the gospel is thus not a moral command or obligation to work harder and do more, but a proclamation of what God in grace has already done for the world in Jesus Christ. It is *good news!*

When Jesus finished reading, "the eyes of everyone in the synagogue were fastened on him" (v. 20). This literary interlude creates masterful suspense. The Greek word for "fastened," *atenizein,* a favorite Lukan expression, denotes looking to someone in expectant trust.[17] If the first word of Jesus' public ministry is a quotation of Scripture, his first word of interpretation is about

---

15. For a full discussion of the whole quotation, see Tannehill, *Narrative Unity of Luke-Acts,* 62-68.

16. Luke may have intended the saving benefits of the Messiah in Isa 61 to counteract the propaganda campaign of Augustus Caesar. Note the similarity of some claims of Augustus: "This [Augustus] is the Caesar who calmed the torrential storms on every side, who healed the pestilences common to Greeks and barbarians, pestilences which descending from the south and east coursed to the west and north sowing the seeds of calamity over the places and waters which lay between. This is he who not only loosed but broke the chains which had shackled and pressed so hard on the habitable world. This is he who exterminated wars both of the open kind and the covert which are brought about by the raids of brigands. This is he who cleared the sea of pirate ships and filled it with merchant vessels. This is he who reclaimed every state to liberty, who led disorder into order and brought gentle manners and harmony to all unsociable and brutish nations. . . . He was also the first and the greatest and the common benefactor" (Philo, *Embassy* 145-49).

17. D. Hill, "The Rejection of Jesus at Nazareth," in Orton, *Composition of Luke's Gospel,* 24.

himself as its fulfillment, "Today this scripture is fulfilled in your hearing" (v. 21). The angelic announcement to the shepherds began on the same note of fulfillment, "Today a savior was born to you, who is Christ the Lord" (2:11). The final word of Jesus to the disciples in 24:44 will repeat the same theme: "Everything must be fulfilled that is written about me in the Law of Moses, the Prophets, and the Psalms." Jesus' life and proclamation are not novel and innovative. They are — and are only understandable as — the expression and fulfillment of the will of the Father attested in Scripture.[18] The one new thing in Jesus' message is *today*. What until now had been potential, promise, hope, and long-awaited, is at this moment present reality. Jesus' interpretation of Isa 61 is a four-word summary of salvation history: "Today Scripture is fulfilled" (v. 21).[19] It is not fulfilled in abstraction, however, but "in your hearing" (v. 21), as a prophetic call of Jesus for listening ears and responsive hearts.[20]

Rarely does a sermon — especially a one-line sermon — elicit such response. On the one hand, there is bated expectation following the reading of Isaiah (v. 20), and praise and amazement "at the gracious words that come from [Jesus'] lips" (v. 22). But there may also be apprehension — not unlike the disquiet of Zechariah (1:18-20) and Mary (1:29) at the divine announcements of Gabriel. "Isn't this Joseph's son?" (v. 22). The question, which mentions Joseph for the last time in the Third Gospel,[21] can be understood in different ways. "Son of Joseph" is a human rather than a christological title, as is "Son of God" (1:35; 3:22). This is not inherently pejorative, for readers of the Third Gospel are privileged with knowledge of Jesus that the townspeople do not have. If Mary kept Jesus' divine sonship to herself (2:51), and if the heavenly voice addressed Jesus alone in the baptismal declaration (3:22), then the townspeople would not have known of Jesus' divine sonship. "Isn't this Joseph's son?" could be taken as an expression of marvel, in concert with the preceding amazement of the crowd. But it could also be defamatory, especially if townspeople suspect that Jesus has presumed "to rise above his circumstances." The antagonistic response of Jesus in vv. 23-24 implies a deeper division between Jesus and the townspeople than we would perceive from their comment, which suggests that

---

18. Irenaeus, *Haer.* 4.23, cites Luke 4:18 as a proof text that the patriarchs and prophets point to Jesus Christ, apart from whom Christ would not be intelligible.

19. The significance of "today" is esp. developed by Schweizer, *Lukas,* 58-60.

20. Green, *Luke,* 214.

21. Joseph was probably older than Mary, and he probably predeceased her by many years. J. Reed, "Instability in Jesus' Galilee: A Demographic Perspective," *JBL* 129/2 (2010): 365, comments on life expectancies in first-c. Galilee thus: "The traditional picture of a young Mary and elderly Joseph who later disappears in the Gospels is absolutely unremarkable in actuarial terms. Men were often much older than their wives, almost no children ever knew their grandfathers; and few adults had fathers who were still alive. It is not odd that the Gospels do not speculate on Joseph's fate; it was assumed that he had passed away."

"Isn't this Joseph's son?" was intended to disparage rather than celebrate Jesus. The NIV subtitles this unit "Jesus Rejected at Nazareth," but the text suggests that Jesus also rejected Nazareth.

Origen, typically, interpreted the conflict allegorically, with Nazareth representing Jews; and Capernaum, Gentiles. Since Jews rejected the prophets, apostles, and Jesus himself, Jesus rejected them in favor of the Gentiles.[22] Joachim Jeremias hypothesized that the Nazarenes were offended because Jesus omitted the all-important final line from the Isaiah quotation, "the day of the vengeance of our God." According to Jeremias, the day of God's vengeance was reserved for Gentiles, and by omitting that line and concluding the quotation with the "year of the Lord's favor," Jesus blessed, rather than cursed, Gentiles. Hence, the displeasure of his Jewish hearers.[23] Enthusiasm for this interpretation outstrips evidence for it, however.[24] "Day of vengeance" is probably a circumlocution for "Day of Yahweh" (Isa 2:12; Joel 2:1-11; Amos 5:18-27), which is certainly not reserved exclusively for Israel's foes.[25] Moreover, the response of Jesus in vv. 23-24 makes no reference to Jews or Gentiles. Somewhat more plausible is Bargil Pixner's suggestion that, in moving to Capernaum, Jesus had violated his kinship bond with the Nazarene clan and, in consequence, reaped their animosity.[26] The taunt of the Nazarenes to "do here in your hometown what we have heard that you did in Capernaum" (v. 23) could support Pixner's thesis. However, it was not uncommon for young men to leave their hometowns, and there is no evidence that those who did were considered to have betrayed kinship allegiances.[27] None of the above suggestions adequately explains the conflict between Jesus and his hometown.

The text suggests that Jesus, not the villagers, provoked the crisis. The Nazarenes admired Jesus (v. 22), but their admiration was tempered by skepticism. Jesus was born and raised in Nazareth (v. 16; Gk. *ēn tethrammenos*), and he knows what his fellow Nazarenes are thinking before they say it. "Surely

---

22. Origen, *Hom. Luc.* 33.1.

23. J. Jeremias, *Jesus' Promise to the Nations* (SBT 24; London: SCM Press, 1954), 44-45.

24. Kenneth Bailey follows Jeremias in *Jesus through Middle Eastern Eyes,* 155. In equating the Nazarenes with the attitudes and actions of modern Jewish "settlers" in Israel, Bailey imposes a very questionable cultural hermeneutic on Luke 4:16-30.

25. Claus Westermann, *Isaiah 40–66: A Commentary* (trans. D. M. G. Stalker; Philadelphia: Westminster Press, 1969), 367.

26. Pixner, *With Jesus through Galilee,* 59.

27. Mobility of young males in first-c. Galilee was common for a variety of reasons: to find work (e.g., fishing on the Sea of Galilee or working in Antipas's massive construction projects at Sepphoris and Tiberias [Josephus, *Ant.* 18.37]); to attend rabbinic schools or to join the various Essene communities, esp. at Qumran; to find a marriageable woman; or as seems most common, to relocate in Jerusalem (Acts 2:41-47; 5:42–6:6; Jas 1:27). See J. Reed, "Instability in Jesus' Galilee: A Demographic Perspective," *JBL* 129/2 (2010): 343-65.

you *will* quote this proverb to me" (v. 23), he says. The two sayings he quotes to them, "Physician, heal yourself!" (v. 23) and "Prophets are not accepted in their hometowns" (v. 24) are not situation-specific. They are general proverbs that were widespread in Judaism and beyond, both of which pertain to the rejection of prophets and sages.[28] This suggests that the conflict in Nazareth is not related to a specific grievance. Rather, the Nazarenes' response to Jesus is a microcosm of the chronic hardness of Israel's heart to the prophets. Like Israel's prophets, Jesus names the thoughts and intentions that barricade hearts from a proper understanding of God's saving grace.[29]

25-30   Jesus does not attempt to mollify the Nazarenes. The preface of v. 25, "I assure you" (Gk. lit. "I tell you the truth"), signals the importance of what follows in the stories of Elijah (1 Kgs 17) and Elisha (2 Kgs 5). Both stories make three crucial points that the Nazarenes must understand if they are to accept Jesus' ministry. First, the presumption that salvation is the exclusive privilege of Israel is revoked in both illustrations. "There were many widows in Israel in Elijah's time. . . . Yet Elijah was not sent to any of them" (vv. 25-26); "there were many in Israel with leprosy in the time of Elisha the prophet, yet not one of them was cleansed" (v. 27). Israelites — very needy Israelites who were starving and suffering and afflicted with leprosy — were passed over in favor of others. Jesus thus echoes the earlier warning of John that Jews should not presume on God's favor by saying, "We have Abraham as our father" (3:8). Second, Israelites were passed over for Gentiles. Elijah was sent to a widow "in the region of Sidon"; and Elisha, to Naaman "the Syrian." Not only were the widow and Naaman Gentiles, they were from regions historically hostile to and loathed by Israel. At the time Elisha was sent to Naaman, the latter was a Syrian general *besieging* Israel. Third and finally, Jesus is not citing an abnormality in Israel's history, but God's will. "Elijah *was sent*" and "Naaman the Syrian *was cleansed*." Both references are "divine passives," i.e., ways of referring to the activity of God without using God's name (for fear of profaning it).

The widow of Zarephath and Naaman the Syrian illustrate the Isaiah text that Jesus just read in the synagogue: they are the poor who receive good news, the captives released, the blind whose sight is restored, the beneficiaries of "the year of the Lord's favor" (v. 19). Most Jews of Jesus' day identified themselves — not Gentiles — as the poor and oppressed to whom God shows favor. The widow of Zarephath and Naaman the Syrian emphatically indicate that the

---

28. "Physician, heal yourself!" is attested in *Gen. Rab.* 23 (15c), *Gos. Thom.* 31, and in a variant form in Matt. 27:42. "Prophets are not accepted in their hometowns" occurs in variant forms in Judaism (John 4:44) and the Greek world (Plato, *Rep.* 6.489).

29. Vinson, *Luke*, 123-24, "Jesus already knows how they will react to his ministry and launches a preemptive prophetic strike against this point of view. . . . The congregation's hostility at the end is proof of Jesus' prescience, not a reaction to his provocation."

divine mercy announced in the Isaiah quotation is extended to Gentiles as well as Jews. If the Jewish people in Nazareth cannot affirm the Isaiah text for Gentiles, then they cannot claim it for themselves.[30] It is certainly true, as many scholars recognize, that, as a result of Israel's rejection of Jesus, the gospel was taken to "all nations" (24:47) and to the Gentiles (Acts 13:46). But the sermon in Nazareth brings a radically new insight to bear on this truth. The extension of the gospel to Gentiles was not an afterthought because Jews rejected Jesus; it was the result of divine election of Gentiles (Eph 1:4-5), already operative in the days of Elijah, indeed, even in the days of Abraham, who at the time of his call was a Gentile.

Before Jesus finishes speaking, the townspeople have cast their vote against him. Their wrath in v. 28 anticipates — and repeats in virtually the same Greek phraseology — the wrath of the Ephesians at Paul's preaching of the gospel (Acts 19:28). The townspeople "drove [Jesus] out of town" (v. 29). The Greek expression behind this phrase, *ekballein exō tēs poleōs,* is used in the LXX for ridding a (Jewish) city of defilement, such as plague (Lev 14:40-41, 45), foreign gods (2 Chr 33:15), or a (supposed) evil person (1 Kgs 21:13). The phrase is a ritual anathema and a gauge of the outrage against Jesus. Jesus has become like a Gentile pollutant. The phrase is also a foreshadowing of the Christian mission, for in Acts both Stephen (Acts 7:58) and Paul (Acts 14:5-6) will be "thrown outside the city" with murderous intent. The rabid reflex of the crowd reminds one of a lynch mob. Nazareth clings to the slopes of the Galilean hills, although the exact "brow" of the hill from which the townspeople attempted to hurl Jesus is unknown.[31] Rabbinic tradition could prescribe stoning a blasphemer or idolater to death, but throwing a person off a cliff was not prescribed.[32] Nevertheless, the brother of Jesus was later thrown from the temple parapet and stoned to death. It is not impossible that the attempt to throw Jesus down the hill was intended as a prelude to stoning.[33] One scholar thinks "it is virtually impossible to imagine that Jesus actually asserted publicly (or even implied) that his ministry must . . . be among non-Israelites."[34] To the contrary, it is virtually impossible to imagine a village turning so violently against a favorite son *unless* he had offended it in the manner described.

---

30. So too J. Siker, "'First to the Gentiles': A Linguistic Analysis of Luke 4:16-30," *JBL* 111/1 (1992): 83.

31. G. Dalman, *Sacred Sites and Ways,* 73, suggests the sixty-foot precipice above the "new well" as a possible location.

32. Str-B 2:157. The single instance in Scripture of execution by throwing off a cliff was reserved for Israel's enemies in battle (2 Chr 25:12).

33. On the death of James, brother of Jesus, see Josephus, *Ant.,* 20.200; Eusebius, *Hist. eccl.* 2.23.

34. D. Hill, "The Rejection of Jesus at Nazareth (Luke iv 16-30)," in Orton, *Composition of Luke's Gospel,* 37.

We should not be surprised if Jesus was rejected by outsiders and enemies. The unsettling truth of this story is that the greatest danger to the way of God in this world is posed by those who are closest to it. Jesus is rejected not in Sodom and Gomorrah, but in Nazareth. He is betrayed not by the devil, but by one of the Twelve whom he chose. He is crucified not in pagan Rome, but in the heart of Israel at Jerusalem. The rejection of Jesus repeats the rejection of God in the history of Israel, whose ultimate adversary was not Baal worship or foreign nations, but "my own people who are bent on turning from me, declares the Lord" (Hos 11:7). "[Jesus] came to that which was his own, but his own did not receive him" (John 1:11).

In the sovereign mystery of God, the work of Jesus goes forward from Nazareth, for Jesus "walked right through the crowd and went on his way" (v. 30; cf. John 10:39). History is not unfamiliar with the power of a courageous individual to avert the intentions of a belligerent crowd. Jesus is depicted as such an individual here. There is more to his deliverance than human courage, however. His life is the fulfillment of God's purposeful work in history, and neither diabolical machinations nor human opposition, even of friends and relatives, can thwart the fulfillment of God's sovereign will through him.

WONDROUS WORKS IN CAPERNAUM (4:31-44)

Luke now focuses on Jesus as an itinerant Galilean preacher based in Capernaum. Luke has taken over the stories and sequence of Mark 1:21-39 with only minor changes, thus preserving a distinctively Markan flavor in 4:31-44. The four episodes in 4:31-44 are narrated in a compressed time frame of two days, leaving readers with a sense of authority and urgency in the mission of Jesus. The tight concatenation of actions rather than sayings depicts a Jesus who does not wait for events to transpire before getting involved. The experiences of Jesus at Capernaum repeat a paradox evident in Israel before him and in the church after him, namely, the rejection of the gospel by insiders and its reception by outsiders.[35] Jesus' life and mission are especially epitomized by the Greek word *exousia,* "authority," which, beginning in vv. 32 and 36, occurs fifteen times in the Third Gospel as a designation of his sovereign freedom to declare and embody the gospel (4:22, 43), to prevail over evil and demons (4:36; 9:1), and to forgive sins (5:24). Unlike the authority of the scribes and religious teachers of Judaism, which derived from Torah, Jesus received his authority directly from the Father at the baptism as the Spirit-filled Son of God (3:22).

31-37   Capernaum was favorably situated for a ministry in Galilee. Lo-

---

35. Tannehill, *Luke,* 96.

cated on the north shore of the lake, Capernaum lay adjacent to the Via Maris, the main trade route between the Mediterranean coastal plain and Damascus in the north. Capernaum was propitiously distant from Tiberias, where Herod Antipas, who was antagonistic to both John and Jesus, made his capital. In the first century a harbor supported by an eight-foot (2.5 m)-wide seawall extended along Capernaum's 2,500-foot (750-m) promenade. Piers extended from the promenade a hundred feet (30 m) into the lake. Capernaum was a border town between the tetrarchies of Philip and Herod, and hence the site of a customs office (5:27). Its inhabitants, primarily Jews, labored as fishermen, farmers, artisans, merchants, and officials, including tax collectors. A small Roman garrison, quartered in better conditions than could be said of the locals, enjoyed a Roman bath with caldarium, tepidarium, and frigidarium. The building of a synagogue in Capernaum by a Roman centurion, who on one occasion even found Jews pleading his case before Jesus (7:1-10), suggests that relations between Jews and Gentiles were cordial. The commercial advantages of a location on a major trade route surrounded by fertile lands and plentiful fishing resulted in an enviable degree of economic prosperity in Capernaum. On the negative side, Capernaum's altitude — 700 feet (215 m) below sea level and surrounded by water — inevitably incubated infectious diseases, especially malaria. The gleaming white limestone synagogue visible today in Capernaum, the most impressive synagogue to be excavated to date in the Holy Land, dates from the fourth century and is thus not the synagogue visited by Jesus. The black basalt foundation of the synagogue Jesus knew is clearly visible, however, at ground level beneath the limestone synagogue.[36]

On the heels of his brush with death at Nazareth, Jesus "went down to Capernaum, a town in Galilee" (v. 31). The Nazarenes had baited Jesus to "Do here in your hometown what we have heard that you did in Capernaum" (v. 23). This implies that Jesus had a prior ministry in Capernaum. If Luke transposed the sermon in Nazareth, which in both Matt 13:53-58 and Mark 6:1-6 occurs later in Jesus' ministry, to a time *before* Jesus had settled and ministered in Capernaum, then this anachronism is reasonably accounted for. Matt 4:13, which was probably written after Mark and Luke, clarifies the abruptness of 4:31 (and Mark 1:21) by reporting, "Leaving Nazareth, [Jesus] went and lived in Capernaum, which was by the lake in the area of Zebulun and Naphtali." Luke, the most positive of the four Evangelists about Jesus' relation to Judaism, omits Mark's addendum that Jesus' authority was "not

---

36. On Capernaum, see S. Loffreda, *Recovering Capernaum* (Jerusalem: Terra Santa, 1985); R. Riesner, "Neues von den Synagogen Kafarnaums," *Biblische Umschau* 40 (1985): 133-35; V. Corbo, "Capernaum," *ABD* 1:866-69; M. Nun, "Ports of Galilee," *BAR* 25/4 (1999): 23-27. J. Murphy-O'Connor's description of Capernaum as poor and undistinguished (*The Holy Land*, 223-25) underestimates the significance of the archaeological remains.

as the teachers of the law" (Mark 1:22). Like a Jewish rabbi, Jesus teaches on the Sabbath. Frequent references to Jesus teaching and even healing on the Sabbath and in synagogues reinforces Luke's salvation-history motif that the gospel arises from the heart of Israel and its worship.[37] The periphrastic construction of "teaching" (v. 31; Gk. *ēn didaskōn*) implies habitual rather than occasional teaching. The construction is also direct and personal: "Jesus was teaching *them*." The Greek behind "his words had authority" (v. 32) does not mean that Jesus made various authoritative pronouncements, but rather that his word was divinely authoritative in both substance and manner.

The account of the healing of the demoniac in the synagogue of Capernaum (vv. 33-37) adheres closely to Mark 1:23-28. Jesus' first miracle, significantly, is an exorcism. Ancient Jewish and pagan sources report very few exorcisms, and those that are reported do not closely resemble the exorcisms of Jesus.[38] The greatest number of exorcisms in Scripture occurs in the Synoptic Gospels, in contrast to their paucity or absence in the OT, John, Acts, and the Epistles. The fact that Jesus' first miracle is an exorcism, and that he frequently encounters and heals the demon-possessed, testifies that vanquishing Satan and dividing his plunder (11:21-22) was central to his mission (1 John 3:8). Jesus is sent into the world not simply as a moral example, but as a heavenly combatant on a mission to rescue those possessed and oppressed by demons. Not surprisingly, demons recognize the power, purpose, and person of Jesus before mortals do.

The narrative begins with the approach of a demoniac in a Sabbath synagogue service. Luke omits "*their* synagogue" (v. 33) to alleviate Mark's possible pejorative reference (1:23). Mark's nondescript "unclean spirit" (1:23) is identified by Luke in a manner nowhere else attested in Scripture, as "a spirit of an unclean demon" (v. 33).[39] Uncleanness and contamination were tantamount to ungodliness in Judaism. The demoniac cries out, "What do you want with us, Jesus of Nazareth? Have you come to destroy us? I know who you are — the Holy One of God!" (v. 34). This plaintive appeal recalls the desperate words of the widow of Zarephath to Elijah (1 Kgs 17:18) alluded to in vv. 26-27. "What do you want with us?" (lit. "What [is it] to us and you?") occurs not infrequently in the LXX and NT.[40] With the exception of John 2:4, the phrase implies that the two parties concerned have nothing to do with one another. The demon's self-reference in the plural, "us," may suggest that it regards the mission of

---

37. Ambrose, *Exp. Luc.* 4.58, further noted that the new creation in Jesus begins where the old creation ceased, on the Sabbath, thus designating Jesus co-creator with the Father.

38. Fitzmyer, *Luke (I–IX)*, 542; Nolland, *Luke 1:1–9:20*, 204.

39. Nolland, *Luke 1:1–9:20*, 206, suggests this means "a spirit, that is, an unclean demon."

40. LXX: Judg 11:12; 2 Sam 16:10; 19:23; 1 Kgs 17:18; 2 Kgs 3:13; 9:18; 2 Chr 16:3; 35:21; NT: Mark 5:7 par.; Matt 27:19; Luke 4:34; John 2:4.

Jesus as an assault on *all* demonic strongholds. The reference to Jesus as "the Holy One of God" may reflect the belief that naming a spiritual foe granted mastery over it. "Holy One of God" not only recalls the divine sonship of Jesus' baptism (3:22) but may liken Jesus to Samson, the mighty vanquisher of the Philistines, the only other person in the Bible to be called "Holy One of God" (Judg 16:17).[41] There may be an added correlation between Samson's "Nazirite" vow and the reference to Jesus from "Nazareth," both of which stem from the same Hebrew root.[42] "Said sternly" (v. 35), a translation of Greek *epitiman,* is a technical term in Judaism "by which evil powers are brought into submission and the way is thereby prepared for the establishment of God's righteous rule in the world."[43] Jesus silences the demon because, in God's kingdom, revelation is dependent on relationship. As a being hostile to God, the demon cannot be a revealer of God's Son.[44] The description that "the demon *threw* [Gk. *rhipsan*] the man down . . . and came out without *injuring* (Gk. *blapsan*) him" (v. 35) alludes to the violence of the demonic attack by use of two Lukan medical terms not found in Mark's account.

Luke omits Mark's climactic exclamation, "A new teaching — and with authority!" (Mark 1:27), perhaps because "*new* teaching" suggests a novel overture of God. Luke emphasizes Jesus as the *fulfillment* of the unified purpose of God throughout salvation history. By replacing "new teaching" with "What words these are! With authority and power he gives orders . . ." (v. 36), Luke repeats the authoritative "word" of v. 32 immediately above. The "word" of Jesus is more than a verbal utterance. It is a divine enactment, a no-contest authority over powerful demonic beings and forces. The *logos* of Jesus is both word and work, one and the same, authoritative and powerful!

38-39 Following the synagogue service, Jesus enters **the home of Simon**. This structure, a stone's throw from the synagogue in the direction of the lake, was part of an "insula" complex in which doors and windows faced an inner courtyard. The courtyard, accessed by a gateway from the street, was

---

41. On "Holy One of God," see Klein, *Lukasevangelium,* 198.

42. The correlation with Samson is made plausible by the designations "Nazarene" (NIV "Nazareth") and "the Holy One of God," both of which are applied to Samson in Judg 16:17 (LXX), who in the A text is called *naziraios theou* and in the B text *hagios theou.* The Hebrew term behind *naziraios* is *nazir,* meaning "to be consecrated or devoted," hence the correlation with "the holy one of God." See E. Schweizer, "Er wird Nazoräer heissen," in *Neotestamentica: Deutsche und Englische Aufsätze, 1951-1963* (Zürich: Zwingli Verlag, 1963), 51-55. Lohmeyer's suggestion in *Das Evangelium des Markus,* 37, that "the Holy One of God" refers to the high priest Aaron is less plausible.

43. H. C. Kee, "The Terminology of Mark's Exorcism Stories," *NTS* 14 (1968): 235.

44. In the fifth c. Cyril of Alexandria, *Comm. Luc.,* Hom. 12, gave three reasons for Jesus silencing the demoniac: (1) the demon was attempting to usurp the apostolic office, (2) it spoke the mystery of Christ in a polluted tongue, and (3) light cannot be revealed by darkness.

the common space of those who lived in the dwellings around it, containing hearths, millstones for grain, handpresses, and stairways to the roofs of dwellings. The dwellings were constructed of heavy walls of black basalt and flat roofs of wood and thatch. Archaeological investigations have determined that the house in question was built in the first century B.C. and in use in the following century, making its occupation contemporary with Jesus and Peter. Late in the first century its walls, ceiling, and floor were atypically plastered and then etched with sacred and devotional graffiti in Greek, Latin, Syriac, and Aramaic. The dwelling was venerated as a gathering place for Christians, and perhaps as a church, from the end of the first century and may preserve Peter's house.[45] Since Scripture makes no reference to Jesus' dwelling place in Capernaum, it is possible that he lived with Peter.

This unassuming story may preserve a personal reminiscence of Peter and may owe its memory in the church to Peter's influence.[46] Along with Simon, the names of Andrew, James, and John are included in Mark 1:29. Luke omits the three additional names, probably because they have not yet been called as disciples. The mention of Simon alone prepares for his appearance in 5:1-11. The narrative radiates outward in ever-widening circles of influence from Peter's mother-in-law (v. 38) to "all" the townspeople (v. 40) and finally to "Judea" (v. 44). It is tempting to suggest that the woman's "high fever" was malaria, a common ailment in low-lying, water-bound Capernaum.[47] If it was malaria, Luke implies it was demonically induced. In both the NT and rabbinic tradition, fevers are often attributed to divine punishment or demon possession. Luke precedes this story (vv. 33-37) and follows it (vv. 40-41) with exorcisms. This is the only healing miracle in which Jesus addresses the illness rather than the ill person, and the rebuke (Gk. *epitiman*) preserves the common Greek technical word reserved for exorcisms. In contrast to Jesus' tender grasp of the ailing woman's hand in Mark 1:31, Luke reports him rebuking the fever itself (v. 39), i.e., he deals with the source of the malady rather than with the victim of it.[48] This

45. V. Corbo, "Capernaum," *ABD* 1:867-68; E. Meyers and M. Chancey, *Alexander to Constantine: Archaeology of the Land of the Bible* (New Haven: Yale University Press, 2012), 190-93.

46. T. Zahn, *Introduction to the New Testament* (trans. M. Jacobus and C. Theyer; 3 vols.; Edinburgh: T&T Clark, 1901), 2:496-97, is followed by many others in suggesting that the Markan account stems from a first-person report of Peter that ran as follows: "We came directly from the synagogue to our house, and James and John accompanied us; and my mother-in-law lay sick of a fever, and we spoke with Him at once concerning her."

47. A centurion's son also suffered from fever in Capernaum according to John 4:52. On Capernaum and malaria, see J. Reed, "Instability in Jesus' Galilee: A Demographic Perspective," *JBL* 129/2 (2010): 357.

48. The miracles of Jesus are frequently reported with a facticity that is absent from miracles attributed to Hellenistic wonder-workers. In many Hellenistic accounts, the verb "to seem,"

brief story portrays a special reciprocity between Jesus and Peter's mother-in-law.[49] Unlike the demon in the previous story, which sought to communicate information about Jesus without knowing and serving him, Luke portrays a saving-serving relationship between Jesus and the woman. The story begins with "Jesus arising [*anistanai*] from the synagogue" (v. 38), and it ends with the woman "arising [*anistanai*] to serve them" (v. 39). The word for "serve" (Gk. *diakonein*; NIV "wait on") is the typical Greek word for Christian service in the NT. Peter's mother-in-law is, literally, the first "deacon" in the church. Her value to the community derives from what Jesus has done for her; her service flows from Jesus' prior service of her.

40-41 Sabbath extends from sunset on Friday to sunset on Saturday, during which time Jews were forbidden to work or travel. The mention of "sunset" (v. 40) signals the end of Sabbath, at which time Jews in Capernaum flock to Jesus. The Greek is emphatic: *all* afflicted with various illness were brought to Jesus. Mark writes that "the whole town gathered at the door, and Jesus healed many who had various diseases" (1:33-34). Luke focuses not on the crowd, but on Jesus' attention to and empathy for each person in it: "laying his hands on each one, he healed them" (v. 40). Laying on of hands was practiced in the OT as a form of blessing (e.g., Gen 48), but laying on of hands for healing was unique to Jesus, and not attested in the OT or rabbinical writings.[50] In the NT, moreover, this is the only instance where laying on of hands is associated with exorcism, perhaps to signal at the outset of Jesus' ministry that his authority is grounded in compassion as well as in might.[51] Exorcised demons exclaimed, "You are the Son of God!" Jesus "rebuked them and would not allow them to speak, because they knew he was the Messiah" (v. 41). Demons are supernatural beings, and as such they recognize Jesus' supernatural character and power before humans do. The appearance of Son of God and Messiah in v. 41 recalls the same titles at the annunciation of Mary in 1:32-35. At the annunciation the offices were foretold; in Capernaum they are demonstrated. As the messianic Son of God, Jesus prevails over Satan and delivers people oppressed by Satan.

The **command to silence** is surprising, for in forbidding the healed to

---

dokein (or similar term), accompanies the miracle description. Thus, the girl whom Apollonius was reputed to have raised from the dead only "seemed" so, according to Philostratus (*Vita Apol.* 4.45). Asclepius "seemed" to have "brought back many to life who had died" (Diodorus, *Bib. hist.* 4.71.1-2). People "assumed" Heracles went to be with the gods after his cremation (ibid., 4.38), and a thunderbolt "seemed" to fall at Apollonius's birth (Philostratus, *Vita Apol.* 1.5).

49. Similar reciprocity is seen in the healed women who support Jesus (8:2-3), the centurion who builds a synagogue because Jesus has healed his son (7:4-5), and the expectation that disciples should receive hospitality from those they serve. See Vinson, *Luke*, 127-28.

50. A lone exception occurs in 1QapGen 20:28-29, where Abram lays hands on pharaoh and heals him (noted by Evans, *Luke*, 81-82).

51. Nolland, *Luke 1:1–9:20*, 213.

make him known, Jesus seems to work at cross purposes with his mission. Terms like "son of God" and "Messiah" (Gk. *Christos,* lit. "anointed"), however, carried political and military connotations in the Greco-Roman and Jewish worlds. Such connotations were inappropriate to Jesus' mission, and they risked negative responses from ruling authorities, both Jewish and Roman. A major model of Jesus' ministry was the Servant of the Lord (Isa 42:1-4; 49:1-6), whose restraint, humility, and even hiddenness would, ironically, be a "light to the nations." The quality of concealment or hiddenness is also attested in the Psalter as a characteristic of the individual through whom God works (Ps 17:8; 27:5; 64:2). No other figure — not Abraham, Moses, Samuel, or any of the kings or prophets — exerts the influence on Jesus' ministry that the Servant of the Lord does (Matt 12:15-21). The profile of the righteous, even *suffering,* Servant (Isa 52:13–53:12) is more effective in evoking faith than a potentate would be in coercing it. The model of the Servant is essential to understanding the divine sonship of Jesus. Since that role is not fulfilled until the cross of Golgotha, all utterances about Jesus' nature and mission are premature until then.

42-44   This episode again closely adheres to Mark (1:35-39) and concludes the narrative of Jesus preaching in and around Capernaum. Jesus regularly repaired to "the wilderness" (Gk. *erēmos;* NIV "a solitary place") to be alone with God in order to remain true to and effective in his calling.[52] Interestingly, Luke does not say Jesus went into the wilderness to *pray,* as does Mark 1:35. Luke includes many more instances of Jesus praying than does Mark or any other Gospel, but in Luke prayer occurs only at critical junctures in Jesus' ministry. This is not such a juncture, and as a consequence Luke likely omitted prayer here. Likewise in Mark, Peter and the disciples pursue Jesus into the wilderness in an effort to restrain him, whereas Luke ascribes the pursuit and restraint to the "crowds" (NIV "the people"), thereby exonerating the disciples. The sense of pursuit is nevertheless present in Greek *epizētein* (NIV "looking for"), which in Luke-Acts signifies seeking to control something or someone.[53] In addition to pursuing Jesus, the crowd wishes to "restrain" him. The Greek behind "restrain," *katechein* (v. 42), means to "hold fast (to something)" (NIV "they tried to keep him"). Luke can use this word positively of adhering to God's word in faith (8:15), but here it describes an attempt to contain Jesus and is therefore neither faithful nor positive. The people of Capernaum thus want to control Jesus. True, Capernaum has received Jesus eagerly, as Nazareth did not; but Capernaum's desire for "exclusive rights" to Jesus misunderstands and impedes his mission, for it prevents him from proclaiming "the good news of the kingdom of God to the other towns." Satan sought to redefine Jesus' mission in the temptation, and the Nazarenes, in threatening to throw Jesus from

52. 5:16; 6:12; 9:18, 28-29; 11:1; 22:40.
53. 4:42; 12:30; Acts 12:19; 13:7.

a cliff, sought to end it.[54] But even Capernaum's desire to "be fed by" Jesus, as we say today, is self-serving and thus an overture of self-will over God's will.

Jesus seizes the misunderstanding to clarify his purpose, "I must proclaim good news of the kingdom of God to the other towns also, because that is why I was sent." And "he kept on preaching in the synagogues of Judea" (vv. 43-44). The three verbs with which Jesus defined his mission from Isa 61:1-2 in vv. 18-19 — sending, proclaiming good news, and preaching — also describe his ministry in vv. 43-44. The central message of John was "a baptism of repentance for the forgiveness of sins" (3:3), but for Jesus it is "the good news of the **kingdom of God**" (v. 43), mentioned here for the first time in Luke. More than any other phrase in the Synoptic Gospels, "the kingdom of God" describes the essential feature of Jesus' mission. The kingdom of God takes its initial shape from Israel's concept of God as king (Exod 15:18; 1 Sam 12:12; Ps 5:2). As creator of the world, God is exalted above his creatures, rules in majestic splendor, mocks gods of wood and stone, and brings kingdoms to naught. The reign of God was initially manifested in Israel's history in the exodus from Egypt and the giving of Torah at Sinai, but it would be supremely manifested in the advent of a future Messiah, whose reign would usher in the eternal and heavenly reign of God. In Jesus' day, Jews generally affirmed God's reign as dividing humanity into the righteous and the unrighteous — "the sons of light and the sons of darkness," in the words of the Qumran community. In Judaism the righteous took the yoke of obedience to Torah on themselves, whereas the unrighteous did not; and because of their obedience, the righteous could expect to be rewarded in the future after God annihilated the ungodly.

The exact phrase "kingdom of God" does not occur in the OT. In developing this theme for his purposes, Jesus goes beyond its understanding in both the OT and rabbinic Judaism by anchoring the kingdom to God's gracious initiative rather than primarily in human obedience. Jesus rarely speaks of God as king or of his sovereignty over Israel or the world. Rather, he speaks of *entering* the kingdom as entering the family of God. The kingdom of God is not a result of human effort, nor does it evolve toward its completion, nor is it associated with Torah obedience. The primary purpose for which the Father sent Jesus the Son was to embody, proclaim, cultivate, and effect the kingdom in those who would receive it.[55] It is an inscrutable mystery of God (8:10) that cannot be deciphered and calculated (17:20); it is God's doing (10:9, 11; 11:20), and it is best portrayed in analogies or parables. At present the kingdom is hidden, although it awaits future manifestations of unprecedented proportions, including power and glory (9:27). Its future manifestation makes it urgent for people to respond to it in its present hiddenness. In a reversal of human

---

54. See Vinson, *Luke,* 129.
55. Bovon, *Lukas 9,51–14,35,* 413.

values, the poor, insignificant, and even children will be offered the kingdom (18:15-17), whereas it will be more difficult for the powerful and rich (18:24-25). Even though the kingdom is not yet fully realized, it is already present *in nuce* wherever people respond to the gospel (17:21; 18:16). The kingdom of God was the substance of Jesus' teaching (4:43; 9:2), and it corresponded in the closest possible way with his own person and ministry. In Jesus of Nazareth the kingdom of God makes a personal appearance.[56]

The kingdom is *God's* doing, not humanity's, and it cannot be taken captive by any people or ideology. The kingdom must reach "the other towns" (v. 43), indeed "the ends of the earth" (Acts 1:8). The proclamation of God's kingdom was the purpose for which Jesus "was sent" (v. 43). The verb *apostellein* ("send") was quoted by Jesus from Isa 61 in v. 18 in reference to himself. The passive form ("[that is why] I was sent") is a divine passive, i.e., an indirect reference to God, meaning "God sent me to proclaim the good news of his kingdom." Luke concludes with a summary of Jesus' ministry in v. 44, "Jesus kept on preaching in the synagogues of Judea," which echoes a similar summary in v. 15. The word for "preaching" *(kēryssein)* is the third defining verb of Isa 61 quoted in vv. 18-19. This word, which first appears in Luke with the preaching of John (3:3), became a technical term in early Christianity for preaching the gospel. The focus of Jesus' ministry in Jewish synagogues indicates he is not an itinerant Greco-Roman philosopher, a wandering Cynic sage, a Qumran rigorist, or even a hermetic moral reformer like John. Jesus proclaims the good news of God's reign in practicing communities of Jewish faith to signify that his message and mission are the fulfillment of God's revelatory history in Israel.[57]

---

56. D. Flusser, *Jesus* (Jerusalem: Magnes Press, Hebrew University, 1997), 110-11, notes that "[Jesus] is the only Jew of ancient times known to us who preached not only that people were on the threshold of the end of time, but that the new age of salvation had already begun. . . . For Jesus, the kingdom of heaven is not only the eschatological rule of God that has dawned already, but a divinely willed movement that spreads among people throughout the earth. The kingdom of heaven is not simply a matter of God's kingship, but also the domain of his rule, an expanding realm embracing ever more and more people, a realm into which one may enter and find one's inheritance, a realm where there are both great and small. That is why Jesus called the twelve to be *fishers of men* and to heal and preach everywhere."

57. "Synagogues of *Galilee*" is to be expected in v. 44, but "synagogues of Judea" is more strongly attested. A number of manuscripts (A D Θ Ψ) read "Galilee," but this appears to be a later accommodation to Galilee in vv. 14 and 31. The oldest and most important manuscripts, esp. 𝔭[75] ℵ B Q, read "Judea." Moreover, there is no satisfactory answer why scribes would have changed "Galilee" (if it were original) to the much more difficult "Judea"; whereas scribes could be expected to change an original "Judea" to the more expected "Galilee." Thus, the more difficult reading, "Judea," which is accepted by a majority of commentators, is more likely to be original. The originality of "Judea" can also be supported by similar uses of the word in Luke-Acts. In 6:17, hearers of the Sermon on the Plain (in Galilee) are identified as Judeans; in 7:17, news of the raising of the dead boy in Nain (also in Galilee) is said to have gone out "to

PETER: THE CATCHER WHO WAS CAUGHT (5:1-11)

The other three Gospels record that Jesus gathered a cohort of disciples — Peter, Andrew, James, and John among them — before embarking on his itinerant ministry. Luke, however, reports a brief solo ministry of Jesus in and around Capernaum, during which he healed, proclaimed the kingdom of God, and was manifested as both Son of God and Messiah (4:31-44), before calling Peter and his first disciples. The Jesus of Luke is thus not a total stranger to those who will become his first disciples, for he has taught among them in Capernaum (v. 31) and has already healed Peter's mother-in-law there (vv. 38-39). This explains why Peter recognizes Jesus in 5:8, even calling him Lord. Particularly in Mark and John, Peter is portrayed as simply one of Jesus' disciples, although "first among equals." In Luke, Peter plays a more prominent role. In 5:1-11 Jesus' call to Peter to follow him eclipses the call of the Zebedees and his brother Andrew in the other Synoptics (Matt 4:18-22; Mark 1:16-20) and assumes a scale comparable to the epic calls of Moses (Exod 3:1–4:17), Isaiah (Isa 6:1-7), and Paul (Acts 9:1-19).[58] At the conclusion of the Gospel, Peter will be named by Jesus apostle preeminent, who will strengthen the other apostles (22:31-32).

As in the sermon in Nazareth (4:16-21), Luke narrates the call of Peter in a "chiastic" structure, proceeding skillfully in a sequence of scenes to the miraculous catch of fish, from which Luke exits by repeating the sequence in reverse order.

A   The boat goes out in the lake and Jesus teaches (v. 3)
  B   Jesus tells Peter to catch fish (v. 4)
    C   Peter speaks to Jesus in defense and faith (v. 5)
      D   The miraculous catch of fish (vv. 6-7)
    C¹   Peter speaks to Jesus in contrition (vv. 8-9)
  B¹   Jesus tells Peter to catch people (v. 10)
A¹   The boat returns to shore, and the disciples follow Jesus (v. 11).[59]

---

all Judea"; in Acts 10:37 Peter refers to Judea inclusive of Galilee. Luke may have used "Judea" to include Galilee because Galilee was more geographically ambiguous than were Judea and Samaria. Matt 4:23-24, e.g., seems to use "Galilee" and "Syria" more or less interchangeably. In pre-Christian times, Galilee is not mentioned as an administrative district alongside Coele-Syria and Phoenicia (Josephus, *Ant.* 12.154; Schürer, *History of the Jewish People,* 1:41). On the extent of Galilee as a region, see Schürer, *History of the Jewish People,* 2:7-10.

58. The description of Peter by Eusebius, *Hist. eccl.* 2.14.6, as "the noble captain of God," who "for his virtues was the leader of all the other Apostles," may be indebted to the call of Peter in 5:1-11. On Peter as the greatest apostolic authority in early Christianity, see M. Hengel and R. Feldmeier, *Studies in the Gospel of Mark* (trans. J. Bowden; Philadelphia: Fortress Press, 1985), 50-53, 59-63.

59. For a fuller elaboration of this schema, see Bailey, *Jesus through Middle Eastern Eyes,* 136-38.

In modern literary conventions, the climax in a series of statements or events normally occurs at the end of the sequence. The chiastic structure widely employed in ancient literature, however, places the climactic point in the middle of the sequence, to which the narrative proceeds and from which it recedes. Many scholars suppose that the postresurrection appearance of Jesus to Peter in John 21 has been transformed into the call of Peter and transposed to 5:1-11. The two accounts display several similarities, but their differences are equally numerous.[60] Moreover, 5:1-11 appears to have been influenced to some extent by Mark 1:16-20 and 4:1, and especially by the Hebrew Gospel.[61] The presence of *nine* Hebraisms in the pericope, five in the introduction in v. 1 and another four in vv. 3-7, strengthen the plausibility of Hebrew influence.[62] The composite evidence suggests that Luke has spliced elements from Mark 1:16-20 and 4:1 into an original story from the Hebrew Gospel that narrated the call of Peter in the context of a miraculous catch of fish.

1-3   The notoriety of Jesus' ministry in and around Capernaum (4:31-44) has drawn a crowd that is pressing around him on the lakeshore to hear "the word of God." The phrase "the word of God" appears only once each in Matt (15:6) and Mark (7:13), but in nearly twenty instances it characterizes the proclamation of the gospel in Luke-Acts.[63] In Luke, Jesus alone preaches the word of God, whereas in Acts the church, in the name and power of Jesus, proclaims the word of God. The word of God is something humanity learns from verbal proclamation rather than from intuition; hence, the word is the object of proclamation (Acts 13:5; 17:13), evangelism (Acts 8:4; 15:35), speech (Acts 4:31; 16:6), teaching (Acts 16:6; 18:11), and hearing (5:1; 8:21; Acts 13:44; 19:10). When the word of God is accepted (Acts 11:1; 15:36; 17:13), it causes growth (Acts 6:7; 12:24). The proclamation of God's word requires hearers, and when it finds hearers, it produces a relational bond between them and Jesus. The word of God is the place where God manifests himself as the gracious God who is bodily present in the person of Jesus.[64]

---

60. R. Brown, *The Gospel according to John (xiii–xxi)* (AB 29A; Garden City: Double-day, 1970), 1070, concludes, on the basis of ten points of similarity between 5:1-11 and John 21, that John and Luke preserve variant forms of the same story; Klein, *Lukasevangelium,* 206, concludes likewise. To the contrary, Plummer, *Luke,* 147, finds seven points of dissimilarity between the two stories that argue for separate stories. For further defenses of the basic historicity of Luke 5:1-11, see Fitzmyer, *Luke (I–IX),* 560-63; and Bock, *Luke 1:1–9:50,* 448-53.

61. See a quotation from the Hebrew Gospel in Epiphanius, *Pan.* 30.13.2-3 with clear similarities to 5:1-11. Nolland, *Luke 1:1–9:20,* 220, does not mention this quotation, but he correctly attributes 5:1-11 to "a complex source history."

62. The Hebraisms are listed in Edwards, *Hebrew Gospel,* 302.

63. 1:2; 5:1; 8:11, 21; 11:28; Acts 4:31; 6:2, 7; 8:14; 11:1; 12:24; 13:5, 7, 44, 46, 48; 16:32; 17:13; 18:11.

64. On "the word of God," see Bovon, *Lukas 1,1–9,50,* 230-31; Klein, *Lukasevangelium,* 207.

Unlike the other Evangelists, Luke never refers to "the Sea of Galilee," but always to "the lake."[65] Luke's nomenclature likely derives from the Hebrew Gospel, which also preferred "lake" to "Sea of Galilee."[66] Exactly where Jesus taught beside the lake cannot be said for sure, but a possible location is a natural amphitheater situated halfway between Capernaum and Tabgha to the south, where the land slopes gently down to a natural bay. Israeli scientists have verified that this bay can transmit a human voice effortlessly to several thousand people on shore.[67]

Two boats are beached on the shore, their owners washing nets from a night's fishing. The description of "washing nets" in v. 2 identifies the exact net in use, the trammel net. A trammel net was the only fishing net used in ancient times on the Sea of Galilee that was referred to in the plural, because it consisted of three layers; and because of its complexity it was also a net that needed "washing." The bottom of a trammel net was rigged with weights and the top with floats so that it created a vertical "wall," extending from the bottom to the surface of the lake. The net wall consisted of three layers, two outer nets of wide mesh with a fine-mesh net between them. Boats would cause turbulence and noise on the surface of the water, driving fish toward the net from either direction. Fish could pass easily through the first net of wide-mesh, but were held fast when, in their drive to escape, they pushed the inner fine-mesh net through the outer wide-mesh net.[68] When the trammel net was hauled aboard the boats, fishermen recovered fish from the fine-mesh "bag" protruding through the outer net.

Like all Jewish rabbis, Jesus taught not only in synagogues but also by roadsides and open areas.[69] As Jesus stood on the lakeshore, he "saw" (v. 2).

---

65. "Sea of Galilee" occurs in Matt thirteen times, in Mark sixteen times, in John nine times, but not in Luke. "Lake" (Gk. *limnē*) occurs five times, uniquely in Luke among the Gospels.

66. In the Hebrew Gospel, the call of the disciples takes place beside "Lake Tiberias" (Epiphanius, *Pan.* 30.13.2-3). The reference to "lake" is a strong refutation of the common hypothesis that Lukan Semitisms are "Septuagintisms," i.e., incorporations of semiticized Greek from the LXX in the Third Gospel. In the LXX, "sea" *(thalassa)* occurs 432 times, whereas "lake" *(limnē)* occurs only five times — and never with reference to the Sea of Galilee. Luke obviously cannot have received this expression from the LXX, but he could — and apparently did — receive it from the Hebrew Gospel. See R. Notley, "The Sea of Galilee: Development of an Early Christian Toponym," *JBL* 128/1 (2009): 188.

67. See B. Crisler, "The Acoustics and Crowd Capacity of Natural Theaters in Palestine," *BA* 39 (1976): 137. On the location of the Bay of Parables, see B. Pixner, *Wege des Messias und Stätten der Urkirche* (ed. R. Riesner; Giessen: Brunnen Verlag, 1991), 88-89; same author, *With Jesus through Galilee*, 41-42.

68. On trammel nets and fishing on the Lake of Galilee, see M. Nun, *The Sea of Galilee and Its Fishermen in the New Testament* (Ein Gev: Kinnereth Sailing Company, 1989), 28-38; further, Lagrange, *Luc*, 157-58.

69. Str-B 2:157.

The (in)sight of Jesus opens a constricted situation to new horizons and possibilities. As the fishermen washed silt and weeds from the nets, Jesus stepped into the boat of Simon and asked him to push back from the shore. Jesus had healed the mother-in-law of Simon shortly before (4:38-39) and was not unknown to him. In asking a favor of Simon, Jesus frees him of any debt he may feel toward Jesus for the healing. In the Greco-Roman and Jewish worlds, teaching was done from a seated position; hence, Jesus *sits* in his floating pulpit to teach the crowds on the shore.[70] The Gospels frequently call Jesus Teacher or, as here (v. 3), describe him in the act of teaching, but they less frequently report what he actually taught. The person of Jesus is more critical than the content of his teaching; and the teaching itself is meaningful only when one knows the Teacher.

4-7   The earliest chapter divisions of the Gospels in Codex Alexandrinus (fifth c.), which were reproduced widely in subsequent Greek manuscripts, begin a new chapter at v. 4. A new chapter at v. 4 interrupts the plotline begun at 5:1, but it accentuates a key organizational principle of the earliest editors of the Gospels, who endeavored to begin chapters at points where Jesus emerges as the speaking or acting subject.[71] Jesus emerges as both the speaking and acting subject in v. 4, hence the new chapter division in the old Greek manuscripts. He directs Peter to "put out into deep water, and let down the nets for a catch" (v. 4). The early church, ever fond of allegory, saw in v. 4 a command to forsake safe harbors and launch out into the deep where there is no safety except the command of the Lord.[72] The Greek verb for "put out" is singular and directed to Peter alone, whereas "let down" is plural in Greek and directed to the crew manning the nets.

Jesus begins Peter's journey of discipleship not by calling him away from his profession, but by challenging him to bolder practice of it. Jesus does not assert his lordship at Peter's weakest point but at his strongest point — his professional expertise as a fisherman! Nor does Jesus wait for an appropriate mood. Few fishermen endure failure in the art admirably, and people who fish for a living rather than for sport may endure it even less admirably. We need not ask what goes through the mind of a professional fisherman in a foul mood when a nonfisherman orders him to do again in bad conditions what he has already tried and failed to do in good conditions. "Master, we've worked hard all night and haven't caught anything. But because you say so, I will let down the nets" (v. 5). Two voices are audible in Peter's reply — the

---

70. C. Schneider, *kathēmai, TWNT* 3:446.

71. See J. Edwards, "The Hermeneutical Significance of Chapter Divisions in Ancient Gospel Manuscripts," *NTS* 56/3 (2010): 413-26.

72. E.g., Maximus of Turin: "The church is called out into the deep . . . where is 'the depth of the riches and wisdom of God' (Rom 11:33)" (Just, *Luke*, 88).

professional fisherman and the fledgling disciple, the man of this world and the man of faith. Peter knows from experience the futility of fishing after sun-up, when fish can see the nets, and he reminds Jesus, who is considerably less experienced in such matters, of this fact. His final word, however, is not based on his experience, reasonable as it may be, but on the authority of Jesus. Like Mary, who submitted to the angelic herald at the annunciation in spite of her bewilderment (1:29), Peter trusts the word of Jesus in spite of all experience to the contrary. And that for him — as for all believers of all time — is faith.[73] When Peter calls Jesus **Master** (v. 5; Gk. *epistatēs*), there is already a hint of his ultimate allegiance. Close in meaning to "rabbi," *epistatēs* occurs in the NT only in Luke, and in every instance but one it comes from the mouths of people endeavoring to follow Jesus.[74] It is less a theological title than acknowledgment of a practical relationship, "You're the boss!"[75] Rather than reporting prosaically, "They caught many fish," Luke describes the *effects* of the catch. The huge shoal of fish threatens to break the valuable trammel nets. Consternation overshadows amazement at the catch, and a signal[76] is sent for more hands and another boat to help with the catch. "Both boats [were] so full that they began to sink" (v. 7).

8-11 The miraculous catch of fish and call of Peter began when Jesus *saw* (v. 2) a boat as a pulpit. The complement of faith occurs when Peter *saw* (v. 8) through the miracle to the Lord behind it.[77] Peter "fell at Jesus' knees and said, 'Go away from me, Lord; I am a sinful man'" (v. 8).[78] Jesus is now more than "Master," *epistatēs*, "Boss" (v. 5); he is "Lord" (v. 8; Gk. *kyrios*) and rightly confessed as such. *Kyrios* can mean "Sir" as well as "Lord," but Luke has prepared readers for a full christological understanding of the term in v. 8. "Lord" has been employed *thirty* times in the Third Gospel so far, all with reference to the Lord God. Luke surely intends readers to hear "Lord" as a divine title,

---

73. Bovon, *Lukas 1,1–9,50*, 232-33, develops this point magnificently; also Vinson, *Luke*, 134.

74. 5:5; 8:24 (2x), 45; 9:33, 49; 17:13.

75. On *epistatēs*, see Bovon, *Lukas 1,1–9,50*, 233; Wolter, *Lukasevangelium*, 213.

76. Commentators enjoy speculating why the fishermen signaled rather than shouted. The miracle left them speechless (so B. Weiss); their comrades were too far away to be heard (Plummer); shouting would be discourteous to Jesus (Bengel) or betray their success and attract other fishermen (Bailey) or scare the fish (Bovon). The last suggestion seems reasonable, although one can imagine that motioning rather than shouting attracted less attention to themselves — and to their wounded dignity as fishermen!

77. Bovon, *Lukas 1,1–9,50*, 233-34, again notes the interplay between the seeing eye of Jesus and that of Peter: "The look of the Lord in v. 2 organizes the church; the look of the believer inaugurates confession of faith."

78. One would expect the text to read that "Peter fell on his knees before Jesus," but the Greek manuscript tradition is secure in the reading of the NIV, that Peter fell before the knees of Jesus.

confessing both Peter's sin and his faith. Peter's confession need not imply a mortal sin obstructing his faith, but rather, like the prophet Isaiah (Isa 6:5), the inevitable awareness of abject unworthiness in the presence of the Holy. If Torah is one's standard of righteousness, one may, like the psalmist, confidently declare, "I have led a blameless life; test me, Lord, and try me, for I have always been mindful of your unfailing love" (Ps 26:1-2). One cannot enter the holy and glorious presence of God, however, nor can one hear the word of Jesus in all its grace and truth without being convicted of one's utter ungodliness. The miraculous catch does not depend on Peter's confession of faith. The source of the catch depends on the will of Jesus, on grace; grace precedes repentance. Only an encounter with the grace of God can evoke true acknowledgment of sin and repentance. Recognition of guilt and unworthiness does not drive one from God. Rather, in a paradox of grace, it draws one to God. Earlier, Jesus drew apart from the villagers who wanted to keep him for themselves (4:42-43); here, as "the friend of sinners" (7:34), he draws near to Peter in the latter's awareness of his unworthiness.[79] Jesus does not call the righteous who seek to justify themselves by some standard other than himself; he calls sinners like Peter who drop their defenses and yield to his transformative love and forgiveness.

Vv. 9-10a seem slightly intrusive in the storyline, due perhaps to Luke's weaving threads of additional source narratives into the account. The verses are important, however, for they guard against an overly individualistic view of discipleship. Peter is not simply a solitary disciple, but also representative of the other fishermen, including James and John.[80] Capitalizing on the miracle, Jesus bestows on Peter a new commission: "From now on you will fish for people" (v. 10). The word for "fish," *zōgrein,* means to "capture *alive*"; what Peter will do in service for Jesus will cause life to flourish. The metaphor of "fishing for people" does not appear in Jewish literature, perhaps because of connotations of scheming and conniving.[81] It is nevertheless an appropriate (if inelegant) incarnational metaphor, for it describes the life of discipleship in everyday human terms. The call of Peter demonstrates what "fishing for people" means: Jesus has "caught" Peter by a miracle of grace, and he commissions Peter to "catch" people likewise. Although Luke does not specifically say that Jesus "called" Peter, the call is implied and inescapable, for when the

---

79. Green, *Luke,* 230-31.

80. According to a variant reading in vv. 10-11 in Codex Bezae (D), Jesus issues the same call to the Zebedees that he issues to Peter: "For James and John, sons of Zebedee, were [Peter's] partners. Jesus said to them, 'Stop angling for fish; I'll make you fishers of people.' When they heard this, they left everything lying on the ground and followed him."

81. Str-B 1:188. "Fishing for people" was no more attractive in the early church, for the Gk. *zōgrein* appears only sparingly, and never of evangelism and mission (see Lampe, *Patristic Greek Lexicon,* 593).

boats reached land, Peter and partners left "everything" and followed Jesus. The other Synoptics record that the disciples left "their boat and father" (Matt 4:22; Mark 1:20), but Luke's account specifies the ultimate claim of Christ on believers: they left *everything* and followed Jesus.

CHAPTER FIVE

Jesus — the Authority of God in Person

Luke 5:12–6:11

This section comprises seven stories, most of which repeat earlier accounts in the same sequence in Mark 1:40–3:6, and all of which are set in Jesus' elective mission field on the northwest quadrant of Lake Gennesaret. Apart from the presence of Jesus in each, the stories are unrelated to each other, although Luke links four of them by Greek *egeneto*, "it happened" (5:12, 17; 6:1, 6), which reflects the ubiquitous OT Hebraic copulative *wehi*. Each story is set in a distinctive Jewish context, and in each Jesus exhibits the divine authority he received at his baptism. In 5:12-16 he demonstrates authority over leprosy and uncleanness; in 5:17-26, authority over sin; in 5:27-39, authority to reconcile the deep and chronic divide between Jews and Gentiles; and in 6:1-11, authority to redefine Sabbath, the longest of the Ten Commandments and the only commandment ordained by God at creation. Jesus is thus not like a radio transmitter or messenger who relays a signal unaltered, a mere transmitter of Jewish tradition. He is like a commander at headquarters who receives, interprets, and reissues tradition with new and transforming authority. Unlike the scribes and Pharisees, whose ministries are defined by Torah, Jesus exercises sovereign authority as an interpreter of Torah and, in so doing, reconstitutes Judaism itself.

TOUCHING THE UNTOUCHABLE (5:12-16)

The healing of the leper reproduces the same story of Mark 1:40-45. Luke's narrative contains minor editorial changes, but the quotations of Jesus are virtually verbatim with those in Mark, suggesting a conscious fidelity to the *ipsissima verba Jesu* in the gospel tradition. Luke's introduction to the narrative in 5:12a is wholly new, however, and wholly Hebraic (as is the introduction in 5:17). Luke frequently adds his own introductions to stories he receives from Mark or the Double Tradition, and the introductions are usually distinctively Semitic. In fourteen instances, hyper-Semitic verses introduce pericopes unique to Luke, and six additional hyper-Semitic verses introduce pericopes that Luke shares in common with Mark and Matthew. These Semitic prefaces suggest that Luke used the Hebrew Gospel to frame material that he received from other sources.[1]

12-13 The several lepers encountered by Jesus in his ministry and the plethora of instructions about the disease in the Mishnah attest to the prevalence of **leprosy** in ancient Palestine. Leprosy (Hansen's Disease) is a chronic infectious disease caused by a bacillus that gravitates to peripheral nerves and cooler regions of the body. As the coolest region of the body, skin is usually affected first and most significantly by leprosy. It is not surprising that in the ancient world leprosy was considered a skin disease, which, like all skin diseases, is difficult to diagnose and heal. Its conditions are discussed in two lengthy chapters in Lev 13–14 that read like an ancient manual on dermatology. Heb. *tsaraath* covers other skin diseases besides Hansen's Disease, including boils (Lev 13:18), burns (Lev 13:24), itches, ringworm, and scalp conditions. Scribes counted as many as seventy-two different afflictions that were defined as leprosy. In the OT leprosy was generally regarded as a divine punishment, the cure of which could be effected only by God (Num 12:10-13; 2 Kgs 5:1-14). The dread of its contagion is reflected in the following passage:

> The person with such an infectious disease must wear torn clothes, let his hair be unkempt, cover the lower part of his face and cry out, "Unclean! Unclean!" As long as he has the infection he remains unclean. He must live alone; he must live outside the camp. (Lev 13:45-46)

Elaborating Lev 13–14, tractate *Negaim* ("Plagues") of the Mishnah discusses the spread of leprosy not only among people but also among garments (*Neg.* 3:7; 11:1-12) and houses (*Neg.* 3:8; 12–13). Lepers were required to make their appearance as repugnant as possible.

Such severe precautions were prescribed to protect the health of the community from a dreaded contagion. The social consequences of leprosy were perhaps worse than the illness itself, however. Leprosy was a sentence of social ostracism. The disease deprived victims not only of health, but of their names, occupations, social habits, families, fellowship, and worshiping communities. Leprosy contaminated Israel's status as a holy people (although it did not contaminate Gentiles, who were already considered unclean, *Neg.* 3:1; 11:1). Other illnesses had to be healed, but leprosy had to be *cleansed,* as thrice attested in

---

1. The specific verses and data are presented in Edwards, *Hebrew Gospel,* 145-46, 302. The Hebraic style of 5:12a is recognized by many scholars, including Bovon, *Lukas 1,1–9,50,* 237, and Wolter, *Lukasevangelium,* 216, although the latter two mistakenly, in my judgment, attribute it to Luke's attempt to imitate the LXX.

vv. 12-14. Josephus speaks of the banishment of lepers as those "in no way differing from a corpse" (*Ant.* 3.264). The reference to Miriam's leprosy in Num
12:12 prompted rabbis to speak of lepers as "the living dead," the cure of which
was as difficult as raising the dead.[2] The reclaiming of an individual from such
a fate was a supreme expression of Jesus' messianic mission (4:18-19).

Lepers were required to "stand at a distance" (17:12) of fifty paces from
healthy society. The law decreed that a leper's entrance into a house contaminated it (*Neg.* 12–13), and a leper's standing under a tree polluted anyone who
passed under it (*Neg.* 13:7). The approach of this man, whom Luke describes
as "covered with leprosy" (v. 12), would therefore compromise Jesus' ritual
cleanliness. The leper breaks both law and social custom on the chance of
being healed by Jesus. No obstacle, not even the decrees of Torah, prevent him
from coming to Jesus. His plea, "Lord, if you are willing, you can make me
clean," betrays the long humiliation of his affliction. The plea contains a germ
of faith, however, for the leper does not question Jesus' *ability* to save him,
only his *willingness* to do so. The reference to Jesus as "Lord" initially strikes
the reader as "a respectful form of address,"[3] but it is probably more than that.
The title is a Lukan addition to Mark's account, it occurs in the context of a
miracle, it is accompanied by language and posture appropriate to worship,
and it echoes Peter's address to Jesus immediately before in 5:8. These factors
argue for a fuller christological understanding of "Lord" in v. 12.[4]

Luke describes the leper's condition (v. 12) more graphically than does
Mark 1:40 (and Matt 8:2): the man is *covered* with leprosy; he falls *on his face*
before Jesus; and he *begs* Jesus rather than merely speaking to him. His un-
touchability is accentuated, thus making the touch of Jesus more scandalous.
An ordinary Jew could be expected to recoil at the intrusion of the leper, but
the compassion of Jesus supersedes social indignation. The outstretched arm of
Jesus was a long reach for his day . . . for any day. It removes the social, physical, and spiritual chasms prescribed by Torah and custom alike. The touch and
verbal declaration confirm Jesus' willingness to cleanse the leper.[5] "And immediately his leprosy left him" (v. 13). A reverse contagion has taken place: rather
than Jesus being polluted by the leper, the leper is cleansed by Jesus' holiness.

14-16   The NIV translates v. 14 as though it is a direct command, "Don't

2. In the litany of humanity's afflictions the prophet Isaiah repeatedly includes deafness,
blindness, and poverty (Isa 29:18; 35:5-6; 42:18; 61:1). This *mélange* of texts is twice quoted by
Jesus according to 7:22 and Matt 11:5, into which he inserts "leprosy." In a third list of afflictions,
Jesus pairs the cleansing of leprosy with raising the dead (Matt 10:8). On leprosy in general,
see Str-B 4/2:743-63.

3. So Marshall, *Luke*, 209.

4. See Rowe, *Early Narrative Christology*, 89-92.

5. The compassion of Jesus is further accentuated by Luke's omission of references to
Jesus' "indignation" and "strong warning" in Mark 1:41, 43.

tell anyone, but go, show yourself to the priest" (on the **Command to Silence**, see at 4:41). The original Greek sentence is more subtle. It begins in third person ("Jesus commanded *him* to tell no one"), then switches to second person ("but to go and show *yourself* to the priest"). The second person seems to preserve the memory of Jesus' actual words. The command alludes to the specification of Lev 14 and rabbinic tradition (*m. Neg.* 14). Priests (on the priesthood, see at 1:5), although officially associated with the temple in Jerusalem, were not required to live in Jerusalem. They often lived, and it was not unusual to find them, in outlying regions, even Galilee. One legal responsibility of priests entailed making pronouncements regarding diseases. Inspection of alleged cases of leprosy played a necessary role in their duty to preserve ritual cleanness in Israel; hence, "only a priest may pronounce [lepers] unclean or clean" (*m. Neg.* 3:1; also Lev 13:50; 14:2-4). If a clean bill of health was rendered and certified in writing (*m. Neg.* 8:10), the healed person was instructed to present two birds, one killed at the temple in Jerusalem, the other dipped in the blood of the slain bird and released. After a waiting period of eight days, the healed person further brought to the priest three lambs — one a sin offering, one a guilt offering, and one a whole offering (Lev 14:10-11; *m. Neg.* 14:7). Reductions in offerings were allowed for suppliants too poor to afford three lambs.

Despite the command to silence, "news about [Jesus] spread all the more" (v. 15). For Mark, the source of the "leak" was the leper himself (1:45), but Luke identifies the source as *ho logos* ("the word"; NIV "the news"). The word of God is not an inert object that, apart from human aid and intervention, is idle and lifeless. Luke attributes active agency to "the word," which "was going forth" (v. 15). When rightly expressed and enacted, the word is infused with the power of the Spirit and takes on an effective life of its own. Thus, Jesus' ministry to one person affects "crowds of people [who] came to hear him and to be healed of their sicknesses" (v. 15). The messianic mission of Jesus is not confined to the religious sphere of Jewish life in synagogues, temple, and rabbinic circles. It encounters fishermen beside the lake and lepers beside the roads. The mission of Jesus is necessarily public, although it is not fueled by publicity and amazement, but, as Luke states in v. 16, by "withdrawing in solitude and prayer" (also 9:10, 28).

ISAIAH'S MESSIANIC PROPHECY IS FULFILLED IN THE HEALING OF A PARALYTIC (5:17-26)

Luke narrates the story of the healing of the paralytic carried by four friends, which he shares with Mark 2:1-12, as a fulfillment of Isaiah's messianic prophecy quoted by Jesus at his inaugural sermon in Nazareth (4:16-21). The "Spirit of the Lord" on Jesus in 4:18 is now the "power of the Lord" at work through him (v. 17); the messianic release and forgiveness promised to the oppressed in 4:18 is here granted to the paralytic (v. 20); and Jesus' pronouncement, "*Today* this scripture is fulfilled in your hearing" (4:21), is echoed by the crowds, "We have seen marvelous things *today*" (v. 26). Luke's narrative includes no fewer than seventeen Hebraisms that are not present in Mark's original story, however, which seems to indicate that Luke supplements his Markan *Vorlage* with a version of the story from the Hebrew Gospel.[6] Luke's narrative elevates Jesus' person and power with unusual emphasis: crowds from Galilee, Judea, and Jerusalem (v. 17) — the most comprehensive geographic description of Jesus' audience in the Gospels — are drawn to Jesus; the "power of the Lord" — the only such reference in the NT — is with Jesus to heal (v. 17); and the final two verses abound with praise and ecstasy, including the glorification of God by both paralytic (v. 25) and crowds (v. 26), for Jesus' miracle and teaching.

EXCURSUS: PHARISEES IN LUKE

The Pharisaic movement arose at the time of the Maccabean Revolt (168 B.C.) and had been in existence some two centuries by Jesus' day. "Pharisee" means either "separated one" or "holy ones," two interpretations that are not incompatible. A defining characteristic of Pharisaism from its inception was its staunch opposition to Hellenism, i.e., the tendency, outright or subtle, to accommodate Jewish life to prevailing Greco-Roman ideals. In contrast to accommodation, Pharisees championed Torah, "the precious instrument by which the world was created," the perfect expression of God's wisdom and will, and the surpassing object of human existence (*Pirke Abot* 3:19). Pharisees were not a political party. Indeed, as long as Pharisees were permitted the pursuit of Torah, they were rather indifferent to politics. Pharisees were regarded as the authorized successors of the Torah, who sat on "Moses' seat" (Matt 23:2). Pharisaism was reputed for high ideals and was, in the words of Josephus, "extremely influential among the common people" (*Ant.* 18.14-15). The strength and adaptability of Pharisaism were evinced by the fact that, of all Jewish parties, Pharisaism alone survived the war with Rome in 66-70. All Judaism subsequent to that catastrophe owed its existence to Pharisaic origins. The foundational beliefs of the Pharisees, expounded by an illustrious tradition of rabbis, included belief in the sovereignty of God, coupled with human accountability for virtue and vice; the resurrection of the dead; angels and demons; and scrupulous adherence both to the written Torah and to the

---

6. See Edwards, *Hebrew Gospel*, 302-3.

oral traditions based on it, coupled with expressed disdain for those who were ignorant, negligent, or violators of Torah.[7]

Pharisaism was a lay movement numbering some six thousand persons in the first century (perhaps 1 percent of the population), according to an estimate of Josephus (*Ant.* 17.42). Pharisees were numerically small, but in the Gospels their influence vastly exceeds that of other Jewish parties. In Luke, Sadducees (20:27) and Zealots (6:15) are mentioned only once each; Essenes and Herodians, not at all. Pharisees, in contrast, are mentioned twenty-five times as the chief Jewish party with which Jesus interacts. Pharisees are frequent antagonists of Jesus, although not always. Unlike the Fourth Gospel, where Pharisees appear in collusion with chief priests throughout Jesus' ministry (7:32; 11:47, 57; 18:3), Pharisees drop out of Luke's narrative in 19:39 and play no role in the Passion Narrative. In the Third Gospel, the arrest, trial, and crucifixion of Jesus are spearheaded by scribes and chief priests (19:47; 20:19; 22:2), the Sanhedrin (20:1; 22:66), and civil authorities (19:47; 20:20; 22:4; 23:13-14), but not by Pharisees. According to Acts, these same authorities, again without the Pharisees, will be the chief antagonists of the apostolic community and early church gathered in Jerusalem.[8] Pharisees, in fact, appear in largely positive roles in Acts. The only Pharisee mentioned in the first half of Acts is Gamaliel, who sympathizes with the apostles (5:34 [in contrast to Sadducees, 5:17!]), and the Pharisaic bloc of the Sanhedrin later sympathizes with Paul (23:6-9). The only other references depict Pharisees as believers, both at the Council of Jerusalem (15:5) and most notably as Paul the Pharisee (26:5). Two stories in the Third Gospel — the meeting in the house of Simon the Pharisee (7:36-50) and the elder brother in the parable of the Loving Father (15:11-32) — leave the fates of two key Pharisees undecided. Perhaps Luke intended their stories to be completed in the conversion of Paul, the final Pharisee mentioned in Luke-Acts (26:5).

17-20 The first twenty Greek words of v. 17 can be easily rendered in biblical Hebrew, thus suggesting a probable Hebrew source.[9] The Gospels portray Jesus in a number of roles, including healer, itinerant preacher, exorcist, miracle worker, and rabbinic antagonist. His most distinctive role, however, was *teaching*, though often, as in v. 17, we are not told what he taught.

---

7. On the Pharisees, see Str-B 4/1:334-52; E. Schürer, *History of the Jewish People,* 2:381-403; S. Cohen, *From the Maccabees to the Mishnah* (LEC; Philadelphia: Westminster Press, 1987), 143-64; G. Moore, *Judaism in the First Centuries of the Christian Era* (Cambridge: Harvard University Press, 1927), 1:56-71.

8. Chief priests: Acts 4:1, 6, 23; 5:17, 21, 24, 27; 7:1; elders: 4:5, 8, 23; 6:12; scribes: 4:5; 6:12; rulers: 3:17; 4:5, 8, 26.

9. Edwards, *Hebrew Gospel,* 302.

Sitting with the Pharisees were **scribes**. Before the advent of universal education and literacy, there was a great demand for scribes throughout the ancient world, and especially in Judaism, where the written code of Torah regulated Jewish life. The Hebrew word for scribes, *sopherim*, has to do with counting, reckoning, and the keeping of written documents, and this function is associated with the first reference to "scribes" as royal officials who were general secretaries and recorders in the Davidic monarchy (2 Sam 8:16-17; 20:24-25; 1 Kgs 4:3). In post-Exilic Judaism "scribe" came to designate an expert in Torah, of whom Ezra was the first in an illustrious line (Ezra 7:6, 11). Torah expertise is clearly intended in v. 17, where Luke, who otherwise refers to scribes by Greek *grammateis* (14x), in this single instance calls them *nomodidaskaloi*, "lawyers." Scribes taught Torah in synagogues and issued binding decisions on its interpretation. "Scribe" thus combined the offices of Torah professor, teacher, moralist, and civil lawyer, in that order. The erudition and prestige of scribes reached legendary proportions by the first century, surpassing on occasion that of the high priest (*b. Yoma* 71b). Only scribes (apart from chief priests and members of the patrician families) could enter the Sanhedrin. Commoners deferred to scribes as they walked through the streets. The first seats in the synagogues were reserved for scribes, and people rose to their feet when they entered a room.[10]

Jesus' reputation attracts people "from every village of Galilee and from Judea and Jerusalem," i.e., from throughout Palestine; and from "Pharisees and lawyers," who were leaders in those areas. The unusual phrase "the power of the Lord was with Jesus to heal" (v. 17) should not be understood to imply that sometimes such power was not with Jesus.[11] The only other occurrence in Scripture of "the power of the Lord" is in Exod 12:41, where it describes God's summary power of releasing Israel from 430 years of bondage in Egypt. "The power of the Lord" equates Jesus' healing ministry with the authority and might of God, signaling that in Jesus a new exodus is at hand (9:31).

As Jesus teaches in a house (identified in v. 19), four men seek to bring a fifth man, a paralytic on a stretcher, to him (v. 18). We are not told that the four anticipated a particular response or acted on preconditions; they simply desire "to lay [their friend] before Jesus" (v. 18). A crowd of people prevents their access to Jesus, however. The crowd is not portrayed pejoratively, as in Mark (where crowds typically impede access to Jesus), but rather as the inevitable result of Jesus' reputation. "When they could not find a way" (v. 19) to reach Jesus, they did not give up but sought another way. Climbing onto

---

10. On scribes, see G. Moore, *Judaism in the First Centuries of the Christian Era* (New York: Schocken, 1971), 37-47; E. Sanders, *Judaism: Practice and Belief, 63 BC–66 AD* (Philadelphia: Trinity Press International, 1992), 170-89; G. Baumbach, *grammateus, EDNT* 1:259-60; Jeremias, *Jerusalem in the Time of Jesus*, 233-45; Schürer, *History of the Jewish People*, 2:322-30.

11. See the thorough discussion in Rowe, *Early Narrative Christology*, 92-98.

the roof, they removed the tiles and lowered the stretcher in front of Jesus. **Palestinian houses** typically had exterior staircases or ladders to their roofs, offering relief from dank quarters below, access to fresh air, and space to dry laundry, eat, and even pray (Acts 10:9). Roofs were typically flat, supported by beams resting on exterior walls. The beams were cross-hatched by smaller poles, which in turn were covered with thatch and mud. Luke does not say the men "dug through" the roof, as we should expect (so Mark 2:4), but that they "lowered him through the tiles" (v. 19). Scholars often suggest that Luke's use of "tiles" is an accommodation to Hellenistic houses with which his readers were familiar. We do not know why Luke alters Mark's account at this point, but it certainly is not implausible to imagine that roof tiles, which were used throughout the Mediterranean, were used in at least some Palestinian houses.

Removal of a roof might appear disrespectful to a teacher below, but Jesus sees it as an example of "faith" (v. 20), the first occurrence of the word in the Third Gospel. We know nothing of the beliefs of the four friends of the paralytic, except that they take action. Faith is first and foremost not knowledge about Jesus or right feeling about him, but a determination to allow nothing, not even crowds and roofs, to impede access to Jesus. "When Jesus saw their faith, he said, 'Man, your sins are forgiven'" (v. 20). The Greek word for "man" in the vocative, *anthrōpe* (NIV "friend"), is unique to Luke, but it also occurs in the Hebrew Gospel, which may be its source here.[12] Reference to *"their* faith" raises the question of vicarious faith. Whether "their faith" includes the paralytic's faith is not addressed in the relevant Gospel texts (v. 20//Matt 9:2// Mark 2:5), although it is difficult to imagine four friends bringing the paralytic to Jesus against his will, and equally difficult to imagine a paralytic not wanting to be healed.[13] There may be a precedent for vicarious faith in intercessory petitions, which are brought to Jesus on more than one occasion.[14] The power of Jesus is actually enhanced in such instances, for the cure cannot be attributed to autosuggestion or to the victim's inner preparedness.[15] The critical element in this and similar encounters with Jesus seems to depend less on *whose* faith — whether the paralytic's or his friends' — than on faith itself.[16]

---

12. *Anthrōpe* appears in 5:20; 6:4(D); 12:14; 22:58, 60. For its use in the Hebrew Gospel, see Origen, *Comm. Matt.* 15.14. On the whole question, see Edwards, *Hebrew Gospel,* 60-62, 334-35.

13. Lagrange, *Évangile selon Saint Marc* (Paris: J. Gabalda, 1947), 35.

14. E.g., the father who petitions Jesus for the healing of his daughter (8:40-56); the Syro-phoenician woman who begs Jesus to heal her demon-possessed daughter (Mark 7:24-30); the official who intercedes with Jesus for his son (John 4:46-53) or servant (Matt 8:5-13).

15. E. Schweizer, *The Good News according to Mark* (London: SPCK, 1971), 61.

16. Note Schlatter's felicitous wording on this point: "A petition is not weakened by becoming an intercession; an intercession even better illustrates the rule of Jesus, which is not to destroy faith" (*Der Evangelist Matthäus* [Stuttgart: Calwer Verlag, 1959], 297-98).

Commentators often treat the question of the possible relation of the paralytic's sin and his illness as nothing more than the inevitable and organic connection between sin and illness characteristic of all humanity.[17] The text invites further consideration of the matter. It is uncharacteristic of Jesus to use a person for an ulterior motive, and hence unlikely that Jesus addresses the paralytic's sins in order to provoke the scribes, thus providing an occasion to demonstrate his authority. Moreover, no other healing of Jesus expressly correlates infirmity with sin. "Your *sins*" thus appears to address specific sins rather than a general condition of sin, although we are given no clue what the paralytic's sins may be.[18] Nothing is more distinctive of a person than his or her sins. If Jesus' response to the paralytic reflects knowledge of his sins and their relationship to his paralysis, then Jesus addresses him at the deepest level of his existence, which may be particularly appropriate, lest the paralytic think the faith of his friends is an acceptable substitute for his own response to Jesus.

The perfect passive form of the Greek word for "forgiveness" (v. 20) is instructive. Mark 2:5 attributes forgiveness to the present moment ("your sins are [now] forgiven"), but Luke's wording, "your sins *have been* forgiven," implies that forgiveness is a prior and accomplished condition. A rabbinic saying from the third century reads, "The patient is not healed of his illness until God has forgiven all his sins."[19] The quotation of Isa 58:6 quoted in Jesus' inaugural sermon at Nazareth at 4:18 links healing with release and forgiveness, both of which are seamlessly combined in Jesus' response to the paralytic.

21-26   Mention of **forgiveness of sins** draws the scribes, who until this point have observed from the anonymity of the crowd, from the wings to center stage. Apart from the single act of absolution on the Day of Atonement, in which the high priest acted *on behalf of* God, not even the high priest could forgive sins. Jesus, however, appropriates the divine prerogative and presumes to forgive sins. He does not pronounce forgiveness in the name of God (e.g., 2 Sam 12:13), but from his own person. It is, of course, the prerogative of a mortal to forgive sins against himself, but the sin in this instance is not against Jesus. Jesus forgives sins of another, which can only be God's prerogative. In the Markan account (2:7), the scribes are offended by the *act* of Jesus, but in Luke they are offended by Jesus *himself*: "Who is this fellow who speaks blasphemy? Who can forgive sins but God alone?" (v. 21). The

---

17. In Jesus' day, Judaism characteristically regarded illness as the result of sin (see Str-B 1:495-96). Some illnesses are clearly the result of sin, but not all (e.g., 13:1-5). In John 9:1-3, Jesus denies a categorical equation of sin with illness.

18. So Tannehill, *Luke*, 106: "The story need not imply that every health problem is caused by sin, only that the man's sins are a significant factor in this case."

19. The saying comes from *b. Ned.* 41a, quoted from Str-B 1:495.

scribes are correct in believing that only God can forgive sins (Exod 34:6-7; Ps 103:3; Isa 43:25; Mic 7:18). In Jewish understanding, not even Messiah would forgive sins. The classic description of Messiah in *Pss. Sol.* 17–18 speaks of his overcoming demons, ushering in a perfect government, judging the godless, and being righteous and even sinless (17:36), but not of his ability to forgive sins. Strack and Billerbeck rightly conclude that "there is no place known to us in which the Messiah has the authority to pronounce forgiveness of sins from his own power. Forgiveness of sins remains everywhere the exclusive right of God."[20] In every sin, even in sins committed ostensibly only against one's neighbor, God is the party most offended. Even in the acts of adultery and murder, David confesses to God, "against you, you only, have I sinned" (Ps 51:4). In saying, "Who can forgive sins except God alone?" (v. 21), the scribes and Pharisees rightly understand that Jesus is speaking and acting as only God can speak and act.[21] To assume a role as rival to God is to commit blasphemy, and blasphemy, along with idolatry, was the gravest sin in Israel (Lev 24:16).[22]

Jesus knows the thoughts of the religious leaders. Luke three times repeats the Greek word *dialogizesthai* in vv. 21-22, which the NIV renders as "thinking." Jesus sees more than their thoughts, however. Like a sword, his insight pierces *their hearts,* exactly as Simeon had prophesied to Mary (2:35). The scribes have nothing to say to the man's physical or spiritual condition. Jesus has something to say to both. Jesus also has something to say to the scribes, who suffer from a form of spiritual paralysis. Like the paralytic, the scribes are also dependent on Jesus for the work of God, but their learning and status make them less aware of their need for it. Jesus wants them to *know* (v. 24), to experience firsthand the authority by which he forgives sins. In v. 21 the scribes ask who "can" (Gk. *dynatai*) forgive sins, i.e., Who has the ability? Jesus declares that the Son of Man has not only the ability but the *authority* to do so (on authority, see at 20:2). From a human perspective it is safe to pronounce forgiveness of sins, since the pronouncement cannot be proved. Jesus' authority to forgive, no less effective because of its invisibility, will be proved by healing the paralytic. The authority to heal and the authority to forgive are the same authority that Jesus received at the baptism by both the endowment of the Holy Spirit and the Father's declaration of divine sonship (3:21-22).

---

20. Str-B 1:495. The uniqueness of Jesus' forgiveness is noted already in Irenaeus, *Haer.* 5.17.3, "For if no one can forgive sins but God alone, while the Lord remitted them and healed people, it is plain that he was himself the Word of God made the Son of Man, receiving from the Father the power of remission of sins."

21. See Rowe, *Early Narrative Christology,* 102-5.

22. The fear of blasphemy caused Jews to avoid pronouncing the divine name whenever possible. Following Num 15:30, the Mishnah decreed expulsion from the community as punishment for taking God's name in vain (*m. Ker.* 1:1-2; *m. Sanh.* 7:5). The same punishment was decreed at Qumran for uttering God's name frivolously (1QS 7).

Jesus says to the paralytic, "I tell you, get up, take your mat and go home" (v. 24). All three Synoptics record the astonishment of the crowds at the healing of the paralytic, although none as emphatically as Luke in vv. 25-26. "Immediately" the paralytic arose, and along with the crowds "glorified God." "Ecstasy" (NIV "amazement") overtook "everyone" (emphatic in Greek), and people were filled with awe. They exclaimed, "We have seen remarkable things today." The Greek word for "remarkable," *paradoxa,* is the basis of the English word "paradox": they beheld a divine paradox (see 1:65). At his inaugural sermon in Nazareth, Jesus declared that "today!" the messianic prophecy of Isaiah was fulfilled in himself. That promise is fulfilled in the exclamation of the crowd at Capernaum: "We have seen a paradox of grace *today.*"

EXCURSUS: SON OF MAN

Son of Man, which occurs in Luke for the first time in v. 24, was largely free of the political and military connotations that were associated with Messiah, thus allowing Jesus to speak of himself in public, and often in the face of opposition and hostility. The title is somewhat ambiguous and does not appear to have made any special claim in the ears of Jesus' contemporaries. Nowhere are people amazed that Jesus calls himself the Son of Man, for example, nor do they take exception to his doing so. Son of Man occurs twenty-five times in Luke, always in the mouth of Jesus. As in the other Gospels, Son of Man appears in three contexts. In eleven instances it occurs in apocalyptic contexts (9:26; 11:30; 12:8, 40; 17:24, 26, 30; 18:8; 21:27, 36; 22:69), like its usage in Dan 7 and *1 En.* 37–69, where it refers to the Son of Man coming in judgment at the end of time. In nine instances the title refers to Jesus' earthly ministry (7:34; 9:58; 12:10; 17:22; 19:10; 22:22, 48), including his authority to forgive sins (5:24) and supersede Sabbath (6:5). In five instances it refers to Jesus' suffering (6:22; 9:22, 44; 18:31; 22:69). In each of these three contexts "Son of Man" refers either to a divine attribute or to the fulfillment of a divinely ordained purpose. This is also true of its uses with reference to Jesus' betrayal and death, in which the Son of Man "must" (Gk. *dei*) suffer (9:22) "in fulfillment of everything written in the prophets" (18:31). "Son of Man" is thus not a mere circumlocution for "the human one." In the present passage "Son of Man" depicts Jesus' authority to forgive sins, thereby alluding to the Son of Man figure in Dan 7:13-14, who likewise is empowered with God's authority ("there before me was one like a son of man. . . . He was given authority [LXX: *exousia*], glory, and sovereign power").[23] Jesus frequently chooses to

---

23. In an article remarkable for its brevity and sensibility, C. Moule, "'The Son of Man': Some of the Facts," *NTS* 41 (1995): 277-79, underscores the association of Son of Man with an

speak of his work as the Son of God by the title "Son of Man." He does not speak of his work and vocation in the first person, i.e., "That is the way I do things," but in the titular third person "Son of Man," which designates a divinely ordained *office* of humiliation, suffering, and exaltation according to God's plan.

MINISTERING TO THOSE WHO NEED IT MOST (5:27-32)

This pericope is a version of the same story related in Matt 9:9-13 and Mark 2:13-17, although Matt and Mark refer to tax collectors as representative of "sinners" in general, whereas Luke focuses more particularly on tax collectors alone (vv. 27 [2x], 28, 30). Levi, a tax collector, becomes the fourth individual, following Peter (5:8) and James and John (5:10), called to follow Jesus in Luke. These four calls are illustrative rather than exhaustive, for in 6:13-16 the names of the Twelve are listed, although only a third of their number have been called at that point. All the Twelve were Jews, although none came from the religious elite of the day. Peter, James, and John belonged to a respected entrepreneurial class of fishermen, and were much less objectionable recruits than Levi, who was a cog in the opprobrious Roman tax juggernaut.

27-28 With a bare-bones transition ("After this"), Luke reports that "Jesus went out and saw a tax collector" (v. 27; on tax collectors, see at 3:12). Anyone familiar with "moles" and informants in Nazi and Communist regimes will appreciate the loathing of tax collectors in first-century Judaism. There cannot have been many Jews in first-century Palestine who expected (or wished!) to see in a tax collector anything other than the husk of an individual whose soul had been eaten away by complicity with Roman repression. Luke's use of Greek *theasthai* (v. 27; NIV "saw") is therefore somewhat unexpected, for it means "to look at intently and purposively," indicating that Jesus was not eying a despised official, but looking at — even *into* — a real person with a name, Levi. It was not uncommon in first-century Palestine for an individual to bear both a Hebrew/Aramaic name and a Greek/Latin name. Simon Peter, Joseph Caiaphas, and Saul/Paul are examples of such in Luke-Acts. The Levi of v. 27 (and Mark 2:14) may therefore be the same individual as "Matthew" (Matt 9:9) in the account of this story in the First Gospel, for the name "Matthew

---

individual (as opposed to a communal understanding of the term) who must suffer: "I still believe that the simplest explanation of the almost entire consistency with which the definite singular is confined to Christian sayings is to postulate that Jesus did refer to Dan 7, speaking of *'the* Son of man [whom you know from that vision]', and that he used Daniel's human figure as not primarily a title so much as a symbol for the vocation to victory through obedience and martyrdom to which he was called and to which he summoned his followers (so that they would together constitute 'the people of the saints of the Most High')."

[the tax collector]" appears in all four NT apostolic lists (6:15; Matt 10:3; Mark 3:18; Acts 1:13), whereas "Levi" appears in none of them.[24] It is worth noting, however, that a quotation from the Hebrew Gospel identifies Levi with the *Matthias* who was elected to the apostolic college after the defection of Judas in Acts 1:23, 26. If this is the case, then Levi is not identical with Matthew (Matt. 9:9), but rather a member added to the apostolic company only after Jesus' ascension.[25]

Jesus summons this individual by saying to him, "Follow me" (v. 27). Luke reports no prior acquaintance of Levi with Jesus, nor is Levi's call probationary, contingent on his forsaking the tax industry.[26] The call does not depend on Levi, but on the sovereign authority of Jesus, to which Levi must respond. Levi's circumstances are patently different from those of Peter, James, and John, but discipleship requires the same of him that it does of them: "he left everything and followed [Jesus]" (v. 28; see 5:11). "Left everything" (in Codex Sinaiticus "everything" is emphatic, *hapanta*) signifies that Levi reoriented his life, perhaps even forsook the tax trade, but he evidently did not divest his possessions, for in the following verse he throws a banquet for Jesus.[27] The imperfect tense of the Greek word for "followed" signifies that Levi's discipleship was not momentary, but enduring.

29-32   In hosting "a great banquet for Jesus at his house" (v. 29), Levi further attests to the sincerity of his discipleship. "Hosting a great banquet" recalls the same or similar Greek phraseology of celebrated banquets in Gen 21:8; 26:30; Esth 1:3; Dan 5:1, and 1 Esd 3:1. Banquets (see further at 11:37) constitute an important and recurring theme in Luke, exhibiting Jesus' commitment to embrace a wide social-spectrum of Palestinian society, especially outliers, in intimate table fellowship. The Lukan banquets at which Jesus presides are

---

24. On this issue, see Fitzmyer, *Luke (I–IX)*, 589-90, and the discussion of "Matthew" at 6:15.

25. Didymus of Alexandria (ca. 310-98; also known as Didymus the Blind) spoke about double names thus: "There are many such name changes [in Scripture]. Matthew appears in the [Gospel] according to Luke under the name of Levi. He is not the same person (mentioned in Matt 9:9), but rather the Matthew who was appointed in place of Judas; he and Levi are the same person under two different names. This is made apparent in the Hebrew Gospel" (quotation from S. Brock, "A New Testimonium to the 'Gospel according to the Hebrews,'" *NTS* 18 [1971]: 220). According to Didymus, Levi was not an apostle during the Lord's earthly lifetime but became an apostle only after the resurrection of Jesus, at which time he took the name Matthias. The postresurrection apostolic college thus had two apostles with virtually the same name, a Matthew who had been called by Jesus (Matt 9:9), who was an apostle throughout Jesus' ministry, and a Matthias who was named to the apostolic guild after the defection and death of Judas. On the whole question, see Edwards, *Hebrew Gospel*, 23-26.

26. John likewise admonished tax collectors to fair practices, but not to abandonment of their profession (3:12-13).

27. Green, *Luke*, 246.

palpable anticipations of the eschatological kingdom of God proclaimed by Jesus. In Lukan banquets, however, Jesus hosts unexpected and sometimes offensive guests — the outcast (5:27-32; 19:1-10), sinners (7:36-50; 15:1-2), and the sick, poor, lame, and blind (14:7-24). He also hosts his disciples (22:7-38; 24:28-35), but Pharisees, who would top most guest lists, were often rebuked (11:37-54; 14:1-6). Banquets hosted by Jesus — like the kingdom of God itself — have very diverse guest lists and unusual outcomes.

The Greek of v. 30 refers to "the Pharisees and *their* scribes" ("their" omitted by NIV). Luke's wording likely derives from Mark's "scribes of the Pharisees" (2:16), designating scribes of Pharisaic (as opposed to Sadducean) persuasion. The agreement between Pharisees and *their* scribes is not unlike the agreement of an American president and *his* political appointees to the federal court system. The irony between vv. 29 and 30 is sharp and unmistakable: Levi, tax collectors, and "others" recline with Jesus in feast and festivity (v. 29), while Pharisees and teachers of the law (on both groups, see at 5:17) stand outside in complaint and judgment (v. 30).[28] The Pharisees view the "others" (v. 29) as blatant "sinners" (v. 30). By **sinners** they think of the "wicked" of the Psalms, which in the LXX appear as "sinners" (Gk. *hamartōloi*). In the Psalms, the "wicked" are not occasional transgressors of Torah, but the reprobate who stand outside it. The Mishnah describes "sinners" as gamblers, money-lenders, people who race doves for sport, people who trade on the Sabbath year, thieves, the violent, shepherds, and, of course, tax collectors (*m. Sanh.* 3:3). Not all the foregoing are obvious criminals. Many are simply common laborers too busy, too poor, or too ignorant to live up to the rules of the religious authorities. Attentiveness to Torah, by contrast, constituted the standard of the "deserving" and "righteous."[29] By inference, those who did not study Torah belonged to "tax collectors and sinners" (v. 30). The Greek word for "complained" (v. 30), *gongyzein*, recurs throughout Exod 15–17 and Num 14–17 with reference to Israelite "murmuring" against Moses and God in the wilderness. *Gongyzein* is not a reaction sparked by ill-temper or circumstance, but an expression of obstinacy and resistance. *Gongyzein*, occurring only here in Luke-Acts,[30] im-

---

28. The Greek of v. 30 reads "Pharisees and *their* teachers of the law" (NIV "Pharisees and the teachers of the law"). "Teachers of the law" (= scribes) constituted a profession, whereas Pharisees denoted lay voluntary members of a religious movement. The wording in v. 30 (as in Mark 2:16, "scribes of the Pharisees") indicates scribal professionals who allied themselves with Pharisaic ideals.

29. So R. Meir: "He that occupies himself in the study of the Law . . . is deserving of the whole world. He is called friend, beloved of God, lover of God, lover of mankind; and it clothes him with humility and reverence and fits him to become righteous, saintly, upright, and faithful; and it keeps him far from sin and brings him near to virtue, and from him men enjoy counsel and sound knowledge, understanding and might" (*m. 'Abot.* 6:1).

30. A compound form of the word, *diagongyzein,* occurs in 15:2 and 19:7.

plies that Pharisaic opposition to Jesus' table fellowship with tax collectors is, like the defiance of the Israelites in the wilderness, a refusal of the redemptive work of God.[31]

In response to the grumbling of the Pharisees, Jesus responds, "It is not the healthy who need a doctor, but the sick. I have not come to call the righteous, but sinners to repentance" (vv. 31-32). This pronouncement was remembered and preserved in a number of early Christian sources, including Clement of Rome (*2 Clem.* 2:4), *Did.* 4:10, *Barn.* 5:9, and Justin Martyr (*1 Apol.* 15.8). The saying does not mean that Jesus is indifferent to righteousness, but rather that his fellowship with the disreputable was an unforgettable hallmark of his ministry, and an enduring lesson to the church to embrace the socially marginalized or outcast. The grace of God extends to and overcomes the worst forms of human depravity. Ironically, in one sense great sinners stand closer to God than those who think themselves righteous, for sinners are more aware of their need of God's transforming grace. "Where sin increased, grace increased all the more" (Rom 5:20). Matt (9:13) and Mark (2:17) report that Jesus called tax collectors and sinners unconditionally, but Luke adds that he called them "to repentance." For Luke, Jesus embraces those whom society shuns, and he seeks the lost, not simply out of compassion, but in order to rescue them (15:7; 19:10). When repentance leads to rescue, it is a cause of great joy. Luke places repentance in the context of feasting rather than mourning and fasting, for "the sign of repentance can be the joy of finding and being found."[32]

FORM FOLLOWS FUNCTION (5:33-39)

The preceding story of Levi offers no antecedent to "they said" in v. 33. This may indicate that 5:33-39, as is recognized by Matt 9:14-17 and Mark 2:18-22, was an independent unit of tradition. Luke may append this story here because it continues the themes of feasting and fasting.

33-35 Jesus is questioned why the disciples of John and the Pharisees fast, but his disciples do not. Only one fast was required in Judaism, on the Day of Atonement (*Yom Kippur,* Lev 16:29-31; *m. Yoma* 8:1-2). Mishnah tractate *Ta'anit,* which is devoted to proper observances of **fasting**, specifies three other types of fasts, however. One was fasts that lamented national tragedies, such as the destruction of the temple by Nebuchadnezzar (Zech 7:3-5; 8:19); another, fasts in times of crises, such as war, plague, drought, famine, etc; and a third was self-imposed fasts for any number of personal reasons (2 Sam 12:16;

---

31. On *gongyzein,* see K. Rengstorf, *TWNT* 1:727-37.
32. Tannehill, *Luke,* 108.

Ps 35:13). The Pharisees normally fasted on Mondays and Thursdays (*Did.* 8:1; *b. Ta'an.* 12a), although this was not required. The required fast on the Day of Atonement lasted a full twenty-four hours, whereas voluntary fasts as a rule extended only from dawn to dusk. Although not a legal requirement except on the Day of Atonement, fasting had become in Jesus' day a prerequisite of religious commitment, a sign of atonement of sin and humiliation and penitence before God, and a general aid to prayer. The rabbis often referred to fasting as "an affliction of the soul," thereby designating it as a characteristic and sacrificial act of piety.[33]

To the abstemious question of fasting, Jesus responds with a wholly contrary and festive image of a **wedding** feast. A wedding celebration in a Jewish village normally lasted seven days for a virgin bride, three days for a remarried widow. Friends and guests had no responsibility but to enjoy the festivities. There was abundance of food and wine, as well as song, dance, and fun both in the house and on the street. Rabbis, too, were expected to suspend Torah instruction and celebrate with their students. "The guests of the bridegroom" (Gk. lit. "sons of the bridegroom," a Semitism) pictures the gathering of the wedding party, waiting impatiently to eat. On such an occasion fasting is entirely out of the question!

Jesus is not opposed to fasting in principle. The reference to "frequent" fasts (v. 33; NIV "often") may suggest that his disciples also fast, although perhaps not as often. The statement that, when the bridegroom is taken away, "in those days [his disciples too] will fast" (v. 35), implies the same.[34] In his chronicle of roughly the first thirty-five years of the Christian movement in Acts, Luke describes the deprivations, hardships, and opposition faced by early Christians after the ascension of Jesus, and the role that fasting played in sustaining the nascent community of faith.[35] The discipline of physical privation in fasting was an aid to watchfulness, contrition, and strength and sensitivity in Christian life. But while the "bridegroom" is present, the "wedding" supersedes and suspends the principle of fasting.[36] The "bridegroom" (v. 34) is normally not a messianic metaphor; nowhere in the OT is the Messiah presented as a bridegroom, and only rarely so outside the OT.[37] This does not diminish its

33. On fasting, see J. Behm, *nēstis*, *TDNT* 4:924-35; Str-B 2:241-44; 4/1:77-114.

34. In *Gos. Thom.* 104 Jesus instructs his hearers to fast and pray when they see him coming from the wedding chamber. This saying conflates two competing sets of imagery and appears to subordinate Jesus to fasting, whereas in the canonical Gospels it is Jesus who subordinates fasting to himself.

35. Acts 13:2-3; 14:23; (27:9). On fasting in Paul, see 1 Cor 7:5; 9:25-27; 2 Cor 6:5; 11:27. Further, *Did.* 8:1.

36. Unlike its parallels in Matt 9:15 and Mark 2:19, the Greek text of v. 34 exhibits several textual variants.

37. A Jewish midrash on Exod 12:2 reads, "In the days of the Messiah the wedding

christological significance, however, for in the OT God is not infrequently described as Israel's husband and lover (Isa 5:1; 54:5-6; 62:4-5; Ezek 16:6-8; Hos 2:19).[38] The same nuptial imagery increases in later Judaism.[39] In this stunning metaphor, which appears in all four Gospels,[40] Jesus does not allude to his messianic office, but presumes the prerogatives of God himself. Similar to the forgiveness of sins in 5:24, Jesus invites hearers to supply their own answer to his identity. Both episodes, powerfully though implicitly, provoke hearers to recognize that, in the mission of Jesus, the *person* of God is present.[41]

Already early in the Galilean ministry, storm clouds of opposition are gathering against Jesus. The image of "the bridegroom [being] taken from them" is alarming. It is the guests, not the groom, who leave in a normal wedding. The Greek word for "taken [away]," *apairein*, does not necessarily denote force,[42] but the unusual circumstance of separating a groom from a bride implies such. Luke has already noted opposition to Jesus from his relations in Nazareth (4:29), and from the scribes and Pharisees at his presumption to forgive sins (5:21) and to eat with tax collectors and sinners (5:30). The reference to the bridegroom being "taken away" reveals that Jesus is aware of such opposition — and its potential consequences (17:22). Luke bookends Jesus' earthly ministry between explicit images of suffering (2:34-35; 24:26), and an explicit reference to Isaiah's Servant of the Lord reminds readers that Jesus "was numbered with the transgressors" (22:37; see Isa 53:12).

36-39   The messianic wedding imagery is followed by the first two crisp parables in the Gospel of Luke. Both parables emphasize the uniqueness of Jesus, and are thus generally rather than specifically related to the preceding teaching on fasting. Like all Jesus' parables, both incorporate images common to his hearers. The first pictures a new patch of cloth sewn on an old garment. When washed, the new patch shrinks, causing a tear in both garment and patch (see Job 13:28).[43] The second pictures used wineskins filled with new

---

will take place" (*Rab. Exod.* 15 [79b]). The NT, of course, is familiar with the bridegroom as a messianic image (Rev 19:7-9), but that is not its sense in *Rab. Exod.* 15.

38. Contra D. Nineham, *The Gospel of St Mark* (London: Adam & Charles Black, 1963), 103, who dismisses the Christological significance of the metaphor.

39. W. Eichrodt, *Theology of the Old Testament* (trans. J. Baker; London: SCM Press, 1961), 250-58; J. Jeremias, *nymphē, TDNT* 4:1101-3.

40. 5:34; Matt 9:15; Mark 2:19; John 3:29.

41. In the gnostic *Tri. Trac.* from Nag Hammadi, the bridegroom imagery, shorn of its relationship with God and Jesus' earthly ministry, is spiritualized as the union of the soul with Christ in the bridal chamber of election (122.14-30).

42. BDAG, 96.

43. Greek manuscripts show unusual diversity in wording of the parable of the New Patch on the Old Garment (see R. Swanson, ed., *New Testament Greek Manuscripts: Variant Readings Arranged in Horizontal Lines against Codex Vaticanus; Mark* [Sheffield: Academic Press, 1995], 32-33). For a reconstruction of the saying, see the discussion in Metzger, *TCGNT,*

wine that ferments and expands, bursting the old and brittle skins (see Job 32:19). Both wine and wineskins come to ruin.

The parallel to the first parable in Matt 9:16 and Mark 2:21 sets Jesus and the gospel in pronounced opposition to their Jewish context. In Luke the opposition is less pronounced.[44] In Matt and Mark, the unshrunken patch tears and destroys the old garment, whereas in Luke the patch only fails to "match" the old. The parable of the Wineskins (v. 37) is closer to its parallels in Matt 9:17 and Mark 2:22. Pouring new wine into old wineskins causes the latter to "burst" (Gk. *apollyein,* "destroyed"), resulting in the loss of both wine and skins. But here too Luke moderates the parable by adding that "new wine must be poured into new wineskins" (v. 38). Luke's clearest moderating influence occurs in the concluding verse, "And none of you, after drinking old wine, wants the new, for you say, 'The old is better'" (v. 39). This verse is not present in the Synoptic parallels, and seems somewhat incongruous with the previous material. It may have existed as an independent maxim (similar to John 2:10?), for sayings on the preference of old wine over new wine were not uncommon in the pagan and Jewish worlds.[45] Its novelty causes many commentators to interpret it in isolation from vv. 36-38, usually with reference to the continuing resistance of Jewish hearers to the gospel, or as a warning against the temptation to hold on to the old and familiar — and thereby miss the new wine of Jesus.[46] The fact that Marcion omits v. 39 would support this interpretation, for Marcion did not want to grant the old covenant any advantage over the new covenant in Jesus, which a straightforward reading of v. 39 seems to do (see Marcion, in Introduction).[47] Is it possible, however, to regard v. 39 as a conclusion to the two foregoing parables, rather than as a novel or even contrary point of view? Only if the old wine, which in v. 38 is regarded negatively, is regarded positively in v. 39, as in Augustine's hermeneutic, for example, that the new covenant is concealed in the old covenant, and the old is revealed in the new. Such a reading allows for the interpretation that the Lukan versions of the parables of the New Patch and New Wine imply the incompatibility of any response that fails to recognize Jesus as the fulfillment of the hope of Israel.

This does not mean that Jesus is simply another link in the chain of sal-

---

67-68. Leaney, *Luke,* 128, thinks Luke has misconstrued the point of the patch parable, but Evans, *Luke,* 98, rightly argues that the 5:36 is not a misreading of the original parable.

44. *Gos. Thom.* 47 includes both parables in a cluster of short parables about the impossibility of riding two horses or stringing two bows or serving two masters. In *Gos. Thom.* the two parables are about divided allegiances, and thus ethical in nature, whereas in the Synoptic Gospels they are Christological.

45. See the instances gathered in Wolter, *Lukasevangelium,* 232-33.

46. Marshall, *Luke,* 228; Schweizer, *Lukas,* 73-74; Tannehill, *Luke,* 109.

47. Despite Marcion's omission of the verse, Metzger, *TCGNT,* 115-16, notes its "almost overwhelming" external attestation.

vation history, an addendum or appendage to the divine work in history. The parables of the Patch and Wineskins illustrate his sovereign role as both the new and the final patch and wine. He cannot be integrated into or contained by preexisting structures, even Judaism, Torah, and synagogue. Rather, structures — and this may be a reminder of Luke to the church of his day — must be conformed to Jesus. Form must follow function. The images in vv. 33-39 of wedding feast, new patch on old garment, and new wine in old wineskins pose crucial questions for followers of Jesus. The question is not whether disciples will, like sewing a new patch on an old garment or refilling an old container, make room for Jesus in their already full agendas and lives. The question is whether they will forsake business as usual and join the wedding celebration; whether they will become entirely new receptacles for the expanding fermentation of Jesus and the gospel in their lives.

JESUS' SOVEREIGNTY OVER SABBATH (6:1-5)

The present pericope and the following one in 6:6-11 continue the half-dozen conflict-stories between Jesus and the religious leaders, particularly the Pharisees and scribes, that constitute Luke 5:12–6:11. The issue at stake in these final two disputations is Sabbath observance. Unlike most religions, which venerate sacred places or sacred objects, Jews venerate sacred *time* — Sabbath. Sabbath is not simply another article of faith in Judaism, on a par, for example, with distinctions between clean and unclean that dominate the disputations in 5:12-32. Sabbath was the defining characteristic of Judaism, the observance of which, even more than circumcision, determined one as an observant Jew. Sabbath raised the stakes between Jesus and the Jewish religious leaders to their zenith. The pronouncements that Jesus makes regarding Sabbath are prime examples of the new versus the old in the two preceding parables (5:36-39).

1-2 The general indifference of Western Christians toward Sabbath observance puts them at a disadvantage in understanding the importance of Sabbath in Judaism. Two observances above all defined Jews and set them apart from the nations: circumcision and **Sabbath**. Both observances marked Jews perceptibly, the first in their flesh and the second in their use of time. Sabbath extended from sunset Friday until sunset Saturday. The Fourth Commandment, the longest of the Ten Commandments (Exod 20:1-17; Deut 5:1-21), enjoins Jews, in imitating the divine Sabbath rest, to abstain from virtually every form of Sabbath labor. According to Jewish tradition, God chose Israel from all the peoples of the earth and instituted the Sabbath as an eternal sign and blessing of Israel's unique status (Ezek 20:12; *Jub.* 2:18-33). The Sabbath commandment is the only one of the Ten Commandments instituted by God at creation (Gen 2:2-3; *Mek. Exod.* 20:17), and its purpose was to set Israel not only in a right relationship with God, but also in a right relationship with creation by observing proper duties to fellow Israelites, foreigners, slaves, animals, and even vegetation (Deut 5:12-15; Philo, *Moses* 2.22). In Sabbath observance righteous Jews became partners with God in the creation of the world and aided in bringing salvation to the world (*b. Shab.* 118-19b). The DSS preserve the most rigorous Sabbath regulations in Judaism, forbidding even the carrying of children, giving of help to birthing animals, or the retrieval of an animal fallen into a pit on the Sabbath (CD 10–11). Sabbath regulations set forth in tractate *Shabbat* in Mishnah and Talmud, which were observed in Pharisaic and rabbinic traditions, were only slightly less rigorous. Amplifying on Exod 35:1-3, Mishnah lists thirty-nine classes of work that profane the Sabbath, including those we might expect, such as plowing, hunting, butchering; and those we would not, such as tying or loosening knots, sewing more than one stitch, or writing more than one letter (*m. Shab.* 7:2). Rabbis endeavored to offer a rule, or at least a precedent, for every conceivable Sabbath question. The metarule of Sabbath observance was not to begin a work that might extend into Sabbath, and not to do any work on the Sabbath that was not absolutely necessary to preserve life (*m. Yoma* 8:6).[48]

The controversy in 6:1-5 reflects the Pharisaic determination to uphold proper Sabbath observance.[49] Matt 12:2 and Mark 2:24 report that the Pharisees as a whole challenged Jesus and the disciples for pilfering grain, but Luke lessens the conflict, saying only "*Some* of the Pharisees" (v. 2) questioned them. Pharisees were offended by Jesus' disregard of distinctions between clean and unclean (5:12-32), and not surprisingly they surveilled his Sabbath activities as well. The plucking of grain on the Sabbath may reflect the practice of eating grain left standing on the edges of fields for the poor (Lev 23:22; *m. Pe'ah*). This would explain why the Pharisees do not accuse Jesus and the disciples of theft

---

48. On Sabbath, see Schürer, *History of the Jewish People,* 2:467-75; Str-B 1:610-22.

49. The qualification of Sabbath in v. 1 by the Greek word *deuteroprōtos* is almost certainly a scribal blunder. The presence of this word in a number of strong manuscripts (A C D Θ Ψ) may indicate that the error occurred early in the manuscript tradition, and in an honored manuscript (tradition) that was followed by subsequent copyists. *Deuteroprōtos,* lit. "second-first," is a linguistic absurdity that occurs nowhere else in Greek literature (LSJ, 381). Attempts to account for it as a reference to "a second (Sabbath) after the first one," i.e., the second Sabbath after the Sabbath mentioned previously in 4:31 (and prior to the third Sabbath in 6:6), are offered by Leaney, *Luke,* 130-31. All attempts to date to salvage the word are "born of despair" (Marshall, *Luke,* 230). Lagrange proposes a possible explanation of this nonword: a copyist qualified the Sabbath in 6:1 as the "first" (Gk. *prōtos,* in comparison with the Sabbath mentioned in 6:6), another copyist qualified it as the "second" (Gk. *deuteros,* in comparison with the Sabbath mentioned in 4:31), and a third copyist combined the two qualifications into a nonword, *deuteroprōtos* (see Lagrange, *Luc,* 175; Metzger, *TCGNT,* 116; Fitzmyer, *Luke [I–IX],* 607-8; Bovon, *Lukas 1,1–9,50,* 266-67; Wolter, *Lukasevangelium,* 233-34).

per se, but only of doing "what is unlawful *on the Sabbath*" v. 2). According to Deut 23:25, pinching grain from a neighbor's field was permissible — but not on the Sabbath, according to later rabbinic ruling (*m. Shab.* 7:2). It might also be supposed that Jesus and the disciples were breaking the Sabbath travel prohibition, for walking more than 1,999 paces (= 875 yards [800 m]) was considered a journey, and hence a breach of Sabbath (CD 11:5-6). If, however, Jesus and the disciples were plucking grain along the edges of fields, again in accordance with *Pe'ah*, they may not have violated the travel prohibition.[50]

3-4 The Pharisees accuse Jesus and the disciples of Sabbath breaking (the "you" in v. 2 is plural in Greek), but Jesus alone answers them. Jesus normally appeals to his *exousia*, or God-given authority, when making pronouncements or judgments. In this instance, however, he follows the rabbinic precedent of appealing to Scripture in settling a controversy. "Have you never read what David did when he and his companions were hungry?" asks Jesus. The precedent to which Jesus appeals comes from the years when David was a fugitive from King Saul (1 Sam 21:1-6). In hunger and desperation, David entered "the house of God" (i.e., the tabernacle) in search of food. The bread in question refers to the twelve loaves that were placed on the altar Sabbath by Sabbath as food for the priests (Exod 40:23; Lev 24:5-9). The messianic implication of the bridegroom imagery in 5:34 is present here in much bolder relief. David was Israel's greatest king and precursor of Messiah (2 Sam 7:11-16; Ps 110:1). "'The days are coming,' declares the Lord, 'when I will raise up to David a righteous Branch, a King who will reign wisely and do what is right in the land. In his days Judah will be saved and Israel will live in safety'" (Jer 23:5; see also *Pss. Sol.* 17:21). The Davidic messianic hope was enshrined in the Eighteen Benedictions recited in the synagogue, "Cause the Branch of David thy servant speedily to sprout, and let his horn be exalted by thy salvation" (Ben. 15 [14]). In Scripture, tradition, and liturgy, David was enshrined as the inaugurator of a messianic reign that would exceed in glory David's historical reign.

Jesus cites David's violation of Torah not as an excuse for his action but as a *precedent* for it. In alluding to David, Jesus invites a comparison between his person and Israel's royal messianic prototype. This is the first of several references or allusions to David in Luke that help define what kind of Son of God Jesus is. A blind man in Jericho will call Jesus the Son of David (18:38-39); later in the temple — at the heart of Israel — Jesus will pursue the issue of Messiah by questioning the religious leaders how it is possible for Messiah to be both David's "son" and David's "lord" (20:41-44). Jews consider Messiah,

---

50. The case for the present story as an example of *Pe'ah* is made by M. Casey, "Culture and Historicity: The Plucking of the Grain (Mark 2:23-28)," *NTS* 34 (1988): 1-23. D. Hagner, "Jesus and the Synoptic Sabbath Controversies," *BBR* 19/2 (2009): 219-25, ably defends the essential historicity of the story from its several detractors.

since he is a descendent of David, to be "son of David," but Jesus asserts the higher authority of Messiah, who is "lord of David." In appealing to David here, Jesus begins to define his authority as the royal Son of God anticipated since the reign of David.[51]

5 By what authority does Jesus contravene Sabbath convention and presume to redefine it? The answer is given in the Promethean pronouncement of v. 5. True lordship over Sabbath is invested in the Son of Man. Some scholars argue that "Son of Man" in v. 5 is a circumlocution for "man," i.e., that humanity retains ultimate authority over Sabbath.[52] This argument may be attractive on humanistic grounds, but it is not supported by evidence within the Gospels. If, as we have noted, Sabbath was grounded in creation and was the most distinctive characteristic in Judaism, it is inconceivable that Jesus or any other rabbi would declare human supremacy over it.[53] It is not given to a mere human to supersede an order of creation. Moreover, "Son of Man" in the Gospels is not used with reference to humanity in general. Luke's first use of Son of Man in 5:24 refers to Jesus' forgiveness of sins, which is a divine rather than a human attribute. "Son of Man" appears only in the mouth of Jesus, and only with reference to himself. Particularly the definite article — *the* Son of Man — refers to Jesus' unique vocation as the Son of Man with divine

51. Codex Bezae (D) preserves a unique version of Luke 6:1-10. It places v. 5 after v. 10 and in its place reads: "On the same day, he [Jesus] saw a certain man working on the Sabbath and said to him, 'Man, if you know what you are doing, you are blessed; but if you do not know, you are accursed and a transgressor of the law.'" Bezae thus preserves a complex of three Sabbath stories — plucking grain (6:1-4), warning of man working on Sabbath (6:5), and healing of man with withered hand (6:6-10) — all of which are concluded by Jesus' pronouncement of the sovereignty of the Son of Man over the Sabbath (see Metzger, *TCGNT,* 117). The warning of the man working on the Sabbath preserved in Bezae appears in no other Gospel, but it bears stylistic similarities to Lukan style, including address in the vocative (5:20; 12:14; 22:58, 60), accusative indefinite pronoun (Gk. *tina*), and the word for "blessed" (Gk. *makarios*). Origen (*Comm. Matt.* 15.14) preserves a saying of Jesus from the Hebrew Gospel somewhat similar to the Bezaen addition, "[Jesus] said to him, 'Man, do the law and prophets.'" The Bezaen addition thus displays linguistic elements common to Luke and the Hebrew Gospel. Even if the Bezaen addition is not original with Luke, its inclusion in the Third Gospel can be plausibly explained as the result of a scribe or copyist who held the Hebrew Gospel in high esteem and recognized the appropriateness of this verse in the context of Luke 6:1-10. See Edwards, *Hebrew Gospel,* 333-35.

52. E.g., R. Funk, R. Hoover, and The Jesus Seminar, *The Five Gospels: What Did Jesus Really Say?* (San Francisco: HarperSanFancisco, 1997), 49, translates Mark 2:27-28 thus: "The sabbath was created for Adam and Eve, not Adam and Eve for the sabbath day. So, the son of Adam lords it ever over the sabbath day." By "Adam and Eve" and "son of Adam," the Jesus Seminar means any member of the human race. See the discussion and critique of this reading in R. Guelich, *Mark 1–8:26* (WBC; Dallas: Word Books, 1989), 125-27.

53. F. Beare, "The Sabbath Was Made for Man," *JBL* 79 (1960); 130-36; D. E. Nineham, *The Gospel of St Mark* (London: Adam & Charles Black, 1963), 108.

authority and power, in accordance with its use in Dan 7:13.[54] Even when "Son of Man" refers to Jesus' human suffering, as it frequently does, it nearly always refers to suffering in fulfillment of *divine* appointment (see on Son of Man at 5:26). "Son of Man" signifies various offices of Jesus, but in the Gospels it does not mean mere "man."

The Greek syntax of v. 5 is bold. "Lord" (Gk. *kyrios*) is shifted prominently to the front of the sentence, and "Son of Man" is placed at the end, thereby accentuating both titles. It could well be rendered, "Just who is Lord of the Sabbath? The Son of Man is!" God instituted the Sabbath (Gen 2:2-3), and Jesus expressly claims God's prerogatives, presuming preeminence over Sabbath! The purpose of the Sabbath, as originally intended by God, cannot be understood by Moses, and especially not by the rabbinic tradition subsequent to Moses, but only by Jesus, who is Lord of the Sabbath.

THE COST OF LEADERSHIP (6:6-11)

This story completes the sequence of seven stories Luke received from Mark 1:40–3:6. In each story Jesus charts a sovereign course, free alike from societal norms and expectations of scribes, Pharisees, and rabbinic interpretation of Torah. In each episode and encounter Jesus embodies the word of God (5:1) and the power of God (5:17) in ministry to people, especially needy people. His sovereign authority to redefine and even supersede Torah, and especially the Sabbath, has aroused opposition to his mission, however. Jesus began his ministry by a harrowing escape from his hometown of Nazareth (4:30), and he must continue it by contending with the fury of scribes and Pharisees (6:11).

6-8 On "another Sabbath" Jesus is in an unspecified synagogue service where a man with "a shriveled" hand is present. The Greek word for "shriveled" (*xēra*) occurs in Luke only here and once again at the crucifixion when Jesus declares, "If people do these things when the tree is green, what will happen when it is *dry*" (23:31; Gk. *xēra*). Luke may utilize this word to symbolize the arid and atrophied Judaism that he encounters in synagogues. Luke intensifies Mark's version of this story (3:1) by identifying the shriveled *right* hand (v. 6). Luke shows a preference for the right side of things.[55] Given the dominant

54. C. Moule, "'The Son of Man': Some of the Facts," *NTS* 41 (1995): 277-79.

55. Luke twice adds "right": to the shriveled hand (6:6; Mark 3:1) and to the lopped-off ear (22:50; Mark 14:47). Additionally, an angel appears at the right side of the altar (1:11), a penitent(?) thief is crucified on Jesus' right (23:33), and God's right hand of power (20:42; 22:69). Similar changes occur in Josephus in the restoration of Jeroboam's hand (1 Kgs 13:4) to his right hand (*Ant.* 8.408); Jonathan strikes Bacchides (1 Macc 9:47) with his right hand (*Ant.* 13.14). See H. J. Cadbury, *The Making of Luke-Acts*, 178.

function of the right hand in the ancient world, to restore one's right hand was to restore one to gainful employment and social propriety.[56] More important, Luke specifies that the scribes and Pharisees "watched [Jesus] closely to see if he would heal on the Sabbath" (v. 7). Jesus has previously healed on the Sabbath (4:31-37), and Luke's expression for "watched closely" (Gk. *paretērounto*; NIV "looking"), in the Greek middle voice, connotes close scrutiny from the authorities. The scrutiny is not impartial, for "they were looking for a reason to accuse Jesus" (v. 7). Jesus is fully aware "what they were thinking" (v. 8; so too 5:22; 9:47; 24:38). The Greek word for "thinking" *(dialogismos)* is a favorite Lukan word, occurring six times as a noun and six as a verb.[57] *Dialogismos* does not connote objective thinking, but thoughts that unsettle and offend. Luke's classic use of the term occurs in Simeon's prophecy that Jesus will be a sign that will be opposed, a piercing sword, exposing "the thoughts [*dialogismoi*] of many hearts" (2:35). All but two of Luke's uses of the term refer to Jesus, not as a placating savior, but as a disquieting savior whose reordering of life according to God's design brings questions, stress, and change into believers' lives.

9-11 Sabbath regulations could be overridden only in cases of endangerment to life (*m. Yoma* 8:6). Otherwise, the various schools of Judaism were agreed that Sabbath must be fully upheld.[58] First aid was deemed permissible to prevent an injury from worsening, but efforts toward a cure were regarded as work that must await the passing of Sabbath. A withered hand was not life threatening and thus did not qualify as an exception to Sabbath rules. Rabbinic tradition, in fact, forbade "straightening a deformed body or setting a broken limb [on the Sabbath]" (*m. Shab.* 22:6). Jesus orders the man to "stand up in front of everyone" (v. 9). He asks, "Which is lawful on the Sabbath: to do good or to do evil, to save life or to destroy it?" The question about doing good or evil obviously refers to healing the handicapped man. For Jesus, human need poses a moral imperative. Where good needs to be done, there can be no neutrality; and failure to do the good is to contribute to evil. It is thus not simply permissible to heal on Sabbath, it is *right* to do so, whether "lawful" or not. A litmus test of true versus false religion is its response to injustice. According to Luke, the religious authorities have nothing to say to Jesus' question. Their silence is self-incriminating, and Jesus returned their searching looks (v. 7), "looking around at them all" (v. 10). The religious authorities are not only willing to tolerate the lamentable condition of another human being, but to

---

56. "Right" was associated with conceptions of fortune, success, and salvation in the ancient (incl. Jewish) world. The right hand executes the main work (6:6), gives alms (Matt 6:3), performs laying on of hands (Rev. 1:17), is raised to heaven in oaths (Rev 10:5), receives the saving mark (Rev. 13:16), and extends it in handshakes of fellowship and trust (Gal 2:9; 2 Macc 12:11-12). See P. von der Osten-Sacken, *dexios, EDNT* 1:286.

57. 1:29; 2:35; 3:15; 5:21, 22 (2x); 6:8; 9:46, 47; 12:17; 20:14; 24:38.

58. See the discussion of Sabbath observance at 6:1-2.

use it as leverage against Jesus. Jesus does not use people for ulterior purposes. The test of all theology and morality is either passed or failed by one's response to the weakest and most defenseless members of society. For Jesus the call of God presents itself urgently in the plight of the man with the shriveled hand.

Jesus' second question — "to save life or destroy it?" — comes as a surprise. It also radically redirects the story. The issue before the synagogue is whether or not Jesus will heal on the Sabbath.[59] Or so it seems. Jesus, however, knows the intentions of some present (v. 8), and to them the second question is posed. This question no longer refers to the disabled man, but to the religious authorities themselves, and to their fierce antagonism to Jesus. If Jesus heals on the Sabbath, then he perpetrates his Sabbath violations, which will give the authorities reason to dispatch him. Both of Jesus' questions link his fate to that of the man with the shriveled hand. The response of Jesus to the man with the shriveled hand thus determines the response of the religious authorities to him. He does not equivocate or weigh his response in light of foreseeable consequences. "Stretch out your hand," he commands. A decision of faith now confronts the man. Most people with physical deformities seek to conceal them. What Jesus commands is the last thing the man wants to do if he is to hide his deformity, but the first thing he must do if he is to be healed of it. "He did so, and his hand was completely restored" (v. 10). The man's infirmity could be healed only by exposing it to Jesus. Faith is a risk that Jesus is worthy of trust when no other hope can be trusted.

Jesus' compassion is free to the man with the shriveled hand, but costly to himself. The hand is restored, but Jesus' opponents were filled with madness.[60] The Greek word for "madness" (NIV "furious"), *anoia*, occurs in the NT only here and in 2 Tim 3:9, where it means "folly." The word means to "take leave of one's senses," "to be swept up in irrational anger."[61] The parallel texts in Matt 12:14 and Mark 3:6 report that opponents wanted to "destroy"

---

59. Matt 12:9-14 omits the reference to "to save life or to kill," thus maintaining the focus of the story on the healing. The same is true of the version of the story preserved in Jerome (*Comm. Matt.* 12:13), who also includes the man's vocation: "In the Gospel which the Nazarenes and the Ebionites use, which we have recently translated out of Hebrew into Greek, and which is called by most people the authentic [Gospel of] Matthew, the man who had the withered hand is described as a mason who pleaded for help in the following words: I was a mason and earned my livelihood with my hands; I beseech thee, Jesus, to restore to me my health that I may not with ignominy have to beg for my bread" (*NTApoc.* 1:160).

60. The rendering of the NIV, "But the Pharisees and the teachers of the law were furious" (v. 11), is overtranslated. The original Greek does not name Pharisees and teachers of the law, and "fury" would be better rendered, "they were filled with madness."

61. J. Behm, *anoia*, *TWNT* 4:960-61; *anoia*, *EDNT* 1:105. Cyril of Alexandria, *Comm. Luc.*, Hom. 23, speaks of Jesus' Sabbath behaviors producing "envy" and "madness" in the Pharisees.

Jesus, whereas Luke softens the resolve to "what they might do to Jesus" (v. 11). Nevertheless, the use of *anoia* signals that Jesus is now the object of destructive rage on the part of the authorities. The reasons for their resolve are not stated, but the evidence against Jesus has been compounding: Sabbath violations (4:31-37; 6:1-5), fraternizing with lepers and sinners (5:12-16, 27-32), disregarding rabbinic custom (5:33-38), and presumption to forgive sins (5:17-26). The life and writings of Dietrich Bonhoeffer have familiarized the Christian world with the expression "the cost of discipleship." This section is a reminder that there is an even greater "cost of leadership." Jesus' mission to the captives and oppressed, as announced in the Nazareth synagogue (4:18-19), has resulted in mortal opposition from religious authorities.

CHAPTER SIX

Jesus Calls and Instructs His Disciples

Luke 6:12-49

In the previous section (5:12–6:11), Luke portrayed Jesus' sovereign authority as Son of God to cleanse lepers, forgive sins, call sinners, challenge religious authorities, and redefine Judaism and the Sabbath. In these matters, he acted not only on behalf of God, but *as* God. In 6:12-49 his ministry expands from a ministry of one to a ministry of many — and to many. The section commences in v. 12 with Jesus in prolonged prayer. In Luke, prayer typically signals a new stage in salvation history, here achieved in the call of the Twelve. The only other Lukan episode introduced with such intense prayer signals another divine revelation, the transfiguration in 9:28-29. Following the call of the Twelve, vv. 17-19 extend the ministry of Jesus and the Twelve to crowds from greater Palestine and beyond. Together, Jesus and the Twelve will minister to greater crowds than Jesus heretofore has ministered to alone (4:44; 5:1). The unit concludes with Jesus teaching disciples and crowds about the kingdom of God (vv. 20-49). This section is thus an outreach of grace, beginning with Jesus in solitary prayer (v. 12), extending to the call of the twelve apostles (vv. 13-16), then to a larger group of disciples (v. 17), and finally to healing and proclaiming the kingdom of God to greater Palestine (vv. 18-19).[1] The whole is orchestrated like a symphony that begins with a single motif, which then weaves its way throughout the orchestra, gathering complementary instruments and melodies, until the full orchestra reaches its finale.

---

1. On the crescendo effect of this unit, see Lagrange, *Luc,* 179-80; Wolter, *Lukasevangelium,* 240.

JESUS REPRODUCES HIMSELF
IN TWELVE APOSTLES (6:12-19)

12-13 Lists of the twelve apostles are found in the NT in 6:14-16, Matt 10:2-4, Mark 3:16-19, and Acts 1:13 (minus Judas).[2] Luke's introduction of the Twelve contains several novel elements not present in other NT lists of the Twelve. The Greek style of vv 12-13 is distinctively Hebraic, suggesting that Luke's introduction of the Twelve may derive from the Hebrew Gospel.[3] The content of the verses is equally distinctive. The phrase "It happened in those days" (NIV "One of those days") appears in the NT only in Luke, and signifies a plot progression (1:39; 6:12; 24:18; Acts 1:15). Above all, Luke prefaces the call of the Twelve with Jesus praying. In calling the Twelve, Jesus prays on a mountain, as he does frequently in Luke (v. 12; 9:28; 19:29, 37; 21:37; 22:39). On mountains he experiences intimate fellowship with God, but he descends to the plain (v. 17) in order to preach, heal, and minister to crowds.[4] Prayer plays a more significant role in the Lukan portrayal of Jesus than it does in the other Gospels, with references to prayer almost always in the verb form, i.e., to the *activity* of praying.[5] In Luke, Jesus prays before or during the most significant events of his life, and especially at decisive junctures in the unfolding of the plan of salvation.[6] We may erroneously assume that Jesus had a link with God that gave him effortless access to the Father's will. How significant that Jesus, the Son of God indwelt by the Holy Spirit (3:21-22), in whom God's presence is powerful to heal (5:17; 6:19), must spend all night praying in discernment of God's will. The uniqueness of Jesus' prayer in v. 12 is signaled by a Greek phrase found nowhere else in Scripture: he spent the night "in the prayer of God" (NIV "praying to God"). This phrase suggests not only prayer to God, but prayer in conformity with the very nature and will of God.[7]

2. Outside the NT, a partial list of Jesus' apostles appears in Epiphanius, *Pan.* 30.13.2-3: "And when Jesus came into Capernaum, he entered the house of Simon who was called Peter, and having opened his mouth, Jesus said, 'As I passed beside the Lake of Tiberias, I chose John and James, the sons of Zebedee, and Simon and Andrew and Thaddaeus and Simon the Zealot and Judas the Iscariot, and you, Matthew, I called while you were sitting at the tax table, and you followed me. You therefore I desire to be twelve apostles for a witness to Israel.'" For a discussion of this text, see Edwards, *Hebrew Gospel*, 66-68. The role of the apostles as authorized envoys of Christ is already celebrated in *1 Clem.* (42), which is one of the oldest extracanonical Christian writings (ca. 90-100).

3. See Edwards, *Hebrew Gospel*, 304.

4. Schweizer, *Lukas*, 75.

5. Prayer as a noun occurs only three times in Luke, but verbal descriptions occur twenty times.

6. Bovon, *Luke 1,1–9,50*, 280-81.

7. Codex Bezae omits "of God," thereby bringing the phrase into conformity with other

At daybreak Jesus chooses twelve men from among his followers, naming them "apostles" (v. 13). Acts 1:21-22 reports that a group of disciples had accompanied Jesus from the time of his baptism. From this group Jesus chooses an elite group of associates. The Greek verbs for "called" *(prosphōnein)* and "chose" *(eklegesthai)* are distinctively Lukan. The first verb emphasizes the authority of Jesus' call (v. 13; 13:12), and the second, which usually has God or Jesus as its subject, signifies divine election.[8] Together they emphasize Jesus' sovereign role in constituting the Twelve. The same sovereignty extends to the naming of the Twelve. In Jesus' day the right to bestow a name belonged to a superior, e.g., maker, master, owner, or parent. The bestowal of a name determined the essence and purpose of the thing named. Thus, the "naming" (Gk. *onomazein;* NIV "designated") of the apostles is essential to their constitution by Jesus.

The word "**apostle**" (Gk. *apostolos*) derives from *apostellein,* "to send," signifying that the sending nature of God is instituted in the mission of the Twelve. The fulfillment of salvation history is a history of divine sending — of Gabriel as its harbinger (1:19, 26), of John as its forerunner (7:27); of Jesus as its atoning embodiment (4:18), and of the Twelve, who proclaim the kingdom of God and heal with Jesus' authority (v. 13; 9:2; 10:1-3, 16; 11:49; 13:34). "Apostle," like the Greek word *agapē* (love), is a word to which Christians imputed a sense not inherent in its secular Greek usage. The word was originally a naval technical term, especially for warfare. The earliest use of the term similar to its Christian sense occurred in the Cynics, who referred to their wandering philosophers as "apostles." The Hebrew *shaliah* likewise referred to an "authorized messenger of an established community." Both of these prior uses may have contributed to the Christian understanding of "apostle." The earliest documented Christian use of the term occurs in Paul, where it refers to one commissioned to proclaim the message of the gospel of Jesus. The designation apostle, as both a name and reference to an office, doubtless derives from Jesus himself. In the early church, "apostle" covered a wider semantic field than only the Twelve apostles called by Jesus; hence, it is not a redundancy for Luke to refer to "the twelve apostles" in 6:13. The emphasis in v. 13 falls on the office of apostleship rather than the name, for in Luke Jesus does not address his elect followers as "apostles," but either as "the Twelve" (8:1; 9:1; 18:31; 22:3, 47), or more frequently as "disciples" *(mathētēs).*[9]

---

references to Jesus praying. "The prayer of God" is evidently not a Hebraism, for the typical Heb. *battipilah le'lohim* means "in prayer to God."

8. 6:13; 9:35; Acts 1:2, 24; 13:17; 15:7, 22, 25.

9. For a full discussion of "apostle," see K. Rengstorf, *apostolos, TWNT* 1:406-48. Regarding the Twelve in Luke, including a citation of relevant literature, see Klein, *Lukasevangelium,* 238-39; Nolland, *Luke 1:1–9:20,* 266-68; Str-B 1:529-38.

With reference to the apostolic cohort, the number **twelve** is more important than "apostle," for although the names in the four NT apostolic lists differ slightly, the names always number twelve.[10] The twelve apostles, and the emphatic symbolic use of the same number in Revelation (7:5-8; 12:1; 21:12-21), make "twelve" a commonplace among Christian readers. Somewhat surprisingly, twelve is not a common number in Jewish literature outside the OT. Apart from a reference to twelve council elders at Qumran (1QS 8:1), for example, the number twelve was not a common number for Jewish assemblies; thus, in Acts 6:3 the apostles chose seven deacons, and in Talmud, Jesus is reputed to have had five disciples.[11] Twelve is more common in the OT, although, when employed with conscious significance, it usually recalls the twelve tribes of Israel (e.g., Gen 35:23-26; 49:1-28) or persons or objects related to them. Thus, Joshua appoints twelve men, one from each tribe in Israel, to place twelve stones in the Jordan before the conquest of Canaan (Josh 4:2); Solomon's personal guard consists of twelve officers (1 Kgs 4:7); Ezra appoints twelve priests (Ezra 8:24). The importance of the twelve tribes may have deterred the use of twelve for other fellowships in Israel. The twelve apostles are consciously symbolic of the twelve tribes of Israel, for the early church understood Jesus to be intentionally reconstituting Israel (Rev 21:12-14).[12] According to 22:30 (and Matt 19:28), the Twelve not only extend Jesus' earthly ministry, but they will sit in judgment over Israel in God's coming kingdom. As a reconstitution of Israel, the choice of twelve apostles signifies to Gentiles that "salvation is from the Jews" (John 4:22), i.e., that salvation comes to the world via the saving line from Abraham to Jesus; and it signifies to Jews that the destiny of Israel is fulfilled in the fellowship and service of Jesus.

14-16 The four apostolic lists in the NT agree in three main features. (1) The names are arranged in three groups of four. (2) The same apostles — (Simon) Peter, Philip, and James of Alphaeus — head each of the three groups. (3) The first group of four apostles always consists of Peter, Andrew, James, and John (although Andrew's name appears last in Mark and Acts; likewise Mark

---

10. The essential importance of twelve is indicated in Acts 1:15-26, where Matthias, an otherwise unknown disciple, is chosen to fill the complement of the Twelve after Judas's defection. Occasionally "twelve" is used when only eleven apostles are meant, e.g., *Gos. Pet.* 59; *Asc. Isa.* 3:17; 4:3. On the Twelve in early Christian literature, see *NTApoc.* 2:16-25.

11. "Jesus had five disciples: Matthai, Nakai, Nezer, Buni, and Todah" (*b. Šabb.* 43a). For a discussion of this text, see G. Dalman, *Jesus Christ in the Talmud, Midrash, and Zohar, and the Liturgy of the Synagogue* (Cambridge: Deighton, Bell, 1893), 71-79.

12. " 'The Twelve' represent proleptically the renewed people of God, whose members are measured by its standard. They are sent by Jesus and proclaim with word and deed the imminent coming of the time of salvation. They prepare the land for the time of salvation by their conduct and they summon it to repentance. They are thus at the same time important witnesses for the character and content of the words of Jesus" (T. Holtz, *dōdeka, EDNT* 1:363).

13:3). With further regard to the third feature, Peter, James, and John form an inner circle among the Twelve that accompany Jesus on special occasions (5:10; 8:51; 9:28). Simon is nicknamed "the rock" (Ar. *Cephas,* Gk. *Petros*), a term that designates his predominant role among the apostles rather than his rock-like character, for firmness and stability do not always characterize Peter, even after Pentecost (Gal 2:11-14). Peter is the cornerstone of the apostolic college not because of his merit but because of Jesus' call and designation.[13] The position of James in the Synoptic lists suggests a status second in command to Peter.[14] James was the first apostle to be martyred, and his show execution by Herod Agrippa I, grandson of Herod the Great, in Acts 12:2 evinces his influential role.[15] Three of the apostles are referenced further in the NT only by the Fourth Gospel: Andrew (John 1:41, 44; 6:8; 12:22), Philip (John 1:44-49; 6:5-7; 12:21-22; 14:8-9), and Thomas (John 11:16; 14:5; 20:24-29; 21:2). Of Bartholomew, James the son of Alphaeus, Thaddaeus, and Simon the Zealot, we hear nothing further in the NT.

Beyond these details, the apostolic lists leave readers with three outstanding problems. The first concerns "Matthew." The "Levi" called by Jesus (5:27; Mark 2:14) is not named in any list of the Twelve. Christian tradition has usually accounted for this by the reasonable assumption that "Matthew" in all apostolic lists refers to Levi, who was also known as Matthew (so Matt 9:9).[16] A second problem concerns Judas of James, who appears in v. 16 and Acts 1:13 in place of Thaddaeus (or Lebbaeus in Codex Bezae) in Matt 10:3 and Mark 3:18. Here again, Judas of James and Thaddaeus may have been the same individual.[17] The third problem is Judas Iscariot, who is furthered referenced mainly in the Fourth Gospel (6:71; 12:4; 13:2, 26; 14:22), and who has become a tradition unto himself in Western literature. The meaning of "Iscariot" is obscure. "The man of Kerioth" (Heb. *ish Kerioth*) is its most probable meaning, identifying Judas with the town of Kerioth, some twenty miles (30 km) due

---

13. On Peter's primacy among the apostles, see M. Hengel, *Saint Peter: The Underestimated Apostle* (trans. T. Trapp; Grand Rapids: Eerdmans, 2010), 1-102.

14. Andrew's name intervenes in Matt 10:2 and Luke 6:14 only because he is Peter's brother.

15. Plummer, *Luke,* 173.

16. This solution commanded assent from most church fathers. Jerome, e.g., regularly equates Levi with Matthew (*Vir. ill.* 3; *Comm. Matt.* Praefatio). Some fathers, however, doubted the equation of Levi and Matthew (Origen, *Cels.* 1.62) or rejected it (Didymus of Alexandria, see at 5:27, n. 25). A review of the problem is offered by D. Dulling, "Matthew (Disciple)," *ABD* 4:618-22.

17. Plummer, *Luke,* 172, suggests that "Lebbaeus" can be explained as an attempt to include Levi among the apostles, the Greek form of which might be *Leb(b)aios.* That leaves the name "Thaddaeus," which, despite any direct evidence, may have been a second name of Judas, son of James.

east of the Dead Sea (Jer 48:24; Amos 2:2). This would make Judas the only apostle of Jesus not from Galilee. An alternative suggestion derives "Iscariot" from the Latin *sicarius* ("dagger [man]"), perhaps an identification of Judas with a radical fringe of Zealot assassins.[18] This suggestion may represent later Christian speculation, for there is no certain evidence that Judas was a Zealot; moreover, it was very uncommon for sons to be named after political parties.

The list of the Twelve is significant in three additional respects. First, apart from various pious but unreliable legends, our knowledge of many names of the apostles is meager or nonexistent.[19] What their specific contributions were to the advancement of the gospel, we do not know. Their names, however, like the even longer list of names in Rom 16:1-16, stand as silent witnesses to the truth that the existence of the church is indebted to the labors of those who for the most part remain unacknowledged, unnamed, or unknown. Second, as far as we know, none of the apostles comes from the upper echelon of Jewish leadership. They all derive from the common folk, the *am-ha'arets,* "people of the land." Within that nondescript category, names like Peter, Andrew, James, and John represent the respectable (or acceptable) middle,[20] with the opposite extremes present in Matthew, the collaborating tax collector, and Simon the Zealot, whose name associates him with a movement committed to holy war against Rome. The differences of the latter two especially exceed anything that might conceivably unite them, except for the authoritative call of Jesus. Finally, the name of "Judas Iscariot, who betrayed [Jesus]" is especially significant. The church must have been tempted to strike from the list of the Twelve a name that had caused such scandal.[21] The enduring presence of Judas's name among the Twelve is a testimony to the historical veracity of the Gospels and

18. On the reading *Ishkarioth* (or *Ishkariotēs*), see Metzger, *TCGNT,* 21-22. For an argument that the name refers to Judas's falsehood, see Marshall, *Luke,* 240-41. B. Pixner makes the intriguing but speculative suggestion that the connection of Judas's name with "Simon the Zealot" (also 6:15-16) can be explained by supposing that both came from Gamala, the eagle's nest of the Zealots northeast of the Sea of Galilee (*Wege des Messias und Stätten der Urkirche* [ed. R. Riesner; Basel: Brunnen Verlag, 1991], 76). M. Hengel, however, cautions against assuming Judas was a Zealot (*The Zealots* [trans. D. Smith; Edinburgh: T&T Clark, 1989], 338). In the wake of the publication of *The Gospel of Judas,* the name of Judas has been revisited by J. Taylor, "The Name 'Iskarioth' (Iscariot)," *JBL* 129/2 (2010): 367-83, who surveys the various hypotheses regarding the name, suggesting (implausibly, in my opinion) that Iskarioth derives from "choking" or "bursting," i.e., referring to the manner of Judas's death.

19. See W. Bienert, "The Picture of the Apostle in Early Christian Tradition," *NTApoc.* 2:5-27.

20. *Barn.* 5.9, on the contrary, says the disciples were "iniquitous above all sin," in order to demonstrate that Jesus called the unrighteous.

21. Ambrose, *Exp. Luc.* 5.42-45, reflecting on the name Judas within the apostolic cohort, writes: "How great is the integrity of the Lord, who preferred to endanger his judgment among us, rather than his compassion."

to the Evangelists' understanding of the church. The fellowship recruited and trained by Jesus is not an untarnished, utopian society. Judas reminds the church that followers of Jesus are not perfect, nor do they have to be in order to accomplish the purposes for which he calls them. But Judas also reminds the church that proximity to Christ does not guarantee immunity from betraying Christ; moreover, when those closest to Christ betray him, they do the greatest damage to the cause of Christ.[22]

17-19   With the Twelve, Jesus descends from the mountain to "a level place" (v. 17) in order to teach the crowds. The Greek *pedinos,* which occurs in the NT only here, means "flat" or "level." This same word regularly occurs in the LXX in contrast to the hill country,[23] and Luke probably intends *pedinos* to mean the lower ground adjacent to the Sea of Galilee. There Jesus meets with "a large crowd of his disciples," indicating once again that his disciples comprised a larger group than the twelve apostles. Luke describes the crowds in vv. 17-19 with two terms that he otherwise rarely uses together. The first, used twice in vv. 17, 19, describes the larger group of disciples just mentioned by Gk. *ochlos* ("crowd"), which includes intermittent sympathizers who gather around Jesus (8:4, 19), follow him (7:9, 11; 9:11; 14:25), wait for him (9:37), hear his word (5:1), and marvel at his works (11:14). The second term, occurring in v. 17, is Greek *laos,* "people" (see discussion of this term at 1:10). This term, occurring nearly forty times in Luke and nearly fifty in Acts, is Luke's preferred term for the people for whom the gospel of salvation is intended. This people is the object of the joyful news of the Savior's birth (2:10), and throughout the Gospel the object of the Savior's teaching (7:1, 29; 9:13; 19:48; 20:1, 9, 45). This people, also, will abandon Jesus in his passion and call for his crucifixion (23:18) — although Luke lays the blame for their defection more on Jewish leaders than on the people themselves. In the Gospel *laos* refers primarily to Jews, but in Acts the people of God will include both Jews and Gentiles (Acts 18:10).[24]

Jesus' earlier audiences were drawn from Galilee and Judea (5:17). His fame has now grown, for people gather to hear him from "Judea, from Jerusalem, and from the coastal region around Tyre and Sidon" (v. 17). The parallel passage in Matt 4:25 and Mark 3:7 includes people from Galilee. Luke omits Galilee from his list, perhaps because the presence of Galileans in Jesus' audience is presupposed. A variant though reputable tradition also includes people from Transjordan.[25] Jesus' audience thus comprises greater Palestine,

---

22. Note the replay of this sorry reality in *Mart. Pol.* 6.2: "those who betrayed [Polycarp] were of his own house."

23. *Pedinos* often translates Heb. *shephelah,* which became a proper noun in later Judaism for the lowlands adjacent to the Mediterranean coast.

24. On these two terms, see Klein, *Lukasevangelium,* 241.

25. So א (original hand!), W, Latin. Transjordan was the region east of the Jordan River.

with diverse ethnicities as well as diverse geographies, for Transjordan was a Jewish-Gentile region, and Tyre and Sidon were predominantly Gentile. People were drawn to Jesus by three preeminent qualities: to hear him teach, to receive healing, and to be freed from evil spirits (v. 18). Jesus' fame is the result of faithfulness to his vocation as Servant of the Lord, for these three qualities summarize the vocation that Jesus applied to himself in his inaugural sermon in Nazareth (4:18-19; Isa 61:1). Luke again reports that "power was coming from Jesus" (v. 19; also 4:14; 5:17; 8:46). The power referred to is "the power of the Holy Spirit" with which Jesus returned from the wilderness temptation (4:14). Power often divides, and great power easily, almost invariably, becomes coercive (22:25). The magnetism of Jesus' unconditional love is a power that unites, however, drawing people into fellowship with himself. People — here crowds (v. 19), later a sinful woman (7:39), later still a humiliated woman (8:44-47) — simply want to "touch" Jesus, for his power is a holy contagion of healing, forgiveness, and wholeness.

COSTLY DISCIPLESHIP (6:20-49)

Following the designation of the twelve apostles, Jesus instructs his disciples — both the Twelve and the larger company from which they are chosen — in behaviors that uniquely distinguish Christians. His instruction is not a treatise on humanistic ethics, or even on religious ethics such as the Ten Commandments or the Eightfold Path of the Buddha. It is a sample of the sacrificial ethics expected of those who heed the call to follow Jesus. Nor is it a treatise on what people must do to enter the kingdom of God, but rather on what is expected of those who already are in the kingdom.[26] The instruction is sometimes referred to as the "Sermon on the Plain," in distinction from the "Sermon on the Mount" of Matt 5–7. The designation mistakenly suggests that 6:20-49 is a Lukan version of the Sermon on the Mount. Matt consciously presents Jesus' Sermon on the Mount (Matt 5:1) as a counterpart to Moses' revealing of the law from Mount Sinai (Exod 19–20; Deut 5:1-22).[27] In Luke, however, the mountain

---

26. Evans, *Luke,* 107.

27. Matt's parallels between Jesus and Moses are clear. Moses climbed Mount Sinai to receive the law from God (Exod 19:3), sat on Sinai to teach (*b. Meg.* 21a), and descended from Sinai after presenting Israel with Torah (Exod. 34:29); likewise Jesus begins the Sermon by ascending a mountain, teaches while sitting on the mountain (Matt 5:1), and afterward descends from the mountain (Matt 8:1). Jesus also addresses similar topics in Matt's Sermon, as does Moses on Sinai, including murder, adultery, divorce, oaths, revenge, and love (D. Allison, *The Sermon on the Mount: Inspiring the Moral Imagination* [New York: Crossroad, 1999], 19).

is gone, as are all references to the law.[28] Luke's instruction comprises only thirty verses, whereas Matt's Sermon comprises more than a hundred. Several topics in 6:20-49 are repeated in the Sermon on the Mount, but the wording is rarely exact enough to require a common exemplar.[29] Moreover, material from Matt 6 is wholly absent in Luke 6 (although similarities with Matt. 6 occur later in Luke). Finally, and most important, a number of elements in Luke 6 appear to represent an earlier and more primitive form than their counterparts in Matt 5–7.[30] Luke 6 does not appear to be a counterpart to Matt's Sermon on the Mount, but an earlier anthology of Jesus' ethical teaching that was widely known and variously quoted in the early church.[31]

Here as elsewhere in the Third Gospel, Luke preserves the didactic tradition he has received with particular fidelity, presumably out of reverence for the words of Jesus.[32] Luke heralds the way of the kingdom of God as a radical antithesis to the ways of the world. The way of the kingdom is one of solidarity with the poor and needy, not the pursuits and indulgences of the wealthy. The way of the kingdom resists conformity to the common denominator of the here-and-now, but allows life's here-and-now to be permeated by the eternal realities of the coming kingdom of God. Luke's sermon addresses disciples directly in second-person plural — "you [all]" — with concrete and sacrificial ways of living in accordance with the call of Jesus.

Blessings and Woes (6:20-26)

20-23 The sermon begins with "Jesus lifting up his eyes" (NIV "looking"), a Hebraic expression that in its three NT uses signals a moment of resolve (v. 20; 16:23; John 17:1). Matt addresses Jesus' sermon to both crowds and disciples (5:1), but Luke addresses it to disciples alone and on behaviors unique to Jesus

---

28. The reference to "level place" (6:17) is probably intended as a contrast to the hill country; hence, it could be translated "lowlands" (see discussion at 6:17). The standard word for "plain" in the LXX, *pedion*, occurring nearly 200 times, does not occur in the NT. The following Matthean material is absent from Luke: Matt 5:17, 19-20, 21-24, 27-28, 29-30, 33-39a, 43; 6:1-8, 16-18; 7:6, 15. See Lagrange, *Luc*, 184; Fitzmyer, *Luke (I–IX)*, 628.

29. For precise comparisons of Lukan and Matthean material, see Klostermann, *Lukasevangelium*, 78; Wolter, *Lukasevangelium*, 245-46; Plummer, *Luke*, 178.

30. For a discussion of the probable priority of Lukan material shared in common with Matt, see Edwards, *Hebrew Gospel*, 246-50.

31. See 1 Pet 3:14; 4:14; *Barn.* 19:4; *1 Clem.* 13:3; Polycarp, *Phil.* 2.3; *Did.* 3:7; *Gos. Thom.* 54, 68, 69; Clement of Alexandria, *Protr.* 10.94.4.

32. "Luke has been quite sparing in altering the text of the Sermon on the Plain, quite obviously out of reverence for the words of Jesus" (Jeremias, *Sprache des Lukasevangeliums*, 151).

alone so that they may be "fully trained like their teacher" Jesus (v. 40). The specific focus on disciples in vv. 20-49, and their unique behaviors in the face of persecution, may suggest that Luke is presenting Jesus' teaching for a persecuted church. The sermon begins with four blessings followed by four contrasting woes, both of which are prefigured in Mary's Magnificat (1:51-53). The Greek word *makarios* carried strong and palpable connotations in Luke's day that are only partially captured by the word "blessing." In classical Greek society *makarios* designated the upper social caste, which, in contrast to the lower class of slaves and servants, enjoyed wealth, prosperity, happiness, blessings, and good fortune. In the NT *makarios* has by and large shed its quantitative reference to goods and things and has become reserved for qualitative characteristics, especially joy, happiness, and well-being that manifest themselves in believers as they participate in God's kingdom. In the LXX, *makarios* translates the Hebrew *asher*, "blessed," which occurs frequently in Pss and Prov. But unlike the wisdom tradition, where blessings are normally a reward of wise conduct, especially conduct in accord with Torah, Jesus' blessings are the surprising eschatological gift of God to those who follow him in costly discipleship.[33]

The blessings and woes set forth the way of Jesus concretely and directly, and in contrast to conventional societal behaviors. Those blessed are not "poor *in spirit*" (Matt 5:3), i.e., blessed because of spiritual humility, but those who have given up everything and are persecuted for Jesus' sake (18:18-30; Acts 2:44-47; 4:32-35).[34] The poor are prominently championed in the Pss and Prophets, but elsewhere in the OT and intertestamental literature their importance diminishes.[35] Strikingly, Jesus *begins* his blessings with the poor, assuring his disciples, "*yours* is the kingdom of God" (v. 20).[36] Luke refers to the poor twice as often as do both Matt and Mark, and often in prominent contexts. In Isa 61:1, the foundational text of Jesus' inaugural sermon in Nazareth, "proclaiming good news to the poor" (4:18) is the first characteristic of God's Spirit-anointed Servant, and it is likewise preeminent in Jesus' sermon. In Wisdom literature the poor can be condemned for bringing poverty on themselves

---

33. On *makarios*, see G. Bertram and G. Hauck, *makarios, TWNT* 4:365-73; Fitzmyer, *Luke (I–IX)*, 632-33.

34. *Gos. Thom.* 54, reproduces Luke's wording more closely than Matt's, "Blessed are the poor, for yours is the kingdom of heaven."

35. J. Pleins, "Poor, Poverty," *IDB* 5:402-14, finds "a notable lack of poverty language," esp. in the Pentateuch and Deuteronomic histories, concluding that "the plight of the poor was not a vital issue for ancient Israel's 'historians'" (413).

36. The conclusion of Str-B 1:190, that "by the 'poor' Jesus means that broad class of belittled and despised among his people, whom the rabbis referred to as 'the am-haaretz' [the people of the land]" may be appropriate for the understanding of the poor in Matt 5:3, but less so for Luke, who identifies the "poor" with the disciples whom Jesus addresses in the sermon.

through sloth (Prov 6:6-8; 10:4) and irresponsibility (Prov 13:18; 23:21); later rabbis likewise ascribed both riches and poverty to (spiritual) merit.[37] Even when poverty is viewed more positively in the OT — for example, in commands to be generous to the poor (Deut 15:1-11) or in the prayer of the poor for deliverance (Pss 12:5; 86:1) — poverty remains a condition to be relieved and remedied. Jesus does not extol poverty per se as an ideal or virtue, i.e., disciples are not happy *because* they are poor. Ambrose rightly understood that "poverty is neutral. The poor can be either good or evil."[38] But poverty does make disciples aware of their need and dependence on God, and their physical wants open them to the abundant love of God and joy of salvation. Poverty is not a reflection of divine displeasure, but rather, like Pascal's "God-created vacuum," something that God uses to increase dependence on himself, and to fill with himself. There can be joy *in* their poverty, for everything contained in the kingdom of God (see on term at 4:43) is their possession.[39]

Besides Jesus' words to the poor, he pronounces blessing over the hungry, the sorrowful, and the persecuted (vv. 21-23). The Sermon on the Mount spiritualizes the reference to hunger as "those who hunger and thirst for *righteousness*" (Matt 5:6), but Luke leaves hunger and tears unqualified (v. 21). Indeed, he intensifies their urgency to those who hunger and weep "now." In the Magnificat, Mary recalled Ps 107:9, extolling God who "filled the hungry with good things but has sent the rich away empty" (1:53). Jesus applies the same divine mercy to his disciples. The three beatitudes related to hunger, sorrow, and persecution (vv. 21-22) are not exactly parallel to the first on poverty. Poverty, as noted above, cannot be relieved, for it is an indispensable condition revealing the need and dependence of Jesus' disciples on God. Such dependence is the essence of the kingdom of God. The last three conditions, by contrast, will be remedied — and extravagantly so. The hungry will be satisfied, the sorrowful will laugh, the persecuted will receive great heavenly reward (vv. 21-23). Hunger and sorrow refer to lamentable conditions for which there may or may not be culpable parties. But the last beatitude describes the undisguised and unrestrained ill will to which disciples will be subjected: they will be hated, excluded, insulted, rejected, and slandered because they follow the Son of Man (Isa 66:5).[40] This beatitude illustrates with particular clarity that Jesus is not

37. *M. Qidd.* 4.14 quotes R. Meir (second c.) that "neither poverty nor wealth is due to the craft [of an individual], but all depends upon one's [spiritual] merit."

38. Ambrose, *Exp. Luc.* 5:62-68; cited in Just, *Luke*, 104.

39. On Luke's Beatitudes, see Schlatter, *Evangelien nach Markus und Lukas*, 221.

40. The version of this beatitude preserved in *Gos. Thom.* 68-69 combines the literal and spiritualized versions of it in both Luke and Matt: "Jesus said, Blessed are you when you are hated and persecuted; and no place will be found where you have not been persecuted. . . . Blessed are those who have been persecuted in their hearts, these are they who have known the Father in truth."

setting forth a universal moral code, but addressing disciples who encounter hardships precisely because they follow the Son of Man. This beatitude, too, applies a promise from the infancy narrative — "salvation from our enemies and from the hand of all who hate us" (1:71) — to Jesus' disciples.

Disciples are not to respond to the foregoing trials and adversities reciprocally and proportionally. Rather, they are to respond in a manner wholly unwarranted: they are to "rejoice" (v. 23). The Greek word for "rejoice" is in the passive voice, "overjoyed," implying that joy in the face of such adversities is given, not self-produced. The source of the joy is not poverty, hunger, sorrow, and ill-treatment themselves, although persecuted believers may take consolation in knowing that they share the fate of the prophets before them. The source of joy is *God,* who has ordained a "great reward in heaven" (v. 23). Because their destinies are determined not by sin, sorrow, and Satan, but by the eternal and triumphant God, believers are to "leap for joy" (v. 23; *skirtan*). This verb refers to the frisking of young goats or lambs. Its only other NT occurrence is in Luke's description of John's joyful movement in the womb of Elizabeth at the news of Mary's pregnancy (1:41, 44). The joy of v. 23 is pure joy, given by God and fulfilled in God.

24-26   The four blessings are followed by four woes (vv. 24-26). The Greek word for "woe," *ouai,* does not denote a mere misfortune, but a deep and inconsolable misery, in contrast to the "blessings" of the previous verses. The precedent for such woes is not found in Jesus' rabbinic contemporaries, but rather in the prophets,[41] who, like Jesus, teach both righteousness and the calamitous consequences of unrighteousness. The behaviors condemned in the woes are expressions of hedonism, broadly speaking: the rich who live for present pleasures, those whose needs are met now, those who laugh now, and those who are roundly applauded. The woes and blessings are set in antithetical parallelism. The rich who have their rewards stand in antithesis to the poor who belong to the kingdom (v. 20). This is the first of eleven references in Luke to the "rich" (Gk. *plousios*),[42] a word that, with the possible exception of Zacchaeus (19:2), is always used pejoratively. Poverty, as noted at v. 20, requires dependence on God, but wealth easily, perhaps inevitably, becomes a comfortable substitute for God (12:16-22; 16:14; 18:23, 25). Likewise, the well-fed who will face hunger stand in antithesis to the hungry who will be satisfied (v. 21). The word for "well fed" (v. 25; *empiplanai*) refers generally to being sated and surfeited with things, although its primary connotation in v. 25 is food. Those who now laugh but later will weep stand in antithesis to those who now weep but later will laugh (v. 21). Laughter occasionally carries positive connotations

---

41. Isa 1:4; 3:9-11; 5:8-22; 10:5; Jer 23:1; Ezek. 24:6; Hos 7:13; Eccl 10:16; Tob 13:12, 14; *2 Bar.* 10:6; *1 En.* 94-100; on "woes," see H. Balz, *ouai, EDNT* 2:540.

42. 6:24; 12:16; 14:12; 16:1, 19, 21, 22; 18:23, 25; 19:2; 21:1.

in Scripture, as it does in v. 21, where it recalls the eschatological joy of Ps 126. But frequently in both OT and NT it connotes scoffing and derision (Gen 17:17; 18:12-15; Mark 5:40; Jas 4:9), as it may in v. 25.[43] This may be the reason why the Evangelists, although they portray Jesus as joyful (10:21), never describe him laughing. Finally, those applauded by all stand in antithesis to those maligned and mistreated (v. 22). The sharp antitheses of the fourth blessing and woe especially invoke the prophets. Throughout history, reputation and honor rank among the highest of human values, in some instances higher than life itself. In v. 22 Jesus praises disciples who are willing to sacrifice even this virtue for fellowship with the Son of Man, for in so doing they join the company of the holy prophets of old. To place acclaim and reputation above discipleship to the Son of Man is actually to gain fellowship with the *false* prophets, who enjoyed acclaim by riding the waves of the status quo. Luke does not regard universal acclaim a virtue (beware "when *everyone* speaks well of you," v. 26). Rather, the nature of one's enemies — or lack thereof — is a critical indicator of one's righteousness!

Agapē — the Heart of Jesus' Ethical Teaching (6:27-36)

The apostle Paul declared that "love is the fulfillment of the law" (Rom 13:10). Luke portrays love as something even greater, which constitutes the essence of discipleship to Jesus. Perhaps to signal its importance, Luke has constructed the love discourse with symmetry, repetition, and parallelism. He begins with an authoritative transition, "But to you who are listening I say" (v. 27). This statement resembles Matt's emphatic refrain in the Sermon on the Mount, "But *I* say to you . . ." (5:22, 28, 32, 34, 39, 44), although Matt's Greek wording places the emphasis on Jesus, whereas Luke's Greek wording places it on *you,* the disciples. What Jesus teaches about love is addressed specifically to his followers. The first love commandment is surely the most difficult, "Love your enemies" (v. 27).[44] This is Luke's first use of the Greek word for **love** (in the verb form). *Agapē* is rightly perceived by Christians as the unique expression of God's love and the behavioral expectation of those who belong to God through Jesus Christ. This understanding is due to the gospel rather than to the Greek etymology of the word. Of the three primary words for "love" in Greek — *erōs* (passionate [often sexual] desire for something or someone), *philia* (friendship), and *agapē* (good-will or benevolence) — the last was the most colorless and indistinct. Biblical and particularly NT writers took over *agapē* and filled

---

43. See K. Rengstorf, *gelaō, TWNT* 1:656-60.
44. On the origin of this teaching in the historical Jesus, see Bovon, *Lukas 1,1–9,50,* 310-11.

it with rich and unsurpassed significance, defined by God's unmerited and unconditional love for Israel (Deut 7:6-11) and Israel's corresponding love for God (Deut 6:5). Above all, *agapē* was defined by the redemptive love of God in the life, death, and resurrection of Jesus (John 3:16).[45] The unique Christian understanding of *agapē* is declared in Jesus' first commandment: "love your enemies" (v. 27).[46] This radical commandment, for which there is no precedent in the OT, sets Jesus' teaching on the subject in a class unto itself.[47] In the infancy narrative, Zechariah spoke of "salvation from our enemies" (1:71), but Jesus commands love for enemies. The example of Jesus' love for enemies and of doing good that could not be repaid impressed itself indelibly in the memory of early Christianity.[48]

27-28 These two verses are a single sentence constructed of four imperatives: love, do, bless, and pray.[49] Each imperative is in the Greek present tense, connoting continual action in accordance with the command. The commandments thus characterize not temporary or occasional activities, but habitual behaviors of Jesus' followers. The commandments are nonintuitive, i.e., they may not seem reasonable, and they enjoin behaviors that do not come naturally. In their ethics, Christians are not to be determined by the

---

45. On *agapē,* see E. Stauffer, *agapaō* etc., *TWNT* 1:20-55; G. Schneider, *agapē* etc., *EDNT* 1:8-12; on love of enemies, Klein, *Lukasevangelium,* 255-56. Particularly revealing is the declaration of a modern Jewish scholar on the uniqueness of Jesus' teaching on love of enemies: "The love of enemies as a moral principle is unknown to Judaism. This imperative is doubtlessly the only imperative in [Matthew's] three chapters of the Sermon the Mount without any parallel or analogy in rabbinic literature. This theme, as theologians say, is a unique characteristic *(Sondergut)* of Jesus" (P. Lapide, "Die Bergpredigt — Theorie und Praxis," *ZEE* 17 [1973]: 371).

46. For a discussion of this precept, esp. in modern scholarship, see A. Kirk, "'Love Your Enemies,' the Golden Rule, and Ancient Reciprocity (Luke 6:27-35)," *JBL* 122/4 (2003): 667-86.

47. Benevolence toward enemies was occasionally taught in the ancient world, particularly among Stoics. Seneca (first c.) spoke of pardoning enemies, and Marcus Aurelius (second c.) spoke of not doing anything that debased the Good by hindering or harming his enemies. Both sentiments were regulated by the principles of Stoicism, e.g., refraining from anger and acting dispassionately and patiently toward contrary individuals. For Jesus, love of enemies is regulated, not by an ethical ideal, but by conformity to the nature of God. Perhaps the closest one comes to Jesus' love of enemies is a statement Plutarch attributes to Ariston of Sparta in the first c. B.C.: when King Cleomenes asked Ariston if a king's duty was to do good to friends and evil to enemies, Ariston replied, "How much better, my good sir, to do good to our friends, and to make friends of our enemies." On these and other examples, see *HCNT,* 195-99.

48. Acts 20:35; P.Oxy. 1224; *Gos. Thom.* 95; *1 Clem.* 2:1; 13:2; *2 Clem.* 13:4; Ign., *Pol.* 2:1; Pol., *Phil.* 12.3; *Did.* 1:2-5; Justin, *1 Apol.* 15.9-13; 16.1-2; *Dial.* 96.3.

49. The asyndetic construction of these four commands is non-Lukan, suggesting that Luke is relying on a non-Markan, pre-Lukan source here as in 12:19 and 15:23 (Jeremias, *Sprache des Lukasevangeliums,* 141-42).

prior behaviors of others toward them, but by the character of God. Hence, believers are not to reciprocate in kind, but to respond in ways unlike and disproportionate to the ways they are treated: enemies are to be loved, haters are to be treated with goodness, revilers are to be blessed, and maligners (NIV "mistreat"; Gk. *epēreazein,* "to act spitefully, to abuse") are to be prayed for. This is not an ethics that can be argued on the basis of reason alone. Such commands were surely as offensive in Jesus' day as they are in ours. There is, however, a power in these principles that is not rationally apparent, for they correspond to the nature of God, whose rule over this world is sovereign. No power in the world is comparable to *agapē* love, both to keep Christians from becoming like their enemies,[50] and to release their enemies from the prisons of their own hatred.

29-31   The four principles of vv. 27-28 are followed by four specific behaviors in vv. 29-30, with three of the four imperatives in the present tense, connoting habitual behaviors. NIV "If someone slaps you on the cheek" (v. 29) is too mild. Gk. *typtein* means "to strike or hit"; and the Greek word for "cheek," *siagōn,* means "jawbone." The phrase is brawny, "to get socked in the jaw." Vv. 29-30 describe various ways believers are maltreated by physical violence, extortion or coercion, being imposed upon, and being robbed. The natural human response to such offenses is to recoil and protect, then retaliate appropriately. The teaching of Jesus is again wholly counterintuitive: believers are not to defend themselves, but *expose* themselves to evil and injustice. This is graphically communicated in the prescriptions. To "turn the other cheek" is not a passive response, but a provocative response, inviting further aggression.[51] Likewise, the instruction to surrender not only your "coat" (Gk. *himation,* outer garment) but also your "shirt" (Gk. *chitōn,* undergarment worn next to skin) is not to arm oneself in the face of evil and injustice, but to become naked in the face of it. The purpose of such calculated vulnerability is not to invite aggression, but, by ceasing to offer resistance, to provide no further cause for aggression.[52] Not surprisingly, such teachings are regularly

---

50. So Marcus Aurelius, *Med.* 6.6, "The best way of avenging thyself is not to become like the wrongdoer"; Pelagius, "Your enemy has overcome you when he has made you like himself" (quoted from C. E. B. Cranfield, *Epistle to the Romans* [ICC; Edinburgh: T&T Clark, 1979], 2.650).

51. Tannehill, *Luke,* 118.

52. Gregory Palamas's insight on 6:29 in *A New Testament Decalogue* (*The Philokalia* [ed. G. Palmer, P. Sherrard, and K. Ware; London: Faber & Faber, 1995], 4:329) seems to capture Jesus' intention: "As murder results from a blow, a blow from an insult, an insult from anger, and we are roused to anger because someone else injures, hits or insults us, for this reason Christ told us not to stop anyone who took our coat from taking our shirt also; and we must not strike back at him who strikes us, or revile him who reviles us. In this manner we will free from the crime of murder both oursel[ves] and him who does us wrong."

considered impractical, even absurd.[53] The twentieth century was powerfully altered, however, by courageous observance of this essential teaching. Gandhi's radical response to injustice, which he inherited from Tolstoy and bequeathed to Martin Luther King Jr., was to "become naked," i.e., put himself in a defenseless posture vis-à-vis powerful aggressors in order to shame them into repentance by the evil in their hearts.[54] The result of Gandhi's unconventional behavior was the liberation of India from British rule; and the result of similar behavior on the part of King, massive gains of civil rights for African Americans in the United States. The peaceful demonstrations that issued from the *Friedensdekade* — a decade-long prayer for peace in Protestant churches in former East Germany — broke ground not only for the fall of the Berlin Wall in 1989, but for the eventual collapse of the Soviet Union. The Truth and Reconciliation movement played the critical role in dismantling apartheid in South Africa and in sparing the nation a bloodbath of racial revenge. In each instance powerful and systemic structures of oppression were undermined by nonreciprocal and nonviolent practices that were informed by and modeled on the essential teaching on love articulated in 6:27-30.

Jesus summarizes the foregoing principles and practices in the well-known Golden Rule, "Do to others as you would have them do to you" (v. 31).[55] The Golden Rule is often regarded as the quintessence of Jesus' ethical teach-

---

53. Plummer, *Luke*, 185, decries these precepts: "It is impossible for either governments or individuals to keep them. A State which endeavored to shape its policy in exact accordance with them would soon cease to exist; and if individuals acted in strict obedience to them society would be reduced to anarchy. . . . The inference is that *they are not precepts, but illustrations of principles.* They are in the form of rules; but as they *cannot* be kept as rules, we are *compelled* to look beyond the letter to the spirit which they embody" (italics in original). For Plummer, the "spirit which they embody" is for believers not to hate or to become like their enemies; thus, "It is right to withstand and even punish those who injure us, but in order to correct them and protect society; not because of any personal *animus*." For further discussion and a similar judgment on this issue, see Bovon, *Lukas 1,1–9,50*, 326.

54. Reflecting the consequences of love of enemies, Bovon, *Lukas 1,1–9,50*, 319-20, writes, "In loving their enemies, Christians act *in behalf of* the future of their enemies. Jesus, the bearers of the tradition, and the Evangelists all hope that this new approach to enemies will present the opportunity and possibility for them to leave their hostility behind. The posture of the Christian presents the enemy not with the opponent he expected, but with a partner he did not expect."

55. The original Greek syntax is inverted: "As you wish people to treat you, treat them." A number of weighty and diverse Greek manuscripts (א A D LW Θ Ξ Ψ) make the rule emphatic: "As you wish people to treat you, *you also* treat them." Metzger, *TCGNT*, 118, dismisses the emphatic form as a probable scribal assimilation to the version of the Golden Rule in Matt 7:12. Evidence for the emphatic form is very strong, however, both textually (the chief witnesses for the shorter, unemphatic form are only p[75] and B) and internally (the emphatic Greek *you* in 27a).

ing. Vv. 27-30 are actually more characteristic of Jesus' ethical teaching, for they appeal to divine grace rather than to the principle of self-interest (". . . as you would have them do to *you*"). The moral standard of the world is, "Do to others what they do to you." Samson, one of Israel's most celebrated judges (Judg 15:11), lived by this standard. Followers of Jesus are called to calculate morality by a different equation. Versions of the Golden Rule abound in the history of religion and philosophy, almost always in the negative form.[56] Jesus' positive version of the rule differs distinctly from the negative version. The command not to do something is easily measured, whereas the command to do something is less easily measured. We know quite definitely when we have not done a particular act, but we never know with the same degree of certainty whether we have done all we should in fulfillment of a positive commandment. Religions that define righteousness by what adherents have *not* done can and do speak quite sincerely of being "good" or "bad" believers. Christians can only rarely and imperfectly speak of being good followers of Christ, for when have Christian believers ever done for others all that they might wish others to do for them? The positive command to love rather than simply to refrain from doing evil causes believers to examine themselves in deep and searching ways. Such examination alters more than behavior; it alters character itself. Even in their most righteous behaviors, followers of Jesus know that they are forever debtors of grace (17:7-9): "So you also, when you have done everything you were told to do, should say, 'We are unworthy servants, we have only done our duty' " (17:10).

32-36   Vv. 32-34 set forth three negative behaviors in contrast to the teachings on love in the foregoing verses. Believers are not to love only those who love them (v. 32); they are not to do good only to those who do good to them (v. 33); they are not to lend only to those who will repay (v. 34).[57] The refrain *poia* (NIV "what credit is that to you?") echoes through each of the three parallel constructions. Jesus calls people who do these things "sinners." They certainly are not sinners according to any ethical system known to humanity. By all ethical canons, people who love, do good, and lend to others are virtuous people. Jesus is thus not contrasting his way with the way of the wicked, but his way with the way of moral righteousness. "Sinners" is Jewish hyperbole on Jesus' part, signifying the way ordinary people behave. Good as their behaviors may be, they are nevertheless not reflective of Jesus' way in the

---

56. "Do not do to others what you would not want them to do to you": Tob 4:15; *Tg. Yer. 1*; Lev 19:18; Rabbi Hillel (*b. Šabb.* 30a) and subsequent Jewish rabbis; Isocrates (*Demon.* 1.17); Homer, *Od.*, 5.188-89; Herodotus, *Hist.*, 3.142; *Let. Aris.* 207; *Did.* 1:2; *Apos. Con.* 7.2.1; Stoicism; Buddhism.

57. The command to lend without hope of repayment is similar to a rabbinic teaching in *Exod. Rab.* 31 (91c), "Whoever possesses wealth and gives alms to the poor without interest is counted by God as though he had fulfilled all the commandments."

world, and thus not *Christian*.[58] The precise distinction between such morality and the way of Jesus hinges on reciprocity. Loving others, doing good to others, and lending money to others are good things to do, but when they are done for ulterior purposes of receiving the same from others, as they are here, they do not reflect the way of Jesus. The NIV ends v. 34 with "being repaid in full," but the Greek reads "being paid in *equal* [Gk. *isa*] measure."[59] That is the crux. Conventional morality does good in accordance with the likelihood of receiving commensurate good in return; Jesus commands disciples to focus on the good act exclusively, regardless of commensurate return.

Jesus completes his teaching on love by repeating, "Love your enemies" (v. 35). "Love" is again in the present tense in Greek, signifying continuous, unrelenting action. Love of enemies is a uniquely Christian commandment, indeed the first and last word of Jesus on the subject of *agapē* (vv. 27, 35). Jesus repeats the three commands again in v. 35 — to love, do good, and lend — but without any reference to reward. A significant textual variant occurs in v. 35, which the NIV (and many English translations) renders, "lend to them *without expecting to get anything back.*" This translation is derived from context (as a corollary to lending "to those from whom you expect payment," v. 34) rather than from lexicography, for the Greek words for "expect" in vv. 34 (*elpizein*) and 35 (*apelpizein*) are not the same. The standard definition of *apelpizein* means "to despair of" something (so Eph 4:19).[60] It makes perfect — perhaps even better — sense to allow *apelpizein* its primary lexical meaning in v. 35: "Love your enemies, do good to them, and lend to them, *never despairing.*"[61] Reason might lead us to despair of doing the unrecompensed good that Jesus commands, but faith knows there are more factors in the Christian moral equation than ourselves and others. God, the chief architect of the moral equation, is also present. Ironically, when the recipients of our benevolence cannot repay, "then your reward will be great" (v. 35). When disciples are *not* repaid in equal measure, they are again "naked" (v. 29) and thus in a position to be rewarded not by the recipients of the benevolence but solely by the One who has issued the commandment. In so doing, believers become "children of the Most High" (v. 35). The Greek word for "children," *huioi,* means "sons." Throughout the ancient world, sons — especially firstborn sons — were accorded chief inheritance and privileged status. The ethics of *agapē* usher believers into fellowship with God as *sons,* and sons partake of the nature of their Father (2 Pet 1:3). God is

---

58. "To give a loan with the hope of receiving it back, is an office of kindness becoming of a man; to do so without such hope, is one becoming a Christian" (Bengel, *Gnomon,* 2:65).

59. On *isa,* see Bovon, *Lukas 1,1–9,50,* 317-18.

60. LSJ, 185; BDAG, 101, defines *apelpizein* in 6:35 as "expect back" on the basis of context rather than on the basis of any pre-Christian evidence for the translation.

61. So Plummer, *Luke,* 187-88; Metzger, *TCGNT,* 118.

kind and merciful, even to "the ungrateful and wicked" (v. 35); "children of the Most High" should likewise be merciful as their Father is merciful.[62]

Ethics within the Family of Faith (6:37-49)

6:27-36 instructs believers on the characteristics of *agapē* owed to those outside the community of faith. The present section lists behaviors owed to those within the family of faith. The instructions are given by placing two things in antithetical parallelism — two blind people, a teacher and a disciple, two brothers, two trees, two types of people (good and evil), and two houses.[63] The dualities focus attention on interpersonal, "I-Thou" ethical responses and responsibility.

37-38   The first unit consists of four commands, two negative and two positive. All four commands are present tense second-person plural (in Greek), thus prescribing habitual behaviors of believers. Each command consists of two parts, an active command followed by a passive response, e.g., "Do not judge, and you will not be judged" (v. 37). The passive response, "you will not be judged," is a Semitic way of avoiding pronouncing the name of God; it means, "Do not judge, and God will not judge you." "Do not judge" — frequently (mis-) quoted — does not mean never to judge. On matters essential to faith and morality, both Jesus (e.g., 11:39-52; Matt 23) and Paul (Gal 2:11-14) expressed clear and forceful judgments. Early Christianity distinguished between essential and nonessential matters of faith; the former (*diapheronta,* Rom 2:18; Phil 1:10), like an egg yolk, were those on which believers could not disagree and maintain fellowship, whereas the latter (*adiaphora,* illustrated in Rom 14:1–15:13), like the surrounding egg white, were matters on which believers could differ without jeopardizing fellowship. The command not to judge is directed to the egg white *(adiaphora),* not to the yolk *(diapheronta),* in which believers are united. Christians should refrain from such judgments because they can be deceived by circumstances. God forbears with human shortcomings, allowing time to repent and mature (Rom 14:4). Moreover, such judgments divide the Christian fellowship on nonessential issues (Rom 14:15). "Do not judge" is thus not a command to refrain from ethical evaluation or spiritual discernment, but a warning against a fault-finding and censorious spirit that binds rather than liberates others in the faith community (Rom 2:1-3).[64]

---

62. All three Abrahamic faiths confess and teach the mercy of God: Judaism (Exod 34:6-7; for later rabbinic confessions of the same, see Str-B 2:159), Christianity (here and throughout the NT), and Islam (Qur'an 1:1 and frequently thereafter).

63. Bock, *Luke 1:1–9:50,* 609. Jeremias, *Sprache des Lukasevangeliums,* 61-62, 146-51, notes that antithetical parallelism is non-Lukan, suggesting a pre-Lukan source of the material.

64. See Lagrange, *Luc,* 197.

The second command, "Do not condemn" (v. 37), employs a Greek word *(katadikazein)* that connotes hard-heartedness and lack of compassion (Matt 12:7; Jas 5:6). The third command is positive, "Forgive, and you will be forgiven" (v. 37). "Forgive" may be too restrictive, for the Greek *apolyein* means generally to pardon and release, i.e., to set people free rather than binding them. The final command, "Give, and it will be given to you" (v. 38), is elaborated with Hebraic hyperbole. Generous believers will not merely receive reciprocal treatment, they will find "a good measure, pressed down, shaken together and running over, poured into your lap." This image, both happy and humorous, pictures a person gathering up his or her garment to receive a quantity of grain that is poured in, packed down, and filled up beyond expectation. This is again a reference to God without using God's name (Gk. *dōsousin,* "they will give"; NIV "will be poured"). God will repay lavishly and abundantly those in the Christian community who are generous.[65] The unit concludes with a Jewish proverb, "With the measure you use, it will be measured to you."[66] The moral enshrined in this proverb is a variant on the Golden Rule: as we treat others, so shall we be treated.

39-40 The parable about the blind leading the blind into a pit (v. 39) was widely known in various forms throughout the ancient world,[67] but it was particularly apropos in Palestine, where the perennial search for water left the land pockmarked with pits and cisterns.[68] Overland travel was perilous for a seeing person, particularly at night; how much more so for a blind person! The parable may warn against presuming leadership in the Christian fellowship before one is spiritually mature, jeopardizing both leader and follower. This complements v. 40, "A disciple is not above his teacher." The NIV (and many commentators) translate the saying as a general proverb ("Students are not above their teacher"), but the saying more likely refers to Jesus and his disciples.[69] Apart from this verse, "teacher" (Gk. *didaskalos*) occurs fifteen times in Luke, thirteen of which refer to Jesus. Twice again in Luke teacher and disciple are paired with reference to Jesus and his disciples (19:39; 22:11). Lexical evidence thus favors interpreting v. 40 with reference to Jesus and his disciples. Context does also. Rabbinic students mastered the teachings of rabbis in hopes of someday exceeding them, but Jesus never suggests his

---

65. Plummer, *Luke,* 189; Str-B 2:160; Jeremias, *Sprache des Lukasevangeliums,* 146.

66. *Tg. Isa.* 27:8; *b. Sanh.* 100a; *m. Soṭah* 1:7; Str-B 1:444-46. Mark 4:25 follows the saying about measures with this saying, "Those who have will be given more; as for those who do not have, even what they have will be taken from them." Luke omits this statement but includes it virtually verbatim in the parable of the Ten Minas in 19:26.

67. Plato, *Rep.* 554; Xenophon, *Mem.* 1.3.4; Dio Chrysostom, *Regn. tyr.* 7; Diogenes Laertius 5.82; Philo, *Virt.* 7; *b. B. Qam.* 52a; *Gos. Thom.* 34; Rom 2:19.

68. Isa 24:17-18; Lagrange, *Luc,* 198-99.

69. So too Wolter, *Lukasevangelium,* 263.

disciples can surpass him. V. 40 preserves a prime example of Jesus' unique self-understanding, for he presents himself as the sole authority who cannot be exceeded (Matt 10:24-25; John 13:16; 15:20), even when his disciples are "fully trained." At best they can be "like" him, as was Stephen in his prayer of forgiveness (Acts 7:60). Vv. 39-40 thus admonish believers not to dominate others in the Christian fellowship, and above all not to replace or exceed Jesus.[70] The latter admonishment cannot be recalled too often by pastors, theologians, and commentators!

41-42   With humor and hyperbole, Jesus uses the caricature of a speck and a log in the eye to warn against judging fellow believers.[71] The caricature recalls the lesson about judging in v. 37. The reference to "brother" (v. 41; Gk. *adelphos;* NIV "friend") connotes a member of the Jesus-fellowship,[72] and the "speck of sawdust" connotes something minuscule, i.e., the *adiaphora,* the things over which believers can disagree without breaking fellowship. The contrast between a "speck" (Gk. *karphos,* "chip, fleck, splinter") and a "plank" (Gk. *dokos*) is comical, for the latter denoted the load-bearing roof beam of an average house.[73] The moral, obviously, is that self-examination and reform are necessary prerequisites for anyone presuming to teach and lead others. We may think we see the fault of the fellow believer clearly, even that we are offended by it, but the log in our eye obscures our perspective and judgment. Jesus calls this "hypocrisy" (v. 42), a word in Greek that referred to wearing a theatrical mask. Only self-reform enables Christians to see the other not only differently, but correctly. The final verb for seeing with the beam removed (Gk. *diablepein*) is different from the previous word for seeing, meaning "to see clearly, to perceive the heart of the matter." The purpose of the saying is not spiritual introspection, however, but making ourselves of service to others, "to remove the speck from the other's eye."

43-45   The prophetic tradition before Jesus relied frequently on the metaphor of fruit trees, which Jesus employs in vv. 43-45.[74] The summary of Jesus' teaching, "Each tree is recognized by its own fruit" (v. 44), may errone-

---

70. See Schweizer, *Lukas,* 83.

71. The same imagery appears in later rabbinic sayings, indicating that Jesus may be repeating rather than inventing a maxim. Complaining about the moral obstinacy of his generation, Rabbi Tarphon (ca. 100) said, "If someone said, 'Take the splinter out of your eye,' people today would probably retort, 'And you take the beam out of yours!'" (Str-B 1:446). *Gos. Thom.* 26 accurately preserves the Jesus saying, "You see the speck that is in your brother's eye, but you do not see the log that is in your own eye. When you take the log out of your own eye, then you will see to take out the speck from your brother's eye."

72. Jeremias, *Sprache des Lukasevangeliums,* 146.

73. Lagrange, *Luc,* 199.

74. Isa 5:1-7; Jer 2:21; 3:10; 17:10; 21:14; Hos 10:13; Prov 1:31; 31:16. For rabbinic variations on this theme, see Str-B 1:466-67.

ously suggest that fruit determines the tree. Each example employed by Jesus actually moves in the opposite direction, however. Each subject — good trees, bad trees,[75] thornbushes, briers, good people, and evil people — is the source of a corresponding product — good fruit, bad fruit, thorns, briers, good things, and bad things. The tree, in other words, determines its fruit. Fruit is not a *work*, i.e., something external from and perhaps disassociated from its source, but a *product* that corresponds to the nature of the tree.[76] The Greek of v. 44 makes this apparent: "Each tree is known *by its own* fruit." Ignatius (*Eph.* 14:2) cites this verse as evidence that a true profession of Christ is testified in deeds as well as words. In more modern and psychological parlance we might say that we inevitably live out what we believe. This teaching advocates a form of virtue or deontological ethics rather than utilitarianism, i.e., the good is the result of character. The emphasis in each example in vv. 43-45 falls on the good *person* — "the good stored up in the heart," rather than simply the good deed. The Greek word for "heart," *kardia,* refers to the source, center, and seat of the acting agent. It is thus not good deeds that make a good person (although good deeds may be a stimulus to becoming a better person), but rather inner virtue, particularly the *agapē* of vv. 27-29, that bears fruit in true *goodness.*

46-49 Luke concludes Jesus' sermon to the disciples, as does Matthew the Sermon on the Mount (7:24-27), with the parable of Two Builders. The parable is introduced by four faith responses to Jesus: calling him Lord, coming to him, hearing him, and doing his will (vv. 46-47). Of the four, the first, ironically, is the least trustworthy, for it is easy to say things — even true things such as "Jesus is Lord" — and not mean or do them (Jas 2:14-26).[77] Speaking of Jesus as Lord but not doing his will is contrary to the point of the previous verse, i.e., speaking from "the overflow of the heart" (v. 45). "Lord, Lord" (v. 46) is understood by many commentators in its mundane sense of "Sir, Master,

75. Gk. *sapros,* translated "bad," can mean "rotten" or "worthless." The second meaning is required here, for a rotten tree produces no fruit.

76. The "nature" of the tree is likened to the work of God in the Greek of v. 44, a literal translation of which reads, "For they do not gather figs from thorns, nor do they harvest grapes from briers." The third person plural "they," a Jewish circumlocution to avoid using the name of God, means "*God* does not bring forth figs from thorns or grapes from briers." See Jeremias, *Sprache des Lukasevangeliums,* 149.

77. The temptation to substitute Christian rhetoric for authentic discipleship remained a problem in early Christianity. Thus, 2 *Clem.* 4:1-2, 5 (second c.), "Let us, then, not merely call him Lord, for this will not save us. For he says, 'Not everyone who says to me Lord, Lord shall be saved, but the one who does righteousness.' . . . For this reason, if you do these things, the Lord said, 'If you are gathered together with me in my bosom, and do not do my commandments, I will cast you out, and will say to you, Depart from me, I do not know where you come from, you workers of iniquity.'" The reference to being gathered in the Lord's bosom is a quotation from *Gos. Naz.* 6, a text from the Hebrew Gospel tradition. For a modern warning against "cheap grace," see D. Bonhoeffer, *The Cost of Discipleship,* part 1, "Grace and Discipleship."

Teacher," rather than in its exalted christological sense. The Greek *kyrios* (similar to German "Herr" or British "Lord") includes the mundane as well as the exalted sense, and thus on the basis of lexicography alone the word may not be christologically significant. Christological imagery, however, appears in neighboring contexts. The Teacher who cannot be exceeded by his disciples implies high (though implicit) Christology in v. 40; and Isaiah's Foundation Stone (Isa 28:16), which is a distinct eschatological image, seems embedded in vv 48-49 (see below). "Lord, Lord" can justifiably be taken christologically in v. 46, in accordance with Luke's typical use of *kyrios*.[78]

What is the antidote to false faith and discipleship? The answer is given in three present tense verbs in v. 47, each of which connotes habitual behaviors: coming to Jesus, hearing his words, doing his will. These three qualities lay the foundation for genuine discipleship. They lay claim to the whole person, the relational, the verbal, and the behavioral — and in that order. All discipleship consists — foremost and forever — in coming to Jesus and being with him (Mark 3:14). Only in relationship with Jesus as Lord do disciples hear him and learn his way. Within the same relationship they do his will — or better, like the foregoing image of the fruit tree, they allow Jesus to bear fruit through them (Rom 2:13). This is the true formula for a saving faith. It is also the true formula for a strong and vibrant church: coming to Jesus in evangelism, hearing his word in preaching and exposition, learning and doing his will in catechesis.

Professing Jesus as Lord but not following Jesus as Lord (v. 46) is entirely different from coming to Jesus, hearing him, and doing his will. Jesus illustrates the difference by a parable about two builders (vv. 48-49). The parable is not about knowing and confessing Jesus, not even about hearing Jesus: both "builders" do both. The parable is about *acting* on what one knows and hears from Jesus. Matthew's version of the parable (7:24-27) is about *where* one builds — on rock or sand? Luke's version is about *how* one builds — with or without a foundation? Soil in Palestine is often hardpan, tempting one to build on soil itself rather than investing time, labor, and money in digging through the hardpan to lay a proper foundation. Isaiah seized on this problem to illustrate the true foundation that God was laying, "a stone in Zion, a tested stone, a precious cornerstone for a sure foundation" (28:16). Jesus likely recalls that image in speaking of the "wise architect" (to use a Pauline term, 1 Cor 3:10) "who dug down deep and laid the foundation on rock. When a flood came, the torrent struck that house but could not shake it, because it was well built" (v. 48). The Greek word for "flood," *plēmmyra*, signifies a body of water that bursts its banks — perhaps the Jordan River or Sea of Galilee — rather than a flashflood in a wadi. Whoever hears the words of Jesus and does not do them,

---

78. Rowe, *Early Narrative Christology*, 111-14, marshals strong evidence for a Christological understanding of 6:46, but Bultmann's contrary judgment softens his conviction.

however, is like a foolish builder who trusts the hardpan rather than laying a foundation. The floodwaters will crush his house; the Greek *sympiptein* ("to collapse, implode") signifies total destruction. In the inaugural sermon at Nazareth, Jesus applied the prophecy of the Lord's "Anointed" from Isa 61:1 to himself (4:18-19). At the conclusion of the sermon he appears to apply a second messianic image from Isaiah to himself: Jesus is the "sure foundation" promised by Isa 28:16. Whoever builds on him and his words will not be shaken.[79]

---

79. See Bailey, *Jesus through Middle Eastern Eyes,* 321-31.

CHAPTER SEVEN

Jesus Ministers and Teaches in Galilee

Luke 7:1–8:56

Following the teaching unit in 6:12-49, Luke resumes Jesus' itinerant ministry of healing and teaching in Galilee. Luke 7–8 exhibits an increase of local color, vaguely suggestive of a travel diary, including place-names — Capernaum (7:1), Nain (7:11), Gerasa (or Gergesa, 8:26); personal names — John the Baptist (7:18-35), Simon the Pharisee (7:43), Mary Magdalene (8:2), Joanna the wife of Chuza (8:3), Susanna (8:3), Jairus (8:41); and unnamed but unforgettable characters — the sinful woman who anoints Jesus' feet (7:36-50), the demoniac among the tombs (8:26-39), and the daring woman with a hemorrhage (8:43-48). Luke 7–8 is characterized by dramatic encounters that result in trust and transformation by Jesus. A clue to the meaning of these encounters is provided by two terms: faith and salvation. Nowhere else in the Third Gospel do these terms appear either in conjunction with one another or as frequently as in this section.[1] Equally distinctive of this section, and continuing into chap. 9, is Luke's employment of prophetic typology to portray Jesus (7:16, 26, 28, 39; 9:8, 19). Elijah and Elisha are not named in Luke 7–9, but the presentation of Jesus, and particularly his miracles, in these chapters is narrated with conspicuous allusions to Israel's two greatest healers (see excursus at 7:17). The Elijah-Elisha typology expresses in a new way the distinctive Lukan theme that Jesus is the fulfillment of the hopes of Israel (24:44), and that the history of Israel is the necessary foundation by which to understand Jesus (24:27).

---

1. Gk. *pisteuein* ("to trust, believe") or *pistis* ("faith") appears in tandem with *sōzein* (meaning either "to heal" or "to save") in 7:50; 8:12, 48, 50. *Pisteuein/pistis* appears singly in 7:9; 8:13, 25, as does *sōzein* in 8:36.

TO BE WORTHY IS TO REALIZE
ONE'S UNWORTHINESS (7:1-10)

The healing of the centurion's servant is commonly considered a "Q" pericope, a story that Matt (8:5-13) and Luke (7:1-10) derived from a prior sayings source common to both. The story is not a saying-unit, however, but a narrative. Moreover, the differences between the Matthean and Lukan versions are remarkable: Luke's version is nearly twice as long as Matt's and replete with stylistic features not shared by Matt.[2] The "Q" hypothesis is particularly unsuitable in explaining the literary origin or theological significance of this pericope.

1-5 Luke commences the story with a signature transition, "When Jesus completed all his words" (v. 1). The NIV translation, "When Jesus had finished saying all this" is a better translation of Matt (7:28) than of Luke.[3] The Greek word for "completed" (v. 1; *eplērōsen*) does not mean to stop speaking, but rather, in accordance with its usage throughout the Third Gospel (1:20; 4:21; 7:1; 9:31; 24:44), the fulfillment and completion of the Scriptures, or Jesus' sayings, as the word of God.

Jesus returns to Capernaum (4:23, 31), where he is informed of the critical illness of a valuable servant of a centurion.[4] The bond between the centurion and the servant is indicated by the reference to the latter as *pais* (v. 7), a Greek word that speaks of a servant endearingly as a child. A **centurion** was a principal officer in the Roman army, responsible for the command of one hundred men, one of sixty such officers in a Roman legion (approx. 6,000 soldiers).[5] Roman centurions were typically persons of economic means, and the use of their means for *munera* — public services and civic projects —

---

2. Jeremias, *Sprache des Lukasevangeliums*, 151-56.

3 The same tendency is evident in the Western text (D), which conflated Matt 7:28 with Luke 7:1, "And when [Jesus] finished saying all these words, he went. . . ."

4. The relation between this story and John 4:46-54 is ambiguous. The two stories share several obvious similarities: both are set in Capernaum, both request healing for a servant/son near death, both attest to the faith of the petitioner, and both attest that Jesus healed the servant/son from a distance. There are as many differences, however. In Luke the petitioner is a centurion, in John a royal official; in Luke the victim is a servant, in John a son; John makes no mention of a delegation sent to Jesus or of a change of mind of the petitioner; and in John the malady is identified as fever. Furthermore, at 700 feet below sea level and adjacent to a large body of water, Capernaum was plagued by fevers, gastrointestinal disorders, and respiratory diseases such as dysentery, typhus, tuberculosis, and esp. malaria (see J. Reed, "Instability in Jesus' Galilee: A Demographic Perspective," *JBL* 129/2 [2010]: 353-60). The proliferation of diseases with similar symptoms in a single locale raises the possibility that the Lukan and Johannine accounts are two different episodes.

5. The favorable assessments of centurions in the NT, and particularly in Luke (7:1-10; 23:47; Acts 10:22; 22:26; 23:17, 23, 24; 24:23; 27:43), indicates the general quality of individuals chosen for the office.

played an important role in their appointment and promotion to the upper ranks of Roman military and political life.[6] Countless inscriptions from the ancient Mediterranean world celebrate them as public benefactors. The centurion's patronage of the Jewish synagogue in Capernaum conforms to this expectation.[7] This fact need not compromise the sincerity of his gift, any more than claiming a tax exemption allowed in the U.S. tax code compromises a charitable contribution. Herod Antipas was invested by Rome with political and military authority over Galilee, and Capernaum, which lay immediately within the border of Galilee, had both a Roman tax station and a Roman army garrison. The centurion was probably, though not necessarily, a Roman (for Antipas employed non-Romans as well as Romans in his army), and certainly a Gentile. Antipas's phobia of the nascent renewal movement represented by John and Jesus was no secret; he had imprisoned John (3:20) and would kill him (9:9), and he resolved a similar fate for Jesus (13:31). A centurion loyal to Antipas (see excursus on Antipas at 23:1) could not automatically be considered a safe inquirer of Jesus.

"The centurion heard of Jesus and sent some elders of the Jews to him, asking him to come and heal his servant" (v. 3). The fact that a Gentile Roman had heard of Jesus testifies that his fame exceeded the confines of Judaism. It was a Jewish custom to dispatch delegations in matters of vital importance (7:18-19; 9:52; 10:1; Acts 25:15).[8] Seizing on this custom in hopes of saving his servant, the centurion sends respected elders of the local Jewish community to plead with Jesus on his behalf. The imperfect tense of the Greek word for "plead" (v. 4; Gk. *parekaloun*) indicates earnestness and persistence. Their request, "This man deserves to have you do this" (v. 4), is a rare NT Latinism,[9]

---

6. D. Potter, *Constantine the Emperor* (New York: Oxford University Press, 2013), 11-17.

7. Excavations in 2005 at Kefar Othnay, an ancient village adjacent to Tel Megiddo, uncovered a third-c. Christian church or prayer hall — the oldest evidence of Christianity in pre-Constantinian Palestine — with a dedicatory inscription to a centurion who sponsored the laying of a mosaic floor. See V. Tzaferis, " 'To God Jesus Christ': Early Christian Prayer Hall Found in Megiddo Prison," *BAR* 33/2 (2007): 38-49; E. Meyers and M. Chancey, *Alexander to Constantine: Archaeology of the Land of the Bible* (New Haven: Yale University Press, 2012), 199-210.

8. The Jewish custom of the embassy is grounded in God's provision of a guardian angel to guide Israel to the land of promise (Exod 23:20). The custom came to vintage expression in the belief that God would send Elijah to prepare the way of the Lord (Mal 3:1; Sir 48:10). The same custom regulated Israel's social and political history. In the late 30s, e.g., Philo of Alexandria sailed to Rome with an embassy seeking to redress Jewish grievances before Emperor Caligula (Philo, *Embassy*, 190, 370; Josephus, *Ant.* 18.257-60). In early Christian tradition Ignatius of Antioch (d. ca. 107) elevates emissaries between him and his churches to a virtual fourth church office in addition to bishops, elders, and deacons.

9. Gk. *axios estin hō parexē touto* (v. 4) renders verbatim Lat. *dignus est cui hoc praestes* (BDF §5[3[b]]).

i.e., a Greek rendering reflecting an original Latin idiom, which appears to preserve the centurion's *ipsissima verba*. Evidence of the centurion's worthiness is supplied in his love for "our nation" and building of the synagogue of Capernaum. The Greek of v. 5 is emphatic — "he himself built the synagogue for us" — indicating personal commitment of funds or effort by the centurion. "Love for our people/culture" and benefaction in building the synagogue distinguish the centurion, like Cornelius (Acts 10:2), as a "God-fearer," i.e., a Gentile who sympathized with Judaism and in varying degrees participated in its life and cult.[10] It hardly needs saying that Jews seldom argued the case of "unclean" Gentiles. The centurion's leverage with the Jewish elders to represent him before Jesus attests to an unusually positive association with the Jewish community of Nazareth. The white limestone synagogue preserved today in Capernaum dates from the fourth century, although its black basalt foundation, still visible at ground level, belongs to the synagogue Jesus knew in Capernaum.[11]

6-10 Implicit in Jesus' consent to visit the centurion is a willingness to include Gentiles in his ministry. As Jesus neared the house, he was met by a second delegation, also dispatched by the centurion, which reversed the appeal of the first: "I did not even consider myself worthy to come to you" (v. 7). The Greek word for "worthy," *axioun,* is the verbal form of the same word *(axios)* in v. 4. A rich and fruitful irony results. The centurion grounded his first appeal in his worthiness, and the second in his *un*worthiness. Practical considerations, of course, may have influenced the change of mind; the centurion, for example, may have wanted to spare an observant Jew from being compromised by entering a ritually polluted Gentile dwelling.[12] But Luke's conscious contrast "worthy"/"unworthy," coupled with the centurion's second address to Jesus as "Lord" (Gk. *kyrie*), invites a fuller explanation. Immediately prior to this story Jesus bade people, "Come to me" (6:47). Like many seekers, both then and now, the centurion imagines himself as good as the next guy. Indeed, his credits (v. 5!) should put him in a pole position with Jesus, and he naturally makes his appeal on the basis of his worthiness. But as Jesus draws

10. Significant numbers of Gentiles were attracted to the monotheism and ethical teachings of Judaism, but without undergoing the Jewish rite of circumcision. Schürer, *History of the Jewish People*, 3:161-71, concludes that Gk. *theosebeis* ("God-fearers") should "be categorized as a formal group attached to a Jewish community, and distinguished both from Jews and from full proselytes" (166). Further, see Wolter, *Lukasevangelium*, 271.

11. See S. Loffreda, *Recovering Capernaum* (Jerusalem: Terra Santa, 1985); R. Riesner, "Neues von den Synagogen Kafarnaums," *Biblische Umschau* 40 (1985): 133-35; V. Corbo, "Capernaum," *ABD* 1:866-69; M. Nun, "Ports of Galilee," *BAR* 25/4 (1999): 23-27. J. Murphy-O'Connor's description of Capernaum as poor and undistinguished (*The Holy Land*, 223-25) is unjustifiably dismissive of the significance of the archaeological remains.

12. Plummer, *Luke*, 196.

near to him, he must revise, indeed reverse, his outlook. He lowers the flag of self-satisfaction and lifts up his hands in contrition — and it is contrition, not status and influence, that evokes the powerfully warm response of Jesus. The semantic ambiguity of "Lord" (v. 6; Gk. *kyrie*), a title equally appropriate and equally employed both for humans ("Sir, Master") and for God ("Lord"),[13] allows the centurion to express his dawning awareness that the Jesus who draws near to him is more than he imagined when he summoned him. That awareness is exclaimed in a veritable profession of faith in v. 7: "Say the word and make my servant well!" This exclamation often seemed too imperious in early Christianity and was given a facelift in the textual tradition, "Say the word, and my servant will be healed."[14] The centurion seems to express faith rather than impertinence, however. The chain of command under which he lived resulted in a world of assured outcomes. A soldier or a servant who was ordered to do something, did it (v. 8). The explanation of v. 8 thus reflects realities of the Roman army as much as virtues on the part of the centurion.[15] The centurion perceives that the presence of Jesus ushers in a similar though more powerful reality. A word from Jesus would do to the disordered world of sickness and death what a word from a Roman officer does in a disordered and rebellious society. Jesus need only say the word, and the servant will be healed.[16]

"When Jesus heard this, he was amazed at him" (v. 9). The verb for "amazed" or "astonished" (Gk. *thaumazein*) proliferates in the Gospels, almost always as a description of the amazement of others toward Jesus. Only here and in Matt 8:10 and Mark 6:6 is it used of Jesus. Jesus is amazed *at the centurion*. The core of this pericope follows the faith of the centurion more than the healing of his servant, for the centurion's faith is celebrated beyond anything Jesus has experienced in Israel, whereas the healing of the servant is appended somewhat anticlimactically. Faith — the combination of humility ("Lord, I am not worthy") and confidence ("Say the word and make my servant well") exhibited by the centurion[17] — is a greater miracle than even physical healing. Faith is found in unexpected quarters — in Gentile centurions, in

---

13. See discussion of the term in Rowe, *Early Christian Narrative*, 114-17.

14. A host of manuscripts (ℵ A C D W Θ Ψ), including the NIV rendering, assimilates v. 7 to the easier reading of Matt 8:8. The blunt imperative is to be preferred to the more polite future passive, however. See Metzger, *TCGNT*, 118. It might be noted in this regard that all the verbs save one in the Matthean (6:9-13) and Lukan (11:2-4) versions of the Lord's Prayer are imperatives!

15. Josephus, *J.W.* 2.195, quotes the Roman general Petronius replying to Jewish insurgents in A.D. 40 in these words, "I too must obey the law of my master; if I transgress it and spare you, I shall be put to death, with justice. War will be made on you by him who sent me, not by me; for I too, like you, am under orders."

16. Grundmann, *Lukas*, 157.

17. Vinson, *Luke*, 207.

alien Samaritans (17:18), in desolate widows (18:8). But wherever it is found, it results in the joy of the incarnation. Faith is of course willed for Israel (2:32), but is not the sole possession of Israel. It is equally willed for outsiders, for Gentiles who are far away and do not belong to Israel. Jesus is not only amazed at the faith of the centurion but *pleased* with it, for it is the firstfruit of Simeon's prophecy to Mary and Joseph, "a light for revelation to the Gentiles" (2:32). The miracle of 7:1-10 is not simply that Jesus healed the servant at a spatial distance; he has spanned a greater cultural distance in bringing a Gentile to faith.

A FUNERAL PROCESSION THAT BECAME A STREET PARTY (7:11-17)

11-12 Luke regularly constructs his narrative by the use of pairs, and often male and female pairs (see excursus at 14:1). In this and the previous narrative, Nain and Capernaum are juxtaposed, as are the widow and the centurion. Both pericopes are also narrated with conscious reference to Elijah-Elisha typology (see excursus at vv. 15-17). In addition, the two narratives are linked temporally by "soon afterward" (v. 11).[18] Luke clearly narrates 7:11-17 as a sequel to 7:1-10.[19] The miracle at Nain, which is not mentioned by the other Evangelists, occurs in the southernmost city of Galilee. Luke customarily refers to settlements, whether large or small, as "cities" (v. 11; Gk. *polis*). Nain belonged to the small category and was situated on the north slope of the Hill of Moreh, with commanding views to Mount Tabor to the northeast and Nazareth to the northwest, both about seven miles (11 km) distant. Nain lay twenty-five miles (40 km) south of Capernaum, making it a full-day's walk from the healing of the centurion's servant.[20]

Accompanied by his disciples and a sizable crowd, Jesus is depicted as an itinerant rabbi with a large following (v. 11).[21] Near the gate of the town, Jesus and his retinue meet a funeral procession coming out of the town. Attending

18. A number of important witnesses (D W ℵ C K) make the temporal link more definite, "the next day." Stronger manuscript evidence, however, favors the less definite "soon afterward." See Metzger, *TCGNT*, 119.

19. For further evidence of correspondence between the two pericopes, see Nolland, *Luke 1:1–9:20*, 313-14.

20. In the late fourth c., Nain was identified by both Eusebius and Jerome (*Onomasticon*, §140 [p. 77]). For modern descriptions of Nain, see G. Dalman, *Sacred Sites and Ways*, 191-92; and esp. J. Strange, "Nain," *ABD* 4:1000-1001.

21. A well-attested textual variant (A C Θ Ψ *f*[13]) at v. 11 reads "[Jesus'] *many* disciples and a large crowd," suggesting a retinue of more disciples than the Twelve, plus a large crowd. For a discussion of the variant, see Metzger, *TCGNT*, 119.

to proper burial etiquette was a "work of mercy" that, on the basis of passages like Exod 18:20 and Mic 6:8, was incumbent on every Israelite. Participation in funeral proceedings was not simply a social expectation but a rabbinic requirement. Even study of Torah, a most inviolable pursuit in Israel, was suspended for funerals, allowing all people associated with the deceased to accompany the body to the place of burial outside the city. In Galilee it was customary for men to walk in front of the deceased and women behind, with hired mourners and musicians with instruments processing with their respective genders.[22] Mention of a gate implies that Nain, although perhaps only a village, was surrounded by a wall. In the biblical world, the city gate was the most important place in a locale, where all official business was conducted. At this decisive point the funeral procession leaving the town met the rabbi and his entourage entering it.

The cause of the funeral procession was the death of an "only son of his mother," who was a "widow." Luke further reports that "a large crowd . . . was with her" and that "[Jesus'] heart went out to her" (vv. 12-13). Each of the above descriptions focuses on the plight of the mother rather than the son, much as in the preceding story Luke focused on the centurion rather than his servant. In the Gospel and first letter of John (1:14, 18; 3:16, 18; 1 John 4:9), "only son" (Gk. *monogenēs huios*) is an epithet of majesty and divine sonship. Elsewhere in Scripture (Heb 11:17; Judg 11:34; Tob 3:15; 8:17), however, including its three occurrences in Luke (7:12; 8:42; 9:38), *monogenēs* refers to an only human child. An only child is an especially beloved child, and its loss especially agonizing. In character with the occasion, the footsteps of the funeral procession fall heavy and mournful in Luke's narrative, recalling the grief of the broken-hearted in Israel (Jer 6:26; Amos 8:10; Zech 12:10).

13-14   Luke includes two data in v. 13 that are quite out of character with the occasion. The first is reference to Jesus as "Lord." Luke does not take this pericope from either Mark or the Double Tradition.[23] Hence, we should understand his intentional reference to Jesus as "Lord," coupled with the exclamation of the crowd that in Jesus "a great prophet, . . . God has come to visit his people" (v. 16), to indicate that the one who meets the funeral procession at the gate is more than a rabbi.[24] In contrast to the "many lords" (1 Cor 8:5) of the Greco-Roman world — rulers, kings, and heroes — who solicited homage for themselves but were predictably indifferent to others, Jesus is a "Lord" with particular compassion "on her," the widow. The reference to Jesus as "Lord" in the context of compassion on the broken-hearted intentionally portrays him as Israel's Lord (Isa 54:7-10).

---

22. On rabbinic rules for burial of the dead, see Str-B 1:488; 4/1:578-610.

23. There are, however, six Hebraisms in 7:11-17, suggesting a possible relation to the Hebrew Gospel (see Edwards, *Hebrew Gospel*, 305).

24. See Rowe, *Early Narrative Christology*, 117-21.

The second element out of character with the occasion is Jesus' command, "Don't cry" (v. 13). To command a widow not to cry at the death of her young son is patently absurd; some people, after all, were *paid* to cry on such occasions. The Greek word for "cry," *klaiein,* appeared in the blessing of 6:21, "Blessed are you who weep [*klaiein*] now, for you will laugh." Jesus now illustrates how he as the Lord of life is the true fulfillment of his commandments, for he will turn the widow's mourning into laughter. Jesus stops the funeral procession, touches the bier, and says, "Young man, I say to you, get up" (v. 14). In halting the funeral procession and disregarding the ritual defilement of touching a dead body (Num 19:11, 16), and in the emphatic command, "I say to *you,* get up!" — or more precisely in Greek, "be raised [by God]" — Jesus displays a divine intolerance of death.

15-17 At the command "Be raised," the dead boy "sat up and began to talk, and Jesus gave him back to his mother" (v. 15).[25] The final phrase seems irrelevant, for the boy already belonged to his mother. This phrase, which is verbatim with 1 Kgs 17:23, links the narrative typologically with the prophet Elijah (see excursus on Elijah-Elisha at v. 17). The phrase is also implicitly christological, however, for those who are resurrected from the dead belong no longer to this world, but to the Lord of Life, who redeemed them. The first face the boy sees on awakening from death is the face of Jesus, a face with which he is unfamiliar, but to which he belongs.[26] Giving the boy back to his mother is a further demonstration of Jesus' compassion for her (v. 13). The miracle was directed to the mother and the son, but it could not be contained by them. A gust of awe and praise seized *all* who were present — the "all" being emphatic *(hapantes)* in a number of weighty Greek manuscripts.[27] "A great prophet has

---

25. "The dead man sat up" is a linguistic contradiction, of which Luke was certainly aware. The contradiction was necessary, however, in order to convey that the boy was biologically dead — not just near death, unconscious, or swooning. There are occasional stories of Greco-Roman wonder-workers who raised the dead, the most famous (or most similar to the raising at Nain) being the story of the raising of the dead bride by Apollonius of Tyana (Philostratus, *Vita Apol.* 4.45), a first-c. peripatetic philosopher in Cappadocia. Philostratus wrote *Life of Apollonius* a century and a half after the latter's death (early third c.) with the apologetic intention of showing Apollonius similar or equal to Jesus in miraculous powers. In the story of the resuscitated bride, Philostratus clearly reveals his doubts about her death, for although "she seemed dead" (Gk. *tēn korēn tou dokountos thanatou*), vapor arose from her face as she lay in the rain. None could decide if she was dead or near death, concludes Philostratus. Similarly, the account of Apuleius, *Flor.* 19.2-6, in which Asclepiades recognizes that a man being prepared for burial is in fact still alive, is clearly (like Acts 20:7-12) a story of resuscitations from swooning or unconsciousness. For further discussion of real versus apparent deaths, see *HCNT,* 203-5; Klein, *Lukasevangelium,* 278.

26. Ephrem the Syrian, *Comm. Tat. Diates.* 6.23, describes the bond between the two as "the Virgin's Son and the widow's son."

27. ℵ A C L W Γ Θ Ξ Ψ.

appeared among us. God has come to help his people" (v. 16). The Greek word for "come to help" *(episkeptesthai)* was the first (1:68) and last word (1:78) of Zechariah's song in the infancy narrative. Its subject is God — not a distant and uninvolved God — but the God who *visits,* even intrudes into, his creation in grace in order to "redeem" (1:68) and raise up a "horn of salvation" (1:69) for his people "from heaven" (1:78). The exclamation of the people in v. 16 is a *confession of faith* that, in the raising of the boy in Nain, this prophet from Capernaum is the fulfillment of the longing of Israel for God's eschatological intervention of salvation.[28] Luke underscores the radical nature of the divine visitation in v. 17 when he says that "this word [Gk. *logos;* NIV 'news'] about Jesus spread throughout Judea and the surrounding country." Judea here, as in 4:44, is used generically of greater Palestine rather than exclusively of the political tetrarch of Judea. "Surrounding country" (Gk. *perichōros*) repeats the same term of 3:3 (see further there; also 4:14, 37; 8:37), recalling the land chosen by Lot in Gen 13:10. Within that territory lay Sodom, which became a byword for sin and depravity in Israel. The concluding references to "Judea" and "surrounding country" *(perichōros)* assert unambiguously that God's visitation — and the prophet who embodies it — is not a reward for the exceptional, elite, or holy. God's visitation is a gift of grace for all Palestine, even the *perichōros,* its meanest and most desperate regions. Jesus is the prophet of that visitation, "to seek and save the lost" (19:10).

EXCURSUS: ELIJAH AND ELISHA TYPOLOGY
IN THE GALILEAN MINISTRY

The dominant purpose of the Third Gospel, woven like a signature motif in a musical score, is that, in the life, death, and resurrection of Jesus, the saving promises of God to Israel are fulfilled. A remarkable characteristic of Jesus' ministry in Galilee was its evidence of God's power (4:14; 5:17; 6:19; 8:46). Luke portrays that power frequently — and in this he is unique among the Evangelists — according to expressions of power by the prophets Elijah and Elisha. The importance of Elijah and Elisha in Luke's presentation of Jesus is initially signaled by their prominence in the programmatic introduction to Jesus' ministry in his inaugural sermon in Nazareth (4:25-27).[29] Elijah and Elisha typology is subsequently alluded to throughout practically the whole of chap. 7, beginning with the healing of the centurion's servant in 7:1-10, which is narrated with reminiscences of Elisha's healing of Naaman (2 Kgs 5). Both

---

28. H. Beyer, *episkeptomai, TWNT* 2:601.
29. Fitzmyer, *Luke (I–IX),* 537-38.

Naaman and the centurion are Gentiles, both have servants, both send emissaries before them, and both change their minds.

The raising to life of the only son of a widow at Nain in 7:11-17 displays an even stronger allusion to the raising of the only son of the widow of Zarephath by Elijah (1 Kgs 17:17-24; Sir 48:4-5), and to a lesser extent to the raising of the only son of the widow of Shunem by Elisha (2 Kgs 4:32-37). Elijah calls on God as Lord (*kyrios*, 1 Kgs 17:21), and Jesus is called Lord (*kyrios*, 7:13) in the healing at Nain. The phrase "[Elijah/Jesus] gave him back to his mother" is exactly the same in both narratives.[30] The healings of Elijah and Elisha, like Jesus' healings of the centurion's son and the widow's son in Nain, are seen as evidence of God's mighty power at work in the healing prophet. The proximity of Nain to the ancient site of Shunem, a half-mile (1 km) to the south, coupled with the similarity of miracles, may explain Luke's choice to include the miracle at Nain, which appears in no other Gospel. Finally, Jesus interprets the ministry of John the Baptizer with reference to Mal 3:1, "I will send my messenger ahead of you, who will prepare your way before you" (7:27), a saying that, as Mal 4:5 indicates, is identified with the prophet Elijah.[31]

Elijah and Elisha typology is not limited to Luke 7, however. The protest of the demon in 4:34, and to a slightly lesser extent the protest of the demoniac in 8:28, both recall the protest of the widow of Zarephath in 1 Kgs 17:18. The restoration of Jairus's daughter to life in 8:55 is described in a manner reminiscent of the raising to life of the widow's son in 1 Kgs 17:21. In the feeding of the five thousand (9:12-17), the command of Jesus for the crowd to recline in groups of "fifty each" (9:14) recalls the Elijah story of 1 Kgs 18:13, which is the only other place in the Greek Bible where the phrase *ana pentēkonta* ("fifty each") occurs. Additionally, in 9:8, 19 John the Baptist is linked to Elijah as the forerunner of Jesus the Messiah; and in 9:30, 33 Elijah expressly anticipates and introduces Jesus in the transfiguration. Luke completes Jesus' Galilean ministry with two further references to Elijah and Elisha. The first occurs in 9:54, when James and John (the "Sons of Thunder," Mark 3:17), citing the precedent of Elijah calling down fire on the soldiers of King Ahaziah (2 Kgs 1:10, 12), wish to call down fire in judgment on Samaria. The final reference occurs in 9:61-62, where Elisha's turning from the plow to follow Elijah forms a model — albeit negative in this instance — for following Jesus. All told, some

---

30. Gk. *kai edōken auton tē mētri autou* (7:15; 1 Kgs 17:23). This phrase is not necessary to the story (the boy always belonged to his mother), thus heightening Luke's intentional linkage of the pericope to Elijah in 1 Kgs 17.

31. On Elijah typology in Luke 7, see T. L. Brodie, "Towards Unraveling Luke's Use of the Old Testament: Luke 7:11-17 as an *Imitatio* of 1 Kings 17:17-24," *NTS* 32 (1983): 247-67; idem, "Luke 7:36-50 as an Internalization of 2 Kings 4:1-37: A Study in Luke's Use of Rhetorical Imitation," *Bib* 64 (1983): 457-85; J. Croatto, "Jesus, Prophet like Elijah, and Prophet-Teacher like Moses in Luke-Acts," *JBL* 124/3 (2005): 451-65.

fifteen references or allusions to Elijah and Elisha appear in Luke's depiction of Jesus' Galilean ministry, from the inaugural sermon in 4:25-27 to the outset of his journey to Jerusalem in 9:61-62.

Elijah and especially Elisha are not the most obvious choices of OT precursors of Jesus, for other personalities such as Abraham, Moses, David, and perhaps Samuel play larger and more significant roles in the history of Israel. Elijah and Elisha were doubtless chosen by Luke because, of all OT figures, their lives and ministries prefigure the ministry of Jesus in at least three ways. The primary prefigurement is in their *prophetic* office.[32] All references to Elijah and Elisha, and all six references to Jesus as a prophet (with the exception of 24:19), occur only in the Galilean ministry in Luke 1–9. As the anointed prophet of Isaiah (4:18), Jesus proclaims the good news (Gk. *kēryssein; euangelizesthai*) of the word (Gk. *logos*) — terms that occur either exclusively or predominantly in Luke 1–9. Jesus is expressly called a prophet in chaps. 4 (v. 24), 7 (vv, 16, 26, 39), and 9 (vv. 8, 19), and in conjunction with these prophetic references Luke clearly alludes to the figures of Elijah and Elisha.[33] When the two travelers on the road to Emmaus are asked to describe Jesus, they declare, "He was a prophet, powerful in word and deed before God and all the people" (24:19).

Second, Elijah and Elisha prefigure Jesus by their *miraculous powers and healings.* In this they are more unique, for apart from these two eighth-century prophets, miraculous powers, and especially healings, are scarce and nontypical of both the OT (see John 9:32) and rabbinic Judaism.[34] Only with the advent of the Messiah would Israel's true healer arise.[35] Luke's typological use of Elijah's and Elisha's healings in the Galilean ministry signals the fulfillment of the messianic ideal in Jesus' healing ministry.[36] At the conclusion of the Gospel when Jesus is described as "a prophet, powerful in word and deed before God and all the people" (24:19), Luke recapitulates the life of Jesus in terminology particularly reflective of Elijah and Elisha.

32. On this theme, see T. L. Brodie, "A New Temple and a New Law: The Unity and Chronicler-Based Nature of Luke 1:1–4:22a," *JSNT* 5 (1979): 21-45; idem, "Towards Unraveling Luke's Use of the Old Testament: Luke 7:11-17 as an *Imitatio* of 1 Kings 17.17-24," *NTS* 32 (1986): 247-67; Fitzmyer, *Luke I–IX*, 213-15.

33. On Jesus as prophet, see Moessner, *Lord of the Banquet,* 47-50.

34. Thus A. Schlatter, "In Palestinian Judaism there were no miracle workers, and also none who were revered as such." Further, H. Beyer, "Reports of the healing of infirmities among the rabbis are very isolated" (for both quotations and further evidence, see H. Beyer, *therapeuō, TWNT* 3:128-32).

35. *Jub.* 23:26-30; *1 En.* 5:8; 25:5-7; *4 Ezra* 7:121; 8:52. Further, see Str-B 1:593-96.

36. In chaps. 7–9, in particular, Luke has narrated the material with allusions and references to Elijah and Elisha, but he has not *invented* stories about Jesus on the basis of a literary template of Elijah and Elisha, as A. Loisy, *Les évangiles synoptiques* (Paris: Ceffonds, 1907), 1:657-58 argues. For a defense of the historicity of the infancy narrative material, see Lagrange, *Luc,* 208-9.

Finally, both Elijah and Elisha prefigure the ministry of Jesus by the *inclusion of Gentiles* within the circumference of their prophetic orbits.[37] Each of the Lukan references to the healing miracles of Elijah and Elisha depicts the healing of Gentiles.[38] The Elijah-Elisha typology is thus another facet of Luke's dominant theological motif, signifying to readers that Jesus' prophetic healing ministry, and its extension to Gentiles, is not an aberration of the mission of Israel, but the germination of a divine seed that, though planted by Israel's first and greatest prophet, lay dormant until its fulfillment in Jesus.

THE TESTIMONY OF JESUS TO JOHN THE BAPTIZER (7:18-35)

The alternating emphases on angelic prophecies related to John and Jesus, followed by alternating stories of their divine conceptions, births, circumcisions, and coming of age in the infancy narrative (Luke 1–2), could imply that John and Jesus both played roughly essential roles in salvation history. Since the beginning of the Gospel proper in Luke 3, the relationship between John and Jesus has not been further defined, not even at the baptism. The present story returns to their relationship, but unlike the infancy narrative, it records the reflections of John and Jesus toward the other rather than of Luke toward them both. Above all, and again unlike the infancy narrative, it emphasizes the qualitative differences between the two.

18-23   Matt 11:2-6 also records the story of John's emissary to Jesus, but Matt's account is leaner, focused on one specific point, "Are you the one who was to come, or should we expect someone else?" (v. 19). Luke includes a summary of Jesus' ministry in v. 21 (omitted by Matt) that provides fuller context from which to consider John's question. The reference to "all these things" (v. 18), of which John has heard, recalls that fuller context. Like Jesus and the rabbis, John also gathered disciples to himself, and since his imprisonment (3:20) some of his disciples have evidently accompanied Jesus. Despite the ardent reports they bring to John, John is troubled by doubts about Jesus and his mission. He cannot doubt the reports of Jesus' miraculous deeds and dynamic teaching that have spread throughout the region (6:17-19). The only

---

37. The significance of Elijah and Elisha for Luke's presentation of Jesus far exceeds the theme of election, to which C. Evans limits his discussion in "Luke's Use of the Elijah/Elisha Narratives and the Ethic of Election," *JBL* 106/1 (1987): 75-83.

38. The only possible exception is Elisha's raising of the dead son of the Shunammite woman. Shunem lay inside the border of Israel in the hill country of Issachar (Josh 19:18), but it was widely associated in Israel with the Philistine encampment of the Philistines and the death of Saul (1 Sam 28:4).

attribute of the messianic mission about which John could harbor doubts is the absence of the element of judgment in Jesus' early Galilean ministry. In the inaugural sermon at Nazareth Jesus omitted reference to "the day of the Lord's vengeance" (4:18-19; Isa 61:1-2), and in the epitome of Jesus' ministry delivered to John in v. 22 — an epitome woven together from a collage of Isaiah texts[39] — there is no reference to cutting down evildoers (Isa 29:20) and punishing sinners (Isa 26:20). John's graphic wilderness warnings of divine reckoning — winnowing forks, clearing of threshing floors, burning of chaff with unquenchable fire (3:17) — attest that judgment of evildoers was a constituent element of his messianic understanding. The silence of Jesus on the matter of judgment could account for the apparent reservations that John harbors about Jesus.[40]

Summoning two of his disciples, John "sent them to the Lord to ask, 'Are you the one who was to come, or should we expect someone else?'" (v. 19). Sending two disciples reflects Jewish conviction that two witnesses are required to certify a matter (Deut 19:15). Reference to Jesus as "the Lord" (not present in Matt 11:2) is a Lukan addition, alerting readers to the qualitative difference between John and Jesus.[41] "The Coming One" is an eschatological metaphor of calculated ambiguity — the ambiguity being the result not of an uncertain hope but of an unspecified fulfillment (e.g., Hab 2:3). In the OT the "Coming One" can refer to God (Isa 40:10; Zech 14:5; Mal 3:1). But since John earlier referred to the Messiah as the "Stronger One" who would come to reveal and to judge (3:16-17), the "one to come" in vv. 19, 20 likely recalls the same messianic figure.

John's disciples relay his question to Jesus. Before Luke records what Jesus says in response, he reports what Jesus *does* in his powerful works of healing and exorcism (v. 21). The answer to John's question cannot be supplied in a mere affirmative, "Yes, I am he!" Jesus is the Messiah, but not the exact *kind* of Messiah his generation expects. Whoever desires to know Jesus, John included, can know and believe in Jesus only on the basis of his incarnate life. John sends emissaries to Jesus in hopes of learning whether John's calling and ministry have been justified and have any continuing validity. John's life and ministry are at stake in Jesus' answer. Grasping that critical reality, Jesus responds not with a propositional answer but with a resume of his own life.[42] John's disciples are sent back to report what they "have seen and heard" (v. 22).

---

39. Isa 26:19; 29:18; 35:5-6; 42:18; 61:1. 4Q521, a messianic apocalypse from Qumran, assembles a similar battery of texts and images signaling the advent of "the anointed one of God."

40. See here Nolland, *Luke 1:1–9:20*, 332.

41. *Kyrios* claims weaker textual attestation than "Jesus," but it is the harder reading and thus to be preferred. It is unlikely that copyists would delete the name of Jesus, and "Lord" is also typical of Lukan style. See Metzger, *TCGNT*, 119.

42. See Klein, *Lukasevangelium*, 282.

"The blind receive sight, the lame walk, those who have leprosy are cleansed, the deaf hear, the dead are raised, and the good news is proclaimed to the poor" (v. 22). These six claims, all direct quotations from Isaiah (29:18; 35:5-6; 42:18; 26:19; 61:1; and Sir 48:5, respectively), are also conspicuous fulfillments of the messianic prophecy of Isa 61:1-2, on which Jesus based his ministry (4:18). Each claim is a claim of *healing*, which is yet a further messianic testimony, for in the age of salvation the Messiah would heal all Israel's diseases.[43] The texts cited in v. 22 exceed the conventional Jewish messianic ideal, however, for Isa 35 attests to the saving effects of the messianic age on *Gentiles* as well as Jews. The inclusion of Gentiles in Jesus' ministry rather than judgment of them is thus not an aberration of the divine will but an embodiment of it. Jesus concludes, "Blessed is anyone who does not stumble on account of me" (v. 23). This is not a generic proverb, for "blessed" is not plural (as in 6:20-22), but singular — referring specifically to John. Something in Jesus' ministry — perhaps, as suggested above, absence of the note of judgment — is a cause of stumbling to John that impedes his full understanding of Jesus.[44] John is another example of a Lukan irony, that even those directly involved in the divine economy must struggle with faith — first the pious priest Zechariah (1:20), then the Virgin Mary (1:29), now John, the divinely ordained forerunner of the Messiah.

24-30 Luke never informs readers of John's response. Like the elder brother of the Prodigal (15:25-32), John's decision — a crucial decision, it would seem — is left hanging. The essential thing about John at this point is not his answer but his question. Even this question designates John in an unexpected and indirect way the forerunner of Jesus, for his question prompts Jesus' question of the crowd, "What did you go out into the wilderness to see?" (see 3:7). Three times Jesus repeats this question to the crowd (vv. 24, 25, 26).[45] In the Hebrew world, repetition signaled emphasis, and Jesus' repeated interrogation of the crowd is calculated to elicit a proper understanding of John as a prerequisite to a proper understanding of himself. The first two questions of Jesus are put as metaphors that communicate readily and effectively. Did crowds go out into the wilderness to see "a reed shaken by the wind" (v. 24)[46] — a weak and wavering figure? Or did they go out to see someone "dressed in fine clothes" (v. 25) — a soft, privileged, and self-indulged individual? Hardly! People do not make an arduous trek into the wilderness to see someone like

---

43. Str-B 1:593-96.

44. Plummer, *Luke*, 203.

45. In reporting Jesus' question once rather than thrice, *Gos. Thom.* 78 deemphasizes its significance.

46. In an Aesop's fable, a reed and an olive branch dispute who is stronger. The slender reed bends before the force of the wind, whereas the brittle olive branch breaks. The moral of the fable emphasizes flexibility and compliance, quite the opposite of the reed in Jesus' metaphor.

any number of people they know at home. Why, then, did the crowds go out? To see a prophet? Yes, a prophet, indeed more than a prophet (v. 26). "More than a prophet" seems to indicate the penultimate superprophet who would be greater than all the prophets before and inaugurate the messianic age (e.g., John 7:40). The Melchizedek figure of Qumran (11Q13 [11QMelch]) who would usher in the eschatological jubilee was such a figure,[47] as was the messenger like Elijah who would precede and prepare the way of the Lord (v. 27; Exod 23:20; Mal 3:1).[48]

In v. 28 Jesus summarizes his interrogation of the crowd with an unqualified declaration, "I tell you, among those born of women there is no one greater than John; yet the one who is least in the kingdom of God is greater than he." This declaration is less straightforward and clear in the original Greek than in the NIV.[49] "Among those born of women" is a Hebraism *(yelud ishah)* that is slightly awkward in Greek *(en gennētois gynaikōn).*[50] The declaration has also undergone various expansions in transmission, most notably the insertion of "prophet" before John's name.[51] The point of the declaration is nevertheless obvious. "Among those born of women" is a universal statement, meaning that John is the best the human race has to offer. If John's preeminence in the human race were based on merit, we might expect Mary to outrank him (1:26-38). His preeminence is not based on merit, however, but on his office as forerunner of the Messiah. In this John exceeds all other members of the human race. The only person who could be greater than John would have to be greater in kind rather than in degree. That person — and this is the point of the second half of v. 28 — cannot, like John, have one foot planted in the old order and one in the new, but must have both feet planted anew in the kingdom of God. John is the critical transition figure between the promise of the kingdom of God and its fulfillment in Jesus. His role is essential and without equal in preparing for the kingdom. But anyone born within the kingdom —

---

47. See F. Hahn, *Christologische Hoheitstitel: Ihre Geschichte im frühen Christentum* (4th ed.; Göttingen: Vandenhoeck & Ruprecht, 1974), 351-71; Bovon, *Lukas 1,1–9,50,* 377.

48. The return of Elijah at the end of time as herald of the age of salvation was *status confessionis* in Second Temple Judaism. See Str-B 1:597. The quotation of v. 27 "was one of the common-places of Messianic prophecy, and had been stereotyped in an independent Greek form before the Evangelists made use of it" (Plummer, *Luke,* 204).

49. *Gos. Thom.* 46 also preserves the essence of the declaration, "From Adam to John the Baptist there is none born of woman who is greater than John the Baptist. . . . But I have said that whoever among you will become a little one will know the kingdom and will be greater than John."

50. See the examples drawn from Midrash and Talmud in Str-B 1:597.

51. Several manuscripts (A D Θ Ψ *f*[13]) add, "among those born of women, no *prophet* is greater than John." The addition of "prophet" ostensibly spares Jesus from the comparison. The apologetic intent of the addition, as well as the dearth of manuscript evidence in its favor, argues against its originality (see Metzger, *TCGNT,* 119).

anyone born of the "Spirit" (to use Pauline and Johannine terminology) — is greater than John.[52]

In contrast to John's ambivalent judgment of Jesus, Jesus' judgment of John is razor-sharp. Like all things honed to a sharp edge, Jesus' judgment divides. On the one hand, "all the people, even the tax collectors" (v. 29) saw in Jesus' judgment of John a vindication of their baptism by him. On the other hand, the Pharisees and scribes who had not been baptized by John rejected Jesus' judgment, which Luke describes as a rejection of the "counsel of God" itself (v. 30; NIV "God's purpose"). The exact interpretation of vv. 29-30 is made somewhat difficult because the key verb (Gk. *dikaioun*, "to make righteous; vindicate"; NIV "acknowledged God to be right") typically appears in Scripture with God as subject, whereas here it appears with human agents as subject. The idea is that the people, even tax collectors, had done the right thing in going out to hear John preach and in submitting to his baptism, for John's teaching and baptism were valid signs of preparation for the inbreaking of God's kingdom.[53] The Pharisees and scribes, by contrast, by refusing to go out and be baptized by John, refused "the counsel of God" (v. 30). Neither party, however, was aware of the rightness or wrongness of their actions at the time. They were only informed of such in retrospect, i.e., in light of what Jesus says. Jesus' judgment of John confirms the prior actions of the one and condemns those of the other. John's preaching and baptism, faithful and sacrificial as it was, was not a final and sufficient testimony to the inauguration of the kingdom of God. John's ministry, like a torchbearer who runs in advance of the Olympic games, is incomplete and ambiguous in itself. Indeed, it has no meaning if it remains independent of what follows. John's ministry requires the ministry of Jesus for its completion and validation. Vv. 29-30 thus portray Jesus not only as the authoritative interpreter of John's ministry, but in light of v. 28 they portray Jesus as the authoritative interpreter of the history of Israel. In Jesus the meaning and purpose of Israel is both revealed and fulfilled.

31-35 Following the authoritative pronouncement on John's relationship to the kingdom of God, Jesus concludes with a similar pronouncement on John's relationship to himself. The people of this age are like fickle children who either do not know what they want or are inconstant in what they want.[54]

---

52. See here Plummer, *Luke*, 205; Bovon, *Luke 1,1–9,50*, 378.

53. So Fitzmyer, *Luke (I–IX)*, 676; Jeremias, *Sprache des Lukasevangeliums*, 165. The rendering of the verse in BDAG, 249, "all the people and tax-collectors affirmed God's uprightness and got baptized" erroneously implies that baptism followed the people's decision, whereas the natural sense of the Greek is that the people's baptism preceded their understanding of its rightness (see Marshall, *Luke*, 298-99).

54. Jesus' lamentation against his contemporaries is not dissimilar to that of Josephus thirty years later. Commenting on the destruction of the Holy City, Josephus *J. W.* 6.408, wrote

Their fickleness is pictured not in the open interpretive space of a parable, but in a tight simile with direct correspondence between the elements of the story and "the people of this generation" (v. 31). On the one hand, "We played the pipe for you, and you did not dance; we sang a dirge, and you did not cry" (v. 32). Playing the pipe, a common form of entertainment in both Greco-Roman and Jewish society, symbolizes Jesus' acceptance of tax collectors and sinners. The Jewish religious establishment, however, reproached him and would not "dance."[55] On the other hand, John "sang a dirge" — pronounced judgment and wrath — but those who should have repented "did not cry." John, continues Jesus, is considered a fanatic, even demon-possessed, for his abstinence from food and alcohol (v. 33), whereas the Son of Man (see excursus at 5:26) is called a "glutton and drunkard," a profligate who associates with tax collectors and sinners (v. 34). The contrast between Jesus and John in vv. 32-34 forms a chiasmus:

> A   Jesus: "Piping but no dancing"
>   B   John: "Dirge but no crying"
>   B¹   John: A radical ascetic who neither eats nor drinks
> A¹ Jesus: The Son of Man, who parties with prodigals.

Jesus has performed a comedy — in the true sense of a story that ends well — and John a tragedy, but the audience is pleased with neither. Had Jesus and John performed similar routines, the audience could legitimately complain that a different act might please them. The routines of Jesus and John are as different as night and day, however, thus raising the legitimate question whether "the people of this generation" will be pleased with anything.

Jesus concludes, "Wisdom is proved right by all her children" (v. 35).[56] The point of this proverb, and its relation to the preceding chiasmus, is not immediately obvious. "Wisdom" and her "children" could possibly be taken as a sarcastic reference to the folly of the fickle and defiant generation. This is improbable, however.[57] Throughout Wisdom literature, "wisdom" typically

---

that Jerusalem was "undeserving of these great misfortunes on any other ground save that she produced a generation such as that which caused her overthrow."

55. On the relation of this image to Jesus' historical ministry, see C. Blomberg, "Jesus, Sinners, and Table Fellowship," *BBR* 19/1 (2009): 48-49.

56. Luke's reference to the *children* of wisdom rather than the "works" of wisdom (so Matt 11:19) is more Hebraic and thus probably the earlier version of the saying.

57. T. Phillips, "'Will the Wise Person Get Drunk?' The Background of the Human Wisdom in Luke 7:35 and Matthew 11:19," *JBL* 127/2 (2009): 385-96, argues on the basis of selected references to drunkenness in Philo and Seneca that "wisdom" is not a reference to God but to an Aristotelian golden mean, i.e., that the wise person would avoid the extremes of John's abstinence and Jesus' drunkenness. This is to miss the forest for a tree — or perhaps

appears as a personification of God (Prov 8; Sir 24; Wis 6:22–9:18), and "wisdom" appears to personify the missions of John and Jesus here (e.g., 11:49).[58] This is further supported by the use of *dikaioun*, which repeats its unusual sense above: as the people and tax collectors were vindicated *(edikaiōsan)* in their judgment of John (v. 29), so is wisdom vindicated *(edikaiōthē)* in her children or effects (v. 35). "The people of this generation" are indeed obdurate, and they are numerous, but despite their predominance, they cannot hold back the kingdom of God. There is a remarkable remnant that acknowledges John's baptism and the truth of Jesus' teaching and ministry. The reference to "*all* [Gk. *pantōn*] her children" emphasizes this remarkable remnant in v. 35.[59] This remnant is "the children of wisdom" — Christians. Despite the critical mass that rejects Jesus, as it earlier rejected his forerunner John the Baptizer, followers of Jesus are living witnesses to the wisdom of God, in the same way that fruit is a living witness to the nature of the tree that bears it (6:44).[60]

OF DEDICATION AND DOUBT (7:36-50)

The story of the sinful woman and a Pharisee (7:36-50) is the fourth interpersonal encounter of Jesus in Luke 7. Unique to Luke, it is normally read as an independent pericope. The story is nevertheless linked to the preceding story of Jesus and John (7:18-35) in several vital ways that inform and determine its proper understanding. In both accounts sinners appear as protagonists of the gospel (7:29, 47-50) and Pharisees as antagonists (7:30, 40-47). In both Jesus makes his decisive point by means of a brief parable in the midst of the story (7:32, 41-42). And finally, in both the fate of Jesus' counterpart — John the Baptizer in the first, and Simon the Pharisee in the second — is left open-ended. The story of the sinful woman and Simon the Pharisee illustrates the generic reference to sinners and Pharisees in 7:29-30 in one of the most memorable stories in the Gospels.[61]

---

a vine. The gist of 7:31-35 is not about drunkenness or even wisdom, but about the respective ministries of John and Jesus.

58. See Lagrange, *Luc,* 225-27.

59. See Metzger, *TCGNT,* 120.

60. See Schweizer, *Lukas,* 89; Klein, *Lukasevangelium,* 291.

61. All four Gospels record a story of a woman who breaks an alabaster jar of ointment at a dinner party in the presence of Jesus (7:36-50; Matt 26:6-13; Mark 14:3-9; John 12:1-8). The Matthean account is virtually identical with the Markan account and almost certainly dependent on it. John's account departs from Matt and Mark in several minor respects, and in major respects by setting the event six days before Passover (Matt/Mark, two days before), and by the woman anointing Jesus' feet (as opposed to his head in Matt/Mark, and Ignatius,

36-39   The banquet table is a favorite Lukan narrative setting (5:29; 7:36; 9:16; 11:37; 14:1; 22:14; 24:30). In the Third Gospel the banquet at Simon's house is second in memorability only to the Last Supper. Luke's first banquet portrayed a sinner as host and Pharisees as intruders (5:29-32); in this his second banquet a Pharisee is the host and a sinner the intruder.[62] A Pharisee invites Jesus to dinner and Jesus accepts.[63] Pharisees (see at 5:17) have been mentioned six times previously (5:17, 21, 30, 33; 6:2, 7), each time in antagonism to Jesus' mission. The fact that a Pharisee would invite Jesus to a banquet in the first place, and that in doing so he was sufficiently assured of Jesus' acceptance,[64] is significant to the outcome of the story. The banquet was ceremonious, for Luke records that Jesus "reclined" (v. 36; *kateklithē*). Reclining — resting on one's left elbow, with head toward food and company and feet extended outward, leaving the right hand free with which to eat — was customary at formal occasions. Invitation to a banquet was an honor, but it also exposed guests to potential risks, for eating at table was the single most intimate social setting in the ancient Jewish world, and the presence of ritually unclean individuals and/or foods inevitably jeopardized Jewish ritual purity and social stratification.

Into a kosher banquet appears an uninvited guest, "a woman in that town who lived a sinful life" (v. 37). The woman introduces into the narrative another of Luke's signature male-female pairs (see at 14:1). The man and woman occupy opposite ends of the social spectrum in first-century Judaism. The man

---

Eph. 17:1). Matt, Mark, and John all agree, however, in setting the episode in Bethany, in the indignation of those present following the anointing, in the value of the ointment (300 denarii), in Jesus' concluding words, and esp. in the verbatim description of the "pure nard, an expensive perfume." These similarities argue rather strongly that these three Evangelists preserve varying renditions of the same account. Luke 7:36-50 is likely a different story, however. It is set in Galilee, not Judea; the Simon of Luke is a Pharisee, not a leper; the pervasive element of the woman's sinfulness and forgiveness in Luke is wholly absent from the other three accounts; in Luke's account Simon objects to the woman's sinfulness, not to her extravagance as in the other accounts; and the motif of anointing for burial is absent in Luke. It is unlikely that the sinful woman of Luke 7 is identical with Mary of John 12, who otherwise is not identified as a sinner. See a full discussion of the matter in R. Brown, *The Gospel according to John (I–XII)* (AB; New York: Doubleday, 1966), 449-54. The conflation of Luke's sinful woman with Mark's unnamed woman led Ephrem the Syrian in the fourth c. (and many since) to identify the woman as Mary Magdalene — a conclusion for which there is no biblical evidence. On this final point, see J. Shaberg, "How Mary Magdalene Became a Whore," *BRev* 8/5 (1992): 30-37, 51-52.

62. Vinson, *Luke*, 227.

63. The imperfect tense of "invite" (*ērōta*, v. 36) implies forethought rather than spontaneity on Simon's part.

64. Two things (among many) incumbent on a Jewish host were (1) not to leave a worthy guest uninvited and (2) not to invite a guest who might decline the invitation (Str-B 4/2:612). The first mistake shamed the guest; the second, the host.

is four times identified as a "Pharisee" (vv. 36 [2x], 37, 39), which guarantees his preeminence in Jewish society, and three times he is identified by his personal name, "Simon" (vv. 40, 43, 44). The woman is not formally introduced or identified, but referred to repeatedly and anonymously as "woman" (37, 39, 44, 50), "sinner" (37, 39 [49]), or simply by the feminine pronoun (44 [2x], 45, 46, 47, 48). Luke does not specify what kind of sinner she was, but popular imagination has branded her with a scarlet letter. Whether prostitution can be demonstrated — and if not, whether it can ever be removed — is another question. Many commentators portray the detailed description of her behavior in vv 37-38 in the most lurid light. "In the city" (v. 37; NIV "in that town") is taken to connote a streetwalker; the expensive alabaster jar of perfume is attributed to her opprobrious professional success; the letting down of her hair and kissing of Jesus' feet are taken as tell-tale eroticisms. This is obsessive, for none of the descriptions, singularly or combined, is necessarily meretricious. "In that town" (Gk. *en tē polei*) occurs seventy-six times in the Greek Bible, only once (Amos 7:17; possibly also Deut 22:24) with reference to prostitution. A woman's possession of a valuable alabaster jar of perfume could easily (and better) be explained as an inheritance. Much ado is made of the woman's unbound hair, but unbound hair does not reveal the nature of her sin. It was shameful for a married woman to appear in public with unbound hair, but unmarried Roman and Greek women — and evidently unmarried Jewish women as well — wore their hair free. Unbound hair could be sexually provocative, to be sure, but perhaps no more so than a woman wearing a short skirt today. Far more often in both Greco-Roman and Jewish literature, loose and disheveled hair symbolizes humility, grief, contrition, and gratitude, particularly when accompanied, as it is here, by tears (e.g., *b. B. Qam.* 8.6).[65] In this instance the woman's unbound hair serves as a towel that Simon, the host, has not provided.[66] Nor is the reference to Jesus' "feet" sexually symbolic.[67] The Hebrew language can indeed use feet with reference to genitals, but like all euphemisms, a specific context is required to convey this sense.[68] It is inconceivable that an afternoon banquet in a Pharisee's house in Galilee would provide a

65. C. Cosgrove's comprehensive and well-documented study of this issue in "A Woman's Unbound Hair in the Greco-Roman World, with Special Reference to the Story of the 'Sinful Woman' in Luke 7:36-50," *JBL* 124/4 (2005): 675-92, concludes soberly that "the woman's gesture with her hair is not sexually provocative, indecent, or even a breach of etiquette" (691).

66. So Bailey, *Jesus through Middle Eastern Eyes*, 249.

67. The relish with which Vinson, *Luke*, 232-33, interprets "feet" in v. 38 as a Hebrew euphemism for genitals ("The woman's numerous kisses on Jesus' feet — his *feet* — went beyond mere hospitality") seems rather prurient.

68. See the article on "foot" by F. Stendebach, *regel* etc., *TDOT* 13:309-24, who finds only two certain uses of "feet" to refer to genitals (Exod 4:25 and Isa 7:20; Ezek 16:25 uses "legs" equally sexually) out of 245 uses of the word in the MT.

context for a prostitute to ply her trade — and that Jesus would commend her for doing so! The *triclinium* itself accounts for the footwashing, for with the feet of guests extending outward to the circumference of the gathering, Jesus' feet were the only part of his body available for an outsider to wash with her tears and anoint with perfume.

All this does not disprove that the woman was a prostitute. She could have been. It merely dispels the prurient assumption that Luke's description of the woman's behavior in vv. 37-38 is full of sexual innuendos, and that she can safely be assumed a prostitute. Both assumptions lack convincing evidence.[69] Luke never pairs "sinner" with "prostitute" — indeed the Third Gospel omits "prostitute" entirely except for a single reference in 15:30. The most common sinner explicitly identified in the Third Gospel is "tax collector" ("tax collectors and sinners" appear in 5:30; 7:34; 15:1). The second of these references occurs only two verses prior to the introduction of the sinful woman in v. 36. If context is a clue to the woman's sinfulness — and the introduction to this section notes several data linking 7:18-35 with 7:36-50 — then it is not impossible that the woman's sinfulness was related to the hated Roman tax system. If so, it would make her sinfulness more loathsome, for the Roman tax system permeated and poisoned Jewish society to a greater extent than did prostitution.

The triple reference to the situation of the woman beside Jesus' "feet" in v. 38 accentuates her humility — or better, humiliation. She is not passive, however. Vv. 37-38 contain eight verbal assertions of her conduct: she *learned* where Jesus was, *brought* a jar of ointment, *stood* behind his feet, *wept, washed* his feet with tears, *wiped* them with her hair, *kissed* them, and *anointed* them with perfume. These verbs attest to her remarkable determination and devotion. The Pharisee's conduct, by contrast, is described in a perfunctory description of social propriety: he *called* him (v. 39). Vv. 44-45 will describe how little he has done for Jesus. In their respective responses to Jesus, the Pharisee and the sinful woman continue to occupy opposite ends of the spectrum. In contrast to the woman's extravagant generosity, the Pharisee festers inwardly,[70] for if Jesus were indeed a prophet,[71] he should know what kind of woman was touching him. The Pharisee is vexed not by the presence of the sinful woman in the room, for in the ancient Jew-

---

69. It is worth recalling that the earliest patristic interpreters of 7:36-50 (e.g., Asterius of Amasea, *Hom.* 13.10.2-3) did not judge the woman a prostitute, but rather a grieving penitent.

70. The Greek expression for "he said to himself" (v. 39), *en heautō,* is a Hebraism referring to an inner dialogue "in one's heart" (see Edwards, *Hebrew Gospel,* 139).

71. Two important ancient Greek manuscripts, Codices Vaticanus (B, fourth c.) and Zacynthius (Ξ, sixth c.), read *the* Prophet, as an allusion to the eschatological Prophet of Deut 18:15. The internal integrity of the narrative does not require an elevated Christological question at this point, however, and textual evidence vastly favors simply *a* prophet.

ish world uninvited persons were permitted at banquets as long as they remained along the walls.[72] He is vexed because Jesus does not know and judge this sinful woman.

40-46   For the first time Jesus speaks, forthrightly and personally, addressing his host not by his office but by his name, "Simon." Jesus knows all people, and he addresses them by their proper names. Jesus tells Simon a compact parable. Two people are indebted to a moneylender, one for five hundred denarii, and the other for fifty. Neither can repay, and the lender graciously cancels both debts. Which of the two, asks Jesus, will love the lender more (vv. 41-42)? A denarius was the standard wage for a day's work in Jesus' day (Matt 20:2). The sums owed the lender translate to debts approximating two years' and two months' wages, respectively. Those are significant debts, and both debtors have reason to be grateful, especially the greater debtor. Until this point the sinful woman has dominated the story, but with Jesus' question the focus shifts unexpectedly to righteous Simon. Luke does not allow readers to dismiss Simon superficially and self-righteously. Simon refers to Jesus honorably as "teacher" (v. 40), an esteemed title in a society of Jewish sages and savants. He does not evade Jesus' question but enters thoughtfully into his parable, following it to the rightful conclusion (v. 43). Reflective interaction with Jesus can be a first human step in a saving direction (1:29; 3:15). "You have judged correctly," Jesus said (v. 43).

Jesus then turns to the woman but continues speaking to Simon. Simon and the woman have stood poles apart, but Jesus triangulates a new relationship between them ("those who once were far away but now have been brought near," Eph 2:13). A scandalous irony ensues. To a woman who three times is openly declared a sinner — and let us remember that sin (whatever its precise nature in this instance) was taken far more seriously in Jesus' day than it is in ours — Jesus breathes not a word of judgment. To Simon, who has not violated an iota of Torah in this narrative, Jesus delivers a blistering denunciation. "I came into your house. You did not give me any water for my feet, but she wet my feet with her tears and wiped them with her hair. You did not give me a kiss, but this woman, from the time I entered, has not stopped kissing my feet. You did not put olive oil on my head, but she has poured perfume on my feet" (vv. 44-46).[73] In socially stratified first-century Palestine, meals and banquets were potentially volatile — and this one has exploded. Jewish feasts were governed by a litany of complex and obligatory protocols. They included invitations delivered to guests by slaves or servants (feasts were normally scheduled in late

---

72. Str-B 4/2:615.

73. "Never in my life," writes K. Bailey in *Jesus through Middle Eastern Eyes*, 256, "in any culture, anywhere in the world have I participated in a banquet where the guest attacked the quality of the hospitality" as here.

afternoons); preparation of proper foods; proper reception of guests, serving of hors d'oeuvres, inviting of guests into the dining room, and seating them in order of age and importance; provision of washbasins and wine, and prayers before meals and various times during it; and lighting of incense candles after the meal, followed by more wine and sweets.[74] Luke's interest, of course, is on the three main participants at the banquet and not on its social etiquette. Jesus' three indictments of Simon — washing of feet, kissing, and anointing the head with oil — were in fact not normally required.[75] Nevertheless, compared to general protocol of Jewish feasts (Gen 18:1-8!), and especially compared to the extravagant hospitality of the sinful woman, "Simon's welcome of Jesus looks decidedly cool."[76] The woman who crashed the party has been Jesus' true host. She is a sinner who "acknowledged God," thus fulfilling the judgment of 7:29, whereas Simon is a Pharisee who has "rejected the counsel of God," fulfilling the judgment of 7:30.

47-50 Jesus receives the woman's hospitality as an eloquent though unspoken confession of faith. "I tell you the truth, her many sins have been forgiven — as her great love has shown" (v. 47). Her sins are not overlooked or unannounced; indeed, Jesus calls them "many." But in vv. 47-48 he twice declares her sins forgiven (on forgiveness of sins, see at 5:21). The Greek verb tense (perfect passive indicative, "have been forgiven") indicates *prior* forgiveness, exactly as in the earlier declaration of forgiveness to the paralytic, "When Jesus saw their faith he said, 'Man, your sins have been forgiven'" (5:20). The original Greek, which reads "because she loved much," could imply that her forgiveness was the result of her love, which would make grace dependent on the quality of her love (e.g., John 9:31). This deduction runs counter to the summary story of Jesus — and to elements within this narrative. It is precisely the unwarranted free conferral of grace to "tax collectors and sinners" that forever scandalizes Pharisees, Simon included. Jesus' foregoing parable in vv. 41-42 declares the gracious forgiveness of the two debtors irrespective of merit on their part. Likewise in v. 50 Jesus attributes the woman's salvation to her faith, not to her love. The woman may have had a prior acquaintance with Jesus (through the baptism of John, 7:29?), which would account for the

74. On Jewish banquets and festivals, see Str-B 4/2:611-39. For a description of table protocol in Hellenistic feasts, similar in many respects to Jewish festivals, see E. Steele, "Luke 11:37-54 — a Modified Hellenistic Symposium?" *JBL* 103/3 (1984): 379-94.

75. The only person who could be compelled to wash a Jew's feet was a Gentile slave; even a Jewish slave could not be compelled to wash another Jew's feet (Str-B 2:557). Public kissing was not condoned in Jewish society with the exception of (1) kisses of homage, (2) kisses before long separations, and (3) kisses after long absences (Str-B 1:995). Anointing of the head of a guest with oil seems to have been more customary, although not strictly required (Str-B 1:986; 4:26-29).

76. Tannehill, *Luke,* 136.

intentional manner by which she sought him out in vv. 37-38. The NIV correctly conveys that her love and gratitude were the *result* of her forgiveness, not the cause of it.[77] It is Jesus — not the woman's love — who is the source of her forgiveness. His unmerited acceptance of her scandalizes both the table guests (v. 49, "they began to say among themselves") and Simon (v. 39, "he said to himself"). What is a scandal to Simon and guests, however, is grace to the woman, to whom Jesus says, "Your faith has saved you; go in peace" (8:48; 1 Sam 1:17; 20:42; Jdt 8:35)!

The saving resolution of grace in the sinful woman's life fascinated the fathers of the early church, as it has readers ever since, who saw in her a quintessential symbol of devotion to Jesus, both individually and ecclesially. By comparison, Simon is a mean figure. Nevertheless, he plays an important role in the Lukan narrative, for his fate is left unresolved, and this mirrors the unresolved fate of John in the previous story. When Luke composed his Gospel, Gentile "sinners" (like the sinful woman) were streaming into the church, but Jews (like Simon) were less enthusiastic, and their fate vis-à-vis the gospel remained an open question. Luke populates the Third Gospel with recurring Jewish leaders whose response to the kingdom of God inaugurated in Jesus is undetermined. John the Baptizer in the previous story is such a figure (7:19), as is Simon the Pharisee here (7:39). The priest and Levite in the parable of the Good Samaritan remain undetermined characters (10:31-32), as do the pious elder brother in the parable of the Prodigal Son (15:25-32) and the self-satisfied Pharisee in the parable of the Pharisee and the Tax Collector (18:9-14). The fate of each figure — all Pharisees or Jewish leaders except for John — is left provocatively open-ended as an existential reminder of the unfinished mission to Israel.

Does Luke leave any clues to the resolution of this momentous question? In the present story there are at least hopeful signs. Simon's correct interpretation of the parable of Two Debtors is an initial positive step. The inclusion of his name is perhaps also significant, for names of persons who joined the Christian movement were remembered and recorded — especially in a Gospel based on "eyewitnesses" (1:2).[78] Above all, Luke knows one Pharisee — Paul — far more antagonistic than Simon, who surrendered to grace. Paul's salvation is a harbinger of hope for Simon and the Elder Brother and "all Israel" (Rom 11:26).

---

77. For a full discussion of this point, see J. Kilgallen, S.J., "John the Baptist, the Sinful Woman, and the Pharisee," *JBL* 104/4 (1985): 675-79. For succinct reviews, see Plummer, *Luke*, 213-14; Marshall, *Luke*, 313. The argument of Wolter, *Lukasevangelium*, 296, that forgiveness depends on the woman's love, is not convincing.

78. R. Bauckham, *Jesus and the Eyewitnesses: The Gospels as Eyewitness Testimony* (Grand Rapids: Eerdmans, 2006), 39-66.

WOMEN AMONG JESUS' DISCIPLES (8:1-3)

Jesus' missionary outreach in proclaiming the good news of the kingdom of God to the towns and villages of Galilee is resumed in 8:1. A previous mission occurred in 4:43, and another follows in 9:1. According to 4:43 and 8:1, itinerancy was the chief characteristic of Jesus' ministry in Galilee, although 9:1 describes an independent mission of the Twelve. The mention of women in 8:1-3 is unique among the Gospels. All four Gospels report named women at the crucifixion (23:49; Matt 27:55-56; Mark 15:40-41; John 19:25) and resurrection (24:1-12; Matt 28:1-8; Mark 16:1-8; John 20:1-18), and Matt 27:55 and Mark 15:41 declare in retrospect that women had followed Jesus from Galilee. But 8:1-3 is the only prepassion reference to a sorority of **women as Jesus' disciples**.[79] Women's names do not appear in the list of the twelve apostles (6:12-16), nor are women sent into mission with the Twelve (9:1-6). Luke differentiates "the Twelve [who] were with [Jesus]" (v. 1) from "the women [who] were helping to support them out of their own means" (v. 3). Nevertheless, the *kai . . . kai* construction in Greek, meaning "*both* the Twelve who were with him *and* certain women who had been healed," combines the Twelve and the women in Jesus' mission. The apostles are set on a similar plane with women disciples in Acts, when Luke reports that the Twelve "continued with one accord (Gk. *homothymadon*) in prayer *with the women and Mary the mother of Jesus and his brothers*" (Acts 1:14). In v. 3 the Gk. *diēkonoun* (NIV "support") — a technical term for "deacon" in Luke's day (Acts 6:1-7; 1 Cor 12:5) — designates the women as an operative support wing, along with the Twelve, in Jesus' ministry. In the crowd at Jesus' crucifixion Luke likewise explicitly mentions "women who mourned and wailed for [Jesus]" (23:27). We do not know that the latter were identical with the women of 8:2-3, but their mention here, and the report in Acts 1, testifies that women disciples belonged to the nucleus of Jesus' ministry and the earliest Christian community in Jerusalem. The chief responsibility of the early church was to "be my witnesses" (Acts 1:8), and women, as Nolland notes insightfully, constitute the only group to witness all four essential components of the early church's confession of 1 Cor 15:3-5: the death, burial, empty tomb, and resurrection of Jesus.[80]

1-3   Like the preceding story of the sinful woman and Simon, vv. 1-3 are unique to Luke and replete with Hebraisms.[81] The oldest Greek manuscript

---

79. For an overview of women in Israel, see P. King and L. Stager, *Life in Biblical Israel* (Louisville: Westminster John Knox Press, 2001), 49-59; for an overview of women in the Jesus movement, see M. Hengel, *Saint Peter: The Underestimated Apostle* (trans. T. H. Trapp; Grand Rapids: Eerdmans, 2010), 103-34.

80. Nolland, *Luke 1:1–9:20*, 366.

81. There are six Hebraisms in 8:1-2. See Edwards, *Hebrew Gospel*, 306; and Jeremias, *Sprache des Lukasevangeliums*, 175.

divisions of the Gospels combine both stories into a single chapter (#21), suggesting that the sinful woman of 7:36-50 was not an exception in Jesus' ministry but typical of the "many other women" who followed and supported him (8:2-3).[82] 8:1-3 perhaps also implies that earlier references to "disciples" (6:13, 17; 7:11) included women as well as men.[83] It was not uncommon for women to support Jewish rabbis (e.g., Josephus, *Ant.* 17.33-45), but it was virtually unknown for women to travel with rabbis. The presence of sizable numbers of women in Jesus' retinue must be regarded as a critically assured fact, for it was not a practice the Evangelists would invent (John 4:27),[84] and evidently one their successors forgot.[85] Luke himself is tutored by Jesus' radically inclusive fellowship, for the Third Gospel is replete with men and women paired in the story of salvation (see excursus at 14:1).

Luke is discreetly ambiguous about who "had been cured of evil spirits and diseases" (v. 2). So far in the Third Gospel only one woman, Simon's mother-in-law, has been cured by Jesus (4:38-39), but the women here mentioned could have been cured at 4:40-41, 6:17-19, or another time. Mary Magdalene, who according to all four Gospels was the first witness and herald of the resurrection, probably came from Magdal Nunaja ("Fishtower") on the west coast of Lake Gennesaret between Tiberias and Capernaum.[86] The reference to "*seven* demons" must signify the gravity of her oppression (11:26; also 17:4). Joanna is identified as the wife of a Chuza, "the manager of Herod's household."[87] The Herod referred to is Herod Antipas, tetrarch of Galilee, who imprisoned and executed John the Baptizer. The Jesus movement has

---

82. On the old Greek chapter divisions and their significance, see J. Edwards, "The Hermeneutical Significance of Chapter Divisions in Ancient Gospel Manuscripts," *NTS* 56/3 (2010): 413-26.

83. It is doubtful that the seventy-two missionaries in 10:1, though unidentified, include women, for gender stratification in first-c. Judaism would scarcely allow women to travel two-by-two with men who were not their husbands.

84. Rabbinic sayings are not complimentary with respect to rabbis speaking to women. Thus, "Talk not much with womankind. They said this of a man's own wife: how much more of his fellow's wife! Hence the Sages have said: He that talks much with womankind brings evil upon himself and neglects the study of the Law and at last will inherit Gehenna" (*m. 'Abot.* 1.5). Likewise, "A man shall not be alone with a woman in a dwelling place, even with his sister or daughter, due to sinful thoughts. A man should not discourse with a woman on the street, even with his own wife, and certainly not with another woman, because of human gossip" (Str-B 2:438).

85. The infrequent references to 8:2-3 in the patristic period suggests a lack of enthusiasm among the Fathers for the active participation of women in Jesus' retinue. Augustine is one of the few Fathers who cites the passage, and he interprets the women's participation in terms of monasticism.

86. See Klein, *Lukasevangelium*, 300.

87. See Fitzmyer, *Luke (I–IX)*, 698; Lagrange, *Luc*, 235.

thus infiltrated the highest echelons of society and influenced a wife to travel without her husband.[88] Susanna is not otherwise known. Of the three women, Mary Magdalene and Joanna reappear at the empty tomb (24:10), and women who traveled with Jesus in Galilee are mentioned again in 23:55-56. Mary, Joanna, Susanna, and other women were both beneficiaries of Jesus' healing and benefactors of his mission, contributing to the Jesus movement[89] from their own possessions (v. 3). Their "ministry" (Gk. *diakonein*) should be understood both materially and spiritually.[90]

THE PARABLE OF THE SOWER (8:4-15)

4-8   Matt 13:1 and Mark 4:1 identify the parable of the Sower with a *place* — beside the Sea of Galilee — whereas Luke focuses on the *audience* streaming to Jesus "from town after town" (v. 4). Jesus made virtually every encounter into a teaching opportunity, and when large crowds were gathered, as here, he often taught in **parables**. His success with parables stamped virtually all subsequent reference to parables with a more specific understanding than was common before him. Greek *parabolē* is the standard translation of Hebrew *mashal,* which throughout the OT and rabbinic literature connotes a brief maxim, saying, or figure of speech that involved a comparison or picture. Instances of *parabolē* used in this generic sense are preserved sporadically in the Gospels (e.g., Matt 15:15; Mark 3:23; 7:17; Luke 4:23). Jesus, however, developed the art of parabolic discourse to a degree unknown in the OT (2 Sam 12:1-14; Ezek 17:1-10) and among the rabbis and in Greco-Roman antiquity.[91] His distinctive alteration of the art accounts for the enduring connotation of "parable" among Christians. The earliest editors of the Gospels regarded parables the most characteristic and insightful form

88. Nolland, *Luke 1:1–9:20,* 367-68.

89. Several manuscripts (א A L Ψ) read that the women supported "him" (= Jesus), but the stronger manuscript evidence reads "them" (= Jesus and disciples). See Metzger, *TCGNT,* 120-21.

90. Tannehill, *Luke,* 139, notes that women's roles in Jesus' ministry may reflect the ancient world's division of labor of men running public affairs and women running households. This division would give women an entrée into leadership roles in the Jesus movement.

91. Parables are found in rabbis from Palestine but not from Babylonia. The subject of such parables is invariably Torah, whereas for Jesus it is the kingdom of God. According to Str-B 1:654, the single rabbinic parable known to antedate Jesus is from Hillel (ca. 20 B.C.). For examples of Hellenistic stories that resemble parables, see *HCNT,* 89-92. The differences in the latter are noteworthy, however. Hellenistic parables are not about the kingdom of God, they nearly always have a moral appended, and they do not need to be "entered" to be understood.

of Jesus' teaching, and they consequently began new chapter divisions with parables, as they also did with Jesus' miracles.[92] The Gospels record some sixty different parables of Jesus, most in Matt and Luke, fewer in Mark, and none in John. Most of Jesus' parables intended to teach something about the kingdom of God, which he illustrated by everyday episodes of fishing and farming, housekeeping and family life, royalty and banquets. No special knowledge or vocabulary was required to understand Jesus' parables. Parables reflect daily life, but they are not simple or easily understood. Jesus' parables often confront hearers with the unexpected, confounding them and forcing them to perceive things in a new light. A few of Jesus' parables have allegorical qualities, but allegory is not their chief characteristic. In allegory an element in a story equates directly with a reality outside the story, and once the equation is made, the story itself ceases to be significant. An allegory can be objectively resolved, but one must enter *into* a parable if one is to understand the kingdom of God. Parables are like stained-glass windows in a cathedral, dull and lifeless from the outside, but brilliant and radiant from within. Parables do not simply dispense good advice. They are good news, but the good news cannot be understood apart from the one who announces it. The life of Jesus is the greatest parable of all.

The original parable in the gospel tradition is about a sower scattering seed on the ground, something with which all people in all times are familiar.[93] Some seed falls on pathways, some on rocky ground, some among thorns, and some on good soil.[94] This typifies the farming conditions prevalent in the austere terrain of Galilee. Farming in Palestine was a hardscrabble affair (Jer 4:3; Jas 1:11), and the farmer sows unsparingly. The Mishnah decrees that farming should be orderly and methodical, with special care given not to mix seeds (*m. Kil.* 2). The sowing in Jesus' parable, by contrast, is profligate, almost wasteful. The indiscriminate scattering of seed has often been explained as a result of plowing *after* sowing in first-century Palestine. This is an attractive hypothesis, for it would help explain why seed is sown in unpromising places. On the whole, however, evidence suggests that ancient farmers plowed before sowing — although they also may have plowed afterward to provide a protective layer of soil for the seed.[95] So intent is the farmer that he sows in every

92. See J. Edwards, "The Hermeneutical Significance of Chapter Divisions in Ancient Gospel Manuscripts," *NTS* 56/3 (2010): 418-22.

93. The parable of the Sower is the first major parable in all three Synoptics (8:4-15; Matt 13:1-17; Mark 4:1-20). According to Mark, it is fundamental to the understanding of all parables: "Don't you understand this parable? How then will you understand any parable?" (Mark 4:13).

94. This same order of sowing in preserved in *Gos. Thom.* 9.

95. J. Jeremias, *The Parables of Jesus* (trans. S. Hooke; rev. ed.; London: SCM Press, 1963), 11, asserts that "in Palestine sowing precedes ploughing." K. White rebuts this assertion forcefully in "The Parable of the Sower," *JTS* 15 (1964): 300-307. The issue has been reexamined

corner of the field, "in hopes that good soil might somewhere be found," said
Justin Martyr in his retelling of the parable over a century later (*Dial.* 125.1-
2).[96] Even so, rocks, thorns, and adverse elements render three-quarters of
the labor lost.[97]

Those are discouraging odds. But the parable does not end on a discouraging note. "Other seed fell on good soil. It came up and yielded a crop, a
hundred times more than was sown" (v. 8). A harvest of one-hundred fold was
extraordinary in Palestine, and if not strictly miraculous, it certainly evinced
divine blessing (Gen 26:12).[98] Not infrequently in Jewish literature, "the harvest" is a metaphor for the inbreaking of the kingdom of God (Isa 9:3; Ps 126:6).
The prolific harvest of the parable illustrates that inbreaking.

The parable is often understood as a parable of Soils, interpreting the
hardened ground, rocks, thorns, and good soil as allegories of wrong or right

---

by P. Payne, "The Order of Sowing and Ploughing in the Parable of the Sower," *NTS* 25 (1978):
123-29. Payne sustains his conclusion that "ploughing regularly follows sowing in order to bury
the seed" (127) only by admitting that spring plowing preceded fall sowing in Palestine. As
Isa 28:24, Hos 10:12, Jer 4:3 and other OT texts indicate, plowing normally preceded sowing,
and sometimes following in order to cover the seed. See J. Drury, *The Parables in the Gospels*
(London: SPCK, 1985), 57-58.

96. The power and the purpose of the sower are lost in the apocryphal *Mem. Apost.*, in
which the disciples accuse Jesus of being a bad farmer for having sown seed where it cannot
grow (see *NTApoc.* 1:376).

97. The enemies of the harvest are legion. See G. Suess, "Enemies of the Harvest," *JerusalemPersp* 53 (1997): 18-23, who lists some 125 species of thistles in Palestine that choke the
harvest. Similarly, M. Knowles, "Abram and the Birds in *Jubilees* 11: A Subtext for the Parable
of the Sower?" *NTS* 41 (1995): 145-51, draws attention to similarities between the ravishing
crows in *Jub.* 11:10 and the role of birds in the parable of the Sower. In *Jub.* the crows are sent
by Mastema/Satan, prince of demons.

98. *Gos. Thom.* 9 increases the harvest in the parable to "sixtyfold and even 120-fold."
The size of an average harvest in first-c. Palestine is still debated. J. Jeremias, *The Parables
of Jesus* (rev. ed.; London: SCM Press, 1963), 150, following G. Dalman, *Arbeit und Sitte in
Palästina* (Hildesheim: G. Olms, 1964), 153-65, maintained that a seven-and-one-half yield was
average in first-c. Palestine, and thirtyfold or more was unheard of. W. D. Davies and D. Allison dispute this judgment in *A Critical and Exegetical Commentary on the Gospel according
to Saint Matthew* (ICC; Edinburgh: T&T Clark, 1991), 2:385, saying that the figures given in
the parable of the Sower "do not seem obviously out of the ordinary." The truth probably lies
between these two positions. Varro, Theophrastus, Strabo, Pliny, and Gen. 26:12 all preserve
evidence that huge crops were possible in some places in some years. But the average harvest
seems to have been far less, perhaps even as low as three- or fourfold (see R. McIver, "One-
Hundred-fold Yield — Miraculous or Mundane? Matthew 13:8, 23; Mark 4:8, 20; Luke 8:8,"
NTS 40 [1994]: 606-8, who surveys the literature and maintains that "a yield of thirty-fold . . .
was not only exceptional, it was miraculous in first-century Palestine"). There is no evidence
in ancient literature that the figures in the parable of the Sower were normal. A hundredfold
signaled a remarkable, if not miraculous, harvest.

discipleship.[99] The parable is more than a metaphor of human responses and responsibilities, however, interesting as those are to our modern, self-help world.[100] The parable is about the miraculous power of germination in a "seed."[101] Not the soil, but the seed and sowing is thrice emphasized in Greek in the opening line: "The sower [Gk. *speirōn*] went out to sow [Gk. *speirai*] the seed [Gk. *sporon*]" (v. 5). In v. 11 the seed is expressly identified as "the word of God." In v. 10 Jesus explains the parable not as a matter of soils but as "the mysteries of the kingdom of God," i.e., the miraculous inbreaking of God's kingdom to do — like the wondrous power of a seed — the unexpected in the world. The astounding harvest is not the result of human activity but of God's providential power.[102] God is at work — hidden and unremarkable as a seed itself — in Jesus and the gospel to produce a yield wholly disproportionate to human prospects and merit. The extravagant sowing that seemed mistaken and futile is vindicated by a bumper crop. Resistance and rejection abound, but there is a disarming power in the ministry of Jesus, like the irrepressible generation of the seed, to break through the opposition of scribes, Pharisees, crowds, and even his own kin and associates.[103]

9-10 Jesus' "disciples" (v. 9) ask him about the meaning of the parable. In Mark 4:10 the question is put to Jesus by the Twelve and his inner circle, i.e., his elite followers. For Luke the parable is significant not only for leaders, but for all disciples — the church. "To you," says Jesus, "it has been given to know the mysteries of the kingdom of God, but parables are reserved for others" (v. 10). This is my rendering of v. 10. In Greek, "to you" is shifted to the front of the declaration, making it emphatic. Knowledge of the mysteries of the kingdom that "has been given" is a "divine passive," i.e., a way of speaking of God without using God's name. V. 10 thus informs and reminds disciples that they occupy a unique position, for to them God has revealed knowledge of the mysteries of his kingdom. Disciples occupy this position not because of merit — Jesus makes no reference to their being "good soil" — but because of grace. The "others" who have not received this revelation must be instructed in parables. In Mark 4:11 the others are called outsiders, but Luke does not

99. So Bock, *Luke 1:1–9:50,* 717-39; Vinson, *Luke,* 246-56.

100. See J. Drury, *The Parables in the Gospels* (London: SPCK, 1985), 51.

101. See J. Jeremias, *Die Gleichnisse Jesu* (7th ed.; Göttingen: Vandenhoeck & Ruprecht, 1965), 149-50; Tannehill, *Luke,* 141-42.

102. The reference to the parable of the Sower in *Ap. Jas.* 8.15 from Nag Hammadi reflects the tendency to separate the parable from the ministry of Jesus and to focus instead on seeds and soils.

103. Near the end of the first c., Clement of Rome saw in the parable of the Sower not only God's providence in Jesus' ministry but an anticipation of Jesus' resurrection: the Master who raises up decayed seeds from parched and barren soil will likewise raise up Jesus from death and the grave (*1 Clem.* 24:5).

separate believers ("you") and nonbelievers ("others") so starkly.[104] The se-
crets, or "mysteries" (Gk. *mystēria*), refer to knowledge of God that cannot be
attained by natural means (Dan 2:27-28; Wis 2:22).[105] The mystery is "given,"
but it cannot be earned or merited.[106] No amount of research can unlock the
mystery of God, for in the NT, as in Judaism, the mystery must be revealed
from heaven in order to be known, and hence it is received by faith as a result
of *hearing*. Because the mysteries of the kingdom are revealed by God, they
cannot be simply imagined or hoped for, but *known* (v. 10; Gk. *gnōnai*).

Parables are reserved for "others" who have not (yet) received what the
disciples have received in the kingdom of God, "so that, though seeing, they
may not see; though hearing, they may not understand" (v. 10). The quotation
comes from Isa 6:9. Luke does not follow either the MT or LXX version, as
does Matt 13:13-15 (LXX), but rather a brief version of Mark's Targumic paraphrase.[107] Isa 6:9-10 was an explicative proof-text of the early church, quoted
more often in the NT than any other OT text apart from Psalm 110:1 in order
to account for the rejection of the gospel by Jews (8:10; Matt 13:14; Mark 4:12;
Acts 28:26; Rom 11:8; John 12:40). Luke gives a full and verbatim LXX quotation of the text at the conclusion of Acts (28:26-27) to explain the Jewish
rejection of Paul's preaching in Rome. His use of the passage in v. 10 is much
less final, however. In Matt 13:13-15 Jesus spoke in parables *because* the crowds

---

104. The giving of the explanation to the disciples and crowds in Luke "insinuates
the degree to which the boundaries between followers of Jesus and the crowds are porous"
(Green, *Luke,* 326).

105. In the NT as a whole *mystērion* does not refer, as it does in Iamblicus, *Vita Pyth.,*
23.104-5, e.g., to esoteric knowledge reserved for select initiates; nor, as in modern detec-
tive stories, to unknown information that must be pried out by stealth and wit. "Mystery,"
rather, means the truth of God that is available only as a revelation of God. Its purpose is not
simply to reduce ignorance but to produce awe, and esp. faith. The mystery and kingdom
of God are inescapably present and fulfilled in the words and works of Jesus. On "mystery,"
H. Krämer, *mystērion, EDNT* 2:446-49; J. Marcus, "Mark 4:10-12 and Marcan Epistemology,"
JBL 103 (1984): 558-61; M. Bockmuehl, *Revelation and Mystery in Ancient Judaism and Pauline
Christianity* (WUNT 2/36; Tübingen: Mohr Siebeck, 1990). K. Barth, *Church Dogmatics* 1/1:188,
says, "*Mysterium* signifies not simply the hiddenness of God, but rather His becoming manifest
in a hidden, i.e., in a non-apparent way, which gives information not directly but indirectly.
Mysterium is the veiling of God in which He meets us by actually unveiling Himself to us:
because He will not and cannot unveil Himself to us in any other way than by veiling Himself."

106. Note, by contrast, *Gos. Thom.* 62, where Jesus discloses his mysteries to the *worthy,*
shifting the focus from God's sovereignty to human merit. See E. Kellenberger, "Heil und Ver-
stockung: Zu Jes 6,9f. bei Jesaja und im Neuen Testament," *TZ* 48 (1992): 268-75, who argues
that Mark, and to a lesser extent Matt and Luke, properly understand Isa 6:9-10 to show the
inseparable tension between salvation and judgment, both of which are proclaimed in Isa
6:9-10 without reference to human merits.

107. Targums were Aramaic paraphrases of OT texts used in synagogue readings.

were hard of heart, and in Mark 4:12 Jesus spoke in parables *so that* outsiders could not believe. Luke quotes Isa 6:9 briefly and inconclusively, implying that parables, like one-way glass, either afford or obstruct vision depending on the sympathy of hearers.

In the inscrutable interplay between the expressed purposes of God and the contrary facts of history, the early church saw more than a tug-of-war between equal and opposite forces. The sovereign God was exercising a teleological purpose. The God who "gives" the mystery (v. 10) is the same God who refuses to coerce those who wish not to see and hear. Parables, like the ministry of the Servant of the Lord (Isa 49:1-6), present the kingdom of God in hiddenness and mystery that both reveals and conceals.[108] Jesus presents the kingdom of God in such a way that it creates a crisis and a division (12:51), for these are the necessary prerequisites of decision and repentance. The Gospel of John well expresses this crisis: "For judgment I have come into this world, so that the blind will see and those who see will become blind" (9:39).

11-15 In vv. 11-15 Jesus shifts from the divine initiative represented in the sowing of the seed to the human responses to it represented in the various soils. The transition from seed to hearers' responses is expressed awkwardly in vv 12-13 where "those along the path/rock" refer not to seeds, as we should expect, but to hearers. Some scholars regard this disagreement as evidence of a later interpretation of the church that was projected onto Jesus.[109] This fact alone does not prove that the interpretation in vv. 11-15 derives from a later period. Parables, by nature, are similes, i.e., they establish likenesses, and likenesses are rarely exact. Parables do not follow strict rules of logic. Indeed, there are several instances where Jewish tradition speaks of the faithful being "planted" as they are here (Hos 2:23; Jer. 31:27; 1 En. 62:8; 2 Esd 8:41).[110] The apostle Paul also speaks of the sowing of people (1 Cor 15:42-48), as does the Shepherd of Hermas (*Herm. Sim.* 9.20.1; *Herm. Vis.* 3.7.3).

Luke's interpretation of the parable of the Sower hangs on the declaration

---

108. Note M. Hengel's insight: "What we have [in the parables] is what I would want to call a 'revelatory concealment.' Revelation can conceal and concealment can reveal. . . . There are circumstances which can only be expressed adequately in the form of a revelation which conceals, and I believe that the 'mysteries' of Jesus are such situations. Not because the one who talks about such circumstances wants to be mysterious, . . . but because the nature of these circumstances does not allow any other kind of language as an adequate expression" (*Studies in the Gospel of Mark* [trans. J. Bowden; Philadelphia: Fortress Press, 1985], 95-96).

109. For a discussion of the relation of the interpretation to the historical Jesus versus the early church, see J. Edwards, *Mark*, 136-37.

110. L. Ramaroson, "Jesus semeur de parole et de peuple en Mc 4:3-9 et par.," *SciEsp* 47 (1995): 287-94, examines nine passages where God sows the people of his kingdom, arguing that the explication of the parable of the Sower is faithful to Jesus' thought.

of v. 11, "The seed is the word of God." The productivity of the various soils depends solely on how the word of God is *heard*. Right hearing is hearing that leads to faith, and right faith is faith that leads to behaviors consistent with the word of God.[111] The three initial hearings — the seed sown on hard earth that the birds/devil take away, the seed sown on rock that does not take root, and the seed sown among thorns that is choked out — are not unproductive because the word has been wrongly or only partially proclaimed. The fourth and final hearing of the good soil, likewise, is not productive because the word has been better and more fully proclaimed. The problem is not the proclamation: the seed — the word of God — is the same life-giving element in all four instances.[112] *How* the word of God is heard is the sole deciding factor in whether the word will bear fruit or not. A superficial hearing that does not hold onto the word, an impermanent hearing in which the word is not allowed to take root, or an anxious hearing that does not "fear, love, and trust God above all things" (Luther) will be unproductive and fruitless. But the hearing of a "noble and good heart," i.e., a humble and sincere faith that hears the word, holds fast to the word, and bears fruit by enduring in the word (v. 15) is a salvific hearing. In the present context the woman who anointed Jesus' feet (7:36-50) and the women who followed him in discipleship (8:1-3) are the most immediate examples of "good soil."

Although Luke's version of the parable of the Sower is shorter and simpler than Mark's, Luke makes four strategic insertions in the parable that define it for his readers and for the church of his day. First and most important, the seed is identified as "the word *of God*." This phrase occurs only once in Matt (15:6) and Mark (7:13), but it is a load-bearing phrase for Luke,[113] as it is for the apostle Paul.[114] For Paul and the early church, the proclamation of the church is the form in which the living and gracious God manifests himself. The proclamation of "the word of God," whether through a parable of Jesus or the kerygma of the church, is the powerful, life-giving seed of salvation.[115] To fail to hear the kerygma is to fail to hear the word of God. A second distinctive Lukan addition appears in v. 12: "the devil comes and takes away the word from their hearts *so that they may not believe and be saved.*" Neither

---

111. Green, *Luke,* 329.

112. Geldenhuys, *Luke,* 245, correctly notes that preachers are forever being criticized by their congregations, but here we have a perfect sermon — and it too is largely rejected.

113. [1:2]; 5:1; 8:11, 21; 11:28; Acts 4:29, 31; 6:2, 7; 8:14; 11:1; 12:24; 13:5, 7, 44, 46, 48; 16:32; 17:13; 18:11.

114. Rom 9:6; 1 Cor 14:36; 2 Cor 2:17; 4:2; Phil 1:14; Col 1:25; 1 Thess 2:13 [2x]; 1 Tim 4:5; 2 Tim 2:9; Titus 2:5.

115. See Bovon, *Lukas 1,1–9,50,* 230-31; Klein, *Lukasevangelium,* 207. Vinson, *Luke,* 251, correctly notes that the sower need not be identified, because "once you know that the seed is the word, then anyone who spreads the word plays the role of the sower."

Matt nor Mark contains this sober admonition to right hearing. Right hearing is essential, for apart from it people cannot be saved. Luke's warning of the potential of perdition generally echoes the equally dire warning in Mark 4:12.[116] The warning not to fall away from faith *in the time of testing* (v. 13) is a third Lukan addition. The final Greek word in the interpretation, that believers must hear the word, hold fast to it, and bear fruit *by persevering* (v. 15), is the fourth. These additions remind the church of Luke's day, as Jesus reminded disciples of his day, that receiving the word of God is a matter of taking up the cross and *daily* following Jesus (9:23).

A LAMP IN THE DARKNESS (8:16-18)

The three sayings in this unit are also found in Matt and Mark, as well as in early church tradition, although they are often employed in different contexts and for different purposes.[117] Despite the thematic similarity of the sayings, their wording varies among the Synoptics and in early church tradition, suggesting that the material circulated in various forms or perhaps in oral tradition. Like Mark, Luke places the sayings immediately following the parable of the Sower, almost certainly as an aid to understanding it. Oil lamps, one of the more common artifacts discovered by archaeologists, provide roughly the same amount of light as a candle. For optimum light they must be elevated rather than "hidden in a jar or placed under a bed" (v. 16).

16-18 This verse may recall the lampstand that illuminated the interior of the tabernacle (Exod 25:37); perhaps that lampstand inspired the original saying. The image of the burning lamp recurs in 11:33 and 12:35 and may reflect a Hebrew figure of speech about "not quenching the lamp" (Prov 31:18; Lev 6:12, 13). In 1 Sam 3:3 and 2 Sam 21:17 the saying refers to not allowing the lamp (of revelation) to go out in Israel. If the "lamp" in v. 16 carries similar connotation — and context suggests it does — then Jesus is exhorting believers not to hide or quench the light of the gospel. To the saying of the lampstand Luke appends an explanation not found in either Matt or Mark: "so that those who enter can see the light" (v. 16). A parable requires those who would understand it to do precisely this — to enter and see the light. Luke repeats v. 16 nearly verbatim in 11:33 following the lesson of Jonah (11:29-32), again suggesting that one must enter into the story to see its inner illumination. The "light" is thus not

---

116. On the significance of this phrase, see W. Robinson Jr., "On Preaching the Word of God (Luke 8:4-21)," in Keck and Martyn, eds., *Studies in Luke-Acts,* 131-38.

117. V. 16: Matt 5:15; Mark 4:21; *Gos. Thom.* 33; v. 17: Matt 10:26; Mark 4:22; *Gos. Thom.* 5-6; P.Oxy. 654, nr. 4; v. 18: Matt 13:12; Mark 4:25; *Gos. Thom.* 41; 4 Ezra 7:25(?).

a general truth but Jesus himself, who calls disciples to "come to me" (6:47). Entering into a parable can be the first step in coming to Jesus.

There is a paradox in a parable, of course, as there is in the life of Jesus and in the appearance of the kingdom of God itself. The external appearance is ordinary rather than spectacular, and hence the ordinary appearance does not immediately seem to have extraordinary significance. The initial work of God in the world is "hidden" and "concealed" (v. 17). The purpose of the concealment is not to obstruct, but to reduce the divine to a proportion that can be "known" and "brought out into the open" (v. 17). If the beginnings of the kingdom look inauspicious and unpromising, that serves God's purpose, for it is the very mundane and earthly quality of Jesus that prevents the glory of God from overwhelming and blinding the world, allowing people to encounter God.[118] Only that which is hidden can be found, and only the concealed can be disclosed.

As in the parable of the Sower (8:11-15), everything depends on hearing, "Therefore consider carefully how you listen" (v. 18). "Listen" (Gk. *akouete*) is present tense, connoting ongoing hearing. The word of God cannot be given superficial attention; it must be engaged, weighed, pondered. Jesus' audience is like a group of prisoners planning an escape, like mountaineers pursuing a perilous and solitary route to the summit. Success depends on hearing, learning, and remembering. Repeating a Hebrew maxim, Jesus charges, "Those who have will be given more; as for those who do not have, even what they think they have will be taken from them" (v. 18).[119] Recognizing the strict illogicality of the maxim, Luke adds "think" (v. 18; Gk. *dokein*) — "even what they *think* they have will be taken from them." The degree to which one hears the parables, the extent to which one allows the kingdom to break upon oneself, will determine the measure of one's understanding. Again, as in 8:10, saving knowledge is not a matter of achieving but of *receiving*: in both instances it must be "given" (Gk. *didonai*). The one to whom the mystery of the kingdom of God is given in Jesus will receive greater capacity to enter it (see Prov 1:5-6; 9:9), but to the one who fails to receive the mystery in Jesus, "even what he has will be taken from him."

---

118. P.Oxy. 654, nr. 4 expands the saying in v. 17 to include ". . . and nothing buried that will not be raised." This addition connotes that the veil and concealment of Jesus' earthly ministry will be lifted at his resurrection from the dead.

119. God "puts more into a full vessel, but not into an empty one; for it says, 'If hearkening you will go on hearkening (Exod. 15.26), implying, If you hearken you will go on hearkening, and if not you will not hearken'" (*b. Ber.* 40a); "According to the standards of mortal man, an empty vessel is able to contain [what is put into it], and a full vessel cannot contain it, but according to the standards of the Holy One, blessed be He, a full vessel is able to contain it while an empty one cannot" (*b. Sukkah* 46a-b). Cited from M. Hooker, *The Gospel according to St Mark* (BNTC; Peabody, Mass.: Hendrickson, 1991), 134.

JESUS' TRUE FAMILY (8:19-21)

19-21 The account of this story in the Second Gospel (Mark 3:31-35) portrays Jesus' family in an oppositional role to his ministry. Luke crops Mark's story and presents Jesus' family in a more neutral light.[120] The placement of the story at the tail of the parable of the Sower implies that Jesus is still teaching in the open air, but the reference to the family "standing outside" (v. 20) suggests an interior location, which would put the story at a different time and place. Jesus' Galilean ministry habitually attracted large crowds, and in this instance they obstruct the mother and brothers of Jesus from meeting with him (v. 19). In the second century Marcion (see Introduction), who believed Jesus was divine but not human, expunged v. 19 from his edition of Luke in an attempt to repudiate Jesus' earthly lineage. Tertullian scored a point against Marcion and other Docetists by rightly insisting on the originality of the verse, assuring readers of Jesus' earthly family and humanity.[121] The crowd announces to Jesus that his mother and brothers are outside and wish to see him (v. 20). Luke reports this objectively, without Mark's insinuation that the family is trying to constrain Jesus. Hearing this, Jesus pronounces, "My mother and my brothers are those who hear God's word, and put it into practice" (v. 21). This leaves the impression (confirmed by Acts 1:14) that Jesus' mother and brothers are included in the greater family of faith. Given Luke's exemplary portrayal of Mary in the infancy narrative (esp. 1:26-38), this is exactly as we should expect.[122] Even Mary does not occupy the epicenter of Jesus' fellowship, however. Luke already established that God and his house — not Mary and Joseph — constituted Jesus' true family (2:48-50), and he twice reaffirms here and nearly verbatim again in 11:27-28 that allegiance to the word of God determines Jesus' true and eternal family. According to v. 21, the Holy Family cannot assume privilege, and

---

120. According to Mark, Jesus' family attempts to take control of him, thinking him "out of his mind" (3:21). Twice Mark portrays the mother and brothers "outside" the fellowship of Jesus, "calling" (Gk. *kalein*) and "seeking" (Gk. *zētein*) him (3:31-32). Both Greek words connote the attempt to lay claim to Jesus. In Mark, Jesus' mother and brothers are not part of the fellowship Jesus redefines as his family. Luke reduces the references to being "outside" from two to one (v. 20), he omits the references to "calling" and "seeking," and he likewise omits Mark's statement (3:34) that only those sitting around Jesus are his mothers and brothers.

121. *Marc.* 4.19. Luke 8:19-21 and parallels left Jesus' full humanity open to attack throughout the patristic era, as the following quotation from Epiphanius (d. 403; *Pan.* 30.14.5) indicates: "Again, they [docetists] deny that [Jesus] was a true man, surely from the word spoken by the Savior when it was announced to him, 'Behold, your mother and your brothers are standing outside,' to which the Savior responded, 'Who is my mother and who are my brothers?' And having stretched out his hand to the disciples he said, 'These are my brothers and my mother, those who are doing the desires of my Father.'"

122. See the evidence for this in Brown, *Birth of the Messiah*, 317-18.

sinners cannot assume rejection. This is at once a warning to the comfortable and complacent, and an encouragement to the dejected. In the kingdom of God true family is determined not by biology or physical proximity to Jesus, but by hearing "the word of God and doing it!" (v. 21; on "the word of God," see at 8:15). Tertullian captured the essence of this narrative, "Jesus transferred the names of blood-relationship to others whom he judged to be more closely related to him by reason of their faith."[123]

THE RIGHT QUESTION . . . (8:22-25)

The "power of the Lord" (5:17), evident throughout Jesus' Galilean ministry, is effective over aberrations of nature as well as infirmities of human nature. In the story of the calming of the storm on the lake, Luke follows Mark's account (4:35-41), but he introduces the narrative in v. 22 with a highly Semitic sentence that has no parallel in Mark or Matt.[124] In six instances Luke introduces Markan narratives with equally Semitic sentences, suggesting that he utilized the Hebrew Gospel in addition to Mark in the construction of these six narratives.[125]

Lake Gennesaret, or the **Sea of Galilee**, is a picturesque lake roughly seven by nine miles (11 × 15 km). Josephus extols its pure sweet water and many species of fish, as well as the surrounding fertile soil and pleasing climate, which supply fruit and produce ten months of the year. "Nature had taken pride" in the whole region, says Josephus (*J.W.* 3.516-21). Lying nearly 700 feet (215 m) below sea level, the sea is confined by a steep bank of mountains on the east, and by gentler slopes on the west. Seen from the heights, the lake is roughly harp-shaped, from which it may have received its name

123. *Marc.* 4.19. Green, *Luke*, 330, rightly concludes, "Jesus neither rejects nor praises his physical family; rather, he uses their arrival as a catalyst to redefine in the hearing of his disciples and the crowds the basis of kinship. Kinship in the people of God is no longer grounded in physical descent, he contends, but is based on hearing and doing the word of God."

124. In addition to the four Hebraisms noted and discussed in Edwards, *Hebrew Gospel*, 145-46, 307, two more deserve mention. The Greek word for "day," *hēmera*, translates *yōm*, the chief designation for a unit of time in Hebrew. The high frequency of *yōm* in the MT (ca. 2,250x) is reflected in the high frequency of *hēmera* in Luke (80x; cf. Matt 45x; Mark 27x; John 30x). The second Hebraism is Luke's references to the Sea of Galilee as "lake" (5:1, 2; 8:22, 23, 33). R. Notley, "The Sea of Galilee: Development of an Early Christian Toponym," *JBL* 128/1 (2009): 188, rightly notes that Luke's "omission of the name Sea of Galilee and preference for the name used by local inhabitants — Lake of Gennesar — lends the impression that he is drawing from sources other than his Synoptic counterparts." See at 5:1-3, n. 66, for evidence in favor of the Hebrew Gospel as the source.

125. The six narratives begin at 5:12, 17; 8:22; 9:18, 28; 20:1.

in Hebrew, Kinnereth ("harp").[126] The interchange of cold air from the surrounding mountains — including Mount Hermon, reaching nearly 10,000 feet (3,000 m) high only thirty miles (50 km) to the north — and warm air rising from the surface of the lake often produces sudden and violent storms on the Sea of Galilee.

22-25 As the boat[127] proceeds eastward across the sea with Jesus asleep onboard, "a squall came down on the lake, so that the boat was being swamped and they were in great danger" (v. 23).[128] The disciples, some of them veteran fishermen, know their imminent danger and awaken Jesus, "Master, Master, we're going to drown!" (v. 24). The description recalls the similar situation of Jonah 1:4-6, in which the captain upbraids Jonah for sleeping while he and the crew are "perishing" (LXX *apollyein*) — the same Greek word translated "we're going to drown" (v. 24: NIV). The word for "Master," *epistatēs,* occurs in the NT only in Luke, always in reference to Jesus, and all save one from the mouth of disciples.[129] Those committed to Jesus as Master can be wholly honest and transparent before him, even with doubts and fears. People who face imminent death are reminded who is Master. Jesus arose and "rebuked" the storm, after which a calm hushed the waves — again like the calm that ensued when Jonah had been thrown overboard (Jonah

---

126. Heb. *kinor,* "harp" or "lyre," probably influenced the Hebrew name of the lake, *kinnereth,* which translated into Greek Chenereth or Gennēsaret (*HALOT* 1:486-87).

127. In 1986 the hull of a fishing boat was recovered from the mud on the northwest shore of the Sea of Galilee, about five miles south of Capernaum. The boat — 26½ feet long, 7½ feet wide, and 4½ feet high — corresponds in design to a first-c. mosaic of a Galilean boat preserved in Migdal only a mile from the discovery site, and to a sixth-c. mosaic of a similar boat from Madeba. Carbon-14 technology dates the boat between 120 B.C. and A.D. 40. The hull of the recovered boat has a relatively deep stern, covered in both fore and aft sections with a deck, under which passengers might take shelter or sleep. The boat was propelled by two rowers per side, four total, and could carry up to fifteen persons. The Galilee boat corresponds to the particulars of the boat described in this story and to depictions in various ancient artistic renderings. A similar boat accommodated Jesus and his disciples on their crossings of the Sea of Galilee. See S. Wachsmann, "The Galilee Boat," *BAR* 14/5 (1988): 18-33; E. Meyers and M. Chancey, *Alexander to Constantine: Archaeology of the Land of the Bible* (New Haven: Yale University Press, 2012), 174.

128. Mendel Nun, who spent his life researching the many harbors of the Sea of Galilee, writes of 8:22-25: "This is an accurate and detailed description of an eastern storm on the Kinneret. It fits precisely the tales of contemporary fishermen who have sailed to fish for sardines at Kursi and were caught in a transit by the well-known eastern storm, called 'Sharkia' in Arabic. . . . Even today this storm, which usually starts in the early evening, is good cause for apprehension among fishermen" (M. Nun, *The Sea of Galilee and Its Fishermen in the New Testament* [Kibbutz Ein Gev: Kinnereth Sailing Co., 1989], 54). Bovon, *Luke 1,1–9,50,* 425, suggests that *katabainō* (v. 23, "the storm *descended*") locates the boat under the precipitous mountains on the west side of the lake (also where Kursi is located).

129. 5:5; 8:24, 45; 9:33, 49; 17:13. The last is the only reference from a nondisciple.

1:15).[130] The word for "rebuke," *epitiman,* occurring frequently in Luke and the Synoptics, derives from the vocabulary of Jewish exorcists with reference to "the commanding word, uttered by God or his spokesman, by which evil powers are brought into submission and the way is thereby prepared for the establishment of God's righteous rule in the world."[131] Jesus' power over aberrant nature — and over aberrant human nature in the following story of the Gerasene demoniac (8:35) — exemplifies his ultimate power as the Strong Man who overpowers Satan and "divides his plunder" (11:21-22).

Once the storm is quelled, Jesus asks the disciples, "Where is your faith?" (v. 25).[132] In the Third Gospel the faith of a number of nondisciples is praised, including the four men carrying the paralytic (5:20) and the centurion in Capernaum (7:9). Likewise, to the sinful woman (7:50), the hemorrhaging woman (8:48), the Samaritan leper (17:19), and the blind man in Jericho (18:42) — all nondisciples — Jesus declares, "Your faith has saved you." Luke also addresses the faith of the disciples, of course, but in each instance their faith is questioned (v. 25; 8:48; 22:32). This should not surprise us. The call to follow Jesus in daily discipleship (9:23!) and enter into "the mysteries of the kingdom of God" (8:10) is harder and more complex than responding to a single encounter with Jesus, even a miraculous encounter. Prolonged experience with Jesus inevitably means that initial understandings must yield to deeper understandings, and deeper understandings often elicit deeper questions. These disciples had surely seen Jesus' healings and works of power, the very things expected of the Messiah. But supremacy over the cataracts of nature far exceeded the words and powers of Israel's expected Messiah. The quelling of the storm is reminiscent of Jonah 1, as we have noted, and the rescue of perishing sailors is a testimony to God's "unfailing love" (Ps 107:23-32). In the OT only *God* stills storms such as this (so too Ps 65:7; 89:9; 104:7; 106:9; *T. Adam* 3:1).[133] On the lake Jesus has done what only God can do; and equally like God, he does it without prayer.[134] This wholly new experience of Jesus evokes new questions from the disciples. "Who is this?" they ask. "He commands even the winds and the water, and they obey him" (v. 25). These are the right questions.

---

130. Ephrem, *Comm. Tat. Diates.* 6.25, notes a supreme role reversal in the narrative: Jesus, who was asleep, is awakened; and he casts the sea, which is awakened, into sleep.

131. H. Kee, "The Terminology of Mark's Exorcism Stories," *NTS* 14 (1968): 323-46.

132. See Vinson, *Luke,* 260, who rightly recognizes that the question is not a rejection of the disciples. "On this day, they cannot do what he expects, but on the other days they will. Those two things — Jesus' patient presence and the disciples' eventual progress in imitating Christ — are much more important than the calming of a storm."

133. Nolland, *Luke 1:1–9:20,* 401, notes that, despite a widespread ancient belief that kings and wise men could exert power over the elements, no Jewish, Greek, or Roman accounts of the period depicts a figure using his own supernatural power to quell a storm.

134. See Bovon, *Lukas 1,1–9,50,* 423-24.

The right questions lead not to pat and ready answers, but to awe and wonder in the presence of Jesus.

. . . AND THE RIGHT ANSWER (8:26-39)

The healing of the demoniac follows the quelling of the storm (8:22-25) in all three Synoptics. Both narratives dramatically portray the power and compassion of Jesus to rescue people from chaos and destruction, whether in nature or in human nature. In so doing, both narratives press readers, as they pressed the original participants, for an adequate and ultimate understanding of Jesus. In the former account the disciples ask, "Who is this man?" who calms the storms (8:25), and in the sequel comes the answer from a demoniac in Gentile territory, "He is the Son of the Most High God" (v. 28).

26 The boat arrives in "the region of the Gerasenes, which is across the lake from Galilee" (v. 26). The region east of the lake and Jordan River was known as the Decapolis (Ten Cities) and was largely Gentile. The city of Gerasa (modern Jerash in Jordan) lay not on the eastern shore of the lake but more than thirty miles (50 km) inland to the southeast. Gerasa is slightly better attested in the manuscript tradition of v. 26 than two other place-names, Gadara and Gergesa. If Gerasa is original, it must mean the *region* of Gerasa, which may have extended to the Sea of Galilee. Gerasa is not an assured reading, however. The manuscript support for Gergesa and its location "across the lake from Galilee" (v. 26) commend it for serious consideration.[135]

---

135. For discussions favoring the originality of Gerasa, see Plummer, *Luke*, 227-28, and Metzger, *TCGNT*, 18-19, 121. Support for "Gergesa," however, is considerable. Gergesa is attested by Codex Sinaiticus (א), as well as by L Θ Ξ. Origen (*Comm. Jo.* 6.41) and Eusebius and Jerome (*Onomasticon*, 74) identified the swine miracle with a town named Gergesa on the east side of the lake. Origen, however, found Gergesa in manuscripts prior to his day, and Fitzmyer, *Luke (I–IX)*, 736-37, correctly notes that its attestation antedates Origen. The name and proper location of Gergesa appear in a midrash to Song of Songs (Zuta 1:4): "The graves of Gog and Magog will be open from south of the Kidron Valley to Gergeshta on the eastern side of Lake Tiberias." The Zuta midrash is late, but this particular saying is ascribed to R. Nehemiah, an acclaimed disciple of R. Akiba in the second c. It thus preserves an independent tradition a century earlier than Origen that a town named Gergesa (or Gergeshta) existed along the northeast shore of the lake. The date is important, for pre-Byzantine site identifications are generally more trustworthy than those that stem from the Byzantine period. For the Zuta reference, see Z. Safrai, "Gergesa, Gerasa, or Gadara?" *JerusalemPersp* 51 (1996): 16-19. In explanation of the variant place-names, Safrai makes the plausible suggestion that Origen's mention of Gergesa as "an ancient city" indicates that already in his day it was in decline. When Gergesa became unknown, it was altered to the well-known "Gerasenes." The great distance of Gerasa from the lake, however, invited the emendation to "Gadarenes" (modern Umm Qeis), closer to the

27-33   Luke follows Mark's account (5:1-20) closely, although he narrates it in his own words. Scripture preserves no more lamentable description of human wretchedness than this demoniac. Luke and Mark agree that the man was demon-possessed, consigned to live among tombs, and possessed with superhuman strength capable of breaking chains and fetters. Mark 5:3-5 describes the demoniac in brute terminology: untamable, crying among the tombs, cutting himself with stones. Luke omits these additions but adds that he was driven into the wilderness naked and homeless. The evil forces that torment the man among the tombs parallel the storm that battered the boat on the lake (8:23).[136]

Luke's account is only slightly less vivid than Mark's, but it differs in two main respects. Mark's description, though graphically explicit about the man's condition, is ambiguous about its origin, attributing it to "an unclean spirit" (3x) and demon-possession (3x). Luke, by contrast, seven times attributes the man's condition to the demonic. This is characteristic of Luke, who twice as often as both Matt and Mark identifies the essential adversary of Jesus, particularly in Galilee, as the demonic.[137] In the ancient world the demonic was usually not regarded as an intermediate stage between human and divine, but rather a power and authority equal to the divine.[138] The repeated emphasis on the demonic in Luke establishes Satan as Jesus' true adversary, and Jesus' subjugation of the demonic establishes his supremacy over satanic power in the created order. Luke reminds readers in five instances that the "name of Jesus" is the sole power capable of vanquishing the demonic.[139] The effectiveness of Jesus' spiritual authority is attested by the demons recognizing Jesus as the strong Son of God (4:41; 8:28) before humans do, including Jesus' disciples.

---

lake. This is an explanation with which Bovon, *Luke 1,1–9,50,* 434, agrees. In 1970 a bulldozer cutting a road along the eastern shore of the lake unearthed the remains of an ancient town immediately south of Wadi Samak in the Valley of Kursi (or "Gersa" or "Gursa," as known in local dialect). The location of the town and similarity in the place-names suggest an identification of Kursi with Gergesa. By the early third c. both archaeology and church tradition were locating the swine miracle at this site. For arguments in favor of Gergesa, see V. Tzaferis, "A Pilgrimage to the Site of the Swine Miracle," *BAR* 15/2 (1989): 45-54; B. Pixner, *Wege des Messias und Stätten der Urkirche* (ed. R. Riesner; Giessen: Brunnen Verlag, 1991), 142-48.

136. For a comprehensive article on spirit possession, see C. Keener, "Spirit Possession as a Cross-cultural Experience," *BBR* 20/2 (2010): 215-36. Surveying a wide range of testimony from anthropological and non-Western sources, Keener argues that "there is no reason to doubt that [spirit possession] occurred in various forms in Mediterranean antiquity as well as today. . . . [W]e should evaluate these reports on a case-by-case basis [involving a work's genre, sources, and similar factors]. . . . Nothing in the early Christian descriptions requires us to assume that they could not depend on genuine eyewitness material" (230-35).

137. 4:33, 35, 41; 7:33; 8:2, 27, 29, 30, 33, 35, 36, 38; 9:1, 42, 49; 10:17; 11:14; 13:32.

138. See W. Foerster, *daimōn, TWNT* 2:8-19.

139. 4:34, 41; 8:28; 9:49; 10:17.

If the essential antagonism to Jesus is the demonic itself, then the essential purpose of the Incarnation is to destroy the works of the devil (1 John 3:8).

Luke's second characteristic feature concerns the interface between Jesus and the demoniac. Mark sets the powerful and tragic description of the demoniac (5:3-6) in stark contrast to Jesus as the strong Son of God (5:7-10). Luke, however, weaves Jesus and the demoniac into a tighter narrative fabric (vv. 27-31). The unclean elements of the region — the Gentile Decapolis on the east shore of the lake, the existence of a Roman settlement and harbor in Kursi/Gergesa, the pollution of tombs[140] and swine[141] — would normally deter Jews from visiting or fraternizing in the region. Luke's antiphonal narration of Jesus and demoniac enhances Jesus' solidarity with a man of unclean spirit living among unclean tombs surrounded by people employed in unclean occupations, all in unclean Gentile territory.

The unclean contagion of region and demoniac does not defile Jesus; rather, the holy contagion of Jesus rescues and transforms the demoniac. "When [the demoniac] saw Jesus, he cried out and fell at his feet, shouting at the top of his voice, 'What do you want with me, Jesus, Son of the most High God? I beg you, don't torture me!'" (v. 28).[142] (On "What do you want with me?" see at 4:34.) The plea "don't torture me!" is a no-contest admission of subservience on the part of the demoniac. The declaration that Jesus is "the Son of the Most High God" is the revelatory answer to the question of the previous story, "Who is this man?" (8:25). "Most High God" is a Jewish epithet emphasizing the transcendence and exaltation of Israel's God over pagan gods, goddesses, and rival powers.[143] The strength of this God is demonstrated in

140. Contact with the dead defiled Israelites for seven days, and those who failed to purify themselves from the pollution of tombs "must be cut off from Israel" (Num 19:11-14). Later rabbis included anything in *contact* with the dead — bier, mattress, pillow, or tombs — as ritual defilements (*m. Kelim* 23:4; *m. 'Ohal.* 17-18). The city of Tiberias had been constructed over graveyards, and this, declares Josephus, "was contrary to the law and tradition of the Jews because [it] was built on the site of tombs, . . . and our law declares that such settlers are unclean for seven days" (*Ant.* 18.38). For the rabbis, signs of madness included running around at night, sleeping among tombs, tearing of one's clothes, destruction of property and self (Str-B 1:491-92).

141. For the OT proscription against swine, see Lev 11:7; Deut 14:8. Likewise, "None may rear swine anywhere" (*m. B. Qam.* 7:7). The staple food of the Roman army was grain and corn, but meat was a prized supplement when available. If the swineherds were supplying the Roman legions with pork, then the raising of unclean food for the hated Roman occupation was doubly offensive.

142. *T. Sol.*, a Jewish-Christian demonological text dating from the first to third centuries, is a folktale concerning a panoply of demons. The exorcism of the Gerasene demoniac fascinated its author and provided grist for several episodes contained therein (e.g., *T. Sol.* 1:13; 11:1-7; 17:2-3).

143. Gen 14:18; Num 24:16; Isa 14:14; Dan 3:26; Luke 1:32, 35, 76; 6:35; Acts 7:48; 16:17;

the vanquishing of a legion of demons powerful enough to destroy a herd of swine. The reference to "Son of the Most High God" rather than "Son of God" is typical of Gentile polytheism, designating Jesus as the Son of the one, true, transcendent God. "Son of the Most High God" identifies the authority of Jesus and the universality of his power as the authority and power of God Almighty.

Greek magical papyri discovered in Egypt preserve complex formulas, spells, conjurations, and catchwords that ancient exorcists employed as they sparred with demonic opponents. Similarly, Philostratus describes an involved conversation of Apollonius with a demon in order to ascertain if the exorcism had been effective.[144] Jesus does not confront the demonic with such protocols, incantations, or magic. His power over the demonic resides within himself.[145] The man identifies himself as "Legion," for "many demons had gone into him" (v. 30). The Roman army stationed the majority of its occupation forces over Palestine in the Gentile Decapolis. The name "Legion" was a painful reminder of Roman domination. A *legio* was the largest military unit in the Roman army, consisting of some 5,600 soldiers.[146] The best analogy of the demoniac's oppression is Palestine's subjugation by Rome.

Why Jesus sends the demons into a herd of swine has been a subject of inconclusive conjecture. Jesus grants no such waivers in Jewish territory, and this allows for the possibility that the plea of the demons may be rooted in the illusion that in Gentile regions they are safe from the authority of Jesus. The demons offer no resistance but plead for Jesus' mercy as the only alternative to experiencing his wrath.[147] Judaism popularly believed the Messiah would rid Palestine of Roman occupation. In this instance Jesus fulfills popular messianic hopes — although the "legions" expelled are of a very different nature.

The demons plead to be allowed to "go into the Abyss" (v. 31). The Greek word for "abyss," *abyssos,* occurs only here in the four Gospels, translating *tehom* in the MT, which denotes the primeval deep of the sea (Gen 1:2; 7:11; Job

---

Heb 7:1; *Acts Thom.* 45. Heb. *el elyon,* "Most High God," is found fifteen times in the DSS and seldom in rabbinic literature. It occurs in the OT thirty-one times, and increases in frequency after the Maccabees in order to show the supremacy of Israel's God over pagan gods and goddesses (G. Bertram, *hypsos, TDNT* 8:602-20; E. Lohmeyer, *Das Evangelium des Markus* [17th ed.; Göttingen: Vandenhoeck & Ruprecht, 1967], 95).

144. See *HCNT,* 69-72, 331-32.

145. The repetition of commands in vv. 29, 32 is the result of Luke's interweaving Jesus' story with the demoniac's rather than evidence of an ineffective first command of Jesus.

146. F. Annen, *legiōn, EDNT* 2:345.

147. R. Bultmann, *The History of the Synoptic Tradition* (trans. J. Marsh; rev. ed.; Oxford: Basil Blackwell, 1972), 210, regards the demoniac's self-identification as a boast, hoping to outwit Jesus by its strength and numbers. Neither dialogue nor context supports this conjecture. The demon's self-identification is not a challenge but an acquiescence to Jesus. So too the recounting of the story in *Ep. Ap.* 5 (cited in *NTApoc.* 1:253).

28:14) or earth (Deut 8:7; Ps 71:20). In the NT *abyssos* connotes the place of the dead (Rom 10:7) or realm of evil spirits (Rev 9:1, 2, 11; 20:1, 3).[148] The hostility and complete incompatibility of evil with Christ is signaled by the demons' preference of chaos and despair over the kingdom inaugurated in Jesus. Grace is so constitutive to the nature of Jesus that, even in acceding to the request of implacable opponents, Jesus exhibits a degree of mercy. The demons enter a herd of grazing swine — Matt calls it "a herd of many swine" (8:30), Mark of "some two thousand" (5:13), Luke simply "a considerable [Gk. *hikanos*] herd" (v. 32) — and hurl it headlong into the lake. About two miles (3.2 km) south of Kursi/Gergesa a ridge extends from the eastern slopes of the hillside to a steep embankment over the lake. This geological formation may be the place referred to in vv. 32-33. The destruction of swine poses a thorny moral question with regard to both the loss of animal life and the economic loss of swineherds and swineowners. The narrative is silent on such matters. In the kingdom of God the rescue and restoration of a wretched individual supersedes even the lives of animals (12:6-7) and vast capital assets (9:25).[149]

34-39 The narrative now shifts to the reaction of the locals. The swineherds reported the event in "town and countryside" (v. 34), drawing people to the lakeside. The town nearest the site of the miracle was Kursi/Gergesa, but Hippos, a dominant city of the Decapolis, commanded the summit of a steep promontory in the vicinity on the east side of the lake. "They found the man from whom the demons had gone out, sitting at Jesus' feet, dressed and in his right mind" (v. 35). "Sitting at Jesus' feet" is a classic description of a Jewish rabbi with his disciples (2 Kgs 4:38; Acts 22:3; *m. 'Abot.* 1:4). Like all rabbis, Jesus attracts disciples, but the disciples at Jesus' feet — a sinful woman (7:38), a restored demoniac (8:35), a desperate father (8:41), a woman who forsakes the kitchen (10:39), a Samaritan (17:16) — are unlike any rabbi's disciples. They are a radically new community — many of them women — comprising individuals who would not qualify for rabbinic schools. The uniqueness of this community requires new structures — new wineskins (5:37) — of mission. The gathering at Jesus' feet is more than a school of learning; it is a school of *salvation*. Luke is the only Evangelist who identifies the demoniac by the Greek word *sōzein* (v. 36), meaning "healed" (so NIV) or "saved," depending on context. The word is employed with both senses in this narrative. The man had many demons

---

148. See Lagrange, *Luc*, 249; Bock, *Luke 1:1–9:50*, 775.

149. St. Diadochos of Photiki (5th c.), reflecting on the difference between justice and redemption, writes, "Human tribunals cannot circumscribe the eternal justice of God. . . . It is therefore better to endure the lawlessness of those who wish to wrong us, and to pray for them, so that they may be released from their guilt through repentance rather than through restoring what they have taken. Divine justice requires that we receive back not the objects of theft, but the thief himself, freed through repentance from sin" ("On Spiritual Knowledge," *Philokalia* 1:273).

(v. 27), but the demons left him (v. 35); he had worn no clothes (v. 27), but he was clothed (v. 35); he lived among tombs (v. 27), but was restored to his home (v. 39); he accosted Jesus and shouted at him (v. 28), and later sat at his feet (v. 35); the demon seized him and he was out of control (v. 29), and he was later in his right mind (v. 35).[150] This man — wretched, rejected, condemned to life among the dead — is Exhibit A of Jesus' saving power.

Despite the saving reversal of the demoniac's fortunes, the locals react in fear rather than faith. Their reaction parallels that of the disciples' in the previous narrative. At the crossing of the lake, the disciples were more terrified of Jesus' power to still the storm than of the storm itself (8:25); here the inhabitants are more frightened by Jesus' power to expel the demons than they are of the demoniac himself (v. 35). The world seeks a direct manifestation of God in signs (23:8), but when God's works are not veiled (8:10), the reaction is inevitably fear, even rejection (5:8; John 1:11).

The healed demoniac begs "to be with Jesus" (v. 38). Given Jewish attitudes toward Gentiles, a disciple from the Decapolis would create serious obstacles for Jesus' mission in Jewish Galilee and Judea. Jesus tells the demoniac, "Return home and tell how much God has done for you" (v. 39). This command is evidence that authentic witness to Jesus is not confined to participation in the Twelve, or even to his larger retinue of disciples. The demoniac is commissioned to genuine evangelical witness, for the word for "tell" (Gk. *diēgeisthai*) is the verb form of *diēgēsis* of the prologue (see at 1:1). The story the man tells will not be merely a personal anecdote, but the essential narrative of salvation that in 9:10 is entrusted to the twelve apostles.[151] "Proclaiming (Gk. *kēryssein*) in every city" (v. 39; also 24:19) further describes the witness in apostolic terminology, for *kēryssein* is used throughout Acts of the distinct *Christian* proclamation. "Tell how much *God* has done for you," commands Jesus. The man then went out and told "how much *Jesus* had done for him" (v. 39). For this man, God and Jesus are one and the same. In Jesus the demoniac experiences the kingdom of God, and from Jesus he receives a commission to proclaim it to the Gentile world.[152] Like Jesus' inaugural sermon in Nazareth (4:16-30), this story attests that the Gentile mission was rooted in the ministry of Jesus.

---

150. Green, *Luke*, 336.

151. "Jesus thus gives the former demoniac the very task that Luke has exercised in the writing of Luke-Acts — namely, the 'narration' of God's mighty acts" (Green, *Luke*, 341-42).

152. See Green, *Luke*, 336. Schweizer, *Lukas*, 98, argues that, because terminology related to the Gentile mission in Mark and John is absent in Luke's narrative of the demoniac, for Luke "the hour for the Gentiles has not yet arrived." This is unpersuasive. The use of *sōzein* (v. 36) to describe the demoniac's restoration, as well as the commission in v. 39 for the demoniac to take the expressly Christian missionary message throughout the Decapolis, clearly extends the mission of Jesus to Gentile regions.

TWO ILLUSTRATIONS OF FAITH THAT
MAKES ONE WHOLE (8:40-56)

Jesus and the demoniac both "return" (Gk. *hypostrephein*) to their respective places: the demoniac to his home (v. 39), and Jesus to Galilee (v. 40). Jesus encounters the problem of "uncleanness" on the western Jewish side of the lake as he did on the eastern Gentile side, however, for he is immediately brought into contact with two unclean bodies, a woman with a menstrual hemorrhage and the corpse of a little girl. As in the previous story, where Luke underscored Jesus' solidarity with the demoniac by intertwining their two stories, in the present story Luke emphasizes Jesus' unrestricted contact with the "unclean" persons by four repetitions that Jesus and the hemorrhaging woman "touched" one another (vv. 44, 45, 46, 47). In a Jewish hierarchy of values, the distinctions of "clean" and "unclean" were of central importance. The "uncleanness" of the hemorrhaging woman and the dead girl, and the "cleanness" of Jairus, are ultimately immaterial in this story, however, for all three need Jesus, and Jesus ministers to all three without reference to *tohoroth,* "uncleanness."

40-42   A crowd expectantly awaits Jesus when he disembarks from the boat in Galilee (v. 40). Crowds are ubiquitous in Jesus' ministry (4:42), but they are also ambiguous, for "the crowds were choking [NIV 'crushing'] him" (v. 42). The Greek word for "choking" *(sympnigein)* occurs only twice in Luke, once of the thorns choking the seed in the parable of the Sower (8:14), and here, in a veritable illustration of the parable, of the crowd choking Jesus.[153] Jairus, a "synagogue leader," approaches Jesus from the crowd.[154] A **ruler of the synagogue** was the president or "head" of a local Jewish worshiping community, *rosh ha-keneset* in Hebrew (*m. Yoma* 7:1; *m. Soṭah.* 7:7-8; on "synagogue," see at 4:16). The term is found throughout the Mediterranean world in the first century, although it does not occur in Josephus or Philo. Synagogue worship, including reading Scripture, preaching, and prayer, was conducted not by a professional class of officials, but by lay synagogue members. The ruler of the synagogue was entrusted by elders of the community with general oversight of the synagogue and orthodoxy of teaching, including building maintenance and security, procuring of scrolls for Scripture reading, and arranging of Sabbath worship by designating Scripture readers, prayers, and preachers. Ordinarily, a synagogue had only one ruler, although Acts 13:15 speaks of at least two rulers

---

153. Further on this thought, see Green, *Luke,* 344.

154. "Jairus" derives from the Heb *Jair* (Num 32:41; Judg 10:3), meaning "YHWH will enlighten" (not "YHWH will awaken" — despite the symbolic significance of the latter). See Bovon, *Luke 1,1–9,50,* 447. In ancient historiography *named* witnesses were important in verifying truthfulness (e.g., Acts 1:15). Jairus's name may indicate that he later became a believing member of the Christian community (see R. Bauckham, *Jesus and the Eyewitnesses* [Grand Rapids: Eerdmans, 2006], 39-66).

in the same synagogue. Inscriptional evidence from the first century ascribes the title to a surprisingly diverse lot of individuals, including individuals who bore Greek names and who wrote in Greek.[155] In this instance, Jairus's role as a synagogue official has nothing to do with his approach of Jesus. He is, rather, a desperate suppliant, "falling at Jesus' feet" (v. 41; see at 8:35) and "pleading"[156] with him to save his only daughter (cf, 7:12!), twelve years old, who was dying (v. 42).[157]

43-48 Luke states objectively and without fanfare that Jesus, whose mission was to minister to needy people (4:18, 43), went "on his way" with Jairus (v. 42). A woman "subject to bleeding for twelve years . . . came up behind Jesus and touched the edge of his cloak" (vv. 43-44).[158] Torah declared a woman unclean for seven days after her monthly period, and a woman with

---

155. See Str-B 4/1:145-47; E. Schürer, *History of the Jewish People*, 2:433-37; and J. Burtchaell, *From Synagogue to Church: Public Services and Offices in the Earliest Christian Communities* (Cambridge: University Press, 1992), 240-46. On rulers of synagogues in first-c. Greek inscriptions, see *HCNT*, 316. The title was occasionally applied to women (and children), although when so applied its significance is difficult to assess. B. Brooten, *Women Leaders in the Ancient Synagogue: Inscriptional Evidence and Background Issues* (BJS 36; Chico, Calif.: Scholars Press, 1982), assembles nearly two dozen inscriptions referring to women as "head of the synagogue," "leader," "elder," "mother of the synagogue," "priestess," and "presiding officer." Brooten argues that such nomenclature is not simply honorific but descriptive, i.e., that women were *bona fide* rulers of synagogues. Burtchaell argues to the contrary that such titles were honorific, indicating only that women bearing such titles were married to men who were rulers of synagogues; and likewise that children bearing such titles were children of rulers of synagogues, but not rulers themselves. Burtchaell reasons that Philo would not have been surprised that the Therapeutae admitted women into their Sabbath assemblies if there were Jewish women rulers of synagogues. Further, "there was absolutely no participation by females in the Jewish priesthood, yet there are epitaphs of Jewish priests in the feminine." Finally, "How is it likely in a culture where women were legally forbidden to be counted as members of the worship fellowship, to study Torah, to join in the communal recitation of grace [and by many rabbis to read Torah in public], that women could have been officers of the community's public affairs?" Beyond the inscriptional evidence there is no evidence that women acted as officers in synagogues. Burtchaell's evidence and reasoning urge caution in affirming that women (and children) were actual rulers of synagogues in ancient Judaism.

156. The imperfect tense of the Greek verb indicates intensity and persistence.

157. Lexically, Gk. *apothnēskein* means "to die," but the imperfect tense here *(apethnēs-ken)* implies an action in progress, i.e., "was dying," "was at the point of death" (so Josephus, *Ant.* 5.4), a meaning required by v. 49. See BDF §§326-27; H. W. Smyth, *Greek Grammar*, §1895. The subject of the verb remains ambiguous in the Greek manuscript tradition, depending on the accenting of the Gk. *autē*. The words accented as "she" in some manuscripts (K L Δ Θ) and "this [girl]" in others (B Ψ), were left unaccented in the key manuscripts (𝔭⁷⁵ ℵ B C W Γ), suggesting that the proper reading of the word was unknown.

158. Later Christian tradition, undoubtedly apocryphal, identified the woman as either Bernice or Veronica, who reputedly lived in Caesarea Philippi (*Acts Pil.* 7; Eusebius, *Hist. eccl.* 7.18).

a protracted gynecological malady, as may be the case with this woman, remained unclean throughout its duration. Accordingly, a menstruating woman — and whoever touched her — was banished from the community until purification.[159] Josephus's testimony that "the temple was closed to women during their menstruation" (*J. W.* 5.227) indicates that this particular Torah ruling was enforced in Jesus' day. Luke (v. 43) reduces the sharp polemic of Mark 5:26 against the medical profession of the day in his account of the hemorrhaging woman.[160] "[The woman] came up behind [Jesus] and touched the hem of his cloak, and immediately her bleeding stopped" (v. 44). "The hem of his cloak" probably refers to the tassels on the corners of the outer garment worn by all observant Jews (Num 15:38-39; Deut 22:12).[161] Luke does not explain the woman's intent in touching Jesus. Rulers in the ancient world were commonly believed to possess power to bless those who touched them. Alexander the Great was often mobbed by crowds who "ran to him from all sides, some touching his hands, some his knees, some his garment" in hopes of being baptized with his aura and power.[162] Sometimes the approach was made in hopes of healing or fulfillment of a request.[163] The woman may have approached Jesus with a similar intent, perhaps mixed with superstition that Jesus, like the altar of the tabernacle, was a representative of God who would render holy those who touched him (Exod 29:37).

The woman's motives are as obscure to Jesus as is her identity. His question, "Who touched me?" (v. 45), is masculine in Greek rather than feminine, indicating that her identity is unknown to him. This is one of the few instances in the Gospels when readers know more than Jesus does. The crowd denies touching Jesus, and Peter cries out, "Master, the people are crowding and pressing around you" (v. 45). The Greek word for "crowding," *synechein*, can refer to restraining a prisoner in jail or a dead-locked siege; and "pressing," *apothlibein*,

159. Lev 15:19-27; 1QSa 2:2-4; 11Q19 48:15-17; Pseudo-Philo 7; Philo, *Spec.* 3:32-33. Menstrual blood, along with other "fluxes" (semen, spittle, urine, and pus), rendered one unclean, a *zab*, according to rabbinic tradition (*m. Zabim* 1-5). Bovon, *Luke 1,1–9,50*, 447-49, offers a good discussion of hematological pollutions.

160. Evidence for and against the originality of "and she had spent all she had on doctors" (v. 43) is evenly divided (Metzger, *TCGNT*, 121). Luke's omission of the negative reference to physicians could argue in favor of his being a physician (Col 4:14). This one instance should not be unduly pressed, however, for Luke omits or abbreviates many details in this and other accounts of Mark.

161. The parallel passage in Matt 9:20 expressly mentions "tassels" (Gk. *ta kraspeda*; Heb. *tsitsit*). Tassels normally consisted of four woolen threads (three white and one blue) worn on outer garments by all observant Jews — priests, Levites, women, and even slaves — as reminders of the commandments of the Lord and Israel's election. See Str-B 4/1:277-92.

162. Arrian, *Anab.* 6.13.3. So too Plutarch, *Sull.* 35 (474C). Both passages are cited from *HCNT*, 78.

163. Tacitus, *Hist.* 4.81.1, also cited from *HCNT*, 78.

refers to the squeeze of a crowd. The mass and pressure of human bodies, in other words, make Jesus' question patently absurd, and for the second time (5:5) Peter addresses Jesus in exasperation and alarm (on "Master," see at 8:24). The woman's healing is not the result of magical manipulation of forces, whether natural or divine, but of personal power resident in Jesus. A hemorrhage flows from the woman's body, but power to heal flows from Jesus' body.[164] Both of their bodies are porous, as it were: the woman's of uncleanness, and Jesus' of grace. In saying "power has gone out from me," Jesus indicates the healing has exacted a personal cost to himself.[165] For Luke "power," *dynamis,* is a primary sign of Jesus' spiritual authority.[166] The word is almost exclusively used of the ministry and mission of Jesus, and especially, as here, of Jesus' power and compassion to heal. The power of Jesus effects not only a physical cure, but a meeting, a *knowing* of Jesus and the woman. Her healing is a creative act of God, and like God's powerful works in creation (Gen 1), Jesus' power *separates* the woman from both the crowd and her infirmity, restoring her as a unique and whole person. Realizing that she can no longer escape notice, the woman comes forth and confesses her healing (v. 47). Her act and confession are an expression of faith, for faith is both a trust in Jesus and a risk to break through conventions and customs to meet Jesus.[167] The woman refers to her healing in physical terms (v. 47; Gk. *iasthai*), but Jesus responds, "Daughter, your faith has healed you. Go in peace" (v. 48). This is the same benediction with which Jesus blessed the sinful woman in 7:50. In both instances the Greek word for "healed" is *sōzein,* meaning either "to heal" or "to save," depending on context. The woman who touched Jesus hoped for a physical cure, but she received a deeper, saving wholeness through Jesus. The word for *sōzein* in Hebrew and Aramaic is *yasha,* which is actually a variant of the Hebrew name of Jesus, Yeshua. Jesus' final word, "Go in peace,"[168] is not a mere formality, but a fulfillment of the peace promised by the angels at Jesus' birth (2:14). The effect of meeting Jesus and in responding to the gospel by faith is always an experience

---

164. W. D. Davies and D. Allison, *A Criticial and Exegetical Commentary on the Gospel according to Saint Matthew* (ICC; Edinburgh: T&T Clark, 1991), 2:130, "Instead of uncleanness passing from the woman to Jesus, healing power flows from Jesus to the woman."

165. Valentinian Gnosticism, seizing on the woman's twelve years of infirmity, attributed her healing not to Jesus but to the twelfth (of thirty) aeons (see Irenaeus, *Haer.* 2.23.1).

166. "Power" occurs fifteen times in Luke and ten times in Acts, including heavenly power (21:26), power and glory (21:27), power and authority (4:36; 9:1; 10:19), power from on high (24:49) and of the Highest (1:35), power of God (22:69; Acts 8:10) or of the Lord Jesus (5:17), great power (Acts 4:33; 8:10, 13), power of the Spirit (4:14), power of signs/wonders (Acts 2:22; 6:8; 8:13), in/with power (1:17; 4:36; 21:27), and receiving divine power (Acts 1:8).

167. See Schweizer, *Lukas,* 98.

168. "Go in peace" was a Hebrew blessing (*leki leshalom:* 1 Sam 1:17; 20:42; 2 Sam 15:9; 2 Kgs 5:19; Luke 7:50; Acts 16:36; Jas 2:16; *Ep. Ap.* 51).

of the peace of God (Rom 5:1). Jesus' healing compassion is finally signaled in the word "daughter." The Judaism of Jesus' day used "daughter" normally to refer to a biological daughter or a younger woman.[169] Calling the woman "daughter" — especially if she was older than Jesus — was unusual and perhaps socially inappropriate. Luke has told readers how precious the sick daughter was to Jairus (v. 42); the use of "daughter" with reference to the woman with the blood flow tells readers how precious she is to Jesus!

49-56 As Jesus speaks to the woman, an aide of the synagogue ruler arrives to announce that the young girl has died. The interruption, so profitable to the woman, has cost the life of Jairus's daughter. The slender thread of hope has broken, and Jesus' mission must be scuttled, "Don't bother the teacher anymore" (v. 49). Jesus overhears the report, but he is not determined by it. He does not refer to what has happened, why, or what might have been. He does not speak of the girl at all, but directly to Jairus. There is still one thing Jairus can do, but he must shift his focus from his daughter's death to Jesus himself. "Don't be afraid; just believe, and she will be healed," says Jesus (v. 50). The challenge of faith before Jairus — and for everyone who meets Jesus — is whether to believe only in what circumstances allow, or in what God declares possible. One thing is necessary — to believe in God rather than surrender in despair. The Greek word for "healed" in the promise of v. 50 — something Luke adds to Mark 5:36 — is not the customary word for physical healing (Gk. *iasthai*), but *sōzein*, the same word with which Jesus described the woman's healing in v. 48. This promise means, despite all circumstances to the contrary, that Jairus's future is still open. Whether or not Jairus has faith we do not know, but Jesus' faith has Jairus, carrying him from despair to hope.[170] With Jesus, the fate of the woman with the blood flow can also be the fate of Jairus's daughter.

Peter, John, and James, the trusted inner circle of Jesus, accompany Jesus, along with the father and mother of the child, to the dead girl's side.[171] Mourn-

---

169. See H. Haag, *bath, TDOT* 2:332-38; Bovon, *Lukas 1,1–9,50*, 450.

170. The second- (or third-) c. *Acts Thom.*, a gnostic Hellenistic romance, tells an apocryphal story of the apostle Thomas's visit to India, where he is thrown into prison for building a palace of good works rather than of stone for King Gundaphorus. As Thomas is delivered to prison, he quotes, "Fear nothing, but only believe."

171. The normal order of the inner circle is Peter, James, and John (Mark 5:37; 9:2; 14:33). In Luke-Acts, however, the name of James never follows Peter. When Peter's name is followed by one or both of the Zebedee brothers, it is followed first by John (8:51; 9:28; 22:8; Acts 1:13; 3:1, 3, 4, 11; 4:13, 19; 8:14). When Luke-Acts refers to the Zebedees alone, however, James usually precedes John (5:10; 9:54; Acts 12:2). Thus, in Luke-Acts the name of John appears second to James when the two are mentioned alone, but it always precedes James and appears second to Peter when the Zebedees are mentioned alongside the chief apostle. Luke-Acts may place John's name second to Peter's because, at the time of writing, James had been martyred (Acts 12:2) and John remained as the more prominent disciple.

ers, usually women, formed an obligatory professional guild in first-century Judaism, accompanying the bier from the house to the grave while clapping their hands and wailing laments. "Even the poorest person in Israel should hire at least two flute players and one wailing woman," said Rabbi Judah a century after Jesus.[172] Jesus' command, "Stop wailing, she is not dead but asleep" (v. 52), runs counter to all basic human instincts in such a situation. The gospel makes some demands that can be believed and followed only by the power of God at work in believers. This is surely an instance of such a demand. Hard-core realists of every age find such demands ludicrous. Professional mourners, who know a dead body when they see one, laugh in scorn (v. 53), just as seasoned intellectuals of Athens laughed when Paul proclaimed a gospel of resurrection from the dead (Acts 17:32). The willingness to bear ridicule for the sake of the gospel is not the lightest cross to bear daily for Christ (9:23). A belief that all phenomena can be explained rationally, a hallmark introduced into Western culture at the time of the Enlightenment, causes some commentators to argue that this story is about a "deliverance from premature burial" rather than a raising from the dead.[173] The obvious implication of the story, however, is that the girl died, and that her death is independently attested by two entities, the messenger and the professional mourners. Jesus' reference to the girl "sleeping" may indicate to Jairus the way God would have believers regard all who die in faith.

Jesus "took [the girl] by the hand" and commanded "get up!" (v. 54). The power of life in Jesus, like the breath of God at creation (Gen 2:7), made the girl a living being. The instruction to feed her (v. 55) signifies a full restoration to physical health. Several details in Luke's narrative recall the raising

---

172. Str-B 1:521-23.

173. H. Paulus, *Das Leben Jesus als Grundlage einer reinen Geschichte des Urchistentums* (Heidelberg: C. F. Winter, 1828). Paulus, a thoroughgoing rationalist, believed in the impossibility of miracle and regarded the laws of nature as coextensive with God. See the discussion of his work in A. Schweitzer, *The Quest of the Historical Jesus* (trans. W. Montgomery; London: Adam & Charles Black, 1911), 48-57. For Paulus, the achievement of Jesus in the present story was the presentiment to know the girl was comatose rather than dead. In this Paulus essentially follows an ancient hermeneutic extending from Celsus (*On Medicine* 2.6) back to Apuleius of Madaura (*Flor.* 19.2-6) and finally back to Pliny (*Nat.* 7.37), who applauded the Greek physician Asclepiades for recognizing by careful observation that a man carried in a funeral procession was actually alive. The Asclepiades tradition is only a distant parallel to the present story, however. Its purpose is to commend a wise physician rather than to appeal for faith in him; indeed, there is no role or necessity of faith in the Asclepiades tradition. The raising of Jairus's daughter, on the contrary, is about a dead child brought back to life. The tradition of Apollonius raising a young girl from "her seeming death" probably belongs in a similar category of heroic resuscitations (Philostratus, *Vita Apol.* 4.45; cited in *HCNT,* 203-4). The Apollonius traditions, which were produced by Philostratus in the third c., were influenced at least in some degree by the Gospels.

of the widow's son at Nain (7:11-17).[174] More important, the phrase "her spirit returned" (v. 55), unique to Luke, is reminiscent of the account of the healing of the dead son of the widow of Zarephath (1 Kgs 17:21), once again recalling the significance of Elijah (and perhaps Elisha, 2 Kgs 4:34), Israel's two greatest healers, as prophetic prototypes of Israel's Messiah. (On the command to silence, see at 4:41.)

174. In both stories only children are brought back to life (7:12; 8:42); Jesus commands those present not to weep (7:13; 8:52); and both are evidence of Jesus' good news to the poor. See Green, *Luke,* 344.

CHAPTER EIGHT

Self-Disclosure of Jesus to the Twelve

Luke 9:1-50

Since the call of the Twelve in 6:12-16, they and a larger group of unnamed disciples have attended Jesus in his teaching (6:17-49) and travels (7:1–8:56). The description of 8:1-3 began to intimate a fuller participation of the disciples in Jesus' ministry, with the expressed inclusion of women who supported Jesus and the Twelve "out of their own means." The role of the Twelve reaches a new stage in 9:1-50, however, for beginning in vv. 1-2, they are endowed with Jesus' authority and proclamation to participate not only as observers but also as missionary agents. The greater involvement of the Twelve in Jesus' ministry results in greater revelation of Jesus' identity and destiny to them. As the Twelve accept fuller responsibility in their apostolic vocation, Jesus reveals the ultimate purpose of his messianic vocation in Jerusalem, which he describes as an "exodus" (9:31) and "being taken up" (9:51; similarly 9:22, 44, 53). This latter expression encompasses all that will be completed in Jerusalem, being "taken up" on the cross and in resurrection, and especially and finally in the ascension. The Twelve are inducted into greater responsibility not simply so they can do more, but so they can also *receive* more. A complementary relationship between discipleship and Christology ensues: true understanding of Jesus is granted to those who entrust their lives in discipleship to him. 9:1-50 describes the all-important first steps of the apostolic ministry: the first mission outreach (vv. 1-6), the participation of the Twelve in the miraculous feeding of the multitude (vv. 12-17), their deeper understanding of Jesus (vv. 18-22) and of the cost of discipleship (vv. 23-27), their witness of his transfiguration (vv. 28-36), and also the first two predictions of his suffering in Jerusalem (vv. 22, 44).

THE FIRST CHRISTIAN MISSION (9:1-6)

The new phase of ministry is signaled by Luke's terminology: "Jesus *summoned* the Twelve, *gave* them power and authority, and *sent* them to proclaim and heal" (vv. 1-2). "Summoned" (Gk. *synkalein;* NIV "called together") denotes intentionally convening a group, e.g., inviting guests to a banquet (15:6, 9; Acts 10:24) or organizing a delegation (23:13; Acts 5:21; 23:17). The Twelve do not "happen" to share in Jesus' ministry; they are *willed* by him to do so. "Gave them power and authority" transfers the endowments of the Spirit that Jesus received at his baptism (3:21-22) to the disciples. "Sent them to proclaim . . . and heal" defines the mission of the Twelve in the programmatic terminology of Isa 61 with which Jesus inaugurated his ministry in Nazareth (4:18-19). These endowments are unique to the Twelve, for the same power and authority are not mentioned in the commission of the seventy(-two) in 10:1-12, with the exception of "healing the sick" (10:9). Until now only Jesus has exhibited "power" (Gk. *dynamis;* [1:35]; 4:14, 36; 5:17; 6:19; 8:46) and "authority" (Gk. *exousia;* 4:6, 32, 36; 5:24); he alone has proclaimed the kingdom of God ([1:33]; 4:5, 43; 6:20; 7:28; 8:1, 10; see at 4:43) and healed (5:17; 6:18-19; 7:7; 8:47). These characteristics are transferred to the Twelve[1] in 9:1-2, signifying their formal investiture with the authority and mission of Jesus.[2] The ministry of the Twelve, like Jesus' ministry, will be one of word and deed (Acts 1:1), with primary emphasis on proclaiming the kingdom of God, for which both Jesus and the Twelve were "sent" (4:43; 9:2). Right proclamation of the kingdom is the source of power to exorcise and heal.[3] There is little evidence that Jewish rabbis sent out disciples, as Jesus does here, in the name but without the person of their master. There were at least some efforts at proselytizing among Jews (Matt 23:15), but these appear to have been voluntary rather than authorized deputations.[4] Not only is Jesus unique in calling the disciples to himself rather than to Torah, he is unique in *sending* them in his name and in his authority.[5]

---

1. A number of manuscripts read "twelve *apostles*" (א C L Θ Ξ Ψ), but "the Twelve" is more strongly attested (𝔭75 A B D W). See Metzger, *TCGNT,* 122. Luke refers to "the Twelve" six times (8:1; 9:1, 12; 18:31; 22:3, 47), but only once (6:13) to the twelve "apostles." "The Twelve" in 9:1 is thus favored on both external and internal grounds.

2. According to the prophecy of *T. Levi* 18:12, the messianic high priest would "grant his children the authority to trample on wicked spirits."

3. So Irenaeus, *Haer.* 2.31.2: the truth of God is corroborated by the power of God.

4. See K. Rengstorf, *apostolos,* TDNT 1:418: "It must be emphasized most strongly that Jewish missionaries, of whom there were quite a number in the time of Jesus, are never called *seluhim* ["apostles"], and that in relation to them the words *selak* ["to send"] and *apostellein* ["to send"] play no part. Their work took place without authorization by the community in the narrower sense, and it thus had a private character. . . . Thus we cannot really speak of Jewish 'apostles' at the time of Jesus."

5. St. Francis of Assisi (1181-1226) initially dressed as a penitent, intending to live a life of comtemplative seclusion. Upon reading Jesus' commission of the Twelve in Luke 9:3-5, however, Francis changed his mission and gathered a group of like-minded disciples for the purpose of preaching the gospel, esp. to the poor and illiterate. See Kealy, *Interpretation of the Gospel of Luke,* 191.

1-6   Mission instructions to the Twelve are negative with reference to things and positive with reference to relationships. With regard to the former, Jesus specifies five things the Twelve are not to take: "Take nothing for the journey — no staff, no bag, no bread, no money, no extra shirt" (v. 3). According to Mark 6:8 the Twelve are allowed a staff, but even this is prohibited in Luke. The Twelve are allowed a tunic, belt, and sandals, but nothing more. Bread, bag, money, and even a second tunic must all be left behind. The word for "bag" (Gk. *pēra*) can refer to a beggar's bag, or even a bag carried by wandering Cynic philosophers, but the generic sense of "travel bag" seems preferable here. The Twelve are not to set out with a bag full of provisions.[6] Everything, in other words, that the Twelve foreseeably need — and that a responsible master would advise them to take — is expressly denied them. Jesus sends them into mission with a calculated deficit, reminding them clearly, perhaps even painfully, that they are prepared for mission only as they depend on him. Service of Jesus is characterized by dependence on Jesus, and dependence on Jesus means going where Jesus sends, despite material shortfalls and unanswered questions. The order to travel sparsely recalls the exodus from Egypt (Exod 12:11): the Twelve must travel light, lest possessions and cares impede the mission and blunt the urgency of the message. Like the reduction of Gideon's troops before the battle with Midian (Judg 6–7), the Twelve must go in dependence on God. Like birds of the air and lilies of the field (Matt 6:25-34), they must trust him alone who sends them. Jesus' rigorous instructions ensure that the Twelve seek not their own advancement, but promote the gospel. If they go with an elaborate support system and provisions for every eventuality, then they need not go in faith, and if they go not in faith, their proclamation is not believable.

The positive instructions concern the relationships they will share with those whom they serve. The gospel is rightly propagated not by campaigning, crusading, or conquering, but within a context of relationships defined by mutual trust and sharing. Trust in the sending Jesus includes trust in the receiving communities to which Jesus sends the disciples. The Israelites were instructed to eat the Passover in one house (Exod 12:46); the Twelve are likewise to be grateful guests in the place where they are received, and not dishonor their hosts by moving from house to house. If rebuffed, the Twelve must "shake the dust off your feet when you leave their town, as a testimony against them" (v. 5). When Jews traveled outside Palestine, they were commanded to shake themselves free of dust when returning to Israel, lest they pollute the Holy Land.[7] The commandment to "shake the dust off your feet" is thus a sharp

---

6. See W. Michaelis, *pēra*, *TWNT* 6:120-21; BDAG, 811. For a discussion of wandering Cynic philosophers in relation to the early Jesus movement, see Edwards, *Mark*, 179-81.

7. See Neh 5:13; Acts 18:6. For further references from Mishnah and Talmud, see Str-B 1:571. According to Ruth 4:6-7, removal of shoes also indicated the *finality* of a judgment!

judgment, declaring an inhospitable Jewish village *heathen,* a judgment the early church remembered and practiced in its missionary outreach (Acts 13:50-51). In applying a Gentile figure of speech to a Jewish village, Jesus desacralizes Eretz Israel, and with it the presumption of salvation on the basis of ethnicity, nation, or race. Even in the Promised Land there will be those who reject the Promised One. "Not all who are descended from Israel are Israel" (Rom 9:6).

The mission of the Twelve[8] is summarized in the Greek words *euangelizomenoi* and *therapeuontes,* "proclaiming the good news and healing people everywhere" (v. 6). The two distinguishing hallmarks of the church in every age are preaching the gospel and works of mercy. The final reference to "everywhere" (Gk. *pantachou*) indicates the thoroughness with which the first mission was pursued. Underprepared and uncomprehending disciples typify believers in every age who are sent out by the Lord of the harvest. No matter how much exegesis, theology, and counseling believers have studied, they are never "prepared for ministry." A genuine call to ministry is a call to that for which one is never adequately prepared. Deficiency, however, teaches one to depend not on human capabilities but on the One who calls and in the power of the proclamation to authenticate itself (Ps 55:22). "This brief description," writes Eduard Schweizer, "shows how important the genuineness of the proclamation is. Everything, even the poverty and simplicity of the messenger, indeed even the courage to be rejected, must conform to the Word that affirms that God is infinitely more important than all else."[9]

FAITH COMES FROM HEARING, NOT SEEING (9:7-9)

7-9 Luke reported John's imprisonment by Herod Antipas immediately before the baptismal narrative (3:19-20). Here he adds factually and without elaboration that Antipas beheaded John in prison (v. 9). Reports of Jesus' ministry raise fears in Antipas that Jesus may be John returned to life, or an apparition of Elijah or one of the prophets. These three opinions were not original to Antipas but widely current in Galilee (9:18-19).[10] By including Antipas's question

---

8. The imperfect tense *diērchonto* (v. 6, "they were going throughout") implies an extended period of time.

9. E. Schweizer, *Evangelium nach Markus* (NTD; Göttingen: Vandenhoeck & Ruprecht, 1968), 73.

10. Leaney, *Luke,* 161, notes the well-attested variant reading at Mark 6:14, "he was saying" (Gk. *elegen*), rather than "they were saying" (Gk. *elegon*), which attributes the rumor connecting John and Jesus to Antipas rather than to the crowds. The singular "he was saying" was probably caused by a scribe harmonizing "he was saying" with "he [Antipas] heard" at the beginning of v. 14. The result, however, is nonsensical, for it makes Antipas's knowledge of

in a unit devoted to the disciples, Luke may imply that fears earlier aroused by Jesus are now also aroused by his disciples.[11] For Matt 14:1-12 and Mark 6:14-29, Herod's anxieties become the occasion to complete the grisly but riveting account of John's martyrdom, the longest story in the Synoptics that is not devoted to Jesus. Luke deals with Herod's anxieties much differently. Rather than diverting the narrative to a flashback on John's death, well known though it was (see Josephus, *Ant.* 18.116-19), Luke omits all further reference to John and focuses on Jesus. "Who, then, is this I hear such things about?" (v. 9), asks Antipas. This question, which is not included in any other Gospel, essentially repeats the question of the disciples after the storm on the lake (8:25). It is the right question, but as the parable of the Sower repeatedly emphasized (8:4-15), its answer can be received only by *hearing*. Antipas, however, "tried to see [Jesus]" (v. 9). Indeed, as his interrogation of Jesus in 23:8 confirms, he wants to see a *sign* from Jesus. Such hopes will be disappointed. Had Antipas desired to *hear* Jesus, perhaps a seed might have been planted that could have led to faith (8:4-15). But he hankers for a spectacle, and if Jesus will not provide one, Antipas will provide one himself by mocking Jesus. Those who require a spectacle will eventually make Jesus to their own liking, and they will both mock and hate what they have made. (See excursus on Antipas at 23:1.)

FEEDING FIVE THOUSAND
AT A WILDERNESS BANQUET (9:10-17)

10-14a When the apostles returned from their mission, "They reported to Jesus what they had done" (v. 10). The Greek word for "reported," *diēgeisthai*, describes the apostolic mission with a word from the same root that Luke used to describe his composite Gospel narrative in the prologue (1:1, *diēgēsis;* NIV "account"). This term is used elsewhere in the Third Gospel only of the proclamation of the demoniac, which Jesus commanded him to make in the Decapolis (8:39). Here, as there, the term is dedicated to the "good news," the apostolic witness to the kingdom of God and the miraculous healings attendant to it.[12]

Following the mission of the Twelve, in which they "proclaimed the good news and healed people everywhere" (9:6), Jesus withdraws with them "to a

---

John derive from his own rumor (v. 14). It also puts the singular *elegen* in contrast to the two plural and obviously parallel uses of *elegon* in v. 15. Further, see Metzger, *TCGNT,* 76.

11. So Green, *Luke,* 361.

12. For comparisons and contrasts of the first apostolic mission with missionary practices of the early church, esp. as reported in the *Did.,* see Edwards, *Mark,* 181-82.

city called Bethsaida" (v. 10). Bethsaida, meaning "house of the fisher," a name derived from its chief industry, lay a thousand yards (less than 1 km) east of the point where the Jordan River empties into the north end of the Sea of Galilee. Bethsaida technically belonged to the tetrarchy of Philip in Gaulanitis, but its proximity to Capernaum only three miles (5 km) to the west, anchored it to Jesus' Galilean ministry. Three of Jesus' disciples, Philip, Andrew, and Peter, came from Bethsaida (John 1:44; 12:21).[13] The exact location of the feeding of the five thousand is difficult to establish. The other Gospels place it vaguely along the unpopulated north shore of the lake (Matt 14:23; Mark 6:32; John 6:1). Luke's description would place the miraculous feeding to the east of the general vicinity suggested in the other Gospels, near "a city called Bethsaida" (v. 10). Luke's geography is thus more precise, but its textual attestation is uncertain.[14] If "a city called Bethsaida" is original, Luke, who routinely refers to towns and villages as "cities," may mean a remote region whose nearest city was Bethsaida.[15] To this region the crowds follow Jesus, and despite his desire to be alone with the Twelve, Jesus "welcomed them" (v. 11) and began to proclaim the kingdom of God and heal them.[16]

As the day wanes, and with it time and opportunity to attend to the needs of the crowd, the disciples implore Jesus to dismiss the crowds to procure provisions in surrounding villages. Given the circumstances, the suggestion of the Twelve seems eminently reasonable. Rather than alleviating the crisis, however, Jesus seems to exacerbate it: "You give them something to eat" (v. 13). The "you" is emphatic, laying responsibility on the disciples to solve the problem. The Twelve are no longer expected to be mere observers of Jesus' ministry, but active participants in it. Two options present themselves: to canvass the crowd for provisions, or to buy food in surrounding villages. The first option yields "only five loaves of bread and two fish" (v. 13), obviously of little consequence for a crowd of "five thousand men" (v. 14). The Greek word for "men," *andres,* means "males," which would amount to a much larger crowd when women and children were counted.[17] With regard to the second option,

---

13. Josephus, *Ant.* 18.28. Josephus says Philip "raised the village of Bethsaida . . . to the status of a city [Gk. *polis*] by adding residents and strengthening its fortifications"; Luke, likewise, calls it a "city" (Gk. *polis*), although other evangelists frequently refer to it as a "village." Although a quarter of the Twelve came from Bethsaida, there is no indication that Jesus' ministry was unusually successful there ("Woe to you, Korazin! Woe to you, Bethsaida!" (10:13 par. Matt 11:21). See M. Avi-Yonah, "Bethsaida," *IDB* 1:397.

14. See Metzger, *TCGNT,* 123.

15. Leaney, *Luke,* 161, rightly notes "Luke's stylistic desire to always locate events in or near nameable towns as opposed to unidentifiable country."

16. The Greek verbs for "speak" and "heal" are both imperfects, implying extended commitment to the crowds.

17. On the possibility that the exclusive reference to "men" may refer to an embryonic

Luke's phrasing, which I would translate "Do you want *us* to go and buy food for all these people?" (v. 13), betrays a decided lack of enthusiasm. The Twelve are overwhelmed. Their impotence in the face of the impending crisis mirrors and indeed accentuates their initial unpreparedness for mission (9:3).

14b-17 Everything now depends on Jesus. "Have them sit down in groups of about fifty each," he orders (v. 14). From the earliest days of the Christian movement, the feeding of the five thousand, the only miracle recorded in all four Gospels and an ever-popular story of the church, was interpreted with reference to "manna": as Moses fed the crowds in the wilderness with heavenly food, so Jesus feeds the crowds with the bread of heaven that will satisfy their hunger forever.[18] Luke doubtless affirms this typological connection, but he adds a unique and decisive clue in the phrase "fifty each." The number "fifty" occurs 160 times in the Greek Bible, but "fifty each" (Gk. *ana pentēkonta*) occurs only once again in the Greek Bible. In 1 Kgs 18:13 Obadiah tells Elijah that he has supplied food and water to "fifty each" *(ana pentēkonta)* of the prophets of the Lord during the famine in the land and the pogrom of Ahab and Jezebel to exterminate them. The use of "fifty each" is yet another Lukan allusion to the prophet Elijah (and perhaps also to the miraculous feeding of Elisha, 2 Kgs 4:42-44) as a prefigurement of Jesus: the salvific care that God showed to the faithful remnant of Yahweh prophets will be shown to the disciples and crowd through Jesus' ministry in the wilderness (see excursus on Elijah-Elisha typology at 7:15-17).

"Taking the five loaves and the two fish and looking up to heaven, [Jesus] gave thanks and broke them. Then he gave them to the disciples to set before the people." This verse is virtually verbatim in the three Synoptics (9:16; Matt 14:19; Mark 6:41) and nearly as close to the wording of John 6:11. It preserves the memory of the church with greater unanimity than perhaps any other single text in the four Gospels. The exactitude with which this verse was preserved in church tradition almost certainly resulted from the fact that the early church perceived a parallel between the accounts of the feeding of the five thousand and the Last Supper, both of which contain the fourfold word sequence: "took (bread)/blessed/broke/gave."[19] To be sure, the Passover significance of the Last Supper is absent in the wilderness banquet, and the two episodes differ in various details.[20] Nevertheless, Jesus' introduces the wilderness banquet in terminology that is unique to himself. The fourfold word sequence is absent

Zealot uprising, see Edwards, *Mark*, 194-95. Luke has omitted most clues of popular messianic fervor in Mark 6:32-44, but the retention of "men" (Gk. *andres*), which is present in all three Synoptics, is a vestige of support for the Johannine report that a movement was afoot to sweep Jesus up as a guerilla leader (John 6:14-15).

18. Cyril of Alexandria, *Comm. Luc.*, Hom. 48.

19. See here Nolland, *Luke 1:1–9:20*, 446.

20. See the contrasts noted by Marshall, *Luke*, 361-62.

from the common Jewish table prayer ("Praise be to you, O Lord our God, king of the world, who makes bread to come forth from the earth and who provides for all that you have created"),[21] but it is present in the feeding of the Five Thousand (9:16), the Last Supper (22:19), and the banquet at Emmaus (24:30).[22] In each banquet the theme of *revelation and recognition* is paramount. The wilderness banquet is sandwiched between Antipas's question, "Who, then, is [Jesus]?" (9:9) and Peter's declaration, "You are the Messiah of God" (9:20). In the Last Supper the fourfold liturgy of institution is repeated in the context of a Passover meal that inaugurates the new covenant of the kingdom of God (22:14-20). And at the fourfold liturgy during the Emmaus banquet "the eyes [of the disciples] were opened and they recognized [Jesus]" (24:30-31). Luke thus employs the formula "took/blessed/broke/gave" in three critical and calculated contexts, in each instance of which the breaking and dispensing of bread to the disciples is a revelatory symbol of Jesus' self-giving for the church in his passion and resurrection, through which disciples recognize him (24:31) as the fulfillment of Scripture (24:32).

"They all ate and were satisfied." The word "satisfied" (Gk. *chortazein*) recalls Luke's second beatitude, "Blessed are you who hunger now, for you will be satisfied" (6:21). The word "all" is equally significant. Nowhere did Torah and oral tradition regulate Jewish life more prescriptively than at table. The effect of kosher was to ensure that proper foods, properly prepared, were properly eaten; unclean foods and unclean persons were necessarily excluded. At the wilderness banquet the ritual of kosher is abandoned in favor of an open invitation and inclusion of all people. "They *all* ate and were satisfied." The meal provided by Jesus does not "tide the crowd over" until something more substantial can be had. The meal is so sufficient and satisfying[23] that a basket of leftovers remains for each of the disciples.[24] The "twelve baskets of leftovers" (v. 17) may symbolize the twelve tribes of Israel, a conjecture that is strengthened by the emphatic placement of *dōdeka*, "twelve," as the final Greek word of the miracle. If so, "twelve" is Luke's final reminder that the bread offered by Jesus not only feeds and satisfies a crowd of five thousand, but all Israel. At the same time, "twelve" reminds the disciples how those sent in mission with a calculated deficit are not abandoned by Jesus but abundantly provided for.

21. Str-B 1:685.

22. So too Tannehill, *Luke,* 155.

23. The second-c. *Ep. Ap.* 5, in attempting to answer the claims of Gnosticism, spiritualizes the bread, making it a metaphor for the doctrines of the creed — Father, Jesus Christ, Holy Ghost, the church, and forgiveness.

24. BDAG, 563, describes the basket (Gk. *kophinos*) as a "large, heavy basket, probably of various sizes, for carrying things." Josephus, *J.W.* 3.95, uses the word for the kind of basket in which Roman soldiers carried daily rations.

PETER DECLARES WHO JESUS IS, JESUS DECLARES WHAT DISCIPLES MUST BECOME (9:18-27)

18-21 V. 18 is one of six instances in the Third Gospel in which Luke supplies a wholly unique introduction to a pericope that he inherits from Mark.[25] This introduction, like the other five, is strongly Semitic, again suggesting Luke's indebtedness to the Hebrew Gospel.[26] Both Matt 16:13 and Mark 8:27 set the story of Peter's confession at Caesarea Philippi, but Luke omits the place-name and sets the scene with Jesus "praying in private" (v. 18).[27] We have noted the prevalence of prayer in Luke-Acts and its importance as a signal of divine revelation. In Jesus' ministry prayer occurs at the baptism (3:21-22), call of the Twelve (6:12), confession of Peter (9:18), transfiguration (9:28-29), temptation on the Mount of Olives (22:41), and crucifixion (23:46). In each instance, prayer precedes and forecasts critical developments in the story of salvation.

Luke 9, as noted at the introduction of this chapter, promotes the Twelve from general observers of Jesus' ministry to actual participants in it. In the feeding of the five thousand, Jesus told the disciples to feed the crowd (9:13); here he poses a question that will require even greater commitment on their part, "Who do the crowds say that I am?" (v. 18). The question must catch the disciples by surprise. We do not know how long they have accompanied Jesus. Until this point, however, Jesus has not pressed them for a personal judgment, for he has willed that their choice be based not on hearsay or feelings but on experience. The question of v. 18 is generally foreign to the rabbinic tradition, for in the latter it was disciples, not rabbis, who were expected to pose questions. Jesus' question requires a level of understanding and personal commitment that exceeds the most rigorous rabbinic expectations. There is, furthermore, an oddity to the question. People normally ask what others *do*, not who they *are*. The question prods the disciples to make a judgment about something they have not consciously considered. Perhaps they have subconsciously anticipated the question, however, for at the calming of the storm they asked, "Who is this? He commands the winds and the water, and they obey him" (8:25). Likewise, when Antipas heard about Jesus, he too asked, "I beheaded John. Who, then, is this I hear such things about?" (9:9).

Jesus puts the question of his identity in two stages: first, what others say (v. 18); then, what the disciples themselves say (v. 20). There seems to have

---

25. 5:12, 17; 8:22; 9:18, 28; 20:1.

26. Three Hebraisms are identified in Edwards, *Hebrew Gospel*, 304. Bovon, *Luke 1:1–9:50*, 477, likewise notes that Luke derives the verse from another source, although he does not name it.

27. On prayer, see at 3:21-22, n. 63.

been a general consensus that Jesus was John the Baptist returned to life or Elijah or a prophet of old, for these three categories were known to Antipas (9:7-8) as well as to the disciples (v. 19). No OT personality held such fascination for first-century Judaism as did Elijah. Luke, as we have noted (see excursus on Elijah-Elisha typology at 7:15-17), sees three elements in Elijah that commended him as a critical precursor of Jesus: his prophetic office, his miraculous healing powers, and his inclusion of Gentiles in the benefits of those powers. In Judaism, however, it was not these three elements that accounted for Elijah's enduring popularity, nor even his dramatic victory over the prophets of Baal on Mount Carmel (1 Kgs 18), but rather the tradition that he had been taken bodily to heaven (2 Kgs 2:11), whence he oversaw the deeds of mortals, comforted the faithful, helped the needy, and above all, would return as forerunner of the great and terrible Day of the Lord (Mal 3:1; 4:5-6; Sir. 48:9-10).[28]

Other opinions regarded Jesus more generally as a reappearance of a prophet "of long ago" (v. 19). The modern world typically regards antiquity as something that has been surpassed and is thus functionally irrelevant. In Jesus' day antiquity was a sign of veracity and genuineness, for the true and indestructible was that which had survived the ages. A prophet "of long ago" was thus a distinction of veracity, not a curse of irrelevance. The same phrase perhaps also recalled the great prophet foretold by Moses: God would "raise up for you a prophet like me from among your brothers" (Deut 18:15, also v. 18). This final prophet would speak for the entire prophetic tradition and declare God's word conclusively to the people.

Comparing Jesus to John, Elijah, or a prophet indicates his preeminence in the popular mind and enshrines him among the stellar figures in Israel's long and illustrious history. Yet even these comparisons are inadequate. To designate Jesus a new Moses or Elijah — or, as we often hear today, the greatest teacher or moral example who ever lived — is ultimately to deny his uniqueness, for it simply identifies him as the reemergence, or greater example, of an earlier prototype. Such thinking is an example of "pouring new wine into old wineskins" (5:37). The authority and power that Jesus has demonstrated since his endowment with the Holy Spirit at the baptism (3:21-22) do not allow him to be defined by something other than himself and his relationship with the Father.

A genuine confession of Jesus requires of believers more than a proxy endorsement of the judgments of others. "But what about you? Who do you say I am?" presses Jesus (v. 20). Peter's answer to that question requires a personal risk in which he stands alone with and before Jesus.[29] His answer

---

28. See Str-B 4/2:764-98.
29. Noted by Cyril of Alexandria, *Comm. Luke. Hom.* 49.

becomes the first voice in the chorus of the apostolic tradition that every follower of Jesus must acknowledge and confess for himself or herself. The categories of John the Baptizer, Elijah, or one of the prophets resemble the various and valiant reconstructions of Jesus since the Enlightenment according to historical, ideological, nationalist, feminist, liberation, racial, and sociological categories. Such restorations may or may not illuminate valid facets of Jesus' personality and mission, but they are insufficient to answer the question Jesus poses to disciples — of all ages.[30] Jesus' question cannot be answered by simply amassing more data. Like all ultimate commitments in life, his question cannot be answered by knowledge alone. It requires risk and trust that either commit one to, or separate one from, his identity and mission. Peter answers that Jesus is "God's Messiah" (v. 20).[31] Peter's confession, as noted early by Cyril of Alexandria and often since, may have been influenced, at least in part, by the miraculous feeding of the multitude in the wilderness.[32] Until this point in Jesus' ministry, God and demons have recognized Jesus as Messiah[33] and Son of God,[34] but no human has recognized or confessed Jesus as either.[35] Now, at last, there is human recognition corresponding to the proclamation of Jesus in the infancy narrative; and like divine proclamations of the infancy narrative, Peter's confession is enabled by the divine efficacy of Jesus' prayer.

---

30. The question "Who do you say I am?" is of central significance with regard to the upsurge of interest in the "historical Jesus." According to the NT, who Jesus is cannot be discovered or recovered by new historical data or theories or better sociological models, but only from the apostolic testimony itself, of which Peter's declaration is the beginning. "One cannot learn who Jesus from Nazareth is by 'the quest of the historical Jesus,' but only by recourse to the apostolic witness to Christ in the New Testament" (O. Hofius, "Ist Jesus der Messias? Thesen," in *Der Messias* [JBTh 8; ed. I. Baldermann; Neukirchen: Neukirchener Verlag, 1993], 104.

31. The historicity of Peter's declaration is supported by Jesus' reserve with regard to the title (v. 21) and by his sharp rebuke of Peter's falsification of it (Mark 8:33). See E. Schweizer, *Theologische Einleitung in das Neue Testament* (GNT 2; Göttingen: Vandenhoeck & Ruprecht, 1989), 19. Likewise Nolland, *Luke 1:1–9:20*, 453-54: "If there is no place somewhere in the ministry of Jesus for the emergence of the view that he was the Messiah, it is difficult to see how that title came to play such a basic role in the early church."

32. Cyril, *Comm. Luke, Hom.* 49.

33. God: 2:11, 26; demons: 4:41.

34. God: 1:35; 3:22; demons: 4:3, 9, 34, 41; 8:28.

35. According to *Gos. Thom.* 13, Thomas declares Jesus an ineffable being who cannot be captured in human thought and words because Jesus escapes and defies human conception. *Gos. Thom.* is unable to define Jesus' identity because it is unable to affirm the incarnation. The apostolic tradition, by contrast, which is represented in the four canonical Gospels, affirms that, in becoming truly human, Jesus enters human categories rather than eschewing them and thus both invites and requires human judgments about himself.

EXCURSUS: CHRIST

"Christ" (from Greek) translates "Messiah" (from Hebrew), meaning "anointed." In the OT, three classes of people received anointing: prophets, priests, and kings. The third class, kings, influenced the development of the concept of the Messiah in Judaism (e.g., 2 Sam 7; Ps 2). With the demise of the monarchy and its capitulation to Nebuchadnezzar in 586 B.C., the messianic hope, rather than suffering corresponding demise, revived with expectation that God would raise up a new and greater king like David. " 'The days are coming,' declares the Lord, 'when I will raise up to David a righteous branch, a King, who will reign wisely and do what is just and right in the land' " (Jer 23:5).[36] The OT does not develop a formal doctrine of the Messiah, and this remains generally true for the subsequent intertestamental period as well, where the concept of Messiah is less frequent and less uniformly developed than often supposed. The absolute use "Messiah" is rare, the single OT exception being Dan 9:26, and the earliest known instance outside the OT coming from Qumran (1QSa 2:12).[37] The most specific form of the otherwise general messianic conception in pre-Christian texts is that of an *eschatological king*. The Messiah would be the perfect king chosen by God from eternity, through whom God would deliver Israel from its enemies and cause Israel to live in peace and tranquility thereafter (*Sib. Or.* 3.286-94). Contrary to popular notions, neither the Servant of Yahweh nor the Son of Man concepts in the OT are associated with messianic expectations.

Disappointment with the Hasmonean princes who ruled Israel after the Maccabean revolt in the second century B.C., and disillusionment following Pompey's seizure of Jerusalem in 63 B.C., fueled messianic expectations in both specificity and compass. Though entirely human,[38] Messiah would nevertheless be far greater than God's earlier messengers to Israel. When the two disciples on the road to Emmaus spoke of Jesus as "powerful in word and deed before God and all the people" (24:19), they may have been tutored by current messianic terminology. Messiah would be mighty and wise in the Holy Spirit, endowed with miraculous powers, holy and free from sin, the final Anointed One and true king of Israel who would destroy God's enemies by the word of his mouth. He would deliver Jerusalem from the

36. OT messianic texts include Isa 9:1-7; 11:1-10; Jer 30:8-11; 33:14-18; Ezek 17:22-24; 34:23-31; 37:15-28; Mic 5:1-5; Zech 9:9-13.

37. See F. García-Martínez, "Messianische Erwartungen in den Qumranschriften," in *Der Messias* (JBTh 8; ed. I Baldermann; Neukirchen: Neukirchener Verlag, 1993), 171-208.

38. The Jew Trypho declares that Messiah will be *anthrōpos ex anthrōpōn genomenos* ("a human born of humans"), Justin Martyr, *Dial.* 67.2 (cf. 48.1; 49.1).

Gentiles, gather the faithful from dispersion, and rule in justice and glory (*Pss. Sol.* 17:23-30).[39]

This seems to have been the prevalent concept of Messiah in Jesus' day, to which Josephus attests in his description of the Sicarii — the revolutionaries who plunged Palestine and especially Jerusalem into a Götterdämmerung in the late 60s, "whose passion for liberty is almost unconquerable, since they think that God alone is their leader and master" (*Ant.* 18.23).[40] The latent messianic expectations of the five thousand men in the wilderness (9:12-17), the references to Jesus as "Son of David" (18:38-39; 20:41, 44), the reference to Jesus as "king" at the triumphal entry (19:38) and before Pilate (23:2), and Rome's execution of Jesus as "king of the Jews" (23:38) — all these reflect the expectation of a militant messianic king. This association with sword and scepter, military might and political dominance, was consciously rejected by Jesus, however; hence, his command to silence immediately following Peter's confession (v. 21).[41] Neither Jesus nor early Christians rejected the concept of God's divinely anointed Messiah, of course, but in the Gospels (though not in Paul) the title is used with caution and control in order to preserve its theological integrity from national triumphalism.

The title "Messiah" rightly belongs to Jesus alone, and he, not extraneous ideologies, must define it.[42] Luke's two uses of the term in the infancy narrative (2:11, 26) tether it to Lord (2:11) and Holy Spirit (2:26), and its use by demons in 4:41 tethers it to the concept of Son of God. As a title, "Messiah" plays no special role in the Galilean ministry, a role, as we have seen, that is assumed by the category (if not actual title) of "prophet" in chaps. 4, 7, and 9. At Peter's confession, however, Luke begins a titular transition away from "prophet," which is abandoned after chap. 9, to "Messiah," which anticipates Jesus' passion in Jerusalem.[43] Occasional uses of "Messiah" in the Galilean ministry increase in frequency and importance in the Passion Narrative. There the title

39. For discussions of the messianic expectation, see Str-B 4/2:799-1015; G. Moore, *Judaism in the First Centuries of the Christian Era* (New York: Schocken Books, 1971), 2:323-76; Schürer, *History of the Jewish People*, 2:488-554; O. Hofius, "Ist Jesus der Messias? Thesen," in *Der Messias* (JBTh 8; ed. I. Baldermann; Neukirchen: Neukirchener Verlag, 1993), 103-29. Qumran expected two messianic figures: a son of David as military deliverer and a son of Aaron as high priest (1QS 9:11). The expectation of a messianic high priest seems to have been limited to Qumran, however, and to have exerted little if any influence on subsequent Judaism.

40. Nolland, *Luke 1:1–9:20*, 453, correctly notes the variety of messianic conceptions current in Jesus' day, but he underestimates the predominance of the military conception in popular Judaism.

41. So Irenaeus, *Haer.* 3.18.4, "[Jesus] rebuked Peter because he supposed Jesus to be the Christ according to the common conception of the people."

42. Thus, identifications by demons that Jesus is Messiah and Son of God (4:41), Holy One of God (4:34), or Son of the Most High (8:28) are all followed by commands to silence.

43. Also noted by Nolland, *Luke 1:1–9:20*, 448.

appears with diametrically opposite meanings, depending on who uses it. The Sanhedrin (22:67) and Pilate (23:2) associate the title with kingship, an association that is sufficient grounds for their condemnation of Jesus. The taunts of bystanders (23:35) and criminals (23:39) at the site of crucifixion for Jesus to save himself may also presuppose kingship ideology. In the mouth of Jesus, however, "Messiah" is consistently associated with *suffering*, a characteristic that made it revered by Christians and offensive to Jews. In the first passion prediction (9:22), the title is expressly defined by the necessity of suffering; and its increased frequency in the Passion Narrative reminds readers that, even though misunderstood by his adversaries, Jesus is fulfilling his divine office as suffering Messiah, for which he was "elected" (Gk. *eklegesthai,* 9:35; *eklektos,* 23:35), i.e., destined by God. The final two uses of "Messiah" in the Third Gospel (24:26, 46), both from the mouth of the resurrected Jesus, validate this understanding. The office of "Messiah" bears greater salvific weight than that of "prophet," although when applied to Jesus, both offices bear witness to God's sovereign will: "This man was handed over to you by God's deliberate plan and foreknowledge . . . to put him to death by nailing him to the cross" (Acts 2:23).

22-27 Peter's confession of "God's Messiah" may distinguish his confession from the popular militant messianic conception. Only Jesus, however, can fully define the title Peter confesses. He does so in v. 22 by four infinitives: the Son of Man (see excursus on Son of Man at 5:26) must suffer, be rejected,[44] be killed, and be raised on the third day. V. 22 is a virtual one-verse summary of the second article of the Apostles' Creed. Jesus is properly understood as God's Messiah when he is understood as the *suffering* and *resurrected* Messiah. The verb "must" (Gk. *dei*) is crucial to Jesus' answer: his suffering and exaltation as Messiah are not the result of fluctuating fortunes, but foreordained by God (24:26, 46!). It is doubtful that any Jew before Jesus ever conceived of Messiah in such terms. Israel was of course familiar with the image of the Suffering Servant in Isaiah, but as noted in the foregoing excursus, there is no evidence that the Servant of the Lord was associated with the Messiah.[45] Nor is there any

44. Gk. *apodokimasthēnai* ("to be rejected") derives from the noun *dokimasia* ("examination"), referring to "the scrutiny which an elected magistrate had to undergo at Athens, to see whether he was legally qualified to hold office. The hierarchy held such a scrutiny respecting the claims of Jesus to be the Christ, and rejected him" (Plummer, *Luke,* 247).

45. Isa 42:1-4; 49:1-6; 50:4-11a; 52:13–53:12. *Tg. Jon.* associates the servant of Yahweh with Messiah in Isa 53, but it interprets the verses that refer to suffering as *not* referring to the Messiah! (See Schürer, *History of the Jewish People,* 2:547-49.) This tradition of interpretation generally continues in Jewish interpretations until today. As one example, A. Heschel's otherwise excellent discussion of prophecy passes over the Suffering Servant passages in silence

notion of expiatory suffering of the Messiah. The suffering foreseen by Jesus is not regarded, as is suffering in the Psalms, for instance, as a misfortune contrary to God's will. Rather, the way to Jerusalem and the bitter end that awaits Jesus there is affirmed as God's ordained way for him: he *must* suffer. Eduard Schweizer perceives the revelatory significance of Jesus' suffering:

> God is therein precisely God in that he can do what humanity cannot do: God can allow himself to be rejected, to be made low and small, without thereby being driven into an inferiority complex. . . . Whoever understands the suffering of the Son of Man understands God. It is there, and not in heavenly splendor, that one sees the heart of God.[46]

The prediction of Jesus' passion conceals a great irony, for the suffering and death of the Son of Man do not come, as we would expect, at the hands of godless and wicked people, but rather at the hands of "the elders, chief priests and teachers of the law" (v. 22). The Son of God will not be a victim of criminal lawlessness and anarchy, but of careful deliberations of lawful and religious leaders who, in rendering their decisions, believe themselves to render service to God (John 16:2). Jesus will be arrested with official warrants, and tried and executed by the envy of jurisprudence in the world of that time — the Jewish Sanhedrin and the *principia iuris Romanorum*.

The Roman Imperium, aware of the fierce religious independence of Jews and their equally fierce antipathy to Gentile occupation, established in the Jewish **Sanhedrin** a proxy buffer governing apparatus that was granted near complete freedom in religious matters and limited freedom in political matters. The Sanhedrin comprised seventy-one members, divided into three groups: chief priests, elders, and scribes. Elders (both Pharisees and Sadducees) and scribes (most of whom were Pharisees) constituted seventy members of the Sanhedrin. The ruling chief priest constituted the seventy-first and lead member of the Sanhedrin, although predecessors and members of his family could also be included in the designation, hence "chief priests" (plural). The chief priests, all of whom belonged to the sect of the Sadducees, included Caiaphas (ruled 18-36), his father-in-law Annas (ruled 6-15), and Caiaphas's successor, Jonathan, and his brother Theophilus (Acts 4:6; Josephus,

---

and never raises the issue of the Messiah (*The Prophets* [2 vols.; New York: Harper Torchbooks, 1962], 1:145-58).

46. *Das Evangelium nach Markus* (NTD; Göttingen: Vandenhoeck & Ruprecht, 1968), 98. Compare a similar thought of the divine humility in Dante:

> Limited man, by subsequent obedience,
> > could never make amends; he could not go
> > as low in his humility as once,
> rebellious, he had sought to rise in pride. (*Paradiso,* canto 7, lines 97-100)

Ant. 18.26, 95, 124). The scribes (see at 5:17) were legal experts and advisers to the Sanhedrin.

The disciples to whom Jesus speaks evidently included Mary Magdalene, Joanna the wife of Chuza, and other women (8:2-3; 24:10), for following the resurrection an angel reminds them to "remember" the passion prediction of v. 22 (24:6-8). Jesus' definition of messiahship has irrevocable consequences for discipleship, which is immediately defined by self-denial and "taking up the cross daily and following me" (v. 23).[47] Faith entails affirming the truth that Jesus is Messiah, but it also entails more than this. It entails acting on that truth by *following* Jesus in daily discipleship. Modern culture is exposed to the symbol of the cross primarily in jewelry or figures of speech (e.g., "bearing one's cross"). In the first century, the **cross** was not a mere symbol or figure of speech but a repugnant instrument of cruelty, pain, dehumanization, and shame.[48] The cross was the most visible and omnipresent aspect of Rome's terror apparatus, designed especially to punish criminals and quash slave rebellions in the most painful, protracted, and public manner possible as a warning against rebellion. In 71 B.C. the Roman general Crassus defeated the slave-rebel Spartacus and crucified him and 6,000 of his followers on the Appian Way between Rome and Capua. A century later Nero crucified and burned Christians who were falsely accused of setting fire to Rome. There are no known survivors of Roman crucifixions. The cross was thus a symbol of absoluteness and totality, and it retains both senses as used by Jesus. The cross signified a total claim on life, a claim that "daily" (v. 23) must be accepted in the lives of Jesus' followers. Only Luke introduces the qualification "daily," which expands the connotation of the cross from physical martyrdom to the metaphor of daily self-denial. The inclusion of "daily" in v. 23 changes the saying of Jesus from the final act of discipleship fulfilled in physical death to the *first* and repeated act of discipleship fulfilled in daily obedience to the claim of Jesus on one's life.[49]

---

47. The substance of v. 23 is preserved in various apocryphal gospels, but often with slight shifts of emphasis. *Gos. Thom.* 55 introduces the concept of becoming worthy: "whoever will not take up his cross as I do, will not be worthy of me." *Ap. Jas.* 5.30–6.10 expounds the idea ("Remember my cross and my death, and you will live") as a formula of salvation. *Ep. Pet. Phil.* 138, on the contrary, states that Jesus does not suffer (although the text is corrupt at this point), whereas disciples must suffer because of their "smallness."

48. See M. Hengel, *Crucifixion in the Ancient World and the Folly of the Message of the Cross* (trans. J. Bowden; Philadelphia: Fortress Press, 1977).

49. St. Makarios of Egypt, a fourth-c. Coptic desert father, spoke of this claim thus: "If we want to share His inheritance we must be willing to share His sufferings with an equal zeal. Those who love the Lord may be recognized by the fact that because of their hope in Him they bear every affliction that comes, not simply courageously but also wholeheartedly" (*Philokalia* [trans. G. Palmer, P. Sherrard, and K. Ware; London: Faber & Faber, 1984], 3:344). D. Bonhoeffer, *The Cost of Discipleship* (trans. R. H. Fuller; London: SCM Press, 1959), 79, interprets Jesus' command of the cross likewise: "The cross is not the terrible end to an otherwise god-fearing

Three statements expound the meaning of discipleship in vv. 24-26. Each is prefaced in Greek with "for," a conjunction of purpose indicating that each statement is adduced in support of v. 23. The first statement in v. 24 is chiastic (A-B-B-A):

A   For whoever wants to **save** his life
  B   will **lose** it,
  B^1 but whoever **loses** his life for me and the gospel
A^1 will **save** it.[50]

The supreme element in a chiastic list is the central element; hence, the emphasis in v. 24 is on *losing* one's life. The word for "life" (Gk. *psychē*) can simply mean physical existence (e.g., Acts 27:37), but its more common and important sense is that of "personhood," "being," or "soul," i.e., the core of one's existence that is not limited to boundaries of time and space. In v. 24 *psychē* carries this latter sense, for the call to take up the cross obviously implies the loss of physical life, at least in one sense of the word, but it cannot connote the loss of one's "soul." The way of the cross is a way of irony, for the one thing that is more important than anything else cannot be saved by preserving it, but only by forsaking it in favor of following Jesus on the way of the cross.[51] To the one for whom the way of Jesus is more important than his own existence, his eternal existence will be secured; to the one whose existence is more important than Jesus, both Jesus and his existence will be lost.[52]

Discipleship is not a form of spirituality severed from historical knowledge of Jesus' life, death, and resurrection. For believers after the incarnation, Jesus Christ is known through the proclaimed word of the gospel. When confronted by the call to discipleship, disciples do not have a "both . . . and" choice — both Christ and their own lives. They stand before an "either . . . or" choice.

---

and happy life, but it meets us at the beginning of our communion with Christ. When Christ calls a person, he bids him come and die. It may be a death like that of the first disciples who had to leave home and work to follow him, or it may be a death like Luther's, who had to leave the monastery and go out into the world. But it is the same death every time — death in Jesus Christ, the death of the old man at his call."

50. *Gos. Thom.* 110 preserves this saying thus: "Jesus said: He who has found the world and become rich, let him deny the world."

51. For a defense of the historicity of this saying according to the criteria of dissimilarity and multiple attestation, see W. Rebell, " 'Sein Leben verlieren' (Mark 8.35 parr.) als Strukturmoment vor- und nachösterlichen Glaubens," *NTS* 35 (1989); 202-18. For a discussion of the relationship between discipleship/apostleship and Christology, see C. Breytenbach, "Christologie, Nachfolge/Apostolat," *BTZ* 8 (1991): 183-98.

52. A point immortally captured in a motto of Jim Elliot, who died a martyr's death at the hands of the Huaorani Indians in South America, "He is no fool who gives up what he cannot keep in order to gain what he cannot lose."

The claim of Jesus is a total and exclusive claim. It does not allow a convenient compartmentalization of secular and sacred, of natural life and religious life. The whole person stands under Christ's claim.

Second, v. 25 places the question of discipleship in the context of ultimate reality: the soul and the world. Suppose one were to gain "the whole world" — everything one could possibly hope for — at the cost of one's soul.[53] It would be a poor bargain, according to Jesus. "The world" one can live without, but when one loses one's personhood or being, what can one give in exchange for it (see Ps 49:6-8; Sir 26:14)? There is a further paradox in this verse, for those who strive desperately to preserve their souls do not in fact know the value of the soul. Apart from God, the soul is the one thing without compare. It takes the word of Jesus both to *teach* the infinite worth of the human soul and to *preserve* it.[54]

Third, Jesus says, "If any of you are ashamed of me and my words, the Son of Man will be ashamed of you when he comes in his glory and in the glory of the Father and of the holy angels" (v. 26; Matt 10:33).[55] In referring to himself in first person ("me") and "the Son of Man" in third person, Jesus is not referring to two different persons. Rather, as noted in the excursus on Son of Man at 5:26, when referring to himself as Son of Man, Jesus refers to his fulfillment of various *offices,* one of which is the second coming in glory and judgment. It is the nature of Jesus, as it is of the Father, to share not only his attributes but also his essence with those who belong to him. Among the attributes Jesus shares with the Father and the holy angels — an attribute he also imparts to his followers (John 17:22) — is his glory. Those who are

---

53. See 2 *Clem.* 6:2; Justin, *1 Apol.* 15.12.

54. For an ancient illustration of this truth, see the story in 2 Macc 6 of Eleazar, an aged scribe who faced martyrdom during the Maccabean Revolt in these words: "It is clear to the Lord in his holy knowledge that, though I might have been saved from death, I am enduring terrible sufferings in my body under this beating, but in my soul I am glad to suffer these things because I fear him" (v. 30). A modern illustration of the same truth occurs in the Stasi files — the voluminous secret police records of former East Germany. A contact who was approached to become an informant writes, "After a thorough and intensive examination of my religious convictions as a Christian I must tell you that I cannot compromise the fundamentals of what I believe by what you are asking me to do. I cannot justify such behavior with what the New Testament requires of me: Matthew 16:26, 'What good will it be for a man if he gains the whole world, yet forfeits his soul?'" (J. Gauck, *Die Stasi-Akten: Das unheimliche Erbe der DDR* [Hamburg: Rowolt, 1991], 59).

55. The omission of "words" from v. 26 in Codex Bezae (D) leaves the somewhat unusual reading: "whoever is ashamed of me and my [followers]." This appears to be an error caused by homoeoteleuton, i.e., a scribe inadvertently omitting the second of two words ending similarly ("my," *emous*; "words," *logous*). See Metzger, *TCGNT,* 84. Apart from Bezae, the manuscript tradition unanimously includes "words." The NIV rightly includes "words," thus preserving the direct link here between Jesus' teaching about suffering messiahship and suffering discipleship.

ashamed to bear dishonor for Jesus' name now will be unable to share Jesus' future glory and exaltation. Participation in Jesus' future glory, in other words, cannot be deferred to the future; it can only be decided now — *daily* (v. 23) — by "rejoicing to be counted worthy to suffer disgrace for the name of Jesus" (Acts 5:41; cf. 2 Tim 1:8, 12; 1 Pet 4:16).

Jesus gives three statements in defense of discipleship defined as denial of self, taking up the cross daily, and following him (v. 23). In v. 27 he summarizes the hard core of his teaching on discipleship with a declaration of his personal authority, "Truly, I tell you." The OT prophets customarily prefaced their sayings with "Thus says the Lord" as a guarantee of Yahweh's authority. Jesus assumes that authority *himself,* earnestly pronouncing, "I tell you the truth, some who are standing here will not taste of death before they see the kingdom of God." The very difficulty of this saying argues for its authenticity, for the early church would scarcely have attributed what appeared to be an unfulfilled prophecy to Jesus. This saying is often combined with sayings of similar effect in the NT[56] that are commonly understood to predict the return of Christ (Parousia) during the lifetime of Jesus' contemporaries.[57] Since Jesus did not physically return during their lifetimes, some scholars conclude that Jesus was in error regarding the expectation of the imminence of the Parousia. We cannot here examine all that Jesus (and the early church) believed and taught about eschatology, but a substantial argument can be made that Jesus, and certainly Mark (9:1) and Luke (v. 27), intended the coming of the kingdom of God to refer not to the Parousia but to the resurrection.[58] The placement of this logion in all three Synoptics between Jesus' teaching on discipleship and the transfiguration (v. 27; Matt 16:28; Mark 9:1) relates it to suffering and exaltation, both of which are more analogous to Jesus' death and resurrection than to his second coming. This interpretation claims a long history of support that goes back to many Fathers in the early church. Like-

---

56. 13:26; 1 Thess 4:15–5:3; 1 Cor 15:51; 16:22; Phil 4:5.

57. See the discussion in T. W. Manson, *The Teaching of Jesus: Studies in Its Form and Content* (Cambridge: University Press, 1963), 277-84. Manson reviews various interpretations of this saying, e.g., that it refers to the transfiguration or to the fall of Jerusalem or to the coming of the Holy Spirit at Pentecost. He rejects these possibilities, however, concluding that "Jesus expected the consummation of the Kingdom to take place at some time in the immediate future, and that this expectation was not realized" (p. 282). The various options open to interpreters of v. 27 are concisely summarized by Plummer, *Luke,* 249-50; and Bock, *Luke 1:1–9:50,* 858-59.

58. Some scholars (e.g., Plummer, *Luke,* 249-50; Geldenhuys, *Luke,* 277) argue that v. 27 must refer to the fall of Jerusalem rather than to the resurrection, since all Jesus' hearers would presumably still be alive at his resurrection, but some would die by 70, when Jerusalem fell to the Romans. The minor merits of this argument cannot compensate for its major weakness, that the fall of Jerusalem — to which there is not one unambiguous reference in the NT — is never asserted in early Christianity as the advent of the kingdom of God.

wise, the transfiguration that immediately follows this logion is a prolepsis of the resurrection.[59]

Luke concluded Peter's confession of Jesus with the phrase "the Messiah of God" (v. 20), and he concludes Jesus' confession about discipleship with the phrase "the kingdom of God" (v. 27). In so doing, Luke unites Christology and discipleship in a unique and symbiotic relationship. Proper confession of Jesus involves a new understanding of discipleship. When believers confess who Jesus is, they also and inevitably confess what they must become. But equally true, when believers follow Jesus in costly discipleship, they see Jesus as he truly is. Antipas hoped "to see" Jesus (9:9; 23:8), but apart from trusting and following Jesus, he could not "see" him. Those who confess Jesus as "the Messiah of God" and deny themselves, take up the cross daily, and follow him will see both Jesus and the kingdom he inaugurates.

JESUS: THE HUMAN TABERNACLE OF GOD (9:28-36)

The transfiguration of Jesus is a unique event with no analogy in the Bible, or in extrabiblical literature from the Apocrypha, Pseudepigrapha, rabbinic literature, Qumran, Nag Hammadi, or in Hellenistic literature as a whole. All three Synoptics link the transfiguration to Peter's confession, Matt 17:1 and Mark 9:2 by an interval of "six days," and Luke by an interval of "about eight days." The number eight normally carries no symbolic import in Judaism.[60] "Eight" is an important number in Luke,[61] however, and the use of "about" (Gk. *hōsei*) for such a low number seems intentionally symbolic.[62] Jewish males were circumcised on the eighth day of life — a point that Luke emphasizes in the cases of John and Jesus (1:59; 2:21; also Phil 3:5). Torah also required an eight-day waiting period before a cleansed leper could sacrifice the appropriate offering in the temple (Lev 14:10; *m. Neg.* 14:7). "Eight days" thus demarcated two important cultic time frames in Judaism. The interval of "eight days" of v. 28 appears to identify the transfiguration as the divine complement to the all-important preceding messianic revelation (vv. 18-27) — the significance of which Luke announces by setting it in the context of prayer. "Eight" also figures prominently in the dimensions of the restored

59. So too the Nag Hammadi tractate *Treat. Res.* 48.9-10, which correlates the transfiguration with the resurrection.

60. *Enc. Jud.* 12:1258.

61. Luke favors the number eight, either alone (1:59; 2:21; 9:28; Acts 7:8; 9:33) or in combination with ten (eighteen: 13:4, 11, 16; Acts 25:6) or in multiples of ten (eighty: 2:37; 16:7).

62. The similar grammatical reference in Greek to "about twelve men" (Acts 19:7) alludes to the Ephesian converts in apostolic nomenclature.

temple in Ezek 40. The image of the restored temple is significant in the transfiguration narrative, for it complements the tabernacle motif of vv. 34-35, in which the divine overshadowing designates Jesus and the disciples as the living "tabernacle" (Exod 40:34-35), the dwelling of God with humanity (John 1:14).

28-31   Vv. 28-29 are similar to the introduction of the transfiguration in Matt 17:1-2 and Mark 9:2-3, but in Luke they are seasoned with six Hebraisms, suggesting influence from the Hebrew Gospel.[63] Taking his inner circle of disciples, Peter, John, and James (see at 8:51, n. 171), Jesus "went up onto a mountain to pray" (v. 28). The frequent prayers of Jesus in the Third Gospel introduce new stages of God's unfolding salvific plan.[64] The reference to prayer (twice, vv. 28-29) on a mountain thus prepares readers for a divine initiative. Mountains figure prominently in Jesus' ministry: on mountains he prays (v. 28; 6:12; 22:39; Mark 6:46; John 6:15), preaches (Mark 3:13; Matt 5:1), performs miracles (Matt 15:29-30; John 6:2-3), is tempted ([4:5]; Matt 4:8), calls his disciples (6:12-13; Mark 3:13), sends them into mission (Matt 28:16), and accomplishes his passion (Mark 11:1; 14:32; 15:22). Of the various references to mountains in Scripture, however, the Mount of Transfiguration, along with Mount Sinai, becomes a site par excellence of divine revelation.[65] From earliest times the Mount of Transfiguration was identified as Mount Tabor, the dome-shaped mountain in the Esdraelon plain that separated Galilee and Samaria.[66] It is more probable, however, that the Mount of Transfiguration was Mount Hermon, which dominates the region of Caesarea Philippi where, according to Matt 16:13 and Mark 8:27, Peter's confession occurred.[67] Mount Tabor is a great distance to the south from that region, and it is not a particularly "high mountain" (Matt 17:1; Mark 9:2). Tabor, moreover, offered no solitude ("they

---

63. See Edwards, *Hebrew Gospel*, 308. V. 28, along with 5:12, 17; 8:22; 9:18; and 20:1, is one of six hyper-Semitic introductions to pericopes that Luke shares with Mark (ibid., 145).

64. 3:21; 5:16; 6:12; 9:18, 28, 29; 11:1; 22:40, 41, 44. On prayers, see at 3:21-22, n. 63, and at 9:18.

65. Gen 22:2; Exod 24:15; Deut 34:1; 1 Kgs 18:20; 19:11; Ezek 40:2; Matt 5:1; 14:23; 28:16; Mark 6:46; John 4:20; 6:3, 15; Acts 1:12; Rev 14:1; 21:10. See H. Riesenfeld, *Jésus transfiguré* (ASNU 16; Copenhagen: Munksgaard, 1947), 243-45.

66. The source of this identification, which was followed by Eusebius, Cyril, and Jerome, seems to have been a quotation from the Hebrew Gospel preserved by Origen, "Just now my mother, the Holy Spirit, took me by a lock of hair and lifted me up to great Mount Tabor" (*Comm. Jo.* 2.12.87). It is not clear, however, whether Origen understands the quotation to refer to the transfiguration or the temptation of Jesus. See the discussion in Edwards, *Hebrew Gospel*, 56-59.

67. The Hebrew radicals of Hermon, *hrm*, meaning "sacred" or "holy," may find an echo in the reference to the Mount of Transfiguration as "the sacred mountain" in 2 Pet 1:18. For arguments favoring Mount Hermon as the site of the transfiguration, see A. M. Ramsay, *The Glory of God and the Transfiguration of Christ* (London: Longmans, Green, 1949), 113.

were all alone," Matt 17:1; Mark 9:2), since in Jesus' day its summit was inhabited and surrounded by a wall.[68]

"As [Jesus] was praying, the appearance of his face changed, and his clothes became as bright as a flash of lightening" (v. 29). Luke's language refers to changes in Jesus' appearance, not in his nature. The impression left is that, for the first time in Jesus' ministry, his brilliant face and garments now accord with his divine nature.[69] The word "appearance" (Gk. *eidos*), which is not present in either Matt or Mark, is important. This is the same word that appears in the description of the tabernacle in Exod 26:30 (LXX), "Set up the tabernacle according to the plan [Gk. *eidos*] shown to you on the mountain."[70] *Eidos* is a rare word in the NT, occurring only five times, but again in Luke at 3:22 at the baptism of Jesus. *Eidos* connects the transfiguration with both the baptism and the tabernacle, which are the two referents that guide a proper understanding of Luke's transfiguration narrative.

In describing Moses and Elijah "talking with Jesus" (vv. 30-31), Luke presents them holding an audience with Jesus as a superior, bearing witness to him. Judaism is not elsewhere familiar with two precursors of the Messiah, nor do Moses and Elijah ever appear together as precursors of the end time.[71] Only once again in the NT do the two appear together (Rev 11:3-11), in an altogether different context. Their presence in the transfiguration is thus not explainable on the basis of pre-Christian Jewish tradition. It is probably too limited to identify Moses strictly with the law and Elijah with the prophets, for each figure was

---

68. Josephus, *Ant.* 13.396. Josephus himself erected a fortress on the site to withstand the siege of Vespasian in the war of A.D. 66-70. Like all cities, Tabor fell to the Roman onslaught (Josephus, *J.W.* 4.54-61). See G. Dalman, *Sacred Sites and Ways* (trans. P. Levertoff; London: SPCK, 1935), 188-89.

69. Brilliant garments often signify heavenly beings in Scripture: Dan 10:5; Matt 28:3; Mark 16:5; John 20:12; Acts 1:10; Rev 3:4; 4:4; 6:11; 7:9, 13; 14:14; 19:14.

70. *Eidos* translates Heb. *mishpat*, which means the entire plan of the temple and everything belonging to it (*HALOT* 1:651-52). Of fifty-two occurrences of *eidos* in the LXX, this is the only place it translates Heb. *mishpat*.

71. See Str-B 1:756; J. Jeremias, *Ēlias*, TDNT 2:938-39; *Mōysēs*, TDNT 4:856-57. Other figures emerge from apocalyptic literature as precursors of the messianic age: Ezra (*4 Ezra* 14:9), Baruch (*2 Bar.* 76:2), Jeremiah (*2 Macc* 2:1), Enoch, Noah, Shem, Abraham, Isaac, and Jacob (*T. Benj.* 10:5-6), and Enoch (*2 Esd* 6:25). We have earlier noted that Elijah appears in the OT not as a forerunner of the Messiah but of the final Day of the Lord. Moses likewise plays only a peripheral role eschatologically in later Judaism. Although a Sifre on Deut 34:5 reads that "Moses did not die, rather he dwells and serves above," the majority tradition in Judaism believed that Moses died like other mortals. He was esteemed as lawgiver and deliverer of Israel, but seldom as an eschatological precursor. Josephus, *Ant.* 4.323-26, also believed that Moses died, but he includes an intriguing legend with some similarities to the transfiguration story: "As Moses dismissed Eleazar and Joshua, and yet while he conversed with them, suddenly a cloud came to stand over him and he disappeared into a certain valley."

associated with both the law and the prophets. According to Deut 18:15, 18 (a passage recalled in v. 35), Moses is considered the prototype of the eschatological Prophet. Moses is also regarded as the representative figure of the prophetic tradition in Judaism. Likewise, Elijah was associated with Mount Sinai (1 Kgs 19:1-18), where he too received the word of God, though in different fashion from Moses. In only one passage do Elijah and Moses appear together before the Day of Yahweh. In Mal 4:4-6 Israel is commanded to remember the "instruction" (Heb. *torah*) of God's servant Moses. Immediately following, Elijah is introduced as the prophet who turns the hearts of people to repentance on the Day of Yahweh. The appearance of Moses and Elijah in the transfiguration narrative likely recalls this passage and their prophetic roles as joint preparers of the final Prophet to come (so Deut 18:15, 18 [see also 4Q175, lines 5-8], Mal 4:5-6). Moses and Elijah should thus be understood as the chief representatives of the prophetic tradition, in which capacity the early church believed they would anticipate Jesus, for "all the prophets testify to [Jesus]" (Acts 10:43).

Luke highlights the significance of Moses in v. 31, however, where, alone of the Gospels, he identifies the subject of the celestial conversation: "They spoke about [Jesus'] exodus which he was about to bring to fulfillment in Jerusalem." There are only three references to the **exodus** in the NT: 9:31; Heb 11:22; 2 Pet 1:15. The reference in Hebrews refers to the exodus of Israel from Egypt, and the other two to human deaths. V. 31 emphasizes Jesus' fulfillment of the history of salvation in his death in Jerusalem. The announcement of Jesus' "exodus" by Moses and Elijah signals its divine determination. The allusion to the exodus that "[Jesus] was about to bring to fulfillment in Jerusalem" redirects attention from the Galilean ministry to the passion in Jerusalem (v. 22). The exodus from Egypt, the foundational episode of redemption and formation of Israel into a people and nation, becomes a prefigurement of Jesus' passion, through which he redeems people from the power of sin and forms them into the church.

32-34 Moses and Elijah reinforce the preeminent Lukan theme that Jesus is not a "walk-on" in the divine economy, but the fulfillment of God's historical purpose for Israel and, through Israel, for the world. The witness of Moses and Elijah does not rival Jesus but points to him and culminates in him. Their word and work are consummately fulfilled in Jesus (Rom 10:4; 2 Cor 1:20). Moses and Elijah depart from Jesus, leaving him alone with Peter and the disciples, who, according to the Greek, were "burdened with sleep" (v. 32). The reference to sleep leads some commentators to surmise that the transfiguration took place at night.[72] More probably the reference links the transfiguration

---

72. A number of scholars (Plummer, Lagrange, Fitzmyer, Wolter, Klein) understand the reference to drowsiness in v. 32 — the only such reference in the Synoptic accounts — to imply a nocturnal transfiguration. Reference to "the next day, when they came down from

with Jesus' prayer on the Mount of Olives (22:39-46), which are the only two events in the Third Gospel where Jesus receives heavenly visitants, and where after both visitations the disciples are found sleeping. Exactly what we are to conclude from the disciples' battle with drowsiness, Luke does not say. What is clear is that in both events the disciples appear weak and insensate in the presence of the heavenly visitants, and thus they do not contribute to the definition or fulfillment of Jesus' mission that occurs in either the transfiguration or the prayer on the Mount of Olives.

The attending disciples nevertheless "saw his glory and the two men standing with him" (v. 32). Peter suggests erecting "three shelters" for Jesus, Moses, and Elijah (v. 33). This suggestion is commonly derided and dismissed as a foot-in-mouth comment of a bumbling fisherman.[73] This is seriously mistaken. The word for "shelters" (v. 33; Gk. *skēnē*) is the word for "tabernacle" in the LXX. Having witnessed Jesus' glory (vv. [29], 31, 32) and being reminded of the glory that suffused the tabernacle at its completion by Moses (Exod 40:34-35), Peter desires, appropriately, to commemorate the event in a tabernacle. All Judaism held onto the hope that God would once again tabernacle with his people as in the exodus. "Make a right confession to the Lord and bless the King of the ages, so that once again his dwelling [Gk. *skēnē*] may be erected with you in joy (Tob. 13:10; likewise Zech 14:16-19). Josephus records the hope of a new and literal tabernacle in the wilderness (*Ant.* 20.167; *J.W.* 2.259). The editorial comment in v. 33, "He did not know what he was saying," does not refute this understanding. Luke does not say Peter "did not know *what to say,*" but he "did not know *what he was saying.*" Luke's wording implies that the full import of Peter's comment escaped him — a very human experience, indeed. Peter's inclination to build tabernacles in consequence of the transfiguration may be no less insightful than his confession of Jesus as "God's Messiah" (v. 20).

As Peter was still speaking, "a cloud appeared and covered them" (v. 34). The cloud, as Origen correctly perceived, was God's provision of the "tents"

---

the mountain" (9:37) is likewise understood as the morning following the (nocturnal) transfiguration. Despite the weight of scholarly opinion in favor of this interpretation, it is not an assured conclusion. For one, Jews reckoned the beginning of a new day from sunset rather than sunrise; thus, dawn did not signify "the next day" but the continuation of the day begun at the previous sunset. Moreover, Luke, who frequently describes nocturnal activity (e.g., 2:8; 5:5; Acts 9:24; 27:27), including nocturnal visions (Acts 16:9; 18:9), makes no explicit reference to night in the transfiguration narrative. Mountaineers, in particular, will find the nocturnal hypothesis somewhat fanciful, for ascending and descending a mountain as high and rugged as Mount Hermon is much more difficult and dangerous in the dark than in daylight.

73. *Apoc. Pet.* 16 likewise misunderstands Peter's comment: "And [Jesus] said to me [Peter] in wrath, 'Satan makes war against you, and has veiled your understanding, and the good things of this world conquer you.'"

Peter had proposed.[74] Before Peter's very eyes God's dwelling with humanity is present, for Jesus is the new tabernacle of God. The word "covered" (v. 34; Gk. *episkiazein;* see at 1:35) is of critical importance for Luke's understanding of the transfiguration. The cloud first "overshadowed" (Gk. *episkiazein*) a *place* — the tabernacle — with God's presence in the wilderness (LXX Exod 40:35); it then overshadowed a *person* — Mary — with God's presence at the incarnation (1:35); now it overshadows *"them"* — Jesus and the disciples — with God's power and authority (v. 34). Jesus is the tabernacle of God, the incarnation of God's glory. The disciples' fear of entering into the cloud of glory (v. 34) repeats the fear of Moses at the completion of the tabernacle: "Moses could not enter the tent of meeting because the cloud has settled on it, and the glory of the Lord filled the tabernacle" (Exod 40:35). The revelation of Jesus' divine nature before the disciples attests that "the dwelling place of God is with men, and he will live with them" (Rev 21:3).

Luke moors his transfiguration narrative repeatedly and firmly to tabernacle imagery to signify that the glory of God that filled the tabernacle (Exod 40:34-35) and temple (1 Kgs 8:10-11) prefigures and is fulfilled by the glory of God in Jesus' transfiguration. Thus, the number "eight" (v. 28) reflects the measurements of the restored temple in Ezek 40 (vv. 9, 31, 34, 37); the "appearance" (v. 29; Gk. *eidos*) of Jesus transfigured recalls the appearance (Gk. *eidos*) of the tabernacle in Exodus 26:30; the "glory" ([29], 31, 32) on the mountain recalls the glory of the tabernacle (Exod 40:34-35); the "tabernacles" (v. 33; Gk. *skēnē*) suggested by Peter reflect the tabernacle of Moses; and the "cloud" (vv. 34-35) that descends on Jesus recalls the cloud of God's glory that descended on and inaugurated the tabernacle in the wilderness (Exod. 40:34). Luke's transfiguration narrative is a visual depiction of John 1:14, "The Word became flesh and lived [Gk. *skēnoun,* lit. 'tabernacled') for a while among us."

35-36   This symbolism is verbalized climactically in the heavenly voice, "This is my Son, whom I have chosen. Listen to Him!" (v. 35). This pronouncement recalls the declaration of Jesus as Son of God at the baptism and carries the full content of meaning discussed at 3:21-22. Three aspects are unique to the declaration at the transfiguration, however, that were not present at the baptism. First, at the baptism the declaration was directed to Jesus ("You are my Son") as a confirmation of his divine sonship, whereas here the voice "from the cloud" (= God) reveals his sonship to the *disciples* ("*This* is my Son"). Second, Jesus is designated the "chosen" Son (v. 35) rather than the "beloved" Son, as he was at his baptism (3:22).[75] The word for "chosen" Gk. *eklegesthai*),

---

74. Origen, *Fr. Luc.* 146 (Luke 9:31).

75. The original reading is doubtless "chosen" (Gk. *eklelegmenos*), which here carries "a quasi-technical sense." Substitute adjectives in the manuscript tradition (Gk. *eklektos* or *agapētos*) are the result of scribal assimilation to more familiar expressions (Metzger, *TCGNT,* 124).

used with reference to the divine appointment of the twelve apostles (6:13), here in the Greek perfect form, signifies that Jesus has been divinely chosen beforehand as Messiah of God (v. 20; 23:35) to fulfill the office of the chosen Servant of the Lord (Isa 42:1). Finally, the command *"listen to him"* (v. 35; Gk. *autou akouete*) recalls Deut 18:15, "The Lord your God will raise up for you a prophet like me. . . . You must listen to him [Gk. *autou akouesthe*]." The divine declaration thus ratifies the earlier word of Jesus in response to Peter's confession that the Messiah — and the disciples in following the Messiah — must suffer (vv. 20, 22).[76] Christology leads to discipleship, and discipleship flows from Christology. "Listen to him" not only designates Jesus as the prophet who would follow Moses, but also as the Son who must suffer, and who calls disciples to share his suffering.[77] The disciples have not come — indeed they *cannot* come — to the recognition of Jesus as God's chosen Messiah on their own (so Matt 16:17; 2 Pet 1:17-18). Only the Father can impart the mystery of Jesus' divine sonship to believers.

The transfiguration, like all numinous experiences with God, ends in solitude and silence. The word of God is no longer heard, but the Son of God is still standing with the disciples. Elijah and Moses, the greatest figures of the OT, have vanished to glory. Jesus has not vanished with them but remains to fulfill his mission in Jerusalem (v. 31).[78] What the disciples have experienced, "they kept to themselves and did not tell anyone at that time what they had seen" (v. 36). They will need a new "tongue" — which also must be both revealed and imparted by God at Pentecost (Acts 2:1-41) — to proclaim the meaning of this event.

AN EPILEPTIC BOY AND THE INADEQUACY OF THE DISCIPLES (9:37-43A)

In 9:1-50 Jesus equips and includes the Twelve in his mission. The unit began with Jesus endowing them with power and authority over demons and diseases. These divine endowments do not magically transform the Twelve into supermen or saints, for in this unit they are made aware of their inabilities and even impotence before some powers: in 9:43-45 they are ignorant of the divine

---

76. By contrast, the Nag Hammadi tractate *Ep. Pet. Phil.* 134.15-19 applies the injunction "Listen to him" to Jesus' eternal existence, not to the necessity of the cross.

77. The necessity of the disciples' suffering is omitted in *Gos. Phil.* 58, where the disciples themselves are elevated along with Jesus.

78. In *Apoc. Pet.* 15-17 the transfiguration is depicted as a return to Eden, at the end of which — in stark contrast to the canonical accounts — Jesus ascends with Moses and Elijah into the second heaven!

plan, in 9:46-50 they contend and conflict with one another, and in 9:51-56 they entertain calling down divine vengeance on an unresponsive Samaritan village.[79] The disciples are making the same journey to Jerusalem with Jesus, but they experience it differently from Jesus. His journey is one of fulfilling who he *is* as Messiah (24:26, 46), whereas their journey is one of *becoming* faithful witnesses of all they have seen and heard (24:48; Acts 1:8; 5:28, 32; 8:1; 10:39).

37-40   Luke's account of the healing of the boy possessed by an "unclean spirit" is half the length of the parallel account in Mark 9:14-29. The dramatic dialogue between Jesus and the boy's father, and the father's existential struggle for faith in Mark 9:21-24, are omitted by Luke in favor of an abridged account focusing on Jesus and the disciples. The day following the transfiguration a large crowd gathers around Jesus (v. 37).[80] A man from the crowd calls to Jesus in desperation, "Teacher, I beg you to look at my son, for he is my only child" (v. 38).[81] This is the third and final reference to an "only child" (Gk. *monogenēs*) in Luke. Unlike the uses of *monogenēs* in John with reference to the saving incarnation of God (1:14, 18; 3:16, 18; 1 John 4:9; also Heb 11:17?), in Luke the term carries a natural biological meaning[82] — and with it the pathos of a parent pleading for the life of an only child. The father asks Jesus not to heal his son, but simply to "look" upon him, trusting that what he sees will move him to greater compassion than words alone could evoke. It is a profound request, one better made of God than of an ordinary rabbi.[83] The man's son is not simply ill, he is assaulted. "A spirit seizes him" (v. 39), exclaims the father, a spirit that is described as a "demon" and "unclean [evil] spirit" (v. 42). The effects of the seizures — sudden convulsions, foaming at the mouth, followed by death-like torpor — are classic symptoms of tonic-clonic (grand mal) seizures, identified as epilepsy in Matt 17:15.[84] Luke's terminology is not as medically precise as Matt's, although his description of the boy's symptoms and the father's distress is more complete, graphic, and empathetic than either Matt 17:15-16 or Mark 9:18.[85] Why Luke, ostensibly a

---

79. Several of these points are noted by Schweizer, *Lukas,* 106.

80. On the possibility that "the next day" (v. 37) implies a nocturnal transfiguration, see at 9:32, n. 72.

81. For a similar situation, see 8:41-42.

82. Jeremias, *Sprache des Lukasevangeliums,* 157.

83. Rightly, Wolter, *Lukasevangelium,* 357.

84. Matt 17:15 identifies the boy's affliction as epilepsy, but in vv. 18-19 the affliction is ascribed to a *daimonion* ("demon"). In this instance Matt thus ascribes epileptic symptoms to demonic possession.

85. A long account of a demon-possessed boy in Philostratus's *Vita Apol.* 3.38 provides an instructive contrast to 9:37-43a, and particularly to Mark 9:14-29. In the Philostratus account, attention is devoted primarily to the demon, and to the child only incidentally. A complete history of the demon and the circumstances contributing to its habitation of the

physician, attributes the malady to a "spirit" rather than to epilepsy, which was widely diagnosed in the ancient world,[86] is difficult to say. Perhaps, as suggested below, he desires to emphasize Jesus' power over hostile spiritual powers than simply over physical illness. Even the disciples are powerless in the face of the child's condition.[87] The father, fortunately, does not rest his case with the disciples but with Jesus himself, in whom there is hope when all human hopes are exhausted.

41-43a   At the father's report, Jesus exclaims, "You unbelieving and perverse generation, how long shall I stay with you and put up with you?" (v. 41). Though the disciples are unable to heal the boy, Jesus does not chastise them. Inability and inadequacy are limitations, not faults. In contrast, disbelief (12:46) and perverse belief (Acts 13:8, 10; 20:30) are willful choices for which people are culpable. The chastising lament in v. 41 closely echoes prophetic grievances against unbelieving Israel (Deut 32:5, 20; Num 14:11; Isa 65:2). Human doubts and disbelief are not the last word, however, nor do they determine Jesus' willingness or ability to act. Jesus calls for the child (v. 41). As the boy is brought, his plight is manifested before Jesus' eyes: "the demon threw him to the ground in a convulsion" (v. 42). The word for "threw" (Gk. *hrēgnynai*) is used of boxers or wrestlers dashing an opponent to the ground.[88] Luke's description differentiates between cause and effect: the latter may be symptomatic of epilepsy, but the symptoms are engineered by a malevolent and demonic force. Here as elsewhere in Luke, demon possession is portrayed more in terms of violence than of fear and horror — throwing a victim to the ground (4:33-35), producing deafness (11:14), afflictions of wretchedness and destruction (8:26-38). The present episode testifies to the mission of Jesus, first manifested in his confrontation with the devil in the wilderness (4:1-13), to confront and to defeat powers of evil. This may be the reason why Luke refers to the malady in terms of spiritual rather than medical causes. Jesus is

---

child is provided, but the child is of interest only as host of the demon. Indeed, the child is not even present, for Apollonius exorcises the demon by a letter! Luke's story, by contrast, is ambiguous about the demon but focused on the pathos of the boy and father, and the disciples. Philostratus did not publish his work until the early part of the third c., so the Gospel accounts cannot have been influenced by him.

86. On knowledge and diagnosis of epilepsy in the ancient world, see Wolter, *Lukasevangelium*, 357.

87. The reference to the disciples' inability to heal the possessed boy argues in favor of the historicity of the account, for the church is unlikely to have invented a story that cast the apostles in a negative light. For two studies that defend the essential historicity of the account, see P. Achtemeier, "Miracles and the Historical Jesus," *CBQ* 37 (1975): 471-91; and G. Sterling, "Jesus as Exorcist: An Analysis of Matthew 17:14-20; Mark 9:14-29; Luke 9:37-43a," *CBQ* 55 (1993): 467-93.

88. Plummer, *Luke*, 255.

the Stronger One who vanquishes the satanic strong man, in proof that "the kingdom of God has come upon you" (11:20-22).

The initial result of Jesus' work, however, is not peace but conflict, as noted by Eduard Schweizer: "This indicates how the presence of God can produce storm and stress before anything constructive is accomplished."[89] The story concludes with three decisive acts: Jesus "rebuked the evil spirit," "healed the boy," and "gave him back to his father" (v. 42). Divine power leads to physical healing, and physical healing leads to the restoration of relationships. In this instance, Jesus again reveals himself to be a restorer of families, giving the boy back to his father as he earlier gave a boy back to his mother (7:15). Luke concludes that the crowd was "amazed at the greatness of God" (v. 43a). The word for "greatness" (Gk. *megaleiotēs*) means the quality of being unsurpassed. 2 Pet 1:16 uses *megaleiotēs* of the "majesty" that the three elite disciples witnessed atop the Mount of Transfiguration; Luke's use of the word here suggests that, in the exorcism and healing of the boy, the same majesty is displayed for all to see at the foot of the mountain.

THE SECOND PASSION PREDICTION AND THE
IGNORANCE OF THE DISCIPLES (9:43B-45)

As "everyone was marveling at all that Jesus did" (v. 43a), Jesus recalls his impending passion in Jerusalem. The paradox between the crowd basking in the sunlight of Jesus' majesty and Jesus' stormy announcement of his impending suffering is abrasive, reminding disciples and readers alike that authentic witness to the word of God and discipleship with Christ is a *theologia crucis* before it is a *theologia gloriae*. Jesus' prediction is prefaced with an unambiguous Hebraism, "Put these words in your ears!" (v. 44; NIV "Listen carefully"). Similar Hebraisms occur in 1:66, 21:14, and Acts 19:21, though here the "you" is emphatic in Greek: "*You* must put these words in your ears!" The lesson of sacrifice and suffering is one that Jesus must teach disciples explicitly and repeatedly. Luke's second prediction of Jesus' death is the most truncated passion prediction in all the Synoptics. "The Son of Man is going to be delivered over to human hands" (v. 44). Unlike Mark 9:31 and Matt 17:22-23, Luke's second prediction makes no mention of Jesus' death or resurrection after three days. "Son of Man" (see excursus at 5:26) and "hands of men" (NIV "human hands") form a play on the Greek word *(anthrōpos),* which would have been more apparent in the Semitic original: "The Son of Man [Heb. *ben ha-adam*] is going

89. *The Good News according to Mark* (trans. D. Madvig; Atlanta: John Knox Press, 1970), 188.

to be delivered into the hands of the sons of men [Heb. *bene adam*]." The man who lives among men will be rejected by them. The first passion prediction attributes Jesus' suffering to Jewish enmity (9:22), but the second attributes it to all humanity. The essential opposition to the work of God, and especially to the incarnation, is not an ethnic condition but a *human* condition — the power of sin in the world and in every human heart.

God is also involved in a way not apparent in the first prediction. The Greek word for "delivered over" can also mean "handed over." The passive voice of the verb is a reference to God without using God's name (for fear of defiling it), i.e., God is handing over his Son to humanity. The verse reflects the language of the Servant of Yahweh in Isa 53:6, 12 (LXX) and hints that Jesus will die for the sins of others. "It is just this meaning that that Christian proclamation finds in Christ's death: His incomprehensible fate is for the benefit of the very ones at whose hands he died, and that benefit is in accordance with God's salvific will for humankind."[90] But here as elsewhere in Scripture, God's will does not absolve humanity of its responsibility. "The Son of Man will go as it has been decreed. But woe to that man who betrays him!" (22:22).

That Luke receives the passion prediction of v. 44 from Mark is suggested by the identical wording of the beginning of v. 45, "But they did not understand."[91] Luke, however, describes the disciples' ignorance more fully and explicitly than does Mark or Matt. "They did not understand . . . it was hidden from them . . . they did not grasp it" (v. 45). Especially the second verb (Gk. *parakalyptein*), meaning "hidden, concealed, veiled," implies ignorance — evidently divinely ordained ignorance — rather than willful resistance.[92] The disciples' ignorance is nevertheless ironic, for the Twelve have had greater access and opportunity to know Jesus, and yet they remain unknowing. In the previous narrative we saw that the call and empowerment to follow Jesus do not make disciples omnipotent; in this narrative the call and empowerment do not make them omniscient. The experience of discipleship, even *apostle*ship, is fraught with human inability and ignorance. The emphasis on ignorance in v. 45 thus does not stress culpability on the part of the disciples. Rather, it is the necessary will of God until the final purpose of the Son of Man is achieved on the cross and empty tomb. The fear of the disciples to ask Jesus about the meaning of the prediction is not the will of God, however, but simply human frailty. The same word for "fear" (Gk. *phobeisthai*) describes the fear of the disciples to enter the cloud of God's presence after the transfiguration (9:34).

90. P. Achtemeier, "Mark 9:30-37," *Int* 30 (1976): 180.

91. The Greek wording of v. 45 and Mark 9:32 is identical: *hoi de ēgnooun to rēma (touto)*.

92. The word for "not understanding" (Gk. *agnoein*) is also used in Acts 17:23 of non-culpable ignorance.

Here, like there, it refers to reluctance — even among the chosen and empowered Twelve — to "come to Jesus" (6:47).

TENSION AND CONTENTION
AMONG THE DISCIPLES (9:46-50)

46-48   Luke's unit on the disciples (9:1-50), which began with Jesus' conferral on the Twelve of authority and power to heal infirmities and exorcise demons, ends with contention among them. Mark 9:33-35 introduces this episode with greater detail and local color, but Luke limits the focus to a **quarrel** among the disciples, which he mentions twice (vv. 46, 47). The Greek word *dialogismos* (NIV "argument" [v. 46]; "thinking" [v. 47]) denotes the process of reasoning, weighing thoughts, and pondering, with an inclination toward doubts and even disputes. Luke frequently employs this term in combination with "the heart" to describe inner reservations or resistance to the word of God. This resistance, ironically, is not a characteristic of the wicked but of the righteous — of Mary, righteous Jews, scribes and Pharisees, and Jesus' own disciples.[93]

The present quarrel is an "inner contention" (v. 47; Gk. lit. "a quarrel in their hearts") pertaining to "who of them might be the greatest" (v. 46). Bonhoeffer describes this "struggle of the natural man for self-justification . . . comparing oneself with others and condemning and judging them" as a life-and-death contest that can destroy a fellowship.[94] Jesus' response reveals the depths of his wisdom and humility. Rather than *speaking* the truth — a truth that in this instance would likely be tolerated but dismissed as a moralism — Jesus *enacts* the truth. He "took a little child and had him stand beside him. Then he said to them, 'Whoever welcomes this little child in my name welcomes me; and whoever welcomes me welcomes the one who sent me. For whoever is least among you all is the greatest'" (vv. 47-48). We are mistaken if we imagine that Greek and Jewish societies extolled the virtues of childhood as is generally true in modern Western society. Societies with high infant mortality rates and high demand for human labor are not sentimental about infants and youth. Until children could contribute to the labor force, they simply had "not arrived."[95] They were, quite literally, "the least among you"

---

93. Verb: 1:29; 3:15; 5:21-22; 12:17; 20:14; noun: 2:35; 5:22; 6:8; 9:46-47; 24:38.

94. D. Bonhoeffer, *Life Together* (trans. J. Doberstein; New York: Harper & Brothers, 1954), 90-91.

95. The negligible value of children is suggested by a comment of R. Dosa ben Harkinas in the Mishnah: "Morning sleep and midday wine and children's talk and sitting in the meetinghouses of ignorant people put a man out of the world" (*m. 'Abot.* 3:11). Girls under the age of twelve could be sold as slaves by their fathers (*m. Ket.* 3:8).

(v. 48). Nor does Jesus reference children, as is often supposed, as a model of humility that disciples should emulate. Rather, the child is an example of the "little" and insignificant ones whom followers of Jesus are *to receive*. Disciples are thus not to be like children, but rather like Jesus, who embraces children — and others like them.[96] God often appears in the world in the small, powerless, and insignificant, and the response of Christians to such — the hungry, thirsty, lonely, naked, sick, and imprisoned — is their response to God. "Whatever you did for one of the least of these brothers of mine, you did for me" (Matt 25:40). The simplest act of kindness begins a chain reaction that reaches heaven itself, for whatever is done to the little and least is done to Jesus, and whatever is done to Jesus is done to God!

49-50 The exclusiveness of the disciples is not limited to the apostolic fellowship. Speaking for all Twelve, John, who nowhere else in the gospel tradition appears solo, addresses Jesus: "Master [see at 5:5], we were hindering [someone from driving out demons in your name] because he does not follow with us" (v. 49).[97] With the exception of Peter, it is unusual for an apostle to be singled out from among the Twelve; John's name in association with this memorable remark likely assures the historicity of this account. The imperfect tense of "hindering" (Gk. *ekōlyomen*) implies that John's response was habitual in such instances.[98] We should expect John to say, "because he does not follow *you*." It seems rather presumptuous for John, or any of the Twelve at this point in their relationship with Jesus, to pose as model disciples and rebuke someone "because he does not follow with *us*."[99] Being in Jesus' inner circle had at least some deleterious effects on John — as inner circles often do — for his elitist attitude is repeated in yet another context, along with his brother James (9:54; also Mark 10:35). John regards his call as a disciple not as a call to service, but

96. Contrary to *Gos. Thom.* 22, which makes *children* the model of discipleship: "Jesus saw children nursing. He said to his disciples: 'These nursing children are like those who enter the kingdom.' The disciples said to Jesus, 'If we are children, shall we enter the kingdom?'" The *Shepherd of Hermas*, likewise, makes the simplicity of children a moral virtue for disciples (*Mand.* 2.1; *Sim.* 11.29.3).

97. This story does not answer the question, frequently asked, whether morally good people who have not heard of Christ are acceptable to God. The unnamed exorcist was not a stranger to the gospel, after all, but acting "in [Jesus'] name," i.e., in his authority and power. The issue raised in this story is whether there can be true followers of Christ who do not share the experience of the Twelve. Or in a slightly broader context perhaps, how should believers regard those who take up the name and mission of Jesus but belong to other traditions?

98. A number of strong manuscripts read "we hindered" in the past tense, but the imperfect reading claims both the earliest (𝔭⁷⁵) and weightiest manuscripts (ℵ B L Ξ), and should be preferred (Metzger, *TCGNT*, 124).

99. The NIV translation of this verse ("Master, we saw someone driving out demons in your name and we tried to stop him, because he is not one of us") inadequately renders both of the above points.

as an entitlement of privilege and exclusion. His attitude is not only a sharp contrast to the lesson of the previous story about acceptance of "children," but it proscribes the independent exorcist for doing precisely what he and the disciples could not do in 9:40.[100]

What constitutes true membership in the community? The issue is a common one to religious communities, especially in their founding stages. The early Hebrews questioned whether the Spirit of God rested on two men who did not belong to the seventy designated elders of Moses (Num 11:24-30). Early Christian communities debated criteria that would distinguish true from false prophets (1 John 4:2; *Did.* 11:8-12; *Herm. Man.* 11.7-16). The present story indicates that such issues were present in the embryonic apostolic fellowship. Must all disciples belong to the Twelve, or can a genuine follower of Christ exist outside their number? As is true of many religious traditions, so also in this instance, the founder shows himself to be more broad-minded than the sectarian inclinations of his disciples.

Jesus charges the disciple not to proscribe the independent exorcist. The present tense of the Greek imperative *kōlyete* (v. 50; "Do not stop him") implies a general rule: "Don't stop such people." "Whoever is not against you is for you," says Jesus (v. 50). The master is more inclusive than his disciples. Making known the name of Jesus is more important than *who* makes it known (see Phil 1:12-18). The difference between Jesus' tolerant attitude in this saying and his intolerant attitude in the similar saying of 11:23, "Whoever is not with me is against me" (also Matt 12:30; similarly *P.Oxy.* 1224: "He who is not with me is against me, and he who does not gather with me scatters"), may depend on the different pronouns. Here in v. 50 the issue is the relationship of disciples *among themselves;* in 11:23 the issue is the relationship of disciples *with Jesus.* There can be no neutrality with regard to the person of Jesus (so 11:23), but disciples must learn tolerance with those who differ from them (so 9:50). The interplay between Jesus and the disciples in 9:1-50 argues for exactness in the church's Christology and broadness in its ecclesiology.

---

100. R. Gundry, *Mark: A Commentary on His Apology for the Cross* (Grand Rapids: Eerdmans, 1993), 510-11.

CHAPTER NINE

Discipleship and Mission

Luke 9:51–11:13

EXCURSUS: THE MISSION OF JESUS AS THE WAY OF SALVATION

The narrative flow of the Third Gospel is more seamless than that of the other three Gospels, and hence outlines of Luke are less uniform than are those of Matt, Mark, and John. The Third Gospel obviously divides the infancy narrative (2:52) from the appearance of John (3:1). Another divide is signaled in multiple ways at 9:51, with Jesus setting his face to Jerusalem. A geographic shift occurs at 9:51, with Jesus and disciples leaving Galilee and entering Samaria on the way to Jerusalem. A source change also occurs at 9:51, with Luke departing from the Markan narrative and commencing nearly ten chapters of material unique to the Third Gospel. 9:51 also introduces a thematic change from Jesus' itinerant ministry at the Sea of Galilee, particularly on its northwest quadrant, to a singular and unwavering focus on Jerusalem as his messianic destiny. The Nestle-Aland Greek text of Luke indicates the transition at 9:51 with a major narrative break, a transition acknowledged and followed by most modern interpreters and commentators. These reasons justify a major division at 9:51, at which point the central section of the Gospel begins, which I believe concludes at 18:34 (see discussion at 18:31-34).[1]

---

1. A major break at 9:51 is widely acknowledged, but not universally so. Reasons can also be cited in favor of concluding the Galilean ministry at 9:62. The whole of chap. 9 is devoted to Jesus and the Twelve, whereas chap. 10 commences a new unit devoted to Jesus and the seventy (-two) disciples. Likewise, the Elijah-Elisha typology, developed by allusion and citation throughout the Galilean ministry, concludes not at 9:51 but with three final links to Elijah in 9:53-62 (see excursus on Elijah-Elisha typology at 7:15-17). Finally, the earliest interpreters of Luke, as signified in the chapter divisions of Codex Alexandrinus, which were adopted by virtually all subsequent ancient manuscripts, began a new chap. at 10:1 rather than at 9:51 (see J. Edwards, "The Hermeneutical Significance of Chapter Divisions in Ancient Gospel Manuscripts," *NTS* 56 [2010]: 413-26). Similarly, and unlike Nestle-Aland, the UBS Greek text

Schleiermacher christened the central section of Luke "the travel narrative."[2] Although widely accepted by commentators, this designation is not
entirely appropriate, for apart from mention of Jerusalem, the central section
is virtually devoid of geographic references, place-names, and movements of
Jesus and the disciples.[3] "Travel narrative" is more appropriate to the Galilean
ministry in 4:14–9:50, and the approach to Jerusalem in 18:35–19:46, than to the
central section, where a travel itinerary toward Jerusalem is lacking or confusing. If 9:51–18:34 is a "travel narrative," it is oddly circuitous,[4] for Luke reports
Jesus entering a Samaritan village in 9:52, yet in 10:13-15 he is still in northern
Galilee, so too evidently in 13:31-33.[5] Only as late as 17:11 does Jesus quit Galilee.
Schlatter regards "travel narrative" a misnomer, although his suggestion that
Jesus is a "wanderer" who has left his beloved Galilee and has no place to lay
his head is misleading. Jesus is not "wandering," but resolutely embracing his
divine *destiny* in Jerusalem.[6] Bengel is more correct in regarding Jerusalem
as the *goal* of the central section of Luke.[7] The Holy City plays a critical role
for Luke, as indicated by the fact that fully two-thirds of the 143 references
to Jerusalem in the NT appear in Luke-Acts. There were of course several
important cities in Palestine in addition to Jerusalem in Jesus' day, including
Sepphoris, Tiberias, Sebaste, Jerash, Caesarea-Maritima. Nearly all were in
regions visited by Jesus. Many of them are mentioned in the NT, especially in
Acts, but no Gospel reports that Jesus visited any of these cities. In "set[ting]
his face toward Jerusalem" (9:51), Jesus is not exercising an elective option but
acting in obedience to divine providence as declared by the prophets (18:31-
34). Like an artist, Luke paints the canvas of the central section from a "linear
perspective" with a single focal point of Jerusalem.

The narrative structure of the central section sets forth *the mission of Jesus
as the way of salvation*. That mission is introduced in the programmatic sermon
of Nazareth (4:18) when Jesus quotes Isa 61, "The Spirit of the Lord is upon me

---

of Luke does not signify a special transition at 9:51, nor did the majority of interpreters until
the premodern period.

2. See the discussion of the issue in Moessner, *Lord of the Banquet*, 1-44; and the exten-
sive bibliography and summary discussion in Klein, *Lukasevangelium*, 357-60.

3. Green, *Luke*, 399, accepts the description of "travel narrative" but qualifies it: "In
short, the 'journey' in which Luke is interested is not about narrative structure or travel itinerary; rather, it concerns the fulfillment of God's redemptive purpose." Bock, *Luke 9:51–24:53*,
963, redefines the narrative similarly.

4. K. Schmidt, *Der Rahmen der Geschichte Jesu: Literarkritische Untersuchungen zur
ältesten Jesusüberlieferung* (Berlin: Trowitsch & Söhne, 1919), 269, summed it up thus: "Though
Jesus is always traveling to Jerusalem, he never makes any real progress on this journey."

5. Jesus would not need to flee from Herod, who ruled Galilee and Perea, if he were
not in either place.

6. Schlatter, *Lukas*, 331-32.

7. Bengel, *Gnomon*, 2:86.

... and has *sent* me." In 9:51 Jesus' mission receives specific definition, and from then on assumes dominant narrative significance via two parallel lines of development. The first line begins with the announcement of Moses and Elijah on the Mount of Transfiguration that Jesus "must fulfill his exodus into Jerusalem" (9:31), an announcement that is followed by seven subsequent repetitions in the central section of the divine necessity of Jesus going to Jerusalem (9:51, 53; 13:22, 33; 17:11, 18:31; 19:28). A second narrative line begins with the passion prediction in 9:22 that Jesus must suffer, which is also followed by seven subsequent references to the passion (9:44; 17:25; 18:32-33; 24:7, 26, 44, 46). The Jerusalem-narrative line contains no references to the necessity of Jesus suffering, and the suffering-narrative line contains no references to Jerusalem. At only one point do the two narrative lines intersect — at the conclusion of the central section in 18:31-34, where Jesus declares that he must *suffer in Jerusalem*. These sixteen combined references prepare for, and must be understood in the context of, Jesus' *way* to his impending suffering and death in Jerusalem. The "way of peace" foreseen by Isaiah (59:8) and reclaimed in the Benedictus of the infancy narrative (1:79) is now fulfilled in Jesus. This "way" of Jesus will become the earliest description of the Christian movement, according to Acts.[8] Luke summarizes and reinforces the theme of the mission of Jesus as the way of salvation at the conclusion of the Gospel when the two disciples confess at Emmaus, "Did not our hearts burn within us as *Jesus spoke to us on the way*, as he opened to us the Scriptures" (24:32).

JESUS SETS HIS FACE TO JERUSALEM, AND THE DISCIPLES SET FIRE TO SAMARIA (9:51-62)

51-56 Beginning in 9:51 Luke departs almost completely from the Markan narrative, converging again with Mark only at the commencement of the Passion Narrative at 18:35. From 18:35 to 24:8 Luke tracks Mark rather closely, but in 24:9-53 Luke again departs from Mark and concludes the Third Gospel with another unique block of material. The material of 9:51–18:34 and 24:9-52 is thus largely unique to Luke, deriving, in my judgment, primarily from Luke's use of the early Hebrew Gospel.[9] The style of the present section in 9:51-62 is particularly Hebraic, v. 51 being entirely Semitic, consisting of eight Hebrew expressions in Greek translation.[10]

---

8. Acts 9:2; 13:10; 16:17; 18:25-26; 19:9, 23; 22:4; 24:14, 22.

9. See "Luke's Sources" in the Introduction and Edwards, *Hebrew Gospel,* esp. chaps. 1-5.

10. Edwards, *Hebrew Gospel,* 309-10. Fitzmyer's description of v. 51 as "almost certainly [a] Lucan composition" (*Luke [I–IX],* 826) is misleading. V. 51 is unique to Luke, and its Greek entirely Hebraic.

V. 51 marks a major thematic change in the Third Gospel, signaling the end of Jesus' *presence* in Galilee, where he crisscrossed the lake and itinerated in villages, and the commencement of the fulfillment of his *purpose* in Jerusalem. That purpose is especially signified by the Greek word *analēmpsis* (v. 51; NIV "being taken up to heaven"), which occurs only here in the NT. In both its noun and verb forms, this word is a semitechnical term in Judaism for being taken up into heaven, used in this sense of Abraham (*T. Ab.* 7:8), Moses (Philo, *Moses* 2.291), Elijah (2 Kgs 2:11; 1 Macc 2:58), and believers in general (*T. Job* 39:12) being assumed into heaven. The term frequently signifies heavenly glory and majesty, but in late Jewish literature (e.g., *Pss. Sol.* 4:18) it can mean "death" as well. Some scholars combine these two meanings, interpreting *analēmpsis* to refer to Jesus' passion *and* resurrection in Jerusalem.[11] Two data, however, argue rather conclusively for understanding *analēmpsis* with reference to Jesus' ascension in v. 51. First, seven occurrences of *analambanein* (the verb form of *analēmpsis*) occur in Acts, each meaning "taking up," three of which refer to Jesus' ascension (Acts 1:2, 11, 22).[12] The consistent use of this term in Luke-Acts with reference to Jesus being taken into heaven therefore confirms its semitechnical use in Judaism noted above. This interpretation is further corroborated by Justin Martyr (*1 Apol.* 1.26) and Eusebius (*Hist. eccl.* 2.13.3; 3.5.2), both of whom use a form of *analēmpsis* with reference to Jesus' ascension.[13] Second, the Greek construction *en tō symplērousthai tas hēmeras* (v. 51; "when the days were fulfilled"; NIV "as the time approached") occurs again with reference to Pentecost in Acts 2:1, *en tō symplērousthai tēn hēmeran*. These are the only two uses of this phrase in the Greek Bible. Both uses inaugurate major movements in salvation history: the first in Luke 9:51 signals the fulfillment of Jesus' ministry in Jerusalem, and the second in Acts 2:1 signals the descent of the Holy Spirit on believers at Pentecost and the commencement of the ministry of the church. The use of the Greek verb "to fulfill" *(symplēroun)* delimits the two consummating events of Luke's two-part history of salvation: the era of the earthly ministry of Jesus, which is fulfilled in the journey to Jerusalem, passion, crucifixion, and resurrection; and the era of the church, which is inaugurated at the descent of the Holy Spirit at Pentecost.[14] The divide between these two eras — a veritable "continental divide" — is Jesus' ascension into heaven.

Jesus "set his face" (v. 51; NIV "resolutely set out") to this destiny in Je-

---

11. Delling, *analēmpsis, TWNT* 4:9; Bovon, *Lukas 9,51–14,35,* 27.

12. Acts 1:2, 11, 22; 10:16; 20:13, 14; 23:31. The use of the term at 10:16 is also "taken up into heaven."

13. For further references of both noun and verb forms referring to assumption into heaven, see BDAG, 66-67.

14. Delling, *symplēroō, TWNT* 6:307.

rusalem. This inimitable Hebraism occurs in Psalms and in a dozen instances in Ezekiel as a metaphor of determination, i.e., setting one's eyes or heart on an object of great desire.[15] Perhaps most important, the Servant of the Lord "sets his face like flint" to the work to which God calls him, trusting that the Lord will vindicate his cause (Isa 50:7). 9:51 does not simply announce Jesus' "exodus," which was foretold by Moses and Elijah at the transfiguration (9:31), but also signifies Jesus' dedication to embrace and pursue the suffering that it will entail in Jerusalem.

For a second time Jesus sends out members of the Twelve, this time not to proclaim his word (9:1-6) but to prepare his way in Samaria (v. 52). The determination and definition of Jesus' ministry are reinforced in the Greek text by a threefold repetition that Jesus' "face" is directed to Jerusalem (vv. 51, 52, 53). The Pentateuch speaks of God or a divine messenger "going before" the Israelites as they enter and inherit the Promised Land (Exod 33:2, 14; Deut 4:37-38). This proleptic imagery is appropriated and elevated by the prophets who apply it to the "preparation for the way of the Lord" (Isa 40:3-5), specifically in a reappearance of Elijah (9:8; Mal 4:5). Early Christian tradition unanimously understood John the Baptizer to fulfill the role of Elijah as the acclaimed forerunner of the way of the Lord (3:4-6; Matt 17:9-13). In v. 52 Jesus reappropriates this forerunner imagery, heretofore claimed exclusively by John the Baptizer, and transfers it to the Twelve, whom "he sent before his face . . . to prepare the way for him";[16] and in 10:1 the same imagery will be expanded to the larger group of seventy(-two) disciples.[17] The disciples, and by extension the church, inherit the role of John to prepare the way of the Lord — like a "fifth column" — in the world. The Twelve and a larger group of disciples thus prepare the way for Jesus' passion in Jerusalem as John prepared the way for Jesus' Galilean ministry. Not surprisingly, perhaps, the mission of the Twelve to Samaria is rejected, as was the mission of John earlier. Antagonism between Jews and Samaritans was pronounced and protracted in the intertestamental period.[18]

15. The Hebraic phrase behind "to set one's face" in 9:51 (Heb. *sim panaw*) is rendered in several different ways in the LXX (e.g., Gen 31:21; 2 Kgs 12:18 [Eng. 17]).

16. Luke reinforces the transferal of John's function to the Twelve by the use of *hetoimazein* ("to prepare"), which in three out of four previous uses in the Gospel referred to John the Baptizer preparing the way for Jesus (1:17, 76; 3:4), whereas here it refers to the Twelve preparing his way (so Bock, *Luke 9:51–24:53*, 969).

17. In employing this imagery, Luke may again allude to Elijah (so Rowe, *Early Narrative Christology*, 124). When King Ahaziah of Israel suffered an injury and turned to pagan gods for healing, the gods failed him. He then sent messengers to Elijah for help. Elijah knew their insincerity, and rebuffed them ("Is it because there is no God in Israel that you are going off to consult Baal-Zebub, the god of Ekron?" 2 Kgs 1:3, 6, 16). Jesus' messengers will be equally rebuffed by Samaria.

18. Sir 50:25-26 refers to Samaritans as "foolish people," and Samaritans responded to

In the mouth of Jews, "Samaritan" was a term of opprobrium (John 8:48). In Jesus' day "Jews did not associate with Samaritans" (John 4:9), and Galilean Jews passing through Samaria en route to festivals in Jerusalem faced particular dangers.[19] The Samaritans, knowing Jesus' ulterior purpose in traversing their territory, "did not welcome him, because he was heading for Jerusalem" (v. 53).

At this affront, James and John, whom Jesus had nicknamed "Sons of Thunder" (Mark 3:17), live up to their reputation. "Lord, do you want us to call down fire from heaven to destroy them?" (v. 54).[20] This flagrant image appeals to the precedent of Elijah, who called down fire to destroy companies of soldiers sent to him by King Ahaziah of Israel (2 Kgs 1:10, 12). Particularly in the prophets, fire appears as a metaphor of the eschatological judgment of God (Lev 10:2; Amos 1; Hos 8:14) and the Day of the Lord (Joel 2:3; Mal 4:1; Isa 66:15-16).[21] In white-hot passion the Zebedee brothers want to incinerate the Samaritans, as surely as Elijah called down fire on Ahaziah's soldiers![22] Their passion may seem wildly inappropriate, but given the precedent of Elijah in 2 Kgs 1, and the fact that some of the OT texts about God going before the Israelites into Canaan are texts of destruction (Exod 23:28; Deut 7:20; Josh 24:12), and above all the chronic animosity of Jews toward Samaritans, their chafing to redress the Samaritan rebuff of Jesus — whom they call Lord — may be understandable.

"Jesus turned and rebuked them" (v. 55). The word for "rebuke" (Gk. *epitiman*) is intense, usually reserved for the rebuke and exorcism of demonic forces.[23] The fanaticism of the Zebedees, who appear willing to employ any force to accomplish God's will, is sharply rejected by Jesus. James and John have appealed to Jesus as "Lord," but Jesus will not exercise the plenipotentiary role of lordship so prevalent in the ancient world, particularly as exhibited in the later Roman emperor cult. The Zebedees are wrong about Jesus: the Son of Man will not accomplish God's will through force and violence, but through weakness, even suffering, rejection, death, and

---

Jews with equal animosity. See Schürer, *History of the Jewish People*, 2:19-20; Klein, *Lukas-evangelium*, 364.

19. For an account of open warfare between Samaritans and Galilean pilgrims to Jerusalem, see Josephus, *Ant.* 20.118-24.

20. An addition to v. 54, "as also Elijah did," enjoyed wide circulation in parts of the ancient church (A C D W Θ Ψ), but a cadre of early and strong witnesses omits the addition (p[45, 75] ℵ B L Ξ). See Metzger, *TCGNT*, 124. The addition may have been added to reinforce the precedent of Elijah and thus further justify the intention of the Zebedees.

21. See F. Lang, *pyr*, *TWNT* 6:933-46.

22. See C. Evans, "Luke's Use of the Elijah/Elisha Narratives and the Ethic of Election," *JBL* 106/1 (1987): 80-81.

23. A number of manuscripts add didactic sayings to the rebuke (e.g., "Jesus said, 'You do not know what spirit you are'"; "The Son of Man did not come to destroy human beings but to save them"). The manuscript support for both readings is relatively weak. The sayings may have been added later in order to soften Jesus' rebuke of the Zebedees.

resurrection (9:22).[24] They are also wrong about the Samaritans: despite this particular rejection, and despite the widespread proscriptions of Samaritans by Jews, Samaritans are distinguished in Luke-Acts as early and important recipients of the gospel. A Samaritan plays a heroic role in a parable (10:29-37), a Samaritan is a paragon of grateful discipleship (17:11-19), and the gospel is preached in Samaria with favor (Acts 8:1-25). Finally, the Zebedees are wrong about discipleship: disciples are not commissioned to commandeer God's role as judge, but to serve the Son of Man, whose face is set to Jerusalem. The alternative of Jesus to righting wrongs, getting even, and perpetuating cycles of vengeance is simple: "He and his disciples went to another village" (v. 56). Rejection, as Paul would recognize (Rom 11:11-12), can lead to greater exposure of others to the gospel and "riches for the Gentiles."

57-62 Luke concludes the theme of Jesus and the Twelve, begun in 9:1, with Jesus in conversation with three would-be followers "on the way" (v. 57). These brief, illustrative exchanges differ from the classic "call" stories in the Synoptics (5:11, 27-28; Mark 1:16-20). In earlier stories each call is issued by Jesus to named persons, and each individual follows without resistance or delay.[25] Here, to the contrary, the first and third conversations are initiated by would-be followers rather than by Jesus, all three parties are anonymous — as is the gender of the first aspirant,[26] the parties negotiate with Jesus about conditions of discipleship, and we are not told whether the parties follow Jesus. These three conversations are thus about *discipleship* rather than the call of three specific disciples. The graphic exchanges between Jesus and the three aspirants translate the metaphoric language of discipleship in 9:23 — self-denial, taking up one's cross "daily," and following Jesus — into real conditions of discipleship. This is, moreover, the first pericope in Luke 9 that does not involve the Twelve. These three unnamed seekers form a bridge to the call and sending of the seventy(-two) in the subsequent pericope (10:1-20), and beyond them to the call and cost of discipleship for all who would hear and follow Jesus.[27]

The first candidate vows, "I will follow you wherever you go" (v. 57). This vow is easier made than kept. The chief apostle will make a similar promise (22:33) — but the Rock himself will be unable to live up to it (22:34, 54-62). Jesus responds in characteristic parabolic imagery: "Foxes have holes and birds have nests, but the Son of Man has no place to lay his head" (v. 58; on Son of Man, see excursus at 5:26). Animals can adapt to nature, but the Son of Man has not

---

24. On this point, see Bovon, *Lukas 9,51–14,35*, 27-28; Rowe, *Early Narrative Christology*, 126-27.

25. The conversation between Jesus and Peter in 5:4-8 is a minor exception to this rule.

26. In v. 57 the NIV overtranslates the indefinite Greek pronoun *tis* as "man." *Tis* includes both masculine or feminine genders and should be translated "someone."

27. See Bovon, *Lukas 9,51–14,35*, 32.

been sent into the world to adapt to it. The Christian doctrine of the incarnation affirms an absolute identification of the divine Word with humanity, and yet the Son of God born of Mary (1:31, 35), the "Word made flesh" (John 1:14), is forever a stranger and alien in this world. How foreign this Jesus to the domesticated Jesus of nineteenth-century liberalism so comfortably conventional and bourgeois! The world may claim shelter as an inalienable human right, but the Son of Man has no place to lay his head; it may claim the right to a better future, but the Son of Man offers hope only in the coming kingdom of God; it may claim the right to rest, peace, and justice, but the Son of Man finds only tribulation in the world.[28] The response of Jesus in v. 58 may seem intolerably harsh, but have not the world's great reformers and moralists said essentially the same, whether Socrates[29] or Epictetus,[30] Bonhoeffer[31] or Martin Luther King Jr.?[32]

"[Jesus] said to another man, 'Follow me.' But he replied, 'Lord, first let me go and bury my father'" (v. 59).[33] Jews regarded proper burial of the dead among the "decrees and instructions" commanded in Torah (Exod 18:20). Burial was a paramount example of a "work of love," enjoining tears, mourning, and fervent wailing.[34] The moral imperative of proper burial is equally attested in Sophocles' *Antigone,* who persists in performing funeral rites for her dead brother at the cost of her life. "Do not neglect burial" (Sir 38:16-23) was for all ancients, Jews and Greeks, a virtually inviolable duty.[35] Jesus' shocking

28. These contrasts derive from Origen, *Hom. Luc.* 9.58.

29. Plato, *Apol.* Socrates declares that the truth he speaks is verified by his want and poverty, the evil of which he is accused, and his being made a wanderer throughout life.

30. Epictetus, *Diatr.* 3.22.45-48, describes his Stoic calling as "a man who has nothing, who is naked, without home or hearth, in squalor, . . . without city, . . . yet free."

31. See Bonhoeffer's poem "Who Am I?" (*Letters and Papers from Prison* [New York: Macmillan, 1967], 188-89), or his more evocative but nearly untranslatable "Von guten Mächten wunderbar geborgen" (*Widerstand und Ergebung* [Munich: Kaiser Verlag, 1961], 275-76; or his circular letter to Confessing Churches in 1935: "Dear brethren, we can only prepare ourselves for the hours which lie ahead by strong and unwearying prayer and by wakefulness in everything. We shall now see whether our prayer and our life has been up till now a preparation for these hours of confession. If we are steadfast in prayer, we may confidently trust that the Holy Spirit will give us the right word at the right time and that we will be found faithful. It is a privilege to be allowed to stand alongside our brothers, but, near or far, each day we are bound together by the prayer that on the day of Jesus Christ we shall stand before him united in joy. Here then each stands or falls by his Lord" (*The Way to Freedom* [London: Collins, 1966], 260).

32. See King's "Letter from a Birmingham Jail."

33. The presence of "Lord" in v. 59 is not entirely certain. The probability of a scribe intentionally omitting *Kyrios,* however, argues in favor of its authenticity (see Metzger, *TCGNT,* 125; Rowe, *Early Narrative Christology,* 128-30).

34. On Jewish burial practices, see Str-B 1:487-90.

35. See the full discussion of this text in M. Hengel, *The Charismatic Leader and His Followers* (trans. J. Greig; New York: Crossroad, 1981), 3-15.

reversal of a universally acknowledged moral duty is an important example of "implicit Christology." "There is hardly one logion of Jesus which more sharply runs counter to law, piety, and custom than does . . . Lk 9:60," writes Martin Hengel.[36] To be sure, Jesus' reply, "Let the dead bury their own dead" (v. 60), employs "the dead" in a figurative rather than literal sense (also 15:24, 32), meaning "spiritually dead," those who have not responded to the gospel. Nevertheless, v. 60 is a powerful testimony to Jesus' self-understanding over against all forms of prior revelation, including Torah. The kingdom of God that Jesus proclaims, indeed that is uniquely present in him, takes precedence over the Mosaic authority received at Sinai.

Finally, another said, "I will follow you, Lord; but first let me go back and say good-by to my family" (v. 61). This candidate, too, appears to be acting on the precedent of sound Jewish tradition, on the basis of which he is hopeful of being approved by Jesus, for Elijah had permitted Elisha to say good-by to parents before following him (1 Kgs 19:19-21). This is the final allusion in the Galilean ministry to Elijah and Elisha, whom Luke repeatedly employs as prototypes of Jesus' prophetic and healing ministry to both Jews and Gentiles. But as the demands of Jesus are more exacting than those of Moses in Torah, so too they are "more stringent than those of Elijah."[37] Discipleship to Elijah is not a valid precedent for discipleship to the Son of Man. Elisha may turn back from the plow to settle affairs at home before following Elijah, but a disciple cannot turn back from the plow and follow Jesus at a more convenient time.[38] This pronouncement, like the others in vv. 57-62, confronts the disciple-inquirer with an existential choice that is focused exclusively on Jesus, a Jesus who does not apologize for or attempt to justify the high cost of discipleship.[39] One cannot call Jesus Lord, as this disciple-aspirant does, and then impose limits on his lordship. A prior commitment to Torah or prophecy cannot simply be transferred to Jesus, for the upward call of Jesus is greater than both. This third discipleship-encounter recalls and completes the transfiguration narrative: as Elijah departed from Jesus on the Mount of Transfiguration (9:33), so too the prophetic model must yield to the authority of Jesus.

The exchanges between Jesus and would-be disciples in vv. 57-62 concern property ("the Son of Man has no place to lay his head"), family ("let me

---

36. Hengel, *Charismatic Leader*, 14.

37. Marshall, *Luke*, 412.

38. St. Peter of Damascus notes the steadfastness (which he describes as "patient endurance") required by this saying: "Patient endurance is the consolidation of all the virtues, because without it not one of them can subsist. For whoever turns back is not 'fit for the kingdom of heaven' (Luke 9:62). . . . Patient endurance is required before anything can come about; and, once something has come about, it can be sustained and brought to perfection only through such endurance" (*Philokalia* [London: Faber & Faber, 1995], 3:222).

39. Rowe, *Early Narrative Christology*, 132.

go and bury my father"), and work ("one who puts a hand to the plow"). These same three claims will again be given as reasons for refusing the invitation to the Great Banquet (14:16-24), and Jesus will assert his call to discipleship in relation to them in 14:25-33. Property, family, and vocation are life's most ultimate obligations. If anything should qualify as a valid exception to Jesus' exclusive call to discipleship — or as a postponement or modification of it — these should. Therein lie their danger and deception, for *no* reasons, no matter how worthy, can compensate for failing to accept the invitation to discipleship. "If anyone comes to me and does not hate father and mother, wife and children, brothers and sisters — yes, even life itself — such a person cannot be my disciple" (14:26).

JESUS SENDS SEVENTY(-TWO) IN MISSION (10:1-16)

The mission of the seventy(-two), which is recorded in no other gospel,[40] is an extension of the prior mission of the Twelve in 9:1-6, but it is not an exact duplication of it. The Twelve were formally endowed with power and authority to subdue demonic forces, heal sickness and diseases, and proclaim the kingdom of God (9:1-2). The seventy(-two) are sent before Jesus with the same proclamation of the kingdom of God (vv. 9, 11), but the power and authority to exorcise demons and heal diseases that were granted to the Twelve are not repeated in the commissioning of the seventy(-two). To be sure, the seventy(-two) also heal (v. 9) and exercise "authority . . . to overcome all the power of the enemy" (v. 19), but the differences both in their commissioning and in the description of their mission imply that the Twelve, Jesus' primary and innermost circle of apprentices, possess Jesus' endowments of divine power and authority in a measure that does not characterize the larger cohort of the seventy(-two).

1-11   "After this . . ." signifies a transition from the mission of the Twelve to that of the seventy(-two), whom Jesus "appointed" (v. 1). The Greek word

---

40. Fitzmyer, *Luke (X–XXIV)*, 843, states that "Luke has clearly created this literary 'doublet' from 'Q' material that is parallel to Mark 6:6a-13." This is overstated. Matt contains no account of the mission of the seventy (-two), and the mission of the Twelve in Matt 9:37-38; 10:7-16, though thematically similar, is very different verbally. There appears to be no "Q" "doublet" to the mission of the seventy (-two). The mission of the seventy (-two), along with virtually the whole of 9:51–19:28, is unique to the Third Gospel. This large block of material likely derives from the eyewitness source(s) alluded to in the prologue (1:1-4). Given the significant verbal correspondences between 9:51–19:28 and the quotations from the Hebrew Gospel in the Fathers, it is plausible to deduce that one of the sources mentioned in the prologue, esp. for the central section of Luke, was the Hebrew Gospel. See Edwards, *Hebrew Gospel*, chap. 4.

for "appointed" *(anadeiknynai)* is common in diplomatic contexts in Greek literature.[41] In Luke-Acts the verb appears with only Jesus or God as subject, and both here and in Acts 1:24 the term implies formal divine appointment, which is reinforced by the reference to Jesus as "the Lord" (v. 1). Whether Jesus sent out **seventy or seventy-two disciples** is a complex question for which only a tentative answer may be given. The manuscript evidence, though slightly favoring "seventy-two," is too evenly divided between the two figures to be decisive.[42] Arguments from internal probability can also be made with equal plausibility for both figures. The number "seventy," like the even more common number "forty," appears frequently and often symbolically in Hebrew tradition as an approximate number for a large quantity.[43] It could thus be that an original "seventy-two" was altered in the transmission process to the more familiar "seventy." The number "seventy-two," however, tends to be specific in the OT and Hebrew tradition and, although not unknown, is much less frequent.[44] But "seventy-two" could have arisen by dittography, i.e., by a scribal accidentally adding "two" (which already occurs twice in v. 1) to an original "seventy." Many scholars favor the originality of "seventy-two" and interpret the mission of seventy-two against the background of the table of nations in Genesis 10.[45] A particular strength of this interpretation is that it accounts for *both* disputed figures, for Gen 10 contains seventy nations in the

41. F. Danker, *Jesus and the New Age: A Commentary on St. Luke's Gospel* (rev. ed.; Philadelphia: Fortress Press, 1988), 211.

42. See the argument in favor of "seventy-two" by K. Aland in Metzger, *TCGNT*, 126-27; also Marshall, *Luke*, 414-15. For an argument in favor of "seventy," see Metzger, "Seventy or Seventy(-two) Disciples?" *NTS* 5/4 (1959): 299-306; idem, *The Text of the New Testament: Its Transmission, Corruption, and Restoration* (New York: Oxford University Press, 1964), 243-45.

43. Most frequently as seventy years (Gen 5:12 and throughout the OT) and seventy sons of Jacob (Gen 46:27; Exod 1:5), but also as seventy days (Gen 50:3), seventy shekels (Num 7 [12x]) or talents of silver (Exod 38:29), seventy elders (Num 11:16), seventy kings (Judg 1:7), seventy sons of Gideon/Jerubbaal (Judg 8:30; 9:24) or sons of Ahab (2 Kgs 10); seventy men (Judg 9; 1 Sam 6:19); seventy brothers of Abimelech (Judg 9:56); seventy jackasses (Judg 12:14) or cattle (2 Chr 29:32); and seventy cubits (Ezek 41:12). Josephus, *J.W.* 2.570; *Vita* 79, also placed seventy elders in charge of the administration of Galilee during the First Jewish Revolt.

44. Seventy-two cattle (Num 31:38) and lambs (1 Esd 8:65), seventy-two languages of the world (*3 En.* 17:8; 18:2; 20:2); seventy-two reputed translators of the LXX (*Let. Aris.* 32); seventy-two nations of Gen 10 (LXX; but seventy in MT). Beyond these examples, "seventy-two" occurs nine times in combination with centenary numerals (172, 272, etc., in 1 Esd, Ezra, and Neh), but not alone in the OT. Even in combination with centenary numerals "seventy" is often variable, however. The 276 passengers en route in Acts 27:37 appear alternatively as 275 (Codex A), 270 (Codex C; 69), 176 (or 876 in Bohairic mss.), 76 (522, Lat.), and 70 (Epiphanius). See Metzger, *TCGNT*, 442.

45. See K. Rengstorf, *hepta*, *TWNT* 2:630-31, who is followed by many modern scholars. Marshall, *Luke*, 414-15, provides careful evidence pro and con on the matter.

MT and seventy-two in the LXX! This interpretation provides a serendipitous solution to the discrepancy of "seventy" versus "seventy-two," but it falters thematically, in my judgment, for the mission of the seventy(-two) in Luke 10 is not directed to Gentiles but to Israel (the towns mentioned in vv. 13-15, for example, are in Galilee).[46] I am more inclined to find a prefigurement of Luke 10 in God's command to Moses in Num 11 to anoint elders (seventy elders, v. 16; but perhaps seventy-two with the addition of Eldad and Medad, vv. 26-29) with "the power of the Spirit" in order to share and extend the ministry of Moses.[47] The narratives of Num 11 and Luke 10 are both initiated by "the Lord" (10:1; Num 11:16), and both closely identify the seventy(-two) with the Spirit and the mission of Moses and Jesus. The institution of the "elders" of Num 11 set a precedent in Second Temple Judaism for the composition of the council of elders, including the Sanhedrin; and although this council was typically numbered at seventy elders (or seventy-one with the high priest),[48] several authorities in rabbinic Judaism numbered it at seventy-two members.[49] To summarize this complex question, although manuscript evidence does not allow us to decide for certain between "seventy" or "seventy-two" missionaries (henceforth, "seventy(-two)"),[50] it would seem that the number likely recalls the elders of Num 11. If Jesus' choice of twelve apostles signified a reconstitution of Israel (22:30!; see at 6:13), it seems equally probable that the commissioning of the seventy(-two) signified an extension of his ministry through a larger secondary cohort analogous to the elders of Num 11. No names of the seventy(-two) are recorded in the NT, and the fourth-century church historian Eusebius, who endeavored to recover all possible literary sources of the Gospels, knew of no extant list of the seventy.[51]

Sending the disciples in pairs probably reflects the necessity of two wit-

---

46. Furthermore, there is no eponymy (naming a people after an ancestor) in Luke 10 as there is in Gen. 10; and perhaps most important, the argument assumes that interpreters would actually count the extended list of nations in Gen 10.

47. For supporting evidence for this interpretation in Judaism, see Str-B 2:166.

48. *M. Sanh.* 1:6; *m. Šebu.* 2:2.

49. *M. Zebaḥ.* 1:3; *m. Yad.* 3:5; 4:2; *y. Ber.* 1cd; *b. Ber.* 27b. On the composition of the Sanhedrin, see Schürer, *History of the Jewish People,* 2:199-226.

50. The choice of the NIV translators to read "seventy-two" seems to overstate the evidence. Metzger, "Seventy or Seventy(-two) Disciples?" 305-6, more cautiously concludes that composite evidence is "so evenly balanced, that the investigator must be content with the conclusion that (1) on the basis of our present knowledge the number of Jesus' disciples referred to in Luke X cannot be determined with confidence, and (2) if one is editing the text the least unsatisfactory solution is to print 'seventy (-two).'"

51. Eusebius, *Hist. eccl.* 1.12.1. Origen (*Hom. Luc.* 10.1) and Eusebius (*Hist. eccl.* 1.12.1) preserve the number "seventy" rather than "seventy (-two)" in their references to Luke 10. A fragmentary, late, and obscure "Gospel of the Seventy" (*NTApoc.* 1:380-81) bears no apparent relationship to 10:1-16.

nesses in capital offenses in Israel (Deut 17:6; 19:15). The requirement of two witnesses to take or preserve a human life may carry the added significance that the mission of the seventy(-two) is a matter of life-and-death importance. Fitzmyer writes that "the custom of traveling in pairs . . . is not found in the OT. . . . [It] becomes famous in the later rabbinical tradition."[52] This is not entirely true. Pairs occasionally occur in the OT, including Moses and Aaron (Num 33:1), Joshua and Caleb (Num 14:6), Eldad and Medad (Num 11:26), Naomi and Ruth (Ruth 1–2), Elijah and Elisha (2 Kgs 2).[53] Likewise, the ten Torah scholars known to have lived prior to Jesus, the last and most famous of whom were Hillel and Shammai, are arranged and discussed in the Mishnah in pairs.[54] There is thus at least limited precedent in Judaism for pairs of witnesses, but Jesus' sending of missionaries in pairs clearly set a widely followed precedent in early Christianity.[55]

The pairs are "to go before his face" (NIV "go ahead of him") to every place Jesus is about to go. The repetition of "face" recalls the same word thrice mentioned immediately before in 9:51-53, thus bonding the seventy(-two) with Jesus' mission to Jerusalem. The overarching mission to Jerusalem does not eclipse or cancel Jesus' preaching and teaching, however. Rather, it seems to intensify both. "He was instructing them, 'The harvest is plentiful, but the workers are few. Ask the Lord of the harvest, therefore, to send out workers into his harvest field. Go!'" (vv. 2-3).[56] "Harvest" is a symbol of God's eschatological judgment in the OT (Joel 3:1-13; Isa 27:11-12) and here signifies the prime season for proclaiming the kingdom of God. The "Lord of the harvest" would appear to be God, but the fact that Jesus is identified as "Lord" in v. 1 and is so identified again in v. 17, suggests that the work of God is so closely identified with the mission of Jesus that he can be taken as "Lord of the harvest."[57] The reminder that the harvest is ripe but the workers few is a sobering, even discouraging, introduction to the mission of the seventy(-two). The seventy(-two) are called to a task for which they are not adequate. Even before they go they must *pray* — that the Lord will send workers for the harvest. The NIV translation "ask" is too anemic for Greek *deisthai* (v. 2), which means "to implore, entreat, pray." Likewise, *ekballein* is stronger than "send" (v. 2; NIV) and slightly unusual, implying that workers will not volunteer for this mission

52. Fitzmyer, *Luke (X–XXIV)*, 846.

53. Some of these pairs are noted by Origen, *Hom. Luc.* 10.1.

54. *M. 'Abot.* 1:4-12; Schürer, *History of the Jewish People*, 2:360-67.

55. Two travelers (24:13), Peter and John (Acts 3:1; 8:14), two messengers (Acts 9:38), Paul and Barnabas (Acts 13:2ff.), Judas and Silas (Acts 15:22), Barnabas and Mark (Acts 15:39), Paul and Silas (Acts 15:40), Timothy and Erastus (Acts 19:22), and possibly Andronicus and Junia(s) (Rom 16:7). See Fitzmyer, *Luke (X–XXIV)*, 846; Wolter, *Lukasevangelium*, 377.

56. This saying reappears nearly verbatim in *Gos. Thom.* 73.

57. See Green, *Luke*, 411-12; Rowe, *Early Narrative Christology*, 133-36.

but must be *dispatched* for it. V. 2 thus emphasizes that the seventy(-two) are commissioned by the "Lord of the harvest."

The mission is not only discouraging, it is also dangerous. "I am sending you out like lambs among wolves" (v. 3). This is a graphic and violent simile. A lamb is not simply the weaker of two antagonists, but utterly defenseless before a wolf. The image was not forgotten in the early church: in Acts 8:3 Luke describes Saul "ravaging" (Gk. *lymainein*) the fledgling church following the martyrdom of Stephen (likewise Acts 9:1-2; 26:11); and at the end of the first century, 2 *Clem* 5:2 depicts (Domitian's?) persecution of the church in the same simile of a lamb among wolves.

In addition to discouragement and danger, the seventy(-two) must embark in mission with calculated deficits. V. 4 contains four prohibitions: "Do not take a purse or bag or sandals; and do not greet anyone on the road." Ancient travelers often bound money in the outer garment under their belt (so Matt 10:9), but the Greek word for "purse," *ballantion,* which occurs in the NT only in Luke (10:4; 12:33; 22:35-36), refers to an actual money bag or purse, such as a well-to-do traveler might carry.[58] The first prohibition thus may not forbid taking money for essentials, but it clearly forbids taking extra or excess money. Nor may the seventy(-two) take a "bag." The Greek *pēra* means a traveler's bag or knapsack for clothing and provisions, common to shepherds and even more to Cynic philosophers.[59] The seventy(-two) are thus not "Christian Cynics," for their sparse gear does not recall that of wandering Cynic preachers.[60] Anyone familiar with the rocky and thorny terrain of Palestine will find the prohibition against wearing sandals a painful deprivation. This prohibition was not made of the Twelve (9:3; Matt 10:9; Mark 6:8). Is it an example of Jewish hyperbole, or perhaps a prohibition of a *second* pair of sandals? Finally, the seventy(-two) are forbidden from "greeting anyone on the road." This prohibition signals the urgency of the task before the disciples, in a similar way that Elisha's order to Gehazi in 2 Kgs 4:29 signaled urgency in saving a boy's life.[61] These rigorous requirements — more rigorous than those required of the Twelve or the early church[62] — appear to be specific to the mission of the seventy(-two). The net effect of Jesus' commands is to accentuate the dependency of the seventy(-two)

58. K. Rengstorf, *ballantion, TWNT* 1:523-34.

59. BDAG, 811.

60. On this point, see Edwards, *Mark,* 179-81.

61. Str-B 2:166.

62. The position of the early church vis-à-vis material possessions seems to have been neither uniform nor prescriptive. Some believers sold homes, fields, and possessions (Acts 2:44; 4:34); others retained them without proscription (Acts 5:4), and Paul engaged in fund-raising for his mission expansion (1 Cor 16:1-4; 2 Cor 9:12-14; Rom 15:25-27). Vinson, *Luke,* 323, seems correct in saying that "Luke probably understood the rules about no supplies and no shoes to have been temporary strategies rather than constitutive principles for the Jesus movement."

on him and the word they proclaim.[63] If they go with an elaborate support apparatus, then they will not be believable. They will be believable only to the extent that they go on want, and thus in dependence on the "Lord of the harvest" and the kingdom they proclaim.

The mission of the seventy(-two) is not a mission to streets and marketplaces, but to homes. The instruction to greet homes in peace (vv. 5-6), sit at table, eating and drinking what is offered by hosts, and not move from place to place (v. 7) depicts a mission of relationships rather than programs. The Jewish home, and particularly the Jewish *table,* was the most cherished and protected sector of Jewish communal life. To enter that space was to be granted access to a most intimate space. The mission of the seventy(-two) is thus not a crusade, strategy, or program, but an interpersonal encounter in which the gospel is proclaimed within the context of trusting relationships; indeed, it will be "at table" that the eyes of unknowing disciples will be opened to recognize Jesus (24:30-31).[64] The Greek word for "peace" (vv. 5-6, *eirēnē*) reflects the Hebrew *shalom,* meaning wholeness and good will, and in the mouths of the seventy(-two) it is a virtual synonym for salvation (1:79; 2:14, 29; 7:50; 8:48; 19:38, 42; 24:36).[65] "If there be a son of peace" (v. 6; NIV "If the head of the house loves peace") is a striking Hebraism, meaning one whose character is shaped by peace, as one is shaped by father and family. Fitzmyer applies the term explicitly to the proclamation of the kingdom of God: a son of peace is "a person open to and receptive of the prime quality of Christian salvation brought by Jesus."[66]

The command to be grateful recipients, repeated twice in vv. 7-8, is expressed in the present tense in Greek, meaning to *continue* eating and drinking what hosts offer. Refusing what people offer insults them, but receiving with gratitude what they offer honors them, and honoring people is a fulfillment of the commandment of *agapē.* The concomitant command to "stay put" and not move from house to house is likewise given with hosts in mind: moving from one house to another insults the first host, imputing inadequacy to his or her (Acts 16:15) hospitality. This practical advice took root in the memory of the early church in *Gos. Thom.* 14 and in *Did.* 11:3-6, both of which apply it to hosts as well as to missionaries: itinerant apostles and prophets are to be received "as the Lord" — but for no more than three days! The principle of the worker being worthy of his wages (v. 7) was also recalled by the apostle Paul.

---

63. Cyril of Alexandria, *Comm. Luc. Hom.* 62, noted that Jesus commanded the disciples to take nothing on the trip, not so that they would learn to despise ordinary things, but so that they would learn to depend solely on him.

64. An insight of Vinson, *Luke,* 323.

65. See Green, *Luke,* 412; Tannehill, *Luke,* 175.

66. *Luke (X–XXIV),* 848.

Only rarely does Paul either cite or allude to a specific teaching of Jesus, but in 1 Cor 9:4-14 he defends his missionary enterprise by reminding his detractors of Jesus' teaching in vv. 7-8, "the Lord has commanded that those who preach the gospel should receive their living from the gospel."

The seventy(-two) are not to be idle guests, but to "heal the sick" and proclaim, "The kingdom of God has come near to you" (v. 9). "Heal the sick" (NIV) may be overly specific. The Greek *therapeuein* usually connotes healing in the NT, but it denotes serving as well as healing;[67] the Greek *asthenēs* likewise often connotes sickness and disease, but its root meaning is simply "weakness" or "inability." V. 9 should thus not be limited to medical cures, but to serving people in their broader needs. The seventy(-two) are not given a new or different message from the message of Jesus; they are to proclaim the same kingdom proclaimed by Jesus (4:43; see discussion of "kingdom of God" there). They are not sent to innovate with the kingdom or adapt it to their circumstances, but to be witnesses and stewards of the kingdom. To hear and receive the message of the seventy(-two) is to hear and receive Jesus; and to reject the message of the seventy(-two) is to reject both Jesus and the Father who sent him (v. 16).

The critical element of the proclamation of the seventy(-two) is that the kingdom of God, whose roots extend back to the announcement of God's eschatological kingdom in Isa 40–66, has "come near" (Gk. *engizein*). Jesus inaugurated his ministry with the declaration, "Today this scripture is fulfilled in your hearing" (4:21); the essential message of the church from Jesus until the second coming is, "The kingdom of God is at hand." The kingdom is not of human origin, for it does not depend on human calculation, enablement, or activity. It is ordained for human salvation, however, and thus it must be actualized in human history. The kingdom is a state inaugurated by divine *activity,* "the great transformation of the world, the promised coming of God's redemptive reign that breaks as a miracle of God into the human present."[68] The kingdom is not only proclaimed by Jesus but actually present in Jesus, although its full realization remains outstanding until the cross and the final consummation of the second coming. Significantly, the "drawing near" of the kingdom is reserved for the second half of Luke. Both the proclamation of the arrival of the kingdom of God by the seventy(-two) (10:9, 11) and Jesus' focus on Jerusalem itself (18:35, 40; 19:29, 37, 41; 21:8, 20, 28) are depicted in the Greek word *engizein,* "to draw near, to be at hand." This word characterizes both the proclamation of the church and the way of Jesus in this world; or put otherwise, the way of Jesus in this world *is* the proclamation of the kingdom of God, and hence the gospel. Since the kingdom is not of human origin, it does not

67. H. Beyer, *therapeuō, TWNT* 3:129-32.
68. H. Preisker, *engizō, TWNT* 2:329-32.

require human acceptance or even acknowledgment to be actualized in this world. Jesus instructs the seventy(-two) that, when a city does not receive it, the disciples are to publicly shake the dust from their feet as a witness against that city and declare, "Be sure of this: the kingdom of God has come!" (v. 11). Seventy years later, Ignatius of Antioch (ca. 35-107) recalled and echoed this truth when he wrote, "There is a judgment even if people do not believe on the blood of Christ" (*Smyrn.* 6:1). The instruction to shake dust from their feet is a searing judgment. Jews traveling outside Palestine were required to shake themselves free from (Gentile) dust when returning home, lest they pollute Eretz Israel.[69] This commandment declares a nonresponsive Jewish village to be, in essence, a *heathen* village. The apostle Paul develops the implications of this same teaching in Rom 2 and 9–11 when he writes that Jews may not presume on salvation on the basis of ethnicity or religion. "Not all who are descended from Israel are Israel" (Rom 9:6).

12-16 Place-names and chronology are virtually absent from Jesus' "itinerary" in the central section of Luke, but the mission of the seventy(-two) is addressed with special intensity to Chorazin, Bethsaida, Tyre, Sidon, and Capernaum (vv. 12-15). All these towns are either in northern Galilee or north of Galilee, reminding readers that the central section includes itineration and preaching in Galilee as well as en route to Jerusalem. Jesus declares that it will be more bearable for Sodom in the day (of judgment) than for a city that rejects the kingdom of God (v. 12). The sharp polemic in vv. 12-15 echoes and alludes to prophetic polemic in the OT. The story of Sodom's depravity and fiery judgment in Gen 19 branded it as the model of infamy in Israel, the most sinful place of the most godless people, in the words of later rabbis.[70] Ezekiel likened Jerusalem to an idolatrous and adulterous wife, "the sister of Sodom" (Ezek 16). In similar prophetic rebuke Jesus declares desolate Sodom *better* than a city that spurns the kingdom of God. Jesus directly indicts Chorazin and Bethsaida, about three miles (5 km) north and three miles east, respectively, of their sister city Capernaum. If Tyre and Sidon had seen the wonders done in Chorazin and Bethsaida, Israel's ancient nemesis to the north "would have repented long ago in sackcloth and ashes" (v. 13).

These stark and graphic judgments further testify to "implicit Christology." In speaking implicitly rather than explicitly about himself, Jesus, like God, who in the OT withholds a direct revelation of himself to humanity, veils the truth, not to obscure it but in order to make it receivable — if it will be received at all. So exceptional is the advent of the kingdom of God in Jesus that Sodom, Tyre, and Sidon — places proverbially beyond hope of salvation — can

---

69. See Neh 5:13; Acts 13:51; 18:6, and Str-B 1:571 for further references in Mishnah and Talmud.

70. Str-B 1:571-74.

still be saved; and places like Chorazin, Bethsaida, and Capernaum — places that have heard with their ears, seen with their eyes, and touched with their hands the Word of Life (1 John 1:1) — will be doomed unless they repent. No place had greater exposure to this Word than Capernaum (4:31-32!), no place, perhaps, had responded with greater "amazement" (9:43). "And *you*, Capernaum," says Jesus in rebuke. In its pride and complacency, Capernaum imagines it "will be lifted up to the skies. No! You will go down to the depths" (v. 15). The imagery of elevation to the heavens and condemnation to the depths is an allusion to "the rise and fall" of the almighty king of Babylon in Isa 14 — an image that Jesus will extend to the fall of Satan immediately following (10:18)! When one truly hears the proclamation of grace in the kingdom of God, one can only repent like the Ninevites (Jonah 3:6), or like Peter (5:8), "sitting in sackcloth and ashes" (v. 13). Despite human sin — and examples like Sodom, Nineveh, and Tyre epitomize the depths of human sin — the proclamation of the kingdom of God offers an opportunity of grace to turn and be saved.

Luke concludes Jesus' address to the seventy(-two) with a summary statement that recalls 10:1 and their mission as a whole: "Whoever listens to you listens to me; whoever rejects you rejects me; but whoever rejects me rejects him who sent me" (v. 16). This statement, like the even more magisterial pronouncement in 10:22, sounds unusually Johannine (e.g., John 5:23; 12:48; 15:23; 1 John 2:23), attesting to a precedent in the Synoptics for the distinctive speech form of Jesus in the Johannine corpus. The seventy(-two) who are appointed and sent by Jesus (v. 1) are not simply representatives of Jesus: they have been made his surrogates and alter egos — his voice, his word, his deed.[71] To hear and respond to his appointed and anointed disciples is to hear and respond to *Jesus* — and to the Father who sent him![72] In Judaism, Torah was considered the word of God, and thus to hear Torah was to hear God.[73] The same could possibly be said of Sabbath.[74] No human being in the OT, however, presumes to liken himself or herself to God. The remarkable and unprecedented declaration of Jesus in v. 16 establishes in a rather scandalous way an unbroken relational line of revelation between Jesus and disciples that reflects the relational line of revelation between Jesus and the Father (10:22).

---

71. A point made at length in Cyril of Alexandria, *Comm. Luc. Hom.* 62.

72. The Lutheran faith tradition, in particular, emphasizes that believers are "Christ to their neighbors," a truth frequently depicted in Lutheran art by placing the preaching Luther on the same level as the crucified Jesus.

73. See Str-B 2:167.

74. *HCNT*, 113 quotes *Te'eraza Sanbat* (an Ethiopic-Jewish Falasha writing, perhaps, first c.), in which God, speaking to the personified Sabbath, says, "Those who honor you honor me, and those who reject you reject me. And those who serve you serve me. And those that I accept are those who accept me, and they do me the honor of observing the Sabbath."

JESUS' JOY AND SELF-DISCLOSURE AT THE RETURN OF THE SEVENTY(-TWO) (10:17-24)

The return of the seventy(-two) parallels the return of the Twelve from mission (9:10). Luke's overwhelming preference for the word "return" (Gk. *hypostrephein*), a word that occurs thirty-two times in Luke-Acts but never in Matthew, Mark, or John, and only thrice elsewhere in the NT, is frequently used, as here, of returning to safety and refuge.[75] For Luke, encountering Jesus is a *returning* to a God-intended state. The mission to which Jesus appointed the seventy(-two) entailed discouragements (10:2), dangers (10:3), and deficits (10:4). The stage seems to have been set, in other words, for the poorly equipped and underprepared disciples to return limping in defeat. How remarkable, then, the report of Luke that "the seventy-two returned with joy and said, 'Lord, even the demons submit to us in your name'" (v. 17). Obedience to the commands and commission of Jesus has not left the disciples spent, cynical, "burned out." Rather, their experience of God's providence and power results in *joy*. The Christian gospel is a true "comedy" in that it begins in sorrow but ends in joy. The infancy narrative resounded with joyful anticipation (1:14, 28, 44, 47, 58; 2:10, 13, 20). Jesus himself taught joy (6:23) — and he certainly both enjoyed and brought joy to people, especially troubled and marginalized people (7:34!). No story in the Gospels emphasizes the disciples' joy (vv. 17, 20 [2x]) — and Jesus' participation in their joy (v. 21) — as expressly as does this story. Luke identifies Jesus as "Lord" at the outset of the mission of the seventy(-two) (10:1), but on their return from mission they personally confess *him* as "Lord" (v. 17). The subjection of demons in Jesus' name (v. 17) was not something they had been promised in their mission contract. The experience of discipleship is *more*, not less, than what Jesus promised. The powers inherent in the gospel they proclaim are greater than they were aware of.[76] If demonic forces are subjected to Jesus, then truly, as Peter will later confess, "Jesus Christ is Lord of all!" (Acts 10:36).[77]

17-20 At the report of the subjection of the demonic in Jesus' name, Jesus declares, "I saw Satan fall like lightning from heaven" (v. 18). This apocalyptic image recalls the downfall of the king of Babylon in Isa 14:13-15 — and repeats the same image applied immediately before to Capernaum (v. 15). In both contexts it declares God's uncompromising judgment on pride, especially pride that would rival God.[78] Second Temple Judaism widely interpreted Isa 14 with reference to the final, precipitous fall of Satan and his demons "like flashes

---

75. See discussion of term in Jeremias, *Sprache des Lukasevangeliums*, 63.
76. A point recognized by Bengel, *Gnomon*, 2:92, and Plummer, *Luke* 277, 79.
77. See Rowe, *Early Narrative Christology*, 135.
78. Lagrange, *Luc*, 302.

of lightning to the earth" (*T. Sol.* 20:16-17).[79] Until this point in the Third Gospel the evil one has been referred to as "the devil" (Gk. *diabolos;* 4:2, 3, 6, 13; 8:12), but from now on the evil one is called Satan (Gk. *Satanas;* 10:18; 11:18; 13:16; 22:3, 31). "Satan" is a transliteration of Heb. *stn,* an unambiguous Hebraism that may derive from Luke's Hebrew source.[80] The Greek tense of "fall" is imperfect, connoting something that Jesus saw happening over a period of time, presumably during the mission of the seventy(-two). The syntactic placement of "fall" at the end of the Greek sentence makes it emphatic; along with the aorist tense of its participle, this indicates a decisive overthrow. The catastrophic defeat of Satan is not the result of the mission of the seventy(-two) but rather of the inbreaking of the kingdom of God that they proclaim in Jesus' name (10:9, 11), and in whose name they heal (v. 17).

The seventy(-two) were not aware of the fall of Satan. They were simply going about the routine of witness and mission assigned to them by Jesus. But during their unsung obedience something decisive happened, though it was not visible or comprehended by them: Satan fell. Whenever the kingdom of God is truly proclaimed, the work of God is accomplished in ways that even its proclaimers are often unaware of. The kingdom is not simply a distant future hope; it has become a present reality in Jesus, and one of the signs of its presence is the overthrow of Satan. "Luke's Jesus declares to the disciples that they, in the microcosm of their experience, have in fact experienced the turning point of world history."[81] "God is again the sole ruler on heaven's throne (Pss 33:13-22; 103:19). What to human beings looks impenetrably dark and evil has now, because of the activity of Jesus, come to an end, unequivocally revealing God's saving work."[82]

According to v. 19, the subjection of demonic powers during the mission of the seventy(-two) is a consequence of the authority of Jesus, which derived from the declaration of Jesus' divine sonship and indwelling of the Holy Spirit at his baptism (3:21-22) and which he conferred on the disciples. The statement about "trampling on snakes and scorpions" (v. 19), although superficially similar to Gen 3:15,[83] is more properly illuminated by *T. Levi* 18:12, "And Beliar [= Satan] shall be bound by him [the messianic Son of God]. And

---

79. See the passages gathered in Str-B 2:167-69; additionally Rev 12:9; *Ascen. Isa.* 7:9-12; *T. Mos.* 10:1; *T. Sim.* 6:6; *T. Zeb.* 9:8.

80. Jeremias, *Sprache des Lukasevangeliums,* 187-88, notes that Luke purges words of Hebrew origin in material he receives from Mark but includes words of Hebrew origin (incl. "Satan") freely in material unique to Luke. This observation indirectly corroborates the Hebraic character of Special Luke, which owes, in my judgment, to the Hebrew Gospel.

81. Bovon, *Lukas 9,51–14,35,* 78.

82. Schweizer, *Lukas,* 118.

83. Contra Bock, *Luke 9:51–24:53,* 1007-8, who sees v. 19 as "reassert[ing] humanity's vice-regent role in creation."

he shall grant to his children the authority to trample on wicked spirits. And the Lord will rejoice in his children." Luke's narrative diction — complete with the downfall of Satan, conferral of authority of the Son of God (v. 22) on his servants, and the joy of messianic victory — conforms in both essence and particulars with the messianic hope set forth in this text, signifying that in Jesus the eschatological kingdom of God is powerfully present. V. 19 should not be understood to promise immunity from bodily injury. Rather, like the same metaphors of the psalmist, it refers to the spiritual protection God provides those who acknowledge his name and the invincible salvation granted to those who take refuge in him (Ps 91:7-16). The assurance of that spiritual protection is emphasized by three Greek negatives in v. 19 (and is thus considerably stronger than the NIV "nothing will harm you"), connoting that absolutely nothing can conquer those who belong to Jesus (Rom 8:31-39).

21-22 "Your names are written in heaven" (v. 20) continues the metaphoric imagery. The passive voice ("are written"), an instance of the reverential Jewish custom of avoiding writing or vocalizing the name of God, means that *God* writes their names in heaven.[84] The metaphor of a heavenly book was widespread in Judaism, sometimes used, as here, of the book of eternal life,[85] but also of books recording the sum of human deeds, final judgment, and God's plans for the world.[86] Jesus uses the image to remind disciples of their true source of joy. Let them not rejoice "that the spirits submit to you," i.e., in your power and accomplishments — even *spiritual* power and accomplishments — but that your names are entered in heaven. Whatever is in heaven belongs irrevocably to God! The kingdom of God is above all a kingdom of relationships and eternal belonging, which are and remain the true joy and hope of believers.

The jubilant return of the seventy(-two) from mission launches Jesus into the most revelatory soliloquy in the Synoptics: "Full of joy through the Holy Spirit, Jesus said, 'I praise you, Father, Lord of heaven and earth, because you have hidden these things from the wise and learned, and revealed them to little children'" (v. 21). The Greek *agallian*, meaning "exceedingly joyful," is the most exultant description of Jesus in all Scripture. "Full of joy *through the Holy Spirit*" clarifies that the source of Jesus' joy is the spiritual significance of the mission of the seventy(-two), which consists in the proclamation of the kingdom of God by Jesus' authorized disciples and the downfall of Satan. Joy in the Holy Spirit need not be understood exclusive to Jesus, for if "spirit" here re-

---

84. Jeremias, *Sprache des Lukasevangeliums*, 188-89.

85. Exod 32:32-33; Ps 56:8; 69:28-29; 87:4-6; Isa 4:3; Dan 12:1; Mal 3:16-17; Phil 4:3; Heb 12:23; Rev 3:5; 13:8; 17:8; *1 En.* 47:3; 108:3; 1QM 12:2 (see Nolland, *Luke 9:21–18:34*, 566; Str-B 2:169).

86. On these various books and their significance, see Str-B 2:169-76.

flects the endowment of God's Spirit on the elders of Num 11:16 (see discussion of "seventy[-two]" at 10:1), then Jesus exults in the work of the Holy Spirit in the disciples as well as in himself.[87] "Spiritual joy" is not simply a consolation in the absence of earthly joy; it is the deepest and most abiding of all joys.

The wisdom of God is both praised and professed (the Gk. *exomologein* includes both senses),[88] for God as almighty creator of heaven and earth has both *hidden* and *revealed* his will. Jesus probably originally spoke vv. 21-22 in Aramaic or perhaps Hebrew, but Luke's Greek wording of the acclamation is masterful, both in alliterative uses of *apekrypsas* ("hidden") and *apekalypsas* ("revealed"), and in irony between "the wise and learned" and "little children." The praise and profession of Jesus expressly declare that spiritual knowledge and understanding are not human achievements of the educated, morally upright, or enlightened, but states alone made possible by the inscrutable will of God, who conceals himself from those who would turn his self-disclosure into an occasion for pride and reveals himself to those whose very unworthiness allows them to receive his revelation in freedom and joy. God Almighty not simply elects to reveal himself to the simple and lowly; like the Son he too finds *joy* in doing so, "for this was your good pleasure" (v. 21). The apostle Paul develops this theme inimitably in 1 Cor 1:18-29, declaring that "God chose the foolish things of the world to shame the wise."[89] Not to be overlooked in the joyful revelation of v. 21 is an intimation of the Trinity, for Jesus' lordship (v. 17) is combined with the Father and mediation of the Holy Spirit. Mention of the Holy Spirit is surprising and unprecedented in this context, for "there is no parallel [to exulting in the Holy Spirit] in the Scriptures."[90] This fact argues against the likelihood of the expression being an editorial addition of the later church and in favor of it deriving from Jesus himself. Naming of the Father, Son, and Holy Spirit in vv. 21-22 does not constitute a liturgical Trinitarian formula (nor at 3:21-22), but it appears to preserve a conscious Trinitarian *assumption* from the mouth of the historical Jesus.

V. 22 is characterized by A. M. Hunter as "perhaps the most important verse in the Synoptic Gospels,"[91] which provides a clearer aperture into the

---

87. Thus Bengel, *Gnomon*, 2:93, "The crowning point of the fruits of Christ's office was reached at that time. He Himself rejoiced in the joy of His disciples described in ver. 20." Likewise, Plummer, *S. Luke*, 280, Jesus exults over "the Divine Preference shown to the Disciples. . . . Nowhere else is anything of this kind recorded of Christ."

88. In the LXX *exomologeisthai* is often the opening ascription in psalms of praise (Nolland, *Luke 9:51–18:34*, 571). Lagrange, *Saint Luc*, 306, notes its use in liturgical contexts, including here from the mouth of Jesus, as an *explosion de louange* ("explosion of praise").

89. Making this the second theme in Luke 10 (see at 10:7) developed by the apostle Paul.

90. Metzger, *TCGNT*, 128.

91. "Crux Criticorum — Matt. XI.25-30, a Re-appraisal," *NTS* 8 (1961/62): 241. For further discussions of the passage, see J. Jeremias, *The Prayers of Jesus* (trans. J. Bowden; Phil-

self-consciousness of Jesus than any dominical saying in the Synoptics, including, perhaps, the Fourth Gospel. Vv. 21-22 closely parallel Matt 11:25-27, apparently deriving from a source common to Matt as well, i.e., the Double Tradition.[92] The noninterchangeable relationship between Father and Son in v. 22 and the style in which the relationship is expressed, like the reciprocal relationship and style of v. 16, remind readers immediately of the Fourth Gospel; indeed, Plummer rhapsodizes that v. 22 "contains the whole of the Christology of the Fourth Gospel."[93] No text from the OT, and no text from the intertestamental period or rabbinic literature, either states or intimates an exclusive and unshared relationship with the Father that Jesus claims for himself in v. 22. Paul Billerbeck's massive five-volume commentary on the NT from Talmud and Midrash finds no parallel to 10:22 in the entire Jewish tradition. David Flusser, a Jewish scholar who devoted his life to the study of Jesus against the background especially of Second Temple Judaism, finds the closest analogy to Jesus' self-consciousness in Hillel, although even that analogy is inadequate.[94] Nineteenth-century liberalism fiercely resisted the exclusive claim of divine sonship in v. 22, for in summarizing the essence of the Christian faith as "the fatherhood of God and the brotherhood of man," it concluded that Jesus' relationship with the Father was in essence no different from the relationship that all humanity naturally share with God.[95] The claim

---

adelphia: Fortress Press, 1978), 45-52; I. H. Marshall, *The Origins of New Testament Christology* (Downers Grove: Intervarsity Press, 1976), 115; R. P. Martin, *New Testament Foundations* (Grand Rapids: Eerdmans, 1975), 1:291-98.

92. On the Double Tradition, see the discussion "Luke's Sources" in the Introduction. For a discussion of this tradition, see Edwards, *Hebrew Gospel*, chap. 7. Although this is the only instance in the Double Tradition in which Jesus calls himself "the Son," Jesus' filial understanding is present in all discernible strata ("the things . . . handed down to us by those who from the first were eyewitnesses and servants of the word," 1:1-2) preceding the written Gospels. For evidence of the Hebraic character of v. 22, see Lagrange, *Luc*, 309; J. Jeremias, *New Testament Theology* (trans. J. Bowden; New York: Scribners, 1971), 56-62; and many scholars subsequently.

93. *Luke*, 282. He cites Johannine parallels in 3:35; 6:46; 8:19; 10:15, 30; 14:9; 16:15; 17:6, 10.

94. D. Flusser, *Entdeckungen im Neuen Testament*, vol. 1: *Jesusworte und ihre Überlieferung* (Neukirchen: Neukirchener Verlag, 1987), 215: "In the last analysis, there is a great difference between Hillel and Jesus. Hillel's self-understanding is not limited to his own person, but is typical for every person. Jesus' self-understanding of his unsurpassable bearing was, like Hillel's, always accompanied by humility and it avoided suggesting anything like a 'personality cult,' but it was also bound up with the knowledge that his own person was not interchangeable with any other human being. He understood himself to be 'the Son', and as such to have a central commission and role in the economy of God."

95. Evidence for the authenticity of v. 22 is considerable. Its textual integrity is secure, apart from a secondary introduction ("Then he turned to his disciples and said") transposed from the introduction of v. 23 (see Metzger, *TCGNT*, 128). The content of v. 22 satisfies the so-called criterion of dissimilarity in that there are no collaborative cultural parallels. The saying

of Jesus in v. 22 both to *universality* ("all things have been committed to me") and *exclusivity* ("no one knows who the Son is except the Father, and no one knows who the Father is except the Son and those to whom the Son chooses to reveal him") could be made of no character in the OT, and to my knowledge has been made by no founder of any other religion.

Jesus' reference to "*my* Father" further echoes his unshared divine sonship. There are fifty-one occurrences (excluding parallels) of "Father" in the mouth of Jesus in the Synoptic Gospels, in twenty-nine of which Jesus speaks of God (as here) as "my Father," and in twenty-two of which he teaches the disciples about God as "your Father." In no instance, however, does Jesus include himself with the disciples in addressing God as "our Father."[96] In v. 22 Jesus claims to stand in a unique and unshared relationship with the Father, as a consequence of which the Father has delivered "all things"[97] to the Son,

---

is typical of Jesus' style, particularly in the bold reference to God as "Father" (see on term at 11:2), and the Hebraic character of the saying argues against its being a later Hellenistic addition. The saying has not been seriously attacked on textual, linguistic, or historical and cultural grounds, but primarily on theological grounds, i.e., the offense of Jesus' claim of exclusive divine Sonship. Lagrange, *Luc,* 306-9, addresses a number of the nineteenth-c. attacks of Loisy, Wellhausen, and Harnack. A modern attack from G. Vermes, *Jesus the Jew: A Historian's Reading of the Gospels* (New York: Macmillan, 1973), 201, echoes earlier theological skepticism: "In removing this hymn from the lips of Jesus and accrediting it instead to the primitive church, contemporary exegetical skepticism joins forces for once with common sense; for no unbiased interpreter can fail to notice how discrepant these words are in both tone and content from the normal sayings of Jesus." Bovon, *Lukas 9,51–14,35,* 72-73, likewise searches for possible sources of the saying in post-Easter theology that may have been retrojected on the historical Jesus, perhaps from an early Christian author or prophet, or in the later historicizing of a parable. How, then, should we respond to a saying such as v. 22 that satisfactorily passes the relevant tests of authenticity but appears to offend modern presentiments against religious exclusivity? In my judgment, if we take the baptismal experience of Jesus seriously, and if we ponder the significance of his several implicit Christological disclosures (see J. Edwards, *Is Jesus the Only Savior?* [Grand Rapids: Eerdmans, 2005], chap. 5), the words and spirit of v. 22 are not "discrepant" but in character with the historical Jesus.

96. The "our Father" of the Lord's Prayer is an instruction to the disciples, not a self-confession of Jesus. T. W. Manson, *The Teaching of Jesus: Studies in Its Form and Content* (Cambridge: University Press, 1963), 102, writes that "the experience of God as Father dominates the whole ministry of Jesus from the Baptism to the Crucifixion." Indeed, for Luke it dominates even Jesus' self-understanding as a boy (2:49).

97. Origen, *Hom. Luc.* 10.22, sees in Jesus' claim to have received "all things" an echo of Matt 28:18 ("All power in heaven and on earth has been given to me") and Col 1:20, that "through his cross he might reconcile both what is upon the earth and what is in heaven." As such, Jesus "is the savior of all humanity" (1 Tim 4:10), "the expiation of all our sins" (1 John 2:2), "so that at the name of Jesus every knee should bend — of those in heaven, on the earth, and under the earth — and every tongue confess that Jesus Christ is Lord to the glory of God the Father" (Phil 2:10-11).

and given the Son exclusive authority to reveal knowledge of himself and the Father to whomever he wills.

23-24   Evidence particularly within the Synoptic Gospels indicates that Jesus allowed such apertures into his self-consciousness only rarely and on guarded occasions, and only then within the confines of his closest confidants. The introduction to v. 23 ("Then Jesus turned to his disciples and said privately") is consistent with this evidence. The reference to "his disciples" probably refers to the Twelve (and perhaps their auxiliaries, so 6:17, 20) rather than to the seventy(-two), for the seventy(-two) are not expressly referred to as disciples in Luke 10, and the use of "privately" (v. 23; Gk. *kat' idian*) often accompanies intimate fellowship with the Twelve alone in the Gospels.[98] The uniqueness of the Twelve consists not only in their special authorization (9:1-2) in contrast to other followers, but particularly in their eyewitness experience of Jesus. It is to such eyewitness experience — and the authority attendant upon it — that Luke appeals in the prologue of the Gospel (1:2).[99] Others greater than the disciples — "prophets and kings" (v. 24) — longed in vain for what the disciples see and hear. The revelation the disciples have received, and for which they are responsible, exceeds that of "prophets and kings" of old — indeed, of Judaism as a whole.[100] The sense here is not that the gospel replaces and dispenses with the old covenant, as might be argued for example from the metaphor of "new wine" and "old wineskins" (5:37-39), but that the completion of salvation history eagerly anticipated in the old covenant (Jer 31:31-34; Ezek 36:24-32) is present in the witness of Jesus' disciples. The relation of the disciples to "prophets and kings" parallels the relation of "little children" to the "wise and learned" in v. 21. What the disciples experience is due not to their merits, but to divine grace and election; they are "those to whom the Son chooses to reveal himself" (v. 22).

THE GOOD SAMARITAN (10:25-37)

In 10:21-22 Luke preserves the unsurpassed revelation of Jesus, who stands in a unique relationship with the Father; in 10:25-37 Luke preserves the parable that supremely expresses that revelation in Christian love. These two passages, set adjacent to one another like Jakin and Boaz, the two temple pillars (1 Kgs 7:15-22), combine theological truth and practical ethics, word and

---

98. Matt 20:17; Mark 4:34; 6:31; 9:28; Luke 9:10; Gal 2:2; see Wolter, *Lukasevangelium,* 389.

99. On eyewitness evidence in the gospels, see R. Bauckham, *Jesus and the Eyewitnesses: The Gospels as Eyewitness Testimony* (Grand Rapids: Eerdmans, 2006).

100. Bovon, *Lukas 9,51–14,35,* 74-75.

deed, faith and works, not unlike Paul's witness of "faith expressed through love" (Gal 5:6).[101]

25-29   "On one occasion an expert in the law stood up to test Jesus" (v. 25). "And behold" (Gk. *kai idou;* NIV "On one occasion") is one of the many indefinite connectives in the central section, meaning simply "sometime later." Luke uses three different Greek words for Jewish scribes, who, in the words of Schürer, were "the undisputed spiritual leaders of the people."[102] The other Evangelists refer to scribes only by the Greek word *grammateus,* which Luke uses in fifteen instances, especially when following Mark. In addition, Luke refers to scribes six times as "lawyers" (Gk. *nomikos*),[103] and once as "teachers of the law" (5:17; Gk. *nomodidaskalos* [again in Acts 5:34]). "Expert in the law" here translates the second term, *nomikos.* Luke does not make a distinction among these terms, but *nomikos* may designate a distinguished category of scribes, a "first among equals," as it were, who both knew the law and were authorized to teach it.[104] V. 25 recalls a typical Jewish teaching scene, with teacher surrounded by disciples and hearers, all seated. Jewish disciples normally honored rabbis by standing when they spoke or asked a question. The description of the scribe as "[standing] to test Jesus" thus suggests either disingenuousness or duplicity on his part, for his intention does not correspond to his respectful posture. The brief exchange between Jesus and the scribe resembles Mark 12:28-31//Matt 22:34-40, but the encounter may derive from a different source or be a different episode altogether, for the question posed to Jesus is entirely different.[105] "What must I do to inherit eternal life?" was not an uncommon question in first-century Judaism, and it is not difficult to imagine that Jesus was asked this or similar questions more than once in his ministry.[106] The verb in Greek is in the aorist tense, implying a pat solitary action: "What *thing* must I do?" If it does not intend a single deed, it intends something that at least can be calculated. Jesus responds, "What is written in the Law? How do you read it?" (v. 26). This question corresponds to the way rabbis engaged students in debate, and references to "written," "Law," and "read" drive the scribe irrevocably to Torah.[107] The counterquestion thus

101. See Klein, *Lukasevangelium,* 388.

102. *History of the Jewish People,* 2:4.

103. Matt 22:35 includes *nomikos* once as well.

104. See Str-B 1:898; Jeremias, *Sprache des Lukasevangeliums,* 165-66; W. Gutbrod, *nomikos, TWNT* 4:1080-81; Schürer, *History of the Jewish People,* 3:2-35.

105. So too Plummer, *Luke,* 283-84; Fitzmyer, *Luke (X–XXIV),* 877; Bovon, *Lukas 9,51–14,35,* 84.

106. Who would inherit eternal life is first voiced in *1 En.* 40:9. The same question is asked of Jesus in another context in 18:18 (par. Mark 10:17). The presence of the question in various forms in the *Mishnah* (e.g., *'Abot* 2.7; 5.19) and *Talmud* (e.g., *b. Soṭah* 7b; *b. Qidd.* 40b) attests to its currency in first-c. Judaism. See Str-B 1:829.

107. Str-B 2:176-77.

implies that the core of the gospel is present and knowable to the scribe in Torah, "concealed in the OT and revealed in the NT," as Augustine would later say.

The scribe responds in v. 27 with a conflation of Deut 6:5 and Lev 19:18: Torah requires both love of God and love of neighbor. The Hebrew and Greek versions of Deut 6:5 enjoin a threefold response to God of "heart," "soul," and "strength." Luke substitutes a different Greek word for "strength" *(ischys,* not *dynamis)* and adds a fourth response of "mind" not present in the Deuteronomic commandment. The only other version of the oft-quoted Shema to include this fourfold response is Mark 12:30, which suggests that Luke here quotes the commandment from Mark. The commandment does not require a different form of love for God than for neighbor, but the same form of love (Gk. *agapan)* for both (on *agapē,* see at 6:27). Disciples are thus not to apply a different or lesser love to others than they apply to God. The fourfold repetition of "all" before each response emphasizes a total commitment of love to the lordship of God. In Deut 6:5 each of the three responses is prefaced by "from" (Gk. *ex),* i.e., love of God *from* heart, *from* soul, etc. In the Lukan version of v. 27, "from" occurs only before the first response: "You shall love the Lord your God *from* your whole heart and *with* [Gk. *en]* all your soul and *with* all your strength and *with* all your mind." In light of the following parable the meaning of "neighbor" is especially important, for in first-century Judaism, as in the OT, "neighbor" designated Israelites (including strangers who shared the land with them [Lev. 19:34]), but not Gentiles.[108]

In Mark 12:30-31 and Matt 22:37-38 the combination of the two commandments to love God and love neighbor occurs in the mouth of Jesus, whereas in Luke it occurs in the mouth of the scribe. Jesus was distinctive for summarizing the totality of the Torah in these two commandments, and his summary defined the subsequent mainstream of Christian tradition.[109] Jesus was not entirely unique in this distinction, for isolated voices in Judaism in the first century (and perhaps even earlier) also prescribed love of God and love of neighbor as the essence of Torah.[110] As far as we know, however, no Jew apart from Jesus identified the cardinal virtues of love of God and love of neighbor in the words of Deut 6:5 and Lev 19:18. This unusual correspondence between the words of the scribe and the words of Jesus suggests that Luke

108. Str-B 2:353-54.

109. Rom 13:8-10; Gal 5:14; Jas 2:8; *2 Clem.* 3:4; *Did.* 1:2; 2:7; *Barn.* 19:5; Justin Martyr, *Dial.* 93:2-3; *1 Apol.* 16.6; *Mart. Pol.* 3.3.

110. *T. Iss.* 5:2, "Love the Lord and the neighbor"; *T. Dan* 5:3, "Love the Lord with all your life and each other with a true heart"; Philo, *Spec.* 2.63, "But among the vast number of particular trusts and principles [related to the Sabbath] there studied, there stand out practically high above the others two main heads: one of duty to God as shown by piety and holiness, one of duty to people as shown by humanity and justice." From Qumran, see 4QTLevi, 4QTNaph. On this question, see Fitzmyer, *Luke (X–XXIV),* 879; Wolter, *Lukasevangelium,* 393.

ascribes the response of the scribe in the words of Jesus himself. Jesus affirms the scribe's answer similar to his earlier affirmation of Simon the Pharisee (7:43) and enjoins him, "Do this and you will live" (v. 28). Had Jesus merely affirmed the scribe's theology, he may have pursued matters no further, for he had "answered correctly" (v. 28). But Jesus commands him, "*Do this.*" The scribe must act on his belief, lest his belief, correct as it is, remains inert and fruitless. Wishing to "justify himself" — or better, wishing a *self*-justification (16:15!) against the possible claim of Jesus' commandment on his life — the scribe asks, "Who is my neighbor?"

30-37   Hoping to evade a possible obligation of faith, the scribe asks to whom he owes the duty of *agapē*. Even in the scribe's resistance, Jesus senses a glimmer of openness, and he "takes up" (v. 30; Gk. *hypolambanein;* NIV "in reply") his challenge by putting a question to the questioner in hopes of convicting him of the fuller ramifications of faith. "A man was going down from Jerusalem to Jericho, when he fell into the hands of robbers. They stripped him of his clothes, beat him and went away leaving him half dead" (v. 30). The elevation of Jerusalem is 2,600 feet (800 m) above sea level, and Jericho, eighteen miles (29 km) to the northeast, lies 825 feet (250 m) *below* sea level. Despite its arid and desolate surroundings, Jericho was a verdant, fertile, and productive oasis of date palms.[111] The serpentine road from Jerusalem to Jericho descended 3,400 feet (1,040 m) through steep and rugged hill country pockmarked with caves, which, especially near the ascent to Jerusalem, offered refuge for brigands. The Greek word for "robbers" (v. 30; *lēstai*) is used by Josephus of the Zealots, but Luke uses it more generally of bandits who, again according to Josephus, were numerous enough that even the Essenes armed themselves when traveling in the region (*J.W.* 2.125). The notoriety of the road from Jerusalem to Jericho provided Jesus with an appropriate setting of the parable: an unnamed Samaritan fell victim to highway robbers, who stripped him, beat him, and left him half-dead.

"By chance a priest was going down the very road" (v. 31). The Greek expression *kata synkyrian* ("by chance"; NIV "happened") means "an unexpected conjunction of events." Coming immediately after the misfortune of the traveler, it raises the prospect of help. The approaching pedestrian is a priest, not wholly surprising, for most priests who served in the temple (see at 1:5) resided not in Jerusalem but in other cities and villages of Judea and beyond. The greatest number of priests who did not live in Jerusalem lived in Jericho, the closest large city. The priest in the parable may have been returning to Jericho after having completed his temple service in Jerusalem; or he may have been returning after conveying provisions from families in Jericho

---

111. On Jericho and its fertility, see Strabo, *Geogr.* 16.2.763; Josephus, *J.W.* 4.459-74; Schürer, *History of the Jewish People*, 1:298-99.

to priests still serving in the temple.[112] The approach of a priest would seem a good omen, for one who served God in the temple could be hoped to serve a wounded traveler on the roadside.[113] The priest saw the wounded traveler, but for reasons we are not told, he "passed by on the other side of the road" (v. 31).[114]

Fortunately, a **Levite** also approached. The tribe of Levi was responsible for oversight of the central sanctuary of Israel by assisting the priests, preparing sacrifices, cleansing and caring for the sacred courts and vessels, serving as porters, gatekeepers, singers, and musicians, and also by interpreting Torah. Because of its ordination to temple service, the tribe of Levi did not receive a land allotment as did other Israelite tribes.[115] Normative Judaism is usually stereotyped in the Gospels by "Pharisees and scribes." Jesus' pairing of "priests and Levites" (elsewhere in the NT only John 1:19) seems particularly significant in the parable, for the two offices frequently occur in a trilogy of "priests, Levites, and people" as a designation for all Israel.[116] "Priests and Levites" thus personifies the distinctive relationship of Israel with God, particularly as it was expressed in the temple cult of Jerusalem.[117] It could thus be hoped that the Levite who assisted in the temple would assist a wounded man beside the road. Like the priest before him, however, the Levite, also for undisclosed reasons, passes by the wounded man.[118] With their receding footsteps, hope from Israel fades for the wounded man.

112. On priests in Jericho, see Str-B 2:66, 182-83.

113. I do not follow Paul Billerbeck's judgment that priests and Levites were popularly considered "idolatrous, quarrelsome, greedy, arrogant, godless, debauched, pederasts, and beastialists" (Str-B 2:182), and thus of no hope or help to the wounded man. Billerbeck grounds his judgment solely on *T. Levi* 17:11, a text whose intent is not to profile the traditional priesthood but rather the corruption of the priesthood immediately prior to the advent of the messianic priest in *T. Levi* 18. The common profile of priests and Levites conveyed in 1–2 Chr, Ezra, Neh, Josephus, *Ant.* 11, and in 1QS, CD, 1QM, and 11Q19 is not pejorative, however, and thus does not conform to or confirm Billerbeck's negative assessment of the priesthood. The presence of priests and Levites in the parable would thus awaken hope in hearers, not cynicism.

114. K. Bailey, *Jesus through Middle Eastern Eyes,* 293, suggests that the priest refrains from contact with the wounded man (who could have been dead) in order to avoid defilement, which would have jeopardized his temple service. Two reasons discount this suggestion. The priest in the parable cannot be worried about rendering himself unclean for temple service because he is going away from Jerusalem, i.e., he has already completed his temple service. Moreover, in Jewish law saving a life supersedes all other laws. In the Mishnah, the earliest compilation of rabbinic law, even a high priest is directed to attend a neglected corpse (*m. Naz.* 7.1).

115. On the Levitical priesthood, see R. Abba, "Priests and Levites," *IDB* 3:876-88; M. Rehm, "Priests and Levites," *ABD* 4:297-310.

116. 1 Chr 28:21; 2 Chr 34:30; 35:2-3, 8, 18; Ezra 2:70; 7:7, 13; 8:15; 9:1; 10:5, 18-22, 25-43; Neh 7:72; 8:13; 9:38; 10:28; 11:3, 20.

117. See Wolter, *Lukasevangelium,* 396.

118. On the Greek textual variants of v. 32, see Metzger, *TCGNT,* 128-29.

"But a certain Samaritan, as he traveled, came to the man" (v. 33). With this statement comes the turning point of the parable. This is a surprising turning point indeed, for if priests, Levites, and people formed the three major sociological divisions of postexilic Israel, we should expect Jesus to include a Jewish layman as the third traveler on the road.[119] The third traveler is not an Israelite, however, but an outsider and alien, a Samaritan. The priest and Levite had passed by at safe distance and made no contact with the wounded man. The Samaritan, however, came either to the *place* where the man was, or directly to the *man* (v. 33; *kat' auton* could mean either, but probably the latter). The Samaritan was presumably as aware as the travelers before him that, in so doing, he was vulnerable to being robbed, or could himself be suspected of having waylaid the wounded man. But the Samaritan does what the priest and Levite do not do: he makes contact with the man and is moved with compassion.[120] Unlike the priest and the Levite, the Samaritan had not come from the temple in Jerusalem, for **Samaritans**, although they worshiped the same God, observed the same rites and festivals, and read the same Torah as Jews, tenaciously worshiped God on Mount Gerizim in Samaria rather than on Mount Zion in Jerusalem. Moreover, the demography of Samaria had been radically altered by two population exchanges — the first following the fall of Samaria in 721 B.C., when the Assyrians resettled Babylonians and other Mesopotamian stock in Samaria, and the second when Alexander the Great resettled Macedonians in Samaria some three centuries later. Centuries of intermarriage had rendered Samaria overwhelmingly Gentile and thus ethnically contaminated in Jewish eyes. This, combined with their renegade sanctuary on Mount Gerizim, made Jews — including Jesus' disciples (9:54) — deeply antagonistic toward Samaritans (John 4:9).[121] To Jews, Samaritans were not simply outcasts, they were enemies (John 8:48).

The inclusion of a Samaritan in the parable would seem to seal the wounded man's fate, for if a priest and Levite offered no help, how much less a Samaritan! Ironically, Jesus makes a Samaritan — whose theology he judged defective on another occasion (John 4:22!) — a moral hero in Israel. The Samaritan treats the victim's wounds with bandages, oil, and wine, puts him on his donkey, brings him to an inn, and cares for him (v. 34). The details of first aid would be of special interest to Luke if, as is traditionally held, he was a physician. Oil and wine — probably mixed — were familiar remedies in Israel

119. See M. Gourgues, "The Priest, the Levite, and the Samaritan Revisited: A Critical Note on Luke 10:31-35," *JBL* 117/4 (1998): 709-13.

120. Plummer, *Luke*, 287.

121. On Samaria and Samaritans, see Schürer, *History of the Jewish People*, 2:15-20. Ben Sira's disparagement of Samaria surely spoke for many Jews: "Two nations my soul detests, and the third is not even a people: Those who live in Seir and the Philistines, and the foolish people that live in Samaria" (Sir 50:25-26).

(Isa 1:6; Jer 51:8), and if poured on *after* the wounds were bandaged, as the sequence of v. 34 suggests, they may have formed a medicinal compress. Inns were not always reputable or safe places in the ancient world — and innkeepers no more so.[122] Travelers usually camped or sought accommodations with friends or members of their same guild, cult, or profession. If these were not available, Jewish travelers would seek accommodations from a synagogue, if present. Public inns and houses were often associated with prostitutes, thieves, bedbugs, and filth. Depositing two denarii — the equivalent of two days' wages (Matt 20:2) — with a proprietor of such a place, attests to the serious condition of the wounded man and the risk incurred by the Samaritan to help him. His resolve to help the man is made emphatic in the Greek of v. 35: whatever the cost overrun for his care, "*I* will repay."

The waylaid traveler is never identified, nor do the priest and Levite figure further in the parable. The decisive turn comes with the entrance of the Samaritan, and the story ends with his intervention on behalf of the wounded man. "Who of the three," asks Jesus, "was neighbor to the man who fell into the hands of the robbers?" (v. 36). The question Jesus asks the lawyer is not the same question the lawyer asked Jesus in v. 29. For the lawyer, "neighbor" is a noun. "Neighbor" is an object to whom one owes duties — burdensome duties that the lawyer desires to avoid (v. 29). For Jesus, "neighbor" is a verb, a way of behaving toward people in need that gives life to both giver and receiver. The Greek word *gegonenai* is crucial to Jesus' question in v. 36: "Who of the three *became* a neighbor [or *showed* neighborliness] . . . ?" For Jesus, one does not *have* a neighbor; one *is* a neighbor, or better, *becomes* a neighbor. The parable does not require hearers to convert enemies into friends, to do everything for everyone, to solve the problems of the world. To be a neighbor is not a condition one inherits, in other words, but a choice one makes to render the tangible assistance one is able to render to those in need of it, and to render

122. The inn, like other details, is important to the parable, but a specific inn between Jerusalem and Jericho is not necessarily implied, nor is the existence of such an inn necessary for the effect of the parable. In the early fifth c., Jerome (d. 420), who spent the final decades of his life in the Holy Land and translated Eusebius's fourth-c. *Onomasticon* into Latin, identified the site of Adummim as the "inn" of the Good Samaritan. Adummim lay roughly midway on the ancient road (not the modern highway) connecting Jerusalem and Jericho. Jerome writes: "In Latin [Adummim] can be called the Ascent of the Reds or the Blood-Stains, because of the blood that has been shed there by thieves. For it is at the border of the tribe of Judah with Benjamin, on the way down to Jericho from Aelia [Capitolina = Jerusalem], where also there is a military post situated to help travellers. The Lord is also recorded as mentioning it as a cruel and blood-stained place in a parable of the man going down to Jericho from Jerusalem" (*Onomasticon,* 21-22). Archaeological excavations begun in 1998 indicate that in the Second Temple period the village of Adummim was a *khan* or *caravansary* (overnight hostel for travelers and pack animals) that was further developed in the Byzantine, Crusader, and Ottoman periods. See Y. Magen, "Inn of the Good Samaritan Becomes a Museum," *BAR* 38/1 (2012): 48-57.

it irrespective of ethnic, religious, cultic, or racial differences.[123] The lawyer does not expect the conclusion to which the parable leads him; the fact that he cannot bring himself to say "the Samaritan" in answer to Jesus' question may betray his difficulty in accepting the full ramifications of the parable. But if he won't acknowledge the neighbor, he at least acknowledges neighborliness, "to show mercy" (v. 37). Anyone who "goes and does likewise" (v. 37) fulfills the heart of the parable.[124]

Already in the second century the Good Samaritan was widely identified as Jesus Christ, and the parable as a whole interpreted as an allegory of the gospel. Allegorical renditions were offered as early as Marcion and Irenaeus (both second c.), but in the third century Origen offered the most elaborate allegory: the man who fell among thieves was Adam coming from Paradise (Jerusalem) into the world (Jericho); the robbers were evil powers; the priest was the law, the Levite, prophets, and the Samaritan, Christ; the wounds were disobedience; the beast of burden, the body of Christ; the inn, the church; the two denarii, the Father and Son (or the two sacraments); the innkeeper, the bishop; and the promise of the Samaritan to return, the promise of the second coming of Christ.[125] Allegorical interpretations prevailed throughout the patristic and medieval periods, and even Luther, who typically rejected allegory, maintained allegorical interpretations of the parable in no fewer than ten sermons.[126] The modern ethical interpretation of the parable began with John Calvin, who rejected allegory, asserting that the fathers "devised this interpretation without regard to the true meaning of the Lord's words."[127] As Bovon suggests, the parable of the Good Samaritan essentially illustrates the second commandment, the love of neighbor (so 10:27; Lev 19:18), whereas the following story of Mary and Martha illustrates the first commandment, the love of God (10:27; Deut 6:5).[128]

MARTHA, MARY, AND JESUS (10:38-42)

38-40　V. 38 resumes the journey of Jesus and his disciples to Jerusalem (9:51), last noted in 9:57. Luke reports that Jesus entered an unnamed village and was received into the home of two sisters, a more dominant woman

---

123. See Lagrange, *Luc*, 315-16; Schweizer, *Lukas*, 122-23; Fitzmyer, *Luke (X–XXIV)*, 884.

124. p[45] emphasizes the final command of Jesus, "Go, and you *also* do likewise."

125. Origen, *Hom. Luc.* 34.

126. For one of Luther's sermons on 10:25-37, see Kealy, *Interpretation of the Gospel of Luke*, 276-77.

127. *Institutes of the Christian Religion*, 2.5.19.

128. On the history of interpretation of the parable, see Bovon, *Lukas 9,51–14,35*, 93-99.

named Martha and a (presumably) younger woman named Mary (vv. 38-39). The description of Jesus' mission and reception in v. 38 exemplifies the instructions he gave the seventy(-two) disciples in 10:5-8.[129] Two sisters in John 11:1 and 12:1-3 also bear the names Martha and Mary, and they too invite Jesus to dinner in their home, with Martha "serving" him (v. 40; John 12:2). The Lukan and Johannine accounts are similar, but they are not carbon copies of one another and it is difficult to know what relation, if any, they share with one another. In John the focus is on a brother named Lazarus and on Mary's anointing Jesus' feet with expensive ointment, neither of which is mentioned in Luke. In Luke the focus is on Martha's distraction while serving and Jesus' affirmation of Mary's choice to be with him, neither of which is mentioned in John. John further identifies the village of Lazarus, Martha, and Mary as Bethany, which lay two miles (3 km) southeast of Jerusalem. In 10:38 Jesus and the disciples are far away from Bethany, which will not be reached until 19:29.[130] It is thus conceivable that the Lukan and Johannine accounts are different episodes altogether.

The skeletal similarities between the two narratives are tantalizing, however, and may suggest a common source. To be sure, "Mary" was the most common female name in Hellenistic Judaism (and "Martha" the fourth most popular female name),[131] so it would not be too unusual for Jesus to meet women of the same names. It would be more unusual, however, for them to be sisters who received him in similar fashion. It would also be very unusual for two unknown women to accept Jesus (and disciples?) into their home,[132] whereas if Jesus knew the family, as John 11:1-5 and 12:1-3 report, his acceptance by Martha and Mary would be more explicable. The fact that Jesus is thrice referred to as "Lord" in the pericope — once by Martha herself (v. 40;

129. A majority of manuscripts reads, "Martha received him into her home" (NIV "Martha opened her home to him"), but three of the oldest and weightiest manuscripts (p[45, 75] B) omit "into her home," reading simply, "Martha received him" (Gk. *hypedexato auton*). The abrupt shorter reading, normally to be preferred as the more original, has evidently undergone scribal expansion: "Martha received him *into her* (or *her own*, or *their*) home." See 19:6, where Luke writes that Zacchaeus "received him gladly" (Gk. *hypedexato auton chairōn*).

130. For fuller comparisons and contrasts between the two stories, see Bovon, *Lukas 9,51-14,35*, 103.

131. According to R. Bauckham, *Jesus and the Eyewitnesses: The Gospels as Eyewitness Testimony* (Grand Rapids: Eerdmans, 2006), 89, literary evidence in the time period 330 B.C.–A.D. 200 shows Mary to have been the most common female name (70 records), followed by Salome (58), Shelamzion (24), and Martha (20), with Joanna (12) and Sapphira (12) tied for the fifth most common name.

132. Schweizer, *Lukas*, 124, asserts that it would be "almost unthinkable" for Martha, as a female head of a household, to invite male company to her house. This is doubtless true of a woman inviting unfamiliar male company into her house, but much less true if Jesus (and disciples) were personal friends of Mary and Martha.

cf. John 11:3) — may also suggest that Jesus was known to the sisters.[133] With regard to the different aspects of the two accounts, three Hebraisms in vv. 38, 39, and 42 may betray Luke's indebtedness to any earlier Hebrew source that differed from John's account.[134] It is not impossible that Luke, or the Hebrew Gospel before him, isolates specific elements of the episode for its narrative purposes, whereas John emphasizes other elements for its purposes. Finally, with regard to the place-name of Bethany, we have seen that Luke does not always follow the other Gospels in matters of chronology and geography. The sermon in Nazareth, for example, which appears midpoint in Matt 13:53-58 and Mark 6:1-6, appears as the programmatic introduction to Jesus' ministry in 4:16-30.[135] Luke's chronology in the central section, as noted in the excursus at 9:51, is characteristically nebulous, and it is not difficult to imagine that he employed the story of Martha and Mary for its particular narrative effect at the end of the unit on discipleship in 10:1-42.

Martha "had a sister called Mary, who sat at the Lord's feet listening to what he said" (v. 39). This seemingly objective statement is actually the description of a model disciple in Judaism. "Sitting at one's feet" is a classic description of a rabbinic disciple (2 Kgs 4:38; 6:1; Acts 22:3; *m. 'Abot.* 1:4). In Luke, "sitting" (or "falling") at Jesus' feet symbolizes faith (8:41). Those who congregate at Jesus' feet — women (7:38; 10:39), Gentiles (8:35), and Samaritans (17:16) — were not permitted at the feet of typical Jewish rabbis, however.[136] The description of Mary "hearing his word" (v. 39; NIV "listening to what he said") is even more important, for "hearing [Jesus'] word" is in Luke-Acts the critical and consummate human response to divine revelation.[137] The Greek imperfect tense of "hearing" in v. 39 means that Mary is *absorbing* Jesus' word.

The Greek text includes an illuminating variant in v. 39 not noted in the NIV: "[Martha] had a sister called Mary, who *also* sat at the Lord's feet." Textual evidence for this variant is virtually evenly divided.[138] The variant might be understood to refer to Jesus' disciples, i.e., "along with Jesus' disciples, Mary *also* sat at the Lord's feet." But since Jesus' disciples are not mentioned

---

133. On the use of "Lord" in the pericope, see Rowe, *Early Narrative Christology,* 142-51.

134. Edwards, *Hebrew Gospel,* 311.

135. Recall that early in the second c. Papias (Eusebius, *Hist. eccl.* 3.39.15) did not consider changes in the chronology of events to jeopardize the accuracy of the Gospel of Mark ("Mark . . . wrote accurately all that [Peter] remembered, though not in the order of the things said and done by the Lord"). Papias does not address the Gospel of Luke in this matter, but the same principle may apply.

136. Note the pronouncement of R. Eliezer (ca. 80-120) that "if any man gives his daughter a knowledge of the Law it is as though he taught her lechery" (*m. Soṭah* 3:4).

137. 4:32; 5:1; 6:47; 8:11, 15, 21; 10:39; 11:28; Acts 2:22; 4:4; 5:5, 24; 10:44; 13:7, 44; 15:7; 19:10. Further on the "word of God," see at 8:15.

138. Inclusion of *hē* ("she"): p[45, 75] ℵ* B² L Ξ 579; omission: ℵ¹ A B* C D W Θ Ψ *f*¹ *f*¹³.

in the account, this assumption seems improbable. *Also* would seem to refer to Martha, and given Jesus' rebuke of Martha and praise of Mary, it is easier to imagine a scribe omitting the variant than adding it. This would argue in favor of its originality; and if so, the variant implies that Martha as well as Mary was a model disciple.[139]

While Mary is absorbed in Jesus' presence, Martha is left with "all the preparations" (v. 40; Gk. lit. "much service") without Mary's help or the help of a servant. In Near Eastern culture, then as now, this was a considerable obligation. Patience decreases as pressure increases, and Martha approaches Jesus, "Lord, don't you care that my sister has left me to do the work by myself? Tell her to help me!" (v. 40). Commentators sometimes note that, in emphasizing *me,* Martha violates the cardinal rule of hospitality, i.e., she is thinking of herself rather than of Jesus, her guest. This may be true, but Martha's aggravation in the circumstances is entirely understandable — and evidently forgivable, for Jesus makes no mention of it in his response. The rhetorical question "Don't you care?" (v. 40; Gk. *ou melei soi*) is a colloquial understatement, implying that Mary (or Jesus?) is responding inadequately (Mark 4:38). Martha speaks of her younger sister as the elder brother speaks of his younger brother in the parable of the Prodigal Son (15:30): both address their siblings through the medium of an authority figure in hopes of vindication.

41-42 "Martha, Martha," Jesus answered, "you are worried and upset about many things" (v. 41). The repetition of Martha's name conveys Jesus' affection for her, and an understanding of her predicament. "All the preparations" (v. 40) have made her anxious and distracted by "many things" (v. 41). Jesus does not condemn Martha, but reminds her with gentleness and firmness of a better way. "One thing is necessary. Mary has chosen what is better, and it will not be taken away from her" (v. 42). The beginning of v. 42 in Greek is unfortunately no longer recoverable with certainty.[140] The reading of the NIV, "Few things are needful — or indeed only one," although well attested in the manuscript tradition, is, in my judgment, a conflation of two readings. The longer reading in the NIV softens the absoluteness of "one thing." It also implies that Jesus' rebuke relates to culinary matters, i.e., Martha should prepare fewer items, or only one, for the meal.[141] A stronger case, in my judgment, can be made for "one thing is needful." The manuscript support for this reading, though slightly weaker than the longer reading, nevertheless combines

---

139. So too M. D'Angelo, "Women in Luke-Acts: A Redactional View," *JBL* 109/3 (1990): 454.

140. See a full discussion of the problem in G. Fee, "'One Thing Needful'? Luke 10:42," in *New Testament Textual Criticism: Its Significance for Exegesis; Essays in Honour of Bruce M. Metzger* (ed. E. Epp and G. Fee; Oxford: Clarendon Press, 1981), 51-75.

141. Origen's several interpretations of the saying in *Hom. Luc.* Frag. 171 reflect the ambiguous state of the textual tradition already in the early third c.

early and weighty evidence.[142] Furthermore, internal evidence argues for the originality of this reading, which is shorter and more difficult. The shorter reading also stands in contrast with "many" immediately before and offers greater interpretive insight into the pericope. "One thing is needful" directs Martha's attention away from the menu to the "one thing" of absolute importance — hearing Jesus' word (v. 39). Preparations and hospitality are indeed important, but they are not as important as "hearing Jesus' word." The gospel of Jesus reprioritizes all of life. Mary has made the gospel primary, to which all other things, even hospitality, are relative. The primacy of the gospel is the "good part," for it alone determines the life of discipleship, and it shall not be taken from Mary.

In the ancient church Martha and Mary emerged as types of the active and contemplative lives, respectively. Greater honor was accorded to Mary, the contemplative. Origen further allegorized Martha as a symbol of the Jew, distracted by "works righteousness," while Mary symbolized faithful Gentile Christianity.[143] The Tübingen School of the eighteenth century maintained this latter uncharitable allegory. Modern readers may be inclined to see in Martha and Mary types of social action on the one hand and evangelism and Bible study on the other. These allegorical interpretations misconstrue Martha and Mary in terms of competing opposites.[144] Jesus' appeal to Martha concerns *diakonein*, which here (v. 40, twice), and frequently in Luke-Acts (4:39; 12:37; 17:8; 22:26-27; Acts 6:1-2), pertains to table hospitality. Jesus does not condemn Martha's hospitality but directs her to a new understanding and employment of it in light of the gospel, an understanding that will prevent it from impeding discipleship

---

142. p[45, 75] A C* W Θ Ξ Ψ *f*[13]. See Metzger, *TCGNT,* 129; Wolter, *Lukasevangelium,* 401. *Herm. Sim.* 4.7 (mid-second c.) appears to affirm this understanding: "If anyone is occupied with one deed [Gk. *mian praxin*], he can also serve the Lord; for his understanding is not corrupted away from the Lord, but he will serve him with a pure mind." Stoicism upheld the sovereign human will rather than the word of God as the one thing of essence in life (see Epictetus, *Diatr.* 1.1.14).

143. Origen, *Hom. Luc.* Frag. 171.

144. A story from the Desert Fathers warns of the dangers of this dichotomy. "A stranger monk came to abbot Silvanus at Mount Sinai, and when the monk saw the brethren busy in the fields he said to them, 'Why do you labor for the meat that perishes? For Mary chose the part that was good.' The abbot then told his assistant to give the monk the Scriptures to read and put him in a cell with nothing in it. By mid-afternoon the monk was gazing out his window hoping for news of dinner. When the hour had come and gone he came to the abbot and asked why he had not been called to eat. Abbot Silvanus replied, 'You are a spiritual man, and you did not think food important. We, on the other hand, are flesh and blood; we need to eat, and that's why we work. You, however, have chosen the good part, for you read all day and don't need to eat.' On hearing this the monk was ashamed and said, 'Forgive me, Father.' The abbot answered, 'So Martha is necessary to Mary, for because of Martha is Mary praised'" (abbreviated from H. Waddell, *The Desert Fathers* [New York: Random House, 1998], 143).

and redeem it on behalf of discipleship. Luke's objective in this story correlates closely with his objective in Acts 6:1-7, in which the apostles, through the establishment of the office of deacon, enable the ministry of food to continue without impeding the more important ministry of the word in preaching and prayer.[145] Luke's objective — and vocabulary[146] — further correlate with 1 Cor 7:32-35, in which Paul differentiates between the married state and its concerns for the world and the celibate state and its concerns for the Lord.

I close by directing attention beyond the meaning of "one thing is needful" to the significance of both Mary and Jesus in this pericope. We have noted at 8:1-3 the special place accorded to women in Jesus' ministry in the Third Gospel. The kingdom of God inaugurated by Jesus is not reserved for one ethnicity or gender, but is open to Jew and Gentile, slave and free, male and female (Gal 3:28). Sitting at Jesus' feet is not reserved exclusively for males but open to those who "hear his word" (v. 39). In joining the company at Jesus' feet, Mary has not betrayed her "place" as a woman or jeopardized the "place" of men. She has chosen the rightful place open to her as well as to men, a place that supersedes all culturally conditioned places for men or women, a place that will not be taken from her. Finally, and most important, in announcing that only "one thing is needful" (v. 42), Jesus has subtly but deliberately placed himself above Torah. The "one thing needful" in the Jewish synagogue — by all accounts — was study of Torah.[147] Jesus does not direct Martha or readers to Torah, but to *himself.* In so doing, he has given a definitive and final answer to the question of the lawyer in vv. 25-26. Not in fulfilling the two greatest commandments — whether love of God or love of neighbor — is eternal life inherited, but in sitting at Jesus' feet and hearing his word.

JESUS TEACHES DISCIPLES TO PRAY (11:1-13)

"The Lord's Prayer" appears in three ancient versions: 11:2-4, Matt 6:9-13, and *Did.* 8:2-3. The last is nearly verbatim with, and clearly derived from, Matt 6:9-

145. See T. Seim, *The Double Message: Patterns of Gender in Luke-Acts* (Edinburgh: T&T Clark, 1994), 107-12; V. Koperski, "Luke 10,38-42 and Acts 6,1-7: Women and Discipleship in the Literary Context of Luke-Acts," in *The Unity of Luke-Acts* (ed. J. Verheyden; BETL 142; Leuven: Peeters, 1999), 517-44; B. Koet, "Luke 10:38-42 and Acts 6:1-7: A Lukan Diptych on ΔIAKONIA," in *Studies in the Greek Bible: Essays in Honor of Francis T. Gignac, S.J.* (ed. J. Corley and V. Skemp; CBQMS 44; Washington, D.C.: Catholic Biblical Association of America, 2008), 163-85.

146. Common words include "the Lord," "anxious(ness)," "distraction," and the theme of constancy.

147. Str-B 2:185.

13, with the exception of the addition of a final ascription of praise, "for thine is the power and the glory for ever." Luke's version of the prayer is one-third shorter than Matt's, however, and the exact relationship between the two is unclear. Matt's version is addressed to "Our Father who art in heaven," whereas Luke omits everything but "Father." Luke includes Matt's first two ascriptions of praise to God, but the third ("thy will be done") is omitted, as well as the summary of the foregoing ascriptions of praise, "on earth as it is in heaven." Luke likewise reduces Matt's four petitions to three, omitting "deliver us from [the] evil [one]." The Matthean form of the prayer, which contains fifty-seven words in Greek, is comparatively short by Jewish standards, but Luke's thirty-eight-word version is leaner yet. To be sure, expansions of Luke's version with the missing Matthean words are well-documented in critical Greek editions of the Lord's Prayer, but these expansions can be accounted for as subsequent assimilations to the Matthean version of the prayer, which predominated in the early church.

The exact relationship between the Lukan and Matthean versions of the prayer remains an unresolved matter in NT scholarship.[148] Among the plethora of information on the subject, the following data seem both important and relevant for a defensible, if provisional, judgment on the matter. First, given the dominance of the Matthean version in the early church, "it is remarkable that such a variety of early witnesses managed to resist what must have been an exceedingly strong temptation to assimilate the Lukan text to the much more familiar Matthean form."[149] This perspective suggests that the Lukan text is not an abridgement of the Matthean text, but a version anchored to strong and early tradition that was regarded as equally or more authoritative than the dominant Matthean version. Furthermore, although it is possible that Jesus taught two different versions of the prayer, the additional material in Matt (as well as the conclusion of the version in the *Didache*) can be reasonably accounted for as expansions of a prior and shorter Lukan version.[150] This premise is strengthened by the view, to which I subscribe, that the Gospel of Luke was written prior to the Gospel of Matthew.[151]

---

148. G. Stanton, *The Gospels and Jesus* (2nd ed.; Oxford: University Press, 2002), 6-11, provides a careful and insightful discussion of the Matthean and Lukan forms of the prayer, with arguments for the priority of the Lukan form.

149. Metzger, *TCGNT,* 130.

150. J. Jeremias, *The Prayers of Jesus* (trans. J. Reumann; Philadelphia: Fortress Press, 1978), 87-89, thinks the two different versions derive from two different church communities in which the prayer was known. This hypothesis seems inconsistent with Jeremias's ruling assumption, however, for it would allow a community a measure of freedom with the Lord's words that Jeremias maintains would never have been allowed an individual, not even an Evangelist.

151. On Matthean posteriority, see Edwards, *Hebrew Gospel,* chap. 8.

Second, the assertion that the Lord's Prayer, in both the Matthean and Lukan versions, derives from a Greek rather than a Hebrew original cannot be maintained. Every article in the prayer can be replicated in the OT or Jewish prayers;[152] indeed, Fitzmyer provides a full reconstruction of the prayer in Aramaic.[153] Fitzmyer even hypothesizes that "the prayer might have been uttered by Jesus in Hebrew, rather than in Aramaic."[154] There is indeed reasonably strong evidence for a Hebrew provenance of the prayer. Hebrew, not Aramaic, was the preferred language in Judaism well into the second century for Scripture, liturgy, and rabbinic teaching. Prayers are the most sacred element of liturgy. The question is not whether a Jewish rabbi would have taught his disciples a prayer in Hebrew, but whether he would have taught a prayer in any language *other* than Hebrew.[155] There is further evidence in favor of an original Hebrew provenance of the prayer. The Lord's Prayer appears especially indebted to a Hebrew source, for it occurs in the central section of Luke, which displays a 400 percent increase in Hebraisms over Lukan material parallel with Mark and/or Matt. A putative Hebrew source is particularly evident in 11:1, which contains three Hebraisms.[156] Finally, according to the testimony of Jerome, the Lord's Prayer was present in the Hebrew Gospel known to him.[157] There is thus considerable support of the thesis that the Lukan form of the Lord's Prayer derives from a Hebrew version of the prayer that ostensibly derived from Jesus himself.

1 Matt 6:7-13 sets the Lord's Prayer within the Sermon on the Mount, but Luke sets it on the journey to Jerusalem while Jesus is praying in an undisclosed place (v. 1; "in a certain place"). Prayers of Jesus typically signal a new stage in the development of the Third Gospel (on prayer, see at 3:21-22, n. 63; and at 9:18). This prayer ostensibly covers the whole focus on Jerusalem in the large central block of Luke's Gospel, for it is the last prayer before Jesus' final and climactic prayer at the Mount of Olives (22:39-46). Rabbinic disciples

152. So Str-B 2:186; Vinson, *Luke*, 361-67. Fitzmyer, *Luke (X–XXIV)*, 900, shows parallels from Jewish prayers with each article of the Lord's Prayer, concluding, "In many respects the 'Our Father' is a thoroughly Jewish prayer, for almost every word of it could be uttered by a devout Jew."

153. Fitzmyer, *Luke (X–XXIV)*, 901. Fitzmyer is followed in this belief by Jeremias, *Sprache des Lukasevangeliums*, 195-96; and M. Black, *An Aramaic Approach to the Gospels and Acts* (Peabody, Mass.: Hendrickson, 1998), 193-94.

154. Fitzmyer, *Luke (X–XXIV)*, 901.

155. Edwards, *Hebrew Gospel*, 166-82. For further evidence of the prayer in Hebrew, see Marshall, *Luke*, 455; J. Carmignac, "Hebrew Translations of the Lord's Prayer: An Historical Survey," in *Biblical and Near Eastern Studies: Essays in Honor of William Sanford LaSor* (ed. G. Tuttle; Grand Rapids: Eerdmans, 1978), 18-79.

156. Edwards, *Hebrew Gospel*, 311.

157. Edwards, *Hebrew Gospel*, 141-48, 311. Jerome's testimony is discussed with reference to *epiousion* ("daily") in v. 3.

were known to request renowned rabbis to teach them prayers that would characterize and differentiate them from other rabbinic schools. The request of "one of [Jesus'] disciples, 'Teach us to pray, just as John taught his disciples'" (v. 1), is such a request.[158] Jesus' disciples earlier asked him to declare himself on the question of fasting, as John had done with his disciples (5:33); for a second time in Luke Jesus' disciples ask him, again following John's example, to instruct them in prayer. John's ministry continues to set an agenda in certain respects for Jesus' ministry, and Jesus responds with a prayer intended to uniquely define his followers.

2-4 The prayer begins with the invocation "Father." This direct, unadorned, even daring address is unique to Jesus, for Jews normally did not refer to God without adding the epithet "heavenly." In the OT God is of course attested as "Father" (Exod 4:22; Deut 32:6; Jer 31:9; Mal 2:10), but he is seldom *addressed* as "Father," and then usually only as Father of the nation rather than of an individual. By contrast, as T. W. Manson correctly observed, "The experience of God as Father dominates the whole ministry of Jesus from the Baptism to the Crucifixion."[159] Jesus' speech about God as Father reveals the heart of his unique filial consciousness, which came to supreme expression in 10:21-22. His divine sonship was both the source of his authority and one of the oldest convictions of the early church (Mark 14:36; Gal 4:6). *Abba* very likely lies behind most or all the references to God as "Father" in the words of Jesus, and was thus the preferred and unique way for Jesus to speak of God. *Abba* is itself an Aramaic word, but it was close to the Hebrew *abbi,* having even worked itself into the Hebrew Mishnah (*m. Ketub.* 2:6; 13:5; *m. Ned.* 2:1). The presence of this word alone is not proof that Jesus' taught the prayer in Aramaic rather than Hebrew. "God" and "Lord" occur in a wide range of public speech forms of Jesus, but "Father" does not. "Father" never occurs in a Scriptural quotation, a narrative description, the discourse of any speaker other than Jesus, or Jesus' words to his adversaries. All references to God as Father come from Jesus, either in his prayers or in his teaching of disciples.[160] Jesus' use of *abba* was unique among Jewish rabbis, for no evidence has yet been found in the literature of Palestine of "my Father" being used by individuals to address God. Jesus, however, not only addressed God confidently and securely as *abba,* but he taught his disciples to do the same.[161]

---

158. On prayer characteristics of rabbinic schools, see Str-B 2:186; Jeremias, *The Prayers of Jesus,* 94.

159. *The Teaching of Jesus: Studies in Its Form and Content* (Cambridge: University Press, 1963), 102.

160. R. L. Mowery, "From Lord to Father in Matthew 1-7," *CBQ* 59/4 (1997): 642-56.

161. Full discussions of Jesus' use of "Father" appear in G. Dalman, *The Words of Jesus* (trans. D. Kay; Edinburgh: T&T Clark, 1909), 184-98; and Jeremias, *The Prayers of Jesus,* 11-65. Recent critiques of Jeremias (e.g., M. D'Angelo, "*Abba* and 'Father': Imperial Theology and the

The first ascription of praise is "hallowed be your name" (v. 2). In the Hebrew world, a name is ordinarily not a merely arbitrary moniker. "Father" is thus a representation of God's nature and character, and it is to be honored as essential to God's self-revelation (Exod 3:14; 6:2-3; Ezek 36:16-32). "Hallowed" means to "sanctify," "make holy," and thus to acknowledge and honor God's holiness, which is one of his defining characteristics in Scripture (Lev 11:44; 21:8; 22:31-33; Ps 99:1-3). The Greek verb *hagiasthētō* is imperative in the prayer, i.e., "let your name be sanctified." In the following ascription, "your kingdom come" is also an imperative, i.e., "let your kingdom come." Neither attribute depends on human works; neither is something that humans are responsible to bring about.[162] God's kingdom is already supremely present in Jesus. It is not a question whether God will reveal it; he has already chosen to do so independently and even contrary (John 1:11) to human volition. The question is whether humanity will receive it. The ascription is both praise of God's holiness and kingdom, and a prayer that God will so make himself known that humanity will rightly acknowledge, confess, and honor him in this world.[163]

The first of Luke's three petitions is "Give us each day our daily bread" (v. 3). The present tense of "give," in contrast to the aorist tense of the same verb in the Matthean version, means to *continue* giving us the bread we need. The word for "bread" (Gk. *artos*) likely derives from the Hebrew *lechem,* which denotes "bread" but regularly connotes food in general. The petition thus includes the food we need for existence, perhaps even necessities beyond food, but not luxuries. Despite the fixed form of the first petition in both English translations and church liturgy, the exact meaning of "daily [bread]" is puzzling. The word so translated, *epiousion,* appears in the Greek NT only here and in the Matthean version of the prayer but is not found with certainty in any extrabiblical text (although it occurs widely in the Fathers' discussions

---

Jesus Traditions," *JBL* (111/4 [1992]: 611-30) modify his conclusions at isolated points but fail to alter his central thesis that there are (as yet) still no examples of the use of *abba* for God in Jewish texts as early as the Gospels.

162. Contra Augustine, *Sermon* 56.6 (Just, *Luke,* 187), "When you pray, 'Thy kingdom come,' you pray for yourself; i.e., you pray that you may live a life worthy of the kingdom and have a share in it."

163. A textual variant following the second praise ascription, "Thy Holy Spirit come upon us and cleanse us," occurs in one eighth-c. and one twelfth-c. manuscript. The phrase may have derived from an original rite of baptism or the laying on of hands, or it may bear some relation to the Holy Spirit mentioned in v. 13. A similar reading occurs in the apocryphal *Acts Thom.* 27, "May the Holy Spirit come and cleanse their dead and their heart." Weak textual attestation of the reading should not obscure the fact that it is quoted by Gregory of Nazianzus, Maximus the Confessor, and Tertullian and was thus known by the early third c. See Metzger, *TCGNT,* 130-31; Marshall, *Luke,* 458; Wolter, *Lukasevangelium,* 406-7. A reading attested by only two late manuscripts is scarcely original, but its presence is further evidence of resistance to assimilating the Lukan version of the Lord's Prayer to the Matthean version.

of this verse). The exact derivation of the word has been widely canvassed but without reaching unanimity on its final meaning.[164] Acquired meanings of words can of course vary from their literal etymologies, and the meaning of *epiousios* is likely determined by acquired meanings. Three data, in my opinion, are important regarding a judgment on its meaning, all of which argue for a futurist sense. First, why would Luke use a rare word to render a mundane concept like "daily" that can be rendered by a half-dozen ordinary Greek words?[165] The employment of *epiousion* may thus signal an atypical meaning. Second and more important is the testimony of Jerome that "in the Gospel called 'According to the Hebrews,' I found *mahar* with reference to the supernatural bread, which means 'tomorrow.'"[166] Jerome cites the Hebrew Gospel again in his *Tractate on the Psalms* with reference to the same issue, "In the Hebrew Gospel according to Matthew it has this: 'Give us today our bread for tomorrow'; that is, the bread that will be given to us in your kingdom, give us today.'"[167] Jerome thus testifies that the early Hebrew Gospel interpreted the first petition in an eschatological sense: disciples are to pray that they may live in the present according to the promises of the future. According to this sense, the first petition coheres with the first two ascriptions of praise in Luke's version of the Lord's Prayer, both of which pray for the realization of God's eternal characteristics, especially the realization of his reign, in the mundane present. A third clue comes from Luke himself. Five times in Acts (7:26; 16:11; 20:15; 21:18; 23:11) Luke uses a form of the same word, *epiousē*, to refer to the "coming" or "next" day. Luke is the only NT writer to use *epiousē*, and his consistent use of the term for "tomorrow" seems relevant for understanding his use of *epiousion*, which is a close cognate of *epiousē*. These data, and especially the second and third, argue in favor of an eschatological understanding of "daily bread," which was widely understood in the ancient Eastern and Western branches of Christianity to mean "bread of salvation," "bread of life," or "heavenly manna." This understanding also accords with the theology of the Psalms (104:14; 136:25; 145:15; 147:9). *Epiousion* is thus the opposite of procrastination. The latter delays until tomorrow, but *epiousion* preempts tomorrow. The petition for "daily bread" is thus more than a prayer

---

164. Two alternatives present themselves: (1) a derivation from Gk. *epienai*, with a future sense of "the coming (day)," or (2) a derivation from Gk. *epiousia*, with a present sense of "this day." See discussions in Plummer, *Luke*, 295-96; E. Lohmeyer, *Das Vater Unser* (4th ed.; Göttingen: Vandenhoeck & Ruprecht, 1952), 98; Marshall, *Luke*, 459-60; Fitzmyer, *Luke (X–XXIV)*, 904-6.

165. "Daily" can be rendered in Greek by *ephēmeros, kathēmerinē, epitēdeios, sēmeron, hēmera kai hēmera*, or *to kath' hēmeran*, which occurs in v. 3 in addition to *epiousion*. See Lohmeyer, *Das Vater Unser*, 99-100.

166. *Comm. Matt.* 6:11 (Heb. *mahar* means "tomorrow").

167. See Edwards, *Hebrew Gospel*, 83-84.

for material blessings in the present; it is a prayer that believers may, by grace, view the present through the promise of the future, and model mundane life according to eternal ethics.[168]

The second petition is "Forgive us our sins, for we also forgive everyone who sins against us" (v. 4). It is obvious that there can be no life without food and necessities, but it is equally true (though perhaps less obvious) that there can be no life without forgiveness. A world of revenge and retaliation is a world of terror and dread; a world of forgiveness is a world where there is renewal of life, peace, and hope. In Matt 6:12 both references to infractions are presented as "debts," i.e., things *owed,* sins of omission rather than sins of commission. In Luke, however, the first infraction is termed *hamartiai* ("sins"), which is the common Greek word for offenses — whether "done" or "left undone" — against God and others. The second infraction is termed *opheilein,* ("debts"), meaning something owed, a sin of omission. Sins of omission are often less culpable than sins of commission. If Luke intends a theological distinction between the two words, it could be that the sins that God must forgive in us are greater than the sins we must forgive in others. Although this point may be speculative, the emphasis on "us" in the second half of the petition is not. A literal translation of the Greek of v. 4b, "for also *we ourselves* forgive everything owed *us,*" clearly implies that we cannot ask or claim God's forgiveness for ourselves while refusing it to others. Believers are not simply objects of forgiveness; they are also *conduits* of forgiveness, extending to others what God in grace has freely extended to them.

The third and final petition is "lead us not into temptation." The Greek *peirasmos* might better be rendered "test" than "temptation." A temptation entices one to sin (which God does not do, Jas 1:12-15), whereas a biblical test is a trial intended to reveal faithfulness (Acts 20:19; Jas 1:12-15; 2 Pet 2:9). *Peirasmos* was a rare word in secular Greek, which would seem to imply that ancient Greeks were concerned with the results of behavior rather than with its causes. The Christian faith has a more holistic understanding of the role of causality in human behavior. The third petition is both a confession of weakness and a prayer for faithfulness. It relieves believers of the pretense of being religious superstars. They need not bait God for opportunities to prove how righteous they are (e.g. Ps 26:1-3). They pray, rather, to be rescued from situations that, apart from God's intervention on their behalf, they would be unable to withstand.[169] In his prayer on the Mount of Olives, Jesus twice admonishes the disciples to pray that they will not enter into such situations (22:40, 46).

---

168. For similar interpretations of v. 3, see Lohmeyer, *Das Vater Unser,* 97-101; Jeremias, *Prayers of Jesus,* 100-104; Marshall, *Luke,* 460; Wolter, *Lukasevangelium,* 407-8. "View the Present through the Promise" is the title of a hymn written by Tom Troeger, music by Ben Brody.

169. See here also Vinson, *Luke,* 374.

The prayer Jesus taught his disciples, both its ascriptions of praise to God as Father and its petitions for daily necessities, assumes throughout God's covenant faithfulness to his people. The prayer comprises past, present, and future and sets both our times and our persons within the one covenantal faithfulness of God. Most of us think of prayer in terms of requests couched in the subjunctive mood; we modify petitions with words like *if, would,* or *might.* The Lord's Prayer invites believers to approach God not in polite timidity but in bold confidence. All the verbs except for "forgive" (v. 4) are in the imperative mood, emboldening disciples to pray expectantly that God wills to act according to his promises. The Lord's Prayer cannot be either understood or prayed, however, apart from the recollection that *Jesus* was its author and teacher. The Lord's Prayer, as we have seen, is in many respects a thoroughly Jewish prayer, but the fact that Jesus taught it transforms it into a quintessential Christian prayer.[170] Disciples are invited to stand with Jesus in a position of intimate trust with *Abba* and, like Jesus, address God as "Father." Because of Jesus, disciples are instructed not to think of forgiveness in terms of deeds and deserts, but in terms of sheer grace freely granted by God's mercy — and freely extended to fellow human beings. Above all, disciples may trust that God's name will be sanctified, God's reign will break forth, and believers will not be put to the test, for Jesus as the Son of God is the human incarnation of God's holiness, his reign, and his saving deliverance.

5-8 The model prayer of Jesus is followed by a parable about prayer. In the original Greek the parable depends somewhat awkwardly on the indefinite subject, "Who among you" (*tis ex hymōn;* NIV "Suppose you have"). This may be a Hebraism, for the same convention occurs in the Hebrew OT,[171] and it is repeated six times in Luke's distinctly Hebraic central section (11:5, 11; 12:25; 14:28; 15:4; 17:7). The effect of the construction is to make the hearer (and reader) the fictional subject of the parable. The chiastic structure of the parable is further evidence of a possible Hebrew background:

A   Even if he will not give to him
  B   and not get up
    C   because of friendship
    C^1 because of shameless audacity
  B^1 he will surely get up
A^1 he will give you as much as you need.[172]

---

170. Contra Nolland, *Luke 9:21–18:34,* 619, "It is notable that the prayer Jesus gives is not particularly 'Christian.'"

171. OT forms appear in 2 Chr 36:23 and Hag 2:6. In the NT, see John 8:46; Heb 3:13; 4:1. On the form as a Semitic construction, see BDF §469.

172. On the chiasmus, see Wolter, *Lukasevangelium,* 411-12. On the Hebraic character of

The imperative mood of the verbs in the Lord's Prayer challenges disciples to pray the prayer of Jesus with the trust of Jesus, that the God who promises is the God who acts on his promises. The present parable builds upon the Lord's Prayer, teaching that true prayer is not only expectant but perseverant. In the Middle East people sometimes travel at night to avoid the heat of day. If a villager receives a surprise visit at midnight, and if the villager goes to a friend to ask for food to feed the visitor, even though the friend is already in bed with his house shuttered, will he not get up and do what the villager asks? Even if the villager is not a friend, will he not offer help simply to gain peace for himself? According to the explanation of the parable in v. 8, the final motive for responding to the request is less the desire to help the neighbor than to end his bothersome request. The point of the parable is similar to the point of Jesus' parable in 18:1-5 about the woman who begs the judge for justice: the judge finally renders justice in order to gain relief from her pleading perseverance. Both parables are about insistence and perseverance. The fact that Jesus made persistence the subject of two different parables indicates its importance in relation to prayer. In the present parable the perseverance of the petitioner is accentuated by *anaideia,* which throughout Greek literature has a thoroughly pejorative meaning: asking rudely — even acting rudely — to get a request at any cost, without thought of propriety or shame.[173] The implication of this word for the parable is both bracing and abrasive: the parable puts no premium on "niceness" in prayers — or on pray-ers. The accent falls on approaching God with a not-to-be-deterred attitude. Prayer is not a polite religious sentiment; it is something on which people must be willing to stake their lives, the determination not to give up until God has heard us.[174]

The point of the parable is not solely about perseverance, however, for God is not like the reluctant sleeper who requires a melodrama of excuses before attending to requests. The sleeper does not want to be "bothered" (v. 7),

---

the verses, note Nolland, *Luke 9:21–18:34,* 623: "The awkward underlying Semitic syntax that holds together vv. 5-7 . . . is hardly likely to have been penned by Luke."

173. See K. Snodgrass, "*Anaideia* and the Friend at Midnight," *JBL* 116/3 (1997): 505-10. Of the roughly 250 uses of the term in Greek literature, Snodgrass finds no instance apart from 11:8, where *anaideia* appears in a positive sense. So too H. Waetjen, "The Subversion of 'World' by the Parable of the Friend at Midnight," *JBL* 120/4 (2001): 720.

174. Lagrange, *Luc,* 326. Nolland, *Luke 9:21–18:34,* 622-27, argues that *anaideia* should not be understood with reference to the villager but to the sleeper, who finally attends to the request not because of the villager's perseverance (Nolland sees no evidence of persistence in the villager's request) but out of shame that not doing so will violate the Middle Eastern custom of hospitality. Nolland is not alone in this interpretation, but I think that "shameless audacity" on the part of the petitioner remains the better interpretation, esp. in the context of the foregoing imperatives in the Lord's Prayer and following verb tenses in vv. 9-10, all of which convey perseverance in prayer.

but God is willing to be "bothered" in ways that humans will not tolerate. This homely parable is thus also about divine humility. Anyone who treats a friend as the villager treats his friend would sooner or later cease to have a friend. But God can be approached with persistence, perseverance, even "shameless audacity," because God is not offended by honest and urgent prayer, for as the following section establishes, it is God's good pleasure to give good gifts to his children.

9-13   Elaboration on the Lord's Prayer continues, but in contrast to the emphasis on perseverance in vv. 5-8, vv. 9-13 emphasize the good and trustworthy character of God to answer prayer. Vv. 9-13 closely parallel Matt 7:7-11, especially vv. 9-11, which are almost verbatim with Matt 7:7-9. The saying in 11:9 about seeking and finding also appears in a quotation from the Hebrew Gospel preserved by Clement of Alexandria: "The one who seeks will not cease until he finds; and having found he will be amazed, and being amazed he will reign, and reigning he will rest."[175] Clement does not reference the quotation to either Matt or Luke; indeed, it can scarcely be drawn from either, since three-fifths of the quotation is absent from them. It appears that the Hebrew Gospel cited by Clement preserved a (fuller) version of the saying than Luke quotes in 11:9. The several Hebraisms in the teaching on prayer, including the two actual quotations from the Hebrew Gospel with reference to v. 3 and v. 9 appear to be residual evidence that the Hebrew Gospel was a source of 11:1-13.

The substance of Jesus' teaching on prayer in vv. 9-10 is also present in the OT (Isa 55:6; Jer 29:12 [LXX 36:12]). Jesus does not simply repeat the OT material, however, but infuses it with his authority. "I say to you" (v. 9) is emphatic in Greek, indicating the importance of the Teacher in understanding prayer. All three verbs — "ask," "seek," and "knock" (vv. 9-10) — are in the Greek present tense, designating ongoing engagement and habitual behaviors rather than sporadic or temporary involvement. The outcome of prayer is not tentative or uncertain but explicit and sure: "For everyone who asks receives, those who seek find, and to those who knock, the door will be opened" (v. 10). Prayer, perhaps more than any other religious activity, is frequently considered a passive activity, recondite, even capricious. Jesus' teaching about prayer is direct and definite, simple, and inviting. Prayer is not a mysterious burden but an interrelational adventure with God, with Jesus as one's example and companion.

Jesus closes with a brief parable, which again (as in 11:5) makes the hearer (or reader) the fictional subject. "Which of you fathers, if your son asks for

---

175. Clement of Alexandria, *Strom.* 5.14.96. Clement does not specifically attribute the saying to the Hebrew Gospel, but the quotation is a fuller version of two earlier quotations of similar effect (*Strom.* 2.9.45; 3.9.63), both of which are attributed to the Hebrew Gospel. A variant of the same quotation in *Strom.* 5.14.96 appears in P.Oxy. 654 and *Gos. Thom.* 2. See Edwards, *Hebrew Gospel*, 12-15.

a fish will give him a snake instead? Or if he asks for an egg, will give him a scorpion?" (vv. 11-12).[176] We can imagine a child asking its father for a fish or an egg. We cannot imagine a father responding by giving the child a snake or a scorpion. A father who so responded would be notorious.[177] The Greek word for "snake" (v. 11; *ophis*) need not denote a poisonous snake,[178] but paired with scorpion, it is a malicious image. The only other place in Luke-Acts where either word appears is in Jesus' commission to the disciples in 10:19, "I have given you authority to trample on snakes and scorpions and to overcome all the power of the enemy." In this context snakes and scorpions are synonymous with the evil one, and they should probably be taken likewise in vv. 11-12. In the second century Marcion considered the God of the OT a malevolent God to be feared and rejected. Some people may desist from praying, or from praying at all, by imputing indifference or even malevolence to God. The odious contrasts between fish and snake, egg and scorpion, show how offensive this thought is to Jesus. God is a good Father — far better than any human father — who wills to give good gifts to his children. God wills to destroy all that is connoted by "snakes" and "scorpions," not give them as gifts! Jesus has just taught believers to address God as "Father" (11:2). No fathers — not even human fathers of ill repute (v. 13) — give such things to their children. They may not be good fathers, but if they give "good gifts" to anyone, they give them to their children. "How much more will your Father in heaven give the Holy Spirit to those who ask him!" (v. 13).

Reference to the "Holy Spirit" in v. 13 gives a more theological understanding to Jesus' teaching on prayer than does the parallel reading in Matt 7:11, which focuses on material requests ("good *things*"; NIV "good gifts").[179] Heretofore in the Third Gospel the Holy Spirit has been referenced in relation to the annunciations of John and Jesus and to Jesus' messianic call, but not to disciples.[180] In the theological architecture of Luke-Acts, the Holy Spirit

---

176. For the relation of Luke's two pairs (fish/snake and egg/scorpion) with Matt's two pairs (7:9-10: bread/stone and fish/snake), plus the presence of the Semitism in 11:11, see Metzger, *TCGNT,* 132-33.

177. Nolland, *Luke 9:21–18:34,* 632, argues that both fish and snakes are slippery, and eggs and scorpions (when curled up) are round. Nolland's point seems to be that God will not trick those who pray to him by offering them something that looks like their request but differs from it dramatically. This explanation seems contrived (nor are snakes slippery). The above discussion is more faithful to the connotations of "snake" and "scorpion," esp. in relation to 10:19, the only other place in Luke where both terms occur.

178. The Gk. *echidna* is normally a poisonous snake, whereas *ophis* is a generic snake.

179. Manuscript evidence for "Holy Spirit" is extremely strong, and the alternative readings of "good gift(s)" (D Θ) or "good spirit" (𝔭⁴⁵ L) can be accounted for as assimilations either to the first half of v. 13 or to Matt 7:11. See Metzger, *TCGNT,* 133.

180. 1:15, 35, 41, 67; 2:25, 26; 3:16, 22; 4:1, 14; 10:21.

will come upon the disciples only after the ascension of the resurrected Jesus (24:49; Acts 1:4, 7-8; 2:1-21). Luke does not have a static understanding of the Spirit, however. The "era" of the Spirit is not inaugurated until Pentecost, but the Spirit permeates the ministry of Jesus and the apostolic cohort prior to Pentecost. Jesus prepares the disciples in his earthly ministry in both 11:13 and 12:12 for their impending reception of the Spirit after his bodily departure. The verbs in both texts assign the Spirit's activity to the future, i.e., the Spirit *will* come upon and *will* teach the disciples. This prophetic promise, like the focus of the Lord's Prayer as a whole, directs disciples' attention to the future fulfillment of God's promises. But even though the bestowal of the Holy Spirit on the church must await Acts 2, the gifts of the Spirit in material blessings, human relationships, and effective calling are already present in the lives of disciples through their fellowship with Jesus.

CHAPTER TEN

Discipleship and Conflict

Luke 11:14-54

In 11:1-13, Jesus taught disciples how to be united with the will and Spirit of the Father through prayer. This would seem a welcome teaching, of benefit both to disciples and the wider society they influence. Jesus is not praised for it, however, but assailed. It is a dangerous thing to teach about God, for no society — and certainly not first-century Palestine — is indifferent to God. God, by definition, is supreme, all-powerful, "that than which nothing greater can be conceived," and any ultimate category as God inevitably challenges and relativizes earthly powers and principalities. Even good deeds done in God's name raise suspicions about their motives and source of power. Good deeds, in fact, seem not to be sufficient testimony in themselves to God's presence, but here require accompanying "signs" of verification. No one has a more jealous stake in the matter of God's redemptive work than the religious leaders, for whom Jesus appears to be a rival. Opposition, however, can have a positive effect of setting the truth of the gospel in sharper contrast. It does so in vv. 14-54 by showing the significance of hearing and obeying the word of God (v. 28) for the Beelzebul controversy (vv. 14-28), seeking signs (vv. 29-36), and the opposition of Pharisees and lawyers (vv. 37-54).

A STRONG MAN AND A *STRONGER* MAN (11:14-28)

14-20 The scene opens abruptly with Jesus "driving out a demon that was mute. When the demon left, the man who had been mute spoke, and the crowd was amazed" (v. 14). The wording of this verse in both the NIV and the Greek confuses the demon and the man, i.e., the demon is called dumb because it made the man dumb. The elliptical grammar is nevertheless theologically perceptive, for the demonic abhors that which is different from itself. It wants to make objects like itself, absorb and consume them. The divine, in contrast, glories in the freedom of creation and its differentiation from the Creator. Gen 1 teaches the profound mystery that humanity, in which the process of differentiation and complexity has reached its greatest extent, is in fact most *like* the Creator! Jesus, as the incarnation of the Creator, releases a victim of demonic ventriloquism, freeing him to speak for himself as an autonomous individual.

The crowds marvel at the miracle, as they often do when Jesus teaches and acts. Marveling is not faith, however. Here, in fact, marveling creates an appetite for a greater spectacle and leads away from both Jesus and faith. "Some of [the crowd]" accuse Jesus of driving out demons because he is acting in league with, or by the power of, Beelzebul, the prince of demons, (v. 15). The other Synoptics identify the accusers as Pharisees (Matt 12:24) and scribes (Mark 3:22), but Luke leaves them unidentified. His vagueness directs focus on Jesus — but without excluding hearers (and readers) from the opposition! The term **Beelzebul** (v. 15) appears nowhere outside the Gospels. A related term, Beelzebub, occurs infrequently as a Syrian god of Ekron (2 Kgs 1:2, 6). Although Beelzebub originally meant something like "Lord of the Dwelling (= Temple)," already in the LXX it is made a term of contempt, *Baal muiōn,* "Lord of the flies," "Lord of the dung heap."[1] The Greek of v. 15, however, does not read Beelzebub but Beel*zeboul.* The word *zebul* occurs only five times in the Hebrew OT (1 Kgs 8:13; Isa 63:15; Hab 3:11; Ps 49:15; 2 Chr 6:2), in each instance with reference to an exalted dwelling place such as a temple or heaven. The Targums corroborate the sense of celestial dwelling, as do the three occurrences of *zeboul* in the DSS (1QM 12:1-2; 1QS 10:3; 1QH3:34//1QpHab 3:34). The best suggested meaning of Beelzeboul is "Baal's abode or dynasty," a meaning reinforced in Matt 10:25, where Jesus calls Beelzebul the "lord of the house." Not only during the OT monarchy but also in the succeeding Hellenistic period, the chief rival of Yahweh faith was the cult of the heavenly Baal. Biblical writers commonly explained foreign gods as demons (Ps 96:5; 1 Cor 10:20), and in this instance Beelzebul is seen as the archruler of a dynasty of demons and evil spirits (v. 15).[2] Although Satan is nowhere called Beelzebul in Jewish literature, Jesus' rhetorical question in v. 18 equates Satan with Beelzebul, "the prince of demons."[3] The understanding of Beelzebul as Baal, ruler of a demonic dynasty, is further reinforced by Jesus' reference to Satan's realm as a "house" and a "kingdom" (vv. 17-18).

It is significant that Jesus' opponents do not deny his authority to expel

---

1. See BDAG, 173; Str-B 1:631-35; V. Taylor, *The Gospel according to St. Mark* (2nd ed.; New York: St. Martin's Press, 1966), 238-39; T. Lewis, "Beelzebul," *ABD* 1:638-40.

2. See L. Gaston, "Beelzebul," *TZ* 18 (1962): 247-55; E. MacLaurin, "Beelzeboul," *NovT* 20 (1978): 156-60; Wolter, *Lukasevangelium,* 416.

3. *Jub.* 10:8 identifies the prince of demons as Mastema. *T. Sol.* 3:5-6; 6:1-11 calls Beelzebul the "Prince of Demons," the highest-ranking angel in heaven. The Beelzebul in *T. Sol.* is a comical figure, however, for when Solomon subdues him with a magic ring, and when the demon complains, Solomon condemns him to cut marble for the construction of the temple!

demons, nor do they accuse him of being an impostor. They acknowledge his miracles but attempt to discredit them by attributing them to Beelzebul rather than to God.[4] People often imagine they would believe in Jesus if they saw his miracles, but this text is evidence that undisputed miracles do not necessarily evoke faith. Other bystanders desired to see a corroborating "sign from heaven" from Jesus (v. 16). The demand for a sign would seem less antagonistic than the accusation that Jesus is in league with Beelzebul, but in the context it is no less offensive. Deut 13:1-2 allows a prophet to prove himself by an accompanying sign, but the demand for a sign immediately following an exorcism, itself powerful evidence of God's activity, betrays latent skepticism.[5] V. 16 agrees in verbal and thematic particulars with Mark 8:11 and is evidence of a residual discontent among the crowds for "proof" that would relieve all doubts (11:29). Satan's third temptation in the wilderness was the demand for a wondrous sign that would compel belief (4:9-12).[6] The word "seek" (Gk. *zētein*) occurs frequently in Luke (26x), sometimes in positive contexts (11:9; 12:31; 19:10), but more often, as here, in pejorative contexts (19:47) of trying to control Jesus or determine the conditions of faith. The use of this verb in the imperfect tense, implying continual seeking, connotes deep dissatisfaction with Jesus' ministry. All these data warrant the conclusion that the demand for a sign is itself a sign of unbelief.

The emphasis on "he" (= Jesus) in v. 17 assures readers that, in this instance, as in others (5:22; 6:8; John 2:24-25), Jesus knows the thoughts of the crowd. "Any kingdom divided against itself will be ruined, and a house divided against itself will fall" (v. 17). In depicting the accusations of the crowds in terms of "kingdoms" and "houses," Jesus profiles the struggle according to the larger matrix of the dominion of Satan and the dominion of God.[7] A struggle between two dominions is not uncommon and perhaps in some instances necessary, but a division or "civil war" *within* a dominion endangers its very existence. This is reinforced in v. 17 by the Greek *erēmoun,* meaning to "lay waste" or "devastate" (NIV "ruined"), and by *piptein,* meaning to "collapse" (NIV "fall"). The counterargument of Jesus is thus one of common sense: how could the conflict of which the crowds accuse Jesus, which in political and domestic life would cause utter destruction, not cause the same for Jesus' mission?

The principle that a house divided against itself cannot stand provides

---

4. This same judgment typifies the Jewish Talmud (*b. Šabb.* 104b), which profiles Jesus as a magician who learned Satanic arts in Egypt. See G. Dalman, *Jesus Christ in the Talmud, Midrash, Zohar, and the Liturgy of the Synagogue* (trans. A. Streane; Cambridge: Deighton, Bell, 1893), 45-50.

5. Nolland, *Luke 9:21–18:34,* 643.

6. Plummer, *Luke,* 301.

7. Green, *Luke,* 455.

the condition for three conclusive "if" clauses in vv. 18-20. The first repeats and summarizes the scandalous accusation that Jesus drives out demons by the power of Beelzebul: "If Satan is divided against himself, how can his kingdom stand?" (v. 18). This statement identifies entities by their proper names, for it is not Jesus who is "prince of demons" (v. 15) but Satan. In the wilderness temptation the evil one was referred to generically as "the devil" (Gk. *diabolos*; 4:2, 5, 9, 13). The first mention of "Satan" in Luke was at the return of the seventy(-two) disciples, when Jesus declared, "I saw Satan fall like lightning from heaven" (10:18). Mention of Satan here may play off this latter passage, i.e., My house has not "fallen" (v. 17; Gk. *piptein*); rather, Satan has "fallen" (10:18; Gk. *piptein*).[8]

The second "if" clause (v. 19) begins emphatically in Greek, "If *I* drive out demons by Beelzebul, in what do your sons drive them out?" The use of "sons" (Gk. *huioi*; NIV "followers") is a Hebraic way of referring to people who belong to a movement. "Your sons" could refer to Jewish exorcists, although this is by no means certain, for exorcisms were a rarity in both Israel and Judaism.[9] Greco-Roman exorcists such as Pythagoras, Asclepius, some Roman rulers, Apollonius of Tyana, Alexander of Abononteichos, and Simon Magus, were more widely known than Jewish exorcists, although the boundary between myth and reality is blurred in many accounts of exorcisms. "Your sons" (v. 19) seems to be included for rhetorical effect more than with specific reference to exorcists, i.e., the exorcisms of "your sons" — whatever the source and outcome of their works — do not signal the inbreaking of God's reign, for that belongs exclusively to the miraculous signs of Jesus.[10]

The final "if" clause explicitly identifies the inbreaking of the reign of God with the ministry of Jesus: "If I drive out demons by the finger of God, then the kingdom of God has come upon you" (v. 20).[11] "The finger of God"

---

8. Green, *Luke,* 455, notes that Jesus' response implies four things: (1) Beelzebul and Satan refer to the same entity, (2) the propriety of referring to Satan as head of a kingdom, (3) the marshaling of demons under the command of Satan and their service of his aim, and (4) the unity of Satan's dominion.

9. 1 Sam 16:14, 23 (= Josephus, *Ant.* 6.166-69); Tob 8:1-3; Acts 19:13; 1QapGen. 20:28-29; Josephus, *Ant.* 8.46-48; *J.W.* 7.178-89; Acts 19:13. On the Jewish conception of demons, see Str-B 4/1:501-35. Josephus's two accounts are related with unbridled superstition, including the use of magic rings common to folklore (on the latter, see J. Edwards, "Magic Rings in C. S. Lewis and J. R. R. Tolkien," *Bulletin of the New York C. S. Lewis Society* 30/9 (September 1999): 1-7. Justin Martyr, *Dial.* 85, argues that Jesus' powers as an exorcist were unrivaled in Judaism.

10. W. D. Davies and D. Allison, *A Critical and Exegetical Commentary on the Gospel according to Matthew* (3 vols.; ICC; London: T&T Clark, 2001-4), 2:339; Wolter, *Lukasevangelium,* 418.

11. Nolland, *Luke 9:21–18:34,* 639-40, offers several reasons for considering "finger of God" to be later Lukan redaction of Matt's more original "Spirit of God." This seems unlikely. It is hard to imagine that Luke would alter an original reference to "Spirit," which is one of Luke's

is not a metaphor of the ease with which Jesus prevails over the demonic, although it could signify "instrumentality."[12] It is a Hebraism that locates supremacy over the demonic not in the charms and incantations of popular exorcists but in the *activity* of Jesus. At the exodus the magicians of Pharaoh were able to repeat the first two signs of Moses and Aaron by their secret arts, but they could not compete with the third plague, that of the gnats, declaring to Pharaoh, "This is the finger of God" (Exod 8:19 [LXX Exod 8:15]). Reference to "the finger of God" may claim that Jesus' miracles are as superior to rival exorcists as were the miracles of Moses and Aaron to the magicians of Egypt. The miracles of the latter presaged Israel's deliverance from "the house of bondage"; the exorcisms of Jesus signify deliverance from "the house (and kingdom) of bondage of Satan." Jesus does not refer to the kingdom of God (see at 4:43) as a promise or a potential, but as a present reality. The Greek *ephthasen* (NIV "has come upon you") is sometimes translated "come near," i.e., the kingdom is drawing near but has not yet arrived. This almost certainly understates its significance. Especially in the present context, Jesus' expulsion of demons means the kingdom is a present reality. In Satan's fall from heaven (10:18), the kingdom was not simply near but actualized (so too 17:21). Paul's use of the same form of the word in Rom 9:31 carries the clear sense not of something *about* to happen, but of something that *has* happened. Jesus' exorcisms are not merely "signs" of the presence of God's kingdom, but concrete experiences of it.[13]

21-23 In vv. 21-26 Jesus illustrates the conflict with Beelzebul in two different ways. The first, in vv. 21-23, appeals to a mighty metaphor from Isaiah.

> Can plunder be taken from warriors, or captives be rescued from the fierce? But this is what the Lord says: "Yes, captives will be taken from warriors, and plunder retrieved from the fierce; I will contend with those who contend with you, and your children I will save." (Isa 49:24-25)

Isa 49 is dedicated entirely to the Servant of the Lord, whose mission is both to redeem Israel and be a light to the Gentiles, so that God's "salvation may reach to the ends of the earth" (v. 6). The Servant's redemption and deliverance are not conferred peacefully but won at the cost of combat with "fierce" and "warrior" powers, "plundering" their goods, i.e., liberating their captives. The Servant's mission is so seamlessly harmonious with God that God claims the

---

preferred terms (Bovon, *Lukas 9,51–14,35*, 175). "Finger of God" appears to be a Hebraic anthropomorphism, preserved perhaps in the Hebrew Gospel (see Edwards, *Hebrew Gospel*, 249).

12. Bovon, *Lukas 9,51–14,35*, 173-74.

13. See G. Fitzer, *phthanō*, TWNT 9:90-94; V. Hasler, *phthanō*, EDNT 3:421-22; Bock, *Luke 9:51–24:53*, 1080; Wolter, *Lukasevangelium*, 419.

Servant's mission as his own, "*I* will contend with those who contend with you, and your children *I* will save" (49:25).

The portrayal of a fully armed strong man controlling his "possessions" until a stronger man "attacks and overpowers him . . . and divides his plunder" (vv. 21-22) repeats the image of Isa 49:24-25 in different vocabulary. The "strong man" is Satan, and his trust in his armor signifies Satan's trust in his own plans and "technology," thus in himself rather than in God. "His possessions" are captive and oppressed humanity. The "Stronger Man" is Jesus, who drives out demons and inaugurates the reign of God by liberating captives of the strong man (Isa 53:12; Col 2:15; 1 John 4:4; *Gos. Thom.* 35). Jesus' primary messianic mission, like the mission of the Servant of the Lord, is not, as nineteenth-century liberalism fondly imagined, to be a great moral example or teacher. The reality of the incarnation is not so tame. The incarnation is nothing short of an assault against the fully armed strong man, a carefully planned offensive to subdue hostile and inimical powers and restore humanity to its intended image and purpose of the Creator (1 John 3:8!).[14] Like the mission of the Servant, God is so identified with the work of Jesus that the work of the Son is equally the work of the Father.[15]

"Whoever is not with me is against me," says Jesus, "and whoever does not gather with me scatters" (v. 23). Jesus made a seemingly contrary statement in 9:50, "whoever is not against you is for you." The statements are not in fact contradictory, for the earlier concerns disciples, and the latter, Jesus himself. 9:50 is a reminder that no disciple stands at the epicenter of faith, and hence disciples do not determine the circumference of faith. Disciples may differ from one another and still be faithful to Jesus; hence, they must extend tolerance to one another. The present saying is about Jesus, and is in fact an example of "implicit Christology," i.e., a claim Jesus makes of himself that no human being could make of himself or herself.[16] Jesus places himself in a separate class from disciples, for only Jesus can bind the strong man (v. 22; Mark 3:27). The

14. For Vinson, *Luke,* 383, the imagery of the strong man and the Stronger Man is not about Satan and Jesus but an allegory "why empires always fall[;] even if they are not divided internally . . . there is always another tyrant, another empire, a bigger fish to swallow the smaller." This interpretation repeats nineteenth-c. attempts to moralize the Gospels. 11:14-26 is not a philosophy of history but a Christological metaphor of Jesus' mission in relation to evil in the world.

15. For a fuller development of this theme, see J. Edwards, "The Servant of the Lord and the Gospel of Mark," in *Biblical Interpretation in Early Christian Gospels,* vol. 1: *The Gospel of Mark* (ed. T. Hatina; London: T&T Clark, 2006), 49-63.

16. An earlier example of implicit Christology occurs in 11:2 with reference to "Father." In the Gospels Jesus speaks of God as "my Father," but with reference to the disciples he speaks of God as "your Father." In no instance does Jesus place himself with the disciples, saying "our Father."

work of Satan and the work of Jesus are not a "both . . . and," two different sides of the same spiritual coin. They are irrevocably and eternally incompatible. With regard to Jesus' struggle against the evil in demonic forces, no one can remain neutral or noncommittal. Jesus gathers the flock (Mark 14:28; John 10:11), Satan scatters it (Mark 14:27; John 10:12). People must decide whether they will join Jesus in gathering it, or serve Satan by scattering it.

24-26 A second illustration of Jesus' conflict with Satan occurs in the parable of vv. 24-26. When an unclean spirit leaves a person, it seeks rest in "arid places," but finding no rest, it returns to its human abode, now cleansed and ordered, which the demon reclaims with seven spirits more wicked than itself. The last state of the person is far worse than the first (2 Pet 2:20-21). "Arid [Gk. *anydros*, 'waterless'] places" refers to the desolate wilderness regions of the Middle East, the proverbial abode of demons (Rev 18:2; Tob 8:3; Bar 4:35); and "seven unclean spirits" (8:2) connotes "full occupancy," complete take-over. From start to finish the parable is about the unclean spirit — restless, rabid, plotting, and ever more malicious and destructive in its quest for control over the "house," its human host (2 Cor 5:1). The parable virtually pleads with hearers: Don't mess with this spirit, don't underestimate its power, and above all, don't imagine that one eviction ends its threat (Mark 9:25)! The departure of the unclean spirit could refer to the man exorcised of a demon (v. 14), or to people who want to remain neutral or "open" regarding religion (v. 23), or to people who crave heavenly "signs" (vv. 16, 29, 30; 23:8). Such people may claim profound spiritual experiences, but if they do not *receive* Jesus by faith and follow him, they are spiritually powerless against more sinister forces. The departure of the unclean spirit is like deleting data from a computer hard drive: the deleted data is still there and can be erased only by *overwriting* it with new data. The place in one's life once controlled by demonic forces must be "overwritten" by Jesus and the gospel or one's life is not secure from the return of a fatal virus. "Whoever is freed of demons and does not decide for Jesus is simply preparing the premises for a more complete mastery by the demons. . . . People who have been healed by Jesus but do not adhere to Jesus are a prize find for demons."[17]

27-28 Luke does not leave disciples helpless, or to the perils of chance in the face of spiritual combat. A brief encounter found in no other Gospel[18] is appended to the Beelzebul controversy, assuring believers of the saving presence of the Stronger Man (vv. 21-22) in the midst of spiritual temptation. "As Jesus was saying these things" links vv. 27-28 to the parable of the Unclean Spirit (vv. 24-26). A woman from the crowd "lifted up her voice and said, 'Blessed is the womb that bore you and the breasts that nursed you'"

---

17. Klein, *Lukasevangelium,* 416.

18. *Gos. Thom.* 79 reproduces a close variant of the saying, however.

(v. 27).[19] An unnamed woman disciple provides the context for Jesus' resolution of the cosmic conflict between the kingdom of evil and the kingdom of salvation in human lives! The insight of this woman is further evidence (e.g., 8:1-3) of the importance of female disciples in the ministry of Jesus and in the architecture of the Third Gospel. The object of the unnamed woman's blessing in v. 27 is, of course, the mother of Jesus, and her blessing accords with Luke's earlier testimony to Mary (1:28, 42). In the Magnificat, Mary proclaimed, "From now on all generations will call me blessed" (1:48); the woman's blessing here is a fulfillment of Mary's prophecy about herself as mother of the Messiah.[20] But the woman's blessing was equally a blessing of Jesus. Maternal blessings similar to v. 27 were proverbial in Judaism and thus not original — although not thereby less heartfelt.[21] Such blessings were not employed primarily to eulogize mothers, but to pay tribute to exceptionally worthy individuals born of them. In the present context the woman's benediction identifies Jesus as a great hope in the face of conflicts, especially of demonic conflicts.

Jesus' response, "Blessed rather are those who hear the word of God and obey it" (v. 28), alters and expands the woman's blessing, however. This expansion is anticipated by Luke's grammar, which casts a spotlight on Jesus ("he" is emphatic in Greek), and by "rather" (Gk. *menoun*), a rare Greek particle with the sense of "yes, but. . . ." Jesus thus affirms the woman's response but defines blessedness with greater particularity: *True* blessedness depends not on the circumstance of blood relationship with himself, but on an elective response to "hear the word of God and obey it." (On "word of God," see at 8:15.) The Greek word for "obey" (*phylassein*) means to "guard" or "value greatly." The original sense of the woman's blessing seems to have been, "Women are blessed by being mothers of great sons," but in v. 28 Jesus promises blessings to women for being more than mothers, for they too must hear and obey God's word. The Virgin Mary was herself a prime example of such a blessing (1:38).

Hearing and obeying the word of God were the sole criterion determining a failed from a robust harvest in the parable of the Sower (8:15). Hearing and obeying the word of God were the deciding factor between belonging to Jesus' biological family or his true family (8:21). Hearing and obeying the word of God is also Jesus' advice for thwarting the predatory nature of the demonic in human life (vv. 24-26). Discipleship is not simply about eliminating bad

---

19. NIV "Blessed is the mother who gave you birth and nursed you."

20. So Plummer, *Luke*, 305.

21. See Judg 5:24; Jdt 13:18; *2 Bar.* 54:10. For renditions of the saying in the rabbinic tradition, see Str-B 2:187-88, esp. Rabbi Abba ben Zutra (ca. A.D. 270), who praised Rachel's birth of Joseph thus, "Blessed are the breasts that nursed you, and the body that bore you."

habits, but about filling the void with Jesus himself. Hearing and obeying the word of God as it is present in Jesus transforms life according to the criteria of the kingdom of God — and where the kingdom is present, there is "No Vacancy" for other kingdoms, dominions, and lords.

JESUS TEACHES ABOUT SIGNS AND LIGHT (11:29-36)

The demand for a sign is more subtle than accusing Jesus of expelling demons in the name of Beelzebul (vv. 14-26). It may be as adversarial, however, for according to v. 16, it too is an expression of disbelief, and because it is less alarming, it is more widespread. "As the crowds increased," Jesus began to teach them (v. 29). Luke repeatedly reminds readers of Jesus' popularity with crowds.[22] His bond with them includes the willingness to confront them: "This is a wicked generation. It asks for a sign, but none will be given it except the sign of Jonah" (v. 29). "Generation" is emphatic in Greek and is repeated seven times in the remainder of the chap. (vv. 29, 30, 31, 32, 50, 51), including twice in v. 29: "This generation is a wicked generation." This generation is not just misled or ignorant; it is *ponēros,* an intense Greek word denoting knowing and intentional wickedness. "Sign" repeats the same request in v. 16. There it was paired with "testing" (Gk. *peirazein*) and "desiring" (Gk. *zētein*), terms of opposition in Luke.[23] The function of a sign is to point to a deeper reality in relation to itself. If the crowds seek a "sign" from Jesus, say in a miracle or prophecy, they may not be concerned with the miracle or prophecy and its relationship to Jesus, but with something separate from Jesus. If they are, the sign will not lead to an encounter with Jesus, but away from him. In seeking a "sign from heaven" (v. 16), the crowds seek something other than Jesus, something more "spiritual." In this Jesus fails to satisfy them. In the second century, Gnosticism promised a more "spiritual" form of Christianity, as did heresies in succeeding centuries. The longing for a more spiritual revelation is the mother of all heresies, the original temptation of the serpent no longer simply to know God, but to *be* god (Gen 3:5).

29-32 "Sign" occurs thrice in v. 29: No sign will be given to the generation that seeks a sign — except the sign of Jonah! The only other NT reference to the "sign of Jonah" is Matt 12:39-40, where Jonah's three-day confinement in the belly of a sea monster symbolizes Jesus' three days in the tomb. Luke

---

22. 4:42; 5:1; 6:17; 7:11; 8:4, 19, 40; 9:11, 37; 11:27; 12:1, 54; 14:25; 15:1; 18:36; 19:37, 48.

23. *Peirazein* appears elsewhere in Luke only with reference to the devil (4:2); *zētein* occurs some twenty-five times in Luke, more than half of which are pejorative (2:48, 49; 9:9; 11:16, 29, 54(?); 12:29; 13:24; 17:33; 19:3, 47; 20:19; 22:2, 6; 24:5).

makes no mention of the three days in either the sea monster or the tomb. Jonah is a "sign" to the Ninevites, as the Son of Man (see at 5:26) will be to his generation. It is possible that Luke, like Matt, intends the "sign of Jonah" to anticipate Jesus' resurrection: scholars who think so frequently interpret the future tenses in vv. 29-30 to signify the future resurrection of the Son of Man.[24] But without the Matthean parallel, would one interpret Luke's indeterminate "sign of Jonah" thus? Jonah's story was popular with generations of Jewish interpreters, not as a symbol of the resurrection, but with reference to the rescue of the righteous individual, or more frequently, to his preaching of judgment against Nineveh.[25] Luke, likewise, does not explicitly correlate the "sign of Jonah" with resurrection but with judgment and repentance. Judgment was the substance of Jonah's preaching to Nineveh (Jonah 3:4), and "judgment" is likewise mentioned four times in vv. 31-32. True, Jonah's pronouncement of judgment resulted in Nineveh's repentance rather than destruction (Jonah 3:5-10), but Jesus' warnings of judgment are likewise concluded with repentance, "[The Ninevites] repented at the preaching of Jonah; and now one greater than Jonah is here" (v. 32). The theme of repentance was typical of Jesus' preaching (5:32; 10:13; 15:7; 19:10). It would appear that Luke's "sign of Jonah" (v. 29) should be understood in terms of "the preaching of Jonah" (v. 32), i.e., in terms of judgment and repentance.[26]

The "Queen of the South" who came to hear the wisdom of Solomon (v. 31) refers to the queen of Sheba (1 Kgs 10:1). Luke's pairing of the queen of Sheba with Jonah is another example of his combining male and female responses to the gospel. The emphasis on analogous gender responses in the Third Gospel may be another example of the way the new covenant completes the old: the image of God consists of both male and female (Gen 1:26), and thus both male and female attest to the true Image of God in Jesus Christ (2 Cor 4:4; Col 1:15; 3:10). Especially important is the queen's coming "from the ends of the earth" to hear Solomon's wisdom. In the OT, and particularly the Psalms, the universal scope of the faith of Israel extends to and gathers people from "the ends of the earth."[27] The queen of Sheba (Sheba was in southern Arabia,

---

24. So Plummer, *Luke*, 306-7; Geldenhuys, *Luke*, 335. Green, *Luke*, 463-64, cites the significance of Jesus' resurrection for the missionary preaching in Acts as additional evidence for this view.

25. Str-B 1:642-49.

26. Two references in early fathers, *1 Clem.* 7:7 and Justin Martyr, *Dial.* 107.1, likewise interpret the "sign of Jonah" with reference to judgment and repentance.

27. Tob 13:13; Pss 2:8; 21:28 (Eng. 22:27); 45:10 (46:9); 47:11 (48:10); 58:14 (59:13); 60:3 (61:2); 64:6 (65:5); 66:8 (67:7); 94:4 (95:4); 97:3 (98:3); Dan 4:21-22. Each passage repeats the same Greek phrase of v. 31, *ek tōn peratōn tēs gēs*. *1 Clem.* 4:7 applies this same concept to the universal scope of the gospel, testifying that the apostle Paul "taught righteousness to the whole world, even going to the limits of the West."

roughly equivalent to modern Yemen) exemplifies this motif, for she, a Gentile foreigner, is drawn to the superior wisdom of Solomon, Israel's wise king. "One greater than Solomon is here" (v. 31) is a claim of implicit Christology on Jesus' part that his wisdom and authority surpass Solomon's. Moreover, the queen's prudent acknowledgment of Solomon's wisdom will judge the folly of "this generation," which fails to recognize Jesus' greater wisdom and authority.[28] "The men of Nineveh" will likewise rise up in judgment against this generation, for Nineveh, no less remote than Sheba, recognized the revelation of God in Jonah's proclamation of judgment and repented, whereas "this generation" does not recognize or honor that, in Jesus, "one greater than Jonah is here" (v. 32).

33-36 In vv. 33-36 Luke appends a series of concise sayings employing the image of the ubiquitous ancient oil lamp (Gk. *lychnos*). "Lamp" interjects a new image into Jesus' teaching, but the theme of light is not new, for it relates to the requests for "signs" in vv. 14-32.[29] Lamp-sayings appear in several different contexts in the Gospels (8:16; 15:8; Matt 5:15; Mark 4:21), suggesting that the theme and imagery were fairly common in Jesus' teaching. Here the sayings contrast inner light and inner darkness. The guiding light in the passage is the Greek word *haplous* (v. 34; NIV "healthy"), meaning "singleness of purpose, sincerity, free from guile." The use of *haplous* in *T. Iss.* 4:1-6 conforms to Jesus' teaching here, namely, that actions done with integrity and sincerity of motive, i.e., with singleness of purpose, affect one's ability to *see*.[30] Such people possess an inner light that does not require "signs." Wis 1:1-2 likewise teaches that singleness of heart is the antithesis of those who require signs in order to believe in God. This same idea culminates in Jesus' foregoing warning against faithless tests for signs in vv. 16, 29-32 and lays the foundation for his case against the Pharisees and lawyers in vv. 37-54, where duplicity and internal corruption are the antithesis of single-minded commitment to the will of God.[31] Seekers of signs, including the Pharisees and lawyers, are *ponēros* (v. 34), the same Greek word of vv. 4, 13, 26, and 29. In all these passages *ponēros* signifies willful evil. Such people possess, indeed are *possessed by*, inner darkness. Since they have no inner light by which to see the gospel, they demand "signs" (v. 29), but signs will not be given to them because the request betrays reticence, perhaps even unwillingness to believe.[32]

28. See here Green, *Luke*, 465.

29. The old Greek chapter divisions of Codex Alexandrinus also designate 11:29-36 a unified pericope.

30. S. Garrett, "'Lest the Light in You Be Darkness': Luke 11:33-36 and the Question of Commitment," *JBL* 110/1 (1991): 96-100. "Luke's reference to 'the single eye' . . . would have conveyed the notion that a given individual *focuses his or her eye on God alone*. No worldly pleasures, no competing masters, no evil spirits can cause the person of 'the single eye' to compromise his or her integrity toward the Lord" (99, emphasis in original).

31. Garrett, "Lest the Light in You Be Darkness," 102-3.

32. See Plummer, *Luke*, 308.

The lamp of v. 33, lighted and placed prominently so that it illumines all who enter, is a reference to Jesus Christ. At 8:16 lamp is used metaphorically and somewhat similarly of the revelation of God that should not be "hidden" or "placed under a bed." The imagery is similar to that of the new patch and the old garment, and the new wine and the old wineskins, of 5:36-39. All these images are commonsense pleas to use things according to their purposes, not contrary to them. Similarly, Jesus' light cannot be hidden or placed under a bowl. The thought again recalls the mission of the Servant of the Lord in Isa 49, to which Jesus alluded in vv. 21-22. The Servant was not sent to Israel alone, but to be "a light for the Gentiles" (Isa 49:6). Jesus, likewise, is not the sole claim of one interest group, not even of Judaism and the temple, but *the* light for all who enter — even for people as far away as Nineveh and Sheba!

The "lamp" is also applied to the eye of the individual in vv. 34-36. The imagery of the lamp and darkness in v. 34 recalls the same imagery of Ps 18:28//2 Sam 22:29. In the psalm, God is the source of light, but in v. 34 the integrity of one's "eye" is made the source of light or darkness. Here the "eye" signifies the center of one's being, the soul or spirit according to the rabbis, or as we say today, one's intentions or "heart."[33] In v. 34 the "healthy eye" signifies a pure heart, and the "unhealthy eye," envy.[34] The "eye" as a conduit of the intentions of the heart was known to ancient Judaism, and in many parts of the Middle East still today, as the "evil eye." Saul's evil glance at David (1 Sam 18:9) led to a belief that an evil look can harm or bewitch another person. By association, an "evil eye" connoted stinginess, selfishness, and jealousy (Prov 28:22). Scores of arts and amulets were developed to protect against the influence of the evil eye, including blue paint and an amulet in the form of an open hand in the Middle East today.[35] In the present context, however, Jesus emphasizes the danger of the "evil eye" for *oneself* rather than for others. The eye is portrayed as an aperture through which either light or darkness enters and fills the body. A sound eye (v. 34; Gk. *haplous;* NIV "healthy") allows the kingdom of God inaugurated by Jesus to enter and infuse one's life. People who are receptive to the kingdom are thus given light and guidance necessary to negotiate a dark world.[36] An evil eye is either not open to the kingdom or is divided, duplicitous, and distracted from the kingdom. This results in self-serving darkness rather than the light of the kingdom. Jesus warns against a perspective that can and will corrupt the heart of an individual unless repented of and resisted.

---

33. On rabbinic uses of "light of the eye," see Str-B 1:432-33.

34. M. Völkel, *ophthalmos, EDNT* 2:552-53.

35. See *Enc. Jud.* 6:998-1000.

36. Bock, *Luke 9:51–24:53,* 1102.

The lamp-sayings conclude in v. 36, "Therefore, if your whole body is full of light, and no part of it dark, it will be just as full of light as when a lamp shines its light on you." There is a certain redundancy to this saying, and this, combined with its obscurity, may be the reason it is omitted in the parallel section of Matt 6:22-23. It is grammatically possible to understand the saying to mean that the virtuous heart that is receptive of truth will ultimately receive the revelation of the gospel in Jesus Christ.[37] The current interest in the modern West in a divine inner light within each individual makes this an attractive interpretation. Such an interpretation, however, seems patently discrepant from Jesus' teaching. Jesus does not identify the source of divine light within the native human heart but in the kingdom of God that he himself inaugurates. Without that source of light the human heart, even if "swept clean and put in order" (v. 25), will not grow increasingly luminous but will succumb to an infinitely worse condition. V. 36 is better understood to accord with Jesus' overall teaching that a disciple who is now illuminated by the light of Jesus (v. 33) will in the future consummation experience the full revelation of God's light.[38]

A TABLE PREPARED IN THE PRESENCE OF HIS ENEMIES (11:37-54)

37-38   In the original Greek a Pharisee (on Pharisees, see at 5:17) extends a dinner invitation "while Jesus was speaking" (v. 37; not "*after* Jesus had finished speaking," so NIV). In extending the invitation while Jesus is teaching on light and darkness, Luke links the meal with the Pharisees and lawyers in vv. 37 54 to the preceding teaching on willful darkness (vv 34-36). This is the fourth of seven **banquet** scenes in Luke (5:29; 7:36; 9:16; 11:37; 14:1; 22:14; 24:29), and one of three hosted by Pharisees (7:36; 11:37; 14:1). The banquet narrative was a familiar genre in ancient Greek literature for showcasing the wisdom of honored guests.[39] It is not surprising that Luke, who commences his Gospel with a formal Hellenistic introduction (1:1-4), should employ this genre to emphasize Jesus' disputes with Jewish religious leaders. Luke does not appropriate the Hellenistic banquet motif unaltered, however, but especially in

---

37. E.g., Klostermann, *Lukasevangelium*, 129.

38. So F. Hahn, "Die Worte vom Licht, Lk 11, 33-36," in *Orientierung an Jesus: Zur Theologie der Synoptiker* (ed. P. Hoffmann; Freiburg: Herder, 1973), 129-31. A full discussion of the issues surrounding the verse is offered by Marshall, *Luke*, 489-90.

39. See Plato, *Symp.*, 86-87; Xenophon, *Symp.*, 380-83. For a discussion of the banquet in 11:37-54, see E. Steele, "Luke 11:37-54 — a Modified Hellenistic Symposium?" *JBL* 103/3 (1984): 379-94; Klein, *Lukasevangelium*, 425.

the present banquet emphasizes the *prophetic* character of Jesus' dispute with the Jewish religious leaders.[40]

The banquet to which Jesus is invited is not an evening meal but an earlier afternoon meal.[41] The reference to "reclining" (v. 37), the protocol at formal meals, indicates the importance of the affair. Given the Pharisees' history of antagonism to Jesus, this prestigious invitation raises apprehensions. Indeed, the Pharisee "was surprised . . . that Jesus did not first wash before the meal" (v. 38). Throughout the Third Gospel, "surprised" (Gk. *thaumazein*) registers the effect of Jesus' actions on observers, but it does not signify a faith response of observers. Here, the Pharisee's "surprise" is a censure of Jesus for not washing before the meal. The Greek word for "dip" or "immerse," *baptizein,* is the normal Lukan word for "baptism" (8x in the Gospel). This is the only instance in the Third Gospel in which the word means "to wash," perhaps because it translates the Hebrew *tabal.* **Washing** was technically necessary only if one had touched a bodily discharge (Lev 15:11), but Pharisees, along with the Qumran community, expanded both the number and significance of washings as signs distinguishing observant Jews from nonobservant Jews and Gentiles.[42] Jesus' involvement with unclean crowds and his failure to wash before eating would have been particularly offensive to a Pharisee. Jewish purity laws, including washings and various categories of "cleanness," were not primarily concerned with germs and hygiene, but with religious propriety.[43] Jacob Neusner writes, "If you touch a reptile, you may not be dirty, but you are unclean. If you undergo a ritual immersion, you may not be free of dirt, but you are clean. A corpse can make you unclean, though it may not make you dirty. A rite of purification involving the sprinkling of water mixed with ashes of a red heifer probably will not remove a great deal of dirt, but it will remove the impurity."[44] Such ritual purity was a dominant trait of Pharisaism prior to 70.[45] Fully 25 percent of the Mishnah is devoted to issues of purity, and archaeological excavations continue to reveal *mikwa'ot,* cleansing baths, in ancient Jewish localities — even on the summit of Masada, one of the hottest and most arid places on earth. A modern analogy to ritual purity occurs in

---

40. The after-dinner drinking bout typical in Hellenistic banquets is absent from Lukan banquets, and Luke focuses only on Jesus' words, in contrast to the Hellenistic banquet genre, in which all guests speak.

41. The Greek word for "meal" in v. 38 is not *deipnon,* signifying a formal evening meal, but *ariston,* which designates either a morning (so the verb in John 21:12) or midday meal in 11:38; 14:12; and Matt 22:4. See BDAG, 131; Str-B 2:204-6.

42. See Str-B 1:695-704.

43. Thus, washing in water produces hygienic cleanliness, but washing in blood produces ritual cleanliness (Heb 9:22)!

44. J. Neusner, *The Idea of Purity in Ancient Judaism* (SJLA 1; Leiden: Brill, 1973), 1.

45. Neusner, *The Idea of Purity,* 65.

authoritarian societies and organizations where people who are under suspicion, for whatever reason, are shunned by those who are not, lest the "tainted" individual jeopardize those associated with them.

39-41   Ritual purity may seem an arcane formality in modern thinking, but it did not seem so to Jesus. His confrontation of the issue is signaled by the reference to him as "Lord," and by his emphatic address, "Now then, you Pharisees, you clean the outside of the cup and dish, but inside you are full of greed and wickedness" (v. 39). "Greed" and "wickedness" are sharp indictments: the first (Gk. *harpagē*) means taking advantage of others by robbery and plunder (see Mark 12:38-40), and the second (Gk. *ponēria*) repeats the theme of wickedness of vv. 13, 26, 29, 34. V. 39, preserved also in Matt 23:25-26 and *Gos. Thom.* 89, accuses Pharisees of meticulous attention to outward appearance and gross neglect of inner integrity. The contrast between cosmetic exterior and decayed interior replays the theme of the healthy eye of v. 34: when the inside is sound, the whole organism is sound, but a good appearance does not necessarily indicate a pure heart. Jesus calls people who follow the latter course "fools" (v. 40; NIV "You foolish people!"), another sharp invective. In OT Wisdom literature, a "fool" signified a type of person or pattern of behavior that rejected the ways of God in favor of one's own destructive ways.[46] Luke is the only Evangelist to use this term from the Jewish Wisdom tradition, which may be due to a Hebraic influence in the Third Gospel. In 1 Cor 15:36 Paul calls his opponents fools, which may also recall the figure of Wisdom literature.[47] In contrast to the fool, the wise person, says Jesus, knows that the God who "made the outside made the inside also" (v. 40).

The Greek wording of v. 41 is very compressed, resulting in both ambiguity of meaning and diversity of translations. The phrase "give alms" (NIV "be generous to the poor") is a Hebraism,[48] and the juxtaposition of words in the first part of v. 41 without showing their syntactic relationship to each other suggests Hebraic influence as well. The Hebraic character of the verse may help explain its meaning. The LXX translators regularly chose to translate *tsedaqah*, the important Hebrew word for "righteousness" and/or "justice," with the Greek word for "alms," *eleēmosynē*.[49] Giving to the poor, in other words, was at the core of God's will for justice in the world. The Hebraism "give alms" seems to signify something similar in v. 41. Giving alms, being generous with the poor, is not only the opposite of "greed" and "wickedness" (v. 39), but a deep and genuine expression of a pure heart. When one's heart is pure, "everything will be clean for you."

46. D. Zeller, *aphrōn*, *EDNT* 1:184-85.

47. See also the interplay between "wisdom" and "folly" in Eph 5:15-17.

48. Gk. *dote eleēmosynēn* = Heb. *nathan tsedaqah*; Str-B 2:188-89.

49. R. Bultmann, *eleēmosynē*, *TWNT* 2:482-83.

42-44   Jesus launches into three denunciations of Pharisees in vv. 42, 43, 44, followed by three denunciations of religious lawyers in vv. 46, 47, 52 (on this term, see at 10:25). Elsewhere in Luke sequences of blessings (6:20-22) or woes (6:24-26) are also presented in balanced numbers, perhaps as a memory aid. Each of the present denunciations of Pharisees and lawyers is emphatic in Greek. The first reads, "Woe to *you* Pharisees, because you give God a tenth of your mint, rue and all other kinds of garden herbs, but you neglect justice and the love of God." Torah required Israelites "to set aside a tenth of all that your fields produce each year" (Deut 14:22) for the support of worship centers and their ministers, as well as foreigners, the fatherless, and widows (Deut 14:28-29). Additional passages in both OT and Mishnah address agricultural tithes,[50] although without specific mention of herbs. Like other matters, including washings, fasts, and prayers, tithing burgeoned in rabbinic tradition as a way of demonstrating religious faithfulness.[51] The tithes of v. 42 may strike moderns as trivial or vain, but Jesus does not reject them. In this he demonstrates respect for the Jewish law — and not only for the moral law but for the ceremonial law as well (see Mark 1:44). He denounces Pharisees, however, because they allow minor external observances, about which the OT is ambiguous, to displace central matters such as "justice and the love of God," about which the OT is unambiguous (1 Sam 15:22; Isa 42:1; Mic 6:8). The Pharisees displace ultimate faith expressions such as justice and love of God by faith expressions of lesser value. The issue, once again, is essential matters versus nonessential matters, i.e., the content of the vessel rather than its appearance (vv. 40-41; 2 Cor 4:7). Marcion, the second-century heretic who rejected the Jewish sacrificial system, expunged the end of v. 42 from his version of Luke.[52] Some proponents of the so-called Third Quest of the Historical Jesus, who portray Jesus as an antinomian reformer who subverted the kind of Jewish legalism mentioned in v. 42, are not dissimilar to Marcion in this respect. Luke's presentation of Jesus does not stress this antinomian profile. In declaring that God made both the outside of the cup and the inside of the cup, Jesus seems to affirm a "both/and" policy. Nevertheless, when the interior of the cup is given priority, i.e., when generosity to the poor is attended to, "everything will be clean for you" (v. 41). The issue is one of priorities of religious values more than competition between them.[53]

A second denunciation of Pharisees concerns their "love [for] the most

---

50. Lev 27:30-33; Num 18:12; Neh 10:37-38; 12:44; 13:5, 12; 2 Chr 31:5-12; Mal 3:8, 10; *m. Šebu.* 9:1.

51. See Str-B 4/2:690-97; Fitzmyer, *Luke (X–XXIV)*, 948.

52. Metzger, *TCGNT*, 134-35.

53. So Plummer, *Luke*, 311, "[The Pharisees'] carefulness about trifles is not condemned, but sanctioned. It is the neglect of essentials which is denounced as fatal. It is not correct to say that Christ abolished the ceremonial part of the Law while retaining the moral part."

important seats in the synagogues and respectful greetings in the market-places" (v. 43). On more than one occasion Jesus criticized the desire of the Pharisees for recognition and reputation (Matt 23:6; Mark 12:38), a desire to which religious leaders of all times and places are not immune. Social acknowl-edgment — honor versus shame — is one of the strongest motivating factors in human behavior, and no less so for those whose recognition is supposed to come from God rather than society (Matt 6:4, 6, 18).

Third and finally, Jesus criticizes Pharisees as "unmarked graves, which people walk over without knowing it" (v. 44).[54] In Israel contact with the dead, including their final resting places, defiled a person for seven days (Lev 21:1-4, 11; Num 19:11-22). It was customary in Israel to whitewash tombs (Matt 23:27-28) in the spring of the year so people would not unknowingly come into contact with them. This was of particular importance for priests and Levites, for whom a seven-day defilement might render them unfit for temple service.[55] In A.D. 20 Herod Antipas replaced Sepphoris as capital of Galilee with Tiberias on the west coast of the Sea of Galilee. Tombs were discovered on the construction site of Tiberias, rendering the city unclean for observant Jews (*y. Šebu.* 9:1; Josephus, *Ant.* 18.36). This may be one reason why Jesus never went to Tiberias, and why the city is mentioned only once in passing in the Bible (John 6:23). In calling Pharisees "unmarked graves," Jesus accuses them of a dangerous deception: they presume to be religious leaders and models, because of which they enjoy great social esteem, but those who are attracted to them, or who would pattern themselves after them, are rendered unclean and defiled in the sight of God.

45 "One of the experts in the law" at the meal realized that Jesus' crit-icisms of Pharisees were applicable to his profession as well. "Teacher," he in-terjected, "when you say these things you insult us also" (v. 45). "Lawyers" (Gk. *nomikos*, see at 5:17; 10:25) were renowned for mastery of Torah, for which they commanded unrivaled esteem in the Jewish religious hierarchy. For a learned professional to call Jesus Teacher is a noteworthy acknowledgment of his rep-utation — a reputation that makes Jesus' denunciation the more trenchant. The Greek word for "insult," *hybrizein*, usually denotes physical mistreatment and suffering (18:32; Matt 22:6; Acts 14:5; 1 Thess 2:2 = Acts 16:22-24), but here it bears the special sense of *ga'ah* in the Hebrew OT (which the LXX regularly translates by *hybrizein*), meaning "arrogance" or "presumption" (Isa 2:12; Jer

---

54. "Pharisee" is omitted in the third denunciation because of ellipsis (the textual variant "scribes and Pharisees, hypocrites" [A (D) W Θ Ψ] is a later scribal harmonization with Matt 23:27). The earliest Gospel chapter divisions in Codex Alexandrinus (A) include v. 44 in 11:37-45 (= chap. 42 in A), indicating that it belonged to the denunciations of Pharisees rather than lawyers, the latter of which are treated in 11:46-54 (= chap. 43 in A).

55. Str-B 1:936-37.

48:29; Ps 94:2; Prov 15:25; 16:19).[56] The lawyer, in other words, reproaches Jesus for haughtiness, which is roundly censored in the OT. This particular reproach is a backhanded testimony to Jesus' implicit christological self-assumption, for his denunciation of the Pharisees could be valid only if made by God, but if merely human would be, as asserted by the lawyer, categorically "haughty."

46-52 Most individuals, when reproached as Jesus is in v. 45, respond either by defending their words and behavior, or by clarifying, moderating, or apologizing for them. Jesus does none of these. He *presses* the point and sharpens the offense (also Matt 15:12). The interjection of the lawyer elicits from Jesus three equally emphatic denunciations of the lawyers. "Woe to you experts in the law, because you load people down with burdens they can hardly carry" (v. 46). Scribal interpretations of Torah create burdens too heavy for people to bear, they set bars too high for them to clear and standards too rigorous to satisfy (see Acts 15:10; Gal 2:14). Moreover, the lawyers "do not lift a finger to help" people meet the standards. This criticism reveals a particularly important insight of Jesus regarding teachers and leaders. Teachers must not only inform people, they must aid people. They must show people what to do, but also support them in doing it — and above all, attempt to live by it *themselves.*

The second denunciation of lawyers resumes the imagery of tombs, although with a different sense from v. 44. Building tombs in reverence of ancestors, and particularly great ancestors, was an important part of Jewish tradition. Herod the Great's epic plans for his burial at Herodium were perhaps the greatest illustration of funerary pomp in Jesus' day.[57] Burial etiquette was not limited to royalty, however. The Mount of Olives, which Jews traditionally associated with the return of the Messiah, was (and still is) covered with literally thousands of tombs. When Rome banned Jews from Jerusalem, following the Bar Kokhba revolt in 132-35, Jews built more elaborate burial caves for the Sanhedrin and other notable leaders at Beth-Shearim in the Jezreel Valley. It is not exactly tombs and monuments that Jesus decries, however,[58] but the hypocrisy of supposedly honoring those whom their fathers had murdered. "Woe to you, because you build tombs for the prophets, and it was your ancestors

---

56. See G. Bertram, *hybris, TWNT* 8:295-307.

57. Josephus, *J.W.* 1.419, 625, 673; *Ant.* 14.360; 15.323-25; 17.199; Pliny the Elder, *Nat.* 5.14.70.

58. Bock, *Luke 9:51–24:53*, 1120, writes, "They killed the prophets; you make sure they stay dead." This expression memorably notes the collusion between the present and past generations, but it misses the *hypocrisy* of the present generation in honoring what the past vilified. Cyril of Alexandria rightly notes that, in building tombs for prophets killed by their ancestors, the Jews of Jesus' day sought to honor the prophets and thus condemn their ancestors' actions. But they themselves were soon to be guilty of worse crimes in killing the Prince of Life and then his followers, such as Stephen (*Hom. Luc.* 85, cited in Just, *Luke,* 201).

who killed them" (v. 47).[59] This denunciation is not limited to first-century Jews, for "the blood of the prophets has been shed since the beginning of the world" (v. 50). No generation, in other words, is exempt from this searing condemnation. Is not the attempt of the American government to discredit the character of Martin Luther King Jr. while he was alive and then declare a national holiday in his honor once he was dead an uncomfortable example of such hypocrisy?

Jesus concludes that the history not only of Israel but of the world is one of violence against the prophets and apostles whom God has sent into this world. The parable of the Vineyard and Tenants (20:9-19) — the final parable in the Third Gospel — is an illustration of this truth. The prophets before Jesus had made an equally summary judgment against Israel (Jer 7:25-26; Rev 18:24). Scripture as a whole delivers the same verdict, for the reference to "the wisdom of God" (v. 49; NIV "God in his wisdom"), according to its only other reference in the Hebrew and Greek Bible (Ezra 7:25), is a circumlocution for Torah, Scripture.[60] In asserting that "the wisdom of God" tells the story of the persecution of the prophets, Jesus implies that *all* Scripture testifies that the history of the world is one of violence against the messengers of God, for which each generation is responsible.[61] The first witness to this shameful truth was written in the blood of Abel (v. 51; Gen 4:1-16), and "the blood of Zechariah, who was killed between the altar and the sanctuary" (v. 51), was the last witness to it in the Hebrew canon of the OT. Solomon's temple in Jerusalem faced toward the east, and in front of the sanctuary and a short distance removed from it stood the great altar of burnt offering on which animal sacrifices were offered (Ezek 44:13-17). Between the altar and the sanctuary proper Zechariah the priest, son of Jehoiada, was "stoned to death in the courtyard of the Lord's temple" (2 Chr 24:20-21) for condemning the people for disobedience — much as Jesus here condemns Pharisees and lawyers.[62] The place of this gruesome

---

59. The phrase "their tombs" in v. 48 ("they killed the prophets, and you build *their tombs*") is absent in the oldest and weightiest manuscripts, and thus probably a later scribal addition in order to provide a suitable object for the verb "build" (see Metzger, *TCGNT,* 135).

60. The rabbis frequently used the expression "the Holy Spirit speaks" or "the divine righteousness speaks" to imply the word of God as it was made known through Scripture (Str-B 2:189). The apostle Paul likewise speaks of "Scripture" as a circumlocution for "God" in Gal 3:8, 22. For a slightly different understanding of "wisdom of God" as a circumlocution for God's name, see Jeremias, *Sprache des Lukasevangeliums,* 208-9.

61. See Wolter, *Lukasevangelium,* 435.

62. Matt 23:35 identifies Zechariah as "son of Berekiah" (so Zech 1:1, 7). Zechariah son of Berekiah, however, was a different Zechariah from the one who suffered the gruesome fate described in Matt 23:35. Luke's omission of "son of Berekiah" may reflect the influence of the Hebrew Gospel, for Jerome attests that "in the Gospel that is used by the Nazarenes, we find 'son of Jehoiada' in place of 'son of Barachias'" (*Comm. Matt.* 23:35). Jeremias, *Sprache des*

deed "between the altar and the sanctuary" should not be overlooked, for it reminds Jesus' hearers that violence against God's messengers occurs not in back alleys but at Israel's holiest site! Not only does such rebellion take place on *terra sancta,* it happens in *"this generation* [which] will be held responsible for it all" (v. 51). The rejection that Jesus experiences from "this evil generation" — a theme repeated throughout his teaching on discipleship and conflict (vv. 29, 30, 31, 32, 50, 51) — is thus not only typical of the rejection of God's prophets and apostles, but the climax of it!

Jesus' third and final denunciation of the lawyers concerns their misuse of Torah. Their expertise in Torah, which Jesus refers to as a "key of knowledge" (v. 52), should have opened the door for themselves and others to knowledge of God and communion with him. The lawyers, however, have used their "key of knowledge" to close doors and prohibit access to God, for "you yourselves have not entered, and you have hindered those who were entering" (v. 52; also Matt 23:13).

53-54   With this denunciation the meal concludes. The meal has not been one of fellowship or bridging differences, but one in which lines of division have become deeper and sharper. The sober conclusion, "Jesus went outside" (v. 53), is both descriptive and symbolic, for even at table Jesus was an outsider among the scribes and Pharisees. The description of the religious leaders' animosity toward Jesus in vv. 53-54 is among the most polemic in the Gospels. They were "extremely hostile" (Gk. *deinōs enechein;* NIV "to oppose [Jesus] fiercely"), seeking "to incriminate him" (Gk. *apostomatizein auton;* NIV "to besiege him with questions"), "plotting to trap him" (Gk. *enedreuontes auton thēreusai;* NIV "waiting to catch him"). The language is premeditative and virulent — only a step shy of violence to Jesus' person (Acts 7:51-60).

The conclusion of Luke 11 may appear offensive to those who hold to a stereotype of "gentle Jesus, meek and mild." Jesus appears to be a rude guest who offends against good manners of ritual purity, who rebukes Pharisees for being internally filthy, and who concludes with an exposé of the worst offenses of both Pharisees and lawyers.[63] Such a profile poses a challenge for an age, like ours, that equates Christianity with "niceness" and "tolerance." The present pericope also gives a fuller understanding of the virtues of 6:27-31. The denunciations of the Pharisees and lawyers demonstrate that "love of enemies" does not mean saying what people want to hear, but telling the truth they may not want to hear.[64] "Doing good to those who hate you" does not mean being nice in the face of hatred and injustice, but speaking and acting in

---

Lukasevangeliums, 210, also recognizes that the reference is pre-Lukan, although he does not attribute it to the Hebrew Gospel. On the whole issue, see Edwards, *Hebrew Gospel,* 86-87.

63. See C. Blomberg, "Jesus, Sinners, and Table Fellowship," *BBR* 19/1 (2009): 58-59.

64. Vinson, *Luke,* 398-99.

ways that have the potential to reduce or eliminate hatred and injustice. The great violation of the *agapē* love-ethic is not confrontation, but indifference. Jesus is not indifferent.

Some may hear anti-Semitic "hate speech" in Jesus' denunciation of the Jewish leaders. It is helpful to be reminded in this regard that Jesus' denunciations of the religious leaders were in character with OT prophetic attacks on Israel's religious and political leaders. Critique is usually sharpest where one is most committed to a cause — and most aware of its abuses.[65] Reform is never born of indifference or mere tolerance, but of engagement and confrontation. Ironically, the polemical Jesus who likely offends modern sensibilities was a great reassurance to early orthodox believers, especially those engaged in the earnest struggle with Marcionism, which endeavored to fashion a new god of infinite forbearance and "niceness" in contrast to the tough love and judgment of the God of the OT. Jesus' posture and persona at the Pharisee's table were seen by such early Christians as "in character" with the God of the OT, as exhibited in the prophetic attack on hypocrisy and moral corruption. The profile of Jesus vis-à-vis the Jewish religious leaders reassured early Christians that divine love is not saccharine and permissive, but a love of costly forgiveness and justice as revealed in salvation history and personified in Jesus.[66]

---

65. Significant studies of Pharisaism by modern Jewish interpreters have concluded that the NT portrait of the Pharisees is not a misrepresentation of the movement or rooted in anti-Jewish biases but is essentially faithful to other first-c. witnesses to Pharisaism. J. Neusner, *The Idea of Purity in Ancient Judaism* (SJLA; Leiden: Brill, 1973), 65, writes: "The legal matters attributed by later rabbis to the pre-70 Pharisees are thematically congruent to the stories and sayings about Pharisees in the New Testament Gospels, and I take them to be accurate in substance, if not in detail, as representations of the main issues of Pharisaic law." E. Rivkin, *A Hidden Revolution* (Nashville: Abingdon Press, 1978), 123-24, 147-79, argues that the picture of the Pharisees in the Gospels and Paul conforms in essential respects with that of the Mishnah and Talmud and, moreover, that various rabbis, Johanan ben Zakkai among them, criticized some rabbis, and particularly Sadducees, no less severely than did Jesus. This understanding is echoed in the article on "Jesus" in *Enc. Jud.* 10:13, which states, "In general, Jesus' polemical sayings against the Pharisees were far meeker than the Essene attacks and not sharper than similar utterances in the Talmudic sources."

66. On the relevance of 11:37-54 for early Christians, esp. Tertullian and the African theologians in their confrontation with Marcionism, see Bovon, *Lukas 9,51–14,35*, 238-41.

CHAPTER ELEVEN

Discipleship: Decisions That Divide

Luke 12:1-59

Luke 12 continues the teaching of 11:14-54, but with special emphasis on bearing witness to faith in the face of opposition, the lure of possessions, and worry and anxiety. Teachings that are the same or similar to the teaching in this unit also appear in the Double Tradition, especially Matt 5–7, 10, and 24, and to a lesser extent in Mark and elsewhere in Luke.[1] The repetition and echo of the teachings of Luke 12 throughout the Synoptic Gospels leave the impression that the sayings preserved in this unit were uttered more than once by Jesus and on various occasions in his ministry.[2] This idea suggests that such teachings were regular themes in Jesus' ministry. The consistency with which the material is presented in the various sources attests to the care of the early church in the preservation of Jesus' teaching.[3]

In relation to the foregoing narrative, Jesus has left the house of the Pharisee in which the teaching of 11:37-54 took place and resumed the open-air preaching of 11:14-36. An interesting interplay between Jesus' disciples and the crowds emerges in chap. 12. Jesus primarily addresses disciples in the discourse, yet crowds are also present and even participate.[4] Luke does not structure the discourse, however, in terms of insider-disciples and outsider-crowds, but more in terms of "insiders" and "onlookers." Theophilus, the recipient of

---

1. **12:2-9** = Matt 10:26-33; Mark 4:22; 8:38; Luke 8:17; 9:26; 12:24; 21:18. **12:10** = Matt 12:31-32; Mark 3:28-30. **12:11-12** = Matt 10:19-20; Mark 13:11; Luke 21:14-15. **12:22-32** = Matt 6:7-8, 25-34; 10:29-31; Luke 12:6-7. **12:33-34** = Matt 6:19-21; 19:21; Mark 10:21; Luke 16:9; 18:22. **12:35-48** = Matt 24:42-51; 25:1-13, 20-21; Mark 13:33-37; Luke 17:7-10. **12:49-53** = Matt 10:34-36; Mark 10:38. **12:54-56** = Matt 16:2-3. **12:57-59** = Matt 5:25-26.

2. On this possibility, see Plummer, *Luke,* 316-17; Bock, *Luke 9:51–24:53,* 1130; Wolter, *Lukasevangelium,* 439-40.

3. Jeremias, *Sprache des Lukasevangeliums,* 219, writes, "This section [12: 1-34] reveals only minimal editorial intervention. It makes particularly clear how reserved Luke was in altering the words of Jesus."

4. Disciples: "disciples" (vv. 1, 22), "my friends" (v. 4), "little flock" (v. 32), Peter (v. 41). Crowds: "crowds" (vv. 13, 54), "parables" (v. 16), which are typically addressed to crowds.

the Third Gospel, may have been such an onlooker (see at 1:4). Thus, Luke does not erect an impermeable partition or barrier between disciples and crowds. The center of Luke's narrative spotlight is directed at the disciples, but its periphery radiates to the surrounding crowds, allowing them to hear Jesus' call to discipleship and inviting them to respond in faith. The resultant picture may be a model for Luke's church, and the church in every age: Jesus' theological discourse is both edifying and challenging for believers, but mindful, responsive, and inviting of the surrounding culture.

THE ETERNAL CONSEQUENCES OF CHRISTIAN WITNESS (12:1-12)

1-3 Luke typically frames material that he has received from "eyewitnesses and servants of the word" (1:2) with his own introductions, and the first half of 12:1, with its emphasis on the size and intensity of the crowds surrounding Jesus, is a further and dramatic example of Luke's editorial hand. The Greek word "first" (v. 1, *prōton*) could modify either the disciples or the commandment to beware of the Pharisees. The NIV opts for the former ("Jesus began to speak first to his disciples"), implying that Jesus is addressing the disciples in particular. The Greek syntactic placement of "first," however, more plausibly modifies the commandment regarding the Pharisees, i.e., "First, be on your guard against the yeast of the Pharisees, which is hypocrisy" (v. 1; similarly 14:28, 31).[5] Nevertheless, Jesus clearly addresses his followers in 12:1-12, for within the multitudes mobbing Jesus he identifies his "disciples" (v. 1), whom he calls "my friends" (v. 4), admonishing them three times directly, "I tell you" (vv. 4, 5, 8).

The warning against the "yeast of the Pharisees" occurs also in Matt 16:6 and Mark 8:15, but only Luke identifies it as **hypocrisy** (see, however, Matt 16:12). The first reference to yeast in Israel's history occurs at the exodus, when the haste in which Israel fled Egypt left no time for their bread to rise (Exod 12:39). The initial mention of yeast is thus negative — a sign of servitude, a hindrance. This negative connotation is retained in the metaphor of hypocrisy. "Hypocrisy" (Gk. *hypokrisis*) was primarily a theatrical term, denoting the mask an actor wore to impersonate a given character. But its obvious applicability to related issues led to a number of secondary associations, including, in this instance, the properties of "yeast," the fermenting sugar that causes dough to expand. Both theatrical masks and yeast create false impressions: masks produce exterior appearances at variance from intrinsic characteristics,

---

5. See Bovon, *Lukas 9,51–14,35*, 248.

and yeast activates a gaseous reaction that increases mass but not substance and weight. The use of "yeast" as a metaphor of hypocrisy was not novel with Jesus, for Jewish rabbis and Greek authors also used "yeast" as a metaphor of evil impulses within people, or of the art of pretense and deception.[6] We should not imagine that hypocrisy was unique to Pharisees — or even in a degree not present in other people of faith. Hypocrisy is an ever-present danger in all religious traditions. It is perhaps most perilous in a religion like Christianity, which calls for radical discipleship and transformation. Pharisees imagined that the privilege of election was due to merit, that the gift of Torah implied worthiness rather than responsibility, and that, in following a higher rule, Pharisees were in fact better people. Jesus condemned no malignancy, whether spiritual or moral, more severely than he condemned hypocrisy. He taught — and he expected his disciples to demonstrate — that call and election were not pretexts for pride but admonitions to humility. "From everyone who has been given much, much will be demanded; and from the one who has been entrusted with much, much more will be asked" (12:48).

The theme of veiling and concealment is continued in vv. 2-3. Hypocrisy is successful to the degree that pretense is taken for reality. The falsehood of hypocrisy cannot be perpetrated forever, however. "There is nothing concealed that will not be disclosed, or hidden that will not be made known" (v. 2; *Gos. Thom.* 5). Powerful natural phenomena such as volcanoes, earthquakes, hurricanes, avalanches, and tidal waves can sometimes be partially or temporarily manipulated, but they eventually and inevitably prevail over all attempts of human control. Nor can the inexorable subterranean realities of nature and human nature be endlessly masked and concealed by the artifice of hypocrisy. V. 3 develops this truth. It begins with a rare Greek expression, *anth' hōn*, a genuine Hebraism signifying purpose.[7] "Accordingly" (Gk. *anth' hōn*), says Jesus, "what you have said in the dark will be heard in the daylight, and what you have whispered in the ear in the inner rooms will be proclaimed from the roof" (v. 3; for a variant form of this saying, see *Gos. Thom.* 33). The reference to "inner rooms" (Gk. *tameion*) refers to compartments, cellars perhaps, that are sequestered and sealed from their environments. Such spaces are not *successfully* sealed from their environments, however, for plans hatched in the bowels of secrecy will eventually be shouted from the rooftops. Humans are unable either fully or finally to disguise the motivating impulses of their lives; indeed, they inevitably and perfectly live out what they actually believe. The

---

6. Str-B 1:728-29; Wolter, *Lukasevangelium*, 440-41.

7. In the LXX *anth' hōn* translates various Hebrew expressions some one hundred times, but the expression occurs only a dozen times in all Greek literature prior to the LXX and Christian era. Of its five occurrences in the NT, four occur in Luke-Acts. See Edwards, *Hebrew Gospel*, 140.

desires and intentions of human hearts come to light in the shape of human character and actions. Thornbushes do not bear figs, briers do not bear grapes; "a tree is recognized by the fruit it bears" (6:43-45).

4-7 What are the ultimate and inescapable dangers facing humanity? Which of our fears are legitimate, and which should we in fact not fear? This is the question of vv. 4-7. The story of the martyrdom of Eleazar in 2 Macc 6:18-26, which incorporates the theme of avoidance of hypocrisy and integrity before the judgment seat of God, is a fitting complement to these verses. A fivefold repetition of "fear" in vv. 4-7 — two more references to "fear" than in the Double Tradition (Matt. 10:28-31) — accentuates the theme. It would seem self-evident that "those who kill the body" (v. 4) should be feared. Surprisingly, Jesus dismisses this fear. "I will show you whom to fear: Fear him who, after your body has been killed, has authority to throw you into hell" (v. 5). Physical death is a season, perhaps painful and protracted or perhaps instantaneous, but a season nonetheless, after which physical life is terminated. Nothing in this experience is deserving of genuine fear. True fear — fear that we are wise to countenance and unwise to disregard — concerns the fate of life *after* physical death. It hardly seems necessary to note that v. 5 assumes the existence of life beyond the grave. By introducing a final authority beyond earthly life, however short or long that life may be, Jesus sets human existence in an entirely new perspective. The purpose of life is not disclosed in the existential Now, but rather by the One who determines its eternal destiny.

The word for "hell" (v. 5) in Greek, *Gehenna* (Heb. *Ge-hinnom*), signifies the valley south of Jerusalem that empties into the Kidron Valley, in which Judahites prior to King Josiah sacrificed their sons and daughters in burned offerings to Baal Molech on a "high place" called Topheth (Jer 7:32; 19:4-6; 32:34-35; 2 Kgs 16:3; 21:6). During King Josiah's reform Topheth was dismantled, desecrated, and turned into a smoldering rubbish dump as a lurid reminder of wickedness, suffering, and shame (Jer 18:1-4; 19:2, 10-13; Neh 2:13; 2 Kgs 23:10). Gehenna was a graphic image of hell to Jesus' audience — as near as a stone's throw from the temple. The one who "has authority to throw you into hell" (v. 5) might seem at first to refer to Satan, but it almost certainly refers to God, for in scriptural tradition "the one who has power to cast into Gehenna is God."[8] Thus God is to be feared (23:40; Ps 119:120; Heb 10:31; Rev 14:7, 10), whereas Satan is not to be feared but resisted (Jas 4:7; 1 Pet 5:9). The reference to Gehenna attests to God's ultimate authority over life beyond the grave, which in Rev 2:11; 20:6, 14; 21:8 is called "the second death."[9]

8. Marshall, *Luke*, 513.
9. See Str-B 4/2:1016-165; O. Böcher, *Gehenna*, EDNT 1:239-40; Fitzmyer, *Luke (X–XXIV)*, 959-60.

Jesus does not end on the note of God's terrible omnipotence, however. Having established the One alone whom we should fear in life and death, Jesus immediately reminds hearers of the tenderness and compassion of the Almighty. "Are not five sparrows sold for two pennies? Yet not one of them is forgotten by God. Indeed, the very hairs of your head are numbered" (vv. 6-7).[10] There is no contest or contradiction in Jesus' mind between the love of God and the justice of God, between God as Father and God as Final Judge. The One who has unrivaled authority to condemn is the One who need not be feared because his omniscience and all-compassion enfold the sparrows of the sky and the hairs of our heads. "Don't be afraid," says Jesus, "you are worth more than many sparrows" (v. 7). Physical death presents no obstacle to God's providential care of disciples, for "if we live, we live to the Lord; and if we die, we die to the Lord" (Rom 14:8). Human destiny is not determined on the anvil of fear but in the tender hands of God's grace, for although "God is the one who should be feared, the character of God is such that one need not fear him."[11] All humanity associates "God" with characteristics of might, glory, and judgment. In these verses Jesus reveals another and perhaps even deeper insight into the divine — the intimacy and tenderness of God, who cherishes humble creatures like sparrows, and who attends to insignificant details like the hair on our heads.

8-9 Jesus now turns from proper fear of the authority and compassion of the Father to proper confession of the Son of Man. The declaration is again prefaced with a solemn warning, "I tell you" (v. 8), followed by, "Whoever publicly acknowledges me, the Son of Man will also acknowledge before the angels of God" (v. 8). The Greek word for "publicly acknowledge," *homologein*, means "to commit oneself to something with a promise or confession." *Homologein* figures prominently in the apostolic vocabulary of the early church, but it derives from the Jesus tradition in the Gospels, especially the Gospel of John.[12] V. 8 could be literally translated, "Whoever confesses in me before man, the Son of Man will confess in him(self) before the angels of God." There is an obvious wordplay on "man" (Gk. *anthrōpos*), and the contrast between *in me* and *in him(self)* derives from the Hebrew influence of confessing or swearing against oneself.[13] *Homologein* is here used in a forensic context, i.e., Jesus swears against himself to confess before the angels of God in heaven those who confess him on earth. The saying asserts an inseverable connection between this world and the world to come (also Matt 5:16; 6:1; Luke 16:15; Rev

---

10. "Penny" (Gk. *assarion*) = one-sixteenth of a denarius, the latter of which was a standard day's wage.

11. Green, *Luke,* 482.

12. See O. Michel, *homologeō, TWNT* 5:206-9.

13. Discussions of the Hebraism can be found in Lagrange, *Luc,* 355; Fitzmyer, *Luke (X–XXIV),* 960; Wolter, *Lukasevangelium,* 444.

13:13; *T. Sim.* 5:5; *T. Levi* 17:8). A genuine confession of Jesus Christ in this world may have the effect of exposing a believer to opposition and persecution, but it *unites* a believer to Jesus Christ and to the holy company of "the angels of God" in the world to come. Some scholars have argued that Luke's use of "Son of Man" in v. 8 refers to someone other than Jesus, but this is virtually impossible on exegetical and theological grounds.[14] Matt's version of this saying (10:32), for instance, replaces "Son of Man" with the first-person singular pronoun "I," thus referring both halves of the saying to Jesus. The distinction between Jesus' human self-reference as "I" and his future self-reference as "Son of Man" is not a description of two different beings, but a distinction between his present earthly humiliation and his future heavenly exaltation (e.g., Rom 1:3-4; Phil 2:8-9; 1 Tim 3:16).

V. 8 is accompanied by a counterpart: "Whoever publicly disowns me will be disowned before the angels of God" (v. 9). The NIV translates vv. 8-9 in antithetic parallelism, but v. 8 is conditional (hence the subjunctive, "whoever would confess me"),[15] and v. 9 is factual (hence the aorist indicative; i.e., "whoever has denied me"). The implication is that condemnation before the judgment seat of God will be rendered on the basis of a pattern in life history. The contrast between acknowledgment and denial (vv. 8-9) recalls the Deuteronomic contrast between the "two ways" of life and death, prosperity and destruction (Deut 30:15-20). The Third Gospel attests that the "two ways" was a recurrent motif in Jesus' ministry: good versus bad tree (6:43-44), pure versus evil heart (6:45), house built on rock versus on sand (6:47-49), good versus bad servants (12:36-40), narrow versus wide gate (13:23-28).[16] In each of the contrasting sets of possibilities, Jesus begins with the positive option, trusting in the transformative appeal of virtue as opposed to the ruin of vice.

10-12 Luke concludes the pericope of 12:1-12 with two teachings on the Holy Spirit. The first occurs in v. 10, "Everyone who speaks a word against the Son of Man will be forgiven, but anyone who blasphemes against the Holy Spirit will not be forgiven." The final verb, "will be forgiven," is "divine passive," a Jewish way of avoiding vocalizing the name of God, meaning "God will forgive." This is an abbreviated, though more Hebraic,[17] version of a longer

---

14. See the discussion of the issue and critique in Marshall, *Luke*, 376-77; Bovon, *Lukas 9,51–14,35*, 258-59.

15. Several important manuscripts (A B D Γ Δ) read the future ("will confess") rather than subjunctive.

16. Bovon, *Lukas 9,51–14,35*, 257.

17. The Lukan wording, *hos erei logon eis ton huion tou anthrōpou* (lit. "whoever says a word *(in)to* [Gk. *eis*] the Son of Man") reflects the Hebraic use of a *beth*-prefix to mean "against." The wording of the same statement in Matt 12:32 reflects proper Greek usage, "whoever says a word *against* [Gk. *kata*] the Son of Man." See Jeremias, *Sprache des Lukasevangeliums*, 214; Edwards, *Hebrew Gospel*, 313.

saying that occurs in different contexts in Matt 12:31-32 and Mark 3:28-30. It is difficult to know in this first reference to blasphemy in the Gospel how Luke intends readers to understand blasphemy against the Holy Spirit. In Mark the saying follows the accusation that Jesus is in league with Beelzebul, the chief of demons (Mark 3:22-30). Mark thus implies that a deliberate association of Jesus with Satan is a denial of God's Holy Spirit and has unforgivable consequences.[18] Luke separates the saying about blasphemy against the Holy Spirit from the charge that Jesus is in league with Beelzebul, which he included earlier in 11:15. Luke's saying here about blasphemy against the Holy Spirit is without context, and thus more difficult to understand.[19] At the very least, the references to the Holy Spirit in vv. 10-12 suggest the important role the Holy Spirit plays in confessing Christ, which has been the theme of 12:1-12. In v. 10 the Spirit appears analogous to "the finger of God" (11:20) "as a way of expressing God's salvific intervention in human activity."[20] To reject the overtures and intervention of God is to reject the very person of God (Acts 7:51).[21]

The role of the Spirit in confessing Christ is made more explicit in vv. 11-12, where the Holy Spirit teaches believers what and how to speak when they are haled "before synagogues, rulers, and authorities" (v. 11). The use of "synagogues" combined with "rulers and authorities" implies that Jesus is preparing disciples for both Jewish and Gentile opposition. The testimony of the Holy Spirit is not something for which one can prepare, but something that comes upon those who bear witness in faith "at the very moment" (NIV "at that time") it is needed.

In appending two references to the Holy Spirit in vv. 10-12, Luke casts genuine confession of Christ, especially under adversity, in a Trinitarian perspective. Unlike the profession of the Pharisees (v. 1), Christian faith must be integrated into one's person (v. 3), rooted in a fear of God the Father that places all other fears in their proper context (vv. 4-7), and confessed in the world in union with Christ and with the angels of God (vv. 8-9) in reliance on the Holy Spirit, who is the inner testimony to the truth of the gospel, and who will instruct, empower, and free believers from anxiety in their public profession of faith.[22]

---

18. See here Edwards, *Mark*, 122-24.

19. Vinson, *Luke*, 406-7, observes that Luke tells us what the sin against the Holy Spirit is *not*, i.e., it is not apostasy, for Peter is restored from that (24:12); it is not killing Jesus, for Jesus prays for forgiveness of his tormentors and killers (23:34); it is not idolatry, for that is a sin of ignorance (Acts 17:30-31). Vinson concludes that it may be lying to God (so Acts 5:1-11).

20. Fitzmyer, *Luke (X–XXIV)*, 966.

21. H. Beyer, *blasphēmeō, TWNT* 1:623, asserts that the sin against the Holy Spirit is "wanton rejection of the saving and redemptive power and grace of God that is given to humanity. Only the one who forsakes forgiveness is excluded from forgiveness."

22. Bovon, *Lukas 9,51–14,35*, 243, is one of the few commentators to note the Trinitarian context of Luke's admonition of Christian confession in the face of opposition and adversity.

THE DANGER OF TRUSTING IN WEALTH
AND POSSESSIONS (12:13-21)

13-15 Following a request to arbitrate a dispute over an inheritance (vv. 13-15), Jesus delivers a parable about the false security of earthly possessions (vv. 16-21). The theme of the wealthy who were ever desirous of more wealth was not unique to Jesus but common to both ancient Hellenism and Judaism.[23] The dispute of the brothers in vv. 13-15 and the subsequent parable are unique to Luke among the Gospels, however. Combined, the two pericopes contain no fewer than ten Hebraisms, suggesting that the material derives from Luke's Hebrew source.[24] "Someone in the crowd said to [Jesus], 'Teacher, tell my brother to divide the inheritance with me'" (v. 13). The indefinite pronoun "someone" (Gk. *tis*) and especially the address to Jesus as "Teacher" may indicate the questioner is a Pharisee or Jewish leader, for ten of eleven addresses to Jesus as "Teacher" in Luke come from such, whereas disciples usually refer to Jesus as "Lord" or "Master." The plea likely comes from the younger of two brothers, for in lieu of an oral or written will from the father, an estate held by two brothers usually required the consent of the elder before it could be divided.[25] Family feuds, especially when they involve money, are among the most difficult disputes to reconcile.[26] According to v. 13, the (younger) brother has already decided what justice in this instance requires, and he enlists the advocacy of Jesus in effecting it.[27]

Whether or not a genuine issue of justice was at stake in the inheritance, we are not told. If there was such an issue, Jesus bypasses it — no doubt to the affront of the brother — in order to teach a more important lesson. "Man, who appointed me a judge or arbiter between you?" (v. 14). The reference "Man" in the vocative (Gk. *anthrōpe*) is unique to Luke in the Gospels (5:20; 12:14; 22:58, 60). It is not exactly harsh,[28] but it is direct and emphatic, very possibly due to Luke's Hebrew source (i.e., Heb. *ben adam*). The reference to being a judge or arbiter echoes Exod 2:14, where Moses intervenes in a dispute between two men.[29] A Pharisee or Jewish religious leader could be expected to catch this

---

23. See Hos 12:8-10; *1 En.* 97:8-10; Sir 11:18-19; and rabbinic material gathered in Str-B 2:190. For Hellenistic similarities, see *HCNT*, 215.

24. Edwards, *Hebrew Gospel*, 313.

25. Str-B 3:545-53; Deut 21:17; Num 27:8-10.

26. It was in attempting to adjudicate an inheritance dispute among the counts of Mansfeld that Martin Luther died of a heart attack in Eisleben, the town in which he was born, on 18 February 1546.

27. See here Bailey, *Jesus through Middle Eastern Eyes*, 300-301.

28. Contra Jeremias, *Sprache des Lukasevangeliums*, 215, and Bailey, *Jesus through Middle Eastern Eyes*, 302.

29. The textual tradition has tended to alter "judge and arbiter" (v. 14) to "ruler and

allusion, and also to hear in it that Jesus was *not* willing to play the role of Moses in his fraternal dispute.

"Watch out!" says Jesus. "Be on your guard against all kinds of greed; life does not consist in an abundance of possessions" (v. 15). Luke refers more frequently to the dangers of material possessions and wealth than do the other Gospels, but this is his only reference to "greed" or "avarice" and, apart from Mark 7:22, the only such reference in the Gospels. Jesus detects a covetous desire behind the man's request for a settlement of the inheritance, and he warns that "life does not consist in an abundance of possessions." Few sayings of Jesus are more relevant to the consumer mentality of the modern world than this statement, for life cannot be measured or judged by the amount of stuff we own, amass, or win.

The Greek language had three words for "life" that Luke could have chosen. One was *bios,* which referred to *quantitative* life, i.e., how long one lived, how many goods one acquired. Another was *psychē,* which referred to *qualitative* life, i.e., to the values and relationships that constitute personhood. The third was *zōē,* which referred to *quintessential* life, i.e., to the life offered to humanity in the call to follow Jesus, and through him to live in a personal relationship with the Father.[30] The first form of "life," *bios,* could, in fact, be measured by one's possessions. Luke does not use *bios,* however, but rather *zōē,* the word that describes God's life and the abundant God-life offered to the world in the gospel (John 10:10). *Zōē* cannot be reduced to, measured by, or satisfied by stuff. We do not earn or merit *zōē* but receive it freely and undeservedly from God through the person of Jesus Christ. *Zōē* is relational rather than material, I-Thou rather than I-It, eternal rather than temporal and fading. *Bios* leaves us restless and insatiable, hungering for more; *zōē* produces contentment, peace, and joy. "Be on your guard," says Jesus, against trying to achieve and satisfy *zōē* with things!

16-21   Jesus follows the admonition to the brother with the first of three parables about rich men recorded in the Third Gospel (12:16-21; 16:1-9, 19-31). "The ground of a certain rich man yielded an abundant harvest" (v. 16). The opening line of this parable is important, for the subject of the sentence is not the rich man but the "ground." The prosperity of the rich man is not his doing but a consequence of the productivity of land. His prosperity derives from a source other than himself. It is, in other words, an inheritance, even a *gift.* But the rich man cannot (or will not) acknowledge this. Instead, he sings a doxology to himself redundant in first-person singular pronouns: "He thought to *himself,* 'What shall *I* do? *I* have no place to store *my* crops. This is what

---

judge" in harmony with Exod 2:14. "Judge and arbiter" is doubtlessly original, accounting for all subsequent readings (Metzger, *TCGNT,* 135).

30. See J. Edwards, "Life in Three Dimensions," *Touchstone* 6/3 (1993): 17-21.

I'll do. *I* will tear down *my* barns and *I* will build bigger ones, and there *I* will store *my* surplus grain. And *I'll* say to *myself,* "*You* have plenty of grain . . ."'" (vv. 17-19). *Gos. Thom.* 63 preserves a summary of this parable, with the rich man equally confused about ownership versus stewardship. Inner monologues such as this are a unique feature of the Third Gospel, occurring nearly a dozen times, and always in sections of Luke not paralleled by Mark or the Double Tradition.[31] Not surprisingly, these soliloquies frequently reflect, as they do here, the human will in defiance of the divine will (also 7:39; 11:38; 12:45; 16:3; 18:4-5, 11-12).

The Middle East was and still is a communal culture where people gather at city gates and tea shops, kitchen tables and roadsides to talk about things great and small. In the midst of an intensely connected culture, this man has no one with whom to share his good fortune. His wealth, like virtually all wealth, has isolated him and eroded his trust in others. He is surrounded by people yet alone, a self-exile, and his isolation has made him foolish rather than wise.[32] "I will say to myself, 'You have plenty of grain laid up for many years. Take life easy; eat, drink and be merry.'" But then God spoke to him, "You fool! This very night your life will be demanded from you" (vv. 19-20).[33]

In what has he been a fool? Not in his foresight and planning; in these he has been exemplary. Nor was he wicked (12:45) or unjust (18:6). His folly is his oblivion to God. There are many forms of pride, but the worst of them is to think that one has no need of God. He does not acknowledge the source of his blessings. Rather, he gathers to himself and serves himself, and as such is a practical atheist. He has succumbed to the wilderness temptation of Jesus to live from bread alone (4:3-4). The word for "life" in vv 19-20 is no longer *zōē*, as it is in v. 15, but *psychē,* i.e., life identified by goals, values, and commitments. Having failed to recognize his wealth as a gift of God, and having thereby rejected the God-life, the rich man rests all his hopes in *things.* Investment in things never pays the dividends one hopes for. He may "eat, drink, and be merry," but he is a fool, "for tomorrow we shall die."[34] For the second and final

---

31. The Greek construction is *en heautō* ("in himself"): 1:29[D]; 7:39; 11:38[D]; 12:17, 32[D]; 16:3; 18:4; similarly 7:30; 15:17; 18:9, 11. See Edwards, *Hebrew Gospel,* 139. Jeremias, *Sprache des Lukas Evangeliums,* 215-16, considers three additional passages, also unique to Luke (5:21; 7:49; 20:13), in which inner monlogues are pursued without *en heautō.*

32. On the role of community in Middle Eastern life, see Bailey, *Jesus through Middle Eastern Eyes,* 303-4.

33. The original Greek reads, "Fool, this very night *they* will demand your soul from you." It is possible to regard the third person pronoun with fatal irony, i.e., the rich man thinks he owns his possessions, but they own him — and demand his life. It is also possible (and more likely) that this is another "divine passive" in which "they" is substituted for the name of God (also 6:38; so Jeremias, *Sprache des Lukasevangeliums,* 216).

34. "Eat, drink, and be merry" was widely known and quoted in antiquity, e.g., *1 En.*

time in Luke Jesus calls someone a fool (11:40; 12:20), in both instances for confusing temporal earthly realities with eternal divine realities.

The parable concludes with a moral, "So it is for everyone who stores to himself rather than is rich for God" (v. 21).[35] Whether v. 21 is Luke's summary or a quotation of Jesus is unclear. It could be from Jesus, but since Jesus leaves most parables open-ended, it more likely derives from Luke. The moral is a helpful reminder that Jesus did not consider wealth per se evil. Indeed, v. 21 commends wealth. The man was a fool not because he sought wealth, but because he imagined that wealth consisted in things, and that things rather than God could satisfy his life. Augustine memorably exposes his folly: "He did not realize that the bellies of the poor are much safer storerooms than his barns."[36]

THE FATHER'S PROVIDENTIAL CARE
OF HIS "LITTLE FLOCK" (12:22-34)

Why should Jesus call one into obedient fellowship with himself, and why should one so called accept the invitation? The answer is that discipleship with Jesus saves one from the disaster of the rich fool in the preceding parable. Consequently, Jesus addresses his instruction on this matter to disciples (v. 22) rather than the crowds (so 12:1-21). The rich fool thought in terms of surplus — tearing down his barns and building bigger ones so he could gather more, store more, hoard more (12:18). Jesus thinks in terms of necessities and God's provision for them. Jesus no longer speaks in parables, for in addressing disciples it was his custom to speak plainly rather than metaphorically (Mark 4:33-34). His address is direct and concentrated, an imploring wisdom lesson, alternating between rhetorical questions and declarations assuring hearers that God is attentive and faithful in providing for the needs of his "little flock" (v. 32). Frequent references to villages as "cities" in the Third Gospel suggest that Luke may have been written primarily for urban dwellers. If so, Luke makes no effort to alter Jesus' rustic imagery for his urbane audience. Jesus teaches in this section in bucolic imagery of farming, land, nature, and wildlife, and is thus another example of

---

97:8-10; Eccl 5:18; 8:15; Tob 7:10; Sir 11:19; 31:3; *Jos. Asen.* 20:8. Tannehill, *Luke,* 206, wryly notes the fool's fatal omission of "for tomorrow we shall die." Tolstoy's pompous baron in "What Men Life By" is the rich fool in more modern dress.

35. The syntax of the original Greek is such that the verse could be misunderstood, i.e., "Thus, the one who stores to himself and not to God is rich." The awkwardness of the verse may be the reason it is omitted in Codex Bezae (D). See the discussion of the problems in E. Schweizer, *Neues Testament und heutige Verkündigung* (Neukirchen: Neukirchener Verlag, 1969), 61-62.

36. Augustine, *Sermon* 36.7; quoted from Just, *Luke,* 208.

Luke's careful preservation of the form of Jesus' teaching.[37] These memorable pastoral images and sayings circulated widely and variously in the early church.[38]

22-26 "Therefore I tell you, do not worry about your life, what you will eat; or about your body, what you will wear. Life is more than food, and the body more than clothes" (vv. 22-23). The word for "life" here is the Greek word *psychē*, the same word used of the rich fool in vv. 19-20, thus applying the lesson of the rich fool to the disciples. The key word is "worry" (Gk. *merimnan*), which three times vocalizes the central theme of this unit (vv. 22, 25, 26; also 10:41). Food, clothing, and shelter represent the indispensable needs of humanity. *Merimnan* does not refer to forethought and planning about such things, but rather to undue concern about them, which results in apprehensiveness and anxiety. *Angst* is a common theme in ancient as well as modern literature, including Jewish Wisdom literature. Hardships and difficulties are undeniably the common lot of humanity, but worry and distress over them result in sleeplessness, physical exhaustion, and bitterness (Eccl 4:4-6; 6:7; 1 Macc 6:10; Sir 29:21-28; 40:1-11; 42:9). "Greater possessions bring greater worries" lamented Rabbi Hillel (*m. 'Abot* 2:7). This leitmotif of Wisdom literature is here accentuated by Jesus: happiness is not a product of human striving, but of learning to surrender all of life into the faithful and caring hands of the Father.[39]

The satisfaction of life's basic necessities still leaves other and even greater human needs unsatisfied, for "life is more than food, and the body more than clothes" (v. 23). "Consider the ravens," says Jesus. "They do not sow or reap, they have no storeroom or barn; yet God feeds them. And how much more valuable are you than birds!" (v. 24). There are valuable lessons to be learned from nature, and Jesus makes *birds* master teachers of nature (Job 12:7-9!). In Matt's version of this saying (6:26) the instructors are "birds of the sky," but in Luke they are "ravens," a word occurring nowhere else in the NT. Torah deems ravens unclean and worthless (Lev 11:15; Deut 14:14; *Barn.* 10:1, 4), yet even they and their helpless young are graciously provided for by God (Job 38:41; Ps 147:9). In saying that ravens "have no storeroom or barn," Jesus is not prohibiting people from providing for their necessities, but warning against surplus and hoarding (vv. 18-19) as signs of distrust in God's provision (Heb 13:5).[40] Ravens do not provide for themselves, yet God provides for them and even sends these clever birds on errands of mercy to Elijah in time of famine (1 Kgs 17:6). Jesus' point could not be simpler or more trenchant: "How much

37. Jeremias, *Sprache des Lukasevangeliums*, 219.

38. Clement of Alexandria (*Strom.* 1.24) and Justin Martyr (*1. Apol.* 15.14-17) both preserve sayings from this section, as does *Gos. Thom.* 36-37. The fullest version comes from farthest afield, from Oxyrhynchus in Egypt. On P.Oxy. 655, see esp. Fitzmyer, *Luke (X–XXIV)*, 976, and Bovon, *Lukas 9,51–14,35*, 299-300.

39. On anxiety and care, see Bovon, *Lukas 9,51–14,35*, 302-3.

40. Bovon, *Lukas 9,51–14,35*, 305.

more valuable are you than birds!" (v. 24). If God has created and called you as disciples, will he not also provide for your food and clothing![41] Worry and anxiety are not simply unhealthy and unfaithful, they are futile, for "who of you by worrying can add a single cubit to your height?" (v. 25).[42] Jesus was no stranger to hyperbole, and in speaking of adding a cubit (= ca. 21") to one's height, he was interjecting a note of humor as a way of underscoring the absurdity of worry. If disciples cannot increase their own height, why should they worry about other things over which they have no control (v. 26)?

27-31 Ravens are not nature's only instructors of humanity. Jesus appeals to the powers of observation of his disciples to "consider how the wild flowers grow" (v. 27). The Greek for "wild flowers," *krina,* is normally translated "lilies," but it may include the autumn crocus, anemone, gladiolus, or simply the happy flowers of Galilee.[43] "Observe them," urges Jesus. The command in v. 27 is the exact word and form of v. 24. Prolonged observation is not required: the aorist imperative *(katanoēsate)* means, "Take one look!" Even nonsentient flowers, which "do not labor or spin,"[44] teach disciples the same lesson the ravens do. They make no provision for themselves but fulfill their God-ordained purpose simply by being beautiful and productive.[45] In so doing, they surpass

---

41. Klein, *Lukasevangelium,* 453.

42. The NIV (and NRSV) read "single hour to your life." This translation reflects the sense that seems required (i.e., it seems more imaginable to add an hour to one's life than a cubit to one's height). "Hour," however, does not reflect the best lexical meaning of Gk. *hēlikian . . . pēchyn.* Whereas *hēlikia* can refer to either age or stature, *pēchys* is a linear rather than temporal measurement, meaning "cubit" (length of forearm from wrist to elbow) and, by association, "centerpiece," "(cross)beam," "bridge," etc. (LSJ, 1402; Jeremias, *Jerusalem in the Time of Jesus,* 11, n. 20). Since the first term can be either temporal or spatial, whereas the denotation of the second is spatial alone, a spatial translation seems preferable for the terms in combination (so BDAG, 812; Schlatter, *Lukas,* 532). The four occurrences of *pēchys* in the NT, two of which are necessarily spatial (John 21:8; Rev 21:17), and two of which are apparently so (Matt 6:27; Luke 12:25), also corroborate a spatial translation.

43. BDAG, 567.

44. The NIV translation "[the wild flowers] do not labor or spin" is supported by a broad spectrum of ancient Greek manuscripts, with the exception of Codex Bezae (D), which reads, "do not spin or weave." The editorial committee of both NA[28] and UBS[3] wisely rejected the substitution of "weave" (which occurs nowhere else in the NT) for "labor" "as a stylistic refinement introduced by copyists in view of the following reference to Solomon's clothing" (Metzger, *TCGNT,* 136).

45. Jesus was not the only Jewish teacher to appeal to nature for lessons about discipleship. Two centuries after Jesus, R. Simeon ben Eleazar said, "In my whole life I have not seen a deer engaged in gathering fruits, a lion carrying burdens, or a fox as a shopkeeper, yet they are sustained without trouble, though they were created only to serve me, whereas I was created to serve my Maker. Now, if these, who were created only to serve me, are sustained without trouble, how much more so should I be sustained without trouble, I who was created to serve my Maker! But it is because I have acted evilly and destroyed my livelihood, as it is

"even Solomon in all his splendor" (v. 27). This lovely metaphor, as beautiful as the wild flowers themselves, is also unrelenting in its logic: if Solomon, the wisest and most munificent of Israel's kings, is outdone by wild flowers, why should disciples follow his example rather than the example of the flowers of the field? God's providence extends to the grass itself, in fact, which is here today and gone tomorrow (see Isa 40:6-8; Ps 37:2; 90:5-6; 103:15). Employing the well-known argument from lesser to greater, Jesus concludes, "How much more will God clothe you — you of little faith!" (v. 28).

Jesus sums up nature's lessons for disciples in vv. 29-32. V. 29 is more direct and emphatic in Greek than in the NIV, emphasizing "you" (plural) five times in one verse: "As for you — you should not seek what you are to eat and what you are to drink, and you are not to be troubled." The "you" is an intensive reference to Jesus' disciples; they are not, as the foregoing illustrations make abundantly obvious, to clamor after food and drink. The command "not to be troubled" is controversial, however. The original Greek, *mē meteōrizesthe*, occurs only here in the NT. Many commentators and translations take it to mean "do not worry" (so NIV), in agreement with the sense of the verse and the emphasis on "worry" in vv. 22, 24, 25.[46] This translation is derived from context rather than lexicography, however, for *meteōrizesthe* is an entirely different word from the word for "worry" *(merimnan)* already used thrice in this passage. Had Luke intended "worry" here, would he not have repeated *merimnan* again? In both denotation and connotation *meteōrizesthai* does not mean "worry"[47] but "to make oneself high" and, by implication, to be "presumptuous, overbearing."[48] The word could carry this sense in v. 29, i.e., in your concern for worldly goods do not — like the rich fool in the parable — overreach or seek more than you need![49] *Meteōrizesthai* also came to describe the condition of a ship sailing on the *high* seas, i.e., being tossed to and fro or blown off course. This derivative meaning is widely attested in Greek literature and may give the best sense of this unique word in v. 29,[50] i.e., that

---

said, 'Your iniquities have turned away these things' " (*b. Qidd.* 82b). Despite his longing to do otherwise, R. Simeon concludes that sin prohibits him from following the example of nature. In contrast to R. Simeon, Jesus makes no reference to sin but proffers the example of nature as a valid antidote for worry and anxiety.

46. See the article and conclusions by K. Deissner, *meteōrizomai*, *TWNT* 4:633-35, followed by BDAG, 642-43 and many exegetes.

47. Klein, *Lukasevangelium*, 455-56, finds only one passage in extant Greek literature (P.Oxy 1679) with this meaning!

48. Heb. *g'h,* frequent in rabbinic usage (e.g. *t. Soṭah* 3:6), which appears to lie beneath the Greek verb (Schlatter, *Lukas*, 534), means to be "high, haughty, arrogant, or proud."

49. So the Vulgate, Luther Bible, and Schlatter, *Lukas*, 532.

50. See the lexical evidence and discussions presented in Plummer, *Luke*, 328; Bovon, *Lukas 9,51–14,35*, 308-10; Wolter, *Lukasevangelium*, 453-54.

Jesus' disciples are not to be undecided, vacillating between faith and doubt whether God will care for them.

Disciples should not seek after food and drink (v. 29) because such are the pursuits of the world, and disciples are not to pattern themselves after the world (v. 30). The contrast of v. 30 is intensified by reference to "the nations of the world" (Gk. *ta ethnē tou kosmou;* NIV "the pagan world"), a Hebraism frequently employed by Jewish rabbis to accentuate the difference between Jews and Gentiles, but which occurs nowhere else in the LXX or Greek NT.[51] The prophet reminded Israel that "[God's] thoughts are not your thoughts, neither are your ways [God's] ways" (Isa 55:8). In v. 30 Jesus repeats this simple, difficult, and truly countercultural lesson for his disciples: God's care for the humble and unassuming life-forms of nature has more to teach disciples about trust in God than do all the sophisticated and enticing nations of the world. "Your Father" (v. 30) — the God who cares for the ravens (v. 24) and adorns the wild flowers of the fields (v. 27) — knows the needs of all his creatures, Jesus' disciples included. "But seek his kingdom and these things will be given to you as well" (v. 31). God's kingdom, his glory, and his reign in the world are to be the defining purpose of Jesus' disciples. When disciples make God's way in this world their primary goal, all other things — the food, clothing, shelter that the world clamors for — will be given to them as well.[52] The rich man vainly imagined that all his wealth was due to his effort and merit (vv. 16-21). Jesus teaches that all that the disciples need will be *given* to them by God if only they seek God above all things. Indeed, God will give something far greater than things to his disciples: he will give the kingdom itself (v. 32). If God gives the greatest of all things to them, can they not trust God for lesser things as well?

32-34   Jesus consoles the disciples with a final warning against anxiety, "Do not be afraid, little flock, for your Father has been pleased to give you the kingdom" (v. 32). The voice of the Good Shepherd is clear and reassuring in this verse, the only verse in this section that has no parallel in Matt's Sermon on the Mount. "Little flock," a metaphor for God's chosen people in the OT (Jer 23:2; Ezek 34:6; Hos 4:16; Mic 7:14; Ps 95:7; 100:3), is here applied to Jesus' chosen people.[53] Like the "Twelve" (see 6:13), this image transfers the principle of divine election in the OT to Jesus' disciples. The tender reference to "little flock" is a reminder that disciples are precious to Jesus, not when or if they become large and powerful, but even in their minority and weakness. It is no

---

51. See Str-B 2:191; Schlatter, *Lukas,* 534. Luke's use of a Hebraism that does not occur in the LXX is evidence that the Hebraism cannot derive from the LXX and is thus not a "Septuagintism." It likely derives from an alternative Hebrew source, presumably the Hebrew Gospel.

52. So Clement of Alexandria, *Strom.* 1.24: "Seek the great things, and the lesser things will be added as well"; Origen, *Or.* 14.1; 2.2: "Seek the great things, and the lesser things will be added to you; and seek the heavenly things and the earthly things will be added."

53. See J. Jeremias, *poimnion, TWNT* 6.498-501.

surprise that this image lived on in the vocabulary of the early church (Acts 20:28-29; 1 Pet 5:2-3). The disciples are aware that Jesus stands in a unique relationship with God as Father (3:21-22; 10:22), and that they too should address God as "Father" (11:2). The declaration that "Your Father has been pleased to give you the kingdom" warmly assures disciples that God is truly *their* Father (1 John 3:1), and that the gift of the kingdom is not outstanding, but already present in Jesus.

Jesus concludes with a radical imperative: "Sell your possessions and give to the poor. Provide purses for yourselves that will not wear out, a treasure in heaven that will never fail" (v. 33). The categorical nature of this command is at least mild hyperbole, for no human being can live without possessions. Like many Jewish teachers, Jesus was no stranger to hyperbole, and he employs it here to good effect. The import of v. 33 is not to define discipleship in terms of deprivation or asceticism, but to warn disciples of the confining and restricting nature of possessions, freedom from which ushers them into an unimaginably greater existence.[54] There is more emphasis in v. 33 on *giving* and *investing* — "giving to the poor," "providing purses for yourselves," "treasures in heaven" — than on doing *without*. Nothing in this world is worthy of an ultimate investment or allegiance. Nothing in this world is safe from theft or decay or corruption. If human allegiances and treasures are to be eternally secured, they must be invested in eternal concerns, in the kingdom of God, which is a "treasure in heaven" (v. 33). "Giving to the poor" is good for the poor, but it is no less good for the giver. In the mission of the seventy(-two), disciples were sent without a "purse" (10:4), but giving to the poor makes a "purse" (same Gk. word, *ballantion*) for disciples that will not wear out, ever fail, or be destroyed. Divesting of possessions and giving to the needy creates capital in God's economy because it directs both resources and allegiances

---

54. A woodenly literal interpretation of 12:22-34, as registered by Bovon, *Lukas 9,51–14:35*, 295, results in a seriously negative judgment of its value. "The wisdom that Jesus expresses in these lines is shocking; so mistaken *(verrucht!)*, in fact, that the position that he denounces is the only reasonable one to support. Is it not our responsibility to give thought to the sustenance and livelihood on which we depend? Furthermore, does the picture of nature shown to us here have any likeness to today's reality? Can we live without possessions? In short, is not this text, which many recall fondly from their childhood and whose truth they follow, irritating or at least distasteful?" That Luke does not understand Jesus' teaching literally, or in terms of absolute asceticism, is evinced by the fact that numerous people in the gospel narrative possess capital or real estate without censure — women with possessions (8:3); Zacchaeus (19:8), Joseph of Arimathea (23:50-53), Ananias and Sapphira (Acts 5:4; further, 14:28-33; 16:1-12, 19-31). Luke presents Jesus' teaching on wealth in terms of critical realism. Discipleship to Jesus cannot avoid the issue of wealth and possessions, not because the latter are evil in themselves, but because they easily and inevitably entice believers to trust in things that are transient and unfulfilling rather than in the eternal and truly fulfilling verities of the kingdom of God. On the role of possessions in Luke-Acts, see Klein, *Lukasevangelium*, 459.

to the Lord rather than to the world (1 Cor 7:32-34). The ultimate concern is treasure, not as humans define it, but as Jesus defines it — "treasure in heaven that will never fail . . . for where your treasure is, there your heart will be also" (vv. 33-34). The exact relation of "treasure" and "heart" is important to note: it is not allegiances that create behaviors, but behaviors that create allegiances, proper habits that create proper dispositions, as Aristotle rightly maintained. If God does not own our possessions, then our possessions will own us.

LIVING IN READINESS (12:35-48)

Fellowship with Jesus calls and equips disciples for the extraordinary. In the previous section (12:22-34), Jesus warned disciples that life's anxieties easily divert attention away from God's faithful care of his children. In the present section Jesus shifts from a warning to an exhortation — to watchfulness, preparedness, and readiness for the unexpected. This exhortation resounds throughout Scripture and the early church.[55]

35-40 Jesus introduces the theme with perhaps the archetypical Israelite image of preparedness — the Israelites with their cloaks tucked into their belts (v. 35; NIV "Be dressed") prior to the exodus from Egypt (Exod 12:11). The verb tenses in v. 35 reflect an underlying Hebraism, alluding to a constant state of readiness[56] — "sleeves rolled up," as we would say today. The image of the cloak tucked into one's belt (1 Kgs 18:46; Eph 6:14; 1 Pet 1:13) signifies speed and agility, and "lamps burning" the ability to move in the dark. The burning lamp imagery likely reflects a Hebrew figure of speech admonishing Israel not to allow the "lamp" (of revelation) to go out in Israel (see at 8:16). If Jesus uses it analogously here, it exhorts disciples not to allow the lamp of the gospel to grow dim.

The state to which Jesus calls disciples is characterized in terms of "waiting" (v. 36), "watching" (v. 37), "opening [the door]" (v. 36), "readiness" (v. 40), and being "blessed" (v. 38; NIV "it will be good for you"). Disciples do not set the agenda or take the lead; rather, they adopt a posture of attentiveness to their master's will and readiness to do it. Jesus speaks no longer in the bucolic imagery of the previous section, but in the gritty imagery of slavery (v. 37),

---

55. Watchfulness in relation to the day of the Lord was a common theme in the OT: Isa 13:6; Ezek 30:3; Joel 1:15; 2:1; Amos 5:18; Obad 15; Zeph 1:14-18 (see Fitzmyer, *Luke (X–XXIV)*, 987). In the NT and early church, 1 Thess 5:2; Rev 16:15; *Did.* 16:1; Justin, *1 Apol.* 1.17.4; *Gos. Thom.* 21, 103.

56. The imperative of the verb "to be," *estōsan*, combined with the participle *periezōsmenai*, connotes watchfulness and preparedness to act (Bock, *Luke 9:51–24:53*, 1174). On the Hebraism, see Schlatter, *Lukas*, 318.

burglary (v. 39), drunkenness (v. 45), dismemberment (v. 46), and beatings (v. 47). These images are distasteful to modern readers. We can be sure they were even more distasteful to those who first heard them, for whom they were not simply metaphors, as they largely are for us, but ugly realities of daily life. The imagery is scandalous, and perhaps inevitably so, for the incarnation, the transformation of the Holy into the human, occurs in a world where hierarchies of allegiances already exist, and the claim of God's Son and Servant to supersede those values and allegiances is an unsettling claim that causes division in the world, as Paul maintains in 1 Cor 1:18-31. Luke reports that these divisions extend to Jesus' hometown (4:28-29) and the very soul of his mother (2:34-35).

Weddings were joyful celebrations in ancient Jewish life (see at 5:34). The wedding imagery in v. 36 is employed in a novel way, however, for it focuses on the slaves who guard the property while the master attends the festivities. On the master's return the slaves are thrice called blessed (Gk. *makarios,* vv. 37, 38, 43). This is a curious oxymoron, for the lot of a slave in the ancient world — indeed in any world — was anything but "blessed." More remarkable, in reward for the vigilance and faithfulness of the slaves, on his return the master "will dress himself to serve, will have [the slaves] recline at the table and will come and wait on them" (v. 37). The master, in other words, will change roles by becoming a *servus servorum* — a servant to his slaves (17:8; John 13:4). The Greek verb for "serve" (v. 37, *diakonein*), particularly in its noun form *diakonia,* characterizes the ministry posture of the early church, which was formalized in the office of "deacon" (Acts 6:1, 4). In the present instance, and twice again in Luke (4:39; 22:27), it refers to Jesus serving his own disciples. Attending the master's property is not mindless waiting: the master may be gone a long time, and he may not return at a convenient time, but rather "in the second or third watch of the night" (v. 38; NIV "in the middle of the night or toward daybreak"). Jews divided night (= 6 P.M.–6 A.M.) into three four-hour watches, but by NT times the Jewish custom had been replaced by the Roman custom of dividing night into four three-hour watches (Mark 13:35).[57] The second or third watch would thus put the master's return in "the dead of night."

The admonition to watchfulness is reinforced by a parable inside a parable in v. 39 about a homeowner who guards his house against a thief. In the original Greek, the owner guards it against "being dug through" *(dioryssein),* referring to digging through a wall of sun-dried bricks to force entry into a Palestinian house. The imagery of both parables is paradoxical, for in the first the returner is a protagonist (the master), and in the second an antagonist (a thief), but the lesson of both is the same: disciples cannot be certain *when* the Son of Man (see excursus at 5:26) will return. They may be certain only *that*

---

57. Str-B, 1.688-89. Luke follows the Roman four-watch custom elsewhere in Acts 12:4.

he will return! Until this point in the Third Gospel Luke has mentioned the return of the Son of Man only twice (9:26; 12:8-9). The eschatological return of the Son of Man is not a recurrent theme in Luke, but a very particular and special theme, and its mention here is a unique admonition to believers to remain vigilant![58]

41-48 "Peter asked, 'Lord, are you telling this parable to us, or to everyone?'" (v. 41). This is the only mention of the Twelve in the central section of Luke (9:51–18:30), and here Peter serves as their spokesman. The reference to Jesus as "Lord" (v. 41) is an important key to understanding Luke's construction of vv. 35-48. "Lord" occurs nine times in this section, the first two of which refer to an earthly master (vv. 36-37). Luke's frequent use of "Lord" for Jesus heretofore in the Third Gospel prepares this mundane use of "Lord" for possible christological significance. Luke's insertion of Peter's question (v. 41), which is not present in the parallel of Matt 24:45-51, skillfully identifies Jesus as "Lord," and the specific christological significance of "Lord," in contrast to its indefinite reference to "master" in the Matthean parallel, governs Luke's seven remaining references to Lord in vv. 41-48. Thus, in vv. 41-48 Jesus is not simply speaking about responsible discipleship (as in the Matthean parallel), but of himself in his future Parousia as the Son of Man, and of the need of *eschatological* attentiveness on the part of his followers.[59]

Jesus responds to Peter's question with a parable about two different choices a slave could make in his master's absence. The slave could choose to be a conscientious steward of the property while the master is away.[60] Such a slave is deemed "faithful," "wise," and "blessed," and when the master returns, he will be "put in charge of all his possessions" (vv. 42-44). The conscientious slave will be promoted into the higher purposes and powers of the owner. A second choice would be for the slave to take advantage of his master's absence by usurping his rights and privileges — and usurping them in the worst possible manner, "by beating the other servants, both men and women, and by eating and drinking and getting drunk" (v. 45).[61] The first is an obedient choice that honors and serves the master, the second is a calculating choice that uses power and opportunity for self-advantage. The latter not simply dishonors the master, it despises his kindness and grace (Rom 2:4), exalts self over the master, and makes a debauchery of his well-ordered house. The second choice is more than simply foolish; it is evil, and it results in one of the harshest recorded

---

58. So Green, *Luke,* 499.

59. For a fuller discussion of this point, see Rowe, *Early Narrative Christology,* 151-57.

60. The Gk. word *oikonomos* (v. 42), as in Matt 24:45, means a steward of the house, who although a slave (vv. 43, 45, 46), was entrusted with the entire operation of the house in his master's absence (Str-B, 2.192).

61. On drunkenness as a characteristic of pride and rebellion in Scripture, see 21:34; Isa 28:1; Joel 1:5; Matt 24:38; 1 Cor 11:21; 1 Thess 5:7; 1 Pet 1:13; 5:8.

condemnations of Jesus.[62] "The master of that servant will come on a day when he does not expect him and at an hour he is not aware of. He will cut him to pieces and assign him a place with the unbelievers" (v. 46).

The extreme treatment of the wicked servant impressed itself in the memory of the early church, for v. 46 appears verbatim in the Double Tradition represented in Matt 24:50-51.[63] The Greek verb *dichotomein* ("cut to pieces, dismember") occurs nowhere else in Scripture (apart from the parallel in Matt 24:51), although various Psalms recall similar imagery (Ps 50:22). The only other reference in Scripture to such violent dismemberment is Samuel's hacking to pieces of the Amalakeite chieftain Agag (1 Sam 15:33). Like *dichotomein*, the Hebrew word describing this deed, *shasaph*, is a *hapax legomenon*, occurring only once in Scripture. It therefore seems unlikely to me that Jesus' reference to this extreme punishment is a coincidence.[64] Agag's fate may have been seized by Jesus as a graphic *eschatological* illustration. The eschatological import of v. 46 is further signaled by reference to "day" (= "Day of the Lord," Joel 2:31), and by the severity of the punishment and final assignment to "a

---

62. The Gk. *dichotomein* means literally "to cut to pieces," "to dismember," "to cleave a body into two (with a sword)" (Str-B, 1.969). The word is sometimes interpreted metaphorically to mean "to cut off" in terms of excommunicate. O. Betz, "The Dichotomized Servant and the End of Judas Iscariot," *RevQ* 5 (1964), 43-58, argues for this sense, citing 1QS 2:16, where indolent believers will "be cut off from the midst of all the sons of light." The Heb. word for "cut off" in 1QS 2:16 is *nikrat*, however, whereas the Heb. word that lies beneath *dichotomein* in the LXX is not *nikrat* but always *nathah* (Exod 29:17 [2x]; Lev 1:8; Ezek 24:4) or *gazar* (Gen 15:17). Klein, *Lukasevangelium*, 464, correctly notes that Betz's argument "contributes little to the understanding of Luke at this point." Moreover, separation from the Jewish community was usually signified by other words (e.g., Gk., *aposynagōgos*, "removal from the synagogue," John 9:22; 12:42; 16:2) or expressions ("let him become a Gentile," Matt 18:17). Plummer, *Luke* 332-33, correctly summarizes the lexical history of the word to denote literal rather than metaphorical "cutting" in the ancient world.

63. The ancient world indulged in cruel punishments, particularly of slaves, that are repugnant to moderns. Punishment by "dismemberment" may not have appeared implausible, perhaps not even terribly startling, to Jesus' audience, however. Slaves were routinely subjected to sexual abuse, flogging, torture, and cruel deaths. A slave who stole silver from a banquet of Caligula had his hands cut off and hung around his neck in punishment in order to deter other slaves from similar behavior. A Roman nobleman fed to his lampreys a boy who broke a crystal cup. In the comedies of Plautus, Menander, and Terence, slaves appear as "whip-worthy" or "gallows birds." On slave punishments, including the above, see K. Bradley, *Slaves and Masters in the Roman Empire* (New York: Oxford University Press, 1987), 113-21.

64. The saying must in fact derive from Luke's Hebrew source, for *dichotomein* is an exact translation of the Heb. *shasaph*. The LXX translates *shasaph* by the Gk. word *sphazein*, meaning "to slay, slaughter." Luke's use of *dichotomein* rather than *sphazein* demonstrates that v. 46 is *not* a "Septuagintism," but an exact Gk. translation of Heb. *shasaph*. The Hebrew New Testaments of Franz Delitzsch (1877) and the United Bible Societies (1976) both render *dichotomein* by Heb. *shasaph*.

place with the unbelievers."[65] In Israel such drastic punishments are the result of divine vengeance.[66] The wicked servant's security is a house without a foundation (6:49), a fleeting mirage that will be taken from him in a moment's time (Rev 18:7-8). V. 46, like John's image of "unquenchable fire" (3:17) and Jesus' later image of slaying of enemies (19:27), should be understood as an eschatological judgment of those who contemptuously refuse God's gracious invitation of the kingdom and abuse God's forbearance before the return of the Son of Man (v. 40).

Vv. 47-48 continue the theme of the guilty slave, although they are unique to Luke and not found in the Matthean parallel (24:43-51). These verses contain two Hebraisms and an anonymous reference to God typical of Judaism and may plausibly derive from Luke's Hebrew source.[67] Two servants again illustrate Jesus' teaching, one who knowingly violates his master, and one who unknowingly violates his master. Jesus assigns culpability in proportion to the degree of knowledge; the slave with knowledge will be "beaten with many blows" (v. 47); the slave with little or no knowledge, with "few blows" (v. 48). Neither of these slaves can refer to the same individual of v. 46, for the punishment of v. 46 is obviously terminal. The Greek transition to v. 47, *ekeinos de ho doulos* ("But that slave . . .") must refer back to the faithful "steward" (also referred to as "slave") of vv. 36-38 and 42-44. Luke's addition of these verses thus provides a fitting conclusion of *both* parables above.

In v. 41 Peter asked Jesus if the foregoing parable was intended for disciples or for outsiders. Here Jesus gives an answer: disciples — those "who know the master's will" but fail to do it — will be judged by a harsher standard than those with less knowledge of it.[68] Jesus' answer echoes the plenary teaching of Israel on willful versus ignorant sin.[69] The relevance of this teaching for Jesus'

---

65. Bovon, *Lukas 9,51–14,35*, 337, understands v. 46 to refer to two successive punishments, a bodily death by dismemberment, followed by final divine spiritual judgment and punishment. This interpretation is appealing, particularly (as Bovon notes) as an illustration of 12:4-5. I am more inclined, however, to take the initial reference to "day" to signal "the day of the Lord," the last judgment, which would encompass the entire verse.

66. Jer 34:18; Sus (Theod.) 55, 59; *3 Bar.* 16:3. See Wolter, *Lukasevangelium*, 465-66.

67. On the Hebraisms, see Edwards, *Hebrew Gospel*, 314. The final Gk. phrase of v. 48, which literally reads "to whom they entrust much, they will ask much in return," means "to whom *God* entrusts much, much will be required in return." Bovon, *Lukas 9,51–14,35*, 340, suggests the possibility that "they" may refer to angels sent in judgment and thus be literal. This is possible, but it would be the only such instance in Luke, whereas the use of the third person plural as an anonymous reference to God occurs in four other instances (6:38; 12:20; 16:9; 23:31). In favor of an anonymous reference to God, see Str-B, 2.221; BDF §130.2; Fitzmyer, *Luke (X–XXIV)*, 974.

68. Wolter, *Lukasevangelium*, 466-67, develops this theme.

69. Num 15:30; Deut 17:12; Ps 19:13; Amos 3:2; 1QS 5:12; 7:3; 8:17, 22, 24; 9:1; CD 8:8; 10:3; Jas 3:1; Str-B, 2.192.

disciples cannot be overlooked: those endowed with positions of authority and leadership in Jesus' mission and church are held to a higher standard. Jesus voiced the same warning earlier in 10:12-14, that it will be better for Sodom in the day of judgment than for those who have heard the gospel and refused it. Here too the differing punishments, in character with both preceding parables, must be understood as eschatological. Augustine understood such punishments as evidence of the purging fire of purgatory awaiting believers, "proportioned to the deserts of the wicked, so that to some it will be more, and to others less painful" (*Civ.* 21.16). This particular passage may seem to comport with a doctrine of purgatory, but Scripture does not propound such a doctrine,[70] and it is not necessary to infer it on the basis of vv. 47-48. The plain sense of the passage is preferable, namely, that in the final assize culpability will depend on the response one has made to the knowledge and revelation one has received.

DECISION AND DIVISION (12:49-59)

49-53 The eschatological motif begun in 12:35 continues in the present passage with references to "fire," "baptism," and divisions within the family, the core human social community. "I have come to bring fire on the earth, and how I wish it were already kindled. And I have a baptism to undergo, and what constraint I am under until it is completed!" (vv. 49-50). These two verses are less parallel in Greek than in the NIV translation because v. 49 contains a Hebraism not present in v. 50.[71] Whereas the saying about "baptism" in v. 50 may stem from a similar saying in Mark 10:38, the saying about "fire" in v. 49 evidently stems from Luke's Hebrew source. The word translated "constraint" in v. 50 (Gk. *synechein*) means "to be caused distress by force of circumstances."[72] The apostle Paul uses this word when he speaks of being "torn between" the desire to depart and be with Christ and yet also remain with the Philippians (Phil 1:23). In v. 50 *synechein* underscores the dominant theme of the central section

---

70. The chief Scriptural text suggesting purgatory is 2 Macc 12:45, although 1 Cor 3:15 and 1 Pet 1:7 have also been understood to refer to the doctrine. Purgatory is mentioned by a number of church fathers, but the doctrine was not formalized in Roman Catholic theology until the thirteenth century (councils of Lyons, 1274; Florence, 1439; and Trent, 1563). Dante's *Purgatorio* remains the most systematic and artistic representation of the doctrine. See *ODCC*, 1349-50; *Catechism of the Catholic Church* (1992), §1030-32.

71. Two words *(ti, ei)* in the phrase *kai ti thelō ei ēdē anēphthē* (v. 49, "how I wish it were already kindled") correspond not to their ordinary Greek meanings, but to Heb. *mah* and *im*, respectively. See Bovon, *Lukas 9,51–14,35*, 351.

72. BDAG, 971.

of Luke that Jesus' face is fixed on Jerusalem, for there he is "constrained to undergo baptism," i.e., complete the primary purpose for which he was sent. Jesus normally speaks of his "sending" in soteriological terms, e.g., "I must proclaim the good news of the kingdom of God, . . . that is why I was sent" (4:43; Mark 1:38). In v. 50, however, he reveals the larger canvas of his mission, of which the soteriological mission is one part. His ultimate mission involves "fire" and "baptism." It is for this mission, which includes the subjection of powers and principalities (1 John 3:8), declares Jesus, that "I have come." The mission of Jesus is not a matter of fate or chance, but of the Father sending the Son in order to bring the divine purpose to completion. The reference to "fire" carries the sense of purging in v. 49 and thus is probably not a reference to the tongues of fire at Pentecost, which connotes anointing for mission. John employed the images of "fire" and "baptism" eschatologically (3:9, 16-17), and Jesus employs them likewise here. All but one of the seven references to "fire" in the Third Gospel are eschatological.[73] "Baptism" (v. 50) also connotes a future occurrence, no longer an initiatory rite (so 3:21-22), but rather Jesus' death, which Luke also refers to as "exodus" (9:31) or "completion" in Jerusalem (18:31!).[74] The use of "baptism" as a metaphor of Jesus' impending death is evidence that he foresaw both his death in Jerusalem and its atoning significance (Mark 10:45). The death of Jesus in Jerusalem is a precondition of the coming fire, and like "fire," "baptism" inaugurates the fulfillment of God's will. Vv. 49-50 are an important window into Jesus' christological self-understanding, for he is conscious that his person and mission cannot be separated from the ultimate "fire" and "baptism" to which the world will be subjected.[75] Jesus plays the central role in the kingdom of God, which is the fulfillment of God's redemptive purpose in the world. One's personal response to Jesus and his mission is the critical factor in one's participation in the kingdom, both now and in the future.

The kingdom that Jesus inaugurates is not coterminous with this world, nor is it the result of an evolutionary process in which the present material world evolves into a future spiritual or even "Christified" world.[76] If the kingdom were simply a greater and more complete version of this world, then it

---

73. 3:9, 16, 17; 9:54; 12:49; 17:29. The one exception is the fire in the courtyard at Peter's denial (22:55). The "fire" in the parallel saying in *Gos. Thom.* 10 is also eschatological. On fire as an eschatological harbinger, see 1 Kgs 18:38; 2 Kgs 1:10, 12; Ezek. 38:22; 39:6; Rev 20:9.

74. On "baptism" as a reference for Jesus' death, see A. Oepke, *baptisma, TWNT* 1.536, 43.

75. See Bovon, *Lukas 9,51–14,35,* 350.

76. On the theories of Hegel and David Friedrich Strauss of evolving Christological speculation, see A. Schweitzer, *Quest of the Historical Jesus* (New York: Macmillan, 1968), 77-80; on Teilhard de Chardin's idea of evolution to "an omega point," see *The Phenomenon of Man,* trans. B. Wall (New York: Harper and Row, 1965).

would essentially sanction this world, and the coming of Jesus would bring peace to it.[77] The kingdom is not an evolutionary extension of this world, however, but a judgment of the world, a *krisis,* according to the Fourth Gospel (John 3:19; 5:22-30; 8:16; 12:31). There is great disparity between the kingdom and this world. The introduction of the kingdom in Jesus awakens the world to its alienated existence from its Creator and points it to its Restorer and Redeemer. In vv. 51-53 Jesus articulates the effect of introducing the kingdom in terms of *division.* Division, and in some instances disunity, are not unfortunate side-effects of the incarnation. As a fetus grows, it eventually separates from its maternal host, and continued growth causes it to separate from infancy, childhood, and adolescence until a more completely separate and divided being exists. The separation or division that Jesus introduces into creation is similar, namely, a state of maturity that divides the disciple from conditions that differ from or impede the wholeness of salvation (v. 51; 2:34-35). Vv. 52-53 remind hearers and readers that Jesus and the kingdom must take precedence over the most intimate and ultimate human social bond — the family. The precedence of Jesus over family does not result in a firmer family bond but in a realigned family, "three against two and two against three." There will not simply be discord between siblings, which is common enough in families, but even discord between parents and children. V. 53 clearly echoes Mic 7:6, a reference that also appears in rabbinic traditions in relation to the coming of the Messiah. The rabbis held that presumption and family dissension would precede the advent of the Messiah, whose coming would heal all divisions (*m. Soṭah* 9:15).[78] Jesus famously departs from this rabbinic tradition. The essential function of the Messiah, according to Luke, is not to heal divisions but to intensify them.

Indecision does not divide, but decision, by its very nature, divides the chosen from the nonchosen. The decision to follow Jesus inevitably concentrates and focuses the lives of disciples: Peter and the Zebedees are divided from nets and homes (5:1-11), the women who follow Jesus from homes, spouses, and possessions (8:1-3), and disciples in mission from their customary securities (9:3; 10:4). The theme of decision and division has of course been latent throughout Luke's narrative, but in chaps. 11–12 it is specifically and repeatedly addressed, signifying that decision and division are essential to the gospel. The theme was broached in 11:17-18, when Jesus reminded opponents that his casting out of demons was not the result of his collaboration with Satan, for "a house divided against itself will fall." Jesus then refused to take sides in a dispute between two sons over the division of their father's inheritance

---

77. Luke's literal wording, "Do you think I came to give peace on earth?" is a Hebraism, in which "give" (Gk., *didōmi*) reflects Heb., *nathan,* which is typically used in the sense of "bring." Note, by contrast, Matt's more Hellenistic "cast (Gk., *balein*) peace" (10:34).

78. Str-B, 1.586.

(12:13-15). He did so, not because he was indecisive, but because he did not want to divert attention away from life's most important decision. Decision was intimated to Mary when the baby Jesus was presented in the temple of Jerusalem. Even as an infant, the significance of his life was foreseen in terms of "division." "The child is destined to cause the falling and rising of many . . . and a sword will pierce your own soul too," declared Simeon (2:34-35). If the mother of Jesus is "constrained" to participate in the division that Jesus brings into the world, then all human families are constrained by the same division, "father against son . . . daughter against mother" (v. 53).

Division may seem discordant and even offensive to our inclusive age, but it is a fundamental property of God's relation to the world. In Gen 1 the Hebrew word *badal* ("to divide, to exclude") occurs five times (vv. 4, 6, 7, 14, 18) — and never again in Genesis. God creates by a process of separation, dividing nature first from chaos, and then successively land from water, light from darkness, and lower life-forms of fish, birds, and mammals from humanity. In the divine economy, the process of division does not result in diminishment or destruction, but in the greater diversity and distinctiveness of creation. This process, when pushed to its final stage, results, ironically, in greatest *likeness* to God — humanity created in "the image of God." Division is an operative principle in creation, and it is no less operative in the process of redemption. It is classically developed in Rom 9–11, where the apostle Paul depicts God separating a smaller Israel from greater Israel, not to save the former and damn the latter, but to use the smaller separated Israel as a redemptive agent in the salvation of "all Israel" (Rom 11:26). Whoever hears the call of Christ and allows the call to take precedence over the otherwise ultimate claims of marriage and family, even of one's own life, is graciously received into the fellowship of Jesus and his mission, which is the kingdom of God. A decision to allow the kingdom's ultimate authority in one's life thus divides one from the world, but it does not alienate one from the world. Fellowship with Jesus endows one with freedom, strength, and love to participate in the world redemptively, to serve the world, and even to suffer in the cause of Christ for the world (Col 1:24).[79] Decision and division are

---

79. C. S. Lewis reflects thus on the interplay of "division" in both creation and redemption: "I sometimes wonder if we have even begun to understand what is involved in the very concept of creation. If God will create, He will make something to be, and yet to be not Himself. To be created is, in some sense, to be ejected or separated. Can it be that the more perfect the creature is, the further this separation must at some point be pushed? It is saints, not common people, who experience the 'dark night.' It is men and angels, not beasts, who rebel. Inanimate matter sleeps in the bosom of the Father. The 'hiddenness' of God perhaps presses most painfully on those who are in another way nearest to Him, and therefore God Himself, made man, will of all men be by God most forsaken" (*Letters to Malcolm: Chiefly on Prayer* [New York: Harcourt Brace, 1964], 44).

not intended to exclude or to doom and damn, but "to make ready a people prepared for the Lord" (1:17).

54-56 Jesus is surprised that his hearers are prescient in some matters pertaining to the future and ignorant in others. They are wise in regard to meteorology, but foolish in regard to history. Jewish rabbis taught that the cosmic plan of God had been predetermined from eternity. The rabbis, not surprisingly, were especially attentive to signs preceding the messianic age and to calculations of its coming. Not all their eschatological schemes agreed; indeed, the more specifically each was considered, the greater were the differences among them.[80] Unlike the rabbis, Jesus does not propose an eschatological scheme or spreadsheet. Rather, he admonishes his hearers to something more basic and less speculative, to knowing "how to interpret this present time" (v. 56). The Greek word here for "time," *kairos,* does not refer to time as duration but to time as opportunity, e.g., time to plant, time to harvest, time to celebrate, time to raise or lower the sails. *Kairos* is not about ages but about *seasons,* and how to recognize them.[81] Every farmer, traveler, shepherd, and sailor knew enough about wind, temperature, and sky to forecast the weather with relative accuracy. "When you see a cloud rising in the west, immediately you say, 'It's going to rain,' and it does. And when the south wind blows, you say, 'It's going to be hot,' and it is" (vv. 54-55).[82] Matt 16:2-3 records a version of this saying, the details of which — red sky at sunset, fair weather in the morning; red sky at sunrise, storms later in the day — differ from Luke's version. Mendel Nun, an Israeli archaeologist who devoted his life to the history and character of the Sea of Galilee, noted that the "weather forecast as it appears in Matthew is accurate, and confirmed by generations of Kinneret residents, including this writer." Of Luke's version, the red sunset portending fair weather in the morning is generally true throughout Israel, according to Nun, but the detail of the south wind holds only for the southern part of Israel rather than for Galilee, where hot winds from the Negev in the south bring warm days.[83] According to Nun, in other words, Luke's version describes a Judean rather than Galilean weather forecast. If so, it could imply that Jesus was in Judea when this saying was delivered. But wherever Jesus is, in appealing to "this present time," he implores hearers to recognize that, in his teaching and healing and mission, in

---

80. See the lengthy discussion of foretelling the messianic age in Str-B, 4/2.977-1015.

81. Schlatter, *Lukas,* 321, notes the importance of *kairos* for understanding vv. 54-56.

82. An embryo of the same maxim is present in 2 Sam 23:4.

83. M. Nun, *The Sea of Galilee and Its Fishermen in the New Testament* (Kibbutz Ein Gev: Kinnereth Sailing Co., 1989), 55-57. Bovon, *Lukas 9,51-14,35,* 360, assumes that Luke's version is foreign to *all* Palestine, which Nun asserts is not true. Bovon concludes unnecessarily that the conditions describe the Aegean Sea rather than Palestine.

his very *person,* the kingdom of God is present — and the kingdom requires a decisive response.[84]

57-59   People are not dependent on external signs, however, to know times and seasons. They need not watch the skies. They do not need to be Jesus' disciples, nor do they need any particular help from Jesus.[85] They only need common sense, to look within and "judge for [yourselves] what is right" (v. 57).[86] All human beings possess the ability to make basic value judgments and act on them. They do not require supportive signs, data, and evidence for such judgments. They simply know what is required of them in a given circumstance, what is the *right* thing to do. Luke cites an example of Peter and John displaying such judgment in Acts 4:19, and the apostle Paul appeals similarly to the common sense of the Corinthians in a different matter (1 Cor 6:5). Jesus illustrates this principle by a story of two persons involved in a dispute. If they are determined to prosecute one another, they can appeal to a magistrate, but a magistrate will call in a judge, and the judge, after hearing the case and pronouncing his verdict, will summon an "officer" to execute the sentence. The Greek word for "officer," *praktōr,* which occurs only here in all of early Christian literature, signifies a bailiff or constable in charge of a debtor's prison. The duty of a *praktōr* was to execute whatever sentence the judge ordered, and by force if necessary.[87] "I tell you," assures Jesus, "you will not get out until you have paid the last penny" (v. 59). In Matt's version of this story (5:26) the Greek word for "penny" is *kodrantēs,* the smallest Roman coin. Luke, however, uses the Greek word *lepton,* which translates the Hebrew *perutah.* The utter insignificance of a *lepton/perutah* — a small copper Jewish coin so worthless that two were required to equal a *kodrantēs* — heightens Jesus' point.[88] How wise is it to initiate a legal process that will squeeze the last penny from you if you lose; and even if you win, it will cost you no less in time and energy? Would you not be better off to settle out of court!

Judge for yourself, says Jesus! If you know how to judge rightly in such a situation, then judge equally rightly in "interpreting the present time" (v. 56). The present time refers to the inbreaking of the kingdom of God in the person and ministry of Jesus. People's response to Jesus and his messengers is here

---

84. Several important manuscripts ($\mathfrak{p}^{45}$ ℵ* D L) omit "know," thus implying people's *unwillingness* to use their knowledge, and therefore heightening Jesus' condemnation. The manuscript evidence favoring "know" is slightly stronger, however, which argues for its inclusion (so TNIV). See Metzger, *TCGNT*[2], 136.

85. This appeal is again addressed to the crowds (see 12:54).

86. Origen, *Hom.* 35.1, begins his discussion of vv. 57-59 by asserting that "we were by nature suited to judge what is just."

87. BDAG, 859.

88. On the value and significance of *lepton* in this illustration, see Schürer, *History of the Jewish People,* 2.66; Jeremias, *Sprache des Lukasevangeliums,* 225.

defined in terms of "fire" and "baptism" (vv. 49-50), that is, the arrival of the long-awaited kingdom of God. The kingdom is personally present in Jesus, and the response of people to Jesus and the messengers in his name determines people's standing in the future and final fulfillment of the kingdom.[89] Like the debtor and his opponent en route to the magistrate, this is the time for Israel to settle accounts with God. Let them recognize the season, let them wake up to common sense and "be reconciled" (v. 58) to their God.[90]

---

89. Luke repeatedly reminds readers of Jesus' essential role in the kingdom: 6:46-49; 9:23-26; 10:1-16; 11:23; 12:8-9; 13:22-27; 16:30-31; 18:22-30.

90. See B. Kinman, "Debtor's Prison and the Future of Israel (Luke 12:57-59)," *JETS* 42/3 (1999), 411-17.

CHAPTER TWELVE

"Jerusalem, Jerusalem"

Luke 13:1-35

The central section of Luke in 9:51–18:34 is particularly defined by the orientation point of Jerusalem (see at 9:51). Luke 13 stands at the mathematical midpoint of the central section,[1] and at this midpoint the relation of Jesus to Judaism, as symbolized in Jerusalem, reaches its most critical dimension. The central section may impress readers as a miscellany rather than ordered unit, but Luke has crafted the material in chap. 13, which is largely unique to the Third Gospel,[2] with a structural symmetry otherwise uncharacteristic of the central section. Luke 13 consists of six sections that form a chiasmus:

> A   The need for Israel to repent (vv. 1-9)
>> B   True versus false children of Abraham (vv. 10-17)
>>> C   The growth of the kingdom from small beginnings (vv. 18-19)
>>> C¹   The expansion of the kingdom from small measure (vv. 20-21)
>> B¹   True versus false children of Abraham (vv. 22-30)
> A¹   Israel's judgment by God (vv. 31-35).

The chiasmus begins and ends with Jerusalem (vv. 4, 34). Ever since the transfiguration, Jerusalem has been the focus of Jesus' destiny,[3] but its character as "killer of the prophets and stoner of those sent to it" (v. 34) discloses what kind of "exodus" (9:31) awaits Jesus there. The chiasmus then focuses on identifying the true children of Abraham, to which Israel's leaders do not belong. The chiasmus climaxes in two brief parables of the kingdom that

---

1. Luke 9:51–12:59 comprises 167 vv. (3,181 Greek words); Luke 14:1–18:34 comprises 168 vv. (3,092 Greek words); the two sections are within eighty-nine words of being the same length in Greek.

2. Distinct parallels exists only with the two brief parables in 13:18-19 (par. Matt 13:31-32; Mark 4:30-32) and 13:20-21 (par. Matt 13:33). Themes in 13:22-30 appear at various places in Matt, but in different forms and wording. 13:34-35 appears verbatim in Matt 23:37-39, but this agreement is almost certainly due to Matthew's reliance on Luke (see at 13:34-35).

3. 9:31, 51, 53; 13:22, 33; 17:11; 18:31; 19:11, 28.

prophesy the growth and influence of the kingdom despite the antagonism of Jerusalem.[4]

PLEA FOR REPENTANCE (13:1-9)

Luke commences chap. 13 with references to two current events of the day and a parable of Jesus, all dedicated to the theme of repentance. The two events are summarized by an identical refrain, "Unless you repent, you too will all perish" (vv. 3, 5), a rendition of which also summarizes the parable, "If [the fig tree] bears fruit next year, fine! If not, then cut it down" (v. 9).

1-5 Jesus typically taught in parables, of which there are nearly sixty in the Synoptic Gospels. He departs from his signature parabolic style in vv. 1-5 in order to illustrate the theme of repentance by references to current events. "There were some present at that time who told Jesus about the Galileans whose blood Pilate had mixed with their sacrifices" (v. 1). Luke not infrequently begins a pericope with a surprise encounter (8:19; 10:25; 11:27, 37), but this is one of the only times in any Gospel where Jesus is taught something he does not know. The massacre of the Galileans is unique to Luke and not attested elsewhere in ancient literature.[5] The announcement has the ring of a recent event, perhaps even "breaking news," and Jesus seizes its immediacy as an illustration. We do not know the cause of the slaying, but Josephus and Philo mention three other instances in which Pilate unleashed (or was prepared to unleash) violence on his subjects, each of which involved his disdain for Jewish religious customs and his intractability in the face of Jewish protests (see excursus on Pilate at 23:1). This first mention of Pilate in the Third Gospel stands in grim conformity with his other notorious dealings with the Jews, for which he was recalled as prefect of Judea in 36. The reference to "sacrifices" (v. 1) implies the Galilean incident was related to religious matters, perhaps at Passover, when the Roman prefect and Roman troops were in Jerusalem and tensions between Jews and Romans ran high. It was the duty of Jewish priests to gather and pour out the blood of animals slain on the altar, but the actual slaughter of the victims was the responsibility of those who offered them.[6]

---

4. On Luke 13, its relation to the central section, and its chiastic structure, see R. Shirock, "The Growth of the Kingdom in Light of Israel's Rejection of Jesus: Structure and Theology in Luke 13:1-35," in Orton, *Composition of Luke's Gospel*, 169-83.

5. Some scholars imagine that the uniqueness of this episode argues either for an invention on Luke's part or confusion with another episode. Fitzmyer, *Luke (X–XXIV)*, 1006-7, seems to overestimate Josephus's importance in taking him as the final authority on Pilate ("It is difficult to think that this incident would have escaped [Josephus's] attention").

6. Str-B 2:192-93.

The macabre note of mixing the blood of slain Galileans with their sacrifices makes sense if Pilate slew pilgrims in the act of slaughtering their own animal offerings. Pilate treats Galilean pilgrims like their sacrificial animals, in other words, attesting to his disdain for pilgrims and animal sacrifices alike.

Jesus' hearers would surely have sympathized with the slain Galileans, especially if their fate was incurred in the act of temple sacrifice. Surprisingly, Jesus does not uphold the Galileans as martyrs, or heroes of Jewish nationalism, as do accounts of the martyrdom of the seven brothers in 2 Macc 7, for example, or Eleazar's famous martyr speech at Masada (Josephus, *J. W.* 7.323-36). No attempt is made to account for their suffering, except twice (vv. 3, 5) to emphasize that it was *not* because they were worse sinners than those who did not suffer such misfortune. Jesus' response expressly rejects any concept of karma, i.e., that the fate of individuals in this life is either a reward for good or punishment for evil in a former life. Jewish theology, although aware that some human suffering was undeserved (e.g., Lament Psalms), as a rule ascribed suffering to prior sin and guilt.[7] For Jesus, however, the death of the Galileans, whatever the cause, is significant as a warning of the coming judgment on all sinners, unless they repent.

The eighteen victims of the collapse of the tower of Siloam are cited to the same effect (v. 4). This, too, is a rogue event, recorded only by Luke. A specific tower of Siloam is unknown, but in describing the oldest wall around Jerusalem Josephus notes that at a point "above the fountain of Siloam" the wall turned east "towards Solomon's pool" (*J. W.* 5.145). At this corner juncture a tower may have stood that, perhaps in construction or repair, collapsed and killed eighteen people. Like the deaths of the Galileans, the sudden and seemingly senseless deaths of the victims is not sensationalized or sentimentalized, not memorialized or moralized. Jesus does not eulogize the victims but addresses his hearers directly in second person: "I tell you, unless you repent, you too will all perish" (vv. 3, 5). This need not imply that Jesus was insensitive or heartless toward the victims of these events. Rather, he tapped into the passionate feelings that such events aroused in his hearers in order to harness those feelings for the salvation of the unrepentant living rather than relegate them to the memory of the noble dead.

Jesus exploits the powerful sentiments associated with Pilate's massacre and the collapse of the tower in order to warn the living and call them to repentance (see at 3:3). The verb "to repent" occurs nine times in Luke, and only in the central section.[8] In calling for such repentance, Jesus echoes and fulfills John's similar call for "fruit in keeping with repentance" (3:8). The call to repentance is a warning light. A problem exists between humanity and God that

---

7. Str-B 2:193-94.

8. 10:13; 11:32; 13:3, 5; 15:7, 10; 16:30; 17:3, 4.

necessitates both acknowledgment and corrective action. An abrupt course change, an about-face, is required — like the younger brother in the parable (15:17-19) — not simply to rectify a bad conscience, but to take the first step in faith in order to receive the promised reconciliation of God.[9]

6-9 Luke further illustrates the need for repentance in a parable about a fig tree. It is not necessary to presume a relationship between this parable and the withering of the fig tree in Matt 21:18-20 and Mark 11:12-14, 20. True, Luke omits the latter in his Gospel, but the fig tree was ubiquitous in the Mediterranean world and a common image in the ministry of Jesus, being the subject of a miracle (Mark 11:12-14), a parable (21:29; Matt 24:32; Mark 13:28), and a third analogy in vv. 6-9. OT prophets often used the fig tree as a symbol of judgment (Isa 34:4; Jer 29:17; Hos 2:12; 9:10; Joel 1:7; Mic 7:1). The fig functions similarly in this parable, indeed emphatically so, for Luke places it (Gk. *sykē*) prominently at the head of the sentence, and thrice repeats its fruitlessness (vv. 6, 7, 9). The fact that the owner "went to look for fruit" on the tree suggests it had earlier been fruitful. The gardener intercedes as an advocate for the tree,[10] "Sir, leave it alone for one more year, and I'll dig around it and fertilize it. If it bears fruit next year, fine! If not, then cut it down" (vv. 8-9). The Greek word for "leave it," *aphienai*, is somewhat awkward, but it anticipates the same word at the end of the chiasmus in 13:35, "Your house is *left to you desolate*." Through the parable of the Fig Tree Luke prepares readers for the fate of the Jewish nation. A fruitless tree is not promising; it would probably be wiser, and certainly simpler, to cut it down. But these are not equal and indifferent options in the mind of the owner. "Fine" (NIV) is too cavalier a translation in v. 9. The Greek *eis to mellon* literally means "for the future," implying hope for a better state of affairs: "Well and good" (so NRSV) or "so much the better!"[11] A cloud of futility has hung over the parable until this point, and one expects the tree to be cut down. Here, finally, there is a ray of hope. The gardener wants the tree to live and bear fruit, and he makes the more costly choice to allow for the possibility. He digs down and fertilizes the root of the tree — where repentance must take place. The repeated desire for "fruit" (6, 7, 9) again recalls the Baptist's mission to see "fruit in keeping with repentance" in Israel (3:8). Like the man who should settle with his accuser before it is too late (12:58), the owner creates a window of opportunity to bear fruit. In the olive tree illustration of Rom 11:22 Paul speaks of the "goodness and severity" of God, precisely the

---

9. On repentance, see Bovon, *Lukas 9,51–14,35*, 377-79.

10. Schlatter, *Lukas*, 323, sees Jesus in the gardener, who gives his final love and sacrifice for Jerusalem, knowing full well that it is lost. "Jesus is here the Paraclete for Israel as he is for Peter in 22:32."

11. On the meaning of this expression, see Wolter, *Lukasevangelium*, 479; Klein, *Lukasevangelium*, 476.

themes of this parable. The parable declares the owner's heart and resolve, but not the tree's response. Like Simon the Pharisee (7:50) or the elder brother in the parable of the Prodigal Son (15:32), the question is left open whether there will be "fruit in keeping with repentance" (3:8).

THE LORD OF THE SABBATH COMPLETES GOD'S WORK ON THE SABBATH (13:10-17)

This pericope is paired with vv. 22-30 in Luke's chiasmus (see introduction to chap. 13). The figure of the synagogue ruler here (v. 14) is complemented by the owner of the house there (v. 25); the "daughter of Abraham" (v. 16), by "Abraham, Isaac, and Jacob" (v. 28); and a reversal of fortune ends both pericopes (vv. 17, 30).[12] The theme of the present episode is the Sabbath, which is repeated five times in the pericope (vv. 10, 14 [2x], 15, 16). This is the final Sabbath synagogue appearance of Jesus in Luke (4:16, 33; 6:6; 13:10), the last three of which narrate healings. The synagogue setting is crucial, for in the synagogue of Nazareth Jesus announced his messianic mission to "set the oppressed free" (4:18). Now in a synagogue at the heart of Luke's central section, Jesus frees a "daughter of Abraham" from satanic bondage (v. 16). In both the first and last synagogue appearances, however, the Jewish leaders are hardened to Jesus' ministry.

10-13 The eight Hebraisms in 13:10-17 suggest that the pericope derives from Luke's Hebrew source.[13] In v. 10, which is entirely Hebraic, Jesus is a rabbinic teacher in a synagogue. He is, in other words, fulfilling a characteristic Jewish role in a characteristic Jewish setting. He does not render a characteristic Jewish interpretation, however. "A woman was there who had been crippled by a spirit for eighteen years. She was bent over and could not straighten up at all" (v. 11). Jesus must have seen the woman after the Sabbath service, since

---

12. R. Shirock, "The Growth of the Kingdom in Light of Israel's Rejection of Jesus: Structure and Theology in Luke 13:1-35," in Orton, *Composition of Luke's Gospel*, 175-78.

13. Edwards, *Hebrew Gospel*, 315. The reference to "Sabbath" in the plural (Gk. *en tois sabbasin*, v. 10) may also be a Hebraism, but this is not certain. In Luke, "Sabbath" occurs in the plural five times and in the singular fourteen times. A similar alternation between singular and plural forms of "Sabbath" occurs in the LXX, although in reverse proportion (plural 22x, singular 8x). See Jeremias, *Sprache des Lukasevangeliums*, 120-21. The "heavy Lukan redaction," by which some scholars characterize vv. 10-17, is in my judgment due to the inordinate number of Hebraisms in the pericope. Rather than evidence of Lukan editorial invention, the style more likely results from reliance on a Hebrew *Vorlage*. For arguments favoring the historicity of the passage on other grounds, see D. Hagner, "Jesus and the Synoptic Sabbath Controversies," *BBR* 19/2 (2009): 229-48.

women were not permitted in the sanctuary of a Jewish synagogue. The diagnosis of her malady, "a spirit of infirmity" (v. 11; NIV "crippled by a spirit"), was a generic Hebraism for ill health,[14] in a similar way, for example, that "dermatitis" covers a wide range of skin diseases today. The description of the malady, however, is specific: she was "bent double, unable to straighten up" (Gk. *synkyptein*). This is the only description of such a malady in the Bible. People with physical deformities were expected to remain socially invisible, especially if they were women. Women rarely if ever approached rabbis, nor did rabbis as a rule speak with women. Personal encounters between rabbis and women were consequently rare occurrences in Judaism. Jesus takes the initiative with this forlorn woman, however, and emphatically so: he *saw* her, *summoned* her, and *said* to her, "Woman, you are set free from your infirmity" (v. 12). His pronouncement (Gk. *apolelysai*, second-person singular, perfect passive indicative) means "you have been released." The woman's release is thus spoken of as an already accomplished condition effected by the redemptive and liberating word of Jesus. The passive voice of the statement attributes the action to God. This pronouncement is therefore christologically significant, for in making it, Jesus presumes to stand in the place of God.

Jesus accompanies the spoken address by "put[ting] his hands on her" (v. 13). In the OT **laying on of hands** signified one of three things: dedication of sacrifices to God (Exod 29:10, 15; Lev 1:4; 3:2, 8, 13), installation of Levites to the priesthood (Num 8:10), or blessing (Gen 48:17-22; Num 27:18, 23; Deut 34:9). The only instance of laying on hands in the OT that relates to healing is Naaman the Syrian's desire for the healing touch of Elisha (2 Kgs 5:11). Jesus, not surprisingly, follows the precedent of Elisha (see excursus on Elijah and Elisha at 7:15-17), for Jesus most frequently places hands on people in healing contexts (4:40; 5:13; 8:54; 13:13; Mark 1:41; 5:23; 7:33; 8:22, 23, 25). In the OT the hand often symbolized power, including the power of God. Hands were laid on animals or persons to consecrate them from the profane to the sacred. With Jesus, however, the power transfer is reversed, for through his hands sacred power is communicated to the profane, including women (13:13), children (8:54), and unclean, sinful, and suffering humanity (4:40), lepers (5:13), and Gentiles (Mark 7:33).

With Jesus' pronouncement and healing touch the woman's physical condition is radically reversed: her bent body became straight and erect (Gk. *anōrthōthē*), and she "praised God" (v. 13). Praise or glorification of God is a signature Lukan characteristic,[15] in every instance coming from those whose

---

14. Wolter, *Lukasevangelium*, 482.

15. "To glorify God" *(doxazein ton theon)* is a Hebraism occurring eight times in Luke (2:20; 5:25, 26; 7:16; 13:13; 17:15; 18:43; 23:47), but only once each in Matt and Mark. See Edwards, *Hebrew Gospel*, 138-39.

afflictions or social conditions place them on the margins of or outside the circle of Jewish ritual cleanness: shepherds (2:20), crowds (5:26), a Roman gentile (23:47), healed paralytic (5:25), widow whose son is raised to life (7:16), severely crippled woman who was healed (13:13), healed Samaritan leper (17:15), and healed blind man (18:43). Except in the infancy narrative (Luke 1–2), praise of God is not heard within established Judaism, but rather in the voices of marginalized and suffering individuals who join the heavenly chorus of angels "praising God" (2:13).

14-17   The synagogue ruler (see at 8:41) was "indignant because Jesus had healed on the Sabbath. 'There are six days for work. So come and be healed on those days, not on the Sabbath'" (v. 14). This is the only place in the Gospels where a specific reason is given why Jewish leaders opposed Jesus' Sabbath healings. The ruler makes this pronouncement not to Jesus but to the crowd, thereby challenging Jesus' authority and seeking to turn the crowd against him. An important word in the ruler's pronouncement is *dei*, "it is necessary" (lit. "There are six days in which it is necessary to work"). The root and essence of religion for the ruler consist in actions that are regulated by Torah, and can be calculated and done with exactitude. This is an "I-It" understanding of faith. This is not exactly faith, however, but religious bureaucracy, for neither people nor God is necessary for the enactment of such religion.

The synagogue ruler had complained to the crowds, but Jesus speaks directly to the ruler in v. 15, and he speaks as "the Lord." This is a strategic title, for Luke has already emphasized that Jesus is "*Lord* of the Sabbath" (6:5). In rebutting the ruler's Sabbath pronouncement, Jesus offers not simply an alternative rabbinic opinion; he speaks with the authority of the very God who established Sabbath (Gen 2:2-3). Jesus declares the synagogue ruler's pronouncement scandalous, for the latter denies to a human being something that rabbis freely granted to animals. The rabbinic tradition was united in understanding Torah to require compassion to animals in distress. A farm animal that was tied or confined, for example, must be freed and led to water — even on Sabbath.[16] Jesus appeals again to this common understanding in 14:5. To show such consideration to an animal that was bound, but to refuse it to a "daughter of Abraham whom Satan had bound for eighteen years," is "Hypocrisy!" (v. 15).[17]

Jesus presses his point. "This woman who is a daughter of Abraham" is shifted prominently to the head of v. 16 in Greek in order to emphasize her qualifications for the exemption of v. 15. In Luke-Acts **Abraham** is a histori-

---

16. *M. Šabb.* 5. According to *m. Šabb.* 7.2, knots could not be untied on the Sabbath, but the Gk. *lyein* does not have to imply untying a knot; it can simply refer to releasing an animal to water it. On the matter, see Str-B 2:199-200.

17. Bock, *Luke 9:50–24:53*, 1218.

cal figure who assumes an eschatological role. In later Christianity Abraham will become a prefigurement for God's covenant with both Jews and Gentiles (e.g., Irenaeus, *Haer.* 4.25), but in Luke-Acts Abraham remains particularly the father of Jews rather than of Gentiles or Christians. He is not presented as a prototype to be imitated but rather as the personification of God's covenant people and intimate family, whose members represent the chief constituency of Jesus' saving mission.[18] As the primary recipient of God's promises, Abraham became the father of God's true children who embodied the promise in history (Isa 45:11; Rom 9:6-9). Two members of the family of "Father Abraham" (16:30) — Zacchaeus, a "son of Abraham" (19:9), and the woman here, a "daughter of Abraham" (v. 16) — are named members of "the children of Abraham" (3:8). A third individual, the rich man in Jesus' parable of Lazarus, presumes on that familial connection by calling on "Father Abraham" (16:24) to have mercy on him in Hades. Jesus does not recognize him as a "son of Abraham," however, for his selfish use of wealth and callousness to the needs of the poor have separated him from Abraham's true family. The crippled woman in this pericope is a member of this elect constituency, however, and as such, she exerts a special claim on Jesus as Savior. Hence, "it is necessary" (Gk. *dei*) for her to be released from her satanic bonds (v. 16). *Dei* repeats the same word in v. 14; there the synagogue ruler attributed final authority regarding Sabbath observance to Torah; here Jesus supersedes Torah. Vanquishing Satan, plundering his cache (Mark 3:27; Isa 49:24), was the central purpose of the sending of the Son (11:20; 1 John 3:8).

It was not coincidental but "necessary" that Jesus should free a woman bound by Satan, and to do so *on the Sabbath,* for Jesus, who is Lord of the Sabbath, must complete his mission of redemption on Sabbath, just as God completed his mission of creation on Sabbath. Jesus intimates this in his initial mission declaration, "It is necessary [Gk. *dei*] for me to proclaim the kingdom of God" (4:43).[19] The mission of Jesus and the Father are one, and thus inseparable, as Jesus declared in 10:22, "All things have been committed to me by my Father. No one knows who the Son is except the Father, and no one knows who the Father is except the Son and those to whom the Son chooses to reveal him." Healing of the severely crippled woman on the Sabbath is not a "violation" of Sabbath, as the synagogue ruler implies, but wholly in character with the filial union of Jesus with the Father and his Spirit-anointed mission to liberate the oppressed (4:18). The prophetic promise of God's release of the captives (Isa 61:1) is fulfilled when Jesus heals this "daughter of Abraham." "At issue here as everywhere else is the person of Jesus himself," who knows the Father, takes

---

18. N. Dahl, "The Story of Abraham in Luke-Acts," in Keck and Martyn, eds., *Studies in Luke-Acts,* 140-42.

19. Wolter, *Lukasevangelium,* 484.

the place of Torah, and both understands and fulfills the essence of Sabbath. For Jesus, the essence of Sabbath is not the postponement or avoidance of the work of God, but the *completion* of the work of God.[20]

The realization of God's saving purpose in Jesus results in yet another division in his ministry: "All his opponents were humiliated, but the people were delighted with all the wonderful things he was doing" (v. 17). The word "all" is repeated thrice in this verse, emphasizing the fulfillment and completeness of Jesus' mission.[21] V. 17 is a paraphrase of Isa 45:16, in which God's opponents are put to shame.[22] In summarizing the work of Jesus in the same theme and even wording in which the work of God is summarized, Luke again signals that in this decisive — and yes, divisive — Sabbath healing, God is present and glorified.

THE INEXORABLE ADVANCE
OF THE KINGDOM OF GOD (13:18-21)

At the center of Luke 13, which itself lies at the center of the central portion of the Third Gospel (9:51–18:34), appear two brief parables likening the kingdom of God to a mustard seed and yeast. If Luke 13 is envisioned in terms of concentric circles, the outer circle narrates the murderous intent of Jerusalem (vv. 1-9, 31-35); the next circle, a judgment against Jewish leaders (vv. 10-17, 23-30); and the innermost circle, two parables of the growth of the kingdom of God. These two parables appear at the heart of the chiasmus in Luke 13 and stand in bold contrast to the remainder of the chapter. Despite polemical opposition from Jerusalem and Jewish leaders, the gospel of the kingdom will grow in redemptive irony, as surely as seeds grow and yeast permeates and expands.

18-21   Luke shows a preference for pairs, especially male-female pairs; in vv. 19, 21 such a pair is highlighted in syntactic parallelism in Greek. The two parables at the center of the chiasmus depict a man sowing a mustard seed and a woman making bread. Both illustrate the kingdom of God, and their placement immediately following the severely crippled woman is a reminder that her healing, and healings like it (14:1-6), herald the inbreaking of the kingdom.[23] The kingdom of God "is like a mustard seed, which a man took

---

20. See here J. Neusner, *A Rabbi Talks with Jesus: An Intermillennial, Interfaith Exchange* (New York: Doubleday, 1993), 72-73; and D. Hagner, "Jesus and the Synoptic Sabbath Controversies," *BBR* 19/2 (2009): 246-47.

21. See Bock, *Luke 9:50–24:53*, 1219-20.

22. Vinson, *Luke*, 456, discusses the full significance of the correlation.

23. Schweizer, *Lukas*, 148; Bock, *Luke 9:50–24:53*, 1222. Vinson, *Luke*, 459, writes that the parables of growth are "a happy resolution to this section that began, like the evening news, with stories of terrible disasters."

and planted in his garden. It grew and became a tree, and the birds perched in its branches" (v. 19). This parable appears similarly in Matt 13:31-32, Mark 4:30-32, and *Gos. Thom.* 20. Jesus' introduction in v. 18, "To what is the kingdom of God like, and to what shall I liken it?" recalls Isa 40:18 ("To what will you liken the Lord, and to what image will you liken him?"). Jesus thus frames the parables of the Mustard Seed and the Yeast in the famous prophetic declaration of Isaiah that God is bringing long-awaited deliverance to Jerusalem. The parable of the Mustard Seed recalls the parable of the Sower (8:4-15), although the parable of the Mustard Seed emphasizes *contrast* in addition to growth. The mustard seed, an annual that proliferates anew each spring, produces a shrub rather than a tree. Unlike the versions of the parable in Matt 13:32 and Mark 4:31, Luke does not mention the microscopic size of the mustard seed, although Jesus capitalizes on its smallness in 17:6 to emphasize that great faith arises from small beginnings. Instead of smallness, Luke specifies that the seed was planted in a "garden" (v. 19). The reference to a garden is unique to Luke and somewhat unexpected, for rabbinic tradition considered mustard a fruit of the field rather than a garden.[24] Jesus may assign the mustard seed to a garden in order to emphasize the point of the extraordinary labor in the vineyard of vv. 6-9 that God wills for the kingdom to bear fruit even in Jerusalem, where opposition to Jesus is most concentrated.

All four versions of the parable end with the refrain that the mustard seed "grew and became a tree, and the birds perched in its branches" (v. 19). This is a reference to Ps 104:12, which, along with other occasional OT texts (Ezek 17:23; 31:6; Dan 4:9-21), speaks of the inclusion of Gentiles in God's chosen people in terms of birds nesting in branches.[25] In addition to the surprising growth of the kingdom, the parable of the Mustard Seed contains a hint of God's grace to *all* peoples. "Out of the most insignificant beginnings, invisible to human eyes, God creates his mighty Kingdom, which embraces all the peoples of the world."[26]

The kingdom is also likened to the role of yeast in making bread. The parable of the Yeast is recorded in the Double Tradition (v. 21//Matt 13:33) as well as *Gos. Thom.* 96. No food is more common to humanity than bread, in its many and various forms. The image of making and baking bread is thus a mundane rather than extraordinary occurrence. In choosing mustard seeds and yeast to illustrate the kingdom of God, Jesus highlights not its extrava-

---

24. Lev 19:19; *m. Kil.* 3:2; *t. Kil.* 2:8. The only mention of a garden in the Synoptics appears in 13:19.

25. A similar idea is preserved in *Jos. Asen.*, a Jewish novella dating from perhaps the first c.: "And your name shall no longer be called Aseneth, but your name shall be City of Refuge, because in you many nations will take refuge with the Lord God, the Most High, and under your wings many peoples trusting the Lord will be sheltered" (15:7).

26. J. Jeremias, *The Parables of Jesus* (rev. ed.; London: SCM Press, 1963), 149.

gance but its necessity to life. These humble parables are intensely "incarnational," identifying the kingdom with the daily routines of Jesus' world. Yeast is a leaven that ferments, causing dough to rise. The image may arise from the feast of unleavened bread at the Exodus (Exod 12:18). An image related to the exodus could be expected to carry positive connotations, but surprisingly, with the exception of this saying, all occurrences of "leaven" in the NT and in rabbinic literature, when used metaphorically, refer to evil intentions of the human heart.[27] In the present parable, Jesus appeals to the physical rather than metaphoric properties of yeast: the kingdom of God, like yeast, is indiscernible at inception, but once introduced, its silent permeation is inevitable and unstoppable. The volume of flour in v. 21 is astonishing: "three measures of flour" (NIV "about sixty pounds [27 kg] of flour") amounts to a whole bushel (40 liters) of flour, enough to feed well over a hundred people.[28] The inauspicious measure of yeast is like the unassuming beginnings of the kingdom; what is initially underwhelming will eventually permeate and transform the entire mass of dough into something unimaginable.

The parables of the Mustard Seed and Yeast both attest to the advent of the kingdom as God's doing, not humanity's. God ordains to introduce his kingdom from obscurity and insignificance. That which one cannot initially see or imagine will, in time, be impossible to ignore. God's reign will not only be more real than the world can imagine, it will also be larger and more encompassing.[29] The emphasis, however, lies on its small and obscure beginnings, which are now hidden and easily overlooked. Had Jesus desired to emphasize the power and glory of the kingdom of God, he could have told a parable about a cedar, which was a symbol of might (Ps 80:10; 92:12; Zech 11:2) and splendor (Cant 1:17; Jer 22:23). But the mystery of the kingdom is not present in the cedar, but rather in a mustard seed and leaven. "What appears to be the smallest is nevertheless the greatest. In that which is hidden, the foundation of a work is laid that will encompass the whole world."[30]

---

27. For rabbinic uses, see Str-B 4/1:466-83. Of the eleven uses of "leaven" in the NT, only 13:20-21 and Matt 13:33 are used positively.

28. BDAG, 917; Marshall, *Luke*, 560; Bovon, *Lukas 9,51–14,35*, 419. The unusual size is also noted in the "large loaves" of *Gos. Thom.* 96. Did Luke intend a correlation between the three measures here and three years in v. 7? The question is interesting but has no conclusive answer.

29. Seneca, a contemporary of Jesus, likened human words and reason to seeds that, when scattered, grow from insignificance to "greatest growth" (*Ep.,* "Letter to Lucilius" 4.38.2; cited in *HCNT*, 94). Seneca's analogy celebrates the power inherent in human reason and language, whereas similar imagery of Jesus affirms the miraculous irony of God to produce his kingdom in the world from insignificant beginnings.

30. Schlatter, *Evangelien nach Markus und Lukas*, 48.

THE NARROW DOOR (13:22-30)

At the heart of the central section Luke again calls attention to Jerusalem as the focal point of Jesus' ministry (v. 22).[31] This is the fourth of nine such announcements in Luke.[32] This one emphasizes that Jesus is *on the move*, not aimlessly or frantically, but steadfastly and purposefully "making his way to Jerusalem."[33] The repeated references to Jesus' destiny remind readers that his suffering and death in Jerusalem is the fulfillment of his purpose (9:22), his "exodus" (9:31).

22-24 Along the way "someone asked [Jesus], 'Lord, are only a few people going to be saved?'" (v. 23). This question was a subject of debate in Jesus' day and could have been asked of any rabbi. Opinions on the question ranged from inclusive to exclusive. Some rabbis taught that "all Israelites have a share in the world to come" (*m. Sanh.* 10:1), whereas others believed that "the Most High . . . made the world to come for the sake of a few" (*4 Ezra* 8:1). Throughout the central section of Luke, Jesus emphasizes the difficulty of entering the kingdom. His questioner is not identified, but the honorary title *kyrie* (either "Lord" or "Sir"), coupled with the question itself, suggests, if not a disciple, someone familiar with Jesus' teaching. Jesus does not reply directly to the questioner but takes the question as an opportunity to instruct "them" (v. 23), the gathering around him. Jesus allows God to determine how many will find salvation. He approaches the question instead from the perspective of the human effort required to enter the kingdom. The questioner may have hoped that Jesus would relax the rigors of discipleship, but he steadfastly maintains them (9:23; 12:33; 14:26-27). "Make every effort to enter through the narrow door," admonishes Jesus (v. 24). The effort specifically required is captured in the Greek word *agōnizesthe*, occurring only here in Luke-Acts, which means to engage in an athletic contest or combat. This same word occurs in a speech of Judas Maccabeus, exhorting his troops "to fight bravely [*agōnizesthai*] to the death for the laws, temple, city, country, and commonwealth" (2 Macc 13:14). In his reply to the questioner, Jesus thus places himself squarely in the company of Moses and Israel's prophets, including the Qumran covenanters, all of whom demanded the dedication of "heart and soul" to God's declared will.[34] This do-or-die resolution must characterize Jesus' followers, for many call him Lord, but few follow him as such.

31. So too Green, *Luke*, 529: "Luke's interest in the journey is less about a travel itinerary and more about the motif of journeying and the identification of Jesus' destination."

32. 9:31, 51, 53; 13:22, 33; 17:11; 18:31; 19:11, 28.

33. Jeremias, *Sprache des Lukasevangeliums,* 231, gives a full analysis of the vocabulary of v. 22.

34. 1QS 5:8-9 summarizes the compliance "with whole heart and whole soul" to all that was commanded by Moses.

25-27 Jesus concludes the parable of the Narrow Door in v. 25: "Once the owner of the house gets up and closes the door, you will stand outside knocking and pleading, 'Sir, open the door for us.' But he will answer, 'I don't know you or where you come from.'" Some scholars consider v. 25 an artless addition that is incompatible with the logion of the "narrow door" (Matt 7:13-14).[35] This judgment imposes an overly rigid constraint on the logia of Jesus, excluding the possibility that he could employ a metaphor in more than one way. In the parable of the Ten Virgins (Matt 25:10), Jesus speaks of a "closed door" similarly to its use here. King Saul's disregard of God's overtures through the prophet Samuel, and Saul's resultant rejection by God, might exemplify such a "closed door" (1 Sam 28:15-18). Strenuous effort is required to pass through the narrow door, and the master within may at any moment close the door. This repeats the same theme broached earlier in 12:58 and 13:6-9, and again in 14:24, that the present offer of salvation is not indefinite. The master who now opens the door may in the future close it. The warning not to presume on the grace of God is repeated more fully — and with equal gravity — in the parable of the Banquet in 14:15-24. People may imagine they can postpone entering the kingdom until a more opportune time. Surely they may return and knock at the door in the future (v. 25).

And why not? "We ate and drank with you, and you taught in our streets" (v. 26). People have comfortably affiliated with Jesus for a long time, and they presume to do so indefinitely. But the master will repeat, "I don't know you or where you come from. Away from me all you evildoers!" (v. 27). In the Third Gospel hospitality is regularly upheld as a chief sign and hallmark of the kingdom of God. In bitter irony, however, God will revoke his hospitality in the final judgment.[36] "Away from me, all you evildoers!" (v. 27) is probably a quotation from Ps 6:8.[37] The Sixth Psalm is a lament of a suffering individual who longs for healing. "Worn out from groaning," the psalmist finally waves aside those who have stood by without mercy or help. "Away from me, all you who do evil," he cries (Ps. 6:6-8). The parable of the Narrow Door is also a lament. The master holds open the door, longing for people to enter. Finally, to those who hang around the door but refuse to enter, he declares, "I don't know you. . . . Away from me, all you evildoers!" (v. 27).

28-30 Those who through either procrastination or refusal pass not

35. R. Bultmann, *The History of the Synoptic Tradition* (rev. ed.; New York: Harper & Row, 1972), 130, considers vv. 24-25 to be "extremely clumsy."

36. A point made by Vinson, *Luke,* 463, who speaks of God's judgment as an "anti-hospitality event."

37. The quotation could possibly recall the heroic achievements of Judas Maccabeus, among which was instilling fear in evildoers (1 Macc 3:6). The use of *agōnizesthai* in v. 24, which recalls 2 Macc 13:14, makes it tempting to imagine a relation to Maccabees here. The wording of the quotation in v. 27 corresponds more fully and closely with Ps 6:9, however.

through the narrow door will be left outside, "weeping and gnashing their teeth" (v. 28). This image of anguish and torment occurs six times in Matt, but only here in Luke. It is the tragic and terrifying opposite of the joy of the kingdom of God attended by "Abraham, Isaac and Jacob, and all the prophets" (v. 28). The repetition of Abraham here corresponds to "daughter of Abraham" (v. 16) in the chiastic counterpart of Luke 13. In both instances, and throughout Luke (see at 13:16), Abraham identifies especially the Jewish community that belongs to "the kingdom of God" (vv. 28, 29). The mention of Abraham and the kingdom of God in v. 29 paints a stark contrast to the eschatological pessimism of v. 23, which, accompanied by the strenuous effort to pass through the narrow door (v. 24) and the anguish of those "thrown out" (v. 28), might imply that heaven will be populated by a grim and skeletal few. In jubilant irony, the kingdom of God will in fact be attended by throngs from the four points of the compass. V. 29 combines two motifs of the coming kingdom, its *universality* and its *banquet festivity.*

Isaiah, in particular, emphasizes that in the last days the nations will stream to the Lord from east and west "like a pent-up flood" (59:19). A number of biblical texts similarly attest to non-Israelite peoples and nations turning to the Lord (v. 29; Isa 43:5; 49:12; 59:19; Ps 107:3; Mal 1:11; Rev 14:15). All points of the compass appear in these texts except for "south."[38] The guest list of the eschatological banquet of Jesus includes people from everywhere, however, including south (so v. 29). The motif of banquet festivity also capitalizes on OT eschatological imagery (Isa 25:6-8; *1 En.* 62:14; 1Q28a 2:11-22), but Luke again adds special emphasis. Banquet scenes are an important motif in the Third Gospel (see at 11:37), but the image of "reclining," the typical posture of guests at ancient Middle Eastern banquets, occurs only thrice (2:7; 12:37; 13:29). The first is the baby Jesus lying in the animal feed trough in Bethlehem; the last is the nations of earth reclining at the eschatological banquet at the end of time. God ordained to recline with humanity in the manger of Bethlehem (2:7), and he ordains that humanity recline with him in the eternal banquet of heaven (13:29). Both "banquets" are orchestrated by God, and as such they radically reverse all human standards: "The first will be last and the last will be first" (v. 30).[39] In answer to the presenting question how many will be saved (v. 23), Jesus responds that "people will come from east and west and north and south, and will take their places at the feast in the kingdom of God" (v. 29). Salvation is entirely God's achievement, "a marvel in our eyes."

---

38. It is possible that "the sea" refers to south in Ps 107:3, although this is not certain, for "sea" (Heb. *yam*) normally signifies "west" in Hebrew rather than "south."

39. Similarly, 14:11, "Those who exalt themselves will be humbled, and those who humble themselves will be exalted." Both reversals are equally stark, although the distinctions in 13:30 are temporal, whereas in 14:11 they are spatial.

PHARISEES, THE FOX, AND THE FATE
OF JERUSALEM (13:31-35)

The Pharisees' warning of Herod's desire to kill Jesus is unique to the Third Gospel. Two Hebraisms occur in the first verse,[40] and five more in vv. 32-35, including a probable wordplay on the Hebrew word "fox."[41] Such verbal DNA likely derives from Luke's Hebrew source. Structurally, this section corresponds to its chiastic counterpart in 13:1-9, in which Israel is called to repentance. "The open door that Jesus mentioned in the previous parable is closing for this generation. The fig tree is about to be uprooted."[42]

31 "At that time some Pharisees came to Jesus and said to him, 'Leave this place and go somewhere else. Herod wants to kill you'" (v. 31). The Herod intended here is Herod Antipas, tetrarch of Galilee and Perea, son of Herod the Great, last mentioned at 9:7-9 in relation to the death of John the Baptizer (see excursus at 23:1). The warning implies that Jesus is still within the political jurisdiction of Antipas, hence in Galilee or Perea. Whether the Pharisees are acting in collusion with Antipas, or are allying themselves (for once) with Jesus, is difficult to say. The mention of Pharisees makes the report immediately suspect, for Pharisees are mentioned twenty-six times elsewhere in the Third Gospel, each time pejoratively. The Pharisees are uncompromising in their opposition to Jesus as an unorthodox rabbi (11:53-54!), and it is not difficult to imagine their entering into collusion with Antipas, who suspects Jesus as John the Baptizer redivivus, who is capable of fomenting insurrection (9:7-9). Indeed, in instructing the Pharisees to report to Antipas (v. 32), Jesus tacitly assigns them to the tetrarch's camp. "Both wished this undesirable mischief-maker removed from their territory," surmises Pixner.[43]

Despite the above evidence, it is not assured that the Pharisees are colluding with Antipas in this instance. Luke's reference to "certain" Pharisees (Gk. *tines;* NIV "some") may indicate that these particular Pharisees are an exception to the norm. More important, there is no indication here, as there is in 14:1, 16:15, or 20:20, of Pharisaic intrigue, of which Jesus is otherwise and without exception intolerant. From a purely theological perspective, Jesus shared more in common with Pharisees than he did with any other Jewish school or sect (see at 5:17), and his acceptance of their report without refuta-

---

40. *En autē tē hōra* ("in that hour"; NIV "at that time") and the Hebraic repetition of *exerchesthai* and *poreuesthai* (lit. "leave and go"). See Schlatter, *Lukas,* 330; Jeremias, *Sprache des Lukasevangeliums,* 234.

41. Edwards, *Hebrew Gospel,* 316.

42. Bock, *Luke 9:51–24:53,* 1243.

43. B. Pixner, *With Jesus through Galilee according to the Fifth Gospel,* 104-5; similarly Klein, *Lukasevangelium,* 492.

tion could imply their collaboration with him. If so, this instance is the classic exception to the proverbial rule.[44]

32-33 Whether ill- or well-intended, however, the report of the Pharisees does not alter Jesus' mission. "Go tell that fox, 'I will keep on driving out demons and healing people today and tomorrow, and on the third day I will reach my goal'" (v. 32). In calling Antipas a fox, Jesus employs a multifaceted metaphor.[45] "Fox" was an epithet for a sly and crafty person in both Jewish and non-Jewish culture,[46] and Herod's corresponding profile in the Gospels makes him a deserving object of the epithet. But the full implications of "fox" are not thereby exhausted. Particularly in Jewish circles, "fox" commonly symbolized an individual who considered himself (or was considered by others) a lion, but was in reality much smaller game.[47] This does not imply outright mockery of Herod.[48] Antipas exercised power erratically and lethally — witness his execution of the Baptist (9:9; Mark 6:14-29), and his recall and exile under Caligula in 39 for amassing weapons.[49] According to the early record in Acts, Antipas, even more than Pilate, was responsible for the death of Jesus, God's "holy, anointed servant" (Acts 4:27). In this latter sense, "fox" implies that, in the grand scheme of things, Antipas was a character of minor significance who would not dissuade or deflect Jesus from his mission. Jesus' fate will be determined in Jerusalem, not by Antipas, and until Jerusalem, it is "business as usual." In this respect, Herod's threat to Jesus mirrors that of Amaziah to Amos (Amos 7:10-17).[50] Both rulers sought to drive the prophets from their territory, but like Amaziah, Herod learns to his dismay that his authority is trumped by the foreordained mission of Jesus.[51] Finally, and perhaps above all, the evident Hebraic background of this episode provides a third insight into the epithet. The Hebrew word for "fox," *shual,* is a virtual homophone of the Hebrew word for "Saul," *sha'ul.* In referring to Herod as a *shual,* Jesus could easily suggest that he was in fact acting like *sha'ul* in plotting against Jesus, as Saul plotted against David.[52] David was nevertheless destined to be

44. So Plummer, *Luke,* 348-49; Schlatter, *Lukas,* 330; Fitzmyer, *Luke (X–XXIV),* 1030.

45. See the overall discussion of the term in Klein, *Lukasevangelium,* 493.

46. See Jewish evidence for this understanding in Str-B 2:200-201, and in Greek and Roman sources in Fitzmyer, *Luke X–XXIV,* 1031; Wolter, *Lukasevangelium,* 496.

47. Str-B 2:201.

48. Vinson, *Luke,* 471-75, trivializes Antipas in referring to him as a "yappy dog," a "Chihuahua."

49. Josephus, *Ant.* 18.252-56; Schürer, *History of the Jewish People,* 1:350-53.

50. Bengel, *Gnomon,* 2:123-24, who has been followed by many subsequent interpreters.

51. On the various interpretations of "fox," see Bock, *Luke 9:51–24:53,* 1247.

52. See O. Betz, "Die Frage nach dem messianischen Bewusstsein Jesu," *NovT* 6 (1963): 42.

inaugurated as the Lord's anointed, and Jesus is likewise destined to fulfill his mission in Jerusalem.

The expression "today and tomorrow, and on the third day" (v. 32) is a Hebraic idiom for a short, indefinite period of time.[53] The expression is an allusion to Hos 6:2, which here implies the near future, and which similarly in 24:46 occurs with reference to Jesus' resurrection on the third day. In the present context the allusion to Hos 6:2 seems to refer to Jesus' *analēmpsis*, his "being taken up" (9:51) in Jerusalem. Neither the Pharisees nor Herod determine Jesus' fate, but Jesus, in obedience to divine providence, determines his fate, his "goal" (v. 32). The Greek verb for "reach a goal," *teleioun*, from which the English word "teleology" is derived, means "to fulfill or perfect an intended purpose." Its present passive form here is a "divine passive," meaning "God must complete his purpose through me." Jesus' course is determined by God, which will be fulfilled in *death*, similar to the sense of Wis 4:13-14. Jesus need not flee Herod prematurely, but will complete his mission in Jerusalem in the fullness of time. His death will not occur at the hands of Herod, but according to the will of God; and it will not be a deprivation of life, but a fulfillment of his life.[54]

Jesus' foreordained course is repeated and emphasized in v. 33: "I must . . . journey . . . to Jerusalem" (Gk. *dei . . . poreuesthai . . . Ierousalēm*). For the second time Jesus declares his prophetic role (4:24), and the necessity of its completion in Jerusalem (9:31). The identification of Jerusalem as a place where prophets perish (vv. 33-34) owes its source as much to Jesus as to historical reality. Some prophets perished in Jerusalem — Uriah (Jer 26:20-23), Zechariah (2 Chr 24:20-22), the later legend of the martyrdom of Isaiah (*Mart. Isa.* 5:1-14). Others were persecuted in the temple sanctuary — Jeremiah in Jerusalem (Jer 38:4-6), and Amos in Bethel (Amos 7:10-17). Under King Manasseh Jerusalem flowed with innocent blood (2 Kgs 21:16; 24:4).[55] Jews did not normally regard Jerusalem as a killer of prophets, however. Such an assertion would surely have struck many Jews as a sacrilege. The declaration of v. 33 and the lament of vv. 34-35 are, above all, a judgment of Jesus as both sage and prophet who fathoms the fundamental character of Jerusalem. As a boy, Jesus defined the purpose

---

53. Most commentators consider the expression Greek, e.g., Epictetus, *Diatr.* 4.10.31, "tomorrow or the third day"; see Wolter, *Lukasevangelium*, 496. Hebrew, however, expresses the same idea similarly. "Yesterday or three days ago" (e.g., Gen 31:2, 5; Exod 5:8; Josh 4:18; 2 Kgs 13:5, etc.) regularly signifies the recent past; likewise, "today and the third day" indicates the immediate future (Hos. 6:2, and similar formulations 23x in the MT, Gen 22:4; Exod 19:11; Lev 7:17; Num 7:24, etc.). Leaney, *Luke*, 209, recognizes the Hebraic sense of the expression.

54. Wolter, *Lukasevangelium*, 496, "In brief: Jesus will not die until he has brought to completion the task entrusted to him by God. The passive verb signifies that it is God who will bring [Jesus'] life to its intended purpose."

55. On the persecution of Israelite prophets in Jerusalem, see Str-B 1:943; Fitzmyer, *Luke (X–XXIV)*, 1032; Klein, *Lukasevangelium*, 494; Wolter, *Lukasevangelium*, 251.

of the temple as the locus of his Father's business (2:49); here he declares its fate to reject the prophet sent to it.

34-35 The lament over Jerusalem (v. 34) evokes David's lament at the death of Absalom (2 Sam 18:33). The double vocative, "Jerusalem, Jerusalem" (similarly 10:41; Jer 22:29), endows the lament with pathos and prophetic quality.[56] Vv. 34-35 appear virtually verbatim in Matt 23:37-39, both pericopes of which are commonly ascribed to the Double Tradition. A distinctive verbal characteristic, however, suggests the Hebrew Gospel as the source of v. 34. "Jerusalem" appears thrice in unbroken succession (vv. 33-34), each time in its Hebraic *(Ierousalēm)* rather than Hellenistic *(Hierosolyma)* spelling. The Hebraic spelling of Jerusalem prevails throughout Luke, but it occurs in the First Gospel only at Matt 23:37.[57] Given the multiple Hebraisms in 13:31-35, it is reasonable to infer that the unique Hebraic spelling of "Jerusalem" in Matt 23:37 derives either from Luke or his Hebrew source.

Jesus' turbulent lament over Jerusalem is the result of his compassion ("I have longed to gather your children together") being met by a stubborn countercurrent of human rejection ("but you were not willing"). God is not infrequently portrayed in the OT as a protective mother bird.[58] Jesus assumes the same image here, perhaps as a hen, "under whose wings you will find refuge; whose faithfulness will be your shield and rampart" (Ps 91:4). The maternal instinct of the hen is powerful, and no less the compassion of Jesus for Jerusalem. Jerusalem spurns Jesus' compassion, however, for Jerusalem "kills the prophets and stones those sent to you." The literal meaning of "apostles" in Greek is "sent ones." Hence the reference to "prophets and those *sent*" (v. 34) repeats Jesus' earlier prophecy of 11:49, "I will send them prophets and apostles, some of whom they will kill." Stoning can be an impulsive expression of wrath in the Bible,[59] but it also was the prescribed form of execution for the sins of idolatry and apostasy.[60] The stoning of v. 34 implies determination rather than impulsiveness. Those whom God sends to Jerusalem, in other words, received the ultimate religious sanction — stoning.[61] The will of God is thus rejected by a perversion of the law of God.

"Look, your house is left to you desolate" (v. 35). The native force of this

---

56. Bock, *Luke 9:51–24:53*, 1248-49.

57. On the Hebraic versus Hellenistic spelling of "Jerusalem" in Luke, see chap. 2, n. 64. In Matt, the Greek spelling of "Jerusalem" occurs eleven times, the Hebraic spelling only at 23:37. Jeremias attributes this fact to the indelible impression that Jesus' lament made on the early church (*Sprache des Lukasevangeliums,* 235). For the likelihood that Matt's version derives from Luke, see Edwards, *Hebrew Gospel,* 136-37.

58. Deut 32:11; Ruth 2:12; Pss 17:8; 36:7; 57:1; 61:4; 63:7; 91:4; Isa 31:5.

59. Exod 17:4; Num 14:10; 1 Sam 30:6; 1 Kgs 12:18.

60. Lev 20:2; Num 15:35; Deut 13:10.

61. *Enc. Jud.* 5:142; Green, *Luke,* 538.

judgment in the original Greek (and Hebrew) is diminished by the passive voice in which it is expressed. "Is left" is a "divine passive," a reference to God without using his name, meaning "God will destroy this place." This doubtless recalls Jeremiah's prophecy "The Lord declares, I swear by myself that this house will become a ruin" (Jer. 22:5).[62] "House" in Hebrew can carry broader connotations than simply the temple (e.g., Jer 12:7), and many commentators understand it as a judgment on "Jerusalem as the centerpoint of practices and institutions that shape life throughout Palestine."[63] The distinction between "your" and "house" (v. 35), however, may imply a more precise interdiction on the temple (or Jerusalem itself), thus corroborating the similar prophecy of the destruction of both temple and Jerusalem in 19:41-44 and 21:20.[64]

The solemnity of Jesus' declaration, "I tell you, you will not see me again until you say, 'Blessed is he who comes in the name of the Lord'" (v. 35), is difficult to interpret. This quotation from Ps 118:26 will be recited at Jesus' entry into Jerusalem (19:38). Some scholars correlate its use here with the entry into Jerusalem,[65] but the present quotation seems inappropriate to the Jerusalem entry, for it is not a joyful declaration here as it is there, nor is the temple "desolate" there as it is here, and above all, the grave pessimism of vv. 34-35 would scarcely comport with Jesus' entry into Jerusalem. V. 35 must therefore refer to the future Parousia. The recitation of Ps 118 could perhaps signify the eschatological exultation of converted Israel at the appearance of her Messiah (Rom 11:26),[66] although that seems improbably optimistic, given the lament of vv. 34-35. The quotation of Ps 118 seems rather to pertain to the context of final judgment. Like v. 24, at Jesus' second coming people will of necessity do what they were invited to do during Jesus' life, but refused to do.[67]

EXCURSUS: JERUSALEM IN THE THIRD GOSPEL

Throughout the Third Gospel "Jerusalem" is almost without exception a metonym for the massive and magnificent temple complex, which was the

---

62. The Greek word *erēmos* is present in several uncial manuscripts (D N Δ Θ Ψ), but its absence in more and older manuscripts argues in favor of a later assimilation to Jer 22:5. See Metzger, *TCGNT,* 138.

63. Green, *Luke,* 539; similarly Bock, *Luke 9:50–24:53,* 1250.

64. So Bovon, *Lukas 9,51–14,35,* 457; Bengel, *Gnomon,* 2:126; Nolland, *Luke 9:21–18:34,* 743.

65. Fitzmyer, *Luke (X–XXIV),* 1037; Schweizer, *Lukas,* 152.

66. So Plummer, *Luke,* 353; perhaps Marshall, *Luke,* 577.

67. So T. W. Manson, *The Sayings of Jesus* (London: SCM, 1949), 128; Wolter, *Lukas-evangelium,* 499.

locus of the Jewish sacrificial system, the heart of which, the Holy Place, symbolized the sacral presence of God in Israel's history and experience. Jerusalem, or the temple, appears throughout the Third Gospel in both positive and negative roles vis-à-vis the mission of Jesus as Messiah. In the infancy narrative (Luke 1–2) Jerusalem signifies the fulfillment of the saving purpose of God in the history of Israel. In the temple the angel Gabriel declares that a son born to Zechariah, a devout and righteous priest, and his wife, Elizabeth, will be the forerunner of the Messiah (1:8-17). Gabriel's annunciation is validated by the Holy Place in which it is delivered. Most important, the angel of the Lord proclaims "the city of David" as the birthplace of Jesus (2:11). All but two references to "city of David" in the OT refer to Jerusalem as the final resting place of Israelite kings. The burial place of the Israelite monarchs thus becomes the birthplace of the Messiah, who is destined to be Israel's "Savior" and "Lord." Jesus is circumcised (2:21) in the temple of Jerusalem, and there presented to the Lord in accordance with the law of Moses (2:22), thus signifying Joseph's and Mary's allegiance to their ancestral faith. In the temple Simeon (2:25-35) and Anna (2:36-38) are appointed by the Holy Spirit to confirm Jesus' role as Israel's Redeemer and Savior. The infancy narrative concludes with the twelve-year-old Jesus debating Israel's sages in the temple, which he identifies as the place of his Father's business (2:46-49).

In the Galilean phase of the Gospel (Luke 3–9), Jerusalem emerges as a menacing backdrop to Jesus' ministry. Though ninety miles (145 km) distant from Galilee, Jerusalem sends people to hear Jesus (6:17), but also, in the Pharisees and scribes, Jesus' archetypical antagonists, to oppose him (5:17). Already in the third wilderness temptation, the devil tests Jesus to perform a spectacular demonstration of his divine sonship in the temple (4:9-12). This test places the temple in opposition to Jesus' faithfulness to his divine calling, in a similar way that the call for Jesus to demonstrate his messiahship by coming down from the cross (23:35-39) places a veritable fourth temptation of Jesus at the crucifixion in Jerusalem. At the conclusion of the Galilean ministry the theme of opposition converges with that of fulfillment in Jesus' first passion prediction that "the Son of Man must suffer many things and be rejected by the elders, the chief priests, and the teachers of the law" (9:22). Elders, chief priests, and lawyers, the three offices constituting the Sanhedrin, are a circumlocution for the temple authority in Jerusalem. At the transfiguration, Jesus is reminded by Moses and Elijah of the necessity of his "exodus" in Jerusalem (9:31), and at the conclusion of the Galilean ministry Jesus predicts his "being taken up" in Jerusalem (9:51). The metaphor of "exodus" certainly includes the necessity of suffering in the fulfillment of the divine plan. Jerusalem marks the "completion" of Jesus' "exodus" (9:31), for as the human tabernacle of God, Jesus fulfills and replaces the sacrificial role of the temple in Jerusalem (see at 9:34). In "setting his face toward Jerusalem" (9:51), Jesus fulfills both the prophetic ideal of Elijah and his own divine destiny, "for no prophet can die outside Jerusalem!" (13:33).

So central is Jerusalem in the Third Gospel that the passion journey is not Jesus' first journey to Jerusalem but his fourth (2:22, 42; 4:9; 19:28). As noted in the excursus "The Mission of Jesus as the Way of Salvation" (see at 9:51), beginning in 9:51 Jesus' mission receives specific definition and from then on assumes dominant narrative significance via two parallel lines of development. The first line begins with the announcement of Moses and Elijah on the Mount of Transfiguration that Jesus "must fulfill his exodus into Jerusalem" (9:31), an announcement that is followed by seven subsequent repetitions in the central section of the divine necessity of Jesus going to Jerusalem (9:51, 53; 13:22, 33; 17:11, 18:31; 19:11). A second narrative line begins with the passion prediction in 9:22 that Jesus must suffer, which is also followed by seven subsequent references to the passion (9:44; 17:25; 18:32-33; 24:7, 26, 44, 46). The Jerusalem-narrative line contains no references to the necessity of Jesus suffering, and the suffering-narrative line contains no references to Jerusalem. At only one point do the two narrative lines intersect — at the conclusion of the central section in 18:31-34, where Jesus declares that he must *suffer in Jerusalem*. These sixteen combined references prepare for, and must be understood in the context of, Jesus' *way* to his impending suffering and death in Jerusalem.

The divine necessity of Jesus' suffering does not alleviate humanity from responsibility, however. Those killed by the collapse of the Tower of Siloam in Jerusalem were no more guilty than those who refuse to repent and receive the kingdom of God (13:4-5). A present window of opportunity for repentance will not remain open indefinitely (13:24-25). Though Antipas wishes to kill Jesus, Jesus knows he must continue to Jerusalem, where the prophets before him have perished (13:33). Jerusalem is at once the object of Jesus' compassion and divine judgment, the former conveyed by the tender image of a hen wishing to gather her young under her wings, the latter by the prophecy that the temple will be left "desolate" because Jerusalem will not receive her Messiah (13:34-35). Jesus weeps for Jerusalem, no longer a city of "peace" but a city of defiance (19:41-42; 23:27-30). The temple in particular is intended as a place of prayer and worship, but in reality it is a place of corruption and love of money (19:45-46). It is constituted as a place of adherence to the will of God, but in reality it questions the authority of Jesus (20:1-8) and tries to trap Jesus on questions of taxes (20:20-26), resurrection from the dead (20:27-38), and Messiah (20:39-44). Its desolation will be complete in the elaborate siege and destruction awaiting Jerusalem in 70 (19:43-44; 21:20-24).

The final rejection of Jesus transpires in Jerusalem. Throughout the passion, crucifixion, and burial, Jerusalem blindly rejects its Messiah, but God works in and through its rejection. Following the crucifixion, two disciples leaving Jerusalem meet the resurrected Jesus incognito, who explains to them that everything written in Moses and the prophets was completed in the suffering of Jesus (24:26-27, 44). Jesus' testimony to his fate as foreordained in Scripture causes the blind eyes of the disciples to be opened (24:31, 32, 45), whereupon they *return* to Jerusalem. Unlike the instruction to the Twelve to return to Galilee after the resurrection (so Matt and Mark), Luke (and John) instructs the Twelve to remain in Jerusalem and await the anointment and appointment of the Holy Spirit, for "beginning in Jerusalem" the gospel must be proclaimed in the name of Jesus to all the nations (24:47-49; Acts 1:8; 23:11). Jerusalem is thus not only the place where Jesus must be "taken up" (9:51), i.e., where he consummates his messianic mission, but also the place from which the apostolic witness commences. Like the neck of an hourglass, Jerusalem is the point *to which* the narrative focus of the Third Gospel irrevocably flows, and *from which* the mission of the early church extends in its sequel in the Book of Acts.

In sum, the temple serves as the point of contact with God's saving purpose in the OT in the infancy narrative. Additionally, the temple serves as a place of temptation where Jesus demonstrates his commitment to the Father's will, and also a place of corruption and punishment because of its failure to recognize its Lord's coming. Despite its unwillingness to recognize its Messiah, however, the temple remains the location of the divine plan for Jesus' life, for in Jerusalem, according to Luke, Jesus is crucified, resurrected, and gathers his disciples. Finally, Jerusalem is not only the necessary terminus of Jesus' life but also the necessary origin of the church, where Jesus' disciples will be anointed by the Holy Spirit, and from which the missionary witness of the church commences.

CHAPTER THIRTEEN

Jesus: Both Guest and Lord of the Banquet

Luke 14:1-35

Already in the infancy narrative Luke introduced the rudiments of what would later become the doctrine of the divine and human natures of the incarnate Son. When Mary found the twelve-year-old Jesus, who had been lost in Jerusalem, she says, "Your father and I have been anxiously searching for you" (2:48). All too human. In the same episode, however, Jesus amazes Torah scholars and replies, "Didn't you know I need [Gk. *dei*] to be about the work of my Father?" (2:49). Not human at all. Jesus appears as the same son of two fathers, one human, one divine. In chap. 14 Luke broaches the "two natures" motif somewhat differently. Jesus is a guest at a dinner party where conversation turns to gossip and judgments. All too human. At the dinner party Jesus tells the story of a greater banquet, the messianic banquet, which he narrates no longer as a guest but as the host — as God himself (14:24). Not human at all. The host's profligate desire that the banquet hall be filled, followed by Jesus' definitive teaching on discipleship in 14:25-35, signifies that in Jesus, the doors of the banquet hall — the kingdom of God — are thrown open to those for whom the old Israel had no place.

The material in chaps. 13–14 is largely unique to the Third Evangelist. 13:10-30 and 14:1-11, in particular, exhibit obvious parallels in structure and details. Both units contain more than a half-dozen Hebraisms each,[1] both begin with Sabbath healings in the presence of Jewish leaders, both describe healing in terms of "release," and Jesus justifies both healings by analogies with domestic animals (13:10-17//14:1-6).[2] Both miracles are followed by parables (13:18-21//14:7-10), and both units conclude with aphorisms (temporal in 13:30,

---

1. Edwards, *Hebrew Gospel*, 315-16.

2. The accounts, however, are not mirror images of one another. The healing in 14:1 takes place at a meal in the house of a leading Pharisee, not in a synagogue (13:10); both ailments (severely crippled woman [13:11] and edema [14:2]) are unparalleled in Scripture; Jesus heals by touch in 14:4 but by word in 13:12; no opposition to Jesus is voiced in 14:4, in contrast to 13:14. See J. Meier, *A Marginal Jew* (New York: Doubleday, 1994), 2:711.

spatial in 14:11) of astonishing reversal. The remainder of chap. 14, though less obviously related to chap. 13, contains further verbal clues that link the two chapters complementarily.[3]

EXCURSUS: PAIRS IN THE THIRD GOSPEL

A unique characteristic of the Third Gospel is the yoking of pairs in the narrative.[4] Things repeatedly appear in twos: two doves (2:24), two pigeons (2:24), two tunics (3:11; 9:3), two boats (5:2), two disciples of John (7:18), two debtors (7:41), two fish (9:13, 16), two denarii (10:35), two pennies (12:6), two copper coins (21:2), two swords (22:38), two angels at the tomb (24:4). Some pairs designate places — Bethlehem and Jerusalem (2:4-21, 22-39), Nazareth and Capernaum (4:14-30, 31-43), Capernaum and Nain (7:1-10, 11-17); Chorazin and Bethsaida (10:13); Tyre and Sidon (10:13). Other pairs appear as illustrations — "picking figs from thornbushes or grapes from briers" (6:44), ravens and lilies of the field (12:24, 27), three against two and two against three (12:52), cloud and wind (12:54-55), death from Pilate and death from a fallen tower (13:1-5), the days of Noah and the days of Lot (17:26-29), including pairs in parables: mustard seed and yeast (13:18-21), building a tower or going to war (14:28-32), lost sheep and lost coin (15:4-10). Most of the pairs are people, often of the same gender — Mary and Elizabeth (1:39-45), James and John (5:10; 9:54), sending disciples in pairs (10:1), Moses and Elijah (9:30), Mary and Martha (10:38-42), Peter and John (22:8), Pilate and Herod (23:1-12), two crucified criminals (23:32), two sons (15:11), two masters (16:13), two people in bed (17:34), two women grinding (17:35), two people in a field (17:36), two women following Jesus (23:55), two people walking to Emmaus (24:13); or two classes of people — tax collectors and soldiers (3:12-14), tax collectors and sinners (15:1), tax collector and Pharisee (18:9-14), priest and Levite (10:31-32), chief priests and lawyers (throughout the Passion Narrative).

Luke's most numerous and unique class of pairs, however, are male/female pairs, usually with the male mentioned first.[5] The parallel features of the healings of the severely crippled woman in 13:10-17 and the man with edema in 14:1-6 exemplify male/female pairs in Luke. Male/female pairs were introduced with special emphasis in the infancy narrative and they continue throughout the Gospel. Annunciations of the angel Gabriel come to both

---

3. "Tower" (13:4; 14:28); "manure" (13:8; 14:35); "kingdom of God" (13:18, 20, 28, 29; 14:15).

4. On Lukan pairs in general, see Wolter, *Lukasevangelium,* 20-21.

5. H. Cadbury, *The Making of Luke-Acts,* 233-34.

Zechariah (1:11-20) and Mary (1:26-38), both of whom subsequently sing psalms of praise, Mary in the Magnificat (1:46-55) and Zechariah in the Benedictus (1:67-79). The circumcision of John is attended by both Elizabeth and Zechariah (1:57-66). The redemptive mission of the newborn Jesus is acknowledged in the temple by Simeon (2:25-35) and Anna (2:36-38); and at age twelve Jesus is again in the temple with Mary and Joseph (2:41-50). At the inaugural sermon in Nazareth, Jesus cites the widow of Zarephath (4:26) and Naaman the Syrian (4:27) as Gentile beneficiaries of Israel's mission. Similarly, in chap. 11 witness is brought against the disbelief of Israel by the Queen of the South (11:31) and the men of Nineveh (11:32). The healings of the centurion's servant (7:2-10) and the widow's son (7:11-17) form twin accounts in the Galilean ministry; and in a different combination, the only son of a mother (7:11-17) and the only daughter of a father (8:40-42, 49-56) are both healed by Jesus. Jesus travels through Galilee proclaiming the kingdom of God with the Twelve and with "certain women" (8:1-3). In the parables at the center of chap. 13, the kingdom of God is illustrated by a man sowing seed (13:18-19) and a woman baking bread (13:20-21); and in chap. 15 Jesus tells parables of a man searching for a lost sheep (15:4-7) and a woman for a lost coin (15:8-10). In chap. 17 Jesus illustrates the sudden surprise of the return of the Son of Man by two men lying in a bed (17:34) and two women grinding at a mill (17:35). Jesus is hosted (Gk. *hypodechesthai*) at separate meals by Martha (10:38) and Zacchaeus (19:6), and Jesus calls a severely crippled woman and Zacchaeus "daughter of Abraham" (13:16) and "son of Abraham" (19:9), respectively. En route to the crucifixion Jesus speaks with the "daughters of Jerusalem" (23:27-31), and on the cross he is flanked by two male criminals (23:32-33); and his death is first attended by women (23:49), followed by Joseph of Arimathea (23:50-52).

In the Jewish world — and Luke framed his narrative to bear witness to that world — two witnesses were required to establish valid testimony (Deut 19:15; Num 35:30; 1 Kgs 21:10, 13; 1 Tim 5:19). The repeated use of pairs assures readers that the life, death, and resurrection of Jesus satisfy Jewish canons of reliability. But Luke's preference for pairs exceeds that requirement alone. Scriptural revelation opens with the testimony that the apex of creation is achieved in a complementary human pair, male and female, both of whom equally reflect the image of God. The emphasis on complementary pairs in the Third Gospel conveys that they too are equal objects of the redemptive work of God in Jesus Christ. Jesus' saving mission is extended to both men and women, and both participate in his mission as disciples. What 1 Pet 3:7 declares as a theological maxim — that women are "fellow heirs of the grace of life" with men — is repeatedly and variously epitomized in the Third Gospel.

A LESSON TO GUESTS (14:1-11)

1-6 "One Sabbath, when Jesus went to eat in the house of a prominent Pharisee, he was being carefully watched" (14:1). This is Jesus' third and final Sabbath healing (6:6; 13:10), and the last Sabbath incident in Luke (4:16-30, 31-37; 6:1-5, 6-11; 13:10-17). The intensity with which Pharisees have opposed Jesus (e.g., 11:53-54) makes an invitation to a Sabbath meal in a Pharisee's home somewhat surprising. Jesus' ministry was clearly and consistently characterized by Pharisaic antagonism (see at 13:31). Despite their vigorous differences, however, Jesus and the Pharisees did not break fellowship with one another, for the Gospels record Jesus' ongoing interactions with Pharisees until the final week in Jerusalem. Moreover, in none of the Gospels does Pharisaic opposition play a prominent role in Jesus' death, for the capital case against Jesus was pressed by scribes and chief priests, not by Pharisees, who are mentioned but once in the Passion Narratives (Matt 27:62).[6]

The Sabbath meal, which would have been prepared the day before, was likely at noon, for it was Jewish custom to eat the Sabbath meal at the sixth hour (= 12 noon).[7] Itinerant rabbis were often invited (as are visiting ministers especially in rural communities today) to the Sabbath meal following worship.[8] "The entire scenario," writes Craig Blomberg, "fits a credible early first-century context."[9] Observant Jews did not invite guests who might compromise the ritual cleanliness of other guests; nor were they inclined to invite guests who might decline an invitation.[10] The Pharisee's invitation thus attests that Jesus was acceptably kosher, and that, for all his differences, Jesus could be counted on to accept his invitation. Why a Pharisee would invite Jesus to a Sabbath meal is debatable, but three clues suggest motives beyond sheer hospitality. Most important, Luke's editorial addition that "[Jesus] was being carefully watched" (v. 1) implies surveillance prompted by malice (see use of term at 20:20).[11] Furthermore, the reference to the Pharisee as "a leader/ruler" (Gk. *archōn;* NIV "prominent") may be relevant, for seven of eight occurrences of *archōn* are pejorative in Luke, and six of the eight refer to *religious* leaders.[12]

---

6. Schlatter, *Lukas,* 334, challenges the negative stereotype of Pharisees in his discussion of Jesus' relationship to Pharisees.

7. Josephus, *Life,* §279; further, see Fitzmyer, *Luke (X–XXIV),* 1040-41.

8. Str-B 1:611-15; 2:202-3.

9. "Jesus, Sinners, and Table Fellowship," *BBR* 19/1 (2009): 59; similarly, K. Bailey, *Jesus through Middle Eastern Eyes,* 309, writes that the setting of the dinner party in 14:15-24 is "authentically Middle Eastern."

10. Str-B 4/2:611-39.

11. BDAG, 771, defines Gk. *paratērein* as scrupulous observance accompanied by intrigue or malice.

12. *Archōn:* 8:41; 11:15; 12:58; 14:1; 18:18; 23:13, 35; 24:20.

In the Third Gospel, religious leaders are normally opponents of Jesus. Finally, the presence of a man suffering from swelling or edema seems irregular at a banquet. Bodily edema is the excessive accumulation of fluid in corporeal tissues and joints, which is usually symptomatic of other (often cardiac-related) factors. It would seem abnormal for such an individual to be included in a Sabbath meal in a Pharisee's house, for rabbinic discussions (although somewhat later than Luke's day) associate edema with vice — sinfulness, fornication, demon possession.[13] Furthermore, an edematous man would seem to compromise Torah rules related to bodily discharges, or offend guests, or both. All three clues allow for the possibility, or even probability, that the edematous man's presence was arranged by the host to test or trap Jesus on matters related to Sabbath observance.

Without their speaking, the thoughts of "the Pharisees and experts in the law" (v. 3) are known to Jesus (see John 2:25). "Is it lawful to heal on the Sabbath or not?" he asks (v. 3). Jesus was of course familiar with attitudes subordinating human need to Sabbath prescriptions (6:6-9). The general rule governing activity on Sabbath pertained to *necessity:* if something could not be delayed, then it was permitted on Sabbath; but if it could be delayed until Sabbath was over, it was forbidden. Assuming the man's edema was not life-threatening, it belonged to the latter category, and hence a healing on Sabbath would be forbidden. The Pharisees are silent in response to Jesus' question (v. 4). Silence normally signifies consent, but since competing opposites cannot be consented to, silence here — especially if the prominent Pharisee hoped to trap Jesus — would seem to imply hardness of heart and judgment of Jesus. However the Pharisee intended the silence, Jesus takes it as an instructive interlude, and "taking hold of the man, he healed him and sent him on his way" (v. 4). The Pharisee was passive and silent, whereas Jesus initiated and engaged with human need. God's power was present not in the Pharisee's religious indifference but in Jesus' active compassion.[14] The Greek verb for "sent him on his way," *apolyein,* can also mean "to release or set free," which recalls a different form of the same word in 13:16, "it is necessary for this woman, bound by Satan, to be set free on the Sabbath!" The Pharisees, who think Torah is honored by scrupulous adherence to its commands, ask what is *permitted* on Sabbath; Jesus, who is Lord of the Sabbath (6:5), asks what is *intended* by Sabbath. From the latter perspective, healing the man with edema is not simply permitted but *required* on Sabbath.

In justification of the healing, Jesus asks, "If one of you has a child or an ox that falls into a well on the Sabbath day, will you not immediately pull it out?" (v. 5). Torah requires giving aid to "someone's donkey or ox fallen on the

---

13. Str-B 2:203-4.
14. Bock, *Luke 9:51–24:53,* 1259.

road" (Deut 22:4),[15] and Jesus' illustration obviously appeals to that precedent. Already in Jesus' day, however, a more rigid interpretation emerged at Qumran, forbidding offering assistance to an animal giving birth on Sabbath or, in contradiction to Deut 22:4, aiding a stranded animal on Sabbath (CD 11:13-14). If the Pharisees had planted the edematous man as a test of Jesus, they may have adhered to this restrictive interpretation. The fact that Jesus appeals to a Torah ruling in justification of his Sabbath healing is evidence that he is not a despoiler of Sabbath, nor indifferent to it, but that as Lord of the Sabbath (6:5), he is invested with the proper understanding of the Fourth Commandment. Once again (v. 4), the Pharisees are mute before the authority of Jesus, this time because they have no answer to his scriptural logic. V. 6 reminds Luke's readers that there are people, like the Pharisees, who call upon Jesus, sit in his presence, and listen to his teaching — yet remain silent in the face of his concrete call to discipleship to help a fellow human being in need.[16]

7-11 Jesus follows the healing of the edematous man, as he does the healing of the severely crippled woman (13:10-17), with a parable. The parable presupposes a culture of honor and shame in ancient Jewish and Hellenistic societies, and illustrates that culture by means of seating order at banquets. The subject of the parable and its intended lesson may have been prompted by the contrast between the contented Pharisee and the afflicted edematous man in the previous story. In the ancient world banquets were public exhibitions of the social status of guests; and not surprisingly, banquets are frequent contexts of Jesus' instruction in the Third Gospel (see at 11:37). Social preeminence was signified by proximity to the host, hence the most coveted seat at a banquet was the seat closest to the host. An obscure seat distant from the host was not an auspicious position. It is human nature to desire to be first, but the desire to be first is risky, for if someone more important arrives, the host will say, "Give this person your seat"; but then, "humiliated, you will have to take the least important place" (v. 9). "Give this person your seat" is a Hebraism, translating *pinah maqom*, "Surrender your seat."[17] Plummer notes the appalling contrast between "the brief self-assumed promotion" of the person who seeks the best seat, and the permanent disgrace of being demoted to an obscure position before the eyes of the guests.[18] Neither the lesson nor the banquet illustration is novel to Jesus. Virtually the same lesson occurs in Prov 25:6-7, which may be the basis for Jesus' teaching, although the same ideal is also present in Hellenistic social

---

15. The presence of "child" (Gk. *huios*) is preserved in the oldest manuscripts ($\mathfrak{p}^{45, 75}$ B N W Γ Δ), but since the combination of "son" and "ox" departed from the obvious allusion to Deut 22:4 and seemed incongruous to scribes, it was evidently later altered either to "donkey" (Gk. *onos*) or "sheep" (Gk. *probaton*). See Metzger, *TCGNT*, 138-39.

16. See Schweizer, *Lukas*, 154.

17. Str-B 2:204.

18. Plummer, *Luke*, 357.

etiquette.[19] Although the parable presupposes an honor-shame culture, it does not exactly subvert that culture, for the parable ends with the humble person "honored in the presence of all the other guests" (v. 10). This warns against the folly of self-promotion — the root problem Jesus sees in Pharisaism. The "one who calls" — the host — is mentioned five times in the parable. It is the host — not the guests — who determines the seating arrangement. Whoever is called to a wedding feast (v. 8) is invited into a context that is larger than self — and hence no longer defined by self. That context is determined by the master of ceremonies. The choice of a wedding ceremony as the theme of the parable is at least suggestive that the "one who calls" is God, for in the OT Israel's husband and lover is God (Isa 5:1-5; 54:5-6; 62:4-5; Ezek 16:6-8; Hos 2:19).

The moral is summarized in v. 11, "Those who exalt themselves will be humbled, and those who humble themselves will be exalted." The theme of eschatological reversal is common to Luke. The same theme concluded the sister passage in 13:30, and the same words reappear almost verbatim in 18:14.[20] One can imagine that such a memorable maxim was repeated more than once in Jesus' ministry. The passive voice here is another "divine passive," a reference to God without using God's name, meaning "God will humble the exalted and exalt the humbled!" The Pharisees seek to exalt themselves, and in so doing they cease being models and rulers of God's people. God's way is not their way, but Jesus' way. And because God's way is Jesus' way, the Pharisees' rejection of Jesus does not reflect God's opinion of Jesus.[21] The Pharisees regard Jesus' intimacy with the social riff-raff as a source of defilement, but Jesus is not worried about associating with "the poor, the crippled, the lame, and the blind" (vv. 13, 21). If anything defiles Jesus, it is his association with *Pharisees,* for they are obsessed with self-promotion rather than surrendering in trust to "the one who calls."[22] Christian discipleship is not self-promotion, but freedom from it, freedom from self-obsession itself. It trusts in "the one who calls," in God rather than in Torah, to bestow personal identity and honor, to establish our place and purpose in life.

A LESSON TO HOSTS (14:12-24)

The theme of "calling" (Gk. *kalein*), which occurs five times in vv. 7-11, continues in the present section with another five occurrences (vv. 12, 13, 16, 17, 24). In v. 7 Jesus addressed the *called* as guests; in parallel wording in v. 12, he

---

19. Plutarch, *Mor.,* "Table-Talk," 1.2.1-5.
20. Elsewhere in Luke, see 1:52-53; 6:21, 25; 10:15.
21. Bock, *Luke 9:51–24:53,* 1260.
22. C. Blomberg, "Jesus, Sinners, and Table Fellowship," *BBR* 19/1 (2009): 60.

addresses the *caller* as the host, with the parable of the Great Banquet (vv. 16-24) appended, which depicts God as the model host.[23]

12-14 The "host" whom Jesus addresses in v. 12 must be the "prominent Pharisee" of v. 1. The Pharisee may expect words of appreciation from his guests, but from Jesus he learns what it means to be a true host. "When you give a luncheon or dinner, do not invite your friends, your brothers or sisters, your relatives, or your rich neighbors" (v. 12). The Greek word for "luncheon," *ariston,* refers to a midday meal, whereas the word for "dinner," *deipnon,* the main meal of the day, refers to a late afternoon or evening meal. The distinction is immaterial for Jesus' lesson, however. The Greek *mē phonei* (v. 12; NIV "do not invite"), a present imperative, connotes that, whatever the occasion, "don't call the people you usually call," i.e., friends, brothers (and sisters), relatives, and rich neighbors. Instead, call "the poor, the crippled, the lame, and the blind" (v. 13). This unconventional guest list reappears almost verbatim in the parable of the Great Banquet in v. 21, which indicates that Jesus enjoins the Pharisee to call to his banquet the people whom God calls to his. In doing so, the Pharisee will be "blessed" (v. 14), for his unusual guests cannot repay him as his usual guests can. The theme of reciprocation appears in vv. 12, 14. If one does something knowing it will be repaid, then it is an exchange rather than a gift. Those who "come to Jesus and hear his words" (6:47) are taught another way, the way of *agapē,* which gives, and gives freely without thought of return. Jesus instructs the Pharisee in the same ethic he taught disciples in 6:32-35. The Pharisee — and all hosts — are taught to think of hospitality in terms of debt rather than repayment. *Agapē* is an expression of faith that puts one in debt to God (Rom 13:8). Other debts can be repaid by other agents, but God alone can repay *agapē* — "at the resurrection of the righteous" (v. 14).

15-24 Someone present at the table interjected, "Blessed are those who will eat at the feast in the kingdom of God" (v. 15). Luke typically uses anonymous interjections, as here, to focus an issue while still allowing Jesus to retain the spotlight.[24] Reference to "the kingdom of God" recalls the same subject in 13:29, and is yet another link between Luke 13 and 14. The topic of the eschatological messianic banquet enjoyed a long rhetorical history in Israel. Isa 25:6-9 depicts the messianic banquet as an outpouring of grace when God will wipe away tears and remove disgrace from his people, and the redeemed will celebrate the joy of salvation. In subsequent centuries participation in the messianic banquet became increasingly dependent on human worthiness rather than on divine grace. The Targum to Isa 25 stresses punishment by plagues that will befall the guilty at the messianic banquet. "The Rule of the Congregation" at Qumran

---

23. For fuller analysis of the parallel structure between advice to guests (vv. 7-11) and hosts (12-14), see Green, *Luke,* 549.

24. Similarly, 11:27, 45; 12:13; 13:1, 23, 31. Further, Green, *Luke,* 554.

assures that Messiah will indeed bless the righteous who participate in the eschatological banquet — but only after the exclusion of Gentiles, the ritually defiled,
and the physically handicapped (1Q28a 2). A later Christian apocalypse warns
that the messianic banquet is no safe haven for those who fail to "put away the
lusts of women" (*Herm. Sim.* 9.14.2). V. 15 constitutes yet another word in the
historic debate about the messianic banquet. The interjector may intend it as the
last word, for he leaves the impression of attempting to trump Jesus. Although
more moderate than some of the above voices, the interjector nevertheless alters
the understanding of "blessedness" taught in Isaiah and by Jesus: for him blessedness is not unrequited *giving*, as Jesus maintains (v. 14), but eternal *receiving*,
"Blessed are those who eat at the feast in the kingdom of God."

To this Jesus tells a parable about a great banquet, which constitutes
Jesus' contribution to the theme of the *messianic* banquet. The theme of the
parable is shared with Matt 22:1-14 and *Gos. Thom.* 64, the latter of which is
closer to the Lukan than the Matthean version. The differences in vocabulary
and details between the Lukan and Matthean versions suggest either that the
two Evangelists employ an earlier parable tradition for their respective purposes, or that they are working with different traditions.[25] The latter case seems
more likely. The versions of the parable in Luke and *Gos. Thom.*, despite their
similarities, do not appear to be dependent on one another; and the same is
true of the Lukan and Matthean versions, despite greater dissimilarities. It
would appear that the Evangelists are working from separate traditions.[26]

"A certain man was preparing a great banquet and invited many guests,"
says Jesus (v. 16). The word for "banquet" (Gk. *deipnon*) refers to the main meal
of the day, usually late afternoon or early evening. The words for "banquet"
and "invite" (Gk. *kalein*, "to call") repeat the same words in the foregoing story,
thus linking the parable to the host who "called" Jesus in v. 12. When the feast
was prepared, the host "sent his servant to tell those who had been invited,
'Come, for everything is now ready'" (v. 17). Plans for the banquet proceed
propitiously: an impressive list of guests has been invited, they have accepted,
and the banquet is now ready. Suddenly things fall apart. The timetable of the
host does not fit that of the guests, and "they all alike began to make excuses"
(v. 18). The Greek expression *apo mias* (NIV "all alike"), occurring nowhere
else in Greek literature, is evidently a Hebraism, translating *kūlām yaḥdāu* (so
Isa 45:16; Neh 4:2). It means to act "in unison or concert, as one."[27] Coupled
with "all" (Gk. *pantes*), it signals a social catastrophe: the guests who initially

---

25. A majority of scholars accepts the former option, which Bovon, *Lukas 9,51–14,35*,
504-7, discusses in detail and favors. For discussions of the second option, which I favor, see
Bock, *Luke 9:51–24:53*, 1269-70.

26. Wolter, *Lukasevangelium*, 509-10.

27. Edwards, *Hebrew Gospel*, 316.

accepted the invitation all beg off — to a person! One asks to be excused because he has bought a field and must inspect it; another because he needs to test five yoke of oxen he has just purchased; and a third just got married, and well . . . obviously, he cannot come (vv. 18-20).

Some scholars find these excuses lame, even contemptuous. They accuse the guests of "thumbing their noses" at the host; indeed, acting in collusion to boycott and "shut down the banquet."[28] The first two excuses seem particularly vulnerable to this accusation. Buyers of real estate and heavy equipment should be expected to test them *before* the purchase. Moreover, if the banquet is late afternoon or early evening, how can people inspect property or test oxen in the dark? If we conclude that the excuses are hollow and disdainful, it seems wholly justified that the host — God — should bar and punish those who wantonly insult him.[29]

In one sense it does not matter whether the excuses are sound or hollow, for they prevent the people who make them from accepting the invitation to the banquet — and missing the banquet is the point of the parable. But are the excuses as lame as some imagine them? The third excuse has the full weight of Torah behind it: a newly married man is exempted from military or any other duty: "for a year he is to be free to stay at home and bring happiness to the wife he has married" (Deut 24:5). To a Pharisee (14:1) — the man to whom Jesus addresses the parable (v. 12) — this excuse should seem quite plausible. A similar case can be made for the first excuse about property and the second about work. When all three are combined — property, occupation, and family — they comprise the essential commitments of life. These commitments constitute the greatest rival to the kingdom of God. In Jesus' exchanges with three would-be disciples in 9:57-62, family, work, and property were asserted as reasons — good reasons — for not following Jesus. The same three claims appear in Jesus' sobering instruction on discipleship in the following pericope (14:25-33), where he expressly teaches that, unless one forsakes "even life itself — such a person cannot be my disciple" (14:26). In the parable of the Sower, Jesus taught that "life's worries, riches, and pleasures" choke out the word of God (8:14; similarly 21:34). If these are not valid excuses for refusing an invitation, what would be?

If the excuses are lame and contemptuous, then the parable has no particular claim on Jesus' hearers. The three guests reveal themselves to be fools, and we (like the Pharisees!) may safely condemn them, and those like them.

---

28. E.g., Vinson, *Luke*, 489; Bailey, *Jesus through Middle Eastern Eyes*, 313-16.

29. Bailey, *Jesus through Middle Eastern Eyes*, 313-14, writes: "Imagine a contemporary Western scene in which the guests arrive and are seated in the living room. When the food is ready the hostess invites the guests to take their places but, to the shock of all, they offer excuses and head for the door. One says, 'I have to mow the lawn.' The second blurts out, 'I must feed the cat.' The third says, 'There are bills on my desk waiting to be paid.' And all three walk out the door!"

If, however, the three guests make the kinds of excuses we ourselves make —
especially when it comes to following and obeying Christ — then the parable
reasserts the scandal of the gospel. A short list of life's obligations certainly
includes property, work, and family, and these can be expected (if only temporarily!) to take precedence over the kingdom of God. From a purely human
perspective — and this is the perspective from which we justify 99 percent of
our actions — good excuses give the characters good reasons for not accepting
the invitation. Therein lies the point of the parable, for even a good excuse for
refusing the banquet is not good enough! From a divine perspective — and
this is the perspective Jesus introduces us to in the parables — work, property,
family, and even life itself are trifles in comparison to the incomparable and
eternal kingdom of God. To refuse the kingdom on their account is sheer folly.

The servant returns with bad news: instead of an entourage of happy
guests, he has merely a handful of excuses. The host is incensed and instantly
dispatches the servant to "the streets and alleys of the town," whence he should
"bring in the poor, the crippled, the blind, and the lame" (v. 21).[30] These four
groups of people repeat the same four groups of v. 13 above, indicating that
the parable is tailored to the host and guests of vv. 12-14. The master's orders
are fulfilled, but there is still room at the banquet. "Go out into the roads and
country lanes and compel them to come in," orders the master, "so that my
house will be full" (v. 23). The three invitations — original guests, poor and
lame inside the gates, people outside the gates — are commonly understood
allegorically to refer to righteous Jews, Jews in general, and Gentiles.[31] This
interpretation corresponds both to prophetic understandings (Isa 56:8) and
to the ministry of Jesus and development of the early Christian mission (Acts
13:46; Irenaeus, *Haer.* 4.36.5). Although this allegorical interpretation seems
justifiable, it is not mandatory.[32] The invitations are not identical, for the first
is more intentional, and the second and third do not differentiate between
inside (Jews in general) and outside the city (Gentiles). More important, an
allegorical interpretation shifts the focus to the guests, whereas throughout the
parable the accent falls on the host and his indefatigable desire for a full and
joyful banquet. The host, like the father in the parable of the Prodigal Son, is
the decisive figure in the parable. He is the first mentioned and last to speak,
and the fate of the banquet depends on him. He plans the banquet, calls the

---

30. The Matthean version of the parable (22:7) inserts at this point, "The king was en-
raged. He sent his army and destroyed those murderers and burned their city." One is tempted
to regard this as a later insertion reflecting the destruction of Jerusalem for the rejection of
Jesus (see G. Stanton, *The Gospels and Jesus* [2nd ed.; Oxford: University Press, 2002], 77).

31. E.g., J. Jeremias, *Die Gleichnisse Jesu* (7th ed.; Göttingen: Vandenhoeck & Ruprecht,
1965), 61-62; Fitzmyer, *Luke (X–XXIV)*, 1053; Bailey, *Jesus through Middle Eastern Eyes*, 318.

32. For nonallegorical interpretations, see Bock, *Luke 9:51–24:53*, 1277; Wolter, *Lukasevangelium*, 513.

guests, and when all is prepared he proclaims, "Come, for everything is now ready" (v. 17). When the first guests don't show, the servant is commanded to "bring in" uninvited guests — the poor, crippled, and blind (v. 21). This is done, but "there is still room" (v. 22). At this point an ordinary host would cut his losses and go with what he's got. Not the master of this banquet. The sorry response fuels his passion for a full house: scour the countryside, he demands, and "compel them to come in, so that my house will be full" (v. 23). The word "compel" has sometimes been interpreted as justification for coercing people to convert to the faith.[33] This is not its intent in the parable. People who are invited to occasions unexpectedly and for which they are unprepared are not surprisingly reticent to accept them. The use of "compel" reflects ancient Near Eastern practices, in which a resolute host takes the hand of a hesitant guest and ushers him or her personally into the house (Gen 19:3).[34] It is an expression of compulsory benevolence (Gen 33:10-11), not wrath.[35]

The parable closes with a shift of emphasis in Greek that is not apparent in English. "I tell you, not one of those who were invited will taste of my banquet" (v. 24). "You" is plural in Greek *(hymin),* signifying that the parable is now over and Jesus is addressing guests rather than the host. V. 24 is robustly christological, for Jesus speaks no longer as a mere Jewish storyteller but as the *master,* himself the host of the messianic feast. "Jesus wishes this feast to be regarded as His feast, the table at which the guests are to recline as His table, and the coming kingdom of God as His kingdom."[36]

There is a lurking prejudice in the minds of some that God arbitrarily and unjustly condemns some people to hell. This parable speaks to that prejudice. The host (= God) excludes no one. It is he who first issues the invitation,

33. The classic example is Augustine's compulsion of Donatists into the Latin fold (*Gaud.* 1.25, 28). Augustine's authority played a regrettable influence in the later Spanish Inquisition. See Fitzmyer, *Luke (X–XXIV),* 1057.

34. Grundmann, *Lukas,* 300.

35. In *Church Dogmatics,* 2/2, Karl Barth's distinction between God's power and God's sovereignty is relevant to a proper understanding of "compel." With reference to God's power, Barth says, "The basis of the divine claim does not consist in the fact that God can overcome and smash and annihilate man. By doing this God cannot and will not compel man to obedience; and He never has. He could certainly compel him — but only to something which falls far short of man's obedience. If He were to compel him in this way, His claim on him would still be without foundation. Even in the depths of hell it could still be flouted and despised" (p. 554). With reference to God's sovereignty, Barth says, "God could not demonstrate and proclaim more clearly than with His grace in Jesus Christ that He is not mocked, that He will not give His glory to another, that 'all that He proposes to do and wills to have will finally achieve its goal and end.' The fact that God is gracious to us does not mean that He becomes soft, but that He remains absolutely hard, that there is no escaping His sovereignty and therefore His purpose for man. To know His grace is to know this sovereignty" (p. 560).

36. T. Zahn, *Lukas,* comment at 14:24, cited by Geldenhuys, *Luke,* 396.

and in the face of refusals repeats the invitation to include others not originally intended. It is the *invited* who, refusing the invitation, exclude themselves. They are excluded not because they are wicked, sinful, or bad. They are good and respectable people; were they not, they would not have been invited in the first place. Their excuses — at least in their minds — seem justified. Like the people in 14:1-6, they know Jesus, they sit at table with him and enjoy his company. Their absence at the banquet is contrary to the will of the host and due solely to the fact that they had other and higher priorities. Their finances, businesses, occupations, and families were more important than the invitation to the feast.[37] The parable concludes with a sobering admonition: those who refuse the host's invitation will not be invited again.[38] The master has extended his invitation to insiders and outsiders, those near and far. His desire for a full house is so great that he pleads for *all* to enter. But some still refuse, and they have only themselves to blame.[39]

THE COST OF DISCIPLESHIP (14:25-35)

Various sayings in vv. 25-35 are parallel or similar to those in Matt, Mark, and *Gos. Thom.*[40] This section, which follows immediately on the parable of the Great Banquet (vv. 16-24), constitutes the clearest and most demanding charge on discipleship in the Third Gospel. A literary analysis indicates that Luke has carefully constructed the charge from his sources (1:1), including Mark, the Hebrew Gospel, and perhaps the Double Tradition.[41] Luke characterizes discipleship in terms of *coming to Jesus,* a theme introduced earlier in 6:47, when Jesus called disciples, "Come to me and hear my words and put them into practice." That call was left open, however, and a disciple might assume that coming to Jesus is one of several relationships he or she might enjoy, and hearing the word of Jesus one of several words that he or she might hear. The full significance of coming to Jesus is sharpened in vv. 25-35 with reference to three exclusive premises. In v. 26 coming to Jesus is defined in terms of "hating" father, mother, wife, children, brothers, sisters, and even self. The call of

37. Schweizer, *Lukas,* 158, offers helpful insights on this matter.

38. Klein, *Lukasevangelium,* 509-10.

39. See T. W. Manson, *The Sayings of Jesus* (London: SCM Press, 1949), 130: "The two essential points of [Jesus'] teaching are that no [one] can enter the Kingdom without the invitation of God, and that no [one] can remain outside it but by his own deliberate choice. Man cannot save himself; but he can damn himself."

40. Vv. 26-27 (par. Matt 10:37-38; *Gos. Thom.* 55, 101); vv. 34-35 (par. Matt 5:13; Mark 9:50).

41. For a discussion of the various sources, see Wolter, *Lukasevangelium,* 516.

Jesus takes precedence even over primary familial and marital relationships of life. In v. 27 coming to Jesus is defined in terms of bearing one's cross, an image of discipleship introduced earlier. The cross (see at 9:23), an instrument of suffering and shame, epitomizes the sacrifices required of a disciple in following Jesus. And in v. 33 coming to Jesus is defined in terms of forsaking earthly possessions. Coming to Jesus, in other words, means acknowledging Jesus as the preeminent *relationship* in one's life, whose costly mission determines the *way* of one's life, and whose presence takes precedent over all *things* in life. In 9:59-62 Jesus spoke of the relationship of disciples to the kingdom of God and to himself in similar terms, but the theme is climactically elaborated here with the requirement of exclusive allegiance to Jesus. Each of the three premises concludes with the refrain that whoever does not do thus "cannot be my disciple" (vv. 26, 27, 33). This refrain is another example of implicit Christology, for Jesus requires allegiance to himself that formerly has been required of the kingdom of God (9:2, 60; 10:9, 11; 11:20).[42] In his Shorter Catechism, Luther summarized the teaching of vv. 25-35 as the essence of the first commandment: "To fear, love, and trust God above all things."

Between the second and third premises appear two illustrations that apply to all three premises. The first illustration is the building of a tower (vv. 28-30), and the second the decision of a king to wage war (vv. 31-32). Both illustrations warn against making rash commitments. Building a great edifice and waging war must be weighed carefully and planned with resolve — and so must following Jesus. A great building project and going to war also involve high costs — as does following Jesus. Chap. 14 concludes with sober earnestness, not because the gospel is ominous or forbidding, but because, like all things in life of surpassing value, the gospel is both costly and worth the cost. True love makes great sacrifices for the beloved, and also great demands on the beloved. Not unlike the jealous love of God in the OT, Jesus here declares the uncompromising essence of his unconditional love.[43]

25-33 The meal in the Pharisee's house (14:1) is over, and Jesus is again on the move (v. 25). This is not a "travel narrative," however, for the journey is not defined by distances and destinations. The reference to movement reasserts Jesus' goal, his *intention* to go to Jerusalem (see excursus at 9:51). In Matt 10:37-38 the charge of vv. 26-27 is addressed to Jesus' disciples (Matt 10:1), but here it is addressed to the "large crowds." Luke thus addresses the charge not to the converted, but to crowds and readers, to all who are contemplating a relationship with Jesus, lest they imagine that familiarity with Jesus, even proximity to him, are substitutes for costly discipleship with him (13:26-27). Churches

---

42. With reference to the three premises, Plummer, *Luke,* 364, correctly asks, "Would any merely human teacher venture to make such claims?"

43. Schweizer, *Lukas,* 160.

may be tempted to attract new members by stressing how little membership will cost. Vv. 26-33 offer Luke's version of an "inquirers' class," in which he emphasizes how much a relationship with Jesus is worth.

"If anyone comes to me and does not hate his own father and mother and wife and children and brothers and sisters — yes, even his own life — such a person is not able to be my disciple" (v. 26). Matt records this saying less offensively, "Anyone who loves father or mother more than me is not worthy of me" (10:37). Scholars debate which form of the saying is closer to the original uttered by Jesus. Several Hebraic echoes in v. 26 commend Luke's version as the earlier.[44] The reference to "hate" likely reflects an original Hebrew *sane'*, which may have been later rendered more positively by Matt. The Lukan version is also more comprehensive, including wives, brothers, sisters, and one's very self, all of which are left unmentioned in Matt. The greater comprehensiveness is more concrete and thus more Hebraic, and the linking of each term by "and" (Gk. *kai*) appears to reflect an original Hebrew sequence linked by *wehi*. Above all, the hatred (Gk. *misein*) of family, friends, and relatives in v. 26 cannot be understood apart from Jesus' teaching in 21:16-17, where he warns disciples that parents, brothers, relatives, and friends will hate (Gk. *misein*) them and betray them to death. The bonds of family and friendship are the strongest of all human social bonds, but even those bonds can be broken and twisted into hatred and death. The bond of fellowship with Christ is stronger than all earthly bonds, and it can never be broken, nor does Christ ever betray a follower. When a choice must be made between even the strongest of earthly bonds and Jesus, the disciple must choose the unbreakable bond with Jesus.

"Hate" in v. 26 should not be understood in terms of emotion or malice, but rather in its Hebraic sense, signifying the thing rejected in a choice between two important claims (Gen 29:30-33; Deut 21:15-17; Judg 15:2; Sir 7:26), e.g., "I have loved Jacob, but Esau I have hated" (Mal 1:2-3; Rom 9:13). The ancient world frequently spoke of the same matters addressed by Jesus in vv. 25-33 not in terms of differences in degree or of competing goods, as we might today, but in terms of categorical contrasts.[45] This does not diminish the force of the teaching of vv. 25-33, but it does mean that the form in which it is presented was understood

---

44. Lagrange, *Luc*, 409; Jeremias, *Sprache des Lukasevangeliums*, 241; Wolter, *Lukasevangelium*, 516-17.

45. Thus Epictetus, *Diatr.* 3.3.5-7, declares that "the good is preferred to every intimate relationship. There is no intimate relationship between me and my father, but there is between me and the good. . . . My father is not my good; my brother is not my good." Likewise, Philo, *Contempl.* 18, commends asceticism over worldliness: "So when they have divested themselves of their possessions and have no longer anything to ensnare them they flee without a backward glance and leave their brothers, their children, their wives, their parents, the wide circle of their kinsfolk, the groups of friends around them, the fatherlands in which they were born and reared . . . and they pass their days outside the city walls pursuing solitude."

to convey the inestimable worth of a choice, not a malicious motive of a choice. What Jesus requires of disciples in v. 26 is essentially what Deut 33:9 required of every Israelite priest — to watch over God's word and guard his covenant, "having no regard for father and mother, neither recognizing brothers nor acknowledging one's children."[46] The point of v. 26 is that good things, even things created and commended by God such as father and mother and the honor due them (Exod 20:12; Mark 7:10), cannot be given precedence over Jesus. When the good rivals the best, then it must be "hated." Gregory Palamas (d. 1359) cited the Fifth Commandment with reference to v. 26: "It is through [your father and mother] that God has brought you into this life and they, after God, are the causes of your existence. Thus after God you should honor them and love them, provided that your love for them strengthens your love for God. If it is does not, flee from them."[47] Schlatter summarizes Jesus' teaching with less compromise and perhaps even more faithfulness to Luke: "Hatred of everything that we are obliged to love, including our own lives, is the requirement of that fellowship with Jesus expressed in costly discipleship. Everything that binds us together by nature is for the disciple an enemy that the disciple must contend against, for it contends against the disciple. The very perfection of love that Jesus requires explodes the bounds of all natural associations."[48]

Coming *to* Jesus (v. 26; Gk. *erchetai pros me*) is repeated in v. 27 as bearing one's cross and coming *after* Jesus (Gk. *erchetai opisō mou*).[49] There is probably little difference between the two expressions, although the latter, combined with the metaphor of "bearing one's cross," which connotes the process of following Jesus through daily trials (9:23), prepares for the theme of constancy and steadfastness, as illustrated in the two parables of vv. 28-32.[50] Both parables admonish hearers to *forethought*. The forethought that the Book of Common Prayer admonishes regarding matrimony, that marriage "is not to be entered into unadvisedly or lightly, but deliberately," captures the gist of the forethought admonished in both parables. The first parable is about building a tower (vv. 28-30). Construction of a tower conjures up mental images of a civic project, but the reference to "one of you" (v. 28) suggests something everyday hearers might

---

46. Monastic vows in both the Catholic and Orthodox traditions still today entail essentially the same expectation.

47. Gregory Palamas, "A New Testament Decalogue," in *Philokalia* (ed. G. Palmer, P. Sherrard, and K. Ware; London: Faber & Faber, 1995), 4:327.

48. *Lukas,* 343-44.

49. V. 27 has been wholly omitted by M (ninth c.), R (seventh c.), Γ (tenth c.), and several minuscule manuscripts owing to homoeoteleuton, i.e., an error caused when a scribe, seeing two lines of text ending in the same word or syllable, mistakes the second line for the first, omitting the intervening material. See Metzger, *TCGNT,* 139; idem, *The Text of the New Testament* (New York: Oxford, 1964), 189-90.

50. See Bock, *Luke 9:51–24:53,* 1284, 1286.

build. The Greek word for "tower," *pyrgos,* can refer to the tower of a fortress or city wall (13:4), but it can equally refer to a common watchtower in a vineyard (Mark 12:1), or any tall structure a landowner might build.[51] The word occurs in Luke only here and in 13:4, and is another Lukan link between Luke 13 and 14. The emphasis is less on the type of structure than on the planning needed to complete it. One must "sit down"[52] and "estimate the cost" (v. 28). The Greek word for "estimate," *psēphizein,* referring to counting with pebbles, was used in antiquity for tallying business assets or casting a vote[53] — both matters to which hearers were advised to give considered attention. This building requires a "foundation" (v. 29), the resolve to dig deep and build on bedrock (6:48). Anyone who undertakes such a project with less resolve may never finish it — and end up the laughingstock of the county. This latter state was far worse in the honor-shame culture of Jesus' day than whatever the capital losses might be.

The second parable of a king waging war (vv. 31-32) also appeals to the forethought of hearers, although the consequences of misjudging here are more disastrous. They no longer involve ridicule, but defeat and death — either in battle or by execution at the hand of the victorious enemy commander. Another Hebraism, "ask for terms of peace" (v. 32), links this parable, as the former, to Luke's Hebrew source.[54] Both parables repeat and reinforce the parable of the Friend at Midnight, who will not be dissuaded from his errand (11:5-8). The accent of both parables falls not on the decision to start a project, but on the determination to finish it. The exclusiveness of the teaching in this section is indeed unique to Jesus, but the rationale by which it is argued is not. The gist of the parables repeats the lesson of Prov 24:3-6, for example, as well as the motto of Caesar Augustus to "Make haste slowly," and the admonishment of Epictetus to forethought before great undertakings.[55] The same practical wisdom would have been as apparent to Jesus' hearers as it is to us.

For the third and final time in v. 33 Jesus repeats that whoever does not forsake all his possessions "cannot be my disciple." This statement repeats more vigorously what Jesus teaches elsewhere, that life does not consist of posses-

---

51. The meaning of *pyrgos* here, declares Bovon, *Lukas 9,51–14,35,* 538, gives commentators gray hair. That may say more about commentators than about the difficulty of this particular term.

52. Another Hebraism in this section; see Jeremias, *Sprache des Lukasevangeliums,* 242.

53. Fitzmyer, *Luke (X–XXIV),* 1065.

54. On the Hebraism, see Wolter, *Lukasevangelium,* 519. Gk. *erōta ta pros eirēnēn* translates Heb. *sha'al leshalom,* Judg 18:15; 1 Sam 10:4; 25:5; 30:21; 2 Sam 8:10; 11:7; 1 Chr 18:10.

55. So Epictetus *Diatr.* 3.15.1, who illustrates a chapter entitled "That we ought to proceed with forethought in everything," with this example: "In every act consider what precedes and what follows, and only then act. If you do not consider, you will begin with spirit, since you have not thought through the things that follow. Afterwards, when difficulties arise, you will abandon the project in shame."

sions (12:15). Hence, sell them (12:33) — especially if they prevent you from following Jesus (18:22). The necessary equipment for ministry with Jesus is, as Jesus has already taught in the call and sending of the disciples (9:3; 10:4), to have no equipment, to depend wholly and solely on Jesus. Jesus, as Bock notes, is not a minimalist when it comes to commitment. "It is not how little one can give that is the question, but how much God deserves."[56] What Jesus teaches in the metaphor of the cross in v. 27 is what Paul teaches in the same metaphor, "I have been crucified with Christ and I no longer live, but Christ lives in me" (Gal 2:20). The threefold call of Jesus to forsake family and self, bear the cross of discipleship, and renounce possessions is nothing less than the summons to a new identity, not on the basis of genetics, race, or social factors, but on the basis of costly discipleship with Jesus.[57] "Let goods and kindred go, this mortal life also," wrote Luther in "A Mighty Fortress Is Our God." Jesus gives all so that he may reign over all; he dies for all, and thus requires all of his followers.

This teaching is not advanced as a mythical fiction or unachievable ideal, but as a genuine characteristic of knowing and loving Jesus. In some instances one must forsake family (v. 26), and in others bring the family into the fellow-ship (Acts 16:33; 1 Cor 7:12; Col 3:18-21); in some instances bear one's own cross (v. 27), and in others bear the burdens of others (Gal 6:2). One must forsake all things (v. 33; 18:29), yet receive all things (12:22-32; 14:1; 18:30); one must give all things to others (10:38; 22:10-12; Matt 25:35-36), and be put in charge of the Master's possessions (12:44). One must come to the Lord and serve him (v. 26), yet the Lord also comes to disciples and serves them (12:36-37). Discipleship consists of both giving and receiving. Not all are called to the same form of discipleship at all times. But whatever form the call takes, all are called to Jesus absolutely and without reserve. Discipleship cannot be an expression of mere civil religion. It does not confuse the gospel with ideologies or cultural norms, nor does it tailor the gospel to our preferences and causes, even the most noble.[58] It is the forsaking of all for Jesus, or retaining all and forsaking Jesus.

34-35 Luke concludes Jesus' teaching on discipleship with a saying about salt, variants of which occur in Matt 5:13 and Mark 9:50. The unusual reference to salt becoming "foolish" (v. 34; Gk. *mōrainein;* NIV "loses its salt-iness") apparently derives from an original Hebrew *taphel,* which literally means "stupid" or "foolish," but with reference to salt, "dull" or "tasteless" (Job 6:6; similarly Job 1:22; 24:12; Jer 23:13; Lam 2:14).[59] Luke does not apply the

---

56. Bock, *Luke 9:51–24:53,* 1290.

57. Green, *Luke,* 565, insightfully recognizes that authentic discipleship involves nothing less than new identity.

58. The influence of Schweizer, *Lukas,* 160, is apparent in the above paragraph.

59. On the Hebraic analysis, see Wolter, *Lukasevangelium,* 520. For analyses of the three Synoptic versions of the saying, see Klein, *Lukasevangelium,* 514; and esp. Schlatter,

saying on salt explicitly to discipleship, as do Matt and Mark. Both of the fore-going observations suggest that Luke may preserve the earliest written version of the saying. "Salt is good," preserved in the Markan and Lukan versions (and assumed in the Matthean), appears to be the backbone of Jesus' original saying, but its context has been lost, with the result that each Evangelist employs the saying for his particular editorial purposes.

Salt was derived from various places and was used for various purposes in first-century Palestine.[60] In the temple cult, salt signified the covenant (Num 18:19) and was a requisite element in all Israelite sacrifices (Lev 2:13). Salt is not used with reference to its cultic function in vv. 34-35, however, but with reference to its two most important mundane functions, the preservation and the seasoning of food. Luke's conclusion that "salt is good" (v. 34) logically applies to Jesus' call to discipleship. Salt is more than a metaphor of disciple-ship; it is a veritable quality of it. Christians are not commanded to be nice, but to be *salty*. Salt is savory, it not only preserves food from putrefaction but makes it enjoyable to eat. Insipid and tasteless salt does none of these and is utterly worthless.[61] So it is with Jesus' disciples. The believers for whom Jesus is more important than family and friends, even their own lives, who take up their crosses as living martyrs, and who forsake the claims of possessions are savory salt who bring joy to God and make palpable differences in the world. Christians who are not salty are not Christian at all, more useless than those who never claimed to follow Jesus in the first place.[62]

Lukas, 546-47 (although his arguments that Matt preserves the earliest form of the saying are not compelling).

60. Ostracine, a town on the Palestinian-Egyptian border, was a major source of salt. Pungent salt from the Dead Sea served in temple sacrifices, and rock salt was used in the preservation of meat. See Str-B 1:232-36.

61. Table salt (sodium chloride, NaCl) is a very stable compound that does not degrade naturally, nor does it lose its physical properties, including flavor, apart from a chemical re-action. How, then, should Jesus' statement be understood? Four suggestions have been advanced. (1) Salt was procured by evaporating water from the Dead Sea, leaving dried beds of salt crystals and carnallite. If the concentration of the latter was too high, the pungency of the former was diluted and compromised. (2) The salt here refers to tablets of salt used for catalytic purposes in ovens. In time the tablets lost effectiveness and were thrown out. (3) In cooking, salt could be used alone or with other spices. When it was used with too many (or the wrong) spices, it lost its effect. (4) Jesus, like people in general, knew that salt does not lose its taste. The metaphor therefore suggests the impossibility of a Christian being anything other than a Christian; i.e., to be anything less than the disciple of vv. 25-33 is to be no Christian at all. See Bovon, *Lukas 9,51–14,35*, 546-47, and G. Bertram, *mōros et al.*, *TWNT* 4:842-44. I, along with Bovon and Bertram, favor number 4; Bock, *Luke 9:51–24:35*, 1290-91, favors number 2.

62. The reference to "manure" (Gk. *kopria*) connotes the worthlessness of something that has lost its purpose. Like several other words in chap. 14, *kopria* links back to the same word in 13:8.

CHAPTER FOURTEEN

Lost and Found

Luke 15:1-32

From chap. 15 through the remainder of the central section (ending at 18:34), Luke alternates between units of material addressed to Pharisees and those addressed to disciples.[1] Luke 15 begins the sequence by addressing three parables to Pharisees and scribes (vv. 1-2). All three parables repeat the elemental themes of need of repentance (vv. 7, 10, 18, 21), finding the lost (vv. 4 [2x], 5, 6, 7, 8, 9 [2x], 24, 28, 32), and above all, God's joy in recovering the lost (vv. 5, 6, 7, 9, 10, 23, 24, 25 [2x], 29, 32 [2x]).[2] Thoughtful readers will note that the shepherd in the first parable (vv. 3-7), the cleaning woman in the second (vv. 8-10), and the father in the third (vv. 11-32) undertake risks that, from the standpoint of wisdom and practicality, may not be advisable. These risks are essential to understanding all three parables, for they are not parables of prudence but parables of the recovery of the lost and God's singular joy in redemption. In the first parable the lost sheep is recovered outside the fold, in the second the lost coin is recovered inside the house, and the third and climactic parable incorporates both motifs: the father must await the return of a rebellious son, and

1. | 15:1-32 | Pharisees and scribes |
   |---|---|
   | 16:1-13 | Disciples |
   | 16:14-31 | Pharisees |
   | 17:1-10 | Disciples, including apostles |
   | 17:20-21 | Pharisees |
   | 17:22–18:8 | Disciples |
   | 18:9-14 | Pharisees (v. 9 describes Pharisees, e.g., 16:14-15) |
   | 18:15-17 | Disciples |
   | 18:18-27 | Pharisees (the ruler unable to divest his money suggests Pharisees of 16:14) |
   | 18:28-34 | Disciples |

See Wolter, *Lukasevangelium*, 514-15.

2. The theme of joy is expressed in a chorus of words and images in the parables, including "celebrate" (Gk. *euphrainein*, vv. 23, 24, 29, 32), "joy" (*chara*, vv. 7, 10), "rejoice" (*chairein*, vv. 5, 32), "rejoice together" (*synchairein*, vv. 6, 9), "music" (*symphōnia*, v. 25), and "dancing" (*chorōn*, v. 25).

he must seek the return of a resentful one. In the first two parables the sheep and coin do nothing to be found; their recovery depends entirely on the initiative of the one who seeks them. The same determination is fundamental to the third parable as well, for apart from the father's waiting- and seeking-love, neither younger nor elder son would be rejoined or reconciled to the family.

The ordering of the three parables, like the material in chaps. 13–14, bears distinctive marks of Luke's editorial hand. This is particularly evident in the vocabulary and style of the parables of the Lost Sheep and Lost Coin in 15:1-10.[3] The parable of the Prodigal Son, in contrast, exhibits a high concentration of Hebraisms — no fewer than twenty — in evidence of its provenance in Luke's Hebrew source.[4] This architectural influence should not be mistaken for invention on Luke's part, however. All three parables, and especially the third, bear witness to the indomitable love of God for the lost, which was the driving impetus of Jesus' ministry, "For the Son of Man came to seek and to save what is lost" (19:10). All three parables are widely recognized as authentic expositions of that impetus.[5]

THE LOST SHEEP AND LOST COIN (15:1-10)

1-2 "Now the tax collectors and sinners were all gathering around to hear Jesus. But the Pharisees and the teachers of the law muttered, 'This man welcomes sinners and eats with them'" (vv. 1-2). The wording and content of this introduction replay closely the wording and content of the call to Levi in 5:29-32.[6] The comment that "all" (Gk. *pantes*) sinners and tax collectors were gathering to Jesus is Jewish hyperbole, reflecting the Hebrew *kāl* (e.g., 2 Sam 15:23). Jesus' habit of fraternizing with sinners and tax collectors, and the aggravation of the religious elite at his — and the early church's (Acts 11:3)

---

3. Jeremias, *Sprache des Lukasevangeliums*, 243-55.

4. Nolland, *Luke 9:21–18:34*, 781; Edwards, *Hebrew Gospel*, 317-18.

5. On the question of authenticity, see J. Jeremias, *The Parables of Jesus* (3rd ed.; London: SCM Press, 1972), 128-36; C. Blomberg, "Jesus, Sinners, and Table Fellowship," *BBR* 19/1 (2009): 60.

6.

5:29	a large crowd	15:1	all
5:30	tax collectors and sinners		tax collectors and sinners
	murmur (Gk. *egongyzon*)	15:2	murmur (Gk. *diegongyzon*)
	Pharisees and teachers of the law		Pharisees and teachers of the law
	saying		saying
5:32	sinners		sinners
5:30	eat with		eat together with

See Jeremias, *Sprache des Lukasevangeliums*, 243.

— doing so are not new themes in Luke. They have characterized Jesus' ministry from its Galilean beginnings (5:30; 7:34). The wording of 15:1-2 informs readers that Jesus intends to address head-on his receptivity of sinners and the Pharisees' opposition to it. The combination of *prosdechesthai* (v. 2; "welcome") with *synesthiein* (v. 2; "eat with") connotes more than table hospitality with Torah defilers — radical though that was. The combination of these two words designates the creation of *fellowship*. In receiving and eating with sinners, Jesus bound himself in community with them.[7]

Why does Jesus invite sinners into community in v. 2, whereas in 14:25-35 he warns against rash discipleship? It was fitting of Jesus, says Plummer, to check the heedless enthusiasm of the crowds in 14:25, lest they follow him and soon afterward turn away; but it would be shameful of Jesus to send away the sinful and needy simply to save himself from legal pollution.[8] The word for "murmur" (Gk. *diagongyzein;* NIV "mutter") occurs in Luke only here and in the Zacchaeus story (19:7), where it is used to the same effect in a similar context. Despite its infrequency in Luke, the word would have recalled to readers the murmuring of the Israelites in the wilderness (Exod 16:2, 7, 8; Num 14:2; Josh 9:18). There, murmuring is a consequence of ingratitude, and an expression of unfaithfulness. What was directed against God in the exodus is here directed against Jesus. The Pharisees' rejection of Jesus' profligate love for the lost is a further expression of Israel's rejection of God. Rabbis issued a summary rule that Jews should not associate with the godless (*Mek. Exod.* 18:1).[9] A prayer of the Pharisees from the first century gives classical expression to this rule:

> I thank you Lord, my God, that you have set my portion with those who sit in the sanctuary, and not with those who sit on street corners. I rise early and they rise early: I rise to attend to the word of Torah, and they to attend to futile things. I exert myself and they exert themselves: I exert myself and receive a reward, and they exert themselves and receive no reward. I run and they run: I run to life in the world to come, and they run to the pit of destruction.[10]

3-7 It is to those, like the Pharisees, who upheld such a formula that Jesus addresses a parable. It is possible that "parable" in the singular (v. 3) refers only to the Lost Sheep immediately following, but since the three parables in Luke 15 are devoted to God's search and recovery of the lost, and since this is

---

7. Wolter, *Lukasevangelium,* 523.

8. Plummer, *Luke,* 367.

9. Str-B 2:208.

10. *B. Ber.* 28b, cited in J. Jeremias, *Die Gleichnisse Jesu* (7th ed.; Göttingen: Vandenhoeck & Ruprecht, 1965), 141-42.

the dominant theme of Jesus' ministry, it is not improper to take the singular with reference to all three parables.[11] Jesus' parables, though hypothetical, tell stories that happen to ordinary people. The only prerequisite needed to understand his parables is life experience. "What person among you . . ." (v. 4; NIV "Suppose one of you"), asks Jesus. The relationship of God and people was commonly depicted in Israel by the image of shepherd and sheep. God is a good shepherd (Ps 23; 80:1; Isa 40:11). David is transformed from a literal shepherd to a figurative shepherd of Israel (2 Sam 5:2), and the same imagery is frequently applied to Israel's subsequent leaders, including kings and priests (Ezek 34:1-10). It is not surprising that Jesus should speak of both himself (John 10:1-16) and God in shepherd-imagery.

Here and in Matt 18:12-14 he tells a parable of a person who had a hundred sheep, one of which became lost.[12] "Doesn't he leave the ninety-nine in the open country and go after the lost sheep until he finds it?" (v. 4). Framing the crux of the parable in the form of a question transforms an objective narrative into an existential dilemma, pulling hearers out of their seats and onto the stage. Scholars debate whether a hundred sheep implies a wealthy shepherd or not.[13] Such a flock was probably above average, but since "one hundred" and "ninety-nine" are frequent stereotypes in rabbinic teaching,[14] Jesus may be resorting to a conventional number. Its precise significance in the parable is that "the loss in comparison to what remains is so small."[15] In a flock of one hundred sheep, the loss of one is, all things considered, inconsequential. Israel's leaders did not go in search for every stray and lost sheep (Ezek 34:4). The lost sheep here, in contrast to the version of the parable in *Gos Thom.*

11. Schweizer, *Lukas,* 162, notes that Jesus himself is the interpretation of his own parables.

12. The relationship between the Matthean and Lukan versions of the parable is difficult to determine. Despite their obvious similarity, Luke's version assumes a successful search, whereas Matt's does not; and the joy of Luke's repentant sinner is greater than Matt's just people who need not repent. See Marshall, *Luke,* 600; Nolland, *Luke 9:21–18:34,* 771. These differences, combined with the different appropriation of the imagery in John 10 and *Gos. Thom.* 107, may imply that Jesus used the imagery on more than one occasion for slightly different purposes (so Klein, *Lukasevangelium,* 521-22).

13. Green, *Luke,* 574, argues that an average family possessed between five and fifteen sheep; hence a flock of one hundred indicates a wealthy shepherd. So too K. Bailey, *Poet and Peasant* and *Through Peasant Eyes* (Grand Rapids: Eerdmans, 1980), 148; A. Hultgren, *The Parables of Jesus: A Commentary* (Grand Rapids: Eerdmans, 2000), 53; Vinson, *Luke,* 504. In contrast, the Talmud considered three hundred sheep a large flock (*b. B. Qam.* 6.20). Jacob had a flock twice the size of the parable (Gen 32:14), and Job had a flock of 7,000 sheep, which at his restoration was doubled (Job 1:3; 42:12). Fitzmyer, *Luke (X–XXIV),* 1076, is probably correct in judging the shepherd prosperous, but not inordinately rich.

14. Str-B 1:784-85.

15. Plummer, *Luke,* 368.

107, is not the largest or most important in the flock. In the forbidding Judean wilderness a lost sheep might not be found; and even if it is, a shepherd who leaves his flock unprotected might lose more sheep than the stray he recovers. Reason would dictate that the shepherd should cut his losses, count his blessings, and go — happily.

This the shepherd does not do. He is not predicating decisions on strategies and outcomes. He is concerned about one lost sheep. One sheep in danger takes precedence over all other sheep well and safe. The shepherd "leaves the ninety-nine in open country and goes after the lost sheep until he finds it" (v. 4). "In the wilderness" (Gk. *en tē erēmō*) may connote a lost cause in the eyes of the world, perhaps even in the eyes of a shepherd, but in the Third Gospel "wilderness" signifies a place of divine rescue (3:2, 3; 4:1; 15:4). "The lost" (Gk. *to apolōlos*), a phrase that occurs only in Luke (15:4, 6; 19:10) and Ezek 34 (vv. 4, 16), links the language of the parable to God's search-and-rescue operation in Israel. God's sheep "were scattered over the whole earth, and no one searched or looked for them" (Ezek 34:6). Israel's leaders abandoned the search, but God declares, "I myself will search for my sheep and look for them. . . . I will search for the lost and bring back the strays" (Ezek 34:11, 16). The emphasis in both Luke and Ezek 34 falls on God's radical resolve not simply to undertake the search, but to complete it — to *find* the lost (v. 4).

"And when [not *if!*] he finds it, he joyfully puts it on his shoulders and goes home" (vv. 5-6). A rabbinic commentary on Exod speaks of Moses seeking for a lost sheep of his father-in-law Jethro, and finding it, he "put it on his shoulders and went home" (*Exod. Rab.* 2 [68b]). A wounded animal would need to be carried, perhaps also a healthy animal simply lost.[16] When one is lost, no thought is dearer than home; when one is searching, no thought more pleasing than finding. The image of a shepherd carrying the lost-and-found lamb on his shoulders is an image of sheer joy. True joy must be shared, hence the shepherd "calls his friends and neighbors together and says, 'Rejoice with me; I have found my lost sheep'" (v. 6). To analyze the economic cost of such a celebration is to miss its role in the parable.[17] The various elements related to the festivity are devoted to a single point: the joy in heaven over a converted sinner. Rabbinic literature also spoke of joy in heaven — joy when irritating people were vanquished, the wicked crushed, the godless condemned.[18] Jo-

---

16. J. Jeremias, *The Parables of Jesus* (rev. ed.; New York: Scribners, 1963), 134, followed by several recent scholars, maintains that a lost sheep will not move on its own but must be carried. Whatever the habits of stray sheep, the purpose of the imagery is to depict the joy of the shepherd.

17. Vinson's concern (*Luke*, 504-5) that a banquet will require the slaughter of a sheep, and that the woman will spend more in hosting a party than the value of the coin recovered, mistakes economic factors for the joy they are meant to convey.

18. Str-B 2:209.

nah longed for such joy in the destruction of Nineveh, and God's mercy on Nineveh caused him grief. The Pharisees would rejoice to see Jesus condemn tax collectors and sinners, and like Jonah, they grieve when he shares table fellowship with them (vv. 1-2). The joy "in heaven" — here a circumlocution for "God" — is caused by repentance of sinners, not by their condemnation; by conversion, not by destruction. Repentance is not the cause of God's love, but the result of God's love. The sheep, and even less the coin, do nothing to warrant being found. The pursuit of the lost and unworthy derives solely from the seeker. The reference to "ninety-nine righteous persons who have no need to repent" (v. 7) is not meant to imply that some have no need of repentance — the "righteous" Pharisees and scribes (vv. 1-2) and the elder brother (15:25-32) dispel that myth — but simply highlight God's joy in the repentance of *one* sinner, the recovery of *one* lost sheep.

8-10 For the third time in as many chapters Luke includes double parables on single themes: chap. 13 presented the growth of the kingdom of God in the parables of the Mustard Seed and Leaven (13:18-21), chap. 14 warned against thoughtless discipleship in the parables of the Rash Builder and the Rash King (14:28-32), and in 15:8-10 Luke follows the parable of the Lost Sheep with that of the Lost Coin. The present doublet consists of another male-female pair (see excursus at 14:1). Here Jesus likens God's redemptive work to that of a woman, a very common woman doing housework.

We all lose things from time to time. In this second parable, a woman has lost one of her ten drachmas. A drachma, a Greek silver coin that varied in weight and value in different times and places in the ancient world, frequently approximated the value of a denarius (= average daily wage, Matt 20:2). A day's paycheck is worth finding.[19] The woman's resolve to find the drachma rivals that of the shepherd to find the sheep (v. 4). Palestinian dwellings were typically constructed of stone or mud bricks, resulting in windowless, dark interiors. Many dwellings did not have stone floors, and a lost coin embedded in an earthen floor was hard to find. Recovering a coin in such a domicile is harder than it may appear. Hence, the woman "lights a lamp, sweeps the house, and searches carefully" (v. 8). The words in this verse are distinctively Lukan,[20] the last, *epimelōs* (NIV "carefully"), conveying a "painstaking" search. No it-will-turn-up-sooner-or-later attitude here. The woman scours the house "until she finds it" (v. 8). And when she does, "she calls her friends and neighbors together and says, 'Rejoice with me; I have found my lost coin'" (v. 9). Schweizer quotes the comment of a boy in a confirmation class when he heard this parable: "What a dumb woman! She spent more on the party than the coin was worth."[21]

19. On the value of a drachma, see Fitzmyer, *Luke (X–XXIV)*, 1081.

20. Jeremias, *Sprache des Lukasevangeliums*, 247.

21. Schweizer, *Lukas*, 162.

Exactly! From an economic point of view the woman's response is folly. The parable is not about economics, however. It is about God's grace, perhaps the *folly* of God's grace, that seeks the lost until they are found and, once found, celebrates their recovery in abandon. The joy of God has no price tag. "There is rejoicing in the presence of the angels of God over one sinner who repents" (v. 10).[22] A great chasm (16:26!) lies between the Pharisees and the kingdom of God at this point: they complain when Jesus eats with many sinners and tax collectors, yet all heaven rejoices when one of them repents!

HOW GREAT THE FATHER'S LOVE FOR US (15:11-32)

The third parable in Luke 15 makes a fresh start at v. 11. Its greater length and detail bring the lost-and-found theme in the first two parables to inimitable and immortal expression. This parable, even more than the parable of the Good Samaritan, has been the object of more theological commentary from the early church to the present, and has commended itself as the subject of more painters and artists, composers and musicians, dramatists, writers and poets than any other parable of Jesus.[23] In English the parable has always been known as The Prodigal Son, an expression indelibly engrained in English parlance, used and recognized even today by moderns who have lost familiarity with the Bible. If one insists on retaining "son" in the title, the parable could as justifiably be called The Lost Son (as it is in German) or "The Two Sons." The uniqueness of the parable does not consist in the sons, however. We all know people like the rebellious younger son or the resentful older one. At one time or another, in fact, most of us have been like the one or the other. But we have never known anyone like the father, nor would we claim to be such ourselves. The father is the first party named and the last to speak, the unique and causal figure in both halves of the parable. The relationship between the two sons has long eroded, as has their relationship to the family, although each in different ways. None of the problems posed in the parable can be solved without the father, who is the last remaining link of each son to the family. In varying ways, neither son's story is complete: we are not told, for instance, how the younger

22. Vinson, *Luke,* 506, praises these "ideal disciples. Each of them works hard to find the lost; neither of them is dissuaded by the cost of discipleship; each of them is a generous host, and ready to think of their own property as a gift to be shared with others." Excellent conclusions — but based on false premises. Neither parable is taught as a moral for discipleship; both are presented as illustrations of the unflagging, profligate love of God for sinners and of the joy of heaven at their repentance!

23. On the influence of the parable, see Fitzmyer, *Luke (X–XXIV),* 1083, and esp. the twelve-page survey in Bovon, *Lukas, 15,1–19,27,* 53-65.

son behaved once he was received back into the family; and more important, we are not told whether the older son overcame his resentment and joined the celebration. The father is the only finished character in the parable. He has done all that can and need be done to restore the family. The parable is about the indomitable love of the Father.

11-24 "There was a man who had two sons" (v. 11). Some people think all Christians are alike. The two sons in the parable, both sons of the one father, demolish that stereotype. Middle Eastern protocol would dictate that the characters in the parable should be heard from in order of seniority: father, older son, younger son. This protocol is disrupted when the younger son speaks first, and in a way that violates his social superiors. "Father, give me my share of the estate" (v. 12). According to Jewish custom, property was bequeathed through the male line, from father to son,[24] the first son being entitled to twice the amount given to other sons (Deut 21:17). A man with two sons would give two-thirds of his estate to the first son, and one-third to the second. The irregularity in the younger son's request is not the amount — he requests his share, not his brother's double share — but the request itself and its timing. Property was customarily disposed by a will executed after a father's death, not by request when he was alive (Num 27:8-11). It was regarded as unwise, though not exactly illegal, to dispose of property during one's lifetime.[25] The younger son's request shames both his father and his family. It is a certified public statement that he no longer wishes to live within or be identified by the family. In requesting what should become available only at his father's death, the son is, in effect, writing his father's death certificate. In ancient Jewish society, that was a virtually unforgivable offense.[26]

The father could have responded variously. He could have put the young man in his place: "I had to wait until my father was lowered in the ground, and you must too." He could have tried appeasement: "If your allowance is not enough, I'll double it." He could have taken a probationary approach: "I'll give you a half-section of property and see how you do with it." He could have appealed to the remaining shreds of his son's honor: "Don't subject our family to such disgrace." The father has authority to do any of these, but he forsakes them all. The son's resolve is such that the father's exercise of power and au-

---

24. *M. B. Bat.* 8:1, "Sons inherit from their father, and brothers by the same father." For discussions of ancient Jewish inheritance rights, see Vinson, *Luke,* 508; Wolter, *Lukasevangelium,* 531.

25. Sir 33:19: "Do not give power over yourself, as long as you live; and do not give your property to another, in case you change your mind."

26. K. Bailey, *Poet and Peasant* (Grand Rapids: Eerdmans, 1983), 161-66; W. Pöhlmann, *Der verlorene Sohn und das Haus: Studien zu Lukas 15,11-32 in Horizont der antiken Lehre von Haus, Erziehung und Ackerbau* (WUNT 68; Tübingen: Mohr Siebeck, 1993), 181-87; G. Forbes, "Repentance and Conflict in the Parable of the Lost Son (Luke 15:11-32)," *JETS* 42/2 (1999): 215.

thority, in whatever form, will likely drive him away forever.[27] The father opts for a more extraordinary and difficult way (1 Cor 12:31), the one remaining way that might reclaim his son — if he can be reclaimed at all. We are not told what the father felt or thought, only what he did. "He divided his property between them" (v. 12). The Greek uses two different words for "property" in v. 12. The son asks for *ousia,* an objective word for financial wealth. The father shares with him *bios,* one of several Greek words for "life." Luke uses *bios* to describe both the woman who "exhausted her (life's) earnings [*bios*] on doctors" (8:43) and the widow in the temple who, "out of her poverty, put in all she had to live on [*bios*]" (21:4). The father does not simply divide his assets; his skin is in the bequest.

The deal done, the parable — like the younger son — proceeds precipitously. "Not long after that" (Gk. lit. "after not many days") is a litotes — the use of a negative for understatement, a signature Lukan expression.[28] "The younger son got together all he had, set off for a distant country and there squandered his wealth in wild living" (v. 13). "Distant country" is a double helix packed with narrative DNA, both literal and metaphoric. In Jewish parlance, "distant land" usually signified a region beyond the sea — a long way off.[29] But in the parable the expression is a high-caliber metaphor: the son's receding footsteps to a far country quickly convert his inner alienation to spatial distance from the father. The word for "wealth" in v. 13 is again *ousia,* not *bios,* i.e., severed from all connection to the father, it is cash to be enjoyed! Money, anonymity, distance — all these release the son's stifled energies. He has it made! For a wise son, that could have been an opportunity. But passion has consumed whatever wisdom this young man once had. There, his dreams realized, "he squandered his wealth in wild living" (v. 13). His downfall was not the result of misfortune — accident, theft, recession, bad business deals, whatever. His circumstances did not *happen* to him, he *caused* them. In Greek, *zōn asōtōs* (v. 13; NIV "wild living") connotes "wasteful and dissolute pleasures." The expression, occurring nowhere else in the Greek Bible, is used by Josephus to describe an equally wasteful son who dissipated with unrestrained passion his father's hard-earned money (*Ant.* 12.203). The younger son gathered it all and lost it all in a hurry, from feast to famine in one verse.

The young man's folly is now compounded by forces beyond his control. Famine hits. In happier days, "distant country" (v. 13), "*that* country" (vv. 14,

27. On the father's options with the son, see E. Schweizer, *Jesus, das Gleichnis Gottes* (Göttingen: Vandenhoeck & Ruprecht, 1995), 66.

28. "The loss was no laughable matter" is an example of litotes. This is the sole litotes in the Third Gospel, but there are eighteen in Acts, including a repeat of the litotes of v. 13 in Acts 1:5. No other NT writer employs as many litotes as Luke (Jeremias, *Sprache des Lukasevangeliums,* 249).

29. Str-B 2:212-13.

15), spelled Land of Opportunity. Suddenly it becomes *alien,* a place far removed from the security and resources of home. Heretofore the young man savored the delights — and squandered his money — in "*that* country" simply by socializing. If he is now to survive, he must to do the repugnant — even for a Jew of loose commitments. The NIV says he "hired himself out to a citizen of that country," but that understates the offense of v. 15. A Jew could be hired by a Gentile without violating dietary laws, and thus without defiling himself. The Greek *kollan* (v. 15) does not mean "hire," but "to bind oneself closely to another, unite with, *cleave to.*" The boy must identify with "*that* country" in such a way that his Jewish identity is not only defiled but expunged. *Kollan* appears only once elsewhere in the Third Gospel, of the defiling dust of unbelief that must be shaken from the feet of missionaries (10:11). The young man, like his boss, has become a bona fide "citizen of that country." The boy is sent into the fields to feed swine, and his hunger is so great that he longs to eat their food (v. 16).[30] The Greek word for "pods," *keration* (= "small horn"), refers to *ceratonia siliqua,* a pod between four and ten inches (10-25 cm) long and up to an inch (2.5 cm) thick used as swine and donkey fodder. It could be — and probably was — consumed by the poor when necessary, but always, in rabbinic lore, as a symbol of bitter poverty.[31] *Keration* is a symbol of bitter poverty in v. 16. Jews considered pigs unclean animals (Lev 11:7; Deut 14:8; 1 Macc 1:47), and the prohibition of pork, along with circumcision and Sabbath observance, constituted an inviolable boundary between Jews and Gentiles. In the second century B.C., Antiochus IV sought to eradicate Judaism by uncircumcising Jews and forcing them to defile the temple by offering swine sacrifices (1 Macc 1:47). For Jews, pigs were a symbol of degradation, and to eat their food — well, no lower could a Jew fall. The son's plight is sealed in the phrase "no one gave him anything" (v. 16). Entirely alone, he is both prodigal and lost.

Loneliness and wretchedness have a salutary effect, however. The young man "came to his senses" (v. 17). "Want," writes Plummer, "rekindles what his revelry had extinguished."[32] The Greek expression behind "came to his senses," *eis heauton,* is a translation of the Hebrew *bilebo,* meaning "in his heart." Luke uses this phrase eleven times — all in Special Luke — to signify

---

30. The NIV translation, "[the boy] longed to fill his stomach," is supported by three strong uncial manuscripts (A Θ Ψ), but the shorter "longed to eat [or be satisfied]" commands stronger support (𝔭75 ℵ B D L). See Metzger, *TCGNT,* 139. Schlatter, *Lukas,* 358, queries whether "stomach" may be original, since "Luke was a physician, and from a physician one might expect a reference to the significance of the stomach." Whatever the value of this conjecture, the shorter reading ("he would have gladly fed on the pods that the swine ate," RSV) is preferable.

31. For discussions of the terms, see Str-B 2:213-14; Bock, *Luke 9:51–24:53,* 1311-12.

32. Plummer, *Luke,* 374.

inner ruminations that result in resolutions to act.[33] "How many of my father's hired servants have food to spare, and here I am starving to death!" (v. 17). The first consequence of "coming to one's senses" is clarity of thought and honest self-appraisal that in his present state he is utterly "perishing" (v. 17). The Greek word behind "perishing," *apollyein,* occurs eight times in Luke 15 with reference to "lost." It is an essential admission, for only the lost can be found. Scholars worry that his repentance was not entirely altruistic, that hunger rather than remorse drove him home.[34] That seems to me like worrying whether people are in church for the "right" reasons. Is it necessary that his motives be perfect for the father to receive him? Fortunately for all of us, the God of Jesus — and the father in the parable — is willing to accept a sinner on almost *any* terms!

The son translates his resolve into action — and into a speech to explain it: "I shall arise and go to my father and I shall say to him, 'I have sinned against heaven and before you'" (v. 18; similarly Hos 2:7). The fourfold repetition of the first-person verbs and a pronoun signifies the resolution to take full responsibility for his plight. The son's attitude to his father has changed. In parting, he spoke coldly, "Father" (v. 12); in returning, he speaks intimately, "*my* father" (v. 18). But one thing has not changed. The father is still *his* father. In his rebellion he addressed his father as such, and the relationship with his father, strained though it was, always admitted the possibility of repentance. The older son, by contrast, will never address his father as such, even though the father addresses him intimately (v. 31; Gk. *teknon,* "child").[35] In his heartless and disgraceful departure, the younger son offended his community, family, elder brother, and father. His confession omits all but the father, and includes another party otherwise unmentioned — heaven itself. The son's violation of his father is more than a social offense; it has a "vertical" as well as a "horizontal" dimension. In the Jewish world, as in the ancient world in general, an offense against one's father was an offense against the orders of creation, against heaven itself (Exod 10:16). If the sin is to be forgiven, it must be confessed to the ultimate parties offended.

So complete is the son's failure, in his mind, that he has forfeited the

---

33. 1:29(D); 7:39; 11:38(D); 12:17, 32(D); 16:3; 18:4; similarly *pros heauton* (18:11), *eis heauton/heautous* (7:30; 15:17); *eph' heautois* (18:9). See Edwards, *Hebrew Gospel,* 139. The expression is recognized as a Semitism by Jeremias, *Gleichnisse Jesu* (Göttingen: Vandenhoeck & Ruprecht, 1965), 129-30; and Marshall, *Luke,* 609; but as an Aramaism by Str-B 2:215.

34. Bailey, *Poet and Peasant,* 173-80, reads v. 17 as a shrewd and self-serving conspiracy on the son's part. This judgment sounds like that of the elder brother (v. 30). There is no evidence that it is true; even if it were, it would be less shrewd than the steward in the following parable (16:8), whom Jesus commends.

35. See here E. Nida, J. Louw, A. Snyman, and J. Cronje, *Style and Discourse* (Cape Town: Bible Society, 1983), 142; Vinson, *Luke,* 513.

right to be a son. "I am no longer worthy to be called your son" (v. 19), he confesses. This is doubtless the only statement in the parable on which both sons agree. The younger son asks not to be received as a son, but hired as a slave. "Make me like one of your hired servants" (v. 19). Despite the outward similarity between the two sons at this point, they stand poles apart from each other. The younger son, reckless in disobedience, confesses his sin; the elder son, ungrateful in obedience, insists on his rights. The younger renounces all claims to sonship and invites servitude; the elder complains of disappointed sonship and despises the servitude to which he thinks himself unfairly reduced. The younger receives mercy from his father; the elder accuses the father in resentful self-righteousness.[36]

The younger son first came to himself (v. 17), and now must come to his father (v. 20). "While he was still a long way off, his father saw him and was filled with compassion for him; he ran to his son, threw his arms around him, and kissed him" (v. 20).[37] The Greek word for "long way off," *makran*, is the same word used for "distant [country]" (v. 13). Its repetition is highly symbolic: the father extends compassion and forgiveness not when he knows of his son's repentance, but when, for all he knows, he is still in the "far" country. Forgiveness is not merited by repentance, but freely and unconditionally bestowed upon his son before he says a word. The son, of course, has no assurance that his father will so respond. The suspense is resolved in v. 20, the vocabulary of which is a key to the parable. The image of running, falling on one's neck, and kissing in forgiveness occurs only once elsewhere in Scripture: in Jacob's reconciliation with Esau. The younger son in the parable has offended both father and older brother on the issue of inheritance, as Jacob offended his father (Isaac) and older brother (Esau) on the same issue. Like Jacob, the younger son faces a day of reckoning: he "comes to himself" and goes back home. Jacob had reason to fear Esau, whom he defrauded; the younger son has reason to fear his father, whom he disgraced. Both fears were mistaken. Esau "ran to meet Jacob and embraced him; he threw his arms around his neck and kissed him" (Gen 33:4). The description of the reconciliation of Jacob and Esau

---

36. The two sons are contrasted differently by E. Nida et al., *Style and Discourse,* 142: "The young son sins and then repents, while the older son does not sin but is unforgiving. The younger son gets possession of his inheritance but wastes it, while the older son also gets possession but never enjoys it. . . . The younger son distances himself from his father but returns, while the older son stays with the father, but in reality distances himself emotionally from his father as well as from his brother."

37. Bailey, *Jesus through Middle Eastern Eyes,* 177, claims that "Middle Eastern adults do not run in public" without being exposed to "public humiliation." However true this may be in the Middle East today, it does not appear to have been the case in ancient Israel. A concordance check of "run" or "ran" reveals dozens of instances of adults running in Scripture without opprobrium (e.g., 19:4; Gen 33:4; Isa 40:31; Mark 10:17).

is unmistakably similar in theme, vocabulary, and syntax to the reconciliation of the younger son and the father.[38] It is not difficult to imagine that this redemptive key in the parable, perhaps the entire parable itself, was fashioned by Jesus on Jacob's inimitable meeting with Esau. So remarkable was Esau's response that Jacob believed he had seen "the face of God" (Gen 33:10). So it is with the younger son: both he and Jacob have been accosted by grace, and grace is the face of God.

The son commences the speech he has rehearsed on the long trek home. We know what he resolved to say when he first came to his senses (v. 18). We should not be surprised if, on further reflection, he qualified the speech. Something, surely, could be said in his defense; his offense, surely, was not as grave as initially thought. Even if the confession were cast in the passive rather than active voice, its intensity — and his guilt — would be softened. Had he done so, we might agree with those who doubt the son's sincerity. The same resolution in the far country, however, passes through his lips at his property line. "Father, I have sinned against heaven and against you. I am no longer worthy to be called your son" (v. 21). The son may wish to say more,[39] but the father cuts him off. The sin, forgiven before it was confessed, needs no further confession.

The father commands the servants with no less vigor than the host in the parable of the Great Banquet "compelled" guests to his banquet (14:23). "Quick! Bring the best robe and put it on him. Put a ring on his finger and sandals on his feet. Bring the fatted calf and kill it. Let's have a feast and celebrate" (vv. 22-23). Robe, ring, and sandals — all three signify status, reputation, and honor. Pharaoh promoted Joseph to vicegerent of Egypt with fine linen, signet ring, and gold necklace (Gen 41:42); King Xerxes promoted Haman by removing the signet ring from his finger and putting it on Haman's (Esth 3:10); King Antiochus made Philip ruler over his kingdom by means of a crown, robe, and signet ring (1 Macc 6:15); and Judith appeared before Holofernes with all these and more (Jud 10:4). Robe and ring signify enhanced status, but sandals signify *new* status, for going barefoot was a sign of humiliation and indignity (2 Sam 15:30; *b. Pesah.* 118a; *b. Šabb.* 152a), and especially slavery.

These gestures far exceed the son's needs. The servants could have satisfied his needs, but only his father can rehabilitate him, and rehabilitation requires honor. The son may return as a slave, but he will not be received as one. The slaughter of a calf in a culture where meat was a rarity signals a celebration.

---

38. Acts 20:37 is sometimes posited as a parallel to v. 20, although the verbal similarities between the two passages are not as close as those between v. 20 and Gen 33:4. More important, the theme of grace in v. 20 and Gen 33:4 is absent in Acts 20:37.

39. Three weighty and diverse manuscripts (ℵ B D) include "make me like one of your hired servants" at the end of v. 21. A longer and stronger manuscript tradition omits the phrase (𝔭[75] A L W Θ Ψ), however, suggesting that the phrase was added by later scribes who endeavored to harmonize v. 21 with v. 19.

The theme of rejoicing is introduced by the Greek *euphrainein*, a word that is unique to Luke among the Evangelists and reverberates through the parable (vv. 23, 24, 29, 32).[40] Some suppose that the death of the calf is symbolic of Christ's death, but this seems overly allegorical and out of character with the parable, for the death of Christ was not a celebration as is the slaughter of the fatted calf.[41] The son may imagine that the father would disown him, but to the contrary, the father distinguishes him, "'*This* my son was dead and is alive again; he was lost and is found.' So they began to celebrate" (v. 24). The son's rebellion and departure were a death, to himself and his father. His return — like the recovery of the lost sheep (v. 6) and lost coin (v. 9) — is a finding of the lost, the return of life itself!

25-32   A literary comedy is a story that begins in sorrow and ends in joy. This parable is a comedy — for all but the older son. He was out "in the field" (v. 25). That minor detail is actually a metaphor of the older son's separation from the father. The younger son was separated overtly, but the older son covertly. To all appearances, the field is a proper place for him to be: he is doing what he is supposed to be doing, and at an appropriate distance from the father. The younger brother's separation was obviously not safe, but the older brother's apparently is. Appearances are misleading, however, for of the two, the older is more dangerously separated. The reminder that the boys are "brothers" is important, for neither refers to the other as such, and the father must twice remind the older son that the renegade younger son is, in fact, his brother (vv. 27, 32). The relationship between the two sons is severed and, left to their powers alone, incapable of reconciliation. The only party capable of reconciling them to one another, and to their father, is the father himself.

Coming in from the field, the older son hears "music and dancing." Both terms contribute to the chorus of joy in the parable, and in chap. 15 as a whole. The lack of joy in the son's heart makes him suspicious of joy elsewhere, and jealous of its possibility at home. The joyless heart finds isolation safer than the risks of participation. He speaks not to the father — and certainly not to the brother — but summons "one of the servants and asked him what was going on" (v. 26). The servant need run no errand to answer, for the farm is abuzz with the news. Is the older son the only one who doesn't know? "Your brother has come," he replied, "and your father has killed the fatted calf because he has him back safe and sound" (v. 27). The older son might have found a way to tolerate the joy, had it concerned anyone but his brother. Mention of the brother and father stoke the embers of hatred and resentment to angry flame. The news could hardly be worse: his brother has returned — and returned *well,* no less. But it can be worse, and is: his father has *celebrated* his return by

---

40. On the theme and words for joy in the parable, see above, n. 2.
41. So Bock, *Luke 9:51–24:53,* 1315.

slaughtering the fattened calf and by receiving him "safe and sound." This last expression (Gk. *hygiainein*) carries both physical and social ramifications: the younger son is in good health, and he has been rehabilitated in the family. The news stops the older son in his tracks. The irony of the scene is unmistakable: the offended insider is himself a resentful outsider. Furious, he refuses to join the celebration (v. 28). His anger at the good fortune of his brother — and his father's celebration of it — is more than mere envy, serious as that is. It exhibits a spiritual dimension that the desert fathers and the Christian monastic tradition know as *acedia*. Also known as the deadly sin of sloth, *acedia* is terribly odd. It is sorrow at spiritual good. The human soul, says Dante, was "created prone to love," but to be slow in love or, worse, to resist love — and to rejoice in resisting it — is to become hideously disfigured. Only the healing gaze of grace, like sunlight thawing ice, can draw straight the deformed limbs and warm the stony face, till the contorted body blooms "as love would wish for its delight."[42]

The older son thinks his anger justified and consequently (unlike the younger son) does not "come to himself" (v. 17). Therefore, father must come to him. As in the case of the younger son, the father again forsakes indignation and reproach. Instead, he "pleads" (v. 28; Gk. *parekalei*), he "invites" and "implores." The imperfect tense of the verb implies constancy in appealing for a change of heart. The father's conciliation does not soften the son — at least not yet. It may even harden him, for grace sets the other free, even allowing retaliation, if that is the necessary precondition of reconciliation. The younger son rehearsed a speech for the father (vv. 18, 21), and the older son has an equally well-rehearsed speech for him as well (v. 29). First-person singular predominates in both speeches. The younger son confessed, "I have sinned without excuse"; the older son complains, "I have served without recompense." The older son launches a counteroffensive against the father — as do the Pharisees with Jesus (15:1-2). His duty has been faultless; he has "served" (Gk. *douleuein*) — for long years — and "never disobeyed your command" (v. 29). Instead of rewarding the son, the father has been mean and unfair. He has divided his "life" (vv. 12, 30) with the younger son and slaughtered a "fattened calf," the best of the flock, for him as well. But for his long-serving, longsuffering, and dutiful older son, the father would not even spare a "goat so I could celebrate with my friends" (v. 29). It is important to note that the coveted celebration of the older son does not include the father.

And of course the older son impugns the younger son: "When this son of yours who has squandered your property with prostitutes comes home, you kill the fattened calf for him!" (v. 30). "This son of yours" is calculated for maximum effect. It repeats "this my son" of v. 24, where it expressed the father's joy. Here it mocks the father for his folly in receiving a son who so

42. Dante, *Purgatory,* cantos 18-19.

egregiously dishonored him and the family. "This son of *yours*" widens the distance between the two sons in an attempt to justify the elder's judgment of the younger. We know the younger son squandered his inheritance, but we do not know for certain that he did so with prostitutes, mentioned here for the first and only time in Luke. In this matter many scholars are willing to give the benefit of the doubt to the younger son, and equally willing to doubt the benefits of the older. They attribute the mention of "prostitutes" to Schaden-freude — malicious delight — on the elder brother's part. The hypothesis may itself be evidence of Schadenfreude on the part of commentators against the elder brother — and the Pharisees he typifies. The facts are the following: the younger son squandered the inheritance, the father does not dispute the in-dictment of prostitutes, a dutiful son — and dutiful Pharisees (15:1-2) — would find prostitution particularly offensive. As for the attraction of prostitutes for a reckless young man with cash in his pocket and anonymity in a far country, well . . . you be the judge. Evidence favors the veracity of the accusation.

The older brother admittedly has a strong case. So do the Pharisees. Righteous people — genuinely righteous people as opposed to hypocrites — usually do. The older son's case is as strong — more so — as those of the guests who begged off from attending the Great Banquet (14:16-24). Why should he go into the banquet? He has his honor to defend! The father is wise to all this. Indeed, his wisdom is the result of his inestimable love, which alone can save his son from himself and his self-righteousness. At this point the parable diverges from the standard Israelite tale — at least as illustrated in the OT — where the younger son is made the hero and object of favor over the elder son.[43] The older son is indeed repellant and unlovable, but so was the younger son. The older son, no less than the younger, is the object of the father's unfath-omable love. The father's invitation of the unworthy to his banquet table is a foreshadowing of the invitation of the unworthy to the table of the Eucharist.

The father does not address or redress the older son's reasons. One issue alone is at stake: the son's relation to the father. Not even the best of reasons is good enough to jeopardize that relationship. "My son," his father said, "you are always with me, and everything I have is yours" (v. 31). This is a direct appeal to *acedia*, mentioned earlier. The older son is like many people who have enjoyed a long relationship with God. His love for the father has grown cold, he has become callous and complaining, he harbors bitterness about the life that passed him by. He has been faithful over the years, and he imagines

---

43. Examples of favor shown to the younger brother over the older abound in Scripture: Cain and Abel, Ishmael and Isaac, Esau and Jacob, the older brothers and Joseph, Manasseh and Ephraim, Aaron and Moses, the older brothers and David, the older brothers and Sol-omon. See G. Forbes, "Repentance and Conflict in the Parable of the Lost Son," *JETS* 42/2 (1999): 223.

that the father owes him a reward. Having not received what he imagines, he thinks himself justified in his bitterness. So bitter is he that he will not address his father as such. The father nevertheless speaks more tenderly to the older brother than to the younger, calling him *teknon* (v. 31). English translations (incl. NIV) usually render the word "son," but that is a disappointing approximation, owing to the fact that English does not have a term of endearment for a grown male. *Teknon* literally means "child," connoting the affection, nurture, and protectiveness of a parent for a child, or even "of a hen that gathers her chicks [Gk. *teknon*] under her wings" (13:34). To the accusation that the father "never" threw a party for the older son (v. 29), the father asserts, "My Son, you are always with me, and everything I have is yours" (v. 31). The description in v. 31 of the relationship of the father to the son — yes, this disgusting elder son — is formulated in the most absolute and unconditional way possible.[44] The only description in the NT analogous to it is that of Jesus and the Father, "All things have been committed to me by the Father" (10:22); "All that I have is yours, and all that you have is mine" (John 17:6, 10).[45]

This reality alone — in comparison with which no excuse in the universe, real or imagined, is worth an ounce of salt — is the reason the older son must "celebrate and be glad, because this brother of yours was dead and is alive again; he was lost and is found" (v. 32). The emphasis on "must" in the father's final speech (v. 32; Gk. *edei*; NIV "had to") recalls the emphasis on "compel" in the parable of the Great Banquet (14:23): deep and undying love is loath to take No for an answer (John 10:28-29). The father has let many angry words pass, but one point must be put right. The older brother referred to his brother dismissively as "this your son" (v. 30), but the father sets the record straight, "This *your* brother was dead and is alive again; he was lost and is found" (v. 32). In restoring the family, the father's love has created a *new* family. The father has regained his son, and hence the older son has regained — or gained for the first time — a brother.

The parable of the Prodigal Son ends unfinished, for the older son's fate is not resolved. This open-endedness follows a pattern that Luke repeats elsewhere in the Gospel, including the story of Simon the Pharisee (7:36-50), the fate of the fig tree (13:6-9), and the Pharisee who hosts Jesus (14:1-6). In each case the unfinished character is a Pharisee (or representative of Judaism, 13:6-9). There can be little doubt that the older son symbolizes Pharisees/Judaism as well. This conclusion is already anticipated in 15:1-2, and it is endorsed by nearly all commentators. The fact that Marcion (see Introduction) omitted this parable from his recension of Luke argues for the same understanding. Had the parable ended with the fate of the younger son (= Gentiles), Marcion

---

44. Marshall, *Luke*, 612.
45. See Schlatter, *Lukas*, 356-57.

would surely have included it, for the redemption of Gentiles fit like a glove with his theology. The gracious treatment of the older brother (= Jews), in contrast, was patently offensive to Marcion — indeed grounds for expunging the parable wholesale.

V. 31 is of revolutionary importance for a Christian understanding of Judaism. All four Gospels report that Jewish opposition attended Jesus' ministry from his baptism in Galilee to his death in Jerusalem. That similar opposition attended the fledgling Christian movement in Luke's day can scarcely be doubted. The fierce opposition (11:53) and grumbling of Pharisees against Jesus (15:2) must describe the historic experience of both Jesus and Luke's audience. How remarkable that, with the exception of the admonition in v. 31, no word of accusation is lodged by the father against the older son. He has not disobeyed the father's orders (v. 29), and no greater service is expected from him. He has always been with the father (v. 31). Their relationship, as noted above, is characterized in terms that elsewhere in the NT characterize the ontological relationship of Jesus and the Father. If the older son symbolizes Pharisees, no portrait of them in all the NT is more positive.[46]

Only one thing is missing: the older son has yet to learn that "righteousness" is not achieved by his worthy obedience. It is a gift conferred by the father's love, and it is received by joining the banquet. In so doing, the son not only bears the family name, he joins the father's mission. His righteousness is not his own, the result of obedience to the law (v. 29!), "but that which comes through faith in Christ" (Phil. 3:9). This description is intentionally drafted in Pauline terminology, for Saul of Tarsus was the quintessential older son, whose self-description ("a Pharisee whose righteousness according to law was faultless," Phil 3:6) is practically interchangeable with the older son's ("all these years I continued serving you and never violated your command," v. 29). According to the virtually unanimous witness of early Christianity, Luke was a protégé of Paul. It seems very possible to imagine that Luke did not intend the stories of Simon the Pharisee, the fig tree, the Pharisee host, and yes, the older brother, to be understood as stories with open or unfinished endings, but rather with *delayed* endings. The intended completion comes in the Acts of the Apostles in the conversion of Saul of Tarsus, whose acceptance of his father's love for him on the road to Damascus enabled him also to accept the Gentile mission of Christ and join the Father's banquet!

---

46. Schlatter, *Lukas*, 356-57.

CHAPTER FIFTEEN

Trust in Wealth versus Wealth in Trust

Luke 16:1-31

Luke 16 begins (vv. 1-8) and ends (vv. 19-31) with parables, although neither is expressly identified as such. Both parables commence with the same formula, "There was a certain rich man . . . ," and both deal with the theme of wealth. The first shows how wealth can be used for one's welfare, and the second how wealth can pave the way for disaster.[1] Between the two parables is included a series of shorter sayings on fidelity regarding "mammon" (vv. 10-12) and masters (v. 13), God's omniscience of the human heart (vv. 14-15), the enduring significance of the law (vv. 16-17), and divorce and remarriage (v. 18). These sayings are not specifically about wealth, although they all share the general theme of fidelity and loyalty. The intervening sayings are not entirely unrelated to the two parables, for vv. 9-13 are appended as interpretations of the first (vv. 1-8); and vv. 14-18 anticipate somewhat less obviously the second (vv. 19-31). With the exception of vv. 13, 16-18,[2] all the material in chap. 16 is unique to Luke or his special source. Luke thus places economics in an editorial package with other primary allegiances of human life, all of which are defined by the overarching theme of trust. Luke 16 teaches that wealth and possessions, like allegiances to masters, spouses, and Torah, are given their rightful place in life and fulfill their purpose when they are made subservient to the sovereignty and service of God.

THE PARABLE OF THE SHREWD MANAGER (16:1-13)

The parable known as the Dishonest Steward (vv. 1-8) presents a unique challenge because it begins with a master dismissing a steward for dishonesty,

---

1. Schlatter, *Lukas*, 363.
2. V. 13 (par. Matt 6:24); vv. 16-17 (par. Matt 11:12-13; 5:18); v. 18 (par. Matt 19:9; Mark 10:11-12).

yet ends with the master praising the steward for an act of greater dishonesty (v. 8; Gk. *adikia,* "unrighteousness"). A bewildering array of proposals has been advanced to explain the parable, some of which are as ingenious as the shrewd steward himself.[3] The interpretive difficulties are related to three problems. First and most obviously, why does the master praise the unjust steward (v. 8)? In conjunction with this, is it possible, as some modern interpreters argue, that the steward was not a villain but a hero — at least of sorts? Second, the Greek *kyrios* (v. 8) could refer either to the rich man in the parable or to Jesus — but which? Third, at what point does the parable end and the interpretation of Jesus (or Luke) begin? Each of these questions will be discussed in the following exposition.

1-9 Jesus' audience is no longer Pharisees (chap. 15) but "disciples" (v. 1) and will remain so through v. 13. No fewer than six parables in Luke begin with "a certain rich man," three of them verbatim (12:16; 16:1, 19), and three stated similarly (10:30; 14:16; 19:12). The rich man in this parable is not significant in himself but only in relation to his "steward" (v. 1; Gk. *oikonomos;* NIV "manager"). Luke mentioned the office of *oikonomos* earlier in 12:42-43 and there made two observations essential to its understanding here. An *oikonomos* could hold responsibilities as an administrator, manager, or superintendent of an owner's estate, affairs, and other slaves (12:42). Nevertheless, an *oikonomos* could still be a slave, albeit an entitled slave (12:43).[4] Readers whose conception of **slavery** has been formed by the institution of slavery in the Americas may be surprised to learn that a slave could be entrusted with such responsibilities. Slaves in Israel were not reduced to the absolute category of chattel, nor to the virtual animal servitude that typified American slavery. Lev 25:40 summed up the general rule governing slavery in Israel: slaves were to be treated as hired workers and were indebted to six years of service. Treatment of non-Hebrew slaves was bleaker than that of Hebrew slaves, but all Israelite slaves were guaranteed control over portions of their personal time. Slaves were not obligated to wash and dress their masters in Israel, although they were obligated to serve them in most other ways, including preparation of food. The greatest difference from American slavery was that first-century Mediterranean slaves — and this included Greco-Roman as well as Jewish slavery — could fulfill professional functions in medicine, education, and busi-

---

3. Bovon, *Lukas 15,1–19,27,* 66-70, lists some 175 books, monographs, and scholarly articles (apart from commentaries) in his bibliography for 16:1-9. Equally remarkable, J. A. Bengel, whose pithy *Gnomon of the New Testament* rarely devotes more than a concise paragraph to a verse, devotes an unprecedented five pages to vv. 8-9 (*Gnomon,* 2:144-49).

4. This description of *oikonomos* holds for the Third Gospel, but Paul's use of the same term, while sometimes describing an entitled slave (Gal 4:2), at others seems to intend an administrator who was either a citizen or freedman (Rom 16:23). On the term, see Str-B 2:193, 217-18; O. Michel, *oikonomos, TWNT* 5:151-55.

ness administration. Included in the last category were slaves who served as authorized deputies of their masters by administering their estates, business transactions, property, and personnel.[5]

The significance in the parable of the Office of Steward, which was introduced in 12:42-43, is signaled by three repetitions of the officeholder (*oikonomos*, vv. 1, 3, 8) and by four repetitions of the office itself (*oikonomia*, vv. 2, 3, 4; *oikonomein*, v. 2).[6] The emphasis on the office of manager is essential for an understanding of its *mismanagement*, which is stressed in the parable even more emphatically. In a peer review, the steward is "accused" (v. 1; Gk. *diaballein*) of "squandering" (v. 1; Gk. *diaskorpizein*; NIV "wasting") his master's possessions. The details need not be rehearsed, for the scandalous behavior of the younger son in 15:13, also characterized by *diaskorpizein*, conveys the degree of the steward's mismanagement. Summoned to give account of his dealings, the steward is sacked from service (v. 2). The master's question, "What is this I hear about you"? (v. 2), appears in variant forms in Acts 14:15 (also Gen 12:18; 20:9; 42:28), in each instance implying the credibility of the charge. The master's summons, "Give an account of your management" (v. 2), need not be restricted to "hand over the account books."[7] The Greek expression, *apodidonai (ton) logon*, regularly in the NT and early Christian literature means, "give an account" or "explain" something.[8] The master knows the steward has no grounds to stand on and terminates him posthaste.

The steward offers no defense but "reflects on his predicament" (*eipen en heautō*, v. 3; NIV "said to himself"). *En heautō*, which occurs nearly a dozen times in Luke, refers to inner monologues that lead to decisive action.[9] Here it means to "come to one's senses." The steward reviews his shrinking options. "My master is taking away my job. I'm not strong enough to dig, and I am

---

5. On slavery in Israel, see Str-B 4/2:698-744; Fitzmyer, *Luke (X–XXIV)*, 1097-98. Cato the Elder (234-149 B.C.) describes the duties and qualifications of a farm steward thus: "He must show good management. The feast days must be observed. He must withhold his hands from another's goods and diligently preserve his own. He must settle disputes among the slaves. . . . He must extend credit to no one without orders from the master, and must collect the loans made by the master. He must lend to no one seed-grain, fodder, spelt, wine, or oil. He must have two or three households, no more from whom he borrows and to whom he lends. He must make up accounts with the master often. . . . He must not want to make any purchases without the knowledge of the master, nor want to keep anything hidden from the master" (*Cato and Varro: On Agriculture* [trans. W. Hooper and H. Ash; Cambridge: Harvard University Press, 1934], 13-15; cited from Vinson, *Luke*, 520).

6. Bovon, *Lukas 15,1–19,27*, 75, also notes the emphatic repetition of *oikonomos*.

7. So Bailey, *Jesus through Middle Eastern Eyes*, 335, who overemphasizes this point in his discussion of the parable.

8. Matt 12:36; Acts 19:40; Rom 14:12; Heb 13:17; 1 Pet 3:15; 4:5; Josephus, *Ant.* 16.120; Justin, *Dial.* 116.1. See Str-B 2:218; BDAG, 600; Bovon, *Lukas 15,1–19,27*, 76.

9. 1:29(D); 7:30, 39; 11:38(D); 12:17, 32(D); 15:17; 16:3; 18:4, 9, 11.

ashamed to beg" (v. 3). The present tense of this saying allows readers/hearers momentarily to eavesdrop on the steward's desperate musings.[10] This is immediately followed by an explosive *egnōn* (v. 4; aorist form), "I've got it!" or "It just came to me!"[11] Optimism quickly dispels the steward's initial desperation. Once discharged by the master, he will use what got him into trouble to get him out of trouble! He will devise a recovery strategy for self-gain (v. 4) that cheats his master by reducing sums debtors owe the master (v. 5-8).

The steward summons each of the debtors and asks what they owe. The steward probably has a good idea what each owes, but by requiring the debtors to declare the exact amount owed and then falsifying the account in their presence, the debtors are made accomplices in fraud, thus ensuring their obligation to the steward in the future.[12] One debtor owes "a hundred baths of oil" (v. 6). A *bath* was a Hebrew liquid measure amounting to some thirty-four liters, or nine gallons. A hundred baths was thus about 900 gallons of oil, worth more than a year's earning. "Slash the figure in half," orders the steward, "and write fifty baths." Another debtor owes "a hundred kors of wheat" (v. 7). *Kor* could be a liquid (1 Kgs 5:25[11]) or, more frequently, a Hebrew dry measure. As the latter, it was the equivalent of 350 to 400 liters, or ten to twelve bushels, nearly 120 bushels in v. 7.[13] The debtor's bill is reduced by one-fifth to eighty kors. This amount of wheat was worth far more than fifty baths of oil, probably amounting to several years' wages. These Hebrew measures, which are not converted to standard Greek *(xestai)* or Roman *(sextarii)* measures, attest to the Hebrew provenance of this parable. The "bill" (Gk. *ta grammata*) refers to the altered promissory note, or IOU.

In the parable, the steward fails every test in the dispatch of his office. A single verbal gavel, *adikia* (v. 8) — "wrongdoing, unrighteousness, wickedness" — sums up his behavior. That comes as no surprise to readers of the parable, and it may have been even less surprising to Luke's original audience, for the venality of slaves was common knowledge (or prejudice) in the Greco-Roman world.[14] What comes as a total surprise is that "the master *praised* the unjust steward because he acted shrewdly" (v. 8, my translation). What is praiseworthy, we ask, and who is praising him? With regard to the second question,

---

10. Gk. *aphairetai* is middle in form but active in meaning (BDAG, 154).

11. See Bock, *Luke 9:51–24:53*, 1329.

12. Bock, *Luke 9:51–24:53*, 1329; Green, *Luke,* 645.

13. These figures are taken from BDAG, 171, 560; Fitzmyer, *Luke (X–XXIV),* 1100-1101; Bock, *Luke 9:51–24:53*, 1330-31; *HALOT* 1:496. On the basis of Josephus, *Ant.* 8.57, Str-B 2:218 calculates a *bath* to be thirty-nine liters; one hundred *baths* would thus be nearly 1,050 gallons.

14. K. Bradley, *Slaves and Masters in the Roman Empire* (Oxford: University Press, 1987), 27-35; M. Beavis, "Ancient Slavery as an Interpretative Context for the New Testament Servant Parables, with Special Reference to the Unjust Steward (Luke 16:1-8)," *JBL* 111/1 (1992): 38-43; F. Udoh, "The Tale of an Unrighteous Slave (Luke 16:1-8 [13])," *JBL* 128/2 (2009): 315-24.

some scholars conclude the parable at v. 7, with Jesus' interpretation beginning in v. 8 following. If this is correct, then "master" in v. 8 (Gk. *kyrios*) refers to Jesus rather than to the master in the parable.[15] Terminating the parable at v. 7 seems premature, however, for it leaves the parable open-ended[16] and without reasonable clues to its meaning. Luke provides an obvious transition in v. 9, where Jesus speaks in first person. This implies a termination of the parable at v. 8 rather than at v. 7. Thus, the *kyrios* of v. 8 (as in vv. 3, 5) reasonably refers to the master of the parable.

Now to the first and major question why the manager is praised. Several new interpretations have been proposed in the past generation in answer to this question. Some argue that the reduction of debts makes the master look generous and thus enhances his honor. When the master learns the ugly facts of the steward's deception, he chooses not to revoke the contractual changes made by the steward (and thereby scotch his reputation for generosity), but ride the wave of the deception in hopes that his enhanced honor will outweigh the losses incurred by the steward's chicanery.[17] In order to be successful, this hypothesis requires that the debtors actually imagine the master to be generous, for whatever honor they accord him will depend on their opinion of his generosity. But given the information in the parable, how could the debtors imagine the master generous? The hurried and deceptive methods of the steward, and the way the debtors are made accomplices in the deception, clearly testify to the fraud of the steward rather than to the generosity of the master.

Others argue that the parable is about the reputation of the master rather than that of the steward. As paterfamilias, the master was expected to exert complete control over his household (wives, children, slaves). News of a rogue steward threatens this reputation, which the master restores by dismissing the steward.[18] This interpretation satisfies the first two verses of the parable, but it does not explain the steward's subsequent fraudulent actions or the master's final praise of him. Moreover, the focus of the parable is not on the master or his reputation, but on the steward and his dilemma. Yet another proposal is that the debt reductions represent the interest that the master was charging on his loans. Since charging interest was legally prohibited in Torah (Deut 23:19) — although tolerated in practice — the steward is praised by

15. So Schlatter, *Lukas,* 365-66; Bultmann, *The History of the Synoptic Tradition* (rev. ed.; New York: Harper & Row, 1972), 175-76; Leaney, *Luke,* 220; Grundmann, *Lukas,* 318; Wolter, *Lukasevangelium,* 544.

16. The case of the older son is left open in 15:31, but the father's concluding words prompt the leading question to resolve the parable: will he join the celebration or not? The conclusion of the parable of the Shrewd Manager at v. 7 leaves no analogous question.

17. E.g., D. Landry and B. May, "Honor Restored: New Light on the Parable of the Prudent Steward," *JBL* 119/2 (2000): 287-309; Bailey, *Jesus through Middle Eastern Eyes,* 338-41.

18. J. Kloppenborg, "The Dishonored Master (Luke 16,1-8a)," *Bib* 70 (1989): 475-79.

the master for bringing his business practices into alignment with Torah.[19] A variant interpretation suggests that the amount reduced was actually the steward's commission rather than his master's money.[20] Whether slaves were allowed a financial commission — a 100 percent commission, no less, in the case of oil! — would need to be established before this interpretation becomes plausible. Moreover, v. 5 ("How much do you owe my *master?*") assumes the entire sum (and not just the principal) is owed the master. With regard to the interest theory in general, scholars rightly question whether an interest rate of 100 percent (v. 6) is plausible in a culture that, in principle, forbade interest?[21]

Each of the foregoing sociological or economic conditions may have existed in one form or another in first-century Palestine. That is not the issue, however. The issue is whether *this parable* bears evidence of such conditions, and whether the outstanding questions in the parable are resolved by such evidence. I am not persuaded that the answer to either question, and particularly the second, is affirmative. Positive appraisals of the steward run aground on the reef of v. 8, for the steward is summarily described as "a steward of *unrighteousness.*" Thus the actions of the steward are not upheld as models in the parable. They are expressly called *adikia,* which in Greek means "wickedness, injustice, wrongdoing." Moreover, the steward is not called a "son of *light,*" but rather a "son of *this world*" (v. 8; NIV "people of this world"). What the steward is praised for is not his unrighteousness but his "shrewdness" or "prudence." This is the key that unlocks the parable.[22] The Greek word for "shrewdly," *phronimōs,* occurs only this once in the Bible, although its adjectival form characterizes "the faithful and wise [Gk. *phronimos*] manager" in 12:42. Throughout the Wisdom literature this same adjective is upheld as the ideal of the wise and prudent person. "Shrewdness," no less than "praise," is a commendation in v. 8. What is praiseworthy about the steward's shrewdness? Unlike the "sons of light," who may retreat into pious passivity in the face of opposition, the shrewd manager forms a plan and acts on it. When all hope seems lost, he does what he can, even if the little he can do may not seem to amount to much. His positive action spares him from resignation and cynicism. In contrast to the parable of the Rich Man who amassed wealth without

<hr />

19. J. Derrett, "Fresh Light on St. Luke XVI: The Parable of the Unjust Steward," *NTS* 7 (1960-61): 198-219.

20. J. Fitzmyer, "The Story of the Dishonest Manager (Lk 16:1-13)," *TS* 25 (1964): 23-42; idem, *Luke (X–XXIV),* 1098.

21. For further discussion and critique of the above, as well as other proposed interpretations, see D. Matthewson, "The Parable of the Unjust Steward (Luke 16:1-13): A Reexamination of the Traditional View in Light of Recent Challenges," *JETS* 38/1 (1995): 29-40.

22. T. W. Manson, *The Sayings of Jesus* (London: SCM, 1964), 292: "There is all the difference in the world between 'I applaud the dishonest steward because he acted cleverly,' and 'I applaud the clever steward because he acted dishonestly.'"

any thought of the future (12:16-21), the master praises the steward, scoundrel though he is, for his ingenuity in figuring out a way of providing for his future by using his soon-to-be-lost financial power. He is indeed a "son of this world," but he is more prudent in planning for the only future he is concerned about than the typical religious person is in planning for his eternal future with God.[23]

The long-standing objection to this interpretation is whether Jesus would praise such a steward. The modern West may frown upon shrewdness as manipulative or deceptive, but the biblical world, like much of the Middle East still today, frequently admired it. A number of stories in the OT commend unjust people who act cleverly.[24] Tamar (Gen 38), Rahab (Josh 2), and Judith (Jdt 8–14) are all praised for ingenuity that is no less morally dubious than the steward's. Abraham deceives Pharaoh and becomes wealthy (Gen 12:10–13:2), Rebecca deceives Isaac and preserves Israel's line (Gen 27), Jacob cheats Laban and prospers (Gen 30:25-43), and the Israelites despoil the Egyptians before the exodus (Exod 3:22). In a mirror plot of the shrewd manager, Absalom succeeds in winning the hearts of all Israel by cutting deals with his father's debtors (2 Sam 15:1-6). The responses of Jesus himself to the questions of his authority (20:1-8), paying taxes to Caesar (20:20-26), and the resurrection (20:27-38) are manifestly shrewd (although not unjust). The interpretation of the parable of the Shrewd Manager follows in this tradition. The scene, to put it in modern terms, is that of a recently terminated middle manager who double-deals with company debtors on the main floor of corporate headquarters while his CEO sits in the boardroom upstairs. When the CEO learns what has happened, he says in admiring disbelief, "I've got to hand it to you. You've turned a pink slip into a promotion!"

The second half of v. 8 explains the master's praise, "For the people of this world are more shrewd in dealing with their own kind than are the people of the light." It is difficult to know for sure who makes this pronouncement. It furthers the thought of v. 8a, and since Jesus does not formally speak until v. 9, it could derive from the master in the parable. V. 8b commences the interpretation of the parable, however, and interpretations are rarely included in Jesus' parables. The presence of Greek *hoti* at the start of v. 8b suggests an explanatory transition similar to 18:6, where Jesus explains the parable of the Unjust Judge. The parable thus appears to end at v. 8a. It is my understanding that Jesus' interpretation of the parable begins in v. 8b, although it appears that

---

23. The foregoing wording is indebted to my predecessor at Jamestown College, Dr. Harold Strandness (personal letter dated January 13, 1981). This general position is also adopted by many scholars, including Schweizer, *Lukas*, 168; Matthewson, "Parable of the Unjust Steward," 40; Bovon, *Lukas*, 15,1–19,27, 78; Klein, *Lukasevangelium*, 538.

24. What Wolter, *Lukasevangelium*, 544, thinks "extremely improbable" is not infrequently attested in Scripture.

the voices of Luke as narrator and Jesus are conflated in v. 8b, similar to the frequent conflation of the voice of the Fourth Evangelist and Jesus.

Four phrases in vv. 8b-9 signal a key change in the narrative — "people of this world," "people of the light," "unrighteous mammon," and "eternal dwellings." All four reflect a Semitic background.[25] The contrast between the first two — conflicting ages or aeons — was typical of Judaism and early Christianity.[26] This contrast is applied to the parable. The rogue steward exhibits more forethought (14:28-32) and "street smarts" than Jesus' own followers. Bengel sees in the contrast between people of light and darkness both a defense of and an admonition for Christians: "The sons of light do not exceedingly care for this world. On this account the sons of this world easily excel them, and carry off from them the commendation of superiority; nor do the sons of the light always evince as much prudence and vigilance even in spiritual matters [as the sons of the world evince in temporal matters]."[27]

Jesus' interpretation is introduced in v. 9, "I tell you," which is emphatic in Greek.[28] "Make friends for yourselves from unrighteous mammon, so that when it is gone they will receive you into eternal dwellings" (v. 9). The accent of this exhortation falls on "yourselves" *(heautois),* which in Greek is placed emphatically at the front of the sentence. Jesus' exhortation is thus not about money per se, but about what disciples do with money. The Greek word for "receive" *(dechesthai)* is used throughout Luke to signal the theme of hospitality, including divine hospitality.[29] "Unrighteous mammon" (lit. "mammon of unrighteousness") is a Hebraic expression occurring in *1 En.* 63:10 and in a variant "wealth of evil" in Qumran (1QS 10:19; see also CD 6:15).[30] It could refer to money procured unjustly, of course, but it should not be restricted to that understanding alone. An inherent characteristic of humans is to place trust in mammon — money and material wealth. That which trusts in something other than God either rivals or replaces God, and is thus "unrighteous."[31]

This understanding is reinforced by the etymology of "mammon," which almost certainly derives from the Hebrew *aman* (from which *amen* is derived), meaning "to place trust in."[32] Jesus earlier warned of the danger

---

25. Fitzmyer, *Luke (X–XXIV),* 1105.

26. John 12:36; 1 Thess 5:5; Eph 5:8; *1 En.* 108:11; 1QS 1:9; 2:16; 3:13, 20; 1QM 1:3, 9, 11, 13.

27. Bengel, *Gnomon,* 2:147.

28. So Lagrange, *Luc,* 433-34; Klein, *Lukasevangelium,* 541; Rowe, *Early Narrative Christology,* 156.

29. 2:28; 9:5, 48, 53; 10:8, 10; 16:4; 18:17.

30. Edwards, *Hebrew Gospel,* 319; BDF §165. Jeremias, *Sprache des Lukasevangeliums,* 232, characterizes "of righteousness" as a "semitisierende Genitivverbindung" (Semitic genitive copulative). On "mammon," see the excursus in Klein, *Lukasevangelium,* 544.

31. Plummer, *Luke,* 385; Bovon, *Lukas 15,1–19,27,* 80.

32. So Fitzmyer, *Luke (X–XXIV),* 1109; Wolter, *Lukasevangelium,* 550.

material possessions pose for disciples (14:33). "Mammon *of unrighteousness*" recalls "steward *of unrighteousness*" immediately preceding in v. 8, implying that believers should make friends with mammon as the steward did. Who are the "friends"? The linking of "friends" with "eternal dwellings" (v. 9) suggests divine beings, perhaps angels as advocates of those who do works of mercy and show financial generosity.[33] This is possible, although a more inclusive understanding according to the imagery of 13:23-30 may be preferable, where God counts works of mercy done to the least of his creatures as works done to himself (e.g., Matt 25:40, 45).[34] This understanding anticipates the wording and thought of v. 10. A further relation with 13:23-30 is implied by the parallel expressions "workers of unrighteousness" (13:27) and "mammon of unrighteousness" (v. 9). The Greek word for "eternal *dwellings*" *(skēnas)* can signify either an earthly tent or the tabernacle of God in the wilderness. Either meaning could apply in v. 9, depending on how one deals with "unrighteous mammon." Trust in mammon draws one into an "eternal (earthly) tent." This expression is an oxymoron, for a tent, like mammon, is not eternal. Yet, mammon entrusted to God leads one into a "tabernacle," for earthly mammon is used for eternal purposes. Thus, disciples, like the unrighteous steward, should use their wits and wealth in ways that please and serve God, for in so doing they will be received into the eternal tabernacle of God, rather than into the transitory earthly tents of debtors.[35]

10-13 To the parable of the Shrewd Manager, Luke appends two further mammon-sayings, one about faithfulness, the other about serving two masters. "Whoever can be trusted with very little can also be trusted with much, and whoever is dishonest with very little will also be dishonest with much" (v. 10). This is a maxim about character. Character is not determined by something external to itself, such as reward, but is of a single and consistent disposition regardless of reward. It is often difficult to judge the importance of a given matter. What may seem important at the time may turn out to be of little importance later on, and vice versa. Character gives attention to matters in proportion to their merit, not to their potential reward. V. 10 is an all-encompassing maxim, which not surprisingly was remembered and repeated in early Christianity (*2 Clem.* 8:5-6; Irenaeus, *Haer.* 2.56.1). A Jewish midrash on Exod 3:1 cites a similar maxim: Moses and David were faithful in shepherding sheep, and God consequently made them shepherds over his people.[36]

The word for "dishonest" (v. 10; Gk. *adikos*) is of the same root as the

---

33. E.g., *m. 'Abot* 4:11, "He that performs one precept gets for himself one advocate; but he that commits one transgression gets for himself one accuser." So Grundmann, *Lukas*, 321.

34. So too Bovon, *Lukas 15,1–19,27*, 80.

35. Plummer, *Luke*, 386.

36. Cited from Bock, *Luke 9:51–24:53*, 1335.

word for "unrighteous" in vv. 8-9 (Gk. *adikia;* NIV "dishonest," v. 8; "worldly," v. 9). *Adikos* is therefore a catchword that resumes the teaching on "unrighteous mammon" from v. 9. "If you have not been trustworthy in handling worldly wealth [Gk. lit. 'unrighteous mammon'], who will trust you with true riches?" (v. 11). We noted above that "mammon" derives from the Hebrew *aman*, "to place trust in." When v. 11 is translated into Hebrew, a triple wordplay occurs on *aman:* "If in unrighteous mammon [Heb. *māmōnāh*] you do not become faithful [Heb. *ne'amānīm*], who will entrust [Heb. *he'amīn*] you with true wealth?" This is compelling evidence for a Hebraic source of v. 11. The argument of vv. 10-12 follows a "lesser-to-greater" genre that was widely employed in ancient rhetoric: if one is faithful/unfaithful in small matters, one will be faithful/unfaithful in great matters. The Greek word for "true riches" is a singular substantive, "the true [good]" *(to alēthinon),* which may allude back to "eternal" in v. 9. This is the only occurrence of the word in this form in Luke, but in John it occurs nine times, always with reference to *divine* truth or God (e.g., John 7:28; 17:3). If one cannot be trusted with earthly wealth, which is here today and gone tomorrow, who would entrust one with the true and eternal wealth of God's kingdom? V. 12 repeats the maxim slightly differently: "If you have not been trustworthy with someone else's property, who will give you property of your own?"[37] "Someone else's property" is a circumlocution for "unrighteous mammon." Both expressions refer to that which is never one's own, and which must inevitably and always be surrendered or lost. "Your own," by contrast, refers to the gift and inheritance of God that is eternal and can never be lost.

The interpretation of the parable concludes in v. 13 with a saying on the impossibility of serving two masters, i.e., of multitasking in matters of ultimate concern. One can, of course, serve two masters at different times or on different matters. But at the same time, and especially on the same matter, one cannot serve two masters simultaneously or equally. Priority must be given to one over the other. The Semitic extremes in v. 13 (also in 14:26) of hatred of the one and love of the other, of devotion to one and despising the other, signify the ultimacy of the choice at hand. The Greek word for "devoted" (v. 13; *antechein*) means to "hold fast, forge a strong attachment," and *kataphronein* means "to despise" or "treat with contempt." The parallelism of v. 13 makes the saying easy to memorize, which accounts for its repetition in Matt 6:24, *2 Clem.* 8:5-6, and in a mélange of similar sayings in *Gos.*

---

37. Two uncial manuscripts (B [Vaticanus], fourth c.; L, eighth c.) read *"our* own," thus implying that true wealth belongs to the Father and Son (or to Jesus and the disciples [Schlatter, *Lukas,* 370]). Marcion supplied the pronoun *"my* own," implying Jesus himself as the source of true wealth. Both the majority manuscript tradition and the context of the saying, however, favor *"your* own." See Metzger, *TCGNT,* 140.

Thom. 47. Variants of the idea appear in the Hellenistic world as well.[38] In v. 13 mammon is elevated to divine status and placed in tension with God. This is a tension that disciples cannot abide. When wealth and possessions control one, one has lost even the shrewdness of "the people of this world" and cannot be counted among "people of the light" (v. 8).[39] The only way "mammon of unrighteousness" can be put in its proper place is to make sure that God *alone* is Lord and Master, and to signify that lordship by using money and wealth in God's service.

THREE SAYINGS IN PREPARATION FOR THE PARABLE OF THE RICH MAN AND LAZARUS (16:14-18)

The change in audience to Pharisees in v. 14 suggests that Luke intends the material in 16:14-31 to be taken as a thematic unit.[40] The overall theme of wealth and possessions continues through Luke 16, but in the latter half of the chapter the theme is considered in relation to Pharisees, whereas in vv. 1-13 it is addressed to disciples. The present unit consists of three sayings of Jesus — a warning to Pharisees (vv. 14-15), the enduring significance of the law (vv. 16-17), a saying on divorce (v. 18) — prefaced to the parable of the Rich Man and Lazarus (vv. 19-31). The last two sayings (vv. 16-18) appear in different contexts in Matt and Mark and may derive from different sources. They do not bear an organic connection to the parable, although minor thematic similarities with the parable may account for Luke's inclusion of the sayings in preparation for the parable. The similarities include the love of money shared by Pharisees (v. 14) and the rich man of the parable (v. 19); "what people value highly" (v. 15) and the rich man's luxury (v. 19); "detestable in God's sight" (v. 15) and the rich man's misery in Hades (v. 23); and knowledge of the law and prophets shared by Pharisees (vv. 16-17) and the brothers of the rich man (v. 29).[41]

14-15 "The Pharisees, who loved money, heard all this and were sneering at Jesus" (v. 14). There is an ironic wordplay here, for rather than using

---

38. Pythagorean Sentences 110, a second-c. Greek source, reads: "It is impossible for the same person to be a lover of success, the body, and God. For whoever loves success, loves also the body. But whoever loves the body also loves money. But whoever loves money is also necessarily unjust. The unjust person however is an offense against the holiness of God and the laws of humanity." Cited from *HCNT,* 227. Similar sayings occur in Dio Chrysostom, *Disc.* 66.13; Seneca, *Ep.* 18.13.

39. See Schweizer, *Lukas,* 170.

40. See at 15:1-32, n. 1.

41. Plummer, *Luke,* 390; Klein, *Lukasevangelium,* 551, 556.

"worldly wealth to make friends" (v. 9), Pharisees are "friends of money."[42] The Greek word for "sneer," *ekmyktērizein,* signals more than an attitude. Meaning "to wrinkle one's nose," it expresses *physical* ridicule (23:35; Ps 2:4; 22:7; 35:16; *1 Clem.* 16:16), frequently used in the wisdom tradition to describe the response of the fool against the wise, or the godless against the righteous.[43] The precise criticism of the Pharisees in v. 15, as elsewhere in the Third Gospel (10:29; 18:9-14; 20:20; also Matt 23:28), concerns religious posturing, attention to appearances over reality. Both "you" and "God" (v. 15) are placed at the beginning of their respective clauses, emphasizing the Pharisees' posture versus God's perception of it. However Pharisees are perceived (and wish to be perceived), "God knows your hearts," says Jesus (v. 15). God's omniscience of the human heart is a constant refrain in Scripture,[44] here underscored by *ginōskein,* the strongest Greek word for "know." God is not simply aware of the human heart, but intensely and intimately knowledgeable of it. Jesus concludes the exposé of the Pharisees with a stark Hebraic contrast reminiscent of the "blessings" and "woes" of 6:20-26: "What people value highly is detestable in God's sight" (v. 15). The Greek word for "detestable," *bdelygma,* as a rule translates the Heb. *toevah* in the OT, the strongest malediction in the Hebrew Bible, meaning "abomination" or "abhorrence."[45] Plummer identifies its original meaning as that which "greatly offends the nostrils" — "stench."[46] If so, it forms a wordplay with *ekmyktērizein* (NIV "sneering") in v. 14: the Pharisees wrinkle their noses at Jesus, but God wrinkles his at their lofty pretenses. The importance of this contrast is difficult to overstate: what is natural to humanity, even noble, may stink in God's nostrils. No hint here of a divine spark within humanity that reflects the eternal light of God. The ways of God are as far removed from human inclinations as are the father's ways from those of his two sons (15:11-32). This God cannot be known by human intuition or analogies, but only in his self-revelation of Jesus Christ. If he is not known in Jesus Christ, he is not known.

V. 14 is the only instance in the NT where Pharisees are explicitly accused of avarice, indeed "constant" *(hyparchontes)* avarice. In later Christian tradition avarice is regarded as one of the seven deadly sins. This sin would seem more appropriate of Sadducees (see at 20:27), who superintended the temple in Jerusalem, which, in addition to its sacred purpose, functioned as the major financial institution of Judaism.[47] Sadducees belonged to the

42. Green, *Luke,* 601.

43. Wolter, *Lukasevangelium,* 553-54.

44. Prov 24:12; 1 Sam 16:7; 1 Kgs 8:39; 1 Chr 28:9; 2 Cor 5:12; 1 Thess 2:4.

45. W. Foerster, *bdelyssomai* etc., *TWNT* 1:598-600.

46. *Luke,* 388.

47. T. W. Manson, *The Sayings of Jesus* (London: SCM, 1964), 295-301, suspects this accusation was originally directed to Sadducees. Marshall, *Luke,* 625, also recognizes its appropriateness to Sadducees.

wealthy aristocracy, and according to the rabbis "used silver and gold vessels all their lives."[48] Pharisees (see at 5:17), in contrast, observed a "simple standard of living, making no concession to luxury," according to Josephus (*Ant.* 18.12). Their principal characteristic, again according to Josephus, was not greed but "exactitude" or "strictness" (Gk. *akribeia; J.W.* 2.162) in interpretation of Torah, a characteristic that, in the eyes of Jesus and early Christianity, resulted in emphases on minutiae. Pharisees were accused of "straining gnats and swallowing camels" (Matt 23:24), of deceptive appearances — "cleansing the outside but not the inside of a cup" (11:39; Matt 23:25), and of "whitewashing tombs" (11:44; Matt 23:27-28). The latter criticism especially forms the basis of Jesus' criticism of the Pharisees in v. 15. Paul later refers to the same as "unenlightened zeal" (Rom 10:2).[49] The love of money appears in early Christian vice catalogs (2 Tim 3:2; *Did.* 3:5), the "root of all kinds of evil" (1 Tim 6:10).[50] The sole reference to Pharisees as money lovers is doubtlessly included here in connection with the foregoing references to the love of unrighteous mammon (vv. 9-13). Why Luke accuses Pharisees of avarice is not immediately obvious. It may be significant that in Israel wealth was often regarded as a reward of righteousness (Gen. 13:2; 1 Kgs 3:13; Ps 112:3; Prov 10:3). The rigor with which Pharisees pursued Torah righteousness may have been matched by shrewdness in material prosperity as well. If so, first-century Pharisees were not unique. Greed is never far from the practice of religion in any age. It is evident today not only in the crass gospel of "health and wealth," but also in subtler ways, such as the temptation to alter the proclamation of the gospel so as to enhance popular and financial support, or the envy of some pastors of the prestige and financial remuneration of their professional counterparts in law, medicine, and business.

16-17 The parable of the Rich Man and Lazarus would naturally follow at this point, but Luke instead includes two further dominical sayings.[51] Vv. 16-17 transition from wealth and religious window-dressing to the question of the relevance of "the Law and the Prophets" in relation to the gospel. "The Law and Prophets were in effect until John, but since then the good news of the kingdom of God is being preached, and all are being pressed into it" (v. 16; my translation). This verse became the drive train for Hans Conzelmann's celebrated thesis that Luke-Acts divides salvation history into three stages: the eras of Israel, Jesus, and the church. Conzelmann assigned John the Baptizer

---

48. L. Feldman (quoting Rabbi Nathan) in Josephus, *Ant.* (LCL, vol. 9; Cambridge: Harvard University Press, 1969), 10, n. *b*.

49. Str-B 4/1:334-52; also Schürer, *History of Jewish People,* 2:381-414, 486-87.

50. The judgment that money is the root of evil is not unique to Christianity but is also attested in Greco-Roman sources. See Wolter, *Lukasevangelium,* 553.

51. A point made by Wolter, *Lukasevangelium,* 554.

to the first of these eras.[52] V. 16, however, mentions only two eras, that of "Law and Prophets" and "gospel," the same two eras that reappear at the end of the Third Gospel in references of the resurrected Jesus to the testimony of the Law and the Prophets to himself as Messiah (24:27, 44).[53] As for John's placement in the scope of salvation history, Luke-Acts is ambiguous. Some texts appear to assign John to a prior age (4:21; 7:28; Acts 10:37?), and others to the age of the gospel (1:76; 3:2; Acts 10:37?; 13:23-25). V. 16 reflects this ambiguity, depending on whether one understands *apo tote* ("from then") to exclude or include John.[54] Taken as a whole, in Luke-Acts John is a pivotal, transitional figure between the promise of the gospel in Israel and its fulfillment in Jesus.[55] John cannot therefore be assigned solely to the era of Israel. There is a further problem with Conzelmann's understanding of "Law and Prophets" in terms of chronology, i.e., a historical epoch coterminous with the history of Israel preceding the advent of Jesus.[56] In each of its nine uses in Luke-Acts, "Law and Prophets" designates not a historical epoch but a body of sacred Jewish

---

52. Conzelmann, *The Theology of Saint Luke* (trans. G. Buswell; New York: Harper, 1960). Conzelmann's three-part schema is set forth on pp. 16-17; his placement of John on p. 161. So too G. Stanton, *The Gospels and Jesus* (2nd ed.; Oxford: University Press, 2002), 183, 211-13.

53. For a discussion and defense of Conzelmann's schema, see Fitzmyer, *Luke (I–IX)*, 181-87; for a criticism, see P. Minear, "Luke's Use of the Birth Stories," in Keck and Martyn, eds., *Studies in Luke-Acts,* 111-30. On the basis of 16:16 and 24:27, 44, a broad division of an era of Israel and an era of the gospel seems viable in Luke-Acts, but nowhere does Luke-Acts identify three eras of salvation history as clearly or necessarily as does Conzelmann, nor is John unequivocally assigned to the era of Israel. Conzelmann's rejection of Luke 1–2 as original to the Third Gospel causes him to dismiss the important testimony to John the Baptizer in the Lukan infancy narrative. The excursus at 2:52 argues that the infancy narrative makes a serious contribution to Lukan theology and introduces major themes that are subsequently developed in the Third Gospel and Acts. In the infancy narrative John (1:76), along with Jesus (1:32), clearly belongs to the inaugural era of salvation, which is confirmed in Acts 10:37-38; 13:23-25. With regard to Conzelmann's second and third eras, it is possible to take Luke's repetition of "when the days had been fulfilled" (Gk. *en tō symplērousthai tas hēmeras*), which occurs only at 9:51 and Acts 2:1, with reference to the ascension of Jesus, thus inaugurating the "era of the church" (see discussion at 9:51). One should beware of conceiving of these "eras" in exclusive terms, however, for important Lukan theological themes such as the Holy Spirit, the forgiveness of sins, and the promise of salvation (among many others) are common throughout salvation history. With regard to Conzelmann's particular interpretation of 16:16, Minear's critique is worth considering: "Rarely has a scholar placed so much weight on so dubious an interpretation of so difficult a logion. . . . This verse achieves a quite unique status in Conzelmann's mind, invulnerable, and undebatable" (ibid., 122).

54. The parallel passage in Matt 11:12 clearly assigns John to the age of the gospel.

55. So Bovon, *Lukas 15,1–19,27,* 99, and Fitzmyer, *Luke (X–XXIV),* 1115-16; Schweizer, *Lukas,* 171, argues decidedly for John's belonging to the gospel era.

56. Irenaeus, *Haer.* 4.4.2, likewise understood v. 16 to signify an epochal break between John and Jesus: "The law originated with Moses, it terminated with John."

literature, "the Old Testament" (16:16, 29, 31; 24:27, 44; Acts 13:15; 24:14; 26:22; 28:23).[57] Conzelmann's three-part scheme of salvation history therefore cannot be determinative for an understanding of v. 16. "The Law and the Prophets were in effect until John" (v. 16) is best understood to mean that the content of John's preaching was a summary of the Law and the Prophets, which of course included the messianic expectations. John lived in the messianic or gospel era, to be sure, but his preaching represented an OT understanding of it.

John and the Pharisees therefore adhered to the theological framework of the "Law and Prophets." The proclamation of "the kingdom of God" does not arise with John, but with Jesus, for whom the "kingdom of God" (see at 4:43) is the dominant theme of his proclamation and ministry, as well as of his disciples (9:2; 10:11). "The good news of the kingdom of God is being preached, and all are being pressed [Gk. *biazetai*] into it" (v. 16; my translation). *Biazetai* (v. 16), a middle/passive form, means "forcing oneself" (middle voice) or "being forced" (passive voice). The meaning of this word in v. 16 has been controversial throughout church history.[58] Rabbinic Judaism taught that certain behaviors could catalyze and even hasten the advent of the messianic era. Usually such behaviors were acts of righteousness, such as repentance: "If Israelites repent for only one day," said Rabbi Levi (ca. 300), "they would be immediately redeemed and the Son of David [= Messiah] would come." Not surprisingly, attempts were made to coerce the advent of the Messiah by militant fervor, against which the rabbis warned.[59] Still today extreme Zionist visions — both Jewish and Christian — of destroying the Dome of the Rock in Jerusalem and rebuilding the temple in its place repeat this misguided zeal. V. 16 does not support this vehement hermeneutic. *Biazetai* is best understood in the passive rather than the middle voice, for a passive understanding makes it parallel to *euangelizetai* immediately preceding, i.e., "the kingdom of God is being proclaimed and all are being pressed into it." A passive translation also concurs with the earliest Syriac translation of the passage, one of the earliest Latin translations, and with all Greek translations of *biazesthai* in the LXX and Greek literature as a whole.[60] The "pressing," in other words, is not

57. Luke's usage of "law [or Moses] and prophets" is also reflected in intertestamental literature (incl. Qumran). See the assembled texts and perceptive discussion in Wolter, *Lukasevangelium*, 555.

58. Codex Sinaiticus (א) omits "and all are being pressed into it."

59. See the material gathered in Str-B 1:599.

60. The research of I. Ramelli, "Luke 16:16: The Good News of God's Kingdom Is Proclaimed and Everyone Is Forced into It," *JBL* 127/4 (2008): 737-58, adduces definitive support for a passive understanding of *biazetai*: "In the whole of the Bible, *biazomai* has only a passive or an intensive meaning, . . . but it never bears the sense of 'to go by force.' . . . [Indeed, in] all of Greek literature, on the basis of my complete search through the TLG, *biazō* means 'I force, I do violence'; . . . *biazomai* means 'I am forced'" (746-47).

something people do. V. 16 is not about muscling one's way into God's favor, fox-hole promises, or resolutions or works intended to merit God's favor. It is about something *done* to people — all people — by the gospel. V. 16 is thus conceptually parallel to 14:23: God's redemptive love "compels" people far and wide to enter the kingdom. The proclamation of God's lavish grace invites — nay pushes and presses — people into the kingdom. The proclamation of the kingdom is an expression of divine persistence, of the indefatigability of God — like the host of the banquet (14:16-23) and the father of the two sons (15:11-32) — inviting, waiting, wooing, and urging people into the kingdom.

What remains of "the Law and the Prophets" with the advent of the gospel era? Are they superseded and supplanted by the fulfillment of the gospel? The concept of salvation unfolding in successive historical stages or dispensations, discussed above, might suggest so. V. 17, however, maintains the validity of "law" in the era of "gospel," the "promise" in the era of "fulfillment": "It is easier for heaven and earth to pass away than to drop a serif from the law" (my translation; cf. Matt 5:18). Solomon's dedicatory prayer at the completion of the temple in Jerusalem declared that not "one word" of God had failed (1 Kgs 8:56); Jesus declares that not "one *keraia*" will fail. *Keraia* means a "little horn," i.e., not one *pen-stroke* of the law will fail. Marcion, the second-century heresiarch who sought to purge the gospel of Jewish elements and influences, substituted "my words" for "the law," thus retaining Jesus and dispensing with Israel. This is a violent misunderstanding of Luke's theology (see excursus at 9:51). Especially in the infancy narrative, but also in the Elijah-Elisha typology of chaps. 7–9 and the recurrent emphasis on Jerusalem throughout the Gospel, Luke reminds readers that "the Law and the Prophets" provide the indispensable pretext and context for the gospel. Israel is the nourishing "root," to use Paul's metaphor (Rom 11:18), from which the olive tree grows, and which supports the tree.[61] The extravagant contrast between "heaven and earth" and a minute pen-stroke, a "little horn" (Gk. *keraia*) of a Hebrew letter in "the Law and the Prophets," expresses the issue in Hebrew hyperbole. The rise of the gospel does not signal the "fall" (Gk. *piptein*) of the law.[62] "Law and Prophets" are more durable than the physical universe. They are the presupposition and promise of the gospel, which is their fulfillment.

18 We know that marriage and divorce were contested issues in Jesus' day. We also know that Jesus upheld a standard of marriage that, so far as we know, no Jewish rabbi upheld. Not surprisingly, Luke includes Jesus' teaching on this particular issue in v. 18 as an example of the enduring validity of the

---

61. For a different Pauline metaphor illustrating the same idea, see the *paidagōgos* image in Gal 3:24.

62. On the various ways in which law and prophets remain valid, see Bock, *Luke 9:51–24:53*, 1355.

law. Marriage is addressed throughout the NT (16:18; Matt 5:32; 19:18; Mark 10:11-12; 1 Cor 7:10-11; Eph 5:21-33; 1 Pet 3:1-7), and the NT witness forms the basis for the Christian understanding of marriage in the early church (Justin, *1 Apol.* 1.15.1-4; *Herm. Mand.* 4.1.6). Jesus declares his will on marriage not on the basis of Deut 24:1-4, the accepted proof-text of the rabbis on the subject,[63] but on the basis of the creation of mankind as male and female in Gen 1-2. Jesus' view on marriage, which is expressed most fully in Mark 10:1-12, is not grounded in the Mosaic law, in other words, but in the will of God as ordered in creation.[64] In v. 18 Luke cites only a portion of the longer tradition preserved by Mark: "Anyone who divorces his wife and marries another woman commits adultery, and the man who marries a divorced woman commits adultery." By grounding his teaching in Gen 1-2, and by expressly referring to male and female in v. 18, Jesus defines marriage as a relationship involving a man and woman rather than two persons of the same sex. Deut 24:1-4 freely granted a man the right to divorce his wife on the grounds of "indecency." The original Hebrew word behind "indecency," *eroth*, literally means "bareness" or "nakedness," which in the Hebrew world was a sign of "disgrace" or "indecency." Rabbis famously declared themselves on the various grounds of indecency, some allowing only adultery and others allowing virtually anything that displeased a husband. All were agreed, however, that divorce was permissible. This sliding scale of permissiveness doubtless resulted in divorce, perhaps even frequent divorce, in first-century Palestine.

The uncompromising pronouncement of v. 18 was thus unique in Jesus' day. Unlike Mark, v. 18 does not address the possibility of a woman divorcing a man. Judaism normally considered male adultery an offense against the woman's father or husband rather than against the woman herself; whereas female adultery was considered an offense against a woman's husband. Third parties are omitted in v. 18, implying that adultery is an offense against the woman herself. The Lukan saying does not condemn divorce per se, which is not surprising, given Jesus' teaching in 14:26 and 18:29. The accent in v. 18 falls rather on remarriage, which results in adultery. The saying preserved by Luke agrees with Paul, who, according to tradition, was Luke's mentor. In 1 Cor 7:10-11 Paul declares that married persons should remain married, but if a man or woman must divorce, both should remain single or reconcile with the original marriage partner, but not remarry. Paul prefaces the above by declaring that his opinion is grounded in the commandment of "the Lord" (1 Cor. 7:10). The commandment of the Lord in which Paul's judgment is grounded is essentially the same as v. 18, namely, that Jesus permitted divorce in cases of extremity,

---

63. See D. Instone-Brewer, "Deuteronomy 24:1-4 and the Origin of the Jewish Divorce Certificate," *JJS* 49 (1998): 230-43.

64. See Edwards, *Mark,* 297-305.

but that remarriage was to be avoided.[65] Luke and Paul therefore agree that Jesus refused to conceive of marriage, as did the rabbis, on the grounds of its possible dissolution. For Jesus, in marriage male and female become "one flesh" (Gen 2:24), which is meant to be permanent and indissoluble. "The law and the Prophets" ordain this state, which represents the divine will expressed in creation. Faithfulness in upholding the divine intent of the marriage union is one of the highest callings of Christian discipleship.

THE PARABLE OF THE RICH MAN
AND LAZARUS (16:19-31)

19-21   Like the parable of the Shrewd Manager, the parable of the Rich Man and Lazarus is not expressly identified as a parable.[66] This is the only parable of Jesus in which a named character appears. Ironically, the named character is not the important person — the rich man — but a poor and wretched man named Lazarus.[67] "The rich man was dressed in purple and fine linen and lived in luxury every day" (v. 19). If clothes make the man, this man has it made. Blue cloth, produced from dye secreted by sea snails *(Murex trunculus),* was the most valuable cloth of the ancient world, the enviable insignia of the ruling caste (1 Macc 8:14; Mark 15:17, 20; John 19:2, 5). A rabbinic prayer shawl *(tallit)* needed to have at least one blue thread in its ritual fringe (Num 15:38-41), but the rich man has an entire garment made of the costly stuff.[68] His robe covered an undergarment of high-quality linen, also costly, the finest of which in first-century Palestine was produced in Beth-shan, just south of Galilee.[69] The Greek describes his garments as "sumptuous" and "resplendent." Most

65. On the agreement of Luke and Paul on this matter, see M. Hengel, *Saint Peter: The Underestimated Apostle* (Grand Rapids: Eerdmans, 2010), 113.

66. Codex Bezae (D, fifth c.) prefaces v. 19, "He said also another parable. . . ."

67. In the course of early Christian tradition a name was supplied to compensate for the anonymity of the rich man. (The name was not "Dives" [which arose from mistaking the Lat. *dives* (= "rich, wealthy") of the Vulgate for a proper name, *Homo quidam erat dives*]). In Egypt the name "Nineveh" was incorporated into the Sahidic version no later than the third c., a form of which is appears in $\mathfrak{p}^{75}$ (third c.). More commonly in the West, again from the third c. onward, the rich man was known as "Phineas," a name that may have arisen from Num 25:7, 11, where Phineas is coupled with Eleazar (from which "Lazarus" is derived). See Metzger, *TCGNT,* 140-41.

68. On *murex trunculus* dye, see F. Danker, "Purple," *ABD* 5:557-60; and esp. A. Greenspan, "The Search for Biblical Blue," *BRev* 19/1 (2003): 32-39; and B. Sterman and J. Sterman, "The Great *Tekhelet* Debate — Blue or Purple?" *BAR* 39/5 (2013): 28, 73, who argue that the dye was blue rather than purple.

69. Str-B 2:222-23. The Greek word for "linen," *byssos,* derives from Heb. *būṣ.*

remarkable, perhaps, they were not exceptional, reserved for special occasions. The rich man's lavish clothes were his "every day" apparel (v. 19)! The rich man is not depicted as a shark, corrupt and decadent. Anyone who has toured the ruins of an ancient Roman city, say Pompei or Ephesus, knows that this man is simply adhering to the social norms of Roman aristocracy — "living according to his means," we might say.

The ancient world was predominantly a two-class world: *patrician* and *plebeian,* free and slave, rich and poor — the latter class being numerically larger than the former. This parable reflects that world. At the gate of the rich man sat a poor man named Lazarus. "Lazarus" is a form of the Hebrew name "Eleazar," meaning "the one God helps."[70] Eleazar was the third most common male name in Jesus' day,[71] a fitting name for a stereotypical poor person. The name itself must be significant, however, for we cannot imagine why Jesus would assign an arbitrary name to the only named character in a parable. Lazarus eventually lives up to his name — no thanks to the rich man — but thanks to God, who receives him securely in heaven in Abraham's arms (v. 22).[72] The wretchedness of Lazarus is described as vividly as is the opulence of the rich man. His placement "at the gate" is telling, for in Israel the gate is the place where judgment is properly rendered. The rich man's gate will be his own court of justice. The Greek word *ebebleto* (v. 20; NIV "was laid") is important but hard to render. From *ballein,* "to throw or cast," the word occurs proportionately less frequently in Luke than in Matt and Mark, often with reference to discarding something: brush to fire (3:9; 12:28), people to prison (12:58; 23:19, 25), manure to refuse (13:8; 14:35). In the passive form here, *ballein* is often a demeaning reference to the afflicted, crippled, and outcast.[73] Lazarus is a "squatter" at the gate. Ulcerous (Job 2:7; 2 Kgs 20:7) and malnourished, a pitiful contrast to the lavish rich man, Lazarus says not a word, longing to "eat what fell from the rich man's table" (v. 21). This last phrase appears also on the lips of the Syrophoenician woman (Matt 15:27; Mark 7:28) and may have been a figure of speech for the barest of essentials. Utterly wretched, even Lazarus's sores are licked by dogs (v. 21).[74]

---

70. Str-B 2:223.

71. R. Bauckham, *Jesus and the Eyewitnesses* (Grand Rapids: Eerdmans, 2006), 85.

72. A relation between the Lazarus of the parable and Lazarus of John 11 or, more remotely, Eleazar of Gen 15, seems speculative and unlikely (so Bock, *Luke 9:51–24:53,* 1366; contra Nolland, *Luke 9:21–18:34,* 833).

73. On the term, see Fitzmyer, *Luke (X–XXIV),* 1131.

74. Bailey, *Jesus through Middle Eastern Eyes,* 385, argues that canine saliva has curative powers and thus aided in healing Lazarus's wounds. He concludes that street mongrels do more for Lazarus than does the rich man. This conclusion is fanciful. It is true that a dog's mouth contains fewer germs than a human's, and a dog's tongue, like other natural remedies such as leeches and maggots, can have a curative effect on human wounds. Nevertheless, a dog's mouth

22-31   "The time came when the beggar died and the angels carried him
to Abraham's side. The rich man also died and was buried" (v. 22). It might
be expected, or hoped, that the inequities and injustices related to the two
men would be made right in this life. They are not. Lazarus and the rich man
both die in the same condition in which they lived. In Judaism angels were
regarded as "ministering spirits" (Heb 1:14), some of whom were believed to
escort the souls of the dead to God. The escort was often the archangel Gabriel
or Michael, but more often Satan, who accused the deceased before the throne
of God.[75] In Jude 9 — the only such instance in the NT — Michael and Satan
contend over the corpse of Moses after his death. In this parable, angels escort
the soul of Lazarus to God, but Satan does not accuse the soul before God.
Lazarus is immediately received into eternal blessedness (v. 22), symbolized
by "Abraham's bosom," and thus joined to the elite company of Moses himself.
The OT regularly refers to death in terms of being "gathered to one's fathers"
(Gen 15:15; 47:30; Deut 31:16; Judg 2:10; 1 Kgs 1:21), which signified the placing
of bones of the deceased in an ossuary with the bones of his or her deceased
ancestors. Occasionally the "fathers" were epitomized by "Abraham, Isaac, and
Jacob" (4 Macc 13:17; *Jub.* 23:2; *T. Ab.* 20:14). These expressions all apply to

----

can also contain bacteria highly infectious to humans, esp. if the dog has eaten feces, which is
not infrequently the case with street mongrels. The medicinal properties of a dog's mouth are
not the decisive issue at v. 21, however. The decisive issues are two: first, whether the licking of
dogs was (or could be) considered positively in the ancient world; and second, whether such
an interpretation is appropriate to understanding the parable. Regarding the first, the ancient
world chiefly revered dogs for hunting, protection of house and herds, and companionship. A
potential role in healing, however, is not attested. The chief medical authorities of the ancient
world were Hippocrates and Galen, neither of whom ascribes a medicinal role to dogs in general or their licking in particular. Hippocrates mentions nearly every cure imaginable in the
treatment of ulcers and sores, except for cures attributed to dogs. Ancient medical treatment
was invariably associated with religious cults, esp. the cult of Asclepius. Dogs do not play a role
in the Asclepius cult, however, including its major centers in Epidaurus and Pergamon, nor
do dogs feature in their known practices or statuary. The Egyptian god Anubis was depicted
with a head like a jackel or dog, but Anubis was associated with mummification of the dead,
not with healing. The claim that the dog cemetery at Ashkelon was related to a canine healing
cult (see L. Stager, "Why Were Hundreds of Dogs Buried at Ashkelon?" *BAR* 17/3 [1991]: 26-
42) is without confirmation and likely overstated (see E. Firmage, "Zoology," *ABD* 6:1143). A
judgment on the first issue regarding a positive interpretation of canine licking in the ancient
world must be rendered in the negative. Regarding the possibility of dogs appearing positively
in this particular parable, it is worth recalling that references to dogs in the Bible are (with the
single exception of a friendly canine traveling companion in Tob 6:1 [S text]) all contemptuous, including the reference to licking blood (1 Kgs 21:19; 22:38). This pejorative perspective
continues in rabbinic literature (see Str-B 4/2:733). Finally, from a rhetorical perspective, dogs
do not appear to function positively in the parable as agents of mercy, but rather to symbolize
Lazarus's abject privation.

75. Str-B 2:223-25.

death and burial, however, with no fixed assumptions about an afterlife. The reference to Lazarus being carried "to Abraham's bosom" (v. 22; Gk. *kolpos;* NIV "Abraham's side") is entirely different. This metaphor depicts Lazarus being gathered into the arms of Abraham with the tender affection of a mother nursing a child.[76] The Fourth Gospel uses *kolpos* to describe the intimacy of Jesus, the only begotten Son, and the Father (John 1:18). The callous treatment of Lazarus at the rich man's gate has been radically reversed in eternity. Lazarus has died and been received in eternal comfort and blessedness.

"The rich man also died and was buried" (v. 22). This statement may be taken in two ways. On the one hand, refusal of burial of a corpse in Judaism signified that, in the eyes of the living, the deceased deserved no honor, but rather God's judgment. The proper burial of the rich man thus assures readers of his honorable discharge in the eyes of the community.[77] On the other hand, and in contrast to the fate of Lazarus, the report of the rich man's burial is curt and unfeeling, like the ground in which he is buried. A great exchange has occurred: the sumptuousness enjoyed by the rich man in life is enjoyed by Lazarus in eternity; the privation that Lazarus suffered in life is the fate of the rich man in eternity.

The rich man does not join Lazarus on Father Abraham's lap but awakes in **Hades**, from where he sees Abraham and pleads for him to send Lazarus to slake his thirst, if only with a drop of water (vv. 23-24). Second Temple Judaism believed that the blessed and damned were able to view one another from their respective outposts, and that their views increased both the joy of the one and the torment of the other (*4 Ezra* 7:85, 93).[78] Following physical death, but prior to final judgment, souls of the departed were believed to inhabit an interim state in Hades that included a separation of the unjust from the blessed, along with their initial punishments and rewards. The eschatological topography of the remainder of the parable describes his interim state (e.g., 10:15). Neither Lazarus nor the rich man is experiencing his final state, although both experience a foretaste or anticipation of it, the "firstfruits (or thistles)" of a fate that cannot be revoked but only increased at the final judgment.[79]

---

76. See Str-B 2:225-27; Wolter, *Lukasevangelium,* 559-560.

77. Str-B 2:227-28. The sentiments of *1 En.* 103:5 about the fate of prosperous sinners is not far from the point of v. 22: "Woe unto you sinners who are dead! When you are dead in the wealth of your sins, those who are like you will say of you, 'Happy are the sinners, and all they have seen in their days! They have died now in prosperity and wealth. They have not experienced struggle and battle in their lifetime. They have died in glory, and there was no judgment in their lifetime.' You yourselves know that they [angels] will bring your souls down to Sheol; and they shall experience evil and great tribulation — in darkness, nets, and burning flame. Your souls shall enter into the great judgment."

78. Str-B 2:228.

79. Second Temple literature on the subject of the afterlife is enormous, as attested by

Looking up in agony, the rich man sees Lazarus blessed in the company of Abraham (v. 23).[80] "Father Abraham," he cries, "have pity on me" (v. 24). John the Baptizer had envisioned precisely such a scene in his wilderness preaching, warning of presuming on Jewish ancestry, even calling Abraham "Father," but neglecting to demonstrate "fruit worthy of repentance" (3:7-8). The rich man's burning appeal to "Father Abraham" and to his mercy are tragically discordant, for his life of luxury attended to neither. The Greek word for "mercy" *(eleos)* forms the root of the concept of almsgiving *(eleēmosynē);* the rich man, ironically, is asking to receive from Lazarus what he denied Lazarus in life. More mystifying is his plea to "send Lazarus" to relieve him, if only for a moment, of his thirst (v. 24). Jesus taught that the kingdom of God breaks into earthly existence and transforms it, "on earth as it is heaven" (see discussion of "daily bread" at 11:3). The rich man resisted that transformation. Mammon was his God. He thought the old order would be the eternal order (Mark 12:25), and even in Hades he imagines Lazarus to be his servant.

Abraham now speaks, "My child, remember . . ." (v. 25). His response is free of rancor or retribution. He in fact addresses the rich man tenderly, *teknon* — the same epithet with which the father addressed the older son (15:31). The rich man has made his choices, and Abraham cannot change their consequences. In the Hades of Latin mythology souls drink "draughts of long forgetfulness" in Lethe, the stream that erases all memory of the past.[81] In Jesus' parable, however, there is a line of cause-and-effect between this world and the world to come that can be remembered. There is no evidence the rich man gave any thought to the future, but now, like Ebenezer Scrooge, who is required by the Ghost of Christmas Past to revisit his early life, the rich man is required to remember his past and realize that it determines his present state. Like many of Luke's teachings in the central section of the Gospel, the decisive eschatological issue is not wickedness but neglect. At the Great Banquet, it was neglect of an invitation (14:16-23); here it is neglect of a man in need whom the rich man could have helped. "In your lifetime you received your good things, while Lazarus received bad things, but now he is comforted here and you are in agony" (v. 25). A "great chasm," says Abraham, "has been set in place" (v. 26) between Lazarus and the rich man that cannot be crossed. The Greek verb *estēriktai,* meaning "to have set firmly in place," is a "divine passive," i.e., a way of speaking of God's activity without using his name. The separation

---

the 155-page excursus on the subject in Str-B 4/1:1016-1165. For condensations, see Schürer, *History of the Jewish People,* 2:538-47; J. Jeremias, *hadēs, TWNT* 1:146-50; G. Moore, *Judaism in the First Centuries of the Christian Era* (New York: Schocken Books, 1971), 2:287-322; S. Cohen, *From the Maccabees to the Mishnah* (LEC; Philadelphia: Westminster Press, 1987), 89-96.

80. The reference to the rich man "looking up and seeing" is a Hebraism, reflecting *nasa enayim* (Gen 13:10, 14; 18:2; 39:7, etc.).

81. Virgil, *Aen.* 6.703-15.

between Lazarus and the rich man has been established by God and cannot be altered. This theme, too, was familiar to intertestamental Jewish literature. *1 En.* 22:2-13 describes souls held in mountain caverns before final judgment or in deep pits (18:11); and in *4 Ezra* 7:85 they are guarded by angels. The finality of judgment is signaled in v. 26 by a Hebraic crescendo in the narrative.[82] "Besides all this" (Gk. *en pasi toutois*), "a great chasm," fixed and unbridgeable, separates the righteous from the damned. The point is as inescapable as the chasm: judgment is irrevocable, with no suggestion of purgatory.[83]

Even across the chasm the rich man continues his appeal. "Father, send Lazarus . . . to warn my five brothers so that they will not also come to this place of torment" (vv. 27-28). The rich man is not the only one separated from blessedness. His family is in equal danger. Lazarus, whom he still imagines his servant, should be sent to warn his brothers. The Greek word for "warn," *diamartyresthai,* is intensive, meaning "to exhort or urge with authority."[84] The plea for his brothers at first seems less selfish than his earlier pleas. The plea is not free from self-justification, however, for it insinuates that in life the rich man did not have adequate opportunity to know and do what he needed to. "If God had warned him sufficiently, he would have escaped this place of torment."[85]

"They have Moses and the prophets," says Abraham. "Let them listen to them" (v. 29). This admonition links the parable back to "the Law and the Prophets" of vv. 16-17, which are an inseparable component of, and preparation for, the kingdom of God. At this, this rich man snaps in exasperation. "No!" The law and prophets — *religion* — is not enough! (Neh 9:26). An inescapable sign is required: "If someone from the dead goes to them, they will repent" (v. 30; cf. 11:16, 29). The request to talk with the dead, especially in dreams, was not an infrequent theme in rabbinic literature, to which the rich man now appeals.[86] On the walk to Emmaus, the resurrected Jesus will testify that everything written "in Moses and all the prophets" bears witness to him (24:27, 44).[87] In dismissing the Law and the Prophets, the rich man also dismisses the gospel. Most Christian heresies result from additions to the gospel not present in the NT; in this instance the rich man demands something *more* than "mere Christianity." Through the storm of protest, Father Abraham maintains a steady course. "If they do not listen to Moses and the Prophets, they will not be convinced even if someone rises from the dead" (v. 31). The Greek present

---

82. On the Hebraism, see Jeremias, *Sprache des Lukasevangeliums,* 261.

83. Marshall, *Luke,* 638.

84. BDAG, 233.

85. Plummer, *Luke,* 396; see also Schweizer, *Lukas,* 173.

86. Str-B 2:233.

87. See also Irenaeus, *Haer.* 4.2.3, who reminds readers that the words of Moses are at the same time the words of Jesus Christ.

tense of "do not listen" implies that the brothers know Moses and the prophets but choose not to believe them. Jesus, it will be remembered, addresses this parable to Pharisees (v. 14), who also know the Law and the Prophets. This final word, much like Rom 10:5-17, reminds the rich man and his brothers — and the Pharisees — that the Law and the Prophets anticipate salvation, and that salvation is not the result of a spectacle or sign, but of a response of faith.[88]

The parable of the Rich Man and Lazarus utilizes a number of elements common to popular Judaism in Jesus' day, including angels of death, Hades, a chasm established by God, meeting with the dead, and the reversal of fortunes in eternity. This last element is often considered the crux of the parable: "Son, remember that in your lifetime you received good things, while Lazarus received bad things, but now he is comforted here and you are in agony" (v. 25). Some scholars take v. 25 in terms of eschatological reciprocity in which those who experience good in earthly life will experience bad in equal measure in the world to come, and vice versa.[89] It is sometimes further maintained that the theme of eschatological reciprocity is imported unaltered into the parable from ancient Near Eastern folk tales.[90] These assumptions must be challenged, for eschatological reciprocity is not the theme of the parable, nor was it a theme affirmed by Jesus (13:1-9; John 9:1-3). Affirming eschatological reciprocity would imply that wealth is inherently evil and poverty inherently good. Indeed, none of the proposed parallels from the ancient Near East espouses a fatalistic determinism that riches in this world spell poverty in the next, and vice versa. Each, in fact, makes the future state dependent on moral categories rather than on wealth and poverty per se. The commonly proposed parallel from Egypt, in which the fate of a rich man and poor man are reversed in the afterlife, attests that the reversal is determined by *deeds:* the poor man's good deeds outweighed his evil deeds in the scale of justice, and the rich man's vice versa.[91] The moral

---

88. Fitzmyer, *Luke (X–XXIV)*, 1129.

89. Wolter, *Lukasevangelium*, 561, writes, "This verse sets forth the conception that God has ordained for each person a carefully measured portion of good and evil, and when in earthly life the equal allotment of the one or other is interrupted, then God sees to its compensation in the afterlife." Further, "Verse 25 makes unmistakably clear that in the Lukan parable assignment of salvation or judgment in the afterlife depends *not* [emphasis original] on good and bad deeds, . . . but solely and only on the wealth of the rich man and the poverty of the poor man" (557-58).

90. Klein, *Lukasevangelium*, 551, cites the Egyptian tale of Setme Chamois, *1 En.* 103:5-8, and Jas 5:1-6 as analogies of the parable.

91. This folk tale, sometimes referred to as Setme Champis, was first cited by H. Gressmann, *Vom reichen Mann und armen Lazarus* (APAW, philosophische-historische Klasse 7; Berlin: Reimer, 1918), 138-60. It is reproduced in *HCNT*, 227-28. Additionally, see J. Jeremias, *Die Gleichnisse Jesu* (7th ed.; Göttingen: Vandenhoeck & Ruprecht, 1965), 182, and Wolter, *Lukasevangelium,* 557-58. The folk tale concludes: "Whoever does good on earth, to that person the underworld is also good, and to whomever is evil on earth, it goes badly [there]" (*HCNT,* 228).

of *1 En.* 103:5-15 and Jas 5:1-6 is the same. In the former, judgment is meted out to those "wealthy *in sin*" versus those who were "righteous and kind" in their lifetimes; in the latter, judgment falls on the rich for exploiting the poor by withholding their wages. To be sure, v. 25 depicts a state of eschatological reversal, but as vv. 30-31 declare — and the concluding verses are the key to the parable — one's future state depends on *repentance.*

Defense of this conclusion is presupposed throughout the parable. The shrewd manager used wealth to gain eternal friendships (16:9), but the rich man fails to use his wealth to help a poor man at his gate — and thus has no eternal "friend" to advocate for him. The rich man complains rather than repents to Father Abraham, and his expectation of Lazarus to serve him, first with water and then with an errand to his brothers, maintains his entitled worldview. His plea for his brothers is a veiled rejection of the will of God: "Moses and the Prophets" are not enough! His brothers need a miraculous tour de force to change. His outlook remains wholly utilitarian: he is concerned with avoidance of "this place of torment" (v. 28) rather than "producing fruit in keeping with repentance" (3:8). What he wants from religion, for himself and his brothers, is not a religion that changes his actions, but one that spares him from the consequences of his actions. During his life he failed to heed the teachings of "Moses and the Prophets," and in Hades it is too late to heed them. The results of his choices are final, for "a great chasm" (v. 26) prohibits altering his destiny. V. 25 thus sets forth a *description* of a state of events that in several respects is similar to ancient Near Eastern final judgment motifs, but the *cause* of the state of events is not wealth and poverty per se. The cause is neglect to "hear Moses and the Prophets" (v. 31). What does it mean to hear "Moses and the Prophets"? In this instance it means to hear the admonishment not to make wealth one's highest good, but to use wealth for good, especially for the poor, whom God favors (Isa 55:13; 60:17; Ezek 17:24).

CHAPTER SIXTEEN

Discipleship and the Kingdom of God

Luke 17:1–18:34

This unit concludes Luke's long central section, which is composed almost entirely of material unique to Luke. Luke, however, concludes the central section in 18:15-34 with three pericopes — Jesus and children, Jesus and a rich ruler, and Jesus' final passion prediction — which are present in the Markan narrative from which he departed at 9:51. In 17:1–18:34 Luke continues to alternate between audiences of disciples and Pharisees, as he has since 15:1, and to intermingle narrative, teaching, and parables. The final overarching theme of the central section is the kingdom of God, which is both a present reality and a future hope. In both its present and future forms the kingdom consists of surprising properties that cannot be understood apart from Jesus' instruction, and not entirely understood until Jesus' resurrection (18:34). As a present reality, the kingdom is already "in the midst" (18:21) of people in Jesus and the proclamation of the gospel, and it comes as a gift of grace to utterly unexpected constituencies — penitent tax collectors (18:13-14), infants (18:15-17), and disciples who are convinced of the impossibility of their pleasing God (18:24-27). As a future reality, the kingdom is guaranteed by the certainty of God's sovereignty, but it will come suddenly and when least expected. The present incognito kingdom and the future triumphant kingdom converge in the final passion prediction of 18:31-34, at which point Jesus affirms his passion in Jerusalem (see excursus at 9:51).

LIFE TOGETHER (17:1-10)

Luke 17 begins with three sets of sayings on sin (vv. 1-4), faith (vv. 5-6), and performing Christian duties without claiming special merit (vv. 7-10). Evidence (discussed below) suggests that Luke derived these sayings largely, if not entirely, from his special Hebrew source. Many scholars see no thematic connection among the sayings, or between the combined sayings and the material preceding or following.[1] Although the present collection of sayings is lacking an apparent thematic unity, it does, like the material in 16:10-18, share a thematic subcurrent, which may account for its collocation. That subcurrent relates to the challenges and responsibilities that inevitably arise as believers share "life together," to use Bonhoeffer's phrase, in the Christian fellowship.[2]

1-4 The audience now changes from Pharisees (16:14-31) to disciples (17:1-19). Appropriate to disciples is a new theme: the inevitability of dissensions. "Things that cause people to stumble are bound to come, but woe to anyone through whom they come" (v. 1). V. 1 of NIV reads, "Things that cause people to stumble are bound to come," but the original Greek is more emphatic, "It is impossible for scandals not to come!" Jesus warns the disciples that Christian community will inevitably be a flawed community, but not thereby a false community. Believers who do not hear and heed this admonition will be ineffective members of the church, for they will be under the illusion that the true church is a perfect church; and not finding a perfect church, they will move from fellowship to fellowship with increasing disillusionment. The Greek word for "impossible," *anendektos*, occurs nowhere else in the Greek Bible. The word for "stumble" or "scandal," *skandalon*, however, is more frequent in both noun and verb forms. It originally meant the bait stick in a trap, and later the trap itself, hence, a "trap," "snare," or "offense" — something that causes one's downfall.[3] The word occurs frequently in Matt, Mark, and Rom, but rarely in Luke. V. 1 teaches that the inevitability of something happening does not absolve people of responsibility for its happening (likewise 22:22). This seems incongruous at first, for if something bad must happen, who can be blamed? It is not incongruous, however, for although sin is inevitable, each sin is freely choosen. The NT does not teach or expect Christians to eradicate evil in the world, but it admonishes Christians, as does Jesus here, to contend earnestly against evil, and above all, not to be a cause of sin to others (Rom 14:13; 1 Cor 8:13; 1 John 2:10; *1 Clem.* 46:8).[4] The scandal here warned against is a two-edged sword, for disciples can alienate others by causing them to sin, but they can also be alienated when others sin against them. In either case, the robe of Christian fellowship is torn.

V. 2 portrays the danger graphically: "It would be better for you to be thrown into the sea with a millstone tied around your neck than for you to

---

1. Fitzmyer, *Luke (X–XXIV)*, 1136, regards the whole as "completely unrelated" isolated sayings; similarly, Plummer, *Luke*, 398.

2. On this theme, see Bovon, *Lukas 15,1–19,27*, 132; and Schlatter, *Lukas*, 382-89.

3. See discussion of the term in G. Stählin, *skandalon*, *TWNT* 7:338-58; Wolter, *Lukasevangelium*, 565; Bock, *Luke 9:51–24:53*, 1384.

4. *Ps-Clem.*, *Hom.* 12.29.1, expands the saying to include a positive counterbalance: "The Prophet of [the] truth says, 'Good things must come, and blessed is the one through whom they come; likewise also bad things necessarily come, but woe through whom they come.'"

cause one of these little ones to stumble." Although "little ones" may include children, it does not primarily intend them.[5] The subject is ordinary Christian fellowship, which Luke elsewhere refers to with diminutives such as "little flock" (12:32) or small children (10:21; further, see Matt 10:42; 18:6, 10, 14; Mark 9:42; Rom 14). "Little ones" carries an additional metaphoric sense, reminding believers that their greatest challenge is the struggle not with evil, but with smallness and weakness — the inability to be what they should be in Christ, and the ease with which they are led astray. A millstone was a massive stone disk that required a beast of burden to turn it, and which, when turned, crushed and pulverized grain. The image of being tossed into the sea with a millstone around one's neck is an example of Jewish hyperbole. The seriousness of the point Jesus makes requires such exaggeration. To lead astray the weak and defenseless is, as Paul declares in 1 Cor 8:12-13, not simply a sin against a Christian, but a "sin against Christ." Schlatter captures the image with magnum force: "Better to be dead than to be a false guide!"[6]

Vv. 1-2 resemble similar sayings in Matt 18:6-7 and Mark 9:42, although the Matthean and Markan sayings agree more closely with one another than either does with Luke. The former read "millstone of donkey" (Gk. *mylos onikos*), whereas Luke reads "stone of a mill" (Gk. *lithos mylikos*). The relationship among these three texts is widely discussed by commentators,[7] although virtually none of them cites a related reference from the Hebrew Gospel. In discussing the commandment not to wrong another person in Ezek 18:7, Jerome cites a passage from "the Gospel according to the Hebrews" that "grieving the spirit of one's brother" is among the gravest of wrongs.[8] This citation is significant for three reasons. First, in addition to the Hebrew Gospel, Jerome cites Eph 4:30, Rom 8:9, and 1 Cor 3:16. The Hebrew Gospel is the only noncanonical source in Jerome's cross-references, attesting to its high standing in his (and his readers') estimation. Second, the brief quotation picks up two foci common to all three Synoptic versions: the gravest of wrongs, and a grievance against one's brother. Third, Jerome cites another reference from the Hebrew Gospel about forgiving a brother "seventy times seven."[9] This is the subject of vv. 3-4 immediately following, suggesting that the material in Luke 17:1-4 formed a similar unit in the earlier Hebrew Gospel.[10]

Vv. 3-4 follow with instructions about a "brother" — a member of the Christian fellowship — who sins against another member and then repents.

---

5. Contra Plummer, *Luke,* 399; Garland, *Luke,* 680.

6. Schlatter, *Lukas,* 383.

7. See the careful source analysis in Wolter, *Lukasevangelium,* 564.

8. Jerome, *Comm. Ezech.* 18:7.

9. Jerome, *Pelag.* 3.2.

10. Further, see Edwards, *Hebrew Gospel,* 91-96.

"If a brother or sister sins against you, rebuke them, and if they repent, forgive them" (v. 3). The version of this statement in Matt 18:15 appears to reflect a similar saying from Lev 19:17,[11] and thus preserve an axiom valid for offenses in general. Luke's saying, pruned to the three elements of sin, repentance, and forgiveness, may reflect a different source altogether.[12] Jerome attributes a saying to the Hebrew Gospel that sheds light on vv. 3-4: "Jesus said, 'If your brother would sin in word and would make restitution to you seven times in one day, receive him.' His disciple Simon said to him, 'Seven times in one day?' The Lord responded and said to him, 'Even, I say to you, as many as seventy times seven.'"[13] It is easy to see how both the Matthean and the Lukan versions could reflect this saying. "Seventy times seven" in Matt 18:22 is verbatim agreement. Although Luke's version is shorter than Matthew's, it agrees in important details more closely with the form of the saying cited by Jerome from the Hebrew Gospel.[14] The combined evidence posits the Hebrew Gospel as a plausible source for 17:1-4.

Personal infractions are an ever-present danger in faith communities, Jewish communities included. Lev 19:17 addresses the issue, and there are long treatments of it in the DSS, including penance, disciplinary measures, and restoration to the Qumran community.[15] The same problem exists in Christian communities. Forgiveness is an important theme in the Third Gospel, although Luke typically addresses the issue from the perspective of God's forgiveness. In the second petition of the Lord's Prayer, "Forgive us our sins, for we also forgive everyone who sins against us" (11:4), readers are reminded that God's forgiveness is a model for believers, and also an obligation for believers to forgive others. Vv. 3-4 stress that obligation in personal terms: personal rebuke of

11. Matt preserves the Greek verb *elenchein* ("to expose, convict") and *ton adelphon sou* (accusative, "your brother"), both of which are present in Lev 19:17 (LXX) but absent in Luke.

12. So Lagrange, *Luc*, 452.

13. Jerome, *Pelag.* 3.2. A variant of this saying, also attributed to "the Jewish [Gospel]," appears in Tischendorf's scholia to Codex 566. Constantin von Tischendorf edited and published 566 in his critical edition of Codex Sinaiticus with the following enthusiastic endorsement of four marginal scholia deriving from the Hebrew Gospel: "But of greatest importance are four notes in our codex, written in the margins of the gospel according to Matthew only. These, indeed, arose from no other source than the Gospel of the Hebrews, and were arranged so as to bring some light to one inquiring regarding what relation there is between the Gospel of Matthew and that celebrated writing" (C. Tischendorf, *Notitia editionis codicis bibliorum, sinaitici* [Leipzig: F. A. Brockhaus, 1860]).

14. Jerome's Latin quotation reflects several elements unique to Luke, including "if your brother sin," "seven times in one day," and the putting of the initial question by Jesus (and in the same verb tense) rather than by Peter (Matt 18:21). The emphases on remission of sins and Jesus as Lord in Jerome's quotation from the Hebrew Gospel are also more common in Luke than in Matt. See Edwards, *Hebrew Gospel*, 94-96.

15. 1QS 5-6; CD 9:1-8.

sins, personal repentance, and personal forgiveness.[16] The obligation to forgive sins is especially necessary when the Christian community is "scandalized" by unforgiveness (vv. 1-2). An unforgiving spirit is a cause of stumbling in the Christian fellowship, and that "scandal" can only be avoided when sins are not counted but forgiven.[17] Vv. 3-4 specify two prerequisites of forgiveness. First, Jesus sees the need to rebuke offenders; and second, the guilty sinner must repent and confess his or her sin. The word for "rebuke," *epitiman,* means to warn or reprove in order to prevent or end an action.[18] Its purpose here is not to humiliate, defeat, or drive out sinners, but to correct and restore them. It is often easier to turn a blind eye to sin in the community. The admonition of fellow believers requires the church to function as a body in the costly work of reconciliation: "If one part suffers, every part suffers with it; if one part is honored, every part rejoices with it" (1 Cor 12:26). Vv. 3-4 make forgiveness conditional upon repentance (so too *Did.* 15:3), but when confession is made, forgiveness must be *unconditional,* given freely and without limit, even "seven times in a day" (v. 4).[19]

5-6 Jesus' teaching on forgiveness is followed by a memorable illustration of faith. "The apostles said to the Lord, 'Increase our faith!'" (v. 5). Luke refers to "apostles" (see at 6:13) and especially "Lord" with great frequency, but only here does he combine the two titles. Ironically, where the disciples are "canonized" as "apostles of the Lord," there they become aware of their deficits! In the Third Gospel Jesus frequently teaches in response to questions of his followers and in personal relationship with them.[20] The tiny mustard seed has already supplied Jesus with an image for a parable recounted in all three Synoptics (13:18-19; Matt 13:31-32; Mark 4:30-32). He again chooses the proverbial mustard seed to respond to the disciples, saying, "If you have faith as small as a mustard seed" (v. 6). Then as now, Christians become aware of the inadequacy of their faith when they are made responsible for leading others. As leaders, they face challenges greater than their faith. They hope for great faith, certainly greater faith than their followers. Surprisingly, Jesus does not require superior spiritual endowments of Christian leaders, even apostles, nor does he offer them such.

---

16. NIV begins v. 3, "If a brother or sister sins *against you.* . . ." "Against you" is probably a later addition. The longer reading is present only in D Ψ and the Byzantine text, whereas the shorter reading is supported by older and weightier uncial manuscripts (ℵ A B L W Θ). Bovon, *Lukas 15,1–19,27,* 139, suggests "against you" might still be original, having been later removed to make the saying more general and applicable to a wider audience. This seems improbable, for a scribe would have been tempted to add "against you" in v. 3 to harmonize it with the same phrase in v. 4 (see Metzger, *TCGNT,* 141).

17. Plummer, *Luke,* 399; Schweizer, *Lukas,* 175.

18. BDAG, 384.

19. Fitzmyer, *Luke (X–XXIV),* 1139-40.

20. See Schlatter, *Lukas,* 385.

He promises, rather, to be present in the smallness of their faith. A mustard seed is so small that, held in the palm of one's hand, it appears as a speck of dust, barely visible. The image of the mustard seed is another hyperbole, but the point is clear. Christians, even *apostles,* are distinguished not by the quantity of faith, but by the employment of faith; not by greatness or smallness of faith, but by acting on faith, even faith the size of a mustard seed.[21]

With "faith as small as a mustard seed, you can say to this mulberry tree, 'Be uprooted and planted in the sea,' and it will obey you" (v. 6). The gospel tradition is familiar with a Jesus-saying about a mountain being cast into the sea (Matt 17:20; Mark 11:22-23; *Gos. Thom.* 48), which derives from the same motif in the OT (Ps 46:3; Job 9:5-6; Isa 54:10), Judaism,[22] and early Christianity (Rev 8:8). Luke preserves a saying about a mulberry tree rather than a mountain being uprooted and cast into the sea (v. 6). Jewish rabbis celebrated the mulberry tree for its vast and tenacious root system, which endowed it with a half-millennium life span. Because of its root system, the Mishnah prescribed that it could not be planted within fifty cubits (= ca. 75 feet [23 m]) of a cistern (*m. B. Bat.* 2:11).[23] A mulberry tree was obviously not a mountain, but its reputation was formidable. Whatever could dislodge such an object — even faith the size of a mustard seed — was mightily impressive.

Why Luke alone preserves the saying with reference to a mulberry tree is difficult to say. Did Jesus innovate on the mountain-saying for some reason?[24] Or did a tree replace a mountain on which it was planted in the course of oral tradition (e.g., Mark 11:13)?[25] However the question is resolved, the following observations seem relevant. First, v. 5 is unique to Luke, with no counterpart in the Synoptics; and v. 6, with the exception of "mustard seed" (a catchword employed more than once by Jesus), is dissimilar to Matt 17:20. Vv. 5-6 thus appear to derive from Luke's special source, which forms a large block of material extending from 16:19 to 17:22. Second, the Greek word for "sea" (v. 6; *thalassa*) is not typical of Luke (only at 17:2, 6; 21:25). Whenever Luke refers to the Sea of Galilee, he uses the Greek word *limnē*, not *thalassa.*[26] *Thalassa* in vv. 2, 6 thus scarcely refers to the Sea of Galilee, although it could refer to the Dead Sea.[27] Third, the Greek word for "mulberry tree," *sykaminos,*

21. Nolland, *Luke 9:21–18:34*, 838, "What is needed is not the increase of faith, but the exercise of faith."

22. See literature gathered in Str-B 1:459.

23. Str-B 2:234; C.-H. Hunzinger, *sykaminos, TWNT* 7:758.

24. So Schweizer, *Lukas,* 175.

25. Lagrange, *Luc,* 453.

26. 5:1, 2; 8:22, 23, 33. On Lukan references to the Sea of Galilee and their relation to the Hebrew Gospel, see at 5:1.

27. All references to the Dead Sea in the LXX refer to it as a *thalassa:* Gen 14:3; Num 34:3, 12; Deut 3:17; Josh 3:16; 12:3; 15:2, 5; 18:19.

occurring only here in the NT, derives from the Hebrew *shiqmāh*. Vv. 5-6 thus contain two loan words, one of which is a definite Hebraism, and they follow a pericope (vv. 1-4) that exhibits verbal and thematic parallels to quotations from the Hebrew Gospel. This is modest but tantalizing evidence that vv. 5-6 also derive from the Hebrew Gospel.

7-10   Luke concludes the catena of Jesus-sayings with a brief parable. Like many shorter parables in Luke, this one is identified as an illustration rather than a parable, "Which one of you?" (v. 7; NIV "Suppose one of you").[28] In all his parables Jesus appealed to the common knowledge and everyday experiences of his hearers. Earlier he spoke of a master who served his slaves (12:37); here he speaks of slaves serving their master (on slavery in Israel, see at 16:1). Included in a slave's responsibilities were serving his master, including serving the master before he served himself. The conditions in the parable reflect these customs.[29]

If a master has a servant who comes in from plowing or tending sheep, the master does not instruct the servant to meet the servant's own needs first. Rather, the servant is expected to tend to the master's need first, and only afterward to his own. The servant should expect no special recognition or reward for so doing, for he is a servant, after all, and has only done what is expected of servants. If he has done everything required of him, he should only say, "We are unworthy servants; we have only done our duty" (v. 10).[30] The reference to

---

28. Luke begins nine parables likewise: 11:5, 11; 12:25; 14:5, 28, 31; 15:4, 8; 17:7.

29. Bovon, *Lukas 15,1–19,27*, 137: "The sharp realism of the speaker as well as the structure and Semitic style of the parable are all arguments in favor of this as an authentic parable of Jesus."

30. Bovon, *Lukas 15,1–19,21*, 140-42, interprets the parable allegorically: thus, master connotes God; slaves and shepherds, church officials; serving, diaconate ministry; eating and drinking, Eucharist; field, mission outreach; plowing, evangelism. Klein, *Lukasevangelium*, 560-61, agrees; Schweizer, *Lukas*, 175, disagrees. Given the typically allergic reaction of modern scholarship to allegory, Bovon's interpretation is unusual. Allegory was unquestionably a major method of interpretation in the ancient world, including Jewish world (e.g., Isa 5:1-7; Jer 18:1-10; Ezek 23; esp. Philo). Allegory dominated patristic exegesis, which in turn influenced the exegetical tradition of Eastern Orthodoxy. On patristic exegesis, A. Coxe notes, "To us there is often a barren bush, where the Fathers saw a bush that burned with fire" (*Ante-Nicene Fathers* [Grand Rapids: Eerdmans, 1977], 1:504). The extent to which allegory influenced Jesus is debated, however. On the whole, Jesus' parables do not exhibit the allegorical tendencies of his contemporaries. There are some exceptions (interpretation of parable of the Sower [8:11-15 par.], parable of Weeds among Wheat [Matt 13:24-30, 36-43]), but modern scholars debate whether these cases derive from Jesus or from early church interpretation. The parable of vv. 7-10 could be allegorical, as Bovon suggests, but it would be unusual if it were. Bovon sees the shift in emphasis from master (vv. 7-9) to servants (v. 10) as evidence that v. 10 is a later oral addition. His reasoning for this is neither clear nor convincing, for the initial attention to the master is necessary in order to emphasize the duty of the servants in conclusion.

doing "what was expected of servants" (v. 9; Gk. *ta diatachthenta*) is a "divine passive," a reference to God without using the name, meaning doing what the *master* (= God) commands.[31] The apostle Paul made a Greek wordplay on an unworthy or useless servant: the runaway slave Onesimus (whose name meant "useful") once was *achrēstos* ("useless"), but having come to faith, he became *euchrēstos* ("useful"; Phlm 11). The word for "unworthy" (v. 10; *achreios*, "useless, of no profit") derives from the same verbal root that Paul used to describe Onesimus. A "useless slave" is an oxymoron, for the purpose of a slave was to be useful. "The groundwork that lies underneath great faith and prayer," says Bengel, "is lowly poverty of spirit, and a profound sense of our *unprofitableness*, and of the debt of duty we owe [Christ]."[32] All true service of Christ inculcates such humility in disciples, for whatever disciples render Christ is not to their merit, but simply their duty (1 Cor 9:16-18). A person making a mountain rescue may be more spectacular than a parent or teacher who sets a moral example, but the former does not necessarily perform a greater service than the latter; and even if mountaineers performed a greater service, they would only be doing their duty — doing for others what they would wish for themselves in similar circumstances — in undertaking a perilous rescue attempt. Rabbi Johanan ben Zakkai (first c.) said the same, "If you have accomplished much in the Law, do not claim merit for yourself, for this was the purpose for which you were created" (*m. 'Abot* 2:8). Even the apostles (v. 5) — apostles who may even consider themselves better than the Pharisees! — are still servants, and whatever they do as apostles is but service due their Lord. Conformity to God's will does not lead to thoughts of "extra credit," self-merit, or entitlement, but to humility; not to pride, but to joy!

A FOREIGNER WHO WAS A "TRUE ISRAELITE" (17:11-19)

11 The references in this verse to Galilee, Samaria, and Jerusalem (= Judea) remind readers that Jesus' ministry encompassed all political and geographical regions of Palestine.[33] For the sixth time since the Transfiguration and the fifth since the commencement of the central section, Luke reminds readers that Jesus' ministry must be completed in Jerusalem (9:31, 51, 53; 13:22, 33; 17:11). V. 11 can be wholly and easily rendered in Hebrew. The concentration of Hebraisms remains unusually high throughout vv. 11-19, and they are complemented by

---

31. Jeremias, *Sprache des Lukasevangeliums*, 264.

32. Bengel, *Gnomon*, 2:159; also Lagrange, *Luc*, 456.

33. So E. Lohmeyer, *Galiläa und Jerusalem* (FRLANT 52; Göttingen: Vandenhoeck & Ruprecht, 1936), 41.

signature Lukan expressions such as "giving glory to God (vv. 15, 16, 18), falling at Jesus' feet (v. 16), and the final benediction (v. 19). The entire pericope is not only unique to Luke but distinctly Hebraic.[34]

The brief itinerary in v. 11 is the most specific travel description in the central section. The grammatical forms of two different verbs for "go" (*poreuesthai* as articular infinitive, "as he was traveling"; and *dierchesthai* in imperfect, "he was going") emphasize Jesus' movement toward Jerusalem. The second verb (often imperfect, as here) is the preferred term in Luke-Acts for interregional travel outside Judea, accompanied in eleven instances by one place-name, and in nine instances by two place-names.[35] The conclusion of the verse, literally translated "through the midst of Samaria and Galilee," requires special consideration. The Greek prepositional phrase *dia meson* ("through the midst") occurs only here in the Greek Bible. When used with the accusative of a spatial reference, as it is here, *dia* carries the sense of "space traversed," meaning "through" or "over."[36] Luke uses virtually the same phrase *(dia mesou)*, again with *dierchesthai*, in 4:30 with reference to Jesus' going through the midst of the crowd. The particular space here traversed would be the region of the Decapolis, which protrudes like an arrowhead into Jewish territory west of the Jordan between Samaria and Galilee, in which Beth-shan was located.[37] The sequence of "Samaria and Galilee" is not backward, as several modern exegetes imagine,[38] if one remembers that in the ancient world the point of *orient*ation was east rather than north, and that it was customary to mention locations to the right (= Samaria) before those to the left (= Galilee). One must further remember that, when traveling south from Galilee, Jews normally skirted Samaria by going eastward to Perea in Transjordan, through which

34. Seventeen Hebraisms are evident in vv. 11-19; see Edwards, *Hebrew Gospel,* 320. Fitzmyer, *Luke (X–XXIV),* 1149, acknowledges a pre-Lukan source of the material, though without identifying it as the Hebrew Gospel. On the signature Lukan expressions in the pericope, see Klein, *Lukasevangelium,* 561, n. 6.

35. *Dierchesthai* occurs ten times in Luke (only twice each in Matt and Mark) and twenty times in Acts (only 5x elsewhere total in the NT). With one place-name: 2:15; 8:22; 19:1; Acts 8:4, 40; 9:32, 38; 13:6; 18:27; 19:1; 20:2. With two place-names: 17:11; Acts 11:19; 13:14; 14:24; 15:3, 41; 16:6; 18:23; 19:21.

36. H. Smyth, *Greek Grammar* (rev. G. Messing; Cambridge: Harvard University Press, 1984), 374.

37. See *TAVO,* B V 18 (N).

38. Too many commentators follow H. Conzelmann's judgment (*Die Mitte der Zeit: Studien zur Theologie des Lukas* [6th ed.; BHT 17; Tübingen: Mohr Siebeck, 1977], 60-66) that Luke's geography in v. 11 is confused and inaccurate (e.g., BDF §222; BDAG, 635; Fitzmyer, *Luke (X–XXIV),* 1152-54; Wolter, *Lukasevangelium,* 571; Vinson, *Luke,* 545-47). As noted above, the unique particulars in v. 11 correspond to the itinerary and description appropriate to an observant Jew traveling from Galilee to Jerusalem. Luke's description reflects the way an ancient Jew making such a journey would describe it.

they then traveled south to Jerusalem. The geographic description of v. 11 is exactly what we should expect with reference to Jesus' itinerary: he is traveling eastward "along the border between Samaria and Galilee" (v. 11; NIV) as he makes his way to Jerusalem.[39]

12-19 As Jesus entered "a certain village," he was met by "ten men who had leprosy" (v. 12). In referring to the ten as *men* rather than as mere "lepers," Luke acknowledges their humanity, thus verbally reclaiming them from the defacement associated with leprosy.[40] The reference to "village" would appear to eliminate Beth-shan, a model Hellenistic city of the Decapolis that lay in the region between Samaria and Galilee, as the place of encounter. It would be natural, however, for ritually unclean lepers to congregate in a small and remote town elsewhere in the Decapolis, for the Decapolis, which hosted many Gentiles, including the Roman army, was considered ritually "unclean." The lepers "stood at a distance and called out in a loud voice, 'Jesus, Master, have pity on us'" (v. 13). Lepers were required to observe a fifty-pace buffer so as not to contaminate people or places (Lev 13:45-46; on leprosy, see at 5:12). Hence, they call to Jesus from "a distance." The reference to "Jesus, Master" suggests an attitude of expectation and trust on their part, for the only persons who refer to Jesus as "Master," an epithet unique to Luke's Gospel, are the Twelve or Jesus' disciples (see on term at 5:5).[41] In so addressing Jesus, the ten are exhibiting the first step in discipleship.

The lepers do not plead for healing — perhaps they have long abandoned such hope. Their plea, though, is a virtual prayer, "Have pity on us" (v. 13). The Greek expression, *eleēson hēmas,* is a petition befitting God, and for the grace and mercy that only God can give.[42] Jesus does not touch them (as he does, for example, in Mark 1:41), promise them healing, or directly acknowledge their request.[43] Rather, he orders them to present themselves to the priests. The relevant priests need not be the ones on duty in the temple at Jerusalem (or perhaps Mount Gerizim) in order to pass a verdict on leprosy. Jesus' command conforms to the traditional rite of cleansing as specified in Torah, demonstrating that he is not a renegade rabbi in such matters.[44] Any Samaritans among

---

39. F. Delitzsch correctly translated Gk. *dia meson* as *ben,* "*between* Samaria and Galilee," in his *Hebrew New Testament* (Berlin, 1931). Plummer, *Luke,* 403, understands Luke properly.

40. Noted by Nolland, *Luke 9:21–18:34,* 846.

41. 5:5; 8:24 (2x), 45; 9:33, 49; 17:13.

42. R. Bultmann, *eleos, TWNT* 2:480-82.

43. The readings of Codex Bezae (D), "You shall be healed," and a note in the margin of p[75], "I wish for you to be cleansed, and immediately they were cleansed," are likely later scribal additions supplying a response of Jesus to their request.

44. Tertullian (*Marc.* 4.25) made this point against Marcion, who asks, "Was it as a despiser of the law" that Jesus sent the ten to the priests? Garland, *Luke,* 691, erroneously

the lepers would present themselves to priests on Mount Gerizim, and Jews among them (if there were any) would present themselves to priests in the temple in Jerusalem.[45] The command itself is curious, for self-presentation to priests was the legal prescription for those who had *already* been healed (Lev 14:2-4). Jesus commands the men to act proleptically, in other words, to act on a reality that is not yet actual. In doing so he repeats an idea taught in the Lord's Prayer, the petition *to live in the presence of the promises* (see at 11:3). As the lepers acted on Jesus' commandment, "they were cleansed" (v. 14). The word for "cleansed" (Gk. *katharizein*) is used throughout Luke with respect to leprosy, for leprosy was both a disease to be healed and a ritual impurity to be cleansed.[46]

"One of them, when he saw he was healed, came back, praising God in a loud voice" (v. 15). Jesus' *exousia* — his power and authority — are so great that, as in the healing of the centurion's servant (7:10), he can heal at a distance.[47] The word for "return" (Gk. *hypostrephein*) is a favorite Lukan word; twenty-one of its twenty-two occurrences in the Gospels are in Luke. Here the concrete act of returning is also symbolic of converting to faith.[48] The man returned to praise Jesus not when he had been declared clean by a priest, but when he "saw that he was healed."[49] Having been healed, he no longer observed the safety zone required of lepers.[50] The description of his returning to praise God (v. 15) is remarkably close in wording to the shepherds praising God after returning from visiting the infant Jesus (2:20).[51] "To praise (or glorify) God" is a quintessential Lukan expression, occurring eight times in the Third Gospel and only once each in Matt and Mark.[52] In Acts 12:23 Luke relates a sobering story about an individual who failed to render glory to God. Sitting or falling at Jesus' feet is also quintessential Lukan, occurring ten times in Luke, and another five times with reference to falling

---

argues that this passage "radically subverts the significance of the temple's rituals." For priestly protocol in the healing of lepers, see at 5:14.

45. The question of R. Bultmann, *The History of the Synoptic Tradition* (New York: Harper & Row, 1972), 33, "What could a Samaritan want with Jewish priests?" is oddly insensitive to Samaritan Judaism.

46. 4:27; 5:12-13; 7:22; 17:14, 17.

47. Additional distance healings in the Gospels occur in Mark 7:29 (par. Matt 15:28); Luke 7:10 (par. Matt 8:13; John 4:50). In each instance the miracle is attested to have occurred at the time when the working word was spoken.

48. H. D. Betz, "The Cleansing of the Ten Lepers (Luke 17:11-19)," *JBL* 90/3 (1971): 318-19, "[The Samaritan's] return to Jesus amounts to his conversion. . . . For the narrator the Samaritan has become a Christian."

49. So Plummer, *Luke*, 404.

50. Bock, *Luke 9:51–24:53*, 1403.

51. Garland, *Luke*, 690.

52. 2:20; 5:25, 26; 7:16; 13:13; 17:15; 18:43; 23:47.

at the apostles' feet in Acts.[53] In Israel one normally fell prostrate in reverence before an altar or at the feet of a king, not before an ordinary human (Acts 10:25-26). The glorification and reverence characteristically rendered to God are here rendered to Jesus — and by a non-Israelite who was a leper, a foreigner, and a Samaritan. "He was a Samaritan" is appended to v. 16 with obvious emphasis, implying "Look who rendered thanks!" Samaritans (see at 10:33) were regarded by Jews not simply as outcasts but as apostates who were loathed. This particular Samaritan, however, in showing glory and reverence to Jesus, fulfills the chief purpose for which Israel exists.

"Were not all ten cleansed?" asked Jesus. "Where are the other nine? Was no one found to return and give praise to God except this foreigner?" (vv. 17-18). If the nine who failed to return were all Jews, then the irony of Jesus' question is biting. Jews, after all, had been tutored to give thanks to God, whereas no such expectation was associated with a Samaritan. We should be cautious about inferring the identity of the other nine, however, for Luke does not say the Samaritan who returned was the only Samaritan, or that the other nine were all Jews.[54] What can be said is that all ten were miraculously healed, but only one returned to glorify and revere Jesus — and the one who returned was the *least* expected to do so. The experience of Jesus reflects that of many ministers, evangelists, and missionaries who invest their lives in other people and situations and often see very little response. Skeptics often assert that, if only they saw a true miracle, they would believe. This story debunks that commonplace. The other nine witnessed a miracle in their own flesh. They were doubtless convinced of the miraculous — and content with it — but it did not lead them to Jesus, faith, or salvation. The Samaritan experienced the same miracle but encountered *God* in it. He returned to Jesus in gratitude, and in returning, Jesus declares him not simply "cleansed," as a priest would, but "whole," even "saved," for the Greek *sōzein* combines both latter meanings.[55]

The narrative provides no further information on the nebulous nine but focuses specifically on the Samaritan, "this foreigner" (v. 18). The Greek word for "foreigner," *allogenēs,* occurs only this once in the NT. The same word occurs occasionally in the LXX, but its most dramatic referent appears in the famous warning in the Jerusalem temple. On the *soreq,* the wall separating the Court of Gentiles from the Jewish sanctuary proper, stones appeared periodically with the following inscription chiseled into them: "No foreigner is

53. 7:38 (3x), 44, 45, 46; 8:35, 41; 10:39; 17:16; Acts 4:35, 37; 5:2, 10; 10:25. See Jeremias, *Sprache des Lukasevangeliums,* 168.

54. Schlatter, *Lukas,* 389, overstates the evidence in assuming the other nine were ungrateful Jews.

55. H. D. Betz, "The Cleansing of Ten Lepers (Luke 17:11-19)," *JBL* 90/3 (1971): 325-26; Schweizer, *Lukas,* 177-78.

permitted inside the partition and wall around the temple. Whoever is caught will have himself to blame for his ensuing death."[56] *Allogenēs,* used both in v. 18 and in the temple warning inscription, does not occur in ancient Greek literature outside Jewish and Christian sources. *Allogenēs* was apparently a catchword word among Jews, a verbal boundary marker like Sabbath, circumcision, and pork, dividing Jew and Gentile, clean and unclean, purity and defilement. In the temple warning inscription it designated a foreigner whose ritual defilement was so odious that, in the precincts of the sanctuary, it would be grounds for death. Not unlike Jesus' reference to the non-Israelite Syrophoenician woman as a "dog" (Mark 7:27; Matt 15:26), Jesus here utters a "street reference" to a non-Israelite in order to intensify the scandal of Jewish ethnocentrism, for a Syrophoenician "dog" and a Samaritan "foreigner," both despised by Jews, are paragons of faith in Israel.[57]

Jesus dismisses the grateful Samaritan with his blessing, "Rise and go; your faith has made you well" (v. 19). This favorite Lukan benediction, like many words and phrases in the pericope, reinforces Jesus' affirmation of the Samaritan. "Your faith has made you well" occurs four times in Luke with reference to a sinful woman (7:50), a hemorrhaging woman (8:48), "this Samaritan" (17:19), and a blind beggar (18:42). The benediction is never used of a Pharisee or Jewish leader, but only of sinners, outsiders, the unclean and needy, for "of such is the kingdom of God" (18:16). The word for "made you well," it must be remembered, is the same Greek word for "saved," *sōzein.* Trust in Jesus — not ritual, sacrifice, or works — brings one into a right relationship with God, making one whole in body and spirit.

THE PROGRESS OF PILGRIMS FROM THE CITY OF DESTRUCTION TO THE CELESTIAL CITY" (17:20-37)

The present section begins with a question of Pharisees about the arrival of the kingdom of God (vv. 20-21), followed by Jesus teaching the disciples about the coming of the Son of Man (vv. 22-37). It is possible to treat the two units separately,[58] but it seems more likely that the two are juxtaposed in order to

---

56. In 1871 in Jerusalem, C. Clermont-Ganneau discovered a finished stone with a complete warning inscription in Greek. The original stone and inscription are today exhibited in the Istanbul Archaeological Museum. This same inscription is thrice referred to by Josephus (*J.W.* 5.194; 6.125-26; *Ant.* 15.417), although with slightly different wording. See Schürer, *History of the Jewish People,* 2:285, n. 57; A. Deissmann, *Light from the Ancient East,* 79-81. The reference in F. Büchsel, *allogenēs, TWNT* 1:266-67, misquotes the Greek inscription.

57. The response of Peter to Cornelius in Acts 10:28 virtually reverses the temple warning!

58. E.g., Bock, *Luke 9:51–24:53,* 1409.

offer a new and fuller revelation of the kingdom of God. This is not the first time the Pharisees have commented on the kingdom (14:15). Jesus now explains that the question of the coming of the kingdom cannot be understood apart from reference to himself, both in his present (v. 21) and in his future (vv. 22-37) appearances.[59] Reference to the future appearance of the Son of Man introduces the theme of eschatology. All three Synoptics set Jesus' major eschatological teaching during Passion Week, either in the temple (21:5-36; Matt 24) or in relation to it (Mark 13). Here, however, Luke sets the ethics of discipleship, which figure prominently in the central section, in the context of an additional (though shorter) eschatological discourse in the midst of Jesus' ministry. Some of the same images and themes of the Passion eschatological discourse reappear here, including "day(s) of the Son of Man," mistaken and premature expectations, the inability to escape, insouciance before the impending *eschaton,* and the disruption of intimate human fellowship.[60] These themes are not always used to the same effects in Luke 17 as they are in Matt and Mark, and their verbal similarities are not close enough to guarantee derivation from a common written source. A comparative analysis of vv. 21-37 suggests that Luke gathered materials from various sources for the purpose of exhorting disciples to proper behavior in light of future judgment.

20-21 The question "when the kingdom of God would come" (v. 20) should not be ascribed to ill will on the Pharisees' part. Jesus himself had spoken earlier of the nearness of the kingdom (10:9; Matt 4:17; Mark 1:15; on the kingdom of God, see at 4:43). Jesus and the Pharisees were agreed that the kingdom would come; hence, the Pharisees do not ask *if* it will come, but *when.* Given Jewish interest in **the day of salvation**, Pharisees could be expected to press Jesus on this point. Divine wisdom "knows the things of old, and infers the things to come" (Wis 8:8). Jesus taught his disciples to pray that God's kingdom, widely attested in the Pss (47; 93; 97–99), would prevail on earth as in heaven (11:2; Matt 6:10). Jews understandably desired to be instructed in the divine plan, which they believed had been determined

---

59. Similar relations between vv. 20-21 and vv. 22-37 are acknowledged by Fitzmyer, *Luke (X–XXIV),* 1167, and Bovon, *Lukas 15,1–19,27,* 183.

60. The following chart relates Luke 17 with counterparts in Matt's and Mark's Passion Narratives (according to Bock, *Luke 9:51–24:53,* 1420-22):

Luke	Matt	Mark
17:21	24:23	13:21
17:23	24:23	13:21
17:24	24:27	—
17:27	24:38-39	—
17:31	24:17-18	13:15-16
17:35	24:41	—
17:37b	24:28	—

from eternity.[61] Beginning with Dan 12:1 and continuing in the Apocrypha, Pseudepigrapha, and rabbinic literature, Jewish tradition was agreed that the day of salvation would necessarily be preceded by great hardship and distress, but that deliverance would follow for those whose names were written in the Book of Life. Attempts to calculate the arrival of the day of salvation were notoriously inconclusive, however.[62] Such attempts easily became obsessive and unhealthy, as they subsequently have in Christianity, prompting one rabbi to declare in reaction, "Whoever forecasts the world to come has no part in it!"[63]

Although less brusque, Jesus declares that the arrival of the kingdom "is not something that can be observed" (v. 20). The Greek word for "observed," *paratērēsis,* occurring only here in the NT,[64] was a technical term in Hellenism for calculating future events by observing the stars.[65] Astrological calculations assume that occurrences in the physical world portend concomitant occurrences in the spiritual world. Jesus does not confirm this assumption, first because it assumes God's kingdom to be exclusively a future entity, and second because it identifies God's kingdom intrinsically with the empirical world.[66] God's kingdom is active in this world, but it is not determined by events in this world, and hence temporal events cannot predict its arrival.

If *time* cannot be used to calculate the arrival of the kingdom, neither can *place.* No one can say, "Here it is" or "There it is," because "the kingdom of God is in your midst" (v. 21). This verse is unique to Luke, although variations of it occur in four early Christian documents.[67] Unlike mystery religions, which were inseparably identified with specific cult sites — Magna Mater with Mount Ida, or Ephesian Artemis with Ephesus — the kingdom of God cannot be limited to site or sanctuary. Rather, the kingdom is "in your midst." This phrase is often understood, as it was by many early church fathers, to refer to a spiritual and ethical kingdom within the soul of the individual believer, analogous to the breath of life breathed into humanity at creation (Gen 2:7).

---

61. See Bovon, *Lukas 15,1–19,27,* 164-65.

62. World history was variously divided into twelve epochs (*4 Ezra* 14:48), ten epochs (*1 En.* 93:1-10), seven days (*2 En.* 33:1-2), different aeons or generations (*As. Mos.* 1:1), or attempts to interpret Judah's seventy years in exile as symbolic of the end time (*2 Bar.* 39:3). The literature is fully surveyed in Str-B 4/2:977-1015. In a related vein, rabbis declared that the day of salvation would arrive if Israel would keep two consecutive Sabbaths according to Torah prescriptions. Conversely, the day of salvation had not come because Israel was not united in the covenant (Str-B 1:600).

63. The quotation is from R. Jose ben Chalaphta (second c.; Str-B 4/2:1015).

64. On possible Hebraic backgrounds of the expression, see Str-B 2:236; G. Dalman, *The Words of Jesus* (trans. D. Kay; Edinburgh: T&T Clark, 1909), 143-45.

65. Wolter, *Lukasevangelium,* 576.

66. Green, *Luke,* 629.

67. Minor variations occur in Mark 13:21, Matt 24:23, and *Gos. Thom.* 3; more major variations, in *Gos. Thom.* 113 and *P.Oxy.* 654:9-16.

The modern appeal of individualism, psychology, and "spiritual experience" makes this an attractive interpretation. Three reasons argue against this understanding, however. First, it is scarcely imaginable that Jesus would assure the Pharisees that the kingdom of God was within them. With one possible exception (13:31), Pharisees are not commended in Luke, and nowhere are they designated as models of the kingdom. Second, the conception of the kingdom of God as an exclusively inner and private possession of individual believers is, as many scholars rightly note, taught neither by Jesus nor by the NT as a whole. Marshall is correct in saying that "Jesus speaks of men entering the kingdom, not of the kingdom entering men."[68] In addition to its "vertical" personal presence, the kingdom of God has a "horizontal" dimension embracing the gathered community of other believers. Third, the vocabulary of this phrase, *entos hymōn* (so too *P.Oxy.* 654), is distinctive in the NT. The preposition *entos,* meaning "inside" or "within," occurs but twice in the NT, and in combination with the plural pronoun *hymōn* must be understood as "among you [plural]" or "in your midst" (NIV).[69] This rare form may derive from an original Hebrew *beqirbekem,* "in your midst" (so Exod 17:7).[70] The sense is that the kingdom is present within a group or community of believers (so 11:20; Matt 18:20). The use of present rather than future tense ("the kingdom of God *is* in your midst") implies that Jesus is referring to the presence of the kingdom *now* rather than in its future and final revelation. "Prior to the incarnation of the Logos of God the kingdom of heaven was as far from us as the sky is from the earth; but when the King of heaven came to dwell amongst us and chose to unite Himself with us, the kingdom of heaven drew near to us all."[71] As Gregory Palamas notes in this quotation, the kingdom is present in the King, Jesus himself (see at 4:43), and hence Jesus can rightly assert to Pharisees and disciples that, in him and his teaching, "The kingdom of God is within your midst" (v. 21).[72]

---

68. Marshall, *Luke,* 655.

69. In Deut 5:14 (LXX) and Isa 45:14 (LXX), even *en soi* (sg.) is used in a plural sense, "in your midst," rather than "in you individually."

70. Franz Delitzsch translates the Gk. *entos hymōn* likewise in his Hebrew NT.

71. Gregory Palamas, "Topics of Natural and Theological Science," in *Philokalia* (London: Faber & Faber, 1995), 4:373.

72. H. Cadbury, "The Kingdom of God and Ourselves," *ChrCent.* 67 (1950): 172-73, following Tertullian (*Marc.* 4.35), offers "within your reach" as a variant translation of the phrase in question. Tertullian took v. 21 to mean that the kingdom of God "is in your hand, within your power, if you hear and do the teaching of God" (*in manu, in potestate vestra, si audiatis, si faciatis Dei praeceptum*). This understanding is favored by a number of modern interpreters (e.g., G. Stanton, *The Gospels and Jesus* [2nd ed.; New York: Oxford University Press, 2002], 210-11; Klein, *Lukasevangelium,* 570-71) because it is consonant with the theology of Luke (and Paul: Rom. 10:5-8 [= Deut 30:11-13]) in calling for a response to the ministry and teaching of

22-25   The Pharisees' question becomes a springboard for Jesus to instruct his disciples on both the future and the present reality of the kingdom. "The time is coming when you will long to see one of the days of the Son of Man, but you will not see it" (v. 22). The original Greek reads lit. "days are coming" (NIV "The time is coming"), which in Second Temple Jewish literature is a technical expression for the advent of the messianic age. "Days are coming" occurs also in 5:35 and 21:6 with reference to a time after Jesus' death, thus assigning a future referent to what follows. According to v. 22 the church will enter a season of discontent in which disciples will long in vain for the presence of Jesus, either in his earthly ministry or more likely in its future glory. The exact meaning of "one of the days of the Son of Man" (on Son of Man, see at 5:24) is uncertain. A Hebraism likely lies behind this Greek rendering, in which "one" refers to "the *first* of days of the Son of Man," just as a similar Greek rendering means "the *first* day of the Sabbath" (e.g., Acts 20:7).[73] This fits the future sense established by "days are coming." Thus, the church will enter a protracted and trying interval in which it will long to see the return of Christ, but will not see it.

In this season of discontent disciples will be susceptible to false rumors, plans, and timetables. It will be said, "There he is!" or "Here he is!" (v. 23).[74] No matter how attractive or enticing the rumors, disciples should not "go after" (Gk. *aperchesthai*) or "pursue" (Gk. *diōkein*) them. The first verb tells them not to be *deceived,* i.e., diverted or distracted from the course of discipleship; and the second verb not to be *deceivers* who pursue such falsehoods and lead others astray. The reason is given in v. 24. Like a bolt of lightning illuminating the expanse of sky in a flash of light, the Son of Man will come, and his coming will be inescapable. In Jewish tradition the identity of Messiah would not be immediately apparent. The rabbis, in particular, taught that Messiah would appear incognito and be recognized only after careful examination, or only when made known by Elijah.[75] In striking contrast to such eschatological tentativeness, Jesus declares the coming of the Son of Man to be sudden, unpredictable, and, above all, universally visible, literally "shining from one end under heaven to the other end under heaven" (v. 24). The first half of the above expression appears in Exod 17:14, Deut 25:19, 29:20, and 2 Macc 2:18, and the second half in Job 38:24. Both halves are combined in v. 24 to signify

---

Jesus. Nevertheless, the lexical character of *entos hymōn* favors the sense "in your midst" (see Bovon, *Lukas 15,1–19,27,* 166-68, who discusses both views at length).

73. So Plummer, *Luke,* 407; Schweizer, *Lukas,* 181.

74. The text of v. 23 cannot be ascertained with certainty because of confusion of several Greek letters, all of which were pronounced similarly, and also due to confusion and perhaps inattention on the part of scribes (see Metzger, *TCGNT,* 142). NIV follows Codex Vaticanus (B) and $\mathfrak{p}^{75}$, which preserve the least-compromised text.

75. Str-B 1:954-55.

the cosmic extent of the Son of Man's appearance.[76] Plummer sums up v. 24: "None will foresee it, and all will see it at once."[77]

With only one exception, Jesus does not attach the coming of the Son of Man to a timetable. The exception is that "first the Son of Man must suffer many things and be rejected by this generation" (v. 25). This statement, nearly verbatim with the first passion prediction in 9:22, is the only passion prediction in the Gospels occurring in an eschatological saying.[78] This is theologically significant, for apocalyptic Christianity often emphasizes religious triumphalism at the expense of costly discipleship, and ascetic Christianity often emphasizes costly discipleship at the expense of ultimate glory. The inclusion of the cross in Jesus' vision of glory gives hope of ultimate triumph to those who suffer, just as it chastens religious triumphalism with the necessity of impending suffering.[79]

26-30   The future coming of the Son of Man is entirely certain, but the exact events that must transpire before the coming are not specified; indeed, according to Mark 13:32, Jesus was as ignorant of such events as are believers. Thus, in response to the Pharisees' question, Jesus calls disciples to be alert, but not at "red alert." If an exact timetable or sequence of preconditions were supplied, believers could simply check them off without faith or spiritual discernment. Believers are taught not to be passive spectators in the tension between present and future, but to be attentive and watchful in events preceding the return of the Son of Man (vv. 22-25). They must be particularly careful to avoid the responses of the generations of Noah and Lot, when people carried on business as usual. They ate, drank, married, gave in marriage, bought, sold, planted, and built — all in oblivion to destruction at the gate. The imperfect tense of these foregoing verbs in vv. 27-28 connotes that the generations of Noah and Lot were chronically and entirely given over to such. Luke again includes a complementary pair in Noah and Lot to emphasize this point, as he does in vv. 34-35 by a complementary male-female pair (see excursus at 14:1). Noah and Lot appear in Jewish tradition as examples of God's judgment on human wickedness.[80] Jesus uses them likewise as examples of what *not* to do. Jesus is atypical, however, in condemning Noah and Lot not for wickedness

---

76. Wolter, *Lukasevangelium*, 580, is correct in noting that Luke's Greek wording follows the LXX verbatim in this expression, while also acknowledging that a Hebrew stereotype lies beneath the Greek wording. Further, see C. Hays, "Hating Wealth and Wives? An Examination of Discipleship Ethics in the Third Gospel," *TynBul* 60/1 (2009): 59, n. 63.

77. Plummer, *Luke*, 407.

78. For a comparison of this saying with counterparts in 9:22 and Mark 8:31, see Jeremias, *Sprache des Lukasevangeliums*, 267-68.

79. So too Plummer, *Luke*, 408.

80. 2 Pet 2:5-8; Jude 6-7; Wis 10:4-7; 3 Macc 2:4-5; Sir 16:8; *Jub.* 20:5; 4Q 180; *T. Naph.* 3:4; Philo, *Mos.* 2.53-56; Str-B 1:574.

and depravity, but for *insouciance* — for inattentiveness and indifference to the dangers at hand.[81] They were attentive to daily business as though it would last forever, and neglectful of eternity as though it would never come. Vv. 26-30 thus reinforce the moral of the parable of the Great Banquet (14:16-23) — people were simply too busy to take the kingdom of God seriously. "It will be just like this on the day the Son of Man is revealed" (v. 30). Only the vigilant few who were prepared for the impending catastrophe were saved. It is these whom Jesus upholds as models for the disciples as they await the coming of the Son of Man. The urgency of the kingdom of God in an age of self-indulgence and moral indifference is the very point at which John Bunyan begins his *Pilgrim's Progress:* a man has a vision of societal indifference to an impending disaster, and with a book in his hand (the Bible) and a burden on his back (sin), he forsakes the City of Destruction, even kindred and family (14:26!), and sets out for the Celestial City.

31-33 On the day when the Son of Man is revealed, "no one who is on the housetop, with possessions inside, should go down to get them. Likewise, no one in the field should go back for anything" (v. 31). "That day" (or "those days") was a technical expression in both Judaism and early Christianity for the arrival of the *eschaton*.[82] Going down from a flat-roofed Palestinian house (see at 5:19) or returning from the field to retrieve something would seem superfluous at the return of the Son of Man. The interjection "Remember Lot's wife!" (v. 32), helps explain v. 31.[83] When fire and brimstone fell on Sodom, when the end was at hand and no further deed or misdeed seemed relevant to one's final fate, Lot's wife looked behind as she fled and, in so doing, became a pillar of salt (Gen 19:17, 26).[84] Her longing look backward to Sodom became proverbial in Israel for disobedience, "a pillar of salt standing as a monument to an unbelieving soul" (Wis 10:7). In vv. 26-30 Jesus warned against indifference to the coming kingdom, but in vv. 31-33, and especially in the haunting image of Lot's wife, he argues *for* indifference to all worldly interests. The latter indifference is the only preparation to receive the Son of Man in his second coming.[85]

---

81. Plummer, *Luke*, 408, describes the theme of these verses as "careless enjoyment suddenly overwhelmed."

82. E.g., Jer 3:16, 18; 31:29; 33:15; Joel 3:1. On the expression in Luke, see Jeremias, *Sprache des Lukasevangeliums*, 139.

83. V. 32 is commonly (though mistakenly) thought to be the shortest verse in the English Bible. V. 32 has three words and seventeen letters in English (four words and twenty-five letters in Greek), whereas 20:30 has two words and nine letters in English (two words and twelve letters in Greek).

84. In narrating this episode, Josephus, *Ant.* 1.203, includes this aside, "I myself have seen this [column of salt] which remains to this day." Several human-shaped rock salt formations at the southern end of the Dead Sea are today nicknamed "Lot's wife."

85. So Plummer, *Luke*, 409.

"Whoever tries to keep one's life will lose it, and whoever loses one's life will preserve it" (v. 33). This verse preserved a sacred and fundamental Christian paradox,[86] a sober reminder that the temptation to secure one's life in something other than the gospel will result not in its preservation but in its loss. The Greek verb for "keep one's life," *peripoiein,* occurring only here in the Gospels, in the present context implies a reliance to the bitter end on possessions and earthly comforts.[87] Even if one, like Lot's wife, escapes the destruction of Sodom but looks back with longing on what "might have been," one's heart belongs to something other than the gospel. The kingdom of God is more than escaping wrath; it is receiving eternal life from the hand of the Son of Man, and whoever receives that life can no longer yearn for the life the world offers. Like vv. 26-30, which furnished Bunyan with the opening theme of *Pilgrim's Progress,* the sober truth of v. 33 furnished him with its final sentence. Christian, Hopeful, and Ignorance have crossed the river of death and are at the gates of Paradise, but Ignorance, even after the long and perilous journey to the Celestial City, had not the certificate of faith and was turned away. "Then I saw," says Bunyan, "that there was a way to hell, even from the gates of heaven, as well as from the City of Destruction."

34-37 In the latter half of Luke 12, Jesus stressed that discipleship requires decisions that divide the most intimate and important of human relationships (12:35-59). He resumes the same theme here, but with reference to the *eschaton* rather than to his earthly ministry. Two people will be lying in the same bed at night,[88] one taken and the other left; two women will be grinding at a mill, one taken and the other left (vv. 34-35).[89] "Two people" (v. 34; NIV) is masculine in Greek, which in the present context may imply two males (although not necessarily, since a Greek masculine plural pronoun could refer to a group that included females), thus complementing the two females in v. 35. Once again Luke provides two witnesses to establish valid testimony (Deut 19:15), in this instance two *pairs* of witnesses, one male and one female (see excursus at 14:1). Modern sensitivities could perceive a same-sex relationship in the analogy of two men sharing a bed; perhaps the analogy suggested the

---

86. 9:24 (par. Mark 8:35; Matt 16:25); 14:26-27 (par. Matt 10:37-38; John 12:24-26; 1 Cor 15:36; Rev 12:11).

87. There is a pronounced inclination in the textual tradition of v. 33 to change *peripoiein* to *sōzein* ("save"), perhaps to harmonize it with 9:24 and/or with the compound verb *zōogonein* in the second half of the verse. See Metzger, *TCGNT,* 142.

88. The suggestion that being taken at night refers to the angel of death at the Passover (Vinson, *Luke,* 556) reads a foreign motif into the illustration (Fitzmyer, *Luke [X–XXIV],* 1172).

89. Codex Bezae (D) includes v. 36 at this point: "Two [men] were in a field; one will be taken and the other will be left behind." Manuscript evidence strongly supports omission of the verse (𝔭⁷⁵ ℵ A B L W Δ Θ Ψ). The probability of v. 36 being a scribal assimilation to Matt 24:40 also argues for the shorter text. See Metzger, *TCGNT,* 142-43.

same to readers of Greco-Romans cultural backgrounds, where homosexual relations were common and celebrated. This is not the intent of the analogy in v. 34.[90] Nowhere in Scripture or in Jesus' teaching on sexuality (Mark 10:2-12) is the practice of homosexuality condoned. Palestinian houses, like most abodes in the ancient Near East, were basic dwellings, and a "bedroom" would be a place where the whole family slept (11:7), including a father and his son(s), or brothers.[91] The analogy of two men in bed illustrates the closest of human ties, as does the analogy of two women grinding *epi to auto* — doing the same thing at the same time and place (v. 35).[92] Outwardly each member of the pair looks the same. Nevertheless, even where a family is bonded or people work in harmony, there the Son of Man knows the heart and soul of each individual and divides accordingly.[93]

Jesus' eschatological lesson ends with the same question with which it began. This time, however, it is asked by disciples rather than Pharisees. "Where, Lord?" (v. 37). The question does not reflect entirely admirably on the disciples, for they request what Jesus has just denied (v. 23). Many conclusions, most of them uncomplimentary, could be drawn from their question. A positive perspective may be the most helpful: the disciples are as impressed by the certainty of the return of the Son of Man as they are by the ambiguity of the events preceding it. Their discontent with the latter — and their discontent anticipates Christian discontent with the issue ever since — elicits an illustration from Jesus. "Where there is a dead body, there the eagles will gather" (v. 37). This image is capable of various interpretations,[94] but assuming that Jesus intends to aid the disciples rather than torment them, the most obvious interpretation commends itself: as eagles are attracted to a dying or dead animal, so the events of vv. 22-26 portend the return of the Son of Man.[95]

---

90. The image of two men lying in one bed reappears in *Gos. Thom.* 61 ("two will be resting on a bed, one will die, and the other will live") and in *Apoc. Zeph.* 2:2-3 ("And I saw two upon a bed, each of them acting [. . . textual corruption]"). *Gos. Thom.* employs the image to illustrate division, as does v. 34, and as does Irenaeus, *Haer.* 5.27.1, who cites v. 34 to the same effect. *Apoc. Zeph.* employs the image to illustrate the heavenly bliss of the righteous.

91. W. McCullough, "Bed," *IDB* 1:372-73.

92. On grinding grain as the work of women in the Jewish world, see Str-B 1:966.

93. See Bovon, *Lukas 15,1–19,27,* 177-78; also Wolter, *Lukasevangelium,* 584.

94. Bock, *Luke 9:51–24:53,* 1439-40, lists seven possible interpretations.

95. Several commentators translate Gk. *aetos* as "vulture" rather than "eagle" (v. 37) on the grounds that eagles do not fly in groups or eat carrion, although vultures do both (so Plummer, *Luke,* 410; Lagrange, *Luc,* 467; Marshall, *Luke,* 669). The translation of *aetos* as "vulture" in NRSV, NIV, and ESV may reflect this thinking. The argument that vultures feed on carrion and eagles on living creatures seems to derive from ancient authorities (Aristotle, *Hist. an.* 9.32 §618a; Pliny, *Nat.* 10.8; and Plutarch, *Mor.,* "The Roman Questions," 93). This is mistaken, however. North American eagles (both bald and golden) do congregate, esp. during nonbreeding season and during migration and wintering. In addition to eating living creatures

Likening the return of the Son of Man to a corpse may seem vulgar, and this is perhaps the reason why Luke used the word "body" (Gk. *sōma*) rather than "corpse" (*ptōma,* so Matt 24:28).[96] Eagles are thus birds of omen, just as events preceding the return of the Son of Man are also omens — not precise time-tables, but certain reminders of the inevitable and ultimate.[97]

By including eschatological instruction in his earthly ministry rather than at the end of it, Jesus signals that eschatology is not an appendage to the gospel, icing on the cake, as it were. Rather, like leaven in dough (13:21) and seed planted in a field (8:8), eschatology is inherent to Jesus' ministry. The future victory of the Son of Man over sin, death, and Satan is therefore essential to the faith and behavior of disciples in the present world. Disciples are not relegated to passive roles as observers or spectators, helplessly longing for the Not Yet. They are given a vision of the One who will come in glory so they may, with hope and resolve, follow the same One who journeys to Jerusalem to "suffer many things and be rejected by this generation" (v. 25). The Son of Man who will come again is the same Son of Man who is now "in your midst" (v. 21). The journey will be long (v. 22), and disciples will be tempted to follow false leads (v. 23). Like the society in which they live, they can easily lapse into neglect and fail in wakefulness and watchfulness (vv. 26-30). They must beware of turning back, even when victory seems assured (vv. 31-34), and of allowing intimate human fellowship and belonging to human communities to replace their allegiance to Jesus and the gospel (vv. 33-36).

The inclusion of eschatology in Jesus' earthly ministry is a robust re-

---

they also feed on carrion, roadkill, and at landfills. The same is true of Eastern Imperial eagles and Steppe (Tawny) eagles, both of which populate the Middle East. (I thank Dr. Anne M. Coyle, professor of biology at the University of Jamestown, Jamestown, N.D., for information on eagle habitat, habits, and diet; see further, www.europeanraptors.org/raptors/eastern _imperial_eagle.html; www.europeanraptors.org/raptors/steppe_eagle.html.) Heb. *nesher* can refer to both eagles and vultures (*HALOT* 1:731-32; T. Kronholm, *nesher, TDOT* 10:77-85). Israel's bird (incl. raptor) population is among the most varied in the world, and bearded, black and griffon vultures and golden, imperial, spotted, and tawny eagles were not always carefully differentiated, esp. when observed in flight (E. Firmage, "Zoology," *IDB* 6:1144). Greek differentiates more precisely between "eagle" *(aetos)* and "vulture" *(gyps),* assigning a different word to each. The use of *aetos* in classical Greek (see LSJ, 29) and its five occurrences in the NT (17:37; Matt 24:28; Rev 4:7; 8:13; 12:14) normally connote "eagle" (BDAG, 22, wrongly allows Aristotle and Pliny to determine its meaning at 17:37 and Matt 24:28). Given that eagles congregate and feed on carrion, that Gk. *aetos* regularly means "eagle" rather than "vulture," and that eagles are ubiquitously associated with swiftness (which repeats the same theme of v. 24), "eagle" should remain the preferred translation of *aetos* in v. 37 (so Fitzmyer, *Luke [X–XXIV],* 1173; Bovon, *Lukas 15,1–19,27,* 179-80; Wolter, *Lukasevangelium,* 585).

96. Heb. *peger* can be equally translated by either "body" or "corpse" (Str-B 2:237).

97. Similarly, Job 39:30; Hab 1:8; Rev 19:17-18. In Greek mythology, eagles function frequently as omens, often sent by Zeus (*Il.* 8.247; *Od.* 2.146).

minder that the kingdom of God is not a detached apocalyptic kingdom of the future, but already present in the costly obedience of discipleship. Nor is the kingdom of God a private inner spiritual sanctuary of the believer, but a living fellowship with Christ, who is "in the midst" of his earthly community. Nor again is the kingdom a utopian dream — whether a reactionary or revolutionary political program — but a kingdom in which God's will is done on earth as in heaven. Nor finally is the kingdom a secularization of the gospel in which the "good life" of financial security, social programs, and retirement funds inoculate the blessed hope and blind believers to the sudden, inescapable, and final return of the Son of Man. Jesus Christ is the human face of God. Whoever recognizes the face of the Crucified One will recognize the same face in the reigning Son of Man; and whoever trusts in the ultimate victory of the Son of Man will receive power through the Holy Spirit to follow Jesus on the road to Jerusalem.[98]

A PARABLE ON BOLD AND PERSISTENT PRAYER (18:1-8)

Luke follows the teaching on eschatology (17:20-37) with the parable of the Unjust Judge (vv. 1-8) and the parable of the Pharisee and the Tax Collector (vv. 9-14). The parables share a symmetrical relationship with one another. Jesus prefaces both with morals and concludes both with authoritative pronouncements. Both parables are related by the theme of prayer. In the first, Jesus warns against faintheartedness, especially in prayer, and the second against overconfidence, especially in virtue.[99] Both faintheartedness and overconfidence endanger faithful discipleship.

The indolent judge who succumbs to the importunate widow (vv. 1-8) is similar in theme to the parable of the visitor who rouses his neighbor from bed at night (11:5-13). Both parables underscore the virtue of persistence and determination in discipleship. In both God is cast in negative stereotypes, as a reluctant paterfamilias in the first, and worse, as a reluctant and *corrupt* judge in the second. This is necessary for the effect of the parable, which exhorts believers to continue with prayer and trust, even when the answer is long in coming. The negative image of the judge is counterbalanced by Jesus' concluding assurance in vv. 6-8, which recalls the plenary teaching of Scripture, that God not only hears the prayers of his elect, but surely responds.

1-5 Luke introduces the parable with a moral: "Then Jesus told his disciples a parable to show them that they should always pray and not give

---

98. See Schweizer, *Lukas*, 183-84.
99. On these two attitudes, see Bengel, *Gnomon*, 2:167.

up" (v. 1). Luke characteristically sets major advances of the Third Gospel in the context of Jesus praying, but the present parable is for the benefit of disciples, not Jesus.[100] The exhortation to "always pray" need not be understood as continuous prayer, but rather to pray consistently and persistently, again and again without losing heart or giving up (21:36; 1 Thess 5:17). Rabbis typically exhorted disciples to limit prayer to three times a day (so Dan 6:10), but not to pray constantly, which was considered tedious to both God and man.[101] A different picture of prayer emerges in this parable. Prayer is beset with opposition and discouragement: pleas for justice go unheard (v. 3), answers are delayed (vv. 4, 7), people cry out day and night (v. 7). Prayer is not a parlor exercise, perfunctory and tidy. It is an existential battle, ongoing and ever present, "hope against hope," as Paul would characterize Abraham's desperate prayer for a son (Rom 4:18), imploring God for the realization of his kingdom on earth as in heaven (11:2).

The parable contains a judge and widow, both familiar characters in Luke.[102] The judge "neither feared God nor cared what people thought" (v. 2). The post-Enlightenment ideal of "blind" jurisprudence holds judges accountable to justice, not to the status of disputants. Jesus describes a judge who neither feared God nor had regard for human beings, and is thus accountable to nothing outside himself, whether to God, human rights, or standards of justice. He acts solely in self-interest. Bengel characterizes this as "the creed of the Atheist in power."[103] The Enlightenment may have introduced the standard of the rule of law, but judgments prior to the Enlightenment were not abandoned to arbitrariness. The dual canons noted by Jesus — honor of God and honor of one's fellow human being — were upheld as ideals throughout the Hellenistic world.[104] Plutarch tells of a poor old woman who begged Philip of Macedon, father of Alexander the Great, unsuccessfully for justice. When Philip told the woman he had no time for her, she burst forth, "Then give up being king!" Amazed, Philip proceeded to hear her case, and others as well.[105] Luke's description of the judge is reminiscent of Josephus's description of a Syrian king named Jehoiakim (or Joakeimos, sixth c. B.C.) who was "neither reverent toward God nor kind to man."[106] Zechariah, father of John the

---

100. On the prayers of Jesus, see at 3:21-22, n. 63; 9:18. The prayers of disciples are treated in 11:1-13; 21:36; 22:40, 46; Acts 2:42; 6:3.

101. Str-B 2:237-38.

102. "Judge" (Gk. *kritēs*) occurs nine times in Luke-Acts and only eight times elsewhere in the NT; "widow" occurs twelve times in Luke-Acts, and only thirteen times elsewhere.

103. Bengel, *Gnomon*, 2:168.

104. See Wolter, *Lukasevangelium*, 587-88.

105. *Mor.* "Sayings of Kings and Commanders: Philip the Father of Alexander," 31; cited in *HCNT*, 230-31.

106. Josephus, *Ant.* 10.83.

Baptizer, had precisely the opposite vision: when the messianic age dawned, people would be delivered from their enemies into a reign of holiness and righteousness (1:74-75).

The counterpart to the judge is a woman,[107] a certain widow who implored the judge for vindication of her cause (v. 3). In an age when social services were almost exclusively dependent on human good will, widows, orphans, and the sick and needy were exposed to a precarious social existence. In Israel a woman's link to the outside community depended largely on a male family member, a father in the case of a daughter, a husband in the case of a wife, a son in the case of a widow. The widow of v. 3 has no male to plead her case, leaving her especially defenseless and vulnerable (20:47!). The OT repeatedly upholds the cause of such, especially widows, and abounds in denunciations of those who oppress them.[108] The obstinacy of the judge and defenselessness of the widow would seem to doom the widow's prospects of success. There is a surprise in store, however. From the opening statement, the widow takes the initiative and is unrelenting in her persistence. The Greek imperfect tense of *ērcheto,* "she kept coming" (v. 3, NIV), connotes repeated attempts to persuade the judge.

The widow's plea, expressed in a Hebraic idiom, is "to be avenged from her enemies."[109] This expression, similar to "deliverance from enemies" in the Psalms, focuses on the principle of justice and honor rather than on a particular incident. The theme of vindication appears four times in this brief parable (vv. 3, 5, 7, 8), designating the seriousness of the cause, and hence the earnestness of prayer.[110] The widow is not pestering the judge about a misdemeanor. The prayer enjoined by the parable is not prayer for a parking place, or that God would bless everyone in the world. One does not "cry out to God day and night" (v. 7) for such matters. The prayer enjoined concerns ultimate and existential issues — life, livelihood, honor. These are not elective but inescapable issues, issues about which one prays earnestly.

The judge initially meets the widow's persistence with stubbornness. The Greek *ouk ēthelen* (imperfect tense) means to have no interest or intention of doing something; thus, "for some time he refused" (v. 4, NIV). The Greek word for "time" here is *chronos* (not *kairos*), implying perhaps that the judge

---

107. On Luke's use of pairs, including male-female pairs, see at 14:1.

108. Exod 22:22-24; Deut 10:18; 24:17; 27:19; Ruth 1:20-21; Job 22:9; 24:3; Ps 68:5; Isa 54:4; Jer 22:3; Lam 1:1; Ezek 22:7; Mal 3:5.

109. The Hebraism "to be avenged from . . . ," *nāqam mīn* . . . , occurs in Josh 10:13; Judg 11:36 (LXX Judg 11:36B), 1 Sam 18:25; 24:13(12). On the Hebraism, see Wolter, *Lukasevangelium,* 588. The same Greek expression appears in Josephus, *Ant.* 6.211; *T. Levi* 2:2; and in Bar Kokhba's *P. Babatha* 20:14-16, 37-39.

110. Klein, *Lukasevangelium,* 577, notes that the kernel of the parable is vindication, but without elaborating its significance.

intended *never* to accede to the widow's request.[111] But her persistence has the same effect that Delilah's pleas had on Samson (Judg 16:15-16). The pleas of the widow are like dripping water on sandstone, wearing down the judge. Like the younger son in dire straits (15:17) or the steward facing impending dismissal (16:3), the judge "said to himself" (v. 4; Gk. *eipen en heautō*). Such inner monologues reflect an underlying Hebraic idiom and are characteristic of Luke, signifying an inner resolve to act (see at 12:17). The resolution of the judge has nothing to do with moral reform; he has no more fear of God or respect for people than he ever had. He is motivated solely by practicality, as was the man tucked in bed with his family (11:7-8). The widow's incessant pleas interrupt his life and exhaust him, tax his patience, and bruise his reputation. Her effect on him is registered in a punishing metaphor: literally, she "is beating me black and blue and will be the end of me" (v. 5). The Greek verb *hypōpiazein*, a boxing term, depicts a face swollen and discolored by blows. NIV translates the expression more literally than necessary (lest she "eventually come and attack me!"). The judge surely has little to fear bodily from the widow, but he has learned to fear her persistence, which, metaphorically at least, leaves him "battered and bruised."[112] Paul uses the same term to refer to the limits to which he pushes himself for the sake of the gospel (1 Cor 9:27). The judge has reached his limit, he is "done in." In order to get her off his case, he must deal with her case.

6-8 This concludes the parable. And "the Lord" said, "Listen to what the unjust judge says" (v. 6). "Lord" is Luke's reference to Jesus, not Jesus' reference to the judge in the parable. The reference to "the unjust judge" parallels the wording and theme of "the unjust steward" earlier (16:8). Both references reflect an original Hebrew construction, as does "unrighteous mammon" (16:11).[113] NIV understands v. 6 as a declarative sentence, but since the original Greek had no punctuation marks, the wording could be understood as a rhetorical question of Jesus, which would make the irony more emphatic: "Do you hear what the unjust judge is saying?" The following verse, at any rate, is clearly rhetorical, "Will not God bring about justice for his chosen ones, who cry out to him day and night?" (v. 7). God is like the judge in that he hears the pleas of his children and vindicates them, but unlike the judge, he is not reluctant to do either. If an indolent and immoral judge finally does the right thing, how much more will God, who is compassionate and merciful, render justice to his children! The certainty of God's doing so is signified in the Greek construction *ou mē poiēsē* (v. 7). *Ou mē* with the subjunctive is the strongest imperative in Greek, used here in a future sense, meaning "Will not

---

111. On Luke's use of *chronos*, see Jeremias, *Spraches des Lukasevangeliums*, 64.
112. On the usage of the term in Greek literature, see Wolter, *Lukasevangelium*, 589.
113. BDF §165; Edwards, *Hebrew Gospel*, 321; Wolter, *Lukasevangelium*, 589.

God *absolutely* bring about justice?" God's involvement is not accidental or indifferent. The pleas are those of God's "chosen ones," and he will hear the deep and desperate prayers of his elect who "cry out to him day and night" (v. 7). The phraseology echoes the cries of distress for salvation in the Psalter, "evening, morning, and noon" (Ps 55:16-17). Jesus' response to the Syrophoenician woman illustrates in his own ministry his willingness to act on behalf of those in need (Matt 15:22-28; Mark 7:24-30).

The concluding phrase of v. 7, "Will [God] keep putting them off?" clashes grammatically with the first part of the verse and is far from clear.[114] Literally translated, the Greek reads, "and he is patient with them." Whether this is intended as a question or a declaration, however, is unclear. The verb "to be patient" (Gk. *makrothymein*) seems ill suited to the context, and its present tense disagrees with the emphatic future sense of *ou mē poiēsē* before. Moreover, Greek *kai* ("and") seems to reflect the Hebrew copulative *wehi*. Most of these problems are resolved if the phrase is understood to recall Sir 35:19, "And the Lord does not delay, nor is he patient with them" (LXX).[115] The parable as a whole is thematically close to Sir 35:14-20, thus making a specific reference to the text plausible. An allusion to Sirach would account for the unusual use of *makrothymein,* and also for a Hebraic *wehi* (Sir was originally written in Heb.). Furthermore, the resultant theme of the immediacy (NIV "quickly") of God's help recurs in the following verse. V. 7b therefore appears to carry forth the theme of 7a, although in different grammatical form, "Will not God bring about justice for his chosen ones. . . . Will he keep putting them off?" (v. 7, NIV).[116]

Jesus concludes the lesson of the parable by shifting from a rhetorical question to an emphatic pronouncement, "I tell you, [God] will see that they get justice, and quickly" (v. 8). This pronouncement creates a problem, for it seems undeniable that God, like the unjust judge, *delays* in vindicating injustice. This brings us to the doorstep of theodicy: "If God is good, why does God allow evil?" More precisely, according to v. 8, "If God is good, why does he *delay* in eradicating evil?" The crux of the problem lies with "quickly," which implies a temporal reference. The Greek prepositional phrase behind "quickly," *en tachei,* occurs twenty times in the Greek Bible, and with four varying connotations. In four instances it connotes "immediately" (Josh 8:18, 19; Acts 12:7; 22:18); in six, "soon" (Acts 25:4; 1 Tim 3:14; Bar 4:22, 24, 25; Sir 27:3);[117] in three, "suddenly" (Ps 2:12; Ezek 29:5; 3 Macc 5:43); and in six, "surely," i.e., assuring

---

114. Bock, *Luke 9:51–24:53,* 1453-54, surveys a dozen possible translations of v. 7b.

115. NRSV, "Indeed, the Lord will not delay, and like a warrior will not be patient until he crushes the loins of the unmerciful" (Sir 35:22).

116. This resolution is favored by Fitzmyer, *Luke (X–XXIV),* 1180, and Wolter, *Lukasevangelium,* 590.

117. So too Bock, *Luke 9:51–24:53,* 1455, who translates the expression "soon."

the certainty of something happening (Deut 11:17; 28:20; 1 Sam 23:22; Rom 16:20; Rev 1:1; 22:6). The first two senses imply a future event that will happen in close proximity to the present, either immediately or soon. The last two senses, having no particular relation to the present, are thus not exactly temporal. Rather, the certainty that something will happen allows it to be spoken of as a present reality — or a near reality, "soon." It is true that the third sense, "suddenly," corresponds with the sense of 17:24 immediately above, and this encourages some commentators to favor this translation.[118] Nevertheless, the rendering "certainly" or "surely," which is frequently attested within the semantic domain of *en tachei,* seems most appropriate to the sense of the parable. Unlike the unprincipled and equivocating judge in the parable, God is not indifferent to injustice. At root, *en tachei* is a confession about the character of God.[119] In the kingdom of God, justice is not a peripheral matter; it is inherent within the character of God. God does not hear the longings and cries of his elect with indifference, but with solidarity. *En tachei* emphasizes that solidarity. In God's sovereign plan of salvation, however, solidarity with the oppressed is combined with forbearance, which is intended to lead sinners to repentance (Rom 2:4). A delay in human reckoning does not in the least imply apathy or inability on God's part, nor is it a "delay" in the divine reckoning (Heb 10:37). The "I tell you" of v. 8a prefaces an authoritative pronouncement of Jesus: "God will surely grant justice!"

The pericope ends, "However, when the Son of Man comes, will he find faith on the earth?" (v. 8). The normal approach to theodicy asks, "Why does a good God allow bad things to happen?" Despite the anguish associated with theodicy, putting the question thus is, in one sense, a comfortable way to put it, for God is in the dock. The onus is on God to deliver, to justify his case. Man is judge, God is on trial. The ultimate concern of Jesus, however, is not with the divine side of the equation; God knows, God cares, God will act, and although it may not happen immediately, it will happen sooner than expected. The ultimate concern rests with the human side of the equation. Jesus is more concerned with *anthropodicy* than with theodicy. "When the Son of Man comes, will he find any faith on the earth?" God is not the only one in the dock; humanity is also in the dock. Greater than the timing of the second coming — for all the problems associated with that question — is the preparedness of humanity to receive it.[120] When the final vindication comes — and it will come — will there be *faith* to receive it? What kind of faith? The kind exhibited by the persistent widow!

---

118. Bovon, *Lukas 15,1–19,27,* 196; and Vinson, *Luke,* 566, favor the sense of "suddenness."

119. See Nolland, *Luke 9:21–18:34,* 871.

120. H. Cadbury, *The Making of Luke-Acts,* 296, aptly notes: "Better God's delay than the unreadiness of men."

THE PARABLE OF THE PHARISEE
AND THE TAX COLLECTOR (18:9-14)

This well-known parable shares several stylistic similarities with its lesser-known predecessor. Both parables contain two characters (on Luke's preference for pairs, see at 14:1), Jesus introduces both with a moral to be taught (18:1, 9) and concludes both with an authoritative pronouncement (18:8, 14), and both depict people praying. The last is important not because either parable is specifically about prayer, but because prayer lays bare the human heart, and Jesus is concerned with the heart. The audience of our parable is no longer disciples (17:22; 18:1), but Pharisees, for v. 14 consciously recalls the description of the Pharisees in 16:15. Both passages remind readers that God knows the difference between a parade of righteousness and the intention of the heart. Several parables of Jesus deal with this same theme, all of them depicting sinful, despised, or outcast people being justified over outwardly righteous people. These parables include those of the Two Sons (Matt 21:28-31), the Two Debtors (7:41-44), the Good Samaritan (10:30-37), the Great Banquet (14:16-23), and especially the Prodigal Son (15:11-32).[121] This theme will receive its orthodox definition in Paul's doctrine of justification by faith (e.g., Rom 10:3; Phil 3:9), but it is not an innovation of Paul. Since several parables suggest this theme, and since in the virtual unanimous judgment of scholars the heart, voice, and even words of the historical Jesus are more audible in the parables than in any other aspect of his teaching, it is proper to conclude that the doctrine of justification by faith is already presupposed and adumbrated in the teaching of Jesus.

9-13 The parable begins with an announcement of its moral: "To some who were confident of their own righteousness and looked down on everyone else, Jesus told this parable" (v. 9). A class of people is described whose behavior, in their estimation, is deemed sufficient evidence of their righteousness, and who "despise" — Gk. *exouthenein* is a term of contempt or rejection (e.g., Ps 118:22) — those who fail to meet their standard. This agrees with Josephus's description of Pharisees as "a class of Jews who consider themselves the godliest of the nation and the most rigorous followers of the law" (*J.W.* 1.111). Jesus (and Luke) may not be thinking exclusively of Pharisees, for scribes and chief priests (the latter of whom were not Pharisees) are similarly described in 20:20. "Confident of their own righteousness" appears to be a Hebraism, which in Jer 7:4 refers to Jews in general. V. 9 should probably be understood with reference to any believers whose pride in their own righteousness is matched by equal contempt for all others.[122] True righteousness is a matter of confidence in God

---

121. On the relation of 18:9-14 to similar parables of Jesus, see Schlatter, *Lukas,* 398; Klein, *Luksasevangelium,* 583.

122. On the Hebraism, see Schlatter, *Lukas,* 401; Edwards, *Hebrew Gospel,* 321.

rather than self (Isa 8:17; 2 Cor 1:9; Heb 2:13), but the gifts of grace in the life of a believer easily tempt one to an attitude of superiority rather than humility and gratitude. This parable is about that temptation.

"Two men went up to the temple to pray, one a Pharisee and one a tax collector" (v. 10). (On Pharisees, see at 5:17; on tax collectors, at 3:12.) The Jerusalem temple was situated at the highpoint of the central hill country of Judea, and it was thus proper to speak of going up to it (v. 10) and down from it (v. 14).[123] The temple was the cultic, ethnic-political, and economic center of Israel, and thus the epicenter of Israelite worship and prayer. Luke began the Third Gospel with Zechariah in prayer in the temple. This parable begins likewise. "The Pharisee stood by himself and prayed, 'God, I thank you that I am not like other people — robbers, evildoers, adulterers — or even like this tax collector. I fast twice a week and give a tenth of all I get'" (vv. 11-12). In most religions, Judaism included, the outward form of religious observance is an essential indicator of inward piety. As such, the Pharisee's prayer is a model in Judaism.[124] "Standing to pray" was the preferred posture of prayer in Judaism.[125] The parable does not specify when the prayer was offered, but it may have been at one of the two periods reserved for public prayer, either 9 A.M. or 3 P.M. (Acts 2:15; 3:1).[126] The Pharisee begins prayer with a customary *Berakah*, "I thank you God. . . ." He stands "by himself," so as not to be contaminated by sin and sinfulness — robbers, evildoers, adulterers.[127] His prayer echoes Ps 26,

> I have led a blameless life;
> I have trusted in the Lord and have not faltered.
> Test me, Lord, and try me, examine my heart and mind;
> for I have always been mindful of your unfailing love. . . .
> I do not sit with the deceitful, nor do I associate with hypocrites.
> I abhor the assembly of evildoers and refuse to sit with the wicked.
> (vv. 1-5)[128]

123. Josephus, *Ant.* 12.164-65, refers to going up to and down from the temple in the same Greek terminology.

124. Schlatter, *Lukas*, 401.

125. Str-B 1:401-2. Bovon, *Lukas 15,1–19,27*, 208, reminds us that the early frescos in the catacomb of Priscilla in Rome portray Christians praying in a standing posture.

126. According to *m. Tamid* 5:1, public prayers consisted of a benediction, recitation of the Ten Commandments, the Shema (Deut 6:4-9), and three benedictions: "True and sure" (*m. Ber.* 1:4; 2:2), "Abodah" (from the Eighteen Benedictions), and the Priestly Blessing (Num 6:24-26).

127. On the textual syntax of Gk. *tauta pros heauton* or *pros heauton tauta*, see Metzger, *TCGNT*, 143.

128. The sentiments of Ps 26 are echoed in other Jewish prayers of Jesus' day. As a Pharisee, Paul prayed a similar prayer before his conversion (Phil 3:4-6); likewise, "I will give thanks to you, O God, who came to my aid for salvation, and who did not count me with the

Christian readers may be inclined to dismiss such prayers as self-righteous, even hypocritical. In Judaism sins were reckoned on the basis of *deeds* rather than on thoughts or intentions, as Jesus later taught (e.g. Matt 5:21-48). It was hence both possible and expected for righteous persons to keep the commandments. In their magnum opus on Judaism, Strack and Billerbeck affirm, "That a person possessed the ability without exception to fulfill God's commandments was so firmly rooted in rabbinic teaching, that in all seriousness they spoke of people who had kept the entire Torah from A to Z."[129]

The Pharisee's piety is not only exemplary, it surpasses Torah requirements. "I fast twice a week," he asserts, "and give a tenth of all I get" (v. 12). (On fasting, see at 5:33.) The only obligatory fast for all Jews was the twenty-four-hour fast on the Day of Atonement (Yom Kippur, Lev 16:29-30; *m. Yoma* 8:1-2). Private fasts could be undertaken at any time, however, especially in cases of war, plague, drought, or famine. As an example of their renown and piety, Pharisees fasted twice per week, on Mondays and Thursdays (*Did.* 8:1; *b. Ta'an.* 12a).[130] Moreover, continues the Pharisee, he tithes all that he gets. Deut 14:22-23 required a tithe on the firstlings of all flocks, as well as on grain, wine, and oil. Rabbinic interpretation extended the tithe to include legumes, vegetables, and herbs, to which reference is made in Matt 23:23. Exactly what is meant by the claim to tithe on "*all* I get" is not clear. It could mean tithes on all the above, i.e., on all agriculture produce, both plants and animals; or it could mean additional tithes on income acquired through commercial interactions. However understood, the Pharisee exceeds the tithing minimum required in Torah.[131] This Pharisee is not invoking legal exemptions or loopholes in meeting his obligations to God (e.g., Mark 7:9-13), but proudly confessing above-and-beyond giving. The Pharisee should not be denigrated for declaring his commendable record, any more than modern contributors to charities should be denigrated for allowing their names and gifts to be publicized. Tobit celebrates his virtue in tithing in equal detail and with equal satisfaction (Tob 1:6-8). The Pharisee's piety would have appeared no less praiseworthy to Jesus' Jewish audience.

Enter the second man in the parable, the tax collector who "stood at

---

sinners for destruction" (*Pss. Sol.* 16:5; first c.); and esp., "I thank you, Lord, my God, that you assigned me a portion with those who sit in the synagogue and not with those who sit on street corners; for I rise early and they rise early: I rise early to attend to the word of Torah and they rise early to do vain things. I work hard and they work hard: I work and receive a reward, and they work and receive no reward. I run and they run: I run to the life of the world to come, and they run to the pit of destruction" (*b. Ber.* 28b; ca. 400).

129. Str-B 1:814.

130. On fasting in Judaism, see Str-B 2:241-44. V. 12 and *Did.* 8:1 are the earliest records in Judaism of Pharisees fasting on Mondays and Thursdays.

131. Str-B 2:244-46.

a distance [and] would not even look up to heaven, but beat his breast and said, 'God, have mercy on me a sinner'" (v. 13). If the Pharisee embodies the confidence of Ps 26, the tax collector embodies the penitence of Ps 51. Unlike the Pharisee's roster of merits, the tax collector is characterized by a litany of deficits. In self-disparagement, he "stood at a distance." We know not where he or the Pharisee were in the sanctuary,[132] so "distance" would appear to be measured not in relation to the altar but in relation to the Pharisee who seemed to him — as the Pharisee seemed himself — so favored by God. Lifting one's eyes and hands to God was customary in Jewish prayer, but the tax collector is too contrite to lift either. Those who are right with God may lift their eyes to him, but the tax collector knows he is a sinner, and sinners cannot "raise their eyes unto heaven as a result of their sins which have been condemned" (*1 En.* 13:5). The gesture of "beating one's breast" is unknown in the OT, but Josephus describes David remorsefully "beating his breast, tearing his hair, and doing himself every kind of injury" at the death of his son Absalom (*Ant.* 7.252). The descriptors of v. 13 obviously symbolize self-deprecation before the Almighty, and the imperfect tenses of *ēthelen* ("*he was not daring* to lift his eyes") and *etypten* ("*he was beating* his breast") connote repeated (not perfunctory) behavior. These gestures come to verbal expression in the plea, "God, have mercy on me, a sinner" (v. 13). In Greek, the tax collector does not refer to himself as a sinner, but as *the* sinner *(tō hamartōlō),* indicating both the degree and his awareness of his sin. Moreover, unlike the Pharisee's parade of virtues before God, the tax collector appeals solely *to* God, who alone can offer such expiation (Ps 25:11; 65:3; 78:38; 79:9). Above all, the Greek verb for "mercy" is not the customary *eleein,* but the highly specialized *hilaskesthai,* which belongs to a word group associated with the most sacred cultic act in Israel on the Day of Atonement (Exod 25:17-22; 38:5-8 [Eng. 37:6-8]; Lev 16).[133] In the NT the verb is used only once again in Heb 2:17, where it refers to Jesus fulfilling the duty of the high priest by atoning for the sins of the people at the Holy of Holies in the temple. In putting a uniquely high priestly prayer of atonement in the mouth of the tax collector in the temple, Jesus suggestively and scandalously casts him in the role of the Jewish high priest.

14 The pericope ends with a pronouncement of Jesus on the parable: "I tell you that this man, rather than the other, went home justified before God" (v. 14). "I tell you" occurs twenty-eight times in Luke as a declaration of Jesus' authority. In dishonorable irony, the Pharisee, so proud of his name and

---

132. Str-B 2:246 places the tax collector in the Court of Women and the Pharisee inside the sanctuary in the Court of Israel. Such precision is not given in the parable, however.

133. J. Hermann and F. Büchsel, *hilaskomai, TWNT* 3:300-324, note that in three-quarters of its occurrences in the OT, *hilaskomai* translates Heb. *kipper* with reference to atonement for sin in the temple.

merits, is summarily dismissed as "the other." In happier irony, the tax collector initially dismissed by the Pharisee is in the end featured by Jesus. This man — yes, this hopeless tax collector — went home justified (v. 14)![134] Indeed, the tax collector "rather than" the Pharisee was justified. The Greek *par' ekeinon* is somewhat unusual, evidently reflecting a Hebraic *min* construction, which has the effect of setting one in a category apart from others.[135] This is the concluding irony of the parable, for Pharisees are proudly distinguished twice as those who are "not like other people" (vv. 9, 11). In truth, declares Jesus, it is the justified tax collector who stands in a class by himself, *not like* the Pharisee![136]

"Two men went up to the temple to pray, but only one of them prayed."[137] The Pharisee mentions God, but does not pray to God, for he rests his case on his catalog of virtues. Jesus earlier instructed disciples, when they had done all they were commanded to do, to say "We are unworthy servants, for we have only done our duty" (17:10). Would that the Pharisee — and all virtuous believers — could follow this advice. Instead, he rehearses his service as above and beyond the call of duty, and puts God in his debt. He is thankful not to God, but simply that he is not like other people whom he considers inferior. In his mind, his virtues are real and his sins illusory. By contrast, the sins of the tax collector are real and his virtues illusory. The tax collector knows his situation to be much different. Without merits to stand on, he must stand humbly before God; without merits to speak for him, he must plead to God; without merits to be rewarded, his only option is to plead for God's mercy. The Pharisee stands before God in self-congratulation, the tax collector stands before God in prayer.

The prayer of the tax collector is one of absolute dependence on God's mercy; as such, he anticipates the later NT doctrine of justification by faith.[138] The Pharisee, imagining himself "justified by works, has something to boast about — but not before God" (Rom 4:2). The tax collector has no works to boast about, "but trusts God who justifies the ungodly, and his faith is credited as righteousness" (Rom 4:5). In Jesus' day, Jewish rabbis taught that atonement

---

134. Similar emphatic irony occurs in 16:8 and 17:18.

135. See its use in Ps 45:8 (MT). The Greek translates Ps 45:8 in Heb 1:9 by means of *para* + accusative, which parallels the *para* + accusative construction in v. 14. See Jeremias, *Die Gleichnisse Jesu* (7th ed.; Göttingen: Vandenhoeck & Ruprecht, 1965), 141; Delitzsch, *Hebrew New Testament*, at 18:14. *Para* with accusative does not normally express contrast in classical Greek (Smyth, *Greek Grammar*, §1692.3). Further on the form *para ekeinon*, BDAG, 758; W. Köhler, *para*, *EDNT* 3:13.

136. On v. 14b, see at 14:11.

137. Caird, *Luke*, 202.

138. Also recognized by J. Jeremias, *Die Gleichnisse Jesu* (7th ed.; Göttingen: Vandenhoeck & Ruprecht, 1965), 140; Fitzmyer, *Luke (X–XXIV)*, 1185; Bailey, *Jesus through Middle Eastern Eyes*, 350.

before God required restitution or appeasement to individuals wronged.[139] Divine forgiveness on the basis of Christ's death on the cross on behalf of sinners rather than on the basis of the works of sinners themselves was, not surprisingly, as Paul would later confess, a "scandal" to Jews" (1 Cor 1:23; Gal 5:11). It would be a mistake, however, to imagine that this understanding of salvation was foreign to Christians before Paul. The death of Christ on the cross was the full payment for the saving grace that had been operative since the days of Abraham, "who believed God, and it was credited to him as righteousness" (Gen 15:6; Rom 4). Justification by faith has *always* been the way sinful humanity — whether Abraham or "*this* tax collector" — is made right before God.

THE KINGDOM AND THE DISPOSSESSED (18:15-17)

15-17   With this story Luke returns to his Markan source, from which he departed at 9:50. The incident in 18:15-17 closely follows the account of Jesus and the children in Mark 10:13-16, and vv. 16-17 follow Mark 10:14-15 verbatim.[140] Luke may have included the account here because children, like the tax collector in the preceding parable, were unlikely candidates for divine favor.[141] The modern West generally regards the qualities of childlikeness — innocence, trustfulness, humility — as inherently praiseworthy, and hence tenderness to children as virtuous. The ancient world did not regard children likewise. In Judaism, women and children derived their position in society primarily in relation to adult males. Sons were of course regarded as blessings from God, but largely because they ensured the continuance of the family for another generation. In general, "childhood" was an unavoidable and uncelebrated interim until the young were mature enough to bear children and contribute to the work force. One will search ancient literature in vain for sympathy toward the young comparable to that shown them by Jesus.[142]

   The imperfect tense of the verb "to bring to" (Gk. *prospherein*) implies

---

139. *M. Yoma* 8:9: "But for transgressions that are between man and his fellow the Day of Atonement effects atonement only if he has appeased his fellow." According to Str-B 2:248, this principle became the norm in Second Temple Judaism for cases of atonement and forgiveness.

140. The narrative of Jesus and the children in Matt 19:13-15 and 18:3 differs slightly from the Markan and Lukan versions. For a discussion of the relationship of the three Synoptic pericopes, plus *Gos. Thom.* 22, see Bovon, *Lukas 15,1–19,27,* 220-21.

141. So too Klein, *Lukasevangelium,* 586-87.

142. Bovon, *Lukas 15,1–19,27,* 225, writes, "The testimony that the NT devotes to children, though modest, is itself one witness for them in the ancient world, which pays little attention to boys and girls other than as a social group that must be brought to adulthood through training and obedience."

that people customarily brought children to Jesus, hence they "were bringing babies to Jesus for him to place his hands on them" (v. 15). Jesus frequently placed hands on people to convey a **blessing**, and in so doing he was following an established ritual in Israel. Noah had blessed Shem and Japheth (Gen 9:26-27), Isaac blessed Jacob and Esau (Gen 27; 28:1-4), and Jacob, his sons and grandsons (Gen 48–49). These blessings primarily concerned the passing on of name or property. "A father's blessing establishes the houses of his children" (Sir 3:9).[143] Laying on of hands was also a priestly rite of investiture in Israel, whereby wisdom (Deut 34:9) and the spirit of office (Num 27:18-20) were conferred on the ordinand. This latter rite was continued in early Christianity (Acts 6:1-6; 13:1-3). The above instances are formal and official, whereas Jesus frequently laid hands to convey personal blessings to common people, and his touch became a distinguishing mark of his ministry. Most frequently he touched people in the process of healing (5:13; 7:14; 22:51), but here he blesses an especially undistinguished element of Jewish society — children.[144] How remarkable that the early church extolled Jesus for concerning himself with a nameless and faceless social group in the ancient world![145] The touch of Jesus was a tangible expression of God's unconditional love for the unclean, foreigners, women, and children. It also became an essential characteristic of the movement he founded, sparing it from the incipient hierarchy and elitism, whether professional or ascetic, so common of religion. "Another gospel would have resulted and not that of Jesus, and another church rather than his church, had children been kept from Jesus and had Christianity been made into something for men alone."[146]

Matt 19:13 and Mark 10:13 call the youngsters "children" (Gk. *paidia*), but Luke calls them *brephē*, which denotes newborn (and even unborn) children, hence "babies" (NIV).[147] The citation of this logion in *Gos. Thom.* 22 follows Luke in referring to them as "nursing children." An infant was more helpless than a child, in a similar way that a tax collector was considered worse than most other sinners. This story, like the previous one, thus lays particular stress

---

143. Later Judaism formalized blessings on Sabbath or holy days, and often in the synagogue. A typical fatherly blessing of a son is that of Gen 48:20, "May God make you like Ephraim and Manasseh," and of a daughter, "May God make you like Sarah, Rebekah, Rachel, and Leah" (see Ruth 4:11), followed by the Aaronic benediction (Num 6:24-26). See *EncJud.,* 4.1087.

144. Bultmann's suggestion in *History of the Synoptic Tradition* (New York: Harper & Row, 1972), 32, followed by Bovon, *Lukas 15,1–19,27,* 221, that this pericope was a later ecclesial invention inspired by 2 Kgs 4:27 is implausible. A culture that frowned on children is unlikely to have invented a narrative of Jesus blessing children.

145. See Bovon, *Lukas 15,1–19,27,* 221.

146. A. Schlatter, *Evangelien nach Markus und Lukas,* 103-4.

147. On *brephos,* see BDAG, 183-84.

on grace rather than merit. "Rebuke" (v. 15; Gk. *epitiman*) is stern and uncompromising, the standard term in the Gospels for demon exorcisms (in Luke, 4:35, 39, 41; 8:24?; 9:42). Here the term connotes censoriousness, as it does also in 9:21, 55; 17:3.[148] Luke does not say why the disciples rebuke the children. Were they merely mirroring conventional Jewish attitudes, or did they think Jesus' attention would better be directed to other needs? Whatever the reason, the will — perhaps even *good* will — of the disciples clashes with Jesus. Christians who presume, as do the disciples here, to know the mission of their Master better than their Master himself, often end up opposing their Master.

According to Mark 10:14, Jesus "reprimanded" (Gk. *aganaktein*) the disciples. Luke omits this rebuttal, reporting instead that Jesus seized the incident as a teaching opportunity. "Let the little children come to me, and do not hinder them, for the kingdom of God belongs to such as these" (v. 16). (On kingdom of God, see at 4:43.) The Greek word for "little children" here is not *brephē*, as in v. 15, but *paidia*, as in Matt 19:14 and Mark 10:14. In his introduction to the pericope Luke appears to prefer the word "infants" (Gk. *brephē*), but his citation of the saying of Jesus according to its received vocabulary, "children" (Gk. *paidia*), demonstrates his honor of prior evangelical tradition.[149] Jesus does not disbar or marginalize children, but commends them as true heirs of the kingdom he inaugurates. This pronouncement again exhibits Jesus' unique authority, for he presumes to correlate the kingdom of God with himself. In coming to Jesus, the children are coming to the one in whom God's present reign is made manifest.

The lesson is concluded and ratified with the same dominical authority: "Truly I tell you, anyone who will not receive the kingdom of God like a little child will never enter it" (v. 17). Children — particularly little children — are often praised for their innocence, spontaneity, and humility. It may be assumed that Jesus commends them because of these qualities. This does not appear to be the reason — or primary reason — why Jesus blesses them.[150] The narrative emphasizes the children themselves rather than their virtues, real or imagined. If we assume that Jesus commends children because of their virtues, then we imply that the acceptability of disciples in God's kingdom depends on similar virtues. Disciples are seldom innocent and eager in the Gospels, however. They are more likely uncomprehending and disbelieving, even cowardly. Jesus does not bless the children for their virtues, but for their deficits. They are important because of what they *lack* — they are small, powerless, without sophistica-

---

148. See E. Stauffer, *epitimaō, TWNT* 2:620-23.

149. So too Bovon, *Lukas 15,1–19,27,* 220.

150. Wolter, *Lukasevangelium,* 596, dismisses the many and frequent attempts to sentimentalize the role of children in the story as "an anthology of bad judgment" on the part of commentators.

tion, overlooked, and dispossessed.[151] Jesus thus emphasizes in the strongest possible way that the kingdom is offered to the helpless, needy, powerless, and weak.[152] Indeed, it belongs to them. Children have no roster of Torah achievements to their credit, as does the Pharisee in 18:11-12. They are, rather, like the tax collector, whose only "merit" is unworthiness. Luke's use of *brephē*, "babies," to introduce the narrative highlights this radical gospel insight, for newborns are too young to exhibit the trust, openness, and receptivity of children. Like the poor of 6:20, they are wholly dependent on God.

Vv. 15-17 are about blessing children rather than baptizing them, but the narrative has nevertheless played a role in Christian history in relation to infant baptism. Calvin argued that, if children were brought to Jesus to receive the kingdom, which is the sum of the blessing sealed through baptism, should they not also be baptized?[153] Cullmann argues that the language of the pericope was chosen in order to answer the question of the propriety of infant baptism.[154] We must wait until the fourth century, however, for this passage to appear in relation to infant baptism,[155] and hence it is more likely that the language of early Christian baptism was taken *from* this logion. Nevertheless, Jesus' blessing and declaration in this pericope establish a positive context in which to consider the question of infant baptism.[156]

THE KINGDOM AND THE WELL-POSSESSED (18:18-30)

Luke refers to wealth and wealthy persons four times as often as do Matt and Mark. Some people of financial means play positive roles in Luke-Acts, including Joseph of Arimathea (23:50-54), Barnabas (Acts 4:37), Roman centurions (7:2-10; Acts 10), perhaps Lydia, a dealer in purple cloth (Acts 16:14). None

151. The uniqueness of Jesus' behavior and teaching is further appreciated by comparing them to *Thom. Cont.* (139.11-12), a gnostic tractate from Nag Hammadi that cites this same story to the effect that babes are simply like beasts *until* they become perfect!

152. A point made by J. Bailey, "Experiencing the Kingdom as a Little Child: A Re-reading of Mark 10:13-16," *WordWorld* 15 (1995): 58-67, who sees children as the epitome of vulnerability, in solidarity with whom disciples also experience the kingdom of God.

153. J. Calvin, *Commentary on a Harmony of the Evangelists* (vol. 2; Edinburgh: T&T Clark, 1945), 390-91.

154. Specifically, Cullmann argues that *mē kōlyete auta* ("do not hinder them," v. 16) is the same wording approving baptisms in the early church (O. Cullmann, *Baptism in the New Testament* [trans. J. Reid; SBT; London, SCM Press, 1950], 72-78). For a counterview, see G. Beasley-Murray, *Baptism in the New Testament* (London: Macmillan, 1962), 320-29.

155. Bovon, *Lukas 15,1–19,27,* 226.

156. Klein, *Lukasevangelium,* 588, is surely correct in asserting that "infant baptism is the next step" to the blessing of children exhibited in the narrative.

of these persons is designated rich (Gk. *plousios*), however. In Acts no one is called *plousios,* whereas in the Third Gospel people are called *plousios* in thirteen instances, but only once positively (Zacchaeus, 19:1-10).[157] Two of the three references to "mammon" are likewise negative (16:9, 11, 13). One cannot say that wealth is a categorical evil in the Third Gospel, but one must say that it poses an unquestionable danger to faith and discipleship.[158] No account of wealth in Luke illustrates the danger better than the present story, for, unlike other Lukan references that link wealth with *unrighteousness* (12:16; 16:11, 13, 19, 21, 22), the rich ruler is *righteous.*

18-22 Luke is indebted to Mark for his version of this story, as he is for the previous and following stories. Luke and Mark agree closely on Jesus' words, especially in vv. 18-23, though Luke prunes Mark's editorial framing of the story. As a result, Luke's account is 30 percent shorter than Mark's. This story is commonly known as "the rich young ruler," a composite title deriving from "rich" in all three Synoptics, "young" in Matt 19:20, and "ruler" in v. 18. "Ruler" (Gk. *archōn*) is a favorite Lukan term, occurring eight times in Luke, compared to five in Matt and one in Mark.[159] What kind of ruler? All but two uses of the word in Luke (11:15; 12:58) designate Jewish religious rulers, and the last three designate members of the Sanhedrin (23:13, 35: 24:20). Josephus uses the same Greek word also with reference to Sanhedrin members.[160] "Ruler" thus connoted religious ruler, and even member of the Sanhedrin.[161] Why does Luke not identify him as such? We cannot say for certain, but generic "ruler" would establish editorial rapport with Theophilus, the patron of the Gospel, who was himself an official (1:3).

The possessions and authority of the ruler are a striking contrast to the simple children of the previous story. Both stories are surprising, the first because incapable infants are offered the kingdom, and the second because a Torah-righteous ruler is not. "Good teacher," the ruler asks, "what must I do to inherit eternal life?" The theme of eternal life was common in Jewish Scrip-

---

157. On riches and rich persons in Luke: 1:53; 6:24; 12:16, 21; 14:12; 16:1, 19, 21, 22; 18:23, 25; 19:2; 21:1.

158. H. Cadbury, *Making of Luke-Acts,* 260-63, concludes a review of Luke's position on wealth thus, "The rebuke of wealth, as of Pharisaic pride . . . and of Jewish national conceit, betokens a concern for the oppressor rather than pity for the oppressed, and, as a technique for social betterment, the appeal to conscience and sense of duty in the privileged classes rather than the appeal to the discontent and to the rights (or wrongs!) of the underprivileged."

159. Luke 8:41; 11:15; 12:58; 14:1; 18:18; 23:13, 35; 24:20.

160. *J.W.* 2.333, 405, 407, 627. In the second reference here, Josephus refers to members of the Sanhedrin as *archontes* ("rulers," the word used in v. 18) and *bouleutai* ("councillors"). *Bouleutēs* ("councillor") is used in 23:50 of Josephus of Arimathea, who, although not expressly identified as a member of the Sanhedrin, is widely considered such.

161. So BDAG, 140; also Schürer, *History of the Jewish People,* 2:212.

tures and Judaism;[162] it was the subject of an earlier question to Jesus (10:25). Torah commandments define right behavior and thus direct one to God. The question "What must I *do*" places the accent where it properly belongs in Judaism: on behavior and conduct rather than on thoughts or intentions. Jesus' typical audiences, disciples included, commonly exhibit blindness, misapprehensions, and even opposition to him. Here, in contrast to the antagonism behind the same question in 10:25, Jesus is asked the right question, with apparently the right motive.

Ironically, Jesus withholds the anticipated answer. Does Jesus sense that the questioner, like the Pharisee in the previous parable (18:11-12), is overconfident or disingenuous? "Why do you call me good?" responds Jesus. "No one is good — except God alone."[163] The Greek *me* (v. 19, "me") in the rhetorical question is positioned emphatically at the front of the sentence, "Why do you call *me* good?" Plummer calls the ruler's address of Jesus "extraordinary," for in Judaism God or Torah are rightly called good, but not rabbis.[164] Jesus does not affirm his goodness but implies that his goodness is the goodness of God, the source of all goodness, working in him: "The Son can do nothing by himself; he can do only what he sees the Father doing" (John 5:19).[165] Given Jesus' servant posture and reticence regarding his messianic status, he directs the ruler unambiguously to God. "No one is good — except God alone" could also be translated "except the *one* God," thus directing the ruler to the Shema (Deut 6:4).[166]

In light of what we learn about the ruler in v. 21, he may have posed his question either in hopes of being commended by Jesus or in hopes of learn-

162. Dan 12:2; 4Q181 1:4; 1QS 4:7; CD 3:20; *Pss. Sol.* 3:12; *1 En.* 37:4; 40:9; 58:3; 2 Macc 7:9; 4 Macc 15:3.

163. "Why do you call me good?" (v. 19; Mark 10:18) appears as "Why do you ask me about what is good?" in Matt 19:17. Matt's wording avoids the question of Jesus' goodness implied in Mark's and Luke's versions. The Matthean wording results in a non sequitur in the following statement, however, "There is only One who is good." Matt's wording argues in favor of his Gospel being produced after both Mark's and Luke's.

164. Plummer, *Luke,* 422, "There is no instance in the whole Talmud of a Rabbi being addressed 'Good Master': the title was absolutely unknown among the Jews. This, therefore, is an extraordinary address, and perhaps a fulsome compliment." Plummer's assertion is qualified slightly but not substantially by the existence of a fourth-c. rabbinic testimony to "Good Master" in *b. Ta'an.* 24b. See G. Dalman, *The Words of Jesus* (Edinburgh: T&T Clark, 1909), 337; Str-B 2:24-25.

165. V. 19 was remembered and quoted by Justin Martyr, *1 Apol.* 16.7, and Hippolytus, *Refut. Om. Haer.* 5.7.25-26. George MacDonald reflects on this verse: "The Father was all in all to the Son, and the Son no more thought of His own goodness than an honest man thinks of his honesty. When the good man sees goodness, he thinks of his own evil: Jesus had no evil to think of, but neither does He think of His goodness; He delights in his Father's" (C. S. Lewis, *George MacDonald. An Anthology* [New York: Macmillan, 1978], 25).

166. Paul uses the same Greek phrase (in different syntax) of the Shema in 1 Cor 8:4.

ing something new from him. Jesus gratifies neither hope. Rather, he directs the ruler to the commandments he already knows (v. 20), saying in effect, "Keep my commandments, and you will live" (Prov 4:4; cf. Lev 18:5; Deut 6:25; 30:16). Jesus directs the ruler to the moral requirements of the second half of the Decalogue (Exod 20:12-16; Deut 5:16-20): not to commit adultery, not to murder, not to steal, not to give false testimony, and to honor father and mother. The commandments are given in the order in which they appear in Deut 5:17-19 (LXX), with the exception of honor of father and mother, which precedes the list in Deut.[167] Mark's account transposes adultery and murder, and adds a commandment not to defraud the poor, which is not in the Decalogue.

A Jewish father was responsible for the deeds of his son until the age of 13, at which age the son was obliged to fulfill all the commandments.[168] In asserting, "All these I have kept since I was a boy" (v. 21), the ruler claims to be a *bar mitzvah,* a "son of the commandment." Christian readers who recall Jesus' teaching that *intent* is equivalent to *deed* (Matt 5:21-48) often doubt the sincerity of the ruler's claim. It is important to recall that, with the exception of the final commandment against coveting, the Ten Commandments require *acts,* and these could indeed be kept — even if one thought or intended otherwise. Paul himself boasted of having been blameless in his moral activity as a Jew (Phil 3:6). As noted earlier, Strack and Billerbeck, in their six-volume work on Judaism, affirm: "That a person possessed the ability without exception to fulfill God's commandments was so firmly rooted in rabbinic teaching, that in all seriousness they spoke of people who had kept the entire Torah from A to Z."[169]

It is often assumed that, if one followed the law perfectly, one would be assured of eternal life. We may assume that the ruler has indeed kept the law, for Jesus does not challenge his claim. Nevertheless, says Jesus, "You still lack one thing. Sell everything you have and give to the poor, and you will have treasure in heaven. Then come, follow me" (v. 22; also 12:33-34).[170] Peter, Andrew, and

---

167. The sequence of commandments in MT Exod 20:13-16 and Deut 5:17-19 is murder, adultery, stealing, bearing false witness; in LXX Exod 20:13-16 the sequence is adultery, stealing, murder, false witness. Luke's list is thus closest to LXX Deut 5:17-19. Decalogue lists in early Christian literature often reveal selectivity, additions, or both. Rom 13:9 includes only adultery, murder, theft, covetousness. *Did.* 2:1-3; 6:1-2 includes the same four plus a dozen additional commandments, including prohibitions against sodomy, abortion, infanticide, and magic. *Barn.* 19:4-8 includes adultery and covetousness and a further eighteen prohibitions, also including abortion, infanticide, and sodomy. On Decalogue lists, see Wolter, *Lukasevangelium,* 599.

168. *EncJud.* 4:243-46.

169. See n. 129 above.

170. The conjecture of Plummer, *Luke,* 424, "that this was a call to become an Apostle," is unnecessarily restrictive. Would Jesus call an apostle at this stage of his ministry? In addition

the Zebedees were not commanded to sell their possessions in order to follow Jesus (5:1-11). This particular command is a clue that the ruler's "exceeding wealth" (v. 23; Gk. *plousios sphodra*) exerts a power over him that the boats and nets did not exert over the first four disciples. "Luke sees a direct relationship between the quantity of one's possessions and the difficulty of one's discipleship."[171] The irony between the ruler and the children in the former story is palpable. The children possess nothing, yet the kingdom of God is theirs; the ruler possesses everything, yet he lacks something. Only when he becomes like a child, i.e., sells all he has, will he possess everything. The ruler appeals to his past record, "All these I have kept since I was a boy." Jesus summons him to an obedient relationship with himself, "Come, follow me."[172] This summons may indicate that the ruler's love of God, which is the subject of the first half of the Decalogue, was not as exemplary as his duties to others in the second half of the Decalogue. True obedience to the law must be rendered in discipleship to Jesus, and unless obedience to the law leads to discipleship with Jesus, something essential is lacking. In following Jesus, the man "will have treasure in heaven" (v. 22). Jesus offers himself as a substitute for the man's possessions.

Origen preserves a version of this narrative from the Hebrew Gospel in which the ruler's wealth is seen to contradict his claim to have kept all the commandments.

> It is written in that Gospel, which is called "According to the Hebrews" (if it pleases one to receive it, not as an authority, but as an example of the proposed question): "Another rich man," it says, "inquired, 'Master, what good must I do to live?'" He said to him, "Man, do the Law and Prophets." He responded to him, "I have done [so]." He said to him, "Go, sell all you possess and distribute it among the poor, and come, follow me." The rich man began to scratch his head in displeasure. The Lord said to him, "How can you say, 'I have done the law and prophets,' since it is written in the law: Love your neighbor as yourself; and behold, your many brothers, who are sons of Abraham, are covered in dung, dying from hunger, while your house is filled with many good things, and not one of the good things

---

to the call to the Twelve (5:11, 27, 28), Gk. *akolouthei moi* is also used with reference to the call of disciples in general (9:23, 57, 59, 61; 18:43).

171. Klein, *Lukasevangelium*, 591.

172. "Although [Jesus] did not oppose the law, he did indicate that what was most important was accepting him and following him. This could eventually lead to the view that the law was unnecessary, but it appears that Jesus himself did not draw this conclusion, nor does this seem to have been an accusation against him. . . . He regarded his own mission as what really counted. If the most important thing that people could do was to accept him, the importance of other demands was reduced, even though Jesus did not say that those demands were invalid" (E. Sanders, *The Historical Figure of Jesus* [London: Penguin Press, 1993], 236-37).

goes out to them." And [Jesus] turned to Simon, his disciple sitting with him, "Simon, son of John, it is easier for a camel to go through the eye of a needle, than for a rich man to enter the kingdom of heaven."[173]

Origen cites the Hebrew Gospel here in order to resolve the conflict over how Jesus could require the rich man to dispense with his wealth after the latter had confessed to keeping all the commandments, including the commandment to love one's neighbor. Or put slightly differently, how could the rich man profess to have kept all the commandments when wealth is contrary to the commandment to love one's neighbor? Origen argues that the commandment "Love your neighbor as yourself" is a redundancy (Origen also believes it a later interpolation), made unnecessary by the commandment to "Go, sell all you possess and distribute it among the poor, and come, follow me," for this commandment contains the substance of the commandment to "love your neighbor as yourself." The Hebrew Gospel, in Origen's judgment, preserves the most original version of the story without the commandment to "love your neighbor as yourself." Despite Origen's opening disclaimer that the Hebrew Gospel is not an authority, it is noteworthy that his exegesis in fact invests it with authority *over* the Synoptic tradition.[174]

23-27   "When [the ruler] heard this, he became very sad, because he was very wealthy" (v. 23). What a contrast to his initial confidence. The ruler leads an exemplary life, even endears himself to Jesus, yet remains an idolater. Matt 19:22 and Mark 10:22 report that he "went away sad." Luke omits "went away," including only his sadness. Is this another example of a Jewish leader, like Simon (7:36-50) or the elder brother (15:25-32), whose story is left open-ended? Will the ruler, like Peter (22:62), proceed from sorrow to repentance

---

173. Origen, *Comm. Matt.* 15:14 (my translation). For the Latin original, see Edwards, *Hebrew Gospel,* 60. The fact that this citation exists only in a Latin translation of a lost Greek original has caused some scholars to doubt its authenticity. It should be remembered that the greater part of Origen's original Greek works now exist only in Latin translations, so this accusation would obviously imperil all Latin versions of Origen's works. G. Dorival, "Un Groupe Judéo-Chrétien Méconnu: les Hébreux," *Apocrypha* 11 (2006): 16-19, defends its authenticity by noting that Origen does not introduce the passage from the Hebrew Gospel as an authority, but only as an illustration, similar to the way he introduces it in *Comm. Jo.* and *Hom. Jer.* More important, the commentary that follows the quotation exhibits Origen's style and manner.

174. Several details of Lukan style echo the version of the Hebrew Gospel quoted by Origen. The use of "son/daughter of Abraham" as a grounds for compassion is esp. Lukan (13:16; 19:9), as is the use of "live" in the sense of "eternal life" (10:28). The command "Sell all you possess and distribute it among the poor, and come, follow me" is nearer in wording to Luke than to either Matt or Mark. The absolute use of "the Lord" in the narrative seems to have been common in the Hebrew Gospel and appears more frequently in Special Luke than in sections paralleled by Matt and/or Mark. Likewise, only in Luke 12:14; 22:58, 60 is "Man" used as a form of address.

and joy?[175] Or is his sadness the final resignation from which there is no return? We do not know. When Jesus saw his response, he spoke — no longer to the ruler but to the disciples — "how hard it is for the rich to enter the kingdom of God" (v. 24).[176] The word for "rich" is not Luke's normal *plousios* (v. 23), but *chrēmata,* which here and in Acts 8:20; 24:26 is used pejoratively of material possessions. "It is easier for a camel to go through the eye of a needle than for the rich [Gk. *plousios*] to enter the kingdom of God!"[177] This memorable metaphor[178] is an example of Jewish hyperbole, humorous in one sense, but its present context — a man turning his back on Jesus — not at all humorous. The suggestion that the original Greek meant "rope" instead of "camel" is based on two late Greek manuscripts of little consequence.[179] The emendation is an unsuccessful improvement, however, for a towrope would scarcely pass through the eye of a needle easier than would a camel. The offense of the received reading of v. 25 is proof of its authenticity. Wealth can of course exist in other than material forms.[180] The ruler's material wealth, however, despite his Torah righteousness, was ultimately his god, for it prevented him from doing the one thing necessary for salvation.

The reaction of the audience is hardly surprising. "Who then can be saved?" The word of Jesus comes to them, as to the rich man, as an offense, and it reveals to them, as to the rich man, their deficiency. Their deficiency is

175. A possibility entertained by Bovon, *Lukas 15,1–19,27,* 236-37.

176. The Greek text of v. 24a is uncertain. A majority of manuscripts reads, "Jesus looked at him being grieved," whereas fewer but weightier manuscripts (א B L) read simply "Jesus looked at him." The longer reading is typically Lukan, for Luke often repeats a word ("grieved") in an adjacent passage; but the shorter reading is also strongly supported (see Metzger, *TCGNT,* 143. NIV opts for the shorter reading.

177. Luke refers to the eye of a *belonē,* whereas the parallel sayings in Matt 19:24 and Mark 10:25 refer to the eye of a *rhaphis.* Both Greek words mean "needle," but *belonē* may reflect better Greek style (BDAG, 904).

178. The recurrence of the metaphor in the Qur'an (7:40) likely recalls Jesus' saying: "For those that have denied and scorned Our revelations the gates of heaven shall not be opened; nor shall they enter Paradise until the camel shall pass through the eye of a needle. Thus shall We reward the guilty" (N. J. Dawood, trans.).

179. The vast majority of Greek manuscripts reads *kamēlon* ("camel"). Only 579 (thirteenth c.) and 1424 (ninth/tenth c.) read *kamilon* ("towrope, ship's cable"). The latter reading obviously reflects a scribal attempt to soften the original statement. The further hypothesis that "eye of the needle" referred to a small city gate through which camels might enter Jerusalem by kneeling — from which a corollary is drawn that the rich may enter the kingdom of God if only they humble themselves — is fictitious. No such gate existed. See O. Michel, *kamēlos,* *TWNT* 3:598; S. Pedersen, *kamēlos, EDNT* 2:247.

180. The Cynic philosopher Diogenes similarly castigated Alexander the Great for concupiscence: "If you wish to become good and upright," said Diogenes, "throw aside the rag you have on your head and come to me. But you certainly cannot, for you are held fast by the thighs of Hephaestion" (*HCNT,* 118).

similar to that with which Jesus sent the disciples into mission, so that they would learn to trust in God (9:3; 10:4). "Who then can be saved?" is a plea of exasperation, but unbeknown to the hearers, it is a doorway of hope. This at last — even more than the ruler's question (v. 18) — is the right question. The disciples, of course, do not consider it such. They understand Jesus' call not simply to be difficult to fulfill, but impossible. The admission of human impossibility, however, opens the door to divine possibility: "What is impossible with human beings is possible with God."[181] "Impossible" (Gk. *adynatos*) appears again in Luke-Acts only with reference to the man in Lystra who could not walk — but who was healed by the proclamation of the gospel (Acts 14:8). The Greek word for "healing" *(sōzein)* the lame man of Lystra is the same word translated as "saved" in v. 26. The disciples respond to their deficiency differently than did the rich ruler. He was confident he could do something to please God, and he went away sad; they are confident they can do nothing to please God, and God does within them what they cannot do. Here again, as in the parable of the Pharisee and the Tax Collector, the kernel of the doctrine of grace as later expounded by the apostle Paul is present.

28-30 "Peter said to him, 'We have left all we had to follow you!'" (v. 28). Peter appears here, as he does frequently in Luke, as the "first among equals" and spokesman of the Twelve.[182] Peter is the one disciple in the Gospels who asks hard questions of Jesus — and questions embarrassing to himself. Here he poses an eternal question: Of what value to faith are human sacrifices? The pronoun "we" is emphatic, indicating that Peter is not merely speaking for himself but in chorus with all disciples: "*We* — who have left all — have followed you!" Jesus responds with an authoritative pronouncement, "Truly I tell you, no one who has left home or wife or brothers or sisters or parents or children for the sake of the kingdom of God will fail to receive many times as much in this age, and in the age to come eternal life" (vv. 29-30). The parallels to this verse in Matt 19:29 and Mark 10:29 include "fields" in the list. Luke omits "fields" and adds "wives," resulting in a list of terms exclusive to home and family relations. Relatives and relationships are the most costly sacrifices disciples can make. Once again (14:26), Jesus declares that life's network of natural relationships and allegiances cannot be given precedence over the call of Christ. The church in the modern West often compromises the gospel by

---

181. Compare Philo's version of Moses' speech to the Israelites trapped at the Red Sea: "'Do not lose heart,' [Moses] said, 'God's way of defense is not as that of men. Why are you quick to trust in the specious and plausible and that only? When God gives help He needs no armament. It is His special property to find a way where no way is. What is impossible to all created beings is possible to Him only, ready to His hand'" (*Mos.* 1.173-74 [LCL, no. 289]).

182. Simon Peter is mentioned more than a dozen times in the Third Gospel, and nearly as often he appears as the spokesman of the Twelve: 5:5; 8:45; 9:20, 33; 12:41; 18:28; (22:58, 60?); 24:12, 34.

proclaiming an "inviting" faith, without costs or demands. Jesus respects both the integrity of the gospel and his hearers by declaring from the outset the demands of discipleship — demands, in fact, that deterred would-be followers in his day (9:57-62). Ironically, these demands do not deprive and deplete those who accept them. In the second mission journey, the disciples are sent out in want (10:4), but they return in joy and empowerment (10:17). Likewise, those who forsake homes and family for Christ receive from Christ many times more than what they forsake (v. 30; Job 42:12). Many Christians have experienced in Christian fellowship and churches the families they never experienced in their birth homes. "I consider that our present sufferings are not worth comparing with the glory that will be revealed in us" (Rom 8:18).

V. 30 is structured as a chiasmus:

A   many times
  B   this age
  B¹   the age
A¹   eternal life

The relation of the present age to the future messianic age was, like the initial question about eternal life in v. 18, much debated in Jewish theology.[183] Jesus' response to this relationship involves a tension. On the one hand, no one can earn salvation by good works; salvation is a human impossibility made possible only by God (v. 27). On the other hand, the ruler and disciples are called to take good works seriously. They are particularly admonished regarding the dangers associated with wealth. Jesus holds divine grace in indissoluble tension with human obedience. Only faith can resolve this paradox: "Command what you will, O Lord, but give what you command."[184] "Eternal life in the age to come" (v. 30) is the one treasure in life (v. 22) that is worth the cost, whatever it takes. Once procured, this treasure renders all costs irrelevant. The "blessed hope" of eternity is the one instance in which the end truly justifies the means.

ALL GOD'S PURPOSES CONVERGE
AT THE CROSS (18:31-34)

The excursus at 9:51 discusses nine references to Jerusalem that, beginning at the transfiguration, guide the development of the narrative in the central section of Luke. Each of these refrains mentions Jerusalem as Jesus' divinely

---

183. See the nearly 200-page discussion in Str-B 4/2:799-976.
184. The substance of this idea is present in Augustine, *Conf.* 6.11.

ordained destiny, although none of them mentions his passion.[185] In addition to these nine references, Luke mentions four passion predictions (9:22, 44; 17:25; 18:32-33) and four postresurrection passion interpretations by either an angel (24:6-7) or the resurrected Jesus (24:27, 44, 46). None of the passion predictions/interpretations, however, mentions Jerusalem. Only in 18:31-34 do these two dominant narrative strands intersect. There Luke ties a knot between them, thereby concluding the central section of the Gospel.

31-33 The final passion prediction is addressed to the disciples, specifically to the "Twelve," here mentioned for the first time since 9:1, 12. The announcement of the necessity of suffering in the messianic purpose is reserved for Jesus' most select followers. "We are going up to Jerusalem." Although Luke is indebted to Mark for this pericope, he substitutes his preferred Hebraic spelling of "Jerusalem" for Mark's Hellenistic spelling.[186] *Up* is the proper word, for Jerusalem, only twenty miles (30 km) from Jericho, is 3,400 feet (1,040 m) higher in elevation. "Going up to Jerusalem" is more than a geographic description, however. For Luke, Jerusalem is the culmination point of the drama of redemption,[187] where "everything that is written by the prophets about the Son of Man will be fulfilled" (v. 31). (On Son of Man, see at 5:24.) This statement, phrased in the "divine passive," signifies that "behind all human activity in the passion, God himself is present."[188]

Nineteenth- and twentieth-century liberal Christianity taught that the essence of Jesus' teaching consisted in his moral teaching and, especially in the latter twentieth century, in his teaching on love. To be sure, morality and love are important in Jesus' teaching, but in both the present declaration of Jesus and the narrative architecture of Luke, the essence of Jesus and his ministry cannot be undertood apart from his *passion*. 18:31-34 is the only passion prediction that characterizes Jesus' death as a fulfillment of Scripture, although in three passion interpretations the resurrected Jesus will do the same (24:27, 44, 46). The second of these in 24:44 associates Jesus' death with all three major divisions of Hebrew Scripture, "Law, Prophets, Psalms." Especially in the infancy narrative Luke rooted every aspect of Jesus' advent in OT prototypes. Jesus now reminds his disciples, as Simeon reminded Mary (2:34-35), that the OT messianic anticipation also includes suffering.[189] The verb "to fulfill" (Gk. *telein*) is a technical term in Luke, used all but once (12:50) with reference to

185. 9:31, 51, 53; 13:22, 33; 17:11; 18:31; 19:11, 28.

186. Also noted by Lagrange, *Luc*, 483; Wolter, *Lukasevangelium*, 604.

187. 2:42; 18:10, 31; 19:28; Acts 3:1; 11:2; 21:12, 15; 24:11.

188. Schweizer, *Lukas*, 191. The insight of Bovon, *Lukas*, *15,1-19,27*, 246, is also important in this regard: "The less sense history makes and the more events defy logic, the more important it is to ground them and hold them in context [with God's redemptive purposes]."

189. The necessity of a suffering Messiah belongs to the core of the kerygma in Acts 2:29-32; 3:18, 21, 24; 13:27, 29, 32-37; 26:22-27; 28:23.

the fulfillment of Scripture, whether law or prophecy (2:39; 18:31; 22:37; Acts 13:29). V. 31 does not specify to which prophetic texts Jesus alludes, but the Suffering Servant passages (esp. Isa 49; 53) are surely presupposed. Although a suffering Messiah was virtually unknown in Judaism (see excursus on "Christ" at 9:18-21), the necessity of animal sacrifice for remission of human sins was deeply ingrained in Israel and indispensable to the temple cult in Jerusalem. Already in the early church the sufferings of Jesus were understood to fulfill temple sacrifices, which prefigured Christ's death on the cross and were consummated by it (Heb 9:23-28).[190] So significant was this fulfillment that the early church could speak of the OT in toto testifying to Christ (John 5:39).[191]

Luke's four passion predictions assign responsibility for Jesus' impending death in Jerusalem to four different parties: "elders, chief priests, and scribes" (= Sanhedrin; 9:22), "human hands" (9:44), "this generation" (17:25), and "the nations" (18:32). Combined, these texts identify all humanity as guilty of the death of Jesus. Both Matt 16:21; 20:18 and Mark 8:31; 10:33 hold Jewish leaders responsible for Jesus' death in two of their three passion predictions. Luke is slightly less condemnatory of Jewish leaders than are the other three Gospels.[192] This is especially true of Pharisees, who are never mentioned in the Passion Narrative. Luke omits the reference to Jewish leaders in the final passion prediction, leaving "the nations," which in this instance connotes Rome, as the responsible agent. Luke's four passion predictions thus attribute Jesus' death to the collective guilt of all humanity — Jews, Gentiles, "this generation," and humanity in general.

Vv. 32-33 describe the passion in seven graphic terms, thus constituting the most detailed of Luke's four passion predictions. The close correspondence between this final prediction and subsequent events in Jerusalem is probably owing to the fact that early Christian tradition, from which Luke received this information, remembered and transmitted Jesus' words in light of events surrounding his passion. Luke has taken over all six of Mark's terms (10:33-34) and added a seventh in *hybrizein* (NIV "insulted"). All six terms in Mark have direct counterparts in the Passion Narrative of the Second Gospel,[193] whereas

---

190. Occasionally in Judaism rabbis transferred the significance of animal sacrifice onto the death of a particularly righteous human being. Thus, a second-c. rabbinic commentary on 1 Kgs 20:37 says, "Every drop of blood from that righteous man atoned for all Israel" (Str-B 2:279).

191. Fitzmyer, *Luke (X–XXIV)*, 1209, is correct that "Luke never gives references to what prophets he has in mind." His suggestion to "leave the *panta ta gegrammena* [all things written] vague and understand it globally," however, is overly dismissive of the rich theological import of this phrase for early Christianity.

192. This moderation continues in Acts 2:23, although Acts 3:13-15 and 13:28 hold Jewish leaders more directly responsible for Jesus' death.

193. See Edwards, *Mark*, 318-19.

only five of the seven Lukan terms have counterparts in the Passion Narrative of the Third Gospel. The Son of Man will be:

"betrayed" (NIV "delivered over") to the Gentiles → 20:20; 23:1
"mocked" → 22:63; 23:11, 36
"treated abusively" (Gk. *hybrizein*; NIV "insulted) → 22:63-64; 23:35
"killed" → 23:46
"resurrected" → 24:1-12.

Luke may have added *hybrizein* in order to incorporate the senses of "spit on" and "flog," neither of which is referred to explicitly in his Passion Narrative. Luke's respect for prior evangelical tradition again appears evident, even when that tradition does not contribute directly to his specific purpose.

Some form and redaction critics frequently describe the passion predictions as *vaticinia ex eventu*, i.e., retrojections after the fact into the life and ministry of Jesus. This hypothesis, sometimes promoted as virtual fact, should be examined critically in each instance that it is asserted. The NT preserves instances of the early church distinguishing between its teaching and that of Jesus (e.g., Acts 15:28; 1 Cor 7:10, 12, 25). If the early church was a careful custodian of tradition in such instances, it is difficult to imagine it being less so with respect to claims as central to Jesus' messianic consciousness as the passion predications. Given the opposition that Jesus' teachings and ministry aroused, it would be surprising if he had no intimation of his impending death. The apostle Paul foresaw his own suffering and imprisonment (Acts 20:22-23), and similar examples are not unknown in recent history.[194] What went on in a Roman prison was no secret to anyone living in the empire. Jesus knew the fate of his predecessors (13:34-35; Pss 22; 69; Isa 50; 53), and he had no reason to expect to be exempted from it.

34 Luke concludes the final passion prediction observing that "the disciples did not understand any of this. Its meaning was hidden from them, and they did not know what he was talking about" (v. 34). This statement is not present in Matt's or Mark's versions of the prediction. It reflects Luke's editorial emphasis, for he concludes both the infancy narrative (2:50) and Jesus' Galilean ministry (9:45) with similar summaries. The observation concludes Luke's central section and anticipates similar responses of disciples in 19:42 and

---

194. Among several examples known to me, two of the most relevant are Corrie ten Boom's vision of her arrest and deportation more than a year before the event (C. ten Boom, *The Hiding Place* [Washington Depot: Chosen Books, 1971], 127) and Sophie Scholl's dream of her imprisonment with "a thick iron ring around her neck" four years before her beheading by guillotine by the Nazis in February 1943 (T. Hartnagel, *Sophie Scholl, Fritz Hartnagel. Damit wir uns nicht verlieren. Briefwechsel, 1937-1943* (Frankfurt: S. Fischer Verlag, 2006), 112.

24:16, 31. These strategic refrains remind readers of the Third Gospel that the meaning and mission of Jesus as the incarnate Son of God (1:35) are not discernible on the basis of human capacities alone, but can be comprehended only by spiritual illumination from the resurrected Lord, who "opens the minds [of disciples] so they can understand" (24:45). The perplexity of the disciples is thus a fitting conclusion to the central section of the Gospel, which has been largely devoted to Jesus' teaching, often in parables. What the disciples must learn at the cross cannot be taught in words, but only demonstrated in Jesus' life.

CHAPTER SEVENTEEN

Arrival of the King

Luke 18:35–19:44

Having concluded the long central section with the final passion prediction (18:31-34), Luke resumes details of Jesus' itineration with place-names and identifiable movements similar to the Galilean narrative of 4:14–9:50. The approach of Jesus to Jerusalem is endowed with gravity as Luke reminds readers four times of Jesus' approach — to Jericho (18:35), then to Bethpage and Bethany (19:29), to the descent from the Mount of Olives (19:37), and finally to the city itself (19:41). Each of these editorial markers is unique to Luke, each is signified by the Greek word *engizein,* "to approach, draw near," and each logs an important stage on the journey to Jerusalem.[1] The long central section has finally brought Jesus "near to Jerusalem" (19:11). This is ceremonially appropriate, for Jesus is not a mere pilgrim to the Passover festival, but the Messiah who is hailed as the "Son of David" in Jericho (18:38) and as "the king who comes in the name of the Lord" (19:38) as he enters Jerusalem.

A HEALED BLIND MAN IN JERICHO IS MADE A DISCIPLE (18:35-43)

Luke commences with another set of pairs (see at 14:1): a blind man (18:35-43) and a tax collector (19:1-10), both from Jericho, and both outcasts — though of very different kinds. Luke continues to follow Mark's narrative, as he has since 18:18, and to crop and sharpen it for his evangelical purposes. Luke omits several details of human interest from Mark's narrative, including the name of the blind man (Mark 10:46), the crowd's encouragement to him (Mark 10:49), and his throwing aside his coat and jumping up to meet Jesus (Mark 10:50). The redactional effect shifts the narrative from the perspective of the

---

1. Bovon, *Lukas 19,28–24,53,* 43, recognizes, but does not elaborate, the importance of *engizein* in the journey from Jericho to Jerusalem.

blind man to that of Jesus. Several minor stylistic changes also result from Luke's editorial hand.[2] Finally, and typical of Luke, the narrative is framed with a Lukan introduction (v. 35a) and conclusion (43), each of which exhibits Hebraic influence.[3]

35-42 From Galilee in the north, Jerusalem was accessible either via a direct north-south route along the crest of the central hill country of Samaria, or via a road through Perea on the east side of the Jordan, which crossed the Jordan at Jericho before climbing up to Jerusalem. Observant Jews often chose the latter route which, though longer, offered the advantage of skirting Samaria (see at 10:33). Luke's geographic reference in 17:11, coupled with mention of Jericho in v. 35, indicates that Jesus followed the latter route.[4] Jericho, one of the oldest continuously inhabited cities on earth, lies 825 feet (250 m) below sea level, some twenty miles (30 km) distant from and 3,400 feet (1,040 m) below Jerusalem to the southwest. Jericho offered weary and parched pilgrims a verdant oasis of water and date palms. As Jesus enters the city, he passes "a blind man sitting by the roadside begging" (v. 35). Matt 20:29 and Mark 10:46 place the encounter as Jesus leaves Jericho, but Luke places it as he enters, perhaps in anticipation of his triumphal procession into Jerusalem.[5] The placement of the beggar beside the road stigmatizes him as a social (and perhaps religious) outcast. Why Luke omits his name (Bartimaeus, Mark 10:46) is unclear,[6] although its omission accentuates Jesus as the only named and titled figure in the narrative.[7]

The blind man hears a commotion and inquires (v. 36). "Jesus of Nazareth is passing by," he is informed (v. 37). "Nazareth" (Gk. *Nazōraios*) should be understood to refer to the town in which Jesus was raised.[8] Bovon's objec-

---

2. "Son of David, Jesus" (Mark 10:47) is altered to "Jesus, Son of David" (v. 38); Gk. *stas* ("having stood," Mark 10:49) is improved by *statheis* (40); "call" (*phōnēsate*, Mark 10:49) is made more specific by "commanded" (*ekeleusen*, 40); "immediately" (*euthys*, Mark 10:52) is improved by the more literary *parachrēma* (43).

3. Edwards, *Hebrew Gospel,* 146-47, 322; H. Cadbury, *Making of Luke-Acts,* 23.

4. Rengstorf, *Lukas,* 192.

5. Rengstorf, *Lukas,* 192.

6. R. Bauckham, *Jesus and the Eyewitnesses* (Grand Rapids: Eerdmans, 2006), 53, suggests his name was dropped "because [the blind man was] not well known when or where [Luke] wrote." "Bartimaeus" does not mean "Son of filth" (so Bailey, *Jesus through Middle Eastern Eyes,* 173). Timaios (variant of "Timothy," so BDAG, 167; Str-B 2:24) derives from the Greek word for "honor" or "praise" (LSJ, 1763), thus meaning "Son of honor."

7. Luke includes twelve names not present in Mark and Matt, all in passages unique to Luke. In passages common to all three Synoptics, Mark mentions eleven names not present in Luke (incl. Bartimaeus), and seven not present in Matt. See R. Bauckham, *Jesus and the Eyewitnesses,* 65-66.

8. The terms "Nazareth/Nazarene" and "Nazirite" are spelled similarly in Greek and are often confused. The adjective *Nazōraios,* used in v. 37 (elsewhere in NT: Matt 2:23; 26:71; John 18:5, 7; 19:19; Acts 2:22; 3:6; 4:10; 6:14; 22:8; 24:5; 26:9), refers to the town of Nazareth,

tion that the term cannot refer to such an insignificant and unknown town is illogical.[9] A popular name like "Jesus"[10] in a large place like Jerusalem or Jericho would have been unremarkable, but "Jesus of *Nazareth*" was unique and precise. The crowd identifies the passerby mundanely, "Jesus of Nazareth," but the blind man "sees" him worthy of a more exalted title, "Jesus, Son of David" (v. 39). Readers are familiar with Jesus' Davidic descent and royal messianic associations from the annunciation (1:27, 32; 2:4), but this is the first time in the Third Gospel that Jesus is called Son of David. It would have been a rare Jew who would have heard or used this title without messianic connotations.[11] The actual title first appears in the middle of the first century B.C. (*Pss. Sol.* 17:21), but messianic associations with David extended back to the promise of 2 Sam 7:11-14 that God would raise up David's offspring and "establish the throne of his kingdom forever." Such associations did not perish with the monarchy; rather, freed from a moribund human institution, they blossomed into fervent messianic expectations.[12] The blind man is no stranger to these expectations, nor to the stories of Jesus' ministry and healings. The use of "Son of David" furnishes Luke with a messianic title as Jesus enters Jericho in preparation for his messianic celebration in Jerusalem (18:38).

Like the lepers in 17:13, the blind man cries out, "Have mercy on me!"[13]

---

mentioned in the NT at 1:26; 2:4, 39, 51; 4:16; Matt 2:23; 4:13; 21:11; Mark 1:9; John 1:45, 46; Acts 10:38. For *Nazōraios* as a reference to Nazareth, see H. Schaeder, *Nazarēnos et al.*, *TWNT* 4:879-83; Fitzmyer, *Luke (X–XXIV)*, 1215-16; Wolter, *Lukasevangelium*, 608-9. When a Nazirite vow is intended (Num 6:2), the term is spelled *naz(e)ir* (Judg 13:5 B), *naz(e)iraios* (Judg 13:5, 7; 16:17 A), or *nazēraios* (Num 6:18, 19 [Sym.]). The reference to the Nazirite vow, esp. as associated with Samson, who is also called "the holy one" (Judg 16:17), appears to play a role in the use of *Nazarēne* in Mark 1:24 and Luke 4:34. Mark 1:24 may influence the subsequent references in Mark 10:47; 14:67; 16:6; and Luke 4:34 may influence the Luke 24:19 reference. The general rule regarding the two terms, observed both in the above NT references and their use in the early church (*PGL*, 896-97), is that a long *ō* in the second syllable refers to "Nazareth," whereas an *i, ei, a*, or *ē* in the second syllable refers to a Nazirite vow.

9. Bovon, *Lukas 15,1–19,27*, 258.

10. R. Bauckham, *Jesus and the Eyewitnesses*, 85, lists "Jesus" as the sixth most common male name among Palestinian Jews.

11. On "Son of David," see E. Lohse, *huios David*, *TDNT* 8:482-92; O. Hofius, "Ist Jesus der Messias? Thesen," in *Der Messias* (JBTh 8; ed. I. Baldermann; Neukirchen: Neukirchener Verlag, 1993), 107.

12. Further messianic texts include Isa 11:1, 10; Jer 23:5; 33:15; Ps 89:4-5(3-4); *Pss. Sol.* 17:21-40; *4 Ezra* 12:32; 1QFlor 1:11-13.

13. R. Bultmann, *History of the Synoptic Tradition* (rev. ed.; New York: Harper & Row, 1972), 213, rejects the historicity of the story on the grounds that expecting miraculous healings of the Messiah is a later Christian invention. The blind man does not ask for a miracle, however. Like the lepers (17:13), he pleads for "mercy" — whatever form it may take in the person of Jesus. Such an expectation — and plea — is entirely consonant with first-c. messianic expectations.

Those in the lead "rebuked him . . . to be quiet" (v. 39), but he is not to be silenced. Like so many who approach Jesus in the Gospels, the blind man does so not out of curiosity but out of desperation. Jesus is the final hope of the otherwise hopeless. He shouts again — and louder, "Son of David, have mercy on me!" (v. 39; on "Son of David," see at 20:41). "Jesus stopped" (v. 40) is both prosaic and remarkable, for Jesus stops for one whom others have relegated to the roadside, ordering "the blind man to be brought to him" (v. 40). "What do you want me to do for you?" he asks. The blind man's need is obvious, of course, but for Jesus the blind man is not a problem to be solved but a person to be honored. He is not "a blind man," but a *person* who is blind, a "Thou," not an "It." Jesus' question honors him.

The blind man reciprocates by honoring Jesus before declaring his request, "Lord, I want to see" (v. 41). Given his earlier address to Jesus as "Son of David," we should understand "Lord" here to imply more than "Sir." Jesus has invited him to declare his heart, and he does so in trust that the one to whom he speaks has the power to grant his request. He asks not for wealth, power, success, or greatness, not for the extraordinary but for the ordinary, for the restoration of the created order, which is the objective of all redemption. In restoring sight, Jesus fulfills the prophecy of Isa 61:1, which he cited in his inaugural sermon in Nazareth, "to give sight to the blind" (4:18). Jesus declares, "Go, your faith has healed you" (on this expression, see at 17:19).[14] In 18:26 the disciples asked in consternation, "Who is able to be saved?" The present healing story provides an answer: whoever has the faith of the blind man can be saved. The word for "healed" (Gk. *sōzein*) also means "saved," combining both physical and spiritual dimensions; thus, "he received his sight" and "followed Jesus, glorifying God." The blind man becomes a model disciple, whose faith results in *following* Jesus.

43 Luke concludes the narrative in v. 43 with three signature themes : "glorifying God," "all the people" (see at 6:17), and "giving praise to God." Glorifying God was a defining characteristic of Israel. The particular phrase used by Luke (Gk. *doxazein ton theon*), although very rare in the MT, occurs eight times in the Third Gospel, apparently deriving from Luke's Hebraic source.[15] The Greek word for "praise," *ainein* (verb)/*ainos* (noun), is also primarily Lukan, in each instance used of praising *God*. Angels praise God (2:13), as do shepherds (2:20), the blind man (v. 43), crowds at the triumphal procession

14. In the apocryphal *Acts Pil.* 6.2, the blind man appears, along with others whom Jesus has healed, as a personal witness for Jesus at his trial before Pilate. "And another Jew hastened forward and said: 'I was born blind; I heard any man's voice, but did not see his face. And as Jesus passed by I cried with a loud voice: *Have mercy on me, Son of David*. And he took pity on me and put his hands on my eyes and I saw immediately.'"

15. *Doxazein ton theon* occurs at 2:20; 5:25, 26, 7:16; 13:13; 17:15; 18:43; 23:47; see Edwards, *Hebrew Gospel*, 138-39.

(19:37), disciples (24:53),[16] and the early church (Acts 2:47; 3:8, 9). For Luke, "glorification" and "praise" of God are distinguishing characteristics of those who experience the saving power of Jesus (5:17). One will note, however, that the disciples (and church!) are not the first to praise God, but late in doing so, reminding readers that disciples do not belong to a precocious elite. Discipleship is a witness to the faithfulness of Jesus Christ rather than to the merits of his followers. Luke places this story immediately following the final passion prediction, which the "disciples did not understand" (18:34). A healed blind man, an outsider beside the way, fulfills the ideal of insider disciples by "following Jesus and praising God" (v. 43); he "sees" what the Twelve do not, that Jesus is "Son of David" and "Lord."[17]

A RICH TAX COLLECTOR IN JERICHO BECOMES A TRUE "SON OF ABRAHAM" (19:1-10)

This story is another of Luke's paired pericopes, indeed doubly paired. Its setting in Jericho makes it a counterpart to the healing of the blind beggar (18:35-43), and the reference to "son of Abraham" (v. 9) makes it a counterpart to the "daughter of Abraham" in 13:10-17. (On Luke's use of pairs, see at 14:1.) The story of Zacchaeus is unique to Luke and especially characteristic of his special source, including a penchant for names[18] and no fewer than eight Hebraisms.[19] This section recapitulates words and themes that distinguish two prior narratives, as here demonstrated:

	Call of Levi (5:27-32)	*Parables of Lost and Found* (15:1-32)	*Call of Zacchaeus* (19:1-10)
Jesus' hospitality with tax collectors and sinners	5:29	15:1	19:5
Jewish leaders "mutter" ([*dia*]*gongyzein*) against Jesus	5:30	15:2	19:7
Jesus defends his table fellowship	5:31-32	15:3-32	19:9-10

16. The presence of *ainein* in 24:53 is subject to doubt. Its textual support is impressive (D A C² W Θ Ψ), although its omission perhaps more so (𝔭⁷⁵ ℵ B C* L).

17. Fitzmyer, *Luke (X–XXIV)*, 1214.

18. Simon (7:36-50), Martha and Mary (10:38-42), Lazarus (16:19-31), Zacchaeus (19:1-10), Cleopas (24:13-35).

19. The Hebraisms are listed in Edwards, *Hebrew Gospel*, 323. Plummer, *Luke*, 432, and Schlatter, *Lukas*, 403, likewise note Luke's indebtedness to a Semitic source.

| Salvation of the lost | 5:31-32 | 15:3-32 | 19:9-10 |
| Rejoicing | 5:32 (implied) | 15:5, 6, 7, 9, 10, 32 | 19:6[20] |

The call of Levi and the parables of the Lost and Found thus prepare readers for Jesus' meeting with Zacchaeus. The encounter of Jesus and the chief tax collector is a thematic capstone not only of the two preceding units, but of Jesus' association with the outcast throughout the Third Gospel.

1-6 The story can be divided into two roughly equal halves, the first (vv. 1-6) set on the road, which is told from Zacchaeus's perspective, and the second (vv. 7-10) at Zacchaeus's house, which is told from Jesus' perspective. Jesus met the blind beggar as he entered Jericho (18:35; on Jericho, see at 10:30, 18:35), and as he "was passing through" (v. 1) he meets an outcast of a very different sort — a man named Zacchaeus, a "chief tax collector" who was "wealthy" (v. 2). The Greek wording of v. 2 is slightly redundant, the result, perhaps, of attempting to render an original Hebrew description faithfully.[21] Zacchaeus, meaning "righteous one," is a Jewish name (2 Macc 10:19),[22] an OT variant of which appears as "Zakkai" (Ezra 2:9; Neh 7:14).[23] Two ancient Christian writers, Clement of Alexandria (d. 215) and Didymus (the Blind) of Alexandria (d. 398), draw a correlation between Zacchaeus and the Levi of 5:27-32 on the basis of the Hebrew Gospel. Didymus argues that Levi (5:27; Mark 2:14) was identical, not with the "Matthew" of Matt 9:9, but with the "Matthias" of Acts 1:23, 26, who was named an apostle after Judas's death.[24] Clement introduces his account of 19:1-10 by the parenthetical note that Zacchaeus was known by some as "Matthias."[25] Theodor Zahn concludes that

---

20. As set forth in D. Hamm, S.J., "Luke 19:8 Once Again: Does Zacchaeus Defend or Resolve?" *JBL* 107/3 (1988): 431-37.

21. Scholars frequently note the Greek pleonasm of v. 2. Leany, *Luke,* 241, notes the Semitic character of v. 2, and Delitzsch's *Hebrew New Testament* (1931) demonstrates the economy with which v. 2 can be rendered in Hebrew.

22. Why Tertullian, *Marc.* 4.37, imagined Zacchaeus a Gentile is unclear.

23. The father of the renowned R. Jochanan ben *Zakkai* lived in Jericho and might have been a descendent of Zacchaeus (Plummer, *Luke,* 432).

24. "Matthew appears in the [Gospel] according to Luke under the name of Levi. He is not the same person [as Matthew the apostle], but rather the Matthew who was appointed [apostle] in place of Judas; he and Levi are the same person under two different names. This is made apparent in the Hebrew Gospel" (my translation); text preserved in S. Brock, "A New Testimonium to the 'Gospel according to the Hebrews,'" *NTS* 18 (1971): 220; also D. Lührmann, *Die apokryph gewordenen Evangelien. Studien zu neuen Texten und zu neuen Fragen* (NovTSup 112; Leiden: Brill, 2004), 184.

25. *Strom.* 4.6.35 ("When Zacchaeus, a chief tax collector, whom some call 'Matthias,' heard that the Lord had consented to come to him, he said, 'Look, I (shall) give half of my possessions for alms,' and 'Lord, if I have defrauded anyone, I (shall) repay fourfold.' The Savior

"Clement apparently knew a complete parallel story to Luke 19:1-10 in a non-canonical gospel."[26] The Hebraisms in the Zacchaeus narrative, its similarities with the call of Levi (5:27-32), and the foregoing references from Didymus and Clement plausibly suggest that the "non-canonical gospel" referred to by Zahn was the Hebrew Gospel.[27]

Zacchaeus is first described simply as "a man." Luke's normal word for "man" is *anthrōpos,* a word occurring a hundred times in the Third Gospel. The word here, however, is *anēr,* occurring one-quarter as often, a hint perhaps that Zacchaeus is a disreputable character.[28] "Tax collector" (see at 3:12), Luke's second description, underscores his disreputability, and "chief tax collector" (Gk. *architelōnēs*), an office mentioned nowhere else in Greek literature until the fourth century, doubly underscores it. Classed with murderers and robbers (*m. Ned.* 3:4), tax collectors were hated in the Jewish world, as are informants in totalitarian societies today. Customs were not collected by civil servants but by tax collectors who leased rights to assess customs in a particular district.[29] Jericho was a large city on Judea's eastern frontier where customs would have been levied. As "chief tax collector," Zacchaeus evidently oversaw the customs franchise there. Luke's final description of Zacchaeus is "wealthy." Wealth and wealthy persons receive greater attention in the Third Gospel than anywhere else in the NT.[30] As noted earlier (see at 18:18), Luke does not earmark wealth as categorically evil, but it nevertheless poses a danger to discipleship that cannot be minimized. The introduction of Zacchaeus in vv. 1-2 is thus compromised, for although Luke depicts Jesus as a "friend of tax collectors and sinners" (7:34), he has not (yet) depicted him as a "friend of the rich." Zacchaeus is described as both, a "rich sinner," and we cannot predict how he will fare with Jesus.

Zacchaeus "wanted to see who Jesus was" (v. 3). The imperfect tense of "wanted" (Gk. *ezētei*) suggests he had wanted to see him *for some time* (John 12:21). The same Greek expression is used of Antipas's desire to see Jesus (9:9). Antipas remained in his comfortable palace, however, whereas Zacchaeus takes the initiative and also a risk in seeking Jesus, for collaborators with Rome were ill-advised to plunge into a crowd that Rome routinely maltreated. Zacchaeus's determination (if not his wisdom) is admirable, for he does not allow "what other people think" to deter him from seeing Jesus.

---

said to him, 'The Son of Man has come today and found the lost' " (my translation). Clement also includes Matthias (along with Zacchaeus) in the retelling of Luke 19:1-10 in *Quis div.* 13.

26. *Geschichte der neutestamentlichen Kanons* (Erlangen: Verlag Deichert, 1888), 2/2:751-53.

27. The issue is discussed in Edwards, *Hebrew Gospel,* 23-26.

28. Plummer, *Luke,* 432, understands *anēr* to imply "no mark of dignity."

29. Schürer, *History of the Jewish People,* 1:374.

30. See F. Hauck and W. Kasch, *ploutos et al., TWNT* 6:326.

As chief tax collector, Zacchaeus was a man to be feared. But alone in the crowd, he is only a man of "little stature" (v. 3; Gk. *hēlikia mikros*). As chief tax collector, he looked down on the crowd, but once in it, "he cannot see over" it (v. 3).[31] Zacchaeus knows Jesus' route and runs ahead to a sycamore tree, which he climbs in order to see Jesus (v. 4). The sycamore fig *(Ficus sycomorus)* can grow sixty feet (18 m) tall. Lateral branches make it easy to climb, and its large evergreen leaves can conceal an onlooker.[32]

Jesus now replaces Zacchaeus as subject of the narrative, for the scripted scheme of the tax collector is fulfilled not by himself but by Jesus. Zacchaeus is set to see Jesus, but Jesus sees him and addresses him by name — almost the same name, and evidently by the same divine power, with which the angel addressed Zechariah in the opening theophany of the Gospel (1:13). "Zacchaeus, come down immediately. I must stay at your house today" (v. 5). This is the only instance in the Gospels in which Jesus invites himself into another person's presence or premises. A self-invitation was not the norm in Judaism, and verged on impropriety. In other respects, however, Jesus' behavior follows the protocol he outlined for the mission of the seventy(-two) (10:5, 8). The injunction to "come down immediately" is urgent: the call of Jesus is not to be put off to a future time, but acted on *today*. Zacchaeus is a man of reputation, wealth, and power, but Jesus appeals to his person rather than his titles or offices. Zacchaeus "came down at once and welcomed [Jesus] gladly" (v. 6). This sentence has only seven words in Greek, four of which are strong verbs: "hurried," "came down," "received," "rejoiced." The word for "welcomed," *hypodechesthai,* a favorite Lukan word, means to receive or entertain as a guest (10:38; 19:6; Acts 17:7). The word for "gladly" (Gk. *chairein*) and the reference to "the lost" (Gk. *to apolōlos*) repeat the load-bearing words and themes of chap. 15. Zacchaeus heard Jesus' unusual invitation not as a judgment but as an occasion of joy — a very unusual response of a tax collector to a meeting with a Jewish rabbi!

7-10   The mood on the street does not match the festivity in the house. "All the people *saw* this and *began* to *mutter,* 'He has *gone* to *be* the guest of a sinner'" (v. 7). The foregoing italicized verbs counteract the positive verbs of v. 6 — and with equal intensity. The use of Greek *katalyein* ("stayed"; NIV "be") is most unusual. *Katalyein* almost without exception in the NT means to "annul," "ruin," or "destroy."[33] Here it means "to lodge," evidently recalling

---

31. Klein, *Lukasevangelium,* 600, apprehends the physical and metaphorical significance of Zacchaeus's "small stature."

32. On sycamore figs, see I. Jacob and W. Jacob, "Flora," *ABD* 2:808.

33. BDAG, 523-24; H. Hübner, *katalyō, EDNT* 2:264. Only here and in 9:12, says Plummer, *Luke,* 434, does the verb have its classical meaning of "loosing one's garments and resting from a journey."

the noun form of the word, *katalyma,* which Luke used at Jesus' birth (2:7; see also 22:11). The "guest room" denied to Jesus at his birth is now found in the home of a sinful tax collector. Jesus' invitation to stay with Zacchaeus evokes two radically opposite responses — praise from Zacchaeus and protest from townspeople.[34] Heretofore Luke has used the Greek verb *(dia)gongyzein* (NIV "mutter") to refer to the censure of Pharisees of Jesus' fraternizing with tax collectors (5:30; 15:2; also Acts 6:1). What earlier typified Pharisees has now spread to the population at large: all "complain" or "grumble" against him. In the parable of the Lost Sheep, ninety-nine sheep were safe and one was lost (15:3-7); in the Zacchaeus story, one is safe and "ninety-nine," as it were, are lost.[35] Moreover, the hostility of the crowd has shifted from Zacchaeus to Jesus. In showing mercy to a tax collector, Jesus has taken the scorn and hatred directed to tax collectors upon himself (Isa 53:4).

The grace of Jesus evokes a transformation within Zacchaeus, who vows, "Look, Lord! Here and now I give half of my possessions to the poor, and if I have cheated anybody out of anything, I will pay back four times the amount" (v. 8). This vow is not made as a precondition of Jesus' acceptance, but as a result of it. Jesus does not require Zacchaeus to change before he takes up residence with him; Jesus takes up residence, and his presence evokes a transformation within Zacchaeus. The Greek word for "cheated," *sykophantein,* refers to the extortion associated with tax collectors (3:14) — the kind of force that the economically and politically powerful exert over the economically and politically weak.[36]

The exact interpretation of v. 8 is complicated by the present tense of the Greek verbs "give" (Gk. *didōmi*) and "pay back" (Gk. *apodidōmi*). Literally, the verse reads, "Zacchaeus stood and said to the Lord, 'Look, Lord, I give half of my possessions to the poor, and if I have defrauded anyone, I pay back fourfold.'" Taken literally, the verse could be understood to describe habitual behavior on Zacchaeus's part, and even a defense of his occupational lifestyle, i.e., he gives half of possessions to the poor, and when he defrauds someone, he makes restitution fourfold.[37] This interpretation faces formidable obstacles, however. First, the Greek word *hyparchonta* refers to "possessions" (so NIV) rather than "income." One could regularly give away half of one's income, but repeatedly divesting half of one's possessions would result in utter destitution. Second, and more problematic, the proposed interpretation implies that Zacchaeus need not confess and renounce his extortion, but *continue* it — provided that he offers

---

34. Similarly, one and the same "aroma" of Christ brings life to those who are being saved and death to those who are perishing (2 Cor 2:15-16).

35. So Klein, *Lukasevangelium,* 601.

36. BDAG, 955; Wolter, *Lukasevangelium,* 614.

37. So Fitzmyer, *Luke (X–XXIV),* 1220-22; Evans, *Luke,* 281, Green, *Luke,* 671-72.

fourfold compensation.[38] This scarcely qualifies as repentance by any moral standard. Torah required a wrongdoer to confess the sin committed, offer full restitution of the wrong, and add one-fifth to the wronged party (Num 5:7). In the case of livestock, five oxen are required in compensation for one lost ox, four sheep for one lost sheep (Exod 22:1; 2 Sam 12:6).[39] An interpretation of v. 8 in the present tense would fail such requirements.[40] Third, the context of vv. 8-10 does not support the "defense" theory. The initial "Look!" (v. 8; Gk. *idou*) implies a change rather than a continuation of behavior on Zacchaeus's part; the forceful "today" (v. 9) implies that salvation is being introduced (rather than being confirmed) to Zacchaeus and his house; and above all, if Zacchaeus is a vindicated righteous person rather than a forgiven sinner, then the climactic pronouncement of v. 10 that the Son of Man seeks and saves the *lost* is meaningless.[41] The two key verbs in v. 8 should be understood in the future tense (so NIV): "will give" and "will repay."[42] Zacchaeus is not defending his actions but repenting of them and making amends in accordance with Torah requirements.[43]

Jesus says to Zacchaeus, "Today salvation has come to this house, because this man, too, is a son of Abraham. For the Son of Man came to seek and to save what was lost" (vv. 9-10). Jesus began his public ministry in Nazareth proclaiming that *today* the messianic salvation announced by Isaiah was fulfilled in him (4:21; Isa 61:1). "Today" is eschatologically charged in v. 5 and especially in v. 9.[44] The incarnation of the Word of God incorporates dimensions of both space and time: in Jesus, the Word is *bodily present*. The message of salvation, consequently, is a space-time proclamation, effectively present wherever and whenever the gospel is declared and practiced (2 Cor 6:2). In Luke, "salvation" (Gk. *sōtēria*) was first announced to Zechariah in the Benedictus (1:69, 71, 77). The term is repeated here for the first time since the Benedictus, and its repetition prepares for the impending Passion Narrative, for the saving forgiveness made available to a sinful man and his house will be completed by Jesus' mission on

---

38. Zahn, *Lukas,* 621, "How hollow and shameless an assurance it would be to promise fourfold restitution to those whom one customarily defrauded."

39. For a fuller discussion of restitution required in the OT, see Plummer, *Luke,* 435-36.

40. So Str-B 2:250-51: In Judaism "honest repentance should express itself above all in one's forsaking the old life of sin."

41. Aware of this last problem, Fitzmyer, *Luke (X–XXIV),* 1221, argues that v. 10 is addressed to the crowd rather than to Zacchaeus. It seems highly implausible that the climax of the pericope would be directed to the crowd, mentioned only once (v. 7), rather than to Zacchaeus, mentioned in every verse except v. 7!

42. So Plummer, *Luke,* 435; Wolter, *Lukasevangelium,* 613-14.

43. This position is well advocated by Schlatter, *Lukas,* 403; Wolter, *Lukasevangelium,* 613-14; Klein, *Lukasevangelium,* 601-2; and particularly, D. Hamm, "Luke 19:8 Once Again," *JBL* 107/3 (1988): 431-37.

44. The eschatological inbreaking of salvation is maintained in the use of *sēmeron* ("today") in 2:11; 4:21; 5:26; 19:5, 9; and 23:43. See Jeremias, *Sprache des Lukasevangeliums,* 81.

the cross.[45] Even sinful Zacchaeus is "a son of Abraham" (on this expression, see at 13:16). The apostle Paul speaks of two types of sons of Abraham, "children of the flesh," who are physical descendents of Abraham, and "children of the promise," who bear the saving promise of salvation from one generation to the next (Rom 9:6-8). In calling Zacchaeus a son of Abraham, Jesus designates him as the latter, a spiritual "son of Abraham." For Jesus to call him a son of Abraham is not to reward him for doing works of repentance, but to fulfill Zacchaeus's Jewish destiny to recognize and rejoice in Jesus the Messiah. Zacchaeus is a model of John's admonition not to presume on sonship to Abraham (3:8). "Those who have faith are sons of Abraham" (Gal 3:7).[46]

Anyone who reads the Gospels — and especially the Third Gospel — knows that Jesus is a friend of the poor and oppressed. The story of Zacchaeus testifies that Jesus is a friend of the rich — even rich oppressors — as well. Luke's story of the incarnation is not developed according to a stereotype of justice in which the poor are befriended and the rich condemned. The fellowship of Jesus is not offered as vindication of poor and condemnation of rich, but as "good news of great joy" (2:20) to all who are lost, whether poor or rich. Grace is forever scandalous because it is forever undeserved. It is doubly scandalous for Zacchaeus, a rich oppressor, who seems so much less deserving of grace than Lazarus, a wretched outcast (16:19-31). Grace is a scandal because it insists on including those whom we wish to exclude. The story of Zacchaeus illustrates such grace. It ends not with Zacchaeus seeking Jesus but in Jesus seeking *him,* not in Zacchaeus's moral perfection, but with his recovery and restoration as a "son of Abraham."[47] The ironic interaction between Zacchaeus and Jesus is not unlike a former student of mine, a Hindu at the time, who began to read the NT — and discovered that the NT was "reading" him! The decisive seeker is not Zacchaeus, but Jesus, who accomplishes God's mission, as foretold by the prophets (Ezek 34:11-16), "to seek and save what was lost" (v. 10).

A PARABLE OF DISCIPLESHIP IN THE INTERIM BETWEEN THE FIRST AND SECOND COMINGS (19:11-27)

A nobleman journeys to a distant land to inherit a kingdom, despite the opposition of some of his subjects. He entrusts equal sums of money to ten servants so they may engage in business while he is gone. On his return he rewards the

---

45. So Schlatter, *Lukas,* 403.

46. Rabbis also differentiated between physical and ethical "sons of Abraham," the latter of which possessed "good eyes, humble spirits, and lowly souls" (*m. 'Abot* 5:19).

47. So Klein, *Lukasevangelium,* 603.

servants according to their use of the trust money, and he orders his opponents to be slain before him. This is the plot of the final parable before Jesus' entry into Jerusalem, a parable that poses some of the most difficult critical issues in the Third Gospel. The theme of servant(s) left in trust during the master's absence is common to Jewish lore,[48] including four parables of Jesus preserved in the Synoptics (12:36-46; 19:11-27; Mark 13:34; Matt 25:14-30). Extracanonical sources preserve two additional parables on the same theme. One may simply be a conflation of 19:23 and Matt 25:30, "You wicked and slothful servant, you ought to have deposited my money with bankers, so that on my return I might have had my gain; cast out the worthless servant into the uttermost darkness" (*Ps.-Clem.* 3.61.1-2).[49] The other is a quotation from the Hebrew Gospel preserved by Eusebius:

> For the Gospel that has come to us in Hebrew characters does not bring condemnation on the man who hid [the money], but on the man who lived a profligate life. For [the master] had three servants: the one who squandered the wealth of the master with prostitutes and flute-players; the one who greatly increased the sum; and the one who hid the talent. One of them was praised; another was merely rebuked; and the other was locked up in prison. It occurs to me that Matthew's condemnation, although it follows the word to the servant who earned nothing, was not intended for him but rather for the former servant who was eating and drinking with the drunkards.[50]

This parable shares superficial similarities with parables of the Talents (Matt 25:14-30) and Minas (19:11-27), but the condemnation of the servant who caroused with prostitutes and drunkards, an element present in neither Matt nor Luke, distinguishes it as a unique and independent tradition.

Many conjectures have been proposed to explain the possible relation of 19:11-27 to the foregoing parables. The most common proposal is that 19:11-27 consists of (1) an original parable similar to Matt 25:14-30 that has been (2) augmented by a story of a nobleman who is made king (19:12b, 14-15b, 27).[51] This is not an implausible hypothesis, although the differences between Luke's parable of the Minas and Matt's parable of the Talents are great enough to cast doubt on a common original to both.[52] I share this skepticism and

---

48. See the story from *Yalqut shim'oni* 267 in *HCNT,* 231; also *b. Šabb.* 152b.

49. *NTApoc.* 2:517.

50. Eusebius, *Theoph.* 4.22 (my translation).

51. Nolland, *Luke 18:35–24:53,* 911, and Bovon, *Lukas 15,1–19,27,* 287, canvas the various options.

52. For discussions of the differences between 19:11-27 and Matt 25:14-30, see Plummer, *Luke,* 437, and Schlatter, *Lukas,* 405-6.

propose a different and slightly simpler hypothesis, namely, that 19:11-27 is an expansion of Jesus' earlier parable of the Returning Master (12:36-46). Both parables feature a righteous master who leaves his property to servants in his absence; both masters reward and punish servants according to their faithfulness in his absence; and most important, both parables end (12:46; 19:27) with retribution of enemies reminiscent of the slaying of Agag by Samuel (1 Sam 15:33). The theme of faithfulness to the master in his absence in 12:36-46 seems to have been expanded and transformed into an allegory on Jesus' ascension to heaven and subsequent return as King to reward the faithful and punish his foes (19:11-27). A relationship between the same two parables is further suggested by elements that each shares in common with the parable from the Hebrew Gospel quoted above. "Eating and drinking and getting drunk," a phrase that occurs nowhere else in the NT apart from 12:45 (par. Matt 24:49),[53] would appear to derive from the same expression in the Hebrew Gospel; and the rebuke but nonjudgment of the servant who hid his sum (19:24; contrast his severe punishment in Matt 25:30) corresponds to the same element in the Hebrew Gospel. A relationship with the Hebrew Gospel is further suggested by the fact that nine Greek terms in the quotation of the Hebrew Gospel are either characteristic of or unique to Luke-Acts among the Gospels. When combined with the eight Hebraisms in 19:11-27, this evidence points to a relationship among the parable in the Hebrew Gospel and the parables of the Returning Master and the Minas. This relationship cannot be determined with further precision, however.[54] Whether the expansions of 19:11-27 derive from Jesus or from Luke (or his source) is impossible to say. The six parables noted above, however, suggest that Jesus crafted more than one parable on the theme of servant(s) left in trust during the master's absence. The allegorical character of 19:11-27 should not be construed as evidence against a dominical source of the parable. Although allegory is not employed as widely in the NT as it is in ancient pagan literature, its occasional presence in the NT testifies that it played at least a measured role in the earliest Christian sources.[55]

11 "While they were listening to this" (v. 11) recalls Jesus' encounter with Zacchaeus and sets the parable of the Minas as the third episode in Jericho since 18:35. Neither Zacchaeus nor Jericho is the focus of the parable, however. The focus, rather, is that "[Jesus] was *nearing Jerusalem* and the people thought that the kingdom of God was going to appear at once" (v. 11). The ref-

---

53. J. Crossan, "Parable," *IDB* 5:149, does not mention the parable of the Returning Master in connection with the Hebrew Gospel, but he characterizes it as the one parable of Jesus that defies classification.

54. Edwards, *Hebrew Gospel*, 63-65, 323. C. Evans, *Ancient Texts for New Testament Studies*, 330-33, also posits a relationship between the Hebrew Gospel and 19:11-27, even suggesting that Luke 19:11-27 is a corruption of the version in the Hebrew Gospel.

55. E.g., Mark 4:13-20; Matt 13:24-30, 36-43; 1 Cor 5:6-8; 9:8-10; 10:1-11; Gal 3:16; 4:22-30.

erence to Jerusalem (again in 19:28), and to the idea of the kingdom appearing "immediately" (Gk. *parachrēma;* NIV "at once"), accentuates both the spatial and the temporal imminence of Jesus' passion. Jerusalem plays a prominent role in the Third Gospel as the place where the divine purpose of Jesus' mission must be fulfilled (see at 9:51; 18:31-34). But what does that purpose have to do with the kingdom of God (on this term, see at 4:43)? Luke's teaching on the kingdom is more nuanced than is his repeated emphasis on the fulfillment of Jesus' destiny in Jerusalem. On the one hand, the kingdom is already present in Jesus. This was earlier made explicit when Jesus taught the Pharisees that the kingdom of God is "among you" (17:20-21). Throughout the Gospel, Luke conveys that the person and ministry of Jesus incarnate and exemplify the kingdom of God. On the other hand, the kingdom present in the historical ministry of Jesus awaits its final fulfillment in the future. Thus, the kingdom has already been conferred on the disciples (22:29), but in the future they will eat and drink with Jesus in his kingdom and judge the twelve tribes of Israel (22:30). The kingdom is already present in Jesus, but not yet fulfilled. Jerusalem plays a pivotal role between the initial and final fulfillments of the kingdom, but not exactly as Jesus' hearers suppose. They expect the full realization of the kingdom to coincide with the fulfillment of Jesus' messianic mission in Jerusalem.[56] In the parable of the Minas, Jesus corrects that misapprehension by instructing disciples on the faithfulness expected of them before the consummation of the kingdom, and by declaring the final judgment of those who oppose his royal mission.[57]

12-14   The parable begins with a signature Lukan expression, "*A certain man* of noble birth went to a distant country to have himself appointed king and then to return (v. 12). In nine of its eleven occurrences in Luke, "a certain man" introduces a parable of Jesus.[58] The custom of client rulers journeying to power brokers in distant lands in order to be appointed (or confirmed) as king was a familiar convention in vassal states like Palestine. Three members of the Herodian dynasty — Herod the Great, Archelaus, and Antipas — had traveled to Rome on such errands. The figure of the nobleman-made-king is portrayed in terms suspiciously reminiscent of Archelaus's royal errand to Au-

---

56. L. Johnson, "The Lukan Kingship Parable (Lk 19:11-27)," in Orton, *Composition of Luke's Gospel,* 69-89, argues that the parable *affirms* rather than corrects the assumption of v. 11. Johnson's two seminal contentions, that *anaphainein* (v. 11) means "declare" rather than "appear" (so NIV), and that the coming of the kingdom in Jesus is dependent on him being called "king," are not persuasive. Rather, Plummer, *Luke,* 439, captures the proper understanding of v. 11: "The Messiah was there; Jerusalem was only a few hours distant; the inauguration of the Kingdom must be *imminent.*"

57. Schlatter, *Lukas,* 405.

58. Gk. *anthrōpos tis,* 10:30; 12:16; 14:2, 16; 15:4, 11; 16:1, 19; 18:2; 19:12; 20:9(?). Only in 14:2, 16 does it not introduce a parable.

gustus after the death of his father, Herod the Great, in 4 B.C. Luke's description of the nobleman and Josephus's description of Archelaus share a half-dozen words or phrases in common; furthermore, like the nobleman, opponents hounded Archelaus to Rome, where they opposed his appointment before Caesar Augustus.[59] Unlike Archelaus, however, who slaughtered three thousand of his Jewish countrymen in the temple precinct,[60] the nobleman in the parable should be understood as a good figure, for in both the NT and classical Greek literature, *eugenēs* connotes nobility of character as well as status.[61] The nobleman, in fact, represents Jesus, who in the following story is declared king (19:38). The reference to "a distant country" (v. 12)[62] is doubly significant as a symbol of Jesus' being "taken up" to heaven (9:51; Acts 1:11), and as a reminder that he will not be returning soon. The use of Luke's preferred term for "return" (v. 12; Gk. *hypostrephein*),[63] likewise symbolizes the second coming of Jesus.[64]

Before leaving, the nobleman summons ten of his servants and entrusts each with a mina to invest "while I am gone."[65] A mina, mentioned only here in the NT, is a Semitic loanword referring to a unit of currency equivalent to one hundred drachmas, or roughly a hundred days' wages. In the Matthean version of the parable (25:15), three servants are given "talents" — five, two, and one. The value of a talent was sixty times that of a mina, which means Matt's servants had won the lottery, so to speak, whereas Luke's, with a single mina each, were only able to buy a Chevy. For Luke, Jesus' disciples are not outfitted with stellar gifts and abilities in his absence. The disciples — and the church — are not left destitute, but neither are they left with exceptional

---

59. Herod the Great's royal errands appear in Josephus, *Ant.* 14.119-22, 158-62, 324-26, 370-89; *J.W.* 1.282-89. Archelaus (*Ant.* 17.299-317; *J.W.* 2.80-100) and Antipas (*Ant.* 17.224-27; *J.W.* 2.20-22) contended as rivals before Augustus for the same kingdom. The following words and expressions appear in common between 19:11-27 and Josephus's description of Archelaus's bid for power: "to receive a kingdom" (Gk. *lambanein basileian* [see Wolter, *Lukasevangelium*, 619], v. 12; *Ant.* 17.317); "hate" (*misos*, v. 14; *Ant.* 17.302); "send" (*apostellein*, v. 14; *Ant.* 17.300); "delegation" (*presbeia*, v. 14; *Ant.* 17.300); "to rule as king" (*basileuein*, vv. 14, 27; *Ant.* 17.304); "citizens" (*politai*, v. 14; *J.W.* 2.89); "slay" ([*kata*]*sphazein*, v. 27; *Ant.* 17.237). Most of these agreements are also noted in C. Evans, *Ancient Texts for New Testament Studies*, 332.

60. Josephus, *Ant.* 17.313.

61. BDAG, 404; LSJ, 708. In the NT, *eugenēs* occurs at 19:12; Acts 17:11; 1 Cor 1:26.

62. The same Greek expression, *eis chōran makran*, appears in 15:13.

63. *Hypostrephein* occurs thirty-two times in Luke-Acts, and only three times elsewhere in the NT.

64. For further discussion of these allegorical details, see Fitzmyer, *Luke (X–XXIV)*, 1229; Wolter, *Lukasevangelium*, 619; Klein, *Lukasevangelium*, 608.

65. The Greek phrase behind "while I am gone" is *en hō erchomai*. The NIV opts for a seemingly required sense, "until I come back," even though there is no instance of *en hō* meaning "until." *En hō* consistently means "while," hence "while I go (*or* am gone)." See BDF §383.1; Fitzmyer, *Luke (X–XXIV)*, 1235.

gifts (1 Cor 1:26-31).[66] They are not instructed or expected to change (or impress, Gal 6:12) the world, but simply to be *faithful* in Jesus' absence with the gift given. The parable illustrates Jesus' aphorism, "Whoever can be trusted with very little can also be trusted with much" (16:10). The mina is a trial sum — not unlike Caesar's appointment of Archelaus as "ethnarch" to test his worthiness to be appointed "king"[67] — to test the servants' faithfulness in the nobleman's absence.[68] They are not instructed or expected to make a profit with the mina, but *pragmateuesthai* — to "do business, engage in trade, put it to work." The imagery of the builder whose work survives (6:48-49), which the apostle Paul also employs in 1 Cor 3:10-17, reflects a similar emphasis to the business analogy of the parable. The accent is not on *gain* but on *witness*, whether they have acted on their calling and gifts. Whether "they have openly and publicly declared their loyalty to the nobleman during the risky period of his absence," as Bailey says,[69] is the point of the gift in the interim absence of the nobleman.

Once the nobleman departs, he faces mutiny from subjects who hate him and reject his rule (v. 14). The parable gives no indication that the nobleman deserves their hatred and antagonism. Vv. 14 and 22 must therefore be understood to reflect negatively on the opponents, not on the nobleman. The Greek terminology for the subjects differs in vv. 13 and 14. In v. 13 they are *douloi*, i.e., those related to Jesus as servants and followers; in v. 14 they are *politai*, "citizens," nominally but not faithfully related. The terminology again reflects the relative disadvantage of believers in the interim between Jesus' first and second comings: both their endowments and their status pale in comparison to "the world." "Citizens" with rights, entitlement, and reputation, however, "hate him" and declare their sovereign independence of his rule. The declaration, "We don't want [Gk. *thelein*] this man to be our king" (v. 14), recalls Jesus' lament over Jerusalem, which was "not willing" (13:34; Gk. *thelein*) to be gathered to Jesus. Both refusals foreshadow the rejection of Jesus by the Sanhedrin, which comprised the moral and religious elite in Judaism. Such rejection is not limited to Jews, of course, for the cultured dismissal of Paul's preaching in Athens came from a similar echelon, the honored philosophical elite. Opposition to the gospel is more probable from "citizens" than from "tax collectors and sinners."

15-27 Having received his kingdom, the nobleman returns as king and calls the servants "to find out what they had gained with [the trust money]"

---

66. So Schlatter, *Lukas*, 406; Schweizer, *Lukas*, 196.

67. Josephus, *Ant.* 17.318.

68. On the theme of testing the servants, see the insights of Bailey, *Jesus through Middle Eastern Eyes*, 397-409.

69. Bailey, *Jesus through Middle Eastern Eyes*, 402.

(v. 15, NIV). This translation implies that the king is interested in gain, but the Greek does not require that sense. *Diapragmateuesthai* is a compound of *pragmateuesthai* in v. 13, and related to it in meaning. The emphasis remains on engaging in business rather than on financial gain and profit, i.e., whether disciples have faithfully dedicated themselves to the call and gifts of Jesus.[70] The sense of v. 15 is thus the master's interest in seeing whether the servants had "acted faithfully with the money entrusted to them." The three servants summoned to account are representative of the remaining seven entrusted with minas. The first servant reports a gain of ten minas — a 1,000 percent increase; the second, a gain of five minas — half as much, but 500 percent profit is still impressive. Socioeconomic theorists sometimes disparage these two venture capitalists, suggesting that in first-century Palestine such profits could be obtained only by exorbitant interest or outright theft.[71] These claims are beside the point. The fabulous growth is to be understood theologically and without insinuating ill-gotten gain, as is the hundredfold yield in the parable of the Sower (8:8). Both parables make the same point: disciples who employ their gifts faithfully and joyfully cannot anticipate the results, but they will be astonished by them. The fruits of the two servants differ, for discipleship is not measured by fixed outcomes or production quotas. The first servant is applauded, "Well done, my good servant. Because you have been trustworthy in a very small matter, take charge of ten cities" (v. 17). The reward is granted on the same principle of Jesus' earlier proverb, "Whoever can be trusted with very little can also be trusted with much" (16:10). The gift of a mina is not the extent of God's blessing, but a test: its faithful employment will lead to greater blessings in the future. The reward is astonishingly disproportionate to the disciple's effort: a mina would scarcely purchase a barn, yet for each mina gained a *city* is given![72] The reward for faithful discipleship is not greater privilege for the disciple — a palace in paradise with servants and a harem, for instance. The reward is rule over ten cities, five cities, etc. This does not mean that a job well done brings on a heavier work load.[73] One should think, rather, of being endowed with greater participation and responsibility in the Master's reign, of Jesus' call to Peter to begin "fishing for people" (5:10), for example, or "sitting on thrones judging the twelve tribes of Israel" (22:30).

70. So Fitzmyer, *Luke (X–XXIV)*, 1236; Bovon, *Lukas 15,1–19,27*, 296; Wolter, *Lukasevangelium*, 620.

71. D. Oakman, *Jesus and the Economic Questions of His Day* (Lewiston, N.Y.: Mellen, 1986); C. Evans, *Ancient Texts for New Testament Studies*, 331.

72. Bengel, *Gnomon*, 2:177.

73. A second-c. rabbi saw a law of progression between faithfulness and disobedience: "Be quick to fulfill a small commandment and flee from transgression . . . , for the reward of fulfilling a commandment is a further commandment, and the reward of a transgression is a further transgression" (Str-B 1:249).

The third servant[74] is simply called "the other" (Gk. *ho heteros,* v. 20), perhaps to signify that there are only two responses to the call of Jesus: faithfulness or disobedience. "Sir," he says, "here is your mina; I have kept it laid away in a piece of cloth. I was afraid of you, because you are a hard man. You take out what you did not put in and reap what you did not sow" (vv. 20-21). Nothing in the parable hints that the king deserves this tirade. The king's unwillingness to punish the servant for such defamation (v. 24) is in fact further evidence of his uprightness. The servant projects his own perversity on the king (Ps 18:26) as a defense of his indolence. But in so doing he impugns himself rather than the king. The Greek for "I have kept it laid away" implies intentionality on his part, "I have kept it just as you left it with me." He is, in other words, not admitting to a fault but professing a virtue.[75] His diatribe reminds one of Cain's insinuation that God is somehow to blame for Abel's death (Gen 4:2-9).

The king does not defend his virtue or enter into dispute with the servant. Wolter rightly observes that the servant's caricature of the master is really a self-description.[76] Hence, his condemnation of the king is a self-condemnation: "I will judge you by your own words, you wicked servant!" says the king (v. 22). Even if the master were guilty of all the servant claims and therefore unworthy of his labor, the servant should have returned the money with the interest it would have earned had it remained in the master's possession (v. 23). As it is, the master receives from the servant less than he lent. "To those standing by the master said, 'Take his mina away from him and give it to him who has ten minas'" (v. 24). An additional mina is of course a negligible gift to a man who already rules ten cities, but this again misses the point of the allegory, which is: "To everyone who has, more will be given, but

---

74. Groups of three are common in Jesus' parables, and also in Luke's editorial structure. In both pagan and Jewish antiquity, three, as represented in a triangle or a temporal sequence (beginning-middle-end), often signified completeness or finality. Many of Luke's uses of threes connote the same. Three groups petition John the Baptizer (3:10-14); three illustrations accompany the Golden Rule (6:31-34); the sinful woman is commended for three kindnesses to Jesus (7:44-46); there are three temptations (4:1-12) and three examples of false discipleship (9:57-62); Peter suggests building three tents on the Mount of Transfiguration (9:33); the parable of the Good Samaritan has three passersby (10:36) and the parable of the Friend at Midnight features three loaves (11:5); and there are three examples of petition (11:9-10), three years in the parable of the Fig Tree (13:7), three parables in chap. 15, three servants in Luke's parable of the Vineyard (20:10-12), three husbands in the story of the Sadducees (20:29-31), three denials of Peter (22:54-61), three appeals of Pilate (23:22). For a proliferation of threes in the crucifixion narrative, see at 23:26. In Acts there are no fewer than a dozen similar uses of threes. See G. Delling, *treis,* TWNT 8:215-25.

75. Plummer, *Luke,* 441.

76. Wolter, *Lukasevangelium,* 623, "The slave is not describing his master but himself, and in the slave's caricature of the master no one is recognizable but himself."

for those who have nothing, even what they have will be taken away" (v. 26; Matt 25:29; *Gos. Thom.* 41). The two passive verbs, "given" and "taken away," are "divine passives," Hebraic ways of speaking of God's giving and taking away. In the world's ledger sheet, to give something away results in subtraction; but the ledger sheet of the kingdom, as St. Francis understood, works differently: "It is in giving, that we receive; it is in pardoning, that we are pardoned; and it is in dying, that we are born to eternal life." The world cannot understand this, and remonstrates, "Sir, he already has ten minas" (v. 25).[77] Grace — receiving what is not deserved — is forever offensive to an ethics of cause and effect. Plummer suggests that v. 25 is an objection of Jesus' *hearers* rather than the characters of the parable, but it coheres with the theme of lavish grace in the parable and should be considered part of it.[78]

In contrast to the indolent servant, the citizens who rejected the king's rule are met with summary punishment: "But those enemies of mine who did not want me to be king over them — bring them here and kill them in front of me" (v. 27). The verdict is even more graphic in Greek, "Bring them here and *slay* them before me." This sentence closely recalls Samuel's hacking Agag to pieces in 1 Sam 15:33.[79] This is not the first instance in Luke where the characters of God or Jesus are illustrated by shocking analogies. The parable of the Returning Master also ends with dismemberment of the unfaithful (12:36-46); the parable of the Great Banquet, with the master "compelling" the guests to enter (14:16-23); the parable of the Unjust Steward, with the steward not only praised but upheld as a model for disciples (16:1-9); the parable of the Unjust Judge, likened to God (18:1-8); and here in the parable of the Minas, a nobleman who represents Jesus is likened to an Archelaus-figure who slays his enemies. Each offensive comparison occurs in a parable, each from the mouth of Jesus. If parables are a signature genre of Jesus' teaching, and only Jesus in early Christianity, who can doubt that we have here his *ipsissima vox* — the very voice and person of Jesus. Who but Jesus would resort to comparisons that offended the sensibilities of the pious in order to prod hearers to understandings they would otherwise shun? Proof of such shunning is the fact that Marcion expunged v. 27.[80] If the kingdom of God is the *one* matter in life to get right (and the teachings of Jesus in the Synoptics verify this premise), then

---

77. This verse is omitted by some ancient manuscripts as superfluous, but it is present in a majority of manuscripts and probably original (see Metzger, *TCGNT,* 144).

78. Plummer, *Luke,* 442.

79. "(Samuel said) 'Lead forth Agag' . . . and Samuel slew Agag before the Lord" (*prosagagete ton Agag . . . kai esphaxen Samouēl ton Agag enōpion kyriou,* 1 Sam 15:32-33); "Lead them here and slay them before me" (*agagete hōde kai katasphaxate autous emprosthen mou,* v. 27).

80. "Augustine more than once points to this sentence in answer to the objection that the severe God of the O.T. cannot be identical with the God of Love in the N.T." (Plummer, *Luke,* 443).

such comparisons as the above might be justified if they succeeded in breaking through the indifference, apathy, and callousness that prevented people — even religious people — from grasping the kingdom.[81] In the allegory of the parable, v. 27 is an allusion to the final judgment, and it corresponds with Jesus' teaching elsewhere on the subject, especially his oft-repeated reference to the final judgment as the "weeping and gnashing of teeth" of the wicked.[82] It may be, as many commentators suspect, that Luke recalls the words of v. 27 in light of the bloody destruction of Jerusalem by the Romans in A.D. 70, an event alluded to shortly in 19:43-44. If so, the desolation of Jerusalem, which was "not willing" to receive its Messiah (13:34-35), prefigures the final judgment of the wicked (Mark 13:14-20).

In contrast to the judgment of the rebel citizens is that of the miserly servant, who is relieved of his gift but not punished. The rebel citizens represent the enemies of Christ, whereas the third servant represents "nominal believers," those who are willing to be identified with Jesus but unwilling to take risks for him.[83] The apostle Paul describes the work and fate of such believers similarly: they will be saved, but their work will perish (1 Cor 3:15). The protagonists of the parable are, of course, the faithful servants. Each receives the same sum, a mina, a practical though not extraordinary sum. There is thus no Christian Hall of Fame and no superstars in the kingdom of God. The miracle is not the mina, the natural endowments of servants, but the providence of God that multiplies the faithful exercise of average gifts to extraordinary effect. The effect of their labors is not determined by the servants, indeed often not even known to them, but solely by the nobleman who will return as king as the final arbiter of their work. His final reward for such servants? "What no eye has seen, what no ear has heard, and what no human mind has conceived — these things God has prepared for those who love him" (Isa 64:4; 1 Cor 2:9).

THE RETURN OF THE KING (19:28-44)

This narrative is commonly known as the triumphal entry and associated with palm branches. In the Third Gospel there is no entry and no palm branches. The narrative might better be called the triumphal *procession*, since Jesus is still

---

81. D. Seccombe, "Incongruity in the Gospel Parables," *TynBul* 62/2 (2011): 171, concludes: "Better to goad the hearers to solemn inquiry: 'What might the King Messiah do to those who oppose his kingdom?'"

82. 12:46; 13:9; 18:8; Matt 25:46; John 5:29. "Weeping and gnashing of teeth," a quotation of Lam 2:16, is attributed to Jesus seven times: 13:28; Matt 8:12; 13:42, 50; 22:13; 24:51; 25:30.

83. So Nolland, *Luke 18:35–24:53*, 918-19.

approaching Jerusalem and first enters Jerusalem, and then only the temple, in v. 45. The narrative appears in all four Gospels (19:28-40; Matt 21:1-9; Mark 11:1-10; John 12:12-19).[84] The Synoptics agree with one another more closely than they agree with John; and among the Synoptics Luke agrees more closely with Mark than with Matt, and in so doing improves Mark's Greek style.[85] The triumphal procession is omitted from *Gos. Thom.,* which reduces Jesus' ministry to sayings alone, as well as from Marcion's edition of Luke, doubtless because it portrays Jesus as the fulfillment (rather than the antithesis) of salvation history. The triumphal procession plays a lesser role in the early church and in its commentators than it does in modern church liturgies, especially Palm Sunday.[86] Jesus is expressly identified as king in v. 38, which connects the triumphal procession to the nobleman who receives his kingdom (vv. 11, 15) in the parable of the Minas immediately before. The nobleman who received a kingdom in a distant land and returned as king in judgment is none other than Jesus, who, in fulfillment of the promise to Mary in the annunciation (1:32-33), enters Jerusalem to the acclamation of the crowds, "Blessed is the king who comes in the name of the Lord" (v. 38).

28-30 "After Jesus said this" (v. 28) connects the entry into Jerusalem with the parable of the Minas. "He approached Bethphage and Bethany" (v. 29) repeats the formulaic construction *engizein* plus specific place-names (18:35; 19:29, 37, 41; see at 18:35), which characterizes Jesus' climactic approach to Jerusalem in 18:35–19:46. Beginning with the transfiguration, where Luke announced the completion of Jesus' "exodus" in Jerusalem (9:31; NIV "fulfillment"), there are nine reminders in the Third Gospel that Jerusalem is Jesus' final destination and destiny (see discussions at 9:51; 18:31). The reference in v. 28 is the ninth and final reference, bringing Jesus to the majestic view of the Holy City from the Mount of Olives.[87] Matt 21:1 and Mark 11:1 depict Jesus and the disciples approaching Jerusalem as a group ("they approached"), whereas Luke accentuates the significance of the event for Jesus personally, "*he* approached Bethphage and Bethany" (v. 29). The modern road to Jerusalem proceeds from Bethany through Bethphage, causing some to question the se-

---

84. Detailed analyses of the relationship among the four accounts are offered by Wolter, *Lukasevangelium,* 627-28, and Bovon, *Lukas 19,28–24,53,* 28-29.

85. Mark and Luke both omit the quotation of Isa 62:11 and Zech 9:9 in Matt 21:4-5, and they both include the conversation of Jesus' disciples with the owners of the colt (19:32-34; Mark 11:4-6), which is omitted by Matt. Fitzmyer, *Luke (X–XXIV),* 1244, is not correct in asserting that "the only significant point of contact different from 'Mk' is the title *ho basileus* added to the acclamation from Ps 118:26." Luke's portrait of the triumphal procession, as discussed in the following exegesis, results in very different emphases from Mark's.

86. See Bovon, *Lukas 19:28–24:53,* 36-38.

87. On the Hebraic versus Hellenistic spelling of "Jerusalem" in Luke, see chap. 2, n. 64. The Hellenistic spelling in v. 28 probably derives from Luke's use of Mark.

quence of place-names in Luke (and Mark 11:1).[88] The Lukan (and Markan) sequence of Bethphage-Bethany is correct, however, for the ancient Roman road followed by pilgrims approaching Jerusalem from the east lay north of the modern road. From Jericho the Roman road ran southwest along what is today Wadi Umm esh Shid, and then directly up to the summit of the Mount of Olives. En route the traveler passed between Bahurim immediately to the north (2 Sam 3:16; 16:5; 17:18; Josephus *Ant.* 7.225) and Bethany further to the south.[89]

The key place-name in the account, mentioned in all three Synoptics, is Bethphage ("house of unripe figs"), which was either near or on the summit of the **Mount of Olives**. Part of a ridge extending north to south on the eastern side of the Holy City, the Mount of Olives rises 300 feet (90 m) higher than Jerusalem to almost 3,000 feet (900 m) above sea level. Already before David's time the Mount of Olives had been a place of worship (2 Sam 15:32). At the fall of Jerusalem in 586 B.C. Ezekiel had a vision of the glory of the Lord departing from Jerusalem and settling on the Mount of Olives (Ezek 11:23). Most important, the prophet Zechariah, followed by Jewish interpreters (e.g., Josephus, *Ant.* 20.169), identified the Mount of Olives as the site of the revelation of the Messiah. On "the Day of the Lord," "the Lord will be king over the whole earth" (Zech 14:1-10). In Luke-Acts, the Mount of Olives is portrayed as the staging site for the fulfillment of Jesus' passion and resurrection in Jerusalem (19:29, 37; 21:37) and ascension into heaven (Acts 1:12). It is thus the place where Jesus, literally, is "taken up" (see at 9:51).

A steep road descends from Bethphage to Bethany, a thousand yards (1 km) south on the eastern side of the Mount of Olives. Jesus sends two disciples down this road to fetch a colt, on which he will ride into Jerusalem. Whether the two disciples are Peter and John, whom he shortly sends to prepare the Passover (22:8), we are not told.[90] The NIV says Jesus directs the disciples "to the village *ahead of* you" (v. 30), but the Gk. *katenanti* probably refers to the village *opposite* you,[91] which could imply Bethphage or per-

---

88. C. Cranfield, *The Gospel according to Saint Mark* (CGTC; Cambridge: University Press, 1985), 348, seems to think of the modern rather than old Roman road in saying, "Bethany would be reached before Bethphage." Schweizer, *Lukas,* 198, also implies Luke is ignorant of geography.

89. Lagrange, *Luc,* 498; R. Beuvery, "La Route Romaine de Jérusalem a Jéricho," *RB* 66 (1957): 72-101; Fitzmyer, *Luke (X–XXIV),* 1247; B. Pixner, *Wege des Messias und Stätten der Urkirche* (Studien zur biblischen Archäologie und Zeitgeschichte 2; Giessen: Brunnen Verlag, 1991), 372-75.

90. Plummer, *Luke,* 446, thinks it "reasonable" to deduce that Peter was one of the two disciples sent, since the details in Mark (which Luke preserves) likely derive from Peter (Mark's traditional source).

91. So BDAG, 530.

haps Bahurim or Bethany. All three Synoptics are imprecise about the village intended.[92]

The two disciples are to retrieve a "colt" (v. 30; Gk. *pōlos*), which can mean the young of either horse or donkey (although the second was more common in Palestine). In contrast to the ambiguity of the village, Luke is precise about the colt, particularly Jesus' knowledge of it. Were this the only instance of Jesus' foreknowledge in the Passion Narrative, we might seek to account for it by his familiarity with the environs of the Mount of Olives, where he camped during his Jerusalem sojourn (21:37; 22:39). This is the first of many predictions in the Passion Narrative, however.[93] Particularly in the Third Gospel Jesus' prescience increases in proportion to his proximity to the cross. "We must not rationalize here," notes Julius Wellhausen. "Jesus has not already ordered the colt, nor made an arrangement with its owners, but he knows beforehand what will happen, because God, who directs what is to happen, is with him."[94] Jesus is not unaware of the storm clouds gathering before him, nor is he an unwilling victim of them. Rather, he possesses foreknowledge and sovereignty over all that "must" transpire in Jerusalem. Jesus' experience in this respect is of course not an exact prototype for believers, for he is Messiah, and believers are not. Nevertheless, if "all right knowledge of God is born from obedience,"[95] then sacrificial obedience and suffering for Christ bring spiritual insight and clarity to believers as well.

The colt plays a further role attesting to Jesus' messianic status, for in the OT the messianic king enters Jerusalem riding "on a colt, the foal of a donkey" (Zech 9:9; Gen 49:11). Jesus' kingly role may be further implied by the fact that the commandeering of a beast of burden was the prerogative of a king in ancient times.[96] And finally, Luke describes the colt as one "which no one has ever ridden" (v. 30). An unbroken beast of burden was regarded as sacred (Num 19:2; Deut 21:3) and thus an appropriate mount for a king, since a king's

---

92. Both Eusebius and Jerome know Bethphage only as "a [Jerome: little] village on the Mount of Olives to which the Lord Jesus came" (Eusebius, *Onomasticon*, 38).

93. The destruction of Jerusalem is foretold (21:20-24); Peter and John are directed to a clandestine meeting to prepare the Passover (22:7-13); the betrayals of Judas (22:21-22) and Simon Peter (22:31-34) are foretold; the "daughters of Jerusalem" are warned of future woes (23:27-31).

94. J. Wellhausen, *Evangelium Marci*, 87 (quoted from Fitzmyer, *Luke [X–XXIV]*, 1249). Plummer, *Luke*, 446, also attributes the event to supernatural knowledge. The several fulfilled predictions in the Passion Narrative and the Christological emphases of Luke's triumphal procession argue against the attempt of Marshall, *Luke*, 710, to eliminate the supernatural from Jesus' knowledge of the colt.

95. John Calvin, *Institutes of the Christian Religion*, 1.6.2.

96. See M. Hooker, *The Gospel according to St Mark* (BNTC; Peabody, Mass.: Hendrickson, 1991), 258.

horse could be ridden by no one but the king.[97] The unridden colt recalls the "two cows that have not had a yoke placed upon them" (1 Sam 6:7) that pulled the cart on which the ark of the covenant was returned to Jerusalem.[98] The ark enters Jerusalem unlike common objects, and Jesus enters Jerusalem unlike ordinary pilgrims, riding on a heretofore unbroken beast. Two episodes of similar nature will also characterize the Passion Narrative. Jesus will suffer the degrading death of a criminal, but he is most emphatically not a criminal; he bears *no* guilt (23:4), there is *no* reason for death (23:15, 22), he has committed *no* crime (23:41). Furthermore, Jesus is "placed in a tomb . . . in which no one had yet been laid" (23:53). Jerusalem may "kill the prophets and stone those sent to it" (13:34), but even prophets and divine envoys are not prototypes of Jesus. Jesus' entry into Jerusalem, as well as his trial and death there, are *singular* events, without precedent and unrepeatable.

31-34   If the two disciples are questioned, they are to assure villagers that the colt is not being stolen by declaring, "The Lord needs it" (vv. 31, 34). The Greek could also be translated, "*Its* Lord has need (of it)."[99] The frequency with which Jesus is called Lord in Luke prepares readers to hear "Lord" with reference to Jesus.[100] That Jesus is "Lord" *(kyrios)* of the colt (vv. 31, 34) is reinforced by a wordplay on "lords" *(kyrioi)* in v. 33. In Mark 11:5 the disciples who fetch the colt are questioned by "bystanders," but in Luke they are questioned by "the colt's owners/masters" (v. 33; Gk. *kyrioi*). The authority of Jesus to be the colt's rightful "Lord," in other words, supersedes that of the colt's owners. For the third time in as many verses, Luke signals Jesus' unique authority in the triumphal procession narrative.

35-38   A subtle element at the beginning of the triumphal procession is important to Luke's royal motif. Mark 11:7 and Matt 21:7 report that Jesus "sat" on the colt (or on both donkey and colt in Matt!), but in Luke Jesus *is placed* on the colt by the crowd (v. 35), which is suggestive of an enthronement. As Jesus proceeds, "people spread their cloaks on the road" (v. 36). This, too, carries royal connotations, for at the inauguration of Jehu the crowd "hurried and took their cloaks and spread them under him on the bare steps. Then

97. "None may ride on [a king's] horse and none may sit on his throne and none may make use of his sceptre" (*m. Sanh.* 5:2).

98. The wording of Luke's description is closer to the MT than the LXX of 1 Sam 6:7.

99. In Greek "it" *(autou)* stands in closer syntactic relation to "Lord" *(kyrios)* than to "need" *(chreia)*, and in identical relation to "masters" (v. 33; *kyrioi*), where it obviously means "its masters." See the discussion in Rowe, *Early Narrative Christology*, 159-60.

100. "Lord," used with reference to Jesus only rarely in Mark (2:28; 5:19; 11:3; 12:36, 37), refers to Jesus no fewer than two dozen times in Luke (1:43; 2:11; 5:8, 12, 17; 6:5, 46; 7:13, 19; 10:39, 40, 41; 12:41, 42; 14:21, 22, 23; 19:8; 20:38, 42, 44; 22:38, 49; 24:3, 34). "The entire Gospel narrative . . . reflects Luke's strategic placement and artful use of *kyrios* in order to shape the auditor/reader's perception of the identity of Jesus as Lord" (Rowe, *Early Narrative Christology*, 203).

they blew the trumpet and shouted, 'Jehu is king!'" (2 Kgs 9:13; Josephus, *Ant.* 9.111).[101] "When [Jesus] came near the place where the road goes down the Mount of Olives," the crowds shouted in joyful praise to God (v. 37). This curious detail, absent in Mark, Matt, and John, is the mirror opposite of King David's tragic flight *up* the Mount of Olives following the rebellion of Absalom that dethroned him: "David continued up the Mount of Olives, weeping as he went; his head was covered and he was barefoot. All the people with him covered their heads too and were weeping as they went up" (2 Sam 15:30).[102] Luke's triumphal procession is a true "comedy" — a story that begins in tragedy and ends in triumph. It is, moreover, a "*divine* comedy," the story not simply of Jesus' royal entry into Jerusalem, but the *return* of the king, who in David fled Jerusalem in defeat and sorrow, and in the "son of David" (18:38) enters Jerusalem in triumph and joy.

The return of the king in the triumphal procession results in three responses that echo the responses in the preceding parable of the Minas (19:11-27). In the procession and parable there are joyful reception of the king (vv. 16-19, 37-38), disgruntlement apart from judgment by the king (vv. 20-26, 39), and utter destruction (vv. 27, 41-44). In both its content and placement in the Third Gospel, the triumphal procession is a historical commentary on the parable of the Minas. The first result is the crowd "joyfully praising God in loud voices" (v. 37), which repeats in similar wording the same motif in 18:43. The blind man of Jericho at the beginning of this unit and the crowd at its end both "glorify and praise God." That God is praised for what Jesus does shows the degree to which the crowd associates the person and work of Jesus with the mission of God. "Blessed is the king who comes in the name of the Lord!" (v. 38), shout the crowds. This acclamation, a quotation from Ps 118:26, was a traditional part of the liturgical ritual of Jewish pilgrims entering Jerusalem. It referred not to the Messiah but to the blessing of pilgrims in God's name as they entered the temple sanctuary.[103] In the Gospel of Mark the quotation remains largely a *pilgrim* psalm. The quotation consummates the theme of the redeemer king in the Third Gospel, however. It summarizes John's prophecy of "the more powerful One to come" (3:16), and his later question whether

---

101. Plutarch records that, when Cato retired from military service, the soldiers honored him by "casting their mantles down for him to walk upon" ("Life of Cato the Younger," 12 [*Plutarch's Lives,* LCL, vol. 8]).

102. The following Greek phrases in v. 37 and 2 Sam 15:30 are closely parallel: "Ascent/descent of the Mount of Olives"; "all the people"; "going up and weeping/rejoicing and praising."

103. The allusion to Ps 118:26 in *Did.* refers to traveling missionaries: "Let grace come and let this world pass away. Hosannah to the God of David. If anyone be holy, let him come! If any one be not, let him repent. Maranatha. Let everyone who 'comes in the Name of the Lord' be received" (10:6; 12:1).

Jesus is "the One to come" (7:19); it repeats Jesus' prophecy over Jerusalem, "Blessed is the One who comes in the name of the Lord" (13:35), with the same acclamation of all the people at his triumphal procession (v. 38). The triumphal procession thus fulfills both Ps 118:26 and Jesus' earlier prediction regarding Jerusalem (13:35).[104] Luke's insertion of "the king" (Gk. *ho basileus*)[105] transforms the quotation into a royal hymn, expressly identifying for the first time what has been inferred throughout the Third Gospel (1:32-33; 18:38; 19:11), that Jesus is king. The nobleman who went to receive a kingdom and returned as king (19:12) is *this* king, Jesus. The approach to Jerusalem on a colt, a messianic mount; Jesus' prescience in knowing the future; his lordship; his reversal of the fortunes of David — all these, too, signify his divine kingship. Jesus is for the first time rightly acclaimed as "the king who comes in the name of the Lord," even though the crowds do not understand — and cannot until the cross — the full meaning of his kingship.[106] The concluding acclamation, "Peace in heaven and glory in the highest!" (v. 38) repeats the similar acclamation of the angels at the birth of Jesus (2:14). This repetition is one of Luke's numerous inclusios linking the infancy narrative with the Gospel proper (see excursus at 2:52). The addition of v. 38b shifts the focus of Ps 118:26 from a present to a future fulfillment. Jesus' enthronement will not occur in Jerusalem, but "in heaven and glory in the highest."[107] The crowd is motivated to praise not by factors associated with "spirituality," but by "all the miracles they had seen" (v. 37), i.e., by evidence from Jesus' life. The life of Jesus, "powerful in word and deed before God" (24:19), is the source of the crowd's joy.

39-44   Matt's triumphal procession ends with crowds proclaiming Jesus the messianic Prophet (21:10-11). Mark's, in stark contrast, ends anticlimactically: Jesus enters an empty and unperceiving temple, which symbolizes his ultimate rejection by Jewish leaders (11:11). Luke appends two vignettes to the triumphal procession that are absent from the other Gospels, both of which

---

104. See Fitzmyer, *Luke (X–XXIV)*, 1246; Rowe, *Early Narrative Christology*, 163-64.

105. Luke's insertion of *ho basileus* into the quotation of Ps 118:26 explains the Greek wording, *ho erchomenos, ho basileus*. Further, see Metzger, *TCGNT*, 144-45.

106. The elements in the triumphal procession narrative stress Jesus' status as Messiah, not, as P. Duff suggests ("The March of the Divine Warrior and the Advent of the Greco-Roman King: Mark's Account of Jesus' Entry into Jerusalem," *JBL* 111/1 [1992]: 55-71), his status as conquering warrior. The similarities of Jesus' entry into Jerusalem with warrior/ruler processions stop at the superficial level of the citizenry meeting the warrior/ruler at the gates and escorting him into the city with hymns of acclamation. Absent from the triumphal procession, in contrast to warrior/ruler processions, are mentions of royal dress, retinue of slaves, speeches, feasting in the city, and temple sacrifice to the gods. Julius Caesar's procession into Rome as king is a marked contrast to Jesus' humble approach to Jerusalem. See C. Maier, *Caesar* (trans. D. McLintock; London: Fontana Books, 1996), 442-47.

107. Nolland, *Luke 18:35–24:53*, 927, develops this idea well.

echo the second and third responses to the returning king of the preceding parable. These vignettes contain a host of Semitisms that suggest an origin in Luke's Hebrew source.[108] The first is a controversy between Jesus and the Pharisees (vv. 39-40), and the second a prediction of the destruction of Jerusalem (vv. 41-44).

As long as Jesus avoided messianic pretense, the Pharisees extended to him a measure of forbearance (13:31; 17:20). The elements of the triumphal procession, however, unite to present Jesus as Israel's Messiah. In the minds of Pharisees, this not only transgresses Torah propriety, but borders on blasphemy.[109] "Teacher, rebuke your disciples" (v. 39), they demand, thus rebuking Jesus no less than his disciples. This is the last appearance of Pharisees in the Third Gospel. Like the disgruntled servant who chastised the nobleman-turned-king (vv. 20-26), and like Simon (7:39) and the elder brother (15:30), both of whom represent Pharisees, the final relationship of Pharisees to Jesus is left unresolved. Perhaps (as noted at 15:32) Paul, Pharisee converted to Christian faith, is a harbinger of Pharisaic believers for Luke.

To the end, Jesus instructs Pharisees that the kingdom, though anticipated in Torah, is not identical with it or determined by it. "I tell you," he avers, "if [my disciples] keep quiet, the stones will cry out" (v. 40). Stones are ubiquitous in Palestine, and it is no surprise that they appear in the NT. The Baptizer earlier warned that God could raise up more faithful followers from stones than from so-called sons of Abraham (3:8). One is tempted to see something similar in Jesus' use of stones here, i.e., that subhuman nature will praise God if human nature is silenced. But this assumes that nature stands in pristine, unbroken continuity with its creator. The immense and ongoing suffering of nature contradicts this assumption, as does the testimony of Scripture. Nature itself is bent, "groaning in the pains of childbirth," and awaits liberation. Nature, too, must be redeemed in order to praise God (Rom 8:18-25). Stones that speak is an eschatological metaphor in Hab 2:11 and *4 Ezra* 5:5, and it appears likewise here.[110] Some stones will declare judgment and destruction on Jerusalem (19:44; 20:18; 21:6), and others, like the stone rolled away from the empty tomb of Jesus (24:2), will shout "Hosanna" to the risen and eternal King. In the age to come, all nature will join in the praise that disciples now sing proleptically.

The prophetic lament of vv. 41-44 corresponds to the third and final

---

108. See Jeremias, *Sprache des Lukasevangeliums,* 281, who recognizes seven sentences connected by *kai* and eight pronouns in enclitic construction, all reflective of Greek translation from Hebrew. For five additional Hebraisms, see Edwards, *Hebrew Gospel,* 323.

109. On the Pharisees, Jerusalem, and Jesus, see Schlatter, *Lukas,* 408-11.

110. On the eschatological and ecological significance of v. 40, see D. Horrell and D. Coad, "'The Stones Would Cry Out' (Luke 19:40): A Lukan Contribution to a Hermeneutics of Creation's Praise," *SJT* 64/1 (2011): 29-44.

response to the returning king in the parable of the Minas. "As [Jesus] approached Jerusalem and saw the city, he wept over it and said, 'If you, even you, had only known on this day what would bring peace — but now it is hidden from your eyes'" (vv. 41-42). For the fourth and final time prior to the Passion Narrative, Luke combines the word "approach" (Gk. *engizein*) with a place-name (18:35; 19:11, 29, 41) to chronicle the journey to Jerusalem. Jerusalem appears in glorious aspect, but the festivity of the crowd (v. 37) becomes "bitter sorrow" (v. 41; Gk. *klaiein*) as Jesus foretells the city's impending destruction. Only once is Jesus said to "rejoice" in the Third Gospel (10:21), and only here is he said to "weep," which in Greek implies deep and audible sorrow. Each element in vv. 41-44 echoes prophetic lamentations.[111] The lack of "peace" that Jesus bewails (v. 42) refers to divine peace, the *shalom* of God, which characterizes Jesus' life (v. 38; 2:14), but not the life of his people. Once again, God's people are undiscerning and nonunderstanding (v. 42; Deut 32:28). Their lack of discernment is not the result of ignorance, or even of immorality. Jerusalem's problem is not that it will not repent, but that its spiritual rebellion has made it *unable* to repent.[112] It does "not recognize the time of God's coming" (v. 44); indeed, its fate is "hidden" from its eyes" (Gk. *kryptein;* v. 42). This is the language of divine agency, which earlier appeared in the final prediction that the meaning of Jesus' passion "was hidden from [the Twelve]" (Gk. *kryptein;* 18:34). Through the various strands of human agency that oppose God's kingdom and his Messiah, the sovereignty of God is weaving a redemptive pattern in the Passion Narrative.

"The days will come" (v. 43), a phrase occurring twenty times in the prophets (all but three in either Jer or Amos), is a Hebraism warning of God's judgment (e.g., Amos 4:2). "Your enemies will build an embankment against you and encircle you and hem you in on every side. They will dash you to the ground, you and the children within your walls" (vv. 43-44). This is one of the most trenchant pronouncements of Jesus in the Gospels, and at the same time an echo of the climax of the parable of Minas (19:27). A dozen repetitions of the singular personal pronoun "you" (Gk. *sou, soi, se*) in vv. 42-44 hammer Jerusalem with personal responsibility for the impending catastrophe. V. 43 is a classic description of a *circumvallatio,* a Roman defense perimeter erected around a city in preparation for a siege.[113] One might suspect that vv. 43-44 are either remembered by Luke's source or narrated by Luke himself to reflect the fatal Roman siege that befell Jerusalem in 66-70. The specific terminology used by Josephus in his various descriptions of the siege of Jerusalem is not

---

111. Also recognized by Bovon, *Lukas 19,28–24,53,* 43; Klein, *Lukasevangelium,* 618.

112. On Jerusalem's lack of recognition of Jesus as a result of God's hardening, see Wolter, *Lukasevangelium,* 634.

113. *EDNT* 3:456.

particularly close to the wording of vv. 43-44, however.[114] Rather, vv. 43-44 are narrated in classic prophetic imagery, especially reminiscent of Isa 29:3, "I will encamp against you on all sides; I will encircle you with towers and set up my siege works against you."[115] References to "dashing children" to death — an atrocity not mentioned by Josephus — recall Ps 137:9; Hos 10:14; 13:16; Nah 3:10; "no stone left on another" (21:6) echoes 2 Sam 17:13; and "not recognizing the time of God's coming to you" recalls similar wording of Jer 6:15. This last phrase is particularly important, for it repeats the seminal word *episkopē* ("visitation"; NIV "God's coming"), which occurs elsewhere only in the Benedictus (1:68, 78), and is thus another of Luke's inclusios linking the infancy narrative and the Passion Narrative (see excursus at 2:52). The sorrow of Jesus in vv. 43-44 could be seen as the obverse of the coin of joy of Zechariah in the Benedictus.[116] Greek *episkopē* translates Hebrew *pequdah,* which typically in the OT signifies God's visitation of Israel in judgment and punishment. In v. 44, however, it refers to Jesus' personal visitation of Jerusalem. In using this term, Jesus employs an OT concept laden with divine agency with special reference to *himself.* Jesus visits Jerusalem not in judgment but in grace, a visitation that the crowd receives with joy. Jerusalem, as evidenced by the rebuke of the Pharisees immediately preceding, does not recognize or receive Jesus, however, and thus his visitation of grace becomes one of judgment — in both the loss of salvation and destruction of the city.[117]

Jesus' prescience, as noted earlier, is more frequently documented in the Passion Narrative than elsewhere in the Third Gospel. Eusebius read vv. 42-44 as a description of "the second year of the reign of Vespasian" (ca. 69-70) that Jesus "foresaw by divine power." Immediately following, Eusebius quotes vv. 43-44 verbatim as a fulfillment of the prophecy.[118] Eusebius may have referred to "divine power" loosely here, for the crisis brewing between Rome and Judea, particularly as foreshadowed by the ever bold and influential

---

114. Josephus thrice refers to the "towers" (Gk. *pyrgos*) of Jerusalem (*J. W.* 7.1, 2, 375), which are not mentioned by Luke; and his words for "walls" (*teichos, J. W.* 7.375), "surround wall" (*peribalon, J. W.* 7.3, 375), and "tear down" (*kataskaptein,* 7.3) differ from corresponding terms in v. 43. Josephus's further description in *J. W.* 5.466-67 is no closer verbally with v. 43.

115. Lukan references to "build" (Gk. *paremballein*) and "encircle" (*perikykloun*) agree with forms of the same words in Isa. 29:3, and the technical reference to "siege works" (*charax;* TNIV "embankment"), a mound fortified by a palisade, is the same in both v. 43 and Isa 29:3. Bovon, *Lukas 19,28–24,53,* is correct in observing that "Luke, who doubtlessly knows details of the siege of Jerusalem by Titus, gives preference to Biblical language over contemporary historical description."

116. For an analysis of vv. 43-44 as an "obverse" of the Benedictus, see Tannehill, *Narrative Unity of Luke-Acts,* 36.

117. H. Beyer, *episkopē, TWNT* 2:602-4. Klein, *Lukasevangelium,* 618, writes, "The rejection of the offer of invisible salvation results in visible disaster."

118. Eusebius, *Hist. eccl.* 3.7.3-4.

Zealot movement, was evident to many by the time Jesus entered Jerusalem; and the graphic imagery with which he predicted it had long been at hand in the prophetic tradition.[119] The calculated procession of Jesus from Jericho to Jerusalem, especially in the triumphal procession, vividly combines the ironic contrasts that determine the Passion Narrative. Jesus is the royal Davidic Messiah who must be rejected, suffer, and die. He is received with joy in Jerusalem at his birth (2:38), but he weeps for Jerusalem at his death (v. 41). Jesus is victor and victim. No understanding or proclamation of Jesus is complete that does not affirm both as essential and inseparable elements in the divine mystery incarnate in Jesus (2:34).

---

119. Josephus, *J. W.* 7.300-301, records a dirge over Jerusalem four years prior to the Jewish War of 66 by a certain Jesus, son of Ananias, who stood in the temple and cried, "A voice from the east, a voice from the west, a voice from the four winds; a voice against Jerusalem and the sanctuary, a voice against the bridegroom and the bride, a voice against all the people." Also prior to the destruction of Jerusalem, a prophecy of doom (of undetermined date) circulated at Qumran, applying the judgment of Hab 2:8a to the priests of Jerusalem, "who will accumulate riches and loot from plundering the nations. However, in the last days their riches and their loot will be given into the hands of the army of the Kittim [= Romans]" (1QpHab 9:4-6). "What is there in these details [vv. 43-44] which is not common to all sieges?", asks Plummer, *Luke,* 451, in defense of Jesus' foreknowledge of the prediction. For a full discussion and defense of the possibility of Jesus uttering vv. 43-44, see Fitzmyer, *Luke (X–XXIV),* 1254-55.

CHAPTER EIGHTEEN

Teacher in the Temple

Luke 19:45–21:4

The journey to Jerusalem, anticipated already in 9:31 and predicted throughout the central section, is finally completed. Jesus arrives in Jerusalem as a king (19:11-44), but once there, he conducts himself, as he has throughout the Gospel (4:14-15), as a teacher. In the Passion Narrative, Jerusalem is a metonym for the temple. The journey to Jerusalem is, practically speaking, a journey to the *temple,* for the Passion Narrative is focused almost exclusively in and around the temple.[1] The temple both symbolized and actualized the central authority of Judaism. The posture of Jesus toward the temple expresses itself in two different attitudes, depending whether the temple is considered according to its purpose or the perversion of its purpose. The structure — the temple proper and its purpose — is presented throughout the infancy narrative as a place of divine revelation, and thus a key locus of salvation history. But its infrastructure, as exemplified in the Sanhedrin and Levitical priesthood, has misappropriated the temple as sacred structure. Luke hinted of its perversion when, as a boy, Jesus referred to the temple as "my Father's house" (2:49). The priest and Levite in the parable of the Good Samaritan (10:30-37) are further intimations of its spurious and unmerciful (Exod 34:6) leaders. Jesus' initial task in Holy Week is to purge the temple infrastructure, which he calls "a den of robbers" (19:46), and through a prophetic action reclaim it as his "Father's house." In this respect, Luke's understanding of the temple differs from Mark's, who understands Jesus to replace the temple rather than cleanse it. Once purged, the temple in Luke becomes the redeemed arena of Jesus' teaching throughout the Passion Narrative (19:47; 20:1, 21; 21:37), even though its infrastructure, the Sanhedrin, continues to oppose Jesus and instigate his death. Luke thus sets Jesus' teaching in bas-relief to the background of opposition from temple authorities. Throughout these encounters Jesus does not endeavor to best, embarrass, or defeat his opponents, but to engage them and, if possible, instruct them regarding the kingdom and his role in it. A similar

---

1. 19:45, 47; 20:1; 21:5, 37, 38; 22:52, 53; 23:45.

scenario repeats itself in Acts, though with reference to Jesus' followers. The temple becomes the home base of the nascent Christian movement, where they pray and proclaim the resurrected Lord (Acts 2:46; 3:1),[2] although not without aggressive opposition of the Sanhedrin (Acts 3–5). This paradoxical role continues throughout the early Christian Gentile mission as well, for in the Book of Acts Paul punctuates his resolute extension of the gospel into Gentile regions with five trips back to Jerusalem and the temple (Acts 9:26; 11:30; 15:2; 19:21; 21:15).

19:45–21:4 consists of nine episodes, all set in the early days of Holy Week. Luke appears to have received all the episodes from Mark (11:15–12:44), which he reproduces in their Markan order.[3] Luke's Passion Narrative proper (19:45–23:56) consists of 216 verses, which represents nearly 20 percent of the Third Gospel. The Passion Narrative contains ten teaching or controversy pericopes (19:45–21:4); a long eschatological discourse (21:5-38); events surrounding the Last Supper (22:1-71, which, although shorter than the Fourth Gospel, are considerably longer than either Matt or Mark); trials by both Pilate (23:1-7, 13-25) and Antipas (23:8-12); and the crucifixion and burial (23:26-56). This is a considerable schedule of events for five days of Holy Week. It is possible that such activity, particularly as recorded in Luke 20–21, transpired over a longer period of time and was later compressed into the traditional Passion Narrative in order to serve the liturgical and catechetical interests of the early church.[4] The Fourth Gospel places Jesus in Jerusalem for the Festival of Dedication (10:22; November-December), after which he retires to trans-Jordan before Passover (10:40–11:54). This would locate Jesus in the environs of Jerusalem for several months prior to Passover. Several references in Luke's Passion Narrative suggest a sojourn in Jerusalem longer than a single week (19:47; 20:1; 21:37; 22:39, 53), thus comporting with the Johannine chronology.

JESUS RETURNS TO HIS "FATHER'S HOUSE" (19:45-48)

45-46   The clearing of the temple, graphically narrated in the other Gospels (Matt 21:12-13; Mark 11:15-17; John 2:13-17[?]), is severely pruned by Luke, who

---

2. Bovon, *Lukas 19,28–24,53,* 48, notes, however, that "there is not one single reference attesting to the first Christians continuing the practice of blood offerings."

3. The only Markan episode not present in 19:45–21:4 is the story of the greatest commandment (Mark 12:28-34), which Luke used earlier (10:25-28) in introduction to the parable of the Good Samaritan.

4. The possibility of Jesus' passion ministry in Jerusalem exceeding a single week is entertained by Schlatter, *Lukas,* 432; Schweizer, *Lukas,* 197; Fitzmyer, *Luke (X–XXIV),* 1269; and Wolter, *Lukasevangelium,* 637.

reduces Mark's sixty-two-word narrative to twenty-five words.[5] The overturning of the tables of money changers and pigeon sellers is omitted in order to focus solely on Jesus' quotation from Isaiah and Jeremiah in v. 46. This again indicates the significance of Jesus' teaching for Luke. Luke does not record a "triumphal entry" into Jerusalem, but only an entry into the temple (on **temple**, see at 2:46). There Jesus "began to drive out those who were selling" (v. 45). By omitting "buyers" (Matt 21:12; Mark 11:15), Luke incriminates temple profiteers rather than worshipers. The precinct of the temple referred to is the **Court of Gentiles**, the outer court accessible to all people, both Jews and Gentiles, which was overseen by the Sadducees. The volume of trade in the Court of Gentiles was conducted on a scale commensurate with the grandeur of Herod's temple itself;[6] it was crucial for the maintenance of proper worship and for the financial gain of the Sadducees and Sanhedrin. In the words of Emil Schürer, the

> huge quantity [of animals], so great as to be almost unbelievable, gave the Temple cults its peculiar stamp. Day after day, masses of victims were slaughtered there and burnt, and in spite of the thousands of priests, when one of the great festivals came round the multitude of sacrifices was so great that they could hardly cope with them.[7]

The enormity of the temple industry may be further appreciated by Josephus's comment that in 66, the year construction of the temple was completed, 255,600 lambs were sacrificed at Passover (*J.W.* 6.422-27).

It is this operation that Jesus interrupts (v. 45), which he justifies by quoting from the prophets, "It is written, 'My house will be called a house of prayer'; but you have made it 'a den of robbers'" (v. 46). "It is written" appears as an authoritative preface to laws and declarations in the Hellenistic world. In the OT the preface specifically designates the authority of God, Torah, king, or prophet.[8] Here it signifies that the quotation to follow expresses God's will. According to *Pss. Sol.* 17:22-30, the Messiah was expected to purge both Jerusalem and the temple of Gentiles, aliens, and foreigners. Jesus reveals himself to be a very different kind of Messiah, for here he clears the temple *for* them.

---

5. For important discussions on the possible relationship of the purging of the temple in the Synoptics with the similar event in John, see R. Brown, *The Gospel according to John* (AB 29; Garden City: Doubleday, 1966), 1:114-25; Fitzmyer, *Luke (X–XXIV)*, 1262-65.

6. H. Betz, "Jesus and the Purity of the Temple (Mark 11:15-18): A Comparative Religion Approach," *JBL* 116 (1997): 464, describes Herod's temple "as a gigantic votive gift for Herod's kingship," with offerings and sacrifices in equal measure.

7. Schürer, *History of the Jewish People*, 2:308.

8. G. Schrenk, *graphō*, *TWNT* 1:747-48. Luke introduces scriptural quotations with *graphein* in 2:23; 3:4; 4:4, 8, 10, 17; 7:27; 10:26; 19:46; 20:17, 28; 22:37.

"My house will be called a house of prayer" is quoted from Isa 56:7, where the prophet declares God's eschatological salvation of all nations, including eunuchs and foreigners, who will stream to God's Holy Mountain for prayer. Jesus claims the quotation, which in Isa denotes a future eschatological reference, for the *present*.[9] Luke first referred to the temple as a place of prayer (1:10), and prayer constitutes its essential purpose, without which it is not God's dwelling.[10] The second part of the quotation in v. 46 comes from Jer 7:11, where the prophet condemns the lies, deception, and false worship perpetrated in the temple. Luke introduces the Jer quotation emphatically, "*You* have made it 'a den of robbers'" (v. 46). "Robbers" (Gk. *lēstēs*), used elsewhere in the Third Gospel of violent criminal activity (10:30, 36; 22:52), attests to Jesus' estimation of the financial operation of the temple and of the Sanhedrin responsible for it. The quotation of v. 46 thus combines the ideal and the real, divine intention and human distortion of the divine intention. The prophetic word of Jesus in v. 46 is the *verbum Dei* for the *locus Dei,* the word of God intended to restore the temple as "my Father's house" (2:49).[11]

47-48 V. 47, which is not present in the other Gospels, describes the ambiguity of the temple as both holy place and hostile place. Having demonstrated his prophetic authority in purging the temple, Jesus may now teach there, and continues teaching there throughout Holy Week (v. 47; 20:1, 21; 21:37). But opposition continues from the temple as well. Luke's summary, "Every day [Jesus] was teaching in the temple," seems to assume a longer length of time than only two or three days of Holy Week. This is the first time since the infancy narrative that Luke records Jesus teaching in the temple. As a boy, Jesus "amazed" the temple authorities (2:46-47), but the former adulation is

---

9. So Klein, *Lukasevangelium,* 620.

10. On the temple as a place of prayer, 1:10; 2:37; 18:10; Acts 3:1; 8:27; 22:17; 24:11. It is unclear why Luke omits from the Isa quotation, "for all nations," which is retained in Mark 11:17. One would expect Luke (esp. if he were a Gentile), who champions the universality of the gospel, to include such a reference. Green, *Luke,* 694, suggests Luke omitted the phrase because he did not want to include the corrupt temple leaders. Marshall, *Luke,* 721, and Bovon, *Lukas 19,28–24,53,* 49, suggest that the fall of Jerusalem in 70 rendered the prophecy irrelevant. Vinson, *Luke,* 606, suggests that, for Luke, the temple is not the locus of the Gentile mission. These suggestions are plausible, if not entirely persuasive. I would venture a linguistic observation in relation to the question. In the original Isa quotation, the Hebrew word for "people" is not *goi,* which generally connotes non-Israelite pagan foreigners, but *'am,* which typically means Israel as God's covenant people (see E. Lipinski, *'am, TDOT* 11:163-73; R. Clements, *goi, TDOT* 2:426-33; *HALOT* 1:837-39, 182-83). This distinction is of course absent in the LXX, *pasin tois ethnesin.* If Luke is using a Hebrew source for the quotation, the narrowing of the original Isa quotation toward Jewish people rather than the nations might incline Luke to omit it.

11. Once the temple was destroyed in 70, early Christianity applied the import of v. 46 to Christians: "If we do not do God's will, we shall be like the saying, 'My house became a den of robbers'" (2 *Clem.* 14:1; similarly, Justin Martyr, *Dial.* 17.3).

not repeated in the Passion Narrative. The authorities now want "to kill him" (v. 47). Luke of course mentions opposition to Jesus prior to the passion (6:11; 11:53-54), but unlike Mark, who discloses the plot to kill Jesus early in the Galilean ministry (3:6), Luke has not recorded an intention to kill Jesus until now. The authorities are identified as "chief priests," "teachers of the law," and "leaders of the people" (see on **Pharisees** and **scribes** at 5:17). In the Third Gospel, opposition to Jesus in the Passion Narrative is spearheaded by scribes and chief priests (19:47; 20:19, 20; 22:2), and by the Sanhedrin (20:1; 22:4-6) and civil authorities (19:47; 20:20; 22:4; 23:13-14), but not by Pharisees. "Chief priests" and "teachers of the law" describe the temple aristocracy and intellectual leadership of the Sanhedrin, and "leaders among the people" sets a third contingent in collusion with them. Luke does not specifically identify "the leaders among the people" (Gk. *hoi prōtoi tou laou*), but similar expressions connote Jewish leaders in general.[12] These three parties constitute the top echelon of temple leadership, the power-holders of Jewish society. Luke does not hold all Jews responsible for the death of Jesus, whether Jews be understood nationally, ethnically, or religiously. Indeed, the posture of the temple leadership toward Jesus conflicts with "the people" — the *Jewish* people — who "hung on his words" (v. 48). That metaphor connotes allegiance, even devotion, to Jesus' teaching that will continue throughout the Passion Narrative. Thus, the Sanhedrin fears being "stoned to death" by the crowds if it impugns John the Baptist's reputation (20:6);[13] the Sanhedrin refrains from seizing Jesus for "fear of the people" (20:19); the people arrive "early in the morning to hear [Jesus] in the temple" (21:38).

Opposition to the messianic mission of Jesus does not come from humanity at its worst, but from humanity at its best, from those knowledgeable about God and authorized to serve in God's house. From the outset of the Passion Narrative Jesus faces "an open door, but many opponents" (1 Cor 16:9), as Paul will later describe his own ministry. The passion of Jesus is a prototype of virtually all expressions of Christian service: great potential on the one hand, and great opposition on the other; limited resources in the face of unlimited needs and opportunities; disappointment by those we overvalue, and surprise by those we overlook; the house of God as both "my Father's house" and "a den of robbers." Within such contrarieties God accomplishes a redemption very different from our expectations, yet greater than we imagine.

---

12. Acts 13:50; 25:2; 28:17; Josephus, *Ant.* 7.53; 11.142; *Vita* 9.

13. *Katalithazein*, occurring in the NT only in 20:6, is intensive, meaning "stoned *to death*" (Klein, *Lukasevangelium*, 622).

A CHALLENGE TO THE TEACHER'S AUTHORITY (20:1-8)

This is the first of six pericopes in which Jesus finds himself in either direct or indirect conflict with the temple administration.[14] In addition, Luke twice informs readers of antagonism from the Sanhedrin toward Jesus (20:1, 19). The sparks of earlier friction between Jesus and the Pharisees now ignite into open conflict with the temple authorities. The intensification of conflict is accompanied by an intensification of Christology. Jesus is presented as the "beloved son" (20:13), the vital cornerstone (20:17), the teacher who cannot be refuted (20:39), the Messiah and "Son of David" (20:41), and Lord (20:42-44). In the divine economy, opposition does not stifle or defeat the revelation of Jesus' divine sonship. In the eschatological discourse Jesus will teach that, when perplexity and terror shake heaven and earth, "lift up your heads, because your redemption is near" (21:28). The same dynamic pervades the Passion Narrative: great travail is counterbalanced by great revelation.

1-2   The challenge to Jesus' authority in vv. 1-8 closely follows the same account in Mark 11:27-33. Luke makes several stylistic improvements to Mark's account, however, and adds his own introduction in v. 1. In style, v. 1 is highly Semitic, corresponding to several other Lukan introductions to Markan pericopes.[15] In content, v. 1 repeats the theme of 19:47-48 immediately before. Jesus continues with the same activities that have characterized his ministry from its inception, "teaching the people . . . and proclaiming the good news" to all the people. These same activities will characterize the ministry of the early church (Acts 5:42; 15:35). And he is again opposed by temple leaders for doing so. The setting of both his teaching and opposition by the Sanhedrin is the temple, making it again a contested arena. The "chief priests, scribes, and elders" (v. 1) were the three groups that comprised the Sanhedrin (see at 9:22), although in this instance a delegation of the Sanhedrin is implied rather than the full council.[16] The appearance of the chief authoritative body of Judaism signifies the gravity of their encounter with Jesus.

---

14. Sanhedrin challenges Jesus' authority (20:1-8); parable of the Vineyard (20:9-18); question about paying taxes to Caesar (20:19-26); Sadducees challenge Jesus on the question of resurrection (20:27-38); question about David's Son (20:39-44); poor widow in the temple (20:45–21:4).

15. 5:12a, 17; 8:22; 9:18a; 20:1. In v. 1 "it happened" *(kai egeneto)* and "on one of those days" (*en mia tōn hēmerōn* [*ekeinōn*]) are both Hebraisms. See Edwards, *Hebrew Gospel*, 144-46, 323; Fitzmyer, *Luke (I–IX)*, 121-22.

16. On the history, composition, and function of the Sanhedrin, see Schürer, *History of the Jewish People*, 2:199-226; E. Lohse, *synedrion*, *TWNT* 7:858-69. B. Metzger, *The Text of the New Testament* (London: Oxford University Press, 1964), 238-39, argues on the basis of *lectio difficilior*, that v. 1 should read "*priests*, scribes, and elders," since "there is no discernible motive for altering 'chief priests' to 'priests.'" ("Priests" appears in A W Byz; "chief priests" in ℵ B C

"Tell us by what authority you are doing these things," they said. "Who gave you this authority?" (v. 2). "These things" ostensibly alludes to the clearing of the temple (19:45-46),[17] although that event was only the most recent incident in a history of provocations, all of which expressed Jesus' unique **authority** (Gk. *exousia*).[18] In the latter portions of the LXX and in intertestamental literature, *exousia* frequently denotes supernatural powers and authorities, especially of God and God's works, representatives, and emissaries, as expressed through kings, priests, and saints. The DSS follow suit, although at Qumran the Hebrew terms that lie behind *exousia* in the LXX *(mashal* and *shalat)* often refer to supernatural powers of a demonic nature. *Exousia* thus typically designates supernatural authority in Jewish literature immediately prior to the Christian era.[19] In Luke, *exousia* can designate extraordinary human authority, especially political authority (7:8; 12:11; 19:17; 20:20; 23:7), but its most distinctive uses are reserved for Jesus. This term, which in 12:5 is used of God's supreme authority, denotes the characteristic of Jesus that left the most lasting impression on his followers and caused the greatest offense to his opponents. The devil, too, possesses supernatural *exousia* and promises to bequeath it to Jesus, if only he will worship him (4:6; 22:53). Jesus maintains fidelity with his divine baptismal commission (3:21-22), however, thereby receiving from the Father *exousia* in word and teaching (4:32), to forgive sins (5:24), and both to vanquish the evil one and his minions (4:36) and to send out disciples with the same power (9:1; 10:19). Jesus' *exousia* is further expressed in his receiving and eating with sinners (15:2), calling tax collectors into fellowship (5:27-32), redefining Sabbath (6:1-5), and superseding Torah (6:1-5; 7:39). The purging of the temple was a further characteristic of Jesus' authority rather than an exception to it. Until this point in the Gospel the source of Jesus' *exousia* has not been divulged. Now, in the temple and before the Sanhedrin, i.e., in Israel's most sacred place and before its authorized leaders, Jesus opens a window of understanding into his own authority.

The question "By what authority?" indicates that the issue for the Sanhedrin is not simply what Jesus did, but his *right* to do it. Was he acting with divine legitimacy or not, i.e., was he a true or false prophet? The punishment

---

D L N Q Θ Ψ). Metzger's conjecture would increase the opposition to Jesus from chief priests to *all* priests. "Chief priests" is probably original, however, because none of Luke's seven references to "priests" sets them in opposition to the gospel (1:5; 5:14; 6:4; 10:31; 17:14; Acts 4:1; 6:7).

17. John 2:13-22 preserves an independent witness linking the question of the religious authorities to Jesus' clearing of the temple.

18. What evidence is there to substantiate the conjecture of Fitzmyer, *Luke (X–XXIV),* 1273, and Wolter, *Lukasevangelium,* 640, that Jesus' teaching in the temple — a commonplace among Jewish rabbis — was the cause of the Sanhedrin's challenge to Jesus?

19. On *exousia,* see J. Edwards, "The Authority of Jesus in the Gospel of Mark," *JETS* 37/2 (1994): 217-22.

prescribed by the Mishnah for the latter was death by strangulation.[20] The question also indicates that Jesus' authority is recognized as exceeding mere human authority; indeed, on an earlier occasion his authority had been attributed to the demonic (11:15). If such power is not innate to humanity, then it cannot come from humanity. A second and related question follows, "Who gave you this authority?" If Jesus attributes his authority to God, then he could be charged with blasphemy — a charge that had earlier been proposed in relation to his presumption to forgive sins (5:21). At the heart of the question about Jesus' *exousia* is his presumption to speak and act in place of God.

3-8   Following rabbinic custom, Jesus responds to a question by posing a counterquestion.[21] Was John's baptism "from heaven, or from men?" he asks.[22] Out of reverence for God, Jews avoided using the divine name, and Jesus follows the custom here, substituting "heaven" in its place. It is important to note that Jesus makes no appeal to the chief sources of authority in Judaism, such as rabbinic tradition, temple, or Torah. He advances only two possible alternatives — divine or human. These are the categories necessary to comprehend his "authority" — his person and his mission. In framing the issue in such a fundamental way, Jesus requires of the Sanhedrin a decision that cannot be answered from their power base in Torah, temple, or Roman authority. When faced with the ultimate question about Jesus, even the Sanhedrin, the most authoritative body in Judaism, cannot avoid a decision of faith.

Jesus' counterquestion in v. 4 may strike readers as irrelevant, perhaps even a diversionary tactic. What, after all, does John's baptism have to do with Jesus' authority? It is important to recall that John's call for baptism, repentance, and preparation for the Coming One was not a negligible influence in first-century Judaism. Allegiance to John was great enough to arouse in Herod Antipas fears of a popular uprising (Mark 6:20; Josephus, *Ant.* 18.118). When Paul visited distant Ephesus in mid-first century, he discovered that John's reputation exceeded that of Jesus (Acts 19:1-7). Josephus's report on John (*Ant.* 18.116-19) surpasses his similar report on Jesus (*Ant.* 18.63-64) in both length and detail.[23] V. 6 itself testifies to John's preeminence, for a wrong decision

---

20. "The false prophet and he that prophesies in the name of a strange god" were to be strangled (*m. Sanh.* 11:1). Although the Mishnah was not codified until a century and a half after Jesus, many of its prescriptions date to Jesus' day and earlier. This one appears to have been in effect in Jesus' day, as the accusation of the chief priest in 22:71 attests.

21. See Str-B 1:861-62.

22. Klein, *Lukasevangelium*, 622, is mistaken in regarding v. 3 a mere defense ("The best defense is also here a good offense, hence the counter question"). The purpose of Jesus' teaching was not *self*-defense, but to enable hearers, even antagonistic hearers, to grasp the truth.

23. For a critical (and positive) assessment of Josephus's report on John, see J. Meier, "John the Baptist in Josephus: Philology and Exegesis," *JBL* 111/2 (1992): 225-37. On John in general, see W. Grundmann, *Evangelium nach Markus* (THKNT; Berlin: Evangelische Verlags-

about John exposes the Sanhedrin to the possibility of stoning, "because [all the people] are persuaded that John was a prophet" (v. 6). Thus, we may assume the Sanhedrin was familiar with John; indeed, the appeal of v. 4 assumes a definite knowledge of John by the Sanhedrin. The counterquestion of Jesus contains the seeds of truth the Sanhedrin pretends to desire. At Jesus' baptism by John heaven was opened, the Spirit descended upon him, and the divine voice declared him God's Son. The baptism inaugurated Jesus' *exousia*, his conscious oneness with the Father, and his sovereign freedom and empowerment for ministry. If the Sanhedrin wants to know whence Jesus received his authority, it must reconsider John's baptism. A decision about John is, indirectly, a decision about Jesus.[24] If John's baptism were solely "of human origin," then Jesus is not acting on behalf of God or with the power of God. He may even be a false prophet, as the Sanhedrin suspects. But if John's baptism was "from heaven," i.e., if it was divinely commissioned and divinely empowered — as the crowds believe and as the Sanhedrin evidently fears — then Jesus teaches and acts with divine authority.

"[The Sanhedrin] discussed it among themselves" (v. 5). The Greek word behind "discussed," *syllogizesthai*, is a rare word, occurring only this once in the NT, and only four times in the LXX. It means "to discuss various possibilities related to a matter."[25] The use of this term in Isa 43:18 is particularly relevant to the present passage: "Do not remember the former things and do not consider [*syllogizesthai*] the things of old." The Sanhedrin would do well not to judge Jesus by old paradigms, but by John's prophetic activity. But this the Sanhedrin is unable to do. Already in v. 5 it shifts from a decision about Jesus to managing the *consequences* of such a decision. A decision for John will appear to support the cause of Jesus; a decision against John will alienate the crowds, for whom John was popularly regarded as a prophet. The Venerable Bede aptly captures the Sanhedrin's dilemma: they fear the possibility of being stoned to death by the crowd, but they fear a true confession even more.[26] The

---

anstalt, 1989), 39-42; J. Jeremias, *New Testament Theology* (New York: Scribner's, 1971), 43-56; G. Stanton, *The Gospels and Jesus* (2nd ed.; Oxford: University Press, 2002), 178-89.

24. "All [Jesus'] actions and words are connected with John and go back to the spirit of God's descent on him after he had accepted baptism at John's hand. Jesus has the right to act the way he does because of what the voice from heaven said to him. He, more than the authorities, is more at home in the temple, because God has called him his dear son" (B. van Iersel, *Reading Mark* [Edinburgh: T&T Clark, 1989], 148).

25. BDAG, 956. Bovon, *Lukas 19,28–24,53*, 61 (relying on G. Mussies, "The Sense of *syllogizesthai* at Luke 20,5," in *Miscellanea Neotestamentica* [ed. T. Baarda et al.; NovTSup 48; Leiden: Brill, 1978], 59-76), defines the word as "cool calculation, a carefully deduced and weighed consideration."

26. Quoted in Plummer, *Luke*, 457. The Greek word for "stone," *katalithazein*, is intensive, meaning "stone *to death*" (Klein, *Lukasevangelium*, 622).

Sanhedrin senses itself checkmated, not by Jesus, but by its own stratagems. "We don't know where it was from," they answer (v. 7). That is not exactly true. They are *unwilling* to know. Their judgment is determined by strategy rather than by the desire for truth. "Neither will I tell you by what authority I am doing these things," declares Jesus (v. 8).

This is the only encounter in the Gospels between a free Jesus and the Sanhedrin. The Sanhedrin comes upon him in the temple, suddenly,[27] to parley as with a foe, to test with a question. His answer, no matter how complete, is unlikely to satisfy them; and no matter how incomplete, almost certain to arouse further suspicion. Jesus refuses to parley, for he will not declare what they are unwilling to hear. As is his custom, he tells a story that might allow them to see for themselves what they are unwilling to hear from another. He brings his interrogators to a threshold that would lead them to the truth they claim to desire, but they refuse to cross the threshold, for they are guided more by self-interest than by truth. When victory is no longer in sight, they calculate how to minimize their losses by "suspending judgment." That is an evasion — but even their evasion is accorded a measure of respect by Jesus. To those unwilling to commit themselves, he commits not himself. Were their faith as small as a mustard seed, he would respond, "Truly I tell you" (Gk. *amēn legō hymin*); but without faith, he responds, "Neither will I tell you" (Gk. *oude egō legō hymin*, v. 8).[28]

John the Baptizer was, to be sure, a preacher of repentance. But above all he was a prophet (1:76; 7:26). Had the Sanhedrin acknowledged John's prophetic call and status, a door would have opened to a proper understanding of Jesus, for John foretold the coming of "the more powerful One," whose deeds would exceed his own (1:16-17, 32-35, 68-76; 3:16).[29] The Sanhedrin is not unaware of the potential ramifications of John's person and preaching with respect to Jesus, for at Jesus' hearing before the Sanhedrin in 22:67-68 the council raises the issue of Jesus' messianic pretensions.[30] The Sanhedrin's predetermination to discount Jesus repeats its same predetermination with respect to John, who, like Jesus, was popularly embraced by the people but

27. The Greek word for "came up to him," *ephistanai,* carries the connotation of suddenness and unexpectedness.

28. "The Sanhedrin has no right to question Jesus' authority, because the question does not motivate them to faith. . . . Whoever does not approach Jesus in faith cannot experience the source of his mission" (Klein, *Lukasevangelium,* 623).

29. Wolter, *Lukasevangelium,* 641.

30. See K. Huber, "Zur Frage nach christologischen Implikationen in den 'Jerusalemer Streitgesprächen' bei Markus," SNT(SU) 21 (1996): 13: "In my judgment, with the reference to John the Baptizer, Jesus lays claim to its content for himself and signifies indirectly that in his own person the announced 'Stronger One' has become reality, i.e., that he himself is this Messianic figure."

summarily rejected by the Jewish leaders (7:29-30). John's significance for Jesus — and in this instance for the Sanhedrin — is as a herald of Jesus' divine sonship. The "these things" of which the Sanhedrin inquires can be understood only if they are seen as consequences of the authority *(exousia)* of Jesus as Son of God, which John's baptism inaugurated. The authority with which Jesus acts as God's servant derives from his declaration and empowerment as God's Son at his baptism by John.

A CHALLENGE TO THE TEACHER'S INHERITANCE (20:9-19)

The parable of the Tenants appears in all three Synoptics (20:9-19; Matt 21:33-46; Mark 12:1-12), a faithful skeleton of which also appears in *Gos. Thom.* 65. Luke follows Mark's version more closely than does Matt, and in both the Second and Third Gospels the parable of the Wicked Tenants is the final and crowning parable of Jesus.[31] The earliest known interpretations of the parable in *Herm. Sim.* 5.2.1-8 and Irenaeus *(Haer.* 4.36.1) interpret it in terms of salvation history.[32] Irenaeus, in particular, emphasizes that the God who sent the prophets is one and the same Father of Jesus Christ.[33] This latter understanding doubtless accounts for the summary omission of the parable from Marcion's version of Luke (see Introduction, Marcion). The parable depicts conditions known to exist between vineyard owners and tenant farmers in first-century Palestine. Both secular records and rabbinic literature depict a widespread system of absentee landowners who employed managers to supervise tenant farmers.[34] A rabbinic commentary dating nearly a century after Jesus illustrated Deut 32:9 ("the Lord's portion is his people") by the same theme:

31. Although 21:29-30 is called a parable, it is more properly an illustration.

32. For a full and informative discussion of the rendition of the parable in *Herm. Sim.* 5, see A. Grillmeier, *Christ in Christian Tradition* (trans. J. Bowden; New York: Sheed & Ward, 1965), 63-68.

33. The versions of the parable in the Synoptics and in *Gos. Thom.* demonstrate that its allegorical character was present in its earliest forms.

34. The judgment of C. F. Evans, *Saint Luke* (London: SCM Press, 1990), 698, that the parable "is so artificial and implausible as not to be intelligible by reference to actual conditions of life, or any likely course of events, but only as an allegory . . . ," is strangely oblivious to both Palestinian agricultural practices and first-c. literary conventions. C. H. Dodd correctly notes that the parable describes "the kind of thing that went on in Galilee during the half century preceding the general revolt of A.D. 66" *(The Parables of the Kingdom* [London: Collins, 1961], 94). A report dating from 257 B.C. discovered in the Zeno Papyri documents an agent who traveled to Galilee to inspect his finance minister's property. Much like our parable, the document includes reports on the production of the vineyard, cisterns, and living spaces. See M. Hengel,

This is like a king who owned a field that he leased to tenants. They began to appropriate it as their own and steal. Thereupon the king took the field from them and gave it to their sons who behaved even worse. When a son was born to the king, the king said to the tenants, "You must leave my property, it is no longer possible for you to remain; render to me my due portion" (*Sipre Deut* 32:9).[35]

This same theme provided raw material for Jesus' teaching on other occasions (11:49; Matt 23:34). Elements of the parable are thus influenced by social circumstances of absentee landowners and tenant farmers, but the subject and plot of the parable as a whole are determined by the parable of the Vineyard in Isa 5:1-7.[36] Isa 5 is an allegory on Israel's relationship to God, and the parable of the Wicked Tenants extends the same allegory to include Israel's relation to the Son of God.[37]

9 Jesus' parables illustrate the basic themes of the kingdom of God by means of everyday Palestinian experiences. In the present parable, Jesus tells Israel's story in terms of the farm crisis of his day.[38] The parable is told to "the

---

"Das Gleichnis von den Weingärtnern Mc 12:1-12 im Lichte der Zenonpapyri und der rabbinischen Gleichnisse," *ZNW* 59 (1968): 12-15, who concludes: "The analogies to our parable are obvious. We encounter a considerable economic domain in Galilee, carried on according to capitalistic methods, which produced large quantities of wine. The system consisted of absentee landowners who employed agents to supervise their property." Further corroboration of the parable's historic plausibility appears in C. A. Evans, "Jesus' Parable of the Tenant Farmers in Light of Lease Agreements in Antiquity," *JSP* 14 (1996): 65-83; and R. MacMullan, *Roman Social Relations, 50 B.C. to A.D. 284* (New Haven: Yale University Press, 1974), 1-27, who documents "the vulnerability of property when its owner was away, [and] the invitation to violence, . . . beatings, maulings, and murder."

35. Str-B 1:874.

36. For hypothetical reconstructions of an original parable, see C. H. Dodd, *The Parables of the Kingdom* (London: Collins, 1961), 96; and esp. B. van Iersel, *"Der Sohn" in den synoptischen Jesusworten* (NovTSup 3; Leiden: Brill, 1964), 140.

37. The history of Israel's response to God is the dominant motif of the OT prophets (e.g., Jer 7:25-26; Hos 11:1-11). It should hardly be surprising if in a parable Jesus should rehearse that history in relation to himself. In this respect, see K. Snodgrass, *The Parable of the Wicked Tenants: An Inquiry into Parable Interpretation* (WUNT 27; Tübingen: Mohr Siebeck, 1983).

38. "Vineyard leases represented a particular type of agricultural lease. Unlike lease of farmland on which the tenant might plant one of several possible annual crops, the lease of a vineyard involved the care of a perennial crop representing significant capital investment. Vines normally took five years to become productive and required constant irrigation. They could suffer damage through neglect, and the proper operation of a vineyard regularly involved care for an adjoining reed plantation, from which supports for the vines were obtained, periodic manuring of the vines and maintenance of water installations" (J. Kloppenborg Verbin, "Isaiah 5:1-7, the Parable of the Tenants, and Vineyard Leases on Papyrus," in *Text and Artifact in the Religions of Mediterranean Antiquity: Essays in Honour of Peter Richardson* [ed. S. Wilson

people" (v. 9) who experienced such conditions, not to condemn them, but to explain how the inheritance of Israel — and hence their inheritance — has been usurped by the temple authorities. V. 19 in conclusion assures readers that the authorities did not fail to get Jesus' point. The parable is cast throughout in OT imagery, including portraying Israel's prophets as servants (Amos 3:7; Zech 1:4-6) and depicting Israel as God's inheritance (Ps 2:8). The dominant theme of the parable — the metaphor of Israel as a vineyard — is also a vintage OT motif.[39] Ps 80:8-13 portrays the exodus as God's bringing "a vine from Egypt." Even more fitting is Isa 5:1-7:

> My loved one had a vineyard on a fertile hillside.
> He dug it up and cleared it of stones
>   and planted it with the choicest vines. . . .
> Then he looked for a crop of good grapes,
>   but it yielded only bad fruit. . . .[40]

Isaiah's metaphor — and the judgment attended by it — was an oft-repeated theme in the OT and thus familiar to Jesus' contemporaries. A similar gavel of judgment was sounded by Jeremiah:

> From the time your ancestors left Egypt until now, day by day, again and again I sent to you my servants the prophets. But they did not listen to me or pay attention. They were stiff-necked and did more evil than their ancestors. (Jer 7:25-26; also 25:4-5)

10-12   The practice of absentee land ownership becomes the occasion of a prophetic judgment against Jewish leaders and temple authorities, who are depicted as tenant farmers. A landowner leases a vineyard to tenants to work in his absence. At harvest season he sends a hired hand to collect his produce (v. 10). But the tenants, in the words of C. H. Dodd, "pay their rent in blows."[41] Another servant is sent, and this one too is beaten, disgraced, and sent away empty (v. 11). A third servant is sent who is "wounded" and thrown out (v. 12). Unlike the versions of the parable in Matt and Mark, Luke's hand in summarizing the parable is evident in the tidy sequence of three servants sent (on threes in Luke, see at 19:20).[42] The vocabulary is also characteristically

---

and M. Desjardins; Studies in Christianity and Judaism 9; Waterloo, Ont.: Wilfrid Laurier University Press, 2000], 125).

39. Rengstorf, *Lukas,* 208, correctly recognizes that "since the time of Isaiah the vineyard is a symbol of Israel."

40. For a comparison of the main elements of Isa 5:1-7 and Jesus' parable, see Bailey, *Jesus through Middle Eastern Eyes,* 414.

41. *Parables of the Kingdom* (London: Collins, 1961), 93.

42. In *Gos. Thom.* 65 the three is inclusive, two servants plus the son.

Lukan. *Traumatizein* (v. 12; from which the word "trauma" derives), occurring in the NT only here and in Acts 19:16, means "to inflict physical injury, to wound or maim." In vv. 11-12 Luke twice repeats the Greek word *prostithenai,* thirteen of eighteen occurrences of which in the NT appear in Luke-Acts.[43] Though untranslated in the NIV, *prostithenai* connotes continuation in a predetermined course of action. In the context of the parable, it signifies that the owner (= God) is not indifferent to the harvest, but attentive to its maturation and indefatigable in securing *his* produce.

13-15a The critical juncture of the parable occurs in v. 13. The "man [who] planted a vineyard" (v. 9) is more precisely identified as "the owner of the vineyard" (NIV), but the Greek *kyrios* can also denote "*lord* of the vineyard." *Kyrios* surely connotes God here.[44] "What shall I do?" asks the owner? This is another of Luke's inner monologues,[45] effectively drawing the hearer/reader into the mind and heart of God. The moral logic of the parable leaves hearers/readers in no doubt what the owner should do: he should send a retaliatory force large enough to seize the vineyard, punish the rebel tenants if they surrender and destroy them if they don't, and give the vineyard over to more worthy tenants. The owner, however, acts otherwise. He resolves, "I will send my son, whom I love" (v. 13). This reveals the owner to be no ordinary human, no human at all, but the Lord God of Israel. The human response would be to get even, settle accounts once and for all; the divine response is one of compassion and unconditional love. The divine response is, of course, a costly gamble. "*Perhaps* they will respect him" (v. 13) indicates that even unconditional love may not succeed where legal rights have failed.

In Jewish law a son possessed legal rights that a slave did not; thus, the son is "the heir."[46] In sending the servants, the owner appealed to the integrity of the tenants; in sending his son, he appeals to the right of law, for the son was the only person, save himself, who possessed legal claim over the vineyard. The owner hopes the tenants will respect this claim. The son goes as the father's

---

43. *Prostithenai* is a Hebraism (Plummer, *Luke,* 460; Bovon, *Lukas* 19,28-24,53, 75; Edwards, *Hebrew Gospel,* 324).

44. C. Rowe, *Early Narrative Christology,* 168: "There is no ambiguity here with respect to the extended referent [of *kyrios*]: it is certainly God."

45. 3:10, 12, 13; 12:14, 17; 15:17; 16:3; Acts 2:37; 4:16. Further on inner monologues, see at 12:17, n. 31.

46. In Jewish law a son possessed legal rights denied to a slave. See J. Derrett, "Fresh Light on the Parable of the Wicked Winedressers," *RIDA* 10 (1963): 31, who writes that, in adjudicating disputes with tenants, "formal 'protest' must be made before witnesses, warning the tenants that legal action would commence against them. Slaves, however, could not make this protest, nor could slaves adjure witnesses — a serious handicap in so involved a matter. By that period it had not yet become possible to plead one's cause through an agent — one must actually transfer one's rights to the 'representative.' Therefore, the son had to be sent."

representative, with the father's authority, to the father's property, to claim the father's due. The version of the parable in *Herm. Sim.* 5.2.1-8 abolishes the singular role of the Son. There the parable illustrates the saving effects of good works (specifically fasting), in which the servant who receives the vineyard does not rebel against the owner but works the field faithfully and industriously, so that on the owner's return he is made coheir of the vineyard with the son. *The Shepherd*, in other words, refashions a parable about the role of Jesus in salvation history into a moral lesson, in which performance of good works makes one equal to the Master's Son.

The Son, however, stands in a unique and unshared relationship with the "owner" and thus bears the hallmarks of Jesus himself.[47] The initial word for "send" (v. 10; Gk. *apostellein*), which establishes the divine initiative in the parable, carries the sense of a divine commission (11:49-51; 13:34-35).[48] The son differs from the servants in the same way that Jesus differs from the prophets: they are many, he is unique; they are not the heirs, he is; they are forerunners, he is the final word of the Father; and above all, they are contractual partners, whereas the son is "beloved." "Beloved" recalls Abraham's love for Isaac (Gen 22:2), Jacob's love for Joseph (Gen 37:3), God's love for Israel (Isa 5:1). "Beloved son" (Gk. *ho huios mou ho agapētos*) is the exact form of divine address to Jesus in the baptism (3:22), recalling the filial relationship of Jesus to the Father. The parable depicts the unprecedented role of Jesus, the Son, in the history of Israel.[49]

The tenants, however, imagine that if they do away with the heir, they will come by the property. The version of the parable in *Gos. Thom.* 65 is ambiguous about the actual guilt of the tenants, suggesting that they mistreated the emissaries because they did not know them. In all three Synoptics, the behavior of the tenants cannot be attributed to ignorance: they kill the son *because* they know him. No longer content with the owner's produce, they go for his prop-

---

47. B. van Iersel, *"Der Sohn" in den synoptischen Jesusworten* (NovTSup 3; Leiden: Brill, 1964), 144, writes: "If one accepts that the parable is authentic, then Jesus himself — though indirectly and very discreetly — designates himself as the son."

48. A further allusion to Isaiah's vineyard is evident here. After the vineyard proves fruitless, the LXX asks the rhetorical question, "What more shall I do for my vineyard?" (Isa 5:4). Jesus gives the answer in this parable: God will send his only Son.

49. W. Bousset, *Kyrios Christos: A History of the Belief in Christ from the Beginnings of Christianity to Irenaeus* (trans. J. Steely; New York: Abingdon Press, 1970), 80, denies that "the son" is a self-designation of Jesus, maintaining that "nowhere else in his parables did Jesus push his own person into the foreground in such a way as here." Bousset's judgment is untenable. If the saying of 10:22 is authentic, as is widely affirmed, then there is no reason that Jesus cannot highlight his definitive role in the history of Israel. "If Jesus spoke of God as his Father, as the evidence of his prayers decisively establishes, it is difficult to see why he could not take the further step of referring to himself as the Son" (I. H. Marshall, "The Divine Sonship of Jesus," *Int* 21 [1967]: 93).

erty as well. "Let's kill him," they say (v. 14), repeating the same words spoken by Jacob's sons when they dispatched Joseph (Gen 37:20).[50] Since the beginning of creation humanity has sought to be like God without obeying God (Gen 3:5), to become lords of Eden rather than stewards of it. What is the sum total of human history if not the attempt to rid the universe of God so that humanity can rule supreme? The tenants of the vineyard are the ultimate expression of human rebellion: they kill the heir and seize the inheritance for themselves.[51]

15b-19 Jesus asks a rhetorical question, "What then will the owner of the vineyard do to them?" (v. 15). The effect of the question, like the inner dialogue in v. 13, forces hearers/readers to see the scandal from God's perspective. The owner will at last intervene decisively, destroying the tenants and leasing the property to others more deserving. It is important to note that the owner takes vengeance on the tenants, not on the vineyard. The parable, in other words, does not lay a blanket of blame on Jewish people, but on their leaders, particularly the Sanhedrin.[52] Moreover, the heroic party is not the tenant farmers (as in *The Shepherd*), but the landowner, who justly settles accounts. The parable thus does not advocate popular retaliation against oppression. Whatever the sentiment about absentee land ownership may have been in Jesus' day, it is the tenants who rebel unjustly against a rightful owner. That must be understood as Jesus' judgment on the Sanhedrin and Jewish leadership.

The vineyard is not a human possession, not even Israel's possession, but God's possession, his work and purpose in history. In the rhetorical question, "What then will the owner of the vineyard do to them?" (v. 15), the Greek

50. The Markan parallel to this verse reads, "They took him and killed him, and threw him out of the vineyard" (12:8). The Lukan sequence (also Matt 21:39) of throwing him out and then killing him corresponds more closely to the actual passion events, i.e., Jesus was arrested, taken out of Jerusalem, and crucified (so John 19:17; Heb 13:12). The alterations in Luke and Matt argue for Markan priority, for it is easier to explain why Luke and Matt would alter Mark in order to correspond to the historical sequence of the passion than to explain why Mark would corrupt an otherwise historical allusion in Luke and Matt. It is possible (though not very likely, in my judgment) that the difference in sequence reflects the Evangelists' understanding of those responsible for Jesus' death: for Mark, Jesus is killed inside the vineyard and then thrown outside, i.e., both rejected and killed by Jews; whereas for Matt and Luke, Jesus is thrown outside and killed, i.e., rejected by Jews but killed by Romans.

51. Some interpreters argue that, in the absence of the landowner, the tenants might expect to acquire ownership by length of tenancy. This theory is based on the custom of usucaption (i.e., in the absence of a title deed, ownership might be claimed on the basis of three years' undisputed possession). According to *m. B. Bat.* 3:3, however, "tenants and guardians cannot secure title by usucaption."

52. In my view, Plummer, *Luke,* 458, and Rengstorf, *Lukas,* 208, are mistaken in maintaining that Jesus directs the parable against the Jewish people rather than against their leaders. It is not the vineyard (as in Isa 5:5) but rather the tenants (= Jewish leaders) who are destroyed, the latter of which are differentiated from "the people" in v. 19.

word for "owner," *kyrios,* is again doubly appropriate, for it means both "owner" and "Lord." The judgment that Jesus pronounces against the vineyard echoes a similar judgment in the DSS, "I will tell you what I am going to do with my vineyard: [I will] remove its fence so that it can be used for pasture, destroy its wall so that you trample it. For I will leave it flattened" and a habitation for brambles and thistles (4Q162[4QpIsa]). "He will come and kill those tenants and give the vineyard to others," says Jesus (v. 16; cf. 19:27). We are not told who the "others" may be. By Luke's day, "others" certainly included Gentiles.[53] We should not think of the Gentile mission, however, as an invention of the later church. Already in the infancy narrative the mission of Jesus is forecast as "a light for revelation to the Gentiles" (2:32), and Jesus' inaugural sermon arouses the wrath of his Jewish kinfolk because he implies that his mission extends beyond the borders of Israel (4:25-30). The frequent recourse to Elijah and Elisha typology in the Galilean ministry (see at 7:17), the parable of the Good Samaritan (10:30-37), and the healing of the Samaritan leper (17:12-19) further evince the universality of Jesus' mission. Nor should Gentiles be understood to exclude Jewish believers. The most obvious referent to "others" — at least for Jesus' original hearers — would be the apostles,[54] or more broadly, his followers, Christians.[55]

Word that the vineyard will be given to others causes the people to exclaim, "God forbid!" (v. 16).[56] The conclusion Jesus draws is unavoidable, yet

---

53. The idea of the "vineyard" passing to Gentiles was apparently not only a Christian concept. An interesting letter from the second c. by a Mara bar Serapion to his son uses the death of Jesus as an example of justice prevailing over tyranny: "What was the murder of Socrates to the Athenians? Their reward for it was hunger and plague. Or what gain did the inhabitants of Samos receive from the burning of Pythagoras? Their land was suddenly covered with sand, in a single hour. Or the Jews, through the murder of their wise king? For it was precisely from this time on that they lost their kingship. God righteously avenged the rejection of the wisdom of these three. The Athenians died of hunger, the people of Samos were covered by the sea, with no chance to be saved. And the Jews, desolated and driven into exile from their own kingdom, are now dispersed throughout every place. But Socrates is not dead after all — because of Plato, and neither is Pythagoras dead, because of the statue of Juno, and neither is the wise king [of the Jews] dead, because of the new laws which he ordained." Although this letter was possibly written by a Jew ("bar Serapion" = Ar. son of Serapion?), it was probably not authored by a Christian, who doubtless would have identified the "wise king" as Jesus and who scarcely would have set him on a par with Socrates and Pythagoras. For the quotation and further analysis, see *HCNT,* 124-25.

54. So Schweizer, *Lukas,* 202; A. Hultgren, *The Parables of Jesus* (Grand Rapids: Eerdmans, 2000), 360; Bailey, *Jesus through Middle Eastern Eyes,* 421.

55. Bovon, *Lukas 19,28–24,53,* 78.

56. "God forbid!" translates Gk. *mē genoito,* a strong negation that occurs nowhere else in the NT except in Paul (in which thirteen of its fourteen occurrences are in Rom and Gal). This may be an example of periodic influence of Pauline vocabulary on the Third Gospel.

people find it unacceptable. That Israel's inheritance could not only be extended to Gentiles, but withdrawn from Israel, is abhorrent to Jesus' audience. Those who have been granted God's favor often think that no offense on their part could cause God to withdraw it. "Jesus looked directly at them and asked, 'Then what is the meaning of that which is written: "The stone the builders rejected has become the cornerstone"?'" (v. 17). The stone referred to is not the keystone of an arch, but a cornerstone uniting two walls. A cornerstone may thus hint at the uniting of Jews and Gentiles in Christ. The Greek word for "looked directly," *emblepein,* occurs elsewhere in Luke only at 22:61. In both instances the word signifies an intense and resolute look. Jews may imagine the vineyard could not possibly be withdrawn from Israel, but the piercing gaze of Jesus assures them otherwise. He concludes the parable with a quotation from Ps 118:22, which in v. 17 appears verbatim with the LXX (Ps 117:22). The reference is to a stone rejected from Solomon's temple, only to become the head of the porch. This quotation played an important role in early Christianity as an explanation of the Jewish rejection of Jesus (Acts 4:11; Rom 9:33; 1 Pet 2:6-8; *Acts Pet.* 24.10).[57] In v. 17 the quotation refers hearers/readers back to the son rejected by the wicked tenants. This correlation is more apparent in Hebrew than in Greek, for "son" (v. 13; Heb. *ben*) and "stone" (vv. 17-18; Heb. *eben*) form a Hebrew wordplay.[58] The rejected stone that becomes the cornerstone is a symbol of the son, rejected and killed, before whom every knee will bow and every tongue confess to the glory of God (Phil 2:5-11). Indeed, "everyone who falls on that stone will be broken to pieces, but he on whom it falls will be crushed" (v. 18). The Greek words for "broken to pieces" *(synthlan)* and "crush" *(likman)* are forceful, meaning "dash to pieces, pulverize." This verse appears to be an allusion to Isa 8:14, where the prophet declares that, for both Judah and Israel, God will be "a stone that causes people to stumble and a rock that makes them fall." Simeon's prophecy (2:34) that Jesus would cause many in Israel to fall was also an allusion to Isa 8:14. Simeon's prophecy and Jesus' declaration in v. 18 form another Lukan inclusio, in which a theme adumbrated in the infancy narrative is completed in the Passion Narrative. The intensity of Jesus' gaze in v. 17 is reinforced by the intensity of the imagery of v. 18. Humanity — even God's chosen people — may cast off the Son and kill him, but they cannot kill God or thwart his mission. The Son of God, like a cornerstone, is either received as the foundation stone of the edifice, or it falls

---

57. In *Gos. Thom.* 66 the saying about the rejected stone is also appended to the parable of the Vineyard. Within rabbinic Judaism the stone was interpreted metaphorically, sometimes with reference to Abraham, sometimes to David, and even on occasion to the Messiah. In the last instance, the builders were regarded as the scribes and the rejected stone as the Messiah. See Str-B 1:875-76.

58. Noted by K. Snodgrass, *The Parable of the Wicked Tenants* (WUNT 27; Tübingen: Mohr Siebeck, 1983), 113-18.

upon those who reject it with crushing force. The Son is either savior or judge of Israel — and humanity.[59]

Luke concludes the parable with an editorial comment, "The teachers of the law and the chief priests looked for a way to arrest him immediately, because they knew he had spoken this parable against them. But they were afraid of the people" (v. 19). The corresponding verse in Mark 12:12 leaves the subject of the saying implied, but Luke, again accentuating the antagonistic role of the Sanhedrin, specifies its two chief constituencies, "teachers of the law and chief priests." The delegation of the Sanhedrin is beginning to act like the tenants in the parable! The temple continues to remain contested ground where the people receive Jesus and his teaching, but also where the Sanhedrin plots to kill him. Jesus is a "contrary sign" (2:34): a source of light and hope, of darkness and fear.

The parable of the Vineyard is a parable of divine sovereignty. The schemes of the rebellious tenants intend to usurp ownership of the vineyard and confiscate its produce, but they do not prevail, nor can they. The perilous mission of the Son furthers the Father's purpose, even in his death and seeming defeat. The vineyard is not dispossessed or destroyed. The wicked tenants are destroyed, and others more worthy are given the vineyard. The parable echoes the providential theme of the parable of the Sower (8:4-8), in which contrary conditions cannot cancel or counteract the harvest of God. Above all, the voice of Jesus is audible in this parable, supremely aware of his role in the divine economy. The preservation of the vineyard is assured not by the self-aggrandizement of the tenants, but by the self-sacrifice of the Son.

A CHALLENGE TO THE TEACHER'S POLITICAL ALLEGIANCE (20:20-26)

The question about paying taxes to Caesar follows the same sequence in Luke's Passion Narrative that it does in Mark 12:13-17. Luke again customizes the introduction (v. 20) and conclusion (v. 26), while following the body of the Markan pericope in vv. 21-25, though amending Mark's Greek throughout. In both Matt 22:15-16 and Mark 12:13 Jesus' antagonists are identified as "Pharisees and Herodians," but Luke omits the names of both parties, noting only that "they" were "keeping a close watch" on Jesus. In surrounding verses, "they" — the watchers — are identified as "teachers of the law" (v. 39; "and chief priests," v. 19) or "Sadducees" (v. 27). These are the implied subjects of the present pericope

---

59. A later rabbinic *Midr. Esth.* 3:6 (ca. 200) proverbializes the same idea: "If a stone falls on a pot, woe to the pot! If a pot falls on a stone, woe to the pot. Either way, woe to the pot!" (Str-B 1:877).

as well.[60] These parties are the dominant constituents of the Sanhedrin, which throughout the Lukan Passion Narrative forms a bloc of antagonism to Jesus.

20 "Keeping a close watch on [Jesus]" (v. 20) replays a signature Lukan theme. The Greek verb *paratērein* is a preferred Lukan term, used twice of Sabbath scrutiny of Jesus (6:7; 14:1), here of spying on Jesus, and in Acts 9:24 of setting guard at the gates of Damascus to apprehend and kill Saul (Paul). In the present context the term refers to gathering evidence for the purpose of arresting Jesus. The aorist tense of the participle in v. 20 indicates that the authorities are not beginning an inquest, but completing one. V. 20 is the final use of *paratērein* in the Third Gospel, and in the context of v. 20 — "they sent spies,[61] who pretended to be sincere, [in order] to catch Jesus" — it denotes the Sanhedrin's sanction of Jesus, the result of which will become apparent in 23:2. The phrase "who intended to be sincere" translates the Greek word *hypokrinesthai,* meaning "to play the hypocrite." The problem with hypocrisy is not that it does not tell the truth, but that it tells the truth without sincerity. Everything in v. 21 is evangelical truth with respect to Jesus, but it is deceptive with respect to the speakers' intent. The intent of the plot, spies, and evidence is to "hand [Jesus] over to the power and authority of the governor." This is the first of ten references to Jesus' betrayal (NIV "hand over"; Gk. *paradido-nai*) in the Passion Narrative. The same word also appears in Jesus' passion predictions (9:44; 18:32). The reference to "the power and authority" of the Roman governor is unique in the Gospels. The only other instance of these two terms occurring together refers to the resurrected Jesus seated at the right hand of God "above all power and authority" (Eph 1:21). The context of these two words in v. 20 testifies to the radical contrast between Jesus' earthly and resurrected states: He who possesses all power and authority in his glorified state is, in his incarnate state, betrayed and made subject to Roman power and authority. The specific authority referred to is Pontius Pilate, Roman ruler of Judea and Samaria from 26 to 36. His official title in Greek was *epitropos* ("guardian, governor") and at times *eparchos* ("prefect, commanding officer"), but in the NT (and frequently in Josephus, e.g., *Ant.* 18.55) he is called *hēgemōn* ("ruler, leader").[62] The office of *hēgemōn* combines Roman political, judicial, and military authority.[63]

21-25 The praise of v. 21 is effusive and insincere. The reference to Jesus not "showing partiality" (v. 21) — in Greek "not receiving one's face" — is a

---

60. Plummer, *Luke,* 464 (on the basis of parallels in Mark and Matt), and Klostermann, *Lukasevangelium,* 195 (on the basis of 18:9), wrongly include Pharisees in v. 20. Luke, however, expressly excludes Pharisees from the Passion Narrative (see at 5:17).

61. This is the only occurrence of "spies" (Gk. *enkathetos*) in the NT.

62. Pilate (20:20; Matt 27:2, 11, 14, 15, 21, 27; 28:14); Felix (Acts 23:24, 26, 33; 24:1, 10); Festus (26:30).

63. A. Weiser, *hēgemōn,* EDNT 2:112.

Hebraism.[64] If Jesus "does not receive the face," i.e., does not succumb to insincere praise, then he is quite unlikely to be influenced by the flattery of v. 21. Fulsome praise can often be dangerous. One recalls Faithful's recollection of meeting the Old Adam in *Pilgrim's Progress:* "Then it came burning hot into my mind, whatever he said and however he flattered, when he got me home to his house, he would sell me for a slave."[65] The Sanhedrin's statement to Jesus, "You teach the way of God" (v. 21), is a proper expression of Jewish theology, for in contrast to Greeks, who sought the "truth of God," Jews sought the "*way of God.*" "Way" denotes not merely right thinking, but right behavior, an entire orientation of life (so 1:79). Not surprisingly, the first recorded designation of the early Christian movement was "the way" (Acts 9:2; 19:9, 23; 22:4; 24:14, 22; also Acts 16:17; 18:25).

The driving question of the authorities is, "Is it right for us to pay taxes to Caesar or not?" (v. 22).[66] The authorities hope to impale Jesus on the horns of a dilemma: support for taxation will be taken as tacit support of the hated Roman occupation, whereas refusal to pay the tax could be grounds for an accusation of sedition against Rome. An affirmative compromises Jesus' standing with the people; a negative, with the governing authorities. A question about paying taxes to Caesar was predictable in Jerusalem, and particularly in the temple, for in Judea money and goods went directly into Roman coffers, whereas in Galilee the same were funneled to Rome through Herod Antipas.[67] The amount required to satisfy the imperial poll tax, first instituted in 6,[68] was a denarius (a Latin loanword). A denarius, the average daily wage in Palestine (Matt 20:2, 9), was a Roman silver coin bearing the semidivine bust of Tiberius Caesar (ruled, 14-37) with an abbreviated Latin inscription, *TI CAESAR DIVI AVG F AVGVSTVS* ("Tiberius Caesar, Son of the Divine Augustus, Augustus"). The obverse bore an image of Tiberius's mother, Livia, with the inscription Pontifex Maximus ("High Priest").

---

64. Plummer, *Luke*, 465; Schlatter, *Lukas*, 712; Fitzmyer, *Luke (I–IX)*, 117; Edwards, *Hebrew Gospel*, 324. The Greek renderings in Mark 12:14 and Matt 22:16 eliminate the Hebraism.

65. J. Bunyan, *The Pilgrim's Progress* (New York: Signet Classics, 1964), 69. Similarly, Plummer, *Luke*, 465, "The falseness of these fulsome compliments in their mouths stamps this as one of the most dastardly of the attacks on Christ."

66. The word for "taxes" in both Matt 22:17 and Mark 12:14 is *kēnsos*, a Latin loanword. Luke uses the more common Greek word *phoros,* also used by Josephus with reference to paying taxes to Rome (*J. W.* 1.154; 2.403; *Ant.* 14.203; *Ag. Ap.* 1.119).

67. On the Roman tax system, see E. Sanders, *The Historical Figure of Jesus* (London: Allen Lane, The Penguin Press, 1993), 252; Wolter, *Lukasevangelium,* 652.

68. Josephus, *J. W.* 2.117; *Ant.* 18.1-10. In reaction to this taxation, Judas the Galilean founded a rebel cause that grew into the Zealot movement. In 66 the Zealots plunged the nation into revolt against Rome, resulting in the annihilation of both the Jewish rebels and the nation.

Immediately, Jesus "saw through their duplicity" (v. 23). Mark says that "Jesus knew their hypocrisy" (12:15). Luke has already called the authorities hypocritical (v. 20), so he describes their intent as *panourgia,* a Greek word that means "readiness to do anything," hence "cunning, scheming."[69] Jesus now shifts from defense to offense.[70] He asks to see a denarius, and then asks, "Whose image and inscription are on it?" (v. 24). There is some irony in the fact that the schemers possess the coin that symbolizes their onerous subjection to Rome. They are thus more compromised by the tax system than their question would suggest. "Caesar's," they replied. The response of Jesus is quintessential: "Then give back to Caesar what is Caesar's, and to God what is God's" (v. 25).[71]

The reply of Jesus does not echo the politics of the Zealots, who were bent on armed combat with Rome; or of the Sadducees, who accommodated to the state; or of the Pharisees, who followed an independent course indifferent to the state. Nor does the judgment of Jesus advocate a separate and perhaps even contrary sacred order within the larger secular society. Both Jesus and his followers situate themselves within their respective political and cultural milieus and advocate service of the common good within them. This political order, according to the early church, could be served irrespective of the rulers' and magistrates' religious beliefs (Rom 13:1-7; 1 Tim 2:1-6; 1 Pet. 2:13-17). However, Jesus does not imply that God and government are two separate and exclusive realms independent of each other. Jesus echoes the OT that God is sovereign over all human affairs, including political affairs. The response of Jesus implies that there are duties to governments that do not infringe on ultimate duties to God, but it also denies that governments may assume total claim over their citizens, "as though the State, over and beyond its special commission, should and could become the single and totalitarian order of human life, thus fulfilling the Church's vocation as well."[72]

Jesus' answer exceeds the exact limits of the question asked him. His addition, "give to God what is God's" (v. 25), is essential to his understanding

---

69. *Panourgia* occurs only here in the Gospels, although it is common to Paul (1 Cor 3:19; 2 Cor 4:2; 11:3; Eph 4:14). The textual variants of v. 23 (substituting "evil intent" for "duplicity"; and adding "why are you trying to trap me"), although reasonably well attested, are best explained as later harmonizations with Matt 22:18.

70. *Eg. Pap.* 2 preserves a fragmentary version of this pericope until this point. Rather than concluding with the request and saying about the coin, however, *Eg. Pap.* 2 concludes with Jesus quoting Isa 29:13, thus apparently conflating the account with Matt 15:7-9 (and Mark 7:6-7).

71. Jesus may be adapting a speech formula to the occasion, for Plutarch, *Mor.* 736c, preserves a similar formula ("it is necessary to render to the Muses all that belongs to them" [cited in Wolter, *Lukasevangelium,* 654]), as does Paul in Rom 13:7.

72. The Theological Declaration of Barmen, art. 5.

of political authority.[73] If ultimate authority belongs to God, then political allegiances must also be subordinated to God. In v. 25 the unmistakable *exousia*, or authority, of Jesus again emerges.[74] Caesar and God vied for ultimate authority in the political and religious climate of Jesus' day, yet Jesus presumes to speak for both. That ultimate authority resided with God is clearly implied in Jesus' use of "image" (v. 24; Gk. *eikōn*), the same word used in Gen 1:26 of humanity's creation in God's image. If coins bear Caesar's image, then they belong to Caesar. The Greek verb *apodidonai* (v. 25) reinforces this point, for it means to give *back* to Caesar what already belongs to him.[75] But the same verb is also applied with reference to God. Humanity bears God's image. Humanity must therefore render ultimate submission to the God in whose image it is made.[76]

26 The pericope concludes in Matt 22:22 and Mark 12:17 with the terse report that the interrogators were "astonished." Luke complements his fuller introduction (v. 20) with a fuller conclusion (v. 26), in both instances framing the pericope with the Greek word *epilambanesthai*. The authorities, Luke noted at the outset, hoped "to *catch* Jesus in something he said" (v. 20). He reports the outcome in his conclusion, "that they were unable to *trap* him in what he said" (v. 26). Both italicized words translate the Greek *epilambanesthai*, meaning to "pounce on something said" or "catch someone off base." The temple is once again the setting of Luke's "passion triangle" comprising the temple authorities, people, and Jesus. The opposition of the authorities to Jesus is firmly established (19:47; 22:2), and in this final initiative they seek to "catch" and "trap" him. But they do not succeed "before the people" (NIV "in public") but are "silenced" by Jesus.[77] The temple, to be sure, is their sphere of influence, but more important, it is Jesus' Father's "sphere of influence" (2:49),[78] where Jesus has the last word.

---

73. Nolland, *Luke 18:35–24:53*, 961, notes a possible connection here between the owner's share in the crop in the preceding parable (20:10) and the "rendering to God called for here."

74. *Gos. Thom.* 100 preserves this saying thus: "They showed Jesus a gold [coin] and said to him: Caesar's agents demand taxes from us. He said to them: Give to Caesar what belongs to Caesar; give to God what belongs to God; and give to me what is mine." This version of the saying differentiates between God and Jesus. The Synoptic version makes no such differentiation, making Jesus the sole spokesman of divine authority.

75. So Marshall, *Luke*, 736.

76. The significance of "image" for the interpretation of v. 25 derives from G. Bornkamm, *Jesus of Nazareth* (New York: Harper & Row, 1960), 123, who credits the idea to D. Cairns, *The Image of God in Man* (London, 1953), 30 (who in turn credits the idea to D. Sayers, *The Man Born to Be King*), and Tertullian, *Idol.* 15 (1.47.25).

77. Wolter, *Lukasevangelium*, 654, writes: "This is the last episode in which Jesus' opponents take the initiative, and with it Luke signals that they will make no further attempts to remove Jesus."

78. The Greek phrase *en tois tou patros mou* (2:49), rendered "in my Father's house" (NIV), is a calculated ambiguity, implying not simply a place but also the purpose for which the place exists, i.e., "the place where my Father accomplishes his work."

A CHALLENGE TO THE
TEACHER'S ESCHATOLOGY (20:27-40)

The dispute over the question of resurrection from the dead is recorded here and in Matt 22:23-33 and Mark 12:18-27. This is the only exclusive meeting in the Gospels between Jesus and the **Sadducees**. Significantly, it is initiated not by Jesus but by the Sadducees. Of the several parties and sects of Judaism in first-century Palestine, the Pharisees (see at 5:17) and Sadducees (see at 16:14) dominated Jewish life in general and the Sanhedrin in particular. Pharisees and Sadducees evidently arose at roughly the same time during the Maccabean revolt against Seleucid tyranny (early second century B.C.). Despite their common origin, they differed greatly in outlook. Pharisees believed in divine sovereignty, while Sadducees affirmed human free will alone; Pharisees believed in angels and demons, both of which Sadducees denied;[79] Pharisees affirmed an understanding of Scripture and revelation that included both written (Torah, Writings, Prophets) and oral traditions, whereas Sadducees accepted only the written Torah; and finally, as this story indicates, Pharisees affirmed the resurrection of the dead, which Sadducees expressly denied (v. 27; Acts 23:8). Sadducees denied angels, demons, and the afterlife because of their exclusive reliance on Torah, which does not set forth these doctrines.[80] Sadducees were thus rationalistic and conservative in theology, whereas the fuller perspective of revelation characteristic of Pharisaism resulted in a more progressive theological outlook. Jesus stood in closer theological alignment with Pharisees than with Sadducees, which may account for his frequent association — and conflicts — with Pharisees, and his lack of association with Sadducees.

In addition to doctrinal matters, Sadducees and Pharisees also differed on social and political issues. Sadducees comprised a clerical and lay aristocracy associated with the priesthood. Prior to the Maccabean Revolt (167

---

79. The proper reading of v. 27 is disputed. *Legontes* ("saying," so NIV) is strongly and broadly attested, and it conforms to Mark 12:18 and Matt 22:23, which Luke follows closely in this pericope. This line of thought favors its originality. However, *antilegontes* ("denying") is typical of Lukan compound verbs, which may have been changed to simple *legontes* by scribal assimilation to Matt 22:23. In addition to being characteristically Lukan, *antilegontes* involves a double negative in v. 27, thus making it the more difficult reading. In sum, *antilegontes*, although claiming weaker manuscript support, may be the more original reading (see BDF §429; Metzger, *TCGNT,* 145-46; Wolter, *Lukasevangelium,* 656).

80. E. Main, "Les Sadducéens et la Résurrection des Morts: Comparaison entre Mc 12,18-27 et Lc 20,27-38," *RB* 103 (1996): 411-32, argues that the Sadducean objection to the doctrine of the resurrection of the dead was due not only to its not being explicitly mentioned in Torah. The formulation of their question to Jesus on the basis of a positive commandment of Torah indicates that, in their thinking, belief in the doctrine of resurrection logically contradicts the teaching of Torah.

B.C.), the priesthood had exerted a dominant influence among Jews, and hence Sadducees, like the priesthood, belonged to the elite social stratum of Jewish society, marked by "wealth" and "men of rank," to quote Josephus. The association of Sadducees with the priesthood meant that their influence was focused above all in the temple and its various operations. The priesthood was an important political as well as religious influence. The Sadducees' close alliance with the priesthood thrust them to the political forefront, as is evidenced by their receptivity to Hellenism and, during Jesus' day, their collaboration with Roman rule.[81]

27 Luke follows Mark's account of the debate with the Sadducees especially closely, without adding his customary introductions and conclusions. Although the Gospels do not record any particular interest of Jesus in the Sadducees, the early church found it necessary to contend with them (Acts 4:1; 5:17; 23:6-8) and Luke's hearers/readers were doubtless familiar with them. Their introduction in v. 27 is attended by their most distinguishing trait in the minds of Pharisees and Christians — their denial of the doctrine of resurrection. Sadducees believed that at death the soul perished along with the body, and hence that there were no future rewards or punishments. References to **resurrection of the dead** in the OT are vague and sporadic. Indeed, as many or more OT texts deny resurrection or forecast a nether world of Sheol, characterized by a pale and joyless existence.[82] By Jesus' day, however, there was a prevailing belief in the resurrection, not only among Pharisees, but among a majority of Jews.[83] "Whoever denies the resurrection of the dead has no share in the world to come," declares the Mishnah (*Sanh.* 10:1). This general belief in resurrection seems to have been extrapolated, at least among the rabbis, from the few OT allusions to it, from reason, and from the precedents of Enoch and Elijah, who were believed not to have died. The Sadducees, however, rejected the majority tradition on this issue, as evidenced by their test of Jesus.

28-33 Like the opponents in the previous account (20:21), the Sadducees address Jesus as "Teacher" (v. 28). Jesus is addressed as teacher a dozen

---

81. Josephus *Ant.* 13.173, 297-98; 18.16-17; *War* 2.164-66. On the Sadducees in general, see Str-B 1:885-86; 4/1:339-52; E. Schürer, *History of the Jewish People*, 2:404-14.

82. OT texts alluding to resurrection are Job 19:26; Ps 16:11; Isa 26:19; Ezek 37; Dan 12:2. Those that deny it or assume Sheol are Ps 6:5; 88:4-5, 11-12; 115:17; Isa 38:18; Eccl 9:4-10. On conceptions of Sheol and Hades, see Fitzmyer, *Luke (X–XXIV)*, 855. Irenaeus, *Haer.* 5.5, typifies much early Christian writing on the subject. Irenaeus does not cite specific proof texts in favor of resurrection but reasons for God's ability to raise human bodies on the basis of the long lives recorded in Genesis, the translations of Enoch and Elijah, and the preservation of lives in danger, such as Jonah's and the three men in Dan 3.

83. See O. Schwankl, *Die Sadduzäerfrage (Mk 12,18-27 parr): Eine exegetisch-theologische Studie zur Auferstehungserwartung* (BBB 66; Frankfurt: Athenäum, 1987), chap. 3.

times in the Third Gospel, but never as such by disciples.[84] For Luke, Jesus is not like the rabbinic and philosophical teachers of Jews and Gentiles, i.e., one teacher among others, but a unique authority.[85] In order to discredit the idea of resurrection — which according to the passion predictions Jesus espoused (9:22; 18:33) — the Sadducees pose an extravagant case of a woman married to seven brothers. Was this a celebrated case of **levirate marriage**, or a wild contrivance? Levirate marriage was a practice whereby a man was obligated to marry a childless widow of his brother in order to preserve the name and memory of his deceased brother and to ensure the establishment of his deceased brother's inheritance within the family line (Gen 38:8; Deut 25:5-6).[86] Various forms of this custom were practiced throughout the ancient Near East; in Judaism, Mishnah tractate *Yebamoth* develops it fully. The practice is first mentioned with reference to Onan (Gen 38:8-10) who, in order to annihilate the line of his brother, refused to have a child by Tamar, wife of his deceased brother Er. Tamar (Gen 38) and Ruth (Ruth 3–4) actually violated prescribed sexual morality to ensure the preservation of their genealogy through levirate marriage. The Book of Tobit tells the story of a woman who married seven men and remained childless (3:7-15) — a story that may have inspired the tale proposed by the Sadducees.[87] The custom of levirate marriage was not devised (as were polygamy and concubinage, for example) for the expressed purpose of allowing a man to have more than one wife, nor to condone sexual promiscuity or immorality. Rather, Levirate marriage was a compensatory social custom designed to prevent intermarriage of Jews and Gentiles and to preserve honor and property within a family line in cases where a woman's husband was deceased.[88]

In the minds of the Sadducees, wit and common sense are sufficient to dispel the superstitions of resurrection and life after death. Their question presumes that the world to come is essentially a materialistic extension of earthly life, including the married state, although under more glorious conditions. In this they reflect Pharisaic and rabbinic assumptions, including the assumption that monogamy is the marriage ideal. In their minds, the impossibility of a woman being married to seven men in heaven renders the concept of resur-

84. 7:40; 8:49; 9:38; 10:25; 11:45; 12:13; 18:18; 19:39; 20:21, 28, 39; 21:7. Jesus' disciples frequently address him as Master (see at 5:5).

85. Bovon, *Luke the Theologian*, 204.

86. V. 28 appears to be a paraphrase or conflation of Gen 38:3 and Deut 25:5-6, rather than a direct quotation of either from the MT or LXX.

87. Tobit may have inspired the Sadducees' story, although in Tobit the seven husbands were not brothers, and each was killed by the wicked demon Asmodeus before the marriage was consummated.

88. Str-B 1:885-97. Further, see S. Frost, "The Memorial of the Childless Man," *Int* 26 (1972): 437-50.

rection an absurd fiction.[89] If Jesus were to accept the assumption that the afterlife stands in unbroken continuity with present life, he would either have to argue on technical grounds that the first husband had rights to the woman in heaven,[90] or concede to the Sadducees.

34-38 Jesus does neither, however, nor does he follow their logic. He begins by negating the assumption of continuity between earthly and heavenly life. In the present age people indeed "marry and are given in marriage" (v. 34), but in the life to come they "will neither marry nor be given in marriage" (v. 35). This pronouncement cuts against the grain of popular Judaism, which assumed conditional continuity between earthly and celestial life, including marriage and sexual relations in the resurrected state.[91] Like the apostle Paul, Jesus asserts that eternal life is not a prolongation of earthly life, but life in an entirely new dimension (1 Cor 15:40-44). In vv. 34-36 he employs the Hebrew word *ben* ("son"), and the connotations inherent within it, to convey the differences between earthly and heavenly existence. Jesus has previously used "sons" with reference to wedding guests ("sons of the bridegroom," 5:34), people of God ("sons of light," 16:8), believers ("sons of the Highest," 6:35, and "son of peace," 10:6), or completed Jews ("daughter/son of Abraham," 13:16; 19:9). Here he refers to earthly existence in terms of "sons of this age," and heavenly existence as "sons of God" and "sons of the resurrection."[92] Luke otherwise follows Mark's account of the question of the Sadducees closely, but the three Hebraic references are not present in Mark 12:24-25 (or Matt 22:29-30). Their presence derives ostensibly from Luke's Hebrew source.

Belief in the immortality of the soul was widely accepted in the Roman and particularly Greek worlds. Throughout vv. 34-38, however, the phenomenon under discussion is not "immortality of the soul" but "resurrection" (vv. 27,

89. Luke again resorts to a series of three husbands in alluding to levirate marriage (on threes, see at 19:20). V. 30 consists of only twelve letters in the Greek, making it the shortest verse in the NT.

90. Plummer, *Luke,* 468, notes that this would have been Jesus' most obvious option, but "while it would have avoided the ridicule to which the Sadducees wish to expose Him, it would not have refuted their doctrine."

91. See Str-B 1:887-89. The rabbinic assumption of continuity was frequently based on Ezek 37. A midrash to Ps 146 from the rabbinic era is a rare exception to the above, arguing that sexual intercourse is forbidden in the world to come.

92. "Sons of this age" (v. 34; NIV "people of this age") = Heb. *beni ha olam;* "sons of God" (v. 36; NIV "God's children") = *beni elohim;* "sons of the resurrection" (v. 36; NIV "children of the resurrection") = *beni hattequmah.* See Edwards, *Hebrew Gospel,* 324; Lagrange, *Luc,* 516. With the exception of "sons of God" (Gen 6:2, 4; Job 1:6; 2:1), none of the above expressions occurs in either the MT or the LXX; hence they cannot be Septuagintisms (i.e., Luke cannot have derived them from the LXX). Bovon, *Lukas 19,28–24,53,* 108-9, acknowledges "their Semitic ring" and ascribes vv. 34-36 to Luke's special source.

33, 35, 36).[93] Resurrection is the result of the gift and power of God, whereas immortality of the soul regards the soul as an eternal element of life that, once freed from mortal flesh, continues an immortal existence. The latter is not a gift of God but simply an inherent reality of nature, as inevitable as dying itself. Moreover, Jesus speaks of those "considered worthy of taking part in the age to come" (v. 35). "Considered worthy" is a divine passive, meaning considered worthy *by God* on the basis of their being in relation to God as "sons of God." Nor does v. 38 ("for to him all are alive") necessarily imply immortality of the soul. This phrase appears to recall 4 Macc 7:19, which, like v. 37, is used with reference to the resurrection of Abraham, Isaac, and Jacob. In both contexts it means "all who are resurrected by God live by and for him."[94]

The life to come constitutes a new taxonomy of existence, "like the angels" (v. 36).[95] The idea that resurrected existence would be angelic in nature was not unknown in the first century (*1 En.* 15:4, 6; *2 Apoc. Bar.* 51.10). The categories of marital and angelic existence repeat those of Gen 6:1-2, in which the "sons of God" condescended to take human wives.[96] But whereas in Gen 6:1-2 the "sons of God" seem to be corrupted by the fall of humanity, in vv. 34-36 the fallen order is redeemed in glorified heavenly existence. God's power to create and restore life bursts the limits of both logic and imagination. Heavenly realities are no more predicated on earthly experience than postpartum life is predicated on life in utero.

Jesus now shifts from assailing the assumption of continuity between earthly and celestial existence to the resurrection itself. Paganism was rife with

93. The judgment that "the Lucan form [of the pericope] clearly becomes an argument for immortality" is uncharacteristically overstated by Fitzmyer, *Luke (X–XXIV),* 1301. Schweizer, *Lukas,* 205, correctly notes that Luke (and Jesus) teach resurrection from the dead, not immortality of the soul.

94. Similarly Lagrange, *Luc,* 516-17. Wolter, *Lukasevangelium,* 660, writes, "Since God is a God of the living, none can be alive who do not owe their life to God."

95. The Greek term, *isangeloi* (v. 36; "like angels"), occurs only here in the Bible. Clement of Alexandria, esp. in his writings against Encratism (a term characterizing several early Christian groups that practiced extreme forms of asceticism), frequently appeals to this word not as a description of the life to come, but to characterize the possibilities present in earthly redemption. For Clement, faith and charity result in "the highest excellence of the flesh" (*Strom.* 7.10), even enabling "apostolic marriages." In the latter, Christian wives became sisters rather than spouses, allowing their husbands to preach and minister without distraction (*Strom.* 3.53). See *PGL,* 676; M. Hengel, *Saint Peter: The Underestimated Apostle* (Grand Rapids: Eerdmans, 2010), 123-25.

96. Justin Martyr's quotation of this passage in *Dial.* 81.4 does not follow the Matthean version (as was customary among the Fathers), but rather the Lukan version. *1 En.* 15:7 (and perhaps also *The Pseudo-Titus Epistle* [*NTApoc.* 2:55, 62-63]) appears to have Gen 6:1-2 in mind when God rebukes the Watchers thus: "I did not make wives for you, for the dwelling of the spiritual beings of heaven is heaven" (*OTP* 1:21).

Corn Kings and Mother Goddesses who oversaw the recurring and eternal cycles of birth, death, and rebirth in nature. Jesus makes no appeal to such, but justifies belief in the resurrection in particularly rabbinic fashion by appealing to Exod 3:6, "I am the God of Abraham, the God of Isaac, and the God of Jacob." In so doing he grounds belief in the resurrection not in nature but in the word of God as revealed in Scripture. The early church will likewise ground its belief in resurrection not in nature but in the historical reality of Jesus' resurrection from the dead. The source of Jesus' quotation is the Torah, and Torah was the putative source of authority for Sadducees. Jesus accepted as axiomatic that the patriarchs and prophets were still alive (16:22-25; Matt 8:11; John 8:56). On the basis of this he argues that the promises of God are made not to the dead but to the living. If Abraham, Isaac, and Jacob are dead, as the Sadducees believe, then God's promise to them was limited to the duration of their earthly lives. God's word is not bound by human limitations, however, nor would God make a pledge to the living that would be terminated by death. For Jesus, the call of God establishes a relationship with God, and once a relationship with God is established, it bears the promise of God that cannot be ended. Indeed, God's promise and power conquer the last enemy — death itself.[97]

39-40 Luke concludes the account with "certain scribes" (NIV "teachers of the law") applauding Jesus, "Well said, teacher" (v. 39). As a rule in the Gospels, scribes oppose rather than praise Jesus. The approval of these particular scribes is an exception, and their approval suggests they were scribes of Pharisaic persuasion (see on **scribes** at 5:17). "Scribe" designates a profession rather than an ideological persuasion, and hence scribes could be either Sadducees or Pharisees. Since the oral tradition (which characterized Pharisees but not Sadducees) was conducted by scribes, and since the scribal tradition continued to thrive after the fall of Jerusalem in 70 (at which point nearly all Sadducees perished), it is safe to assume that the majority — perhaps large majority — of scribes were Pharisees.[98] The scribes who congratulate Jesus in v. 39 probably belong to this majority. Their rare approval can be explained by the fact that Jesus has silenced their arch rivals, the Sadducees (Matt 22:34!).[99] Indeed, for the moment Jesus has silenced all rivals, for "no one dared to ask [Jesus] any more questions" (v. 40). The ultimate answer to the Sadducees, of course, is not exegesis or even Jesus' authority, for they accept neither. The Sadducees' question will only be answered by the empty tomb of Jesus, for he *is* the resurrection (John 11:25).

---

97. Plummer, *Luke*, 471, writes: "Dead things can have a Creator . . . : only living beings can have a God. If Abraham or any of the patriarchs had ceased to exist when he died, God would have ceased to be his God."

98. On Pharisaic and Sadducean scribes, see Schürer, *History of the Jewish People*, 2:329.

99. The assumption of Fitzmyer, *Luke (X–XXIV)*, 1307, that the scribes were embarrassed and humbled Sadducees, seems improbable. Lagrange, *Luc*, 518, and Bovon, *Lukas 19,28–24,53*, 124, correctly infer that the scribes of v. 39 are likely of Pharisaic persuasion.

THE TEACHER POSES THE
QUESTION OF THE DAY (20:41-44)

The tests of the temple authorities are now concluded, for "no one dared ask [Jesus] any more questions" (20:40). Debate is not over, however. Since 20:1 the authorities have dominated the agenda with questions to Jesus they wished to ask; Jesus now asks a question they need to *hear.* The questions and categories of the temple authorities have represented their interests, but their interests, like old wineskins (5:37-38), are inadequate to apprehend the person and mission of Jesus. Jesus now takes the initiative to determine both wine and wineskins, so to speak. Ralph Martin sums up the significance of the moment: "After a day of questions comes the question of the day."[100]

41 "Then Jesus said to them, 'Why is it said that the Messiah is the son of David?'" (v. 41). "Them" must again (as in the foregoing section) imply scribes of Pharisaic persuasion, for whom the Davidic background of Messiah was important.[101] The setting of the question in the temple is particularly important, for the temple was the religious center of Israel and the seat of the Sanhedrin's authority. Here, where religious policy is determined and executed, Jesus chooses to test conventional understandings of messiahship by the larger categories of "Lord" and "Son." The issue about *identity* that Jesus raised privately with the disciples (9:18) is now raised publicly in the temple of Jerusalem.

Jesus invites the audience to consider whether "**Son of David**" (see at 18:38) is conceptually adequate to explain the Messiah (see at 9:20).[102] The Israelite hope of a Davidic deliverer first arises in 2 Sam 7:12 (also Isa 9; 11; Jer 30:9; Ezek 34:23). It is not absolutely certain that "son of David" was correlated with Messiah in Jesus' day, but it very likely was.[103] *Pss. Sol.* 17:21, probably to be dated near the time of the birth of Jesus,[104] makes the correlation thus: "O

---

100. *Where the Action Is* (Glendale: Regal Books, 1977), 106.

101. Bovon, *Lukas 19,28–24,53,* 137, notes the equal interest of the Qumran community in the same question.

102. The Greek placement of "David" *(Dauid)* and "son" *(huion)* in apposition without case markers is typical of Hebrew and may reflect original Hebrew diction.

103. The claim of Fitzmyer, *Luke (X–XXIV),* 1311, "There is simply no evidence of the Davidic messianic interpretation of Psalm 110 in pre-Christian Palestinian Judaism," cannot be affirmed; indeed, his assertion that "the tradition about an expected Davidic Messiah was so strong by the first c. A.D. that it is inconceivable that Jesus would have sought to deny it" (p. 1312) seems to refute such a claim. Str-B 4/1:452-60 offers a more defensible summary of the available evidence; i.e., Ps 110 was interpreted messianically in the first c. A.D.; then, in order to avoid correlating Son of David and Jesus, it was interpreted by rabbis nonmessianically for nearly two centuries (usually with reference to Abraham rather than to David); and only after 250, when the rift between synagogue and church was irreconcilable, did Jewish rabbis again entertain messianic interpretations of Ps 110.

104. R. Wright, "Psalms of Solomon," *OTP* 2:641.

Lord, raise up their king, the son of David, that he may reign over Israel thy servant." The prevalence of the concept of a Davidic Messiah in Jesus' day is further implied by daily recitation in personal prayers and weekly synagogue liturgy of the Amidah ("Eighteen Benedictions"), "Have mercy, Lord our God, over the kingdom of the house of David, the Messiah of your righteousness" (Ben. 14); and by messianic references to 2 Sam 7:12-14 at Qumran.[105] The fact that every early Christian writer who mentions Ps 110 interprets it messianically also implies a pre-Christian association of Son of David and Messiah. Finally, the question of Jesus in vv. 41-44 seems not to introduce a messianic understanding of Ps 110, but to *presuppose* it. Jesus and the early church did not accept the military-political connotations normally associated with Messiah, but early Christianity certainly affirmed that the Messiah would come from David's "house" (1:69), "throne" (1:32), or "seed" (Rom. 1:3; 2 Tim 2:8).

42-44 The preface to the quotation of Ps 110, "David himself declares in the Book of Psalms" (v. 42), is itself noteworthy. Luke's Markan exemplar has David speaking by "the Holy Spirit" (Mark 12:36; also Matt 22:43) rather than "by the Psalms." The change from Holy Spirit to Psalms implies an understanding of Psalms as an expression of the Holy Spirit, hence an equation of Scripture and inspiration. V. 42 thus designates David as a mouthpiece of the Holy Spirit (2 Sam 23:2!).[106] Equally significant is mention of the Book of Psalms, which appears in the NT twice in Luke (20:42; 24:44), twice in Acts (1:20; 13:33), and only three times again in Paul. Only rarely in ancient Jewish literature is the Book of Psalms mentioned in addition to the Law and the Prophets; 24:44, in fact, along with 4Q394 (4QMMT), is one of the few — and earliest — references to a three-part division of the OT.[107]

Ps 110 is the most frequently quoted OT text in the NT.[108] The crux of the quotation is the first line, "The Lord [Heb. *YHWH*] said to my Lord [Heb. *adonai*]. . . ." The psalm was originally a coronation hymn that was sung,

---

105. 4Q174 (4QFlor), 10-11: "a branch of David . . . who will be a son to me"; 4Q252, 5.3-4: "the messiah of righteousness, . . . the branch of David." See E. Lohse, *huios Dauid*, *TWNT* 8:483-86.

106. On the relationship of the Holy Spirit to prophecy and inspiration, see Str-B 2:126-38.

107. K. Schmid, "The Canon and the Cult: The Emergence of Book Religion in Ancient Israel and the Gradual Sublimation of the Temple Cult," *JBL* 131/2 (2012): 298. 4QMMT (= 4Q397/98, 14-21) uses "Moses" and "David" as metonyms for "Law" and "Psalms," i.e., "the book of Moses and the books of the prophets and David." Further, see p. 733.

108. According to D. Hay, *Glory at the Right Hand: Psalm 110 in Early Christianity* (Nashville: Abingdon Press, 1973), 15, 45-47, Ps 110 is quoted or alluded to thirty-three times in the NT and seven times in early Christian authors. The most important quotations are 20:42; Matt 22:44; Mark 12:36; Acts 2:34; 1 Cor 15:25; Heb 1:13; and the most obvious allusions are 22:69; Matt 26:64; Mark 14:62; 16:19; Rom 8:34; Eph 1:20; Col 3:1; Heb 1:3; 8:1; 10:12.

chanted, or recited at the inauguration of the kings of Judah and Israel, in which the first "Lord" (= God) inducted the second "Lord" (= Israelite king) to be seated symbolically at his right hand as vicegerent. The right hand signified honor and proximity to God, thus both an obligation and legitimacy to rule with dominion and justice. Following the destruction of the monarchy in 586 B.C., Ps 110 was frequently reinterpreted to refer to the Messiah, whose kingdom — unlike David's — would not fail. This subsequent interpretation is reflected in the quotation of Ps 110:1 in vv. 42-43, where the first "Lord" refers to God and the second to Messiah. To our way of thinking this might seem a misappropriation of the original meaning of the text. In Jesus' day — and the intent of his question indicates he shared the view of his day — the original reference to the earthly Israelite monarchy was seen as a mere foreshadowing of the ultimate meaning of Ps 110, which pertained to God and the Messiah. Thus, to paraphrase Jesus' question, if David (believed to be the author of the Psalm) said, "The Lord [= God] said to my Lord [= Messiah]: Sit at my right hand until I put your enemies under your feet," then David calls the Messiah his Lord, not his son. The Messiah is thus not a descendent — and thus an inferior — of David, but his superior, indeed his Lord.

In the encounter with the Sadducees (vv. 27-40), Jesus argued that the resurrection is not a mere extension of earthly existence; in vv. 41-44 he argues that Messiah is not a mere extension of the Davidic monarchy.[109] To be sure, Messiah will come *from* the Davidic lineage, but that lineage does not encapsulate the essence of Jesus as Messiah, for Messiah is greater than David.[110] The question of Jesus in vv. 42-44 allows Luke to recapitulate earlier themes related to David and divine sonship in the Third Gospel and subsume them under the exalted title "Lord."[111] **David** is mentioned in the infancy narrative only with reference to Jesus, either with respect to his Davidic lineage (1:27, 69; 2:4, 11) or to his royal sonship in 2 Sam 7:11-14 (1:32). The latter

109. The concept of "David" comprises another inclusio between Luke's infancy and passion narratives.

110. Schlatter, *Lukas*, 128, and T. W. Manson, *The Teaching of Jesus* (Cambridge: University Press, 1963), 266-67, following the lead of the Tübingen school a century earlier, assert that, because Jesus questioned the adequacy of the Davidic lineage to explain the concept of Messiah, he denied the Davidic lineage altogether. This is an argumental fallacy, for denying one element of an argument does not necessarily falsify the whole argument. "Son of David" is not used by Jesus as a contrast to Messiah, but to argue that line of derivation does not explain meaning and significance. Messiah both comes from David and surpasses David (so Rom 1:3; 2 Tim 2:8).

111. Marshall, *Luke*, 745 (apparently echoing E. Lohse, *huios Dauid, TWNT* 8:486-87) believes Jesus' question "was regarded by Luke as a mystery which found its solution in the resurrection." This judgment may reflect the testimony of Acts, but it neglects earlier teachings related to (Son of) David and Son of God in the Third Gospel that are subsumed under the Christological title of Lord in vv. 42-43. Bovon, *Lukas 19,28–24,53*, 140-41, is aware of the significance of Luke's early teaching on David for vv. 42-43.

theme of divine sonship is reinforced in Luke's genealogy, where Jesus, who is "supposed" to be son of Joseph (3:23), is in reality son of Adam, "the son of God" (3:38). Also in the genealogy, Luke associates Jesus more directly with David (see at 3:23-38) by removing the long line of unfaithful Davidic kings (with the exception of Zerubbabel and Shealtiel, 3:27) who are mentioned in the genealogy in Matt 1:6-16. Luke thus distinguishes Jesus as the true heir of "the throne of David his father" (1:32), and also as "the Son of the Most High" (1:32) and "Son of God" (1:35), who fulfills the promise of royal sonship to David (1 Sam 7:12).

The issue of divine sonship is the crux of the verbal gauntlet to which Jesus is subjected in the temple. The Sanhedrin's initial challenge to Jesus in 20:1-8 concerns his *exousia*, "authority" (20:1-8). In the parable of the Tenants immediately following (20:9-19), Jesus hints that his authority derives from being "the beloved son" (v. 13).[112] The combination of "authority" (vv. 2, 8), "beloved son" (v. 13), "Messiah" (v. 41), "son of David" (v. 41), and "Lord" (vv. 42, 44) effects an exalted Christology in Luke 20.[113] Indeed, Jesus "seemingly attains a status close to that of God himself."[114] This may be the reason the quotation of Ps 110 in vv. 42-43 is distinguished in Codex Sinaiticus (ℵ) by arrows in the margin, left of each of the six lines of text cited.[115] If Messiah is David's Lord rather than his "son," (v. 44), then Messiah is the Son of God and transcendent Lord who sits at the right hand of God (v. 42).[116]

---

112. For the above reasons I do not share the judgment of Fitzmyer, *Luke (X–XXIV)*, 1313, and Rowe, *Early Narrative Christology*, 172, that Son of God should be excluded from consideration in vv. 41-44.

113. These same titles are correlated already in *Barn.* 12:10, "See again Jesus, not as son of man, but as Son of God, but manifested in a type in the flesh. Since therefore they are going to say that the Christ is David's son, David himself prophesies, fearing and understanding the error of the sinners, 'The Lord said to my Lord sit thou on my right hand until I make thy enemies thy footstool.'"

114. J. Marcus, *The Way of the Lord: Christological Exegesis of the Old Testament in the Gospel of Mark* (Edinburgh: T&T Clark, 1992), 139-45; similarly J. Kingsbury, *The Christology of Mark's Gospel* (Philadelphia: Fortress Press, 1983), 108-14.

115. These arrows (referred to by D. Parker as "diples") "are the standard marks used to indicate OT quotations throughout [Sinaiticus]" (D. Jongkind, personal correspondence, July 3, 2013). Their sporadic use in manuscripts goes back at least to the second c.; they appear, e.g., in P.Oxy. 405 (late second c./early third c.). They are not employed consistently in Sinaiticus, occurring only in Matt (10x), Luke (1x), Acts (11x), and Rom (7x). They also designate the quotation of Ps 110 in Acts 2:34, although none of the remaining five quotations of Ps 110 in Sinaiticus is so designated.

116. See D. Hay, *Glory at the Right Hand*, 155. Ps 110 is used in vv. 42-43, as it was throughout early Christian writings (e.g., Irenaeus, *Haer.* 3.6.1), not simply as a description of Jesus' purpose and work but as a description of his transcendent status, sitting at God's honored and authoritative right hand.

THE TEACHER, A POOR WIDOW,
AND AN OBJECT LESSON OF FAITH (20:45–21:4)

The final episode in the confrontation with temple authorities consists of Jesus' condemnation of the scribes (20:45-47) and contrasting praise of the gift
of a poor widow (21:1-4). In both episodes Luke continues to follow Mark
(12:37b-44) with fidelity similar to that which is exhibited throughout 19:45–
21:4. Both episodes contain widows — the first as victims of the rapacity of
scribes (20:47), and the second as an example of sacrificial giving (21:4). The
temple again remains the arena of both corrupt and genuine religion, for in
the temple the self-aggrandizement of the scribes and the entrenchment of the
Sanhedrin are denounced, and also in the temple the widow's offering, despite
its ostensible insignificance, is praised.

45-47   This pericope includes the three parties — Jesus, temple authorities, and crowds — that have been the main players in 19:45–21:4. The
disciples, who were last mentioned in the triumphal entry (19:39) and who
have been present but unmentioned throughout the temple controversies, are
now warned by Jesus about the scribes (NIV "teachers of the law," see at 5:17).
Scribes commanded unrivaled authority in first-century Palestine. In contrast
to the colorful common Jewish dress, the "flowing robes" (v. 46) of the scribes
were full-length prayer shawls with tassels attached to the four corners. Made
of wool or linen, these shawls, known as *talliths,* distinguished scribes as men
of wealth and eminence.[117] The scribal concern for appearance and impression
in v. 46 contrasts sharply with Jesus' earlier reminder to disciples that the birds
of the air and flowers of the field display no concern for such matters, yet they
surpass "Solomon in all his splendor" (12:22-32).[118] "The most important seats
in the synagogues" (v. 46) refers to the benches along the walls of the synagogues, and especially the dais at the front of the synagogue, that faced the
congregation. These "first seats," as they were called in Greek, were reserved for
teachers and persons of rank, affording the best position from which to address
the congregation. When a scribe walked down the street or passed through a
marketplace, everyone (with the exception of laborers) was expected to rise.
Such position and privilege invited the desire to make an impression, "to be
greeted in the marketplaces . . . and have places of honor at banquets" (v. 46).
The construction and content of v. 46 depict scribal behavior as calculated to
gain maximum exposure and adulation from the populace.

Luke earlier described Pharisees as "lovers of money" (16:14); here he de-

---

117. On scribes and their clothing, see Str-B 2:31-33. On scribes in general, including
their popular esteem, see Jeremias, *Jerusalem in the Time of Jesus,* 233-45.
118. Clement of Alexandria, *Paed.* 2.11, upholds the instruction of Jesus in Luke 12 rather
than the dress of scribes in v. 46 to admonish believers to modesty in clothing.

nounces scribes for "devouring widows' houses" (v. 47). In 18:2-5 a widow is taken advantage of by an unscrupulous judge; here widows are taken advantage of by scribes, although we are not told how. Jesus' denunciation of the scribes echoes that of Israelite prophets, who railed against the powerful and wealthy for preying on the poor and weak, including widows (Isa 10:2; Amos 2; Mic 3). Josephus (*Ant.* 18.81-84) tells of a Jewish imposter in Rome who "played the part of an interpreter of the Mosaic law and its wisdom" and succeeded in persuading a high-standing woman named Fulvia to make substantial gifts to the temple in Jerusalem, which were then embezzled. When the scandal broke, Tiberius, emperor of Rome, expelled Jews en masse from the capital. A pseudepigraph (*T. Mos.* 7:6) likewise condemns the godless as those who "consume the goods of the poor, saying their acts are according to justice."[119] Unlike Sadducees, scribes were not as a rule wealthy, and thus they were in varying degrees dependent for their livelihood on gifts of worshipers and benefactors. Some scribes exploited their esteem and abused the generosity shown to them by others. In an earlier exchange with a scribe (10:27), Jesus defined genuine religion by quoting Deut 6:5 and Lev 19:18: the sum of the law is love of God and neighbor. Some people, however, harm others rather than help them, and the worst of these use religion as both a means and a justification of their harm. The judgment of Jesus on those who traffic in piety for the purpose of self-aggrandizement is uncompromising: they will be "punished most severely" (v. 47).[120]

21:1-4   The scene now shifts to the temple treasury, where Jesus observes the crowd. The religious authorities have exhibited unrelieved antagonism to Jesus since his arrival in the temple, but that antagonism has not been reflected by the crowds who have received his teaching. The temple has thus been host to both false piety, predicated on might and mammon, and true piety of humility, trust, and sacrifice that honors God. "As Jesus looked up, he saw the rich putting their gifts into the **temple treasury**" (v. 1).[121] The Greek participle for "putting" is present, signifying a common and continual practice. In addition to worship, the temple in Jerusalem, like nearly all temples in the ancient world, functioned as a depository for, and the administration of, vast amounts of wealth. Unlike other tribes of Israel, the tribe of Levi possessed no

119. On these and other examples of preying on widows, see Plummer, *Luke,* 474; Wolter, *Lukasevangelium,* 663-64.

120. One recalls John Bunyan's exposé of such religiosity. Mr. By-Ends, a fair-weather Christian, asks if a minister should not use his position "to get the good blessings of this life." Mr. Money-Love agrees: it is not only permissible but a virtue to use religion to cash in on all possible benefits. Christian condemns their sham piety: "Whoever takes up religion for the world will throw religion away for the world" (*The Pilgrim's Progress* [New York: Signet, 1964], 93-99).

121. "Having looked up, he saw" (v. 1; Gk. *anablepsas . . . eiden*) is a Hebraism, *wayisāh . . . wayarah.*

land. In place of land, Levites were made responsible for superintending the temple, which accrued great quantities of wealth in the form of dues, taxes, and donations of valuable objects and money (2 Kgs 12:4). The vessels used for sacrificial worship were required by Torah to be made of gold or silver. In addition, there were stocks of priceless curtains and priestly garments, and stores of flour, oil, grain, wine, incense, and other valuable commodities. The temple also functioned as a repository of individual wealth, in the belief that a sacred place was a safe place. Not surprisingly, the *gazophylax,* the officer in charge of administering the financial resources and treasures of the temple, was proximate to the chief priest in authority.

The temple treasury (Gk. *gazophylakion*) was located in the Court of Women, the first enclosure of the sanctuary in which Jewish women and children were allowed to worship (Josephus, *J.W.* 5.198-200),[122] where thirteen shofar-chests (*m. Šeqal.* 6:5) were dedicated to special offerings.[123] As their name suggests, these receptacles were shaped like a shofar, a ram's horn, and positioned with the tapered end upward in order to prevent theft. Into one of these receptacles (designated for freewill offerings?) "a poor widow" deposits "two very small copper coins" (v. 2). The widow in this story is the seventh and final widow mentioned in Luke. In Israel widows were not simply women whose husbands were deceased, but women who were thereby made vulnerable, and made to seek their protection and comfort in God.[124] This typifies widows in the Third Gospel, all but two of whom are expressly cited as models of faith.[125] The poverty of the widow is described by the Greek word *penichran,* "needy, in want," occurring nowhere else in the NT or early Christian literature.[126] This particular word, in contrast to Mark's *ptōchos* (12:42), which connotes poverty in things, focuses on impoverished *persons.*[127] The word draws attention not simply to the circumstance of poverty, but to its effect on the widow. It was not lawful to offer less than two lepta, which referred to the smallest coinage in circulation.[128] Hence, the widow's gift was "the smallest

122. On the temple treasury, see Str-B 2:37-45; Schürer, *History of the Jewish People,* 2:279-87.

123. New shekel dues, old shekel dues, bird offerings, young birds for the whole offering, wood, frankincense, gold for the mercy seat, and six shofar chests for freewill offerings (*m. Šeqal.* 6:5). On the particular purposes of each offering, see Str-B 2:38-40.

124. Bovon, *Lukas 19,28–24,53,* 144.

125. Anna (2:37), widows in Elijah's day (4:25), widow of Zarephath (4:26), widow of Nain (7:12), widow in the parable of the Unjust Judge (18:3, 5), defrauded widows (20:47), widow in the temple treasury (21:2, 3). On the special role widows play in Luke-Acts, see G. Stählin, *chēra, TWNT* 9:438-40.

126. A rare Greek word, *penichros* may translate Heb. *'ānī,* "poor, wretched, needy."

127. Bovon, *Lukas 19,28–24,53,* 155-56.

128. A denarius was the standard wage of a day's labor (Matt 20:8-10); a lepton was

offering ever made by anyone."[129] As noted at 19:30, Jesus' prescience increases in the Passion Narrative of the Third Gospel. His knowledge of the amount of the woman's gift could be the result of supernatural knowledge, as perhaps was his knowledge of the colt in the triumphal entry (19:30). Other means might also account for his knowledge, however. In cases where a contribution was rendered for priestly service, the attending priest examined the currency for genuineness, inquired about the purpose of the gift, and verified that the contribution corresponded to the prescribed sacrifice. The priest then directed the worshiper to deposit the amount in the appropriate receptacle. All this was spoken aloud and would have been audible to bystanders. If, however, the gift were a simple freewill offering, the sound of the coin in the shofar, or perhaps the appearance of the woman, may have betrayed her poverty.[130]

In purely financial terms, the value of the widow's offering is negligible. But in the divine scale of value, her gift is inestimable. "Truly I tell you," declares Jesus, "this poor widow has put in more than all the others. All these people gave their gifts out of their wealth; but she out of her poverty put in all she had to live on" (vv. 3-4).[131] The widow's life has been defined in terms of *less* — in comparison with the "rich" (v. 1), scribes (20:46), even common people.[132] Jesus defines her life in terms of *more* — her gift is a sacrificial testimony to her piety and faith, for "she put in more than all the others" (v. 3). The sense in which Jesus celebrates her gift is second only to his joy in 10:21.[133] Ironically,

---

1/64th of a denarius. Codex Bezae (D) defines the two lepta as the equivalent of "a quadrans," but this is doubtless a harmonization with Mark 12:42.

129. Plummer, *Luke,* 475.

130. For a discussion of temple offerings, see Str-B 2:37-46. Some commentators suggest the widow's offering was originally a parable of Jesus, following *Rab. Lev.* 3:5: "A woman once brought a handful of flour for an offering. The priest rejected the offering and said, 'Look what this woman brings! How can such an offering qualify as a sacrifice or provide a priest enough to live on?' Then the priest was warned in a dream, 'Do not despise her, for she is like a person who has sacrificed her whole life'" (cited in Str-B 2:46). The likeness notwithstanding, there is no evidence the widow's offering was originally a parable.

131. Compare the saying of R. Jonathan, "He that fulfills the Law in poverty shall in the end fulfill it in wealth; and he that neglects the Law in wealth shall in the end neglect it in poverty" (*m. 'Abot.* 4.9).

132. On the contrast between the scribes and the widow, see G. Smith, "A Closer Look at the Widow's Offering: Mark 12:41-44," *JETS* 40 (1997): 30-31.

133. A. Wright, "The Widow's Mites: Praise or Lament? — a Matter of Context," *CBQ* 44 (1982): 256-65, declares that Jesus does not praise the widow but laments her gift as an example of the corruption of the value system taught by the scribes, which Jesus condemns in 20:45-47. Wright is followed by Fitzmyer, *Luke (X–XXIV),* 1321; Evans, *Luke,* 306-7; and Green, *Luke,* 728-29. I am unpersuaded by this interpretation. This interpretation infers that Jesus praises those who "gave their gifts out of their wealth," but this cannot be sustained, for the tone of the pericope celebrates the widow's sacrifice ("Truly I tell you, this poor widow has put in *more*

this widow — not the wealthy — is said to give "all" (v. 4; Gk. *panta*).[134] For Jesus, the value of a gift is not the amount given, but the cost to the giver; not how much is given, but how much is retained for self. Others gave what they could spare; the widow spares nothing. Others gave from their surplus; the widow gives from her need, "all she had to live on."

21:1-4 forms a bookend of the Third Gospel in two respects, the first of which involves the widow. The widow of 21:1-4 forms a counterpart to Anna, the first widow in the Gospel (2:36-38). Both appear in the temple, both are characterized by what they lack (2:37; 21:4), and both bear witness in different ways to "redemption" (2:38). The second respect involves the worshiping cult in Israel. Jesus declared the good news of salvation in the synagogue of Nazareth at the outset of his ministry (4:16-30). The modern world tends to be skeptical, sometimes even cynical, of religious institutions. Qualified allegiance to religious institutions may have characterized Jesus' day as well, for the prophets warned against Israelite cult corruption, the Baptizer maintained distance from synagogue and temple, and temple leaders opposed Jesus. Nevertheless, Luke sets Jesus' programmatic declaration of salvation in a synagogue, and perhaps the greatest example of discipleship in the temple. Synagogue and temple constitute the heart of worshiping Israel.[135] Both institutions, to be sure, vigorously opposed Jesus (4:28-29; 19:47; 20:20). Yet both remain a venue of faith for "the people." There, the word of the Anointed One goes forth "to make ready a people prepared for the Lord" (1:17).

---

than all the others"). The interpretation also implies that the widow is a misled fool, which is condescending, for it regards her as too ignorant or cowardly to resist the influence of the scribes. The bravery of her gift suggests she is neither. Finally, the scale of values suggested by the interpretation would reduce Jesus' proclamation to a very bourgeois gospel that makes no unreasonable demands, rather like Aristotle's Golden Mean of nothing in excess. Such a scale of values would also condemn the shepherd who searches for a lost sheep (15:3-7) and tax collectors who repent (18:9-14; 19:1-10). For further discussion and critique, see Bovon, *Lukas 19,28–24,53*, 157.

134. Vinson, *Luke*, 641.

135. Nolland, *Luke 18:35–24:53*, 937-38, writes: "Luke is concerned to minimize any sense in which Jesus might be seen as critical of the Jerusalem temple. . . . The Lukan Jesus acts to purify the worship of the temple . . . [and] is straightforwardly in favor of the temple."

CHAPTER NINETEEN

The Fall of Jerusalem and the Coming of the Son of Man

Luke 21:5-36

The material in 21:5-36, which takes the form of a speech, constitutes the last public address of Jesus in the Third Gospel.[1] Its closest counterpart in the Synoptics is Mark 13, which Luke likely utilized. Luke alters Markan material significantly and shifts the focus more prominently to the fall of Jerusalem than does any other Gospel. Into his Markan exemplar Luke regularly weaves material from his special source. The new material contains a dozen Hebraisms in the thirty-one-verse pericope, which suggests the Hebrew Gospel as one of the sources of the additional material.[2]

The subject of the address is eschatology, the doctrine of "last things." The special feature of eschatological discourse in 21:5-36 is that a final but distant future event is prefigured in a near and realized event. The distant future event is the coming of the Son of Man (v. 27), the final goal of history, which is symbolized and anticipated in the destruction of the Jerusalem temple and fall of the Holy City in the year 70. The fall of Jerusalem stood in the immediate and inescapable future at the time Jesus was speaking, and in the immediate and unforgettable past in the memory of Luke's readers. It therefore functions as a preliminary realization of the final goal of history in the distant and imperfectly known future. The speech was likely compiled from earlier addresses on the same subject at various times and places in Jesus' ministry. This is evident from the fact that the same or similar teachings of Jesus in the eschatological discourse appear in different contexts of his ministry. Sayings in 21:12-19, for example, also appear in 12:11-12, as well as in Matt 10:17-22 and Mark 13:9-13. The Third Gospel itself includes earlier eschatological sayings of Jesus in 12:35-48, 13:34-35, 17:20-37, and 19:41-44. Themes from these earlier teachings are repeated, developed, and culminated in the present eschatological discourse

---

1. The unity of the speech was already recognized in the earliest Greek divisions of the Gospels in Codex Alexandrinus, which designates 21:5-38 as a single discourse.

2. Edwards, *Hebrew Gospel*, 324-25. Schlatter, *Lukas*, 413-15, attributes the Lukan additions to his "Quelle" (special source), of Hebraic/Aramaic provenance.

in 21:5-36.[3] The earlier sayings were addressed to disciples, whereas here they are addressed to all of Jesus' audience. The fulfillment of the earlier sayings was left ambiguous, whereas here their preliminary fulfillment occurs in the destruction of Jerusalem.

The discourse is sometimes inappropriately called The Synoptic Apocalypse.[4] **Apocalyptic** (Gk. lit. "unveiling") is a generic term for a type (as well as a theme and style) of Jewish literature that concerns final events before the end of time, including visions (often in bizarre imagery) of the defeat of chaos and the restoration of creation, and of the coming of the Son of Man to judge the wicked and establish a kingdom of righteousness. Apocalyptic imagery in Luke 21 is generally limited to cataclysmic events (v. 11) and the coming of the Son of Man (v. 27), and several features of Christian apocalyptic such as contrasts between this age and the age to come, heaven and earth, and the church versus the world are absent.[5] Characteristic features of Jewish apocalyptic are also absent, such as bizarre visions and references to resurrection, final judgment, punishment of Satan and his minions, and idyllic descriptions of resurrection existence. Jewish apocalypses generally relate visions in the first-person singular, whereas Jesus' discourse consists largely of second-person plural imperatives. Moreover, first-person apocalyptic is generally revelatory, whereas the final exhortations to waiting and watchfulness in vv. 34-36, in confident trust of the outworking of God's sovereign purpose in history, is hortatory. Luke 21 is properly understood as an *eschatological* rather than apocalyptic discourse. Its primary purpose is to provide a view of the ultimate End in the distant future through the lens of the destruction of Jerusalem in the immediate future.

THE DESTRUCTION OF THE TEMPLE (21:5-24)

5-6   Unlike the Markan narrative, where Jesus leaves the temple, ascends the Mount of Olives, and delivers his eschatological discourse "opposite the temple" (13:1-3), Luke places Jesus' eschatological discourse *in* the temple. More-

---

3. The theme of preparedness in 12:35-48 is repeated in vv. 34-36; "the desolation of your house" in 13:35 and allusions to the fall of Jerusalem in 19:41-44 are repeated and described more fully in vv. 20-24; the various trials preceding the end of 17:25-32 are taken up in vv. 10-17; the suddenness of the end in 17:24 is repeated in vv. 34-35. So too Fitzmyer, *Luke (X–XXIV)*, 1323-25.

4. E.g., *SQE*, 396.

5. W. A. Meeks, "Social Functions of Apocalyptic Language in Pauline Christianity," in *Apocalypticism in the Mediterranean World and the Near East: Proceedings of the International Colloquium on Apocalypticism, August 12-17, 1979* (ed. D. Hellholm; Tübingen: Mohr [Siebeck], 1983), 689.

over, chap. 21 is not specifically identified as a private discourse with disciples (Mark 13:1; Matt 24:1), but as a general discourse. "Some of those" (v. 5) must refer back to 20:45, where "all the people" and the "disciples" are mentioned together. "Some of those" likely includes both groups ("some of his disciples" in NIV is overly specific).[6] Once again in the Lukan Passion Narrative, despite the adversarial role its leaders play in relation to Jesus, the temple remains the proper locus of Jesus' teaching, including his final public address.

The audience marvels at the adornment and immensity of the temple (v. 5). Even today ruins of the Jerusalem temple (see at 2:46) impress visitors with its former mass and grandeur. Reference to "gifts dedicated to God" (v. 5; Gk. *anathēma*) is new to Luke and not in the Markan parallel. The addition draws attention not simply to the stupendous exterior of the temple (as in Mark), but also to its interior, which comports with Luke's emphasis on placing the eschatological discourse in the temple.[7] The grandeur of the temple was celebrated by Josephus:

> The gate opening into [the temple] was completely overlaid with gold, as was the whole wall around it. It had above it golden vines from which hung grape clusters as tall as a man; and it had golden doors fifty-five cubits high and sixteen broad. Before these hung a veil of equal length of Babylonian tapestry, with embroidery of blue and fine linen, of scarlet also and purple, wrought with marvelous skill. (*J. W.* 5.210-11)

This rhapsody is echoed by other ancient authors who were equally impressed with the temple.[8] The Roman historian Tacitus described the temple as *immensae opulentiae*, "immensely opulent."[9] With regard to its immensity, the southeast corner of the retaining wall hung some fifteen stories above the ground that sloped down to the Kidron Valley. The blocks of stone used in construction were enormous; Josephus reports that some were forty cubits (approx. 60 feet [18 m]) in length (*J. W.* 5.189). No block that size has been found in the existing foundation, but stones north of Wilson's Arch measure forty-two feet long, eleven feet high, fourteen feet deep (12.8 × 3.4 × 4.3 m), and weigh over a million pounds. The magnitude of the Temple Mount and the stones used to construct it exceed in size any other temple in the ancient world.[10]

The above merely describes the retaining wall. The temple proper

6. Luke omits reference to the disciples in the eschatological discourse, according to Bovon, *Lukas 19,29–24,53*, 168, because his parting address during the Last Supper in 22:15-38 is reserved for them.

7. See Marshall, *Luke*, 759.

8. Philo, *Embassy* 157, 319; Tacitus, *Hist.* 5.5; 2 Macc 9:16.

9. *Hist.* 5.8.1.

10. See Fitzmyer, *Luke (X–XXIV)*, 1330-31; Wolter, *Lukasevangelium*, 670.

built upon it was "a striking spectacle," to quote Josephus. The Royal Portico perched on the south end of the Temple Mount was forty-five feet (14 m) wide and consisted of three aisles supported by four rows of columns. The columns were crowned with Corinthian capitals and rose to a height of forty feet (12 m), supporting a cedar-paneled ceiling above. "The thickness of each column was such that it would take three men with outstretched arms touching one another to envelop it," reports Josephus (*Ant.* 15.413). In the center of the complex stood the sanctuary, which as ancient writers noted, was shaped like a lion, broader in the front (165 feet [50 m]) and narrower in back (100 feet [30 m]). It rose to a height of 165 feet and presented a gleaming collage of gold and silver, crimson and purple, radiating the morning sunlight like a snow-clad mountain. The figures Josephus gives for the blocks of stone in the sanctuary exceed in size even those of the foundation (*J. W.* 5.222-24).

Whenever I walk among the majestic ruins of the Temple of Apollo in Didyma (Turkey) — one of the only places where a column the size of those in the Jerusalem temple still stands — and imagine the vast complex of such towering columns in the Jerusalem temple, I have the same feeling of awe that I experience when walking among the redwoods of California. How different was the impact of such grandeur on Jesus! "As for what you see here, the time will come when not one stone will be left on another; every one of them will be thrown down" (v. 6). What for worshipers and visitors was sacred astonishment, was for Jesus a premonition of disaster. His response is a sobering reminder of the divine perspective — and judgment — on human culture. "The time will come" (v. 6) is a technical eschatological reference to *God's* decisive intervention.[11] Like a once-healthy system of cells that has become malignant, the temple has forsaken its intended purpose. Jesus warned in the parable of the Fig Tree that, if the tree does not bear fruit, it will be cut down (13:8). The fig tree, a symbol of the temple, will be destroyed — stone by stone.[12] Josephus's lamentation over "that splendid city of worldwide renown"

---

11. The expression, lit. "days are coming" (Gk. *eleusontai hēmerai*), is a Hebraism (*yāmīm bāʾīm*). Eighteen of its twenty OT occurrences appear in prophetic references to divine judgment (Isa 39:6; Amos 4:2; 8:11; 9:13; 14x in Jer). The expression appears in Luke 5:35; 17:22; 19:43; 23:29 (in 19:43 it refers also to the fall of Jerusalem). Further, Wolter, *Lukasevangelium*, 579.

12. Jesus' prediction of the temple's destruction echoes a chorus of similar Jewish predictions, not only in the OT (Ps 74:4-7; Jer 7:14; 9:11; 26:6; Mic 3:9-12; 2 Macc 14:33), but also in extracanonical Jewish literature (*T. Jud.* 23:1-5; *T. Levi* 10:3; 14; 15:3; *1 En.* 90:28-29; 91:11-13; *Sib. Or.* 3.665; 11Q19 (11QT) 30; *Lives of the Prophets* 12:11). As far as we know, all these texts antedate A.D. 70. Added to those who foresaw the temple's destruction are Josephus himself (*J. W.* 3.351-52; 6.311) and at least two rabbis, Yohanan ben Zakkai and Zadok. The corruption of the Herodian temple was widespread and widely recognized. There is every reason to believe that Jesus could predict the temple's destruction. On the subject, see C. A. Evans, "Predictions of the Destruction of the Herodian Temple in the Pseudepigrapha, Qumran Scrolls, and Re-

forty years later attests to the fulfillment of Jesus' judgment: "Caesar ordered the whole city and the temple to be razed to the ground. . . . All the rest of the wall encompassing the city was so completely leveled to the ground as to leave future visitors to the spot no ground for believing that it had ever been inhabited" (*J. W.* 7.3).

7-9 The audience of this dire prediction responds, "Teacher, when will these things happen? And what will be the sign that these things are about to take place?" (v. 7). The reference to "teacher" reinforces the suggestion at v. 5 that Jesus was teaching publicly rather than speaking privately with the Twelve, for in the Third Gospel Jesus is called Teacher by nonfollowers rather than by disciples.[13] Jesus is asked a double question: When will *"these things"* happen, and What will be the *sign* of their happening? "These things" (Gk. *tauta*) must refer to the same word in v. 6, which there designated the destruction of Jerusalem; hence, the first question inquires about that event. The second question inquires about a portending "sign" before the destruction of Jerusalem. Without a sign the disaster would be but a massive misfortune. The question about a sign, therefore, relates to the fall of Jerusalem not simply as a disaster, but as God's expressed will. "Many will come in my name, claiming, 'I am he,' and, 'The time is near,'" responds Jesus (v. 8). By "I am he" and "the time is near," Jesus appears to designate messianic claimants. The Greek of v. 8 reads simply, "I am," which is the name for God in the OT (Exod 3:14). "I am" appears in the Third Gospel only with reference to divinity, either by Gabriel (1:19) or relating to the divine sonship of Jesus (22:70; 24:39). "I am" thus signifies someone claiming to be Jesus, the Son of God. There is no material difference, however, between Jesus' claim "I am" and the same claim of impostors. Believers must therefore be alert to more than words. Does "I am" truly represent God, or does it merely use God and the articles of orthodoxy for ulterior purposes? Impostors will even come "in my name" with powers and credentials that will give the impression that they are messianic. These impostors will have no small effect. The spate of gnostic literature contained in both the Nag Hammadi corpus and the NT Apocrypha testifies to the proliferation of Jewish and especially gnostic sects that purveyed an alien message in the name of Jesus. In the second Jewish revolt (132-35), Bar Kokhba claimed to be the Messiah, and his claim swept many devout Jews into revolt.

We know of at least two such claimants prior to the fall of Jerusalem.

---

lated Texts," *JSP* 10 (1992): 89-147; M. Hengel, *Studies in the Gospel of Mark* (trans. J. Bowden; London: SCM Press, 1985), 14-16.

13. Contra Green, *Luke,* 735, who regards Jesus' questioners as his disciples. Each reference to Jesus as teacher in Luke (7:40; 8:49; 9:38; 10:25; 11:45; 12:13; 18:18; 19:39; 20:21, 28, 39; 21:7; 22:11) from the mouth of a person we can identify comes from a nonfollower, not a disciple or one of the Twelve. See on "Master" at 5:5.

Acts 5:36 records a certain Theudas, who gathered four hundred followers and "claimed to be somebody." Josephus placed the appearance of Theudas under the prefecture of Fadus (44-46), regarding him a prophetic "impostor" who presumed to lead his followers across the parted waters of the Jordan as did Joshua (*Ant.* 20.97-99). A decade later, under the prefecture of Felix (52-60), an Egyptian, whom Josephus also calls a false prophet, mustered a much larger army (4,000 according to Acts 21:38, 30,000 according to Josephus) in an attempt to storm Jerusalem from the Mount of Olives (*J.W.* 2.261). Felix anticipated the stratagem and shattered the rebellion. Neither Theudas nor the Egyptian is specifically called a messianic pretender, but Josephus's descriptions of them as "impostors," "magicians," and "deceivers" who gathered followers "under the belief that God would give them deliverance" (*J.W.* 2.259) imply messianic pretense. Prior to the Roman invasion and siege of Jerusalem, Palestine witnessed an increase in the number of "deceivers and impostors who, under the pretenses of divine inspiration, fostered revolutionary changes" (*J.W.* 2.259).[14] Josephus leaves no doubt that Jewish defense strategies were motivated by religious considerations, in hopes that, in the heat of battle over the temple, Messiah would come.

In response to these desperate and deadly initiatives, Jesus gives a triple warning in vv. 8-9: "do not be deceived" *(mē planēthēte)*,[15] "do not follow them" *(mē poreuthēte)*, and "do not be frightened" *(mē ptoēthēte)*. The last two of these forms echo OT prophetic warnings not to "go after" false prophets (2 Kgs 2:18; Ezek 20:18) and not to be frightened.[16] Each warning in vv. 8-9 begins with the Greek letter pi, and each ends with the identical suffix, making the warnings easy to memorize.[17] Vv. 8-9 are not simply warnings of the dangers attending the military and political situation befalling Jerusalem. They are specific warnings to followers of Jesus — and Christian believers of Luke's day — regarding those who "will come in *my* name." The greatest threats to believers are not external dangers, cataclysmic though they are, but dangers inside the household of faith. Dangers to faith will not be merely sporadic and occasional; there will be many who appear in messianic guise, and they will lead many astray. Prophetic pretenders, along with wars and uprisings, are necessary precedents of the fall of Jerusalem, but they do not signal its immediate arrival. Jesus' followers must resist the temptation to believe, be misled by, and follow false leads and leaders.

14. For discussions of these and other messianic pretenders, see A. Y. Collins, "The Apocalyptic Rhetoric of Mark 13 in Historical Context," *BR* 41 (1996): 14-18.

15. A similar admonition is found in *Gos. Mary,* where, in the annunciation, the angel warns Mary, "Beware that no one lead you astray [*planan*]" (*NTApoc.* 1:392).

16. The final warning not to be frightened appears twenty-five times in the OT and may be a Hebraism, *al-tir'u.*

17. See here Schweizer, *Lukas,* 209.

The word for "sign" (Gk. *sēmeion*) is used predominantly in the Third Gospel with reference to portents of the end time.[18] The signs of vv. 7-9 are not as apparent as they may seem, however, and they must be viewed with extreme caution. Some signs derive from false prophets, and thus deceive rather than inform. Even legitimate signs are not free from ambiguity, for the end "will not come right away" (v. 9). Josephus records similar phenomena prior to the fall of Jerusalem. "Numerous false prophets" assured inhabitants of Jerusalem that deliverance from the Romans awaited them in the temple, but when people fled there, they were slaughtered and incinerated (*J. W.* 6.281-87). Josephus records other omens — stars resembling swords suspended over the city, comets, brilliant lights shining on the altar, temple gates opening of their own accord, cows giving birth to lambs in the sanctuary — which, though they were "the plain warnings of God," were nevertheless ambiguous (*J. W.* 6.288-300).[19]

According to vv. 7-9, various phenomena, including signs that are both true and false, will also portend the fall of Jerusalem referred to in vv. 5-6. There will be wars and "uprisings" (Gk. *akatastasia*). This last term likely refers to political instabilities and disturbances, revolts and insurrection.[20] "Wars and insurrection" could summarize many ages, but they pertain especially well to the first Christian generation. Josephus uses a phrase very similar to v. 9 to describe the rumors of war circulating when Caligula (Roman emperor, 37-41) attempted to erect a statue of himself in the temple of Jerusalem (*J. W.* 2.187). Those rumors turned out to be only that, but twenty-five years later, in 66, total war broke out when the Zealots plunged Palestine into a catastrophic war with Rome. The language of v. 9 finds striking parallels in Tacitus's description particularly of the last years of Nero's megalomania and the civil wars that followed his suicide in 68.[21] Such things "must happen" (v. 9; Gk. *dei*), i.e.,

---

18. 11:16, 29, 30; 21: 7, 11, 25. Otherwise, only at 2:12, 34; 23:8.

19. The Roman historian Tacitus, *Hist.* 5.13, corroborates each of Josephus's portents except for the cow birthing a lamb. Tacitus also notes the ambiguity of the signs, which in his view portended Roman victory. The superstitious populace in the besieged city, he writes, mistakenly understood them as signs of God's favor "and could not be turned to the truth even by adversity."

20. *Akatastasia* occurs in no other Gospel and may derive from Paul (1 Cor 14:33; 2 Cor 6:5; 12:20; elsewhere in NT only Jas 3:16). Further on this term, Schweizer, *Lukas,* 209; Klein, *Lukasevangelium,* 647; Wolter, *Lukasevangelium,* 672.

21. Tacitus commences his *Histories* in 68 with this prologue: "The history on which I am entering is that of a period rich in disasters, terrible in battles, torn by civil struggles, horrible even in peace. Four emperors fell by the sword; there were three civil wars, more foreign wars, and often both at the same time. There was success in the East [referring to the Vespasian-Titus victory in Judea], misfortune in the West. Illyricum was disturbed, the Gallic provinces wavering, Britain subdued and immediately let go. The Sarmatae and Suebi rose against us . . . even the Parthians were almost aroused to arms through the trickery of a pretended Nero. Moreover, Italy was distressed by disasters unknown before or returning

they are so ordered by God (13:33; 17:25; 19:5; 24:7, 26, 44). They are symptoms, a first alert, a divine early warning system. They inform *that* the end is near, but not exactly *when* it will occur. The final consummation of the kingdom of God cannot be calculated (17:20).

10-11 These verses correspond closely with vv. 25-27, which depict the final *eschaton*. Vv. 10-11 thus extend the perspective of the near *eschaton* in the fall of Jerusalem (vv. 7-8) to the distant and final *eschaton* in the return of the Son of Man in glory. The fall of Jerusalem functions as a precursor or prototype of the final eschatological fulfillment. The opening phrase hints of the transition to the distant future, "Then [Jesus] was saying to them" (v. 10). The events depicted are no longer earthly — wars, famines, and pestilence — but cosmic, "fearful events and great signs from heaven" (v. 11). Such language and imagery are standard features of Jewish eschatology and apocalyptic, which Luke sets forth in careful parallelism and in a wordplay on "famines and pestilence" (Gk. *limoi kai loimoi*).[22] In intertestamental literature the catastrophes of vv. 10-11 portend the end of history and the final judgment of God, including nations and kingdoms rising up against one another in warfare,[23] earthquakes,[24] famines, and pestilence.[25] "Fearful events" (v. 11) are graphically summarized in the woes attending the reign of the Antichrist in *Apoc. Dan.* 14, as are "great signs from heaven" (v. 11) in *Sib. Or.* 3.796-806. Vv. 10-11 are thus a flash-forward to events immediately preceding the return of the Son of Man at the Parousia. The Markan parallel to v. 11 includes the phrase, "These are the beginning of birth pains" (13:8). Luke omits this phrase, probably because he regards eschatological "birth pains" to begin with the fall of Jerusalem, not at a later point. Catastrophic events ever after the fall of Jerusalem are but aftershocks, further repercussions that anticipate the second coming, although it "will not come right away" (v. 9).

12-19 The material in this section is roughly parallel to Mark 13:9-13, with additions in vv. 14, 15b, and 18; and deletions of Mark 13:10, and 11d. The

---

after the lapse of ages. Cities on the rich fertile shores of Campania were swallowed up or overwhelmed; Rome was devastated by conflagrations, in which her most ancient shrines were consumed and the very Capitol fired by citizens' hands. Sacred rites were defiled; there were adulteries in high places. The sea was filled with exiles, its cliffs made foul with the bodies of the dead. In Rome there was more awful cruelty. . . . Informers were no less hateful than their crimes; for some, gaining priesthoods and consulships as spoils, others obtaining positions as imperial agents and secret influence at court, made havoc and turmoil everywhere, inspiring hatred and terror. Slaves were corrupted against their masters, freedmen against their patrons; and those who had no enemy were crushed by friends" (*Hist.* 1.2 [LCL]).

22. Bovon, *Lukas 19,28–24,53*, 169-70, sees in the content and structure of these verses evidence of a source other than Mark.

23. Gk. *Apoc. Ezra* 3:13; *4 Ezra* 13:29-31; *2 En.* 70:5, 23; 2 Chr 15:6; Isa 19:2.

24. Ezek 38:19; *Apoc. Ab.* 30:6; *Gk. Apoc. Ezra* 3:11; *2 Bar.* 70:8; Rev 6:12; 11:13; 16:18.

25. *Sib. Or.* 3.332. On these eschatological signs, see Wolter, *Lukasevangelium*, 673.

material remaining in common with Mark is significantly altered by Luke. It seems likely, as several scholars suggest,[26] that Luke is augmenting his Markan exemplar with his special source. Vv. 12-19 reel attention back from the final *eschaton* to the fall of Jerusalem. The change in perspective is signaled in the opening words, "But before all this . . ." (v. 12). The Greek reads, "But before all these things [*tauta*]." *Tauta* recalls the same word of vv. 6 and 7 (NIV translates *tauta* "here" in v. 6), where it refers to the fall of Jerusalem.[27] "They will lay hands on you and persecute you" (v. 12), says Jesus. The "you" refers to believers, the Christian community, which will be persecuted "on account of [Jesus'] name" (v. 12). Believers will be betrayed, beaten, and arraigned before "synagogues, prisons, kings, and governors" (v. 12). These institutions and offices include persecution from both Jewish and Gentile authorities. The gospel will not arouse antagonism only within religious circles, but also from secular powers. The parallels to this verse in Mark 13:9 and Matt 10:17 include "sanhedrins" in addition to "synagogues"; Luke may omit "Sanhedrin" because it no longer existed when he wrote the Third Gospel.[28] The remainder of the Gospel, and especially its sequel in Acts, abound in references to the imprisonment of believers: John the Baptizer is the first witness to the gospel in the Gospel to be imprisoned (3:20), followed by no fewer than sixteen instances of the same in Acts. What was the history of the fledgling Christian movement if not a litany of trials before "kings and governors"? Jesus was haled before Antipas and Pilate (23:1-12), Peter, John, and Stephen before the Sanhedrin (Acts 4:1-22; 6:12), James before Herod Agrippa I (12:2), and Paul before Gallio (Acts 18:12-17), Felix (Acts 23:24, 26, 33; 24:1, 10), and Agrippa and Festus (26:30). In every instance the offense was not a malefaction but was due to bearing witness to "the name of Jesus."

Remarkably, such opposition and adversities do not weaken the church but provide an opportunity for *martyrion* — "testimony" or "witness" (v. 13). The parallels in Mark 13:9 and Matt 10:18 speak of believers standing and bearing witness *to them* (i.e., to hostile authorities). Luke shifts the emphasis to the witnesses themselves, "This will be an opportunity *for you* to bear witness."[29] The Lukan wording is slightly more ambiguous. "Witness" could and certainly does indicate a verbal testimony to the gospel, but it could also include the sufferings of believers as a witness. In all the persecutions that befall them, believers will not only *give* a witness, they will *be* a witness.[30] God

26. BDF §392; Schweizer, *Lukas*, 210; Bovon, *Lukas 19,28–24,53*, 170.

27. Contra Wolter, *Lukasevangelium*, 674, who sees in vv. 12-19 a continuation of the perspective of vv. 10-11.

28. So Schweizer, *Lukas*, 209.

29. The Greek of v. 13 does not include "to me" (so NIV).

30. Marshall, *Luke*, 768, distinguishes between the "activity" of witness and the "evidence" of witness.

will not abandon believers in the hour of crisis but will enable and empower their witness.

"Make up your mind not to worry beforehand how you will defend yourself" (v. 14). The Greek phrase behind "make up your mind" is "place in your hearts," a Hebraism (e.g., Hag 2:15; Mal 2:2; *Sipre Deut.* 34), which Luke has used twice before (1:66; 9:44). It means to be utterly determined, to resolve at the center of one's being. Disciples need not be anxious about what they will say or how they will defend themselves because in the storms of persecution they will have an advocate far superior to their own devices and defenses. "I will give you words and wisdom" (v. 15). Indeed, if they prepare speeches and defenses beforehand, there will be no room for Christ to speak through them.[31] Mark 13:11 and Matt 10:20 assign the advocacy to the Holy Spirit, to which the Book of Acts will also attest through the pouring out of the Holy Spirit on the early church. But Luke assigns the advocacy to Jesus himself (v. 15), thus identifying the presence of the Spirit specifically with the person of Jesus, who will give a "mouth [*stoma*] and mind [*sophia*]" (so too Eph 6:19).[32] V. 15 is strongly emphatic in Greek: "*I myself* will give you words and wisdom that *none* of your adversaries will be able to resist or contradict."[33] Stephen's self-defense in Acts 6–7 is a prime example of courage and wisdom under trial, presided over by "Jesus standing at the right hand of God" (Acts 7:55). Faithfulness does not consist in forecasting the future and determining preemptive responses. Rather, disciples are commanded to trust that God will give them grace to complete their service in his name and that he will speak through them in their deepest need. "The best preparation," says Bovon, "consists in not being prepared, and the only worry is not to worry at all."[34] In earlier missions Jesus' disciples spoke for God (9:2; 10:9), but in their sufferings for God Jesus will speak *through* them.

Believers will be persecuted not only from external sectors — synagogues, kings, and governors (v. 12) — but from near and nourishing communities. "You will be betrayed even by parents, brothers, sisters, relatives and friends, and they will put some of you to death" (v. 16). V. 16 is a prophetic oracle of Jesus similar to Mic 7:6 and *Gk. Apoc. Ezra* 3:12. Persecution will come from families, and it will break up families: siblings against siblings, parents against children, children against parents. The ancient world, including the Jewish world, rooted personal identity in the larger social group — household,

---

31. Bovon, *Lukas 19,28–24,53*, 179.

32. Given Luke's emphasis on the Holy Spirit, Bock, *Luke, 9:51–24:53*, sees in the substitution of Jesus for the Holy Spirit in v. 15 evidence of reliance on a source other than Mark.

33. The Greek words for "none," "adversaries," "resist," and "contradict" (v. 15) all begin with the letter alpha, revealing alliteration from Luke's editorial hand.

34. *Lukas 19,28–24,53*, 179.

family, clan, tribe — more than in the individual: "As for me and my household, we will serve the Lord" (Josh 24:15). An attack on the family — or worse, *from* the family — jeopardized existence at the most intimate and formative level. Jesus' inner circle is rent by such betrayal in the defection of Judas.[35] Family betrayals might even include *Christian* families (8:19-21), for example, Christians informing on one another under interrogation.[36] In his description of the Neronian persecution in 64, Tacitus writes that Christians were first arrested, and *on their disclosures* other Christians were arrested (*Ann.* 15:44). A generation later (ca. 110), Pliny the Younger testifies to the interrogation of Christians "who have been denounced" (by fellow Christians?, *Ep. Tra.* 10.96). The declaration that "everyone will hate you because of me" (v. 17) is echoed again by Tacitus, who refers to Christians as "a class of persons who were loathed, . . . hated by the human race" (*Ann.* 15:44). V. 17 appears to include the church as well as "the world": fallible and false believers within the community of faith will conspire with the world to persecute true disciples. It is important for believers to remember that the word describing their experience of betrayal (Gk. *paradidonai*) is the same word describing Jesus' experience of betrayal (18:32; 22:4; 23:25). "Students are not above their teacher, but all who are fully trained will be like their teacher" (Matt 10:24-25; John 13:16).

"Not a hair of your head will perish" (v. 18) is a Lukan addition to his Markan source. This concrete figure of speech is a proverbial OT saying (1 Sam 14:45; 2 Sam 14:11; 1 Kgs 1:52) that may derive from Luke's Hebrew source. It bears unconditional witness to divine sovereignty in the believer's life and is used with the same assurance by the apostle Paul in Acts 27:34. It means that *God* will not allow a hair to fall from the head of his children apart from his will. Given the context of v. 16, it cannot mean that no physical harm will befall believers. It must be understood spiritually, that, without God's will, nothing can befall believers; and even if death befall them, "their souls will be absolutely safe."[37] V. 18 is not simply spiritual assurance,[38] but a graphic reconfigurement of the meaning of life: from the perspective of eternity, the loss of one's earthly life is no greater than the loss of a single hair.[39]

---

35. Nolland, *Luke 18:35–24:53*, 998.

36. On inner-church betrayals, see T. Radcliffe, "'The Coming of the Son of Man': Mark's Gospel and the Subversion of 'the Apocalyptic Imagination,'" in *Language, Meaning, and God: Essays in Honour of Herbert McCabe O.P.* (ed. B. Davies; London: Chapman, 1987), 167-89; and B. van Iersel, "Failed Followers in Mark: Mark 13:12 as a Key for the Identification of the Intended Readers," *CBQ* 58 (1996): 244-63.

37. Plummer, *Luke*, 480.

38. See Heidelberg Catechism, question 1: "God protects me so well that without the will of my Father in heaven not a hair can fall from my head; indeed, that everything must fit his purpose for my salvation."

39. Wolter, *Lukasevangelium*, 675.

Jesus concludes vv. 12-19 with the exhortation, "Stand firm, and you will win life" (v. 19). This rendering of the NIV is idiomatic. A literal translation of Greek v. 19 is, "For by your endurance you will make your lives secure." The Greek word for "endurance" or "perseverance" *(hypomonē)* occurs only twice in Luke-Acts, first with reference to those in the parable of the Sower who, like good seed, "hear the word, retain it, and by persevering produced a crop" (8:15). *Hypomonē* is used similarly here: by steadfast endurance, believers will receive the promises of God. This repeats a familiar OT refrain: "If you do not stand firm in your faith, you will not stand at all" (Isa 7:9).[40] Believers are not commanded to be superhuman, to feel good in all circumstances, or to emerge victorious from all adversities. They are commanded to do the one thing they can do in every crisis — to endure and be steadfast. Luke places a stronger accent on "endurance" than do Matt 24:13 and Mark 13:13, both of whom say that those who endure "will be saved." For Luke, those who endure will procure — "win" — their eternal souls. The Lukan wording emphasizes gain over loss. The life of faithful obedience is not a grim and dreary existence. True, believers must suffer hardships for their faith, as did Jesus (17:25). But in adversities of faith Jesus himself is strongly present, personally promising, "I shall give you" resources for all your needs.[41] His promise to be with them and for them is something they can "take to heart" (v. 14), for the losses of this life, whatever they may be, indeed the loss of earthly life itself, are but a fallen hair compared to the life to come.

The Book of Acts provides a commentary on nearly every verse in this section.[42] That commentary is not limited to Acts, for these verses are descriptive in varying degrees of the church in every age. However long the time lapse of these verses may be, it is not viewed as a delay — a lateness due to inability — but as a necessary interim before the Parousia. Believers are not given a blueprint of the future, but are reminded that the interim is characterized by "taking up the cross daily and following Jesus" (9:23), in confidence that God is both present in such trials and effecting his saving purpose through them. A critical — and in some instances *heroic*[43] — aspect of bearing the cross of

---

40. See also *4 Ezra* 6:25, "It shall be that whoever remains after all that I have foretold to you shall be saved and shall see my salvation and the end of my world."

41. Schweizer, *Lukas,* 210.

42. Vinson, *Luke,* 647, sees these verses as a "template" for the subsequent experience of the early church.

43. Note God's commendation of Abdiel's steadfast opposition to Satan's rebellion, in *Paradise Lost* 6:29-37:

Servant of God, well done, well hast thou fought
The better fight, who single hast maintaind
Against revolted multitudes the Cause
Of Truth, in word mightier than they in Armes;

Christ is simply standing firm in endurance (v. 19; Dan 12:12). The life of faith is not an exemption from adversity but a reliance on the promise of God to bear witness to the gospel in adversity, and to be saved for eternal life through it.

20-24   These verses recapitulate an earlier allusion in 17:31, and an explicit reference in 19:43-44, to the fall of Jerusalem. Mark 13:14 and Matt 24:15 refer to an enigmatic "abomination that causes desolation" (Dan 9:27; 11:31; 12:11), which signifies the fall of Jerusalem. In place of this cryptic reference Luke supplies lurid details of the Roman siege, the embers of which were still glowing in the memory of his readers. The references to Jerusalem "surrounded by [Roman] armies" (v. 20), to its total subjugation either by sword or imprisonment (v. 24), and to its "trampling by the Gentiles" (v. 24) repeat and expand earlier references to the encirclement of Jerusalem with palisades, slaughter of children (23:28-31!), and pulling down the walls of the temple of 19:43-44.[44] The "desolation" (v. 20; Gk. *erēmōsis*) of Jerusalem recalls Jeremiah's repeated and identical reference to the fall of the city by Nebuchadnezzar in the sixth century B.C.[45] The disciples had been expecting an imminent messianic enthronement of Jesus in Jerusalem (Mark 10:35-40), but it is the *desolation* of Jerusalem that is imminent (similarly Amos 5:18-20).[46]

When Jerusalem is surrounded, "Let those who are in Judea flee to the mountains, let those in the city get out, and let those in the country not enter the city" (v. 21). The exact meaning of this verse is difficult to determine, for the original Greek reads "let those in the country not enter *it*." NIV interprets "it" to mean "the city" (i.e., Jerusalem). Historical circumstances support this interpretation. Once Titus erected the siege perimeter *(circumvallatio)* around Jerusalem, flight into or out of the city became impossible. Those who earlier had fled into the city were not thereby assured of safety, but rather almost certainly of death — either by the Romans or the rebel bandits, who were equally murderous (Josephus, *J.W.* 6.366). "It" could also refer to "Judea," however, for Judea is the subject of v. 21, and this "it" agrees with Judea in gender and number.[47] If Judea

---

And for the testimonie of Truth hast born
Universal reproach, far worse to beare
Then violence; for this was all thy care
To stand approv'd in sight of God.

44. Two second-c. gnostic texts, *2 Apoc. Jas.* 5.4 and *Testim. Truth* 9.3, allude to Titus's siege and destruction of Jerusalem. Likewise, *2 Bar.* 7:1–8:5; 48:34-47 and *4 Ezra* 10:21-24, stemming from the late first c., and *m. Soṭah* 9:15 allude to the fall of Jerusalem (cited in *HCNT*, 133-35).

45. Jer 4:7; 7:34; 22:5; 25:18 (LXX 32:18); 44:6 (LXX 51:6); 44:22 (LXX 51:22).

46. Plummer, *Luke*, 481.

47. So too Schlatter, *Lukas*, 415. The repeated emphasis on flight of v. 21 seems more important than the place of flight (whether Jerusalem or Judea). In this respect it corresponds to prophetic texts such as Jer 4:6; 6:1; 49:8; 1 Macc 2:28.

is the proper understanding, then v. 21 warns the faithful from seeking refuge in Judea itself. We know that prior to the siege of Titus a number of Christians had fled from Jerusalem and Judea to Pella in Transjordan. Eusebius reports that "the church in Jerusalem was commanded by an oracle given by revelation before the war . . . to depart and dwell in one of the cities of Pella" (*Hist. eccl.* 3.5.3). Thus, both grammatical and historical circumstances support a broader understanding of v. 21 warning believers to flee Judea itself.

The "time of punishment" befalling Jerusalem and Judea will "fulfill all that has been written" (v. 22). The fulfillment of Scripture plays an important role in the Third Gospel (4:21; 18:31; 21:22; 24:44). In his inaugural sermon in the synagogue of Nazareth, Jesus said, "This scripture [Isa 61:1] is fulfilled in your hearing" (4:21). Now in the closing address of his public ministry, Jesus declares that the punishment to befall Jerusalem occurs "in fulfillment of all that has been written." Dread of the catastrophe is highlighted by the fate of "pregnant women and nursing mothers" (v. 23; also 23:29-31; *Sib. Or.* 2.190-92). Even these, the most defenseless and vulnerable of Jerusalem's inhabitants, will not be spared. "There will be great distress in the land and wrath against this people" (v. 23). The "distress" of the fall of the city will be the result of God's "wrath against this people," which repeats the theme of the "time of punishment" (v. 22). "Punishment" translates the Greek word *ekdikēsis,* frequently used of divine justice or vengeance. The passive voice is a "divine passive," referring to punishment of God.[48] This common OT theme is here applied to the fall of Jerusalem.[49] The setting of the fateful events of 70 in the context of the fulfillment of Scripture signifies that the fall of Jerusalem is not simply a national tragedy, but the judgment of God.

"They will fall by the sword and will be taken as prisoners to all the nations. Jerusalem will be trampled on by the Gentiles until the times of the Gentiles are fulfilled" (v. 24).[50] These ominous words conclude Luke's report of the fall of Jerusalem. Three aspects of the disaster are emphasized: slaughter by the "mouth of the sword,"[51] captivity by the Romans, and the trampling of Jerusalem by Gentiles. This is a description of total defeat: the people will be killed or captured, the Holy City will be desecrated. One recalls the triumphal procession of Titus into Rome with prisoners captured from the fall of Jerusalem, commemorated on the Arch of Titus, still visible today in Rome.

48. Eusebius, *Hist. eccl.* 3.7.7-9, along with other Fathers, saw the destruction of Jerusalem as divine recompense for the crucifixion of Jesus. Nevertheless, Eusebius adds that Providence withheld the destruction of Jerusalem as long as James, the Lord's brother, remained bishop there. According to Eusebius, the dwelling of early Christians in the temple protected Jerusalem, offering a last opportunity for the city to repent and be saved.

49. Lev 26:31-33; Deut 28:49-57; 32:35; 1 Kgs 9:6-9; Hos 9:7; Mic 3:12; Zech 11:6.

50. Quoted verbatim by Eusebius, *Hist. eccl.* 3.7.5.

51. A Hebraism, Gen 34:26; Josh 19:47; 2 Sam 15:14; Jer 21:7; Sir 28:18; *T. Jud.* 5:5.

All this appears at the hands of the *ethnē*, a Greek word meaning "nations" or "Gentiles," which appears three times in v. 24.

Commentators commonly regard all three references to *ethnē* as negative: the first two referring to the final subjugation of Jerusalem by Rome, and the last ("until the times of the Gentiles are fulfilled") referring to Gentile domination in the interim between the fall of Jerusalem and the coming of the Son of Man (v. 27). The first two references clearly refer to the subjugation of Jerusalem by Rome, and are thus negative. The final reference, however, may introduce a new and positive theme. Several reasons support this suggestion. First, the Greek word for "fulfill," *plēroun,* occurs eight times elsewhere in Luke, always positively, often of the fulfillment of the divine purpose. This favors a positive reference to Gentiles in v. 24. More important, "until the times of the Gentiles are fulfilled" recalls Rom 11:25, where Paul declares that "the full number of Gentiles must come in," after which "all Israel will be saved" (Rom 11:26). This reference to the Gentiles in Rom 11:25 seems to recall Gen 48:19, where Jacob places his hand on the head of the young Ephraim and pronounces that "his seed will become the fullness of the nations."[52] The three references in v. 24, Rom 11:25, and Gen 48:19 share closer wording in Hebrew than in Greek.[53] Like Paul, Luke may recall the theme of Gen 48:19 to signify that Gentile reception of the gospel fulfills the promise to Abraham. Luke's final statement from the mouth of Paul in Acts in fact affirms this theme: "Therefore, I want you to know that God's salvation has been sent to the Gentiles, and they will listen" (Acts 28:28). It seems plausible to understand "until the times of the Gentiles are fulfilled" in v. 24 similarly, i.e., that the Gentile mission must precede the return of the Son of Man.

It might be asked, by way of objection, whether Luke would use Gentiles twice negatively and once positively in the same verse. The force of this objection is diminished by the fact that Mark 13, which Luke references throughout his eschatological discourse, also references Gentiles both negatively and positively. On the one hand, the distress caused by Gentiles will be so severe that, unless God "cut short those days," no one would survive (Mark 13:20); nevertheless, the "gospel must first be preached to all the Gentiles" (Mark 13:10). Luke omits both of these Markan references in the eschatological discourse of chap. 21, but he includes similar references to Gentiles, both negatively and positively, in v. 24: Gentiles will be both the cause of the fall of Jerusalem and the object of the proclamation of the gospel, which must be preached to them

---

52. On the relation between Gen 48:19 and Rom 11:25, see J. Staples, "What Do the Gentiles Have to Do with 'All Israel'? A Fresh Look at Romans 11:25-27," *JBL* 130/2 (2011): 385-89.

53. Gen 48:19: *yihyeh milo haggoyim;* Rom 11:25: *ad ki-yikkanem milo' haggoyim;* Luke 21:24: *ad asher-yimle'u aitot haggoyim.* The NT Hebrew renderings follow Delitzsch's *Hebrew New Testament* (1931).

as a fulfillment of God's saving mission within Israel before the return of the Son of Man.[54]

V. 24 is a unique Lukan addition to Mark, and highly significant for his overall theological perspective. Jerusalem plays a critical role in Luke-Acts as the point *to* which the Gospel narrative flows, and *from* which the Acts narrative flows (see at 9:51, 13:35, and 18:31-34). Jerusalem is central to Luke's theological metanarrative and salvifically significant for both Jews and Gentiles. Jerusalem is associated with the Davidic kingdom, whose fulfillment in Jesus (1:32-33; 2:11) signifies the full salvation of Jews. Jerusalem symbolizes not only the fulfillment of God's saving work *for* Israel, however, but also the fulfillment *through* Israel for the salvation of the Gentile world. Luke's Jerusalem motif combines both elements, which are also contained in the promise to Abraham in Gen 12:1-3: the blessing of Israel, and the blessing of "all the peoples on earth" through Israel. The important point here, which Luke stresses throughout the infancy narrative, is not that Israel is absorbed into the Gentile-Christian church, but that the proclamation of the gospel makes Gentiles heirs in *Israel's* salvation.[55] Luke's emphatic threefold inclusion of Gentiles in v. 24, and especially the final proleptic reminder, "until the times of the Gentiles are fulfilled," assures readers that the fall of Jerusalem is not a miscarriage of the divine purpose, but a fulfillment of the divine purpose for the salvation of Gentiles. The fall of Jerusalem necessitates the extension of the promise to Israel to the nations. "God's salvation has been sent to the Gentiles, and they will listen" (Acts 28:28).

ATTENTIVENESS IN FAITH UNTIL THE SUDDEN COMING OF THE SON OF MAN (21:25-36)

The misuse of eschatology — not least in contemporary America — has resulted in skepticism of eschatology among many Christians. Misuse of a doctrine usually results in its neglect, and neglect of a theological doctrine weakens the church. Without eschatology, the purpose and destiny of history fall into the hands of humanity alone. No one, I think, takes solace in that prospect. Unless history can be redeemed, the fallen greatness of human life is the final and tragic word. The longing that things *ought not be* as they are, and *cannot be accepted* in the state they are, is an eschatological longing. The Gospels proclaim that there is a sure hope for the future. This hope is grounded

---

54. The same paradox in v. 24 is noted by Plummer, *Luke*, 483; Green, *Luke*, 739; Bovon, *Lukas 19,28–24,53*, 185. So too Origen, *Cels.* 1.27.

55. J. Beker, *Paul the Apostle: The Triumph of God in Life and Thought* (Philadelphia: Fortress Press, 1980), 334-35.

not in history, logic, or intuition, but in Jesus' declaration that in the final day the Son of Man will return in glory and power to judge evil, end suffering, and gather his own to himself.

25-28 With the exception of v. 27, the material in vv. 25-28 is unique to Luke. Vv. 25-28 return to the properly eschatological theme of vv. 10-11, which was earlier broached in 17:22-37. This final stage of Jesus' prophecy is lacking in specific time references or timetables.[56] The coming of the Son of Man will be attended by "signs in the sun, moon and stars" (v. 25), but *what* signs are not announced. On earth, nations will be "in anguish and perplexity at the roaring and tossing of the sea" (v. 25). These natural phenomena are more definite, but not more precise, for natural disasters have perplexed nations since time immemorial. Vv. 25-26 repeat OT prophetic language and imagery associated with "the Day of the Lord."[57] These violent changes, both natural and cosmic, will come upon humanity like a blow to the solar plexus. They will produce such anxiety and dread that people will faint, or die from "lack of breath" (v. 26; Gk. *apopsychein*). Terror and death will come not from the cataclysmic events themselves, but from mere *dread* of them. The upheavals will not be limited to local occurrences, nor will they affect believers alone. They will be universal, befalling "the whole inhabited world" (v. 26; Gk. *oikoumenē*). The reference to the whole inhabited world, which is added by Luke, separates this event from what befalls Jerusalem, signifying that the judgment of the world is distinct from the judgment of Jerusalem.[58] The structure of vv. 25-26 forms a chiastic A-B-B-A pattern — heaven-earth-earth-heaven. In both structure and content, vv. 25-26 convey the universal and cosmic reach of the end phenomena.

"At that time they will see the Son of Man coming in a cloud with power and great glory" (v. 27).[59] "They" suggests a future, rather than the present, generation. V. 27 is the only saying in vv. 25-28 that Luke takes over virtually unaltered from Mark (13:26; followed by Matt 24:30). V. 27 derives from the vision of Dan 7:13, in which the Son of Man comes on clouds of power and glory to establish an everlasting kingdom.[60] Luke's only alteration is to render

---

56. Johnson, *Luke*, 330.

57. Isa 13:10; 24:19; 28:2; 29:6; 30:30; Ezek 38:22; Ps 46:3; Dan 8:10.

58. Fitzmyer, *Luke (X–XXIV)*, 1349-50.

59. Modern scholars (e.g., Bock, *Luke 9:51–24:53*, 1684-85) often interpret Son of Man in Dan 7:13 as a collective of Israel. The material gathered in Str-B 1:956 argues against this conclusion: "Dan 7:13f is never understood in early Judaism as a collective expression for 'the people of the Holy One' (= Dan 7:27), but always as the individual Messiah."

60. The Lukan wording of v. 27 agrees nearly verbatim with the wording of Mark 13:26 and Matt 24:30. The wording of the Synoptics, however, does not correspond to the Greek syntax of Dan 7:13 (in either the 𝔊 or θ versions), or with the syntax of the Aramaic of Dan 7:13. Does the close agreement of the Synoptic wording in contrast to the Greek and Aramaic of Dan 7:13 argue for a different version of Daniel used by the Synoptics?

"clouds" (so Synoptics and Dan [Ⴁ, θ, and MT]) in the singular. This slight alteration is significant, for it changes "clouds" from the means by which the Son of Man comes, to a representation of God himself. In Exod 40:34, and many times elsewhere, "cloud" signifies God-present-with-humanity; Luke reappropriates this image and its meaning in the transfiguration (9:34, 35) and ascension (Acts 1:9). Thus, the Son of Man does not come *on* clouds, but *in the form of a cloud*. Son of Man and the cloud are thereby effectively made synonymous: the "power and great glory" of the Son of Man are the "power and great glory" of God.

V. 28, also a Lukan addition, calls for a surprising response to the ca-lamitous natural and supernatural phenomena attending the End. In contrast to the fear and dread of vv. 25-26, believers are to "stand up and lift up your heads" when the Son of Man comes, "because your redemption is drawing near." "Drawing near" (Gk. *engizein*) is used throughout Luke (10:9, 11; 21:8, 20, 28, 31), and also in intertestamental literature (*1 En.* 51:2; *2 Bar.* 23:7),[61] with reference to the dawning of the kingdom of God. The reference to "stand up" (Gk. *anakyptein*) is uniquely Lukan.[62] Elsewhere, Luke uses the word only with reference to Jesus restoring the woman bent double to erect posture (13:11). At the return of Christ, believers are to behave as the woman healed by Christ: they are to heave off the weight of sin and oppression, stand erect, and receive Christ as their heavenly liberator. "Lift up your heads" is a Hebraism that enjoins believers to optimism and hope.[63] They are to stand erect and lift up their heads because the second coming is not an hour of judgment, but the dawn of final redemption. "Redemption" (Gk. *apolytrōsis*) is a Pauline word that occurs only here in the four Gospels.[64] The promises of redemption fore-seen by Zechariah (1:68) and Anna (2:38; Gk. *lytrōsis* in both instances) in the infancy narrative find their eternal fulfillment in the return of the Son of Man in glory. "All longings for eternal salvation are summed up in this word," says Büchsel.[65] Such saving liberation is not something to fear, but something to welcome with rejoicing.

29-33   The parable of the Fig Tree and the warnings of vv. 29-33 return hearers/readers to the time period prior to the fall of Jerusalem that broke off at v. 24. This is apparent from the warnings of the nearness of the end ("know that the summer is near," v. 30; "the kingdom of God is near," v. 31), which would

---

61. Str-B 2:256.

62. Codex D inserts v. 28 verbatim at the end of Matt 24:31, though *anakyptein* ("stand up") is changed to *anablepein,* perhaps because the latter word was more common.

63. Luke's Greek phrase, *eparate tas kephalas,* is a faithful rendering of Heb. *nāsā' rō'sh* (Judg 8:28; Ps 24:7; 83:3[2]; Job 10:15), but it does not repeat the LXX *airein kephalēn,* and is therefore not a Septuagintism.

64. In Paul, Rom 3:24; 8:23; 1 Cor 1:30; Eph 1:7, 14; 4:30; Col 1:14; elsewhere Heb 9:15; 11:35.

65. *TWNT* 4:354.

be superfluous once the Son of Man arrives. The lesson of the fig tree repeats the essence of Mark 13:28-31, but Luke expands it by adding that the lesson taught by the fig is taught by *"all* the trees" (v. 29). The fig tree loses its leaves in winter, and only late in spring, when winter is past and warm weather is at hand, does its branch grow tender with buds. When buds and leaves appear, no further authorities need be consulted. "You can see for yourselves and know that summer is near" (v. 30). In v. 30, the leaves do not signify that summer is about to come, but is *already* here. Similarly, the events of vv. 7-9 and 12-24 point to the irrevocable nearness of the fall of Jerusalem.

"Even so . . . you" (Gk. *houtōs kai hymeis;* "So also you yourselves") at the beginning of v. 31 is an emphatic exhortation of the present generation. Similar summary exhortations are addressed to present hearers/readers throughout Luke (12:21; 14:11, 33; 15:7, 10; 17:10). The opening admonition of v. 31 thus addresses the generation contemporary with Jesus. This conclusion is further confirmed by the immediate reference to *"these things,"* which throughout Luke's eschatological discourse (vv. 6, 7 [2x], 9, 31, 36) follows its similar usage in Mark's eschatological discourse in referring to the things that will transpire in the fall of Jerusalem and not in the final *eschaton.*[66] "When you see these things happening, you know that the kingdom of God is near" (v. 31). The placement of "these things" in direct relationship to the kingdom of God in v. 31 is critical for Luke's eschatology. Since the announcement of Jesus' "exodus" in 9:31 and "setting his face toward Jerusalem" (9:51), Luke has reminded readers that "the kingdom of God is near" (10:9, 11; 11:20; 17:20; 19:11). Luke clearly stresses the significance of Jerusalem for the fulfillment of the kingdom of God. Jerusalem is where Jesus must die and be "taken up" (9:51), thus inaugurating the kingdom of God. But Jerusalem is equally significant with regard to the final fulfillment of the kingdom, for its destruction is a sober admonition for hearers and readers of the nearness of the final *eschaton.* Like birth contractions, the fall of Jerusalem is a sign of the End. Also like contractions, the fall of Jerusalem signifies *that* the End is near, but not precisely *when* it will appear. Jerusalem is a "climax point" for both (1) the inauguration of the kingdom of God in the death, resurrection, and ascension of Jesus and (2) the consummation of the kingdom in the final coming of the Son of Man.[67]

"Truly I tell you, this generation will not pass away until all these things have happened" (v. 32). Despite the exegetical controversy associated with this verse,[68] "this generation" cannot well mean any generation other than the generation hearing Jesus, and Luke's first readers. As noted above, Luke uses "these things" with reference to the fall of Jerusalem. There is some doubt whether

---

66. On the function of "these things" in Mark 13, see Edwards, *Mark,* 385.

67. "Climax point" is the description of Nolland, *Luke 18:35–24:53,* 1010.

68. For a survey of interpretative options, see Bock, *Luke 9:51–24:53,* 1689-91.

"these things" recurs in v. 32, for the Greek manuscript tradition favors "all things" rather than "all *these* things."[69] Nevertheless, the placement of the logion in the context of vv. 29-33, along with its apparent reference to "these things" in the previous verse, favors the understanding that this generation will not pass away until Jerusalem is destroyed.[70] If Jesus pronounced these words in the early thirties, then the generation to which he spoke would still have been alive when the Romans invaded Palestine and destroyed Jerusalem in 66-70.

Beyond the cataclysm, however, stands Jesus himself. "Heaven and earth will pass away, but my words will never pass away" (v. 33). For Jesus to assert that his words will outlive heaven and earth is a remarkable claim of authority. The only being who could reasonably make such a claim is God (Isa 51:6). If Jesus' words will outlive the cosmos, then in ways that we who are bound to the treadmill of time cannot understand, his words encompass past, present, and future. Hence, Jesus can speak of the "nearness" of the kingdom in his Galilean ministry (10:9, 11; 11:20; 17:21), and also of its final eschatological "nearness" (21:8, 20, 28, 31). In God's saving plan, the first advent of God's Son in the incarnation, crucifixion, resurrection, and ascension represents *one* saving event in combination with the second coming of God's Son in the Parousia. Cranfield captures their unity thus: "It was, and still is, true to say that the Parousia is at hand. . . . Ever since the Incarnation men have been living in the last days."[71]

34-36 Jesus concludes the eschatological discourse in vv. 34-36. He gives no further instruction regarding how and when the Son of Man will return; and of subjects associated in the modern mind with the second coming — millennium, rebuilding of the temple, battle of Armageddon, Zionism, restoration of Israel, or the State of Israel — there is no hint. Jesus delivers but two concluding exhortations, neither of which directs attention to the future. Rather, both focus attention to the present, indeed to *ourselves*. The End cannot be prepared for by anticipating and forecasting, but by watchfulness and faithfulness in the present. "Give heed to yourselves" (v. 34; NIV "Be careful") is a Mosaic warning not to transgress Mount Sinai on pain of death (Exod 19:12), not to forget the covenant (Deut 4:23), not to commit apostasy by worshiping other gods (Deut 11:16).[72]

---

69. "All things" is attested by the majority tradition, whereas "all these things" appears in D (5th cent.), Ψ (9/10th cent.), f^{13}, three minuscules, and the Syriac version.

70. So Plummer, *Luke,* 485; Fitzmyer, *Luke (X–XXIV),* 1353.

71. C. Cranfield, *The Gospel according to St Mark* (CGTC; Cambridge: University Press 1985), 408. On the oneness of all aspects of the Christ-event in the divine economy, see same author, "St. Mark 13," *SJT* 7 (1954): 288; and esp. K. Barth, *Church Dogmatics: The Doctrine of Creation* 3/2:485-511.

72. "Give heed to yourselves" (Gk. *prosechete heautois*) is a faithful rendering of Heb. *hishāmru lākem* in Exod 19:12; Deut 4:23; 11:16. The same Hebrew phrase appears in Delitzsch's Hebrew NT at v. 34. It is a Hebraism, not a Septuagintism, which translates Deut. 4:23 with *prosechete hymeis*.

Coming from the mouth of Moses, Israel's preeminent leader, this admonition is a warning of utmost gravity.

In the introduction to Jesus' closing statement on eschatology (v. 34), it carries equal gravity. Jesus warns against lives "weighed down with dissipation, drunkenness and the anxieties of life" (v. 34). Two conditions are the objects of this final warning. The first is a life of "unbridled indulgence" (Gk. *kraipalē;* NIV "dissipation"), typified and expressed in extravagant carousing and drunkenness. The vice of drunkenness and profligacy was widely condemned by the prophets ("Woe to those who are heroes at drinking," Isa 5:22), and by both Jewish and pagan moralists. Luke's description of such as "weighed down" may include not only drunkenness itself but the hangovers that follow.[73] Contrasted to dissipation is a second warning about "anxieties of daily life," which is less obviously harmful. Routine cares, after all, are a normal part of life. Precisely because they are routine, they are, like the similar claims of property, work, and family (see at 9:57-62; 14:12:24), the more dangerous, because routine things are easily justifiable, and they are done without thought. Luke repeatedly warns against allowing the persistent and obligatory cares of life to eclipse the *one* thing of unsurpassable importance — following Jesus (8:14: 12:13-34; 17:26-30).

Debauchery and daily anxieties, though vastly different, impress one's existence with a similar effect: they "weigh down one's heart" (v. 34). Jesus commenced his final exhortation in vv. 34-36 by recalling the words of Moses; his reference to the weighed-down heart may also recall Moses, for "weighed down" (Gk. *barein;* Heb. *kabed*) describes the heart of Pharaoh (Exod 7:14; 8:15, 32; 9:7, 34). The weighed-down heart is burdened and unresponsive, numb to signs of the times, to the day that "will close on you suddenly like a trap" (v. 34).[74] "That day" is a typical prophetic reference to the final *eschaton* (Jer 3:16, 18; 31:29; 33:15; Joel 3:1). The emphasis on the *suddenness* of the day is unique in Luke; indeed, the Greek word for "suddenness" *(aiphnidios)* occurs only five times in the Greek Bible. The prophets too warned of the element of surprise. Amos graphically describes the suddenness and unexpectedness of "that day": "It will be as though a man fled from a lion, only to meet a bear" (Amos 5:19). The suddenness, says Luke, will spring "like a trap that will come on all those who live on the face of the whole earth" (v. 35). The image of a trap or snare is a picturesque figure of speech common to the OT. V. 35 is a summary of the image in Isa 24:17, "Terror and pit and snare will await you,

---

73. On *kraipalē,* see BDAG, 564; Plummer, *Luke,* 486.

74. For St. Diadochos of Photiki (fifth c.), the burdened heart erases the memory of God: "When the soul is disturbed by anger, confused by drunkenness, or sunk in deep depression, the intellect cannot hold fast to the remembrance of God no matter how hard we try to force it" ("On Spiritual Knowledge," *Philokalia,* 1:271).

people of the earth."[75] This final warning is not reserved for only Jesus' hearers or Jerusalem, but is emphatically universal, "for *all* those who live on the face of the *whole* earth" (v. 35).

The second and final admonition is to "Watch, praying at all times" (v. 36). The admonition is not to know the future, but to be vigilant and perseverant in the present. One watches by praying — intelligently, diligently, at all times (Rom 12:12; Eph 6:18; 1 Thess 1:2; 2:13; 5:17; 1 Pet 4:7). The End does not simply come "by and by," "whenever and whatever." The End is already here in the present existence of believers.[76] It is already present because the earthly Jesus who inaugurates the kingdom of God and who calls believers in obedient discipleship is the same Jesus whose return at the end of time as Son of Man in power and glory completes the kingdom of God. Preparedness for *then* depends on watchfulness *now*. Watchfulness provides the ability to "escape" the upheavals that can be escaped. The accent falls not on cowardly flight, but on fleeing from all harms that would distract us "from the hope set before us" (Heb 6:18). Above all, watchfulness causes us "to stand before the Son of Man" (v. 36). The reference to "stand" should be understood positively. It refers not to standing before a judgment seat, but "standing up and lifting up your heads" (v. 28) in confidence, "because your redemption is drawing near" (v. 28). It is now — finally and forever — present in the glorious and triumphant Son of Man.

---

75. The triple alliteration and rhyme of Isa 24:17 in Hebrew (*pachad* [dread] *wāpachath* [trap] *wāpāh* [net]) is impossible to capture in either Greek or English.

76. Schweizer, *Lukas,* 215; Bovon, *Lukas 19,28–24,53,* 209: "The future rules the present: it brings an end to the present order of things."

CHAPTER TWENTY

Last Supper and Arrest

Luke 21:37–22:71

Beginning in 21:37 and continuing through 24:8, Luke follows the climactic events of Jesus' passion that are common to the canonical Gospels, including the betrayal by Judas, preparation for and celebration of the Last Supper, arrest and trial of Jesus before the Sanhedrin and Pilate, denial of Peter, Jesus' crucifixion and burial, and resurrection. In all four Gospels these events bear greater resemblance in both sequence and wording than do any other events or teachings of Jesus' ministry. This unusual similarity extends even to the division of the material in the earliest manuscripts of the Gospels,[1] suggesting the particular interest of the early church in shaping the Passion Narrative for catechetical purposes and missionary proclamation (1 Cor 15:3-4). All four Evangelists supplement the anchor events of the Passion with material distinctive of each, and the supplements assume greater significance in light of the overall harmony of the Passion Narratives. Luke's major supplements to the Markan exemplar are a four-part discourse following the Last Supper (22:21-23, 24-30, 31-34, 35-38) and Jesus' appearance before Herod Antipas (23:6-12) as well as Pilate (23:13-16). The foremost thematic distinctive of Luke's Passion Narrative is the presentation of Jesus as the suffering righteous man, familiar to the Pss and Isa 40–66, who willingly embraces the divine plan, even in crucifixion. From the opening scene and throughout chap. 22, Luke announces that Jesus will be "betrayed" (vv. 4, 6, 21, 22, 48), the same catchword used throughout the Third Gospel of the fulfillment of Jesus' messianic purpose through rejection, suffering, death, and resurrection (9:44; [17:25]; 18:32; 20:20; 21:12, 16; 24:7, 20). The willingness of Jesus to face martyrdom (22:39-46) stands in distinct contrast to the weakness, incomprehension, rivalry, and even treachery of his disciples. Worse than the failings of Jesus' disciples is the antagonism and enmity of the Jewish leaders, and finally Satan himself, for both the leaders and Satan plot to kill Jesus. Jesus' suffering and death do not represent the fate of a

---

1. J. Edwards, "The Hermeneutical Significance of Chapter Divisions in Ancient Gospel Manuscripts," *NTS* 56/4 (2010): 422-26.

tragic hero, however. Jesus is innocent and wholly free from guilt, and because of this he dies as no other human being can die, as the obedient Son of God, who embraces "his exodus in Jerusalem" (9:31) in certainty and trust that, by his suffering as God's righteous Messiah, he becomes the rightful heir of the "throne of David" (1:32) and consummates God's "glory" in the resurrection (24:26).[2]

PREPARATION FOR PASSOVER (21:37–22:13)

Luke prepares readers for the Passover, as he prepared them for Jesus' approach to Jerusalem, with mounting suspense. The approach to Jerusalem is narrated with increasing specification of place,[3] while Passover is introduced with increasing specification of time: the approach of Passover (v. 1), the day of Passover (v. 7), the hour of Passover (v. 14).

21:37–22:2 "Each day Jesus was teaching at the temple" (v. 37). As noted in the introduction to the Passion Narrative (see at 19:45), the summary descriptions of Jesus' activity in Jerusalem make no reference to the days of "Holy Week"[4] and may imply a longer sojourn than merely seven days. The hallmark of Jesus' final ministry in Jerusalem was daily teaching in the temple. Luke emphasizes the importance of "daily" (Gk. *kath' hēmeran*) disciplines in the lives of believers with regard to discipleship (9:23), prayer (11:3), and spiritual practices (Acts 2:46; 17:11). Jesus' teaching in the temple is a further example of this emphasis (19:47; 21:37; 22:53). His arrest and trial are not the result of a provocative act on his part, but of a plot of his opponents who interrupt his discipline of teaching in the temple. The repeated references to "how" (vv. 2, 4; Gk. *pōs*) they might seize Jesus attests to the resolution of the plotters. The other Synoptics report that Jesus and his disciples spent nights in Bethany, some two miles (3 km) east of Jerusalem on the far side of the Mount of Olives (Matt 21:17; 26:6; Mark 11:1, 11, 12; 14:3). Luke omits Bethany in favor of "spending the night on the Mount of Olives" (v. 37; on Mount of Olives, see at 19:29). The Greek verb *aulizesthai* suggests an open-air encampment, perhaps a "bivouac,"[5] in the Kidron Valley or on

2. On Luke's Passion Narrative, see Marshall, *Luke* 785–86; Fitzmyer, *Luke (X–XXIV)*, 1359–68; Wolter, *Lukasevangelium*, 686–88.

3. Luke reminds readers first of Jesus' approach to Jericho (18:35), then to Bethphage and Bethany (19:29), to the descent from the Mount of Olives (19:37), and finally to Jerusalem (19:41).

4. By contrast, note Mark's demarcation of days: 10:46–11:11, Sunday; 11:12–11:19, Monday; 11:20–?, Tuesday.

5. LSJ, 276; BDAG, 150.

the ascent of the Mount of Olives, although the term can also refer to temporary lodgings in a town (Matt 21:17; *Did.* 11:6; Ps 30:6 [LXX]). The term could thus include Bethany in v. 37, and may have.[6] The Mount of Olives, however, places Jesus within the bounds of Jerusalem, with which Luke specifically identifies Jesus' passion. The physical boundaries of Jerusalem were delimited by its walls, but its religious boundaries extended to the Mount of Olives in order to accommodate the throngs of festival pilgrims (*m. Menaḥ.* 11:2). Luke's frequent references to the Mount of Olives in the Passion Narrative (19:29, 37; 21:37; 22:39) keep Jesus within the Holy City, "for no prophet can die outside Jerusalem!" (13:33). From the Mount of Olives, Jesus commutes daily into Jerusalem, as do "all the people [who] came early in the morning to hear him at the temple" (v. 38).[7]

Matt 26:2 and Mark 14:1 both commence the Last Supper narrative "two days" prior to Passover. Luke maintains his temporal ambiguity regarding Holy Week, reporting only that "Passover was approaching" (22:1). The phrase "Festival of Unleavened Bread" appears to be a Hebraism, for it occurs frequently in the OT (Heb. *hag hammatsoth;* Exod 23:15; 34:18; Deut 16:16, 2 Chron 8:13, etc.), but nowhere else in the NT.[8] **"The Festival of Unleavened Bread called Passover,"** one of the great pilgrimage festivals for which Jews gathered annually in Jerusalem, is associated with the exodus from Egypt (Exod 12). A year-old unblemished male lamb or goat (Exod 12:5) was ritually sacrificed in the temple on the afternoon of 14 Nisan (March/April) and eaten after sunset (i.e., on 15 Nisan) in family gatherings in private houses (Exod 12:6-20; Num 9:2-14; Deut 16:1-8). The Passover commenced the week-long Feast of Unleavened Bread (Exod 12:15-20; 23:15; 34:18; Deut 16:1-8), commemorating the hasty departure of the Israelites from Egypt when there was no time to allow dough to rise. The Feast of Unleavened Bread required Israelites to rid their homes of all foods, including yeast. Because of its connection with the Feast of Unleavened Bread, the Passover can refer either to the sacrifice of the lamb and

---

6. E.g., Mark 11:1 associates Bethany and Bethphage with the Mount of Olives. It is scarcely imaginable that Luke, as conjectured by J. Jeremias (*Jerusalem in the Time of Jesus,* 61), places Jesus on the Mount of Olives because "he is ignorant of local geography."

7. Eight Greek manuscripts belonging to family f^{13} include the story of the adulteress (John 7:53–8:11) following Luke 21:38. On the origin and location of this pericope in the Gospels, see Metzger, *TCGNT,* 187-89; R. Brown, *The Gospel according to John* (AB; Garden City: Doubleday, 1966), 332-38. Elements in the *pericope adulterae* that are either characteristic of Luke ("all the people" [see at 6:17], frequency of aorist participles) or unique to Luke ("early" [Gk. *orthros;* 24:1; Acts 5:21], "stand up" [Gk. *anakyptein;* 13:11; 21:28]) could argue for a Lukan provenance of the pericope. If it is of Lukan provenance, its native home can scarcely be 21:38, for Pharisees (mentioned in John 8:3) are expressly omitted from Luke's Passion Narrative. A placement of the pericope following Luke 19:48 would be more plausible.

8. Plummer, *Luke,* 490.

the meal on Nisan 14-15 or to the entire seven-day observance.[9] Luke mentions both events in 22:1, but focuses specifically on the Passover.[10]

The other Synoptics could leave the impression that the plot of the chief priests and scribes did not occur until two days before Passover (Matt 26:2-3; Mark 14:2). Luke gives the impression that the betrayal plot incubated throughout the approach of Passover. The conspirators are specifically identified as "the chief priests and teachers of the law" (v. 2; also 19:47; 20:19), thus designating them leaders of the Sanhedrin (see at 9:22). V. 2 should not be interpreted as a blanket incrimination of "the Jews," or even of the most celebrated Jewish opponents of Jesus, the Pharisees.[11] The plot of "the chief priests and teachers of the law" was an official resolve rather than popular initiative, emanating from the top echelon of the temple leadership. In contrast to Matt 26:4 and Mark 14:1, which report that the Sanhedrin wished "to kill" Jesus, Luke's wording "to get rid of" (v. 2; Gk. *anairein*) is somewhat euphemistic, not uncommon of the way authorities cloak brutalities. Mention of Jesus' death in v. 2 already associates it with the Feast of Unleavened Bread, hinting that he will be the Passover sacrifice. Reference to the *necessity* of the sacrifice (v. 7; Gk. *dei;* NIV "the Passover lamb had to be sacrificed") may reinforce the implication of Jesus as the Passover sacrifice, for throughout Luke-Acts *dei* reminds readers that Jesus must die in accord with his predetermined messianic purpose.[12]

The Sanhedrin has opposed Jesus since the triumphal entry, and its opposition is frequently understood to include the Jewish audience daily attending Jesus in the temple. V. 2 refutes this latter assumption, for Luke reports that the Sanhedrin was "afraid of the people." Indeed, the imperfect tense of the verb in Greek implies a *standing* fear. The enormous influx of Passover pilgrims to Jerusalem prompted massive security precautions on the part of the Roman occupation. The fear of Jesus' popularity with such pilgrims was a factor about which the Sanhedrin could not afford to be indifferent. Hence, it "looked for some way to get rid of Jesus" without arousing the crowds loyal to Jesus.

3-6 In order to arrest Jesus by stealth (v. 6), the Sanhedrin gains a foothold in his inner circle through Judas.[13] This is the first of three references in

---

9. Str-B 2:813-15; 4/1:41-76; H. Patsch, *pascha, EDNT* 3:50-51; J. Rylaarsdam, "Passover," *IDB* 3:663-68.

10. The two festivals are combined in 2 Chr 35:17 and in Josephus, *J.W.* 2.10; *Ant.* 3.249; 10.70; 14.21; 18.29.

11. Pharisees are last mentioned in 19:39 and thus play no role in Luke's Passion Narrative (see at 5:17).

12. See J. Green, "Preparation for Passover (Luke 22:7-13): A Question of Redactional Technique," in Orton, *Composition of Luke's Gospel,* 161.

13. For two important and thorough discussions of Judas, see K. Barth, *Church Dogmatics,* 2/2:458-506, and R. Brown, *Death of the Messiah,* 2:1394-1418.

chap. 22 to Judas, who is mentioned nowhere else in the Third Gospel except in the list of the Twelve in 6:16. Each reference depicts Judas in a position of intimacy with Jesus. In v. 3 he is identified as "one of the Twelve," thus one of Jesus' elect and trusted adherents. In v. 21 the hand of Judas is next to the hand of Jesus at the Passover table, which commemorated the most intimate religious and social rite in Judaism. In vv. 47-48 Judas betrays Jesus to armed authorities with the sign of a kiss. This triangle of intrigue signifies that treachery, even the presence of Satan himself, are not necessarily relegated to distant and alien spheres, but may stand in close proximity to Jesus himself. With regard to v. 3, some scholars suggest that "of the number [Gk. *arithmos*] of the Twelve" (v. 3; NIV "one of the Twelve") implies that Judas, although technically a member of the Twelve, was not *of* them. The implication of this interpretation is to dissociate Judas from Jesus.[14] The two further references to Judas in chap. 22 in even more intimate postures do not argue in favor of this suggestion,[15] but rather strongly against it: Luke is emphasizing the very nearness of Judas to Jesus, and thus the greater danger of his betrayal.

Majority Christian tradition has associated the name of Judas with infamy.[16] Although the betrayal of Judas is unequivocally condemned in the NT, his story is told with "remarkable calm . . . without throwing stones at Judas."[17] The only major addition to the otherwise sparse betrayal narrative comes from the report of Luke (v. 3) and John (13:2, 27) that Satan "entered" Judas. The reappearance of Satan is no surprise in the Third Gospel, for Luke concluded the wilderness temptation with the note that "the devil left [Jesus] until an opportune time" (4:13). That time arrives in the preparation

14. Marshall, *Luke*, 788; Klein, *Lukasevangelium*, 658. Schlatter, *Lukas*, 135, regards "of the number" a Hebraism, as in *Sipre Deut.* 318, *hāyāh min hamminyāh*.

15. So Wolter, *Lukasevangelium*, 693.

16. In Dante's hierarchy of sin, Judas's treachery lands him in the deepest pit of hell, along with Brutus and Cassius (*Divine Comedy, Inferno*, canto 34). The name of Judas is condemned throughout the patristic period as a warning against apostasy. The tide of rejection of Judas may have been less severe in gnostic sects, but attempts to argue on the basis of ambiguous and often fragmentary texts that Judas was a friend of Jesus (e.g., W. Klassen, *Judas: Betrayer or Friend of Jesus?* [Minneapolis: Fortress Press, 1996]) are unsuccessful. The recent recovery of *The Gospel of Judas* (ed. R. Kasser, M. Meyer, and G. Wurst; Washington, D.C.: National Geographic Society, 2006) is no more successful in rehabilitating Judas. The key (though fragmentary) line originally translated "You [Judas] will exceed all of them. For you will sacrifice the man that clothes me" has been exposed as a mistranslation; it should read, "You will do worse than all of them . . ." (see P. Head, "The Gospel of Judas and the Qarara Codices," *TynBul* 58/1 [2007]: 1-24; A. DeConick, *The Thirteenth Apostle: What the Gospel of Judas Really Says* [London: T&T Clark, 2007]; B. Pearson, "Judas Iscariot among the Gnostics: What the Gospel of Judas *Really* Says," *BAR* 34/3 [2008]: 52-57; C. Evans, "Understanding the Gospel of Judas," *BBR* 20/4 [2010]: 561-74).

17. K. Barth, *Church Dogmatics*, 2/2:459-60.

for Passover, when "[Judas] watched for an opportunity to hand Jesus over to them" (v. 6).[18] Moreover, the betrayer — as Jesus predicted in 21:16 — is a "friend," Judas.[19] The other Synoptics mention Satan sporadically, always as a personification of evil. Luke retains this understanding (8:12; 10:18; 11:18) but adds several instances of Satan seeking to establish a claim on believers — on "a daughter of Abraham," 13:16, and especially on Jesus' disciples, including Judas (v. 3), Peter (22:31), and Ananias and Sapphira (Acts 5:3). Satan thus "targets" some individuals, especially those close to Jesus or the Christian mission, for uniquely diabolical purposes. These initiatives should not be understood as irresistible, for none of those targeted is absolved of guilt. Judas is not "possessed" by Satan in the sense that he cannot do otherwise, nor does Satan *cause* Judas, Peter, or Ananias and Sapphira to sin.[20] Each individual remains responsible for his or her moral failure.[21] Judas fails to do the one thing commanded of disciples at the conclusion of the eschatological discourse: "Watch!" (21:36).

"Judas went to the chief priests and officers of the temple guard and discussed with them how he might betray Jesus" (v. 4). Judas's personal responsibility is made explicit by the fact that *he* initiated the betrayal plot. The Greek word for "agreed" (v. 5; *syntithenai*) also implies mutual agreement, not unilateral coercion from one party.[22] Reference to the "temple guard" (Gk. *stratēgos*) is preserved only in Luke-Acts, in all five instances in conjunction with chief priests (22:4, 52; Acts 4:1; 5:24, 26). The *stratēgos* is mentioned by Josephus (*J.W.* 6.294; *Ant.* 20.131) and the Mishnah[23] as "the captain [Heb. *sagan*] of the priests." The extent of this officer's duties, and of those in his charge, is not fully known, but two duties are clear from the above sources. First, the "temple guard" stood second to the chief priest in rank and attended the chief priest when he read Scripture or offered sacrifices. Second, he was also captain of the police force in charge of temple

---

18. The Greek word for "opportunity" (v. 6; *eukairia*) is a compound form of the word for "opportune time" (cf. 4:13, where *achri kairou* carries similar meaning).

19. Green, *Luke,* 753.

20. Plummer, *Luke,* 490: "There is no hint that Judas is . . . unable to control his own actions. Judas opened the door to Satan. He did not resist him, and Satan did not flee him. Jesus must suffer, but Judas need not become the traitor." Likewise, Lagrange, *Luc,* 539, "Judas accepts (only in Luke) the consequences of his free choice and guilt."

21. According to *Herm. Mand.* 12.5.1-2, the angel of repentance assures believers, "I am with you who repent with all your heart, and I strengthen you in faith. Believe in God, though you have renounced your life through your sins, and have added to your sins, and have made our life heavy. 'Turn to the Lord with all your heart, and do righteousness' for the rest of the days of your life, and serve him in uprightness, according to his will, and he will heal your former sins, and you shall have power to master the works of the devil."

22. BDAG, 975.

23. *M. Yoma* 1:1; 2:1; 3:1, 9; 4:1; 7:1; *Soṭah* 7:7-9; *Tamid* 7:3.

security.[24] The chief priests and the temple guard are "delighted" with Judas's initiative. Their joy is one of the bitter ironies in the Gospels. No Hamlet-like lament comes forth from Judas, only his premeditated resolve to "watch for an opportunity to hand Jesus over to them when no crowd was present" (v. 6). Judas is free to choose evil, but he cannot determine the consequences of the evil he chooses. We do not know what Judas hoped to accomplish in the betrayal of Jesus, but we do know how the sovereignty of God used his betrayal: "The Messiah will suffer and rise from the dead on the third day, and repentance for the forgiveness of sins will be preached in his name to all nations, beginning in Jerusalem" (24:46-47).

The Gospels do not explore Judas's motives in betraying Jesus. A popular modern hypothesis is that Judas was a political activist, perhaps a Zealot, who did not intend to betray Jesus but only awaken him from his messianic lethargy and force his hand to drive out the Roman oppressor.[25] We cannot judge this or any putative motive with certainty. The one constant in the Synoptic accounts is that an exchange of money was involved (v. 5; Matt 26:15; Mark 14:11), which may be relevant in light of John's note that Judas was treasurer of the Twelve, and a thief (John 12:6; 13:29). That money — mammon (12:15; 16:13-15) — played a role in Judas's decision seems inescapable. The best way to detect the source of evil in practically any matter is to ask who profits from it financially. Judas profited from the betrayal of Jesus. Other priorities in Judas's life were more important than Jesus, for some of which he was willing to sell Jesus. The role of money in Judas's betrayal may have caused the early church to declare, "The love of money is the root of all evil" (1 Tim 6:10).

Satan entered Judas (v. 3), and Judas left Jesus (v. 4). A more disastrous exchange cannot be imagined. A member of Jesus' inner circle chooses outer darkness (22:53). Jesus has been sent to free "those living in darkness and in the shadow of death" (1:79), but he must now be overshadowed by that darkness (23:44) if he is to free those engulfed by it, and even those who serve it.[26] Other disciples will also fail Jesus by denial (22:56-60) and abandonment (Matt 26:56; Mark 14:50). The premeditated betrayal of Judas is more reprehensible, but even this sin must be submitted to Jesus' final prayer

24. Str-B 2:628-31; Jeremias, *Jerusalem in the Time of Jesus*, 160-63; Schürer, *History of the Jewish People*, 2:277-79; Wolter, *Lukasevangelium*, 693-94.

25. B. Pixner, *Mit Jesus in Jerusalem*, 82-83. F. Gingrich, "Judas Iscariot," *IDB* 2:1006-8, surveys many possible motives of Judas's betrayal.

26. Grundmann, *Lukas*, 415, writes, "The one who came to free those who sit in darkness . . . came under their power himself through those who served it. Their hour will be ended through his hour, and the power of darkness will be conquered by his victory." (One wonders if Grundmann's words about Judas were informed by his own surrender to the darkness of Nazism.)

from the cross, "Father, forgive them, for they do not know what they are doing" (23:34).[27]

7-13   Passover was technically celebrated from sundown until midnight on 15 Nisan. "Then came the day of Unleavened Bread" (v. 7) is regarded by some commentators as evidence of a Greek reckoning of time from daylight rather than a Jewish reckoning from nightfall. This is possible, but by no means certain from the wording of v. 7. Luke's wording is virtually the same as Mark 14:12 ("the first day of the Festival"); moreover, the reference to "day" seems predicated on the day "on which the Passover lamb had to be sacrificed" (v. 7). This appropriately describes the Jewish custom of slaughtering Passover lambs during the day (and particularly the afternoon) of 14 Nisan. Exod 12:6 stipulated sacrifice of the Passover lamb on the afternoon of 14 Nisan, although rabbinic evidence suggests that Passover lambs were also sacrificed earlier.[28] According to Deut 16:5-8, Passover could be celebrated only within the walls of Jerusalem.[29] This produced a great influx of pilgrims into Jerusalem each spring, causing the population to swell to many times its normal size. Josephus reports that at Passover in 66, the year the temple was completed, 255,600 lambs were slaughtered in the temple. Allowing an average of ten diners per lamb, Josephus calculates that two and one-half million people were present in Jerusalem — not counting pilgrims who for various reasons were unclean and could not partake (*J. W.* 6.420-27). One questions how first-century Jerusalem could accommodate such numbers of people.[30] However this question is resolved, the number of pilgrims would practically require the slaughter of lambs to begin prior to the afternoon of Nisan 14. The mood of expectancy and urgency pervades Jesus' band of followers as well, as signified by the fourfold mention of "preparation" (Gk. *hetoimazein;* vv. 8, 9, 12, 13). The reference to eating "the Passover with *my* disciples" (v. 11) establishes Jesus as the presiding head of the meal and anticipates the words of institution, "This is *my* body" (v. 19).

27. The long and probing discussion of Judas Iscariot by K. Barth, *Church Dogmatics,* 2/2:458-506, advises against an easy dismissal of Judas in Christian thinking.

28. "If a Passover offering was slaughtered on the morning [instead of the afternoon] of the 14th [of Nisan] under some other name, R. Joshua declares it valid, as though it had been slaughtered on the 13th" (*m. Zebaḥ.* 1.3). The ruling of R. Joshua (ben Hananiah), a pre-70 Jerusalem rabbi, indicates that sacrifice during "twilight" (= afternoon, so Exod 12:6) was more important than the date of the sacrifice. See M. Casey, "The Date of the Passover Sacrifices and Mark 14:12," *TynBul* 48 (1997): 245-47, who argues that sacrifice on 13th Nisan was "accepted practice."

29. For religious purposes, however, the "walls" of Jerusalem extended to Bethphage on the Mount of Olives (*m. Menaḥ.* 11:2).

30. Jeremias, *Jerusalem in the Time of Jesus,* 57, describes Passover as an "invasion of the city by multitudes of pilgrims." He adds, "Certainly the figure [of Passover lambs] ran into many thousands," according to Jeremias, but he considers Josephus's figure of 255,600 sacrificial lambs "grossly exaggerated."

Jesus does not *re*act to the intricate web of intrigue woven by his adversaries in vv. 1-6, but *pro*acts by initiating a course of action in accord with his purpose and on behalf of his community (vv. 8-12). Mark 14:13 reports that Jesus sent two disciples to prepare the Passover. Alone of the Gospels, Luke identifies the two as "Peter and John." Peter and John are another example of Luke's penchant for pairs. Whenever Peter's name is followed by one or both of the Zebedee brothers, it is always followed first by John in Luke-Acts (8:51; 9:28; 22:8; Acts 1:13; 3:1, 3, 4, 11; 4:13, 19; 8:14). In Luke-Acts the name of John appears second to James when the two are mentioned apart from Peter (5:10; 9:54; Acts 12:2), but John's name always precedes that of James and appears second to Peter when the Zebedees are mentioned alongside the chief apostle. "Peter and John" may be named together here because, at the time of writing, James had been martyred (Acts 12:2), leaving John the remaining prominent disciple next to Peter. The names of Peter and John prepare readers for the important role both will play in Acts. The treason of Judas may have led Jesus to select his two most trusted apostles.[31]

The two are given stealth instructions: "A man carrying a jar of water will meet you" (v. 10) and show you the house. The reference to a jar of water may locate the meeting in the vicinity of the pool of Siloam on Mount Zion, to which water was diverted by Hezekiah's tunnel from Jerusalem's only water source, the Gihon spring. Carrying water was normally the labor of women or slaves; a male water carrier would therefore catch the eye of the disciples. The reference to the contact individual "meeting" Peter and John implies that the water carrier had been prepared in advance.[32] Did Jesus arrange the meeting? If so, his self-introduction as "the Teacher" (v. 11) implies that the owner of the dwelling was not one of his followers, for in Luke "Teacher" is used of Jesus by outsiders rather than insiders.[33] One thing, however, seems clear: the arrangements are made to ensure an uninterrupted Passover celebration with the Twelve before his arrest (John 11:57).[34] The instructions for preparation of the

---

31. So Plummer, *Luke*, 492.

32. B. Pixner, *Wege des Messias und Stätten der Urkirche* (ed. R. Riesner; Giessen: Brunnen Verlag, 1991), 219-21, reasons that, since carrying water was customarily women's work, and the Essene community did not permit women members, the man carrying water was necessarily an Essene. Pixner further argues that the site of the Last Supper was in the Essene Quarter in the southwest corner of Jerusalem (1) because the disciples (being non-Essenes) could not enter the Essene compound (hence, the instructions to inquire of "the owner of the house" in v. 11); and (2) because the Essenes, who were known for hospitality (Josephus, *J.W.* 2.124), could be expected to have a guest room. Pixner's claim cannot be proven, but his chain of reasoning is plausible, for the traditional site of the Last Supper, which has received considerable archaeological attention, neighbors the reputed Essene Quarter.

33. See chap. 19, n. 13. On "Master," see 5:5.

34. B. Pixner, *Mit Jesus in Jerusalem*, 88, suggests that the secrecy of the instructions

Passover, like those for the entry into Jerusalem (19:29-31), demonstrate Jesus' ability to predict and control the events of Passion Week; and also like those of 19:29-31, they demonstrate that he is not an unknowing victim of events. "Jesus remains supremely in charge even as he goes to his death."[35]

Peter and John are to follow the water carrier and inquire of the owner of the house about "the guest room" for the Passover celebration (vv. 11-12). Jewish residents of Jerusalem were expected to make spare rooms in their houses available to Passover pilgrims. The "guest room" (Gk. *katalyma*) requested by Jesus was evidently such a room. The disciples will be shown a large, furnished, upstairs room for the Passover meal (v. 12). The only other time *katalyma* is mentioned in Luke is with reference to the guest room at Bethlehem (see discussion at 2:7), but the guest room referred to here must certainly exceed in size and appointment its Bethlehem counterpart. In addition to furniture, "furnished" (v. 12; Gk. *strōnnyein*) should be understood to include the "spreading out" of rugs and carpets on which to recline. The banquet room is well-appointed and belonged to a person of means. Mount Zion is the probable location of this meeting room, where a number of upscale dwellings have been excavated.[36] The definite article of "*the* upper room" in Acts 1:13 may allude to the same meeting place.[37] Peter and John follow Jesus' instructions, and as they (or two other disciples) discovered prior to the triumphal entry (19:32), "they found things just as Jesus had told them. So they prepared the Passover" (v. 13).

The narrative of the Passover preparation is laden with irony in which elements of free will commingle with divine providence. A score of words and concepts that will later constitute the load-bearing theological terminology of early Christian kerygma are interwoven in this pericope. Some of them —

---

was intended to prevent Judas, the betrayer, from knowing the site of Passover. According to Pixner, Judas, as treasurer, should have made the arrangements assigned to the two disciples. Pixner's thesis must be regarded as tentative, for the NT does not hint that Jesus tried to deceive Judas. Judas was well informed about Jesus' whereabouts (John 18:2), and the introduction to the Last Supper in Matt 26:21-22 and Mark 14:18-21 implies that Judas must be present, not excluded, at the Passover.

35. Nolland, *Luke 18:35–24:53*, 1016.

36. The Cenacle is identified for modern tourists to Jerusalem as the site of the Last Supper. The present structure, a mosque remodeled from a fourteenth-c. church, obviously dates from a much later period, but the site was attested in the fourth c. by Cyril of Jerusalem and the Pilgrim of Bordeaux, and in the sixth c. by the Madaba Map. According to Epiphanius, the emperor Hadrian identified the same site as the place of the Upper Room in 135. See O. Sellers, "Upper Room," *IDB* 4:735; and B. Pixner, "Church of the Apostles Found on Mt. Zion," *BAR* 16/3 (1990): 16ff.

37. Acts 12:12 refers to a Jerusalem dwelling, also a meeting place of the early church, that belonged to Mary, the mother of John Mark, who was the probable author of the Second Gospel. We do not know, however, whether this is the same or a different meeting place.

"hear" (Gk. *akouein;* 21:38), "send" (*apostellein;* v. 8), "follow" (*akolouthein;* v. 10), "prepare" (*hetoimazein;* vv. 8, 9, 12, 13) — belong to the strong current of Jesus' mission. Others — "called" (*kalein;* v. 3), "confess" (*exomologein;* v. 6), and above all "hand over" (*paradidonai;* vv. 4, 6) — describe a violent countercurrent in collision with Jesus' mission. It is the conviction of the early Christian kerygma — and Luke's employment of its signature vocabulary in this pericope signals his awareness of that conviction — that God works his sovereign and saving plan not only in the current of faith, but also in the countercurrent of evil. Judas "hands over" Jesus to the Sanhedrin, yet God "hands over" Jesus for the salvation of the world (Rom 4:25; 8:32; 1 Cor 11:23; John 3:16). Both of the foregoing uses of "hand over" are translations of the same Greek word, *paradidonai.*

The slain Passover lamb prepares for the confession, "Christ died for us" (Rom 5:8). The powerful proclamation of the kerygma, here attested in Luke's Gospel narrative, cannot be "proven." Life's ultimate convictions can never be weighed and counted, measured and calculated to constitute "proof." Trust, hope, love, and obedience are choices made on the basis, not of proof, but of conviction. The history of God's faithfulness in Israel, consummated in the life of Jesus of Nazareth, is the sure foundation of the kerygmatic conviction that preparation for the Passover sacrifice is ultimately preparation for "the Lamb of God who takes away the sins of the world" (John 1:29).

THE NEW COVENANT IN JESUS' BLOOD (22:14-20)

The Lukan Passover tradition is longer than any recorded in earliest Christianity (Mark 14:22-25; Matt 26:26-29; 1 Cor 11:23-26; *Did.* 9:1-5). It also displays notable differences from its counterparts in the Synoptics. The relevant facts related to Luke's Passover narrative are the following. (1) It contains two blocks of material not present in Mark or Matt, the first (1a) occurring in vv. 15-17. This addition contains a cup-bread-cup Passover sequence that differs from the bread-cup sequence in Mark and Matt. The second addition (1b) is vv. 19b-20, the so-called longer text, also absent from Mark and Matt.[38] This longer text is

---

38. The textual tradition favoring the longer reading of 19b-20 is vastly superior in terms of number and weight of manuscripts (p^{75} ℵ A B C K L T W X Δ Θ Π Ψ 063 f^1 f^{13}) in comparison to the shorter reading, which is attested by Codex Bezae (D), a small number of Italian versions, and three Syriac versions (Curetonian, Sinaitic, Peshitta). The authenticity of the longer reading seems secured beyond reasonable doubt. For full discussions, see J. Jeremias, *The Eucharistic Words of Jesus* (Minneapolis: Fortress Press, 1966), 138-73; Metzger, *TCGNT,* 148-50; B. Billings, "The Disputed Words in the Lukan Institution Narrative (Luke 22:19b-20): A Sociological Answer to a Textual Problem," *JBL* 125/3 (2006): 507-26.

unique in containing nineteen Greek words in agreement with 1 Cor 11:24-26.[39] (2) The Lukan Passover narrative contains a host of words that appear only in Luke, many of which appear to have been taken over from a prior source.[40] Included in these words are three evident Hebraisms: *kai egeneto* (v. 14; "and it happened"), *epithymia epethymēsa* (v. 15; "I have eagerly desired"), and *tou genēmatos tēs ampelou* (v. 18; "the fruit of the vine").[41] (3) "For I tell you I will not drink again of the fruit of the vine until the kingdom of God comes" is transposed in Luke from its order in the other Synoptics. In Mark 14:25 and Matt 26:29 this saying concludes the Passover meal, whereas in Luke (v. 18) it appears in the middle of the Passover meal after the giving of the first cup.

Commentators often explain the Lukan Passover narrative as a combination of the Markan narrative and the Pauline tradition in vv. 19b-20, with the rearrangement of v. 18. This solution accounts for (1b) and (3) above, but fails to account for (1a) and (2). In order to account for the latter, many commentators infer that the base text of Luke's Passover narrative is not Mark but a separate Passover tradition that is combined with a Pauline tradition.[42] This is a reasonable inference, and in my judgment virtually required. The probability of Luke's following a separate base text of the Passover is reinforced by two further pieces of evidence, both of which point to a prior Hebrew source, probably the Hebrew Gospel. The first arises from the Passover tradition it-

---

39. *Eucharistēsas* ("having given thanks"); *to hyper hymōn* ("in behalf of you"); *touto poieite eis tēn emēn anamnēsin* ("do this in remembrance of me"); *to [potērion]* ("the cup"); *hōsautōs meta to deipnēsai* ("likewise, after the supper"); *kainē [diathēkē]* ("new covenant"); *en tō haimati* ("in [my] blood").

40. *Kai egeneto* (v. 14, "and it happened"); *epithymia epethymēsa* (v. 15, "I have eagerly desired"); *pathein* (v. 15, "suffer"); *heōs hotou* (v. 16, "until"); the absolute use of *eucharistēsas* (v. 17, "having given thanks") and *eklasen* (v. 19, "he broke"); *hē basileia tou theou elthē* (v. 18, "the kingdom of God may come"), *tou genēmatos tēs ampelou* (v. 18, "the fruit of the vine"). See Jeremias, *Sprache des Lukasevangeliums,* 286-88.

41. The expressions are Hebraisms, not Septuagintisms (i.e., taken over from the LXX). *Kai egeneto* derives from Hebrew rather than Aramaic (G. Dalman, *The Words of Jesus* [Edinburgh: T&T Clark, 1909], 32; BDF §442.5). *Epithymia epethymēsa* reflects the Hebrew infinitive absolute, a grammatical convention that is unique to Hebrew and has no parallel in Aramaic, Syriac, Greek, or Latin (Edwards, *Hebrew Gospel,* 136). *Tou genēmatos tēs ampelou* reflects Isa 32:12; see also *m. Ber.* 6:1 (Heb. *gepen pōrīyāh* and Wolter, *Lukasevangelium* 702).

42. Fitzmyer, *Luke (X–XXIV),* 1365-66, discusses the various options, including lists of commentators favoring each. Commentators who favor Luke's use of a special source include Plummer, *Luke,* 494; Bultmann, *The History of the Synoptic Tradition* (rev. ed.; New York: Harper & Row, 1972), 279; Jeremias, *Eucharistic Words of Jesus* (Philadelphia: Fortress Press, 1977), 97-100, 186; Marshall, *Luke,* 785; Klein, *Lukasevangelium,* 663; Bovon, *Lukas 19,28–24,53,* 238; Wolter, *Lukasevangelium,* 691. See esp. Schweizer, *Lukas,* 221, and his conclusion regarding Luke's special source: "The scene in the Upper Room contains a host of non-Lukan expressions and above all the tensions regarding the two cups and the word about the sword. These are scarcely to be accounted for without acceptance of a written source" (236).

self, which consisted of (a) a family head blessing a first cup of wine, which is then shared by all at the table, followed by herbs dipped in sauce; (b) the family head, in response to a question of the youngest son present, retelling the exodus story from Deut 26:5-11, after which Ps 113 was sung and a second cup of wine was drunk; (c) the family head blessing, breaking, and distributing unleavened bread to the gathering, which is eaten with the meal; and (d) the drinking of two concluding cups of wine and the singing of Pss 114-18.[43] Luke's longer two-cup account preserves more of the Jewish Passover tradition and may be supposed to derive from it.

A second and more important piece of evidence in favor of a Hebrew exemplar occurs in Epiphanius (*Pan.* 30.22.4-5). Eight Greek words that are verbatim with v. 15 are quoted (four times!) by Epiphanius to show that the original Hebrew Gospel had been corrupted by a later Jewish sect called the Ebionites.[44] Epiphanius does not say that the Ebionites took the words of v. 15 from Luke. The discussion in *Pan.* 30 assumes throughout that the Ebionites corrupted an early Hebrew Gospel that existed *prior* to Luke. The Epiphanius quotation and the Hebraisms in Luke's Passover narrative provide both historical and lexical evidence in favor of the inference that a Hebrew source, and perhaps the Hebrew Gospel referenced by Epiphanius, was the base text of Luke's Passover narrative. The above evidence provides a satisfactory, if not conclusive, explanation of the three distinctive characteristics of Luke's Passover narrative. Vv. 14-20 appear to reflect a longer Hebrew tradition of Jesus' final Passover, to which Luke added the saying of v. 18 following the drinking of the first cup, and words from the Pauline Passover tradition in vv. 19b-20 following the drinking of the second cup.[45]

14-18 "When the hour came, Jesus reclined at the table, and his disci-

43. Oldest sources for the Passover meal are Exod 12-13; Philo, *QE 1; m. Pesaḥ.* 10. The composite evidence is synthesized in Str-B 4/1:41-76; Green, *Luke,* 758; Plummer, *Luke,* 495. *M. Pesaḥ.,* the most complete source of the Passover, reflects the celebration as known in ca. 200. We do not know if the Passover custom of first-c. Palestine was exactly the same.

44. The Greek phrase is *epithymia epethymēsa touto to pascha phagein meth hymōn.* The relevant Epiphanius quotation reads: "Next the Lord himself says, 'I earnestly desired to eat this Passover with you.' . . . [The Ebionites], however, destroyed the true order and changed the passage; that is clear to everyone because of the words that belong to each other and they made the disciple say: 'Where do you wish that we prepare the Passover to eat for you?' And they made [Jesus] answer: 'I do not earnestly desire to eat meat with you this Passover.' . . . For instead of saying: 'I earnestly desired,' they added the word 'not.' Actually, [Jesus] said, 'I earnestly desired to eat this Passover with you.' They, however, added 'meat' and deceived themselves recklessly speaking the words, 'I did not desire earnestly to eat meat with you this Passover'" (*Pan.* 30.22.4-5; for the Greek text, see *SQE,* 437). For a discussion of this text, see Edwards, *Hebrew Gospel,* 74-75.

45. Bovon, *Lukas 19,28–24,53,* 239-42, also regards the Lukan version as a separate tradition (although he does not identify it as a Hebrew tradition) combined with a Pauline tradition.

ples with him" (v. 14). Luke tapers the narrative time frame from the *approach* of Passover (v. 1), to the *day* of Passover (v. 7), to the *hour* of the Passover meal (v. 14). It was customary in the ancient world to recline at feasts and formal meals, if not at all meals. Jesus and the apostles would have leaned on their left elbows, with heads toward the table and feet extended outward (see **banquets** at 11:37).[46] V. 14 shines the narrative spotlight specifically on Jesus; it is he (in Greek) who is reclining, "and the apostles with him."[47] Likewise, in v. 39, Jesus goes to the Mount of Olives, followed by the disciples with him. In both instances Luke's wording reminds readers that the substance of discipleship is being "with Jesus."[48] The reference to "apostles" narrows the participants in the Passover meal from the larger group of disciples daily attending Jesus in the temple to the Twelve alone (see at 6:13). Banquets were familiar settings in antiquity for farewell speeches of famous men before their deaths. Jesus delivers a longer speech at Passover than he does in other Lukan banquet scenes, but in Luke it remains a scene typical of a Jewish Passover rather than a farewell speech in Judaism or Hellenism.[49]

Jesus' introductory words, "I have eagerly desired to eat this Passover with you before I suffer" (v. 15), occur only in the Third Gospel. "I have eagerly desired" translates a Hebrew infinitive absolute, which intensifies a statement. The introduction is another and emphatic reminder that Jesus is not playing a defensive endgame in order to escape (or delay) a checkmate from the authorities. He is intentionally presiding over his final earthly Passover meal, which he has convoked. The knowledge of the intensity of the suffering before him does not cancel the intensity of his desire to be with the Twelve.[50] If the word for "Passover" (Gk. *pascha*) connotes Passover *lamb* (as in v. 7) rather than the meal itself,[51] then the slain lamb contributes to the intensification of Jesus' introductory words by symbolizing his impending suffering (1 Cor 5:7).

The Lukan Last Supper was a Jewish Passover meal (vv. 1, 7, 8, 11, 13, 14). It is not Jesus' last Passover, however, for he will again celebrate Passover when "it finds fulfillment in the kingdom of God" (v. 16). The Greek word for "finds fulfillment," an aorist passive subjunctive, is a "divine passive" that refers to

---

46. On the reclining position, see Str-B 4/2:618.

47. The wording of the NIV, "Jesus and his apostles reclined at the table," diffuses the focus from Jesus to the group as a whole.

48. See Green, *Luke,* 759.

49. So too Fitzmyer, *Luke (X–XXIV),* 1407; Bovon, *Lukas 19,28–24,53,* 257-59. R. Brown, *The Gospel according to John (XIII–XXI),* 598-601, lists thirteen characteristics of farewell speeches in Jewish literature, only two (or possibly three) of which are evident in Luke 22. The characteristics of Hellenistic banquets discussed in C. Dodd, *The Interpretation of the Fourth Gospel* (Cambridge: University Press, 1968), 420-23, are no closer to Luke's Passover narrative.

50. Plummer, *Luke,* 494.

51. So Schweizer, *Lukas,* 223.

the perfect Passover that Jesus will celebrate in the eschatological kingdom of God.[52] V. 16, along with v. 18 and Paul's reminder that the Last Supper anticipates Jesus' return (1 Cor 11:26), exhorts believers to "look both ways" in the Last Supper. They are to look to the past in "remembrance" (v. 19) and to the future in anticipation (vv. 16, 18). The atoning death of Jesus Christ is a saving past event that anticipates the future hope of the return of Jesus as the Son of Man (21:27). When believers share the Lord's Supper, they stand in the interim between past and future, in the "already" and "not yet," receiving by faith the self-sacrifice of Jesus for them on the cross, and awaiting by faith the self-return of Jesus for them in the cloud of glory.

Luke sets the first cup of wine (v. 17) between the eschatological sayings of vv. 16 and 18, thus symbolizing the future hope of Passover. The reference to the cup as "the fruit of the vine" (v. 18), an unmistakable Hebraism, may recall the first of four cups of wine that the family head introduced thus, "Blessed are you, Lord our God, eternal King, who have created the fruit of the vine" (*m. Pesaḥ.* 10:2; *b. Pesaḥ.* 103a, 106a).[53] In the Last Supper, however, Jesus does not bless the contents of the cup but gives thanks to God in prayer.[54] The command to "divide it among you" (v. 17) is no more precise in Greek than in English. Greek *diamerizein* can mean either to divide into separate units or to distribute from one source among several recipients. The wording of v. 17 thus does not allow us to say for certain whether the Twelve drank from a common cup or separate cups. The Mishnah implies a separate cup for each Passover participant, and if this custom prevailed, we may assume the same among the Twelve.[55] We are not expressly told that Jesus either drank the cup or ate the bread. This is not conclusive, however, because Luke's Passover account focuses on Jesus' provision of bread and wine for the Twelve, "for you" (vv. 19, 20). Given Jesus' ardent desire to eat the Passover (v. 15), it would be surprising if he did not eat with the Twelve. His statements in v. 16 ("I will not eat [the Passover] again") and in v. 18 ("I will not drink again") further imply his participation in the meal.[56] The conclusion of the eschatological saying of v. 18, "until the kingdom of God comes," is a surprise, "for this expression is not attested in the OT or in ancient Judaism."[57] It appears in the Lord's Prayer (11:2), of course, but the phrase there stems from Jesus. The declaration of the "kingdom of God *coming*" parallels "the Son of Man *coming*" (21:27) and seems

---

52. Klein, *Lukasevangelium*, 665.

53. Bock, *Luke 9:51–24:53*, 1723, and Nolland, *Luke 18:35–24:53*, 1051, also see v. 17 as a reference to the first cup of the traditional Passover meal.

54. So Marshall, *Luke*, 798.

55. So Str-B 4/1:58. Plummer, *Luke*, 495, and Wolter, *Lukasevangelium*, 702, argue for a single cup.

56. See Plummer's (*Luke*, 495-96) lucid defense of Jesus' participation.

57. Jeremias, *Die Sprache des Lukasevangeliums*, 287.

synonymous with it. Jesus does not merely teach about the kingdom of God (see at 4:43) or even bring it; he is the embodiment of the kingdom in his first coming and the consummation of it in his second coming.

19-20   "And [Jesus] took bread, gave thanks and broke it, and gave it to them, saying, 'This is my body given for you; do this in remembrance of me'" (v. 19). The rich and symbolic elements of the Passover are here subsumed in Jesus' simple but momentous words of institution. Already before Luke, the Lord's Supper had achieved liturgical form in the early church, although slight variations are still evident.[58] The liturgy is constructed of load-bearing transitive verbs: "took," "gave thanks," "broke," "gave," "poured out," "do." As in the exodus, which is narrated in similar transitive verbs (God "sees," "hears," "knows," "comes down," "rescues," and "brings out the Israelites," Exod 3:7-10), the Last Supper recounts the saving engagement of Jesus on behalf of the Twelve. The only intransitive verb is in the words of institution, "This *is* my body." The phrase itself is striking, for "none of the Jewish festivals contains a similar formulation."[59] The reference to the bread as Jesus' body reflects his unique innovation to the Passover celebration. The verb "to be" in the words of institution has been the subject of much debate and cause of much division in the history of the church. The language for Jewish religious literature, worship, and liturgy in first-century Palestine remained Hebrew rather than Aramaic,[60] and both the scriptural readings and the Passover liturgy would doubtless have been spoken in Hebrew. "This is my body" could either contain or omit the verb "to be" in the original Hebrew,[61] but even if omitted, the statement implies more than mere sign or symbol. In the NT and Hellenistic world "body" (Gk. *sōma*) designates the whole person, in this instance the very person of Jesus. "Given for you" (v. 19), a phrase not present in Matt or Mark, carries a strong vicarious sense. The phrase, "for you" (Gk. *hyper hymōn*, "on your behalf"), which occurs with reference to both bread (v. 19) and wine (v. 20), imputes to the Last Supper and the crucifixion it anticipates a sense of substitutionary atonement. In conjunction with the transitive verbs in vv. 19-20, "my body given for you" (v. 19) signifies the self-offering of Jesus for the disciples, wholly and without reserve. The accent falls not on ideas, not even on signs and symbols, but on saving activity and agency on behalf of others that will be consummated in Jesus' death on the place called the Skull (23:33).[62]

---

58. *Did.* 9:1-5; Epiphanius, *Pan.* 30.22.4-5; Justin Martyr, *1 Apol.* 66.3; *Dial.* 111.3. For a discussion of the various forms of the words of institution, see Bock, *Luke 9:51-24:53*, 1716-17.

59. Bovon, *Lukas 19,28-24,53*, 245.

60. Edwards, *Hebrew Gospel*, 166-74.

61. The Hebrew NTs of Delitzsch (1931) and the UBS (1976) omit "to be" in v. 19.

62. See Wolter, *Lukasevangelium*, 704-5; Johnson, *Luke*, 338-42. Also L. Boughton, "'Being Shed for You/Many': Time-Sense and Consequences in the Synoptic Cup Citations," *TynBul* 48 (1997): 249-70.

The injunction to "do this in remembrance of me" (v. 19), not present in Matt or Mark, ostensibly derives from the Pauline tradition (1 Cor 11:24). Remembrance belongs among the chief virtues of Judaism (Deut 4; 8). The bread of presentation, called "bread of remembrance" (Lev 24:7), that was placed on the golden table in the tabernacle Sabbath by Sabbath institutionalized the command to "remember and never forget" God's saving deeds and covenant (Deut 9:7). The Passover meal was the quintessential feast of remembrance (Exod 12:14; 13:8-9; Deut 16:3) in which the family head recounted the story, "A wandering Aramean was my father . . ." (Deut 26:5-11; *m. Pesaḥ.* 10:4). The purpose of remembrance was not simply to recall the past, but to *re*present the past in order to participate in it and extend its effects into the present. Passover thus contemporized the exodus for Jews. "In every generation," taught the rabbis, "a man must so regard himself as if he came forth himself out of Egypt, for it is written, 'And you shall tell your son in that day, saying "It is because of that which the Lord did for me when I came forth out of Egypt"'" (*m. Pesaḥ.* 10:5; Exod 13:8). In *re*presenting the Passover, the Last Supper becomes the *new* covenant (v. 20). Jesus' disciples are now not to remember the exodus, but Jesus himself. The presumption of Jesus to substitute himself for the exodus, the foundational event of Israel's existence, is a clue to his messianic self-consciousness.[63] That the meal now recalls Jesus rather than the exodus is powerfully illustrated in the Emmaus story, where "Jesus was made known to [Cleopas and his companion] in the breaking of the bread" (24:30, 35). The second-person plural present tense verb "do" (Gk. *poieite*) signifies that the Last Supper, like the Passover, is both a communal and a continual remembrance: "all of you, continue doing this." Finally, if the imperative of Jesus, "Do this in remembrance of me," resulted in the Eucharist as the backbone of early Christian worship, is it not likely that the same imperative influenced the careful transmission of the early Christian gospel tradition?[64]

"In the same way, after the supper he took the cup, saying, 'This cup is the new covenant in my blood, which is poured out for you'" (v. 20). Since the cup of v. 20 is given "after the supper," it must be either the third or fourth Passover cup. If, as Nolland suggests, Jesus shares his own personal cup with the Twelve in v. 20, then that cup is a concrete illustration of the disciples' participation in Jesus' self-sacrifice.[65] The Lukan wording includes two elements absent from Matt and Mark but present in Paul's account of the Last

---

63. It may be true, as Bovon, *Lukas 19,28–24,53,* 245, notes, that Jesus does not speak of "replacing" Passover with the Lord's Supper. On the basis of vv. 19-20, however, it seems clear that the eschatological Passover to which Jesus looks forward is one in which his death, not the exodus, is commemorated.

64. See here M. Bockmuehl, *Simon Peter in Scripture and Memory* (Grand Rapids: Baker Academic, 2012), 13.

65. Nolland, *Luke 18:35–24:53,* 1054.

Supper in 1 Cor 11:25. The first is reference to the *"new* covenant" (also Rom 11:27; 2 Cor 3:6). This is a direct allusion to the prophet Jeremiah, who, having contemplated the history of Israel, declared that in the days to come God "will make a new covenant with the house of Israel," not like the covenant that God made with their ancestors and that they broke, but a new covenant "put in their minds and written on their hearts" (31[LXX 38]:31, 33).[66] The second element is "the new covenant *in my blood.*" Like the old covenant at Mount Sinai, the new covenant must also be ratified by blood. In Hebrew thought the life of a creature resided in its blood; Jesus' reference to the cup as "my blood" thus implies his very life. In the OT, the shedding of blood nearly always signifies violent death (Gen 9:6; 37:22; Prov 6:17; Ezek 18:10), and the same implication is present in v. 20. Jewish rabbis spoke of "blood of the covenant" only with reference to circumcision.[67] Jesus uses the expression with reference to the first covenant, instituted when Moses threw blood on the people (Exod 24:3-8). The new covenant instituted by Jesus is not ratified by the blood of a surrogate sacrificial animal, but by Jesus' blood, which is not thrown *onto* believers as in Exod 24:8, but received *into* believers.[68] In both the bread and wine "the whole Jesus is present: his person in the bread, and his life in the cup."[69]

FOREWARNINGS FOLLOWING PASSOVER (22:21-38)

Luke follows the Last Supper with four discourses of Jesus (vv. 21-23, 24-30, 31-34, 35-38), each initiated by Jesus and each a forewarning of the imminent challenges awaiting the Twelve. The first two discourses occur in Matt (26:21-25; 20:25-28) and Mark (14:18-21; 10:42-45) prior to the Passover rather than following it. The third is similar in one respect with Matt and Mark (vv. 33-34// Matt 26:33-34//Mark 14:29-30), and the fourth is unique to Luke. In Mark and Matt the Last Supper is concluded with a hymn, followed by immediate adjournment to the Mount of Olives. Luke's discourses following the Last Supper bring his narrative into closer conformity with the long Johannine passion dis-

---

66. *"New* [or *everlasting*] covenant" is present in the OT only in Isa 55:3; 61:8; Jer 31:31; 32:40; Ezek 16:60, 62; 37:26, also 2 *Bar* 2:35 and Qumran (4Q 385; CD 6:19; 8:21; 19:33-34).

67. Str-B 1:991.

68. The assertion of Vinson, *Luke,* 677, that Luke's Last Supper does not envision Jesus' self-sacrifice as an atonement for sins fails to recognize the substitutionary imagery of "the new covenant in my blood" and, above all, the two references to his impending death "in behalf of you" (vv. 19, 20). Bovon, *Lukas 19,28–24,53,* correctly states: "Luke does not refrain from adopting the Biblical tradition of the atoning effects of the suffering righteous person. In the context of Jesus' passion he takes over the teaching and applies it to Christians."

69. Wolter, *Lukasevangelium, 707.*

course, although Luke's narrative is not cast in the farewell genre as is John's.[70] The Lukan warnings in vv. 21-38 exemplify the increasing foreknowledge that Jesus possesses as his crucifixion draws near (see at 19:30). V. 21 begins with a brusque contrast (Gk. *plēn;* NIV "but"; occurring again in v. 22), signaling that the intimacy of the Passover must now give way to the serious business of preparing a foundation of faith capable of weathering the storms awaiting the Twelve (6:48).[71]

21-23 "The hand of him who is going to betray me is with mine on the table" (v. 21). This is the second of three references to Judas in chap. 22 (vv. 3, 21, 47-48), all of which accentuate his nearness to Jesus. The use of "hand" as a causal agent, here as a synecdoche of the person, is typically Hebraic. The betraying back-stabbing or throat-slitting hand is normally hidden. In Judas's case the betraying hand is visible and trusted — indeed, it is a ritually washed hand of the sacred Passover festival. Later artistic depictions of the Last Supper often paint Judas as swarthy, hook-nosed, malevolent. The fact that none of the disciples seems to have suspected Judas of treachery dispels the error of this easy stereotype.[72] The betraying hand of Judas at table with Jesus is poignant and tragic, for the table is a place of intimate and trusted fellowship in Judaism. Many people have experienced the betraying hand in equally trusted relationships — in marriages, from parents, siblings, children, best friends, their own teachers or students. Those who have, know to some extent the sense of betrayal Jesus feels in Judas's betrayal, and they also know that Jesus has experienced what they are going through.

"They began to question among themselves which of them it might be who would do this" (v. 23). Judas evidently played the role of disciple convincingly (Ps 41:9!). Matt and Mark speak of the betrayer's hand with the hand of Jesus in "the bowl" (Gk. *tryblion*). Luke speaks of his hand with Jesus "at the table." The Passover table in particular was the central image of the gathered community of the elect in Judaism. In v. 30 Jesus will speak of eternal felicity as "eating and drinking at my table in the kingdom of God." The Passover table was to be a foretaste of that glorious and victorious table in the future. The table is not a safe zone, however, for Satan is present in Judas, planted in the midst of the trusted Passover fellowship.[73] According to Mark and Matt, the saying of v. 21 occurred immediately before the Last Supper, leaving doubt whether Judas participated in the final meal or not. Luke's placement of the

---

70. See n. 49 above.

71. On the sharp contrast in v. 21, see Fitzmyer, *Luke (X–XXIV),* 1409; Nolland, *Luke 18:35–24:53,* 1060.

72. An insight of Plummer, *Luke,* 500.

73. Marshall, *Luke,* 807, "Even presence at the Lord's table is no guarantee against apostasy, and a warning is laid before the readers of the Gospel."

saying after the Passover relieves all ambiguity: the hand of the betrayer has been with Jesus throughout the sacred gathering. Judas's betrayal is not the result of ignorance, but a knowing and willful act.

"The Son of Man will go as it has been decreed. But woe to that man who betrays him" (v. 22). The first sentence of v. 22 gives us a rare insight into the mind of Jesus. That the saying represents the mind of Jesus is evinced by the presence of "Son of Man" (see at 5:24), a title used only by Jesus of himself and not by the early church of Jesus. Particularly revealing is the statement that the Son of Man must "go as it has been decreed" (v. 22). "Decreed" (Gk. *horizein*) is a "divine passive," meaning what God has predetermined. This is the only instance of *horizein* in Luke, but both the word and the concept occur in Acts with reference to divine providence generally (Acts 10:42; 17:26, 31), and specifically to the necessity of Jesus' suffering (Acts 1:16-20; 2:23; 4:27-28). In no pre-Christian tradition is the Son of Man destined to suffer vicariously for others. That role is reserved exclusively for the Servant of the Lord (Isa 53:6, 10). The idea that the Son of Man must be betrayed and suffer is meaningful only if Jesus, as the Son of Man, identifies himself with the Suffering Servant of the Lord,[74] and sees in his passion the fulfillment of the vicarious atonement of others (Isa 53:4, 12).

The combined sentences of v. 22 afford a rare insight into the paradox of divine providence and human free will. The church fathers insisted that God could not redeem a nature that he had not assumed. God must become a man if he is to redeem man. This mystery is addressed in the two men of v. 22: the Son of Man and the man Judas. Both are described by the same Greek verb, *paradidonai*, meaning "to deliver up" or "hand over" (NIV "betray"). The word means something different of each man, however. In Jesus' case it refers to handing over in fulfillment of the divine will; in Judas's, to handing Jesus over for betrayal. Both currents of divine foreordination and human free will intersect in this verb. In these two men, one serving God and the other Satan, the inscrutable sovereignty of God effects a single saving end. Neither Jesus nor Judas is an instrument of blind fate or a pawn of divine strategy. Divine providence neither cancels human freedom nor relieves responsibility for moral choices. On the Mount of Olives (22:39-46) Jesus engages in a supreme struggle in which he is free not to obey; at the table Judas is equally free not to betray. The Son of Man becomes the effective sin-bearer of the world because his self-offering is freely chosen out of love and obedience; the man Judas becomes the consummate sinner because he freely rejects both. "Woe to that man *through whom* [the Son of Man] is betrayed" (lit. in Gk.; also *1 Clem.* 46:8; *Herm. Vis.* 4.2.6).

24-30 The magnitude of the forces playing out in the Son of Man

---

74. V. Taylor, *The Gospel according to St. Mark* (London: Macmillan, 1966), 541-42.

and the man Judas may perhaps be reflected in the Twelve, for "a dispute also arose among them" (v. 24). The Greek word for "dispute," *philoneikia*, occurring only here in the NT, is a compound word literally meaning "love of victory, desire for glory," here meaning "contention" or "invidiousness." Talk of appointed destinies in v. 22 may have awakened dormant ambitions in the Twelve, whetted now by talk of the imminent kingdom and looming danger. "Which of them was considered to be the greatest?" they debated (v. 24). This is a subject about which the disciples argued earlier (9:46). Their doing so again in the wake of the nadir to which Judas has sunk is especially bitter. We should perhaps like to know whose names were put forth, but the Gospel does not indulge our fancies any more than Jesus indulged theirs. There is perhaps no subject on which Scripture is less tolerant than on that of self-adulation. "The Lord Almighty has a day in store for all the proud and lofty, for all that is exalted" (Isa 2:12).

Jesus interrupts their vanity with a warning, "The kings of the Gentiles lord it over them; and those who exercise authority over them call themselves benefactors" (v. 25). Vv. 25-30 are pervaded by the vocabulary of domination: "kings" (v. 25), "kingdom" (vv. 29-30), "lord it over" (v. 25), "exercise author-ity" (v. 25), "benefactors" (v. 25), "the one who rules" (v. 26), "sit on thrones" (v. 30), "judging" (v. 30).[75] The point of this emphasis is obvious enough: the world both recognizes and rewards power and prominence. "Benefactors" seems to be the tip of the semantic iceberg of these verses. This word, *eu-ergetai* in Greek, fails to deliver the voltage to modern readers that it would have to Luke's first readers. *Euergetai* is among the half-dozen most common epithets of rulers and leaders occurring in monumental Greek inscriptions in the eastern half of the Roman Empire from the NT period to late antiq-uity.[76] This epithet, in fact, was used with reference to Augustus Caesar in the Priene inscription cited on p. 68. "Benefactors" identifies a widespread class of individuals of power, position, and means who celebrated themselves and were celebrated by others in public spaces.[77] The meaning of the Greek verb

---

75. Wolter, *Lukasevangelium*, 710-11.

76. Other epithets include "Great" (Gk. *megistēs* [usually adjectivally — "Artemis the Great," "Ephesus the Great"]), "Master" *(autokratōr)*, "Excellence" *(kratistos)*, "August" *(sebas-tos)*, "Savior" *(sōtēr)*, and "Son of God" *(huios tou theou)*. With the exception of the last two titles, these epithets are avoided or used only rarely and with caution in the NT. "Son of God" and "Savior" occur more frequently in the NT, but they too are used judiciously, specifically of Jesus (or the latter of God, in the Pastorals).

77. Nearly a century ago (1922), A. Deissmann wrote, "It would not be difficult to col-lect from inscriptions, with very little loss of time, over a hundred instances [of *euergetēs*], so widespread was the custom" (*Light from the Ancient East*, 253). The number of inscriptions that has surfaced since Deissmann allows us to speak of *many* hundreds of occurrences of *euergetēs*. See evidence gathered in Wolter, *Lukasevangelium*, 712.

for "call," *kalountai,* can be either middle ("call themselves") or passive ("are called"), thus capturing both senses of self-promotion and desire for recognition. The cult of benefactors was not restricted to Hellenism, for the same epithet also appears as early as the second century B.C. of native rulers of Judea.[78] This posture of prominence evokes a sharp rebuttal from Jesus: "You are not to be like that" (v. 26, NIV). The actual Greek wording of v. 26, like the Greek wording of the beatitudes and woes of 6:20-26, does not contain a verb. Literally, it reads, "You [are] not like that," which should be understood as both imperative and indicative. The rebuttal, in other words, identifies not simply a behavior to be avoided but an alternative way of life to be embraced.[79] The criteria of greatness are radically reversed in the kingdom of God. "The greatest among you should be like the youngest, and the one who rules like the one who serves" (v. 26). The Christian life is a divine paradox, for Jesus enjoins "infant maturity" and "servant leadership." Jesus taught essentially the same thing earlier (9:48), as does the apostle Paul in saying that "God chooses the foolish things of the world to shame the wise, and the weak things of the world to shame the strong" (1 Cor 1:27).

Indeed, in v. 27 the very concept of greatness is questioned. "For who is greater, the one who is at table or the one who serves? Is it not the one who is at table? But I am among you as one who serves." The Greek word for "greater," *meizōn,* could actually be translated as a substantive ("[a] great [one]") rather than a comparative ("greater"), since in both vv. 26 and 27 it is not followed by a genitive of comparison.[80] Various forms of the Greek word for "great" *(megas/megalē/megistēs)* proliferated alongside "benefactor" in the cult of prominence and self-promotion, especially in the later emperor cult. V. 27 presses the case against the cult of superiority. "Who, after all, is great?" or "What is greatness?" is the gist. From the world's perspective, the answer seems obvious: honored guests at banquets are great, . . . certainly greater than those who serve them. This is indeed the case in the world. But not in the kingdom Jesus proclaims. "I am among you as one who serves" (v. 27; also 12:35-48; 17:7-10). "Among you" is particularly personal and relational. Jesus does not simply bear the title "servant"; he performs the duties of a servant among the Twelve themselves. V. 27 ends without any reference to "greatness." Jesus does not say, for example, "The one who serves *is greater than the one who reclines.*" This makes v. 27 seem incomplete. It is not incomplete, however,

---

78. The earliest record is of Onias III (early second c. B.C., 2 Macc 4:1-2), followed by Simon Maccabee (mid-second c. B.C., 1 Macc 14:25-49) and John Hyrcanus I (late second c. B.C., Josephus, *Ant.* 14.149). See G. Gardner, "Jewish Leadership and Hellenistic Civic Benefaction in the Second Century B.C.E.," *JBL* 126/2 (2007): 327-43.

79. So too Bovon, *Lukas* 19,28–24,53, 266-67.

80. See BDF §244; Fitzmyer, *Luke (X–XXIV),* 1416; Wolter, *Lukasevangelium,* 711; Bovon, *Lukas* 19,28–24,53, 265.

because the Son of God is the Servant of the Lord, and as the Servant, Jesus sets an incomparable standard with equals or superiors.

Vv. 28-30 address the Twelve directly. "You are those who have stood by me in my trials" (v. 28). Mention of Jesus' "trials" raises questions for H. Conzelmann's celebrated thesis that Jesus has enjoyed divine protection in a "Satan-free" environment since the temptation.[81] We are not told that Judas has left the gathering, but it is hard to imagine Jesus saying v. 28 if Judas were still present. This verse defines "the cost of discipleship" as well as any in Scripture. "You" is shifted prominently to the front of the sentence in Greek, emphasizing its importance for the disciples. Jesus describes their discipleship not with nouns or adjectives, but with a verb, *diamemenēkotes* (NIV "have stood"), a perfect participle that carries the sense of endurance and solidarity with him. The Twelve joined Jesus at an earlier point in time, and from then until the present they have stood with him. Vv. 27-28 reflect a relational dialectic between Jesus and his followers: he serves in their midst, they remain with him in his trials. V. 28 is a strong critique of discipleship conceived as *theologia gloriae,* all benefits and blessings. The true test of discipleship is not participation in Christ's glory, but commitment to endure "with him in his trials," "to deny self and take up the cross daily and follow me" (9:23). Shallow faith, like seed sown on rock, receives the gospel gladly but forsakes it in times of trial (8:13). "The person who takes up religion for the world will throw away religion for the world."[82] Those who receive the gospel solely for its benefits will abandon it for its costs. Luke 22 is the chapter of trials (vv. 28, 40, 46) for both Jesus and the Twelve.

Discipleship is more than enduring trials, however. Its ultimate purpose, according to vv. 29-30, is to participate in the mission of Christ and to share in the responsibility of his rule. The word for "confer" in v. 29 is the Greek verb form of the word for "covenant" (Gk. *diatithenai*). Participation of disciples in the mission of Christ is thus formalized covenantally. V. 29 is reminiscent of the frequent Johannine theme of reciprocity among the Father, Jesus, and disciples. The disciples will eat and drink with Jesus in the coming kingdom conferred on him by the Father (vv. 29-30). Fellowship with Jesus will be more than celebrating in an eschatological winner's circle, for the Twelve "will sit on thrones judging the twelve tribes of Israel" (v. 30). Judgment over the tribes of Israel was a common reward for the elect in Israel.[83] "Sitting on thrones" does not denote a holiday but a work day, ruling with and on behalf of Jesus Christ, the enthroned Lord of glory. The call and formation of the apostolic college is not an epilogue to the story of Israel, but the completion of the foreordained

---

81. Bovon, *Lukas 19,28–24,53*, 268. Further on Conzelmann's thesis, see p. 131, n. 115.

82. John Bunyan, *The Pilgrim's Progress* (New York: Signet Classic, 1964), 99.

83. See the passages gathered in Wolter, *Lukasevangelium*, 714-15.

messianic task of Jesus. The church is not a scissors-and-paste remedy when Israel failed to receive its Messiah, but the rightful consummation of the work of God in Israel. The church does not replace or nullify the history of Israel; it fulfills the purpose for which Israel was created.[84] Rulership implies that the Twelve, and believers that follow them, will not be relegated to subservient roles, but participate as peers in the mission and reign of Jesus Christ. Paul intimates the same in saying that Jesus Christ "might be the firstborn among many *brothers and sisters*" (Rom 8:29). The ultimate goal of the redemptive work of Christ is not simply to save sinners, but to transform them to become servants of Christ, and as servants to be made siblings who rule for and with Christ.

Finally, the repeated use of the first-person pronoun in vv. 28-30 deserves special attention. The Twelve remain "with *me* in *my* trials" (v. 28). Jesus covenants with the Twelve "as *my* Father covenanted with *me*" (v. 29). The Twelve will sit at "*my* table in *my* kingdom" (v. 30). A pronounced Christology emerges in this emphatic repetition. Jesus does not speak of *our* Father, but exclusively of "*my* Father" (so too 2:49; 10:21-22; 24:49). This is a simple but important observation. The Synoptic Gospels preserve fifty-one instances of Jesus calling God "Father." In twenty-nine instances he speaks of God as "my Father," and in twenty-two he teaches the disciples about God as "your Father," but never does he include himself with the disciples in addressing God as "our Father." This statistic, combined with the repeated first-person pronouns in vv. 29-30, attests to Jesus' unique messianic and filial consciousness. The resultant picture is not that Christ is transfusing nature, humanity, or even Christians, thereby transmogrifying them into a new transcendent order of existence, an "omega point," as Teilhard de Chardin imagined. The emphasis, rather, is emphatically christological. Discipleship is always and only life *with* Jesus, "continuing *with* me [Gk. *met' emou*] in my trials" (v. 28). Disciples are heirs, participants, even partners with Jesus in his earthly and eschatological mission.

31-34   This third post-Passover discourse offers a unique perspective on Peter in the Gospels. V. 31 has no parallel in any other Gospel and lacks characteristic Lukan vocabulary and motifs, which suggests that it stems from Luke's special source. V. 32, in contrast, is signature Lukan,[85] and vv. 33-34

---

84. Fitzmyer, *Luke (X–XXIV)*, 1419, writes, "The apostles will thus become the rulers of reconstituted Israel, the reconstituted people of God. The sense is not that they will sit on thrones in judgment of the Jews who had persecuted them and have been involved in the death of Jesus."

85. Four key words are strongly Lukan: *ekleipein*, "fail" (16:9; 22:32; 23:45; elsewhere only Heb. 1:12); *stērizein*, "strengthen" (9:51; 16:26; 22:32; Acts 18:23; elsewhere only Pauline and General Epistles); *deisthai*, "pray" (fifteen of twenty-two occurrences in NT are in Luke-Acts); and *epistrephein*, "return" (eighteen of thirty-six occurrences are in Luke-Acts).

preserve Peter's boastful claim of loyalty that appears in all four Gospels (Mark 14:29-30//Matt 26:33-34//John 13:37-38).

As the crucifixion approaches, Satan is particularly active in the apostolic company, and with Jesus himself (22:39-46; 23:35-39). Satan earlier "entered" Judas to betray Jesus (22:3); here Jesus informs Peter that Satan has set his sights on all twelve apostles. In addressing the Twelve through Peter, Jesus sees Peter as representative of them and responsible for them. "Simon, Simon, Satan has asked to sift all of you as wheat" (v. 31).[86] This verse and v. 34 are the only two instances in the Gospels where Jesus addresses Peter personally, first as Simon, and the second as Peter. In Jewish and rabbinic literature the repetition of a name often signifies deep feeling, of either affection or sadness.[87] The admonishing repetition of Simon's name here recalls the repetition of Jerusalem in 13:34. Jesus' ministry has been one of conflict with Satan (10:18; 11:15-22), and that conflict now includes the archapostle. Direct discourse with Peter signifies the danger at hand. Satan "asks" to "sift" the disciples (v. 31). The Greek word for "ask," *exaitein,* occurs only here in the Greek Bible, meaning "to demand, to ask as though one has a right to do so." This is the way Satan approaches God with respect to Job and is thus reminiscent of Satan's demand to test Job (Job 1:6-12; 2:1-6).[88] It is often assumed that proximity to Jesus assures immunity from the evil one. The various temptations of Jesus (4:1-11; 22:39-46; 23:37) and the warning here that Satan is preying on the Twelve dispel that assumption. If Peter, the disciple for whom Jesus specifically prays and whom he ordains to "strengthen the brothers," is "sifted," then no follower of Christ should imagine him- or herself immune from Satan's attacks. The chief apostle stands between Satan and Christ, Satan preying on him and Christ praying for him.[89] The image of "sifting" was used earlier by the Baptizer (3:17), but here may derive from Amos 9:9, "I will shake the house of Israel among all the nations as grain is shaken in a sieve, and not a pebble will reach the ground." As this verse states, and as v. 31 implies, the purpose of "sifting" is not refinement but "of utterly destroying the faith of the apostles."[90]

86. A majority of Greek manuscripts preface v. 31 with "The Lord said," but a respectable minority tradition ($\mathfrak{p}^{75}$ B L T), plus the likelihood of the new subject of v. 31 being augmented by an identifying phrase, argues in favor of the shorter reading adopted by the NIV. See Metzger, *TCGNT,* 150-51.

87. Str-B 2:258. Luke's preference for double vocatives appears in "Martha, Martha" (10:41); "Lord, Lord," (6:46); "Master, Master," (8:24); "Jerusalem, Jerusalem" (13:34); and "Saul, Saul" (Acts 9:4; 22:7).

88. See Bovon, *Lukas 19,28–24,53,* 271-72.

89. Bengel, *Gnomon,* 2:198-99, attributes a vicarious role to Peter with regard to both Satan and Christ. If Satan can overcome Peter, he can overcome all the disciples; if Christ can preserve Peter from ruin, he can preserve all the disciples.

90. Bengel, *Gnomon,* 2:199.

Satan can provoke a conflict, but he cannot determine its outcome.[91] Like the strong vanquisher of Isa (49:24; 53:12) and the strong man of Jesus' own parable (11:22), Jesus prays that Peter's "faith may not fail" (v. 32; Jer 7:28 [LXX]; Josephus, *Ant.* 19.273). Jesus' word to Peter in vv. 31-32 contains a warning and a promise, and is thus the gospel in miniature, which comes to believers as a word of both judgment and grace. Jesus' intercession on behalf of Peter and all his disciples (John 17:7, 11, 15) demonstrates the pastoral oversight and edification to which Peter will be called as leader of the Twelve. That does not spare Peter from the test, however, nor from the fall that he will undergo in the house of the high priest (vv. 54-62). Peter will "be knocked down, but not knocked out" (2 Cor 4:9). "And when you have turned back, strengthen your brothers" (v. 32). "Turning back" (Gk. *epistrephein*) should be understood as Peter's repentance, turning away from his denial, and his rehabilitation by Jesus (John 21:15-17).[92] V. 32 invests Peter with dominical authority not to command but to serve and strengthen the apostolic college as "first among equals" (1 Pet 5:1-2) and "pillar" (Gal. 2:9), as the chief apostolic authority in the early Jewish Christian community and beyond (e.g., 1 Pet 1:1). Peter is the prime example of the ministry of strengthening in faith that characterizes God, Christ, Paul, Timothy, and the church in general in the NT. How instructive that the one ordained to strengthen Jesus' followers will not be strong and invincible, but weak and fallen (1 Cor 1:27; 2:3; 2 Cor 11:30; 12:5-10). Usefulness in the kingdom, even leadership in the church, does not depend on perfection but on a journey inward and a journey outward, on (re)turning to Jesus and on strengthening the faithful.

Peter replied, "Lord, I am ready to go with you to prison and to death" (v. 33). Jesus earlier admonished disciples to be "ready" (12:40). Indeed, in God's providence, Peter will be both imprisoned (Acts 12:3-5) and martyred for Jesus, evidently by crucifixion.[93] At the present moment, however, he is ready for neither. Boasts of great feats for Christ and his kingdom are perilous

---

91. See M. Bockmuehl, *Simon Peter in Scripture and Memory* (Grand Rapids: Baker Academic, 2012), 120-22.

92. So Plummer, *Luke,* 504; Hengel, *Saint Peter: The Underestimated Apostle* (trans. T. Trapp; Grand Rapids: Eerdmans, 2010), 44; Wolter, *Lukasevangelium,* 716. M. Bockmuehl's (*Simon Peter in Scripture and Memory,* 156-63) understanding of *epistrephein* as the need for "conversion" is mistaken. Peter does not lose his faith (v. 32); the search for a later "conversion" experience of Peter is fruitless. Similarly, conversion would better be signified by "repentance" (*metanoia*) than "returning" (Klein, *Lukasevangelium,* 675).

93. On the martyrdom of Peter, see Eusebius, *Hist. eccl.* 2.25.5; 3.1.2. In both texts Eusebius substitutes *anaskolopizein,* "to fix on a stake, to impale," for *stauroun,* the customary Greek word for crucifixion. The second passage is the earliest reference to Peter's legendary crucifixion head downward. For a discussion of Peter's martyrdom, see M. Hengel, *Saint Peter: The Underestimated Apostle,* 5-7.

because they presume the strength for self that can come only from Christ. The same Peter who in the comfort of the Last Supper vows readiness to go with Jesus to prison and death will, in the crucible of Caiaphas's courtyard, swear with equal vigor that he never knew Jesus. The grace of God comes in many forms, in this instance in Jesus' refraining from berating Peter for shameless bluster. Jesus mercifully allows the crowing cock to convict Peter of his folly. "I tell you, Peter, before the rooster crows today, you will deny three times that you knew me" (v. 34). Rabbinic texts from a later time will forbid keeping chickens under certain conditions in Jerusalem, but whether these prohibitions existed, or were carefully observed, in Jesus' day is doubtful.[94] The sound of a cockcrow, at any rate, carries a great distance. The prediction of v. 34 is another example of Jesus' prescience of events to come in the Passion Narrative (see 19:30). "Today" fits with the Jewish custom of reckoning a new day beginning at sunset. All four Gospels preserve this searing prediction of Peter's denial (v. 34; Matt 26:34; Mark 14:30; John 13:38).[95] The other three say, "You will deny me three times," but Luke worsens the denial, "You will thrice deny *knowing* me." The third of four Roman night watches was called cock crow (Gk. *alektorophōnia*; Lat. *gallicinium*), and in appealing to this sign, Jesus predicts that Peter will deny him before the night is past.

35-38 The fourth and final Passover discourse about swords is unique to Luke, without parallel in the other Gospels and with surprisingly few allusions in early Christian literature.[96] The Topkapı Palace in Istanbul proudly displays the swords of the fathers of Islam — Abu Bakr, Ali, even Muhammad himself. Swords will also play a prominent role among Christian rulers from the Byzantines onward. A discussion of swords seems inappropriate to the Founder and Fathers of Christianity, however, and has generated considerable controversy.

---

94. The chief (and earliest) witness regarding chickens in Jerusalem is *m. B. Qam.* 7:7, which forbids "rearing fowls in Jerusalem." Chickens and "fowls" were prohibited in Jerusalem not because of noise but because their scratching exposed things considered unclean in Torah. We cannot say, however, whether this rule, which is first attested ca. 200, was observed in first-c. Jerusalem. Additional doubt arises in the Tosefta (*t. B. Qam.* 8:10), which stipulates that chickens could be kept within Jerusalem if a garden or dung heap was available for them to scratch in. See the rabbinic material gathered in Str-B 1:992-93. Jeremias, *Jerusalem in the Time of Jesus*, 47-48, finds the alleged prohibition against keeping chickens in Jerusalem questionable.

95. On the importance of the rooster in relation to the denial of Peter in both the NT and early church, see Bovon, *Lukas 19,28–24,53*, 277-78.

96. Marcion omitted vv. 35-38 entirely from his version of Luke. Only Ambrose, Augustine, Gregory the Great, and Bede are known to have commented on the role of the sword in the early church. In the medieval period, esp. in Pope Boniface VIII and later in Luther, the sword becomes a justifiable instrument in theological politics. See Bovon, *Lukas 19,28–24,53*, 283-89.

The discourse begins with a recollection. "When I sent you out without purse, bag or sandals, did you lack anything?" (v. 35). The question recalls the mission of the seventy(-two) in 10:4, when disciples were sent out without travel necessities and in haste. Despite their calculated deprivations, they lacked nothing. Jesus uses the recollection not as a precedent for the present, but as a contrast to it. "But now . . ." (v. 36). The Greek *alla nyn* is strongly contrastive. From now on the disciples will have few friends and many enemies.[97] The equipment left behind on the earlier mission — purse and bag — must be taken up — and more besides. The Greek of v. 36b is awkward, but NIV renders the sense rightly, "If you don't have a sword, sell your cloak and buy one."[98] Earlier Jesus ordered them, "Sell your possessions and give to the poor" (12:33); now they must sell them to prepare for the future. When one needs a sword more than a cloak, serious danger is at hand.

Different times require different means, hence Jesus commands them to "buy a sword." In none of the Gospels do swords play a role prior to this. The appeal to the fate of the Suffering Servant of the Lord helps us in understanding this startling command. "Buy a sword" is a metaphor of admonition and preparedness, not a sanction for violence and retaliation, and certainly not a sanction to spread the gospel by violence. If Jesus were a Zealot, "sword" might conceivably be taken literally, but nothing in his ministry or teaching identifies him with this militant movement. A literal understanding of "sword" would render the majority of Jesus' teaching in chap. 6 null and void, including his testimony to being a servant leader immediately prior to this (vv. 26-27). Had Jesus intended the Twelve to take up real swords, would he have reprimanded the disciples for calling down fire on Samaria (9:54-55) or for resorting to swords ("No more of this!" v. 51) when he was arrested? The disciples draw attention to two swords in their midst, and he responds, "That is enough" (v. 38). This somewhat enigmatic phrase cannot mean the disciples should rest content with two weapons. If Jesus seriously intended armed resistance, two swords would be pitifully insufficient. "That is enough" means "Enough talk of swords!" — drop the subject, dismiss the matter.[99]

---

97. Schweizer, *Lukas*, 227, understands v. 36 to announce a new context of Christian missions. In the earlier Palestinian mission (chap. 10) disciples could presume on fellow Jews to provide for their necessities, but the extension of Christian missions into Gentile regions would require disciples to provide for themselves. Thus Paul must work to support his mission journeys.

98. This sense is followed in the NRSV, RSV, NAB, NEB. Fitzmyer, *Luke (X–XXIV)*, 1431-32, discusses four possible translations of v. 36 but opts for a translation that distorts the sense of the verse: "But now the one who has a purse had better carry it; and his knapsack too. If one does not have them, he must sell his cloak and buy a sword."

99. Plummer, *Luke*, 507, suggests that "the reply is probably the equivalent of a Hebrew

Overattention to swords obscures the essential issue in this passage.[100] "For I tell you, this scripture must be fulfilled in me, 'And he was counted among the lawless'; and indeed what is written about me is being fulfilled" (v. 37; NRSV).[101] Luke's quotation is slightly more faithful to the Hebrew than is the LXX.[102] The gravity of v. 37 is signified in its decisive language: the singular Greek participle *to gegrammenon* implies "that which is written specifically about me";[103] it "*must* be fulfilled" signifies divine necessity; the two references to fulfillment (Gk. *telein/telos*) mean "to bring to a rightful and final end" (12:50; 18:31; Acts 13:29). The saying is a citation of Isa 53:12 (similarly *Pss. Sol.* 16:5), the concluding verse in the last of the Servant of the Lord passages in Isaiah, and the only direct reference to the Servant of the Lord in the Third Gospel. This citation discloses the prophetic understanding of Jesus' life and death. In the Book of Acts Luke will frequently refer to Jesus as *pais* (3:13, 26; 4:27, 30), the same word used to translate "*Servant* of the Lord" (Heb. *ebed*; Gk. *pais*). The key word in the citation — and ostensibly the reason the passage is cited — is "lawless."[104] On the one hand, "lawless" is a counterpart for "sword." On the other, and more important, it signifies that he who is disgraced — counted among the lawless (22:52; 23:32-33) — is none other than the Servant of the Lord. In the first three centuries of Christianity Jesus was typically regarded by both Jews and Romans as a deceiver and malefactor who was deservedly crucified. The church in the modern West has until recently enjoyed a privileged status as a positive force in personal and social welfare. That approbation is waning. Indeed, Christianity is as often maligned as it is applauded. What the future holds we cannot say, but it is not difficult to imagine the church finding itself in a situation similar to its infant years, in which Jesus is looked on as a malefactor rather than as a benefactor. If so, the church will be called on to learn anew the meaning of discipleship to the one "who was numbered with the transgressors."

---

formula for dismissing the subject" (e.g., *rav-lāk*, Deut 3:26). Fitzmyer, *Luke (X–XXIV)*, 1434, and Wolter, *Lukasevangelium*, 719, do not think the saying a Hebraism.

100. So Klein, *Lukasevangelium*, 679-80.

101. "For I tell you" is inexplicably omitted from v. 37 of the NIV, although it is attested in the plenary Greek manuscript tradition. The full text of v. 37 in the NRSV (here quoted) is considerably more faithful to the Greek than is the NIV.

102. So too Fitzmyer, *Luke (X–XXIV)*, 1432; Wolter, *Lukasevangelium*, 719.

103. The singular participle occurs in Luke only in 20:17 and 22:37, both of which are strongly Christological. Luke otherwise uses the more general plural, "the things written" (18:31; 21:22; 24:44), or the formulaic *gegraptai*, "it is written" (8x).

104. The conjecture of P. Minear, "A Note on Luke 22:36," *NovT* 7 (1964-65): 132, and Vinson, *Luke*, 688, that "lawless" refers to the disciples (because they are armed with swords) is scarcely plausible.

TEMPTATION AND PRAYER
ON THE MOUNT OF OLIVES (22:39-46)

The critical junctures in Jesus' ministry are set in the context of prayer in the Third Gospel (see at 3:21; 9:18). Of Luke's score of prayer accounts, the prayer on the Mount of Olives, which follows the Last Supper and occurs immediately prior to Jesus' arrest, is the most important. The prayer is shared in common with Matt and Mark, but Luke's version is 40 percent shorter than either. Luke omits the name "Gethsemane," as well as the names of the disciples, the quotation from Ps 42:6 ("My soul is overwhelmed with sorrow"), and references to Jesus "falling on the ground" and the "hour." Also omitted are the second and third visits of Jesus to the indolent disciples, and the descriptions of Jesus' profound emotional and spiritual torment in Matt 26:38 and Mark 14:34. New in Luke's account are details of Jesus "kneeling in prayer" "a stone's throw" away from the disciples (v. 41), attributing the disciples' drowsiness to "fear" (v. 45), and a major addition of a ministering angel strengthening Jesus in his agony (vv. 43-44). The other Synoptics focus principally on Jesus, who prays intensely in solitude for strength to do the Father's will. Luke places Jesus and the (unnamed) disciples in more dynamic relation: both he and they pray (vv. 40, 41, 44, 45, 46), and both face temptation (vv. 40, 44, 46). Jesus' twice-repeated command to "pray not to fall into temptation" frames his own prayer in the middle of the account, although his faithfulness stands in stark contrast to the disciples' lethargy. The result is a compact, chiastic narrative:

> A   "Pray not to enter into temptation" (v. 40)
> > B   Jesus separates from the disciples to pray alone (v. 41)
> > > C   Jesus prays in agony (vv. 42-44)
> > B¹   Jesus returns from prayer to the sleeping disciples (v. 45)
> A¹   "Pray not to enter into temptation" (v. 46)

A major controversy in the pericope relates to the authenticity of vv. 43-44. Old and diverse Greek manuscripts line up on both sides of the issue. The witnesses are so closely divided that a convincing case for or against the inclusion of these verses cannot be made on the basis of external evidence alone.[105] We know, however, that the verses in question are very old, as attested in their allusion in Heb 5:7 (late first c.) and citation in Justin (second c.), Irenaeus (second c.), Hippolytus (third c.) and Eusebius (fourth c.). Arguments

---

105. Uncial manuscripts omitting the verses are 𝔭⁷⁵ ℵ²ᵃ A B N T W; those including it are ℵ*²ᵇ D K L Q Γ Δ Θ Ψ. The evidence of Codex Sinaiticus (ℵ) reflects the ambiguity of the manuscript tradition as a whole: the original hand of Sinaiticus (ℵ*) included vv. 43-44, the first corrector (ℵ²ᵃ) omitted them, the second corrector (ℵ²ᵇ) restored them.

on the basis of internal probability can also be made with nearly equally force both for and against the authenticity of the verses. The verses may have been absent in the original but added later in order to counteract incipient docetic tendencies in the early church. (Docetism was an early heresy maintaining that Jesus was not fully human.) However, they may have been original but later omitted because their inclusion was thought to compromise Jesus' deity. Evidence based on external textual witnesses and arguments based on internal probability are too evenly matched to be conclusive.[106] The antiquity and diversity of the external evidence may slightly favor omission of vv. 43-44,[107] whereas the probability of the verses having been original but later omitted out of deference to Jesus' deity seems the stronger of the two arguments based on internal probability.[108]

Two additional pieces of evidence tip the scale moderately in favor of the authenticity of vv. 43-44 in my judgment. First, vv. 43-44 contain a half-dozen words or expressions that are either unique to or characteristic of Luke.[109] This favors the originality of the verses, for if they were later additions, we should not expect such stylistic harmony. Second, two of the foregoing expressions are Hebraisms, one certainly (v. 44; *kai egeneto*, untranslated in NIV), and the other probably (v. 43; *enischyōn*, "strengthened").[110] This suggests that vv. 43-44 may have derived from Luke's special Hebrew source rather than from Mark. A tradition ascribed to the Hebrew Gospel supplies a missing puzzle piece of vv. 43-44, in fact. A medieval Latin text, *Historia passionis Domini* ("History of the Lord's Passion"), alludes to the angelic comfort of Jesus in his agony thus: "An angel from heaven appeared to [Jesus] comforting him, as it is reported in the Gospel of the Nazarenes, 'An angel comforted Christ in the agony of his prayer.'"[111] Since Luke alone records the angelic consolation

---

106. A scorecard of scholars on each side of the issue (several names could be added on both sides) appears in Wolter, *Lukasevangelium,* 723. The number of scholars favoring originality slightly exceeds those doubting it.

107. Metzger, *TCGNT,* 151.

108. E.g., the late second-c. Jewish skeptic Celsus ridiculed Jesus as a mere human precisely because of the kinds of weaknesses and agonies described in vv. 43-44 (Origen, *Cels.* 2.24-25). Further, see K. Madigan, "Ancient and High-Medieval Interpretations of Jesus in Gethsemane: Some Reflections on Tradition and Continuity in Christian Thought," *HTR* 88 (1995): 157-73.

109. "Appeared" (Gk. *ōphthē*), "from heaven" *(ap' ouranou)*, "strengthen" *(enischyōn)*, double use of *ginesthai* (untranslated in NIV), "earnestly" *(ektenesteron)*, and "like" *(hōsei)* are all preferred Lukan terms, some occurring only in Luke. See Jeremias, *Sprache des Lukasevangeliums,* 294.

110. See Edwards, *Hebrew Gospel,* 327.

111. My translation of the Latin, quoted in *SQE,* 457. The Hebrew Gospel was alternatively known in the early church as "Gospel of the Hebrews," "Gospel of the Nazarenes," or "Gospel of the Ebionites." The value of this quotation is not its source, the *Historia passionis*

of Jesus, the only text in the four Gospels to which this text can refer is Luke 22:43-44. The material in vv. 43-44 thus appears analogous to that in v. 15 considered above; in both instances the material is unique to Luke, and in both the material is externally attested in a source identified as the Hebrew Gospel. Thus, although external textual evidence and arguments of internal probability are roughly counterbalanced on vv. 43-44, the pronounced stylistic harmony of vv. 43-44 with the Third Gospel, the presence of at least one and perhaps two Hebraisms in the text in question, and the ascription of this text to the Hebrew Gospel preserved in the *Historia passionis Domini* tilt the balance of evidence in favor of the authenticity of vv. 43-44.

39-42 "Jesus went out as usual to the Mount of Olives, and his disciples followed him" (v. 39). "Went out" refers to leaving the upper room where Jesus and the disciples celebrated the Passover (vv. 14-38). "As usual" (v. 39; Gk. *kata to ethos,* also at 1:9; 2:42) recalls Luke's earlier report that "each evening Jesus went out to spend the night on the Mount of Olives" (21:37; on Mount of Olives, see at 19:29). In choosing to pray at the encampment on the Mount of Olives familiar to all the disciples, Jesus is obviously not trying to escape Judas (John 18:2).[112] Jesus and the disciples maintain the same relationship they have throughout his temple teaching: he leads and they follow. This is the last instance in the Third Gospel of the apostolic band (now only eleven, for Judas has departed) following Jesus — a reminder that the call to discipleship ultimately entails following Jesus in trials (9:23). When they came to "the place" (v. 40) — another indication of the familiarity of the site — Jesus commands the disciples, "Pray that you will not fall into temptation" (v. 40). This same commandment concludes the Mount of Olives prayer pericope (v. 46), thus framing the narrative. A similar commandment concluded Jesus' eschatological discourse in 21:36, and constitutes one of the pillars of the Lord's Prayer (11:4). In none of these instances does Jesus teach disciples that God will spare them from temptation. Only moments earlier in the upper room Jesus

---

Domini, a fourteenth/fifteenth-c. theological miscellany of German origin (see P. Vielhauer and G. Strecker, "Jewish-Christian Gospels," *NTApoc.* 1:151), but the reminiscence that the passage in question belonged to the early Hebrew Gospel. Bovon, *Lukas 19,28–24,53,* 299, accords that reminiscence priority over the Third Gospel itself: "It is possible — although hardly likely — that [the text in the *Historia*] is directly dependent on Luke (in which case it would constitute part of the reception of the Gospel rather than gospel tradition itself). I think, rather, that vv. 43-44, and indeed the entire pericope itself [22:15-46], belong to Luke's special source, and that the author of the Gospel of the Nazarenes was inspired by this source rather than by Luke's gospel. The result is that both the Gospel of Luke and the Gospel of the Nazarenes were witnesses of a very old tradition."

112. The familiarity of the place refutes the derision of Celsus, the second-c. detractor of Christianity, that "Jesus attempted to make his escape by disgracefully concealing himself" (Origen, *Cels.* 2.10).

alerted Peter that Satan had demanded to test him (v. 31). Jesus intercedes for the chief apostle, not that he would be spared the trial, but that the trial would not result in the loss of his faith (v. 32). The same sense governs vv. 40 and 46, namely, that the disciples would not be subjected to circumstances that would be ruinous to their faith.

Jesus "withdraws" (v. 41) to pray — although "withdraw" is perhaps too voluntary. The Greek *apospan* is more compulsory: Jesus is "drawn" or "pulled" away (Act 21:1; 2 Macc 13:18) "by the violence of his emotion, which was too strong to tolerate the sympathy of even the closest friends."[113] Mark 14:35 and Matt 26:39 report that Jesus removed himself "a little further," but Luke signifies the distance more concretely (and perhaps Hebraically, Gen 21:16): "about *a stone's throw* beyond them, he knelt down and prayed" (v. 41). The normal posture of prayer in Judaism was standing, often with upheld hands,[114] but kneeling in prayer, as here, was the pose of intense supplication (1 Kgs 8:54; Ezra 9:5; Dan 6:10). The imperfect tense of "pray" (v. 41) implies protracted prayer, of which v. 42 can only be a summary: "Father, if you are willing, take this cup from me; yet not my will, but yours be done." Among the ten-odd references to Jesus praying in the Third Gospel, this is the first reporting *what* he prayed. This prayer, atomic in compactness, is quintessentially Jesus, quintessentially Jewish, and quintessentially human. The invocation to God as "Father" identifies the prayer as unique to Jesus. Jews rarely if ever addressed God informally as "Father," but Jesus addressed God as such in all his prayers, even boldly and directly calling God "Abba" (Mark 14:36; Rom 8:15; Gal 4:6) and commanding his disciples to address God likewise (11:2).[115] The God to whom Jesus prays is not a cosmic force, an aesthetic or moral sense, or a feeling of sublimity. This God is "Father," *his* Father — near, hearing, compassionate. This prayer both models and testifies that Jesus does not face death alone, unknown, and unloved, but that he and his disciples may appeal to God as "Father" in the hour of doubt, fear, sorrow, and need.

The prayer is also quintessentially Jewish. "If you are willing" is a characteristic invocation in ancient Jewish prayers.[116] "Father" claims God person-

---

113. Plummer, *Luke,* 508.

114. Str-B 2:259-62.

115. Evidence in Jewish Palestine is extremely rare of "Abba" or "my Father" being used in individual address to God. The foremost treatment of the subject remains J. Jeremias, *The Prayers of Jesus* (trans. J. Bowden; Philadelphia: Fortress, 1978), 11-65; also his *New Testament Theology* (trans. J. Bowden; New York: Scribner's, 1971), 62-68. Critiques of Jeremias (G. Vermes, *Jesus and the World of Judaism* [London, 1983], 39-43; M. R. D'Angelo, "*Abba* and 'Father': Imperial Theology and the Jesus Traditions," *JBL* 111/4 [1992]: 611-30) modify Jeremias's conclusions at isolated points but do not rebut his central thesis that there are (as yet) no examples of the use of *abba* for God in Jewish texts as early as the Gospels.

116. Str-B 1:607; 2.262.

ally; "if you are willing" honors God to be forever sovereign and redemptive. The reference to "cup," equally Jewish, is a metaphor of what lies in store for one, whether good (Ps 16:5) or bad (Jer 49:12). When used with reference to Jesus' passion in the Gospels, "cup" is a metaphor of the death he must suffer.[117]

Finally, the prayer is intensely human. "Take this cup from me" is a window of crystal clarity into the soul of Jesus, in whom every human being recognizes his own soul.[118] The prayer of v. 42 is not the prayer of a resigned Stoic or dispassionate ascetic. It is the prayer of one who experiences the fierce claim of his human will over against the divine will. This prayer is Jesus' incarnate testimony that faith is a struggle to submit to the divine will in the face of counterclaims of the human will. The tension produced by these two wills engulfs Jesus not simply in mental anguish but in "anguish of soul" (v. 44; so 2 Macc 3:16).[119]

43-46 In the whirlpool of angst, "an angel from heaven appeared to [Jesus] and strengthened him" (v. 43). The description of an angel appearing to Jesus recalls the appearance of the angel to Zechariah in the infancy narrative (1:11).[120] The angel does not rescue Jesus or exempt him from temptation but "strengthens him" in it. What Jesus experiences from the angel on the Mount of Olives is what he prayed for Peter at the Last Supper (vv. 31-32): to be made strong and faithful (Dan 10:18). Although angels regularly appear in Scripture as guiding figures,[121] and more so, as figures of aid and succor,[122] no other Gospel records an appearance of an angel to Jesus prior to the crucifixion. Readers may doubt the genuineness of the appearance, for such things do not happen in "real life." What is normative for humanity is not normative for Jesus in this particular event, however, for human suffering, no matter how terrible, can never be a true analogy of the suffering of Jesus on the Mount of Olives. The cause of Jesus' intense anguish is not the prospect of his own

---

117. Matt 20:22-23 (par. Mark 10:38-39); Matt 26:39 (par. Mark 14:36; Luke 22:42); John 18:11; see Klein, *Lukasevangelium*, 683. The metaphor of "baptism" in 12:50 similarly refers to Jesus' impending crucifixion.

118. "Nowhere else in the gospel tradition is the humanity of Jesus so evident as here" (Fitzmyer, *Luke [X–XXIV]*, 1442).

119. The agony of Jesus' prayer on the Mount of Olives played a crucial role in the orthodox understanding of Christ, which eventuated in the so-called Chalcedonian Definition (451), esp. over against Apollinarianism, which denied the existence of a human soul in Jesus capable of suffering. See A. Grillmeier, S.J., *Christ in Christian Tradition* (trans. J. Bowden; New York: Sheed & Ward, 1965).

120. Gk. *ōphthē de autō angelos* is verbatim in 1:11 and 22:43. This is another Lukan inclusio of a theme in the infancy narrative corresponding to a similar theme in the Passion Narrative.

121. Gen 24:7, 40; Exod 14:19; 23:20, 23; 32:34; 33:2; Num 20:16; 22:1-41.

122. Hagar (Gen 16:7ff.; 21:17), Abraham (Gen 22:11), Jacob (Gen 31:11; 48:16), Gideon (Judg 6), Manoah (Judg 13), Daniel (Dan 6:22; 10:18), Zechariah (1–6).

death, but that of becoming the sin-bearer of the world, bearing "the sins of many, interceding for transgressors" (Isa 53:12), as Luke has noted immediately before in v. 37.[123] This is the cause of his agony, manifested traumatically in sweat "like drops of blood falling to the ground" (v. 44). If the Father spoke to the Son as he prayed at the baptism (3:21-22), and if the Father glorified the Son as he prayed on the Mount of Transfiguration (9:28-36), can the Father not strengthen the Son in his final prayer on the Mount of Olives?

The word for "anguish" (v. 44; *agōnia*) derives from the Greek word for struggle or striving (so 13:24). The accent here falls on the "stress," or "distress," that Jesus experiences in the prayer of submission.[124] As a consequence, he must "pray more earnestly" (v. 44). The imperfect tense of the verb for "pray" signifies duration: in addition to praying harder, Jesus must pray *more*. Both result in "sweat like drops of blood falling to the ground" (v. 44). Jesus' inner torment manifests itself in physical trauma. Dripping blood would be expected to describe the crucifixion, but no blood attends that narrative. The most intense description of Jesus' suffering in the Gospels occurs not at Golgotha but at Gethsemane, in his decision to submit to the Father's redemptive will.[125] On the Mount of Olives, Jesus' soul is crucified; on the Mount of Calvary, his body is surrendered.[126]

"When Jesus rose from prayer and went back to the disciples, he found them asleep, exhausted from sorrow. 'Why are you sleeping?' he asked. 'Get up and pray so that you will not fall into temptation'" (vv. 45-46).[127] These words conclude Luke's prayer account, omitting the longer versions of Matt and Mark that contain two more visits of Jesus to the disciples. The "sorrow" of the disciples (v. 45), noted only by Luke, makes Luke's Jesus more tolerant of the sleeping disciples than the Jesus of the other Synoptics. Grief is enervating. Jesus understands the disciples, including their sorrow and exhaustion. He appears "like his brothers and sisters in every way, ... merciful and faithful in service to God" on their behalf (Heb 2:17; 5:7-10). He admonishes, prepares, and strengthens them, "Pray that you will not fall into temptation" (v. 46).

---

123. On the fulfillment of the Servant of the Lord motif in the prayer on the Mount of Olives, see W. Larkin, "The Old Testament Background of Luke xxii.42-45," *NTS* 25/2 (1979): 250-54.

124. See the discussion in Bovon, *Lukas 19,28–24,53*, 309.

125. "Jesus' struggle on the Mount of Olives is presented by Luke as the watershed in the passion narrative, the critical point at which faithfulness to the divine will is embraced definitively in the strenuousness of prayer" (Green, *Luke*, 777).

126. Fitzmyer's dismissal of the pathos of this story from the Passion Narrative ("the first real episode of Jesus' passion is the story of his arrest on the Mount of Olives" [*Luke (X–XXIV)*, 1447]) is an absolute conundrum.

127. On the sleeping disciples, see comment at 9:32.

THE ARREST (22:47-53)

Like the foregoing material in chap. 22, the arrest of Jesus in vv. 47-53 appears to be a combination of Mark's narrative and Luke's special source.[128] The various Hebraisms noted subsequently again suggest a Hebrew source. The arrest of Jesus follows the prayer on the Mount of Olives more seamlessly in Luke than in the other Synoptics. Like the prayer, which was framed by Jesus' admonitions to the disciples to pray not to enter into temptation (vv. 40, 46), the arrest is framed by the betrayal of Jesus with a kiss (v. 47) and Jesus' declaration of its meaning (v. 53). The arrest scenes of Mark 14:43-49 and Matt 26:47-56 portray Jesus as acted upon by more powerful forces; Mark, for example, refers four times to Jesus being "seized" (Gk. *kratein*; 14:44, 46, 49, 51). In Luke, Jesus appears in a more sovereign profile. He calls Judas by name, asking if he would betray the Son of Man with a kiss (v. 48). All four Gospels record that an ear was severed in the arrest of Jesus, but only Luke records that Jesus healed the ear. Even in this desperate hour, Jesus remains a healing savior. In the other Synoptics the dominical fellowship is broken when the disciples scatter and Jesus is led away. Luke does not report the flight of the disciples, or even the actual arrest (mentioned in passing only in 22:54), but rather the final judgment of Jesus on his arrest: "This is your hour — when darkness reigns" (v. 53). The early church found in the arrest narrative, and particularly Luke's version of it, a model of behavior for Christians facing persecution and martyrdom.[129]

47-50 "While [Jesus] was still speaking, behold a crowd appeared, and the one called Judas, one of the Twelve, was leading them and he approached Jesus to kiss him" (v. 47, my translation). No respite follows the prayer as the mob emerges from the darkness. Judas is leading the throng, allowing Jesus opportunity first to deal with him, and later with the crowd. The word for "behold" (Gk. *idou*) is not strictly necessary but is typical of Hebrew narrative, suggesting an original Hebrew *hineh*.[130] The reference to Judas as "the one called Judas, one of the Twelve" is needlessly precise, for Judas has been mentioned twice before, once by name (vv. 3-6) and once by allusion (vv. 21-22). "One called" (passive voice of Gk. *legein*) normally either introduces

---

128. Rengstorf, *Lukas*, 233; Grundmann, *Lukas*, 413; Marshall, *Luke*, 834.

129. The mid-second-c. *Mart. Pol.* preserves several reminiscences of the arrest narratives in the Gospels. As Jesus was betrayed by "one of the Twelve" (v. 47), Polycarp was betrayed "by those who were of his own house" (*Mart. Pol.* 6.2). Also like Jesus, Polycarp is taken from an "upper room" (7.1), he is seized as a "robber" (7.1), and his death occurs "on the day of preparation of the meal" (7.1). In his suffering, Polycarp becomes a partaker of Christ, and his persecutors undergo the same punishment of Judas (6.2). Of particular relevance for the Lukan account, the police captain "called [Gk. *epilegomenos*] Herod" may be modeled on the betrayer "called [*legomenos*] Judas" (v. 47).

130. So Wolter, *Lukasevangelium*, 726.

a character or a second name of a character (e.g., 22:1; Acts 6:9), neither of which applies here. Marshall wonders whether the reference is contemptuous,[131] but given the reserve with which the Evangelists refer to Judas, it seems unlikely. Even though Judas has not been mentioned since the Last Supper, the emphasis here is not necessary to reintroduce him.[132] It is possible that the reference derives from Luke's special source, which may have introduced Judas here for the first time.[133]

The note that Judas "approached Jesus to kiss him" (v. 47) is both infamous and puzzling, since Jesus is not otherwise greeted by a kiss, nor is it certain, as some commentators maintain, that a kiss was a customary greeting between rabbis and disciples. Kisses of homage and respect were practiced in Israel (1 Sam 10:1; 2 Sam 19:39; Luke 7:38; Acts 20:37), but this is a kiss of treachery, not of love.[134] It may recall Joab's kiss-and-dagger ruse with Amasa (2 Sam 20:9-10), or even more probably, Jacob's kiss of his father, Isaac, in deceiving him and gaining Esau's blessing (Gen 27:27).[135] Luke records only two instances of Jesus being kissed: by the sinful woman (7:38, 45) and by Judas (v. 47). The kiss of the sinful outsider, ironically, epitomizes love and faith, whereas the kiss of the chosen insider epitomizes betrayal. The one who was far off is brought near (Eph 2:17-19), and the one who was near is cast into outer darkness (v. 53). The other Synoptics report only cursory formalities between Judas and Jesus. Luke records a direct question to Judas by Jesus, not present elsewhere in the Gospels. "Judas, are you betraying the Son of Man with a kiss?" (v. 48). Every word is emphatic. The second-person singular pronoun "you" accentuates Judas's responsibility for the betrayal, thus heightening his guilt. Judas is betraying not simply a person but a divine office, "the Son of Man" (see at 5:24). And all this by means of a kiss — a gesture of love as a cloak of treachery!

"When Jesus' followers saw what was going to happen, they said, 'Lord, should we strike with our swords?'" (v. 49). "Jesus' followers" is overly specific. The original Greek is more ambiguous: "those around [Jesus]" (same Gk. phrase in Mark 3:34; 4:10). This is probably a calculated ambiguity. It may be, as many commentators suggest, another example of Luke shielding the disciples from blame, but it may equally likely reflect the inherent realities of such a situation. Anyone who has been part of a brawl or riot — especially at night — knows how quickly confusion blurs persons and events. There is nothing

---

131. Marshall, *Luke*, 835; so too Bovon, *Luke 19,28–24,53*, 327.

132. So Wolter, *Lukasevangelium*, 726.

133. So F. Rehkopf, *Die lukanische Sonderquelle* (Tübingen: Mohr Siebeck, 1959), 37-38.

134. On the kiss of Judas, see G. Stählin, *phileō*, *TDNT* 9:140-41.

135. The Greek wording of the kisses of Judas and Jacob are close: *kai ēngisen tō Iēsou philēsai auton* (v. 47); *kai* [Jacob] *engisas ephilēsen auton* (Gen 27:27 LXX).

ambiguous, however, about "Should we strike with our swords?" a statement
not present in the other Gospels. The construction of this sentence in Greek
indicates that Jesus is not being asked for permission, but being informed that
the moment for action has arrived![136] Nor is this mere bluster. "One of them
struck the servant of the high priest, cutting off his right ear" (v. 50). This is
another example of Luke's penchant for the "right" side of things (see at 6:6).
Why Luke would note a right ear is unclear, although such a detail might be
expected of a physician. The severing of the ear is preserved in all four Gospels,
although only in John 18:10 is the assailant identified as Peter and the servant
of the high priest as Malchus. That the servant of the high priest is the object
of the first blow could suggest that the defendants regarded the high priest
as the instigator of the arrest. Whether Peter was the swordsman cannot be
affirmed for certain. What can be affirmed is that the flash of swords, especially
given the doubtless superior numbers behind Judas, displays courage on the
part of Jesus' allies.

51-53 The first of Jesus' two responses is to quell the retaliation. His
verbal response in v. 51 is obscure, which may indicate that the original was an
Aramaic or Hebrew idiom. The most common (and preferred) translation of
eate heōs toutou (lit. "allow until this") is "No more of this!" but the response
could possibly mean, "This, and no more," or even "Let them [the police]
have their way."[137] Whatever the precise meaning, the response censures the
blow — although the degree of censure is debatable. Jesus' second response
corroborates the censure: "He touched the man's ear and healed him" (v. 51).
Luke is the only Evangelist to report the healing of the severed ear. From the
outset of his Galilean ministry, Luke portrays Jesus as a prophetic healer, like
Elijah and Elisha (see excursus at 7:15-17). V. 51 testifies that "even in his arrest,
Jesus is a bringer of salvation in both word and deed."[138] In healing the ear of
the servant of the high priest, Jesus exemplifies the love he commanded his
disciples — "Love your enemies, do good to them" (6:35).

Jesus' second response is to address "the chief priests, the temple guard,
and the elders, who had come for him" (v. 52). To all three constituencies
Jesus speaks authoritatively. We know that Judas entered into collusion with
the chief priests and temple guard (see at v. 4), but mention of "elders," i.e.,
members of the Sanhedrin, whether Pharisees or Sadducees, is new. Given
that Luke omits Pharisees from the Passion Narrative, and that the high priest

---

136. So Marshall, *Luke,* 837. The introduction of the question by *ei* in Greek reflects an
original Heb. *'im* (so BDF §440.3), designating the whole question as a probable Hebraism.

137. The translation of the NIV is affirmed by BDAG, 269, as well as by many commentators. The second translation is favored by J. Creed, *The Gospel according to St. Luke*
(London: Macmillan, 1930), 274; the third by Marshall, *Luke,* 837. See discussion of the phrase
in Plummer, *Luke,* 512; Fitzmyer, *Luke (X–XXIV),* 1451.

138. Klein, *Lukasevangelium,* 685.

was a Sadducee, this third group may connote primarily or entirely Sadducean elders. Chief priests, temple guard, and elders were either members or affiliates of the Sanhedrin, thus unambiguously identifying that body as the source and force behind Jesus' arrest. John 18:3, 12 report that Roman soldiers were also present at the arrest, thus suggesting collusion on the part of the Sanhedrin with the Roman governor. Luke makes no reference to Romans, but a Roman presence at the arrest scene cannot be excluded. The question at the end of v. 52, "Have you come out with swords and clubs as though I were a revolutionary?" etched itself deeply into the memory of the early church and is reported verbatim in Greek in all three Synoptics. The word for "revolutionary" (Gk. *lēstēs;* NIV "leading a rebellion") refers to a criminal, a "bandit" or "robber" (10:30, 36; 19:46), especially a violent criminal. Those who plunged Judea into war with Rome in 66 were labeled *lēstēs* by Josephus, by which he meant "insurrectionists, terrorists."[139] Whether use of the term here implies that the Sanhedrin and Romans (?) suspected Jesus of Zealot ties is unclear. V. 52, however, along with the notice on Jesus' cross (23:38), implies that the Sanhedrin was not only aware of Jesus' messianic pretensions but assumed them to be militant.[140]

The concluding declaration of Jesus strips any pretensions of rectitude from the intentions of the Sanhedrin. "Every day I was with you in the temple courts, and you did not lay a hand on me" (v. 53). The fact that the Sanhedrin did not arrest Jesus earlier, and that there are no further grounds for doing so now, condemns his arrest as infamy under the guise of religious and political sanction. "This is your hour, the authority of darkness," concludes Jesus (v. 53). Luke laid the groundwork for this judgment back in 20:19-20, when Jesus described the desire of the scribes and high priests to deliver him to "the authority of the governor" as "their hour." "The authority of darkness" also anticipates the reference to "the authority of Herod" in 23:7, and finally "the authority of Satan" in Acts 26:18. All four phrases are parallel in the original Greek. The ultimate source of "the authority of darkness" in Luke-Acts is Satan (22:31; Acts 26:18). Although Satan corrupts Judas to betray Jesus (22:3), none of the four "authority" sayings refers to Judas. Each refers to political-religious powers, which Jesus names at his arrest. What transpires through the Sanhedrin, Pilate, and Herod is no less "the authority of darkness" than what transpires through Judas. The "hour" has arrived, when these climactic forces conspire against Jesus. They are free to kill God's Son and Servant — and they will — but they are not free to determine the consequences of killing him.

---

139. *J. W.* 2.253-54; 4.504; *Ant.* 14.159-60; 20.160-67.
140. See A. Schlatter, *Der Evangelist Matthäus* (Stuttgart: Calwer Verlag, 1948), 756; K. Rengstorf, *lēstēs, TWNT* 4:267.

THE TESTING OF PETER AND THE TRIAL OF JESUS IN THE HOUSE OF THE HIGH PRIEST (22:54-71)

All four Gospels record a trial of Jesus following his arrest, in which he was taken to the house of the high priest and there denied by Peter, mistreated and interrogated by the Sanhedrin, and finally delivered to Pilate, the Roman governor. The Gospels record these events differently. Mark 14:53-72 (followed by Matt 26:57-75) creates a "sandwich" narrative in which the trial and abuse of the Sanhedrin are inserted into the middle of Peter's denials. Peter's refusal to bear witness in the flanking halves is set in stark contrast to Jesus' faithful witness under greater persecution from the Sanhedrin in the middle of the sandwich. John's account consists of a longer chain of events beginning with Peter in the courtyard of the high priests Annas and Caiaphas (18:12-18), followed by questioning of Jesus by Annas (18:19-24), two denials of Peter (18:25-27), and Jesus' deliverance to Pilate (18:28–19:5).

In the other Gospels the above narrative alternates between Peter and Jesus, but Luke trains the narrative more specifically on Jesus. Peter follows the arrested Jesus to the house of the high priest, where he denies Jesus (22:54-62), after which Jesus is abused by guards of the high priest (22:63-65), arraigned before the Sanhedrin (22:66-71), and delivered to Pilate (23:1). Peter's denial in Luke is less vociferous than it is in Matt or Mark, and once Peter is removed from the scene, the focus on Jesus is undivided. Jesus utters not a word against his mockers and beaters (vv. 63-65), thus fulfilling the prophecy related to the Servant of God, "As a sheep before its shearers is silent, he did not open his mouth" (Isa 53:7). More important, Luke omits from the Sanhedrin trial the testimony of false witnesses and the charge of sedition against the temple (Matt 26:59-63; Mark 14:55-61). These questions will be raised subsequently before Pilate (23:2-5). The whole Sanhedrin speaks with one voice to one issue: is Jesus the Messiah (v. 67) and Son of God (v. 70)? The issue before the Sanhedrin, as before readers of the Gospel, is christological — who *is* Jesus?

54-62 The plot against Jesus, hatched and nurtured since his arrival in Jerusalem (19:47; 22:2), is not resisted, and hence the arrest is anticlimactic, noted only in passing (v. 54; NIV "Then seizing him . . ."). Luke records the arrest in a Greek technical term, *syllambanein,* meaning "taking into custody" (1 Sam 23:26; Acts 1:16; 12:3; 23:27; 26:21), which he follows with a redundancy (v. 54; Gk. *auton ēgagon kai eisēgagon,* "led him away and took him into"). This latter expression is a probable Hebraism, one of ten words or expressions in vv. 54-71 that can be explained as such.[141] Hebraic echoes appear here in similar

---

141. Bovon, *Lukas 19,28–24,53,* 347, describes the redundancy as "an unbelievable repetition." On its probable Hebraic character, see F. Rehkopf, *Die lukanische Sonderquelle* (WUNT 5;

proportions as they have throughout chap. 22, again suggesting that Luke has augmented the Gospel of Mark with a Hebrew source.[142] "Peter followed at a distance" (v. 54) can be interpreted differently, depending on whether one accents "followed" or "at a distance." If "follow" determines the sense, then it is qualified acclaim of Peter, for the other apostles seem to have vanished. If "at a distance" determines the sense — and Peter's earlier boast (v. 33) makes this sense immediately apparent — then we have an apprehensive disciple with second thoughts, which will lead to betrayal. Peter follows to "the house of the high priest" (v. 54; Mark 14:53). The high priest at the time of Jesus' death, Joseph Caiaphas, ruled from 18 to 36. The Fourth Gospel reports that Jesus was taken "first to Annas, who was the father-in-law of Caiaphas" (18:13). John's testimony is worthy of serious consideration, for his account of the arrest and interrogation contains several details, the name of Annas among them, that seem reminiscent of first-person testimony. If early Christian tradition associated only the office of high priest with Jesus' arrest, it would be natural to supply the name of Caiaphas (so Matt 26:57), who was in fact high priest at the time. Since the name of Annas is not the obvious name to supply, its presence in John 18:13 argues for its historicity.

The "house" of the high priest was a villa, even a palace, although its exact location is uncertain. The anonymous Pilgrim of Bordeaux (fourth c.) identified a villa on the eastern slope of Mount Zion as the site of "the house of the High Priest Caiaphas, where the pillars to which Jesus was bound and whipped are still evident."[143] In the sixth century a church was established on the same site, which is commemorated today as the church of St. Peter in Gallicantu (cock-crow).[144] Continued excavations have unearthed beneath the church a series of cisterns and grottos that date to the Herodian period (37 B.C.–A.D. 70), which would have offered maximum security for brief internment of prisoners. The location of this site, which lay little more than 1,000 yards (1 km) southwest of the traditional site of Gethsemane and which is well-attested in Christian tradition, makes it a reasonable site of Peter's denial.[145] Josephus, however, reports that the house of Annas (and Caiaphas?) lay in "the upper city" of Jerusalem, near the palace of Agrippa and Bernice located in the Hasmonean royal palace, only a hundred yards (90 m) west of the south

---

Tübingen: Mohr Siebeck, 1959), 41; Wolter, *Lukasevangelium*, 730. For the remaining Hebraisms in vv. 54-71, see Edwards, *Hebrew Gospel*, 327-28.

142. See the survey of vocabulary unique to Luke in vv. 54-71 in Jeremias, *Sprache des Lukasevangeliums*, 296-300.

143. Cited in Pixner, *Mit Jesus in Jerusalem*, 103.

144. This church is featured behind the Zion church in the Madaba Map (sixth c.).

145. Dalman, *Sacred Sites and Ways*, 328-34, locates the house of Caiaphas in the traditional location.

end of the Temple Mount.[146] If this latter site is correct, then the house of the chief priest would be approximately 550 yards (500 m) north of the Church of St. Peter in Gallicantu.[147]

Spring nights in Jerusalem are cold, and a fire is kindled in the courtyard of the high priest. The Greek word for "courtyard," *aulē*, signifies an interior open area surrounded by walls or living spaces. "When they had lit a fire . . . Peter sat in the midst of them." The identity of "they" and "them" is ambiguous, for Luke's focus is on Peter. The Greek imperfect tense of "sit" indicates that Peter remained there for some time. The double use of *mesos*, "middle, midst" (v. 55), situates Peter squarely in the company of the arrest party. Peter is thus *not* with Jesus (v. 61). The symbolism is low-key, but not to be overlooked. Peter evidently hopes to remain inconspicuous. A servant girl spies him and studies him in the light of the fire (v. 56). Her piercing gaze defrocks his anonymity, and in a classic example of guilt by association, she exclaims, "This man was also with him." Peter has obviously not followed at sufficient distance! Peter may wish to be disassociated from Jesus, but in the eyes of the world his existence is defined in relation to Jesus. He will later again be recognized as "being with him" (Acts 4:13), and then he confesses it boldly. The unassuming presence of Greek *kai*, "also" or "even" (v. 56; omitted in NIV), suggests there was a lookout for other followers of Jesus (22:38). The unwelcome disclosure of the "servant girl" burned itself into the record of all four Gospels. The accusation of an unnamed, unentitled servant girl does not compare with the more powerful accusations of the Sanhedrin against Jesus, but even this test Peter cannot withstand.

Peter is not unprepared with a response. The aorist tense of "deny" (v. 57) implies decisiveness, "I do not know him, woman!" The Greek word for "know" is not the expected *ginōskein*, meaning to know something or someone by experience, but a less frequent word — and also a less-thorough form of knowledge — *oida*, meaning to have information about something. Use of this word implies that Peter neither knows Jesus nor knows about him. The vocative "woman!" at the end of the denial is reprimanding, perhaps insinuating that, as a mere woman, her testimony is invalid. Peter's protests are unable to halt the chain reaction of questions. "A little later a man saw him and said, 'You are also one of them.' 'Man, I am not!' Peter replied" (v. 58). This second accusation is not whether Peter knows Jesus, but whether he is one of "them," i.e., one of his disciples (John 18:25). Peter's second denial is in essence a *self*-denial, for it denies the fellowship, mission, and witness he has shared with Jesus since he was called to "catch people" (5:10).

"After the interval of about an hour another witness" came forward

---

146. Josephus, *J. W.* 2.344, 426; *Ant.* 20.189-90.
147. Murphy-O'Connor, *The Holy Land*, 107, favors this view.

(v. 59). Jewish law required "the testimony of two or three witnesses" to establish a verdict (Deut 19:15). V. 59, which bears throughout the mark of Luke's editorial hand,[148] satisfies the Jewish criterion of credibility by supplying three witness, among them — in accord with Luke's penchant for pairs — a male and female witness (see at 14:1). All three witnesses "sift" Peter (v. 31). The interval between the second and third accusations is longer and more precise in Luke than in Matt 26:73 and Mark 14:70 ("after a little while").[149] Does the interval give Peter false hopes of a reprieve? Or perhaps a chance to reconsider his denials? Or does it simply supply the narrative time lapse necessary for the morning cockcrow?[150] Whatever its effect on Peter, the interval hardens the conviction of the bystanders. The final witness no longer suggests but "asserts . . . in truth" (Gk. *diïschyrizesthai . . . ep' alētheias*) that "this man was with him, because he is a Galilean" (v. 59). The force of the final witness is conclusive that Peter is lying, for he is betrayed by his Galilean speech patterns.[151] Peter denies the accusation emphatically (but not abusively as in Mark 14:71 and Matt 26:74), as he has the first two. "Man, I don't know what you're talking about!" He is barely able to complete the sentence, for "as he was speaking, the rooster crowed" (v. 60).

"The Lord turned and looked straight at Peter. Then Peter remembered the word the Lord had spoken to him: 'Before the rooster crows today, you will disown me three times'" (v. 61). This is another demonstration of Jesus' foreknowledge in the Passion Narrative. The penetrating look that conveys it is absent from the other Gospels, however. We are not told where Jesus saw Peter, perhaps through an opening, or as Jesus was being led to or from interrogation. The word "turned" (Gk. *strephein*) is used seven times in the Third Gospel — always in the same form, always with Jesus as subject, always denoting a decisive word or action.[152] This is the only instance of the seven where Jesus is identified as Lord, and nowhere does it cause a greater turn of events. The last time Peter called Jesus Lord, he swore undying allegiance (v. 33); now the look of Jesus as Lord convicts Peter of betrayal. The relation of Jesus to the disciple is always and only that of Lord.[153] Jesus knows exactly what is happening to Peter, even if Peter does not know what is happening to himself. Like Judas, Peter stands in close proximity to Jesus and is thus in a position to do great harm. The critical encounter is intensified by Jesus' piercing and transformative gaze (Gk. *emblepein;* NIV "looked straight at"), which occurs in

---

148. Jeremias, *Sprache des Lukasevangeliums,* 297.

149. Note the similar concrete image in 22:41, "a stone's throw away."

150. Wolter, *Lukasevangelium,* 731, favors the last option.

151. In the Babylonian Talmud, R. Eliezer (ca. 270) comments that in Galilee "*alefs* were pronounced like *'ayins* and *'ayins* like *alefs*" (cited in Str-B 1:156-59).

152. 7:9, 44; 9:55; 10:23, 14:25; 22:61; 23:28.

153. See here Rowe, *Early Narrative Christology,* 178-79.

Luke only here and in 20:17.[154] Peter could defend himself from the look of the servant girl (v. 56), but not from the look of Jesus.[155] Jesus speaks no word; his solitary gaze causes Peter to "remember the word the Lord had spoken to him" (v. 34).[156] "Remembering the word of the Lord" is an important discipline of Jesus' followers; in this instance it calls sin to remembrance, but in others it is a remembrance of grace (24:8; Acts 11:16; John 2:22). The look of Jesus is thus one of judgment and grace, of condemnation and forgiveness.[157] Peter's bitter sorrow in v. 62[158] signifies repentance that leads to transformation. V. 62 may reflect the poignant prophecy of Isa 22:4, where the destruction of Jerusalem causes the prophet to cry aloud, "Turn away from me; let me weep bitterly." Peter's remorse in the courtyard repeats his confession when he was first called by Jesus, "I am a sinful man" (5:8).

63-65 With the departure of Peter, Luke focuses on Jesus alone, first on his mistreatment in the high priest's villa (vv. 63-65), followed by his hearing before the entire Sanhedrin after daybreak (vv. 66-71). "The men who were guarding Jesus were mocking and beating him" (v. 63). The identity of the abusers is left as unspecific as was that of the gathering in the courtyard (v. 55). The Greek word for "guarding" (*synechein*), like the word for "seizing" (see at v. 54), is a technical term for "guarding in custody," referring here to (male; Gk. *andres*) soldiers or servants of the high priest in charge of Jesus.[159] The primary word Luke uses to describe the mistreatment of Jesus is "mockery." The Greek word *empaizein* literally means "to dance around (someone)," with the derivative meaning, "to mock, scorn, or ridicule." Mockery is especially hurled at the righteous person in Wisdom literature. In the NT the word occurs only in the Synoptics, and there almost exclusively of the mockery of Jesus in the passion. The other Synoptics report that the guards "spit in [Jesus'] face," "struck him with their fists," and "slapped him" (Mark 14:65; Matt 26:67). Luke summarizes these tortures in one word, "they beat him" (v. 63). To pass the time, they turned to sadism, "blind-folding him and demanding, 'Prophesy! Who hit you?'" (v. 64).[160] "And they said many other insulting things [Gk. *blasphēmein*,

---

154. Klein, *Lukasevangelium*, 690, calls Jesus' gaze "transcendental."

155. A point made by Nolland, *Luke 18:35–24:53*, 1095.

156. The exact phrase in Greek appears, again from the mouth of Peter, in Acts 11:16.

157. One of the oldest icons in the world, the sixth-c. "Christ Pantocrator" of St. Catherine's Monastery (Mount Sinai), is famous for its two eyes of Christ — a stern right eye of judgment, and a weeping left eye of mercy.

158. From a textual viewpoint, the authenticity of v. 62 is beyond reasonable doubt (contra Bovon, *Lukas 19,28–24,53*, 353). Its absence from several Italian versions and its doubt in 0171 (ca. 300, the reading of which is uncertain) do not seriously jeopardize its otherwise unanimous attestation in the manuscript tradition. See Metzger, *TCGNT*, 151.

159. BDAG, 971; Plummer, *Luke*, 517.

160. The tormenters were not inventing a new form of humiliation but were resorting

'blaspheme'] to him."[161] In all this, Jesus is silent before his abusers (Isa 53:7). That Luke summarizes their cruelties by what was *said* rather than what was done underscores the deep and abiding offense of mockery.[162]

66-71 At daybreak a formal meeting of the Sanhedrin is convened. A new day is not in view here, but rather the dawn of Nisan 15 or Passover, which began at sunset the night before. The Gospel of Mark records two hearings by the Sanhedrin, one at night (14:55-64) and a second at daybreak (15:1). Luke records only one daytime hearing before the Sanhedrin, perhaps because Jewish law stipulated that a night trial was invalid in capital cases. The most common name of the highest council of the Jews was the **Sanhedrin** (see at 9:22), but it was also known in Greek as *gerousia* ("[council of] elders"; 1 Macc 12:6; Acts 5:21; Josephus, *Ant.* 12.142; 13.166), *boulē* ("council"; Josephus, *J.W.* 2.331), or *presbyterion* ("council of elders"; v. 66; Acts 22:5).[163] In all Greek literature only Luke uses the last term as a designation for the Jewish Sanhedrin.[164] In v. 66 both *presbyterion* (a Hellenistic designation) and *synedrion* (the common Hebrew designation) occur. If they are synonymous, both refer to the council that consisted of chief priests, scribes, and elders. It is possible, however, that *presbyterion* refers to the council and *synedrion* to the *place* where the council met. Luke appears to use *synedrion* elsewhere with reference to place (Acts 4:15; 23:20, 28), and the context of v. 66 (lit. "they led him into their Sanhedrin") allows a similar understanding.[165] According to the later Mishnah (*Sanh.* 11:2),

---

to an old one. See D. Miller, "*Empaizein:* Playing the Mock Game (Luke 22:63-64)," *JBL* 90 (1971): 309-13; Wolter, *Lukasevangelium*, 733.

161. Vv. 65, 71 summarize the Sanhedrin's case against Jesus in generalities rather than specifics. The oldest full manuscript Talmud, the Munich Talmud of 1343, includes the following reference to Jesus of Nazareth and two grounds for his execution that have been expurgated from later versions of the Talmud: "On the eve of Passover they hung Yeshu the Notzri for sorcery and enticing Israel [to idolatry]." According to the Gospels, Jewish charges of sorcery (11:15; Mark 3:22; Matt 12:24) and leading Israel astray (John 7:12) are lodged against Jesus during his ministry, but not specifically at his trial. In the mid-second c. Justin Martyr quotes these same two charges: "For they dared to call him a sorcerer and a deceiver of the people" (*Dial.* 69:7). Justin appears to be quoting a text with which Trypho, his Jewish opponent, is familiar, perhaps the very tradition preserved in the unexpurgated version of the Munich Talmud. For a discussion of the possibility of this reference dating to the time of Jesus, see D. Instone-Brewer, "Jesus of Nazareth's Trial in the Uncensored Talmud," *TynBul* 62/2 (2011): 269-94.

162. See G. Bertram, *empaizō, TWNT* 5:632-35. Luke employs four different words for "mockery" in the trial and crucifixion scene: *empaizein* ("mock," 22:63; 23:11, 36), *blasphēmein* ("blaspheme," 22:65; 23:39), *exouthenein* ("despise," 23:11), and *ekmyktērizein* ("sneer," 23:35).

163. On the Sanhedrin, see Schürer, *History of the Jewish People*, 2:195-226; G. Bornkamm, *presbyterion, TWNT* 6:654; Jeremias, *Sprache des Lukasevangeliums*, 299.

164. Wolter, *Lukasevangelium*, 735.

165. BDAG, 967, and Bovon, *Lukas 19,28–24,53*, 365-66, favor an understanding of place, though Lagrange, *Luc*, 571, disputes it.

the Sanhedrin met in the Hall of Hewn Stones in the temple. If this is the meaning of the term, v. 66 presupposes that Jesus has been transferred from the high priest's house to the chambers of the Sanhedrin in the temple.

The earliest record of Jewish law with regard to capital cases is found in the Mishnah (ca. 200). There twenty-three members of the Sanhedrin are decreed necessary to judge capital cases, with reasons for acquittal preceding those for conviction. Capital cases required a second sitting the following day in order to sustain a verdict of guilt. Both sittings had to take place during daytime, and neither on the eve of Sabbath or a festival (*m. Sanh.* 4:1). Witnesses were to be warned against rumor and hearsay (*m. Sanh.* 4:5). A charge of blasphemy could not be sustained unless the accused cursed God's name itself, in which case the punishment prescribed was death by stoning, with the corpse then hung from a tree (*m. Sanh.* 7:5). As noted above, the prescribed meeting hall was the Hall of Hewn Stones in the temple (*m. Sanh.* 11:2). There is no evidence that the Sanhedrin met formally in the house of the high priest.

Several details of Luke's account conflict with the above protocol. A second hearing is lacking, as are reasons for acquittal. Jesus does not blaspheme God. And as noted above, the hearing may have taken place in the temple, but that is not certain; all other Gospels, at any rate, imply it occurred in the house of the high priest. How should these discrepancies be explained? The Mishnah sets forth the status of Jewish jurisprudence around the year 200, and we cannot be certain the same status prevailed in Palestine 170 years earlier. If it did, we should reckon with something on the order of a grand jury, i.e., a private session to hear accusations in order to determine if just cause existed to refer the case to a higher court. According to Luke, the Sanhedrin placed a contract on Jesus' life before the hearing in the house of the high priest (19:47; 22:2).[166] The Sanhedrin appears to waive or short-circuit whatever legal procedures would prevent an appeal for Jesus' execution by the Roman governor. A similar contravention of legal proceedings probably prevailed in the death of Stephen (Acts 7:54-60), and certainly prevailed in the trial and death of James, brother of the Lord, under the high priest Ananus in 62 (Josephus, *Ant.* 20.200-203).

Two features in particular dominate Luke's description of the hearing before the Sanhedrin, the first being its plenary opposition to Jesus. In Mark 14:60 and Matt 26:62 the interrogation is pressed by the high priest alone, but in Luke Jesus is confronted by the united opposition of the Sanhedrin. The Sanhedrin is gathered (v. 66), puts both questions to Jesus in concert (vv. 67, 70), and is united in its verdict against him (v. 71). We are not told how cacophony results in concert in this matter, but Luke is clear that the case against Jesus is not limited to a radical fringe. The Sanhedrin has been united in opposition

---

166. Mark 3:6, Matt 12:14, and John 5:18 lay the plot against Jesus much earlier in his ministry.

to Jesus throughout the Passion Narrative, and in the trial in the high priest's house it succeeds in enlisting in that opposition the authority of the temple and the people the Sanhedrin ostensibly represent.

Second and more important, Luke's trial narrative focuses exclusively on Christology. Absent are false witnesses (Mark 14:56-60; Matt 26:59-62), and surprisingly even a formal death sentence (Mark 14:64; Matt 26:66). The guards earlier mocked Jesus' reputation as a prophet (v. 64), but the Sanhedrin demands a response from him regarding his reputation as Messiah (v. 67; see on the term at 9:20) and Son of God (v. 70). The last two of these titles would not describe Israel's rabbis, sages, and prophets. Combined, the three titles imply Jesus' unique authority from God and a self-consciousness on his part as the one sent by God to redeem Israel (20:13).

In the lead-up to the Jewish War of 66-70, Jewish revolutionaries appeared in increasing numbers, some of whom harbored messianic pretensions. The Sanhedrin could not afford to be indifferent to these potentially powerful figures, and thus the question of Jesus' messiahship is not wholly unexpected.[167] Jesus responds, "If I tell you, you will not believe me, and if I asked you, you would not answer.[168] But from now on, the Son of Man will be seated at the right hand of the mighty God" (vv. 67-69). In 20:1-8 the Sanhedrin challenged Jesus' authority but refused to declare its own judgment. According to John 10:24-26, insinuations and evasiveness characterized the Jewish leaders' attitude toward Jesus long before Passion Week (cf. Jer 38:15). The distance between Jesus and the religious leaders has become unbridgeable, and Jesus therefore refuses a direct answer. He is indeed Messiah, but his messiahship will not be realized in national aspirations and political hegemony. If he were to answer the question directly, he would have to say, "Did not the Messiah have to suffer these things and then enter his glory?" (24:26). The religious leaders are unprepared to affirm the role of suffering in the fulfillment of the messianic mission, however. Hence, they must await the *eschaton* for their answer, when "the Son of Man is seated at the right hand of the mighty God." In v. 69 Jesus combines two powerful offices in the OT — the return of the Son of Man in glory (Dan 7:13) and the royal Messiah sitting at God's right hand (Ps 110:1). He applies both offices to his future reign. His enthronement in heaven will be the ultimate vindication of his messianic office![169] Already in the mar-

---

167. Barabbas (23:18-19) may have been considered among their number, and Theudas (Acts 5:36; Josephus, *Ant.* 20.97-98), Judas the Galilean (Acts 5:37; Josephus, *Ant.* 18.4-10); and James and Simon, sons of Judas the Galilean (Josephus, *Ant.* 20.102) certainly were.

168. Manuscripts A D K N W Γ Δ Ψ add "you would not answer *me or release* [*me*]" to v. 68, whereas p⁷⁵ ℵ B L T omit the italicized words (so NIV). The manuscripts omitting the words, though fewer in number, are older and more diverse, and their witness argues against the authenticity of the italicized words. See Metzger, *TCGNT*, 152.

169. See Nolland, *Luke 18:35–24:53*, 1110.

tyrdom of Stephen (Acts 7:56), Jesus will be recognized and acknowledged as the heir of these two offices.

EXCURSUS: SON OF GOD

The Sanhedrin's second question to Jesus raises the ontological bar. "Are you then the Son of God?" (v. 70). The title "Son of God" does not play the climactic role in Luke's crucifixion scene that it does in Mark 15:39, nor in Luke's account of Peter's confession as it does in Matt 16:16. In the Third Gospel, the special role of Son of God is reserved for the annunciation (1:35), where, as in the Sanhedrin trial, it appears in conjunction with Messiah (1:32-33), and also as in the Sanhedrin trial, it appears as the final and supreme christological title. At the annunciation (1:35), "Son of God" is introduced in the context of the glorification of the tabernacle in Exod 40:34-35: as God overshadowed the tabernacle and filled it with his presence so that even Moses could not enter, so the Holy Spirit overshadows Mary's womb and fills it with Son of God so that Joseph's seed is not necessary. "Son of God" is thus the primary category by which to understand the incarnation, signifying that as God was present in a holy *place,* the tabernacle, so he is fully and finally present in a holy *person,* Jesus of Nazareth.

This christological foundation at the outset of the Third Gospel determines the subsequent understanding of Jesus' relation to the Father and mission as Son in the remainder of the Gospel. In two further instances — the baptism (3:22) and the transfiguration (9:35) — the Father reconfirms Jesus divine sonship of 1:35, although without developing the concept further. In three instances Jesus himself attests to his unique consciousness of divine sonship. The first is as a boy in the temple when he says, "I must be about the things of my Father" (2:49). The second and most important is when he confesses that, as the Son (which he repeats three times in one verse), he has received "all things" from the Father and is himself the sole revealer of the Father (10:22). The unshared sonship of Jesus with the Father in 10:22 far exceeds an adoptive understanding of sonship (such as king [e.g., 2 Sam 7:14] or "divine man"). Rather, it clearly implies Jesus' unique knowledge of the Father, which endows him with exclusive authority to reveal the Father. Jesus' third reference to himself as the Son occurs in the parable of the Tenants (20:13), where "the beloved Son" must be understood as a testimony to his role in the history of salvation. In comparison to the "servants" who have gone before him, Jesus is the Son, and as such he is the "heir" and fulfillment of Israel. As a consequence of the Son's unique relationship with the Father, Jesus is able to withstand temptations from the devil to employ his divine sonship in ways that would violate the Father's will (4:3, 9). That same filial relationship empowers Jesus with authority to release those bound by the power of the devil (4:41; 8:28). Jesus' divine sonship also determines the critical overture in the Third Gospel, where "as the time approached for him to be taken up to heaven, Jesus resolutely set out for Jerusalem" (9:51). The ultimate meaning of "being taken up" refers to his enthronement as Son of God at the right hand of the Father (see on the term at 9:51), which is subsequently attested in 24:51 and Acts 2:33; 3:19-21; 7:55-56.

"Messiah/Christ" and "Son of God" are frequently (but erroneously) understood to be more or less equivalent titles. In the NT — and in the mouth of the Sanhedrin — these terms differ greatly. Various messianic expectations circulated in first-century Palestine, including a messianic king, apocalyptic Son of Man, eschatological high priest, and eschatological prophet.[170] Whatever the exact messianic expectation, all Jews were agreed that Messiah would supersede God's earlier messengers in his endowment with divine wisdom and power. He would not be a divine being, however, and hence he would not forgive sins, nor would he be raised from the dead. In comparison with Son of God, an exalted figure who would be essentially united to God's nature and authority, Messiah was a lesser and subsidiary figure and office.[171] Jewish literature occasionally brought Messiah and Son of God into relationship with one another, as Luke does in 1:32-35 and 4:41. A commentary on 2 Sam 7:12-14 at Qumran, for example, interprets the phrase "I will be a father to him and he will be a son to me" with reference to "the branch of David" (i.e., Messiah), who will arise to rebuild the fallen house of David (4Q174 = 4QFlor). In bringing Son of God and Messiah together, however, Jews did not equate the two titles. Son of God was the rarer and greater of the two.

The description of the Son of Man in v. 69 far exceeds the attributes ascribed to Messiah. The Sanhedrin perceives the difference and immediately asks, "Are you then the Son of God?" The question could be translated more directly and consequentially, "You are then the Son of God?" It was no sin to claim to be Messiah.[172] It was blasphemous, however — and blasphemy was one of two sins (along with idolatry) for which Jews reserved capital punishment — to claim divine sonship. Jesus does not directly claim to be Son of God, but he answers this second and more important question *less indirectly*

170. For a review of these concepts, see H. Riesenfeld, *The Gospel Tradition* (trans. E. Rowley and R. Kraft; Philadelphia: Fortress Press, 1970), 32-40.

171. So I. Marshall, "The Divine Sonship of Jesus," *Int* 21 (1967): 99; R. Fuller, *The Mission and Achievement of Jesus* (SBT 12; London: SCM Press, 1954), 85; C. Cranfield, "A Study of Mark 1:9-11," *SJT* 8 (1955): 62.

172. In the Second Jewish Revolt (132-35) Bar Kokhba was referred to as Messiah by R. Akiba and also in messianic imagery (e.g., Star of Jacob, Scepter of Israel, Num 24:17) without the title being considered blasphemous. See Schürer, *History of the Jewish People*, 1:543-45.

than he did the first.[173] "You said that I am." The insinuation of the question and the suggestiveness of Jesus' answer result in the Sanhedrin concluding that Jesus acknowledged his divine sonship. This is assured by their conclusion, "Why do we need any more testimony? We have heard it from his own lips" (v. 71).[174] The second "we" is emphatic in Greek: "we *ourselves* have heard it." In refusing to deny the claim of Son of God, Jesus has in effect affirmed it. For the Sanhedrin, that is a blasphemous claim; for Jesus, it is the deepest truth of his existence and the ground of his followers' faith.[175] What Simeon predicted at Jesus' birth has transpired: Jesus is an offense, "destined to cause the falling and rising of many in Israel" (2:34).

---

173. Brown, *Death of the Messiah*, 1:493, sees Jesus' response in v. 70 as "a full affir-mative. . . . Jesus has turned the question of the Jewish authorities into an affirmation of the highest Christian title." Luke, to be sure, holds such a confession, but I am not persuaded that Jesus' answer in v. 70 is as explicit as Brown suggests.

174. "From his own mouth" appears to be a Hebraism for "he himself" (so BDF §217.3; Wolter, *Lukasevangelium*, 737).

175. See Klein, *Lukasevangelium*, 694.

CHAPTER TWENTY-ONE

Trial and Crucifixion

Luke 23:1-49

EXCURSUS: PONTIUS PILATE AND HEROD ANTIPAS

Pontius Pilate was the fifth Roman governor of Palestine (ruled 26-36), and the only governor discussed in any detail by Philo and Josephus. His official title was "prefect," and his residence was Caesarea Maritima.[1] Pilate's three chief responsibilities as prefect were command of Roman troops in Palestine, supervision of judiciary functions, and administration of financial affairs. At Jewish festivals, and especially at Passover, when pilgrims streamed to the temple with religious fervor, the presence of the governor was required in Jerusalem. There Pilate presumably lodged at Herod's Palace on the western wall of the city, and it was probably there that Jesus appeared before him.[2]

Pilate tied for the longest tenure of any of the fourteen Roman governors of Judea prior to the Jewish War of 66-70.[3] Given the challenge of ruling a people that in principle rejected Roman hegemony, his eleven years in office are testimony that he was not an incompetent ruler.[4] Philo nevertheless describes Pilate as "inflexible, stubborn, and cruel" (*Embassy* 301-2), a

---

1. Various titles were used of Roman governors. Josephus, writing in Greek, uses *hēgemōn* ("ruler"), *epitropos* ("guardian/governor"), and *eparchos* ("prefect"). The NT uses only the first term of Pilate, and Philo the second. Tacitus, writing in Latin, uses *procurator*. A Latin inscription discovered in Caesarea Maritima in 1961 refers to Pilate as *praefectus*, "prefect," and this seems to have been the proper title of pre-Claudian governors. See D. Schwartz, "Pontius Pilate," *ABD* 5:397.

2. On the location of the Praetorium in Herod's Palace, see Brown, *Death of the Messiah*, 1:705-10.

3. Pilate's predecessor, Valerius Gratus, also served eleven years (15-26).

4. "Judea was better run under Pilate and in the early prefecture than it had been in the last years of Herod the Great or would be in the last years of the Roman prefecture" (R. Brown, *Death of the Messiah*, 1:683).

judgment with which Josephus agrees. Pilate's contempt for Jewish religion, custom, and privileges not only tarnished his tenure as governor but accounted for his eventual banishment by Emperor Gaius (Caligula). On one occasion he introduced military standards into Jerusalem bearing the bust of the Emperor Tiberius, violating the Jewish ban on images. Offended Jews proceeded en masse to Caesarea, nearly seventy miles (110 km) distant, and staged a five-day nonviolent protest at Pilate's residence. Pilate initially gave orders to slay the protesters in the stadium, but when "they bared their throats, welcoming death rather than transgression of their law," he withdrew the images from Jerusalem (*Ant.* 18.55-59; *J.W.* 2.169-71; Philo, *Embassy* 299-304). His concession was the result of Realpolitik rather than goodwill. On another occasion he financed the construction of a twenty-three-mile aqueduct to sluice water to Jerusalem with funds from the temple treasury. Jews protested the use of temple funds for public works. Pilate exchanged blows for protests, and in the ensuing melee large numbers were slain by military brutality that exceeded Pilate's orders, and still others were trampled to death in attempted flight (*Ant.* 18.60-62; *J.W.* 2.175-77). Luke records a third outrage in which Pilate, having slain a number of Galileans who had brought offerings to Jerusalem, mixed their blood with their sacrifices (13:1). The final straw in Pilate's tenure was an unprovoked attack on a group of Samaritans making a pilgrimage to Mount Gerizim, of whom some were killed, others put to flight, and others captured. Of the captured, the most respected and distinguished were executed. Samaritan survivors pursued their case against Pilate before Vitellius, governor of Syria, who relieved him of his governorship and sent him to Rome to answer for his conduct (*Ant.* 18.85-88).[5]

Pilate was not wantonly brutal, certainly not on the scale of Caligula or Nero, and by standards of the day he was not overly corrupt. He was capable of constructive endeavors on behalf of Jews, as the aqueduct project attests, but equally dismissive of Jewish traditions, as the same incident exhibits. When confronted by (perceived) opposition, he responded with obstinacy and force rather than with wisdom. His Jewish subjects were themselves stubborn and defiant, but his contempt for their religious customs exacerbated rather than ameliorated the conflicts between them and him.

The portrait of Pilate in the Passion Narratives, not least in the Third Gospel, tends to be more sympathetic than the unfavorable picture of Pilate in Philo and Josephus.[6] Luke, for example, omits the brutal whipping account preserved

---

5. See the discussion of Pilate in Schürer, *History of the Jewish People,* 1:383-87; Brown, *Death of the Messiah,* 1:693-705.

6. For a survey of early Christian apocryphal portraits of Pilate that rehabilitate him as a tragic hero of the Christian cause, see Schürer, *History of the Jewish People,* 1:387, n. 144; Brown, *Death of the Messiah,* 1:696.

in the other Gospels (Matt 27:27-31; Mark 15:16-20; John 19:2-3), and Luke depicts Pilate appealing to the high priests, Jewish leaders, and crowds for Jesus' innocence and their clemency (23:4, 14, 16, 20, 22). How should Luke's portrait of Pilate be understood? The Gospels and Christian tradition are unanimous that Jesus was crucified. Crucifixion was a Roman form of execution, hence Roman authority, personified in Pontius Pilate, was ultimately responsible for Jesus' death. According to John 18:3, 12, Roman soldiers participated in the arrest of Jesus, and the haste with which the case against Jesus was prosecuted suggests that Pilate was a knowing and less-than-reluctant accomplice. It might be supposed that the guarded sympathy accorded Pilate in the crucifixion narratives is politically motivated (or partly so), namely, by the unenviable task of the Evangelists of reporting the death of Jesus at the hands of Rome in such a way that Romans were not offended and Christians living under their jurisdiction were not endangered. It has also often been assumed, to the contrary, that the Passion Narratives place the blame for Jesus' death wholly on the Jews — or at least on Jewish leaders — and that the Roman governor, despite his efforts to the contrary, was helpless to prevent it. Both of these views distort the historical circumstances of Jesus' crucifixion, and Luke's record of it. With regard to the first, we should scarcely expect that the Evangelists, who insist that true discipleship is inevitably expressed in faithful witness under persecution, would misrepresent Roman responsibility for Jesus' death in order to avert the possible consequences of suffering for the sake of the gospel. With regard to the second, the Gospels testify that the case against Jesus, though instigated by some Jewish leaders, did not include them all (Nicodemus and Joseph of Arimathea are named exceptions). As for the guilt of Jewish people as a whole, Luke notes that "a large number" of Jews followed Jesus to the cross and mourned for him (23:27-31, 48). As for the view that Pilate heroically though vainly appealed for Jesus' release, no ancient witness — certainly not Josephus or Philo — portrayed Pilate as a friend of the underdog.

With reference to Jesus' death, Luke's four passion predictions lay responsibility at the feet of the Sanhedrin (9:22), "humanity" (9:44), "this generation" (17:25), the nations/Gentiles (18:32). The fourth constituency obviously includes Romans, but the combined accent of all four predictions holds all "sinful humanity" (24:7) responsible for Jesus' death.[7] This does not exempt Pilate from responsibility, however, nor does Luke portray him as a good man. His single judgment of Pilate declares him a murderer (13:1), the same judgment he renders of Antipas (13:31).[8] Luke's overall moderation regarding

---

7. "Judas gave Jesus over to the Jewish authorities; the Jewish authorities gave Jesus over to Pilate; now Pilate gives Jesus over to be crucified. That chain scarcely delivers Pilate from participation" (Brown, *Death of the Messiah*, 1:854).

8. For a full review of Pilate in Luke-Acts, see K. Yamazaki-Ransom, *The Roman Em-*

the Roman governor is typical of the moderation he exhibits toward others involved in the death of Jesus. The disciples are repeatedly exonerated in the Passion Narratives, and the injured servant of the most offending party, the high priest, is healed by Jesus (22:50-51). Judas, as we have seen, is spared vilification. As for Pilate, Luke portrays him as a reluctant and intolerant ruler who, following his abortive transfer of Jesus to Antipas (23:7), forsakes the claims of justice and surrenders Jesus to the implacable mood of the chief priests (23:13-16) and crowds (23:18-23).[9]

Herod Antipas, the son of Herod the Great and Malthace (the fourth of Herod's ten wives!), was both less able and less cruel than his father. During his forty-year-plus reign (4 B.C.–A.D. 39) Antipas respected Jewish sensibilities by not issuing offensive coins, and his building programs in Tiberias and Sepphoris contributed to an impressive and lasting legacy. With the exception of the divorce of his wife in order to marry Herodias — a divorce that led to a war with his deposed wife's father, the King of Nabatea, and his subsequent ouster as tetrarch — Antipas avoided the kind of provocations that resulted in Pilate's recall.[10]

Antipas is referred to in the NT as "Herod" (or occasionally as "Herod the Tetrarch" or "Herod the king"). He is mentioned in Matt 14:1-12 and Mark 6:14-29 only in relation to the martyrdom of the Baptist, and in John not at all. Luke omits the account of the martyrdom of John, yet includes seven references to Antipas not mentioned elsewhere in the Gospels, and two more in Acts. Antipas constitutes a minor figure in the Third Gospel who periodically emerges from the background shadows. He first appears in 3:1-2, along with Tiberius Caesar, two other tetrarchs, and two chief priests, as a datum of information to date and locate the advent of the messianic era. Luke con-

---

pire in *Luke's Narrative* (LNTS 404; New York: T&T Clark, 2010), chap. 4. Yamazaki-Ransom concludes that "Luke's portray of Pilate is essentially negative."

9. H. Conzelmann, *Die Mitte der Zeit* (6th ed.; BHT 17; Tübingen: Mohr Siebeck, 1977), 79-80, followed by Klein, *Lukasevangelium,* 702, argues that Luke's exoneration of Pilate in the Passion Narrative can be attributed to the Jewish War of 66-70, i.e., the early Christian church found Roman hegemony (in both Titus and Pilate) more tolerable than Jewish fanaticism (in both the Zealot revolutionaries and the Jewish crowd at Jesus' crucifixion). This argument is objectionable on several counts. Most obviously, it does not account for Luke's comparable benevolence to the disciples, high priest, and Judas, as well as to Pilate. More problematic, it assumes an easy and — as Western history has tragically illustrated — dangerous dichotomy between righteous Gentiles and wicked Jews. As noted above, a judgment that attributes to Jews sole responsibility in the death of Jesus is a distortion of the Gospels, and particularly the Third Gospel.

10. For overall assessments of Antipas, see Schürer, *History of the Jewish People,* 1:340-53; M. Jensen, *Herod Antipas in Galilee: The Literary and Archaeological Sources on the Reign of Herod Antipas and Its Socio-Economic Impact on Galilee* (WUNT 2/215; Tübingen: Mohr Siebeck, 2006).

cludes the story of John in chap. 3 with a note that Antipas was "convicted" by John's preaching about Herodias, and about "all the evils done by Antipas" (3:19). This note assumes a fuller knowledge of John and his fate on the part of Luke's readers, but by enclosing the biographical sketch of John between two references to Antipas in chap. 3, Luke inextricably links John's fates with Herod Antipas.

Antipas next occurs with reference to a certain Joanna, the wife of Chuza, "the manager of Herod's household" (8:3). This reference, and a similar reference to Manaen (Acts 13:1, "who had been brought up with Herod the tetrarch"), identifies two named Christians within Herod's inner circle. Joanna and Manaen, another of Luke's male-female pairs, are doubtless key sources of Luke's knowledge of Antipas.[11] The terse report that Herod decapitated John (9:7-9) is a startling abridgement of the virtual novellas of John's martyrdom in Mark 6:14-29 and Matt 14:1-12. In omitting the account of John's martyrdom under Antipas, Luke assumes fuller knowledge of John's fate on the part of his readers. Above all, the omission of John's martyrdom retains narrative focus on Jesus. Rather than informing readers of details of John's death, 9:7-9 anticipates the appearance of Antipas in the Passion Narrative (23:8-12).

Antipas again haunts the Lukan narrative in the Pharisees' warning to Jesus, "Flee, for Herod wants to kill you" (13:31). This warning reminds readers that, unlike Matt and Mark, Luke does not dispense with Antipas at the death of John. John's death, in fact, was only a prelude — a forerunner! — to his dealings with Jesus. In Jerusalem Jesus must inevitably meet with Antipas, which Luke alone reports (23:8-12). In 9:9 Luke reports that Antipas longed to "see" Jesus, and he introduces Antipas in 23:8 with *three* further references to his desire to "see" Jesus or a sign from him. His hopes are disappointed, for Jesus remains silent and, perhaps even more disappointing for Antipas, unspectacular. Had Antipas desired to *hear* Jesus, a fertile seed might have been planted (8:4-15). Antipas desires a spectacle, however. Those who are only interested in "seeing" Jesus or a sign from him will make Jesus in their own image and likeness, and they will mock him.

Antipas remained as hostile to the followers of Jesus as to Jesus himself. The warning in Jesus' eschatological discourse that believers "will be brought before kings and governors" (21:12) anticipates the persecution of the disciples

---

11. Following B. Weiss and M. Dibelius, Klein, *Lukasevangelium,* 697, accounts for the name of Antipas in Luke-Acts as a "Christological interpretation" of Ps 2:2 (quoted in Acts 4:26), which mentions the "kings of the earth" (= Pontius Pilate) and "rulers" (= Herod Antipas) conspiring against "the Lord's Anointed" (= Jesus Christ). This fragile hypothesis might possibly account for the presence of Antipas in the trial scene, but it cannot account for the presence of Antipas as a background figure throughout the Third Gospel. Luke's plenary testimony to Antipas is better accounted for by the testimonies of Joanna and Manaen (so too Fitzmyer, *Luke [X–XXIV],* 1479).

in Acts 4. With reference to the arrest of Peter and John by the Sanhedrin (Acts 3–4), Luke quotes from Ps 2, which mentions "the rulers who band together against the Lord and against his Anointed One" (Acts 4:26). That prophecy is fulfilled by "Herod and Pontius Pilate [who] met together with the Gentiles and the people of Israel in this city [= Jerusalem] to conspire against your holy servant Jesus, whom you anointed" (Acts 4:27; cf. Ignatius, *Smyrn.* 1:2).[12] Mention of Antipas's name before Pilate's may suggest that, of the two, the Herodian prince was the more deadly opponent of Jesus and nascent Christianity. According to Luke, Antipas was the only individual outside the circle of Jesus' family and disciples who was personally exposed to both John, "the prophet of the Most High" (1:76), and Jesus, "the Son of the Most High" (1:32). Even firsthand experience of Jesus and John is no guarantee of faith. It can, in fact, result in hardened opposition, in the face of which the proclamation of the gospel must forge its way.[13]

JESUS APPEARS BEFORE PONTIUS PILATE AND HEROD ANTIPAS (23:1-25)

Luke's trial scene compares with the other Synoptics in roughly the same proportion that material since 21:37 has compared with them. In the present section a Markan backbone (vv. 3, 17-22a, 24-25) is fleshed out with large amounts of material either new or revised by Luke (vv. 1-2, 4-12, 13-16, 22b-23).[14] The

---

12. Brown, *Death of the Messiah*, 1:779-81, argues cogently that 23:6-12 rests on a historical reminiscence of Luke rather than a fabrication based on Ps 2.

13. The three official opponents of Jesus and the early Christian movement — Caiaphas, Pilate, and Herod Antipas — are all mentioned roughly a dozen times each in the Third Gospel (the office of high priest is usually mentioned in place of the name "Caiaphas," however). All three were deposed by Vitellius, governor of Syria, within the same period (36-39), and the depositions of all three may bear at least indirect relation to John and Jesus. Regarding the Herodian prince, when Antipas divorced his wife (Shaudat?), daughter of Aretas, in order to marry Herodias (a liaison criticized by John [Mark 6:17-18]), Aretas attacked Antipas, thereby drawing Vitellius into the conflict, who subsequently deposed Antipas (Josephus, *Ant.* 18:101-19). Regarding the Roman governor, Pilate was deposed by Vitellius because of his slaughter of the Samaritans (Josephus, *Ant.* 18.85-89). The slaughter of the Samaritans was cited by Jesus (13:1-3), and it exemplifies the cruelty Pilate exhibited in executing Jesus. Regarding the chief priest, we are not told why "Caiaphas was removed from his sacred office as high priest" by Vitellius (*Ant.* 18:95), but it could be imagined that, in purging Palestine of inept or contrary leadership, the governor of Syria would remove from office a high priest who overexerted his influence in the sentence against Jesus (John 18:28-31).

14. For an inventory of Lukan vocabulary unique to vv. 1-25, see Jeremias, *Sprache des Lukasevangeliums*, 300-304.

presence of at least seven Hebraisms in vv. 5-15 again suggests that a Hebrew source plays a role in the new or revised material.[15]

1-5   Luke begins the trial by emphasizing that the whole Sanhedrin (lit. "all of their multitude") delivered Jesus to Pilate (v. 1). The united front with which the Sanhedrin confronted Jesus in the Passion Narrative (19:47; 20:19; 22:2, 52, 66; 23:10) continues in his trial. The entirety of the Sanhedrin is accentuated in v. 1, but it does not mean absolute unanimity, for Joseph of Arimathea (23:50-51, plus Nicodemus, John 19:39-40) will be named as exceptions to it. It is almost certain that the right of inflicting capital punishment was reserved exclusively for the Roman prefect (John 18:31; Josephus, *J.W.* 2.117).[16] This accounts for the necessity of the Sanhedrin delivering Jesus to the authority of Pilate in order to execute Jesus.

Vv. 2-5 form a chiasmus:

A   Accusation of Sanhedrin (v. 2)
　　B   Pilate questions Jesus (v. 3a, b)
　　　　C   Jesus answers (v. 3c)
　　B¹   Pilate declares Jesus innocent (v. 4)
A¹   Intensified accusation of Sanhedrin (v. 5).[17]

"The [Sanhedrin] began to accuse [Jesus], saying, 'We have found this man subverting our nation and opposing payment of taxes to Caesar and claiming to be Messiah, a king'" (v. 2).[18] A not dissimilar set of charges is leveled against Paul and Silas in Acts 17:6-7. The accusations that the Sanhedrin presents to Pilate are different from their own accusations to Jesus, which concerned christological issues (22:67, 70). All three of their accusations are engineered

---

15. Edwards, *Hebrew Gospel,* 328. The similarities that Schweizer, *Lukas,* 236, and esp. Klein, *Lukasevangelium,* 696-97, note between the trial scenes of Luke and John do not seem to me either numerous or specific enough to warrant positing literary dependence of one Evangelist on the other.

16. The stoning of Stephen (Acts 7:58-60), death of James (*Ant.* 20.200), and perhaps woman taken in adultery (John 8:3-5) are exceptions, but they appear to be irregular rather than legal executions. A. Sherwin-White, *Roman Society and Roman Law in the New Testament* (Oxford: University Press, 1963), 36-37, argues cogently that Rome zealously guarded the right of capital punishment in order to protect pro-Roman factions in occupied territories from vigilante reprisals, and that Judea would have been the last place where an exception to this right would have been allowed. Further, see R. Brown, *The Gospel according to John (XIII–XXI)* (AB; New York: Doubleday, 1970), 849-50.

17. Wolter, *Lukasevangelium,* 738.

18. Marcion's quotation of this verse adds accusations that Jesus "opposed the law and prophets" and "led astray women and children" (Epiphanius, *Marc.* 316-17, 346). Marcion was accused of both offenses, and the additions may derive from him. If so, they profile Marcion as one who suffered the same fate as Jesus. See Plummer, *Luke,* 521.

to tap sensitive political nerves (John 11:48-50) and elicit maximum reaction from Pilate. "This fellow" (Gk. *touton;* NIV "this man"), which is shifted to the front of the Greek sentence for emphasis, is a derogatory way of refusing to acknowledge Jesus by name. Jesus is first accused of being an agitator who "misleads" (v. 2; Gk. *diastrephein;* NIV "subverts") Jews under Roman occupation. Especially in his early Galilean ministry, Jesus attracted large and enthusiastic crowds, but there is zero evidence that he used — or intended to use — his influence to incite them to rebellion.[19] Totalitarianism is ever anxious of insurrection. Even an accusation of such, regardless of lack of evidence, is not without effect. The second accusation — that Jesus opposes payment of taxes to Caesar — is patently false, for he did not forbid paying taxes (20:22, 25) and he notoriously associated with tax collectors (5:27-30; 7:34; 15:1; 18:9-14). Despite its falsity, this particular accusation was not harmless, for all known messianic pretenders prior to the Jewish War were in one way or another tax protesters. The very charge implied that Jesus was a political messianic pretender. Whether Jesus had *yet* refused taxation was immaterial, for the claim to messiahship inevitably included opposition to Roman taxation.[20] The third accusation, that Jesus is Messiah, is the only charge in common with his appearance before the Sanhedrin (22:67). But unlike the earlier charge, where "Messiah" was left undefined, and unlike 2:11, where it is defined by "Lord," Messiah is here defined by "king." Claims of human kingship were categorically anti-imperial, and thus grounds for high treason (John 19:12, 15).[21] The linkage of "king" to "Messiah" in v. 2 is particularly lethal. Josephus canvassed many would-be leaders, kings, prophets, and revolutionaries, yet he applied the term "Messiah" to none of them except Jesus (*Ant.* 20.200).[22] Of the score of named individuals he discusses, none was subjected prior to execution to a legal trial, whether Jewish or Roman, as was Jesus.[23] The accusation that Jesus claimed to be Messiah not only caused his name to be recalled in Josephus's monumental history of the Jews, but doubtless distinguished the trial of Jesus from all others in Pilate's career.

Pilate's question, "Are you the king of the Jews?" and Jesus' answer, "You

---

19. Nolland, *Luke 18:35–24:53*, 1119, notes that Jesus "created a stir throughout Judea, but nothing that smacked of sedition."

20. Schlatter, *Lukas*, 439; Bovon, *Lukas 19,28–24,53*, 384: "All anti-Roman liberation movements regarded every census and every tax levy as an intolerable measure of the ruling occupation force."

21. See Str-B 2:263; Wolter, *Lukasevangelium*, 739.

22. Scholars debate the genuineness of "Messiah" as attributed to Jesus in *Ant.* 18.63-64, but the authenticity of the title in *Ant.* 20.200 is beyond reasonable doubt.

23. The named individuals include Judas son of Ezechias, Simon, Athrongaeus, Menahem, Simon, son of Giora, a Samaritan, Theudas, and "the Egyptian." See Brown, *Death of the Messiah*, 1:472-80, 681.

have said so," are verbatim in all four Gospels (v. 3; Matt 27:11; Mark 15:2; John 18:33, 37). The title affixed to Jesus' cross, "The King of the Jews," is likewise verbatim in all four Gospels (v. 38; Matt 27:37; Mark 15:26; John 19:19). Evangelical tradition is agreed that the accusation of kingship was paramount in Jesus' crucifixion. Josephus uses "King of the Jews" (occasionally "King of the Hebrews") with reference to every Israelite king from Saul to Herod.[24] "King of the Jews" was thus the default expression for every sovereign in Israel. Its ubiquity in the Gospel trial narratives suggests that Pilate suspected — or better perhaps, the religious leaders encouraged him to suspect — that Jesus endeavored to reestablish a kingship over Judea and Jerusalem similar to that exercised by the Hasmoneans and Herod the Great. This would obviously rival the Roman prefect.

"You have said so" strikes one as a noncommittal response to an inevitable fate, and thus a continuance of the messianic ambiguity of Jesus' responses to the Sanhedrin (22:67-70). The reply almost certainly signifies more than this. It was not typical of rabbinic speech, and its ten-odd OT occurrences invariably *affirm* what a speaker has said.[25] Its closest and most dramatic OT referent may be the reply of Moses to Pharaoh, "As you have said [Heb. *kēn dibartāh*], I shall not see your face again!" (Exod 10:29). We cannot know for certain how Pilate understood the response, but in the mouth of Jesus — and in Luke's usage — the phrase is not noncommittal and ambiguous. It avoids answering Pilate's question directly (which would give Pilate grounds for execution), but it implies an affirmation of his question.[26]

Pilate addresses the chief priests and crowd, "I find no basis for a charge against this man" (v. 4). This response presupposes more interrogation than Luke records.[27] It should be remembered that, since Jesus was not a Roman citizen, Pilate was not constrained by Roman law but allowed full discretionary exercise of his imperial authority. Luke telescopes events in order to highlight two points. The first relates to "the chief priests and the crowd." The "crowd" probably includes the various constituencies that are being summoned into the power bloc of the chief priests. The former clearly specifies the chief priests as the driving force in Jesus' trial. They have led the charge against Jesus throughout the Passion Narrative, and they lead it before Pilate. The issue throughout the trial is not one of justice but one of power. The two principals in the power struggle are Pilate and the chief priests (v. 4). Other entities are involved, in-

---

24. *Ant.* 6.98; 7.72; 14.9, 36; 15.373, 409; 16.291, 311; *J. W.* 6.103, 439; 7.171. See Wolter, *Lukasevangelium,* 739.

25. Gk. *sy legeis* ("You say so"): 1 Kgs 3:23 (2x); 18:11, 14; Neh 5:12; 6:8; Amos 7:16; Jer 39[32]:25, 36, 43; 47[40]:16.

26. Str-B 1:990-91 offers a cogent explanation of the expression.

27. Plummer, *Luke,* 521, writes that v. 3 "condenses a conversation given at greater length by J[oh]n, without whose narrative that of the three [Synoptics] is scarcely intelligible."

cluding Jesus, the council, people, and Antipas. Still others will be drawn into the stream as it gathers momentum — Simon of Cyrene (v. 26), women (vv. 27-31), criminals (vv. 39-43), a centurion (v. 47), Joseph of Arimathea (vv. 50-54), and the inevitable *hoi polloi* — acquaintances, observers, and bystanders. None of these, even Jesus himself, is critical in the power struggle, however. The contest is between Pilate and the chief priests, one of whom must prevail over the other. The battle line is drawn in v. 4 — and this is Luke's second point — by the word "find" (Gk. *heuriskein*). In declaring, "I find no basis for a charge," Pilate anticipates a series of declarations to follow in Luke-Acts, all of which exonerate Jesus and his followers, including Paul.[28] The Sanhedrin finds against Jesus (v. 2), whereas Pilate finds for him.

"They insisted, 'He stirs up the people all over Judea by his teaching. He started in Galilee and has come all the way here'" (v. 5). The Greek word for "insisted" *(epischyein)* means "to persist in something." The tense here is imperfect and thus intensified: the chief priests are *unrelenting*. Pilate's bluster has not blown away the Sanhedrin. Rather, like a sail in a stiff wind, the Sanhedrin drafts from it and gains momentum. The accusation of "stirring up" (Gk. *anaseiein*), slightly different from "subverting" (v. 2; Gk. *diastrephein*), carries revolutionary overtones: the teaching of Jesus "incites" the crowds and foments rebellion. As noted above, no evidence exists for this charge. The charge is calculated to magnify Jesus' danger throughout the extent of Pilate's jurisdiction. The reference to "Judea," especially when accompanied by "all over" (Gk. *holē*), must refer to Palestine as a whole (as in 4:44; 7:17), not simply to the province of Judea. The implication of v. 5 is that the pestilence broke out in Galilee but spread throughout Pilate's jurisdiction. Luke uses a virtually verbatim expression in Acts 10:37 to summarize the spread of the gospel in Peter's speech before the Sanhedrin.

A note on "the people" in the trial scene is in order. The Greek word for "people," *laos,* is a favorite Lukan expression, occurring thirty-seven times in the Gospel (see at 6:17). In nearly one-half of its occurrences the word is coupled with "all" or a similar intensifier, implying a vast majority, the entire populace. Its three uses in the trial account (vv. 5, 13, 14) all lack the intensifier, suggesting less than "all the people." Luke's use of *laos* in the trial scene does not permit the conclusion that "all the Jews" sided with the chief priests and clamored for Jesus' death. Not surprisingly, "the people" were divided. The references to "the large number of people following Jesus" to crucifixion (v. 27), and the people at the cross who "beat their breasts and went away" (v. 48), indicate that a sizable population of Jews opposed the sway of the chief priests.

6-12   When Pilate learned that Jesus hailed from Galilee (also John

---

28. 23:14, 22; Acts 17:7-9; 18:12-15; 19:40; 23:9; 26:32; 28:5. See Klein, *Lukasevangelium,* 698.

7:52), he transferred the case to Herod Antipas, tetrarch of Galilee and Perea. Antipas was present in Jerusalem at the Passover festival, if not for reasons of piety, then certainly in order to surveil the throngs of pilgrims and their latent revolutionary potential. Antipas was familiar with that potential, for Galilee was home to several insurgent factions that later coalesced in the Zealot movement and revolted against Roman rule in 66. "The man is a Galilean" (v. 6) may insinuate Jesus' association with such aims and movements.[29] The language of vv. 6-7 is appropriate to political protocol: acknowledging that primary authority (Gk. *exousia*) over the accused belongs to Antipas, Pilate remands (Gk. *anapempein*) Jesus to his jurisdiction.[30] *Anapempein* implies delivering a prisoner to a proper (and often higher) authority. In this gesture Pilate displays deference to Antipas, even though in both principle and practice Pilate was not his subordinate but his superior. We cannot be certain of Pilate's motives in referring Jesus to Antipas.[31] Even if the referral was honorable, ulterior motives likely played a role. Pilate may hope that circumstances will absolve him of dealing with Jesus. Remanding Jesus to Antipas serves a strategy of creating such circumstances. If Antipas rules on Jesus, Pilate will be free of an unwelcome confrontation with the Sanhedrin. Even if Pilate must eventually deal with Jesus, he may gain Antipas as an ally — a *Jewish* ally (v. 15).[32] Severe punishment of Jesus (v. 16), or an amnesty policy (vv. 18-19), may also contribute to such circumstances. In all these eventualities Antipas plays the initial role.

"When Herod saw Jesus, he was greatly pleased, because for a long time he had been wanting to see him. From what he had heard about him, he hoped to see him perform a sign of some sort" (v. 8). The imperfect tenses of the verbs in v. 8 imply that Antipas had long been intent on "seeing" Jesus (repeated three times), or a "sign" from him. Similar wording of 9:9 indicates that Antipas had desired to "see" Jesus since the death of the Baptist. A man whose life hangs in the balance can surely be expected to put on a show. Antipas was ethnically Jewish, but his fascination with paranormal spectacle (e.g., 9:9; Mark 6:14-16) seems more pagan than Jewish. Pagan religion was ultimately a manipulative affair, sampling the altars of many gods, visiting groves of sacred trees, and consulting stars, fires, innards, and mountains, all in order to benefit from the largesse of the gods and placate their vengeance. The Christian faith offers a wholly different understanding of the spiritual world, and those who come to Jesus for any purpose other than knowing, loving, and following him will inevitably be disappointed. The desire for "signs," in particular, has

---

29. So Schweizer, *Lukas*, 234.

30. On the Hebraic versus Hellenistic spelling of "Jerusalem," see chap. 2, n. 64.

31. See Fitzmyer, *Luke (X–XXIV)*, 1480.

32. So Marshall, *Luke*, 855.

already been associated with diabolical intent (4:9-12) or lack of faith (4:23-24). To desire Jesus because of signs and wonders, health and wealth, powers and privilege, or any other ulterior purposes is not to desire Jesus. Jesus does not gratify religious curiosity (11:29). Antipas "plied [Jesus] with many questions" (v. 9). The Greek is literally "with many words." The stress on verbiage rather than value indicates the poverty of the questions. Jesus did not reply to the Sanhedrin because it was too hostile (22:67); he does not reply to Antipas because he is too trivial. The emphatic Greek reference to Jesus in v. 9 allows the verse to be translated thus: "Antipas pressed him hard, but as for Jesus — he answered not a word." The silence of Jesus is not dissimilar to the emphatic silence of God before the frantic prophets of Baal at Mount Carmel — "There was no response, no one answered, no one paid attention" (1 Kgs 18:29).[33] Antipas is not alone in pressing Jesus. The executive committee of the Sanhedrin, ever-present in the trial scene, was on its feet "vehemently [Gk. *eutonōs*] accusing [Jesus]" (v. 10). Once it is clear that Jesus will not perform a spectacle for Antipas, the ruler trifles with Jesus. The Sanhedrin does not trifle. Now is the time to press their case without restraint. Luke emphasizes (as he did with Antipas, v. 9) the passion of their accusations rather than the content.

The audience ends with Antipas and his soldiers "ridiculing and mocking [Jesus], dressing him in an elegant robe, and sending him back to Pilate" (v. 11).[34] In commenting on the prayer on the Mount of Olives (22:39-46), we noted that the trial and crucifixion narratives in the Synoptics accentuate the mockery of Jesus over his physical suffering. That accentuation is doubly present in v. 11, first in Greek *exouthenein*, meaning "to despise, reject disdainfully," and second in *empaizein*, meaning "to mock, scorn, or ridicule." The mockery extends to "dressing [Jesus] in an elegant robe" (v. 11). Unlike modern clothing tailored to general body shapes, the robe described here is a loose-fitting shawl draped over Jesus. In Greek the word for "elegant" *(lampran)* means "majestic" or "magnificent." Luke describes Agrippa I arrayed in similar attire as king (Acts 12:21), as does Josephus, Solomon (*Ant.* 8.183). In light of the reference to Jesus as "Messiah *King*" (v. 2), the attire must be a royal lampoon of Jesus.[35] In

---

33. According to Josephus, *Ant.* 15.235, Mariamne also displayed her innocence by "not speaking a single word" prior to her execution by Herod the Great.

34. A number of strong Greek manuscripts (A B D K Γ Δ Θ) include "Herod and his soldiers *also* ridiculed . . . ," implying that both the Sanhedrin and Antipas disdained and mocked Jesus. A shorter but perhaps heftier list of Greek manuscripts (𝔭⁷⁵ ℵ L N T Ψ) omits the copulative, suggesting that the Sanhedrin accused Jesus, whereas Herod and soldiers mocked him. The evidence, however, is too evenly divided to make a definite judgment on the original reading. So also Metzger, *TCGNT*, 152.

35. On the elegant robe, see Bovon, *Lukas 19,28–24,53*, 406-7. The accusation of Jesus as a royal messianic pretender (v. 2) and the similar use of "elegant robe" with reference to King Herod Agrippa I (Acts 12:21) clearly suggest, in contrast to Wolter, *Lukasevangelium*, 743-44,

the crucifixion Jesus will be subjected to unmitigated physical suffering, but in the prelude to it he is stripped of dignity and reduced to an object of ridicule. Frustrated curiosity turns to revenge, the inevitable response, perhaps, of those whose interest in Jesus consists in their projections onto him rather than in their response to his sovereign call. "Those who are not free of the world are not only separated from Jesus but from truth itself."[36]

Antipas and Pilate became friends on account of Jesus. In spite of themselves, their silent adversary has been a reconcilier. Apart from this verse we know nothing of the depth or duration of their relationship.[37] It is human experience, attested in literature, fables, adages, and history, that the enemy of one's enemy often becomes a friend — at least as long as the enemy of both is in the picture. So it seems with Antipas and Pilate. Conflict between a Roman prefect and Herodian prince was hardly surprising. The later and apocryphal *Gos. Pet.*, desiring to shift guilt regarding Jesus' death from Pilate to Antipas, has the latter addressing the prefect as "Brother Pilate."[38] In sending Jesus back to Pilate, Antipas forces the prefect to face the "Jesus question" anew. Pilate's relation to Jesus will not be solved by circumstances or by shifting a decision about Jesus to others. Nevertheless, the two rulers now agree on Jesus' innocence (v. 15), thereby fulfilling the Jewish prerequisite for legal credibility (Deut 19:15).

13-25 Pilate retakes the reins of the increasingly volatile situation and seeks, with the added support of Antipas's judgment, to reassert (v. 4) the innocence of Jesus. The reference to "the chief priests and the rulers" is an umbrella expression for the Sanhedrin, including scribes, elders, and temple guard (v. 13, so 19:47; 24:20; Acts 3:17; 4:5-8; 13:27-29). We know, however, from vv. 4-5, 13 that the influence of the Sanhedrin was also at work on the people. As noted above, "the people" is not accompanied by Luke's frequent modifier "all," implying less-than-total opposition to Jesus on the part of the Jewish populace.[39] Pilate recapitulates the case by collapsing the three initial charges against Jesus in v. 2 into the single charge that Jesus "incites the people to rebellion." Pilate finds this charge unsubstantiated and attempts to assert his authority as prefect to the contrary, "*I* [emphatic in Greek] have examined him in your presence and have found no basis for your charges" (v. 14). The reference to "examined" (Gk. *anakrinein*) again reflects the vocabulary of juris-

---

who concludes that Gk. *esthēs lampra* is "semantically imprecise," that the attire is intended to mock Jesus' royal pretensions.

36. Rengstorf, *Lukas*, 246.

37. See here Fitzmyer, *Luke (X–XXIV)*, 1480.

38. *Gos. Pet.* 2.5 (*NTApoc.* 1:223).

39. Brown, *Death of the Messiah*, 1:790-91, discusses Luke's use of "people," although he allows its usage in Acts rather than its more specific use in chap. 23 to argue for "a Jewish collectivity opposed to Jesus."

prudence (Acts 4:9; 12:19; 24:8; 25:26; 28:18). Pilate introduces corroborating testimony of Antipas that Jesus "has done nothing to deserve death" (v. 15).[40] The fact that Luke omits reference to the "elegant robe" (v. 11) indicates that the return of Jesus, not his clothing, signaled Jesus' innocence.[41] "Therefore, I will punish him and then release him" (v. 16). How deceptively innocuous this verse! The word for "punish" (Gk. *paideuein*) is a euphemism for whipping. Whether it was the dreaded *verberatio* prior to crucifixion — flogging a bound and naked prisoner with a leather whip woven with bits of bone or metal — or a lesser punishment, we cannot say for sure.[42] Given the fact that Jesus was not a Roman citizen, and that Pilate was caught in brinksmanship with the chief priests, the prefect may have intended a very severe beating as something of a plea bargain. The overture is repeated in v. 22. This extreme bargain should rid readers of any illusion that Pilate's appeal on Jesus' behalf is motivated by kindness. In his power struggle with the religious leaders, and because of his ultimate indifference to Jesus, Pilate is willing to subject Jesus to extreme cruelty.

Pilate's final card in the tense standoff is played with reference to Barabbas (vv. 18-19). The criminal's name, Barabbas (v. 18), is an Aramaic name meaning "son of the father." Along with several church fathers, Jerome believed the name meant "son of the teacher," which is not impossible, since rabbis were often called abba, and also since "Barabbas" and "Bar-Rabban" are practically homophones.[43] A number of Greek manuscripts preface the Barabbas episode with v. 17, "He [Pilate] was under obligation to release someone to them at the festival." This verse is probably a gloss (based on Matt 27:15 and Mark 15:6) added later in order to introduce the Barabbas affair. It is rightly omitted from NIV.[44] "With one voice they cried, 'Away with his man! Release Barabbas to us!'

---

40. Scribal errors have garbled the textual tradition at this point in the trial narrative, several significant manuscripts reading "I sent you to him [Herod]" (A D N W X Γ Δ Ψ, Textus Receptus), or "I sent him [Herod] to you" (f^{13} 579 vg). The most reasonable reading, "He [Herod] sent him [Jesus] back to us" (so NIV), is also the best attested ($\mathfrak{p}^{75}$ ℵ B K L T Θ). See Metzger, *TCGNT*, 153.

41. Noted by Wolter, *Lukasevangelium*, 746.

42. Brown, *Death of the Messiah*, 1:792-93, assumes it was a "minor beating." M. Hengel, *Crucifixion* (Philadelphia: Fortress Press, 1977), 34, cites an example of the flogging of a slave as a punishment rather than as prelude to crucifixion.

43. "[Barabbas] signifies 'the son of their teacher' in the Gospel that is written 'According to the Hebrews,' because he had been condemned for sedition and murder" (*Comm. Matt.* 27:16). For Jerome, Bar-Rabban is a nickname meaning that, as an insurrectionist and murderer, Barabbas is a "son" of his Jewish teachers. The First Gospel makes no mention of Barabbas as an insurrectionist and murderer. Hence, Jerome's quotation links the Hebrew Gospel with Luke rather than Matthew.

44. The inclusion of v. 17 claims strong external textual support (ℵ D W Γ Δ Θ Ψ), although support for its exclusion is stronger ($\mathfrak{p}^{75}$ A B K L T). Arguments from internal evi-

(Barabbas had been thrown into prison for an insurrection in the city, and for murder)" (vv. 18-19). The vehement assertion of will and power in "Away with this man!" has eclipsed all pretenses of justice. The prisoner release to which Luke alludes is referenced in Matt 27:15 and Mark 15:6, and most specifically in John 18:39, "It is your custom for me [Pilate] to release to you one prisoner at the time of the Passover." There is no explicit evidence outside the Gospels for a Passover amnesty as described here, although there is evidence that rulers occasionally released prisoners (often for the duration of the festival) in both Jewish and pagan societies.[45] As prefect, Pilate possessed authority to commute or pardon the sentence of any criminal he chose. All four Gospels mention Barabbas, but only Luke reports that he committed insurrection and murder "in the city" (v. 19) — Jerusalem. He was, in other words, a violent criminal. His notoriety in Jerusalem may be a reason why Luke thinks he needs no introduction. More important for the Third Gospel, however, is that Jerusalem is where Jesus must fulfill his predestined mission (see at 9:51; 18:31-34): Jesus is murdered in Jerusalem for a man who has committed murder in Jerusalem. It is frequently assumed that Barabbas was a Jewish freedom fighter (whether Zealot, Sicarius, or another faction), but we are not told such, and it is debatable whether such groups were organized as early as the year 30. Even if they were, we do not know that Barabbas was associated with them.[46] Indeed, if Barabbas was associated with such groups, we should be very surprised that Pilate would release an enemy of the state. This prisoner exchange already anticipates Jesus' passion as a vicarious and atoning event, and is seen as such in early Christian literature, for Luke refers to the Barabbas affair in Acts 3:13-14 as an exchange of "the Holy and Righteous One . . . for a murderer," and Eusebius writes that the crowd thundered for a murderer of life to be given to them, and for the Author of Life be taken from them (*Hist. eccl.* 3.7.7).

In a wordplay, Luke reports that Pilate calls *to* the crowd (v. 20; Gk. *prosphōnein;* NIV "appealed") for the release of Jesus, but the crowd shouts back more strongly *against* him (v. 21; Gk. *epiphōnein;* NIV "they kept shouting"), "Crucify him! Crucify him!" (v. 21). The aorist tense of the first verb

---

dence also favor its exclusion. The Barabbas episode invites the kind of introduction that v. 17 supplies (and is thus the more difficult reading without it), and the placement of the verse in question following v. 19 in Codex Bezae (D) attests to its dubious location in Luke. See Metzger, *TCGNT*, 153; Fitzmyer, *Luke (X–XXIV)*, 1485-86; Wolter, *Lukasevangelium*, 747.

45. See E. Lohmeyer, *Das Evangelium des Markus* (KEK 2; Göttingen: Vandenhoeck & Ruprecht, 1967), 336-37; and R. Merritt, "Jesus Barabbas and the Paschal Pardon," *JBL* 104 (1985): 57-68.

46. M. Hengel, *The Zealots* (trans. D. Smith; Edinburgh: T&T Clark, 1989), 340-41, thinks it likely that Barabbas was associated with such groups, whereas Brown, *Death of the Messiah*, 1:686-88, finds no evidence that bandits like Barabbas were regarded as revolutionaries in Jesus' lifetime or that Jesus himself was regarded as a revolutionary by his enemies.

indicates isolated appeals of Pilate, whereas the imperfect tense of the second verb indicates the inexorable shouts of the crowd. Crucifixion was a particularly Roman form of execution that was notorious for the affliction of both pain and shame (see at v. 33). In Judaism, hanging someone on a tree was also a sign that the victim was cursed by God (Deut 21:23). In calling for Jesus' crucifixion, the crowd designates him as an enemy of both Gentiles and Jews. In his passion predictions Jesus foretold his death at the hands of Jews (9:22), humanity (9:44), and Gentiles (18:32). All three of these now join in chorus for his crucifixion. "With loud shouts they insistently demanded that he be crucified" (v. 23).[47] Pilate's cunning diplomacy has failed. The prefect and commander of Roman forces in Palestine is once again faced with a situation in which he must either resort to military force or stand down. Pilate was an autocratic Roman ruler, but even as such, he had learned at Caesarea and Jerusalem on earlier occasions that indifference to the will of the crowd could lead to worse consequences.[48] "Their shouts prevailed" (v. 23), and Pilate stands down (v. 24; 24:20). "He released the man who had been thrown into prison for insurrection and murder, the one they asked for, and surrendered Jesus to their will" (vv. 25). Luke does not mention Barabbas by name in v. 25. Rather, he recounts for readers the exact nature of the injustice that has just transpired: an imprisoned murderer has been set free, and a man in whom no fault has been found is surrendered to death. Further insight into the exact historical processes and motives of the parties that have brought about this monstrous injustice cannot be known. In the end, the power and authority of the Roman prefect and the mob incited by the religious leaders are one. The only party who remains truly free in this deadly intrigue is "this man" (v. 14), who, apart from a mere two words (v. 3), has remained silent throughout.

THE CRUCIFIXION: JESUS COMPLETES HIS "EXODUS" IN JERUSALEM (23:26-49)

Luke's account of the crucifixion appears indebted to Mark's account, although Luke has freely altered and appropriated the latter for his own purposes.[49]

---

47. The transmission of the Greek text of v. 23 displays a tendency to identify "their shouts" as those of "the rulers and chief priests" (A D K N P W Γ Δ Θ Ψ), i.e., specifically indemnifying Jews. A leaner but weightier manuscript tradition ($\mathfrak{p}^{75}$ ℵ B L) favors the shorter and vaguer reading adopted by NIV.

48. A Roman proconsul in Asia Minor a century later would learn the same at the execution of Polycarp (*Mart. Pol.* 12).

49. Wolter, *Lukasevangelium*, 753, provides a helpful chart illustrating the similarities and differences between Mark's and Luke's crucifixion narratives.

Omitted are the flagellation of Jesus and crown of thorns (Mark 15:16-20; Matt 27:27-31; John 19:2-3), reference to "Golgotha" (Mark 15:22; Matt 27:33; John 19:17), spiked wine (Mark 15:23; Matt 27:34), accusations that Jesus wished to destroy the temple (Mark 15:29; Matt 27:39-40), the cry of dereliction and association of Jesus with Elijah (Mark 15:34; Matt 27:46), and the centurion's declaration of Jesus as Son of God (Mark 15:39; Matt 27:54). Material not present in the other Gospels includes the women following Jesus to the place of crucifixion (vv. 27-32), the conversation between Jesus and the penitent criminal (vv. 40-43), the quotation of Ps 31:5 in Jesus' dying breath (v. 46), the centurion's declaration of Jesus as "righteous" (v. 47), and the mourning crowd (v. 48). The first two of these additions contain concentrations of Hebraisms that are not evident elsewhere in the crucifixion narrative, suggesting their provenance in Luke's special Hebraic source.[50]

Luke's editorial hand results in a carefully shaped crucifixion narrative with repetitions of threes and fours.[51] The pattern began with Peter's three denials (22:54-62), followed by Pilate's three declarations of Jesus' innocence (23:4, 14, 22). Threes are multiplied in the crucifixion narrative: the women of v. 29 are identified by three forms of barrenness; Jesus is thrice mocked as Messiah (vv. 35, 37, 39); the malefactors are thrice called criminals (Gk. *kakourgoi*, vv. 32, 33, 39); three groups of people mock Jesus to "save" (people, v. 35; soldiers, v. 37; criminals, v. 39); Jesus makes three declarations (vv. 34, 43, 46); and the effect of Jesus' death is registered on the parties (the centurion, v. 47; bystanders, v. 48; and acquaintances, v. 49).[52] In addition, four groups either confess or empathize with Jesus (women, vv. 27-29; penitent criminal, v. 42; centurion, v. 47; crowd, v. 48), and four titles are attributed to Jesus ("Messiah," v. 35; "chosen," v. 35; "king of the Jews," v. 38; "righteous," v. 47). Repetitions of three, in particular, often connote completeness or finality in Judaism.[53] Luke has emphasized the theme of completeness (Gk. *plēroun*, 9x, e.g., 24:44) and fulfillment (Gk. *telein/teleioun*, 6x, e.g., 18:31; 22:37) throughout the Gospel. The finale of repetitions in the crucifixion narrative functions as a literary complement to the theme of fulfillment of Jesus' "exodus" in Jerusalem (9:31).

The sequences of threes and fours serve the overarching themes of *procession* and *intercession* in Luke's crucifixion narrative. The narrative is depicted as a procession to the cross, in which Jesus leads Simon (v. 26), mourning women (vv. 27-31), two criminals (vv. 32), a crowd of revilers (vv. 35-39), mourners (48), and women sympathizers from Galilee (v. 49). This procession

---

50. Hebraisms are listed in Edwards, *Hebrew Gospel,* 329.

51. On repetitions of threes, see at 19:20.

52. Luke's emphasis on threes is clearly recognized by Bovon, *Lukas 19,28–24,53,* 441; and partially by Tannehill, *Luke,* 342-46.

53. G. Delling, *treis, TWNT* 8:215-25.

continues the theme of the "way," which dominated the long central section of the Gospel. It now completes the journey to the cross itself. The "king" who entered Jerusalem on Palm Sunday (19:38) is the same "king of the Jews" who is crucified on Good Friday (23:38). The final and rightful "exodus" of Jesus, foretold at the transfiguration (9:31), is the cross.

The second emphasis is on intercession. In contrast to Jesus' silence before the Sanhedrin, Antipas, and Pilate (vv. 1-25), he now speaks. A common feature of martyr accounts in both pagan and Jewish literature is a final defense of the hero's innocence, or an expression of the hero's convictions. The final speeches en route to or on the cross do not conform to this stereotype, however, for they are not about Jesus, but addressed to and on behalf of others. His last words are intercessory. He bears the grief of mourning women (vv. 27-31), prays for the forgiveness of those who kill and mock him (v. 34), assures a penitent of salvation (v. 43), and finally entrusts himself confidently into the hands of the Father (v. 46). To the very end Jesus remains what he has been from the beginning — the one who forgives and summons to faith, the bearer of iniquities (Isa 53:11), "the man for others."

The man for others is accentuated in the structure of Luke's crucifixion narrative. In the other Gospels the crucifixion and baptismal narratives are focused almost exclusively on Jesus, but in the Third Gospel these two events, which bracket the public ministry of Jesus, are crowded with people. Luke sets Jesus' baptism in the context of "all the people" being baptized (3:21). In the crucifixion narrative the various groups are named or identified: Simon of Cyrene (v. 26), "daughters of Jerusalem" (vv. 27-31), two criminals (vv. 32, 39-43), rulers (vv. 35), soldiers (v. 36), centurion (v. 47), crowd of observers (v. 48), acquaintances (v. 49), Galilean women (v. 49), Joseph of Arimathea (vv. 50-54). A mere Jewish rabbi, even a rabbi as renowned as Gamaliel or Akiba or ben Zakkai, would scarcely attract so many different people. A crosscut of urban Jerusalem is gathered at the foot of the cross of Jesus of Nazareth. They are not merely neutral observers. Each person or party is either for or against Jesus. As in his infancy (2:34-35) and ministry (12:49-53), so too in his death, Jesus is a cause of division.

26-32 For Jesus (9:22) and disciples (9:23), all roads lead to the cross. The final journey begins with somber finality, "And they led him away" (v. 26). The NIV reads "the *soldiers* led him away," but "led away" lacks a definite subject in Greek, and "soldiers" is overly specific in v. 26.[54] In the preceding verse, Pilate "surrenders Jesus to their will" (v. 25). "Their" must refer to the

---

54. The verb "to lead away" lacks a definite subject in all three Synoptics (v. 26; Matt 27:31; Mark 15:20). The presumed subject in Matt and Mark is "the soldiers," who in the preceding story have beaten and mocked Jesus. Luke omits this story, however, and with it the obvious antecedent of soldiers. V. 25 ends with Pilate "surrendering Jesus to [the crowd's will]," and hence the (Jewish) crowd is more reasonably the subject of v. 26.

religious leaders and clamoring crowds. Roman soldiers were of course necessarily present at a crucifixion (v. 36), and since only Romans would compel a bystander like Simon of Cyrene to carry the cross of a condemned criminal, "they" in v. 26 must connote the united conspiracy against Jesus — Jewish leaders, Romans, and crowds.

"Simon from Cyrene" (v. 26) is presumably a Jew. According to Josephus (*Ant.* 14:114-15), Jews constituted one of four dominant classes in Cyrene (modern Libya in North Africa). Cyrene plays a further role in Acts, including mention of a synagogue consisting of "Jews of Cyrene" (6:9), and Christian believers of Cyrenaic background who first proclaimed the gospel to Gentiles in Antioch (11:20), including a Cyrenaic Christian named Lucius, who was a member of the earliest missionary society in Antioch (13:1). What Simon's relation was to these movements, if any, we are not told, but mention of his name, country, and the suggestive note that "he carried [the cross] behind Jesus" (v. 26) may indicate that he was known to readers as a (later) disciple of Jesus.[55] The coercing of Jews for compulsory service was a particularly odious aspect of Roman occupation; indeed, provincials such as Simon may have been more freely and frequently coerced to this loathsome duty than native Palestinians. "On his way in from the country" is a calculated ambiguity in Greek that could refer to entering Jerusalem for any number of reasons; the suggestion of Jeremias that Simon lived outside the city walls and was coming in for 9 A.M. worship is not implausible.[56] The reference to Simon bearing the "cross" of Jesus must refer to the crossbeam. A condemned man normally carried his own *patibulum,* the heavy crossbeam, to the crucifixion site; "every criminal condemned to death bears his cross on his back," declared Plutarch (*Mor.* 554A/B). At the place of crucifixion the *patibulum* was lashed or nailed to the *stipes,* the upright post, which was normally left implanted in the ground. That Jesus would need aid in carrying the *patibulum* is due to weakness and blood loss suffered during the beating of the Sanhedrin (22:63-65), or of the Romans (Mark 15:16-20; Matt 27:27-31). The introduction to the crucifixion narrative ends with reference to Simon "bearing his cross behind Jesus" (v. 26). In 9:23 and 14:27 Luke has twice mentioned the necessity of disciples bearing their crosses "daily." The present tense of the Greek verb "to carry" *(pherein)* connotes ongoing activity, thus underscoring Luke's insistence on constancy in discipleship. "Taking up the cross and following Jesus" is not an imaginary ideal, and not always metaphoric. Simon of Cyrene literally fulfills Jesus' injunction![57]

---

55. The mention of his sons, Alexander and Rufus, in Mark 15:21 suggests the latter were known to Mark's readers. The Rufus in Rom 16:13, who was a member of the church(es) to which Paul wrote, was likely the son of Simon.

56. J. Jeremias, *The Eucharistic Words of Jesus* (Philadelphia: Fortress Press, 1977), 77.

57. Schweizer, *Lukas,* 237, speaks of Simon as a "model of discipleship."

In addition to Simon (v. 26) and two condemned criminals (v. 32), the procession to the cross includes "a large number of people, including women who mourned and wailed for [Jesus]" (v. 27). The women's mourning and wailing exemplifies the conspicuous mourning deemed proper and necessary in Middle Eastern dirges (7:11-13). The structure of this verse recalls frequent descriptions of crowds following Jesus in Galilee and Judea (7:9, 11; 9:11; 14:25; 18:36). The importance of these summaries is the repeated reminder of *following* Jesus, whether in festivity or in sorrow, indeed following him to the cross. Only Luke includes the pericope of mourning women following Jesus in vv. 27-31. There is no instance in any of the four Gospels of a woman being hostile to Jesus.[58] Throughout the infancy narrative and ministry of Jesus, women have played regular and important roles in the Third Gospel,[59] but beginning with this verse they play heightened roles as witnesses of the crucifixion and resurrection (23:27, 49, 55-56; 24:1-11, 22, 24). Vv. 27-31 are a tapestry of Scripture allusions and quotations, prophetic speech forms, and figures of speech. Overall, the unit echoes the lament of Zech 12:10-14, "the weeping in Jerusalem will be great" for "one they have pierced." In Zechariah's prophecy, the mourners consist of the heads of various clans "and their wives," whereas in vv. 28-31 the focus falls on women alone who mourn Jesus' impending crucifixion. Occasional references in Roman literature forbid people from mourning the execution of infamous criminals.[60] There is no indication, however, that this was a general rule in Roman executions.[61]

The reference to "daughters of Jerusalem" is a prophetic speech form that in this instance is doubly significant for the women and Jerusalem.[62] With regard to the former, "Do not weep for me; weep for yourselves and for your children" (v. 28) is obviously addressed to the women. Jesus' sufferings, violent though they are, will soon be over, and they will end in glory. The sufferings of the women, however, and those of their children, will be protracted and will end in shame and destruction. The admonition is a reminder to "daily" discipleship (9:23). It is far more difficult to live faithfully in season and out of season than it is to die heroically in a moment of time.

---

58. Although Herodias was deadly hostile to John the Baptizer (Mark 6:19, 24; Matt 14:8).

59. 1:39-56; 2:36-38; 7:11-15, 37-50; 8:1-3; 10:38-42; 11:27; 13:11-16.

60. Tacitus, *Ann.* 6.19; Suetonius, *Tib.* 61.

61. Plutarch reports a not dissimilar execution to that of Jesus in which a king of Sparta, being led out for strangulation, commanded mourners, "Stop your weeping for me. For in spite of my being put to death in such defiance of law and justice, I am superior to those who are taking my life" (*Mor.* 216; cited in *HCNT*, 233-34).

62. Brown, *Death of the Messiah*, 2:921, writes, "Like the prophets of old who uttered oracles against the nations, Jesus is speaking to Jerusalem as representative of Israel — the last of a series of words of woe."

Here the reminder of Bonhoeffer is relevant: the cross — dying to the old person as a result of an encounter with Jesus Christ — is not "the terrible end" to an otherwise God-fearing and happy life. The cross, rather, meets us at the beginning of our communion with Christ and defines each step of the way with Christ.[63]

If "daughters of Jerusalem" addressed only the women, however, we should expect Jesus to call them daughters of *Abraham.* The epithet also includes the Holy City, or better, the women as personifications of Jerusalem. In the OT, when used with reference to a metropolis, "daughters" (Heb. *banoth*) refers to its suburbs or satellite settlements (e.g., Num 21:25, 32; Josh 15:45, 47; Neh 11:25-31; 2 Chr 28:18).[64] "Daughters of Jerusalem" appears to pick up the lament of 13:34, "Jerusalem, Jerusalem, you who kill the prophets and stone those sent to you, how often I have longed to gather your children together, as a hen gathers her chicks under her wings, and you were not willing." In instructing the women to turn their sorrow away from him to themselves and their children, Jesus issues a final appeal to Jerusalem, similar to the appeal to Israel in Hos 2 or Jer 7, to mourn its apostasy and turn to God's visitation in the person and ministry of Jesus. The lament of v. 28 thus repeats the similar lament of 19:41-44. Schweizer adeptly observes, "Jesus is not looking for sympathy, but for conversion!"[65]

Not surprisingly, the gravity of Jesus' appeal invokes eschatological terminology. "Days will come" (v. 29; NIV "For the time will come") resumes the prophetic eschatological speech form (see at 17:22) in which anarthrous "days" signifies the Day of the Lord (e.g., Jer 7:32; 9:25; 16:14). That day will be so fearful that barren women — "wombs that never bore and breasts that never nursed" (v. 29) — will be called blessed. Childlessness was typically a shame and dishonor in Israel (1:25; 11:27; Gen 15:2; 16:1-6; 1 Sam 1:2-11).[66] To declare childlessness a *blessing,* as Jesus does here, signifies an apocalyptic reversal of values. There are occasions in history when death seems preferable to life: the Soviet Gulag, for example, was known as the place where the living envied the dead. The quotation of Hos 10:8 (v. 30) — a quotation used in a similar context in Rev 6:16 — addresses the theme of catastrophe, again in the voice of prophetic judgment: disobedient Jerusalem will choose to be

63. D. Bonhoeffer, *The Cost of Discipleship* (trans. R. Fuller; London: SCM Press, 1959), 79.

64. On the use of Heb. *banoth* in the OT, see H. Haag, *bath, TDOT* 2:332-38.

65. Schweizer, *Lukas,* 238.

66. *Gos. Thom.* 79 combines 11:27 and 23:29 into a single saying of Jesus: "A woman in the crowd said to him: 'Blessed is the womb which bore you, and the breasts which nourished you!' [Jesus] said to her: 'Blessed are those who have heard the Word of the Father and have kept it in truth! For the days will come when you will say, "Blessed is the womb which has not conceived, and the breasts which have not given milk!"'"

buried alive rather than face divine wrath.[67] This fearful declaration repeats in different imagery the ominous catastrophe awaiting disobedient Jerusalem (19:41-44; 21:20-24). Vv. 27-31 conclude, "If people do these things when the tree is green, what will happen when it is dry?" (v. 31). This saying is a variant of several Jewish maxims illustrating the principle that, if something great can happen, how much easier something lesser (e.g., "If the righteous are judged, how much more the ungodly and sinners!" Prov 11:3; further, 1 Pet 4:1).[68] The point of v. 31 is that fire hot enough to burn wet wood will *devour* dry wood! If God allows his righteous Son to suffer crucifixion, what fate must await unrighteous Jerusalem and those who crucify him!

33-39 "When they came to the place called the Skull, they crucified him there." This laconic pronouncement, devoid of drama and sentimentality, stands in striking contrast to the pathos of the prayer on the Mount of Olives (22:39-46). The crucifixion as *historical event* — not as a symbolic or emotional event — stands in austere witness to Jesus' "exodus" (9:31). The omission of the names "Golgotha" (Mark 15:22; Matt 27:33; John 19:17) — as well as "Gethsemane" (Mark 14:32; Matt 26:36), "Gabbatha" (John 19:13), and "Abba" (Mark 14:36) — is likely due to Luke's avoidance of foreign words.[69] The **Skull** (Heb. *gulgoltah*; Lat. *"calvus"*) is a fitting description of the barren and deadly reality of crucifixion.[70] It was both Jewish and Roman custom to execute victims outside the city limits (Lev 24:14; Num 15:35-36; Heb 13:12). The earliest identification of the site of the crucifixion, *The Onomasticon* of Eusebius (fourth c.), locates Golgotha only approximately, "in Aelia north of Mount Sion."[71] In the nineteenth century Otto Thenius of Dresden proposed a skull-shaped hill outside the walls of Jerusalem as the probable site (visible today overlooking the Arab bus station). Thenius's proposal was popularized by Charles Gordon in 1885, who also discovered what today is known as the Garden Tomb beneath the outcropping. Despite the tranquility and beauty of "Gordon's Calvary," the Church of the Holy Sepulchre has greater claim to be the historical site of the crucifixion and burial of Jesus (on burial, see at 23:53). From the earliest days

---

67. The Lukan quotation of Hos 10:8 does not follow either the MT or LXX, which read that the mountains will cover and the hills fall, whereas v. 30 reads that the mountains will fall and the hills cover. The allusion to Hos 10:8 in Rev. 6:16 is even less exact.

68. See the Jewish and rabbinic examples in Str-B 2:263-64; Bovon, *Lukas 19,28–24,53*, 458-59. Various possible interpretations are set forth in Plummer, *Luke*, 529; Bock, *Luke 9:51–24:53*, 1847.

69. Jeremias, *Sprache des Lukasevangeliums*, 306. The suggestion of Schweizer, *Lukas*, 228, that the omission of the names indicates the places were not holy sites at the time Luke wrote is less likely.

70. "Place of the Skull" appears in *T. Sol.* 12:3 (*OTP* 1:973; first c.?), where "[Christ] will dwell publicly on the cross."

71. *Onomasticon*, 45.

of Christianity the natural rock outcropping that in Jesus' day lay outside the walls of Jerusalem, on which the Church of the Holy Sepulchre was erected in 335, has been venerated as the site of Jesus' crucifixion. Excavations from 1961 to 1980 under the Church of the Holy Sepulchre have added further support to its authenticity as the site of the crucifixion.[72]

Cicero described **crucifixion** as the "most cruel and horrifying punishment."[73] Every totalitarian regime needs a terror apparatus, and crucifixion was Rome's terror apparatus *ad horrendum,* infamous alike for its infliction of pain and shame. Reserved for non-Roman citizens, crucifixion unleashed maximum cruelty on the lowest and most defenseless classes of society — slaves, violent criminals, and prisoners of war. At the defeat of the slave rebellion under Spartacus in 71 B.C., Crassus crucified more than 6,000 slaves along the Via Appia between Capua and Rome. To enhance the deterrent effect of crucifixion, victims were executed as public spectacles. "Whenever we crucify the guilty, the most crowded roads are chosen, where the most people can see and be moved by this fear," wrote Quintillian (*Decl.* 274). Men were normally crucified naked, as the gambling for Jesus' clothes attests (although Jewish sensitivities may have prescribed a loin-cloth).[74] Slave and lower-class women could also suffer the horrors of crucifixion.[75] Western art typically portrays an elevated cross with Jesus' feet nailed together. In reality, most crosses were probably near or slightly above eye-level, and Josephus reports that Romans crucified captives before the walls of Jerusalem in different postures and in different ways (*J.W.* 5.449-51). A tomb discovered in Jerusalem in 1968 revealed the first authenticated evidence of a crucifixion in antiquity. In this particular instance, the arms of the victim appear to have been tied rather than nailed to the *patibulum* (crossbeam), and the legs straddled the *stipes* (vertical post), one leg on each side, with a nail penetrating each heel bone laterally.[76] The Gospels

72. Murphy-O'Connor, *The Holy Land,* 45-50; V. Corbo, "Golgotha," *ABD* 2:1071-73; R. Riesner, "Golgota und die Archaeologie," *BibKir* 40 (1985): 21-26. Less likely is the view propounded by W. Grundmann, *Das Evangelium nach Markus* (THKNT; Berlin: Evangelische Verlagsanstalt, 1977), 431, and Schlatter, *Der Evangelist Matthäus* (Stuttgart: Calwer Verlag, 1948), 779, that "Skull" should be understood theologically as an unclean place where Jesus dies for unclean sinners.

73. *Verr.* 2.5.165. For this and other diatribes against crucifixion by ancient authors, see M. Hengel, *Crucifixion in the Ancient World and the Folly of the Message of the Cross* (Philadelphia: Fortress, 1977), 7-10.

74. On the shame of crucifixion, note Cicero's words: "The very word 'cross' should be far removed not only from the person of a Roman citizen but from his thoughts" (*Rab. Perd.* 5.15-16 [cited in *HCNT,* 157]).

75. K. Corley, "Women and the Crucifixion of Jesus," *Forum,* n.s., 1 (1998): 189.

76. J. Zias and E. Sekeles, "The Crucified Man from Giv'at ha-Mivtar: A Reappaisal," *IEJ* 35/1 (1985): 22-27; H. Shanks, "New Analysis of the Crucified Man," *BAR* 11/6 (1985): 20-21. Ben Witherington III cites three graffiti of crucifixions that also portray the victim with feet

do not say whether Jesus was tied or nailed to the cross, but the reference to marks in his hands and feet following the resurrection (24:39) suggest the latter. Depending on the severity of flogging beforehand, some victims survived on crosses several days. Since no major arteries or organs were compromised, death came not by blood loss, but from hypovolemic shock, exhaustion, asphyxia, dehydration, heart failure, or a combination of the above.[77]

That God's Messiah could suffer "a cross of shame" (Heb 12:2) was of course scandalous, "a stumbling block to Jews and foolishness to Gentiles," as Paul told the Corinthians (1 Cor 1:23). The gnostic Basilides (second c.), aghast at the idea of a crucified Messiah, proposed that Simon of Cyrene was crucified in Jesus' place.[78] The Qur'an similarly declares the idea of a crucified Messiah "a monstrous falsehood."[79] Later apocryphal gospels also insulate Jesus from the horrors of crucifixion.[80] The canonical Gospels and the apostolic kerygma do not spare Jesus from the cross. The cross is, rather, the means by which Jesus "bore the sin of many, and made intercession for the transgressors" (Isa 53:12). Martin Hengel writes, "In the death of Jesus of Nazareth God identified himself with the extreme of human wretchedness, which Jesus endured as a representative of us all, in order to bring us to the freedom of the children of God" (Rom 8:32).[81]

In Luke's baptismal scene Jesus is baptized with the people (3:21), and in the crucifixion scene he is crucified "along with the criminals" (v. 33).[82] In both scenes Jesus appears not only with others, but vicariously *for* them. On the cross, with "one criminal on his right, the other on his left," Jesus becomes a righteous intermediary between them. Jesus' first word from the cross verbalizes his vicarious intercession, "Father, forgive them, for they do not know

---

on each side of the *stipes* ("Images of Crucifixion: Fresh Evidence," *BAR* 39/2 [2013]: 28, 66-67). Brown, *Death of the Messiah,* 2:947, is overly dismissive of graffiti evidence.

77. W. Edwards, W. Gabel, and F. Hosmer, "On the Physical Death of Jesus Christ," *JAMA* 255/11 (March 21, 1986): 1455-63; F. Zugibe, "Two Questions about Crucifixion. Does the Victim Die of Asphyxiation? Would Nails in the Hand Hold the Weight of the Body?" *BRev* 5/2 (1989): 35-43. On crucifixion in general, see G. O'Collins, "Crucifixion," *ABD* 1:1207-10, and esp. Brown, *Death of the Messiah,* 2:945-58.

78. Irenaeus, *Haer.* 1.24.4. The same idea appears in *Treat. Seth* 55-56 and *Apoc. Pet.* 81, where Jesus stands by laughing as Simon dies in his stead on the cross.

79. "They did not kill [Jesus], nor did they crucify him, but he was made to resemble another for them" (Qur'an 4:157).

80. *Gos. Pet.* 10, for instance, says Jesus was silent on the cross because he felt no pain.

81. *Crucifixion in the Ancient World and the Folly of the Message of the Cross* (Philadelphia: Fortress Press, 1977), 89.

82. Later traditions liberally supplied names to the two criminals: Joathas and Maggatras (Codex Rehdigeranus), Zoatham and Camma (Codex Colbertinus at Matt 27:38; Metzger, *TCGNT,* 57-58; 153); Titus and Dumachus (*Arabic Gospel of the Infancy* [23]; Plummer, *Luke,* 534); Dysmas and Gestas (*Acts Pil.* 10).

what they are doing" (v. 34).[83] This prayer fulfills Jesus' teaching on love of enemies in 6:27-28 and 11:2-4 and is echoed in Stephen's death prayer in Acts 7:59-60.[84] The textual authenticity of the prayer (at least in its present location) is contested, however. It is contained in weighty manuscripts (ℵ* C D K L N Q Γ Δ Ψ), but omitted by weightier and more diverse manuscripts ($\mathfrak{p}^{75}$ ℵ[2] B D W Θ). The first set of manuscripts is not as weak as often supposed, however, for among them exist all four text types, and they are augmented by important patristic evidence.[85] External evidence cannot be the deciding factor in the authenticity of the prayer, for better reasons exist for a scribe to have omitted the saying if it were original than for a scribe to have added it if it were not.[86] The fall of Jerusalem was widely considered in early Christianity as evidence of God's judgment on Jerusalem; hence, copyists would be tempted to omit the saying, since the fall of Jerusalem would indicate that Jesus' prayer for its forgiveness had not been answered. Moreover, the prayer seems to run counter to Jesus' previous predictions of the judgment awaiting Jerusalem (13:34-35; 19:41-44; 20:16; 21:20-24; 23:27-33). We also can easily imagine a scribe, believing that some sins should not be forgiven, omitting the verse. Finally, who but Jesus would pray for the forgiveness of those mocking and crucifying him?[87] Such reasons argue for the authenticity of the prayer and its subsequent omission

83. This saying is the second of the traditional seven last words of Jesus: (1) "My God, My God, why have you forsaken me?" (Mark 15:34 par. Matt 27:46); (2) "Father, forgive them, for they do not know what they are doing" (23:34a); (3) "Truly I tell you, today you will be with me in paradise" (23:43); (4) "Father, into your hands I commit my spirit" (23:46); (5) "Woman, here is your son. . . . Here is your mother" (John 19:26-27); (6) "I am thirsty" (John 19:28); (7) "It is finished" (John 19:30).

84. An event from World War II exemplifies Jesus' prayer. Following the destruction of Coventry Cathedral by the German Luftwaffe on November 14, 1940, Provost Richard Howard inscribed "Father Forgive" on the wall behind the altar. Howard also made a cross from three nails taken from the collapsed roof truss of the Cathedral. Today, more than 160 nail crosses can be found around the world. One of them is in the Frauenkirche of Dresden, which was destroyed by Anglo-American bombers on February 13-14, 1945. Nail crosses are now symbols of peace and reconciliation.

85. The Hebrew Gospel may belong to the patristic evidence. Jerome quotes the prayer in *Ep.* 120.8.9, and in a medieval text the whole is attributed to the Hebrew Gospel (see *NTApoc.* 1:164).

86. External evidence is fully set forth and discussed in Fitzmyer, *Luke (X–XXIV)*, 1503-4. Metzger, *TCGNT*, 154, thinks the verse original to Jesus ("it bears self-evident tokens of dominical origin"), but not to the Gospel of Luke; many others, including Brown, *Death of the Messiah*, 2:971-81, Wolter, *Lukasevangelium*, 757-58, and Bovon, *Lukas 19,28-24:53*, 461-62, argue for its authenticity at v. 34. N. Eubank, "A Disconcerting Prayer: On the Originality of Luke 23:34a," *JBL* 129/3 (2010): 521-36, argues strongly from both external and internal evidence in favor of the authenticity of the saying.

87. Vinson, *Luke*, 726, rightly notes the uniqueness of Jesus' prayer for forgiveness of his executioners.

by later copyists, whereas reasons of equal weight cannot be adduced for the prayer's inauthenticity and its later addition.

The exact meaning of the clause on ignorance in the prayer ("for they do not know what they are doing") is debated. Judaism was aware of the problem of sinning unconsciously or in ignorance (Lev 4:2; Num 15:25-26; John 9:41). If the prayer includes those responsible for Jesus' death, which it seems to, their sin is not unconscious. If Jesus is praying only for the soldiers crucifying him, however, it is not clear they are actually sinning, for they are only doing their duty. Such questions, important as they are, cannot be definitively answered by the prayer itself. It is most appropriately understood in its deepest and fullest sense, that on the cross Jesus prays for the forgiveness of those responsible for his death — Sanhedrin, Antipas, Pilate, Jewish leaders, and others of ill will. In so doing, he prays for the forgiveness of the sins of all people, and thus fulfills the commission of the Servant of the Lord in Isa 53:12, who makes intercession for all without distinction.[88] Those responsible for the crucifixion know what they are doing to Jesus, but they do not know what God is doing through Jesus, including praying for their forgiveness. The redemptive and self-sacrificing love of the Father that is demonstrated in the cross surpasses even their evil and envelops them in prayer. The conclusion of v. 34, "And they divided up his clothing by casting lots," is a quotation of Ps 22:18, a psalm that played an important role in the christological thinking of the early church (e.g., *1 Clem.* 16:15-17). Its quotation here reminds readers that suffering is an essential component of Jesus' messianic office. Crucifixion is thus not outside of or contrary to God's providential will, but the saving consequence of the history of redemption in Israel.

Three parties now ridicule Jesus on the cross, each taunting him to "save" himself — and others too. These taunts recall the three temptations of the devil in the wilderness (4:1-13). Luke ended the temptation narrative with a note that the devil "left [Jesus] until an opportune time" (4:13). The taunts of vv. 35-39 resume the wilderness temptation with a climactic fourth temptation of Jesus on the cross. In the first ridicule, "The people stood watching and the rulers even sneered" (v. 35). This description is an allusion to Ps 22:7. Luke follows the quotation from Ps 22 in v. 34 with an allusion to Ps 22 in v. 35 in order to reinforce that Jesus' mockery on the cross fulfills the maltreatment of God's Righteous One predicted in Scripture. Ps 22 "speaks of one whose status is less than human, 'a worm,' scorned, despised, and mocked. This is the very picture painted by Luke."[89] The imperfect tense of the Greek verb for "sneered" (*exemyktērizon*) implies sustained ridicule. "Let him save himself if he is God's

---

88. For the range of possible interpretations of Jesus' prayer, see Bock, *Luke 9:51–24:53,* 1849.

89. Green, *Luke,* 820.

Messiah, the Chosen One," mock the rulers (v. 35). In itself, "Chosen One" is not a messianic title, but it functions as an attributive of Messiah here.[90] "The Chosen One" (Gk. *ho eklektos*) recurs repeatedly in *1 En.* 39–62 with reference to God's Elect One (and elect ones) who will sit with God in glory. Like other conceptions of the Messiah, the Elect One was associated in Jewish thinking with triumph and glory, not with suffering. The presence of Jesus on a cross of shame is proof for the mockers of v. 35 that he is neither Messiah nor God's Elect One. The same assumption is present in the mockery of the soldiers (v. 37) and the criminal on the cross (v. 39).

Luke has prepared readers for a different understanding of Jesus' suffering, however. Already in the Galilean ministry Jesus taught disciples of the necessity of his suffering (9:22), of which he reminds them after the resurrection, "Did not the Messiah have to suffer these things and then enter his glory?" (24:26). Luke earlier identified Jesus as "the Chosen One" (9:35; Gk. *ho eklelegmenos*), but unlike Enoch's glorified "Chosen One," Luke's "Chosen One" is modeled on the Suffering Servant of the Lord in Isa 42:1, whose vocation Jesus fulfills in his "exodus" in Jerusalem (9:31). Thus, the reference to "God's Messiah, the Chosen One" (v. 35) stands in diametrical opposition in the mouths of the rulers and in the words of Luke: for the rulers, the title is flatly denied by Jesus' presence on the cross; for Luke, it is perfectly fulfilled by Jesus' presence on the cross.

The second and third parties of revilers are soldiers who "offered him wine vinegar" (v. 36) and a criminal also suffering crucifixion (v. 39). The Greek word for "wine vinegar," *oxos,* means "sharp," referring to ordinary cheap wine as opposed to sweet table wine, *oinos.* This wine, *oxos,* known in Hebrew as *homets,* was frequently diluted with water and drunk by commoners and soldiers. "The drink was itself a mockery — sour wine suffices for 'the king of the Jews'!" says Hans Heidland.[91] The wine also recalls the scorn heaped on the suffering of the righteous man, "They gave me vinegar [*oxos;* LXX Ps 68:22; *homets;* MT] for my thirst" (Ps 69:21; similarly Prov 31:6). According to Talmud, such wine served as a primitive narcotic offered to deaden the pain of crucifixion victims and was administered as a charitable service by women.[92]

---

90. On the title "God's Messiah, the Chosen One," see Fitzmyer, *Luke (X–XXIV),* 1504-5; Wolter, *Lukasevangelium,* 758-59.

91. H. Heidland, *oxos, TWNT* 5:289, followed by Marshall, *Luke,* 870. Further on sour wine, Fitzmyer, *Luke (X–XXIV),* 1505; Wolter, *Lukasevangelium,* 759.

92. "When one is led out to execution, he is given a goblet of wine containing a grain of frankincense, in order to benumb his senses, for it is written, *Give strong drink unto him who is ready to perish, and wine unto the bitter in soul.* And it has also been taught: The noble women in Jerusalem used to donate and bring it" (*b. Sanh.* 43a). The Babylonian Talmud was compiled five centuries after Jesus, but this testimony purports to relay first-c. execution customs when Jerusalem was still standing.

Like the rulers, the soldiers hail Jesus in scorn as "king of the Jews" (v. 37), the title in the accusation affixed to the cross (v. 38). A literal rendering of the wording of the title is itself suggestive of mockery, "The king of the Jews — this man!" "King" was of course the title that echoed through the crowd as Jesus entered Jerusalem (19:38), and later at the hearing before Pilate (23:2).

A criminal crucified with Jesus hurls the final insult at him, "Aren't you the Messiah? Save yourself and us" (v. 39). There is no evidence that the criminal is a Zealot.[93] Jewish revolutionaries/freedom fighters existed in the year 30, but Zealotism as an organized movement did not. Nothing either in the text (Gk. *kakourgos,* "criminal, malefactor") or context suggests he was anything other than a lawbreaker. Luke is interested not in his identity but in his insult, "Save yourself and us." "Save yourself" recalls the disbelief that Jesus first encountered in Nazareth at his inaugural sermon, "Physician, heal yourself!" (4:23). The addendum ". . . and us" sets signs and miracles as a prerequisite of faith — signs and miracles that benefit the petitioner! The final taunt is the most brazen of the three. Not surprisingly, Luke labels it "blasphemous" (Gk. *blasphēmein;* NIV "hurled insults").[94]

40-43 Luke again relies on pairs (see at 14:1) — two criminals — to advance the narrative. The criminals were in the motley procession to the cross (v. 32), Jesus is crucified between them (v. 33), and one of them has joined the chorus of taunters, "Aren't you the Messiah? Save yourself and us!" (v. 39). Jesus converses with the other criminal, as he earlier conversed with the women mourners (vv. 28-31). Jesus' conversation partners on the cross are only the Father (vv. 34, 46) and a criminal (vv. 40-43). Luke does not quote Isa 53 at the crucifixion, but the presence of two criminals throughout the narrative recalls and seems to fulfill the earlier reference in the Passover discourse to the fate of the Servant of the Lord who "was numbered with the transgressors" (22:37; Isa 53:12).

One of the criminals, silent to this point, rebukes the other criminal for insulting Jesus.[95] "Don't you fear God, since you are under the same sentence? We are punished justly for we are getting what our deeds deserve. But this man has done nothing wrong" (vv. 40-41).[96] The self-confession of the second criminal and acceptance of his punishment as just is received by Jesus as an act of confession. This criminal has done what the rich in the parables of 12:16-21 and 16:19-31 failed to do: he repents before it is too late. If the jeering at Jesus

---

93. So Rengstorf, *Lukas,* 254; Marshall, *Luke,* 871.

94. On the taunt of the criminal, see Schlatter, *Lukas,* 448; Schweizer, *Lukas,* 240.

95. On the various names attributed to the criminals in the early church, see n. 82 above.

96. *Gos. Pet.* 13 records only the speech of the penitent criminal, "We have landed in suffering for the deeds of wickedness which we have committed, but this man, who has become the savior of men, what wrong has he done you?"

on the cross is a revisitation of the devil (4:13), a veritable "fourth temptation," then the penitent criminal's "rebuke" (Gk. *epitiman*) of the impenitent criminal may function in accordance with half its uses in the Third Gospel — as a rebuke of demonic forces.[97] At the least, the rebuke of the reviler, and the grammatical and syntactic construction of vv. 40-41, set the innocence of Jesus in sharp contrast to the criminals' just punishment.

Turning his head to Jesus, the penitent said, "Jesus, remember me when you come into your kingdom" (v. 42). The exact wording of v. 42 varies in the Greek manuscript tradition. The best-attested reading is, "Remember me when you come *in* your kingdom." Here the criminal petitions Jesus to remember him when he returns in eschatological glory at the Parousia. This reading commands strong manuscript support,[98] but it may reflect the theological interests of the early church because it is the kind of alteration one would expect of a Christian copyist. Another variant reads, "Remember me when you come *into* your kingdom." This version is a spatial rather than temporal petition. The criminal is not asking to be remembered at the second coming — of which he is presumably ignorant.[99] He is asking to be received in the place where Jesus is going — in heaven, or Paradise. Although this reading claims weaker manuscript support ($\mathfrak{p}^{75}$ B L), it should probably be preferred (it is accepted by NIV) because it is consonant with Jewish and Lukan theology (24:26), and because we can imagine one in the criminal's position making such a petition.[100]

The criminal acknowledges two things of Jesus in v. 42 — that he believes Jesus to be innocent, and that he trusts Jesus' power to save him. Luke would have us understand the latter as trust in Jesus' *divine* power, for in the OT the exact form of this petition ("remember me"; LXX *mnēsthēti mou*) always occurs (ten times) with reference to God. His plea is grounded neither in good works nor in extraordinary knowledge of Jesus. The time for moral reform is past for him, and the request may exhaust his knowledge of Jesus. Nevertheless, his plea reflects the boldness and absolute trust that Jesus taught in the Lord's Prayer (see at 11:1-4). He believes Jesus to be the arbiter of eternal hope and eternal judgment, and he entrusts his fate entirely into his hands. The scandal of grace is operative both in his petition and in Jesus' response (v. 43).[101] Plummer reminds us that "some saw Jesus raise the dead and did

---

97. 4:35, 39, 41; 8:24; 9:42. Elsewhere (9:21, 55; 17:3; 18:15, 39; 19:39) the verb is used of rebuking humans, and often Jesus' disciples.

98. This reading is attested in ℵ A C D K W Γ Δ Θ Ψ.

99. That the criminal's petition refers "to the parousia of Jesus as the Son of man as a future event associated with the rising of the dead" (so Marshall, *Luke*, 872) assumes remarkable theological sophistication on his part.

100. See Schlatter, *Lukas*, 447; Metzger, *TCGNT*, 154; Wolter, *Lukasevangelium*, 761.

101. Subsequent textual tradition attempts to mitigate this scandal by assigning Jesus' promise of salvation only to the criminal "who rebuked [the reviler]" (D). Codex Colbertinus

not believe. The robber sees him being put to death, and yet believes."[102] For the unrepentant criminal, Jesus must come down from the cross to save (v. 39); for the penitent criminal Jesus must remain on the cross and fulfill his divine duty to save.[103] The petition of the penitent criminal is a witness that Jesus' death is not a defeat but a means of salvation. Luke's use of "remember" (Gk. *mimnēskesthai*) is significant, for it recalls Mary's prayer in the Magnificat that God will "help his servant Israel to remember mercy" (1:54). On the cross, his Suffering Servant Jesus fulfills that prayer.

In the inaugural sermon in Nazareth Jesus declared that, in his person and ministry, the messianic promise of Isa 61 was fulfilled, "Today this scripture is fulfilled in your hearing" (4:21). Similar emphasis is present in Jesus' promise to the criminal, "Truly I tell you, today you will be with me in paradise" (v. 43). "Truly" (Gk. *amēn*) occurs in Jesus' teachings as an authoritative preface, a conviction of his right to speak on God's behalf. "Paradise" occurs only thrice in the NT (v. 43; 2 Cor 12:4; Rev. 2:7) as the opposite of *Gehenna*, the place of condemnation and punishment. In Jewish literature, "paradise" is a transcendent place of blessedness, a celestial Garden of Eden (Gen 2:8; 13:10; Josephus, *Ant.* 1.37), reserved for the righteous after death (*T. Levi* 18:10-11; *Ps. Sol.* 14:3; *1 En.* 17–19; 60–61).[104] Some imagine "paradise" to signify a lower heavenly echelon or temporary eschatological state until the second coming. The term, however, appears to signify the full presence of God, the highest heaven. The criminal phrased his petition vaguely, "when you come," but Jesus answers it specifically, "*today* you will be with me."[105] The emphatic placement of "today" at the head of the final clause assures the criminal — and Luke's readers — that the promise of salvation is not merely a future possibility but an assured and present reality in Jesus.

The governing element in the promise of v. 43 is the phrase "with me." The criminal is not assured of an eternal state in which he is sovereign, but of

---

includes a catechetical question ("Do you believe?") before the assurance of salvation. See Metzger, *TCGNT,* 155.

102. Plummer, *Luke,* 535.

103. A point made by Brown, *Death of the Messiah,* 2:1001.

104. On the meaning of "paradise," see Str-B 2:264-69; J. Jeremias, *paradeisos, TWNT* 5:763-71; Fitzmyer, *Luke (X–XXIV),* 1510-11.

105. Fitzmyer, *Luke (X–XXIV),* 1510. The Curetonian Syriac reorders the syntax of v. 43, "Truly I say to you today, you will be with me in paradise" (Metzger, *TCGNT,* 155). This understanding of the verse, which has influenced the eschatological doctrines of some churches, allows for an understanding of eternal life that begins not at the moment of death but rather at the final resurrection of the dead. This translation (and understanding) strains the obvious sense of the Greek of v. 43 and robs Jesus' declaration of its force. Jews (with the exception of Sadducean Jews) already believed in a final resurrection. The unique force of the declaration binds the criminal's fate existentially to Jesus' very death and resurrection.

an eternal relationship of belonging with Christ. His very existence, and the meaning of his existence, is defined *in Christ*. He lives not unto himself, but with Christ (Gal 2:20). Where Jesus is, he will also be (John 17:24) — in paradise. In Lukan theology v. 43 is a veritable illustration of Paul's teaching in Rom 6:5, "those united with Christ in a death like his, will certainly also be united with him in a resurrection like his."[106] In Jesus' promise to the penitent criminal, Luke's soteriology, which is often muted, is shouted from the rooftops.

44-49 Luke omits the cry of dereliction from the cross (Mark 15:34-35; Matt 27:46-47) and places the offering of sour wine to Jesus at the beginning (v. 36) rather than at the end of the crucifixion (so Mark 15:36; Matt 27:48). In conjunction with the other Synoptics, Luke retains the darkness at midday and the tearing of the temple curtain as Jesus dies on the cross. "It was now about noon, and darkness came over the whole land until three in the afternoon, for the sun stopped shining. And the curtain of the temple was torn in two" (vv. 44-45). Jews reckoned daytime in twelve-hour increments, and nighttime in three watches of four hours each. Day extended from dawn (ca. 6 A.M.) to dusk (ca. 6 P.M.); hence, events from the "sixth" to "ninth" hours (v. 44, in Greek) refer to 12 noon to 3 P.M. Reports of extraordinary occurrences often accompanied deaths of important persons in ancient literature. Rabbinic reports of such include the appearance of stars at midday, weeping of statues, lightning, thunder, even the dividing of the Sea of Tiberias.[107] At the death of Julius Caesar, two Roman historians report the appearance of a seven-day comet.[108] Such portents were usually regarded as divine eulogies for the noble dead. Darkness at midday, by contrast, fulfills a portent attending the Day of the Lord foretold by the prophet Amos. " 'In that day,' declares the Sovereign Lord, 'I will make the sun go down at noon and darken the earth in broad daylight' " (Amos 8:9; also Joel 2:10, 30-31; Zeph 1:15).[109] Darkness at midday is a particularly appropriate cataclysm of divine judgment in light of Luke's earlier description of the opposition of the temple authorities as "your hour — when darkness reigns" (22:53).

Luke reports that darkness covered "the whole *land* [Gk. *gē*]," which could also be translated *earth* (Acts 1:8), thus implicating all humanity in responsibility for Jesus' death. *Gos. Pet.* 15 reports that darkness covered "the land of Judea," apparently symbolizing God's judgment on Jews for Jesus' death.[110]

---

106. Noted by Schweizer, *Lukas,* 241.

107. Str-B 1:1040-42.

108. Suetonius, *Jul.* 88-89; Plutarch, *Caes.* 69.3-5. For further examples of such events, see Wolter, *Lukasevangelium,* 761-62.

109. Likewise *Gos. Pet.* 15-21, which equates the darkness at the cross with blindness and fear. *Gos. Phil.* 68 equates darkness with destruction.

110. *Gos. Pet.* 17 reads: "And they [who gave Jesus gall to drink] fulfilled all things and completed the measure of their sins on their head."

The Lukan phraseology for "the sun stopped shining" (v. 45) is standard diction for an eclipse in ancient literature.[111] Ancient writers do not mention an eclipse in the time frame around Jesus' death. Astronomers consider an eclipse at Passover (= full moon) — and of three hours' duration — an astronomical impossibility.[112] Luke apparently intends the portents attending Jesus' death to signify the consummation of salvation history rather than to describe scientific phenomena. Plummer's view of the imagery as "the sympathy of nature with the sufferings of the Son of God"[113] may be understood similarly.

The second image, also theologically symbolical, is the tearing of the temple **curtain** (v. 45). There were many curtains in the temple complex (Gk. *naos*), the two most important of which (see Heb 9:1-5) were the (outer) curtain before the Court of Israel and the (inner) curtain before the Holy of Holies. Only Jewish men thirteen years of age and older were admitted into the Court of Israel, which was also known as the Holy Place, and contained a seven-branch lampstand, a table set with twelve loaves of bread, and an altar of incense (see at 1:8-12). The curtain before the Court of Israel was a beautifully embroidered Babylonian tapestry, mystically depicting the earth, sea, and heavens that "typified the universe," according to Josephus (*J. W.* 5.210-14). The second or inner curtain (Exod 26:31-37), which Josephus mentions but does not describe, separated the Court of Israel from the "unapproachable, inviolable, and invisible" Holy of Holies, a cubicle some twenty cubits (= thirty feet) square that the high priest entered once a year on the Day of Atonement (*J. W.* 5.219).

None of the Evangelists specifies which of the two curtains is intended.[114] The word for "curtain" (v. 45; Gk. *katapetasma*) is used by Josephus of both curtains (*Ant.* 8.75, 90; *J. W.* 5.212, 219), whereas in *Let. Aris.* 86 it refers to the outer curtain, and in Philo (*Mos.* 2.101) to the inner curtain. *Katapetasma* is also used in the LXX of both curtains; when used without qualification, it typically refers to the inner curtain, but when syntactically qualified, it refers to the outer curtain.[115] In the NT, the only uses of *katapetasma* outside the Synoptic crucifixion narratives occur in Heb 6:19; 9:3; 10:20, all with reference to the inner curtain. *Katapetasma* is thus generally the default term for the

---

111. BDAG, 306. Ancients knew that an eclipse at full moon was an astral impossibility, which may explain why many Greek copyists altered the reading to "the sun was darkened" (Gk. *eskotisthē ho hēlios*, A C³ D K Q W Γ Δ Θ Ψ). The preferred reading, "the sun's light failed (or was eclipsed)" (Gk. *tou hēliou eklipontos*), is supported by 𝔭⁷⁵ ℵ C L B (*ekleipontos*).

112. On eclipses in the ancient world, see Brown, *Death of the Messiah*, 2:1039-43.

113. Plummer, *Luke*, 536-37.

114. *Gos. Pet.* 20, *T. Levi* 10:3, and *T. Benj.* 9:4 also mention the curtain without further identification.

115. D. Gurtner, *The Torn Veil: Matthew's Exposition of the Death of Jesus* (SNTSMS 139; Cambridge: University Press, 2007), chap. 2.

inner veil before the Holy of Holies. Of the two curtains, this veil is the more theologically significant, for its rending would symbolize direct access to God.[116] Because of its heightened cultic significance, the inner veil is usually favored by NT scholars as the curtain torn at the crucifixion.[117]

Despite this probability, there is good reason to believe that Luke intends the outer curtain in v. 45. The word for "sanctuary" (Gk. *naos;* NIV "temple") in v. 45 is thrice used with reference to the Holy Place in the Zechariah story (1:9, 21, 22).[118] If Luke is consistent in his use of *naos* in v. 45, which is the only other instance of the word in the Third Gospel, then *to katapetasma tou naou* ("the curtain of the sanctuary") would seem to imply the magnificent outer curtain described by Josephus that hung before the Court of Israel, or Holy Place. More than any other, the outer curtain signified the temple proper, which throughout the Passion Narrative has been the epicenter of opposition to Jesus and the plot to kill him. The outer curtain was also the only curtain visible to the majority of Luke's readers (unless they were priests or adult Jewish males). The passive voice of "was torn" (Gk. *eschisthē*) is a "divine passive," signifying God's rending of the curtain.[119] The destruction of this curtain,

116. So *Gos. Phil.* 85: "Therefore the perfect things have been opened to us, together with the hidden things of truth. The holies of the holies were revealed, and the bridal chamber invited us in."

117. So C. Schneider, *katapetasma, TWNT* 3:630-33; O. Hofius, *katapetasma, EDNT* 2:266; Bovon, *Lukas 19,28–24,53,* 490.

118. Luke's repetition of *naos* at the crucifixion is another of his inclusios (see chap. 2, n. 140).

119. Three times Jerome cites evidence of a tradition in the early church of the breaking of the temple lintel rather than the tearing of the temple curtain at the crucifixion (v. 45; Matt 27:51; Mark 15:38). "In the Gospel we often mention we read that the immense temple lintel fell and broke to pieces" (*Comm. Matt.* 27:51). In subsequent citations of the same evidence Jerome identifies the source as the Hebrew Gospel (*Epist.* 120.8.2, *ad Hedybiam; Hist. pass. Dom.* f.65 [cited from *SQE* 489]). This tradition may be related to the earthquake in Matt 27:51, for an earthquake is more likely to dislodge a stone lintel than tear a curtain. Jerome refrains from any attempt to harmonize or explain the two different traditions. Rather, in each citation he mentions an apocalyptic vision related by Josephus (*J. W.* 6.290) that, prior to the destruction of the temple by Titus, heavenly powers hovered over the temple, warning "Leave this place!" The portents attending the destruction of the temple by Titus were perhaps regarded by Jerome as fulfillments of the shaking of the temple foundations in Isa 6:4. Evidence for this conclusion can be found in his letter to Pope Damasus, written earlier in 378-80, when, in commenting on Isa 6:1-8, Jerome wrote, "The removal of the lintel and filling of the temple with smoke were signs of the razing of the Jewish temple and incineration of all Jerusalem" (*Epist.* 18.9, *ad Damasum*). Jerome thus evidently cites the tradition of the collapse of the temple lintel, not as a rival tradition to the tearing of the temple curtain, but as supplementary attestation to the destruction of the temple. At the death of Jesus, in other words, not only the temple curtain but the whole portal was destroyed. The fall of the lintel and tearing of the temple curtain thus signify the total destruction of the temple. Further, see Edwards, *Hebrew Gospel,* 88-90.

therefore, continues Jesus' prophetic warnings of God's impending judgment on Jerusalem and the temple (13:34-35; 19:41-44; 21:20-24).[120]

At 3 P.M. — the hour of prayer in Judaism (Acts 3:1; 10:3) — Jesus prays the fourth of the traditional seven last words from the cross, a quotation of Ps 31:5.[121] "Jesus called out with a loud voice, 'Father, into your hands I commend my spirit.' When he had said this, he breathed his last" (v. 46). Ps 31 is a hymn of trust in the midst of deep sorrow, sleep, and death — things over which one has no control, and for which one must trust in God. That steadfast trust is signified by the invocation, "Father." It was highly unusual for Jews to address God as "Father," but Jesus always addressed God as such (10:21), and probably with the intimate and trusting Aramaic invocation, *Abba*.[122] The reference to "my spirit" is not to be understood in the Platonic sense of a disembodied spiritual afterlife, but as a total relinquishment of Jesus to God.[123] This prayer of trust and confidence marks the fulfillment of Jesus' "exodus," first mentioned by heavenly visitants at the transfiguration (9:31). The way of the one filled with the Holy Spirit as Son of God and destined to rule over the throne of his father David (1:32-35) has from the outset been a way of suffering (2:34-35; 9:22) that must lead to Jerusalem and the cross. Only by embracing the cup of suffering (22:42) can Jesus complete the exodus, thereby entering into his glory (24:26) and opening the gates of paradise (23:43).[124] The final prayer of Jesus on the cross is one of total submission and complete peace. Luke will narrate the death of Stephen in Acts 7:59-60 in similar style and terminology. Both prayers of Jesus and Stephen in their hours of death are models for believers as they too face persecution and death.[125] Luke captures this paradox of triumph

120. So too Marshall, *Luke*, 873. Green, *Luke*, 825-26, argues that the tearing of the veil does not signify the temple's destruction (for Jesus' followers continue to relate to it in the early chapters of Acts), but rather "God's turning away from the temple in order to accomplish his purposes by other means."

121. The LXX (Ps 30:6) translates the Hebrew verb *'apqîd* (MT, Ps 31:6, hiphil) as a future *(parathēsomai)*. Luke's present *(paratithemai)* is a more exact translation of the MT than of the LXX.

122. J. Jeremias, *The Prayers of Jesus* (Philadelphia: Fortress Press, 1978), 108-9.

123. Schweizer, *Lukas*, 241.

124. Fitzmyer, *Luke (X–XXIV)*, 1514-15, is one of the few commentators to recognize the cross as the fulfillment of Jesus' "exodus."

125. Both Jesus and Stephen utter great cries, they address their respective prayers to "Father"/"Lord" in the vocative, and they pray for the divine reception of their "spirit" and the forgiveness of their persecutors. Likewise, in the second c., Justin looked to Luke's depiction of Jesus' death as a model for believers: "Hence, God also teaches us by his Son that we should struggle [Gk. *agōnia* → 22:44] in all ways to become righteous and at our departure [Gk. *exodos*, → 9:31] to ask that our souls may not fall under any such [evil] power. For when Christ was giving out his spirit on the cross, he said, 'Father, into your hands I place my spirit.' This also I have learned from the memoirs" (*Dial.* 105).

in death with a wordplay on Greek *pneuma* (v. 46), which means both "spirit" and "breath": Jesus entrusts his spirit *(pneuma)* to the Father, and having done so, he breathes his last *(exepneusen)*.

For the centurion, the cross does not lead to a void of darkness and despair. For this officer (on centurions, see at 7:2) assigned with responsibility for Jesus' execution — and thereby literally a "Christ-killer" — the death of Jesus leads to the glorification of God and confession of Jesus' righteousness (v. 47).[126] Luke provides two subtle linguistic clues based on the Greek word *ginesthai* ("happened) that help explain the different reactions on the part of the centurion, on the one hand (v. 47), and on the part of the crowd and women, on the other (vv. 48-49). The reaction of the centurion is based on "seeing *what had happened*" (v. 47; *to genomenon,* neuter singular), whereas the reaction of the crowd is based on "seeing the *things* that had happened" (v. 48; *ta genomena,* neuter plural). The centurion's reaction is based on a single event — Jesus' death — whereas the people's reaction is based on the several signs accompanying Jesus' death. In witnessing the horror and "scandal of the cross" (Gal 5:11), in seeing not simply Jesus but "Jesus Christ *crucified*" (1 Cor 2:2), the centurion "glorifies God" (NIV "praised God") and pronounces Jesus "righteous." The phrase "to glorify God" (Gk. *doxazein ton theon*) is a Hebraic idiom that occurs rarely in the OT. It plays an important role in the Third Gospel, however, occurring eight times (but only once each in Matt and Mark).[127] The expression forms another of Luke's inclusios in which a word or phrase introduced in the infancy narrative is repeated in conclusion in the Passion Narrative; thus, the shepherds glorify God at Jesus' birth (2:20), the centurion at his death (23:47). For Luke, God is glorified when people recognize his presence and activity in the person and work of Jesus.[128] The use of this expression at the crucifixion signifies that the centurion perceives divine agency in the death of Jesus, the righteous sufferer. Throughout the Passion Narrative Jesus has been "mocked" (*empaizein,* 18:32; 22:63; 23:11, 36), "despised" (*exouthenein,* 23:11), "scorned" (*ekmyktērizein,* 23:55), and "blasphemed" (*blasphēmein,* 22:65; 23:39) because of what *ought* to have happened. Jesus ought to have saved himself, and others (vv. 35-39); and above all, he ought to have been something other than a suffering Messiah. For Luke, if Jesus is not glorified as a suffering Messiah, he will inevitably be mocked and rejected. The centurion does not project his ideal or expectation on Jesus. He allows "what had happened" on the cross to stand in absolute

---

126. Along with the names of criminals on the cross, Christian apocryphal tradition assigned the name of Longinus to the centurion (*Acts Pil.* 11.2). Plummer, *Luke,* 539, suggests the name may derive from the soldier with the spear (Gk. *lonchē,* John 19:34).

127. Edwards, *Hebrew Gospel,* 138-39.

128. 2:20; 5:25, 26, 7:16; 18:43; Acts 4:21; 11:18; 21:20.

and factual reality. In the suffering of the Son of God on the cross, he sees the truth (v. 47; Gk. *ontōs*): Jesus "was a righteous man."

According to the other Synoptics, at Jesus' death the centurion declared, "Truly, this man was the Son of God" (Mark 15:39; Matt 27:54). Luke records a less-exalted christological declaration, "Truly, this man was righteous" (v. 47). It is often suggested that Luke wished to avoid the many and varied associations inherent in "Son of God" in the Hellenistic world. Alternatively, it has been suggested that Luke relied on the Greek word *dikaios* ("righteous"; Heb. *tsadiq*), which carries overtones of Palestinian piety and appears elsewhere in Luke-Acts with reference to moral virtue, in order to imply that Jesus was "innocent." Neither of these suggestions adequately explains the use of "righteous" at v. 47. With regard to the first, Luke has manifestly affirmed Jesus as God's Son (1:35; 3:22; 4:41; 8:28; 9:35; 22:70; see further at 22:70) in the Third Gospel. Echoes of Jesus' divine sonship are also implicit in Luke's crucifixion scene, for in his dying breath Jesus addresses God as "Father." Moreover, in Jewish piety the "righteous one" is precisely he who may "boast that God is his father" (Wis 2:16).[129] One can scarcely argue that Luke's use of "righteous" at the crucifixion is a rejection or avoidance of the title "Son of God." With regard to the second suggestion, had Luke wished to stress Jesus' innocence, he would have used another word than Greek *dikaios*, which means "righteous" rather than "innocent."[130]

In light of this, it is precarious to conclude that "righteous" is a compensatory title in v. 47. It is, rather, consciously elected to emphasize that Jesus fulfills the office of the righteous sufferer in Israel as set forth in Isa 53. The "righteous one" plays a strategic role in Luke-Acts in relation to the mission of Christ. Already in 1:17 John is cast as the forerunner of Jesus, who, in the spirit of Elijah, will restore Israel according to the wisdom of the righteous (one). In his inaugural sermon, Jesus defines his mission in terms of the Servant of the Lord in Isa 61. In Acts 3:14, 7:52, and 22:14, Jesus is specifically designated God's "righteous one." In the Passion Narrative Luke refers to the righteous servant whose suffering will atone for evildoers (22:37; Isa 53:11-12). For Luke, the centurion's declaration that Jesus is righteous designates the cross as the fulfillment of the mission of Isaiah's Suffering Servant, and the accomplishment of Jesus' "exodus" in Jerusalem (9:31).[131]

---

129. Brown, *Death of the Messiah*, 2:1165, writes, "Luke could regard *dikaios* as an interchangeable alternative for Mark's *huios theou* in the centurion's reaction to Jesus' death prayer."

130. *Dikaios* ("righteous") occurs in 1:6; 2:25; 5:32; 14:14; 15:7; 23:50; Acts 10:22; 24:15. On its use in Palestinian Judaism, see Schlatter, *Lukas*, 156; Jeremias, *Sprache des Lukasevangeliums*, 22-23. It is important to recognize that the semantic field of *dikaios* is strongly determined by "just" and "righteous." LSJ, 429 does not give "innocent" as a translation for *dikaios;* and of the seventy-five occurrences of *dikaios* in the NT, BDAG, 246-47, offers "innocent" as a *possible* translation only at Luke 23:47.

131. On Isa 53 as a key to Lukan soteriology, see U. Mittmann-Richert, *Der Sühnetod des*

What for the centurion was a revealing event, was for the beholding crowds (v. 48) and women (v. 49) only a series of confounding events. "When all the people who had gathered to witness this sight saw what took place, they beat their breasts and went away" (v. 48). "What took place" *(ta genomena)* is neuter plural, implying "the *things* that took place." The centurion beheld the death of Christ, but the bystanders seem to have witnessed the *signs* — the cataclysms of darkness and torn temple curtain — attending it. The signs were indeed impressive, but in themselves they are not revealing, and they are not a substitute for faith (11:16, 29, 30). In perplexity, the crowds "beat their breasts and they went away" (v. 48).[132] Even "those who knew Jesus, including the women who had followed him from Galilee, stood at a distance, watching these things" (v. 49).[133] Unlike the crowds of v. 48, the women knew Jesus. They had followed him in Galilee and supported his ministry (8:1-3), and they will be part of the nucleus of the first church in Jerusalem (Acts 1:14). Despite their familiarity with Jesus, and for reasons we are not told, they saw "things" (v. 49) rather than Jesus. The cross was an "I-it" rather than an "I-Thou" encounter. Even familiarity with Jesus is not a substitute for faith, as Judas (6:16; Acts 1:16-20) and Jesus' own family (8:19-21) illustrate. The women are left "standing at a distance." They do not leave, as do the crowds, but they will require a meeting with the resurrected Christ before they believe.

Gottesknechts: Jesaja 53 im Lukasevangelium (WUNT 220; Tübingen: Mohr Siebeck, 2008), 54-85. Mittmann-Richert sees the death of the Servant as the secret of Jesus' messianic existence, a vicarious death "for others" (22:20) that is salvific, freeing humanity from the bondage of sin and death (313).

132. The consternation of the crowds is heightened in the Greek manuscript tradition. Codex Bezae (D) augments v. 48, "they beat their breasts *and their foreheads*"; several versions (Old Syriac, Old Latin, *Gos. Pet.* 7) add the lament, "Woe unto us for our sins and the judgment befalling Jerusalem." See Metzger, *TCGNT,* 155-56.

133. The theme of "knowing Jesus" forms another inclusio between infancy narrative and Passion Narrative, for the same Greek term *(hoi gnōstoi)* appears in 2:44.

CHAPTER TWENTY-TWO

Burial and Resurrection

Luke 23:50–24:53

One of the oldest divisions of the Gospels, the fifth-century tradition begun by Codex Alexandrinus (A), which became the prototype of chapter divisions in most ancient Greek manuscripts,[1] begins the resurrection chapters of all four Gospels not with Easter morning but with the burial of Jesus by Joseph of Arimathea on Good Friday (Matt 27:57–28:20; Mark 15:42–16:8; Luke 23:50–24:12; John 19:38–21:25). In so commencing the final chapter of the Gospels, the early editors signify that the proper understanding of the resurrection begins with the placement of Jesus' body in a tomb, for the body raised on Easter morning was necessarily understood to be the transformed body that was buried by Joseph of Arimathea three days earlier.[2] The Gospel accounts, in other words, cannot be understood to espouse a docetic understanding in which the Easter Jesus was a disembodied spiritual presence without continuity with his premortal physical body.[3] The gospel tradition and the earliest kerygma do not proclaim a resuscitation, but a resurrection of a dead body that had been buried: "They took [Jesus] down from the cross and laid him in a tomb. But God raised him from the dead" (Acts 13:29-30). The Pauline tradition regards baptism as theological identification with both the burial and resurrection of Christ (Rom 6:4; Col 2:12). The importance of the burial in the evangelical narratives is signified by the several names associated with it. Apart from Jesus, the last name to appear in the twenty-four-verse crucifixion narrative is Simon of Cyrene (23:26). In the seven-verse burial narrative, by contrast, three proper nouns appear — Joseph of Arimathea (vv. 50-51), Pilate (v. 52), and the women of Galilee (v. 55). "The women of Galilee" are subsequently identified

---

1. See J. Edwards, "The Hermeneutical Significance of Chapter Divisions in Ancient Greek Manuscripts," *NTS* 56/3 (2010): 413-26.

2. See here Talbert, *Reading Luke,* 225.

3. M. Hengel, *Crucifixion* (Philadelphia: Fortress Press, 1977), chap. 3, speaks of Docetism as a way of removing the scandal of the cross, but Docetism equally removes the scandal of the grave.

as "Mary Magdalene, Joanna, Mary the mother of James, and the others with them" (24:10). These named witnesses "and the others with them" are etched in early Christian tradition as a testimony of the importance and veracity of Jesus' burial. The names of the women in the resurrection narrative are particularly important because they represent eyewitness testimony of the same women — the only witnesses from the apostolic circle — who were present at both Jesus' crucifixion (v. 49) and his burial (vv. 55-56).

JOSEPH OF ARIMATHEA BURIES JESUS (23:50-54)

50-54 The body of Jesus is recovered from the cross and buried in a tomb neither by a relative of Jesus nor by a disciple, but by an otherwise stranger to the evangelical narrative, Joseph of Arimathea, "a member of the Council, a good and upright man" (vv. 50-51). Joseph "came from the Judean town of Arimathea" (v. 51). Arimathea is probably a variant of Ramah (also known as Ramathaim-zophim), some twenty miles (30 km) northwest of Jerusalem.[4] The Greek identifies Joseph as "a counselor" *(bouleutēs),* and this, combined with the following reference to *boulē* (v. 51), which in Greek can refer either to "council" or to "decision [of a council]" (NIV opts for the latter), designates him a member of the Jewish Council, the Sanhedrin (similarly, Josephus, *J. W.* 2.405). The description of Joseph as "good and righteous" (v. 50) recalls similar descriptions of Zechariah and Elizabeth (1:6) and Simeon (2:25). That Joseph was "waiting for the kingdom of God" (v. 51) — *long* "waiting," as signified by the Greek imperfect tense — likewise recalls the similar descriptions of Simeon (2:25) and Anna (2:38) waiting for the redemption of Israel. Apart from Jesus (18:18-19), no person in the Third Gospel is called good except for Joseph of Arimathea. In the sermon beside the sea Jesus taught, "The good person brings forth the good from the good stored up in his or her heart" (6:45). The description of Joseph fulfills that ideal. The confession of a Gentile centurion (v. 47) and kindness of a Jewish Council member (vv. 50-51) — both offices that typically opposed Jesus — may foreshadow the saving effects of Jesus' death for both Gentiles and Jews.[5]

Matt 27:57 and John 19:38 describe Joseph as a covert disciple. Luke's declaration that Joseph "had not consented to [the Sanhedrin's] decision and ac-

---

4. The identification is suggested by 1 Sam 15:34, where Heb. "Ramah" is translated by the LXX as "Armathaim" (see also Josephus, *Ant.* 13.127). The same identification was made in the fourth c. by Eusebius and Jerome, *Onomasticon,* 26. Further, see J. Pattengale, "Arimathea," *ABD* 1:378.

5. Hinted at by Schweizer, *Lukas,* 242.

tion" (v. 51) likewise marks him as a protagonist in the otherwise antagonistic Jewish Council. The Greek word for "consented to" *(synkatatithenai)* appears in Exod 23:1, 32 in a similar context of not consenting to unjust witnesses. This description of Joseph designates him a man of Torah righteousness and is another reminder (see Mark 12:34) that not all Jewish religious authorities opposed Jesus (so too 20:39; Acts 5:34). Joseph's rectitude in the midst of the adversarial Sanhedrin exemplifies the good soil in the parable of the Sower: "a noble and good heart, who hears the word, retains it, and by persevering produces a crop" (8:15).

In order to deter would-be rebels, Romans often allowed the bodies of crucified criminals to hang on crosses until they decayed. If requested, however, corpses might be handed over to relatives or friends for proper burial. Jews considered burial of the dead — including even the dead of enemies — a ritual piety (2 Sam 21:12-14). In Jewish law, a criminal executed for a capital offense (usually by stoning) whose body was hung on a tree in disgrace deserved to be buried before sunset (Deut 21:23).[6] Jews took this commandment seriously. Recounting a slaughter in Jerusalem, Josephus testifies that "[The Idumeans] actually went so far in their impiety as to cast out the corpses without burial, although the Jews are so careful about funeral rites that even malefactors who have been sentenced to crucifixion are taken down and buried before sunset" (*J.W.* 4.316-17). Joseph's behavior in the case of Jesus exemplifies this custom (John 19:31; *Gos. Pet.* 5, 15).[7] Hasty interments, of course, ran the risk of burying someone who had swooned but not died. Jewish custom safeguarded against this possibility by prescribing periodic visits to the tomb following death.[8]

"Going to Pilate, [Joseph] asked for Jesus' body" (v. 52). The retrieval of Jesus' body spares it from further indignities at the hand of the Romans. It took courage to request from the governor the body of a man executed as an enemy of Rome. Joseph's request of Pilate further attests to his integrity: he was willing to stand against the majority on the Sanhedrin, as Gamaliel would later (Acts 5:34); but unlike Gamaliel, he was also willing to risk the ire of the

---

6. According to *Gos. Pet.* 3, Herod (Antipas), of Jewish descent, begs Pilate on the basis of Deut 21:23 to allow Jesus to be buried before Sabbath.

7. The testimony of all four Gospels, combined with Jewish customs regarding burial, rebuts the conjectures of J. Crossan, *Jesus: A Revolutionary Biography* (San Francisco: Harper-SanFrancisco, 1994), 128-29, that Jesus' body was thrown to dogs, and also of M. Borg (Internet posting on "Jesus2000@info.harpercollins.com," 25 March 1996 [no longer available]) that the body of Jesus was "devoured by scavengers or buried in a common/mass grave." There is no evidence in the NT or in surviving early Christian literature for Crossan's and Borg's assertions in this regard. The six-page discussion of Jesus' death by Brown, *Death of the Messiah,* 2:1240, concludes: "That Jesus was buried is historically certain."

8. Str-B 1:1047-48.

Roman governor. Having obtained permission, Joseph wrapped the corpse in linen sheets, perhaps with which he lowered it from the cross, and "placed it in a tomb cut in the rock, one in which no one had yet been laid" (v. 53; Acts 13:29).[9] Matt 27:60 and John 19:41 describe the tomb as "new," but Luke identifies it as "one in which no one had yet been laid." This echoes the description of the triumphal entry in which Jesus rode "a colt on which no one had ever sat" (19:30). Both phrases signify the unique, regal status of Jesus' entry into Jerusalem, and his burial there.[10]

The Greek of v. 53 displays a curious ambiguity with reference to Jesus' body. Having taken the body down from the cross, Joseph "wrapped *it* [Gk. *auto*] in linen cloth and placed *him* [Gk. *auton*] in a tomb." The Greek antecedent of both pronouns (it/him) is "body" (*sōma*), which is neuter. The corresponding pronouns should therefore be "it." The change of the second pronoun to "him" (also present in Mark 15:46, though corrected in Matt 27:59-60) suggests that Luke, like Mark, prefers a personal and reverential reference to Jesus' body over an impersonal (though grammatically correct) reference.[11] The one who conquered death is a "being," not an "it."

Jewish law required that corpses be buried at least fifty cubits (ca. 75 feet) outside the walls of Jerusalem (*m. B. Bat.* 2:9). Unlike modern Western **burial customs** of sealing corpses in coffins and lowering them into the ground, Jews cut burial tombs (or enlarged natural caves) in the limestone hillsides of Palestine. The Mishnah specifies a burial vault six by nine feet (1.8 × 2.7 m) in dimension, with shelf-like niches on which bodies could be placed (*m. B. Bat.* 6;8). Nearly a thousand such "kokhim" (Heb. lit. "niche") tombs have been discovered in and around Jerusalem, some of which have body-shaped depressions carved in their flat surfaces. After the flesh of the corpse decomposed, the bones were removed and deposited in ancestral burial places (often ossuaries hewn out beneath the niches), thus freeing the niche above for repeated use (*m. Sanh.* 6:6). The OT refers to depositing the bones in ossuaries as being "gathered to their fathers" (e.g., 2 Kgs 22:20). In the late Second Temple period, tomb entrances were normally plugged with square or

---

9. Some commentators question whether Joseph could have purchased material on Passover. Rabbinic tradition made provision for such emergencies on holy days (e.g., *m. Šabb.* 23:1). With reference to the linen cloth and the Shroud of Turin, see Fitzmyer, *Luke (X–XXIV)*, 1527-29.

10. Noted by Brown, *Death of the Messiah*, 2:1255.

11. The textual tradition attempts in various ways to alleviate the discrepancy between "it" and "him" in v. 53. Codex Bezae (D) alters "it" to "the body of Jesus," and a twelfth-c. minuscule manuscript (1241) at St. Catherine's Monastery in the Sinai alters "it" to "him." Likewise, a strong tradition seeks to change "him" to grammatically correct "it" ($\mathfrak{p}^{75}$ A K L P W Γ Δ Θ Ψ). "Him" is the preferred reading because it is attested by weighty and diverse witnesses (א B C D lat.) and because, as grammatically incorrect, it is the more difficult reading.

rectangular blocks, which sealed ritual impurities within the tomb and kept animals and grave robbers out. A rolling stone disc in a channel in front of the entrance (24:2) was much rarer, signifying Joseph's elite social status.[12]

None of the Synoptics mentions the location of the tomb, whereas John 19:41-42 reports that "at the place where Jesus was crucified, there was a garden, and in the garden a new tomb, . . . [and] they laid Jesus there." Modern visitors to Jerusalem are customarily shown "the Garden Tomb" as the site of Jesus' burial and resurrection. The tranquility of the garden and reverence of its hosts offer visitors of faith a welcome place for prayer and reflection. The Garden Tomb was first venerated only in 1883, however, and has virtually no historical claim to be the site of Jesus' burial and resurrection. The Church of the Holy Sepulchre, despite its dark, confusing, and cacophonous interior, almost certainly stands on the site where Jesus was crucified and buried. The church stands inside the present-day walls of Jerusalem, but at the time of Jesus' death the site on which it was built lay outside the city walls. Two important data in favor of the authenticity of the site, both from the first century, are (1) testimony of Christian liturgical celebrations, and (2) burial of Christian dead at the site prior to the fall of Jerusalem in 66. Hadrian's attempt to desecrate the site in 135 by erecting two temples on it — one to Aphrodite! — further attests to its historical authenticity. The site was carefully scrutinized in the fourth century when Constantine began building the first Church of the Holy Sepulchre in 326 (dedicated in 335). Thus, from the first century until the present (or until popularizing of the Garden Tomb), the Church of the Holy Sepulchre has a strong and unbroken claim to preserve the site of Jesus' crucifixion and burial.[13]

---

12. Several later minuscule manuscripts and versions harmonize v. 53 with the Synoptic tradition by adding Matt 27:60 and Mark 15:46, "Then he [i.e., Joseph] rolled a great stone against the entrance of the tomb." Bezae (D) and two versions (Italian and Sahidic) add that the stone was so large that "scarcely twenty men could roll it." See Metzger, *TCGNT*, 156. A. Kloner, "Did a Rolling Stone Close Jesus' Tomb?" *BAR* 25/5 (1999): 22ff., argues that the stone blocking Jesus' tomb would have been a square block rather than a round disk. He bases his argument (1) on the fact that 98 percent of burial caves in the Jerusalem area (= ca. 900 tombs) used square blocks, and (2) on the claim that Gk. *kyliein*, "to roll," can mean "dislodge" rather than "roll." Regarding (1), although normal tombs may have used blocks, wealthy tombs (as in the case of tombs of the Herodian family and the families of the Sanhedrin) used rolling disks. Joseph of Arimathea, a prosperous ("rich," Matt 27:57) and distinguished council member, can be expected to belong to the latter category. With regard to (2), neither BDAG, 574, nor LSJ, 1008, gives any definition for *kyliein* except "to roll." All the Synoptics speak of the stone being rolled away (24:2; Matt 27:60; 28:2; Mark 15:46; 16:3), as do *Gos. Pet.* 36 and *Ep. Ap.* 9. Contrary to the arguments of Kloner, the unanimous witness of early Christian tradition is that a stone disc sealed the tomb offered by Joseph of Arimathea. See E. Meyers and M. Chancey, *Alexander to Constantine: Archaeology of the Land of the Bible* (New Haven: Yale University Press, 2012), 177.

13. See Dalman, *Sacred Sites and Ways*, 344-81; J. Murphy-O'Connor, *The Holy Land*,

THE WOMEN WITNESS THE BURIAL (23:55-56)

55-56 The narrative now shifts from Joseph's responsibility for the burial of Jesus to the women's witness of it. Luke ascribes a greater role to the women at the tomb, and gives a fuller description of it, than do the other Evangelists.[14] "The women who had come with him from Galilee followed, and they saw the tomb and how his body was laid" (v. 55, NRSV, ESV).[15] This verse recalls the same women at the crucifixion (v. 49) and anticipates their visit to the empty tomb (24:1-11). According to Luke, the Galilean women are the only party to witness all three events that constitute *status confessionis* of church proclamation: death, burial, and resurrected Jesus (1 Cor 15:3-5; Apostles' and Nicene Creeds). "**Galilee**" is significant in Luke's narrative.[16] In Galilee Mary receives Gabriel's announcement of the birth of God's Messiah and Son (1:26; 2:4, 39). Galilee is the home of Jesus and focus of his early ministry (4:14, 31, 44; 5:17; 8:26; 17:11), and he is identified as Galilean (23:5-6). The chief apostle is also identified as Galilean (22:59), as are the women disciples ([8:2-3]; 23:49, 55). Unlike the other Evangelists (Matt 28:7; Mark 16:7; John 21), Luke places the resurrection appearances in Jerusalem rather than in Galilee, but even in Jerusalem the Twelve and early disciples retain Galilean identity (Acts 1:11; 2:7). Galilean origins of Christianity characterize early Christian proclamation (Acts 10:37) and constitute an important credential of apostolic witness (24:6; Acts 1:21-22; 13:31). In identifying the women as followers from Galilee (vv. 49, 55), Luke endows their witness with unique authority. The Christian movement will expand inexorably beyond Galilee, but it is not impossible that the flight

---

45-58; R. Brown, *Death of the Messiah*, 2:1279-83; R. Ousterhout, "The Church of the Holy Sepulchre," *BAR* 26/6 (2000): 21-35: E. Meyers and M. Chancey, *Alexander to Constantine: Archaeology of the Land of the Bible* (New Haven: Yale University Press, 2012), 181-84.

14. See Brown, *Death of the Messiah*, 2:1256-58.

15. I follow the NRSV and ESV translation of v. 55, which preserves the ambiguity of the Greek. The rendering of the NIV, "The women who had come with Jesus from Galilee followed Joseph and saw the tomb and how his body was laid in it," adds the names of Jesus and Joseph, resulting in an interpretation rather than precise translation.

16. Contra M. Hengel, *Acts and the History of Earliest Christianity* (Philadelphia: Fortress Press, 1979), 18; M. Völkel, *Galilaios, EDNT* 1:234; and E. Lohmeyer, *Galiläa und Jerusalem* (FRLANT 52; Göttingen: Vandenhoeck & Ruprecht, 1936), all of whom dismiss Galilee too freely from Luke's narrative purpose. W. Grundmann, on the contrary, wrote two books (*Wer ist Jesus von Nazareth?* [Weimar: Verlag Deutsche Christen, 1940] and *Jesus der Galiläer und das Judentum* [Leipzig: Wigand, 1940]) that were published in conjunction with the Institute for Research into and Elimination of Jewish Influence in German Church Life, arguing that Jesus was a Galilean and, as such, non-Jewish(!). Both the institute and Grundmann's two volumes subordinated critical scholarship and Christian faith to the Nazi ideology of racial hatred. For brief and balanced discussions of Luke's emphasis on Galilee, see Marshall, *Luke* 878, and Johnson, *Luke*, 385.

of portions of the early church during the Jewish War (66-70) from Jerusalem to Pella, only twenty miles (30 km) south of the Sea of Galilee, may have been connected to the Galilean leadership of the nascent Christian community.[17]

The second half of v. 55 is particularly important, "[The women] saw the tomb and how his body was laid." The word for "saw" (Gk. *theasthai*) is intensive, denoting looking intently at something, "taking it in." The several witnesses present and their careful attention to the burial argue strongly against the possibility that they mistook a different (empty) tomb on Easter morning. "It was Preparation Day, and the Sabbath was about to begin" (v. 54). This statement dates Jesus' death to Friday afternoon. The Greek word for "begin," *epiphōskein,* literally means "to dawn," which is technically inappropriate, since the onset of Sabbath begins at sunset. Luke may use the word apart from its technical sense, or perhaps with reference to the appearance of the first star on Sabbath,[18] but it is not impossible that he employs the word to symbolize that the light of God's promise is present at the grave of Jesus, as it was in the darkness of the crucifixion (v. 44).[19] If Jesus died on the cross about 3 P.M. on Friday and Sabbath began at sundown the same day, haste was required if the necessary procedures — removal of the body from the cross, wrapping in cloth, transportation to and placement in the tomb — were to be completed by sundown. As "needful for the dead," the Mishnah (*m. Šabb.* 23:5) prescribes anointing and washing the corpse, removing it from the deathbed, binding up the chin, closing the eyes. Because of the lateness of the hour, washing Jesus' body (e.g., Acts 9:37) was dispensed with. Likewise, anointing the body, which v. 56 ascribes to the women and which, according to John 19:39-40, was done at the time of interment, would have to await completion of Sabbath.[20] After witnessing the placement of the body in the tomb, the women purchased spices in preparation for anointing Jesus' body after Sabbath.[21] The purpose of anointing was not to embalm and prevent bodily decay (as was the custom in Egypt), but to perfume the decaying corpse as an act of devotion. "Spices" (v. 56; Gk. *arōmata*) and "perfumes" *(myra)* refer to a variety of fragrant vegetable ex-

---

17. On the Christian flight to Pella, see Eusebius, *Hist. eccl.* 5.3.5; Epiphanius, *Pan.* 29.7.7-9. On Pella, see R. Smith, "Pella," *ABD* 5:219-21; on its possible association with early Galilean church leaders, see S. Bourke, "The Christian Flight to Pella: True or Tale?" *BAR* 39/3 (2013): 30ff.

18. E. Lohse, *sabbaton, TWNT* 7:20.

19. So Schweizer, *Lukas,* 242.

20. The Gospels are not entirely agreed on the preparations for Jesus' burial. John 19:39-40 reports that Joseph (and Nicodemus) wrapped Jesus' body "with the spices"; *Gos. Pet.* 24 reports a washing of the body: "He [Joseph] took the Lord, washed him, wrapped him in linen, and brought him into his own sepulchre, called Joseph's Garden."

21. On the role of women in caring for the dead in both Hellenism and Judaism, see K. Corley, "Women and the Crucifixion of Jesus," *Forum* 1 (1998): 181-217.

tracts, either dry or liquid, including salves, oil, ointments, or perfumes. Luke's conclusion to the visit to the tomb is especially noteworthy: "They rested on the Sabbath in obedience to the commandment" (v. 56; Exod 20:10; Deut 5:12-14). That the women would continue to observe Sabbath rather than making an exception to anoint Jesus' body is a remarkable testimony of Torah faithfulness.

THE WOMEN WITNESS THE EMPTY TOMB AND TESTIFY TO THE DISCIPLES (24:1-12)

Luke's Easter morning narrative consists of (1) primary elements shared by the other Gospels, (2) secondary details shared by at least one other Gospel but not by all four of them, and (3) details unique to the Third Gospel. The primary elements are the early visit to the tomb by women on Easter morning (v. 1; Matt 28:1; Mark 16:2; John 20:1), the name(s) of the women (v. 10; Matt 28:1; Mark 16:1; John 20:1), the stone rolled away from the entrance of the tomb (v. 2; Matt 28:2; Mark 16:4; John 20:1), the appearance of angel(s) in radiant clothing (v. 4; Matt 28:2-3; Mark 16:5; John 20:12), and the empty tomb itself (vv. 3, 6; Matt 28:6; Mark 16:6; John 20:6). Of the women, the name of Mary Magdalene is the only name in common with all four Gospels; all four mention her first, and John mentions no other woman.[22] The other Gospels introduce the narrative of the empty tomb with the women's name(s), whereas Luke concludes the narrative with their names. Secondary details include the doubt/fear of the women (v. 5; Matt 28:8; Mark 16:5, 8), the angelic declaration, "He is not here, he is risen" (v. 6; Matt 28:6; Mark 16:6), the departure of the women from the tomb to tell the men disciples (v. 9; Matt 28:8; John 20:2), and the association of the name of Peter with the empty tomb (v. 12; Mark 16:7; John 20:2). The two major particulars unique to Luke are the inclusion of a passion prediction (v. 7) and the accentuated role of the women as credible witnesses contrasted with the expressed disbelief of the Eleven (vv. 8-11).

These various elements are not always arranged in the same sequence in the Gospels, and they are augmented by elements unique to each Gospel. As a result, the four Gospels exhibit greater variations in the Easter narratives than in their crucifixion narratives.[23] The narratives of Mark and Matt are the most similar, whereas Luke and John follow more independent courses. John's

---

22. "Mary Magdalene, a woman disciple of the Lord" also appears at the empty tomb in *Gos. Pet.* 50.

23. Plummer, *Luke,* 546, writes, "The difficulty of harmonizing the various narratives is in itself a security for their general truthfulness. Dishonest witnesses would have made the evidence more harmonious."

additions result in a substantially new narrative, including a race between Peter and the Beloved Disciple to the tomb, followed by a dialogue between Jesus and Mary (John 20:14-17). Luke's more moderate additions result, by contrast, in new emphases.

1-8   "On the first day of the week, very early in the morning, they took the spices they had prepared and went to the tomb" (v. 1).[24] Luke begins chap. 24 with only a feminine pronoun ("they") referring back to the Galilean women at both the cross (23:49) and the tomb (23:55-56). The grammatical dependence of v. 1 on 23:55-56 links the resurrection to the burial, thus corroborating the early Greek chapter divisions that commence the resurrection narrative with the burial of Jesus (see introduction of this chapter). The first day following Sabbath was "day 1 of the Sabbaths" (v. 1, lit. in Gk.).[25] This specifies Sunday as the day of Jesus' resurrection.[26] All four Gospels agree on the women's early arrival at the tomb, although they express it differently.[27] Luke's Greek phrase *orthrou batheōs* (v. 1) means "the extreme point of earliness," perhaps "the crack of dawn." The apocryphal *Gos. Pet.* 50-54 attributes the women's visit in early morning darkness to fear, lest they be seen by the Jews. None of the canonical Gospels repeats this motive. The impression left in all four, rather, is that the early arrival testifies to the women's dedication to anoint the body of Jesus with spices they had prepared before the onset of Sabbath (23:56).

The description of the empty tomb is sparse and objective: "They found the stone rolled away from the tomb, but when they entered, they did not find the body of the Lord Jesus" (vv. 2-3).[28] Especially in Greek Jewish scriptures,

---

24. Whether Luke referred to "tomb" (v. 1) with *mnēma* or *mnēmeion* is difficult to decide. The former is better attested textually and, if original, probably derives from reliance on Mark 16:2. The latter, however, is more characteristic of Luke (vv. 2, 9, 12, 22, 24; see Jeremias, *Sprache des Lukasevangeliums,* 207) and is well attested textually ($\mathfrak{p}^{75}$ ℵ C* Δ).

25. Plummer, *Luke,* 547, notes, "This use of the cardinal ['day one'] for the ordinal ['first day'] is Hebraistic." So too BDF §247.1.

26. The significance of Sunday for Christians was noted by later rabbis, who occasionally referred to it as "the day of the Nazarenes" or "the day of the Christians" (Str-B 1:1052-53).

27. Matt 28:1, "the dawn of the first day of the week"; Mark 16:1, "when the sun had risen"; John 20:1, "in early morning darkness."

28. Apocryphal Gospels attempt explanations of the resurrection not present in the canonical Gospels. According to the Old Latin Codex Bobiensis, "Suddenly at the third hour of the day there was darkness over the whole circle of the earth, and angels descended from the heavens and as [the Lord] was rising in the glory of the living God, at the same time they ascended with him" (Metzger, *TCGNT,* 101-2). *Gos. Pet.* 35-45 relates how the guards at the tomb heard a loud voice from heaven and saw two men come down in great brightness to the tomb. The stone rolled away of its own accord, and the men entered the tomb. They exited, "two of them sustaining the other [i.e., Jesus], and a cross following them, and the heads of the two reaching to heaven, but that of him who was led of them by the hand overpassing the heavens." The guards at the tomb are then converted, and they declare Jesus to be God's Son.

"not find" does not mean the women had not yet found a corpse that existed, but that no corpse existed to be found (Gen 5:24 [LXX]; Sir 44:19-21; *Jub.* 23:10; *T. Job* 39:12; Rom 4:1).[29] The same expression occurs with the same sense in v. 23. Only here in all the Gospels does "the Lord Jesus" (Gk. *tou kyriou Iēsou*) occur, although it occurs fourteen times in Acts and more frequently in the Epistles. Reference to Jesus as "Lord" was absent throughout the trial and crucifixion narrative. For the first time at the empty tomb Luke unites "Lord" with "Jesus" to signify that the crucified Jesus is now the exalted *Lord* Jesus.[30] In Matt 28:2 the tomb is opened by the agency of an earthquake and angels. In the other Gospels the reference to the "stone rolled away" (v. 2; Mark 16:4; John 20:1) is a "divine passive," implying that it was rolled away by God.[31] The women witness an event they neither expected nor effected. NIV says "they were *wondering* about it" (v. 4), but such wording is a generally positive connotation, whereas Greek *aporein* means to be "confused, in doubt, uncertain."[32] They are at a loss to understand the empty tomb; it is beyond their comprehension. Their confusion is a reminder that a fact as irrefutable as the empty tomb does not lead to faith. The empty tomb does not prove the resurrection of Jesus, nor does the NT adduce it as proof of such. Already in Matthew's day opponents of the resurrection explained the empty tomb as evidence that Jesus' body had been stolen (Matt 28:13). Although the empty tomb does not prove the resurrection, it is nevertheless an important datum of faith, for it signifies that the Jesus who died as a bodily being was raised as a bodily being. For the women, faith begins not with the empty tomb, but with the testimony of the angels, and finally by meeting the resurrected Lord.

The appearance of "two men in clothes that gleamed like lightning" (v. 4) does not reassure the women, but leaves them frightened, "their faces to the ground" (v. 5). The description of the lightning-effect of the angelic clothing is superb: lightning breaks in from the sky, and angels break in from heaven. This is one of the few angelic appearances in Scripture not accompanied by the assurance "Do not fear." Matt 28:2 and John 20:12 call the being(s) angel(s) — one in Matt and two in John; Mark 16:5 and Luke v. 4 call the being(s) men, one in Mark and two in Luke. "Two men" again exhibits Luke's penchant for pairs and recalls the "two men" at the transfiguration (9:30; Moses and Elijah),

---

29. See Wolter, *Lukasevangelium,* 770-71.

30. Contra Plummer, *Luke,* 547, the omission of "Lord" in two late minuscules (579, 1241) and two versions (Syriac, Bohairic) is no argument against its originality. Rowe, *Early Narrative Christology,* 182-83, n. 86, offers a detailed defense of its authenticity.

31. Both *Gos. Pet.* 37 and *Ep. Ap.* 9 imply the stone was removed by divine agency. On the rolling away of the stone, Klein, *Lukasevangelium,* 721, writes, "The dead man is denied his eternal rest. Someone disturbed him!"

32. The first half of v. 4 in Greek is strongly Hebraic (Plummer, *Luke,* 547-48; Edwards, *Hebrew Gospel,* 330).

and anticipates the "two men" at the ascension (Acts 1:10). In each appearance the men are gloriously arrayed. We are not told they are the same two heavenly visitants, but their number and similar descriptions in all three episodes confer divine sanction on Jesus' earthly ministry, resurrection, and ascension. The resurrected Lord is not a different being from the earthly Jesus, nor is the mission of the church different from the mission in which the disciples were instructed by the earthly Jesus.[33]

Luke frequently describes angelic appearances in terms of "bright clothing," "light," or "glory" (2:9; 9:29, 31; 24:4; Acts 1:10; 9:3; 12:7), although not always (1:11, 26; Acts 23:11). The different terms attributed to angelic beings and the different descriptions of their appearances imply that angelic appearances are unique rather than uniform. The address of the two angels instructs the fearful and confused women in the first stages of belief. "Why do you look for the living among the dead? He is not here; he has risen! Remember how he told you, while he was still with you in Galilee" (vv. 5-6). There is mild rebuke in the angelic words (cf. 2:49). To seek the living among the dead is absurd (Isa 8:19); indeed, the women are doing what Jesus earlier warned disciples not to do: "Let the dead bury their own dead" (9:60).[34] The word for "living" is not generic but a specific reference to the resurrected Jesus, "the living *One*" (Gk. *ton zōnta*). The living do not inhabit tombs, hence, the women will not find the resurrected Jesus among the dead. "He has risen!" (v. 6; NIV) could be misleading, suggesting that the source of Jesus' resurrection was himself. The dead — and the Scriptures testify that Jesus was truly dead — can do nothing of themselves. The Greek *ēgerthē*, "he was raised," is the most divine passive in the NT, indicating *God raised him from the dead.* Apart from one instance (John 10:17-18), the many references to Jesus' resurrection in the NT all imply that he was raised or resurrected from the dead by the Father.

The angels offer no proof of Jesus' resurrection to the women. They *proclaim* the resurrection, and their proclamation makes faith possible, for faith is not a logical deduction from the fact of the empty tomb but a response of trust to declared truth.[35] The angelic command to "remember" (v. 6) — and the

---

33. On the continuity of identity between the pre- and post-Easter Jesus, see C. Talbert, "The Place of the Resurrection in the Theology of Luke," *Int* 46 (1992): 19-30.

34. *Exod. Rab.* 5 (71) recounts a story relevant to seeking the living among the dead with even stronger rebuke. When Moses and Aaron begged Pharaoh to be allowed to worship YHWH in the wilderness (Exod 5:1), Pharaoh consulted his royal annals, where he found the names of the gods of Moab, Ammon, and Sidon listed, but no name for Israel's God. When he informed Moses and Aaron of this, they responded, "Only a fool seeks the dead among the living and the living among the dead. Our God is a living God, the other gods of which you speak are dead. Our God is a living God and everlasting King!" See Str-B 2:269.

35. See here Bovon, *Luke 19,28–24,53*, 527.

act of "remembering" (v. 8) — lead the women from darkness to the dawn of understanding and faith. The act of remembering may be the most important virtue in Judaism. In the OT, and especially in Deut, Israel is exhorted to "remember" the mercy and faithfulness of God as the essential first step in faith, and the all-important step in maintaining faith (22:61!).[36] The angels remind the women of Jesus' prediction of his suffering, crucifixion, and resurrection on the third day (v. 7). At 18:31-34 the eight Passion sayings in the Third Gospel are discussed, four passion predictions prior to the crucifixion (9:22, 44; 17:25; 18:32-33) and four passion interpretations following the resurrection (24:7, 27, 44, 46). Luke is the only Evangelist to include passion sayings in the resurrection narratives. V. 7, the first of the four, reminds hearers/readers that Jesus' suffering is essential to understanding and believing his resurrected state, for his suffering is a fulfillment of Scripture (vv. 27, 44, 46), and his resurrection is a once-for-all victory over sin and death.

9-12 "When they came back from the tomb, they told all these things to the Eleven and to all the others" (v. 9). Remembrance (v. 8) leads to belief, and belief leads to announcement (v. 9). The women become the first heralds of the gospel, and their congregation the most illustrious in history — the eleven apostles (Judas having departed) and "all the others" gathered with them. V. 9 again reminds us that Jesus' followers exceeded the Twelve, including Cleopas and companion (v. 13), women (23:49, 55-56; 24:1-12), Jesus' family (Acts 1:14), Matthias and Justus (Acts 1:21-23), and unnamed "others" (vv. 9, 33). In much of the ancient world, including Judaism, veracity of testimony was proportional to named witnesses. Luke names at this point "Mary Magdalene, Joanna, Mary the mother of James, and the others with them" (v. 10). The other Gospels name the women prior to the discovery of the empty tomb (Matt 28:1; Mark 16:1; John 20:1), but Luke withholds the names of the three women until the conclusion of the empty tomb narrative in order to set their eyewitness testimony in juxtaposition with the apostles, who are twice mentioned in vv. 9-10. Mary Magdalene and Joanna were mentioned as followers of Jesus from Galilee (8:2-3; see on their names there). The third, "Mary the mother of James," is new to Luke's narrative. If the name derives from Mark, where she is named "Mary the mother of James the younger and Joses" (15:40) and "Mary the mother of Joses" (15:47), then she is possibly also "Mary the wife of Clopas" in John 19:25.[37] These three were not the only women to report to the apostles, for "the *others* with them" (v. 10) is feminine, indicating other women in addition to the three named women. "Mary Magdalene, Joanna, Mary the mother

---

36. See H. Eising, *tsakar*, *TDOT* 4:64-82; O. Michel, *mimnēskomai* etc., *TWNT* 4:678-87.

37. For an argument that John 19:25 lists four women, "his mother, and his mother's sister, Mary the wife of Clopas, and Mary Magdalene," see R. Brown, *The Gospel of John xiii–xxi* (AB; Garden City: Doubleday, 1970), 904-6.

of James" are singled out for special mention.[38] The first two are mentioned twice by name in Luke (v. 10; 8:2-3) and twice by implication (cross, 23:49; empty tomb, vv. 55-56). As wife of the manager of Antipas's household (8:3) and a likely source of Luke's account of Jesus' interview by Antipas (23:6-12), Joanna, along with Mary Magdalene, would qualify as "eyewitness" sources of the Third Gospel (1:2). The gospel tradition may be more indebted to these women than we know.

The names of only women witnesses at an event as momentous as the resurrection is wholly remarkable. Jewish opinion of women, especially in religious matters, was not always positive.[39] In Mark and Matt the women are the sole witnesses of the empty tomb, whereas Luke (v. 12) and John (20:3-10) include the witness of Peter and "the other disciple," although neither of the latter is (yet) a believing witness. The presence of names of women who had followed Jesus from Galilee (v. 6) attests to the early dating of their testimony,[40] and also argues in favor of the veracity of the resurrection narrative, for the fabrication of resurrection testimony involving women (in all four Gospels!) would be incredible. Some two centuries after the Gospels were written the pagan philosopher Celsus could still needle Origen that the Christian doctrine of the resurrection was based on the testimony of "half-frantic . . . self-deceived women" (Origen, *Cels.* 2.55).

A stronger testimony than the women's witness of the crucifixion, burial, empty tomb, and angelic announcement can scarcely be imagined, for the women have been veteran followers of Jesus and supporters of the disciples (8:3!) from the beginnings of the Galilean ministry. The Eleven and others, however, dismiss it as "nonsense" (v. 11). Like the dwarfs in C. S. Lewis's *Last Battle* who "won't be taken in!",[41] the Eleven stand before light, but they choose darkness.

---

38. Several manuscripts omit any introduction of the names (A D W Γ), but the majority tradition prefaces v. 10 either with "the (women)" (Gk. *hai;* ℵ² K Θ Ψ) or, more frequently, with "and they were" (*ēsan de;* 𝔭⁷⁵ ℵ* A B D L W Γ Δ). Which of these readings is followed by the NIV ("*It was* Mary Magdalene . . .") is unclear.

39. The OT does not specifically prohibit female witnesses, but Judaism generally disqualified women as competent witnesses in matters of strict law, or unless no male witnesses were available. Thus, "From women let no evidence be accepted" (Josephus, *Ant.* 4.219). "This is the general rule: any evidence that a woman is not eligible to bring, these [= dice-players, usurers, pigeon-flyers, traffickers in Sabbath Year produce, and slaves] are not eligible to bring" (*m. Roš Haš.* 1:8). "Sooner let the words of the Law be burned than delivered to women" (*b. Soṭah* 19a). See H. Cohn, "Witness," *EncJud* 16:590.

40. I do not share C. Osiek's ambiguity about the historicity of the resurrection ("The Women at the Tomb: What Are They Doing There?" *HvTSt* 53 [1997]: 103-18), although Osiek is correct in asserting that the presence of women at the empty tomb almost certainly anchors the narrative to the earliest layer of tradition.

41. C. S. Lewis, *The Last Battle* (London: Bodley Head, 1956), chap. 13, "How the Dwarfs Refused to Be Taken In."

Lagrange thinks the report was disbelieved because it was brought by women.[42] If so, this is another and most celebrated example of Paul's declaration that in the divine economy, "God chose the foolish things of the world to shame the wise" (1 Cor 1:27). Whether the gender of the messengers was the main reason — or a reason at all — is unclear. Had the report been brought by men, would the Eleven have reacted differently? Resurrection surpasses human comprehension. It seems probable that nothing short of meeting the resurrected Jesus, including strong testimony, could convince the disciples. The Greek word *lēros*, used only here in the NT, is a coarse rejection, signifying "that which is totally devoid of anything worthwhile."[43] Like Ebenezer Scrooge, the apostles judge the witness "humbug" and the witnesses incredible. If the call of the Twelve at 6:12-16 signified a reconstitution and fulfillment of Israel, then the initial response of the Eleven in v. 11 recalls another propensity of the same Israel to disbelieve God and spurn his messengers (20:9-16). Faith is not the inevitable result of "evidence," even good evidence like empty tombs. Faith cannot be proven. It must be chosen, "reckoned" on the basis of trust (Rom 3:28). Peter runs to the tomb and "peering in" (Gk. *parakyptein*) sees the discarded grave cloths (v. 12).[44] The empty tomb causes "amazement" in Peter (Gk. *thaumazein*), but not faith. The implication (repeated in the retelling of the incident in v. 24) is that Peter verifies the empty tomb. This makes him a second and corroborating witness of the same, but not a believer. The note that "[Peter] did not see [Jesus]" (v. 24) is revealing. Faith must await meeting the resurrected Jesus (vv. 34-35) — and even then, belief will not entirely dispel unbelief (v. 41).

THE ROAD TO EMMAUS (24:13-32)

Luke departs from his Markan exemplar for the remainder of the Gospel. Nearly fifty Hebraisms occur in 24:13-53, strongly suggesting reliance upon a

---

42. Lagrange, *Luc*, 601, "Scorn for an extraordinary testimony of women is no more astounding in the Orient than it is anywhere."

43. BDAG, 594.

44. This verse is omitted by the Western text (Codex Bezae [D]) and is regarded by some scholars to be a later addition to Luke derived from John 20:3, 5, 6, 10. See the discussion in Metzger, *TCGNT,* 157-58 (and further the section "Western Non-interpolations," 164-66). I judge the verse likely to be original because (1) its vocabulary (Gk. *anastas* ["having arisen"], *epi to mnēmeion* ["to the tomb"], *thaumazein* ["amazed"], *to gegonos* ["that which had happened"]) is predominantly Lukan, (2) the phrase "Peter arose and ran" is a Hebraism (BDF §419), and (3) if it derives from John 20, why is the second disciple unmentioned in Luke (esp. since v. 24 mentions more than one disciple)? and why is no angel present in the tomb in v. 12 (nor in v. 23) as in John 20:12? See also Schweizer, *Lukas,* 243.

Hebrew source.[45] Equally numerous are words and constructions unique to the Third Gospel, revealing Luke's editorial hand in conveying the Hebraic source material.[46] The resurrection appearance of Jesus in the Emmaus story is unique in artistry and insight, without which the biblical narrative as a whole would be impoverished. Luke portrays the resurrected Jesus as the keystone in the arch of the divine plan for Israel, and he continues its accentuation in the kerygma of the early church in Acts.[47] The resurrected Jesus presents himself as the fulfillment of Scripture, and his life as both the interpretation and actualization of Scripture (vv. 27, 44-45).[48] The Third Gospel is a dramatic triptych, in which the ministry of Jesus in the body of the Gospel is flanked by an introductory infancy narrative that anticipates it and a concluding resurrection narrative that interprets it. In the infancy narrative Luke portrays the history of Israel as the prefigurement of the coming of John and Jesus; in the resurrection narrative (vv. 13-53), Luke portrays the life of Jesus as the fulfillment of the history of Israel.

13-27 "Now that same day two of them were going to a village called Emmaus, about seven miles (11 km) from Jerusalem" (v. 13). "That same day" places the walk to Emmaus on "(day) 1 of the Sabbaths" (v. 1) — Sunday — the day the women discovered the empty tomb. "Two of them" is the last and perhaps most important of Luke's frequent reference to pairs (see at 14:1), for this pair become the first, though unknowing, human witnesses of the resurrection. Two witnesses fulfill the legal requirement of credibility in Judaism (Num 35:30; Deut 19:15; 1 Kgs 21:10, 13), an important requirement to fulfill in the case of an alleged resurrection. "Two *of them*" refers readers to "the Eleven and all the other [disciples]" gathered after the crucifixion (v. 9). Whether the "them" includes women is ambiguous. One of the two, "Cleopas" (v. 18), was not of the Twelve, and the other is not identified, leaving his or her identity a matter of conjecture (see further at v. 18).

Their destination, "Emmaus," is probably located west of Jerusalem, but precisely where is uncertain. Problems exist with both the name, which means "warm well" and was given to many sites in Israel and the ancient Mediterranean world, and with the distance of "seven miles" (11 km; Gk. lit. "sixty stadia"; one *stadion* = 200 yards [180 m]). The distance is the greater problem of the two, for of the two most probable sites, one is half the distance stipulated by Luke, and the other twice the distance. Four main sites have been proposed.

---

45. All Hebraisms are listed in Edwards, *Hebrew Gospel,* 330-32.

46. On the evidence of Lukan vocabulary and style, see Jeremias, *Sprache des Lukasevangeliums,* 313-23; Fitzmyer, *Luke (X–XXIV),* 1554-55; Klein, *Lukasevangelium,* 726, n. 6.

47. Cadbury, *Making of Luke-Acts,* 279, "No New Testament writer more often refers to the resurrection as predicted in Scripture or cites more texts in its support than does Luke."

48. On this point, see H. Betz, "Ursprung und Wesen christlichen Glaubens nach der Emmauslegende (Luc 24,13-32)," *ZTK* 66 (1969): 7-21; Green, *Luke,* 834.

Two of them, Qubeiba and Abu Ghosh, the first west and the second slightly northwest of Jerusalem, are almost exactly seven miles from Jerusalem. Despite their propitious locations, neither site was identified as "Emmaus" until the Middle Ages, and in the case of Abu Ghosh (known in the OT as Kiriath Jearim), not until the Crusader period (eleventh c.). The earliest tradition associating either site with Emmaus, in other words, is a millennium removed from the event. A third and stronger possibility is an "Emmaus" where, according to Josephus (*J.W.* 7.217), Vespasian settled eight hundred veterans following the defeat of Jerusalem by Rome in 70. Josephus locates this Emmaus "thirty stadia" (= 3.75 miles, 6.0 km) west of Jerusalem, roughly as far west of the city as Bethlehem is south of it. The name "Emmaus" is likely preserved in references to "Mozah" (Josh 18:26) or "Motza" (*m. Sukkah* 4:5), which archaeological excavations have identified as modern *Qaluniya* (from Lat. *colonia*). This "Emmaus" is only half the distance from Jerusalem stated in v. 13 (although a round trip from Jerusalem would equal "sixty stadia"). This site, though favored by many modern scholars, was not identified with the Emmaus in question in antiquity, nor have Christian archaeological remains been found there. A fourth possibility is "Emmaus-Nicopolis," which was identified by Eusebius, Jerome, and Sozomen with the Emmaus of v. 13.[49] Literary and numismatic evidence verify the name of the site in the first century,[50] and Christian pilgrim texts from the fourth century assume Emmaus-Nicopolis the proper site of the story at hand. Christian church remains there date to the fifth or sixth centuries.[51] This site has the strongest historical claim to be the "Emmaus" of v. 13, although it lies seventeen miles (27 km = ca. 150 *stadia*) west of Jerusalem, more than twice the distance stipulated by Luke.[52] Many modern scholars think it "absurd" that wayfarers could log a round trip of thirty-five-odd miles (55 km) in a day and dismiss Emmaus-Nicopolis out of hand.[53] The distance that seems insuperable to moderns (who do comparatively little walking) does not appear to have seemed so to ancients (who did much walking).[54] Ancients

---

49. See *Onomasticon*, 53; Jerome, *Vir. ill.* 63; *Epist.* 108.8.2; Sozomen, *Hist. eccl.* 5.21.5.

50. 1 Macc 3:40, 57; frequently by Josephus, *J.W.* 1.222, 319, etc.; *Ant.* 12.298 etc.; Pliny, *Nat.* 5.70. For numismatic evidence, Schürer, *History of the Jewish People*, 1:512-13, n. 142.

51. H. Shanks, "Emmaus: Where Christ Appeared," *BAR* 34/2 (2008): 41-51.

52. A textual variant at v. 13 reads, "*one hundred* and sixty stadia" (so ℵ K N Θ). The attestation of this reading by Codex Sinaiticus (ℵ) is significant, esp. since "one hundred" (Gk. *hekaton*) is naturally embedded in the text and not a marginal or interlinear addition. If correct, it would remove a major obstacle to affirming Emmaus-Nicopolis. The composite textual tradition favoring "sixty stadia" is stronger, however (see Metzger, *TCGNT*, 158). If "*one hundred* and sixty stadia" is a later addition, it attests to a very early identification of Emmaus-Nicopolis as the site intended in v. 13.

53. So Plummer, *Luke*, 551.

54. "Anyone familiar with Palestinian bedouin or Arabs in a pre-automotive culture

reckoned thirty stadia as an hour's march,[55] which equates to ten-odd hours for a roundtrip of three hundred stadia. That is neither impossible, nor perhaps too unusual, in ancient travel. In recording the transfer of Paul to safe custody in Caesarea, Luke reports a night march from Jerusalem to Antipatris, a distance of some forty-five miles (72 km), as though it were standard procedure (Acts 23:31). Eusebius, Jerome, and Sozomen all identified Emmaus-Nicopolis as the intended site of v. 13. That does not verify the site, but it weakens the argument of distance against its authenticity, for all three traveled throughout Palestine by foot and knew its geography intimately.[56]

On their way to Emmaus the wayfarers talk "about everything that had happened" (v. 14) in Jerusalem. Judaism valued the ideal of discussing religious matters while walking (Deut 6:7).[57] These pedestrians were dwelling on the past — what *was;* and on disappointed hopes — what *might have been.* "Everything that had happened" refers to events surrounding the death of Jesus (vv. 18, 21), which is now complicated by perplexing news of the empty tomb. The two are trying "to figure out" (Gk. *syzētein*) what had transpired. As they are underway, Jesus approaches and joins them, although they do not recognize him. Did they fail to recognize him because they were engrossed in conversation, or because he was in a different form (e.g., Mark 16:12; John 20:14-15)?[58] The Greek of v. 16 says, "Their eyes were prevented from recognizing him." The Greek for "prevented," *kratein,* meaning "to control, hold, restrain," suggests an operative beyond human eyesight. The two are not simply imperceptive or, worse, blinded by Satan.[59] This is confirmed by v. 31, which reverses v. 16, "Their eyes were opened and they recognized him." "Prevented" and "opened" are "divine passives," i.e., both their lack of understanding and their subsequent recognition are due to divine agency.[60] Only those who otherwise would have

---

would not doubt the disciples' ability to walk forty miles in a day" (C. Miller, "Emmaus," *Harper's Bible Dictionary* [ed. P. Achtemeier; San Francisco: Harper & Row, 1985], 261-62).

55. See evidence in Bovon, *Lukas 19,28–24,53,* 557.

56. In addition to the sources cited above regarding Emmaus, see Str-B 2:269-71; G. Dalman, *Sacred Sites and Ways,* 226-31; Marshall, *Luke,* 892-93; Fitzmyer, *Luke (X–XXIV),* 1561-62; J. O'Connor, *The Holy Land,* 319-21; Wolter, *Lukasevangelium,* 776-77. It is perhaps worth mentioning that the Madaba Map situates Nicopolis and Modein (both approximately eighteen miles from Jerusalem) within the immediate orbit of Jerusalem, along with Bethlehem, for example.

57. Str-B 2:273.

58. So Plummer, *Luke,* 552, "There is no *need* to assume a special act of will on the part of Christ. . . . They were preoccupied and had no expectation of meeting Him, and there is good reason for believing that the risen Saviour had a glorified body which was not at once recognized."

59. So Nolland, *Luke 18:35–24:53,* 1207; entertained also by Vinson, *Luke,* 750.

60. In rabbinic writings, "to control the eyes" is a Hebraism (Heb. *'akhīzath 'ēnayīm*) suggesting a divine spell. See Str-B 2:271-73.

known Jesus could be prevented from seeing him. Similar to 9:45 and 18:34, Luke reminds readers that recognition of Jesus and confession of him as Christ and Lord are not matters of human insight but of divine enablement — of revelation.

The unrecognized Jesus asks, "What are you discussing together as you walk along?" (v. 17). The NIV translation stresses "you" — the disciples — whereas the Greek stresses the subject of their conversation, "What are *these things* that you are discussing as you walk together?" "These things" recalls the events of vv. 18, 21. The word for "discussing," *antiballein,* occurring only here in the NT, means "to throw back and forth," "to exchange views" on a matter. The question brings the disciples — and the conversation — to a standstill. "They stood still, their faces downcast" (v. 17).[61] The word for "downcast," *skythrōpos,* sums up the scene in one word: the pair is "sad, gloomy" — "bummed out." The two address the Stranger impatiently. "One of them, named Cleopas, asked him, 'Are you the only visitor to Jerusalem who does not know what has happened there in these last few days?'" (v. 18).[62] The placement of Greek *sy* ("you") at the head of the sentence signifies astonishment on their part, "Are *you* the only one in the dark around here?" Insult is one of the inevitable consequences of the incarnation. If only God would remain in heaven where he belongs. When God dares to involve himself in Israel's affairs or become a human being in Jesus of Nazareth, the consequence is ridicule (8:53), mockery (23:36), or, as here, insult (v. 18).

Exactly who Cleopas was we cannot say. Eusebius identified him as the "Clopas" of John 19:25. Following Hegesippus, Eusebius believed Clopas to be a brother of Joseph, Jesus' father, thus making him Jesus' uncle. Eusebius further believed the partner of Clopas on the road to Emmaus to be his son "Simon," who succeeded James, brother of Jesus, as leader of the church in Jerusalem (*Hist. eccl.* 3.11.1).[63] Older scholars also identified Cleopas with Clopas.[64] According to John 19:25, the wife of Clopas, a woman named Mary, was present at the resurrection (John 19:25), perhaps the same "Mary the mother of James" mentioned in v. 10. If these hypotheses are correct — a big "if" — the partner of Cl(e)opas (if not his son Simon) may have been his wife, Mary — another

---

61. A majority of Greek manuscripts offer the following reading of v. 17: "What are these words that you exchange with one another while you are walking and are gloomy?" A minority of manuscripts, older and weightier (p[75] ℵ A B), should be followed, however, resulting in the NIV rendering of v. 17. See Metzger, *TCGNT,* 158.

62. An overly literal rendering of v. 18 results in a confusing NIV translation: "Are you only a visitor to Jerusalem and do not know the things that have happened there in these days?"

63. Schlatter, *Lukas,* 454, repeats the same testimony of Eusebius regarding Cleopas (and only this testimony), though without affirming or denying it.

64. A. Deissmann, *Bibelstudien* (Marburg, 1895), 184, n. 1; with reservation by G. Dalman, *Grammatik des jüdisch-palästinischen Aramäisch* (2nd ed.; Leipzig, 1905), 179.4.

big "if." Most modern scholars doubt all this. "Cleopas" appears to be a Greek name (abbreviated form of Cleopatros, the feminine form of Cleopatra), and "Clopas" an Aramaic name unrelated to it, thus names of separate persons.[65] Caution is in order when judging names on the basis of Greek and Semitic etymologies, however, since personal names frequently defy precise etymology. The name of Cleopas is thus subject to several hypothetical explanations. The one certainty is that he is not named in any list of the Twelve (see at 6:13) and hence belongs to "the other [disciples]" (v. 9).

Hypotheses regarding the identity of his companion are equally prolific. The possibility of the companion being Cleopas's wife has been noted above. In addition to the opinion of Eusebius, also noted above, a gloss in the margin of Codex S (tenth c.) identifies the companion as "Simon, not Peter but the other [Simon]."[66] Origen regularly identified the companion as Simon (with no further identification), which suggests "Simon" (Peter) of v. 34.[67] Epiphanius considered him Nathanael,[68] and Jerome argued for James the Just, brother of Jesus, as the companion.[69] Luke may not have known the name of the companion, for he gives no clues to this person's identity other than, like Cleopas, being one of "the other" disciples (v. 9). Further speculation on his identity is wasted ingenuity.

Jesus does not defend himself against the untoward insinuation of Cleopas in v. 18, but asks "What things?" (v. 19). His question invites the pair to open their hearts so he may instruct them in truth that only their hearts may receive. "'About Jesus of Nazareth,' they replied" (v. 19). "They replied" indicates that Jesus engaged not only Cleopas but both disciples in conversation. The original Greek identifies Jesus as "the Nazarene" *(Nazarēnos).* The Greek spelling may indicate Luke derives the name from his special source, for when he writes without influence from another source, he spells "Nazarene" *Nazōraios.*[70] "He was a prophet, powerful in word and deed before God and all the people" (v. 19) is a one-sentence summary of the disciples' understanding of Jesus' life and ministry. "He was a prophet" (Gk. *anēr prophētēs*) is a Hebraism (Judg 6:8; Heb. *ish nabi*), and "powerful in word and deed" recalls other Lukan descriptions of preeminent figures in Israel, including

---

65. BDF §125, followed by a majority of modern scholars.

66. Metzger, *TCGNT,* 158.

67. *Cels.* 2.62, 68; *Hom. Luc.* 24.32; *Hom. Jer.* 20; *Comm. Jo.* 1.5.30; 1.8.50.

68. *Pan.* 33.6.

69. Jerome, *Vir. ill.* 2. For discussion of Jerome's views, see Edwards, *Hebrew Gospel,* 79-82.

70. BDAG, 664; a fuller discussion of the two terms is in H. Kuhli, *EDNT* 2:454-56. This conjecture is reinforced by the fact that many Greek manuscripts replace the less frequently used word *Nazarēnos* (6x in NT) by the more frequently used word *Nazōraios* (13x, incl. 8x in Luke-Acts). See Metzger, *TCGNT,* 159; Klein, *Lukasevangelium,* 730, n. 41.

Moses (Acts 7:22), Zechariah and Elizabeth (1:6), Apollos (Acts 18:24). Such descriptions are typical in ancient Jewish and Hellenistic biographies,[71] including Josephus's description of Jesus himself, "a wise man . . . and worker of remarkable feats" (*Ant.* 18.63). In v. 19 Cleopas and his companion assign Jesus a rank among Israel's preeminent figures. Nevertheless, absence of words like "Lord," "Messiah," or "Son of God" also indicates that Jesus was considered no greater than these same figures. Like so many who had gone before, Jesus too suffered rejection from "chief priests and our rulers" (23:13). Even if Jesus' star had risen higher than his predecessors, his death by crucifixion made his demise the more bitter and final.

Cleopas possesses the beginnings of a proper understanding of Jesus — the cross, evidence for the empty tomb, even a possible relation between these facts and "the redemption of Israel" — but he remains bewildered and despondent. Faith and hope are not assured by correct knowledge, nor even by gaining more knowledge, but by knowledge that enlightens understanding of the living Jesus — "faith seeking understanding," as both Augustine and Anselm decreed. Cleopas has not yet recognized the living Jesus, and until he does, his knowledge of Jesus does not lead to understanding. "We had hoped that he was the one who was going to redeem Israel" (v. 21). The Greek "we" is emphatic. The forlorn plea of the wayfarers, "*We* had hoped," echoes through all humanity. Human beings — including Jesus' disciples — inevitably associate human causes with the will of God. The succinct lamentation of Cleopas sums up the feelings of believers through the ages who conclude that, when God does not fulfill their hopes, all hope is lost. Luke set the stage for the redemption of Israel in Zechariah's hymn at John's birth, "The God of Israel . . . has come to his people and has redeemed them" (1:68, 77). Anna, a temple prophetess, repeats the theme when the baby Jesus awakens hope of "the redemption of Jerusalem" (2:38). The theme of "the redemption of Israel" may initially derive from the exodus from Egypt, but the use of the phrase in Luke 1–2 also seems to reflect characteristic uses of the phrase in Servant of the Lord texts (Isa 41:14; 43:14; 44:24). "Redemption of Israel" should not be limited to nationalistic, political, and sociological aspirations, but should also include hopes for forgiveness of sins and spiritual blessings of Israel.[72] The medium of suffering accompanies the theme of redemption in Isa 40–55, and the same medium is present in Simeon's words that Jesus would face opposi-

---

71. For Jewish examples, Str-B 2:273; for Jewish and Hellenistic examples, Wolter, *Lukas-evangelium,* 780.

72. Str-B 1:67-70 surveys primarily Isaianic references to God as savior. For a discussion of "redemption of Israel" from a largely nationalistic perspective, see Bock, *Luke 9:51–24:53,* 1913-14. For a discussion of the same phrase from a largely spiritual perspective, see Johnson, *Luke,* 394.

tion and sword (2:34-35). The important point here is that suffering *precedes* glory; Jesus must die before he can live (Rom 14:9; Rev 1:18; 2:8). The role of suffering in redemption escapes the pair on the road to Emmaus, as it escaped many if not most of their Jewish contemporaries. For them, suffering and death are the abnegation of hope. They cannot conceive, nor can humanity as a whole conceive, that suffering and death are the necessary means of divine redemption and eternal hope.

The loss of hope in v. 21 is not quite final, for the two report that "some of our women" (v. 22), followed by "some of our companions" (v. 24), went to the tomb and discovered it empty. Mention of the women recalls the narrative of vv. 1-11. "*Our* women" emphasizes known and trusted associates whose report, despite its audacity, should not be discounted.[73] The report of Cleopas and companion on the women's visit to the tomb in v. 23 is revealing, for it omits their confusion (v. 4), fears (v. 5), recollections (v. 8), and angelic conversation (vv. 5-7). The only thing of importance (10:42!) is whether Jesus is alive.[74] The astounding report that the tomb was empty had been substantiated by "some with us." According to v. 12, other than the women, only Peter went to investigate the empty tomb. Vv. 1-12 are evidently selective rather than exhaustive, for the datum of the empty tomb is now attested by *apostolic* confirmation of the women's report (also v. 24). Evidence for the empty tomb is thus considerable, yet still inconclusive on the one thing that matters: "him they did not see" (v. 24). NIV follows the Greek in shifting "him" emphatically to the front of the sentence. The first twenty-five verses of Luke's resurrection narrative effectively convey that belief in the resurrection does not depend on objective evidence, no matter how solid. Until the disciples *meet* the resurrected Jesus, they remain "bewildered, utterly astounded" (Gk. *existanai*), neither their worst fears confirmed nor their faint hopes revived. Saved from despair but unable to believe, they wait in a limbo of conflicting and unconfirmed reports.

On the ironic journey to Emmaus living disciples talk about a dead Jesus, while a living Jesus speaks with lifeless disciples. The disciples bemoan that others have not seen Jesus while they fail to recognize him in their midst. The voice of the disciples is one of human possibilities and their inevitable finitude, weakness, and failures; the voice of Jesus is one of divine confirmation of his sacrificial and saving suffering on the cross, and thus of forgiveness and transformation to eternal life. Jesus now speaks, and his words are an invective of grace. "How foolish you are, and how slow to believe all that the prophets have spoken!" (v. 25). Jesus does not rebuke the disciples for disbelieving the evidence associated with the resurrection, or for disbelieving the witness of

---

73. The Western text (D) omits "our" (Gk. *ex hēmōn*), but its otherwise universal inclusion in the manuscript tradition virtually affirms its authenticity.

74. See here Wolter, *Lukasevangelium*, 782.

the women, or even for not recognizing himself. He rebukes them for reading the Scriptures without understanding and belief.[75] The disciples' problem is not one of head, but of heart. Mary was blessed because she believed the Lord would fulfill his promises to her (1:45). Paul, too, believed that God would act in accordance with all he had spoken (Acts 27:25). The lament that Jesus was yet another defeated Israelite prophet (v. 19) was the result of the disciples' failure to understand and believe the prophetic witness of Scripture.[76] The place in Scripture that makes the truth of this witness most powerfully explicit is Isa 53.[77] It is hard to imagine Isa 53 not being in the forefront of Jesus' thinking in v. 25. He expands the explicit witness to his suffering in Isa 53, however, to include the implicit witness of the entire OT, of "Moses and all the prophets" (v. 27). The plenary witness of Scripture, in other words, is a metanarrative of the Christ-event. The pronouncement of v. 25, which in particular describes Luke's use of the OT and the angelic proclamations of the infancy narrative (Luke 1–2), portrays the OT as *praeparatio evangelica* — the promises of God that point to, and are fulfilled in, the coming of Jesus the Christ.

The disciples' picture of Jesus does not correspond to the real Jesus because they fail to recognize the necessity of his crucifixion (v. 20), his suffering.[78] The thought of a suffering Messiah was foreign to pre-Christian Judaism, including first-century Judaism. No canonical OT text, and no pre-Christian Jewish text that we know of, associates suffering with the Messiah. Even the Pseudepigrapha, which develops messianic conceptions well beyond those of the OT, makes no mention of a suffering Messiah. There, on the contrary, Messiah will be a holy conqueror who will consummate the era of salvation, vanquish all enemies by the word of his mouth, subject the nations to the yoke of Israel, and sit on his glorious throne to judge earthly kings and rulers. True, the Servant of the Lord texts in Isa (esp. 52:13–53:12) depict a suffering righteous one, but the Servant of the Lord is never identified as Messiah, and Judaism never understood Servant of the Lord texts to refer to Messiah.[79] Schürer sums up the issue absolutely: "In none of the

---

75. In the second c., Marcion, who rejected the OT, altered v. 25 from a rebuke of disbelieving "all that the prophets have spoken," to a rebuke of disbelieving "all that *Jesus* has spoken."

76. Wolter, *Lukasevangelium*, 782-83.

77. Nestle-Aland[27], 794, cites Isa 53 in toto with v. 25, although this citation is removed from Nestle-Aland[28].

78. So Schweizer, *Lukas*, 247.

79. *Tg. Isa.* 53:12 associates Messiah with the Servant of the Lord but reinterprets the sufferings of the Servant as *not* referring to Messiah. The precise dating of the Targumim is debated (see Evans, *Ancient Texts for New Testament Studies*, 185-96), though scholarly opinion is generally agreed that they are post-Christian. The general Jewish interpretation of Isa 53, which prevails still today, is that the Servant is a metaphor for Israel as a people. So Origen,

many works discussed here is there the slightest allusion to an expiatory suffering of the Messiah."[80]

For Jesus, suffering is a *necessity* for Messiah to enter into his glory. "Did not the Messiah have to suffer these things and then enter his glory?" And then, "beginning with Moses and all the Prophets, [Jesus] explained to them what was said in all the Scriptures concerning himself" (vv. 26-27). Jesus earlier instructed the disciples on the necessity of his suffering (9:22, 44; 17:25; 18:31-34). All these references involved the enigmatic figure of the Son of Man, however. For the first time Jesus now informs the two disciples that his suffering is the suffering of *Messiah*. The suffering of Jesus as Messiah will become the substance of the early Christian kerygma (Acts 3:18), yet only in Luke 24:26-27 and 1 Cor 15:3-5 are the death, burial, and resurrection of the Messiah identified with the plenary witness of Scripture.[81]

In his earthly ministry Jesus not infrequently said and assumed things of himself that made sense only from the perspective of "implicit Christology." In v. 27 the veil is removed, and we encounter a prime example of explicit Christology in Jesus' declaration that the summary testimony of Scripture "concerns himself." Jesus twice before taught that Moses and the prophets are the foundation of saving truth (16:29, 31), but now he declares that "from one end of the Hebrew Scriptures to the other"[82] they bear plenary testimony to the truth revealed in *him*. Erasmus was so impressed with the significance of v. 27 that he developed it into a summary of salvation history extending to sixteen folio columns in length.[83] The Greek word for "*explained* all the Scriptures," *diermēneuein,* from which "hermeneutics" is derived, means "to translate or interpret," to bridge the two distant realities of the history of Israel and Jesus himself. The resurrected Lord is the authoritative interpreter of the history of Israel that anticipates his messianic appearance. The resurrected Lord is the living Word who alone can enlighten and interpret the written word.[84] This same conviction lay at the heart of early Christian understanding of revelation. In Acts 8 an Ethiopian eunuch asks Philip how to understand the reading of

---

Cels. 1.55, "My Jewish opponent replied that these predictions [Isa 53] bore reference to the whole people regarded as one individual."

80. Schürer, *History of the Jewish People,* 2:547-49; Fitzmyer, *Luke (X–XXIV),* 1565-66; Str-B 2:273-99. The discussion of Str-B is uncharacteristically imprecise, devoted for the most part to the role of suffering in Israel, but with scant reference to suffering of Messiah. With regard to the latter, Str-B concludes that "the thought of a suffering Messiah was far removed from the ancient synagogue in Jesus' day."

81. See Klein, *Lukasevangelium,* 732.

82. Fitzmyer, *Luke (X–XXIV),* 1567.

83. Kealy, *Interpretation of the Gospel of Luke,* 265-66.

84. This latter phrase, reminiscent of Reformation theology, is also attested in the patristic era (Ignatius, *Phld.* 8:2; Irenaeus, *Haer.* 5.1.1).

Isa 53:7, to which Philip "opened his mouth and, beginning with this Scripture, declared to him the good news of *Jesus*" (v. 35).

28-32   The conversation between Jesus and the two travelers is over, but the journey is not. As they approach the village (on the location of "Emmaus," see at v. 13), Jesus gives the impression of intending to go further (v. 28). The two disciples prevail upon him to stay with them, "for it is nearly evening; the day is almost over" (v. 29). The Greek word for "prevail upon," *parabiazesthai*, is forceful, meaning to "urge strongly," even "coerce." Again in Acts 16:15, and similarly in Gen 18:3 and 19:2, the word expresses the Middle Eastern ethos of compelling (14:23!) guests to accept hospitality. Eusebius and Jerome identified Emmaus as the home of Cleopas, and Plummer sees "stay with us" as an invitation to stay at his home.[85] That is possible, but not certain. What is more certain and significant is the thrice repetition of "with us" in vv. 29-30, testifying to the growing bond between the two and Jesus. People often sense the presence of God before they recognize or articulate it. The disciples sense in Jesus something they cannot verbalize or identify. The Resurrected One, vicariously and unbeknownst to them, is having an effect on their faith (Hos 6:2; Rom 6:4). The two disciples do not know who Jesus is, but they know they do not want to be without him. Jesus indulges their desires rather than his and remains with them. Like the Christ of Rev 3:20, he enters and eats with them, and they with him.[86]

"When he was at the table with them, he took bread, gave thanks, broke it and began to give it to them. Then their eyes were opened and they recognized him, and he disappeared from their sight" (vv. 30-31). The obscure and confounding is now enlightened and revealed for what it is. Jesus, the guest at table, now becomes host of the meal. He who seemed blind to events in Jerusalem (v. 18) now opens the eyes of the disciples. The disciples who lament not seeing Jesus (v. 24) now recognize him. The setting is not simply another Lukan banquet scene, nor is it a simple precursor of early Christian communal meals in Acts (e.g., 2:42). This table belongs to three distinctive meals in Luke, along with the feeding of the five thousand (9:16) and the Passover celebration (22:19). All three share six elements in common, and in the same sequence: Jesus (1) took (2) bread, (3) blessed/gave thanks, (4) broke it, and (5) gave it (6) to them. Although the liturgical elements are the same, the results are not. In the feeding of the five thousand, "all were satisfied" (9:17); at the Passover, the apostles "remember Jesus" (22:19); now "their eyes are opened and they recognize him" (v. 31). The effects of the three meals progress from satisfaction to recollection to revelation. We cannot presume that the resurrected Jesus intended the meal in Emmaus to be a Eucharist, or even that Luke understood it

---

85. On Eusebius and Jerome, see *Onomasticon*, 53; Plummer, *Luke*, 556.

86. The connection with Rev 3:20 was made by Erasmus (cited in Kealy, *Interpretation of the Gospel of Luke*, 299).

as such, for no NT Eucharist text contains the single element of bread without wine, as here. Nevertheless, the formulaic narration of all three meals echoes early Christian eucharistic liturgies in important respects (1 Cor 11:23-25).[87] The revelatory effect of the meal at Emmaus (vv. 30-31), following immediately on the interpretative teaching of Jesus that all the Scriptures anticipate his person and ministry (vv. 25-27), foreshadows the ministries of Word and Sacrament.

"Their eyes were opened" is another "divine passive," indicating that the disciples' ability to recognize the resurrected Jesus is made possible by divine revelation, and by contrast, that their inability to recognize Jesus in v. 16 was divinely ordained. Their blindness was not their fault, and their perception is not their accomplishment. Both are the result of spiritual dimensions beyond human abilities and capabilities (e.g., 2 Kgs 6:17, 20). The verb "to open" (Gk. *dianoigein*) occurs six times in Luke-Acts (24:31, 32, 45; Acts 7:56; 16:14; 17:3), all with reference to divine revelation, and in all but two (v. 31; Acts 7:56) of divine revelation via Scripture or kerygma. This one word thus comprises both Word and Sacrament mentioned above: eyes are opened to recognize Jesus as Lord as he breaks bread (vv. 30-31) and interprets Scripture (v. 32).[88]

Once recognized, "[Jesus] disappeared from their sight" (v. 31). His sudden and inexplicable disappearance is the only (obviously) supernatural element in the Emmaus episode. The opening of the minds and eyes of the disciples to understand Scripture and see Jesus is the result not of miracle but of Christian fellowship in which the resurrected Jesus is present as Lord. Jesus' resurrected body is a spiritually transformed body no longer subject to physical properties alone. His body defies the tomb (v. 3), disappears (v. 31), reappears (v. 36), and impresses his followers with ghost-like qualities (v. 37).[89] Although this is the only instance in biblical Greek of the particular word for "disappeared" *(aphantos)*, the sudden and mysterious disappearance of Jesus is similar to the disappearance of Philip after the baptism of the Ethiopian eunuch in Acts 8:39, and the disappearance of an angel following the release of Peter in Acts 12:10. The divinely ordained disappearance occurs in all three instances following the accomplishment of the essential task. Jesus reveals enough of himself to make faith possible, but only enough to make faith nec-

---

87. Jeremias, *Sprache des Lukasevangeliums,* 318: "The reference of v. 30 to the Eucharist is unmistakable."

88. One recalls the expressed relation between Jesus and Scripture in the first article of the Barmen Declaration: "Jesus Christ, as he is attested for us in Holy Scripture, is the one Word of God which we have to hear and which we have to trust and obey in life and in death."

89. See Michael Welker's amicable critique of N. T. Wright's understanding of Jesus' resurrected body as a "robustly physical body" ("Wright on the Resurrection," *SJT* 60/4 [2007]: 458-75). Jesus is indeed resurrected in bodily form, but his resurrection body is not a resuscitated earthly body; rather, it is a new spiritual body that both participates in space-time dimensions and supersedes them.

essary. The disappearance is an object lesson that henceforth Jesus will abide with the disciples not in his precrucifixion body, but as a spiritual presence. The disciples' testimony implies an awareness of their new relationship with Jesus. "Were not our hearts burning within us while he talked with us on the road and opened the Scriptures to us?" (v. 32). Loss, grief, and disappointment are past. Burdened hearts are now burning hearts! The disciples now know why they did not want the Stranger to part from them (v. 29). No more essential calling is set before preachers, teachers — indeed the church itself — than that of v. 32: to open Scripture so that hearts are set aflame![90]

"HE APPEARED TO CEPHAS, AND THEN TO THE TWELVE" (24:33-49)

With this affirmation Paul commences his treatise on the resurrection in 1 Cor 15. With the same affirmation Luke concludes his Gospel. The appearance of several Hebraisms in vv. 33-43, plus the possibility that Luke draws key aspects of the pericope from the Hebrew Gospel (see at v. 39), argues for the provenance of these verses in Luke's special source.[91] Vv. 44-49, by contrast, contain only one Hebraism, and their characteristic style and vocabulary argue for Luke's editorial hand.[92] The entire unit (vv. 33-49) constitutes Jesus' farewell address in the Third Gospel, which, like the previous episodes of chap. 24, is set on the day of the resurrection, Sunday (vv. 1, 13, 33). The farewell address is dissimilar to that of Matt 28:16-20, although the secondary ending of Mark 16:9-20 is repeatedly and unmistakably similar to Luke's farewell address, and

---

90. Pascal's dramatic encounter with God, written and sewn into the liner of his coat, is recounted in terms of "fire."

> The year of grace 1654, Monday, 23 November, feast of Saint Clement, Pope and Martyr, and of others in the Martyrology. Eve of Saint Chrysogonus, Martyr and others. From about half past ten in the evening until half past midnight. Fire!
> "God of Abraham, God of Isaac, God of Jacob," not of philosophers and scholars.
> Certainty, certainty, heartfelt, joy, peace.
> God of Jesus Christ.
> God of Jesus Christ.
> *My God and your God.*
> "Thy God shall be my God."
> The world forgotten, and everything except God.
> He can only be found by the ways taught in the Gospels.

91. Hebraisms include "that same hour" (v. 33; NIV "at once"), "peace be with you" (v. 36), "doubts rising in your hearts" (v. 38), and "before" (v. 43). See Edwards, *Hebrew Gospel,* 331.

92. For a similar linguistic analysis of this section (though without specific allusion to the Hebrew Gospel), see Klein, *Lukasevangelium,* 735, and esp. Bovon, *Lukas 19,28–24,53,* 578-79.

almost certainly reliant on it.[93] There are also similarities between Luke's farewell address and John 20:19-23, although it is difficult to say whether these similarities, which are less exact than the secondary ending of Mark, are due to the reliance of the Fourth Gospel on Luke, or use of common tradition by both.[94]

The resurrection appearances and farewell discourse are not the beginning of a new work, but the completion of Jesus' earthly ministry in which earlier teachings and themes are recalled, interpreted, and concluded. Most immediately, the farewell address displays several parallels with the Emmaus episode: in both, Jesus is at first uncomprehended, his instructions to the disciples are based on Scripture, his instruction leads to revelation of himself, he eats, and he departs supernaturally.[95] The farewell address is the final link in a narrative chain that connects the resurrected Lord with the earthly Jesus. The resurrected Jesus does not appear in proof to Herod or Pilate or Jewish leaders, but to the disciples whom he gathered in his earthly ministry. His primary objective is to enable them to understand that his sufferings as Messiah were the necessary prelude to his glorification, on the basis of which they are sent as "witnesses," empowered by the Holy Spirit, to proclaim repentance and the forgiveness of sins "to all nations" (vv. 46-49).

33-43 Following the meal in Emmaus, Cleopas and companion "returned at once to Jerusalem, where they found the Eleven and those with them assembled" (v. 33). The lateness of the hour had seemed determinative earlier (v. 29), and under any other circumstances the distance of Emmaus from Jerusalem, no matter how far (see at v. 13), would have prohibited further activity that day. Their encounter with the resurrected Jesus now trumps all obstacles, however, and they return to Jerusalem with hearts aflame. Although Galilee was the locus of the majority of Jesus' ministry, the singular importance of his resurrection in Jerusalem determines it henceforth (vv. 33, 49, 52) as the centripetal locus of early Christian community and the centrifugal locus of early Christian mission. Luke provides a fuller description of ecclesial life in Acts 2:42, including apostolic teaching, fellowship, common meals (Eucharist), and prayer. All these are possible, however, only where the church exists as the gathered community described in v. 33. The reference to "the Eleven and those with them" (v. 33) is practically identical to the same description in v. 9, again indicating that the Twelve (minus Judas) and unnamed others constituted the earliest nucleus of the Christian community.[96]

---

93. Vv. 13-32 → Mark 16:12; vv. 33-35 → Mark 16:13; v. 41 → Mark 16:14; v. 47 → Mark 16:15; vv. 50-51 → Mark 16:19.

94. V. 36b → John 20:19c; v. 36c → John 20:19d; v. 40 → John 20:20a.

95. See Fitzmyer, *Luke (X–XXIV)*, 1573.

96. How should reference to the "Eleven" (v. 33) be understood in relation to the absence of Thomas reported in John 20:24? Plummer, *Luke*, 558, suggests Thomas was present through the events of v. 35, after which he departed, missing the farewell speech of vv. 36ff. Or

Given the significance of the Emmaus episode, we should expect a report of Cleopas and companion to the Jerusalem gathering. Before bringing a report, however, the Emmaus pair receive a report from the Jerusalem community: "The Lord was truly raised and was seen by Simon" (v. 34).[97] This abrupt shift in narrative focus is theologically significant in two respects. First, v. 34 credits the apostolic community, and particularly Peter its leader, with the authoritative testimony to the resurrection of Jesus. In so doing, Luke corroborates the tradition of the early church, particularly as recounted by Paul in 1 Cor 15:5, that the witness of Jesus' resurrection is not an occasional truth, but the apostolic nucleus of the early church, and hence foundational Christian dogma. The second theologically significant aspect of v. 34 concerns the use of "truly" (Gk. *ontōs*). The only other time Luke uses this word is in the centurion's confession at the crucifixion, "Truly this man was righteous" (23:47). The two events in Luke-Acts that are designated with absolute verification are thus the death of Jesus on the cross as the righteous Servant of the Lord and his resurrection from the dead. The use of "truly" with regard to the cross and resurrection is Luke's narrative corroboration of vv. 26 and v. 46 that "the Messiah must suffer and be raised to glory on the third day."

We are not told when Jesus appeared to Peter, who was last seen in wonderment at the empty tomb (v. 12). Perhaps Jesus appeared to him subsequently as he appeared to Mary Magdalene in similar circumstances (John 20:11-18). When and how Jesus appeared to him we do not know, but *that* he appeared to him we are assured. The appearance marks the grace promised to Peter at the Last Supper, which would effect his "return" (22:32). The reference to Peter by his Hebrew name "Simon" may reflect "living memory inherited from Luke's 'eyewitnesses' [1:2]," attesting to Peter as lead shepherd of the apostolic cohort.[98] Peter's name is anchored to the resurrection witness in a similar affirmation from Ignatius, which dates from no later than 107, when Ignatius was martyred in Rome. "Jesus truly raised himself . . . and came to those with Peter" (*Smyrn.* 2:1–3:2). The similar stress on the "reality" of the resurrection (Luke, *ontōs*; Ignatius, *alēthōs*) is unique in the Gospel resurrection accounts and may reflect a common tradition (see at v. 39). Jesus did not appear in a vision or as an apparition but "was seen" (Gk. *ōphthē*). In the LXX *ōphthē* frequently

---

should "Eleven" be understood as a general reference to the apostles without Judas, regardless of the precise number gathered (so Bock, *Luke 9:51–24:53*, 1921)? Or was Luke unaware of or unconcerned about the discrepancy?

97. Codex Bezae (D) attributes v. 34 to the Emmaus pair. This reading would account for Origen's belief that the unnamed companion of Cleopas was "Simon Peter" (see at v. 18). The reading of D is opposed by the overwhelming majority of manuscripts, however, which attribute v. 34 to the Eleven.

98. On the name of Peter in v. 34, see M. Bockmuehl, *Simon Peter in Scripture and Memory* (Grand Rapids: Baker, 2012), 123, from which the quotation is taken.

connotes divine or angelic revelations from heaven, as do all but one of its eight uses in Luke-Acts.[99] An essential article of early Christian testimony to the resurrection is that Jesus was seen by named witnesses (John 20:18, 25, 29; 1 Cor 9:1). The lingering doubts associated with reports of the empty tomb are dispelled only by *meeting* the resurrected Jesus.

"Then the two told what had happened on the way, and how Jesus was recognized by them when he broke the bread" (v. 35). The report of the Emmaus pair is appended as supplementary testimony to the apostolic witness. "By subordinating their report Luke guarantees that the appearance of the resurrected Jesus to Peter is the confirmation of the Christian Easter faith, and not his meeting with the Emmaus disciples."[100] The Greek word for "told," *exēgeisthai*, appears five times in Luke-Acts with reference to recounting the mighty works of God in Jesus as a foundation for belief (v. 35; Acts 10:8; 15:12, 14; 21:19). The catechetical lesson on the walk to Emmaus was of course important for the Emmaus disciples' understanding, but it was in the breaking of the bread that "[Jesus] was made known to them" (v. 35). No reference is made to their eating. Their recognition of Jesus did not depend on anything they did, but was due solely to Jesus' self-revelation in the breaking of the bread.[101]

"While they were still talking about this, Jesus himself stood among them and said to them, 'Peace be with you'" (v. 36). The translation "Jesus himself" is probably too strong, for, although important manuscripts include "Jesus" (thus supporting "Jesus himself stood in their midst"), the stronger manuscript tradition omits "Jesus" (thus simply "he stood in their midst").[102] The most probable textual reading thus suggests an unpretentious rather than a dramatic appearance of Jesus. Jesus appears not to impress the disciples, but to edify them. The sudden appearance of Jesus, following his similar disappearance (v. 31), demonstrates the difference between his earthly and resurrection bodily capabilities. The verb "said" (v. 36; Gk. *legei*) is a "historical present," i.e., the narration of a past event in present tense to "contemporize" it. The historical present is common in the Second Gospel, but it occurs only twice in the Third (v. 36; 11:45). Its use here suggests that the words of the resurrected Lord are forever alive and present.[103] Codex Bezae deletes Jesus' greeting, "He said to them, 'Peace be with you'" (v. 36), and a number of scholars follow the deletion, suspecting the greet-

---

99. For *ōphthē* ("was seen") in Luke-Acts, 1:11; 22:43; 24:34; Acts 7:2, (26), 30; 13:31; 16:9. Further, Schweizer, *Lukas*, 247; Wolter, *Lukasevangelium*, 786.

100. Wolter, *Lukasevangelium*, 786-87.

101. Fitzmyer, *Luke (X–XXIV)*, 1569: "What is above all important is that the disciples report that they knew him 'in the breaking of the bread' (v. 35) and not by seeing him."

102. "*Jesus* stood among them" (A K W Γ Δ Ω Ψ); "*he* stood among them" (𝔭75 ℵ B D L).

103. On the historical present, see BDF §321. Wolter, *Lukasevangelium*, 789, describes its present usage as "lebhaft Vergegenwärtigen der Erzählung" ("a vivid representation of the narrative").

ing to be an addition by later copyists in harmony with the same greeting in John 20:19. This is possible, but not certain. The inclusion of the greeting is attested by the majority manuscript tradition; and "Peace be with you" was a common Semitic greeting appropriate for the occasion. "Peace" also signifies "salvation" in Luke, making it doubly appropriate.[104] With regard to the same greeting in John 20:19, it should be recalled that the passion and resurrection narratives of the Third and Fourth Gospels contain many points of contact, which are more likely due to a common source for both than to reliance of one on the other.[105]

People are not infrequently startled by something they actually believe in. A child thought lost, for example, or a loved one not expected to live both arouse wonderment after the crisis is past. Something similar occurs with the disciples in v. 37. Despite their acknowledgment of the resurrection, "they were startled and frightened, thinking they saw a ghost" when Jesus appeared among them (v. 37). The Greek word *pneuma* means "spirit" or "ghost" (so NIV), but Codex Bezae (D) reads *phantasma*, meaning "apparition of the dead." *Phantasma* is doubtless a later addition,[106] but it conveys what the apostles thought they saw — and feared: a wraith without flesh and bone.[107] When Jesus walked on water on the Sea of Galilee, the disciples feared the same (Gk. *phantasma*) and shrieked in terror (Mark 6:49; Matt 14:26). Belief in the resurrection was not a wish-fulfillment of the first disciples, as moderns sometime imagine. Jesus' disciples did not expect him to be raised, and his appearance now sparks panic among them, as the appearance of the angels at the empty tomb frightened the women (v. 5). Knowing their dismay, Jesus asks reassuringly, "Why are you troubled, and why are doubts arising in your heart?" (v. 38). The verbal form of "troubled" (perfect participle plus finite verb "to be") conveys an ongoing "troubled *state*." The wording of "doubts arising in your heart" is a Hebraic formulation.[108] The presence of "troubles" and "doubts" at the conclusion of the Gospel recalls the same two responses of Zechariah (1:12) and Mary (1:29) at its beginning. In each instance the consternation results from an encounter with the supernatural. In the final analysis, the struggle of faith is not a problem of knowledge, for the disciples acknowledge the risen Jesus; nor is faith the banishment of all doubt and uncertainties, for these too are dormant in the disciples. Faith is the choice to believe what they know to be true even in the face of "bewilderment, astonishment, and incredulity."[109]

---

104. On "peace" and "salvation," 1:79; 2:14, 29; 7:50; 8:48; 10:5-7; 19:38.

105. See Metzger, *TCGNT,* 160; Fitzmyer, *Luke (X–XXIV),* 1575; Green, *Luke,* 854; Bovon, *Lukas 19,28–24,53,* 584.

106. The overwhelming majority of manuscripts reads *pneuma.*

107. See Klein, *Lukasevangelium,* 736.

108. Str-B 2:299; Schlatter, *Lukas,* 711; Wolter, *Lukasevangelium,* 789; Edwards, *Hebrew Gospel,* 331.

109. To quote Fitzmyer, *Luke (X–XXIV),* 1572.

"Look at my hands and my feet. It is I myself! Touch me and see; a ghost does not have flesh and bones, as you see I have" (v. 39). This is the only biblical text describing the resurrection body of Jesus in terms of "flesh and bones." 1 John, which speaks of seeing and hearing Jesus and "touching him with our hands" (1 John 1:1), may recall this passage, for "touch" (Gk. *psēlaphan*), an unusual word occurring only four times in the NT, is used in both passages. The confession of "the resurrection of the flesh" (Lat. *carnis resurrectionem*) in the Old Roman baptismal creed (late second c.), which formed the basis of the later Apostles' Creed, may derive from v. 39. In both Luke and John the resurrected Jesus invites the disciples to inspect his body. According to John, Jesus "showed them his hands and side" (20:20); in Luke, Jesus said, "Look at my hands and my feet" (v. 39), thus inviting inspection of the nail marks of crucifixion. Only John 20:25 specifically mentions "nail marks," but Luke seems to presuppose them. The nail marks of the crucified Jesus were regarded by early Christian apologists as fulfillment of the prophecy of Ps 22:16 (Justin, *Dial.* 97.3-4; *1 Apol.* 35.5-7). They also verify the bodily reality of the risen Christ, whose glorified body is the transformation of his earthly crucified body. Both Luke and John stress properties of empirical physicality in Jesus' resurrection body such as seeing and touching, and they also stress its supra-physical properties such as sudden appearances and disappearances, the ability to be recognized or not, and to be in different places nearly simultaneously. V. 39 confirms the identity and bodily reality of the risen Christ. The identity is made in the strongest possible Greek affirmation, "It is I myself" (*egō eimi autos*). The crowning effect of the resurrection is not a *that* — a mighty work of God, a victorious miracle of life over death; it is a *who* — the revelation of Jesus as the suffering Messiah, now glorified by God as eternal Lord.

V. 39 plays an important role in the patristic era that is seldom noted by NT scholars.[110] Four Fathers — Ignatius, Origen, Eusebius, and Jerome — know of Jesus' invitation to "touch me and see that I am not a phantom without a body."[111] Jerome refers to the saying four different times.[112] None of the four attributes the saying to Luke 24:39, nor is the saying reproduced by any of them in a form that is obviously derived from v. 39. Ignatius reproduces the saying no later than 107 (the year of his martyrdom) but does not name its source. Since Ignatius never quotes directly from any of the Gospels, nor

---

110. This negligence is the more remarkable, since v. 39 is "the most popular passage in Luke 24, and perhaps in the Gospel" quoted by the church fathers (Just, *Luke,* xxv).

111. The earliest form of the saying is produced by Ignatius, *Smyrn.* 3:1-2: "For I know and believe that he was in the flesh even after the resurrection. And when he [Jesus] came to those with Peter he said to them, 'Take, touch me and see that I am not a disembodied ghost.' And immediately they touched him and believed." Similarly, Origen, *Princ.* Praefatio 8; Eusebius, *Hist. eccl.* 3.36.11.

112. Jerome, *Comm. Mich.* 7:6; *Comm. Matt.* 12:13; *Vir. ill.* 2, 16.

reveals any particular knowledge of the Third Gospel, it is unlikely that v. 39 is the source of the saying he quotes in *Smyrn.* 3:1-2. The three subsequent fathers reproduce the saying in a form that conforms more closely to the Ignatian than Lukan version, suggesting that they too are not relying on Luke. Origen and Eusebius claim either to be uncertain of its source or not know it, whereas Jerome, who gives the most complete witness to the saying, ascribes it to the Hebrew Gospel, which he claims more than once to having translated into Greek and/or Latin. Ignatius, who preferred oral over written tradition, is probably relying on eyewitness testimony (Luke 1:2) for this saying, which, as Jerome attests, was preserved in the Hebrew Gospel.[113] The above suggests that Luke received v. 39 from the same Hebrew Gospel as did Ignatius, Origen, Eusebius, and Jerome, and probably also the material in vv. 34 and 37, which shares distinctives with the Ignatian material.[114]

The event of Jesus showing the disciples his hands and feet is repeated in v. 40. This verse is omitted by Codex Bezae (D), and its authenticity is doubted by many modern scholars because of its obvious redundancy with v. 39. V. 40 is further suspected as an interpolation from John 20:20, with which (except for two words) it is verbatim. V. 40 is nevertheless included in all the best Greek manuscripts, and its likeness with John 20:20 is not conclusive evidence against its originality, since Luke and John share a large number of similarities and duplications in their Passion Narratives.[115] Considering all the evidence, the originality of v. 40 should be cautiously affirmed.

The effect of Jesus' bodily disclosure leaves the disciples in a pell-mell state of disbelief, joy, and amazement (v. 41). Exactly how we are to understand "disbelief" is not clear. It could imply skepticism, but given its combination with joy and amazement, it more likely describes an extraordinary reality that has yet to be comprehended (e.g., Acts 12:14).[116] Jesus does not reason with the disciples, argue with them, or reproach them. He allows them further op-

---

113. For a full discussion of the saying, see Edwards, *Hebrew Gospel*, 45-55. Bovon, *Luke 19,28–24,53*, 582, also recognizes that the Ignatius-Origen-Eusebius-Jerome tradition of the saying does not derive from Luke, although Bovon ascribes it to a free-floating agraphon rather than to the Hebrew Gospel.

114. The reference to the Lord "really" (Gk. *ontōs*) being resurrected (v. 34) corresponds to the "really [Gk. *alēthōs*] resurrected" of *Smyrn.* 2:1, as the reference to the appearance to Peter in v. 34 corresponds to the same in *Smyrn.* 3:2. The reference to Jesus being a "ghost" (v. 37; Gk. *pneuma*) is similar to his being a "phantom" (*Smyrn.* 3:2; Gk. *daimonion*), and the emphasis on touching Jesus' hands and feet (v. 39) corresponds to his being "in the flesh even after the resurrection" (*Smyrn.* 3:1).

115. Discussions of the originality of v. 40 can be found in Metzger, *TCGNT*, 160; Jeremias, *Sprache des Lukasevangeliums*, 321; Fitzmyer, *Luke (X–XXIV)*, 1576, all of whom lean in favor of its authenticity.

116. For discussions of the term in its present context, see Nolland, *Luke 18:35–24:53*, 1214-15.

portunity to experience his resurrection reality. "Do you have anything here
to eat?" he asks (v. 41). The Greek is off-handed, perhaps, "Do you have any
leftovers?" The request is important to understanding Jesus' bodily reality,
for Jews believed that ghosts and angels neither ate nor drank.[117] The request
demonstrates that Jesus is not a ghost or an angel but the resurrected Lord in
a glorified human body, similar perhaps to the bodies of the Three Visitants
in Gen 18:8, who also ate. "They gave him a piece of broiled fish, and he took
it and ate it in their presence" (vv. 42-43).[118] That fish would be eaten in inland Jerusalem should not be found improbable. At the intersection of the
Tyropoeon valley and the north wall of Jerusalem lay the Fish Gate, where
fish merchants from the Sea of Galilee and Tyre in the north sold dried and
salted fish.[119] This episode forms a parallel with the revelatory meal of Jesus
with the Emmaus pair (v. 30), both of which complement the Feeding of the
Five Thousand (9:16).

44-49 These verses constitute Luke's "Great Commission." They consist of Jesus' declaration that all Scripture is about him and fulfilled in him
(v. 44), followed by the opening of the minds of the apostolic community to
understand the Scriptures (v. 45) as prophecies of the sufferings and resurrection of Jesus as Messiah (v. 46). The elements of vv. 44-46 repeat Jesus' prior
self-disclosure to the Emmaus disciples (vv. 26-32). They are followed by the
declaration that "you are witnesses of these things" (v. 48). As witnesses of the
incarnation, the apostolic community constitutes "those who from the first
were eyewitnesses and servants of the word" (1:2). Proclamation of the gospel
in its oral and written form is founded not on persuasive reasoning, winsome
personality, or impressive results, but on personal witness. On the basis of
what the apostolic community has personally experienced (1 John 1:1), it will
be sent according to the promise of the Father and empowerment of the Holy
Spirit to proclaim repentance and forgiveness of sins in the name of Jesus to all
the nations, beginning from Jerusalem (vv. 47-49). The final commission thus
invests the Jerusalem community with apostolic authority and commissions
it for kerygmatic mission to the nations.

---

117. Judg 13:15-16; Tob 12:19; *Apoc. Ab.* 13:3. See here Wolter, *Lukasevangelium,* 790.

118. A number of uncial manuscripts and several early versions report that, in addition
to broiled fish, Jesus was given "honeycomb" (K N Γ Δ Ψ Θ). "Honeycomb" is probably not
original, for an element so distinctive is unlikely to have fallen out of so many of the best
manuscripts. In parts of the ancient church, honeycomb (and sometimes fish) appeared in
Eucharist celebrations in addition to bread and wine. This practice likely accounts for the
inclusion of honeycomb in the manuscripts listed above. Honey was regarded as paradisiacal
food, the presence of which in the Eucharist carried obvious eschatological significance. On
this variant, see Metzger, *TCGNT,* 161, and esp. Bovon, *Lukas 19,28–24,53,* 588-89.

119. On the sale of fish in Jerusalem, see Neh 3:3; 12:39; 13:16; Zeph 1:10; 2 Chr 33:14.
Further, Str-B 1:683-84; Jeremias, *Jerusalem in the Time of Jesus,* 20; Marshall, *Luke,* 903.

The commission begins in v. 44 by appealing to Jesus' earthly teaching. "These are my words" (NIV "This is what I told you") is shifted emphatically to the head of the sentence. Its Greek form is a clarion echo of the Hebrew "These are the words," which characteristically introduces divine revelation in the OT (e.g., Exod 19:6; 35:1; Deut 1:1; Isa 42:5; Zech 8:16).[120] The reference to Jesus as both content and fulfillment of Scripture repeats the similar declaration of v. 27, except here Scripture is characterized in the tripartite categories of Law, Prophets, and Psalms (v. 44). The biblical manuscripts recovered from the Dead Sea remind us that the exact contents of the OT were still in flux in the first century. Some texts such as Ps 151, Tobit, Sirach, and the Letter of Jeremiah are present at Qumran but absent from the OT, and others such as Esth and Neh are absent from Qumran but present in the OT.[121] The typical designation among ancient Jews for what we call the Old Testament or the Hebrew Scriptures was the bipartite designation Law and Prophets (so v. 27), without specifying exact texts belonging to each category. V. 44 is one of the earliest references to the OT in terms of a tripartite corpus, thus anticipating the same division of the traditional Hebrew Bible as Torah, Nebi'im, and Kethubim.[122]

All these Scriptures, says Jesus, bear witness to me (4:21; John 5:39, 46). The reference to "while I was still with you" (v. 44), reminds the disciples that the final commission is not a new teaching or program, but a continuation of Jesus' earthly teaching and ministry. Jesus is no longer present in his earthly form, but he commissions the apostles to continue and extend his earthly ministry.[123] In declaring that "everything must be fulfilled that is written about me" (v. 44), Jesus does not cite specific messianic proof texts, but he does affirm the global witness of Israel's Scriptures to his messianic ministry. The witness is manifested variously: in the need of payment for sin, including sacrificial victims; the pervasive theme of suffering in the Psalter; the comprehensive testimony of the OT to God's mercy, love, and forgiveness of the penitent; the increasing specification of the OT covenants, culminating in Jer 31:31-34 and Ezek 36:25-28, to mention but two. The OT is *in totum* a primer on the nature and character of God, and those so tutored in that nature and character will

120. The Hebraic form of the Greek is *eleh hadebarim;* see Wolter, *Lukasevangelium,* 791.

121. See J. VanderKam, *The Dead Sea Scrolls Today* (Grand Rapids: Eerdmans, 1994), chap. 2.

122. The closest tripartite division of the OT otherwise known is 4Q397 (4QMMT), "the book of Moses, and the books of the prophets, and in David" ("David" presumably being metonymic for "Psalms of David"). Similarly, Philo, *Contempl.,* 25, "the Law and the Oracles given by inspiration through the Prophets, and the Psalms and other books"; and Josephus, *Ag. Ap.* 1.7-8, 37-43, "Books of Moses, the Prophets after Moses, Hymns and Precepts for the conduct of life." See K. Schmid, "The Canon and the Cult: The Emergence of Book Religion in Ancient Israel and the Gradual Sublimation of the Temple Cult," *JBL* 131/2 (2012): 289-305.

123. On this point, see Schweizer, *Lukas,* 250.

recognize its manifestation in Jesus of Nazareth. As the Son of God, Jesus rightly declares that what testifies to the Father equally testifies to the Son.

"Then he opened their minds so they could understand the Scriptures" (v. 45). In v. 25 Jesus faulted the Emmaus pair for not believing Scripture; here he enables disciples not only to believe but to *understand* Scripture. V. 45 should not be interpreted in isolation from v. 44; Jesus opened the minds of the disciples to understand Scripture because he is its center. Bonhoeffer saw that Jesus Christ rightly and necessarily mediates *all* relationships in the Christian community, not only the vertical relationship of believers and God (1 Tim 2:5), but also horizontal relationships among believers, and with all humanity.[124] V. 45 extends the mediation of Christ to include temporal as well as spatial dimensions. Jesus Christ is the mediator between God and the believer, between the believer and all other human relationships, and between the believer and the scriptural testimony to him in Israel. The Living Word interprets the Written Word.[125] If one does not know Christ, one cannot understand Scripture (John 5:45-47).[126]

For the fourth time in the resurrection narrative, messiahship is defined in terms of crucifixion and resurrection, suffering and glory (vv. 7, 26, 44, 46). The four postresurrection passion interpretations complement the four preresurrection predictions (9:22, 44; 17:25; 18:31-34). We noted earlier (see at v. 26) that no pre-Christian Jewish text speaks of the Messiah suffering; similarly, no known pre-Christian Jewish text mentions the Messiah rising from the dead.[127] Jesus' description of the messianic office is fuller and more complete than its adumbrations in Israel's Scriptures. Jesus presents himself as the authoritative interpreter of both Scripture and the messianic ideal in Scripture. For the first time in v. 46, "what is written about Jesus" in Scripture leads to kerygma. Fact leads to proclamation. V. 46 sums up the Christ-event in the nuclear categories of death and resurrection, without mention of Jesus' birth, ministry, miracles, teachings, or relationships.[128] One could appeal to

---

124. D. Bonhoeffer, *Life Together* (trans. J. Doberstein; New York: Harper Brothers, 1954), chap. 1, "Community."

125. M. Bates, "Closed-Minded Hermeneutics? A Proposed Alternative Translation for Luke 24:45," *JBL* 129/3 (2010): 537-57, is unsuccessful in the attempt to argue that *nous* refers to the meaning of Scripture rather than the mind of the disciples ("Then Jesus exposited the Scriptures so that the disciples could understand their meaning"). Syntax and sense virtually require *nous* to refer to the minds of the disciples. Bates himself concedes that there are no instances of v. 45 being interpreted in accord with his proposed alternative. Above all, the proposed translation would remove Jesus from the living center of Scripture to a mere expositor of it.

126. See here Wolter, *Lukasevangelium*, 792.

127. See Fitzmyer, *Luke (X–XXIV)*, 1583-84; Klein, *Lukasevangelium*, 739-40.

128. Noted by Bovon, *Lukas 19,28–24,53*, 593.

Jesus as the greatest teacher, miracle-worker, or human being who ever lived and still miss his single defining purpose: to die for the sins of the world and be raised from the dead for its redemption (Rom. 4:25). These two events constitute the essence of the mission of the early church and of the church in every age: the proclamation of repentance and forgiveness of sins in Jesus' name to all nations (v. 47). Several articles of v. 47 are repeated in Acts 22:16 with reference to the conversion of Paul, suggesting that Luke presents Paul as the "firstfruits" of the apostolic mission of the church.

V. 47 is a key transition in the narrative of Luke-Acts, for it sums up the life of Christ and anticipates the mission of the church. The forgiveness of sins promised in the sending of Messiah (1:77; 3:3; 4:18) is now fulfilled in the proclamation *in his name* to the nations (v. 47). Jesus assures disciples that the Christ-event consists not only of his historical life, but also when the church speaks and acts in "in his name."[129] The Reformation teaching that in the rightful exposition of Scripture Jesus Christ is salvifically present — symbolized, for example, by Cranach's portraits that place the crucifix on the same level with Martin Luther in the pulpit — is a correct understanding of this truth.

In addition to summarizing the Gospel of Luke, v. 47 anticipates the Book of Acts. For the first time Jerusalem appears as the starting point of the church's mission rather than as the terminus of Jesus' mission (Acts 1:8; Rom 15:19). Had it not been necessary for the Messiah to suffer, the death of Jesus at the hands of the temple leadership in Jerusalem would have alienated the early believers from both Judaism and Jerusalem. Jesus' final commission puts them at peace with his fate and reconciles them with both Judaism and Jerusalem. As a consequence, the early believers make the temple — the very heart of Judaism — their communal base, from which the Spirit will lead them outward in mission (Acts 1:8).

EXCURSUS: UNIVERSAL SCOPE OF THE GOSPEL

The work and witness of Jesus is presented by Luke as unbounded by human borders of ethnicity, gender, age, culture, race, religion, or national and political allegiances.[130] In v. 47, "to all nations" is set at the end of the sentence, emphasizing the universal extent of Jesus' mission. Jesus' parting summons to

---

129. So Schweizer, *Lukas,* 251.

130. Rengstorf, *Lukas,* 3, writes, "The work of Jesus is in no way bound by national [*völkisch*] or religious borders." That was a courageous sentence to write in Germany in 1937, for in denying *völkisch* borders, Rengstorf was explicitly denying the anti-Semitism of National Socialism and the German-Christian movement.

the disciples fulfills the call to Abraham, which concluded with the promise that "all peoples on earth will be blessed through you" (Gen 12:3). That promise lay fallow through most of Israel's history, for "the nations" normally appear in the OT as a place where Israel is "scattered" and judged (Deut 28:64; Zech 7:14; Mal 2:9; Acts 14:16). Only rarely do the prophets portray Gentile "nations" as an object of redemption (Amos 9:12; Jonah). Equally significant, the rabbinic tradition is virtually devoid of a positive assessment of "the nations."

Luke, however, presents the proclamation of the gospel to Gentiles as the expressed and necessary consequence of the election of Israel. The summons to preach the gospel in the name of Jesus to all nations (v. 47) is another Lukan inclusio, complementing the prediction of Simeon in the infancy narrative that, in Jesus, God's salvation has appeared to "all nations: a light for revelation to the Gentiles, and the glory of your people Israel" (2:30-32). That Jesus' significance for Gentiles is reported before his significance for Israel — especially when the infancy narrative is dedicated to portraying the birth of Jesus as a fulfillment of *Israel's* hopes — should not be overlooked or underestimated. Luke reinforces this universal theme in the genealogy in 3:23-38, which traces Jesus' lineage back to Adam, portraying Jesus as "the second man" (1 Cor 15:47), "the last Adam" (1 Cor 15:45), in whom God completes the work begun in Adam, which includes all humanity (Rom 5:12-21). Hints of the future Gentile mission appear in Jesus' inaugural sermon in Nazareth (4:24-27), in which Elijah and Elisha include Gentiles within Israel's vocation, and in his final eschatological discourse (21:24), which includes Gentiles in God's saving election. Jesus' healing of the servant of a Roman centurion (7:1-10) may be seen as a firstfruits of the church's subsequent Gentile mission.

Jesus' social arena was naturally determined by the demography of Galilee, Judea, and Jerusalem. The majority of persons in these areas were Jewish, or related to Jews. Jesus, however, frequently consorted with persons Jewish rabbis would not consort with. He crosses ethnic borders and enters into Samaritan territory (17:11; note instructions to the contrary in Matt 10:5!), healing Samaritans (17:12-19) and upholding them as models of godly behavior (10:30-37). Women play leading roles in the Third Gospel, not anonymously but as named individuals, especially Elizabeth and Mary in the infancy narrative; Mary Magdalene, Joanna, Susanna, and "others" as disciples (8:1-3); Mary and Martha (10:38-42); and above all Mary Magdalene, Joanna, Mary the mother of James, and other women, who were the only remnants of the apostolic fellowship present at the cross, burial, and empty tomb (23:49–24:11). The excursus on Luke's use of pairs (see at 14:1), especially male-female pairs, emphasizes the significance of women in the witness and mission of Jesus and the early church. Jesus includes children in his company and compassion (18:15-17), and always people with manifold needs (6:20-23), especially the poor (16:19-31; 21:1-4) and the sick and lame (13:10-17; 14:2-6; 18:35-43). Jesus sees *persons* within and behind sinful social structures in which they operate as both victims and oppressors: the rich (18:18-23; 19:1-10; 23:50-54), righteous Pharisees (14:1; 15:25-32) and scribes (20:39), unrighteous tax collectors (5:27-32) and sinners (7:36-50; 15:1-2).

There appears to be evidence of social selectivity on Jesus' part, however, for there is no record of his meeting with an Essene, unless the room in which the Last Supper was held was related to Essene connections (see at 22:10). The powerful Sadducees twice initiate meetings with Jesus (20:27-38; 22:52ff.), although never he with them; and with them he appears more guarded than with any other Jewish constituency. In none of the Gospels does Jesus visit Tiberias or Sepphoris, the most Romanized cities in Galilee, although both lay within regions in which he ministered. Nevertheless, the social calendar of no rabbi or Stoic preacher or itinerant philosopher of whom we know anything can compare with the number and diversity of Jesus' social contacts. In this Jesus is a model for the faithful, as Pentecost will demonstrate when the Holy Spirit directs the focus of the church outward from Jerusalem to "every nation under heaven" (2:5). The redemptive outreach of the gospel "to all nations" is virtually without parallel in any other religion, and Luke-Acts is among its foundational witnesses in early Christianity.

The final commission designates two conditions necessary for disciples to participate in the kerygmatic and missionary work of the risen Christ.[131] The first is contained in the declaration "You are witnesses of these things" (v. 48). For the first time in the Third Gospel disciples are called witnesses, and their witness is governed by "these things" — the resurrection appearance and teaching of Jesus. The objective of witness is not self, but the resurrected Lord and his teachings. One must know the resurrected Jesus in order to be a witness to the gospel. As noted above, one can know Jesus as a great teacher, miracle-worker, or model of humanity, but if one does not know Jesus resurrected from the dead, one cannot witness to Jesus. "*You* are witnesses" is emphatic, reminding disciples of the crucial role that they play in the mission of the church to the nations.[132]

Second, witnesses must be clothed with "power from on high," as promised by the Father (v. 49). The promise directs attention to Luke's sequel in Acts, where the disciples are commanded to remain in Jerusalem (Acts 1:4) until the Holy Spirit directs and empowers them for mission (Acts 2:33). As Jesus was endowed with spiritual power to heal and teach (4:14; 5:17; 9:1), so too will disciples be endowed with spiritual power. The wording of v. 49 is strongly reminiscent of the prophetic expectation of the outpouring of the Spirit from on high in Isa 32:15. It is equally reminiscent of the Holy Spirit's overshadowing

---

131. See Wolter, *Lukasevangelium*, 794.
132. See Acts 1:8, 22; 2:32; 3:15; 5:32; 10:39, 41; 13:31; 22:15; 26:16.

of Mary with power from on high (1:35). The similarity with the annunciation is striking, for it applies incarnational language to the missionary witness of the church. The two prerequisites of discipleship thus augment the human witness of disciples and with supernatural outpouring of the Holy Spirit, as promised by the Father.

BENEDICTION AT BETHANY (24:50-53)

The Third Gospel closes on the theme of "blessing," thrice repeated (Gk. *eulogein*, vv. 50, 51, 53). Jesus offers a priestly blessing to the disciples as he ascends from the Mount of Olives, after which the disciples joyfully return to the temple in Jerusalem, blessing God. Like the greater part of Luke's resurrection narrative, the closing benediction in vv. 50-53 incorporates several Hebraisms in a narrative otherwise characterized by Lukan style and vocabulary.[133] The reference to Bethany may also derive from Luke's Hebrew source, for "Bethany" is a loanword that appears elsewhere in Luke-Acts only in 19:29 in reliance on Mark 11:1, whereas Luke's normal reference to the vicinity is "the Mount of Olives" (19:29, 37; 21:37; 22:39; Acts 1:12).

Luke 24 is often understood to place all events, including the ascension of Jesus in v. 51, on resurrection Sunday.[134] Obvious problems are involved in restricting the events of Luke 24 to a single twenty-four-hour day. Doing so implies a nighttime ascension of Jesus in v. 51, which seems unlikely,[135] and it conflicts with Luke's reference to a forty-day interval between Jesus' resurrection and ascension in Acts 1:3. For two reasons I do not understand the events of Luke 24 to be contained within a single day. First, although the events of vv. 1-35 are set on resurrection Sunday (see vv. 1, 13, 33), vv. 36-53 are absent time references. These latter verses do not demand that the events reported in them — the revelation of Jesus to the apostles (vv. 36-43), his teaching on Scripture and final commission (vv. 44-49), and benediction and ascension (vv. 50-53) — be ascribed to the same day as vv. 1-35. Indeed, other NT texts related to the

---

133. Hebraisms are Gk. *kai egeneto* (v. 51; "it happened"), *en tō eulogein* (v. 51; "as [Jesus] blessed [them]"), *kai autoi* (v. 52, "and they"), *Ierousalēm* (v. 52; Semitic spelling of "Jerusalem"), *ēsan . . . eulogountes ton theon* (v. 53; "they were blessing God"); see Edwards, *Hebrew Gospel,* 332. Characteristic of Luke's hand are *exēgagen* (v. 50; "he was leading [them] out"), *heōs pros* (v. 50; "as far as"), *diestē* (v. 51; "he departed [from them]"), *ouranos* (v. 51; "heaven"), *hypestrepsan* (v. 52; "they returned"), *chara megalē* (v. 52; "great joy"), *dia pantos* (v. 53; "continually"); see Plummer, *Luke,* 565; Jeremias, *Sprache des Lukasevangeliums,* 323; Klein, *Lukasevangelium,* 741, n. 2.

134. See Fitzmyer, *Luke (X–XXIV),* 1588-89.

135. See Lagrange, *Luc,* 616.

ascension, most notably Acts 1:3-12, also authored by Luke, forbid their being ascribed to the same day.[136] It seems reasonable to take vv. 36-43 with reference to events subsequent to Easter Sunday that extended over days or even weeks.

Second, neither the NT nor early church differentiated precisely between the glorification of the resurrected Jesus and his ascension. Early Christians were probably influenced in their understanding of Jesus' glorification and ascension by the precedent of Elijah's translation to heaven in 2 Kgs 2:11, and especially by Ps 110:1, the most frequently cited OT text in the NT, "The Lord said to my lord: 'Sit at my right hand until I make your enemies a footstool for your feet.'"[137] In 2 Kgs 2:11 and Ps 110:1 glorification and ascension merge in a single complex, and the NT and early church (at least until about 200) often merge them likewise.[138] Clear-cut temporal distinctions among resurrection, glorification, and ascension, logical as they seem to modern interpreters, may create false dichotomies about matters that the early church often consolidated within the larger complex of Jesus' exaltation.[139]

In relation to this last point, a final word is in order about the narrative overlap between Luke and Acts. The end of the Gospel and beginning of Acts both describe Jesus' final bodily separation from the disciples, both are penned by the same author, but their narrative elements and styles are distinctive and not immediately reconcilable.[140] The conclusion of the Gospel is highly compressed, and its genre, as noted above, is a liturgical priestly benediction. The commencement of Acts, by contrast, is expanded in time and circumstance. The difference between the two narratives may be ascribed to the different purposes of Luke in each instance: at the conclusion of the Gospel the ascension

---

136. Schlatter, *Lukas,* 457, writes, "It is unthinkable that Luke would create a conflict between the end of the Gospel and beginning of Acts that would result in the beginning of Acts contradicting the end of the Gospel."

137. The testimony of *2 En.* 67 may also have contributed to this precedent, which speaks of the angels grasping Enoch and carrying him to the highest heaven.

138. NT texts that fuse the glorification and ascension of Jesus, or fail to differentiate between them, are 9:51; Mark 16:19; John 3:13; 6:62; 7:33; 8:14, 21; 13:33; 14:2, 4, 12, 28; 16:5, 7, 10, 17, 28; 20:17; Acts 1:2, 11, 22; 2:32-35; 5:31-32; Eph 1:20; 4:8-10; Phil 2:9; 1 Tim 3:16; Heb 1:3; 6:20; 8:1; 9:12, 24; 10:12; 12:2; 1 Pet 3:22. In the early church the glorification and ascension are also conflated in *Barn.* 15:19; *Gos. Pet.* 55-56; *T. Benj.* 9:5. On the close connection in early Christianity among Jesus' resurrection, ascension, and session at God's right hand, see A. Grillmeier, *Christ in Christian Tradition* (trans. J. Bowden; New York: Sheed & Ward, 1965), 89-90; B. Metzger, "The Ascension of Jesus Christ," in *Historical and Literary Studies: Pagan, Jewish, and Christian* (NTTS 8; Grand Rapids: Eerdmans, 1968), 79-82.

139. Metzger, "Ascension of Jesus Christ," 82. Bovon, *Lukas 19,28–24,53,* 611-12, is likewise sensitive to the distinction between glorification and ascension in the relevant early Christian references.

140. Johnson, *Luke,* 404, rightly summarizes the matter: "Ancient historians were less fastidious in such matters of overlap than are some contemporary scholars."

is narrated, appropriately, as a divine blessing, whereas at the commencement of Acts it is narrated, also appropriately, as a divine commission of the early church for Spirit-inspired witness for the gospel.

50-53   The village of Bethany (v. 50) was located on the eastern slope of the Mount of Olives. From the Mount of Olives, according to prophetic tradition (Ezek 11:23; Zech 14:4), the glory of the Lord would ascend. Jesus now leads the disciples to his divine appointment on the Mount of Olives, just as he earlier led them to Jerusalem (9:51; 19:28), both in fulfillment of what had been written about him in the prophets (v. 44). There "he lifted up his hands and blessed them" (v. 50). Only here in the NT is such a benediction ascribed to Jesus. This description, like the patriarchal blessings of Jacob (Gen 49:1) and Moses (Deut 33:1), and even more the priestly blessing of Aaron (Lev 9:22; Num 6:22-27), is both a visible and an audible blessing. Lifting hands in blessing, like kneeling in prayer, is liturgical body language in which the body enacts what the will resolves and mouth declares. The Book of Sirach concludes with a similar blessing of the high priest Simon II, son of Onias, who "raised his hands over the whole congregation of Israelites, to pronounce the blessing of the Lord with his lips, and to glory in his name" (Sir 50:20). The departing blessing of the disciples forms another of Luke's many inclusios between the infancy narrative and passion and resurrection narratives: as Simeon blessed the parents of Jesus in the temple before his death (2:34), so Jesus blesses the disciples on the Mount of Olives before his ascension.

"While he was blessing them, he left them and was taken up into heaven" (v. 51). The ascension is not an appendix to the Third Gospel. The nearness and necessity of the ascension play a defining role in 9:51, orienting Jesus resolutely to his divinely ordained fate in Jerusalem. The ascension also fulfills the declaration of Jesus to the Sanhedrin at his trial, "From now on the Son of Man will be seated at the right hand of the mighty God" (22:69). One would expect Luke to employ Greek *analambanein* ("taken up") in v. 51 in correspondence with its distinct uses in 9:51 and Acts 1:2, 11, 22 to designate the glorification of Jesus. Surprisingly, the less distinctive *diistanai*, "left," occurs in v. 51. This may be due to Luke's reliance on his (Hebrew) source. The phrase "[he] was taken up into heaven" (v. 51) is omitted from Codex Bezae (D) and, more important, from Codex Sinaiticus (א). Several reasons can be given for its originality, however. Textual support for its originality is vastly superior (𝔭75 A B C K L W X Θ Π Ψ), Luke's testimony in Acts 1:2 to "the day he was taken up to heaven" presupposes the longer reading of v. 51, and it is hard to imagine the disciples returning to Jerusalem with "great joy" (v. 52) if Jesus had simply "left," rather than ascending to heaven.[141]

---

141. See the several arguments in favor of the longer reading, "[he] was taken up into heaven," in Metzger, *TCGNT*, 162-63; also Fitzmyer, *Luke (IX–XXIV)*, 1590; Wolter, *Lukas-evangelium*, 795-96; Bovon, *Lukas 19,28–24,53*, 615.

Ascension Day falls on the Thursday following the sixth Sunday after Easter — the very day, in fact, on which I write these lines. The **ascension** may be the least-observed event from the life of Christ in the church liturgical year. This is due, perhaps, to the unease and even embarrassment that moderns who are familiar with astrophysics feel when they think of a physical body being levitated into the sky. Whatever qualms moderns may bring to this event, Luke regards the ascension as the rightful and necessary conclusion to the Gospel. First, the ascension of Jesus follows logically from his bodily resurrection. If Jesus rose from the dead with a glorified body that superseded the physical properties governing mortal bodies, then it would appear inappropriate for him to remain permanently subject to those physical properties on earth. His translation to his essential celestial state follows both naturally and inevitably. The ascension thus signals the transition from Jesus' earthly embodied existence to his heavenly embodied existence. Second, the crude objectivity of the ascension, offensive though it may be to modern sensibilities, may have been necessary to convey that Jesus would not again appear in the spiritually embodied state in which the disciples had experienced him as resurrected Lord. It is hard to imagine that the disciples would have believed or grasped the finality of his departure, even if he had instructed them accordingly, had he not performed an empirical object lesson such as the ascension. In this respect, the ascension was not necessary for Jesus; he had, after all, entered into human existence without similar drama. It was necessary for the disciples to acknowledge his future spiritual rather than bodily presence. Finally and most important, Jesus did not discard his body and return to the Father, in contrast to the incarnation, in which he had "departed" from the Father as a purely spiritual being to take on human flesh. His identification and embracing of humanity are so complete that he returns to the Father as the *incarnate* Son. Jesus is not simply the savior of humanity, but in his bodily ascension he exalts humanity with himself. Humanity is now present in the Godhead through Jesus the incarnate Son. As the Lord Jesus now is, believers will someday be. "What we will be has not yet been made known. But we know that when Christ appears, we shall be like him" (1 John 3:2).[142]

"Then the disciples worshiped him and returned to Jerusalem with great joy. And they stayed continually at the temple, praising God" (vv. 52-53; see Acts 1:10-11). Luke rarely employs the language of worship, and when he does, it is due to God alone (4:8). Individuals may fall at Jesus' feet in veneration (5:8, 12; 8:28, 41, 47; 17:16), but until this point he is never the object of worship in the Third Gospel. Following the resurrection, Jesus receives the worship

---

142. The first two points on the ascension have been influenced by Metzger, "The Ascension of Jesus Christ," 83-87.

due to God alone, for he is the glorified Son of God.[143] In obedience to the commandment of Jesus in v. 49, the disciples return to Jerusalem in great joy. Their joy implies a major transition in their understanding of Jesus. His earlier appearances and disappearances evoked confusion and fear (vv. 37-38). The disciples now experience the great joy proclaimed by the angel at Jesus' birth (2:10), for his bodily departure portends their spiritual empowerment from on high (v. 49).[144] The resurrection and ascension of Jesus in Jerusalem establish Jerusalem rather than Galilee as the home of the nascent Christian church. The disciples gather "continually at the temple" (v. 53; Acts 2:46; 5:12, 21, 42), "blessing God."[145] The Gospel has come full circle: the disciples make the temple the base of their communal life, as did Zechariah (1:8); in the temple they bless God, as did Zechariah (1:68) and Simeon (2:28). The completed circle signifies that, in the apostolic proclamation of repentance and forgiveness of sins in Jesus' name (v. 47), Israel is not rejected or discarded, but fulfilled. The final exhortation to "bless God" will become a liturgical greeting in early Christian worship and literature: "Blessed be the God and Father of our Lord Jesus Christ" (2 Cor 1:3; Eph 1:3; 1 Pet 1:3). The exhortation declares the purpose of the gospel for the church in Luke's day and for the church in every age.

143. Codex Bezae (D), perhaps aware that Luke has refrained from ascribing worship to Jesus and that Jesus ascribed worship to God alone (4:8; Deut 6:13), omits "worshiped him" in v. 52. The manuscript tradition, however, strongly attests to its originality (see Metzger, *TCGNT,* 163).

144. Plummer, *Luke,* 565, takes the joy of the disciples as evidence of the historical veracity of the event, for "a writer of fiction would have made them lament the departure of their Master."

145. A number of manuscripts, finding "blessing God" awkward, substitute either "praising God" (D) or "praising and blessing God" (A C K W Γ Δ Θ Ψ). Although "praising God" (Gk. *ainountes ton theon*) is characteristic of Luke (2:13, 20; 19:37; Acts 2:47; 3:8, 9), "blessing" (Gk. *eulogein*), including "blessing God" (1:64; 2:28), occurs three times more frequently in Luke-Acts. The superior manuscript evidence in its support in v. 53 (𝔭[75] ℵ B D L) and its repetition of the theme of blessing (vv. 50, 51, 53) argue in favor of the originality of "blessing God." See also Metzger, *TCGNT,* 163-64.

Index of Subjects

Index of Authors

Index of Scripture References

Index of Extrabiblical Literature

DEAD SEA SCROLLS AND RELATED TEXTS